State Rankings 2017

⑤SAGE stats

Featuring State Stats, Local Stats, and Business Stats

What is **SAGE Stats**? **SAGE Stats** is an exciting online destination for finding, mapping, comparing, and exporting statistics across a number of topics and geographic areas. In its three modules, **SAGE Stats** draws together the statistics from the *State Rankings* series of books by CQ Press (SAGE State Stats); a broad collection of data by county, city, and metro area (SAGE Local Stats); and a collection of highly detailed demographic data (including projections) and industry and labor measures available across geographical areas including ZIP Codes (SAGE Business Stats).

Featuring data from more than 180 different government and nongovernment sources and backed by a rich collection of thousands of historical, current, and projected data series on popular topics of research interest, **SAGE Stats** uniquely allows users to discover, view, and export key information measures for the 50 states and the District of Columbia, over 1,400 cities, over 3,000 counties, over 900 metro areas, and thousands of ZIP Codes.

SAGE Stats makes research easy by providing in one place annual measures dating back decades. Data series are displayed in a clear and consistent format with detailed source information. An intuitive interface lets users easily browse by location or by topic, and then compare across locations or across time.

Users can:

- Analyze data patterns by comparing across locations, data series, and time

- Create and export custom visuals including line charts, scatter plots, and maps

- Generate tables and download data for statistical research

- Toggle user display between interactive visual and tabular data view

- Engage a moveable timeline to discover trends

- Explore interactive maps featuring zoom and hover functions

- Export data across multiple years and data series

Ongoing updates to **SAGE Stats** throughout the year ensure that users have the most current data available.

Check it out online at http://data.sagepub.com/.

State Rankings 2017

A Statistical View of America

Editors

Kathleen O'Leary Morgan
and
Scott Morgan

For information:

CQ Press
An Imprint of SAGE Publications, Inc.
2455 Teller Road
Thousand Oaks, California 91320
E-mail: order@sagepub.com

SAGE Publications Ltd.
1 Oliver's Yard
55 City Road
London, EC1Y 1SP
United Kingdom

SAGE Publications India Pvt. Ltd.
B 1/I 1 Mohan Cooperative Industrial Area
Mathura Road, New Delhi 110 044
India

SAGE Publications Asia-Pacific Pte. Ltd.
3 Church Street
#10-04 Samsung Hub
Singapore 049483

ISBN 978-1-5063-7179-5 (cloth)
ISBN 978-1-5063-7180-1 (paper)
ISSN 1057-3623

Acquisitions Editor: Andrew Boney
Assistant Editor: Diana Aleman
Production Editor: Tracy Buyan
Cover Designer: Michael Dubowe
Marketing Manager: Leah Watson

17 18 19 20 21 10 9 8 7 6 5 4 3 2 1

Contents

Detailed Table of Contents

VI. EMPLOYMENT AND LABOR

VII. ENERGY AND ENVIRONMENT

VIII. GEOGRAPHY

IX. GOVERNMENT FINANCES: FEDERAL

X. GOVERNMENT FINANCES: STATE AND LOCAL

XI. HEALTH

Introduction and Methodology

State Rankings 2017 provides an easily accessible collection of data in a broad range of quality of life factors in the United States. In this latest 2017 edition, *State Rankings* compares data from the fifty states and the District of Columbia in 566 tables in the following fifteen different livability categories: agriculture, crime and law enforcement, defense, economy, education, employment and labor, energy and environment, geography, federal government finances, state and local government finances, health, households and housing, population, social welfare, and transportation.

Purpose of This Book

State Rankings 2017 translates complicated and often convoluted statistics into meaningful, easy-to-understand information. Too often there is an abundance of data but far too little information putting those data into context. This book allows researchers, legislators, policy analysts, journalists, and the general public to access information in a manner that not only provides basic facts about a state's quality of life but also gives a meaningful framework by comparing individual states against the rest of the country.

These data and rankings can be used in a variety of ways, by a variety of audiences, including the following examples:

- Policy makers can use the data to help identify areas warranting further study.
- Journalists can easily find impartial state information that puts stories into context.
- The general public can see how a particular state is faring compared to other states.
- Librarians can use the data as a quick reference to assist patrons in research and offer the sources and websites included as a starting point for finding other related data.

The comparison rankings in *State Rankings 2017* provide an annual snapshot of how the states are doing in the fifteen livability categories mentioned above. There are two principle approaches to using these rankings. The first is to examine how a state is doing compared to all other states via the comparison rankings in this book. The second approach is to compare a state to itself over a given period of time. Both approaches are

important to achieving a good understanding of how and whether a state is making progress. It is important to keep in mind that the rankings are not a definitive determination of which state is the "best." However, since so many issues are surrounded by emotions, tracking them by the numbers can help bring the discussion back to a more balanced, unbiased review that in the end leads to better decisions.

Data and Limitations

The data featured in *State Rankings 2017* were chosen specifically by the editors from a variety of government and private sector sources. The statistics presented are intended to cover a broad array of quality-of-life subject areas, giving users of the book a solid collection of state information. Nonetheless, the statistics are not inclusive of all the possible data that might be available. The statistics in the book are the latest available from the sources. In a few cases, we have retained tables that have not been updated for several years because we believe our readers will find the data relevant, even if updates are not available. In other cases, we replaced obsolete data with new tables. Longtime users should note in particular that we have updated Government Finances: Federal with new government spending data from the OMB's USASpending.gov, but differences in methodology make those data difficult to compare with past editions.

Previous editions of the book have used the term *most livable* when describing states with the highest livability ranking. This term is no longer being used because it is purely descriptive—at no time do we attempt to explain *why* a particular state is ranking higher or lower in livability factors than others or against the national average. This explanation—currently sought by social science researchers—is beyond the scope of this book. While our selection of factors clearly affects the rankings, we believe the rankings provide a solid measurement of how the fifty states and Washington, D.C., are faring with regard to quality of life in the United States. Researchers, practitioners, and others can confidently use the data to understand livability issues and guide policy decisions.

Methodology

The comparison rankings for *State Rankings 2017* are determined using the same methodology as we have used for the past twenty-plus years. The editors used the previously mentioned fifteen livability categories to select forty-three quality of life factors from a broad range of economic, educational, health-oriented, public safety, and environmental statistics. Overall comparison rankings were determined by averaging each state's ranking for each category. The scale is one to fifty, the higher the number, the higher the state is in the rankings (i.e., 50 is the best score to receive). Data used are for the most recent year for which comparable numbers are available from most states. All factors are given equal weight.

While the 566 tables provided in *State Rankings 2017* are ranked highest to lowest without any subjective determination as to whether a subject is "positive" or "negative," for the state comparison rankings, the editors do make a subjective determination as to whether something is "positive" or "negative." Twenty-five of the forty-three factors were determined to be negative, and the remaining eighteen were viewed as positive.

The reason for this division between positive and negative is that if a state ranks first in crime rate (i.e., it has the highest crime rate), its comparison ranking is reduced. Whereas if a state ranks first in per-capita personal income (i.e., it has the highest income), its comparison ranking is increased. To account for this, we subtract the rankings for the positive factors from 51 so that a state with the highest ranking in a positive factor ends up with a 50 for that factor (remember, high numbers are best).

Once we have chosen the factors and divided them into positive and negative groupings, we simply average the ranking for each state in all forty-three factors. If a state is missing data for a given factor, its standing is based on the average ranking for the remaining factors. The book uses the latest available data for each livability factor.

As an example, Maine ranks 46th in crime rate (negative factor), 45th in personal bankruptcy rate (negative factor), and ranks 7th in percent of population graduated from high school (positive factor). The 46th and 45th rankings go straight into the comparison formula, whereas the number seven ranking in percent of population graduated from high school is first subtracted from 51 with the resulting 44 going into the ranking. For these three factors for Maine, we would average 46, 45, and 44 with the result being 45. If these three factors were the only ones we used, then the resulting average of 45 would be the figure we would use to compare Maine to the other forty-nine states. However, for the *State Rankings* comparison rankings, an additional forty factors are added into the calculations before the final results are determined.

Designed with the researcher in mind, the numbers shown in *State Rankings* require no additional calculations to convert them from millions, thousands, and so on. All states are ranked on a high-to-low basis, with any ties among the states listed alphabetically for a given ranking. Negative numbers are shown in parentheses. For tables displaying national totals (as opposed to rates, per capita, etc.), a separate column is included that shows what percent of the national total each individual state's total represents. This column is headed by "% of USA." This percentage figure is particularly interesting when compared with a state's population in a given year. Rates may be per 10,000 persons, per 100,000 persons, or per some other denominator; these are clearly explained by the text following the national rate and, if necessary, the footnotes.

To further assist readers, source information and footnotes clearly are shown at the bottom of each page, while national totals, rates, and percentages are prominently displayed at the top of each table. Every other line is shaded in gray for easier reading. Numerous information-finding tools are provided: a thorough table of contents, table listings at the beginning of each chapter, and a detailed index. In addition, a roster of sources with addresses, phone numbers, and websites is found in the back of the book.

About the Editors

Kathleen O'Leary Morgan and **Scott Morgan** founded Morgan Quitno Press in 1990. They edited more than 2,700 annual state and city statistical reference publications before selling the titles to CQ Press in 2007. They also edited a monthly journal, *State Statistical Trends*, for six years. They have continued to edit a number of the publications continued by CQ Press, as well as an ever-growing online database.

Kathleen received a BS and a master's in Public Administration from the University of Kansas. She served in a number of media and legislative positions within the U.S. Department of Transportation, where she also served as deputy director of congressional affairs.

Scott received both a BS and a law degree from the University of Kansas. He previously worked on the staffs of two U.S. senators as well as the Senate Judiciary Committee. He represented the Senate on the Federal Election Commission and served as Chief Counsel for Senator Bob Dole's presidential campaign in 1988. He was Chief Counsel for Governor Mike Hayden in Kansas until 1990.

The 2017 State Rankings

ALPHA ORDER

RANK	STATE	AVG	16 RANK	CHANGE
46	Alabama	18.93	47	1
36	Alaska	22.44	26	-10
40	Arizona	21.16	40	0
45	Arkansas	19.09	42	-3
26	California	25.28	23	-3
10	Colorado	29.88	10	0
12	Connecticut	29.26	12	0
25	Delaware	25.35	29	4
33	Florida	23.60	38	5
37	Georgia	22.33	41	4
21	Hawaii	26.40	19	-2
23	Idaho	26.12	20	-3
24	Illinois	25.37	31	7
34	Indiana	23.37	36	2
5	Iowa	32.19	3	-2
18	Kansas	27.63	14	-4
44	Kentucky	19.95	43	-1
50	Louisiana	15.77	49	-1
13	Maine	29.05	15	2
19	Maryland	27.53	20	1
4	Massachusetts	32.40	4	0
22	Michigan	26.37	25	3
2	Minnesota	33.63	2	0
49	Mississippi	15.88	50	1
27	Missouri	24.88	33	6
28	Montana	24.84	28	0
7	Nebraska	31.35	4	-3
43	Nevada	20.12	39	-4
1	New Hampshire	36.33	1	0
9	New Jersey	30.49	11	2
47	New Mexico	18.14	46	-1
30	New York	24.60	30	0
39	North Carolina	22.07	37	-2
8	North Dakota	30.88	4	-4
35	Ohio	23.09	35	0
42	Oklahoma	20.51	34	-8
28	Oregon	24.84	22	-6
32	Pennsylvania	24.40	32	0
20	Rhode Island	26.47	23	3
41	South Carolina	20.81	44	3
11	South Dakota	29.47	13	2
38	Tennessee	22.14	45	7
31	Texas	24.53	27	-4
6	Utah	31.74	9	3
3	Vermont	32.53	8	5
17	Virginia	27.74	18	1
16	Washington	27.98	16	0
48	West Virginia	17.58	48	0
14	Wisconsin	28.95	17	3
15	Wyoming	28.37	7	-8

RANK ORDER

RANK	STATE	AVG	16 RANK	CHANGE
1	New Hampshire	36.33	1	0
2	Minnesota	33.63	2	0
3	Vermont	32.53	8	5
4	Massachusetts	32.40	4	0
5	Iowa	32.19	3	-2
6	Utah	31.74	9	3
7	Nebraska	31.35	4	-3
8	North Dakota	30.88	4	-4
9	New Jersey	30.49	11	2
10	Colorado	29.88	10	0
11	South Dakota	29.47	13	2
12	Connecticut	29.26	12	0
13	Maine	29.05	15	2
14	Wisconsin	28.95	17	3
15	Wyoming	28.37	7	-8
16	Washington	27.98	16	0
17	Virginia	27.74	18	1
18	Kansas	27.63	14	-4
19	Maryland	27.53	20	1
20	Rhode Island	26.47	23	3
21	Hawaii	26.40	19	-2
22	Michigan	26.37	25	3
23	Idaho	26.12	20	-3
24	Illinois	25.37	31	7
25	Delaware	25.35	29	4
26	California	25.28	23	-3
27	Missouri	24.88	33	6
28	Montana	24.84	28	0
28	Oregon	24.84	22	-6
30	New York	24.60	30	0
31	Texas	24.53	27	-4
32	Pennsylvania	24.40	32	0
33	Florida	23.60	38	5
34	Indiana	23.37	36	2
35	Ohio	23.09	35	0
36	Alaska	22.44	26	-10
37	Georgia	22.33	41	4
38	Tennessee	22.14	45	7
39	North Carolina	22.07	37	-2
40	Arizona	21.16	40	0
41	South Carolina	20.81	44	3
42	Oklahoma	20.51	34	-8
43	Nevada	20.12	39	-4
44	Kentucky	19.95	43	-1
45	Arkansas	19.09	42	-3
46	Alabama	18.93	47	1
47	New Mexico	18.14	46	-1
48	West Virginia	17.58	48	0
49	Mississippi	15.88	50	1
50	Louisiana	15.77	49	-1

Date Each State Admitted to Statehood*

ALPHA ORDER

RANK	STATE	DATE OF ADMISSION
22	Alabama	December 14, 1819
49	Alaska	January 3, 1959
48	Arizona	February 14, 1912
25	Arkansas	June 15, 1836
31	California	September 9, 1850
38	Colorado	August 1, 1876
5	Connecticut	January 9, 1788
1	Delaware	December 7, 1787
27	Florida	March 3, 1845
4	Georgia	January 2, 1788
50	Hawaii	August 21, 1959
43	Idaho	July 3, 1890
21	Illinois	December 3, 1818
19	Indiana	December 11, 1816
29	Iowa	December 28, 1846
34	Kansas	January 29, 1861
15	Kentucky	June 1, 1792
18	Louisiana	April 30, 1812
23	Maine	March 15, 1820
7	Maryland	April 28, 1788
6	Massachusetts	February 6, 1788
26	Michigan	January 26, 1837
32	Minnesota	May 11, 1858
20	Mississippi	December 10, 1817
24	Missouri	August 10, 1821
41	Montana	November 8, 1889
37	Nebraska	March 1, 1867
36	Nevada	October 31, 1864
9	New Hampshire	June 21, 1788
3	New Jersey	December 18, 1787
47	New Mexico	January 6, 1912
11	New York	July 26, 1788
12	North Carolina	November 21, 1789
39	North Dakota	November 2, 1889
17	Ohio	March 1, 1803
46	Oklahoma	November 16, 1907
33	Oregon	February 14, 1859
2	Pennsylvania	December 12, 1787
13	Rhode Island	May 29, 1790
8	South Carolina	May 23, 1788
39	South Dakota	November 2, 1889
16	Tennessee	June 1, 1796
28	Texas	December 29, 1845
45	Utah	January 4, 1896
14	Vermont	March 4, 1791
10	Virginia	June 26, 1788
42	Washington	November 11, 1889
35	West Virginia	June 20, 1863
30	Wisconsin	May 29, 1848
44	Wyoming	July 10, 1890

RANK ORDER

RANK	STATE	DATE OF ADMISSION
1	Delaware	December 7, 1787
2	Pennsylvania	December 12, 1787
3	New Jersey	December 18, 1787
4	Georgia	January 2, 1788
5	Connecticut	January 9, 1788
6	Massachusetts	February 6, 1788
7	Maryland	April 28, 1788
8	South Carolina	May 23, 1788
9	New Hampshire	June 21, 1788
10	Virginia	June 26, 1788
11	New York	July 26, 1788
12	North Carolina	November 21, 1789
13	Rhode Island	May 29, 1790
14	Vermont	March 4, 1791
15	Kentucky	June 1, 1792
16	Tennessee	June 1, 1796
17	Ohio	March 1, 1803
18	Louisiana	April 30, 1812
19	Indiana	December 11, 1816
20	Mississippi	December 10, 1817
21	Illinois	December 3, 1818
22	Alabama	December 14, 1819
23	Maine	March 15, 1820
24	Missouri	August 10, 1821
25	Arkansas	June 15, 1836
26	Michigan	January 26, 1837
27	Florida	March 3, 1845
28	Texas	December 29, 1845
29	Iowa	December 28, 1846
30	Wisconsin	May 29, 1848
31	California	September 9, 1850
32	Minnesota	May 11, 1858
33	Oregon	February 14, 1859
34	Kansas	January 29, 1861
35	West Virginia	June 20, 1863
36	Nevada	October 31, 1864
37	Nebraska	March 1, 1867
38	Colorado	August 1, 1876
39	North Dakota	November 2, 1889
39	South Dakota	November 2, 1889
41	Montana	November 8, 1889
42	Washington	November 11, 1889
43	Idaho	July 3, 1890
44	Wyoming	July 10, 1890
45	Utah	January 4, 1896
46	Oklahoma	November 16, 1907
47	New Mexico	January 6, 1912
48	Arizona	February 14, 1912
49	Alaska	January 3, 1959
50	Hawaii	August 21, 1959

Source: U.S. Bureau of the Census
    "1980 Census of Population" (vol. 1, part A, PC80-1-A)
*First thirteen states show date of ratification of Constitution.

STATE FAST FACTS

STATE	NICKNAME	CAPITAL	POPULATION*	AREA**
Alabama	Heart of Dixie	Montgomery	4,863,300	52,420
Alaska	The Last Frontier	Juneau	741,894	665,384
Arizona	Grand Canyon State	Phoenix	6,931,071	113,990
Arkansas	The Natural State	Little Rock	2,988,248	53,179
California	Golden State	Sacramento	39,250,017	163,695
Colorado	Centennial State	Denver	5,540,545	104,094
Connecticut	Constitution State	Hartford	3,576,452	5,543
Delaware	First State	Dover	952,065	2,489
Florida	Sunshine State	Tallahassee	20,612,439	65,758
Georgia	Peach State	Atlanta	10,310,371	59,425
Hawaii	Aloha State	Honolulu	1,428,557	10,932
Idaho	Gem State	Boise	1,683,140	83,569
Illinois	Land of Lincoln	Springfield	12,801,539	57,914
Indiana	Hoosier State	Indianapolis	6,633,053	36,420
Iowa	Hawkeye State	Des Moines	3,134,693	56,273
Kansas	Sunflower State	Topeka	2,907,289	82,278
Kentucky	Bluegrass State	Frankfort	4,436,974	40,408
Louisiana	Pelican State	Baton Rouge	4,681,666	52,378
Maine	Pine Tree State	Augusta	1,331,479	35,380
Maryland	Free State	Annapolis	6,016,447	12,406
Massachusetts	Bay State	Boston	6,811,779	10,554
Michigan	Great Lake State	Lansing	9,928,300	96,714
Minnesota	North Star State	St. Paul	5,519,952	86,936
Mississippi	Magnolia State	Jackson	2,988,726	48,432
Missouri	Show Me State	Jefferson City	6,093,000	69,707
Montana	Treasure State	Helena	1,042,520	147,040
Nebraska	Cornhusker State	Lincoln	1,907,116	77,348
Nevada	Silver State	Carson City	2,940,058	110,572
New Hampshire	Granite State	Concord	1,334,795	9,349
New Jersey	Garden State	Trenton	8,944,469	8,723
New Mexico	Land of Enchantment	Santa Fe	2,081,015	121,590
New York	Empire State	Albany	19,745,289	54,555
North Carolina	Tar Heel State	Raleigh	10,146,788	53,819
North Dakota	Peace Garden State	Bismarck	757,952	70,698
Ohio	Buckeye State	Columbus	11,614,373	44,826
Oklahoma	Sooner State	Oklahoma City	3,923,561	69,899
Oregon	Beaver State	Salem	4,093,465	98,379
Pennsylvania	Keystone State	Harrisburg	12,784,227	46,054
Rhode Island	Ocean State	Providence	1,056,426	1,545
South Carolina	Palmetto State	Columbia	4,961,119	32,020
South Dakota	Mount Rushmore State	Pierre	865,454	77,116
Tennessee	Volunteer State	Nashville	6,651,194	42,144
Texas	Lone Star State	Austin	27,862,596	268,596
Utah	Beehive State	Salt Lake City	3,051,217	84,897
Vermont	Green Mountain State	Montpelier	624,594	9,616
Virginia	Old Dominion	Richmond	8,411,808	42,775
Washington	Evergreen State	Olympia	7,288,000	71,298
West Virginia	Mountain State	Charleston	1,831,102	24,230
Wisconsin	Badger State	Madison	5,778,708	65,496
Wyoming	Equality State	Cheyenne	585,501	97,813

*U.S. Bureau of the Census, "Population Estimates" (December 2016, http://www.census.gov/programs-surveys/popest.html)

**Total of land and water area in square miles.

STATE FAST FACTS

STATE SONG	STATE FLOWER	STATE TREE	STATE BIRD
Alabama	Camellia	Southern Pine	Yellowhammer
Alaska's Flag	Forget-Me-Not	Sitka Spruce	Willow Ptarmigan
Arizona	Saguaro Cactus Blossom	Palo Verde	Cactus Wren
Arkansas	Apple Blossom	Pine	Mockingbird
I Love You, California	Golden Poppy	California Redwood	California Valley Quail
Where the Columbines Grow	Rocky Mountain Columbine	Colorado Blue Spruce	Lark Bunting
Yankee Doodle Dandy	Mountain Laurel	White Oak	American Robin
Our Delaware	Peach Blossom	American Holly	Blue Hen Chicken
Swanee River	Orange Blossom	Sabal Palmetto Palm	Mockingbird
Georgia On My Mind	Cherokee Rose	Live Oak	Brown Thrasher
Hawaii Ponoi	Yellow Hibiscus	Candlenut	Nene
Here We Have Idaho	Syringa	White Pine	Mountain Bluebird
Illinois	Purple Violet	White Oak	Cardinal
On the Banks of the Wabash, Far Away	Peony	Tulip Poplar	Cardinal
The Song of Iowa	Wild Rose	Oak	Eastern Goldfinch
Home on the Range	Sunflower	Cottonwood	Western Meadowlark
My Old Kentucky Home	Goldenrod	Tulip Tree	Cardinal
Give Me Louisiana	Magnolia	Cypress	Eastern Brown Pelican
State of Maine Song	White Pine Cone and Tassel	Eastern White Pine	Chickadee
Maryland, My Maryland	Black-eyed Susan	White Oak	Baltimore Oriole
All Hail to Massachusetts	Mayflower	American Elm	Chickadee
Michigan, My Michigan	Apple Blossom	White Pine	Robin
Hail! Minnesota	Pink and White Lady's Slipper	Red Pine	Common Loon
Go, Mississippi!	Magnolia	Magnolia	Mockingbird
Missouri Waltz	Hawthorn	Dogwood	Bluebird
Montana	Bitterroot	Ponderosa Pine	Western Meadowlark
Beautiful Nebraska	Goldenrod	Cottonwood	Western Meadowlark
Home Means Nevada	Sagebrush	Single-Leaf Pinon	Mountain Bluebird
Old New Hampshire	Purple Lilac	White Birch	Purple Finch
Ode to New Jersey	Purple Violet	Red Oak	Eastern Goldfinch
O Fair New Mexico	Yucca	Pinon	Roadrunner
I Love New York	Rose	Sugar Maple	Bluebird
The Old North State	Dogwood	Pine	Cardinal
North Dakota Hymn	Wild Prairie Rose	American Elm	Western Meadowlark
Beautiful Ohio	Scarlet Carnation	Buckeye	Cardinal
Oklahoma!	Mistletoe	Redbud	Scissortailed Flycatcher
Oregon, My Oregon	Oregon Grape	Douglas Fir	Western Meadowlark
Hail! Pennsylvania	Mountain Laurel	Hemlock	Ruffed Grouse
Rhode Island	Violet	Red Maple	Rhode Island Red
Carolina	Yellow Jessamine	Palmetto	Carolina Wren
Hail, South Dakota	Pasque Flower	Black Hills Spruce	Ringnecked Pheasant
The Tennessee Waltz	Iris	Tulip Poplar	Mockingbird
Texas, Our Texas	Bluebonnet	Pecan	Mockingbird
Utah, We Love Thee	Sego Lily	Blue Spruce	Seagull
Hail, Vermont	Red Clover	Sugar Maple	Hermit Thrush
Carry Me Back to Old Virginia	Dogwood	Dogwood	Cardinal
Washington, My Home	Western Rhododendron	Western Hemlock	Willow Goldfinch
The West Virginia Hills; This Is My West Virginia; and West Virginia, My Home, Sweet Home	Big Rhododendron	Sugar Maple	Cardinal
On Wisconsin!	Wood Violet	Sugar Maple	Robin
Wyoming	Indian Paintbrush	Cottonwood	Meadowlark

I. Agriculture

Number of Farms in 2015

National Total = 2,067,000 Farms*

ALPHA ORDER

RANK	STATE	FARMS	% of USA
21	Alabama	42,700	2.1%
50	Alaska	750	0.0%
36	Arizona	19,500	0.9%
20	Arkansas	43,500	2.1%
5	California	77,500	3.7%
27	Colorado	34,200	1.7%
45	Connecticut	6,000	0.3%
48	Delaware	2,500	0.1%
18	Florida	47,300	2.3%
22	Georgia	40,500	2.0%
44	Hawaii	7,000	0.3%
33	Idaho	24,400	1.2%
8	Illinois	73,600	3.6%
14	Indiana	57,700	2.8%
3	Iowa	87,500	4.2%
12	Kansas	60,400	2.9%
6	Kentucky	76,400	3.7%
31	Louisiana	26,900	1.3%
41	Maine	8,200	0.4%
38	Maryland	12,200	0.6%
42	Massachusetts	7,800	0.4%
15	Michigan	51,500	2.5%
8	Minnesota	73,600	3.6%
23	Mississippi	36,700	1.8%
2	Missouri	97,100	4.7%
30	Montana	27,500	1.3%
17	Nebraska	48,700	2.4%
47	Nevada	4,200	0.2%
46	New Hampshire	4,400	0.2%
40	New Jersey	9,100	0.4%
32	New Mexico	24,700	1.2%
25	New York	35,500	1.7%
16	North Carolina	48,800	2.4%
29	North Dakota	30,000	1.5%
7	Ohio	74,400	3.6%
4	Oklahoma	78,000	3.8%
26	Oregon	34,600	1.7%
13	Pennsylvania	57,900	2.8%
49	Rhode Island	1,250	0.1%
33	South Carolina	24,400	1.2%
28	South Dakota	31,300	1.5%
11	Tennessee	67,300	3.3%
1	Texas	242,000	11.7%
37	Utah	18,100	0.9%
43	Vermont	7,300	0.4%
19	Virginia	44,700	2.2%
24	Washington	36,000	1.7%
35	West Virginia	20,900	1.0%
10	Wisconsin	68,900	3.3%
39	Wyoming	11,600	0.6%

RANK ORDER

RANK	STATE	FARMS	% of USA
1	Texas	242,000	11.7%
2	Missouri	97,100	4.7%
3	Iowa	87,500	4.2%
4	Oklahoma	78,000	3.8%
5	California	77,500	3.7%
6	Kentucky	76,400	3.7%
7	Ohio	74,400	3.6%
8	Illinois	73,600	3.6%
8	Minnesota	73,600	3.6%
10	Wisconsin	68,900	3.3%
11	Tennessee	67,300	3.3%
12	Kansas	60,400	2.9%
13	Pennsylvania	57,900	2.8%
14	Indiana	57,700	2.8%
15	Michigan	51,500	2.5%
16	North Carolina	48,800	2.4%
17	Nebraska	48,700	2.4%
18	Florida	47,300	2.3%
19	Virginia	44,700	2.2%
20	Arkansas	43,500	2.1%
21	Alabama	42,700	2.1%
22	Georgia	40,500	2.0%
23	Mississippi	36,700	1.8%
24	Washington	36,000	1.7%
25	New York	35,500	1.7%
26	Oregon	34,600	1.7%
27	Colorado	34,200	1.7%
28	South Dakota	31,300	1.5%
29	North Dakota	30,000	1.5%
30	Montana	27,500	1.3%
31	Louisiana	26,900	1.3%
32	New Mexico	24,700	1.2%
33	Idaho	24,400	1.2%
33	South Carolina	24,400	1.2%
35	West Virginia	20,900	1.0%
36	Arizona	19,500	0.9%
37	Utah	18,100	0.9%
38	Maryland	12,200	0.6%
39	Wyoming	11,600	0.6%
40	New Jersey	9,100	0.4%
41	Maine	8,200	0.4%
42	Massachusetts	7,800	0.4%
43	Vermont	7,300	0.4%
44	Hawaii	7,000	0.3%
45	Connecticut	6,000	0.3%
46	New Hampshire	4,400	0.2%
47	Nevada	4,200	0.2%
48	Delaware	2,500	0.1%
49	Rhode Island	1,250	0.1%
50	Alaska	750	0.0%
	District of Columbia	0	0.0%

Source: U.S. Department of Agriculture, National Agricultural Statistics Service
"Farms and Land in Farms" (http://usda.mannlib.cornell.edu/MannUsda/viewDocumentInfo.do?documentID=1259)
*A farm is any establishment from which $1,000 or more of agricultural products were sold or would normally be sold during the year. This includes places with five or more horses, except horses in boarding stables or racetracks.

Land in Farms in 2015

National Total = 912,000,000 Acres*

RANK	STATE	ACRES	% of USA
31	Alabama	8,800,000	1.0%
44	Alaska	830,000	0.1%
14	Arizona	26,000,000	2.9%
22	Arkansas	13,800,000	1.5%
16	California	25,500,000	2.8%
9	Colorado	31,700,000	3.5%
49	Connecticut	440,000	0.0%
47	Delaware	500,000	0.1%
29	Florida	9,450,000	1.0%
30	Georgia	9,300,000	1.0%
43	Hawaii	1,120,000	0.1%
24	Idaho	11,800,000	1.3%
13	Illinois	26,900,000	2.9%
18	Indiana	14,700,000	1.6%
10	Iowa	30,500,000	3.3%
3	Kansas	46,000,000	5.0%
23	Kentucky	13,000,000	1.4%
34	Louisiana	7,750,000	0.8%
41	Maine	1,450,000	0.2%
40	Maryland	2,020,000	0.2%
46	Massachusetts	520,000	0.1%
28	Michigan	9,950,000	1.1%
15	Minnesota	25,900,000	2.8%
27	Mississippi	10,800,000	1.2%
12	Missouri	28,300,000	3.1%
2	Montana	59,700,000	6.5%
4	Nebraska	45,200,000	5.0%
37	Nevada	5,960,000	0.7%
48	New Hampshire	470,000	0.1%
45	New Jersey	720,000	0.1%
6	New Mexico	43,200,000	4.7%
36	New York	7,200,000	0.8%
32	North Carolina	8,300,000	0.9%
7	North Dakota	39,200,000	4.3%
21	Ohio	14,000,000	1.5%
8	Oklahoma	34,200,000	3.8%
17	Oregon	16,400,000	1.8%
35	Pennsylvania	7,700,000	0.8%
50	Rhode Island	70,000	0.0%
38	South Carolina	5,000,000	0.5%
5	South Dakota	43,300,000	4.7%
26	Tennessee	10,900,000	1.2%
1	Texas	130,000,000	14.3%
25	Utah	11,000,000	1.2%
42	Vermont	1,250,000	0.1%
33	Virginia	8,100,000	0.9%
18	Washington	14,700,000	1.6%
39	West Virginia	3,600,000	0.4%
20	Wisconsin	14,400,000	1.6%
11	Wyoming	30,400,000	3.3%

RANK	STATE	ACRES	% of USA
1	Texas	130,000,000	14.3%
2	Montana	59,700,000	6.5%
3	Kansas	46,000,000	5.0%
4	Nebraska	45,200,000	5.0%
5	South Dakota	43,300,000	4.7%
6	New Mexico	43,200,000	4.7%
7	North Dakota	39,200,000	4.3%
8	Oklahoma	34,200,000	3.8%
9	Colorado	31,700,000	3.5%
10	Iowa	30,500,000	3.3%
11	Wyoming	30,400,000	3.3%
12	Missouri	28,300,000	3.1%
13	Illinois	26,900,000	2.9%
14	Arizona	26,000,000	2.9%
15	Minnesota	25,900,000	2.8%
16	California	25,500,000	2.8%
17	Oregon	16,400,000	1.8%
18	Indiana	14,700,000	1.6%
18	Washington	14,700,000	1.6%
20	Wisconsin	14,400,000	1.6%
21	Ohio	14,000,000	1.5%
22	Arkansas	13,800,000	1.5%
23	Kentucky	13,000,000	1.4%
24	Idaho	11,800,000	1.3%
25	Utah	11,000,000	1.2%
26	Tennessee	10,900,000	1.2%
27	Mississippi	10,800,000	1.2%
28	Michigan	9,950,000	1.1%
29	Florida	9,450,000	1.0%
30	Georgia	9,300,000	1.0%
31	Alabama	8,800,000	1.0%
32	North Carolina	8,300,000	0.9%
33	Virginia	8,100,000	0.9%
34	Louisiana	7,750,000	0.8%
35	Pennsylvania	7,700,000	0.8%
36	New York	7,200,000	0.8%
37	Nevada	5,960,000	0.7%
38	South Carolina	5,000,000	0.5%
39	West Virginia	3,600,000	0.4%
40	Maryland	2,020,000	0.2%
41	Maine	1,450,000	0.2%
42	Vermont	1,250,000	0.1%
43	Hawaii	1,120,000	0.1%
44	Alaska	830,000	0.1%
45	New Jersey	720,000	0.1%
46	Massachusetts	520,000	0.1%
47	Delaware	500,000	0.1%
48	New Hampshire	470,000	0.1%
49	Connecticut	440,000	0.0%
50	Rhode Island	70,000	0.0%
	District of Columbia	0	0.0%

Source: U.S. Department of Agriculture, National Agricultural Statistics Service
"Farms and Land in Farms" (http://usda.mannlib.cornell.edu/MannUsda/viewDocumentInfo.do?documentID=1259)
*A farm is any establishment from which $1,000 or more of agricultural products were sold or would normally be sold during the year. This includes places with five or more horses, except horses in boarding stables or racetracks.

Average Number of Acres per Farm in 2015

National Average = 441 Acres*

<table>
<tr><td colspan="3">ALPHA ORDER</td><td colspan="3">RANK ORDER</td></tr>
<tr><td>RANK</td><td>STATE</td><td>ACRES</td><td>RANK</td><td>STATE</td><td>ACRES</td></tr>
<tr><td>29</td><td>Alabama</td><td>206</td><td>1</td><td>Wyoming</td><td>2,621</td></tr>
<tr><td>8</td><td>Alaska</td><td>1,107</td><td>2</td><td>Montana</td><td>2,171</td></tr>
<tr><td>6</td><td>Arizona</td><td>1,333</td><td>3</td><td>New Mexico</td><td>1,749</td></tr>
<tr><td>22</td><td>Arkansas</td><td>317</td><td>4</td><td>Nevada</td><td>1,419</td></tr>
<tr><td>21</td><td>California</td><td>329</td><td>5</td><td>South Dakota</td><td>1,383</td></tr>
<tr><td>10</td><td>Colorado</td><td>927</td><td>6</td><td>Arizona</td><td>1,333</td></tr>
<tr><td>48</td><td>Connecticut</td><td>73</td><td>7</td><td>North Dakota</td><td>1,307</td></tr>
<tr><td>32</td><td>Delaware</td><td>200</td><td>8</td><td>Alaska</td><td>1,107</td></tr>
<tr><td>32</td><td>Florida</td><td>200</td><td>9</td><td>Nebraska</td><td>928</td></tr>
<tr><td>27</td><td>Georgia</td><td>230</td><td>10</td><td>Colorado</td><td>927</td></tr>
<tr><td>44</td><td>Hawaii</td><td>160</td><td>11</td><td>Kansas</td><td>762</td></tr>
<tr><td>14</td><td>Idaho</td><td>484</td><td>12</td><td>Utah</td><td>608</td></tr>
<tr><td>18</td><td>Illinois</td><td>365</td><td>13</td><td>Texas</td><td>537</td></tr>
<tr><td>26</td><td>Indiana</td><td>255</td><td>14</td><td>Idaho</td><td>484</td></tr>
<tr><td>20</td><td>Iowa</td><td>349</td><td>15</td><td>Oregon</td><td>474</td></tr>
<tr><td>11</td><td>Kansas</td><td>762</td><td>16</td><td>Oklahoma</td><td>438</td></tr>
<tr><td>40</td><td>Kentucky</td><td>170</td><td>17</td><td>Washington</td><td>408</td></tr>
<tr><td>25</td><td>Louisiana</td><td>288</td><td>18</td><td>Illinois</td><td>365</td></tr>
<tr><td>37</td><td>Maine</td><td>177</td><td>19</td><td>Minnesota</td><td>352</td></tr>
<tr><td>42</td><td>Maryland</td><td>166</td><td>20</td><td>Iowa</td><td>349</td></tr>
<tr><td>49</td><td>Massachusetts</td><td>67</td><td>21</td><td>California</td><td>329</td></tr>
<tr><td>34</td><td>Michigan</td><td>193</td><td>22</td><td>Arkansas</td><td>317</td></tr>
<tr><td>19</td><td>Minnesota</td><td>352</td><td>23</td><td>Mississippi</td><td>294</td></tr>
<tr><td>23</td><td>Mississippi</td><td>294</td><td>24</td><td>Missouri</td><td>291</td></tr>
<tr><td>24</td><td>Missouri</td><td>291</td><td>25</td><td>Louisiana</td><td>288</td></tr>
<tr><td>2</td><td>Montana</td><td>2,171</td><td>26</td><td>Indiana</td><td>255</td></tr>
<tr><td>9</td><td>Nebraska</td><td>928</td><td>27</td><td>Georgia</td><td>230</td></tr>
<tr><td>4</td><td>Nevada</td><td>1,419</td><td>28</td><td>Wisconsin</td><td>209</td></tr>
<tr><td>46</td><td>New Hampshire</td><td>107</td><td>29</td><td>Alabama</td><td>206</td></tr>
<tr><td>47</td><td>New Jersey</td><td>79</td><td>30</td><td>South Carolina</td><td>205</td></tr>
<tr><td>3</td><td>New Mexico</td><td>1,749</td><td>31</td><td>New York</td><td>203</td></tr>
<tr><td>31</td><td>New York</td><td>203</td><td>32</td><td>Delaware</td><td>200</td></tr>
<tr><td>40</td><td>North Carolina</td><td>170</td><td>32</td><td>Florida</td><td>200</td></tr>
<tr><td>7</td><td>North Dakota</td><td>1,307</td><td>34</td><td>Michigan</td><td>193</td></tr>
<tr><td>35</td><td>Ohio</td><td>188</td><td>35</td><td>Ohio</td><td>188</td></tr>
<tr><td>16</td><td>Oklahoma</td><td>438</td><td>36</td><td>Virginia</td><td>181</td></tr>
<tr><td>15</td><td>Oregon</td><td>474</td><td>37</td><td>Maine</td><td>177</td></tr>
<tr><td>45</td><td>Pennsylvania</td><td>133</td><td>38</td><td>West Virginia</td><td>172</td></tr>
<tr><td>50</td><td>Rhode Island</td><td>56</td><td>39</td><td>Vermont</td><td>171</td></tr>
<tr><td>30</td><td>South Carolina</td><td>205</td><td>40</td><td>Kentucky</td><td>170</td></tr>
<tr><td>5</td><td>South Dakota</td><td>1,383</td><td>40</td><td>North Carolina</td><td>170</td></tr>
<tr><td>43</td><td>Tennessee</td><td>162</td><td>42</td><td>Maryland</td><td>166</td></tr>
<tr><td>13</td><td>Texas</td><td>537</td><td>43</td><td>Tennessee</td><td>162</td></tr>
<tr><td>12</td><td>Utah</td><td>608</td><td>44</td><td>Hawaii</td><td>160</td></tr>
<tr><td>39</td><td>Vermont</td><td>171</td><td>45</td><td>Pennsylvania</td><td>133</td></tr>
<tr><td>36</td><td>Virginia</td><td>181</td><td>46</td><td>New Hampshire</td><td>107</td></tr>
<tr><td>17</td><td>Washington</td><td>408</td><td>47</td><td>New Jersey</td><td>79</td></tr>
<tr><td>38</td><td>West Virginia</td><td>172</td><td>48</td><td>Connecticut</td><td>73</td></tr>
<tr><td>28</td><td>Wisconsin</td><td>209</td><td>49</td><td>Massachusetts</td><td>67</td></tr>
<tr><td>1</td><td>Wyoming</td><td>2,621</td><td>50</td><td>Rhode Island</td><td>56</td></tr>
<tr><td></td><td></td><td></td><td></td><td>District of Columbia**</td><td>NA</td></tr>
</table>

Source: U.S. Department of Agriculture, National Agricultural Statistics Service
"Farms and Land in Farms" (http://usda.mannlib.cornell.edu/MannUsda/viewDocumentInfo.do?documentID=1259)
*A farm is any establishment from which $1,000 or more of agricultural products were sold or would normally be sold during the year. This includes places with five or more horses, except horses in boarding stables or racetracks.

Average per-Acre Value of Farmland in 2016

National Average = $3,010 per Acre*

ALPHA ORDER			RANK ORDER		
RANK	STATE	PER-ACRE VALUE	RANK	STATE	PER-ACRE VALUE
32	Alabama	$2,700	1	Rhode Island	$13,800
NA	Alaska**	NA	2	New Jersey	12,800
20	Arizona	3,800	3	Connecticut	11,200
26	Arkansas	3,050	4	Massachusetts	10,400
6	California	7,900	5	Delaware	8,400
44	Colorado	1,420	6	California	7,900
3	Connecticut	11,200	7	Iowa	7,850
5	Delaware	8,400	8	Illinois	7,400
13	Florida	5,300	9	Indiana	7,150
22	Georgia	3,400	10	Maryland	7,060
NA	Hawaii**	NA	11	Ohio	5,700
34	Idaho	2,500	12	Pennsylvania	5,500
8	Illinois	7,400	13	Florida	5,300
9	Indiana	7,150	14	Michigan	4,800
7	Iowa	7,850	15	Wisconsin	4,750
41	Kansas	1,880	16	Minnesota	4,700
24	Kentucky	3,350	17	North Carolina	4,450
30	Louisiana	2,900	18	New Hampshire	4,350
38	Maine	2,090	19	Virginia	4,300
10	Maryland	7,060	20	Arizona	3,800
4	Massachusetts	10,400	21	Tennessee	3,700
14	Michigan	4,800	22	Georgia	3,400
16	Minnesota	4,700	22	Missouri	3,400
35	Mississippi	2,470	24	Kentucky	3,350
22	Missouri	3,400	25	Vermont	3,320
46	Montana	900	26	Arkansas	3,050
29	Nebraska	2,950	27	South Carolina	3,000
45	Nevada	1,110	28	New York	2,980
18	New Hampshire	4,350	29	Nebraska	2,950
2	New Jersey	12,800	30	Louisiana	2,900
48	New Mexico	520	31	Washington	2,850
28	New York	2,980	32	Alabama	2,700
17	North Carolina	4,450	33	West Virginia	2,570
42	North Dakota	1,830	34	Idaho	2,500
11	Ohio	5,700	35	Mississippi	2,470
43	Oklahoma	1,800	36	South Dakota	2,250
37	Oregon	2,200	37	Oregon	2,200
12	Pennsylvania	5,500	38	Maine	2,090
1	Rhode Island	13,800	39	Utah	2,040
27	South Carolina	3,000	40	Texas	1,960
36	South Dakota	2,250	41	Kansas	1,880
21	Tennessee	3,700	42	North Dakota	1,830
40	Texas	1,960	43	Oklahoma	1,800
39	Utah	2,040	44	Colorado	1,420
25	Vermont	3,320	45	Nevada	1,110
19	Virginia	4,300	46	Montana	900
31	Washington	2,850	47	Wyoming	660
33	West Virginia	2,570	48	New Mexico	520
15	Wisconsin	4,750	NA	Alaska**	NA
47	Wyoming	660	NA	Hawaii**	NA
				District of Columbia**	NA

Source: U.S. Department of Agriculture, National Agricultural Statistics Service
"Land Values and Cash Rents" (http://usda.mannlib.cornell.edu/MannUsda/viewDocumentInfo.do?documentID=1446)
*Value of farmland and buildings in nominal dollars.
**Not applicable or available.

Percent Change in Average per-Acre Value of Farmland: 2015 to 2016

National Percent Change = 0.3% Decrease*

ALPHA ORDER			RANK ORDER		
RANK	STATE	PERCENT CHANGE	RANK	STATE	PERCENT CHANGE
7	Alabama	2.7	1	Oklahoma	5.9
NA	Alaska**	NA	2	Washington	5.6
21	Arizona	0.5	3	Georgia	4.0
22	Arkansas	0.0	4	Oregon	3.8
9	California	2.6	5	Louisiana	3.6
39	Colorado	(1.4)	6	Kentucky	3.1
34	Connecticut	(0.9)	7	Alabama	2.7
7	Delaware	2.7	7	Delaware	2.7
42	Florida	(1.9)	9	California	2.6
3	Georgia	4.0	10	Mississippi	2.1
NA	Hawaii**	NA	11	New Mexico	2.0
15	Idaho	1.2	12	New Hampshire	1.6
38	Illinois	(1.3)	13	Missouri	1.5
22	Indiana	0.0	14	Tennessee	1.4
42	Iowa	(1.9)	15	Idaho	1.2
48	Kansas	(7.4)	16	Montana	1.1
6	Kentucky	3.1	16	Wisconsin	1.1
5	Louisiana	3.6	18	Texas	1.0
22	Maine	0.0	19	Maryland	0.9
19	Maryland	0.9	20	Vermont	0.6
22	Massachusetts	0.0	21	Arizona	0.5
44	Michigan	(2.0)	22	Arkansas	0.0
22	Minnesota	0.0	22	Indiana	0.0
10	Mississippi	2.1	22	Maine	0.0
13	Missouri	1.5	22	Massachusetts	0.0
16	Montana	1.1	22	Minnesota	0.0
46	Nebraska	(3.3)	22	Pennsylvania	0.0
41	Nevada	(1.8)	22	Rhode Island	0.0
12	New Hampshire	1.6	22	Wyoming	0.0
40	New Jersey	(1.5)	30	South Carolina	(0.3)
11	New Mexico	2.0	31	Utah	(0.5)
33	New York	(0.7)	31	Virginia	(0.5)
36	North Carolina	(1.1)	33	New York	(0.7)
47	North Dakota	(4.7)	34	Connecticut	(0.9)
34	Ohio	(0.9)	34	Ohio	(0.9)
1	Oklahoma	5.9	36	North Carolina	(1.1)
4	Oregon	3.8	37	West Virginia	(1.2)
22	Pennsylvania	0.0	38	Illinois	(1.3)
22	Rhode Island	0.0	39	Colorado	(1.4)
30	South Carolina	(0.3)	40	New Jersey	(1.5)
45	South Dakota	(3.0)	41	Nevada	(1.8)
14	Tennessee	1.4	42	Florida	(1.9)
18	Texas	1.0	42	Iowa	(1.9)
31	Utah	(0.5)	44	Michigan	(2.0)
20	Vermont	0.6	45	South Dakota	(3.0)
31	Virginia	(0.5)	46	Nebraska	(3.3)
2	Washington	5.6	47	North Dakota	(4.7)
37	West Virginia	(1.2)	48	Kansas	(7.4)
16	Wisconsin	1.1	NA	Alaska**	NA
22	Wyoming	0.0	NA	Hawaii**	NA
				District of Columbia**	NA

Source: U.S. Department of Agriculture, National Agricultural Statistics Service
"Land Values and Cash Rents" (http://usda.mannlib.cornell.edu/MannUsda/viewDocumentInfo.do?documentID=1446)
*Value of farmland and buildings in nominal dollars.
**Not applicable or available.

Net Farm Income in 2015

National Total = $80,878,549,000*

ALPHA ORDER

ALPHA ORDER

RANK	STATE	FARM INCOME	% of USA
17	Alabama	$1,602,359,000	2.0%
NA	Alaska**	(6,272,000)	0.0%
24	Arizona	1,107,328,000	1.4%
20	Arkansas	1,299,147,000	1.6%
1	California	14,606,384,000	18.1%
18	Colorado	1,499,780,000	1.9%
44	Connecticut	99,770,000	0.1%
35	Delaware	406,804,000	0.5%
7	Florida	3,014,374,000	3.7%
10	Georgia	2,530,844,000	3.1%
41	Hawaii	156,759,000	0.2%
14	Idaho	1,870,307,000	2.3%
NA	Illinois**	(86,814,000)	-0.1%
21	Indiana	1,254,834,000	1.6%
3	Iowa	5,581,067,000	6.9%
15	Kansas	1,759,502,000	2.2%
16	Kentucky	1,664,352,000	2.1%
32	Louisiana	594,063,000	0.7%
40	Maine	159,865,000	0.2%
34	Maryland	506,677,000	0.6%
48	Massachusetts	2,631,000	0.0%
29	Michigan	766,510,000	0.9%
5	Minnesota	3,426,024,000	4.2%
27	Mississippi	846,931,000	1.0%
19	Missouri	1,355,941,000	1.7%
26	Montana	960,916,000	1.2%
4	Nebraska	4,884,316,000	6.0%
42	Nevada	126,338,000	0.2%
46	New Hampshire	63,126,000	0.1%
37	New Jersey	267,425,000	0.3%
28	New Mexico	788,947,000	1.0%
25	New York	1,004,958,000	1.2%
8	North Carolina	2,924,077,000	3.6%
39	North Dakota	188,364,000	0.2%
23	Ohio	1,166,888,000	1.4%
11	Oklahoma	2,167,978,000	2.7%
22	Oregon	1,214,148,000	1.5%
13	Pennsylvania	1,893,287,000	2.3%
47	Rhode Island	27,532,000	0.0%
43	South Carolina	105,076,000	0.1%
12	South Dakota	2,068,238,000	2.6%
30	Tennessee	730,021,000	0.9%
2	Texas	6,516,887,000	8.1%
33	Utah	584,833,000	0.7%
38	Vermont	196,761,000	0.2%
31	Virginia	709,328,000	0.9%
6	Washington	3,292,941,000	4.1%
45	West Virginia	74,957,000	0.1%
9	Wisconsin	2,547,480,000	3.1%
36	Wyoming	354,561,000	0.4%

RANK ORDER

RANK	STATE	FARM INCOME	% of USA
1	California	$14,606,384,000	18.1%
2	Texas	6,516,887,000	8.1%
3	Iowa	5,581,067,000	6.9%
4	Nebraska	4,884,316,000	6.0%
5	Minnesota	3,426,024,000	4.2%
6	Washington	3,292,941,000	4.1%
7	Florida	3,014,374,000	3.7%
8	North Carolina	2,924,077,000	3.6%
9	Wisconsin	2,547,480,000	3.1%
10	Georgia	2,530,844,000	3.1%
11	Oklahoma	2,167,978,000	2.7%
12	South Dakota	2,068,238,000	2.6%
13	Pennsylvania	1,893,287,000	2.3%
14	Idaho	1,870,307,000	2.3%
15	Kansas	1,759,502,000	2.2%
16	Kentucky	1,664,352,000	2.1%
17	Alabama	1,602,359,000	2.0%
18	Colorado	1,499,780,000	1.9%
19	Missouri	1,355,941,000	1.7%
20	Arkansas	1,299,147,000	1.6%
21	Indiana	1,254,834,000	1.6%
22	Oregon	1,214,148,000	1.5%
23	Ohio	1,166,888,000	1.4%
24	Arizona	1,107,328,000	1.4%
25	New York	1,004,958,000	1.2%
26	Montana	960,916,000	1.2%
27	Mississippi	846,931,000	1.0%
28	New Mexico	788,947,000	1.0%
29	Michigan	766,510,000	0.9%
30	Tennessee	730,021,000	0.9%
31	Virginia	709,328,000	0.9%
32	Louisiana	594,063,000	0.7%
33	Utah	584,833,000	0.7%
34	Maryland	506,677,000	0.6%
35	Delaware	406,804,000	0.5%
36	Wyoming	354,561,000	0.4%
37	New Jersey	267,425,000	0.3%
38	Vermont	196,761,000	0.2%
39	North Dakota	188,364,000	0.2%
40	Maine	159,865,000	0.2%
41	Hawaii	156,759,000	0.2%
42	Nevada	126,338,000	0.2%
43	South Carolina	105,076,000	0.1%
44	Connecticut	99,770,000	0.1%
45	West Virginia	74,957,000	0.1%
46	New Hampshire	63,126,000	0.1%
47	Rhode Island	27,532,000	0.0%
48	Massachusetts	2,631,000	0.0%
NA	Alaska**	(6,272,000)	0.0%
NA	Illinois**	(86,814,000)	-0.1%
	District of Columbia	0	0.0%

Source: U.S. Department of Agriculture, Economic Research Service
  "Farm Sector Financial Indicators, State Rankings"
   (http://www.ers.usda.gov/data-products/farm-income-and-wealth-statistics.aspx)
*Net farm income is a measure of the net value of production in a given year. It is determined by subtracting total production expenses from gross farm income.

Net Farm Income per Operation in 2015

National Average = $39,249 per Operation*

<table>
<tr><th colspan="3">ALPHA ORDER</th><th colspan="3">RANK ORDER</th></tr>
<tr><th>RANK</th><th>STATE</th><th>PER OPERATION</th><th>RANK</th><th>STATE</th><th>PER OPERATION</th></tr>
<tr><td>15</td><td>Alabama</td><td>$37,492</td><td>1</td><td>California</td><td>$188,517</td></tr>
<tr><td>50</td><td>Alaska</td><td>(8,856)</td><td>2</td><td>Delaware</td><td>162,800</td></tr>
<tr><td>11</td><td>Arizona</td><td>57,319</td><td>3</td><td>Nebraska</td><td>100,224</td></tr>
<tr><td>24</td><td>Arkansas</td><td>29,798</td><td>4</td><td>Washington</td><td>91,392</td></tr>
<tr><td>1</td><td>California</td><td>188,517</td><td>5</td><td>Idaho</td><td>76,956</td></tr>
<tr><td>13</td><td>Colorado</td><td>43,569</td><td>6</td><td>South Dakota</td><td>66,384</td></tr>
<tr><td>38</td><td>Connecticut</td><td>16,571</td><td>7</td><td>Iowa</td><td>63,867</td></tr>
<tr><td>2</td><td>Delaware</td><td>162,800</td><td>8</td><td>Florida</td><td>63,800</td></tr>
<tr><td>8</td><td>Florida</td><td>63,800</td><td>9</td><td>Georgia</td><td>62,560</td></tr>
<tr><td>9</td><td>Georgia</td><td>62,560</td><td>10</td><td>North Carolina</td><td>59,840</td></tr>
<tr><td>32</td><td>Hawaii</td><td>22,400</td><td>11</td><td>Arizona</td><td>57,319</td></tr>
<tr><td>5</td><td>Idaho</td><td>76,956</td><td>12</td><td>Minnesota</td><td>46,464</td></tr>
<tr><td>49</td><td>Illinois</td><td>(1,095)</td><td>13</td><td>Colorado</td><td>43,569</td></tr>
<tr><td>36</td><td>Indiana</td><td>21,675</td><td>14</td><td>Maryland</td><td>41,666</td></tr>
<tr><td>7</td><td>Iowa</td><td>63,867</td><td>15</td><td>Alabama</td><td>37,492</td></tr>
<tr><td>26</td><td>Kansas</td><td>28,956</td><td>16</td><td>Wisconsin</td><td>36,993</td></tr>
<tr><td>35</td><td>Kentucky</td><td>21,760</td><td>17</td><td>Oregon</td><td>35,076</td></tr>
<tr><td>33</td><td>Louisiana</td><td>22,176</td><td>18</td><td>Montana</td><td>34,736</td></tr>
<tr><td>37</td><td>Maine</td><td>19,470</td><td>19</td><td>Pennsylvania</td><td>32,718</td></tr>
<tr><td>14</td><td>Maryland</td><td>41,666</td><td>20</td><td>Utah</td><td>32,224</td></tr>
<tr><td>48</td><td>Massachusetts</td><td>335</td><td>21</td><td>New Mexico</td><td>31,482</td></tr>
<tr><td>41</td><td>Michigan</td><td>14,861</td><td>22</td><td>Wyoming</td><td>31,452</td></tr>
<tr><td>12</td><td>Minnesota</td><td>46,464</td><td>23</td><td>Nevada</td><td>29,799</td></tr>
<tr><td>31</td><td>Mississippi</td><td>22,932</td><td>24</td><td>Arkansas</td><td>29,798</td></tr>
<tr><td>43</td><td>Missouri</td><td>13,968</td><td>25</td><td>New Jersey</td><td>29,309</td></tr>
<tr><td>18</td><td>Montana</td><td>34,736</td><td>26</td><td>Kansas</td><td>28,956</td></tr>
<tr><td>3</td><td>Nebraska</td><td>100,224</td><td>27</td><td>New York</td><td>28,420</td></tr>
<tr><td>23</td><td>Nevada</td><td>29,799</td><td>28</td><td>Oklahoma</td><td>27,594</td></tr>
<tr><td>42</td><td>New Hampshire</td><td>14,338</td><td>29</td><td>Texas</td><td>26,850</td></tr>
<tr><td>25</td><td>New Jersey</td><td>29,309</td><td>30</td><td>Vermont</td><td>26,847</td></tr>
<tr><td>21</td><td>New Mexico</td><td>31,482</td><td>31</td><td>Mississippi</td><td>22,932</td></tr>
<tr><td>27</td><td>New York</td><td>28,420</td><td>32</td><td>Hawaii</td><td>22,400</td></tr>
<tr><td>10</td><td>North Carolina</td><td>59,840</td><td>33</td><td>Louisiana</td><td>22,176</td></tr>
<tr><td>45</td><td>North Dakota</td><td>6,535</td><td>34</td><td>Rhode Island</td><td>22,008</td></tr>
<tr><td>40</td><td>Ohio</td><td>15,604</td><td>35</td><td>Kentucky</td><td>21,760</td></tr>
<tr><td>28</td><td>Oklahoma</td><td>27,594</td><td>36</td><td>Indiana</td><td>21,675</td></tr>
<tr><td>17</td><td>Oregon</td><td>35,076</td><td>37</td><td>Maine</td><td>19,470</td></tr>
<tr><td>19</td><td>Pennsylvania</td><td>32,718</td><td>38</td><td>Connecticut</td><td>16,571</td></tr>
<tr><td>34</td><td>Rhode Island</td><td>22,008</td><td>39</td><td>Virginia</td><td>15,928</td></tr>
<tr><td>46</td><td>South Carolina</td><td>4,305</td><td>40</td><td>Ohio</td><td>15,604</td></tr>
<tr><td>6</td><td>South Dakota</td><td>66,384</td><td>41</td><td>Michigan</td><td>14,861</td></tr>
<tr><td>44</td><td>Tennessee</td><td>10,854</td><td>42</td><td>New Hampshire</td><td>14,338</td></tr>
<tr><td>29</td><td>Texas</td><td>26,850</td><td>43</td><td>Missouri</td><td>13,968</td></tr>
<tr><td>20</td><td>Utah</td><td>32,224</td><td>44</td><td>Tennessee</td><td>10,854</td></tr>
<tr><td>30</td><td>Vermont</td><td>26,847</td><td>45</td><td>North Dakota</td><td>6,535</td></tr>
<tr><td>39</td><td>Virginia</td><td>15,928</td><td>46</td><td>South Carolina</td><td>4,305</td></tr>
<tr><td>4</td><td>Washington</td><td>91,392</td><td>47</td><td>West Virginia</td><td>3,612</td></tr>
<tr><td>47</td><td>West Virginia</td><td>3,612</td><td>48</td><td>Massachusetts</td><td>335</td></tr>
<tr><td>16</td><td>Wisconsin</td><td>36,993</td><td>49</td><td>Illinois</td><td>(1,095)</td></tr>
<tr><td>22</td><td>Wyoming</td><td>31,452</td><td>50</td><td>Alaska</td><td>(8,856)</td></tr>
<tr><td></td><td></td><td></td><td></td><td>District of Columbia**</td><td>NA</td></tr>
</table>

Source: CQ Press using data from U.S. Department of Agriculture, Economic Research Service
"Farm Sector Financial Indicators, State Rankings"
(http://www.ers.usda.gov/data-products/farm-income-and-wealth-statistics.aspx)
*Calculated by multiplying average acres per farm by average net farm income per acre.
**Not applicable.

Net Farm Income per Acre in 2015

National Average = $89 per Acre*

<table>
<tr><td colspan="3">ALPHA ORDER</td><td colspan="3">RANK ORDER</td></tr>
<tr><td>RANK</td><td>STATE</td><td>PER ACRE</td><td>RANK</td><td>STATE</td><td>PER ACRE</td></tr>
<tr><td>13</td><td>Alabama</td><td>$182</td><td>1</td><td>Delaware</td><td>$814</td></tr>
<tr><td>50</td><td>Alaska</td><td>(8)</td><td>2</td><td>California</td><td>573</td></tr>
<tr><td>39</td><td>Arizona</td><td>43</td><td>3</td><td>Rhode Island</td><td>393</td></tr>
<tr><td>24</td><td>Arkansas</td><td>94</td><td>4</td><td>New Jersey</td><td>371</td></tr>
<tr><td>2</td><td>California</td><td>573</td><td>5</td><td>North Carolina</td><td>352</td></tr>
<tr><td>38</td><td>Colorado</td><td>47</td><td>6</td><td>Florida</td><td>319</td></tr>
<tr><td>10</td><td>Connecticut</td><td>227</td><td>7</td><td>Georgia</td><td>272</td></tr>
<tr><td>1</td><td>Delaware</td><td>814</td><td>8</td><td>Maryland</td><td>251</td></tr>
<tr><td>6</td><td>Florida</td><td>319</td><td>9</td><td>Pennsylvania</td><td>246</td></tr>
<tr><td>7</td><td>Georgia</td><td>272</td><td>10</td><td>Connecticut</td><td>227</td></tr>
<tr><td>17</td><td>Hawaii</td><td>140</td><td>11</td><td>Washington</td><td>224</td></tr>
<tr><td>15</td><td>Idaho</td><td>159</td><td>12</td><td>Iowa</td><td>183</td></tr>
<tr><td>49</td><td>Illinois</td><td>(3)</td><td>13</td><td>Alabama</td><td>182</td></tr>
<tr><td>26</td><td>Indiana</td><td>85</td><td>14</td><td>Wisconsin</td><td>177</td></tr>
<tr><td>12</td><td>Iowa</td><td>183</td><td>15</td><td>Idaho</td><td>159</td></tr>
<tr><td>40</td><td>Kansas</td><td>38</td><td>16</td><td>Vermont</td><td>157</td></tr>
<tr><td>21</td><td>Kentucky</td><td>128</td><td>17</td><td>Hawaii</td><td>140</td></tr>
<tr><td>29</td><td>Louisiana</td><td>77</td><td>17</td><td>New York</td><td>140</td></tr>
<tr><td>22</td><td>Maine</td><td>110</td><td>19</td><td>New Hampshire</td><td>134</td></tr>
<tr><td>8</td><td>Maryland</td><td>251</td><td>20</td><td>Minnesota</td><td>132</td></tr>
<tr><td>47</td><td>Massachusetts</td><td>5</td><td>21</td><td>Kentucky</td><td>128</td></tr>
<tr><td>29</td><td>Michigan</td><td>77</td><td>22</td><td>Maine</td><td>110</td></tr>
<tr><td>20</td><td>Minnesota</td><td>132</td><td>23</td><td>Nebraska</td><td>108</td></tr>
<tr><td>28</td><td>Mississippi</td><td>78</td><td>24</td><td>Arkansas</td><td>94</td></tr>
<tr><td>36</td><td>Missouri</td><td>48</td><td>25</td><td>Virginia</td><td>88</td></tr>
<tr><td>45</td><td>Montana</td><td>16</td><td>26</td><td>Indiana</td><td>85</td></tr>
<tr><td>23</td><td>Nebraska</td><td>108</td><td>27</td><td>Ohio</td><td>83</td></tr>
<tr><td>41</td><td>Nevada</td><td>21</td><td>28</td><td>Mississippi</td><td>78</td></tr>
<tr><td>19</td><td>New Hampshire</td><td>134</td><td>29</td><td>Louisiana</td><td>77</td></tr>
<tr><td>4</td><td>New Jersey</td><td>371</td><td>29</td><td>Michigan</td><td>77</td></tr>
<tr><td>44</td><td>New Mexico</td><td>18</td><td>31</td><td>Oregon</td><td>74</td></tr>
<tr><td>17</td><td>New York</td><td>140</td><td>32</td><td>Tennessee</td><td>67</td></tr>
<tr><td>5</td><td>North Carolina</td><td>352</td><td>33</td><td>Oklahoma</td><td>63</td></tr>
<tr><td>47</td><td>North Dakota</td><td>5</td><td>34</td><td>Utah</td><td>53</td></tr>
<tr><td>27</td><td>Ohio</td><td>83</td><td>35</td><td>Texas</td><td>50</td></tr>
<tr><td>33</td><td>Oklahoma</td><td>63</td><td>36</td><td>Missouri</td><td>48</td></tr>
<tr><td>31</td><td>Oregon</td><td>74</td><td>36</td><td>South Dakota</td><td>48</td></tr>
<tr><td>9</td><td>Pennsylvania</td><td>246</td><td>38</td><td>Colorado</td><td>47</td></tr>
<tr><td>3</td><td>Rhode Island</td><td>393</td><td>39</td><td>Arizona</td><td>43</td></tr>
<tr><td>41</td><td>South Carolina</td><td>21</td><td>40</td><td>Kansas</td><td>38</td></tr>
<tr><td>36</td><td>South Dakota</td><td>48</td><td>41</td><td>Nevada</td><td>21</td></tr>
<tr><td>32</td><td>Tennessee</td><td>67</td><td>41</td><td>South Carolina</td><td>21</td></tr>
<tr><td>35</td><td>Texas</td><td>50</td><td>41</td><td>West Virginia</td><td>21</td></tr>
<tr><td>34</td><td>Utah</td><td>53</td><td>44</td><td>New Mexico</td><td>18</td></tr>
<tr><td>16</td><td>Vermont</td><td>157</td><td>45</td><td>Montana</td><td>16</td></tr>
<tr><td>25</td><td>Virginia</td><td>88</td><td>46</td><td>Wyoming</td><td>12</td></tr>
<tr><td>11</td><td>Washington</td><td>224</td><td>47</td><td>Massachusetts</td><td>5</td></tr>
<tr><td>41</td><td>West Virginia</td><td>21</td><td>47</td><td>North Dakota</td><td>5</td></tr>
<tr><td>14</td><td>Wisconsin</td><td>177</td><td>49</td><td>Illinois</td><td>(3)</td></tr>
<tr><td>46</td><td>Wyoming</td><td>12</td><td>50</td><td>Alaska</td><td>(8)</td></tr>
</table>

District of Columbia**   NA

Source: CQ Press using data from U.S. Department of Agriculture, Economic Research Service
   "Farm Sector Financial Indicators, State Rankings"
   (http://www.ers.usda.gov/data-products/farm-income-and-wealth-statistics.aspx)
*Net farm income is a measure of the net value of production in a given year. It is determined by subtracting total production expenses from gross farm income.
**Not applicable.

Farm Income: Cash Receipts from Commodities in 2015

National Total = $376,250,405,000*

ALPHA ORDER

RANK	STATE	FARM INCOME	% of USA
25	Alabama	$5,561,876,000	1.5%
50	Alaska	34,261,000	0.0%
29	Arizona	4,134,082,000	1.1%
16	Arkansas	8,878,935,000	2.4%
1	California	47,007,704,000	12.5%
21	Colorado	7,337,457,000	2.0%
46	Connecticut	569,345,000	0.2%
39	Delaware	1,282,440,000	0.3%
17	Florida	8,367,569,000	2.2%
15	Georgia	9,122,127,000	2.4%
45	Hawaii	697,010,000	0.2%
20	Idaho	7,390,275,000	2.0%
6	Illinois	15,827,219,000	4.2%
10	Indiana	11,042,782,000	2.9%
2	Iowa	27,674,193,000	7.4%
7	Kansas	15,554,250,000	4.1%
24	Kentucky	5,829,204,000	1.5%
33	Louisiana	3,319,881,000	0.9%
42	Maine	739,918,000	0.2%
36	Maryland	2,222,888,000	0.6%
47	Massachusetts	412,047,000	0.1%
18	Michigan	7,786,937,000	2.1%
5	Minnesota	16,348,311,000	4.3%
26	Mississippi	5,391,888,000	1.4%
12	Missouri	9,759,057,000	2.6%
30	Montana	3,756,027,000	1.0%
4	Nebraska	23,093,470,000	6.1%
44	Nevada	729,369,000	0.2%
48	New Hampshire	249,711,000	0.1%
40	New Jersey	1,043,360,000	0.3%
34	New Mexico	3,035,501,000	0.8%
27	New York	5,334,055,000	1.4%
8	North Carolina	11,666,532,000	3.1%
22	North Dakota	7,170,648,000	1.9%
13	Ohio	9,258,125,000	2.5%
23	Oklahoma	7,061,050,000	1.9%
28	Oregon	4,937,469,000	1.3%
19	Pennsylvania	7,438,890,000	2.0%
49	Rhode Island	80,782,000	0.0%
35	South Carolina	2,430,622,000	0.6%
14	South Dakota	9,185,004,000	2.4%
32	Tennessee	3,679,798,000	1.0%
3	Texas	23,609,735,000	6.3%
37	Utah	1,988,137,000	0.5%
41	Vermont	821,857,000	0.2%
31	Virginia	3,751,121,000	1.0%
11	Washington	10,049,097,000	2.7%
43	West Virginia	738,405,000	0.2%
9	Wisconsin	11,139,567,000	3.0%
38	Wyoming	1,710,416,000	0.5%

RANK ORDER

RANK	STATE	FARM INCOME	% of USA
1	California	$47,007,704,000	12.5%
2	Iowa	27,674,193,000	7.4%
3	Texas	23,609,735,000	6.3%
4	Nebraska	23,093,470,000	6.1%
5	Minnesota	16,348,311,000	4.3%
6	Illinois	15,827,219,000	4.2%
7	Kansas	15,554,250,000	4.1%
8	North Carolina	11,666,532,000	3.1%
9	Wisconsin	11,139,567,000	3.0%
10	Indiana	11,042,782,000	2.9%
11	Washington	10,049,097,000	2.7%
12	Missouri	9,759,057,000	2.6%
13	Ohio	9,258,125,000	2.5%
14	South Dakota	9,185,004,000	2.4%
15	Georgia	9,122,127,000	2.4%
16	Arkansas	8,878,935,000	2.4%
17	Florida	8,367,569,000	2.2%
18	Michigan	7,786,937,000	2.1%
19	Pennsylvania	7,438,890,000	2.0%
20	Idaho	7,390,275,000	2.0%
21	Colorado	7,337,457,000	2.0%
22	North Dakota	7,170,648,000	1.9%
23	Oklahoma	7,061,050,000	1.9%
24	Kentucky	5,829,204,000	1.5%
25	Alabama	5,561,876,000	1.5%
26	Mississippi	5,391,888,000	1.4%
27	New York	5,334,055,000	1.4%
28	Oregon	4,937,469,000	1.3%
29	Arizona	4,134,082,000	1.1%
30	Montana	3,756,027,000	1.0%
31	Virginia	3,751,121,000	1.0%
32	Tennessee	3,679,798,000	1.0%
33	Louisiana	3,319,881,000	0.9%
34	New Mexico	3,035,501,000	0.8%
35	South Carolina	2,430,622,000	0.6%
36	Maryland	2,222,888,000	0.6%
37	Utah	1,988,137,000	0.5%
38	Wyoming	1,710,416,000	0.5%
39	Delaware	1,282,440,000	0.3%
40	New Jersey	1,043,360,000	0.3%
41	Vermont	821,857,000	0.2%
42	Maine	739,918,000	0.2%
43	West Virginia	738,405,000	0.2%
44	Nevada	729,369,000	0.2%
45	Hawaii	697,010,000	0.2%
46	Connecticut	569,345,000	0.2%
47	Massachusetts	412,047,000	0.1%
48	New Hampshire	249,711,000	0.1%
49	Rhode Island	80,782,000	0.0%
50	Alaska	34,261,000	0.0%
	District of Columbia	0	0.0%

Source: U.S. Department of Agriculture, Economic Research Service
"Farm Sector Financial Indicators, State Rankings" (www.ers.usda.gov/data-products/farm-income-and-wealth-statistics.aspx)
*Commodities include crops and livestock.

Farm Income: Crops in 2015

National Total = $186,484,535,000

ALPHA ORDER					RANK ORDER			
RANK	STATE	FARM INCOME	% of USA		RANK	STATE	FARM INCOME	% of USA
33	Alabama	$1,045,833,000	0.6%		1	California	$35,053,611,000	18.8%
50	Alaska	28,272,000	0.0%		2	Illinois	13,288,516,000	7.1%
24	Arizona	2,343,364,000	1.3%		3	Iowa	12,968,883,000	7.0%
17	Arkansas	3,659,648,000	2.0%		4	Nebraska	9,142,447,000	4.9%
1	California	35,053,611,000	18.8%		5	Minnesota	8,631,871,000	4.6%
26	Colorado	2,093,110,000	1.1%		6	Washington	7,112,732,000	3.8%
41	Connecticut	374,702,000	0.2%		7	Texas	7,036,328,000	3.8%
44	Delaware	265,127,000	0.1%		8	Indiana	6,822,249,000	3.7%
9	Florida	6,103,356,000	3.3%		9	Florida	6,103,356,000	3.3%
20	Georgia	3,076,020,000	1.6%		10	North Dakota	5,820,175,000	3.1%
38	Hawaii	515,208,000	0.3%		11	Kansas	5,532,698,000	3.0%
21	Idaho	2,838,278,000	1.5%		12	South Dakota	5,310,439,000	2.8%
2	Illinois	13,288,516,000	7.1%		13	Ohio	5,157,386,000	2.8%
8	Indiana	6,822,249,000	3.7%		14	Missouri	4,729,818,000	2.5%
3	Iowa	12,968,883,000	7.0%		15	Michigan	4,354,790,000	2.3%
11	Kansas	5,532,698,000	3.0%		16	North Carolina	3,701,408,000	2.0%
23	Kentucky	2,489,828,000	1.3%		17	Arkansas	3,659,648,000	2.0%
28	Louisiana	2,046,326,000	1.1%		18	Wisconsin	3,272,535,000	1.8%
40	Maine	386,636,000	0.2%		19	Oregon	3,168,212,000	1.7%
36	Maryland	858,145,000	0.5%		20	Georgia	3,076,020,000	1.6%
43	Massachusetts	283,978,000	0.2%		21	Idaho	2,838,278,000	1.5%
15	Michigan	4,354,790,000	2.3%		22	Pennsylvania	2,518,638,000	1.4%
5	Minnesota	8,631,871,000	4.6%		23	Kentucky	2,489,828,000	1.3%
27	Mississippi	2,064,009,000	1.1%		24	Arizona	2,343,364,000	1.3%
14	Missouri	4,729,818,000	2.5%		25	Tennessee	2,113,153,000	1.1%
30	Montana	1,886,551,000	1.0%		26	Colorado	2,093,110,000	1.1%
4	Nebraska	9,142,447,000	4.9%		27	Mississippi	2,064,009,000	1.1%
45	Nevada	187,831,000	0.1%		28	Louisiana	2,046,326,000	1.1%
48	New Hampshire	109,308,000	0.1%		29	New York	1,968,434,000	1.1%
35	New Jersey	889,359,000	0.5%		30	Montana	1,886,551,000	1.0%
37	New Mexico	713,715,000	0.4%		31	Oklahoma	1,214,035,000	0.7%
29	New York	1,968,434,000	1.1%		32	Virginia	1,182,126,000	0.6%
16	North Carolina	3,701,408,000	2.0%		33	Alabama	1,045,833,000	0.6%
10	North Dakota	5,820,175,000	3.1%		34	South Carolina	957,160,000	0.5%
13	Ohio	5,157,386,000	2.8%		35	New Jersey	889,359,000	0.5%
31	Oklahoma	1,214,035,000	0.7%		36	Maryland	858,145,000	0.5%
19	Oregon	3,168,212,000	1.7%		37	New Mexico	713,715,000	0.4%
22	Pennsylvania	2,518,638,000	1.4%		38	Hawaii	515,208,000	0.3%
49	Rhode Island	50,170,000	0.0%		39	Utah	451,614,000	0.2%
34	South Carolina	957,160,000	0.5%		40	Maine	386,636,000	0.2%
12	South Dakota	5,310,439,000	2.8%		41	Connecticut	374,702,000	0.2%
25	Tennessee	2,113,153,000	1.1%		42	Wyoming	341,722,000	0.2%
7	Texas	7,036,328,000	3.8%		43	Massachusetts	283,978,000	0.2%
39	Utah	451,614,000	0.2%		44	Delaware	265,127,000	0.1%
46	Vermont	182,473,000	0.1%		45	Nevada	187,831,000	0.1%
32	Virginia	1,182,126,000	0.6%		46	Vermont	182,473,000	0.1%
6	Washington	7,112,732,000	3.8%		47	West Virginia	142,305,000	0.1%
47	West Virginia	142,305,000	0.1%		48	New Hampshire	109,308,000	0.1%
18	Wisconsin	3,272,535,000	1.8%		49	Rhode Island	50,170,000	0.0%
42	Wyoming	341,722,000	0.2%		50	Alaska	28,272,000	0.0%
						District of Columbia	0	0.0%

Source: U.S. Department of Agriculture, Economic Research Service
"Farm Sector Financial Indicators, State Rankings" (www.ers.usda.gov/data-products/farm-income-and-wealth-statistics.aspx)

Farm Income: Livestock in 2015

National Total = $189,765,870,000*

<table>
<tr><td colspan="4">ALPHA ORDER</td><td colspan="4">RANK ORDER</td></tr>
<tr><td>RANK</td><td>STATE</td><td>FARM INCOME</td><td>% of USA</td><td>RANK</td><td>STATE</td><td>FARM INCOME</td><td>% of USA</td></tr>
<tr><td>16</td><td>Alabama</td><td>$4,516,043,000</td><td>2.4%</td><td>1</td><td>Texas</td><td>$16,573,407,000</td><td>8.7%</td></tr>
<tr><td>50</td><td>Alaska</td><td>5,989,000</td><td>0.0%</td><td>2</td><td>Iowa</td><td>14,705,310,000</td><td>7.7%</td></tr>
<tr><td>30</td><td>Arizona</td><td>1,790,718,000</td><td>0.9%</td><td>3</td><td>Nebraska</td><td>13,951,023,000</td><td>7.4%</td></tr>
<tr><td>12</td><td>Arkansas</td><td>5,219,287,000</td><td>2.8%</td><td>4</td><td>California</td><td>11,954,093,000</td><td>6.3%</td></tr>
<tr><td>4</td><td>California</td><td>11,954,093,000</td><td>6.3%</td><td>5</td><td>Kansas</td><td>10,021,552,000</td><td>5.3%</td></tr>
<tr><td>11</td><td>Colorado</td><td>5,244,347,000</td><td>2.8%</td><td>6</td><td>North Carolina</td><td>7,965,124,000</td><td>4.2%</td></tr>
<tr><td>44</td><td>Connecticut</td><td>194,643,000</td><td>0.1%</td><td>7</td><td>Wisconsin</td><td>7,867,032,000</td><td>4.1%</td></tr>
<tr><td>39</td><td>Delaware</td><td>1,017,313,000</td><td>0.5%</td><td>8</td><td>Minnesota</td><td>7,716,440,000</td><td>4.1%</td></tr>
<tr><td>28</td><td>Florida</td><td>2,264,213,000</td><td>1.2%</td><td>9</td><td>Georgia</td><td>6,046,107,000</td><td>3.2%</td></tr>
<tr><td>9</td><td>Georgia</td><td>6,046,107,000</td><td>3.2%</td><td>10</td><td>Oklahoma</td><td>5,847,015,000</td><td>3.1%</td></tr>
<tr><td>45</td><td>Hawaii</td><td>181,802,000</td><td>0.1%</td><td>11</td><td>Colorado</td><td>5,244,347,000</td><td>2.8%</td></tr>
<tr><td>15</td><td>Idaho</td><td>4,551,997,000</td><td>2.4%</td><td>12</td><td>Arkansas</td><td>5,219,287,000</td><td>2.8%</td></tr>
<tr><td>26</td><td>Illinois</td><td>2,538,703,000</td><td>1.3%</td><td>13</td><td>Missouri</td><td>5,029,239,000</td><td>2.7%</td></tr>
<tr><td>17</td><td>Indiana</td><td>4,220,533,000</td><td>2.2%</td><td>14</td><td>Pennsylvania</td><td>4,920,252,000</td><td>2.6%</td></tr>
<tr><td>2</td><td>Iowa</td><td>14,705,310,000</td><td>7.7%</td><td>15</td><td>Idaho</td><td>4,551,997,000</td><td>2.4%</td></tr>
<tr><td>5</td><td>Kansas</td><td>10,021,552,000</td><td>5.3%</td><td>16</td><td>Alabama</td><td>4,516,043,000</td><td>2.4%</td></tr>
<tr><td>22</td><td>Kentucky</td><td>3,339,376,000</td><td>1.8%</td><td>17</td><td>Indiana</td><td>4,220,533,000</td><td>2.2%</td></tr>
<tr><td>38</td><td>Louisiana</td><td>1,273,555,000</td><td>0.7%</td><td>18</td><td>Ohio</td><td>4,100,739,000</td><td>2.2%</td></tr>
<tr><td>43</td><td>Maine</td><td>353,282,000</td><td>0.2%</td><td>19</td><td>South Dakota</td><td>3,874,565,000</td><td>2.0%</td></tr>
<tr><td>36</td><td>Maryland</td><td>1,364,743,000</td><td>0.7%</td><td>20</td><td>Michigan</td><td>3,432,147,000</td><td>1.8%</td></tr>
<tr><td>48</td><td>Massachusetts</td><td>128,069,000</td><td>0.1%</td><td>21</td><td>New York</td><td>3,365,621,000</td><td>1.8%</td></tr>
<tr><td>20</td><td>Michigan</td><td>3,432,147,000</td><td>1.8%</td><td>22</td><td>Kentucky</td><td>3,339,376,000</td><td>1.8%</td></tr>
<tr><td>8</td><td>Minnesota</td><td>7,716,440,000</td><td>4.1%</td><td>23</td><td>Mississippi</td><td>3,327,879,000</td><td>1.8%</td></tr>
<tr><td>23</td><td>Mississippi</td><td>3,327,879,000</td><td>1.8%</td><td>24</td><td>Washington</td><td>2,936,365,000</td><td>1.5%</td></tr>
<tr><td>13</td><td>Missouri</td><td>5,029,239,000</td><td>2.7%</td><td>25</td><td>Virginia</td><td>2,568,995,000</td><td>1.4%</td></tr>
<tr><td>29</td><td>Montana</td><td>1,869,476,000</td><td>1.0%</td><td>26</td><td>Illinois</td><td>2,538,703,000</td><td>1.3%</td></tr>
<tr><td>3</td><td>Nebraska</td><td>13,951,023,000</td><td>7.4%</td><td>27</td><td>New Mexico</td><td>2,321,786,000</td><td>1.2%</td></tr>
<tr><td>42</td><td>Nevada</td><td>541,538,000</td><td>0.3%</td><td>28</td><td>Florida</td><td>2,264,213,000</td><td>1.2%</td></tr>
<tr><td>47</td><td>New Hampshire</td><td>140,403,000</td><td>0.1%</td><td>29</td><td>Montana</td><td>1,869,476,000</td><td>1.0%</td></tr>
<tr><td>46</td><td>New Jersey</td><td>154,001,000</td><td>0.1%</td><td>30</td><td>Arizona</td><td>1,790,718,000</td><td>0.9%</td></tr>
<tr><td>27</td><td>New Mexico</td><td>2,321,786,000</td><td>1.2%</td><td>31</td><td>Oregon</td><td>1,769,257,000</td><td>0.9%</td></tr>
<tr><td>21</td><td>New York</td><td>3,365,621,000</td><td>1.8%</td><td>32</td><td>Tennessee</td><td>1,566,645,000</td><td>0.8%</td></tr>
<tr><td>6</td><td>North Carolina</td><td>7,965,124,000</td><td>4.2%</td><td>33</td><td>Utah</td><td>1,536,523,000</td><td>0.8%</td></tr>
<tr><td>37</td><td>North Dakota</td><td>1,350,473,000</td><td>0.7%</td><td>34</td><td>South Carolina</td><td>1,473,462,000</td><td>0.8%</td></tr>
<tr><td>18</td><td>Ohio</td><td>4,100,739,000</td><td>2.2%</td><td>35</td><td>Wyoming</td><td>1,368,694,000</td><td>0.7%</td></tr>
<tr><td>10</td><td>Oklahoma</td><td>5,847,015,000</td><td>3.1%</td><td>36</td><td>Maryland</td><td>1,364,743,000</td><td>0.7%</td></tr>
<tr><td>31</td><td>Oregon</td><td>1,769,257,000</td><td>0.9%</td><td>37</td><td>North Dakota</td><td>1,350,473,000</td><td>0.7%</td></tr>
<tr><td>14</td><td>Pennsylvania</td><td>4,920,252,000</td><td>2.6%</td><td>38</td><td>Louisiana</td><td>1,273,555,000</td><td>0.7%</td></tr>
<tr><td>49</td><td>Rhode Island</td><td>30,612,000</td><td>0.0%</td><td>39</td><td>Delaware</td><td>1,017,313,000</td><td>0.5%</td></tr>
<tr><td>34</td><td>South Carolina</td><td>1,473,462,000</td><td>0.8%</td><td>40</td><td>Vermont</td><td>639,384,000</td><td>0.3%</td></tr>
<tr><td>19</td><td>South Dakota</td><td>3,874,565,000</td><td>2.0%</td><td>41</td><td>West Virginia</td><td>596,100,000</td><td>0.3%</td></tr>
<tr><td>32</td><td>Tennessee</td><td>1,566,645,000</td><td>0.8%</td><td>42</td><td>Nevada</td><td>541,538,000</td><td>0.3%</td></tr>
<tr><td>1</td><td>Texas</td><td>16,573,407,000</td><td>8.7%</td><td>43</td><td>Maine</td><td>353,282,000</td><td>0.2%</td></tr>
<tr><td>33</td><td>Utah</td><td>1,536,523,000</td><td>0.8%</td><td>44</td><td>Connecticut</td><td>194,643,000</td><td>0.1%</td></tr>
<tr><td>40</td><td>Vermont</td><td>639,384,000</td><td>0.3%</td><td>45</td><td>Hawaii</td><td>181,802,000</td><td>0.1%</td></tr>
<tr><td>25</td><td>Virginia</td><td>2,568,995,000</td><td>1.4%</td><td>46</td><td>New Jersey</td><td>154,001,000</td><td>0.1%</td></tr>
<tr><td>24</td><td>Washington</td><td>2,936,365,000</td><td>1.5%</td><td>47</td><td>New Hampshire</td><td>140,403,000</td><td>0.1%</td></tr>
<tr><td>41</td><td>West Virginia</td><td>596,100,000</td><td>0.3%</td><td>48</td><td>Massachusetts</td><td>128,069,000</td><td>0.1%</td></tr>
<tr><td>7</td><td>Wisconsin</td><td>7,867,032,000</td><td>4.1%</td><td>49</td><td>Rhode Island</td><td>30,612,000</td><td>0.0%</td></tr>
<tr><td>35</td><td>Wyoming</td><td>1,368,694,000</td><td>0.7%</td><td>50</td><td>Alaska</td><td>5,989,000</td><td>0.0%</td></tr>
<tr><td></td><td></td><td></td><td></td><td></td><td>District of Columbia</td><td>0</td><td>0.0%</td></tr>
</table>

Source: U.S. Department of Agriculture, Economic Research Service
   "Farm Sector Financial Indicators, State Rankings" (www.ers.usda.gov/data-products/farm-income-and-wealth-statistics.aspx)
*Includes livestock products.

Farm Income: Government Payments in 2015

National Total = $10,804,486,000*

ALPHA ORDER

RANK	STATE	FARM INCOME	% of USA
25	Alabama	$96,556,000	0.9%
43	Alaska	11,301,000	0.1%
37	Arizona	43,516,000	0.4%
9	Arkansas	379,345,000	3.5%
14	California	235,434,000	2.2%
16	Colorado	218,644,000	2.0%
48	Connecticut	5,204,000	0.0%
46	Delaware	8,440,000	0.1%
30	Florida	68,912,000	0.6%
13	Georgia	305,483,000	2.8%
40	Hawaii	24,841,000	0.2%
27	Idaho	86,249,000	0.8%
8	Illinois	417,077,000	3.9%
15	Indiana	220,742,000	2.0%
1	Iowa	1,408,333,000	13.0%
6	Kansas	531,766,000	4.9%
24	Kentucky	127,707,000	1.2%
20	Louisiana	175,667,000	1.6%
42	Maine	12,369,000	0.1%
39	Maryland	26,786,000	0.2%
49	Massachusetts	4,306,000	0.0%
19	Michigan	187,155,000	1.7%
2	Minnesota	976,584,000	9.0%
21	Mississippi	174,356,000	1.6%
17	Missouri	209,237,000	1.9%
23	Montana	131,273,000	1.2%
4	Nebraska	795,198,000	7.4%
38	Nevada	36,609,000	0.3%
47	New Hampshire	7,001,000	0.1%
45	New Jersey	8,498,000	0.1%
28	New Mexico	80,312,000	0.7%
29	New York	70,421,000	0.7%
26	North Carolina	91,137,000	0.8%
10	North Dakota	363,039,000	3.4%
11	Ohio	305,915,000	2.8%
5	Oklahoma	534,310,000	4.9%
22	Oregon	144,569,000	1.3%
32	Pennsylvania	63,709,000	0.6%
50	Rhode Island	4,013,000	0.0%
33	South Carolina	63,037,000	0.6%
7	South Dakota	425,790,000	3.9%
31	Tennessee	63,799,000	0.6%
3	Texas	944,830,000	8.7%
36	Utah	51,978,000	0.5%
44	Vermont	10,272,000	0.1%
34	Virginia	62,031,000	0.6%
18	Washington	207,741,000	1.9%
41	West Virginia	17,390,000	0.2%
12	Wisconsin	305,627,000	2.8%
35	Wyoming	59,971,000	0.6%

RANK ORDER

RANK	STATE	FARM INCOME	% of USA
1	Iowa	$1,408,333,000	13.0%
2	Minnesota	976,584,000	9.0%
3	Texas	944,830,000	8.7%
4	Nebraska	795,198,000	7.4%
5	Oklahoma	534,310,000	4.9%
6	Kansas	531,766,000	4.9%
7	South Dakota	425,790,000	3.9%
8	Illinois	417,077,000	3.9%
9	Arkansas	379,345,000	3.5%
10	North Dakota	363,039,000	3.4%
11	Ohio	305,915,000	2.8%
12	Wisconsin	305,627,000	2.8%
13	Georgia	305,483,000	2.8%
14	California	235,434,000	2.2%
15	Indiana	220,742,000	2.0%
16	Colorado	218,644,000	2.0%
17	Missouri	209,237,000	1.9%
18	Washington	207,741,000	1.9%
19	Michigan	187,155,000	1.7%
20	Louisiana	175,667,000	1.6%
21	Mississippi	174,356,000	1.6%
22	Oregon	144,569,000	1.3%
23	Montana	131,273,000	1.2%
24	Kentucky	127,707,000	1.2%
25	Alabama	96,556,000	0.9%
26	North Carolina	91,137,000	0.8%
27	Idaho	86,249,000	0.8%
28	New Mexico	80,312,000	0.7%
29	New York	70,421,000	0.7%
30	Florida	68,912,000	0.6%
31	Tennessee	63,799,000	0.6%
32	Pennsylvania	63,709,000	0.6%
33	South Carolina	63,037,000	0.6%
34	Virginia	62,031,000	0.6%
35	Wyoming	59,971,000	0.6%
36	Utah	51,978,000	0.5%
37	Arizona	43,516,000	0.4%
38	Nevada	36,609,000	0.3%
39	Maryland	26,786,000	0.2%
40	Hawaii	24,841,000	0.2%
41	West Virginia	17,390,000	0.2%
42	Maine	12,369,000	0.1%
43	Alaska	11,301,000	0.1%
44	Vermont	10,272,000	0.1%
45	New Jersey	8,498,000	0.1%
46	Delaware	8,440,000	0.1%
47	New Hampshire	7,001,000	0.1%
48	Connecticut	5,204,000	0.0%
49	Massachusetts	4,306,000	0.0%
50	Rhode Island	4,013,000	0.0%
	District of Columbia	0	0.0%

Source: U.S. Department of Agriculture, Economic Research Service
"Farm Sector Financial Indicators, State Rankings" (www.ers.usda.gov/data-products/farm-income-and-wealth-statistics.aspx)
*Government payments made directly to farmers in cash.

Acres Planted in 2016

National Total = 319,257,000 Acres*

ALPHA ORDER

RANK	STATE	ACRES	% of USA
30	Alabama	2,360,000	0.7%
NA	Alaska**	NA	NA
38	Arizona	672,000	0.2%
15	Arkansas	7,297,000	2.3%
27	California	3,208,000	1.0%
17	Colorado	6,170,000	1.9%
46	Connecticut	70,000	0.0%
40	Delaware	457,000	0.1%
35	Florida	1,148,000	0.4%
25	Georgia	3,629,000	1.1%
48	Hawaii	15,000	0.0%
22	Idaho	4,163,000	1.3%
4	Illinois	22,770,000	7.1%
10	Indiana	12,080,000	3.8%
1	Iowa	24,455,000	7.7%
3	Kansas	23,594,000	7.4%
18	Kentucky	6,125,000	1.9%
26	Louisiana	3,315,000	1.0%
44	Maine	243,000	0.1%
32	Maryland	1,605,000	0.5%
45	Massachusetts	108,000	0.0%
16	Michigan	6,423,000	2.0%
6	Minnesota	19,887,000	6.2%
21	Mississippi	4,177,000	1.3%
9	Missouri	13,404,000	4.2%
13	Montana	9,217,000	2.9%
7	Nebraska	19,544,000	6.1%
41	Nevada	356,000	0.1%
47	New Hampshire	68,000	0.0%
42	New Jersey	319,000	0.1%
37	New Mexico	908,000	0.3%
28	New York	3,015,000	0.9%
20	North Carolina	4,438,000	1.4%
2	North Dakota	23,686,000	7.4%
12	Ohio	10,000,000	3.1%
11	Oklahoma	10,018,000	3.1%
31	Oregon	2,149,000	0.7%
24	Pennsylvania	3,668,000	1.1%
49	Rhode Island	9,000	0.0%
33	South Carolina	1,505,000	0.5%
8	South Dakota	17,341,000	5.4%
19	Tennessee	5,030,000	1.6%
5	Texas	21,564,000	6.8%
36	Utah	938,000	0.3%
43	Vermont	280,000	0.1%
29	Virginia	2,680,000	0.8%
23	Washington	3,718,000	1.2%
39	West Virginia	670,000	0.2%
14	Wisconsin	7,885,000	2.5%
34	Wyoming	1,441,000	0.5%

RANK ORDER

RANK	STATE	ACRES	% of USA
1	Iowa	24,455,000	7.7%
2	North Dakota	23,686,000	7.4%
3	Kansas	23,594,000	7.4%
4	Illinois	22,770,000	7.1%
5	Texas	21,564,000	6.8%
6	Minnesota	19,887,000	6.2%
7	Nebraska	19,544,000	6.1%
8	South Dakota	17,341,000	5.4%
9	Missouri	13,404,000	4.2%
10	Indiana	12,080,000	3.8%
11	Oklahoma	10,018,000	3.1%
12	Ohio	10,000,000	3.1%
13	Montana	9,217,000	2.9%
14	Wisconsin	7,885,000	2.5%
15	Arkansas	7,297,000	2.3%
16	Michigan	6,423,000	2.0%
17	Colorado	6,170,000	1.9%
18	Kentucky	6,125,000	1.9%
19	Tennessee	5,030,000	1.6%
20	North Carolina	4,438,000	1.4%
21	Mississippi	4,177,000	1.3%
22	Idaho	4,163,000	1.3%
23	Washington	3,718,000	1.2%
24	Pennsylvania	3,668,000	1.1%
25	Georgia	3,629,000	1.1%
26	Louisiana	3,315,000	1.0%
27	California	3,208,000	1.0%
28	New York	3,015,000	0.9%
29	Virginia	2,680,000	0.8%
30	Alabama	2,360,000	0.7%
31	Oregon	2,149,000	0.7%
32	Maryland	1,605,000	0.5%
33	South Carolina	1,505,000	0.5%
34	Wyoming	1,441,000	0.5%
35	Florida	1,148,000	0.4%
36	Utah	938,000	0.3%
37	New Mexico	908,000	0.3%
38	Arizona	672,000	0.2%
39	West Virginia	670,000	0.2%
40	Delaware	457,000	0.1%
41	Nevada	356,000	0.1%
42	New Jersey	319,000	0.1%
43	Vermont	280,000	0.1%
44	Maine	243,000	0.1%
45	Massachusetts	108,000	0.0%
46	Connecticut	70,000	0.0%
47	New Hampshire	68,000	0.0%
48	Hawaii	15,000	0.0%
49	Rhode Island	9,000	0.0%
NA	Alaska**	NA	NA
	District of Columbia**	NA	NA

Source: U.S. Department of Agriculture, National Agricultural Statistics Service
   "Crop Production: 2016 Summary" (January 2017)
      (http://usda.mannlib.cornell.edu/MannUsda/viewDocumentInfo.do?documentID=1047)
*Estimated totals.
**No acreage or not available.

Acres Harvested in 2016

National Total = 306,161,000 Acres*

<table>
<tr><td colspan="4">ALPHA ORDER</td><td colspan="4">RANK ORDER</td></tr>
<tr><th>RANK</th><th>STATE</th><th>ACRES</th><th>% of USA</th><th>RANK</th><th>STATE</th><th>ACRES</th><th>% of USA</th></tr>
<tr><td>30</td><td>Alabama</td><td>2,248,000</td><td>0.7%</td><td>1</td><td>Iowa</td><td>24,250,000</td><td>7.9%</td></tr>
<tr><td>NA</td><td>Alaska**</td><td>NA</td><td>NA</td><td>2</td><td>Kansas</td><td>23,071,000</td><td>7.5%</td></tr>
<tr><td>39</td><td>Arizona</td><td>658,000</td><td>0.2%</td><td>3</td><td>North Dakota</td><td>23,022,000</td><td>7.5%</td></tr>
<tr><td>15</td><td>Arkansas</td><td>7,138,000</td><td>2.3%</td><td>4</td><td>Illinois</td><td>22,574,000</td><td>7.4%</td></tr>
<tr><td>28</td><td>California</td><td>2,806,000</td><td>0.9%</td><td>5</td><td>Minnesota</td><td>19,585,000</td><td>6.4%</td></tr>
<tr><td>18</td><td>Colorado</td><td>5,881,000</td><td>1.9%</td><td>6</td><td>Nebraska</td><td>19,223,000</td><td>6.3%</td></tr>
<tr><td>47</td><td>Connecticut</td><td>66,000</td><td>0.0%</td><td>7</td><td>Texas</td><td>18,204,000</td><td>5.9%</td></tr>
<tr><td>40</td><td>Delaware</td><td>439,000</td><td>0.1%</td><td>8</td><td>South Dakota</td><td>16,887,000</td><td>5.5%</td></tr>
<tr><td>35</td><td>Florida</td><td>1,121,000</td><td>0.4%</td><td>9</td><td>Missouri</td><td>13,107,000</td><td>4.3%</td></tr>
<tr><td>25</td><td>Georgia</td><td>3,286,000</td><td>1.1%</td><td>10</td><td>Indiana</td><td>11,990,000</td><td>3.9%</td></tr>
<tr><td>48</td><td>Hawaii</td><td>15,000</td><td>0.0%</td><td>11</td><td>Ohio</td><td>9,905,000</td><td>3.2%</td></tr>
<tr><td>22</td><td>Idaho</td><td>4,027,000</td><td>1.3%</td><td>12</td><td>Montana</td><td>8,809,000</td><td>2.9%</td></tr>
<tr><td>4</td><td>Illinois</td><td>22,574,000</td><td>7.4%</td><td>13</td><td>Oklahoma</td><td>8,196,000</td><td>2.7%</td></tr>
<tr><td>10</td><td>Indiana</td><td>11,990,000</td><td>3.9%</td><td>14</td><td>Wisconsin</td><td>7,705,000</td><td>2.5%</td></tr>
<tr><td>1</td><td>Iowa</td><td>24,250,000</td><td>7.9%</td><td>15</td><td>Arkansas</td><td>7,138,000</td><td>2.3%</td></tr>
<tr><td>2</td><td>Kansas</td><td>23,071,000</td><td>7.5%</td><td>16</td><td>Michigan</td><td>6,313,000</td><td>2.1%</td></tr>
<tr><td>17</td><td>Kentucky</td><td>5,985,000</td><td>2.0%</td><td>17</td><td>Kentucky</td><td>5,985,000</td><td>2.0%</td></tr>
<tr><td>26</td><td>Louisiana</td><td>3,184,000</td><td>1.0%</td><td>18</td><td>Colorado</td><td>5,881,000</td><td>1.9%</td></tr>
<tr><td>44</td><td>Maine</td><td>239,000</td><td>0.1%</td><td>19</td><td>Tennessee</td><td>4,920,000</td><td>1.6%</td></tr>
<tr><td>32</td><td>Maryland</td><td>1,474,000</td><td>0.5%</td><td>20</td><td>North Carolina</td><td>4,271,000</td><td>1.4%</td></tr>
<tr><td>45</td><td>Massachusetts</td><td>106,000</td><td>0.0%</td><td>21</td><td>Mississippi</td><td>4,114,000</td><td>1.3%</td></tr>
<tr><td>16</td><td>Michigan</td><td>6,313,000</td><td>2.1%</td><td>22</td><td>Idaho</td><td>4,027,000</td><td>1.3%</td></tr>
<tr><td>5</td><td>Minnesota</td><td>19,585,000</td><td>6.4%</td><td>23</td><td>Washington</td><td>3,645,000</td><td>1.2%</td></tr>
<tr><td>21</td><td>Mississippi</td><td>4,114,000</td><td>1.3%</td><td>24</td><td>Pennsylvania</td><td>3,561,000</td><td>1.2%</td></tr>
<tr><td>9</td><td>Missouri</td><td>13,107,000</td><td>4.3%</td><td>25</td><td>Georgia</td><td>3,286,000</td><td>1.1%</td></tr>
<tr><td>12</td><td>Montana</td><td>8,809,000</td><td>2.9%</td><td>26</td><td>Louisiana</td><td>3,184,000</td><td>1.0%</td></tr>
<tr><td>6</td><td>Nebraska</td><td>19,223,000</td><td>6.3%</td><td>27</td><td>New York</td><td>2,950,000</td><td>1.0%</td></tr>
<tr><td>41</td><td>Nevada</td><td>346,000</td><td>0.1%</td><td>28</td><td>California</td><td>2,806,000</td><td>0.9%</td></tr>
<tr><td>46</td><td>New Hampshire</td><td>67,000</td><td>0.0%</td><td>29</td><td>Virginia</td><td>2,593,000</td><td>0.8%</td></tr>
<tr><td>42</td><td>New Jersey</td><td>309,000</td><td>0.1%</td><td>30</td><td>Alabama</td><td>2,248,000</td><td>0.7%</td></tr>
<tr><td>37</td><td>New Mexico</td><td>756,000</td><td>0.2%</td><td>31</td><td>Oregon</td><td>2,101,000</td><td>0.7%</td></tr>
<tr><td>27</td><td>New York</td><td>2,950,000</td><td>1.0%</td><td>32</td><td>Maryland</td><td>1,474,000</td><td>0.5%</td></tr>
<tr><td>20</td><td>North Carolina</td><td>4,271,000</td><td>1.4%</td><td>33</td><td>South Carolina</td><td>1,448,000</td><td>0.5%</td></tr>
<tr><td>3</td><td>North Dakota</td><td>23,022,000</td><td>7.5%</td><td>34</td><td>Wyoming</td><td>1,390,000</td><td>0.5%</td></tr>
<tr><td>11</td><td>Ohio</td><td>9,905,000</td><td>3.2%</td><td>35</td><td>Florida</td><td>1,121,000</td><td>0.4%</td></tr>
<tr><td>13</td><td>Oklahoma</td><td>8,196,000</td><td>2.7%</td><td>36</td><td>Utah</td><td>917,000</td><td>0.3%</td></tr>
<tr><td>31</td><td>Oregon</td><td>2,101,000</td><td>0.7%</td><td>37</td><td>New Mexico</td><td>756,000</td><td>0.2%</td></tr>
<tr><td>24</td><td>Pennsylvania</td><td>3,561,000</td><td>1.2%</td><td>38</td><td>West Virginia</td><td>665,000</td><td>0.2%</td></tr>
<tr><td>49</td><td>Rhode Island</td><td>9,000</td><td>0.0%</td><td>39</td><td>Arizona</td><td>658,000</td><td>0.2%</td></tr>
<tr><td>33</td><td>South Carolina</td><td>1,448,000</td><td>0.5%</td><td>40</td><td>Delaware</td><td>439,000</td><td>0.1%</td></tr>
<tr><td>8</td><td>South Dakota</td><td>16,887,000</td><td>5.5%</td><td>41</td><td>Nevada</td><td>346,000</td><td>0.1%</td></tr>
<tr><td>19</td><td>Tennessee</td><td>4,920,000</td><td>1.6%</td><td>42</td><td>New Jersey</td><td>309,000</td><td>0.1%</td></tr>
<tr><td>7</td><td>Texas</td><td>18,204,000</td><td>5.9%</td><td>43</td><td>Vermont</td><td>275,000</td><td>0.1%</td></tr>
<tr><td>36</td><td>Utah</td><td>917,000</td><td>0.3%</td><td>44</td><td>Maine</td><td>239,000</td><td>0.1%</td></tr>
<tr><td>43</td><td>Vermont</td><td>275,000</td><td>0.1%</td><td>45</td><td>Massachusetts</td><td>106,000</td><td>0.0%</td></tr>
<tr><td>29</td><td>Virginia</td><td>2,593,000</td><td>0.8%</td><td>46</td><td>New Hampshire</td><td>67,000</td><td>0.0%</td></tr>
<tr><td>23</td><td>Washington</td><td>3,645,000</td><td>1.2%</td><td>47</td><td>Connecticut</td><td>66,000</td><td>0.0%</td></tr>
<tr><td>38</td><td>West Virginia</td><td>665,000</td><td>0.2%</td><td>48</td><td>Hawaii</td><td>15,000</td><td>0.0%</td></tr>
<tr><td>14</td><td>Wisconsin</td><td>7,705,000</td><td>2.5%</td><td>49</td><td>Rhode Island</td><td>9,000</td><td>0.0%</td></tr>
<tr><td>34</td><td>Wyoming</td><td>1,390,000</td><td>0.5%</td><td>NA</td><td>Alaska**</td><td>NA</td><td>NA</td></tr>
<tr><td></td><td></td><td></td><td></td><td></td><td>District of Columbia**</td><td>NA</td><td>NA</td></tr>
</table>

Source: U.S. Department of Agriculture, National Agricultural Statistics Service
  "Crop Production: 2016 Summary" (January 2017)
    (http://usda.mannlib.cornell.edu/MannUsda/viewDocumentInfo.do?documentID=1047)
*Estimated totals.
**No acreage or not available.

Acres Harvested: Corn in 2016

National Total = 86,748,000 Acres*

ALPHA ORDER					RANK ORDER			

RANK	STATE	ACRES	% of USA		RANK	STATE	ACRES	% of USA
28	Alabama	315,000	0.4%		1	Iowa	13,500,000	15.6%
NA	Alaska**	NA	NA		2	Illinois	11,450,000	13.2%
36	Arizona	50,000	0.1%		3	Nebraska	9,550,000	11.0%
19	Arkansas	745,000	0.9%		4	Minnesota	8,000,000	9.2%
30	California	100,000	0.1%		5	Indiana	5,470,000	6.3%
15	Colorado	1,170,000	1.3%		6	South Dakota	5,130,000	5.9%
NA	Connecticut**	NA	NA		7	Kansas	4,920,000	5.7%
29	Delaware	164,000	0.2%		8	Missouri	3,500,000	4.0%
38	Florida	40,000	0.0%		9	Ohio	3,300,000	3.8%
26	Georgia	340,000	0.4%		10	North Dakota	3,270,000	3.8%
NA	Hawaii**	NA	NA		11	Wisconsin	3,220,000	3.7%
30	Idaho	100,000	0.1%		12	Texas	2,550,000	2.9%
2	Illinois	11,450,000	13.2%		13	Michigan	2,040,000	2.4%
5	Indiana	5,470,000	6.3%		14	Kentucky	1,400,000	1.6%
1	Iowa	13,500,000	15.6%		15	Colorado	1,170,000	1.3%
7	Kansas	4,920,000	5.7%		16	Pennsylvania	950,000	1.1%
14	Kentucky	1,400,000	1.6%		17	North Carolina	940,000	1.1%
22	Louisiana	550,000	0.6%		18	Tennessee	830,000	1.0%
NA	Maine**	NA	NA		19	Arkansas	745,000	0.9%
23	Maryland	400,000	0.5%		20	Mississippi	720,000	0.8%
NA	Massachusetts**	NA	NA		21	New York	570,000	0.7%
13	Michigan	2,040,000	2.4%		22	Louisiana	550,000	0.6%
4	Minnesota	8,000,000	9.2%		23	Maryland	400,000	0.5%
20	Mississippi	720,000	0.8%		24	Oklahoma	350,000	0.4%
8	Missouri	3,500,000	4.0%		24	South Carolina	350,000	0.4%
35	Montana	55,000	0.1%		26	Georgia	340,000	0.4%
3	Nebraska	9,550,000	11.0%		26	Virginia	340,000	0.4%
NA	Nevada**	NA	NA		28	Alabama	315,000	0.4%
NA	New Hampshire**	NA	NA		29	Delaware	164,000	0.2%
33	New Jersey	71,000	0.1%		30	California	100,000	0.1%
37	New Mexico	41,000	0.0%		30	Idaho	100,000	0.1%
21	New York	570,000	0.7%		32	Washington	85,000	0.1%
17	North Carolina	940,000	1.1%		33	New Jersey	71,000	0.1%
10	North Dakota	3,270,000	3.8%		34	Wyoming	69,000	0.1%
9	Ohio	3,300,000	3.8%		35	Montana	55,000	0.1%
24	Oklahoma	350,000	0.4%		36	Arizona	50,000	0.1%
39	Oregon	39,000	0.0%		37	New Mexico	41,000	0.0%
16	Pennsylvania	950,000	1.1%		38	Florida	40,000	0.0%
NA	Rhode Island**	NA	NA		39	Oregon	39,000	0.0%
24	South Carolina	350,000	0.4%		40	West Virginia	35,000	0.0%
6	South Dakota	5,130,000	5.9%		41	Utah	29,000	0.0%
18	Tennessee	830,000	1.0%		NA	Alaska**	NA	NA
12	Texas	2,550,000	2.9%		NA	Connecticut**	NA	NA
41	Utah	29,000	0.0%		NA	Hawaii**	NA	NA
NA	Vermont**	NA	NA		NA	Maine**	NA	NA
26	Virginia	340,000	0.4%		NA	Massachusetts**	NA	NA
32	Washington	85,000	0.1%		NA	Nevada**	NA	NA
40	West Virginia	35,000	0.0%		NA	New Hampshire**	NA	NA
11	Wisconsin	3,220,000	3.7%		NA	Rhode Island**	NA	NA
34	Wyoming	69,000	0.1%		NA	Vermont**	NA	NA
						District of Columbia**	NA	NA

Source: U.S. Department of Agriculture, National Agricultural Statistics Service
"Crop Production: 2016 Summary" (January 2017)
(http://usda.mannlib.cornell.edu/MannUsda/viewDocumentInfo.do?documentID=1047)
*Estimated totals. Acres harvested for grain.
**No acreage or not available.

Acres Harvested: Soybeans in 2016

National Total = 82,736,000 Acres*

ALPHA ORDER

RANK	STATE	ACRES	% of USA
23	Alabama	410,000	0.5%
NA	Alaska**	NA	NA
NA	Arizona**	NA	NA
11	Arkansas	3,100,000	3.7%
NA	California**	NA	NA
NA	Colorado**	NA	NA
NA	Connecticut**	NA	NA
27	Delaware	163,000	0.2%
30	Florida	29,000	0.0%
26	Georgia	240,000	0.3%
NA	Hawaii**	NA	NA
NA	Idaho**	NA	NA
1	Illinois	10,050,000	12.1%
5	Indiana	5,640,000	6.8%
2	Iowa	9,450,000	11.4%
10	Kansas	4,010,000	4.8%
15	Kentucky	1,780,000	2.2%
18	Louisiana	1,190,000	1.4%
NA	Maine**	NA	NA
21	Maryland	515,000	0.6%
NA	Massachusetts**	NA	NA
12	Michigan	2,060,000	2.5%
3	Minnesota	7,500,000	9.1%
13	Mississippi	2,020,000	2.4%
6	Missouri	5,540,000	6.7%
NA	Montana**	NA	NA
8	Nebraska	5,150,000	6.2%
NA	Nevada**	NA	NA
NA	New Hampshire**	NA	NA
29	New Jersey	98,000	0.1%
NA	New Mexico**	NA	NA
25	New York	320,000	0.4%
16	North Carolina	1,660,000	2.0%
4	North Dakota	6,000,000	7.3%
9	Ohio	4,840,000	5.8%
22	Oklahoma	470,000	0.6%
NA	Oregon**	NA	NA
20	Pennsylvania	575,000	0.7%
NA	Rhode Island**	NA	NA
24	South Carolina	405,000	0.5%
7	South Dakota	5,170,000	6.2%
17	Tennessee	1,630,000	2.0%
28	Texas	145,000	0.2%
NA	Utah**	NA	NA
NA	Vermont**	NA	NA
19	Virginia	600,000	0.7%
NA	Washington**	NA	NA
31	West Virginia	26,000	0.0%
14	Wisconsin	1,950,000	2.4%
NA	Wyoming**	NA	NA

RANK ORDER

RANK	STATE	ACRES	% of USA
1	Illinois	10,050,000	12.1%
2	Iowa	9,450,000	11.4%
3	Minnesota	7,500,000	9.1%
4	North Dakota	6,000,000	7.3%
5	Indiana	5,640,000	6.8%
6	Missouri	5,540,000	6.7%
7	South Dakota	5,170,000	6.2%
8	Nebraska	5,150,000	6.2%
9	Ohio	4,840,000	5.8%
10	Kansas	4,010,000	4.8%
11	Arkansas	3,100,000	3.7%
12	Michigan	2,060,000	2.5%
13	Mississippi	2,020,000	2.4%
14	Wisconsin	1,950,000	2.4%
15	Kentucky	1,780,000	2.2%
16	North Carolina	1,660,000	2.0%
17	Tennessee	1,630,000	2.0%
18	Louisiana	1,190,000	1.4%
19	Virginia	600,000	0.7%
20	Pennsylvania	575,000	0.7%
21	Maryland	515,000	0.6%
22	Oklahoma	470,000	0.6%
23	Alabama	410,000	0.5%
24	South Carolina	405,000	0.5%
25	New York	320,000	0.4%
26	Georgia	240,000	0.3%
27	Delaware	163,000	0.2%
28	Texas	145,000	0.2%
29	New Jersey	98,000	0.1%
30	Florida	29,000	0.0%
31	West Virginia	26,000	0.0%
NA	Alaska**	NA	NA
NA	Arizona**	NA	NA
NA	California**	NA	NA
NA	Colorado**	NA	NA
NA	Connecticut**	NA	NA
NA	Hawaii**	NA	NA
NA	Idaho**	NA	NA
NA	Maine**	NA	NA
NA	Massachusetts**	NA	NA
NA	Montana**	NA	NA
NA	Nevada**	NA	NA
NA	New Hampshire**	NA	NA
NA	New Mexico**	NA	NA
NA	Oregon**	NA	NA
NA	Rhode Island**	NA	NA
NA	Utah**	NA	NA
NA	Vermont**	NA	NA
NA	Washington**	NA	NA
NA	Wyoming**	NA	NA
	District of Columbia**	NA	NA

Source: U.S. Department of Agriculture, National Agricultural Statistics Service
"Crop Production: 2016 Summary" (January 2017)
(http://usda.mannlib.cornell.edu/MannUsda/viewDocumentInfo.do?documentID=1047)
*Estimated totals.
**No acreage or not available.

Acres Harvested: Wheat in 2016

National Total = 43,890,000 Acres*

ALPHA ORDER

RANK	STATE	ACRES	% of USA
26	Alabama	170,000	0.4%
NA	Alaska**	NA	NA
33	Arizona	103,000	0.2%
30	Arkansas	115,000	0.3%
23	California	217,000	0.5%
6	Colorado	2,200,000	5.0%
NA	Connecticut**	NA	NA
34	Delaware	65,000	0.1%
39	Florida	17,000	0.0%
32	Georgia	110,000	0.3%
NA	Hawaii**	NA	NA
11	Idaho	1,115,000	2.5%
16	Illinois	470,000	1.1%
20	Indiana	280,000	0.6%
39	Iowa	17,000	0.0%
1	Kansas	8,200,000	18.7%
17	Kentucky	400,000	0.9%
38	Louisiana	20,000	0.0%
NA	Maine**	NA	NA
21	Maryland	260,000	0.6%
NA	Massachusetts**	NA	NA
13	Michigan	570,000	1.3%
10	Minnesota	1,268,000	2.9%
35	Mississippi	50,000	0.1%
13	Missouri	570,000	1.3%
3	Montana	5,025,000	11.4%
9	Nebraska	1,310,000	3.0%
41	Nevada	9,000	0.0%
NA	New Hampshire**	NA	NA
37	New Jersey	21,000	0.0%
24	New Mexico	205,000	0.5%
30	New York	115,000	0.3%
18	North Carolina	355,000	0.8%
2	North Dakota	7,410,000	16.9%
15	Ohio	560,000	1.3%
4	Oklahoma	3,500,000	8.0%
12	Oregon	797,000	1.8%
27	Pennsylvania	150,000	0.3%
NA	Rhode Island**	NA	NA
35	South Carolina	50,000	0.1%
8	South Dakota	2,157,000	4.9%
19	Tennessee	335,000	0.8%
5	Texas	2,800,000	6.4%
29	Utah	120,000	0.3%
NA	Vermont**	NA	NA
25	Virginia	175,000	0.4%
6	Washington	2,200,000	5.0%
42	West Virginia	4,000	0.0%
22	Wisconsin	250,000	0.6%
28	Wyoming	125,000	0.3%

RANK ORDER

RANK	STATE	ACRES	% of USA
1	Kansas	8,200,000	18.7%
2	North Dakota	7,410,000	16.9%
3	Montana	5,025,000	11.4%
4	Oklahoma	3,500,000	8.0%
5	Texas	2,800,000	6.4%
6	Colorado	2,200,000	5.0%
6	Washington	2,200,000	5.0%
8	South Dakota	2,157,000	4.9%
9	Nebraska	1,310,000	3.0%
10	Minnesota	1,268,000	2.9%
11	Idaho	1,115,000	2.5%
12	Oregon	797,000	1.8%
13	Michigan	570,000	1.3%
13	Missouri	570,000	1.3%
15	Ohio	560,000	1.3%
16	Illinois	470,000	1.1%
17	Kentucky	400,000	0.9%
18	North Carolina	355,000	0.8%
19	Tennessee	335,000	0.8%
20	Indiana	280,000	0.6%
21	Maryland	260,000	0.6%
22	Wisconsin	250,000	0.6%
23	California	217,000	0.5%
24	New Mexico	205,000	0.5%
25	Virginia	175,000	0.4%
26	Alabama	170,000	0.4%
27	Pennsylvania	150,000	0.3%
28	Wyoming	125,000	0.3%
29	Utah	120,000	0.3%
30	Arkansas	115,000	0.3%
30	New York	115,000	0.3%
32	Georgia	110,000	0.3%
33	Arizona	103,000	0.2%
34	Delaware	65,000	0.1%
35	Mississippi	50,000	0.1%
35	South Carolina	50,000	0.1%
37	New Jersey	21,000	0.0%
38	Louisiana	20,000	0.0%
39	Florida	17,000	0.0%
39	Iowa	17,000	0.0%
41	Nevada	9,000	0.0%
42	West Virginia	4,000	0.0%
NA	Alaska**	NA	NA
NA	Connecticut**	NA	NA
NA	Hawaii**	NA	NA
NA	Maine**	NA	NA
NA	Massachusetts**	NA	NA
NA	New Hampshire**	NA	NA
NA	Rhode Island**	NA	NA
NA	Vermont**	NA	NA
	District of Columbia**	NA	NA

Source: U.S. Department of Agriculture, National Agricultural Statistics Service
   "Crop Production: 2016 Summary" (January 2017)
   (http://usda.mannlib.cornell.edu/MannUsda/viewDocumentInfo.do?documentID=1047)
*Estimated totals.
**No acreage or not available.

Cattle on Farms in 2017

National Total = 93,584,600 Cattle*

ALPHA ORDER

RANK ORDER

RANK	STATE	CATTLE	% of USA		RANK	STATE	CATTLE	% of USA
25	Alabama	1,300,000	1.4%		1	Texas	12,300,000	13.1%
49	Alaska	13,000	0.0%		2	Nebraska	6,450,000	6.9%
31	Arizona	970,000	1.0%		3	Kansas	6,400,000	6.8%
17	Arkansas	1,750,000	1.9%		4	California	5,150,000	5.5%
4	California	5,150,000	5.5%		5	Oklahoma	5,000,000	5.3%
10	Colorado	2,850,000	3.0%		6	Missouri	4,350,000	4.6%
44	Connecticut	48,000	0.1%		7	Iowa	3,850,000	4.1%
48	Delaware	16,000	0.0%		7	South Dakota	3,850,000	4.1%
18	Florida	1,700,000	1.8%		9	Wisconsin	3,550,000	3.8%
30	Georgia	1,100,000	1.2%		10	Colorado	2,850,000	3.0%
42	Hawaii	142,000	0.2%		11	Montana	2,650,000	2.8%
13	Idaho	2,350,000	2.5%		12	Minnesota	2,400,000	2.6%
27	Illinois	1,220,000	1.3%		13	Idaho	2,350,000	2.5%
32	Indiana	890,000	1.0%		14	Kentucky	2,160,000	2.3%
7	Iowa	3,850,000	4.1%		15	Tennessee	1,830,000	2.0%
3	Kansas	6,400,000	6.8%		16	North Dakota	1,810,000	1.9%
14	Kentucky	2,160,000	2.3%		17	Arkansas	1,750,000	1.9%
36	Louisiana	780,000	0.8%		18	Florida	1,700,000	1.8%
43	Maine	84,000	0.1%		19	Pennsylvania	1,620,000	1.7%
41	Maryland	186,000	0.2%		20	Virginia	1,520,000	1.6%
45	Massachusetts	38,000	0.0%		21	New York	1,490,000	1.6%
28	Michigan	1,180,000	1.3%		22	New Mexico	1,430,000	1.5%
12	Minnesota	2,400,000	2.6%		23	Wyoming	1,330,000	1.4%
32	Mississippi	890,000	1.0%		24	Oregon	1,320,000	1.4%
6	Missouri	4,350,000	4.6%		25	Alabama	1,300,000	1.4%
11	Montana	2,650,000	2.8%		25	Ohio	1,300,000	1.4%
2	Nebraska	6,450,000	6.9%		27	Illinois	1,220,000	1.3%
37	Nevada	445,000	0.5%		28	Michigan	1,180,000	1.3%
46	New Hampshire	35,000	0.0%		29	Washington	1,150,000	1.2%
47	New Jersey	28,000	0.0%		30	Georgia	1,100,000	1.2%
22	New Mexico	1,430,000	1.5%		31	Arizona	970,000	1.0%
21	New York	1,490,000	1.6%		32	Indiana	890,000	1.0%
34	North Carolina	830,000	0.9%		32	Mississippi	890,000	1.0%
16	North Dakota	1,810,000	1.9%		34	North Carolina	830,000	0.9%
25	Ohio	1,300,000	1.4%		35	Utah	820,000	0.9%
5	Oklahoma	5,000,000	5.3%		36	Louisiana	780,000	0.8%
24	Oregon	1,320,000	1.4%		37	Nevada	445,000	0.5%
19	Pennsylvania	1,620,000	1.7%		38	West Virginia	405,000	0.4%
50	Rhode Island	4,600	0.0%		39	South Carolina	340,000	0.4%
39	South Carolina	340,000	0.4%		40	Vermont	260,000	0.3%
7	South Dakota	3,850,000	4.1%		41	Maryland	186,000	0.2%
15	Tennessee	1,830,000	2.0%		42	Hawaii	142,000	0.2%
1	Texas	12,300,000	13.1%		43	Maine	84,000	0.1%
35	Utah	820,000	0.9%		44	Connecticut	48,000	0.1%
40	Vermont	260,000	0.3%		45	Massachusetts	38,000	0.0%
20	Virginia	1,520,000	1.6%		46	New Hampshire	35,000	0.0%
29	Washington	1,150,000	1.2%		47	New Jersey	28,000	0.0%
38	West Virginia	405,000	0.4%		48	Delaware	16,000	0.0%
9	Wisconsin	3,550,000	3.8%		49	Alaska	13,000	0.0%
23	Wyoming	1,330,000	1.4%		50	Rhode Island	4,600	0.0%
						District of Columbia	0	0.0%

Source: U.S. Department of Agriculture, National Agricultural Statistics Service
"Cattle" (http://usda.mannlib.cornell.edu/MannUsda/viewDocumentInfo.do?documentID=1017)
*As of January 1, 2017.

Milk Cows on Farms in 2015

National Total = 9,317,000 Milk Cows*

ALPHA ORDER

RANK	STATE	MILK COWS	% of USA
43	Alabama	8,000	0.1%
50	Alaska	300	0.0%
13	Arizona	195,000	2.1%
44	Arkansas	7,000	0.1%
1	California	1,778,000	19.1%
15	Colorado	146,000	1.6%
34	Connecticut	19,000	0.2%
47	Delaware	5,000	0.1%
18	Florida	125,000	1.3%
25	Georgia	83,000	0.9%
48	Hawaii	2,200	0.0%
4	Idaho	585,000	6.3%
22	Illinois	94,000	1.0%
14	Indiana	182,000	2.0%
12	Iowa	211,000	2.3%
16	Kansas	143,000	1.5%
26	Kentucky	61,000	0.7%
37	Louisiana	14,000	0.2%
32	Maine	30,000	0.3%
28	Maryland	49,000	0.5%
40	Massachusetts	12,000	0.1%
8	Michigan	408,000	4.4%
7	Minnesota	460,000	4.9%
41	Mississippi	11,000	0.1%
24	Missouri	88,000	0.9%
37	Montana	14,000	0.2%
27	Nebraska	57,000	0.6%
33	Nevada	29,000	0.3%
37	New Hampshire	14,000	0.2%
44	New Jersey	7,000	0.1%
9	New Mexico	323,000	3.5%
3	New York	618,000	6.6%
29	North Carolina	47,000	0.5%
35	North Dakota	16,000	0.2%
11	Ohio	267,000	2.9%
31	Oklahoma	39,000	0.4%
18	Oregon	125,000	1.3%
5	Pennsylvania	530,000	5.7%
49	Rhode Island	900	0.0%
36	South Carolina	15,000	0.2%
20	South Dakota	106,000	1.1%
30	Tennessee	45,000	0.5%
6	Texas	463,000	5.0%
21	Utah	96,000	1.0%
17	Vermont	132,000	1.4%
23	Virginia	91,000	1.0%
10	Washington	277,000	3.0%
42	West Virginia	9,000	0.1%
2	Wisconsin	1,279,000	13.7%
46	Wyoming	6,000	0.1%

RANK ORDER

RANK	STATE	MILK COWS	% of USA
1	California	1,778,000	19.1%
2	Wisconsin	1,279,000	13.7%
3	New York	618,000	6.6%
4	Idaho	585,000	6.3%
5	Pennsylvania	530,000	5.7%
6	Texas	463,000	5.0%
7	Minnesota	460,000	4.9%
8	Michigan	408,000	4.4%
9	New Mexico	323,000	3.5%
10	Washington	277,000	3.0%
11	Ohio	267,000	2.9%
12	Iowa	211,000	2.3%
13	Arizona	195,000	2.1%
14	Indiana	182,000	2.0%
15	Colorado	146,000	1.6%
16	Kansas	143,000	1.5%
17	Vermont	132,000	1.4%
18	Florida	125,000	1.3%
18	Oregon	125,000	1.3%
20	South Dakota	106,000	1.1%
21	Utah	96,000	1.0%
22	Illinois	94,000	1.0%
23	Virginia	91,000	1.0%
24	Missouri	88,000	0.9%
25	Georgia	83,000	0.9%
26	Kentucky	61,000	0.7%
27	Nebraska	57,000	0.6%
28	Maryland	49,000	0.5%
29	North Carolina	47,000	0.5%
30	Tennessee	45,000	0.5%
31	Oklahoma	39,000	0.4%
32	Maine	30,000	0.3%
33	Nevada	29,000	0.3%
34	Connecticut	19,000	0.2%
35	North Dakota	16,000	0.2%
36	South Carolina	15,000	0.2%
37	Louisiana	14,000	0.2%
37	Montana	14,000	0.2%
37	New Hampshire	14,000	0.2%
40	Massachusetts	12,000	0.1%
41	Mississippi	11,000	0.1%
42	West Virginia	9,000	0.1%
43	Alabama	8,000	0.1%
44	Arkansas	7,000	0.1%
44	New Jersey	7,000	0.1%
46	Wyoming	6,000	0.1%
47	Delaware	5,000	0.1%
48	Hawaii	2,200	0.0%
49	Rhode Island	900	0.0%
50	Alaska	300	0.0%
	District of Columbia	0	0.0%

Source: U.S. Department of Agriculture, National Agricultural Statistics Service
  "Milk Production, Disposition and Income: 2015 Summary" (April 2016)
   (http://usda.mannlib.cornell.edu/MannUsda/viewDocumentInfo.do?documentID=1105)
*Average number during year. Excludes heifers not yet fresh.

Milk Production in 2015

National Total = 208,633,000,000 Pounds of Milk*

ALPHA ORDER

RANK	STATE	POUNDS	% of USA
45	Alabama	101,000,000	0.0%
50	Alaska	3,500,000	0.0%
13	Arizona	4,773,000,000	2.3%
47	Arkansas	91,000,000	0.0%
1	California	40,898,000,000	19.6%
15	Colorado	3,750,000,000	1.8%
34	Connecticut	396,000,000	0.2%
46	Delaware	98,500,000	0.0%
18	Florida	2,582,000,000	1.2%
23	Georgia	1,797,000,000	0.9%
48	Hawaii	35,000,000	0.0%
3	Idaho	14,114,000,000	6.8%
22	Illinois	1,892,000,000	0.9%
14	Indiana	4,030,000,000	1.9%
12	Iowa	4,841,000,000	2.3%
16	Kansas	3,179,000,000	1.5%
27	Kentucky	1,074,000,000	0.5%
40	Louisiana	188,000,000	0.1%
33	Maine	594,000,000	0.3%
29	Maryland	983,000,000	0.5%
39	Massachusetts	217,000,000	0.1%
7	Michigan	10,253,000,000	4.9%
8	Minnesota	9,466,000,000	4.5%
41	Mississippi	165,000,000	0.1%
25	Missouri	1,365,000,000	0.7%
36	Montana	299,000,000	0.1%
26	Nebraska	1,307,000,000	0.6%
32	Nevada	669,000,000	0.3%
37	New Hampshire	282,000,000	0.1%
44	New Jersey	127,000,000	0.1%
9	New Mexico	7,831,000,000	3.8%
4	New York	14,100,000,000	6.8%
28	North Carolina	986,000,000	0.5%
35	North Dakota	332,000,000	0.2%
11	Ohio	5,493,000,000	2.6%
31	Oklahoma	720,000,000	0.3%
19	Oregon	2,551,000,000	1.2%
5	Pennsylvania	10,805,000,000	5.2%
49	Rhode Island	15,900,000	0.0%
38	South Carolina	261,000,000	0.1%
20	South Dakota	2,359,000,000	1.1%
30	Tennessee	742,000,000	0.4%
6	Texas	10,295,000,000	4.9%
21	Utah	2,222,000,000	1.1%
17	Vermont	2,666,000,000	1.3%
24	Virginia	1,771,000,000	0.8%
10	Washington	6,606,000,000	3.2%
42	West Virginia	141,000,000	0.1%
2	Wisconsin	29,030,000,000	13.9%
43	Wyoming	135,400,000	0.1%

RANK ORDER

RANK	STATE	POUNDS	% of USA
1	California	40,898,000,000	19.6%
2	Wisconsin	29,030,000,000	13.9%
3	Idaho	14,114,000,000	6.8%
4	New York	14,100,000,000	6.8%
5	Pennsylvania	10,805,000,000	5.2%
6	Texas	10,295,000,000	4.9%
7	Michigan	10,253,000,000	4.9%
8	Minnesota	9,466,000,000	4.5%
9	New Mexico	7,831,000,000	3.8%
10	Washington	6,606,000,000	3.2%
11	Ohio	5,493,000,000	2.6%
12	Iowa	4,841,000,000	2.3%
13	Arizona	4,773,000,000	2.3%
14	Indiana	4,030,000,000	1.9%
15	Colorado	3,750,000,000	1.8%
16	Kansas	3,179,000,000	1.5%
17	Vermont	2,666,000,000	1.3%
18	Florida	2,582,000,000	1.2%
19	Oregon	2,551,000,000	1.2%
20	South Dakota	2,359,000,000	1.1%
21	Utah	2,222,000,000	1.1%
22	Illinois	1,892,000,000	0.9%
23	Georgia	1,797,000,000	0.9%
24	Virginia	1,771,000,000	0.8%
25	Missouri	1,365,000,000	0.7%
26	Nebraska	1,307,000,000	0.6%
27	Kentucky	1,074,000,000	0.5%
28	North Carolina	986,000,000	0.5%
29	Maryland	983,000,000	0.5%
30	Tennessee	742,000,000	0.4%
31	Oklahoma	720,000,000	0.3%
32	Nevada	669,000,000	0.3%
33	Maine	594,000,000	0.3%
34	Connecticut	396,000,000	0.2%
35	North Dakota	332,000,000	0.2%
36	Montana	299,000,000	0.1%
37	New Hampshire	282,000,000	0.1%
38	South Carolina	261,000,000	0.1%
39	Massachusetts	217,000,000	0.1%
40	Louisiana	188,000,000	0.1%
41	Mississippi	165,000,000	0.1%
42	West Virginia	141,000,000	0.1%
43	Wyoming	135,400,000	0.1%
44	New Jersey	127,000,000	0.1%
45	Alabama	101,000,000	0.0%
46	Delaware	98,500,000	0.0%
47	Arkansas	91,000,000	0.0%
48	Hawaii	35,000,000	0.0%
49	Rhode Island	15,900,000	0.0%
50	Alaska	3,500,000	0.0%
	District of Columbia	0	0.0%

Source: U.S. Department of Agriculture, National Agricultural Statistics Service
"Milk Production, Disposition and Income: 2015 Summary" (April 2016)
(http://usda.mannlib.cornell.edu/MannUsda/viewDocumentInfo.do?documentID=1105)
*Excludes milk suckled by calves.

Milk Production per Milk Cow in 2015

National Average = 22,393 Pounds of Milk per Cow*

ALPHA ORDER

RANK	STATE	POUNDS
49	Alabama	12,625
50	Alaska	11,667
3	Arizona	24,477
48	Arkansas	13,000
9	California	23,002
1	Colorado	25,685
22	Connecticut	20,842
34	Delaware	19,700
24	Florida	20,656
19	Georgia	21,651
43	Hawaii	15,909
5	Idaho	24,126
31	Illinois	20,128
18	Indiana	22,143
10	Iowa	22,943
17	Kansas	22,231
40	Kentucky	17,607
47	Louisiana	13,429
33	Maine	19,800
32	Maryland	20,061
38	Massachusetts	18,083
2	Michigan	25,130
25	Minnesota	20,578
46	Mississippi	15,000
45	Missouri	15,511
20	Montana	21,357
11	Nebraska	22,930
8	Nevada	23,069
30	New Hampshire	20,143
37	New Jersey	18,143
4	New Mexico	24,245
12	New York	22,816
21	North Carolina	20,979
23	North Dakota	20,750
26	Ohio	20,573
36	Oklahoma	18,462
27	Oregon	20,408
28	Pennsylvania	20,387
39	Rhode Island	17,667
41	South Carolina	17,400
15	South Dakota	22,255
42	Tennessee	16,489
16	Texas	22,235
7	Utah	23,146
29	Vermont	20,197
35	Virginia	19,462
6	Washington	23,848
44	West Virginia	15,667
13	Wisconsin	22,697
14	Wyoming	22,567

RANK ORDER

RANK	STATE	POUNDS
1	Colorado	25,685
2	Michigan	25,130
3	Arizona	24,477
4	New Mexico	24,245
5	Idaho	24,126
6	Washington	23,848
7	Utah	23,146
8	Nevada	23,069
9	California	23,002
10	Iowa	22,943
11	Nebraska	22,930
12	New York	22,816
13	Wisconsin	22,697
14	Wyoming	22,567
15	South Dakota	22,255
16	Texas	22,235
17	Kansas	22,231
18	Indiana	22,143
19	Georgia	21,651
20	Montana	21,357
21	North Carolina	20,979
22	Connecticut	20,842
23	North Dakota	20,750
24	Florida	20,656
25	Minnesota	20,578
26	Ohio	20,573
27	Oregon	20,408
28	Pennsylvania	20,387
29	Vermont	20,197
30	New Hampshire	20,143
31	Illinois	20,128
32	Maryland	20,061
33	Maine	19,800
34	Delaware	19,700
35	Virginia	19,462
36	Oklahoma	18,462
37	New Jersey	18,143
38	Massachusetts	18,083
39	Rhode Island	17,667
40	Kentucky	17,607
41	South Carolina	17,400
42	Tennessee	16,489
43	Hawaii	15,909
44	West Virginia	15,667
45	Missouri	15,511
46	Mississippi	15,000
47	Louisiana	13,429
48	Arkansas	13,000
49	Alabama	12,625
50	Alaska	11,667

District of Columbia**   NA

Source: U.S. Department of Agriculture, National Agricultural Statistics Service
   "Milk Production, Disposition and Income: 2015 Summary" (April 2016)
   (http://usda.mannlib.cornell.edu/MannUsda/viewDocumentInfo.do?documentID=1105)
*Excludes milk suckled by calves.
**Not applicable.

Hogs and Pigs on Farms in 2016

National Total = 71,500,400 Hogs and Pigs*

ALPHA ORDER

RANK	STATE	HOGS AND PIGS	% of USA
31	Alabama	40,000	0.1%
47	Alaska	1,500	0.0%
26	Arizona	115,000	0.2%
25	Arkansas	142,000	0.2%
28	California	89,000	0.1%
16	Colorado	670,000	0.9%
43	Connecticut	3,600	0.0%
38	Delaware	7,000	0.0%
33	Florida	18,000	0.0%
29	Georgia	65,000	0.1%
36	Hawaii	10,000	0.0%
NA	Idaho**	NA	NA
4	Illinois	5,100,000	7.1%
5	Indiana	4,100,000	5.7%
1	Iowa	22,400,000	31.3%
10	Kansas	1,910,000	2.7%
18	Kentucky	430,000	0.6%
38	Louisiana	7,000	0.0%
40	Maine	4,600	0.0%
32	Maryland	21,000	0.0%
37	Massachusetts	8,000	0.0%
13	Michigan	1,110,000	1.6%
3	Minnesota	8,300,000	11.6%
17	Mississippi	530,000	0.7%
7	Missouri	3,100,000	4.3%
23	Montana	175,000	0.2%
6	Nebraska	3,400,000	4.8%
48	Nevada	1,200	0.0%
44	New Hampshire	3,200	0.0%
35	New Jersey	11,000	0.0%
45	New Mexico	1,700	0.0%
30	New York	46,000	0.1%
2	North Carolina	9,300,000	13.0%
24	North Dakota	146,000	0.2%
8	Ohio	2,700,000	3.8%
9	Oklahoma	2,150,000	3.0%
34	Oregon	13,000	0.0%
12	Pennsylvania	1,210,000	1.7%
46	Rhode Island	1,600	0.0%
22	South Carolina	200,000	0.3%
11	South Dakota	1,450,000	2.0%
21	Tennessee	225,000	0.3%
14	Texas	880,000	1.2%
15	Utah	700,000	1.0%
41	Vermont	4,000	0.0%
20	Virginia	250,000	0.3%
NA	Washington**	NA	NA
41	West Virginia	4,000	0.0%
19	Wisconsin	325,000	0.5%
27	Wyoming	92,000	0.1%

RANK ORDER

RANK	STATE	HOGS AND PIGS	% of USA
1	Iowa	22,400,000	31.3%
2	North Carolina	9,300,000	13.0%
3	Minnesota	8,300,000	11.6%
4	Illinois	5,100,000	7.1%
5	Indiana	4,100,000	5.7%
6	Nebraska	3,400,000	4.8%
7	Missouri	3,100,000	4.3%
8	Ohio	2,700,000	3.8%
9	Oklahoma	2,150,000	3.0%
10	Kansas	1,910,000	2.7%
11	South Dakota	1,450,000	2.0%
12	Pennsylvania	1,210,000	1.7%
13	Michigan	1,110,000	1.6%
14	Texas	880,000	1.2%
15	Utah	700,000	1.0%
16	Colorado	670,000	0.9%
17	Mississippi	530,000	0.7%
18	Kentucky	430,000	0.6%
19	Wisconsin	325,000	0.5%
20	Virginia	250,000	0.3%
21	Tennessee	225,000	0.3%
22	South Carolina	200,000	0.3%
23	Montana	175,000	0.2%
24	North Dakota	146,000	0.2%
25	Arkansas	142,000	0.2%
26	Arizona	115,000	0.2%
27	Wyoming	92,000	0.1%
28	California	89,000	0.1%
29	Georgia	65,000	0.1%
30	New York	46,000	0.1%
31	Alabama	40,000	0.1%
32	Maryland	21,000	0.0%
33	Florida	18,000	0.0%
34	Oregon	13,000	0.0%
35	New Jersey	11,000	0.0%
36	Hawaii	10,000	0.0%
37	Massachusetts	8,000	0.0%
38	Delaware	7,000	0.0%
38	Louisiana	7,000	0.0%
40	Maine	4,600	0.0%
41	Vermont	4,000	0.0%
41	West Virginia	4,000	0.0%
43	Connecticut	3,600	0.0%
44	New Hampshire	3,200	0.0%
45	New Mexico	1,700	0.0%
46	Rhode Island	1,600	0.0%
47	Alaska	1,500	0.0%
48	Nevada	1,200	0.0%
NA	Idaho**	NA	NA
NA	Washington**	NA	NA
	District of Columbia	0	0.0%

Source: U.S. Department of Agriculture, National Agricultural Statistics Service
   "Quarterly Hogs and Pigs" (http://usda.mannlib.cornell.edu/MannUsda/viewDocumentInfo.do?documentID=1086)
*As of December 1, 2016.
**Not available. Figures for Idaho and Washington withheld to avoid disclosing data for individual operations. The two states combined had 30,000 hogs and pigs.

Chickens in 2015

National Total = 8,686,600,000 Chickens*

ALPHA ORDER					RANK ORDER			
RANK	STATE	CHICKENS	% of USA		RANK	STATE	CHICKENS	% of USA
2	Alabama	1,082,900,000	12.5%		1	Georgia	1,339,600,000	15.4%
NA	Alaska***	NA	NA		2	Alabama	1,082,900,000	12.5%
NA	Arizona***	NA	NA		3	Arkansas	962,000,000	11.1%
3	Arkansas	962,000,000	11.1%		4	North Carolina	822,700,000	9.5%
NA	California**	NA	NA		5	Mississippi	722,500,000	8.3%
NA	Colorado***	NA	NA		6	Texas	608,700,000	7.0%
NA	Connecticut***	NA	NA		7	Kentucky	307,700,000	3.5%
11	Delaware	244,300,000	2.8%		8	Maryland	303,500,000	3.5%
18	Florida	65,100,000	0.7%		9	Missouri	294,600,000	3.4%
1	Georgia	1,339,600,000	15.4%		10	Virginia	262,800,000	3.0%
NA	Hawaii***	NA	NA		11	Delaware	244,300,000	2.8%
NA	Idaho***	NA	NA		12	South Carolina	242,600,000	2.8%
NA	Illinois**	NA	NA		13	Oklahoma	217,000,000	2.5%
NA	Indiana**	NA	NA		14	Pennsylvania	190,400,000	2.2%
NA	Iowa**	NA	NA		15	Tennessee	185,200,000	2.1%
NA	Kansas***	NA	NA		16	West Virginia	93,700,000	1.1%
7	Kentucky	307,700,000	3.5%		17	Ohio	80,400,000	0.9%
NA	Louisiana**	NA	NA		18	Florida	65,100,000	0.7%
NA	Maine***	NA	NA		19	Wisconsin	53,900,000	0.6%
8	Maryland	303,500,000	3.5%		20	Minnesota	46,400,000	0.5%
NA	Massachusetts***	NA	NA		NA	Alaska***	NA	NA
NA	Michigan**	NA	NA		NA	Arizona***	NA	NA
20	Minnesota	46,400,000	0.5%		NA	California**	NA	NA
5	Mississippi	722,500,000	8.3%		NA	Colorado***	NA	NA
9	Missouri	294,600,000	3.4%		NA	Connecticut***	NA	NA
NA	Montana***	NA	NA		NA	Hawaii***	NA	NA
NA	Nebraska**	NA	NA		NA	Idaho***	NA	NA
NA	Nevada***	NA	NA		NA	Illinois**	NA	NA
NA	New Hampshire***	NA	NA		NA	Indiana**	NA	NA
NA	New Jersey***	NA	NA		NA	Iowa**	NA	NA
NA	New Mexico***	NA	NA		NA	Kansas***	NA	NA
NA	New York**	NA	NA		NA	Louisiana**	NA	NA
4	North Carolina	822,700,000	9.5%		NA	Maine***	NA	NA
NA	North Dakota***	NA	NA		NA	Massachusetts***	NA	NA
17	Ohio	80,400,000	0.9%		NA	Michigan**	NA	NA
13	Oklahoma	217,000,000	2.5%		NA	Montana***	NA	NA
NA	Oregon**	NA	NA		NA	Nebraska**	NA	NA
14	Pennsylvania	190,400,000	2.2%		NA	Nevada***	NA	NA
NA	Rhode Island***	NA	NA		NA	New Hampshire***	NA	NA
12	South Carolina	242,600,000	2.8%		NA	New Jersey***	NA	NA
NA	South Dakota***	NA	NA		NA	New Mexico***	NA	NA
15	Tennessee	185,200,000	2.1%		NA	New York**	NA	NA
6	Texas	608,700,000	7.0%		NA	North Dakota***	NA	NA
NA	Utah***	NA	NA		NA	Oregon**	NA	NA
NA	Vermont***	NA	NA		NA	Rhode Island***	NA	NA
10	Virginia	262,800,000	3.0%		NA	South Dakota***	NA	NA
NA	Washington**	NA	NA		NA	Utah***	NA	NA
16	West Virginia	93,700,000	1.1%		NA	Vermont***	NA	NA
19	Wisconsin	53,900,000	0.6%		NA	Washington**	NA	NA
NA	Wyoming***	NA	NA		NA	Wyoming***	NA	NA
						District of Columbia***	NA	NA

Source: U.S. Department of Agriculture, National Agricultural Statistics Service
"Poultry - Production and Value: 2015 Summary" (April 2016)
(http://usda.mannlib.cornell.edu/MannUsda/viewDocumentInfo.do?documentID=1130)
*Broilers. Total includes numbers for states not shown separately but excludes states producing less than 500,000 birds. **These states produced a combined total of 560,600,000 chickens. They are combined to avoid disclosing individual operations. National total does not include chickens used for egg production. ***Produces fewer than 500,000 chickens or are not available.

Eggs Produced in 2015

National Total = 96,437,000,000 Eggs*

ALPHA ORDER

RANK	STATE	EGGS	% of USA
15	Alabama	2,185,000,000	2.2%
NA	Alaska**	NA	NA
NA	Arizona**	NA	NA
10	Arkansas	3,277,000,000	3.3%
9	California	3,306,000,000	3.3%
21	Colorado	1,325,000,000	1.3%
NA	Connecticut**	NA	NA
NA	Delaware**	NA	NA
13	Florida	2,463,000,000	2.5%
6	Georgia	4,832,000,000	4.8%
NA	Hawaii**	NA	NA
NA	Idaho**	NA	NA
20	Illinois	1,359,000,000	1.4%
3	Indiana	8,005,000,000	8.0%
1	Iowa	12,463,000,000	12.5%
NA	Kansas**	NA	NA
22	Kentucky	1,280,000,000	1.3%
30	Louisiana	561,000,000	0.6%
NA	Maine**	NA	NA
25	Maryland	772,000,000	0.8%
34	Massachusetts	47,000,000	0.0%
7	Michigan	3,846,000,000	3.9%
12	Minnesota	2,876,000,000	2.9%
18	Mississippi	1,407,000,000	1.4%
11	Missouri	3,058,000,000	3.1%
33	Montana	142,000,000	0.1%
14	Nebraska	2,291,000,000	2.3%
NA	Nevada**	NA	NA
NA	New Hampshire**	NA	NA
NA	New Jersey**	NA	NA
NA	New Mexico**	NA	NA
17	New York	1,527,000,000	1.5%
8	North Carolina	3,661,000,000	3.7%
NA	North Dakota**	NA	NA
2	Ohio	9,316,000,000	9.3%
28	Oklahoma	702,000,000	0.7%
27	Oregon	732,000,000	0.7%
4	Pennsylvania	7,751,000,000	7.8%
NA	Rhode Island**	NA	NA
24	South Carolina	1,166,000,000	1.2%
29	South Dakota	603,000,000	0.6%
31	Tennessee	347,000,000	0.3%
5	Texas	5,118,000,000	5.1%
23	Utah	1,252,000,000	1.3%
35	Vermont	36,000,000	0.0%
26	Virginia	752,000,000	0.8%
16	Washington	2,095,000,000	2.1%
32	West Virginia	274,000,000	0.3%
19	Wisconsin	1,405,000,000	1.4%
NA	Wyoming**	NA	NA

RANK ORDER

RANK	STATE	EGGS	% of USA
1	Iowa	12,463,000,000	12.5%
2	Ohio	9,316,000,000	9.3%
3	Indiana	8,005,000,000	8.0%
4	Pennsylvania	7,751,000,000	7.8%
5	Texas	5,118,000,000	5.1%
6	Georgia	4,832,000,000	4.8%
7	Michigan	3,846,000,000	3.9%
8	North Carolina	3,661,000,000	3.7%
9	California	3,306,000,000	3.3%
10	Arkansas	3,277,000,000	3.3%
11	Missouri	3,058,000,000	3.1%
12	Minnesota	2,876,000,000	2.9%
13	Florida	2,463,000,000	2.5%
14	Nebraska	2,291,000,000	2.3%
15	Alabama	2,185,000,000	2.2%
16	Washington	2,095,000,000	2.1%
17	New York	1,527,000,000	1.5%
18	Mississippi	1,407,000,000	1.4%
19	Wisconsin	1,405,000,000	1.4%
20	Illinois	1,359,000,000	1.4%
21	Colorado	1,325,000,000	1.3%
22	Kentucky	1,280,000,000	1.3%
23	Utah	1,252,000,000	1.3%
24	South Carolina	1,166,000,000	1.2%
25	Maryland	772,000,000	0.8%
26	Virginia	752,000,000	0.8%
27	Oregon	732,000,000	0.7%
28	Oklahoma	702,000,000	0.7%
29	South Dakota	603,000,000	0.6%
30	Louisiana	561,000,000	0.6%
31	Tennessee	347,000,000	0.3%
32	West Virginia	274,000,000	0.3%
33	Montana	142,000,000	0.1%
34	Massachusetts	47,000,000	0.0%
35	Vermont	36,000,000	0.0%
NA	Alaska**	NA	NA
NA	Arizona**	NA	NA
NA	Connecticut**	NA	NA
NA	Delaware**	NA	NA
NA	Hawaii**	NA	NA
NA	Idaho**	NA	NA
NA	Kansas**	NA	NA
NA	Maine**	NA	NA
NA	Nevada**	NA	NA
NA	New Hampshire**	NA	NA
NA	New Jersey**	NA	NA
NA	New Mexico**	NA	NA
NA	North Dakota**	NA	NA
NA	Rhode Island**	NA	NA
NA	Wyoming**	NA	NA
	District of Columbia	0	0.0%

Source: U.S. Department of Agriculture, National Agricultural Statistics Service
"Poultry - Production and Value: 2015 Summary" (April 2016)
(http://usda.mannlib.cornell.edu/MannUsda/viewDocumentInfo.do?documentID=1130)
*Includes hatching and market (table) eggs. **These states produced a combined 4,205,000,000 eggs. They are combined to avoid disclosing individual operations.

II. Crime and Law Enforcement

I. Arrests:

Important Note Regarding Arrest Numbers

The state arrest numbers reported by the FBI and shown on page 57 are only from those law enforcement agencies that submitted complete arrests reports for 12 months in 2015. The arrest rates were calculated by the editors using population totals provided by the FBI for those jurisdictions reporting. Reports from law enforcement agencies in Illinois and the District of Columbia were insufficient to calculate rates. Reports from Louisiana, Mississippi, New York, Oregon, and West Virginia represented less than 60 percent of their state population. Rates for these states should be interpreted with caution.

V. Juveniles:

Important Note Regarding Juvenile Arrest Rates

The juvenile arrest rates shown on page 58 were calculated by the editors as follows:

The state arrest numbers reported by the FBI are only from those law enforcement agencies that submitted complete arrests reports for 12 months in 2015. Included in the FBI report are population totals of these reporting jurisdictions by state. Using these FBI population figures, we first determined what percentage the FBI numbers represented of each state's total resident population. Next, using 2015 Census state estimates for 10- to 17-year-olds, we multiplied the percentages derived from the FBI population figures into the Census Bureau's total juvenile population counts. The resulting juvenile population is the base that was used to determine juvenile arrests per 100,000 juvenile population. The national rate was calculated in the same manner.

Reports from law enforcement agencies in Illinois and the District of Columbia were insufficient to calculate rates. Reports from Louisiana, Mississippi, New York, Oregon, and West Virginia represented less than 60 percent of their state population. Rates for these states should be interpreted with caution.

Crimes in 2015

National Total = 9,191,335 Crimes*

ALPHA ORDER

ALPHA ORDER

RANK	STATE	CRIMES	% of USA
20	Alabama	167,115	1.8%
43	Alaska	25,947	0.3%
11	Arizona	234,305	2.5%
28	Arkansas	111,731	1.2%
1	California	1,188,373	12.9%
22	Colorado	160,771	1.7%
35	Connecticut	72,720	0.8%
42	Delaware	30,077	0.3%
3	Florida	661,773	7.2%
5	Georgia	346,438	3.8%
37	Hawaii	58,386	0.6%
40	Idaho	32,265	0.4%
8	Illinois	303,811	3.3%
15	Indiana	196,885	2.1%
36	Iowa	72,588	0.8%
34	Kansas	90,188	1.0%
29	Kentucky	105,543	1.1%
17	Louisiana	181,374	2.0%
44	Maine	25,936	0.3%
21	Maryland	166,028	1.8%
23	Massachusetts	140,966	1.5%
13	Michigan	226,045	2.5%
24	Minnesota	134,668	1.5%
32	Mississippi	92,703	1.0%
14	Missouri	203,204	2.2%
41	Montana	30,595	0.3%
38	Nebraska	47,486	0.5%
30	Nevada	96,805	1.1%
45	New Hampshire	25,715	0.3%
19	New Jersey	168,226	1.8%
33	New Mexico	90,318	1.0%
4	New York	391,009	4.3%
7	North Carolina	310,290	3.4%
48	North Dakota	17,763	0.2%
6	Ohio	333,428	3.6%
26	Oklahoma	128,887	1.4%
27	Oregon	128,758	1.4%
9	Pennsylvania	271,241	3.0%
46	Rhode Island	22,484	0.2%
16	South Carolina	185,355	2.0%
47	South Dakota	19,915	0.2%
12	Tennessee	233,486	2.5%
2	Texas	887,641	9.7%
31	Utah	95,802	1.0%
50	Vermont	9,530	0.1%
18	Virginia	172,022	1.9%
10	Washington	268,251	2.9%
39	West Virginia	43,230	0.5%
25	Wisconsin	131,015	1.4%
49	Wyoming	12,405	0.1%

RANK ORDER

RANK	STATE	CRIMES	% of USA
1	California	1,188,373	12.9%
2	Texas	887,641	9.7%
3	Florida	661,773	7.2%
4	New York	391,009	4.3%
5	Georgia	346,438	3.8%
6	Ohio	333,428	3.6%
7	North Carolina	310,290	3.4%
8	Illinois	303,811	3.3%
9	Pennsylvania	271,241	3.0%
10	Washington	268,251	2.9%
11	Arizona	234,305	2.5%
12	Tennessee	233,486	2.5%
13	Michigan	226,045	2.5%
14	Missouri	203,204	2.2%
15	Indiana	196,885	2.1%
16	South Carolina	185,355	2.0%
17	Louisiana	181,374	2.0%
18	Virginia	172,022	1.9%
19	New Jersey	168,226	1.8%
20	Alabama	167,115	1.8%
21	Maryland	166,028	1.8%
22	Colorado	160,771	1.7%
23	Massachusetts	140,966	1.5%
24	Minnesota	134,668	1.5%
25	Wisconsin	131,015	1.4%
26	Oklahoma	128,887	1.4%
27	Oregon	128,758	1.4%
28	Arkansas	111,731	1.2%
29	Kentucky	105,543	1.1%
30	Nevada	96,805	1.1%
31	Utah	95,802	1.0%
32	Mississippi	92,703	1.0%
33	New Mexico	90,318	1.0%
34	Kansas	90,188	1.0%
35	Connecticut	72,720	0.8%
36	Iowa	72,588	0.8%
37	Hawaii	58,386	0.6%
38	Nebraska	47,486	0.5%
39	West Virginia	43,230	0.5%
40	Idaho	32,265	0.4%
41	Montana	30,595	0.3%
42	Delaware	30,077	0.3%
43	Alaska	25,947	0.3%
44	Maine	25,936	0.3%
45	New Hampshire	25,715	0.3%
46	Rhode Island	22,484	0.2%
47	South Dakota	19,915	0.2%
48	North Dakota	17,763	0.2%
49	Wyoming	12,405	0.1%
50	Vermont	9,530	0.1%
	District of Columbia	39,838	0.4%

Source: CQ Press using reported data from the Federal Bureau of Investigation
"Crime in the United States 2015" (Uniform Crime Reports, September 26, 2016, http://www.fbi.gov/about-us/cjis/ucr/)
*Includes murder, rape (legacy definition), robbery, aggravated assault, burglary, larceny-theft, and motor vehicle theft.

Crime Rate in 2015

National Rate = 2,859.7 Crimes per 100,000 Population*

ALPHA ORDER

RANK	STATE	RATE
9	Alabama	3,439.3
8	Alaska	3,513.8
10	Arizona	3,431.5
5	Arkansas	3,751.7
23	California	3,035.9
26	Colorado	2,946.4
44	Connecticut	2,025.1
19	Delaware	3,179.7
15	Florida	3,264.6
11	Georgia	3,391.5
2	Hawaii	4,078.3
47	Idaho	1,949.6
32	Illinois	2,362.5
24	Indiana	2,974.2
35	Iowa	2,323.5
21	Kansas	3,097.5
31	Kentucky	2,385.0
3	Louisiana	3,883.2
46	Maine	1,951.0
28	Maryland	2,764.2
42	Massachusetts	2,074.8
37	Michigan	2,278.2
30	Minnesota	2,453.1
20	Mississippi	3,098.1
13	Missouri	3,340.2
25	Montana	2,961.9
29	Nebraska	2,504.3
12	Nevada	3,348.7
48	New Hampshire	1,932.6
49	New Jersey	1,878.0
1	New Mexico	4,331.7
45	New York	1,975.2
22	North Carolina	3,089.7
33	North Dakota	2,346.9
27	Ohio	2,871.0
14	Oklahoma	3,295.2
18	Oregon	3,195.9
40	Pennsylvania	2,118.7
39	Rhode Island	2,128.5
4	South Carolina	3,785.7
36	South Dakota	2,319.9
7	Tennessee	3,537.6
16	Texas	3,231.5
17	Utah	3,197.8
50	Vermont	1,522.2
43	Virginia	2,052.1
6	Washington	3,741.1
34	West Virginia	2,344.2
38	Wisconsin	2,270.2
41	Wyoming	2,116.5

RANK ORDER

RANK	STATE	RATE
1	New Mexico	4,331.7
2	Hawaii	4,078.3
3	Louisiana	3,883.2
4	South Carolina	3,785.7
5	Arkansas	3,751.7
6	Washington	3,741.1
7	Tennessee	3,537.6
8	Alaska	3,513.8
9	Alabama	3,439.3
10	Arizona	3,431.5
11	Georgia	3,391.5
12	Nevada	3,348.7
13	Missouri	3,340.2
14	Oklahoma	3,295.2
15	Florida	3,264.6
16	Texas	3,231.5
17	Utah	3,197.8
18	Oregon	3,195.9
19	Delaware	3,179.7
20	Mississippi	3,098.1
21	Kansas	3,097.5
22	North Carolina	3,089.7
23	California	3,035.9
24	Indiana	2,974.2
25	Montana	2,961.9
26	Colorado	2,946.4
27	Ohio	2,871.0
28	Maryland	2,764.2
29	Nebraska	2,504.3
30	Minnesota	2,453.1
31	Kentucky	2,385.0
32	Illinois	2,362.5
33	North Dakota	2,346.9
34	West Virginia	2,344.2
35	Iowa	2,323.5
36	South Dakota	2,319.9
37	Michigan	2,278.2
38	Wisconsin	2,270.2
39	Rhode Island	2,128.5
40	Pennsylvania	2,118.7
41	Wyoming	2,116.5
42	Massachusetts	2,074.8
43	Virginia	2,052.1
44	Connecticut	2,025.1
45	New York	1,975.2
46	Maine	1,951.0
47	Idaho	1,949.6
48	New Hampshire	1,932.6
49	New Jersey	1,878.0
50	Vermont	1,522.2

District of Columbia   5,926.2

Source: CQ Press using reported data from the Federal Bureau of Investigation
"Crime in the United States 2015" (Uniform Crime Reports, September 26, 2016, http://www.fbi.gov/about-us/cjis/ucr/)
*Includes murder, rape (legacy definition), robbery, aggravated assault, burglary, larceny-theft, and motor vehicle theft.

Percent Change in Crime Rate: 2014 to 2015

National Percent Change = 2.6% Decrease*

ALPHA ORDER

RANK	STATE	PERCENT CHANGE
29	Alabama	(4.3)
6	Alaska	4.4
22	Arizona	(3.4)
16	Arkansas	(1.7)
2	California	7.3
7	Colorado	4.2
40	Connecticut	(6.3)
46	Delaware	(8.1)
22	Florida	(3.4)
47	Georgia	(9.2)
1	Hawaii	17.7
35	Idaho	(5.4)
26	Illinois	(3.8)
12	Indiana	(1.1)
13	Iowa	(1.4)
10	Kansas	0.1
22	Kentucky	(3.4)
18	Louisiana	(2.3)
43	Maine	(7.3)
41	Maryland	(6.5)
44	Massachusetts	(7.6)
42	Michigan	(7.2)
20	Minnesota	(2.5)
18	Mississippi	(2.3)
11	Missouri	0.0
4	Montana	5.5
48	Nebraska	(10.2)
8	Nevada	3.0
48	New Hampshire	(10.2)
37	New Jersey	(5.7)
5	New Mexico	5.1
36	New York	(5.6)
21	North Carolina	(3.3)
17	North Dakota	(2.2)
39	Ohio	(6.0)
28	Oklahoma	(3.9)
31	Oregon	(4.6)
34	Pennsylvania	(5.3)
50	Rhode Island	(10.9)
31	South Carolina	(4.6)
3	South Dakota	5.9
25	Tennessee	(3.6)
33	Texas	(5.2)
9	Utah	2.9
45	Vermont	(7.7)
26	Virginia	(3.8)
38	Washington	(5.9)
13	West Virginia	(1.4)
30	Wisconsin	(4.4)
15	Wyoming	(1.6)

RANK ORDER

RANK	STATE	PERCENT CHANGE
1	Hawaii	17.7
2	California	7.3
3	South Dakota	5.9
4	Montana	5.5
5	New Mexico	5.1
6	Alaska	4.4
7	Colorado	4.2
8	Nevada	3.0
9	Utah	2.9
10	Kansas	0.1
11	Missouri	0.0
12	Indiana	(1.1)
13	Iowa	(1.4)
13	West Virginia	(1.4)
15	Wyoming	(1.6)
16	Arkansas	(1.7)
17	North Dakota	(2.2)
18	Louisiana	(2.3)
18	Mississippi	(2.3)
20	Minnesota	(2.5)
21	North Carolina	(3.3)
22	Arizona	(3.4)
22	Florida	(3.4)
22	Kentucky	(3.4)
25	Tennessee	(3.6)
26	Illinois	(3.8)
26	Virginia	(3.8)
28	Oklahoma	(3.9)
29	Alabama	(4.3)
30	Wisconsin	(4.4)
31	Oregon	(4.6)
31	South Carolina	(4.6)
33	Texas	(5.2)
34	Pennsylvania	(5.3)
35	Idaho	(5.4)
36	New York	(5.6)
37	New Jersey	(5.7)
38	Washington	(5.9)
39	Ohio	(6.0)
40	Connecticut	(6.3)
41	Maryland	(6.5)
42	Michigan	(7.2)
43	Maine	(7.3)
44	Massachusetts	(7.6)
45	Vermont	(7.7)
46	Delaware	(8.1)
47	Georgia	(9.2)
48	Nebraska	(10.2)
48	New Hampshire	(10.2)
50	Rhode Island	(10.9)

District of Columbia (7.4)

Source: CQ Press using reported data from the Federal Bureau of Investigation
   "Crime in the United States 2015" (Uniform Crime Reports, September 26, 2016, http://www.fbi.gov/about-us/cjis/ucr/)
*Includes murder, rape (legacy definition), robbery, aggravated assault, burglary, larceny-theft, and motor vehicle theft.

Violent Crimes in 2015

National Total = 1,197,704 Violent Crimes*

ALPHA ORDER

RANK	STATE	CRIMES	% of USA
20	Alabama	22,369	1.9%
38	Alaska	5,141	0.4%
13	Arizona	27,198	2.3%
27	Arkansas	14,895	1.2%
1	California	163,459	13.6%
24	Colorado	16,635	1.4%
35	Connecticut	7,654	0.6%
40	Delaware	4,622	0.4%
3	Florida	91,503	7.6%
9	Georgia	37,715	3.1%
41	Hawaii	4,040	0.3%
43	Idaho	3,407	0.3%
5	Illinois	48,082	4.0%
16	Indiana	25,038	2.1%
33	Iowa	8,631	0.7%
30	Kansas	10,989	0.9%
32	Kentucky	9,181	0.8%
17	Louisiana	24,745	2.1%
48	Maine	1,609	0.1%
14	Maryland	26,980	2.3%
15	Massachusetts	26,095	2.2%
8	Michigan	38,944	3.3%
29	Minnesota	12,684	1.1%
34	Mississippi	7,913	0.7%
12	Missouri	29,562	2.5%
42	Montana	3,495	0.3%
39	Nebraska	4,991	0.4%
22	Nevada	19,668	1.6%
45	New Hampshire	2,486	0.2%
19	New Jersey	22,525	1.9%
28	New Mexico	13,224	1.1%
4	New York	73,480	6.1%
10	North Carolina	34,107	2.8%
47	North Dakota	1,743	0.1%
11	Ohio	32,903	2.7%
25	Oklahoma	16,009	1.3%
31	Oregon	10,039	0.8%
7	Pennsylvania	39,156	3.3%
46	Rhode Island	2,441	0.2%
18	South Carolina	24,110	2.0%
44	South Dakota	3,235	0.3%
6	Tennessee	39,690	3.3%
2	Texas	109,902	9.2%
36	Utah	6,524	0.5%
50	Vermont	724	0.1%
26	Virginia	15,552	1.3%
21	Washington	19,882	1.7%
37	West Virginia	5,979	0.5%
23	Wisconsin	17,091	1.4%
49	Wyoming	1,254	0.1%

RANK ORDER

RANK	STATE	CRIMES	% of USA
1	California	163,459	13.6%
2	Texas	109,902	9.2%
3	Florida	91,503	7.6%
4	New York	73,480	6.1%
5	Illinois	48,082	4.0%
6	Tennessee	39,690	3.3%
7	Pennsylvania	39,156	3.3%
8	Michigan	38,944	3.3%
9	Georgia	37,715	3.1%
10	North Carolina	34,107	2.8%
11	Ohio	32,903	2.7%
12	Missouri	29,562	2.5%
13	Arizona	27,198	2.3%
14	Maryland	26,980	2.3%
15	Massachusetts	26,095	2.2%
16	Indiana	25,038	2.1%
17	Louisiana	24,745	2.1%
18	South Carolina	24,110	2.0%
19	New Jersey	22,525	1.9%
20	Alabama	22,369	1.9%
21	Washington	19,882	1.7%
22	Nevada	19,668	1.6%
23	Wisconsin	17,091	1.4%
24	Colorado	16,635	1.4%
25	Oklahoma	16,009	1.3%
26	Virginia	15,552	1.3%
27	Arkansas	14,895	1.2%
28	New Mexico	13,224	1.1%
29	Minnesota	12,684	1.1%
30	Kansas	10,989	0.9%
31	Oregon	10,039	0.8%
32	Kentucky	9,181	0.8%
33	Iowa	8,631	0.7%
34	Mississippi	7,913	0.7%
35	Connecticut	7,654	0.6%
36	Utah	6,524	0.5%
37	West Virginia	5,979	0.5%
38	Alaska	5,141	0.4%
39	Nebraska	4,991	0.4%
40	Delaware	4,622	0.4%
41	Hawaii	4,040	0.3%
42	Montana	3,495	0.3%
43	Idaho	3,407	0.3%
44	South Dakota	3,235	0.3%
45	New Hampshire	2,486	0.2%
46	Rhode Island	2,441	0.2%
47	North Dakota	1,743	0.1%
48	Maine	1,609	0.1%
49	Wyoming	1,254	0.1%
50	Vermont	724	0.1%
	District of Columbia	8,403	0.7%

Source: CQ Press using reported data from the Federal Bureau of Investigation
"Crime in the United States 2015" (Uniform Crime Reports, September 26, 2016, http://www.fbi.gov/about-us/cjis/ucr/)
*Violent crimes are offenses of murder, rape (legacy definition), robbery, and aggravated assault.

Violent Crime Rate in 2015

National Rate = 372.7 Violent Crimes per 100,000 Population*

ALPHA ORDER				RANK ORDER		
RANK	STATE	RATE		RANK	STATE	RATE
10	Alabama	460.4		1	Alaska	696.2
1	Alaska	696.2		2	Nevada	680.4
16	Arizona	398.3		3	New Mexico	634.3
6	Arkansas	500.2		4	Tennessee	601.4
13	California	417.6		5	Louisiana	529.8
29	Colorado	304.9		6	Arkansas	500.2
44	Connecticut	213.1		7	South Carolina	492.4
8	Delaware	488.7		8	Delaware	488.7
11	Florida	451.4		9	Missouri	486.0
24	Georgia	369.2		10	Alabama	460.4
32	Hawaii	282.1		11	Florida	451.4
46	Idaho	205.8		12	Maryland	449.2
22	Illinois	373.9		13	California	417.6
19	Indiana	378.2		14	Oklahoma	409.3
34	Iowa	276.2		15	Texas	400.2
20	Kansas	377.4		16	Arizona	398.3
45	Kentucky	207.4		17	Michigan	392.6
5	Louisiana	529.8		18	Massachusetts	384.1
49	Maine	121.0		19	Indiana	378.2
12	Maryland	449.2		20	Kansas	377.4
18	Massachusetts	384.1		21	South Dakota	376.9
17	Michigan	392.6		22	Illinois	373.9
39	Minnesota	231.0		23	New York	371.2
35	Mississippi	264.5		24	Georgia	369.2
9	Missouri	486.0		25	North Carolina	339.6
26	Montana	338.3		26	Montana	338.3
36	Nebraska	263.2		27	West Virginia	324.2
2	Nevada	680.4		28	Pennsylvania	305.9
47	New Hampshire	186.9		29	Colorado	304.9
37	New Jersey	251.5		30	Wisconsin	296.2
3	New Mexico	634.3		31	Ohio	283.3
23	New York	371.2		32	Hawaii	282.1
25	North Carolina	339.6		33	Washington	277.3
41	North Dakota	230.4		34	Iowa	276.2
31	Ohio	283.3		35	Mississippi	264.5
14	Oklahoma	409.3		36	Nebraska	263.2
38	Oregon	249.3		37	New Jersey	251.5
28	Pennsylvania	305.9		38	Oregon	249.3
39	Rhode Island	231.0		39	Minnesota	231.0
7	South Carolina	492.4		39	Rhode Island	231.0
21	South Dakota	376.9		41	North Dakota	230.4
4	Tennessee	601.4		42	Utah	217.8
15	Texas	400.2		43	Wyoming	213.9
42	Utah	217.8		44	Connecticut	213.1
50	Vermont	115.6		45	Kentucky	207.4
48	Virginia	185.6		46	Idaho	205.8
33	Washington	277.3		47	New Hampshire	186.9
27	West Virginia	324.2		48	Virginia	185.6
30	Wisconsin	296.2		49	Maine	121.0
43	Wyoming	213.9		50	Vermont	115.6
					District of Columbia	1,250.0

Source: CQ Press using reported data from the Federal Bureau of Investigation
   "Crime in the United States 2015" (Uniform Crime Reports, September 26, 2016, http://www.fbi.gov/about-us/cjis/ucr/)
*Violent crimes are offenses of murder, rape (legacy definition), robbery, and aggravated assault.

Percent Change in Violent Crime Rate: 2014 to 2015

National Percent Change = 3.1% Increase*

ALPHA ORDER

RANK ORDER

RANK	STATE	PERCENT CHANGE		RANK	STATE	PERCENT CHANGE
8	Alabama	10.8		1	Hawaii	25.2
4	Alaska	14.9		2	South Dakota	21.0
21	Arizona	5.1		3	Vermont	18.6
13	Arkansas	8.1		4	Alaska	14.9
14	California	7.6		5	Wyoming	14.1
24	Colorado	4.4		6	Missouri	12.4
49	Connecticut	(8.3)		7	Kansas	11.6
29	Delaware	2.8		8	Alabama	10.8
36	Florida	0.7		9	Rhode Island	9.9
45	Georgia	(1.9)		10	New Mexico	9.8
1	Hawaii	25.2		11	Nevada	9.3
26	Idaho	3.3		12	Montana	8.2
26	Illinois	3.3		13	Arkansas	8.1
16	Indiana	6.1		14	California	7.6
20	Iowa	5.2		15	Utah	6.3
7	Kansas	11.6		16	Indiana	6.1
34	Kentucky	1.3		17	West Virginia	5.7
23	Louisiana	4.5		18	Minnesota	5.5
28	Maine	3.2		19	North Carolina	5.4
30	Maryland	2.1		20	Iowa	5.2
42	Massachusetts	(0.7)		21	Arizona	5.1
48	Michigan	(4.3)		22	Wisconsin	4.6
18	Minnesota	5.5		23	Louisiana	4.5
43	Mississippi	(1.3)		24	Colorado	4.4
6	Missouri	12.4		25	Ohio	3.5
12	Montana	8.2		26	Idaho	3.3
40	Nebraska	(0.2)		26	Illinois	3.3
11	Nevada	9.3		28	Maine	3.2
37	New Hampshire	0.6		29	Delaware	2.8
47	New Jersey	(2.3)		30	Maryland	2.1
10	New Mexico	9.8		30	Oklahoma	2.1
43	New York	(1.3)		32	South Carolina	1.7
19	North Carolina	5.4		33	Texas	1.4
50	North Dakota	(10.0)		34	Kentucky	1.3
25	Ohio	3.5		35	Washington	0.9
30	Oklahoma	2.1		36	Florida	0.7
37	Oregon	0.6		37	New Hampshire	0.6
41	Pennsylvania	(0.3)		37	Oregon	0.6
9	Rhode Island	9.9		39	Tennessee	0.3
32	South Carolina	1.7		40	Nebraska	(0.2)
2	South Dakota	21.0		41	Pennsylvania	(0.3)
39	Tennessee	0.3		42	Massachusetts	(0.7)
33	Texas	1.4		43	Mississippi	(1.3)
15	Utah	6.3		43	New York	(1.3)
3	Vermont	18.6		45	Georgia	(1.9)
46	Virginia	(2.2)		46	Virginia	(2.2)
35	Washington	0.9		47	New Jersey	(2.3)
17	West Virginia	5.7		48	Michigan	(4.3)
22	Wisconsin	4.6		49	Connecticut	(8.3)
5	Wyoming	14.1		50	North Dakota	(10.0)

District of Columbia   2.1

Source: CQ Press using reported data from the Federal Bureau of Investigation
"Crime in the United States 2015" (Uniform Crime Reports, September 26, 2016, http://www.fbi.gov/about-us/cjis/ucr/)
*Violent crimes are offenses of murder, rape (legacy definition), robbery, and aggravated assault.

Murders in 2015

National Total = 15,696 Murders*

ALPHA ORDER

RANK	STATE	MURDERS	% of USA
19	Alabama	348	2.2%
39	Alaska	59	0.4%
20	Arizona	309	2.0%
26	Arkansas	181	1.2%
1	California	1,861	11.9%
28	Colorado	176	1.1%
32	Connecticut	117	0.7%
37	Delaware	63	0.4%
3	Florida	1,041	6.6%
6	Georgia	615	3.9%
47	Hawaii	19	0.1%
42	Idaho	32	0.2%
4	Illinois	744	4.7%
17	Indiana	373	2.4%
35	Iowa	72	0.5%
30	Kansas	128	0.8%
25	Kentucky	209	1.3%
13	Louisiana	481	3.1%
45	Maine	23	0.1%
10	Maryland	516	3.3%
30	Massachusetts	128	0.8%
8	Michigan	571	3.6%
29	Minnesota	133	0.8%
21	Mississippi	259	1.7%
11	Missouri	502	3.2%
41	Montana	36	0.2%
38	Nebraska	62	0.4%
27	Nevada	178	1.1%
49	New Hampshire	14	0.1%
18	New Jersey	363	2.3%
32	New Mexico	117	0.7%
7	New York	609	3.9%
9	North Carolina	517	3.3%
46	North Dakota	21	0.1%
12	Ohio	500	3.2%
23	Oklahoma	234	1.5%
34	Oregon	99	0.6%
5	Pennsylvania	658	4.2%
44	Rhode Island	29	0.2%
15	South Carolina	399	2.5%
42	South Dakota	32	0.2%
14	Tennessee	406	2.6%
2	Texas	1,316	8.4%
40	Utah	54	0.3%
50	Vermont	10	0.1%
16	Virginia	383	2.4%
24	Washington	211	1.3%
36	West Virginia	70	0.4%
22	Wisconsin	240	1.5%
48	Wyoming	16	0.1%

RANK ORDER

RANK	STATE	MURDERS	% of USA
1	California	1,861	11.9%
2	Texas	1,316	8.4%
3	Florida	1,041	6.6%
4	Illinois	744	4.7%
5	Pennsylvania	658	4.2%
6	Georgia	615	3.9%
7	New York	609	3.9%
8	Michigan	571	3.6%
9	North Carolina	517	3.3%
10	Maryland	516	3.3%
11	Missouri	502	3.2%
12	Ohio	500	3.2%
13	Louisiana	481	3.1%
14	Tennessee	406	2.6%
15	South Carolina	399	2.5%
16	Virginia	383	2.4%
17	Indiana	373	2.4%
18	New Jersey	363	2.3%
19	Alabama	348	2.2%
20	Arizona	309	2.0%
21	Mississippi	259	1.7%
22	Wisconsin	240	1.5%
23	Oklahoma	234	1.5%
24	Washington	211	1.3%
25	Kentucky	209	1.3%
26	Arkansas	181	1.2%
27	Nevada	178	1.1%
28	Colorado	176	1.1%
29	Minnesota	133	0.8%
30	Kansas	128	0.8%
30	Massachusetts	128	0.8%
32	Connecticut	117	0.7%
32	New Mexico	117	0.7%
34	Oregon	99	0.6%
35	Iowa	72	0.5%
36	West Virginia	70	0.4%
37	Delaware	63	0.4%
38	Nebraska	62	0.4%
39	Alaska	59	0.4%
40	Utah	54	0.3%
41	Montana	36	0.2%
42	Idaho	32	0.2%
42	South Dakota	32	0.2%
44	Rhode Island	29	0.2%
45	Maine	23	0.1%
46	North Dakota	21	0.1%
47	Hawaii	19	0.1%
48	Wyoming	16	0.1%
49	New Hampshire	14	0.1%
50	Vermont	10	0.1%
	District of Columbia	162	1.0%

Source: Reported data from the Federal Bureau of Investigation
"Crime in the United States 2015" (Uniform Crime Reports, September 26, 2016, http://www.fbi.gov/about-us/cjis/ucr/)
*Includes nonnegligent manslaughter.

Murder Rate in 2015

National Rate = 4.9 Murders per 100,000 Population*

ALPHA ORDER

RANK	STATE	RATE
7	Alabama	7.2
6	Alaska	8.0
25	Arizona	4.5
11	Arkansas	6.1
21	California	4.8
35	Colorado	3.2
33	Connecticut	3.3
8	Delaware	6.7
18	Florida	5.1
12	Georgia	6.0
49	Hawaii	1.3
44	Idaho	1.9
14	Illinois	5.8
16	Indiana	5.6
43	Iowa	2.3
26	Kansas	4.4
23	Kentucky	4.7
1	Louisiana	10.3
47	Maine	1.7
3	Maryland	8.6
44	Massachusetts	1.9
14	Michigan	5.8
42	Minnesota	2.4
2	Mississippi	8.7
4	Missouri	8.3
32	Montana	3.5
33	Nebraska	3.3
9	Nevada	6.2
50	New Hampshire	1.1
29	New Jersey	4.1
16	New Mexico	5.6
36	New York	3.1
18	North Carolina	5.1
38	North Dakota	2.8
27	Ohio	4.3
12	Oklahoma	6.0
41	Oregon	2.5
18	Pennsylvania	5.1
39	Rhode Island	2.7
5	South Carolina	8.1
31	South Dakota	3.7
9	Tennessee	6.2
21	Texas	4.8
46	Utah	1.8
48	Vermont	1.6
24	Virginia	4.6
37	Washington	2.9
30	West Virginia	3.8
28	Wisconsin	4.2
39	Wyoming	2.7

RANK ORDER

RANK	STATE	RATE
1	Louisiana	10.3
2	Mississippi	8.7
3	Maryland	8.6
4	Missouri	8.3
5	South Carolina	8.1
6	Alaska	8.0
7	Alabama	7.2
8	Delaware	6.7
9	Nevada	6.2
9	Tennessee	6.2
11	Arkansas	6.1
12	Georgia	6.0
12	Oklahoma	6.0
14	Illinois	5.8
14	Michigan	5.8
16	Indiana	5.6
16	New Mexico	5.6
18	Florida	5.1
18	North Carolina	5.1
18	Pennsylvania	5.1
21	California	4.8
21	Texas	4.8
23	Kentucky	4.7
24	Virginia	4.6
25	Arizona	4.5
26	Kansas	4.4
27	Ohio	4.3
28	Wisconsin	4.2
29	New Jersey	4.1
30	West Virginia	3.8
31	South Dakota	3.7
32	Montana	3.5
33	Connecticut	3.3
33	Nebraska	3.3
35	Colorado	3.2
36	New York	3.1
37	Washington	2.9
38	North Dakota	2.8
39	Rhode Island	2.7
39	Wyoming	2.7
41	Oregon	2.5
42	Minnesota	2.4
43	Iowa	2.3
44	Idaho	1.9
44	Massachusetts	1.9
46	Utah	1.8
47	Maine	1.7
48	Vermont	1.6
49	Hawaii	1.3
50	New Hampshire	1.1

District of Columbia	24.1

Source: Reported data from the Federal Bureau of Investigation
"Crime in the United States 2015" (Uniform Crime Reports, September 26, 2016, http://www.fbi.gov/about-us/cjis/ucr/)
*Includes nonnegligent manslaughter.

Percent of Murders Involving Firearms in 2015

National Percent = 71.5% of Murders*

RANK	STATE	PERCENT
NA	Alabama***	NA
23	Alaska	68.4
38	Arizona	61.5
29	Arkansas	67.1
22	California	68.5
31	Colorado	65.3
24	Connecticut	68.2
3	Delaware	82.5
NA	Florida***	NA
4	Georgia	82.1
48	Hawaii	21.1
5	Idaho	80.0
1	Illinois**	88.5
10	Indiana	76.8
25	Iowa	68.1
14	Kansas	72.8
27	Kentucky	67.5
5	Louisiana	80.0
21	Maine	69.6
12	Maryland	75.0
32	Massachusetts	64.3
25	Michigan	68.1
40	Minnesota	59.4
8	Mississippi	79.2
2	Missouri	83.8
44	Montana	50.0
19	Nebraska	70.5
34	Nevada	63.8
41	New Hampshire	57.1
15	New Jersey	72.2
39	New Mexico	59.6
36	New York	62.7
20	North Carolina	69.8
42	North Dakota	52.9
30	Ohio	65.8
33	Oklahoma	63.9
45	Oregon	47.9
11	Pennsylvania	76.3
47	Rhode Island	37.0
8	South Carolina	79.2
46	South Dakota	44.4
13	Tennessee	73.9
18	Texas	71.0
35	Utah	63.0
5	Vermont	80.0
16	Virginia	71.8
27	Washington	67.5
43	West Virginia	52.6
17	Wisconsin	71.4
37	Wyoming	62.5

RANK	STATE	PERCENT
1	Illinois**	88.5
2	Missouri	83.8
3	Delaware	82.5
4	Georgia	82.1
5	Idaho	80.0
5	Louisiana	80.0
5	Vermont	80.0
8	Mississippi	79.2
8	South Carolina	79.2
10	Indiana	76.8
11	Pennsylvania	76.3
12	Maryland	75.0
13	Tennessee	73.9
14	Kansas	72.8
15	New Jersey	72.2
16	Virginia	71.8
17	Wisconsin	71.4
18	Texas	71.0
19	Nebraska	70.5
20	North Carolina	69.8
21	Maine	69.6
22	California	68.5
23	Alaska	68.4
24	Connecticut	68.2
25	Iowa	68.1
25	Michigan	68.1
27	Kentucky	67.5
27	Washington	67.5
29	Arkansas	67.1
30	Ohio	65.8
31	Colorado	65.3
32	Massachusetts	64.3
33	Oklahoma	63.9
34	Nevada	63.8
35	Utah	63.0
36	New York	62.7
37	Wyoming	62.5
38	Arizona	61.5
39	New Mexico	59.6
40	Minnesota	59.4
41	New Hampshire	57.1
42	North Dakota	52.9
43	West Virginia	52.6
44	Montana	50.0
45	Oregon	47.9
46	South Dakota	44.4
47	Rhode Island	37.0
48	Hawaii	21.1
NA	Alabama***	NA
NA	Florida***	NA

District of Columbia 74.7

Source: CQ Press using reported data from the Federal Bureau of Investigation
"Crime in the United States 2015" (Uniform Crime Reports, September 26, 2016, http://www.fbi.gov/about-us/cjis/ucr/)
*Of the 13,414 murders in 2015 for which supplemental data were received by the F.B.I. There were an additional 2,282 murders for which the type of murder weapon was not reported to the F.B.I. Includes nonnegligent manslaughter. National and state percents based on reporting jurisdictions only. **Illinois's percent is for Chicago and Rockford only.
***Not available.

Rapes in 2015

National Total = 90,185 Rapes*

ALPHA ORDER					RANK ORDER			
RANK	STATE		RAPES	% of USA	RANK	STATE	RAPES	% of USA
21	Alabama		1,456	1.6%	1	California	9,387	10.4%
37	Alaska		650	0.7%	2	Texas	8,925	9.9%
11	Arizona		2,294	2.5%	3	Florida	5,430	6.0%
23	Arkansas		1,300	1.4%	4	New York	4,389	4.9%
1	California		9,387	10.4%	5	Michigan	4,163	4.6%
9	Colorado		2,377	2.6%	6	Ohio	4,154	4.6%
38	Connecticut		582	0.6%	7	Illinois	3,549	3.9%
48	Delaware		243	0.3%	8	Pennsylvania	3,122	3.5%
3	Florida		5,430	6.0%	9	Colorado	2,377	2.6%
10	Georgia		2,296	2.5%	10	Georgia	2,296	2.5%
44	Hawaii		400	0.4%	11	Arizona	2,294	2.5%
39	Idaho		533	0.6%	12	Washington	2,193	2.4%
7	Illinois		3,549	3.9%	13	Tennessee	1,966	2.2%
16	Indiana		1,789	2.0%	14	North Carolina	1,939	2.2%
35	Iowa		851	0.9%	15	Missouri	1,854	2.1%
25	Kansas		1,251	1.4%	16	Indiana	1,789	2.0%
33	Kentucky		997	1.1%	17	South Carolina	1,707	1.9%
24	Louisiana		1,260	1.4%	18	Minnesota	1,686	1.9%
45	Maine		354	0.4%	19	Massachusetts	1,608	1.8%
29	Maryland		1,184	1.3%	20	Virginia	1,493	1.7%
19	Massachusetts		1,608	1.8%	21	Alabama	1,456	1.6%
5	Michigan		4,163	4.6%	22	Oklahoma	1,352	1.5%
18	Minnesota		1,686	1.9%	23	Arkansas	1,300	1.4%
34	Mississippi		862	1.0%	24	Louisiana	1,260	1.4%
15	Missouri		1,854	2.1%	25	Kansas	1,251	1.4%
42	Montana		431	0.5%	26	Nevada	1,238	1.4%
36	Nebraska		652	0.7%	27	Wisconsin	1,224	1.4%
26	Nevada		1,238	1.4%	28	New Mexico	1,215	1.3%
40	New Hampshire		461	0.5%	29	Maryland	1,184	1.3%
32	New Jersey		1,019	1.1%	30	Oregon	1,164	1.3%
28	New Mexico		1,215	1.3%	31	Utah	1,098	1.2%
4	New York		4,389	4.9%	32	New Jersey	1,019	1.1%
14	North Carolina		1,939	2.2%	33	Kentucky	997	1.1%
47	North Dakota		276	0.3%	34	Mississippi	862	1.0%
6	Ohio		4,154	4.6%	35	Iowa	851	0.9%
22	Oklahoma		1,352	1.5%	36	Nebraska	652	0.7%
30	Oregon		1,164	1.3%	37	Alaska	650	0.7%
8	Pennsylvania		3,122	3.5%	38	Connecticut	582	0.6%
46	Rhode Island		338	0.4%	39	Idaho	533	0.6%
17	South Carolina		1,707	1.9%	40	New Hampshire	461	0.5%
41	South Dakota		441	0.5%	41	South Dakota	441	0.5%
13	Tennessee		1,966	2.2%	42	Montana	431	0.5%
2	Texas		8,925	9.9%	43	West Virginia	420	0.5%
31	Utah		1,098	1.2%	44	Hawaii	400	0.4%
50	Vermont		121	0.1%	45	Maine	354	0.4%
20	Virginia		1,493	1.7%	46	Rhode Island	338	0.4%
12	Washington		2,193	2.4%	47	North Dakota	276	0.3%
43	West Virginia		420	0.5%	48	Delaware	243	0.3%
27	Wisconsin		1,224	1.4%	49	Wyoming	125	0.1%
49	Wyoming		125	0.1%	50	Vermont	121	0.1%
					District of Columbia		366	0.4%

Source: Reported data from the Federal Bureau of Investigation
"Crime in the United States 2015" (Uniform Crime Reports, September 26, 2016, http://www.fbi.gov/about-us/cjis/ucr/)
*Although the definition of rape was revised in 2013 the FBI continues to release estimates based on the legacy definition for comparison purposes to previous years. The legacy definition used for these figures is "Forcible rape is the carnal knowledge of a female forcibly and against her will. Assaults or attempts to commit rape by force or threat of force are included. However, statutory rape without force and other sex offenses are excluded."

Rape Rate in 2015

National Rate = 28.1 Rapes per 100,000 Population*

RANK	STATE	RATE
24	Alabama	30.0
1	Alaska	88.0
17	Arizona	33.6
4	Arkansas	43.7
37	California	24.0
5	Colorado	43.6
49	Connecticut	16.2
35	Delaware	25.7
33	Florida	26.8
40	Georgia	22.5
28	Hawaii	27.9
19	Idaho	32.2
29	Illinois	27.6
31	Indiana	27.0
30	Iowa	27.2
6	Kansas	43.0
40	Kentucky	22.5
31	Louisiana	27.0
34	Maine	26.6
45	Maryland	19.7
38	Massachusetts	23.7
8	Michigan	42.0
21	Minnesota	30.7
27	Mississippi	28.8
23	Missouri	30.5
9	Montana	41.7
16	Nebraska	34.4
7	Nevada	42.8
14	New Hampshire	34.6
50	New Jersey	11.4
2	New Mexico	58.3
42	New York	22.2
46	North Carolina	19.3
11	North Dakota	36.5
12	Ohio	35.8
14	Oklahoma	34.6
26	Oregon	28.9
36	Pennsylvania	24.4
20	Rhode Island	32.0
13	South Carolina	34.9
3	South Dakota	51.4
25	Tennessee	29.8
18	Texas	32.5
10	Utah	36.6
46	Vermont	19.3
48	Virginia	17.8
22	Washington	30.6
39	West Virginia	22.8
44	Wisconsin	21.2
43	Wyoming	21.3

RANK	STATE	RATE
1	Alaska	88.0
2	New Mexico	58.3
3	South Dakota	51.4
4	Arkansas	43.7
5	Colorado	43.6
6	Kansas	43.0
7	Nevada	42.8
8	Michigan	42.0
9	Montana	41.7
10	Utah	36.6
11	North Dakota	36.5
12	Ohio	35.8
13	South Carolina	34.9
14	New Hampshire	34.6
14	Oklahoma	34.6
16	Nebraska	34.4
17	Arizona	33.6
18	Texas	32.5
19	Idaho	32.2
20	Rhode Island	32.0
21	Minnesota	30.7
22	Washington	30.6
23	Missouri	30.5
24	Alabama	30.0
25	Tennessee	29.8
26	Oregon	28.9
27	Mississippi	28.8
28	Hawaii	27.9
29	Illinois	27.6
30	Iowa	27.2
31	Indiana	27.0
31	Louisiana	27.0
33	Florida	26.8
34	Maine	26.6
35	Delaware	25.7
36	Pennsylvania	24.4
37	California	24.0
38	Massachusetts	23.7
39	West Virginia	22.8
40	Georgia	22.5
40	Kentucky	22.5
42	New York	22.2
43	Wyoming	21.3
44	Wisconsin	21.2
45	Maryland	19.7
46	North Carolina	19.3
46	Vermont	19.3
48	Virginia	17.8
49	Connecticut	16.2
50	New Jersey	11.4
	District of Columbia	54.4

Source: Reported data from the Federal Bureau of Investigation
   "Crime in the United States 2015" (Uniform Crime Reports, September 26, 2016, http://www.fbi.gov/about-us/cjis/ucr/)
*Although the definition of rape was revised in 2013 the FBI continues to release estimates based on the legacy definition for comparison purposes to previous years. The legacy definition used for these figures is "Forcible rape is the carnal knowledge of a female forcibly and against her will. Assaults or attempts to commit rape by force or threat of force are included. However, statutory rape without force and other sex offenses are excluded."

Rapes (Revised Definition) in 2015

National Total = 124,047 Rapes*

RANK	STATE	RAPES	% of USA
21	Alabama	2,039	1.6%
36	Alaska	901	0.7%
11	Arizona	3,108	2.5%
22	Arkansas	1,931	1.6%
1	California	12,811	10.3%
9	Colorado	3,257	2.6%
38	Connecticut	773	0.6%
48	Delaware	341	0.3%
3	Florida	7,553	6.1%
10	Georgia	3,224	2.6%
42	Hawaii	561	0.5%
39	Idaho	694	0.6%
7	Illinois	4,821	3.9%
16	Indiana	2,404	1.9%
35	Iowa	1,156	0.9%
30	Kansas	1,615	1.3%
32	Kentucky	1,492	1.2%
25	Louisiana	1,723	1.4%
45	Maine	474	0.4%
28	Maryland	1,666	1.3%
20	Massachusetts	2,075	1.7%
4	Michigan	6,450	5.2%
18	Minnesota	2,321	1.9%
34	Mississippi	1,203	1.0%
15	Missouri	2,553	2.1%
43	Montana	547	0.4%
37	Nebraska	873	0.7%
26	Nevada	1,688	1.4%
41	New Hampshire	627	0.5%
33	New Jersey	1,373	1.1%
27	New Mexico	1,672	1.3%
5	New York	6,074	4.9%
13	North Carolina	2,684	2.2%
47	North Dakota	345	0.3%
6	Ohio	5,149	4.2%
23	Oklahoma	1,849	1.5%
31	Oregon	1,593	1.3%
8	Pennsylvania	4,305	3.5%
46	Rhode Island	459	0.4%
19	South Carolina	2,297	1.9%
44	South Dakota	495	0.4%
14	Tennessee	2,676	2.2%
2	Texas	12,250	9.9%
29	Utah	1,645	1.3%
50	Vermont	136	0.1%
17	Virginia	2,340	1.9%
12	Washington	2,705	2.2%
40	West Virginia	672	0.5%
24	Wisconsin	1,780	1.4%
49	Wyoming	173	0.1%

RANK	STATE	RAPES	% of USA
1	California	12,811	10.3%
2	Texas	12,250	9.9%
3	Florida	7,553	6.1%
4	Michigan	6,450	5.2%
5	New York	6,074	4.9%
6	Ohio	5,149	4.2%
7	Illinois	4,821	3.9%
8	Pennsylvania	4,305	3.5%
9	Colorado	3,257	2.6%
10	Georgia	3,224	2.6%
11	Arizona	3,108	2.5%
12	Washington	2,705	2.2%
13	North Carolina	2,684	2.2%
14	Tennessee	2,676	2.2%
15	Missouri	2,553	2.1%
16	Indiana	2,404	1.9%
17	Virginia	2,340	1.9%
18	Minnesota	2,321	1.9%
19	South Carolina	2,297	1.9%
20	Massachusetts	2,075	1.7%
21	Alabama	2,039	1.6%
22	Arkansas	1,931	1.6%
23	Oklahoma	1,849	1.5%
24	Wisconsin	1,780	1.4%
25	Louisiana	1,723	1.4%
26	Nevada	1,688	1.4%
27	New Mexico	1,672	1.3%
28	Maryland	1,666	1.3%
29	Utah	1,645	1.3%
30	Kansas	1,615	1.3%
31	Oregon	1,593	1.3%
32	Kentucky	1,492	1.2%
33	New Jersey	1,373	1.1%
34	Mississippi	1,203	1.0%
35	Iowa	1,156	0.9%
36	Alaska	901	0.7%
37	Nebraska	873	0.7%
38	Connecticut	773	0.6%
39	Idaho	694	0.6%
40	West Virginia	672	0.5%
41	New Hampshire	627	0.5%
42	Hawaii	561	0.5%
43	Montana	547	0.4%
44	South Dakota	495	0.4%
45	Maine	474	0.4%
46	Rhode Island	459	0.4%
47	North Dakota	345	0.3%
48	Delaware	341	0.3%
49	Wyoming	173	0.1%
50	Vermont	136	0.1%
	District of Columbia	494	0.4%

Source: Reported data from the Federal Bureau of Investigation
"Crime in the United States 2015" (Uniform Crime Reports, September 26, 2016, http://www.fbi.gov/about-us/cjis/ucr/)
*The definition of rape was revised in 2013 to "Penetration, no matter how slight, of the vagina or anus with any body part or object, or oral penetration by a sex organ of another person, without the consent of the victim. Attempts or assaults to commit rape are also included; however, statutory rape and incest are excluded." This revised definition includes both male and female victims and drops "forcible" from the title.

Rape Rate (Revised Definition) in 2015

National Rate = 38.6 Rapes per 100,000 Population*

ALPHA ORDER				RANK ORDER		
RANK	STATE	RATE		RANK	STATE	RATE
21	Alabama	42.0		1	Alaska	122.0
1	Alaska	122.0		2	New Mexico	80.2
16	Arizona	45.5		3	Michigan	65.0
4	Arkansas	64.8		4	Arkansas	64.8
39	California	32.7		5	Colorado	59.7
5	Colorado	59.7		6	Nevada	58.4
49	Connecticut	21.5		7	South Dakota	57.7
35	Delaware	36.0		8	Kansas	55.5
30	Florida	37.3		9	Utah	54.9
40	Georgia	31.6		10	Montana	53.0
27	Hawaii	39.2		11	Oklahoma	47.3
23	Idaho	41.9		12	New Hampshire	47.1
29	Illinois	37.5		13	South Carolina	46.9
34	Indiana	36.3		14	Nebraska	46.0
31	Iowa	37.0		15	North Dakota	45.6
8	Kansas	55.5		16	Arizona	45.5
37	Kentucky	33.7		17	Texas	44.6
32	Louisiana	36.9		18	Ohio	44.3
36	Maine	35.7		19	Rhode Island	43.5
46	Maryland	27.7		20	Minnesota	42.3
43	Massachusetts	30.5		21	Alabama	42.0
3	Michigan	65.0		21	Missouri	42.0
20	Minnesota	42.3		23	Idaho	41.9
25	Mississippi	40.2		24	Tennessee	40.5
21	Missouri	42.0		25	Mississippi	40.2
10	Montana	53.0		26	Oregon	39.5
14	Nebraska	46.0		27	Hawaii	39.2
6	Nevada	58.4		28	Washington	37.7
12	New Hampshire	47.1		29	Illinois	37.5
50	New Jersey	15.3		30	Florida	37.3
2	New Mexico	80.2		31	Iowa	37.0
42	New York	30.7		32	Louisiana	36.9
47	North Carolina	26.7		33	West Virginia	36.4
15	North Dakota	45.6		34	Indiana	36.3
18	Ohio	44.3		35	Delaware	36.0
11	Oklahoma	47.3		36	Maine	35.7
26	Oregon	39.5		37	Kentucky	33.7
38	Pennsylvania	33.6		38	Pennsylvania	33.6
19	Rhode Island	43.5		39	California	32.7
13	South Carolina	46.9		40	Georgia	31.6
7	South Dakota	57.7		41	Wisconsin	30.8
24	Tennessee	40.5		42	New York	30.7
17	Texas	44.6		43	Massachusetts	30.5
9	Utah	54.9		44	Wyoming	29.5
48	Vermont	21.7		45	Virginia	27.9
45	Virginia	27.9		46	Maryland	27.7
28	Washington	37.7		47	North Carolina	26.7
33	West Virginia	36.4		48	Vermont	21.7
41	Wisconsin	30.8		49	Connecticut	21.5
44	Wyoming	29.5		50	New Jersey	15.3
					District of Columbia	73.5

Source: Reported data from the Federal Bureau of Investigation
 "Crime in the United States 2015" (Uniform Crime Reports, September 26, 2016, http://www.fbi.gov/about-us/cjis/ucr/)
*The definition of rape was revised in 2013 to "Penetration, no matter how slight, of the vagina or anus with any body part
or object, or oral penetration by a sex organ of another person, without the consent of the victim. Attempts or assaults to commit
rape are also included; however, statutory rape and incest are excluded." This revised definition includes both male and female
victims and drops "forcible" from the title.

Robberies in 2015

National Total = 327,374 Robberies*

RANK	STATE	ROBBERIES	% of USA	RANK	STATE	ROBBERIES	% of USA
22	Alabama	4,611	1.4%	1	California	52,862	16.1%
40	Alaska	761	0.2%	2	Texas	31,934	9.8%
16	Arizona	6,360	1.9%	3	New York	23,936	7.3%
33	Arkansas	2,098	0.6%	4	Florida	21,137	6.5%
1	California	52,862	16.1%	5	Illinois	14,910	4.6%
26	Colorado	3,323	1.0%	6	Pennsylvania	13,003	4.0%
29	Connecticut	2,892	0.9%	7	Ohio	12,554	3.8%
36	Delaware	1,235	0.4%	8	Georgia	12,247	3.7%
4	Florida	21,137	6.5%	9	Maryland	9,863	3.0%
8	Georgia	12,247	3.7%	10	New Jersey	9,729	3.0%
37	Hawaii	1,203	0.4%	11	North Carolina	8,825	2.7%
47	Idaho	192	0.1%	12	Michigan	7,796	2.4%
5	Illinois	14,910	4.6%	13	Tennessee	7,474	2.3%
14	Indiana	7,111	2.2%	14	Indiana	7,111	2.2%
38	Iowa	1,047	0.3%	15	Missouri	6,376	1.9%
34	Kansas	1,818	0.6%	16	Arizona	6,360	1.9%
27	Kentucky	3,307	1.0%	17	Nevada	6,287	1.9%
18	Louisiana	5,550	1.7%	18	Louisiana	5,550	1.7%
44	Maine	311	0.1%	19	Washington	5,449	1.7%
9	Maryland	9,863	3.0%	20	Massachusetts	5,288	1.6%
20	Massachusetts	5,288	1.6%	21	Wisconsin	5,232	1.6%
12	Michigan	7,796	2.4%	22	Alabama	4,611	1.4%
25	Minnesota	3,771	1.2%	23	Virginia	4,441	1.4%
31	Mississippi	2,294	0.7%	24	South Carolina	3,931	1.2%
15	Missouri	6,376	1.9%	25	Minnesota	3,771	1.2%
46	Montana	210	0.1%	26	Colorado	3,323	1.0%
39	Nebraska	994	0.3%	27	Kentucky	3,307	1.0%
17	Nevada	6,287	1.9%	28	Oklahoma	3,005	0.9%
43	New Hampshire	468	0.1%	29	Connecticut	2,892	0.9%
10	New Jersey	9,729	3.0%	30	New Mexico	2,485	0.8%
30	New Mexico	2,485	0.8%	31	Mississippi	2,294	0.7%
3	New York	23,936	7.3%	32	Oregon	2,146	0.7%
11	North Carolina	8,825	2.7%	33	Arkansas	2,098	0.6%
48	North Dakota	148	0.0%	34	Kansas	1,818	0.6%
7	Ohio	12,554	3.8%	35	Utah	1,326	0.4%
28	Oklahoma	3,005	0.9%	36	Delaware	1,235	0.4%
32	Oregon	2,146	0.7%	37	Hawaii	1,203	0.4%
6	Pennsylvania	13,003	4.0%	38	Iowa	1,047	0.3%
42	Rhode Island	556	0.2%	39	Nebraska	994	0.3%
24	South Carolina	3,931	1.2%	40	Alaska	761	0.2%
45	South Dakota	216	0.1%	41	West Virginia	760	0.2%
13	Tennessee	7,474	2.3%	42	Rhode Island	556	0.2%
2	Texas	31,934	9.8%	43	New Hampshire	468	0.1%
35	Utah	1,326	0.4%	44	Maine	311	0.1%
49	Vermont	101	0.0%	45	South Dakota	216	0.1%
23	Virginia	4,441	1.4%	46	Montana	210	0.1%
19	Washington	5,449	1.7%	47	Idaho	192	0.1%
41	West Virginia	760	0.2%	48	North Dakota	148	0.0%
21	Wisconsin	5,232	1.6%	49	Vermont	101	0.0%
50	Wyoming	59	0.0%	50	Wyoming	59	0.0%
					District of Columbia	3,742	1.1%

ALPHA ORDER

RANK ORDER

Source: Reported data from the Federal Bureau of Investigation
"Crime in the United States 2015" (Uniform Crime Reports, September 26, 2016, http://www.fbi.gov/about-us/cjis/ucr/)
*Robbery is the taking or attempting to take anything of value by force or threat of force.

Robbery Rate in 2015

National Rate = 101.9 Robberies per 100,000 Population*

ALPHA ORDER				RANK ORDER		
RANK	STATE	RATE		RANK	STATE	RATE
19	Alabama	94.9		1	Nevada	217.5
17	Alaska	103.1		2	Maryland	164.2
20	Arizona	93.1		3	California	135.0
32	Arkansas	70.4		4	Delaware	130.6
3	California	135.0		5	New York	120.9
35	Colorado	60.9		6	Georgia	119.9
24	Connecticut	80.5		7	New Mexico	119.2
4	Delaware	130.6		8	Louisiana	118.8
16	Florida	104.3		9	Texas	116.3
6	Georgia	119.9		10	Illinois	115.9
23	Hawaii	84.0		11	Tennessee	113.2
49	Idaho	11.6		12	New Jersey	108.6
10	Illinois	115.9		13	Ohio	108.1
14	Indiana	107.4		14	Indiana	107.4
43	Iowa	33.5		15	Missouri	104.8
34	Kansas	62.4		16	Florida	104.3
31	Kentucky	74.7		17	Alaska	103.1
8	Louisiana	118.8		18	Pennsylvania	101.6
45	Maine	23.4		19	Alabama	94.9
2	Maryland	164.2		20	Arizona	93.1
27	Massachusetts	77.8		21	Wisconsin	90.7
26	Michigan	78.6		22	North Carolina	87.9
33	Minnesota	68.7		23	Hawaii	84.0
29	Mississippi	76.7		24	Connecticut	80.5
15	Missouri	104.8		25	South Carolina	80.3
46	Montana	20.3		26	Michigan	78.6
39	Nebraska	52.4		27	Massachusetts	77.8
1	Nevada	217.5		28	Oklahoma	76.8
42	New Hampshire	35.2		29	Mississippi	76.7
12	New Jersey	108.6		30	Washington	76.0
7	New Mexico	119.2		31	Kentucky	74.7
5	New York	120.9		32	Arkansas	70.4
22	North Carolina	87.9		33	Minnesota	68.7
47	North Dakota	19.6		34	Kansas	62.4
13	Ohio	108.1		35	Colorado	60.9
28	Oklahoma	76.8		36	Oregon	53.3
36	Oregon	53.3		37	Virginia	53.0
18	Pennsylvania	101.6		38	Rhode Island	52.6
38	Rhode Island	52.6		39	Nebraska	52.4
25	South Carolina	80.3		40	Utah	44.3
44	South Dakota	25.2		41	West Virginia	41.2
11	Tennessee	113.2		42	New Hampshire	35.2
9	Texas	116.3		43	Iowa	33.5
40	Utah	44.3		44	South Dakota	25.2
48	Vermont	16.1		45	Maine	23.4
37	Virginia	53.0		46	Montana	20.3
30	Washington	76.0		47	North Dakota	19.6
41	West Virginia	41.2		48	Vermont	16.1
21	Wisconsin	90.7		49	Idaho	11.6
50	Wyoming	10.1		50	Wyoming	10.1
				District of Columbia		556.7

Source: Reported data from the Federal Bureau of Investigation
"Crime in the United States 2015" (Uniform Crime Reports, September 26, 2016, http://www.fbi.gov/about-us/cjis/ucr/)
*Robbery is the taking or attempting to take anything of value by force or threat of force.

Aggravated Assaults in 2015

National Total = 764,449 Aggravated Assaults*

ALPHA ORDER

RANK	STATE	ASSAULTS	% of USA
16	Alabama	15,954	2.1%
38	Alaska	3,671	0.5%
13	Arizona	18,235	2.4%
24	Arkansas	11,316	1.5%
1	California	99,349	13.0%
25	Colorado	10,759	1.4%
36	Connecticut	4,063	0.5%
40	Delaware	3,081	0.4%
3	Florida	63,895	8.4%
9	Georgia	22,557	3.0%
44	Hawaii	2,418	0.3%
42	Idaho	2,650	0.3%
6	Illinois	28,879	3.8%
17	Indiana	15,765	2.1%
31	Iowa	6,661	0.9%
29	Kansas	7,792	1.0%
34	Kentucky	4,668	0.6%
15	Louisiana	17,454	2.3%
49	Maine	921	0.1%
19	Maryland	15,417	2.0%
12	Massachusetts	19,071	2.5%
7	Michigan	26,414	3.5%
30	Minnesota	7,094	0.9%
35	Mississippi	4,498	0.6%
11	Missouri	20,830	2.7%
41	Montana	2,818	0.4%
39	Nebraska	3,283	0.4%
21	Nevada	11,965	1.6%
45	New Hampshire	1,543	0.2%
23	New Jersey	11,414	1.5%
27	New Mexico	9,407	1.2%
4	New York	44,546	5.8%
8	North Carolina	22,826	3.0%
47	North Dakota	1,298	0.2%
18	Ohio	15,695	2.1%
22	Oklahoma	11,418	1.5%
32	Oregon	6,630	0.9%
10	Pennsylvania	22,373	2.9%
46	Rhode Island	1,518	0.2%
14	South Carolina	18,073	2.4%
43	South Dakota	2,546	0.3%
5	Tennessee	29,844	3.9%
2	Texas	67,727	8.9%
37	Utah	4,046	0.5%
50	Vermont	492	0.1%
28	Virginia	9,235	1.2%
20	Washington	12,029	1.6%
33	West Virginia	4,729	0.6%
26	Wisconsin	10,395	1.4%
48	Wyoming	1,054	0.1%

RANK ORDER

RANK	STATE	ASSAULTS	% of USA
1	California	99,349	13.0%
2	Texas	67,727	8.9%
3	Florida	63,895	8.4%
4	New York	44,546	5.8%
5	Tennessee	29,844	3.9%
6	Illinois	28,879	3.8%
7	Michigan	26,414	3.5%
8	North Carolina	22,826	3.0%
9	Georgia	22,557	3.0%
10	Pennsylvania	22,373	2.9%
11	Missouri	20,830	2.7%
12	Massachusetts	19,071	2.5%
13	Arizona	18,235	2.4%
14	South Carolina	18,073	2.4%
15	Louisiana	17,454	2.3%
16	Alabama	15,954	2.1%
17	Indiana	15,765	2.1%
18	Ohio	15,695	2.1%
19	Maryland	15,417	2.0%
20	Washington	12,029	1.6%
21	Nevada	11,965	1.6%
22	Oklahoma	11,418	1.5%
23	New Jersey	11,414	1.5%
24	Arkansas	11,316	1.5%
25	Colorado	10,759	1.4%
26	Wisconsin	10,395	1.4%
27	New Mexico	9,407	1.2%
28	Virginia	9,235	1.2%
29	Kansas	7,792	1.0%
30	Minnesota	7,094	0.9%
31	Iowa	6,661	0.9%
32	Oregon	6,630	0.9%
33	West Virginia	4,729	0.6%
34	Kentucky	4,668	0.6%
35	Mississippi	4,498	0.6%
36	Connecticut	4,063	0.5%
37	Utah	4,046	0.5%
38	Alaska	3,671	0.5%
39	Nebraska	3,283	0.4%
40	Delaware	3,081	0.4%
41	Montana	2,818	0.4%
42	Idaho	2,650	0.3%
43	South Dakota	2,546	0.3%
44	Hawaii	2,418	0.3%
45	New Hampshire	1,543	0.2%
46	Rhode Island	1,518	0.2%
47	North Dakota	1,298	0.2%
48	Wyoming	1,054	0.1%
49	Maine	921	0.1%
50	Vermont	492	0.1%
	District of Columbia	4,133	0.5%

Source: Reported data from the Federal Bureau of Investigation
"Crime in the United States 2015" (Uniform Crime Reports, September 26, 2016, http://www.fbi.gov/about-us/cjis/ucr/)
*Aggravated assault is an attack for the purpose of inflicting severe bodily injury.

Aggravated Assault Rate in 2015

National Rate = 237.8 Aggravated Assaults per 100,000 Population*

ALPHA ORDER

RANK	STATE	RATE
9	Alabama	328.3
1	Alaska	497.1
17	Arizona	267.1
5	Arkansas	380.0
21	California	253.8
29	Colorado	197.2
46	Connecticut	113.1
10	Delaware	325.7
11	Florida	315.2
27	Georgia	220.8
35	Hawaii	168.9
38	Idaho	160.1
26	Illinois	224.6
23	Indiana	238.2
28	Iowa	213.2
16	Kansas	267.6
48	Kentucky	105.5
6	Louisiana	373.7
50	Maine	69.3
19	Maryland	256.7
14	Massachusetts	280.7
18	Michigan	266.2
43	Minnesota	129.2
39	Mississippi	150.3
8	Missouri	342.4
15	Montana	272.8
33	Nebraska	173.1
4	Nevada	413.9
45	New Hampshire	116.0
44	New Jersey	127.4
3	New Mexico	451.2
25	New York	225.0
24	North Carolina	227.3
34	North Dakota	171.5
41	Ohio	135.1
13	Oklahoma	291.9
37	Oregon	164.6
32	Pennsylvania	174.8
40	Rhode Island	143.7
7	South Carolina	369.1
12	South Dakota	296.6
2	Tennessee	452.2
22	Texas	246.6
41	Utah	135.1
49	Vermont	78.6
47	Virginia	110.2
36	Washington	167.8
20	West Virginia	256.4
30	Wisconsin	180.1
31	Wyoming	179.8

RANK ORDER

RANK	STATE	RATE
1	Alaska	497.1
2	Tennessee	452.2
3	New Mexico	451.2
4	Nevada	413.9
5	Arkansas	380.0
6	Louisiana	373.7
7	South Carolina	369.1
8	Missouri	342.4
9	Alabama	328.3
10	Delaware	325.7
11	Florida	315.2
12	South Dakota	296.6
13	Oklahoma	291.9
14	Massachusetts	280.7
15	Montana	272.8
16	Kansas	267.6
17	Arizona	267.1
18	Michigan	266.2
19	Maryland	256.7
20	West Virginia	256.4
21	California	253.8
22	Texas	246.6
23	Indiana	238.2
24	North Carolina	227.3
25	New York	225.0
26	Illinois	224.6
27	Georgia	220.8
28	Iowa	213.2
29	Colorado	197.2
30	Wisconsin	180.1
31	Wyoming	179.8
32	Pennsylvania	174.8
33	Nebraska	173.1
34	North Dakota	171.5
35	Hawaii	168.9
36	Washington	167.8
37	Oregon	164.6
38	Idaho	160.1
39	Mississippi	150.3
40	Rhode Island	143.7
41	Ohio	135.1
41	Utah	135.1
43	Minnesota	129.2
44	New Jersey	127.4
45	New Hampshire	116.0
46	Connecticut	113.1
47	Virginia	110.2
48	Kentucky	105.5
49	Vermont	78.6
50	Maine	69.3
	District of Columbia	614.8

Source: Reported data from the Federal Bureau of Investigation
   "Crime in the United States 2015" (Uniform Crime Reports, September 26, 2016, http://www.fbi.gov/about-us/cjis/ucr/)
*Aggravated assault is an attack for the purpose of inflicting severe bodily injury.

Property Crimes in 2015

National Total = 7,993,631 Property Crimes*

ALPHA ORDER

RANK	STATE	CRIMES	% of USA
20	Alabama	144,746	1.8%
45	Alaska	20,806	0.3%
11	Arizona	207,107	2.6%
28	Arkansas	96,836	1.2%
1	California	1,024,914	12.8%
21	Colorado	144,136	1.8%
35	Connecticut	65,066	0.8%
42	Delaware	25,455	0.3%
3	Florida	570,270	7.1%
5	Georgia	308,723	3.9%
37	Hawaii	54,346	0.7%
40	Idaho	28,858	0.4%
8	Illinois	255,729	3.2%
15	Indiana	171,847	2.1%
36	Iowa	63,957	0.8%
32	Kansas	79,199	1.0%
29	Kentucky	96,362	1.2%
17	Louisiana	156,629	2.0%
43	Maine	24,327	0.3%
22	Maryland	139,048	1.7%
25	Massachusetts	114,871	1.4%
13	Michigan	187,101	2.3%
23	Minnesota	121,984	1.5%
31	Mississippi	84,790	1.1%
14	Missouri	173,642	2.2%
41	Montana	27,100	0.3%
38	Nebraska	42,495	0.5%
33	Nevada	77,137	1.0%
44	New Hampshire	23,229	0.3%
19	New Jersey	145,701	1.8%
34	New Mexico	77,094	1.0%
4	New York	317,529	4.0%
7	North Carolina	276,183	3.5%
48	North Dakota	16,020	0.2%
6	Ohio	300,525	3.8%
27	Oklahoma	112,878	1.4%
24	Oregon	118,719	1.5%
10	Pennsylvania	232,085	2.9%
46	Rhode Island	20,043	0.3%
16	South Carolina	161,245	2.0%
47	South Dakota	16,680	0.2%
12	Tennessee	193,796	2.4%
2	Texas	777,739	9.7%
30	Utah	89,278	1.1%
50	Vermont	8,806	0.1%
18	Virginia	156,470	2.0%
9	Washington	248,369	3.1%
39	West Virginia	37,251	0.5%
26	Wisconsin	113,924	1.4%
49	Wyoming	11,151	0.1%

RANK ORDER

RANK	STATE	CRIMES	% of USA
1	California	1,024,914	12.8%
2	Texas	777,739	9.7%
3	Florida	570,270	7.1%
4	New York	317,529	4.0%
5	Georgia	308,723	3.9%
6	Ohio	300,525	3.8%
7	North Carolina	276,183	3.5%
8	Illinois	255,729	3.2%
9	Washington	248,369	3.1%
10	Pennsylvania	232,085	2.9%
11	Arizona	207,107	2.6%
12	Tennessee	193,796	2.4%
13	Michigan	187,101	2.3%
14	Missouri	173,642	2.2%
15	Indiana	171,847	2.1%
16	South Carolina	161,245	2.0%
17	Louisiana	156,629	2.0%
18	Virginia	156,470	2.0%
19	New Jersey	145,701	1.8%
20	Alabama	144,746	1.8%
21	Colorado	144,136	1.8%
22	Maryland	139,048	1.7%
23	Minnesota	121,984	1.5%
24	Oregon	118,719	1.5%
25	Massachusetts	114,871	1.4%
26	Wisconsin	113,924	1.4%
27	Oklahoma	112,878	1.4%
28	Arkansas	96,836	1.2%
29	Kentucky	96,362	1.2%
30	Utah	89,278	1.1%
31	Mississippi	84,790	1.1%
32	Kansas	79,199	1.0%
33	Nevada	77,137	1.0%
34	New Mexico	77,094	1.0%
35	Connecticut	65,066	0.8%
36	Iowa	63,957	0.8%
37	Hawaii	54,346	0.7%
38	Nebraska	42,495	0.5%
39	West Virginia	37,251	0.5%
40	Idaho	28,858	0.4%
41	Montana	27,100	0.3%
42	Delaware	25,455	0.3%
43	Maine	24,327	0.3%
44	New Hampshire	23,229	0.3%
45	Alaska	20,806	0.3%
46	Rhode Island	20,043	0.3%
47	South Dakota	16,680	0.2%
48	North Dakota	16,020	0.2%
49	Wyoming	11,151	0.1%
50	Vermont	8,806	0.1%
	District of Columbia	31,435	0.4%

Source: Reported data from the Federal Bureau of Investigation
   "Crime in the United States 2015" (Uniform Crime Reports, September 26, 2016, http://www.fbi.gov/about-us/cjis/ucr/)
*Property crimes are offenses of burglary, larceny-theft, and motor vehicle theft.

Property Crime Rate in 2015

National Rate = 2,487.0 Property Crimes per 100,000 Population*

ALPHA ORDER			RANK ORDER		
RANK	STATE	RATE	RANK	STATE	RATE
10	Alabama	2,978.9	1	Hawaii	3,796.2
17	Alaska	2,817.6	2	New Mexico	3,697.4
7	Arizona	3,033.2	3	Washington	3,463.8
6	Arkansas	3,251.5	4	Louisiana	3,353.4
25	California	2,618.3	5	South Carolina	3,293.3
23	Colorado	2,641.5	6	Arkansas	3,251.5
44	Connecticut	1,812.0	7	Arizona	3,033.2
21	Delaware	2,691.0	8	Georgia	3,022.3
18	Florida	2,813.2	9	Utah	2,980.0
8	Georgia	3,022.3	10	Alabama	2,978.9
1	Hawaii	3,796.2	11	Oregon	2,946.6
46	Idaho	1,743.8	12	Tennessee	2,936.2
35	Illinois	1,988.6	13	Oklahoma	2,885.9
26	Indiana	2,596.0	14	Missouri	2,854.2
33	Iowa	2,047.3	15	Mississippi	2,833.6
20	Kansas	2,720.1	16	Texas	2,831.3
31	Kentucky	2,177.6	17	Alaska	2,817.6
4	Louisiana	3,353.4	18	Florida	2,813.2
42	Maine	1,830.0	19	North Carolina	2,750.1
28	Maryland	2,315.0	20	Kansas	2,720.1
47	Massachusetts	1,690.7	21	Delaware	2,691.0
40	Michigan	1,885.6	22	Nevada	2,668.3
30	Minnesota	2,222.1	23	Colorado	2,641.5
15	Mississippi	2,833.6	24	Montana	2,623.6
14	Missouri	2,854.2	25	California	2,618.3
24	Montana	2,623.6	26	Indiana	2,596.0
29	Nebraska	2,241.1	27	Ohio	2,587.7
22	Nevada	2,668.3	28	Maryland	2,315.0
45	New Hampshire	1,745.7	29	Nebraska	2,241.1
48	New Jersey	1,626.5	30	Minnesota	2,222.1
2	New Mexico	3,697.4	31	Kentucky	2,177.6
49	New York	1,604.0	32	North Dakota	2,116.5
19	North Carolina	2,750.1	33	Iowa	2,047.3
32	North Dakota	2,116.5	34	West Virginia	2,020.0
27	Ohio	2,587.7	35	Illinois	1,988.6
13	Oklahoma	2,885.9	36	Wisconsin	1,974.0
11	Oregon	2,946.6	37	South Dakota	1,943.0
43	Pennsylvania	1,812.8	38	Wyoming	1,902.6
39	Rhode Island	1,897.5	39	Rhode Island	1,897.5
5	South Carolina	3,293.3	40	Michigan	1,885.6
37	South Dakota	1,943.0	41	Virginia	1,866.5
12	Tennessee	2,936.2	42	Maine	1,830.0
16	Texas	2,831.3	43	Pennsylvania	1,812.8
9	Utah	2,980.0	44	Connecticut	1,812.0
50	Vermont	1,406.6	45	New Hampshire	1,745.7
41	Virginia	1,866.5	46	Idaho	1,743.8
3	Washington	3,463.8	47	Massachusetts	1,690.7
34	West Virginia	2,020.0	48	New Jersey	1,626.5
36	Wisconsin	1,974.0	49	New York	1,604.0
38	Wyoming	1,902.6	50	Vermont	1,406.6
				District of Columbia	4,676.2

Source: Reported data from the Federal Bureau of Investigation
    "Crime in the United States 2015" (Uniform Crime Reports, September 26, 2016, http://www.fbi.gov/about-us/cjis/ucr/)
*Property crimes are offenses of burglary, larceny-theft, and motor vehicle theft.

Percent Change in Property Crime Rate: 2014 to 2015

National Percent Change = 3.4% Decrease*

ALPHA ORDER			RANK ORDER		
RANK	STATE	PERCENT CHANGE	RANK	STATE	PERCENT CHANGE
36	Alabama	(6.3)	1	Hawaii	17.2
8	Alaska	2.1	2	California	7.2
26	Arizona	(4.4)	3	Montana	5.2
17	Arkansas	(3.0)	4	New Mexico	4.4
2	California	7.2	5	Colorado	4.2
5	Colorado	4.2	6	South Dakota	3.4
32	Connecticut	(6.0)	7	Utah	2.7
46	Delaware	(9.8)	8	Alaska	2.1
23	Florida	(4.1)	9	Nevada	1.6
47	Georgia	(10.0)	10	North Dakota	(1.2)
1	Hawaii	17.2	11	Kansas	(1.3)
36	Idaho	(6.3)	12	Missouri	(1.9)
28	Illinois	(5.0)	13	Indiana	(2.1)
13	Indiana	(2.1)	14	Iowa	(2.2)
14	Iowa	(2.2)	15	Mississippi	(2.4)
11	Kansas	(1.3)	15	West Virginia	(2.4)
21	Kentucky	(3.8)	17	Arkansas	(3.0)
19	Louisiana	(3.3)	18	Wyoming	(3.1)
42	Maine	(7.9)	19	Louisiana	(3.3)
43	Maryland	(8.0)	19	Minnesota	(3.3)
44	Massachusetts	(9.0)	21	Kentucky	(3.8)
41	Michigan	(7.8)	22	Virginia	(4.0)
19	Minnesota	(3.3)	23	Florida	(4.1)
15	Mississippi	(2.4)	24	North Carolina	(4.2)
12	Missouri	(1.9)	25	Tennessee	(4.3)
3	Montana	5.2	26	Arizona	(4.4)
48	Nebraska	(11.2)	27	Oklahoma	(4.7)
9	Nevada	1.6	28	Illinois	(5.0)
48	New Hampshire	(11.2)	28	Oregon	(5.0)
35	New Jersey	(6.2)	30	South Carolina	(5.5)
4	New Mexico	4.4	31	Wisconsin	(5.7)
39	New York	(6.6)	32	Connecticut	(6.0)
24	North Carolina	(4.2)	33	Pennsylvania	(6.1)
10	North Dakota	(1.2)	33	Texas	(6.1)
40	Ohio	(7.0)	35	New Jersey	(6.2)
27	Oklahoma	(4.7)	36	Alabama	(6.3)
28	Oregon	(5.0)	36	Idaho	(6.3)
33	Pennsylvania	(6.1)	38	Washington	(6.4)
50	Rhode Island	(12.9)	39	New York	(6.6)
30	South Carolina	(5.5)	40	Ohio	(7.0)
6	South Dakota	3.4	41	Michigan	(7.8)
25	Tennessee	(4.3)	42	Maine	(7.9)
33	Texas	(6.1)	43	Maryland	(8.0)
7	Utah	2.7	44	Massachusetts	(9.0)
45	Vermont	(9.3)	45	Vermont	(9.3)
22	Virginia	(4.0)	46	Delaware	(9.8)
38	Washington	(6.4)	47	Georgia	(10.0)
15	West Virginia	(2.4)	48	Nebraska	(11.2)
31	Wisconsin	(5.7)	48	New Hampshire	(11.2)
18	Wyoming	(3.1)	50	Rhode Island	(12.9)

District of Columbia   (9.6)

Source: Reported data from the Federal Bureau of Investigation
"Crime in the United States 2015" (Uniform Crime Reports, September 26, 2016, http://www.fbi.gov/about-us/cjis/ucr/)
*Property crimes are offenses of burglary, larceny-theft, and motor vehicle theft.

Burglaries in 2015

National Total = 1,579,527 Burglaries*

ALPHA ORDER

RANK	STATE	BURGLARIES	% of USA
15	Alabama	35,255	2.2%
45	Alaska	3,511	0.2%
13	Arizona	37,957	2.4%
24	Arkansas	22,640	1.4%
1	California	197,404	12.5%
23	Colorado	23,454	1.5%
36	Connecticut	10,053	0.6%
41	Delaware	4,773	0.3%
3	Florida	109,268	6.9%
6	Georgia	66,374	4.2%
38	Hawaii	6,557	0.4%
40	Idaho	6,124	0.4%
8	Illinois	46,443	2.9%
17	Indiana	34,410	2.2%
34	Iowa	14,892	0.9%
33	Kansas	15,362	1.0%
26	Kentucky	22,260	1.4%
14	Louisiana	35,453	2.2%
42	Maine	4,684	0.3%
21	Maryland	25,678	1.6%
27	Massachusetts	21,890	1.4%
11	Michigan	40,041	2.5%
30	Minnesota	19,299	1.2%
22	Mississippi	24,799	1.6%
18	Missouri	34,006	2.2%
44	Montana	3,838	0.2%
39	Nebraska	6,422	0.4%
25	Nevada	22,360	1.4%
46	New Hampshire	3,467	0.2%
20	New Jersey	27,960	1.8%
32	New Mexico	17,085	1.1%
9	New York	44,276	2.8%
4	North Carolina	74,841	4.7%
47	North Dakota	2,997	0.2%
5	Ohio	69,303	4.4%
19	Oklahoma	28,406	1.8%
31	Oregon	18,336	1.2%
12	Pennsylvania	39,664	2.5%
43	Rhode Island	3,947	0.2%
16	South Carolina	34,551	2.2%
48	South Dakota	2,960	0.2%
10	Tennessee	43,247	2.7%
2	Texas	153,054	9.7%
35	Utah	12,468	0.8%
49	Vermont	1,968	0.1%
28	Virginia	21,340	1.4%
7	Washington	50,993	3.2%
37	West Virginia	9,170	0.6%
29	Wisconsin	19,554	1.2%
50	Wyoming	1,762	0.1%

RANK ORDER

RANK	STATE	BURGLARIES	% of USA
1	California	197,404	12.5%
2	Texas	153,054	9.7%
3	Florida	109,268	6.9%
4	North Carolina	74,841	4.7%
5	Ohio	69,303	4.4%
6	Georgia	66,374	4.2%
7	Washington	50,993	3.2%
8	Illinois	46,443	2.9%
9	New York	44,276	2.8%
10	Tennessee	43,247	2.7%
11	Michigan	40,041	2.5%
12	Pennsylvania	39,664	2.5%
13	Arizona	37,957	2.4%
14	Louisiana	35,453	2.2%
15	Alabama	35,255	2.2%
16	South Carolina	34,551	2.2%
17	Indiana	34,410	2.2%
18	Missouri	34,006	2.2%
19	Oklahoma	28,406	1.8%
20	New Jersey	27,960	1.8%
21	Maryland	25,678	1.6%
22	Mississippi	24,799	1.6%
23	Colorado	23,454	1.5%
24	Arkansas	22,640	1.4%
25	Nevada	22,360	1.4%
26	Kentucky	22,260	1.4%
27	Massachusetts	21,890	1.4%
28	Virginia	21,340	1.4%
29	Wisconsin	19,554	1.2%
30	Minnesota	19,299	1.2%
31	Oregon	18,336	1.2%
32	New Mexico	17,085	1.1%
33	Kansas	15,362	1.0%
34	Iowa	14,892	0.9%
35	Utah	12,468	0.8%
36	Connecticut	10,053	0.6%
37	West Virginia	9,170	0.6%
38	Hawaii	6,557	0.4%
39	Nebraska	6,422	0.4%
40	Idaho	6,124	0.4%
41	Delaware	4,773	0.3%
42	Maine	4,684	0.3%
43	Rhode Island	3,947	0.2%
44	Montana	3,838	0.2%
45	Alaska	3,511	0.2%
46	New Hampshire	3,467	0.2%
47	North Dakota	2,997	0.2%
48	South Dakota	2,960	0.2%
49	Vermont	1,968	0.1%
50	Wyoming	1,762	0.1%
	District of Columbia	2,971	0.2%

Source: Reported data from the Federal Bureau of Investigation
"Crime in the United States 2015" (Uniform Crime Reports, September 26, 2016, http://www.fbi.gov/about-us/cjis/ucr/)
*Burglary is the unlawful entry of a structure to commit a felony or theft. Attempts are included.

Burglary Rate in 2015

National Rate = 491.4 Burglaries per 100,000 Population*

ALPHA ORDER

RANK	STATE	RATE
8	Alabama	725.6
25	Alaska	475.5
16	Arizona	555.9
4	Arkansas	760.2
21	California	504.3
28	Colorado	429.8
47	Connecticut	280.0
20	Delaware	504.6
17	Florida	539.0
12	Georgia	649.8
26	Hawaii	458.0
35	Idaho	370.0
36	Illinois	361.1
19	Indiana	519.8
24	Iowa	476.7
18	Kansas	527.6
22	Kentucky	503.0
5	Louisiana	759.0
37	Maine	352.4
29	Maryland	427.5
42	Massachusetts	322.2
31	Michigan	403.5
38	Minnesota	351.6
1	Mississippi	828.8
14	Missouri	559.0
34	Montana	371.6
41	Nebraska	338.7
3	Nevada	773.5
48	New Hampshire	260.6
44	New Jersey	312.1
2	New Mexico	819.4
50	New York	223.7
6	North Carolina	745.2
32	North Dakota	395.9
13	Ohio	596.7
7	Oklahoma	726.2
27	Oregon	455.1
45	Pennsylvania	309.8
33	Rhode Island	373.7
10	South Carolina	705.7
39	South Dakota	344.8
11	Tennessee	655.2
15	Texas	557.2
30	Utah	416.2
43	Vermont	314.4
49	Virginia	254.6
9	Washington	711.2
23	West Virginia	497.3
40	Wisconsin	338.8
46	Wyoming	300.6

RANK ORDER

RANK	STATE	RATE
1	Mississippi	828.8
2	New Mexico	819.4
3	Nevada	773.5
4	Arkansas	760.2
5	Louisiana	759.0
6	North Carolina	745.2
7	Oklahoma	726.2
8	Alabama	725.6
9	Washington	711.2
10	South Carolina	705.7
11	Tennessee	655.2
12	Georgia	649.8
13	Ohio	596.7
14	Missouri	559.0
15	Texas	557.2
16	Arizona	555.9
17	Florida	539.0
18	Kansas	527.6
19	Indiana	519.8
20	Delaware	504.6
21	California	504.3
22	Kentucky	503.0
23	West Virginia	497.3
24	Iowa	476.7
25	Alaska	475.5
26	Hawaii	458.0
27	Oregon	455.1
28	Colorado	429.8
29	Maryland	427.5
30	Utah	416.2
31	Michigan	403.5
32	North Dakota	395.9
33	Rhode Island	373.7
34	Montana	371.6
35	Idaho	370.0
36	Illinois	361.1
37	Maine	352.4
38	Minnesota	351.6
39	South Dakota	344.8
40	Wisconsin	338.8
41	Nebraska	338.7
42	Massachusetts	322.2
43	Vermont	314.4
44	New Jersey	312.1
45	Pennsylvania	309.8
46	Wyoming	300.6
47	Connecticut	280.0
48	New Hampshire	260.6
49	Virginia	254.6
50	New York	223.7
	District of Columbia	442.0

Source: Reported data from the Federal Bureau of Investigation
   "Crime in the United States 2015" (Uniform Crime Reports, September 26, 2016, http://www.fbi.gov/about-us/cjis/ucr/)
*Burglary is the unlawful entry of a structure to commit a felony or theft. Attempts are included.

Larceny-Thefts in 2015

National Total = 5,706,346 Larceny-Thefts*

ALPHA ORDER					RANK ORDER			
RANK	STATE	THEFTS	% of USA		RANK	STATE	THEFTS	% of USA
22	Alabama	99,156	1.7%		1	California	656,517	11.5%
45	Alaska	15,249	0.3%		2	Texas	557,200	9.8%
11	Arizona	152,365	2.7%		3	Florida	420,341	7.4%
28	Arkansas	68,424	1.2%		4	New York	257,940	4.5%
1	California	656,517	11.5%		5	Georgia	215,867	3.8%
20	Colorado	104,682	1.8%		6	Ohio	213,993	3.8%
34	Connecticut	48,675	0.9%		7	Illinois	191,634	3.4%
42	Delaware	19,501	0.3%		8	North Carolina	187,907	3.3%
3	Florida	420,341	7.4%		9	Pennsylvania	180,287	3.2%
5	Georgia	215,867	3.8%		10	Washington	170,509	3.0%
37	Hawaii	42,010	0.7%		11	Arizona	152,365	2.7%
40	Idaho	20,863	0.4%		12	Tennessee	137,679	2.4%
7	Illinois	191,634	3.4%		13	Michigan	131,296	2.3%
15	Indiana	123,918	2.2%		14	Virginia	127,019	2.2%
35	Iowa	44,723	0.8%		15	Indiana	123,918	2.2%
31	Kansas	56,880	1.0%		16	Missouri	122,637	2.1%
30	Kentucky	66,320	1.2%		17	South Carolina	113,724	2.0%
18	Louisiana	111,435	2.0%		18	Louisiana	111,435	2.0%
44	Maine	18,829	0.3%		19	New Jersey	105,963	1.9%
21	Maryland	100,219	1.8%		20	Colorado	104,682	1.8%
25	Massachusetts	84,912	1.5%		21	Maryland	100,219	1.8%
13	Michigan	131,296	2.3%		22	Alabama	99,156	1.7%
23	Minnesota	94,704	1.7%		23	Minnesota	94,704	1.7%
32	Mississippi	55,748	1.0%		24	Oregon	89,836	1.6%
16	Missouri	122,637	2.1%		25	Massachusetts	84,912	1.5%
41	Montana	20,844	0.4%		26	Wisconsin	83,385	1.5%
38	Nebraska	32,072	0.6%		27	Oklahoma	74,022	1.3%
36	Nevada	43,426	0.8%		28	Arkansas	68,424	1.2%
43	New Hampshire	18,871	0.3%		29	Utah	68,103	1.2%
19	New Jersey	105,963	1.9%		30	Kentucky	66,320	1.2%
33	New Mexico	51,483	0.9%		31	Kansas	56,880	1.0%
4	New York	257,940	4.5%		32	Mississippi	55,748	1.0%
8	North Carolina	187,907	3.3%		33	New Mexico	51,483	0.9%
48	North Dakota	11,440	0.2%		34	Connecticut	48,675	0.9%
6	Ohio	213,993	3.8%		35	Iowa	44,723	0.8%
27	Oklahoma	74,022	1.3%		36	Nevada	43,426	0.8%
24	Oregon	89,836	1.6%		37	Hawaii	42,010	0.7%
9	Pennsylvania	180,287	3.2%		38	Nebraska	32,072	0.6%
46	Rhode Island	14,707	0.3%		39	West Virginia	25,842	0.5%
17	South Carolina	113,724	2.0%		40	Idaho	20,863	0.4%
47	South Dakota	12,532	0.2%		41	Montana	20,844	0.4%
12	Tennessee	137,679	2.4%		42	Delaware	19,501	0.3%
2	Texas	557,200	9.8%		43	New Hampshire	18,871	0.3%
29	Utah	68,103	1.2%		44	Maine	18,829	0.3%
50	Vermont	6,660	0.1%		45	Alaska	15,249	0.3%
14	Virginia	127,019	2.2%		46	Rhode Island	14,707	0.3%
10	Washington	170,509	3.0%		47	South Dakota	12,532	0.2%
39	West Virginia	25,842	0.5%		48	North Dakota	11,440	0.2%
26	Wisconsin	83,385	1.5%		49	Wyoming	8,797	0.2%
49	Wyoming	8,797	0.2%		50	Vermont	6,660	0.1%
						District of Columbia	25,200	0.4%

Source: Reported data from the Federal Bureau of Investigation
    "Crime in the United States 2015" (Uniform Crime Reports, September 26, 2016, http://www.fbi.gov/about-us/cjis/ucr/)
*Larceny-theft is the unlawful taking of property without use of force, violence, or fraud. Attempts are included. Motor vehicle thefts are excluded.

Larceny-Theft Rate in 2015

National Rate = 1,775.4 Larceny-Thefts per 100,000 Population*

ALPHA ORDER

RANK ORDER

RANK	STATE	RATE		RANK	STATE	RATE
15	Alabama	2,040.7		1	Hawaii	2,934.5
13	Alaska	2,065.1		2	New Mexico	2,469.1
8	Arizona	2,231.5		3	Louisiana	2,385.8
6	Arkansas	2,297.5		4	Washington	2,378.0
28	California	1,677.1		5	South Carolina	2,322.7
20	Colorado	1,918.5		6	Arkansas	2,297.5
44	Connecticut	1,355.5		7	Utah	2,273.2
14	Delaware	2,061.6		8	Arizona	2,231.5
12	Florida	2,073.6		9	Oregon	2,229.7
10	Georgia	2,113.3		10	Georgia	2,113.3
1	Hawaii	2,934.5		11	Tennessee	2,086.0
47	Idaho	1,260.7		12	Florida	2,073.6
35	Illinois	1,490.2		13	Alaska	2,065.1
22	Indiana	1,872.0		14	Delaware	2,061.6
38	Iowa	1,431.6		15	Alabama	2,040.7
19	Kansas	1,953.5		16	Texas	2,028.5
34	Kentucky	1,498.7		17	Montana	2,017.9
3	Louisiana	2,385.8		18	Missouri	2,015.8
40	Maine	1,416.4		19	Kansas	1,953.5
29	Maryland	1,668.5		20	Colorado	1,918.5
48	Massachusetts	1,249.7		21	Oklahoma	1,892.5
45	Michigan	1,323.2		22	Indiana	1,872.0
26	Minnesota	1,725.2		23	North Carolina	1,871.1
24	Mississippi	1,863.0		24	Mississippi	1,863.0
18	Missouri	2,015.8		25	Ohio	1,842.6
17	Montana	2,017.9		26	Minnesota	1,725.2
27	Nebraska	1,691.4		27	Nebraska	1,691.4
32	Nevada	1,502.2		28	California	1,677.1
39	New Hampshire	1,418.2		29	Maryland	1,668.5
49	New Jersey	1,182.9		30	Virginia	1,515.2
2	New Mexico	2,469.1		31	North Dakota	1,511.4
46	New York	1,303.0		32	Nevada	1,502.2
23	North Carolina	1,871.1		33	Wyoming	1,500.9
31	North Dakota	1,511.4		34	Kentucky	1,498.7
25	Ohio	1,842.6		35	Illinois	1,490.2
21	Oklahoma	1,892.5		36	South Dakota	1,459.8
9	Oregon	2,229.7		37	Wisconsin	1,444.8
41	Pennsylvania	1,408.2		38	Iowa	1,431.6
43	Rhode Island	1,392.3		39	New Hampshire	1,418.2
5	South Carolina	2,322.7		40	Maine	1,416.4
36	South Dakota	1,459.8		41	Pennsylvania	1,408.2
11	Tennessee	2,086.0		42	West Virginia	1,401.3
16	Texas	2,028.5		43	Rhode Island	1,392.3
7	Utah	2,273.2		44	Connecticut	1,355.5
50	Vermont	1,063.8		45	Michigan	1,323.2
30	Virginia	1,515.2		46	New York	1,303.0
4	Washington	2,378.0		47	Idaho	1,260.7
42	West Virginia	1,401.3		48	Massachusetts	1,249.7
37	Wisconsin	1,444.8		49	New Jersey	1,182.9
33	Wyoming	1,500.9		50	Vermont	1,063.8

District of Columbia 3,748.7

Source: Reported data from the Federal Bureau of Investigation
"Crime in the United States 2015" (Uniform Crime Reports, September 26, 2016, http://www.fbi.gov/about-us/cjis/ucr/)
*Larceny-theft is the unlawful taking of property without use of force, violence, or fraud. Attempts are included. Motor vehicle thefts are excluded.

Motor Vehicle Thefts in 2015

National Total = 707,758 Motor Vehicle Thefts*

ALPHA ORDER

RANK	STATE	THEFTS	% of USA
24	Alabama	10,335	1.5%
41	Alaska	2,046	0.3%
9	Arizona	16,785	2.4%
35	Arkansas	5,772	0.8%
1	California	170,993	24.2%
10	Colorado	16,000	2.3%
33	Connecticut	6,338	0.9%
46	Delaware	1,181	0.2%
3	Florida	40,661	5.7%
5	Georgia	26,482	3.7%
34	Hawaii	5,779	0.8%
42	Idaho	1,871	0.3%
6	Illinois	17,652	2.5%
13	Indiana	13,519	1.9%
36	Iowa	4,342	0.6%
32	Kansas	6,957	1.0%
31	Kentucky	7,782	1.1%
25	Louisiana	9,741	1.4%
48	Maine	814	0.1%
15	Maryland	13,151	1.9%
29	Massachusetts	8,069	1.1%
11	Michigan	15,764	2.2%
30	Minnesota	7,981	1.1%
37	Mississippi	4,243	0.6%
8	Missouri	16,999	2.4%
39	Montana	2,418	0.3%
38	Nebraska	4,001	0.6%
20	Nevada	11,351	1.6%
47	New Hampshire	891	0.1%
19	New Jersey	11,778	1.7%
27	New Mexico	8,526	1.2%
12	New York	15,313	2.2%
14	North Carolina	13,435	1.9%
43	North Dakota	1,583	0.2%
7	Ohio	17,229	2.4%
23	Oklahoma	10,450	1.5%
22	Oregon	10,547	1.5%
18	Pennsylvania	12,134	1.7%
44	Rhode Island	1,389	0.2%
16	South Carolina	12,970	1.8%
45	South Dakota	1,188	0.2%
17	Tennessee	12,870	1.8%
2	Texas	67,485	9.5%
26	Utah	8,707	1.2%
50	Vermont	178	0.0%
28	Virginia	8,111	1.1%
4	Washington	26,867	3.8%
40	West Virginia	2,239	0.3%
21	Wisconsin	10,985	1.6%
49	Wyoming	592	0.1%

RANK ORDER

RANK	STATE	THEFTS	% of USA
1	California	170,993	24.2%
2	Texas	67,485	9.5%
3	Florida	40,661	5.7%
4	Washington	26,867	3.8%
5	Georgia	26,482	3.7%
6	Illinois	17,652	2.5%
7	Ohio	17,229	2.4%
8	Missouri	16,999	2.4%
9	Arizona	16,785	2.4%
10	Colorado	16,000	2.3%
11	Michigan	15,764	2.2%
12	New York	15,313	2.2%
13	Indiana	13,519	1.9%
14	North Carolina	13,435	1.9%
15	Maryland	13,151	1.9%
16	South Carolina	12,970	1.8%
17	Tennessee	12,870	1.8%
18	Pennsylvania	12,134	1.7%
19	New Jersey	11,778	1.7%
20	Nevada	11,351	1.6%
21	Wisconsin	10,985	1.6%
22	Oregon	10,547	1.5%
23	Oklahoma	10,450	1.5%
24	Alabama	10,335	1.5%
25	Louisiana	9,741	1.4%
26	Utah	8,707	1.2%
27	New Mexico	8,526	1.2%
28	Virginia	8,111	1.1%
29	Massachusetts	8,069	1.1%
30	Minnesota	7,981	1.1%
31	Kentucky	7,782	1.1%
32	Kansas	6,957	1.0%
33	Connecticut	6,338	0.9%
34	Hawaii	5,779	0.8%
35	Arkansas	5,772	0.8%
36	Iowa	4,342	0.6%
37	Mississippi	4,243	0.6%
38	Nebraska	4,001	0.6%
39	Montana	2,418	0.3%
40	West Virginia	2,239	0.3%
41	Alaska	2,046	0.3%
42	Idaho	1,871	0.3%
43	North Dakota	1,583	0.2%
44	Rhode Island	1,389	0.2%
45	South Dakota	1,188	0.2%
46	Delaware	1,181	0.2%
47	New Hampshire	891	0.1%
48	Maine	814	0.1%
49	Wyoming	592	0.1%
50	Vermont	178	0.0%
	District of Columbia	3,264	0.5%

Source: Reported data from the Federal Bureau of Investigation
"Crime in the United States 2015" (Uniform Crime Reports, September 26, 2016, http://www.fbi.gov/about-us/cjis/ucr/)
*Includes the theft or attempted theft of a self-propelled vehicle. Excludes motorboats, construction equipment, airplanes, and farming equipment.

Motor Vehicle Theft Rate in 2015

National Rate = 220.2 Motor Vehicle Thefts per 100,000 Population*

RANK	STATE	RATE
19	Alabama	212.7
9	Alaska	277.1
14	Arizona	245.8
26	Arkansas	193.8
1	California	436.8
6	Colorado	293.2
28	Connecticut	176.5
40	Delaware	124.9
24	Florida	200.6
13	Georgia	259.2
3	Hawaii	403.7
43	Idaho	113.1
36	Illinois	137.3
23	Indiana	204.2
34	Iowa	139.0
16	Kansas	238.9
29	Kentucky	175.9
22	Louisiana	208.6
49	Maine	61.2
18	Maryland	218.9
42	Massachusetts	118.8
30	Michigan	158.9
32	Minnesota	145.4
33	Mississippi	141.8
8	Missouri	279.4
17	Montana	234.1
20	Nebraska	211.0
4	Nevada	392.7
48	New Hampshire	67.0
38	New Jersey	131.5
2	New Mexico	408.9
47	New York	77.4
37	North Carolina	133.8
21	North Dakota	209.1
31	Ohio	148.4
10	Oklahoma	267.2
12	Oregon	261.8
46	Pennsylvania	94.8
38	Rhode Island	131.5
11	South Carolina	264.9
35	South Dakota	138.4
25	Tennessee	195.0
15	Texas	245.7
7	Utah	290.6
50	Vermont	28.4
45	Virginia	96.8
5	Washington	374.7
41	West Virginia	121.4
27	Wisconsin	190.3
44	Wyoming	101.0

RANK	STATE	RATE
1	California	436.8
2	New Mexico	408.9
3	Hawaii	403.7
4	Nevada	392.7
5	Washington	374.7
6	Colorado	293.2
7	Utah	290.6
8	Missouri	279.4
9	Alaska	277.1
10	Oklahoma	267.2
11	South Carolina	264.9
12	Oregon	261.8
13	Georgia	259.2
14	Arizona	245.8
15	Texas	245.7
16	Kansas	238.9
17	Montana	234.1
18	Maryland	218.9
19	Alabama	212.7
20	Nebraska	211.0
21	North Dakota	209.1
22	Louisiana	208.6
23	Indiana	204.2
24	Florida	200.6
25	Tennessee	195.0
26	Arkansas	193.8
27	Wisconsin	190.3
28	Connecticut	176.5
29	Kentucky	175.9
30	Michigan	158.9
31	Ohio	148.4
32	Minnesota	145.4
33	Mississippi	141.8
34	Iowa	139.0
35	South Dakota	138.4
36	Illinois	137.3
37	North Carolina	133.8
38	New Jersey	131.5
38	Rhode Island	131.5
40	Delaware	124.9
41	West Virginia	121.4
42	Massachusetts	118.8
43	Idaho	113.1
44	Wyoming	101.0
45	Virginia	96.8
46	Pennsylvania	94.8
47	New York	77.4
48	New Hampshire	67.0
49	Maine	61.2
50	Vermont	28.4

District of Columbia	485.5

Source: Reported data from the Federal Bureau of Investigation
"Crime in the United States 2015" (Uniform Crime Reports, September 26, 2016, http://www.fbi.gov/about-us/cjis/ucr/)
*Includes the theft or attempted theft of a self-propelled vehicle. Excludes motorboats, construction equipment, airplanes, and farming equipment.

Rate of Consumer Fraud Complaints in 2015

National Rate = 808.1 Complaints per 100,000 Population*

ALPHA ORDER			RANK ORDER		
RANK	**STATE**	**RATE**	**RANK**	**STATE**	**RATE**
10	Alabama	738.1	1	Florida	1,510.2
46	Alaska	395.0	2	Georgia	1,208.3
16	Arizona	623.5	3	Michigan	1,143.6
33	Arkansas	478.4	4	Texas	941.3
8	California	750.2	5	Nevada	836.9
20	Colorado	592.6	6	Delaware	807.8
23	Connecticut	554.1	7	Rhode Island	764.7
6	Delaware	807.8	8	California	750.2
1	Florida	1,510.2	9	Maryland	749.0
2	Georgia	1,208.3	10	Alabama	738.1
47	Hawaii	371.3	11	Tennessee	670.3
41	Idaho	423.1	12	Louisiana	663.7
27	Illinois	517.2	13	Virginia	645.3
29	Indiana	511.1	14	New Jersey	626.5
49	Iowa	349.2	15	Pennsylvania	626.3
40	Kansas	426.9	16	Arizona	623.5
34	Kentucky	467.2	17	Missouri	609.3
12	Louisiana	663.7	18	Ohio	606.8
35	Maine	447.1	19	New Mexico	594.1
9	Maryland	749.0	20	Colorado	592.6
22	Massachusetts	557.6	21	New Hampshire	572.0
3	Michigan	1,143.6	22	Massachusetts	557.6
39	Minnesota	438.2	23	Connecticut	554.1
28	Mississippi	516.3	24	South Carolina	553.3
17	Missouri	609.3	25	North Carolina	550.3
37	Montana	442.6	26	New York	524.9
44	Nebraska	403.3	27	Illinois	517.2
5	Nevada	836.9	28	Mississippi	516.3
21	New Hampshire	572.0	29	Indiana	511.1
14	New Jersey	626.5	30	Oregon	506.0
19	New Mexico	594.1	31	Washington	505.7
26	New York	524.9	32	Oklahoma	493.6
25	North Carolina	550.3	33	Arkansas	478.4
50	North Dakota	278.8	34	Kentucky	467.2
18	Ohio	606.8	35	Maine	447.1
32	Oklahoma	493.6	36	West Virginia	446.8
30	Oregon	506.0	37	Montana	442.6
15	Pennsylvania	626.3	37	Wisconsin	442.6
7	Rhode Island	764.7	39	Minnesota	438.2
24	South Carolina	553.3	40	Kansas	426.9
48	South Dakota	356.0	41	Idaho	423.1
11	Tennessee	670.3	42	Wyoming	415.5
4	Texas	941.3	43	Vermont	406.7
45	Utah	396.2	44	Nebraska	403.3
43	Vermont	406.7	45	Utah	396.2
13	Virginia	645.3	46	Alaska	395.0
31	Washington	505.7	47	Hawaii	371.3
36	West Virginia	446.8	48	South Dakota	356.0
37	Wisconsin	442.6	49	Iowa	349.2
42	Wyoming	415.5	50	North Dakota	278.8
				District of Columbia	1,328.1

Source: Federal Trade Commission, Consumer Sentinel
"Consumer Sentinel Network Data Book for January - December 2015" (February 2016, http://www.ftc.gov/sentinel/)
*National rate includes complaints not shown by state. Rates include "other" complaints but do not include identity theft or "Do Not Call" registry complaints.

Rate of Identity Theft Complaints in 2015

National Rate = 152.8 Complaints per 100,000 Population*

ALPHA ORDER

RANK	STATE	RATE
30	Alabama	102.3
40	Alaska	94.3
14	Arizona	133.8
37	Arkansas	97.7
10	California	141.3
21	Colorado	123.2
2	Connecticut	225.0
20	Delaware	124.9
3	Florida	217.4
7	Georgia	149.1
50	Hawaii	62.6
32	Idaho	101.3
5	Illinois	158.7
41	Indiana	93.9
42	Iowa	89.7
27	Kansas	112.7
46	Kentucky	80.9
39	Louisiana	94.4
26	Maine	113.9
4	Maryland	183.2
18	Massachusetts	125.5
6	Michigan	158.1
36	Minnesota	97.8
35	Mississippi	98.8
1	Missouri	364.3
43	Montana	87.2
34	Nebraska	100.5
19	Nevada	125.0
9	New Hampshire	142.0
17	New Jersey	125.8
33	New Mexico	101.1
23	New York	122.0
29	North Carolina	106.0
48	North Dakota	76.0
12	Ohio	134.4
24	Oklahoma	120.0
15	Oregon	126.1
25	Pennsylvania	116.2
11	Rhode Island	141.2
30	South Carolina	102.3
49	South Dakota	63.1
28	Tennessee	107.9
8	Texas	144.3
44	Utah	85.7
45	Vermont	83.9
21	Virginia	123.2
15	Washington	126.1
47	West Virginia	79.9
12	Wisconsin	134.4
38	Wyoming	96.6

RANK ORDER

RANK	STATE	RATE
1	Missouri	364.3
2	Connecticut	225.0
3	Florida	217.4
4	Maryland	183.2
5	Illinois	158.7
6	Michigan	158.1
7	Georgia	149.1
8	Texas	144.3
9	New Hampshire	142.0
10	California	141.3
11	Rhode Island	141.2
12	Ohio	134.4
12	Wisconsin	134.4
14	Arizona	133.8
15	Oregon	126.1
15	Washington	126.1
17	New Jersey	125.8
18	Massachusetts	125.5
19	Nevada	125.0
20	Delaware	124.9
21	Colorado	123.2
21	Virginia	123.2
23	New York	122.0
24	Oklahoma	120.0
25	Pennsylvania	116.2
26	Maine	113.9
27	Kansas	112.7
28	Tennessee	107.9
29	North Carolina	106.0
30	Alabama	102.3
30	South Carolina	102.3
32	Idaho	101.3
33	New Mexico	101.1
34	Nebraska	100.5
35	Mississippi	98.8
36	Minnesota	97.8
37	Arkansas	97.7
38	Wyoming	96.6
39	Louisiana	94.4
40	Alaska	94.3
41	Indiana	93.9
42	Iowa	89.7
43	Montana	87.2
44	Utah	85.7
45	Vermont	83.9
46	Kentucky	80.9
47	West Virginia	79.9
48	North Dakota	76.0
49	South Dakota	63.1
50	Hawaii	62.6

District of Columbia   228.0

Source: Federal Trade Commission, Consumer Sentinel
"Consumer Sentinel Network Data Book for January - December 2015" (February 2016, http://www.ftc.gov/sentinel/)
*National rate includes complaints not shown by state. Rates do not include consumer fraud or "Do Not Call" registry complaints.

Reported Arrest Rate in 2015

National Rate = 3,398.2 Reported Arrests per 100,000 Population*

ALPHA ORDER

RANK	STATE	RATE
20	Alabama	3,833.5
13	Alaska	4,273.4
11	Arizona	4,431.1
7	Arkansas	4,729.7
38	California	2,977.4
10	Colorado	4,442.5
46	Connecticut	2,584.6
24	Delaware	3,667.0
21	Florida	3,822.2
39	Georgia	2,976.0
33	Hawaii	3,229.9
28	Idaho	3,442.2
NA	Illinois**	NA
34	Indiana	3,202.5
26	Iowa	3,591.7
31	Kansas	3,301.2
9	Kentucky	4,459.6
8	Louisiana	4,516.4
29	Maine	3,408.2
27	Maryland	3,502.0
49	Massachusetts	1,878.3
44	Michigan	2,597.6
42	Minnesota	2,815.3
2	Mississippi	5,987.8
14	Missouri	4,149.3
40	Montana	2,878.5
19	Nebraska	3,912.8
18	Nevada	4,001.4
25	New Hampshire	3,626.5
32	New Jersey	3,255.6
3	New Mexico	5,534.2
45	New York***	2,591.2
17	North Carolina	4,005.8
12	North Dakota	4,374.9
43	Ohio	2,733.6
36	Oklahoma	3,105.6
16	Oregon	4,010.1
35	Pennsylvania	3,147.5
47	Rhode Island	2,572.3
23	South Carolina	3,699.0
1	South Dakota	6,079.0
4	Tennessee	5,288.4
37	Texas	2,993.8
15	Utah	4,076.3
48	Vermont	1,916.3
30	Virginia	3,383.6
41	Washington	2,855.6
22	West Virginia	3,784.3
6	Wisconsin	4,827.4
5	Wyoming	5,164.5

RANK ORDER

RANK	STATE	RATE
1	South Dakota	6,079.0
2	Mississippi	5,987.8
3	New Mexico	5,534.2
4	Tennessee	5,288.4
5	Wyoming	5,164.5
6	Wisconsin	4,827.4
7	Arkansas	4,729.7
8	Louisiana	4,516.4
9	Kentucky	4,459.6
10	Colorado	4,442.5
11	Arizona	4,431.1
12	North Dakota	4,374.9
13	Alaska	4,273.4
14	Missouri	4,149.3
15	Utah	4,076.3
16	Oregon	4,010.1
17	North Carolina	4,005.8
18	Nevada	4,001.4
19	Nebraska	3,912.8
20	Alabama	3,833.5
21	Florida	3,822.2
22	West Virginia	3,784.3
23	South Carolina	3,699.0
24	Delaware	3,667.0
25	New Hampshire	3,626.5
26	Iowa	3,591.7
27	Maryland	3,502.0
28	Idaho	3,442.2
29	Maine	3,408.2
30	Virginia	3,383.6
31	Kansas	3,301.2
32	New Jersey	3,255.6
33	Hawaii	3,229.9
34	Indiana	3,202.5
35	Pennsylvania	3,147.5
36	Oklahoma	3,105.6
37	Texas	2,993.8
38	California	2,977.4
39	Georgia	2,976.0
40	Montana	2,878.5
41	Washington	2,855.6
42	Minnesota	2,815.3
43	Ohio	2,733.6
44	Michigan	2,597.6
45	New York***	2,591.2
46	Connecticut	2,584.6
47	Rhode Island	2,572.3
48	Vermont	1,916.3
49	Massachusetts	1,878.3
NA	Illinois**	NA
	District of Columbia**	NA

Source: CQ Press using reported data from the Federal Bureau of Investigation
  "Crime in the United States 2015" (Uniform Crime Reports, September 26, 2016, http://www.fbi.gov/about-us/cjis/ucr/)
*By law enforcement agencies submitting complete reports to the F.B.I. for 12 months in 2015. These rates based on population estimates for areas under the jurisdiction of those agencies reporting. Arrest rate based on the F.B.I. estimate of total arrests is 3,359.2 reported and unreported arrests per 100,000 population.
**Not available. ***New York's figure does not include New York City.

Reported Juvenile Arrest Rate in 2015

National Rate = 2,828.0 Reported Arrests per 100,000 Juvenile Population*

ALPHA ORDER

RANK	STATE	RATE
45	Alabama	1,435.1
33	Alaska	2,570.4
16	Arizona	3,898.7
27	Arkansas	2,839.3
44	California	1,677.6
6	Colorado	4,671.6
41	Connecticut	2,087.4
13	Delaware	4,048.3
19	Florida	3,340.4
31	Georgia	2,633.6
23	Hawaii	3,067.2
11	Idaho	4,136.2
NA	Illinois**	NA
29	Indiana	2,760.5
12	Iowa	4,057.2
36	Kansas	2,371.5
46	Kentucky	1,367.5
10	Louisiana	4,198.4
26	Maine	2,847.8
20	Maryland	3,305.5
47	Massachusetts	1,237.3
43	Michigan	1,768.4
14	Minnesota	3,966.7
28	Mississippi	2,791.1
18	Missouri	3,608.6
8	Montana	4,222.8
5	Nebraska	4,878.9
21	Nevada	3,119.6
25	New Hampshire	2,853.3
42	New Jersey	1,955.4
22	New Mexico	3,068.0
40	New York***	2,112.1
30	North Carolina	2,726.7
4	North Dakota	5,343.1
34	Ohio	2,556.0
32	Oklahoma	2,600.5
7	Oregon	4,430.6
9	Pennsylvania	4,202.8
35	Rhode Island	2,468.7
24	South Carolina	3,028.5
2	South Dakota	6,003.1
17	Tennessee	3,692.6
39	Texas	2,180.6
15	Utah	3,948.0
49	Vermont	1,143.6
38	Virginia	2,185.9
37	Washington	2,320.6
48	West Virginia	1,156.7
1	Wisconsin	7,784.9
3	Wyoming	5,832.3

RANK ORDER

RANK	STATE	RATE
1	Wisconsin	7,784.9
2	South Dakota	6,003.1
3	Wyoming	5,832.3
4	North Dakota	5,343.1
5	Nebraska	4,878.9
6	Colorado	4,671.6
7	Oregon	4,430.6
8	Montana	4,222.8
9	Pennsylvania	4,202.8
10	Louisiana	4,198.4
11	Idaho	4,136.2
12	Iowa	4,057.2
13	Delaware	4,048.3
14	Minnesota	3,966.7
15	Utah	3,948.0
16	Arizona	3,898.7
17	Tennessee	3,692.6
18	Missouri	3,608.6
19	Florida	3,340.4
20	Maryland	3,305.5
21	Nevada	3,119.6
22	New Mexico	3,068.0
23	Hawaii	3,067.2
24	South Carolina	3,028.5
25	New Hampshire	2,853.3
26	Maine	2,847.8
27	Arkansas	2,839.3
28	Mississippi	2,791.1
29	Indiana	2,760.5
30	North Carolina	2,726.7
31	Georgia	2,633.6
32	Oklahoma	2,600.5
33	Alaska	2,570.4
34	Ohio	2,556.0
35	Rhode Island	2,468.7
36	Kansas	2,371.5
37	Washington	2,320.6
38	Virginia	2,185.9
39	Texas	2,180.6
40	New York***	2,112.1
41	Connecticut	2,087.4
42	New Jersey	1,955.4
43	Michigan	1,768.4
44	California	1,677.6
45	Alabama	1,435.1
46	Kentucky	1,367.5
47	Massachusetts	1,237.3
48	West Virginia	1,156.7
49	Vermont	1,143.6
NA	Illinois**	NA
	District of Columbia**	NA

Source: CQ Press using reported data from the Federal Bureau of Investigation
"Crime in the United States 2015" (Uniform Crime Reports, September 26, 2016, http://www.fbi.gov/about-us/cjis/ucr/)
*By law enforcement agencies submitting complete reports to the F.B.I. for 12 months in 2015. Arrests of youths 17 years and younger divided into population of 10 to 17 year olds.
**Not available.
***New York's figure does not include New York City.

Prisoners in State Correctional Institutions: Year End 2015

National Total = 1,330,337 State Prisoners*

ALPHA ORDER				RANK ORDER			
RANK	STATE	PRISONERS	% of USA	RANK	STATE	PRISONERS	% of USA
15	Alabama	30,810	2.3%	1	Texas	163,909	12.3%
42	Alaska	5,338	0.4%	2	California	129,593	9.7%
9	Arizona	42,719	3.2%	3	Florida	101,424	7.6%
27	Arkansas	17,707	1.3%	4	Ohio	52,233	3.9%
2	California	129,593	9.7%	5	Georgia	52,193	3.9%
24	Colorado	20,168	1.5%	6	New York	51,727	3.9%
28	Connecticut	15,816	1.2%	7	Pennsylvania	49,858	3.7%
38	Delaware	6,654	0.5%	8	Illinois	46,240	3.5%
3	Florida	101,424	7.6%	9	Arizona	42,719	3.2%
5	Georgia	52,193	3.9%	10	Michigan	42,628	3.2%
40	Hawaii	5,879	0.4%	11	Virginia	38,403	2.9%
35	Idaho	8,052	0.6%	12	North Carolina	36,617	2.8%
8	Illinois	46,240	3.5%	13	Louisiana	36,377	2.7%
18	Indiana	27,355	2.1%	14	Missouri	32,330	2.4%
34	Iowa	8,849	0.7%	15	Alabama	30,810	2.3%
33	Kansas	9,857	0.7%	16	Oklahoma	28,547	2.1%
20	Kentucky	21,701	1.6%	17	Tennessee	28,172	2.1%
13	Louisiana	36,377	2.7%	18	Indiana	27,355	2.1%
48	Maine	2,279	0.2%	19	Wisconsin	22,975	1.7%
22	Maryland	20,764	1.6%	20	Kentucky	21,701	1.6%
32	Massachusetts	9,922	0.7%	21	South Carolina	20,929	1.6%
10	Michigan	42,628	3.2%	22	Maryland	20,764	1.6%
31	Minnesota	10,798	0.8%	23	New Jersey	20,489	1.5%
25	Mississippi	18,911	1.4%	24	Colorado	20,168	1.5%
14	Missouri	32,330	2.4%	25	Mississippi	18,911	1.4%
43	Montana	3,685	0.3%	26	Washington	18,284	1.4%
41	Nebraska	5,372	0.4%	27	Arkansas	17,707	1.3%
30	Nevada	13,071	1.0%	28	Connecticut	15,816	1.2%
46	New Hampshire	2,897	0.2%	29	Oregon	15,245	1.1%
23	New Jersey	20,489	1.5%	30	Nevada	13,071	1.0%
36	New Mexico	7,169	0.5%	31	Minnesota	10,798	0.8%
6	New York	51,727	3.9%	32	Massachusetts	9,922	0.7%
12	North Carolina	36,617	2.8%	33	Kansas	9,857	0.7%
49	North Dakota	1,795	0.1%	34	Iowa	8,849	0.7%
4	Ohio	52,233	3.9%	35	Idaho	8,052	0.6%
16	Oklahoma	28,547	2.1%	36	New Mexico	7,169	0.5%
29	Oregon	15,245	1.1%	37	West Virginia	7,118	0.5%
7	Pennsylvania	49,858	3.7%	38	Delaware	6,654	0.5%
45	Rhode Island	3,248	0.2%	39	Utah	6,492	0.5%
21	South Carolina	20,929	1.6%	40	Hawaii	5,879	0.4%
44	South Dakota	3,564	0.3%	41	Nebraska	5,372	0.4%
17	Tennessee	28,172	2.1%	42	Alaska	5,338	0.4%
1	Texas	163,909	12.3%	43	Montana	3,685	0.3%
39	Utah	6,492	0.5%	44	South Dakota	3,564	0.3%
50	Vermont	1,750	0.1%	45	Rhode Island	3,248	0.2%
11	Virginia	38,403	2.9%	46	New Hampshire	2,897	0.2%
26	Washington	18,284	1.4%	47	Wyoming	2,424	0.2%
37	West Virginia	7,118	0.5%	48	Maine	2,279	0.2%
19	Wisconsin	22,975	1.7%	49	North Dakota	1,795	0.1%
47	Wyoming	2,424	0.2%	50	Vermont	1,750	0.1%
					District of Columbia**	NA	NA

Source: U.S. Department of Justice, Bureau of Justice Statistics
"Prisoners in 2015" (December 2016, NCJ 250229, http://bjs.ojp.usdoj.gov/)
*As of December 31, 2015. Totals reflect all prisoners, including those sentenced to a year or less and those unsentenced.
National total does not include 196,455 prisoners under federal jurisdiction. State and federal prisoners combined total 1,526,792.
**Responsibility for sentenced felons in D.C. was transferred to the Federal Bureau of Prisons in 2001.

State Prisoner Imprisonment Rate in 2015

National Rate = 402 State Prisoners per 100,000 Population*

ALPHA ORDER

RANK	STATE	RATE
3	Alabama	611
36	Alaska	306
5	Arizona	596
6	Arkansas	591
33	California	329
27	Colorado	364
35	Connecticut	312
15	Delaware	441
10	Florida	496
9	Georgia	503
39	Hawaii	262
16	Idaho	436
28	Illinois	360
22	Indiana	412
37	Iowa	281
34	Kansas	328
11	Kentucky	489
1	Louisiana	776
50	Maine	132
31	Maryland	339
49	Massachusetts	179
17	Michigan	429
48	Minnesota	196
4	Mississippi	609
8	Missouri	530
29	Montana	355
38	Nebraska	279
14	Nevada	444
44	New Hampshire	217
43	New Jersey	228
32	New Mexico	335
40	New York	260
30	North Carolina	352
42	North Dakota	233
13	Ohio	449
2	Oklahoma	715
26	Oregon	376
23	Pennsylvania	387
47	Rhode Island	204
19	South Carolina	414
20	South Dakota	413
18	Tennessee	425
7	Texas	568
45	Utah	215
46	Vermont	206
12	Virginia	457
41	Washington	252
24	West Virginia	386
25	Wisconsin	377
20	Wyoming	413

RANK ORDER

RANK	STATE	RATE
1	Louisiana	776
2	Oklahoma	715
3	Alabama	611
4	Mississippi	609
5	Arizona	596
6	Arkansas	591
7	Texas	568
8	Missouri	530
9	Georgia	503
10	Florida	496
11	Kentucky	489
12	Virginia	457
13	Ohio	449
14	Nevada	444
15	Delaware	441
16	Idaho	436
17	Michigan	429
18	Tennessee	425
19	South Carolina	414
20	South Dakota	413
20	Wyoming	413
22	Indiana	412
23	Pennsylvania	387
24	West Virginia	386
25	Wisconsin	377
26	Oregon	376
27	Colorado	364
28	Illinois	360
29	Montana	355
30	North Carolina	352
31	Maryland	339
32	New Mexico	335
33	California	329
34	Kansas	328
35	Connecticut	312
36	Alaska	306
37	Iowa	281
38	Nebraska	279
39	Hawaii	262
40	New York	260
41	Washington	252
42	North Dakota	233
43	New Jersey	228
44	New Hampshire	217
45	Utah	215
46	Vermont	206
47	Rhode Island	204
48	Minnesota	196
49	Massachusetts	179
50	Maine	132

District of Columbia**   NA

Source: U.S. Department of Justice, Bureau of Justice Statistics
"Prisoners in 2015" (December 2016, NCJ 250229, http://bjs.ojp.usdoj.gov/)
*Figures as of December 31, 2015. Includes only inmates sentenced to more than one year. Does not include federal imprisonment rate of 55 prisoners per 100,000 population. State and federal combined imprisonment rate is 458 prisoners per 100,000 population.
**Responsibility for sentenced felons in D.C. was transferred to the Federal Bureau of Prisons in 2001.

Percent Change in Number of State Prisoners: 2014 to 2015

National Percent Change = 1.6% Decrease*

ALPHA ORDER

RANK	STATE	PERCENT CHANGE
36	Alabama	(3.0)
46	Alaska	(7.9)
13	Arizona	1.1
21	Arkansas	(0.9)
40	California	(4.8)
35	Colorado	(2.3)
41	Connecticut	(4.9)
38	Delaware	(4.3)
27	Florida	(1.4)
27	Georgia	(1.4)
17	Hawaii	0.2
NA	Idaho**	NA
NA	Illinois**	NA
43	Indiana	(6.5)
18	Iowa	0.1
19	Kansas	(0.2)
NA	Kentucky**	NA
38	Louisiana	(4.3)
7	Maine	1.7
22	Maryland	(1.2)
44	Massachusetts	(7.4)
31	Michigan	(1.8)
10	Minnesota	1.5
16	Mississippi	0.6
12	Missouri	1.2
20	Montana	(0.4)
24	Nebraska	(1.3)
2	Nevada	4.3
33	New Hampshire	(2.2)
42	New Jersey	(5.1)
6	New Mexico	2.1
29	New York	(1.5)
24	North Carolina	(1.3)
1	North Dakota	4.5
11	Ohio	1.4
3	Oklahoma	3.2
13	Oregon	1.1
30	Pennsylvania	(1.6)
37	Rhode Island	(3.3)
33	South Carolina	(2.2)
22	South Dakota	(1.2)
32	Tennessee	(2.1)
24	Texas	(1.3)
45	Utah	(7.7)
47	Vermont	(11.6)
5	Virginia	2.3
15	Washington	0.9
3	West Virginia	3.2
7	Wisconsin	1.7
7	Wyoming	1.7

RANK ORDER

RANK	STATE	PERCENT CHANGE
1	North Dakota	4.5
2	Nevada	4.3
3	Oklahoma	3.2
3	West Virginia	3.2
5	Virginia	2.3
6	New Mexico	2.1
7	Maine	1.7
7	Wisconsin	1.7
7	Wyoming	1.7
10	Minnesota	1.5
11	Ohio	1.4
12	Missouri	1.2
13	Arizona	1.1
13	Oregon	1.1
15	Washington	0.9
16	Mississippi	0.6
17	Hawaii	0.2
18	Iowa	0.1
19	Kansas	(0.2)
20	Montana	(0.4)
21	Arkansas	(0.9)
22	Maryland	(1.2)
22	South Dakota	(1.2)
24	Nebraska	(1.3)
24	North Carolina	(1.3)
24	Texas	(1.3)
27	Florida	(1.4)
27	Georgia	(1.4)
29	New York	(1.5)
30	Pennsylvania	(1.6)
31	Michigan	(1.8)
32	Tennessee	(2.1)
33	New Hampshire	(2.2)
33	South Carolina	(2.2)
35	Colorado	(2.3)
36	Alabama	(3.0)
37	Rhode Island	(3.3)
38	Delaware	(4.3)
38	Louisiana	(4.3)
40	California	(4.8)
41	Connecticut	(4.9)
42	New Jersey	(5.1)
43	Indiana	(6.5)
44	Massachusetts	(7.4)
45	Utah	(7.7)
46	Alaska	(7.9)
47	Vermont	(11.6)
NA	Idaho**	NA
NA	Illinois**	NA
NA	Kentucky**	NA
	District of Columbia***	NA

Source: U.S. Department of Justice, Bureau of Justice Statistics
   "Prisoners in 2015" (December 2016, NCJ 250229, http://bjs.ojp.usdoj.gov/)
*From December 31, 2014 to December 31, 2015. Includes inmates sentenced to more than one year and those sentenced to a year or less or with no sentence. The percent change in number of prisoners under federal jurisdiction during the same period was an 6.7% decrease. The combined state and federal decrease was 2.3%. **Not available.
***Responsibility for sentenced felons in D.C. was transferred to the Federal Bureau of Prisons in 2001.

Prisoners under Sentence of Death in 2013

National Total = 2,923 State Prisoners*

ALPHA ORDER

RANK	STATE	PRISONERS	% of USA
4	Alabama	190	6.5%
NA	Alaska**	NA	NA
8	Arizona	122	4.2%
17	Arkansas	37	1.3%
1	California	735	25.1%
30	Colorado	3	0.1%
24	Connecticut	10	0.3%
20	Delaware	17	0.6%
2	Florida	398	13.6%
10	Georgia	82	2.8%
NA	Hawaii**	NA	NA
22	Idaho	12	0.4%
NA	Illinois**	NA	NA
21	Indiana	14	0.5%
NA	Iowa**	NA	NA
25	Kansas	9	0.3%
19	Kentucky	33	1.1%
9	Louisiana	84	2.9%
NA	Maine**	NA	NA
29	Maryland	5	0.2%
NA	Massachusetts**	NA	NA
NA	Michigan**	NA	NA
NA	Minnesota**	NA	NA
13	Mississippi	50	1.7%
15	Missouri	45	1.5%
32	Montana	2	0.1%
23	Nebraska	11	0.4%
11	Nevada	81	2.8%
34	New Hampshire	1	0.0%
NA	New Jersey**	NA	NA
32	New Mexico	2	0.1%
36	New York	0	0.0%
6	North Carolina	151	5.2%
NA	North Dakota**	NA	NA
7	Ohio	136	4.7%
14	Oklahoma	48	1.6%
18	Oregon	34	1.2%
4	Pennsylvania	190	6.5%
NA	Rhode Island**	NA	NA
15	South Carolina	45	1.5%
30	South Dakota	3	0.1%
12	Tennessee	75	2.6%
3	Texas	273	9.3%
27	Utah	8	0.3%
NA	Vermont**	NA	NA
28	Virginia	7	0.2%
25	Washington	9	0.3%
NA	West Virginia**	NA	NA
NA	Wisconsin**	NA	NA
34	Wyoming	1	0.0%

RANK ORDER

RANK	STATE	PRISONERS	% of USA
1	California	735	25.1%
2	Florida	398	13.6%
3	Texas	273	9.3%
4	Alabama	190	6.5%
4	Pennsylvania	190	6.5%
6	North Carolina	151	5.2%
7	Ohio	136	4.7%
8	Arizona	122	4.2%
9	Louisiana	84	2.9%
10	Georgia	82	2.8%
11	Nevada	81	2.8%
12	Tennessee	75	2.6%
13	Mississippi	50	1.7%
14	Oklahoma	48	1.6%
15	Missouri	45	1.5%
15	South Carolina	45	1.5%
17	Arkansas	37	1.3%
18	Oregon	34	1.2%
19	Kentucky	33	1.1%
20	Delaware	17	0.6%
21	Indiana	14	0.5%
22	Idaho	12	0.4%
23	Nebraska	11	0.4%
24	Connecticut	10	0.3%
25	Kansas	9	0.3%
25	Washington	9	0.3%
27	Utah	8	0.3%
28	Virginia	7	0.2%
29	Maryland	5	0.2%
30	Colorado	3	0.1%
30	South Dakota	3	0.1%
32	Montana	2	0.1%
32	New Mexico	2	0.1%
34	New Hampshire	1	0.0%
34	Wyoming	1	0.0%
36	New York	0	0.0%
NA	Alaska**	NA	NA
NA	Hawaii**	NA	NA
NA	Illinois**	NA	NA
NA	Iowa**	NA	NA
NA	Maine**	NA	NA
NA	Massachusetts**	NA	NA
NA	Michigan**	NA	NA
NA	Minnesota**	NA	NA
NA	New Jersey**	NA	NA
NA	North Dakota**	NA	NA
NA	Rhode Island**	NA	NA
NA	Vermont**	NA	NA
NA	West Virginia**	NA	NA
NA	Wisconsin**	NA	NA
	District of Columbia**	NA	NA

Source: U.S. Department of Justice, Bureau of Justice Statistics
"Capital Punishment 2013" (Bulletin, December 2014, NCJ 248448, http://bjs.ojp.usdoj.gov/)
*As of December 31, 2013. Does not include 56 federal prisoners under sentence of death. There were 39 executions in 2013.
**No death penalty as of December 31, 2013.

Rate of State and Local Police Officers in 2015

National Rate = 22 Officers per 10,000 Population*

ALPHA ORDER				RANK ORDER		
RANK	STATE	RATE		RANK	STATE	RATE
9	Alabama	23		1	New York	38
45	Alaska	16		2	New Jersey	29
22	Arizona	21		3	Louisiana	28
13	Arkansas	22		4	Illinois	26
35	California	18		4	Tennessee	26
28	Colorado	20		6	Wyoming	25
13	Connecticut	22		7	Massachusetts	24
13	Delaware	22		7	Mississippi	24
28	Florida	20		9	Alabama	23
13	Georgia	22		9	Maryland	23
13	Hawaii	22		9	Missouri	23
37	Idaho	17		9	South Carolina	23
4	Illinois	26		13	Arkansas	22
35	Indiana	18		13	Connecticut	22
37	Iowa	17		13	Delaware	22
22	Kansas	21		13	Georgia	22
37	Kentucky	17		13	Hawaii	22
3	Louisiana	28		13	New Hampshire	22
37	Maine	17		13	New Mexico	22
9	Maryland	23		13	North Carolina	22
7	Massachusetts	24		13	Rhode Island	22
37	Michigan	17		22	Arizona	21
45	Minnesota	16		22	Kansas	21
7	Mississippi	24		22	Oklahoma	21
9	Missouri	23		22	Pennsylvania	21
37	Montana	17		22	Virginia	21
33	Nebraska	19		22	Wisconsin	21
37	Nevada	17		28	Colorado	20
13	New Hampshire	22		28	Florida	20
2	New Jersey	29		28	North Dakota	20
13	New Mexico	22		28	Ohio	20
1	New York	38		28	Texas	20
13	North Carolina	22		33	Nebraska	19
28	North Dakota	20		33	South Dakota	19
28	Ohio	20		35	California	18
22	Oklahoma	21		35	Indiana	18
48	Oregon	15		37	Idaho	17
22	Pennsylvania	21		37	Iowa	17
13	Rhode Island	22		37	Kentucky	17
9	South Carolina	23		37	Maine	17
33	South Dakota	19		37	Michigan	17
4	Tennessee	26		37	Montana	17
28	Texas	20		37	Nevada	17
49	Utah	14		37	West Virginia	17
45	Vermont	16		45	Alaska	16
22	Virginia	21		45	Minnesota	16
49	Washington	14		45	Vermont	16
37	West Virginia	17		48	Oregon	15
22	Wisconsin	21		49	Utah	14
6	Wyoming	25		49	Washington	14
					District of Columbia	59

Source: CQ Press using data from U.S. Bureau of the Census, Governments Division
"Government Employment and Payroll" (http://www.census.gov/govs/apes/index.html)
*Full-time equivalent as of March 2015. Does not include employees of police departments who are not officers.

Per Capita State and Local Government Expenditures for Police Protection in 2014
National Per Capita = $320*

ALPHA ORDER

RANK	STATE	PER CAPITA
36	Alabama	$249
1	Alaska	506
24	Arizona	290
44	Arkansas	221
4	California	409
13	Colorado	336
15	Connecticut	323
11	Delaware	360
10	Florida	370
39	Georgia	239
18	Hawaii	320
35	Idaho	252
6	Illinois	388
49	Indiana	183
41	Iowa	233
33	Kansas	260
50	Kentucky	162
16	Louisiana	321
48	Maine	194
3	Maryland	428
12	Massachusetts	349
38	Michigan	242
16	Minnesota	321
40	Mississippi	235
27	Missouri	281
25	Montana	288
45	Nebraska	220
5	Nevada	400
23	New Hampshire	304
8	New Jersey	376
14	New Mexico	325
2	New York	477
20	North Carolina	311
36	North Dakota	249
26	Ohio	282
31	Oklahoma	266
21	Oregon	305
28	Pennsylvania	276
9	Rhode Island	371
42	South Carolina	230
46	South Dakota	212
28	Tennessee	276
32	Texas	263
43	Utah	229
19	Vermont	312
30	Virginia	271
34	Washington	253
47	West Virginia	196
21	Wisconsin	305
7	Wyoming	384

RANK ORDER

RANK	STATE	PER CAPITA
1	Alaska	$506
2	New York	477
3	Maryland	428
4	California	409
5	Nevada	400
6	Illinois	388
7	Wyoming	384
8	New Jersey	376
9	Rhode Island	371
10	Florida	370
11	Delaware	360
12	Massachusetts	349
13	Colorado	336
14	New Mexico	325
15	Connecticut	323
16	Louisiana	321
16	Minnesota	321
18	Hawaii	320
19	Vermont	312
20	North Carolina	311
21	Oregon	305
21	Wisconsin	305
23	New Hampshire	304
24	Arizona	290
25	Montana	288
26	Ohio	282
27	Missouri	281
28	Pennsylvania	276
28	Tennessee	276
30	Virginia	271
31	Oklahoma	266
32	Texas	263
33	Kansas	260
34	Washington	253
35	Idaho	252
36	Alabama	249
36	North Dakota	249
38	Michigan	242
39	Georgia	239
40	Mississippi	235
41	Iowa	233
42	South Carolina	230
43	Utah	229
44	Arkansas	221
45	Nebraska	220
46	South Dakota	212
47	West Virginia	196
48	Maine	194
49	Indiana	183
50	Kentucky	162
	District of Columbia	896

Source: CQ Press using data from U.S. Bureau of the Census, Governments Division
"2014 State and Local Government Finances" (http://www.census.gov/govs/local/)
*Direct general expenditures.

Per Capita State and Local Government Expenditures for Corrections in 2014

National Per Capita = $235*

ALPHA ORDER

RANK	STATE	PER CAPITA
48	Alabama	$146
1	Alaska	465
15	Arizona	244
30	Arkansas	191
2	California	370
18	Colorado	227
29	Connecticut	193
5	Delaware	315
25	Florida	200
21	Georgia	219
45	Hawaii	153
26	Idaho	196
41	Illinois	163
44	Indiana	157
49	Iowa	143
37	Kansas	172
38	Kentucky	169
11	Louisiana	261
47	Maine	149
7	Maryland	300
33	Massachusetts	179
13	Michigan	255
40	Minnesota	166
38	Mississippi	169
42	Missouri	160
16	Montana	238
22	Nebraska	214
14	Nevada	245
50	New Hampshire	130
17	New Jersey	234
4	New Mexico	317
6	New York	313
35	North Carolina	175
36	North Dakota	173
42	Ohio	160
28	Oklahoma	194
8	Oregon	284
12	Pennsylvania	258
26	Rhode Island	196
45	South Carolina	153
24	South Dakota	203
34	Tennessee	177
23	Texas	210
32	Utah	183
20	Vermont	223
9	Virginia	276
18	Washington	227
30	West Virginia	191
10	Wisconsin	262
3	Wyoming	359

RANK ORDER

RANK	STATE	PER CAPITA
1	Alaska	$465
2	California	370
3	Wyoming	359
4	New Mexico	317
5	Delaware	315
6	New York	313
7	Maryland	300
8	Oregon	284
9	Virginia	276
10	Wisconsin	262
11	Louisiana	261
12	Pennsylvania	258
13	Michigan	255
14	Nevada	245
15	Arizona	244
16	Montana	238
17	New Jersey	234
18	Colorado	227
18	Washington	227
20	Vermont	223
21	Georgia	219
22	Nebraska	214
23	Texas	210
24	South Dakota	203
25	Florida	200
26	Idaho	196
26	Rhode Island	196
28	Oklahoma	194
29	Connecticut	193
30	Arkansas	191
30	West Virginia	191
32	Utah	183
33	Massachusetts	179
34	Tennessee	177
35	North Carolina	175
36	North Dakota	173
37	Kansas	172
38	Kentucky	169
38	Mississippi	169
40	Minnesota	166
41	Illinois	163
42	Missouri	160
42	Ohio	160
44	Indiana	157
45	Hawaii	153
45	South Carolina	153
47	Maine	149
48	Alabama	146
49	Iowa	143
50	New Hampshire	130

District of Columbia   299

Source: CQ Press using data from U.S. Bureau of the Census, Governments Division
"2014 State and Local Government Finances" (http://www.census.gov/govs/local/)
*Direct general expenditures.

Per Capita State and Local Government Expenditures for Judicial and Legal Services in 2014
National Per Capita = $138*

ALPHA ORDER

RANK	STATE	PER CAPITA
46	Alabama	$82
1	Alaska	329
18	Arizona	137
49	Arkansas	71
2	California	221
19	Colorado	134
5	Connecticut	210
4	Delaware	218
31	Florida	115
35	Georgia	108
3	Hawaii	219
26	Idaho	124
30	Illinois	116
45	Indiana	83
32	Iowa	114
33	Kansas	110
27	Kentucky	122
11	Louisiana	159
48	Maine	74
17	Maryland	143
9	Massachusetts	162
28	Michigan	119
24	Minnesota	126
44	Mississippi	84
43	Missouri	87
14	Montana	154
42	Nebraska	88
10	Nevada	161
39	New Hampshire	101
8	New Jersey	165
13	New Mexico	155
6	New York	200
47	North Carolina	75
20	North Dakota	128
15	Ohio	153
41	Oklahoma	96
12	Oregon	157
16	Pennsylvania	149
20	Rhode Island	128
50	South Carolina	67
40	South Dakota	98
37	Tennessee	105
38	Texas	102
24	Utah	126
28	Vermont	119
36	Virginia	107
22	Washington	127
22	West Virginia	127
34	Wisconsin	109
6	Wyoming	200

RANK ORDER

RANK	STATE	PER CAPITA
1	Alaska	$329
2	California	221
3	Hawaii	219
4	Delaware	218
5	Connecticut	210
6	New York	200
6	Wyoming	200
8	New Jersey	165
9	Massachusetts	162
10	Nevada	161
11	Louisiana	159
12	Oregon	157
13	New Mexico	155
14	Montana	154
15	Ohio	153
16	Pennsylvania	149
17	Maryland	143
18	Arizona	137
19	Colorado	134
20	North Dakota	128
20	Rhode Island	128
22	Washington	127
22	West Virginia	127
24	Minnesota	126
24	Utah	126
26	Idaho	124
27	Kentucky	122
28	Michigan	119
28	Vermont	119
30	Illinois	116
31	Florida	115
32	Iowa	114
33	Kansas	110
34	Wisconsin	109
35	Georgia	108
36	Virginia	107
37	Tennessee	105
38	Texas	102
39	New Hampshire	101
40	South Dakota	98
41	Oklahoma	96
42	Nebraska	88
43	Missouri	87
44	Mississippi	84
45	Indiana	83
46	Alabama	82
47	North Carolina	75
48	Maine	74
49	Arkansas	71
50	South Carolina	67

District of Columbia	181

Source: CQ Press using data from U.S. Bureau of the Census, Governments Division
"2014 State and Local Government Finances" (http://www.census.gov/govs/local/)
*Direct general expenditures. Includes courts, prosecution and legal services, and public defense.

III. Defense

Homeland Security Grants in 2016

National Total = $982,000,000*

ALPHA ORDER

RANK	STATE	GRANTS	% of USA
28	Alabama	$3,734,500	0.4%
28	Alaska	3,734,500	0.4%
13	Arizona	9,998,000	1.0%
28	Arkansas	3,734,500	0.4%
2	California	184,836,500	18.8%
18	Colorado	6,941,000	0.7%
22	Connecticut	3,978,000	0.4%
28	Delaware	3,734,500	0.4%
8	Florida	19,432,500	2.0%
9	Georgia	12,237,000	1.2%
28	Hawaii	3,734,500	0.4%
28	Idaho	3,734,500	0.4%
3	Illinois	85,018,500	8.7%
22	Indiana	3,978,000	0.4%
28	Iowa	3,734,500	0.4%
28	Kansas	3,734,500	0.4%
22	Kentucky	3,978,000	0.4%
22	Louisiana	3,978,000	0.4%
28	Maine	3,734,500	0.4%
15	Maryland	9,115,500	0.9%
7	Massachusetts	23,415,000	2.4%
10	Michigan	12,088,000	1.2%
14	Minnesota	9,408,000	1.0%
28	Mississippi	3,734,500	0.4%
19	Missouri	6,940,000	0.7%
28	Montana	3,734,500	0.4%
28	Nebraska	3,734,500	0.4%
21	Nevada	6,696,500	0.7%
28	New Hampshire	3,734,500	0.4%
6	New Jersey	28,888,000	2.9%
28	New Mexico	3,734,500	0.4%
1	New York	255,572,000	26.0%
16	North Carolina	8,451,000	0.9%
28	North Dakota	3,734,500	0.4%
12	Ohio	10,660,000	1.1%
28	Oklahoma	3,734,500	0.4%
20	Oregon	6,799,000	0.7%
5	Pennsylvania	31,279,500	3.2%
28	Rhode Island	3,734,500	0.4%
28	South Carolina	3,734,500	0.4%
28	South Dakota	3,734,500	0.4%
22	Tennessee	3,978,000	0.4%
4	Texas	60,493,000	6.2%
28	Utah	3,734,500	0.4%
28	Vermont	3,734,500	0.4%
17	Virginia	7,445,500	0.8%
11	Washington	11,923,000	1.2%
28	West Virginia	3,734,500	0.4%
22	Wisconsin	3,978,000	0.4%
28	Wyoming	3,734,500	0.4%

RANK ORDER

RANK	STATE	GRANTS	% of USA
1	New York	$255,572,000	26.0%
2	California	184,836,500	18.8%
3	Illinois	85,018,500	8.7%
4	Texas	60,493,000	6.2%
5	Pennsylvania	31,279,500	3.2%
6	New Jersey	28,888,000	2.9%
7	Massachusetts	23,415,000	2.4%
8	Florida	19,432,500	2.0%
9	Georgia	12,237,000	1.2%
10	Michigan	12,088,000	1.2%
11	Washington	11,923,000	1.2%
12	Ohio	10,660,000	1.1%
13	Arizona	9,998,000	1.0%
14	Minnesota	9,408,000	1.0%
15	Maryland	9,115,500	0.9%
16	North Carolina	8,451,000	0.9%
17	Virginia	7,445,500	0.8%
18	Colorado	6,941,000	0.7%
19	Missouri	6,940,000	0.7%
20	Oregon	6,799,000	0.7%
21	Nevada	6,696,500	0.7%
22	Connecticut	3,978,000	0.4%
22	Indiana	3,978,000	0.4%
22	Kentucky	3,978,000	0.4%
22	Louisiana	3,978,000	0.4%
22	Tennessee	3,978,000	0.4%
22	Wisconsin	3,978,000	0.4%
28	Alabama	3,734,500	0.4%
28	Alaska	3,734,500	0.4%
28	Arkansas	3,734,500	0.4%
28	Delaware	3,734,500	0.4%
28	Hawaii	3,734,500	0.4%
28	Idaho	3,734,500	0.4%
28	Iowa	3,734,500	0.4%
28	Kansas	3,734,500	0.4%
28	Maine	3,734,500	0.4%
28	Mississippi	3,734,500	0.4%
28	Montana	3,734,500	0.4%
28	Nebraska	3,734,500	0.4%
28	New Hampshire	3,734,500	0.4%
28	New Mexico	3,734,500	0.4%
28	North Dakota	3,734,500	0.4%
28	Oklahoma	3,734,500	0.4%
28	Rhode Island	3,734,500	0.4%
28	South Carolina	3,734,500	0.4%
28	South Dakota	3,734,500	0.4%
28	Utah	3,734,500	0.4%
28	Vermont	3,734,500	0.4%
28	West Virginia	3,734,500	0.4%
28	Wyoming	3,734,500	0.4%
	District of Columbia	57,450,500	5.9%

Source: CQ Press using data from U.S. Department of Homeland Security
"FY 2016 Homeland Security Grant Program (HSGP)" (https://www.fema.gov/media-library/assets/documents/114411)
*For fiscal year 2016. National total includes $7,150,500 in grants to U.S. territories. The Homeland Security Grant Program (HSGP) includes three sub-grant programs: State Homeland Security Program (SHSP), Urban Area Security Initiative (UASI), and Operation Stonegarden (OPSG). Law Enforcement Terrorism Prevention Activities (LETPA) allocations are a 25 percent subset of the SHSP and UASI allocations.

Per Capita Homeland Security Grants in 2016

National Per Capita = $3.02*

<table>
<tr><td colspan="3">ALPHA ORDER</td><td colspan="3">RANK ORDER</td></tr>
<tr><td>RANK</td><td>STATE</td><td>PER CAPITA</td><td>RANK</td><td>STATE</td><td>PER CAPITA</td></tr>
<tr><td>46</td><td>Alabama</td><td>$0.77</td><td>1</td><td>New York</td><td>$12.94</td></tr>
<tr><td>5</td><td>Alaska</td><td>5.03</td><td>2</td><td>Illinois</td><td>6.64</td></tr>
<tr><td>28</td><td>Arizona</td><td>1.44</td><td>3</td><td>Wyoming</td><td>6.38</td></tr>
<tr><td>30</td><td>Arkansas</td><td>1.25</td><td>4</td><td>Vermont</td><td>5.98</td></tr>
<tr><td>7</td><td>California</td><td>4.71</td><td>5</td><td>Alaska</td><td>5.03</td></tr>
<tr><td>30</td><td>Colorado</td><td>1.25</td><td>6</td><td>North Dakota</td><td>4.93</td></tr>
<tr><td>38</td><td>Connecticut</td><td>1.11</td><td>7</td><td>California</td><td>4.71</td></tr>
<tr><td>9</td><td>Delaware</td><td>3.92</td><td>8</td><td>South Dakota</td><td>4.32</td></tr>
<tr><td>40</td><td>Florida</td><td>0.94</td><td>9</td><td>Delaware</td><td>3.92</td></tr>
<tr><td>35</td><td>Georgia</td><td>1.19</td><td>10</td><td>Montana</td><td>3.58</td></tr>
<tr><td>16</td><td>Hawaii</td><td>2.61</td><td>11</td><td>Rhode Island</td><td>3.54</td></tr>
<tr><td>19</td><td>Idaho</td><td>2.22</td><td>12</td><td>Massachusetts</td><td>3.44</td></tr>
<tr><td>2</td><td>Illinois</td><td>6.64</td><td>13</td><td>New Jersey</td><td>3.23</td></tr>
<tr><td>49</td><td>Indiana</td><td>0.60</td><td>14</td><td>Maine</td><td>2.80</td></tr>
<tr><td>35</td><td>Iowa</td><td>1.19</td><td>14</td><td>New Hampshire</td><td>2.80</td></tr>
<tr><td>29</td><td>Kansas</td><td>1.28</td><td>16</td><td>Hawaii</td><td>2.61</td></tr>
<tr><td>42</td><td>Kentucky</td><td>0.90</td><td>17</td><td>Pennsylvania</td><td>2.45</td></tr>
<tr><td>44</td><td>Louisiana</td><td>0.85</td><td>18</td><td>Nevada</td><td>2.28</td></tr>
<tr><td>14</td><td>Maine</td><td>2.80</td><td>19</td><td>Idaho</td><td>2.22</td></tr>
<tr><td>27</td><td>Maryland</td><td>1.52</td><td>20</td><td>Texas</td><td>2.17</td></tr>
<tr><td>12</td><td>Massachusetts</td><td>3.44</td><td>21</td><td>West Virginia</td><td>2.04</td></tr>
<tr><td>33</td><td>Michigan</td><td>1.22</td><td>22</td><td>Nebraska</td><td>1.96</td></tr>
<tr><td>24</td><td>Minnesota</td><td>1.70</td><td>23</td><td>New Mexico</td><td>1.79</td></tr>
<tr><td>30</td><td>Mississippi</td><td>1.25</td><td>24</td><td>Minnesota</td><td>1.70</td></tr>
<tr><td>37</td><td>Missouri</td><td>1.14</td><td>25</td><td>Oregon</td><td>1.66</td></tr>
<tr><td>10</td><td>Montana</td><td>3.58</td><td>26</td><td>Washington</td><td>1.64</td></tr>
<tr><td>22</td><td>Nebraska</td><td>1.96</td><td>27</td><td>Maryland</td><td>1.52</td></tr>
<tr><td>18</td><td>Nevada</td><td>2.28</td><td>28</td><td>Arizona</td><td>1.44</td></tr>
<tr><td>14</td><td>New Hampshire</td><td>2.80</td><td>29</td><td>Kansas</td><td>1.28</td></tr>
<tr><td>13</td><td>New Jersey</td><td>3.23</td><td>30</td><td>Arkansas</td><td>1.25</td></tr>
<tr><td>23</td><td>New Mexico</td><td>1.79</td><td>30</td><td>Colorado</td><td>1.25</td></tr>
<tr><td>1</td><td>New York</td><td>12.94</td><td>30</td><td>Mississippi</td><td>1.25</td></tr>
<tr><td>45</td><td>North Carolina</td><td>0.83</td><td>33</td><td>Michigan</td><td>1.22</td></tr>
<tr><td>6</td><td>North Dakota</td><td>4.93</td><td>33</td><td>Utah</td><td>1.22</td></tr>
<tr><td>41</td><td>Ohio</td><td>0.92</td><td>35</td><td>Georgia</td><td>1.19</td></tr>
<tr><td>39</td><td>Oklahoma</td><td>0.95</td><td>35</td><td>Iowa</td><td>1.19</td></tr>
<tr><td>25</td><td>Oregon</td><td>1.66</td><td>37</td><td>Missouri</td><td>1.14</td></tr>
<tr><td>17</td><td>Pennsylvania</td><td>2.45</td><td>38</td><td>Connecticut</td><td>1.11</td></tr>
<tr><td>11</td><td>Rhode Island</td><td>3.54</td><td>39</td><td>Oklahoma</td><td>0.95</td></tr>
<tr><td>47</td><td>South Carolina</td><td>0.75</td><td>40</td><td>Florida</td><td>0.94</td></tr>
<tr><td>8</td><td>South Dakota</td><td>4.32</td><td>41</td><td>Ohio</td><td>0.92</td></tr>
<tr><td>49</td><td>Tennessee</td><td>0.60</td><td>42</td><td>Kentucky</td><td>0.90</td></tr>
<tr><td>20</td><td>Texas</td><td>2.17</td><td>43</td><td>Virginia</td><td>0.89</td></tr>
<tr><td>33</td><td>Utah</td><td>1.22</td><td>44</td><td>Louisiana</td><td>0.85</td></tr>
<tr><td>4</td><td>Vermont</td><td>5.98</td><td>45</td><td>North Carolina</td><td>0.83</td></tr>
<tr><td>43</td><td>Virginia</td><td>0.89</td><td>46</td><td>Alabama</td><td>0.77</td></tr>
<tr><td>26</td><td>Washington</td><td>1.64</td><td>47</td><td>South Carolina</td><td>0.75</td></tr>
<tr><td>21</td><td>West Virginia</td><td>2.04</td><td>48</td><td>Wisconsin</td><td>0.69</td></tr>
<tr><td>48</td><td>Wisconsin</td><td>0.69</td><td>49</td><td>Indiana</td><td>0.60</td></tr>
<tr><td>3</td><td>Wyoming</td><td>6.38</td><td>49</td><td>Tennessee</td><td>0.60</td></tr>
<tr><td></td><td></td><td></td><td></td><td>District of Columbia</td><td>84.34</td></tr>
</table>

Source: CQ Press using data from U.S. Department of Homeland Security
   "FY 2016 Homeland Security Grant Program (HSGP)" (https://www.fema.gov/media-library/assets/documents/114411)
*For fiscal year 2016. National per capita does not include grants to U.S. territories. The Homeland Security Grant Program (HSGP) includes three sub-grant programs: State Homeland Security Program (SHSP), Urban Area Security Initiative (UASI), and Operation Stonegarden (OPSG). Law Enforcement Terrorism Prevention Activities (LETPA) allocations are a 25 percent subset of the SHSP and UASI allocations.

U.S. Department of Defense Expenditures in 2015

National Total = $279,116,223,000*

ALPHA ORDER

RANK	STATE	EXPENDITURES	% of USA
9	Alabama	$8,520,869,230	3.1%
32	Alaska	1,453,640,332	0.5%
10	Arizona	8,062,352,454	2.9%
42	Arkansas	578,898,465	0.2%
1	California	30,931,781,746	11.1%
18	Colorado	4,869,412,086	1.7%
5	Connecticut	12,236,821,483	4.4%
43	Delaware	226,750,475	0.1%
7	Florida	10,178,412,595	3.6%
16	Georgia	5,212,729,663	1.9%
29	Hawaii	1,791,010,922	0.6%
44	Idaho	220,043,631	0.1%
15	Illinois	5,455,911,440	2.0%
21	Indiana	2,995,529,911	1.1%
35	Iowa	1,192,013,960	0.4%
38	Kansas	893,793,344	0.3%
14	Kentucky	5,670,093,809	2.0%
28	Louisiana	1,904,055,129	0.7%
31	Maine	1,470,345,526	0.5%
4	Maryland	13,429,863,003	4.8%
8	Massachusetts	9,758,445,272	3.5%
25	Michigan	2,370,302,440	0.8%
20	Minnesota	3,653,660,840	1.3%
23	Mississippi	2,410,098,631	0.9%
11	Missouri	6,581,807,752	2.4%
45	Montana	204,864,713	0.1%
40	Nebraska	777,485,179	0.3%
30	Nevada	1,494,922,216	0.5%
36	New Hampshire	1,163,759,839	0.4%
17	New Jersey	5,111,347,790	1.8%
37	New Mexico	1,142,490,086	0.4%
12	New York	6,277,819,763	2.2%
22	North Carolina	2,760,543,727	1.0%
49	North Dakota	143,919,568	0.1%
19	Ohio	3,773,645,625	1.4%
26	Oklahoma	2,250,610,294	0.8%
39	Oregon	848,553,948	0.3%
6	Pennsylvania	10,552,352,270	3.8%
41	Rhode Island	615,925,607	0.2%
24	South Carolina	2,385,808,443	0.9%
48	South Dakota	158,785,340	0.1%
33	Tennessee	1,420,994,465	0.5%
3	Texas	29,725,323,855	10.6%
34	Utah	1,354,045,776	0.5%
47	Vermont	180,234,734	0.1%
2	Virginia	29,798,511,570	10.7%
13	Washington	6,035,112,042	2.2%
46	West Virginia	190,619,406	0.1%
27	Wisconsin	2,061,885,999	0.7%
50	Wyoming	80,777,982	0.0%

RANK ORDER

RANK	STATE	EXPENDITURES	% of USA
1	California	$30,931,781,746	11.1%
2	Virginia	29,798,511,570	10.7%
3	Texas	29,725,323,855	10.6%
4	Maryland	13,429,863,003	4.8%
5	Connecticut	12,236,821,483	4.4%
6	Pennsylvania	10,552,352,270	3.8%
7	Florida	10,178,412,595	3.6%
8	Massachusetts	9,758,445,272	3.5%
9	Alabama	8,520,869,230	3.1%
10	Arizona	8,062,352,454	2.9%
11	Missouri	6,581,807,752	2.4%
12	New York	6,277,819,763	2.2%
13	Washington	6,035,112,042	2.2%
14	Kentucky	5,670,093,809	2.0%
15	Illinois	5,455,911,440	2.0%
16	Georgia	5,212,729,663	1.9%
17	New Jersey	5,111,347,790	1.8%
18	Colorado	4,869,412,086	1.7%
19	Ohio	3,773,645,625	1.4%
20	Minnesota	3,653,660,840	1.3%
21	Indiana	2,995,529,911	1.1%
22	North Carolina	2,760,543,727	1.0%
23	Mississippi	2,410,098,631	0.9%
24	South Carolina	2,385,808,443	0.9%
25	Michigan	2,370,302,440	0.8%
26	Oklahoma	2,250,610,294	0.8%
27	Wisconsin	2,061,885,999	0.7%
28	Louisiana	1,904,055,129	0.7%
29	Hawaii	1,791,010,922	0.6%
30	Nevada	1,494,922,216	0.5%
31	Maine	1,470,345,526	0.5%
32	Alaska	1,453,640,332	0.5%
33	Tennessee	1,420,994,465	0.5%
34	Utah	1,354,045,776	0.5%
35	Iowa	1,192,013,960	0.4%
36	New Hampshire	1,163,759,839	0.4%
37	New Mexico	1,142,490,086	0.4%
38	Kansas	893,793,344	0.3%
39	Oregon	848,553,948	0.3%
40	Nebraska	777,485,179	0.3%
41	Rhode Island	615,925,607	0.2%
42	Arkansas	578,898,465	0.2%
43	Delaware	226,750,475	0.1%
44	Idaho	220,043,631	0.1%
45	Montana	204,864,713	0.1%
46	West Virginia	190,619,406	0.1%
47	Vermont	180,234,734	0.1%
48	South Dakota	158,785,340	0.1%
49	North Dakota	143,919,568	0.1%
50	Wyoming	80,777,982	0.0%
	District of Columbia	4,128,609,715	1.5%

Source: U.S. Office of Management and Budget, USAspending.gov
"Prime Award Spending Data Summary" (https://www.usaspending.gov/, as of February 16, 2017)
*Total includes $22,408,629,000 in U.S. territories and in expenditures not distributed by state. Expenditures allocated based on place of performance of a contract. Includes Contracts, Grants, Direct Payments, Insurance, and "Other." This source replaces a previous data series, "Atlas/Data Abstract for the United States", and definitions may differ.

Per Capita U.S. Department of Defense Expenditures in 2015

National Per Capita = $800*

<table>
<tr><td colspan="3">ALPHA ORDER</td><td colspan="3">RANK ORDER</td></tr>
<tr><td>RANK</td><td>STATE</td><td>PER CAPITA</td><td>RANK</td><td>STATE</td><td>PER CAPITA</td></tr>
<tr><td>5</td><td>Alabama</td><td>$1,755</td><td>1</td><td>Virginia</td><td>$3,561</td></tr>
<tr><td>4</td><td>Alaska</td><td>1,970</td><td>2</td><td>Connecticut</td><td>3,414</td></tr>
<tr><td>9</td><td>Arizona</td><td>1,183</td><td>3</td><td>Maryland</td><td>2,240</td></tr>
<tr><td>45</td><td>Arkansas</td><td>194</td><td>4</td><td>Alaska</td><td>1,970</td></tr>
<tr><td>18</td><td>California</td><td>793</td><td>5</td><td>Alabama</td><td>1,755</td></tr>
<tr><td>13</td><td>Colorado</td><td>894</td><td>6</td><td>Massachusetts</td><td>1,438</td></tr>
<tr><td>2</td><td>Connecticut</td><td>3,414</td><td>7</td><td>Kentucky</td><td>1,281</td></tr>
<tr><td>40</td><td>Delaware</td><td>240</td><td>8</td><td>Hawaii</td><td>1,257</td></tr>
<tr><td>26</td><td>Florida</td><td>503</td><td>9</td><td>Arizona</td><td>1,183</td></tr>
<tr><td>25</td><td>Georgia</td><td>511</td><td>10</td><td>Maine</td><td>1,106</td></tr>
<tr><td>8</td><td>Hawaii</td><td>1,257</td><td>11</td><td>Texas</td><td>1,084</td></tr>
<tr><td>49</td><td>Idaho</td><td>133</td><td>12</td><td>Missouri</td><td>1,083</td></tr>
<tr><td>30</td><td>Illinois</td><td>425</td><td>13</td><td>Colorado</td><td>894</td></tr>
<tr><td>28</td><td>Indiana</td><td>453</td><td>14</td><td>New Hampshire</td><td>875</td></tr>
<tr><td>33</td><td>Iowa</td><td>382</td><td>15</td><td>Washington</td><td>843</td></tr>
<tr><td>37</td><td>Kansas</td><td>307</td><td>16</td><td>Pennsylvania</td><td>825</td></tr>
<tr><td>7</td><td>Kentucky</td><td>1,281</td><td>17</td><td>Mississippi</td><td>806</td></tr>
<tr><td>32</td><td>Louisiana</td><td>408</td><td>18</td><td>California</td><td>793</td></tr>
<tr><td>10</td><td>Maine</td><td>1,106</td><td>19</td><td>Minnesota</td><td>666</td></tr>
<tr><td>3</td><td>Maryland</td><td>2,240</td><td>20</td><td>Rhode Island</td><td>583</td></tr>
<tr><td>6</td><td>Massachusetts</td><td>1,438</td><td>21</td><td>Oklahoma</td><td>576</td></tr>
<tr><td>41</td><td>Michigan</td><td>239</td><td>22</td><td>New Jersey</td><td>572</td></tr>
<tr><td>19</td><td>Minnesota</td><td>666</td><td>23</td><td>New Mexico</td><td>549</td></tr>
<tr><td>17</td><td>Mississippi</td><td>806</td><td>24</td><td>Nevada</td><td>518</td></tr>
<tr><td>12</td><td>Missouri</td><td>1,083</td><td>25</td><td>Georgia</td><td>511</td></tr>
<tr><td>44</td><td>Montana</td><td>198</td><td>26</td><td>Florida</td><td>503</td></tr>
<tr><td>31</td><td>Nebraska</td><td>411</td><td>27</td><td>South Carolina</td><td>487</td></tr>
<tr><td>24</td><td>Nevada</td><td>518</td><td>28</td><td>Indiana</td><td>453</td></tr>
<tr><td>14</td><td>New Hampshire</td><td>875</td><td>28</td><td>Utah</td><td>453</td></tr>
<tr><td>22</td><td>New Jersey</td><td>572</td><td>30</td><td>Illinois</td><td>425</td></tr>
<tr><td>23</td><td>New Mexico</td><td>549</td><td>31</td><td>Nebraska</td><td>411</td></tr>
<tr><td>36</td><td>New York</td><td>318</td><td>32</td><td>Louisiana</td><td>408</td></tr>
<tr><td>39</td><td>North Carolina</td><td>275</td><td>33</td><td>Iowa</td><td>382</td></tr>
<tr><td>46</td><td>North Dakota</td><td>190</td><td>34</td><td>Wisconsin</td><td>357</td></tr>
<tr><td>35</td><td>Ohio</td><td>325</td><td>35</td><td>Ohio</td><td>325</td></tr>
<tr><td>21</td><td>Oklahoma</td><td>576</td><td>36</td><td>New York</td><td>318</td></tr>
<tr><td>43</td><td>Oregon</td><td>211</td><td>37</td><td>Kansas</td><td>307</td></tr>
<tr><td>16</td><td>Pennsylvania</td><td>825</td><td>38</td><td>Vermont</td><td>288</td></tr>
<tr><td>20</td><td>Rhode Island</td><td>583</td><td>39</td><td>North Carolina</td><td>275</td></tr>
<tr><td>27</td><td>South Carolina</td><td>487</td><td>40</td><td>Delaware</td><td>240</td></tr>
<tr><td>47</td><td>South Dakota</td><td>185</td><td>41</td><td>Michigan</td><td>239</td></tr>
<tr><td>42</td><td>Tennessee</td><td>215</td><td>42</td><td>Tennessee</td><td>215</td></tr>
<tr><td>11</td><td>Texas</td><td>1,084</td><td>43</td><td>Oregon</td><td>211</td></tr>
<tr><td>28</td><td>Utah</td><td>453</td><td>44</td><td>Montana</td><td>198</td></tr>
<tr><td>38</td><td>Vermont</td><td>288</td><td>45</td><td>Arkansas</td><td>194</td></tr>
<tr><td>1</td><td>Virginia</td><td>3,561</td><td>46</td><td>North Dakota</td><td>190</td></tr>
<tr><td>15</td><td>Washington</td><td>843</td><td>47</td><td>South Dakota</td><td>185</td></tr>
<tr><td>50</td><td>West Virginia</td><td>104</td><td>48</td><td>Wyoming</td><td>138</td></tr>
<tr><td>34</td><td>Wisconsin</td><td>357</td><td>49</td><td>Idaho</td><td>133</td></tr>
<tr><td>48</td><td>Wyoming</td><td>138</td><td>50</td><td>West Virginia</td><td>104</td></tr>
<tr><td></td><td></td><td></td><td></td><td>District of Columbia</td><td>6,159</td></tr>
</table>

Source: CQ Press using data from U.S. Office of Management and Budget, USAspending.gov
"Prime Award Spending Data Summary" (https://www.usaspending.gov/, as of February 16, 2017)
*National per capita excludes expenditures and population for territories and undistributed amounts. Expenditures allocated based on place of performance of a contract. Includes Contracts, Grants, Direct Payments, Insurance, and "Other." This source replaces a previous data series, "Atlas/Data Abstract for the United States", and definitions may differ.

U.S. Department of Defense Expenditures as a Percent of Total Federal Government Expenditures in 2015
National Percent = 9.3%*

ALPHA ORDER

RANK	STATE	PERCENT
9	Alabama	13.8
5	Alaska	18.2
12	Arizona	12.8
42	Arkansas	2.6
14	California	11.8
10	Colorado	13.6
3	Connecticut	18.5
36	Delaware	3.6
26	Florida	6.6
18	Georgia	9.6
6	Hawaii	17.3
47	Idaho	2.0
22	Illinois	7.7
44	Indiana	2.5
28	Iowa	5.7
33	Kansas	5.1
23	Kentucky	7.4
27	Louisiana	6.5
10	Maine	13.6
2	Maryland	21.7
7	Massachusetts	16.7
36	Michigan	3.6
30	Minnesota	5.5
16	Mississippi	11.1
8	Missouri	14.1
42	Montana	2.6
24	Nebraska	6.9
21	Nevada	8.5
13	New Hampshire	12.7
19	New Jersey	8.7
31	New Mexico	5.2
35	New York	4.2
34	North Carolina	4.5
50	North Dakota	0.2
31	Ohio	5.2
20	Oklahoma	8.6
40	Oregon	2.7
29	Pennsylvania	5.6
24	Rhode Island	6.9
39	South Carolina	3.2
40	South Dakota	2.7
47	Tennessee	2.0
3	Texas	18.5
17	Utah	9.9
36	Vermont	3.6
1	Virginia	32.7
15	Washington	11.3
49	West Virginia	1.2
44	Wisconsin	2.5
46	Wyoming	2.2

RANK ORDER

RANK	STATE	PERCENT
1	Virginia	32.7
2	Maryland	21.7
3	Connecticut	18.5
3	Texas	18.5
5	Alaska	18.2
6	Hawaii	17.3
7	Massachusetts	16.7
8	Missouri	14.1
9	Alabama	13.8
10	Colorado	13.6
10	Maine	13.6
12	Arizona	12.8
13	New Hampshire	12.7
14	California	11.8
15	Washington	11.3
16	Mississippi	11.1
17	Utah	9.9
18	Georgia	9.6
19	New Jersey	8.7
20	Oklahoma	8.6
21	Nevada	8.5
22	Illinois	7.7
23	Kentucky	7.4
24	Nebraska	6.9
24	Rhode Island	6.9
26	Florida	6.6
27	Louisiana	6.5
28	Iowa	5.7
29	Pennsylvania	5.6
30	Minnesota	5.5
31	New Mexico	5.2
31	Ohio	5.2
33	Kansas	5.1
34	North Carolina	4.5
35	New York	4.2
36	Delaware	3.6
36	Michigan	3.6
36	Vermont	3.6
39	South Carolina	3.2
40	Oregon	2.7
40	South Dakota	2.7
42	Arkansas	2.6
42	Montana	2.6
44	Indiana	2.5
44	Wisconsin	2.5
46	Wyoming	2.2
47	Idaho	2.0
47	Tennessee	2.0
49	West Virginia	1.2
50	North Dakota	0.2
	District of Columbia	13.7

Source: CQ Press using data from U.S. Office of Management and Budget, USAspending.gov

"Prime Award Spending Data Summary" (https://www.usaspending.gov/, as of February 16, 2017)

*National percent excludes expenditures and population for territories and undistributed amounts. Expenditures allocated based on place of performance of a contract. Includes Contracts, Grants, Direct Payments, Insurance, and "Other." This source replaces a previous data series, "Atlas/Data Abstract for the United States", and definitions may differ.

U.S. Active Duty Military Personnel Stationed in the United States in 2015

National Total = 1,132,106 Personnel*

ALPHA ORDER

RANK	STATE	PERSONNEL	% of USA
24	Alabama	7,556	0.7%
18	Alaska	17,851	1.6%
17	Arizona	18,533	1.6%
30	Arkansas	4,501	0.4%
1	California	150,563	13.3%
10	Colorado	35,712	3.2%
28	Connecticut	5,979	0.5%
32	Delaware	3,320	0.3%
6	Florida	59,376	5.2%
5	Georgia	68,191	6.0%
8	Hawaii	45,367	4.0%
33	Idaho	3,306	0.3%
16	Illinois	19,294	1.7%
43	Indiana	890	0.1%
48	Iowa	201	0.0%
13	Kansas	23,044	2.0%
11	Kentucky	34,083	3.0%
20	Louisiana	14,877	1.3%
47	Maine	272	0.0%
12	Maryland	28,531	2.5%
40	Massachusetts	1,972	0.2%
42	Michigan	1,092	0.1%
46	Minnesota	492	0.0%
22	Mississippi	11,120	1.0%
19	Missouri	15,387	1.4%
34	Montana	3,251	0.3%
27	Nebraska	6,148	0.5%
23	Nevada	10,311	0.9%
41	New Hampshire	1,131	0.1%
29	New Jersey	5,972	0.5%
21	New Mexico	11,811	1.0%
14	New York	20,908	1.8%
4	North Carolina	99,981	8.8%
25	North Dakota	7,113	0.6%
26	Ohio	6,469	0.6%
15	Oklahoma	19,768	1.7%
45	Oregon	548	0.0%
38	Pennsylvania	2,281	0.2%
35	Rhode Island	3,159	0.3%
9	South Carolina	36,521	3.2%
36	South Dakota	3,144	0.3%
39	Tennessee	2,028	0.2%
3	Texas	116,549	10.3%
31	Utah	3,885	0.3%
50	Vermont	110	0.0%
2	Virginia	124,197	11.0%
7	Washington	57,008	5.0%
49	West Virginia	181	0.0%
44	Wisconsin	617	0.1%
37	Wyoming	3,107	0.3%

RANK ORDER

RANK	STATE	PERSONNEL	% of USA
1	California	150,563	13.3%
2	Virginia	124,197	11.0%
3	Texas	116,549	10.3%
4	North Carolina	99,981	8.8%
5	Georgia	68,191	6.0%
6	Florida	59,376	5.2%
7	Washington	57,008	5.0%
8	Hawaii	45,367	4.0%
9	South Carolina	36,521	3.2%
10	Colorado	35,712	3.2%
11	Kentucky	34,083	3.0%
12	Maryland	28,531	2.5%
13	Kansas	23,044	2.0%
14	New York	20,908	1.8%
15	Oklahoma	19,768	1.7%
16	Illinois	19,294	1.7%
17	Arizona	18,533	1.6%
18	Alaska	17,851	1.6%
19	Missouri	15,387	1.4%
20	Louisiana	14,877	1.3%
21	New Mexico	11,811	1.0%
22	Mississippi	11,120	1.0%
23	Nevada	10,311	0.9%
24	Alabama	7,556	0.7%
25	North Dakota	7,113	0.6%
26	Ohio	6,469	0.6%
27	Nebraska	6,148	0.5%
28	Connecticut	5,979	0.5%
29	New Jersey	5,972	0.5%
30	Arkansas	4,501	0.4%
31	Utah	3,885	0.3%
32	Delaware	3,320	0.3%
33	Idaho	3,306	0.3%
34	Montana	3,251	0.3%
35	Rhode Island	3,159	0.3%
36	South Dakota	3,144	0.3%
37	Wyoming	3,107	0.3%
38	Pennsylvania	2,281	0.2%
39	Tennessee	2,028	0.2%
40	Massachusetts	1,972	0.2%
41	New Hampshire	1,131	0.1%
42	Michigan	1,092	0.1%
43	Indiana	890	0.1%
44	Wisconsin	617	0.1%
45	Oregon	548	0.0%
46	Minnesota	492	0.0%
47	Maine	272	0.0%
48	Iowa	201	0.0%
49	West Virginia	181	0.0%
50	Vermont	110	0.0%
	District of Columbia	8,346	0.7%

Source: U.S. Department of Defense
   "Demographics 2015" (http://www.militaryonesource.mil/footer?content_id=279104)
*Includes 6,052 not shown by state. Numbers reflect where the personnel are stationed.

U.S. Selected Reserve Personnel Stationed in the United States in 2015

National Total = 801,492 Personnel*

ALPHA ORDER

RANK	STATE	PERSONNEL	% of USA
11	Alabama	20,517	2.6%
42	Alaska	4,799	0.6%
25	Arizona	14,625	1.8%
30	Arkansas	12,042	1.5%
1	California	57,791	7.2%
27	Colorado	13,687	1.7%
37	Connecticut	6,846	0.9%
41	Delaware	5,161	0.6%
3	Florida	36,491	4.6%
7	Georgia	27,225	3.4%
34	Hawaii	9,446	1.2%
39	Idaho	5,453	0.7%
9	Illinois	24,821	3.1%
14	Indiana	19,347	2.4%
31	Iowa	11,162	1.4%
32	Kansas	11,011	1.4%
28	Kentucky	13,053	1.6%
12	Louisiana	19,954	2.5%
49	Maine	4,091	0.5%
19	Maryland	18,437	2.3%
22	Massachusetts	15,776	2.0%
23	Michigan	15,289	1.9%
17	Minnesota	18,835	2.3%
21	Mississippi	16,987	2.1%
13	Missouri	19,749	2.5%
44	Montana	4,533	0.6%
38	Nebraska	6,378	0.8%
36	Nevada	7,729	1.0%
47	New Hampshire	4,190	0.5%
20	New Jersey	17,679	2.2%
40	New Mexico	5,186	0.6%
5	New York	29,673	3.7%
10	North Carolina	22,976	2.9%
45	North Dakota	4,465	0.6%
6	Ohio	28,330	3.5%
26	Oklahoma	14,039	1.8%
33	Oregon	9,917	1.2%
4	Pennsylvania	31,703	4.0%
46	Rhode Island	4,448	0.6%
18	South Carolina	18,458	2.3%
43	South Dakota	4,707	0.6%
15	Tennessee	19,316	2.4%
2	Texas	53,701	6.7%
29	Utah	12,062	1.5%
48	Vermont	4,110	0.5%
8	Virginia	26,115	3.3%
16	Washington	19,190	2.4%
35	West Virginia	8,246	1.0%
24	Wisconsin	14,652	1.8%
50	Wyoming	2,937	0.4%

RANK ORDER

RANK	STATE	PERSONNEL	% of USA
1	California	57,791	7.2%
2	Texas	53,701	6.7%
3	Florida	36,491	4.6%
4	Pennsylvania	31,703	4.0%
5	New York	29,673	3.7%
6	Ohio	28,330	3.5%
7	Georgia	27,225	3.4%
8	Virginia	26,115	3.3%
9	Illinois	24,821	3.1%
10	North Carolina	22,976	2.9%
11	Alabama	20,517	2.6%
12	Louisiana	19,954	2.5%
13	Missouri	19,749	2.5%
14	Indiana	19,347	2.4%
15	Tennessee	19,316	2.4%
16	Washington	19,190	2.4%
17	Minnesota	18,835	2.3%
18	South Carolina	18,458	2.3%
19	Maryland	18,437	2.3%
20	New Jersey	17,679	2.2%
21	Mississippi	16,987	2.1%
22	Massachusetts	15,776	2.0%
23	Michigan	15,289	1.9%
24	Wisconsin	14,652	1.8%
25	Arizona	14,625	1.8%
26	Oklahoma	14,039	1.8%
27	Colorado	13,687	1.7%
28	Kentucky	13,053	1.6%
29	Utah	12,062	1.5%
30	Arkansas	12,042	1.5%
31	Iowa	11,162	1.4%
32	Kansas	11,011	1.4%
33	Oregon	9,917	1.2%
34	Hawaii	9,446	1.2%
35	West Virginia	8,246	1.0%
36	Nevada	7,729	1.0%
37	Connecticut	6,846	0.9%
38	Nebraska	6,378	0.8%
39	Idaho	5,453	0.7%
40	New Mexico	5,186	0.6%
41	Delaware	5,161	0.6%
42	Alaska	4,799	0.6%
43	South Dakota	4,707	0.6%
44	Montana	4,533	0.6%
45	North Dakota	4,465	0.6%
46	Rhode Island	4,448	0.6%
47	New Hampshire	4,190	0.5%
48	Vermont	4,110	0.5%
49	Maine	4,091	0.5%
50	Wyoming	2,937	0.4%
	District of Columbia	4,157	0.5%

Source: U.S. Department of Defense
   "Demographics 2015" (http://www.militaryonesource.mil/footer?content_id=279104)
*Numbers reflect where the personnel are stationed.

Veterans in 2014

National Total = 21,999,108 Veterans*

ALPHA ORDER

RANK	STATE	VETERANS	% of USA
21	Alabama	413,618	1.9%
45	Alaska	73,397	0.3%
13	Arizona	532,206	2.4%
29	Arkansas	249,274	1.1%
1	California	1,851,470	8.4%
22	Colorado	413,271	1.9%
34	Connecticut	213,420	1.0%
44	Delaware	78,099	0.4%
3	Florida	1,583,697	7.2%
9	Georgia	752,882	3.4%
41	Hawaii	121,007	0.6%
39	Idaho	132,395	0.6%
10	Illinois	721,575	3.3%
16	Indiana	476,283	2.2%
30	Iowa	231,655	1.1%
32	Kansas	221,206	1.0%
27	Kentucky	330,599	1.5%
28	Louisiana	330,145	1.5%
40	Maine	127,234	0.6%
17	Maryland	437,762	2.0%
23	Massachusetts	379,772	1.7%
11	Michigan	658,469	3.0%
24	Minnesota	369,149	1.7%
33	Mississippi	220,389	1.0%
15	Missouri	494,346	2.2%
43	Montana	99,646	0.5%
38	Nebraska	143,375	0.7%
31	Nevada	228,027	1.0%
42	New Hampshire	113,660	0.5%
18	New Jersey	428,396	1.9%
35	New Mexico	171,528	0.8%
5	New York	892,221	4.1%
8	North Carolina	775,020	3.5%
48	North Dakota	57,395	0.3%
6	Ohio	866,481	3.9%
25	Oklahoma	337,571	1.5%
26	Oregon	331,632	1.5%
4	Pennsylvania	939,069	4.3%
47	Rhode Island	71,966	0.3%
19	South Carolina	417,554	1.9%
46	South Dakota	72,030	0.3%
14	Tennessee	506,340	2.3%
2	Texas	1,680,418	7.6%
37	Utah	151,719	0.7%
50	Vermont	48,602	0.2%
7	Virginia	781,388	3.6%
12	Washington	603,623	2.7%
36	West Virginia	167,355	0.8%
20	Wisconsin	413,723	1.9%
49	Wyoming	49,708	0.2%

RANK ORDER

RANK	STATE	VETERANS	% of USA
1	California	1,851,470	8.4%
2	Texas	1,680,418	7.6%
3	Florida	1,583,697	7.2%
4	Pennsylvania	939,069	4.3%
5	New York	892,221	4.1%
6	Ohio	866,481	3.9%
7	Virginia	781,388	3.6%
8	North Carolina	775,020	3.5%
9	Georgia	752,882	3.4%
10	Illinois	721,575	3.3%
11	Michigan	658,469	3.0%
12	Washington	603,623	2.7%
13	Arizona	532,206	2.4%
14	Tennessee	506,340	2.3%
15	Missouri	494,346	2.2%
16	Indiana	476,283	2.2%
17	Maryland	437,762	2.0%
18	New Jersey	428,396	1.9%
19	South Carolina	417,554	1.9%
20	Wisconsin	413,723	1.9%
21	Alabama	413,618	1.9%
22	Colorado	413,271	1.9%
23	Massachusetts	379,772	1.7%
24	Minnesota	369,149	1.7%
25	Oklahoma	337,571	1.5%
26	Oregon	331,632	1.5%
27	Kentucky	330,599	1.5%
28	Louisiana	330,145	1.5%
29	Arkansas	249,274	1.1%
30	Iowa	231,655	1.1%
31	Nevada	228,027	1.0%
32	Kansas	221,206	1.0%
33	Mississippi	220,389	1.0%
34	Connecticut	213,420	1.0%
35	New Mexico	171,528	0.8%
36	West Virginia	167,355	0.8%
37	Utah	151,719	0.7%
38	Nebraska	143,375	0.7%
39	Idaho	132,395	0.6%
40	Maine	127,234	0.6%
41	Hawaii	121,007	0.6%
42	New Hampshire	113,660	0.5%
43	Montana	99,646	0.5%
44	Delaware	78,099	0.4%
45	Alaska	73,397	0.3%
46	South Dakota	72,030	0.3%
47	Rhode Island	71,966	0.3%
48	North Dakota	57,395	0.3%
49	Wyoming	49,708	0.2%
50	Vermont	48,602	0.2%
	District of Columbia	29,825	0.1%

Source: U.S. Department of Veteran Affairs
"Veteran Data and Information" (http://www.va.gov/vetdata/Veteran_Population.asp)
*Estimates based on 2014 data. Includes 207,515 veterans in U.S. territories or other countries.

Percent of Adult Population Who Are Veterans in 2014

National Percent = 9.0%*

ALPHA ORDER

RANK ORDER

RANK	STATE	PERCENT		RANK	STATE	PERCENT
12	Alabama	11.1		1	Alaska	13.4
1	Alaska	13.4		2	Montana	12.6
20	Arizona	10.6		3	Virginia	12.2
12	Arkansas	11.1		4	Maine	11.9
48	California	6.3		5	Oklahoma	11.6
22	Colorado	10.3		6	West Virginia	11.4
44	Connecticut	7.6		7	South Carolina	11.3
16	Delaware	10.8		7	South Dakota	11.3
23	Florida	10.2		9	Idaho	11.2
29	Georgia	10.0		9	Washington	11.2
14	Hawaii	11.0		9	Wyoming	11.2
9	Idaho	11.2		12	Alabama	11.1
46	Illinois	7.3		12	Arkansas	11.1
34	Indiana	9.6		14	Hawaii	11.0
30	Iowa	9.8		15	New Mexico	10.9
23	Kansas	10.2		16	Delaware	10.8
30	Kentucky	9.8		16	New Hampshire	10.8
37	Louisiana	9.4		16	Oregon	10.8
4	Maine	11.9		19	Nevada	10.7
36	Maryland	9.5		20	Arizona	10.6
47	Massachusetts	7.2		20	Missouri	10.6
42	Michigan	8.6		22	Colorado	10.3
40	Minnesota	8.9		23	Florida	10.2
30	Mississippi	9.8		23	Kansas	10.2
20	Missouri	10.6		23	Nebraska	10.2
2	Montana	12.6		23	North Carolina	10.2
23	Nebraska	10.2		23	North Dakota	10.2
19	Nevada	10.7		28	Tennessee	10.1
16	New Hampshire	10.8		29	Georgia	10.0
49	New Jersey	6.2		30	Iowa	9.8
15	New Mexico	10.9		30	Kentucky	9.8
50	New York	5.8		30	Mississippi	9.8
23	North Carolina	10.2		33	Ohio	9.7
23	North Dakota	10.2		34	Indiana	9.6
33	Ohio	9.7		34	Vermont	9.6
5	Oklahoma	11.6		36	Maryland	9.5
16	Oregon	10.8		37	Louisiana	9.4
38	Pennsylvania	9.3		38	Pennsylvania	9.3
42	Rhode Island	8.6		38	Wisconsin	9.3
7	South Carolina	11.3		40	Minnesota	8.9
7	South Dakota	11.3		41	Texas	8.7
28	Tennessee	10.1		42	Michigan	8.6
41	Texas	8.7		42	Rhode Island	8.6
44	Utah	7.6		44	Connecticut	7.6
34	Vermont	9.6		44	Utah	7.6
3	Virginia	12.2		46	Illinois	7.3
9	Washington	11.2		47	Massachusetts	7.2
6	West Virginia	11.4		48	California	6.3
38	Wisconsin	9.3		49	New Jersey	6.2
9	Wyoming	11.2		50	New York	5.8

District of Columbia 5.6

Source: CQ Press using data from U.S. Department of Veteran Affairs
    "Veteran Data and Information" (http://www.va.gov/vetdata/Veteran_Population.asp)
*Estimates based on 2014 data. National figures does not include veterans in U.S. territories or other countries. Percent calculated with population 18 years old and older in 2013.

U.S. Military Fatalities in Iraq and Afghanistan as of February 15, 2017

National Total = 6,895 Fatalities*

ALPHA ORDER

RANK	STATE	FATALITIES	% of USA
25	Alabama	105	1.5%
46	Alaska	23	0.3%
13	Arizona	154	2.2%
29	Arkansas	89	1.3%
1	California	742	10.8%
26	Colorado	104	1.5%
39	Connecticut	47	0.7%
49	Delaware	19	0.3%
3	Florida	348	5.0%
9	Georgia	218	3.2%
43	Hawaii	37	0.5%
36	Idaho	50	0.7%
7	Illinois	255	3.7%
12	Indiana	156	2.3%
32	Iowa	73	1.1%
31	Kansas	76	1.1%
23	Kentucky	113	1.6%
20	Louisiana	125	1.8%
36	Maine	50	0.7%
22	Maryland	122	1.8%
17	Massachusetts	127	1.8%
8	Michigan	227	3.3%
27	Minnesota	97	1.4%
30	Mississippi	80	1.2%
15	Missouri	144	2.1%
40	Montana	40	0.6%
33	Nebraska	61	0.9%
35	Nevada	54	0.8%
40	New Hampshire	40	0.6%
21	New Jersey	124	1.8%
34	New Mexico	57	0.8%
4	New York	297	4.3%
11	North Carolina	189	2.7%
48	North Dakota	20	0.3%
6	Ohio	280	4.1%
19	Oklahoma	126	1.8%
24	Oregon	109	1.6%
5	Pennsylvania	293	4.2%
50	Rhode Island	17	0.2%
28	South Carolina	96	1.4%
45	South Dakota	24	0.3%
16	Tennessee	140	2.0%
2	Texas	609	8.8%
38	Utah	48	0.7%
44	Vermont	26	0.4%
10	Virginia	200	2.9%
14	Washington	151	2.2%
40	West Virginia	40	0.6%
17	Wisconsin	127	1.8%
47	Wyoming	22	0.3%

RANK ORDER

RANK	STATE	FATALITIES	% of USA
1	California	742	10.8%
2	Texas	609	8.8%
3	Florida	348	5.0%
4	New York	297	4.3%
5	Pennsylvania	293	4.2%
6	Ohio	280	4.1%
7	Illinois	255	3.7%
8	Michigan	227	3.3%
9	Georgia	218	3.2%
10	Virginia	200	2.9%
11	North Carolina	189	2.7%
12	Indiana	156	2.3%
13	Arizona	154	2.2%
14	Washington	151	2.2%
15	Missouri	144	2.1%
16	Tennessee	140	2.0%
17	Massachusetts	127	1.8%
17	Wisconsin	127	1.8%
19	Oklahoma	126	1.8%
20	Louisiana	125	1.8%
21	New Jersey	124	1.8%
22	Maryland	122	1.8%
23	Kentucky	113	1.6%
24	Oregon	109	1.6%
25	Alabama	105	1.5%
26	Colorado	104	1.5%
27	Minnesota	97	1.4%
28	South Carolina	96	1.4%
29	Arkansas	89	1.3%
30	Mississippi	80	1.2%
31	Kansas	76	1.1%
32	Iowa	73	1.1%
33	Nebraska	61	0.9%
34	New Mexico	57	0.8%
35	Nevada	54	0.8%
36	Idaho	50	0.7%
36	Maine	50	0.7%
38	Utah	48	0.7%
39	Connecticut	47	0.7%
40	Montana	40	0.6%
40	New Hampshire	40	0.6%
40	West Virginia	40	0.6%
43	Hawaii	37	0.5%
44	Vermont	26	0.4%
45	South Dakota	24	0.3%
46	Alaska	23	0.3%
47	Wyoming	22	0.3%
48	North Dakota	20	0.3%
49	Delaware	19	0.3%
50	Rhode Island	17	0.2%
	District of Columbia	10	0.1%

Source: U.S. Department of Defense, Defense Casualty Analysis System
"U.S. Military Casualties" (https://www.dmdc.osd.mil/dcas/pages/report_sum_all.xhtml)
*Total includes 114 deaths of soldiers from U.S. territories. Total does not include deaths of United Kingdom soldiers or other coalition nations. Includes 5,390 combat and 1,505 noncombat deaths. Includes 4,484 deaths in Iraq, 2,377 deaths in Afghanistan, and 34 deaths fighting Islamic State in Syria and Iraq.

Rate of U.S. Military Fatalities in Iraq and Afghanistan as of February 15, 2017

National Rate = 2.1 Fatalities per 100,000 Population*

ALPHA ORDER

RANK	STATE	RATE
27	Alabama	2.2
7	Alaska	3.1
27	Arizona	2.2
8	Arkansas	3.0
38	California	1.9
38	Colorado	1.9
50	Connecticut	1.3
35	Delaware	2.0
45	Florida	1.7
32	Georgia	2.1
16	Hawaii	2.6
8	Idaho	3.0
35	Illinois	2.0
20	Indiana	2.4
24	Iowa	2.3
16	Kansas	2.6
19	Kentucky	2.5
12	Louisiana	2.7
2	Maine	3.8
35	Maryland	2.0
38	Massachusetts	1.9
24	Michigan	2.3
43	Minnesota	1.8
12	Mississippi	2.7
20	Missouri	2.4
2	Montana	3.8
5	Nebraska	3.2
43	Nevada	1.8
8	New Hampshire	3.0
49	New Jersey	1.4
12	New Mexico	2.7
48	New York	1.5
38	North Carolina	1.9
16	North Dakota	2.6
20	Ohio	2.4
5	Oklahoma	3.2
12	Oregon	2.7
24	Pennsylvania	2.3
46	Rhode Island	1.6
38	South Carolina	1.9
11	South Dakota	2.8
32	Tennessee	2.1
27	Texas	2.2
46	Utah	1.6
1	Vermont	4.2
20	Virginia	2.4
32	Washington	2.1
27	West Virginia	2.2
27	Wisconsin	2.2
2	Wyoming	3.8

RANK ORDER

RANK	STATE	RATE
1	Vermont	4.2
2	Maine	3.8
2	Montana	3.8
2	Wyoming	3.8
5	Nebraska	3.2
5	Oklahoma	3.2
7	Alaska	3.1
8	Arkansas	3.0
8	Idaho	3.0
8	New Hampshire	3.0
11	South Dakota	2.8
12	Louisiana	2.7
12	Mississippi	2.7
12	New Mexico	2.7
12	Oregon	2.7
16	Hawaii	2.6
16	Kansas	2.6
16	North Dakota	2.6
19	Kentucky	2.5
20	Indiana	2.4
20	Missouri	2.4
20	Ohio	2.4
20	Virginia	2.4
24	Iowa	2.3
24	Michigan	2.3
24	Pennsylvania	2.3
27	Alabama	2.2
27	Arizona	2.2
27	Texas	2.2
27	West Virginia	2.2
27	Wisconsin	2.2
32	Georgia	2.1
32	Tennessee	2.1
32	Washington	2.1
35	Delaware	2.0
35	Illinois	2.0
35	Maryland	2.0
38	California	1.9
38	Colorado	1.9
38	Massachusetts	1.9
38	North Carolina	1.9
38	South Carolina	1.9
43	Minnesota	1.8
43	Nevada	1.8
45	Florida	1.7
46	Rhode Island	1.6
46	Utah	1.6
48	New York	1.5
49	New Jersey	1.4
50	Connecticut	1.3

| | District of Columbia | 1.5 |

Source: CQ Press using data from U.S. Department of Defense, Defense Casualty Analysis System
"U.S. Military Casualties" (https://www.dmdc.osd.mil/dcas/pages/report_sum_all.xhtml)
*National rate does not include deaths of soldiers from U.S. territories. Includes combat and noncombat deaths. Calculated with 2016 population estimates.

U.S. Military Wounded in Iraq and Afghanistan as of February 15, 2017

National Total = 52,524 Wounded*

ALPHA ORDER

RANK	STATE	WOUNDED	% of USA
18	Alabama	863	1.6%
46	Alaska	158	0.3%
14	Arizona	1,154	2.2%
29	Arkansas	647	1.2%
1	California	4,852	9.2%
22	Colorado	818	1.6%
35	Connecticut	423	0.8%
50	Delaware	84	0.2%
3	Florida	2,500	4.8%
9	Georgia	1,486	2.8%
43	Hawaii	208	0.4%
36	Idaho	389	0.7%
7	Illinois	1,751	3.3%
15	Indiana	1,102	2.1%
31	Iowa	624	1.2%
30	Kansas	626	1.2%
27	Kentucky	747	1.4%
21	Louisiana	832	1.6%
41	Maine	323	0.6%
28	Maryland	679	1.3%
20	Massachusetts	834	1.6%
8	Michigan	1,629	3.1%
26	Minnesota	752	1.4%
33	Mississippi	442	0.8%
13	Missouri	1,185	2.3%
40	Montana	324	0.6%
39	Nebraska	336	0.6%
37	Nevada	376	0.7%
42	New Hampshire	297	0.6%
24	New Jersey	768	1.5%
34	New Mexico	425	0.8%
4	New York	2,328	4.4%
10	North Carolina	1,441	2.7%
49	North Dakota	117	0.2%
5	Ohio	2,038	3.9%
19	Oklahoma	856	1.6%
23	Oregon	791	1.5%
6	Pennsylvania	1,998	3.8%
45	Rhode Island	169	0.3%
25	South Carolina	755	1.4%
44	South Dakota	194	0.4%
16	Tennessee	1,017	1.9%
2	Texas	4,361	8.3%
32	Utah	455	0.9%
47	Vermont	152	0.3%
12	Virginia	1,200	2.3%
11	Washington	1,290	2.5%
38	West Virginia	364	0.7%
17	Wisconsin	915	1.7%
48	Wyoming	150	0.3%

RANK ORDER

RANK	STATE	WOUNDED	% of USA
1	California	4,852	9.2%
2	Texas	4,361	8.3%
3	Florida	2,500	4.8%
4	New York	2,328	4.4%
5	Ohio	2,038	3.9%
6	Pennsylvania	1,998	3.8%
7	Illinois	1,751	3.3%
8	Michigan	1,629	3.1%
9	Georgia	1,486	2.8%
10	North Carolina	1,441	2.7%
11	Washington	1,290	2.5%
12	Virginia	1,200	2.3%
13	Missouri	1,185	2.3%
14	Arizona	1,154	2.2%
15	Indiana	1,102	2.1%
16	Tennessee	1,017	1.9%
17	Wisconsin	915	1.7%
18	Alabama	863	1.6%
19	Oklahoma	856	1.6%
20	Massachusetts	834	1.6%
21	Louisiana	832	1.6%
22	Colorado	818	1.6%
23	Oregon	791	1.5%
24	New Jersey	768	1.5%
25	South Carolina	755	1.4%
26	Minnesota	752	1.4%
27	Kentucky	747	1.4%
28	Maryland	679	1.3%
29	Arkansas	647	1.2%
30	Kansas	626	1.2%
31	Iowa	624	1.2%
32	Utah	455	0.9%
33	Mississippi	442	0.8%
34	New Mexico	425	0.8%
35	Connecticut	423	0.8%
36	Idaho	389	0.7%
37	Nevada	376	0.7%
38	West Virginia	364	0.7%
39	Nebraska	336	0.6%
40	Montana	324	0.6%
41	Maine	323	0.6%
42	New Hampshire	297	0.6%
43	Hawaii	208	0.4%
44	South Dakota	194	0.4%
45	Rhode Island	169	0.3%
46	Alaska	158	0.3%
47	Vermont	152	0.3%
48	Wyoming	150	0.3%
49	North Dakota	117	0.2%
50	Delaware	84	0.2%
	District of Columbia	30	0.1%

Source: U.S. Department of Defense, Defense Casualty Analysis System
"U.S. Military Casualties" (https://www.dmdc.osd.mil/dcas/pages/report_sum_all.xhtml)
*Total includes 4,269 wounded soldiers from U.S. territories. Total does not include wounded soldiers of United Kingdom or other coalition nations. Only includes wounded in action. Includes 32,249 wounded in Iraq, 20,244 wounded in Afghanistan, and 31 wounded fighting the Islamic State in Syria and Iraq.

IV. Economy

Gross Domestic Product in 2015

National Total = $17,919,651,000,000*

ALPHA ORDER

RANK	STATE	G.D.P.	% of USA
27	Alabama	$199,656,000,000	1.1%
46	Alaska	52,747,000,000	0.3%
22	Arizona	290,903,000,000	1.6%
34	Arkansas	118,907,000,000	0.7%
1	California	2,481,348,000,000	13.8%
19	Colorado	313,748,000,000	1.8%
23	Connecticut	252,930,000,000	1.4%
41	Delaware	68,724,000,000	0.4%
4	Florida	888,087,000,000	5.0%
9	Georgia	497,944,000,000	2.8%
38	Hawaii	80,376,000,000	0.4%
42	Idaho	65,549,000,000	0.4%
5	Illinois	776,882,000,000	4.3%
16	Indiana	336,053,000,000	1.9%
30	Iowa	174,030,000,000	1.0%
31	Kansas	149,641,000,000	0.8%
28	Kentucky	193,274,000,000	1.1%
24	Louisiana	239,305,000,000	1.3%
43	Maine	57,297,000,000	0.3%
15	Maryland	365,356,000,000	2.0%
11	Massachusetts	484,943,000,000	2.7%
13	Michigan	468,334,000,000	2.6%
17	Minnesota	328,340,000,000	1.8%
36	Mississippi	105,819,000,000	0.6%
21	Missouri	294,491,000,000	1.6%
48	Montana	45,237,000,000	0.3%
35	Nebraska	113,282,000,000	0.6%
33	Nevada	139,724,000,000	0.8%
40	New Hampshire	73,867,000,000	0.4%
8	New Jersey	567,738,000,000	3.2%
37	New Mexico	93,339,000,000	0.5%
3	New York	1,433,531,000,000	8.0%
10	North Carolina	495,402,000,000	2.8%
45	North Dakota	55,860,000,000	0.3%
7	Ohio	610,928,000,000	3.4%
29	Oklahoma	185,981,000,000	1.0%
25	Oregon	217,629,000,000	1.2%
6	Pennsylvania	709,762,000,000	4.0%
44	Rhode Island	56,052,000,000	0.3%
26	South Carolina	201,005,000,000	1.1%
47	South Dakota	47,244,000,000	0.3%
18	Tennessee	315,857,000,000	1.8%
2	Texas	1,630,082,000,000	9.1%
32	Utah	147,503,000,000	0.8%
50	Vermont	30,038,000,000	0.2%
12	Virginia	481,084,000,000	2.7%
14	Washington	445,413,000,000	2.5%
39	West Virginia	74,321,000,000	0.4%
20	Wisconsin	302,076,000,000	1.7%
49	Wyoming	39,864,000,000	0.2%

RANK ORDER

RANK	STATE	G.D.P.	% of USA
1	California	$2,481,348,000,000	13.8%
2	Texas	1,630,082,000,000	9.1%
3	New York	1,433,531,000,000	8.0%
4	Florida	888,087,000,000	5.0%
5	Illinois	776,882,000,000	4.3%
6	Pennsylvania	709,762,000,000	4.0%
7	Ohio	610,928,000,000	3.4%
8	New Jersey	567,738,000,000	3.2%
9	Georgia	497,944,000,000	2.8%
10	North Carolina	495,402,000,000	2.8%
11	Massachusetts	484,943,000,000	2.7%
12	Virginia	481,084,000,000	2.7%
13	Michigan	468,334,000,000	2.6%
14	Washington	445,413,000,000	2.5%
15	Maryland	365,356,000,000	2.0%
16	Indiana	336,053,000,000	1.9%
17	Minnesota	328,340,000,000	1.8%
18	Tennessee	315,857,000,000	1.8%
19	Colorado	313,748,000,000	1.8%
20	Wisconsin	302,076,000,000	1.7%
21	Missouri	294,491,000,000	1.6%
22	Arizona	290,903,000,000	1.6%
23	Connecticut	252,930,000,000	1.4%
24	Louisiana	239,305,000,000	1.3%
25	Oregon	217,629,000,000	1.2%
26	South Carolina	201,005,000,000	1.1%
27	Alabama	199,656,000,000	1.1%
28	Kentucky	193,274,000,000	1.1%
29	Oklahoma	185,981,000,000	1.0%
30	Iowa	174,030,000,000	1.0%
31	Kansas	149,641,000,000	0.8%
32	Utah	147,503,000,000	0.8%
33	Nevada	139,724,000,000	0.8%
34	Arkansas	118,907,000,000	0.7%
35	Nebraska	113,282,000,000	0.6%
36	Mississippi	105,819,000,000	0.6%
37	New Mexico	93,339,000,000	0.5%
38	Hawaii	80,376,000,000	0.4%
39	West Virginia	74,321,000,000	0.4%
40	New Hampshire	73,867,000,000	0.4%
41	Delaware	68,724,000,000	0.4%
42	Idaho	65,549,000,000	0.4%
43	Maine	57,297,000,000	0.3%
44	Rhode Island	56,052,000,000	0.3%
45	North Dakota	55,860,000,000	0.3%
46	Alaska	52,747,000,000	0.3%
47	South Dakota	47,244,000,000	0.3%
48	Montana	45,237,000,000	0.3%
49	Wyoming	39,864,000,000	0.2%
50	Vermont	30,038,000,000	0.2%
	District of Columbia	122,146,000,000	0.7%

Source: U.S. Department of Commerce, Bureau of Economic Analysis
   "Gross Domestic Product Data" (http://www.bea.gov/iTable/index_regional.cfm)
*G.D.P. is the market value of goods and services produced by the labor and property located in a state. It is the state
counterpart to the nation's Gross Domestic Product. This was formerly known as Gross State Product (G.S.P.).

Percent Change in Gross Domestic Product: 2011 to 2015
(Adjusted to Constant 2009 Dollars)
National Percent Change = 8.5% Increase*

ALPHA ORDER

ALPHA ORDER

RANK	STATE	PERCENT CHANGE
41	Alabama	2.8
50	Alaska	(3.2)
22	Arizona	5.6
30	Arkansas	4.5
5	California	13.4
4	Colorado	13.7
49	Connecticut	(1.3)
32	Delaware	4.2
8	Florida	9.9
15	Georgia	7.6
24	Hawaii	5.2
12	Idaho	8.1
29	Illinois	4.8
19	Indiana	6.4
10	Iowa	8.5
38	Kansas	2.9
33	Kentucky	3.8
47	Louisiana	(0.4)
42	Maine	1.8
36	Maryland	3.6
18	Massachusetts	6.5
16	Michigan	7.2
12	Minnesota	8.1
43	Mississippi	1.6
27	Missouri	5.0
28	Montana	4.9
20	Nebraska	5.8
38	Nevada	2.9
31	New Hampshire	4.4
21	New Jersey	5.7
33	New Mexico	3.8
26	New York	5.1
24	North Carolina	5.2
1	North Dakota	30.2
16	Ohio	7.2
3	Oklahoma	16.4
43	Oregon	1.6
11	Pennsylvania	8.3
37	Rhode Island	3.4
14	South Carolina	7.8
35	South Dakota	3.7
9	Tennessee	9.5
2	Texas	21.7
7	Utah	10.7
46	Vermont	(0.1)
38	Virginia	2.9
6	Washington	11.3
45	West Virginia	1.4
22	Wisconsin	5.6
48	Wyoming	(0.9)

RANK ORDER

RANK	STATE	PERCENT CHANGE
1	North Dakota	30.2
2	Texas	21.7
3	Oklahoma	16.4
4	Colorado	13.7
5	California	13.4
6	Washington	11.3
7	Utah	10.7
8	Florida	9.9
9	Tennessee	9.5
10	Iowa	8.5
11	Pennsylvania	8.3
12	Idaho	8.1
12	Minnesota	8.1
14	South Carolina	7.8
15	Georgia	7.6
16	Michigan	7.2
16	Ohio	7.2
18	Massachusetts	6.5
19	Indiana	6.4
20	Nebraska	5.8
21	New Jersey	5.7
22	Arizona	5.6
22	Wisconsin	5.6
24	Hawaii	5.2
24	North Carolina	5.2
26	New York	5.1
27	Missouri	5.0
28	Montana	4.9
29	Illinois	4.8
30	Arkansas	4.5
31	New Hampshire	4.4
32	Delaware	4.2
33	Kentucky	3.8
33	New Mexico	3.8
35	South Dakota	3.7
36	Maryland	3.6
37	Rhode Island	3.4
38	Kansas	2.9
38	Nevada	2.9
38	Virginia	2.9
41	Alabama	2.8
42	Maine	1.8
43	Mississippi	1.6
43	Oregon	1.6
45	West Virginia	1.4
46	Vermont	(0.1)
47	Louisiana	(0.4)
48	Wyoming	(0.9)
49	Connecticut	(1.3)
50	Alaska	(3.2)

	District of Columbia	3.8

Source: CQ Press using data from U.S. Department of Commerce, Bureau of Economic Analysis
   "Gross Domestic Product Data" (http://www.bea.gov/iTable/index_regional.cfm)
*G.D.P. is the market value of goods and services produced by the labor and property located in a state. It is the state counterpart to the nation's Gross Domestic Product. This was formerly known as Gross State Product (G.S.P.). Adjusted for inflation using chained 2009 dollars.

Average Annual Change in Gross Domestic Product: 2011 to 2015
(Adjusted to Constant 2009 Dollars)
National Annual Percent Change = 1.6% Increase*

ALPHA ORDER

RANK	STATE	PERCENT CHANGE
41	Alabama	0.5
50	Alaska	(0.7)
20	Arizona	1.1
29	Arkansas	0.9
5	California	2.5
4	Colorado	2.6
49	Connecticut	(0.3)
32	Delaware	0.8
8	Florida	1.9
14	Georgia	1.5
24	Hawaii	1.0
10	Idaho	1.6
29	Illinois	0.9
18	Indiana	1.3
10	Iowa	1.6
38	Kansas	0.6
33	Kentucky	0.7
47	Louisiana	(0.1)
42	Maine	0.4
33	Maryland	0.7
18	Massachusetts	1.3
16	Michigan	1.4
10	Minnesota	1.6
43	Mississippi	0.3
24	Missouri	1.0
24	Montana	1.0
20	Nebraska	1.1
38	Nevada	0.6
29	New Hampshire	0.9
20	New Jersey	1.1
33	New Mexico	0.7
24	New York	1.0
24	North Carolina	1.0
1	North Dakota	5.4
16	Ohio	1.4
3	Oklahoma	3.1
43	Oregon	0.3
10	Pennsylvania	1.6
33	Rhode Island	0.7
14	South Carolina	1.5
33	South Dakota	0.7
9	Tennessee	1.8
2	Texas	4.0
7	Utah	2.1
46	Vermont	0.0
38	Virginia	0.6
6	Washington	2.2
43	West Virginia	0.3
20	Wisconsin	1.1
48	Wyoming	(0.2)

RANK ORDER

RANK	STATE	PERCENT CHANGE
1	North Dakota	5.4
2	Texas	4.0
3	Oklahoma	3.1
4	Colorado	2.6
5	California	2.5
6	Washington	2.2
7	Utah	2.1
8	Florida	1.9
9	Tennessee	1.8
10	Idaho	1.6
10	Iowa	1.6
10	Minnesota	1.6
10	Pennsylvania	1.6
14	Georgia	1.5
14	South Carolina	1.5
16	Michigan	1.4
16	Ohio	1.4
18	Indiana	1.3
18	Massachusetts	1.3
20	Arizona	1.1
20	Nebraska	1.1
20	New Jersey	1.1
20	Wisconsin	1.1
24	Hawaii	1.0
24	Missouri	1.0
24	Montana	1.0
24	New York	1.0
24	North Carolina	1.0
29	Arkansas	0.9
29	Illinois	0.9
29	New Hampshire	0.9
32	Delaware	0.8
33	Kentucky	0.7
33	Maryland	0.7
33	New Mexico	0.7
33	Rhode Island	0.7
33	South Dakota	0.7
38	Kansas	0.6
38	Nevada	0.6
38	Virginia	0.6
41	Alabama	0.5
42	Maine	0.4
43	Mississippi	0.3
43	Oregon	0.3
43	West Virginia	0.3
46	Vermont	0.0
47	Louisiana	(0.1)
48	Wyoming	(0.2)
49	Connecticut	(0.3)
50	Alaska	(0.7)

	District of Columbia	0.8

Source: CQ Press using data from U.S. Department of Commerce, Bureau of Economic Analysis
    "Gross Domestic Product Data" (http://www.bea.gov/iTable/index_regional.cfm)
*G.D.P. is the market value of goods and services produced by the labor and property located in a state. It is the state counterpart to the nation's Gross Domestic Product. This was formerly known as Gross State Product (G.S.P.). Adjusted for inflation using chained 2009 dollars.

Per Capita Gross Domestic Product in 2015

National Per Capita = $55,842*

ALPHA ORDER				RANK ORDER		
RANK	STATE	PER CAPITA		RANK	STATE	PER CAPITA
45	Alabama	$41,133		1	North Dakota	$73,807
4	Alaska	71,501		2	Delaware	72,795
44	Arizona	42,670		3	New York	72,594
48	Arkansas	39,930		4	Alaska	71,501
8	California	63,634		5	Massachusetts	71,481
16	Colorado	57,581		6	Connecticut	70,558
6	Connecticut	70,558		7	Wyoming	67,963
2	Delaware	72,795		8	California	63,634
40	Florida	43,867		9	New Jersey	63,538
32	Georgia	48,821		10	Washington	62,206
18	Hawaii	56,398		11	Maryland	60,944
49	Idaho	39,659		12	Illinois	60,509
12	Illinois	60,509		13	Minnesota	59,889
29	Indiana	50,819		14	Nebraska	59,818
19	Iowa	55,743		15	Texas	59,428
27	Kansas	51,481		16	Colorado	57,581
42	Kentucky	43,682		17	Virginia	57,494
28	Louisiana	51,254		18	Hawaii	56,398
43	Maine	43,098		19	Iowa	55,743
11	Maryland	60,944		20	New Hampshire	55,534
5	Massachusetts	71,481		21	Pennsylvania	55,485
38	Michigan	47,222		22	South Dakota	55,068
13	Minnesota	59,889		23	Oregon	54,074
50	Mississippi	35,398		24	Rhode Island	53,099
33	Missouri	48,466		25	Ohio	52,643
41	Montana	43,831		26	Wisconsin	52,372
14	Nebraska	59,818		27	Kansas	51,481
34	Nevada	48,452		28	Louisiana	51,254
20	New Hampshire	55,534		29	Indiana	50,819
9	New Jersey	63,538		30	North Carolina	49,366
39	New Mexico	44,867		31	Utah	49,322
3	New York	72,594		32	Georgia	48,821
30	North Carolina	49,366		33	Missouri	48,466
1	North Dakota	73,807		34	Nevada	48,452
25	Ohio	52,643		35	Vermont	47,977
37	Oklahoma	47,597		36	Tennessee	47,893
23	Oregon	54,074		37	Oklahoma	47,597
21	Pennsylvania	55,485		38	Michigan	47,222
24	Rhode Island	53,099		39	New Mexico	44,867
46	South Carolina	41,065		40	Florida	43,867
22	South Dakota	55,068		41	Montana	43,831
36	Tennessee	47,893		42	Kentucky	43,682
15	Texas	59,428		43	Maine	43,098
31	Utah	49,322		44	Arizona	42,670
35	Vermont	47,977		45	Alabama	41,133
17	Virginia	57,494		46	South Carolina	41,065
10	Washington	62,206		47	West Virginia	40,369
47	West Virginia	40,369		48	Arkansas	39,930
26	Wisconsin	52,372		49	Idaho	39,659
7	Wyoming	67,963		50	Mississippi	35,398
					District of Columbia	182,205

Source: CQ Press using data from U.S. Department of Commerce, Bureau of Economic Analysis
    "Gross Domestic Product Data" (http://www.bea.gov/iTable/index_regional.cfm)
*G.D.P. is the market value of goods and services produced by the labor and property located in a state. It is the state counterpart to the nation's Gross Domestic Product. This was formerly known as Gross State Product (G.S.P.).

Percent Change in Per Capita Gross Domestic Product: 2011 to 2015 (Adjusted to Constant 2009 Dollars)
National Percent Change = 5.2% Increase*

ALPHA ORDER

RANK	STATE	PERCENT CHANGE
33	Alabama	1.5
50	Alaska	(5.3)
40	Arizona	0.1
26	Arkansas	3.1
4	California	9.2
6	Colorado	6.7
45	Connecticut	(1.3)
41	Delaware	0.0
19	Florida	3.6
23	Georgia	3.4
35	Hawaii	1.3
22	Idaho	3.5
13	Illinois	4.8
13	Indiana	4.8
9	Iowa	6.5
33	Kansas	1.5
30	Kentucky	2.4
47	Louisiana	(2.5)
32	Maine	1.7
39	Maryland	0.8
19	Massachusetts	3.6
6	Michigan	6.7
12	Minnesota	5.3
37	Mississippi	1.1
18	Missouri	3.7
35	Montana	1.3
28	Nebraska	2.8
48	Nevada	(3.2)
23	New Hampshire	3.4
15	New Jersey	4.4
23	New Mexico	3.4
19	New York	3.6
37	North Carolina	1.1
1	North Dakota	17.9
8	Ohio	6.6
3	Oklahoma	12.7
46	Oregon	(2.4)
5	Pennsylvania	7.8
27	Rhode Island	3.0
28	South Carolina	2.8
43	South Dakota	(0.4)
10	Tennessee	6.1
2	Texas	13.7
17	Utah	4.1
41	Vermont	0.0
43	Virginia	(0.4)
11	Washington	5.9
31	West Virginia	2.0
15	Wisconsin	4.4
49	Wyoming	(4.1)

RANK ORDER

RANK	STATE	PERCENT CHANGE
1	North Dakota	17.9
2	Texas	13.7
3	Oklahoma	12.7
4	California	9.2
5	Pennsylvania	7.8
6	Colorado	6.7
6	Michigan	6.7
8	Ohio	6.6
9	Iowa	6.5
10	Tennessee	6.1
11	Washington	5.9
12	Minnesota	5.3
13	Illinois	4.8
13	Indiana	4.8
15	New Jersey	4.4
15	Wisconsin	4.4
17	Utah	4.1
18	Missouri	3.7
19	Florida	3.6
19	Massachusetts	3.6
19	New York	3.6
22	Idaho	3.5
23	Georgia	3.4
23	New Hampshire	3.4
23	New Mexico	3.4
26	Arkansas	3.1
27	Rhode Island	3.0
28	Nebraska	2.8
28	South Carolina	2.8
30	Kentucky	2.4
31	West Virginia	2.0
32	Maine	1.7
33	Alabama	1.5
33	Kansas	1.5
35	Hawaii	1.3
35	Montana	1.3
37	Mississippi	1.1
37	North Carolina	1.1
39	Maryland	0.8
40	Arizona	0.1
41	Delaware	0.0
41	Vermont	0.0
43	South Dakota	(0.4)
43	Virginia	(0.4)
45	Connecticut	(1.3)
46	Oregon	(2.4)
47	Louisiana	(2.5)
48	Nevada	(3.2)
49	Wyoming	(4.1)
50	Alaska	(5.3)

District of Columbia (4.2)

Source: CQ Press using data from U.S. Department of Commerce, Bureau of Economic Analysis
   "Gross Domestic Product Data" (http://www.bea.gov/iTable/index_regional.cfm)
*G.D.P. is the market value of goods and services produced by the labor and property located in a state. It is the state counterpart to the nation's Gross Domestic Product. This was formerly known as Gross State Product (G.S.P.). Adjusted for inflation using chained 2009 dollars.

State Exports in 2015

National Total = $1,504,597,490,000*

RANK	STATE	EXPORTS	% of USA
23	Alabama	$19,369,520,000	1.3%
39	Alaska	4,675,200,000	0.3%
19	Arizona	22,563,230,000	1.5%
35	Arkansas	5,874,320,000	0.4%
2	California	165,367,010,000	11.0%
33	Colorado	7,977,920,000	0.5%
25	Connecticut	15,255,890,000	1.0%
37	Delaware	5,403,040,000	0.4%
6	Florida	53,843,760,000	3.6%
11	Georgia	38,548,130,000	2.6%
47	Hawaii	1,895,680,000	0.1%
40	Idaho	4,295,520,000	0.3%
5	Illinois	63,402,310,000	4.2%
12	Indiana	33,652,460,000	2.2%
28	Iowa	13,113,620,000	0.9%
30	Kansas	10,685,940,000	0.7%
17	Kentucky	28,052,530,000	1.9%
9	Louisiana	49,183,230,000	3.3%
45	Maine	2,724,100,000	0.2%
31	Maryland	10,029,750,000	0.7%
18	Massachusetts	25,205,990,000	1.7%
7	Michigan	53,171,400,000	3.5%
22	Minnesota	19,988,330,000	1.3%
29	Mississippi	10,785,880,000	0.7%
26	Missouri	13,616,730,000	0.9%
49	Montana	1,386,280,000	0.1%
34	Nebraska	6,555,850,000	0.4%
32	Nevada	8,658,320,000	0.6%
41	New Hampshire	4,006,840,000	0.3%
14	New Jersey	32,076,380,000	2.1%
43	New Mexico	3,771,650,000	0.3%
4	New York	80,059,470,000	5.3%
16	North Carolina	30,017,530,000	2.0%
42	North Dakota	3,863,160,000	0.3%
8	Ohio	50,694,150,000	3.4%
38	Oklahoma	5,257,790,000	0.3%
21	Oregon	20,083,830,000	1.3%
10	Pennsylvania	39,402,720,000	2.6%
46	Rhode Island	2,124,630,000	0.1%
15	South Carolina	30,861,290,000	2.1%
48	South Dakota	1,404,520,000	0.1%
13	Tennessee	32,430,880,000	2.2%
1	Texas	251,087,320,000	16.7%
27	Utah	13,281,640,000	0.9%
44	Vermont	3,176,210,000	0.2%
24	Virginia	18,136,740,000	1.2%
3	Washington	86,353,160,000	5.7%
36	West Virginia	5,722,220,000	0.4%
20	Wisconsin	22,445,120,000	1.5%
50	Wyoming	1,174,000,000	0.1%

RANK	STATE	EXPORTS	% of USA
1	Texas	$251,087,320,000	16.7%
2	California	165,367,010,000	11.0%
3	Washington	86,353,160,000	5.7%
4	New York	80,059,470,000	5.3%
5	Illinois	63,402,310,000	4.2%
6	Florida	53,843,760,000	3.6%
7	Michigan	53,171,400,000	3.5%
8	Ohio	50,694,150,000	3.4%
9	Louisiana	49,183,230,000	3.3%
10	Pennsylvania	39,402,720,000	2.6%
11	Georgia	38,548,130,000	2.6%
12	Indiana	33,652,460,000	2.2%
13	Tennessee	32,430,880,000	2.2%
14	New Jersey	32,076,380,000	2.1%
15	South Carolina	30,861,290,000	2.1%
16	North Carolina	30,017,530,000	2.0%
17	Kentucky	28,052,530,000	1.9%
18	Massachusetts	25,205,990,000	1.7%
19	Arizona	22,563,230,000	1.5%
20	Wisconsin	22,445,120,000	1.5%
21	Oregon	20,083,830,000	1.3%
22	Minnesota	19,988,330,000	1.3%
23	Alabama	19,369,520,000	1.3%
24	Virginia	18,136,740,000	1.2%
25	Connecticut	15,255,890,000	1.0%
26	Missouri	13,616,730,000	0.9%
27	Utah	13,281,640,000	0.9%
28	Iowa	13,113,620,000	0.9%
29	Mississippi	10,785,880,000	0.7%
30	Kansas	10,685,940,000	0.7%
31	Maryland	10,029,750,000	0.7%
32	Nevada	8,658,320,000	0.6%
33	Colorado	7,977,920,000	0.5%
34	Nebraska	6,555,850,000	0.4%
35	Arkansas	5,874,320,000	0.4%
36	West Virginia	5,722,220,000	0.4%
37	Delaware	5,403,040,000	0.4%
38	Oklahoma	5,257,790,000	0.3%
39	Alaska	4,675,200,000	0.3%
40	Idaho	4,295,520,000	0.3%
41	New Hampshire	4,006,840,000	0.3%
42	North Dakota	3,863,160,000	0.3%
43	New Mexico	3,771,650,000	0.3%
44	Vermont	3,176,210,000	0.2%
45	Maine	2,724,100,000	0.2%
46	Rhode Island	2,124,630,000	0.1%
47	Hawaii	1,895,680,000	0.1%
48	South Dakota	1,404,520,000	0.1%
49	Montana	1,386,280,000	0.1%
50	Wyoming	1,174,000,000	0.1%
	District of Columbia	1,089,290,000	0.1%

Source: U.S. Bureau of the Census
   "State Trade Data" (http://www.census.gov/foreign-trade/statistics/state/)
*Based on the state from which the merchandise starts its journey to the port of export; that is, the data reflect the transportation origin of exports. Total includes exports from Puerto Rico, Virgin Islands, and exports with unidentified origin.

Per Capita State Exports in 2015

National Per Capita = $4,468*

ALPHA ORDER

RANK	STATE	PER CAPITA
21	Alabama	$3,991
5	Alaska	6,337
30	Arizona	3,310
43	Arkansas	1,973
18	California	4,241
47	Colorado	1,464
17	Connecticut	4,256
7	Delaware	5,723
36	Florida	2,660
23	Georgia	3,779
50	Hawaii	1,330
37	Idaho	2,599
13	Illinois	4,938
10	Indiana	5,089
19	Iowa	4,200
25	Kansas	3,676
4	Kentucky	6,340
2	Louisiana	10,534
40	Maine	2,049
45	Maryland	1,673
24	Massachusetts	3,715
8	Michigan	5,361
26	Minnesota	3,646
27	Mississippi	3,608
38	Missouri	2,241
49	Montana	1,343
29	Nebraska	3,462
34	Nevada	3,002
33	New Hampshire	3,012
28	New Jersey	3,590
44	New Mexico	1,813
20	New York	4,054
35	North Carolina	2,991
9	North Dakota	5,104
16	Ohio	4,368
48	Oklahoma	1,346
12	Oregon	4,990
32	Pennsylvania	3,080
41	Rhode Island	2,013
6	South Carolina	6,305
46	South Dakota	1,637
14	Tennessee	4,917
3	Texas	9,154
15	Utah	4,441
11	Vermont	5,073
39	Virginia	2,167
1	Washington	12,060
31	West Virginia	3,108
22	Wisconsin	3,891
42	Wyoming	2,002

RANK ORDER

RANK	STATE	PER CAPITA
1	Washington	$12,060
2	Louisiana	10,534
3	Texas	9,154
4	Kentucky	6,340
5	Alaska	6,337
6	South Carolina	6,305
7	Delaware	5,723
8	Michigan	5,361
9	North Dakota	5,104
10	Indiana	5,089
11	Vermont	5,073
12	Oregon	4,990
13	Illinois	4,938
14	Tennessee	4,917
15	Utah	4,441
16	Ohio	4,368
17	Connecticut	4,256
18	California	4,241
19	Iowa	4,200
20	New York	4,054
21	Alabama	3,991
22	Wisconsin	3,891
23	Georgia	3,779
24	Massachusetts	3,715
25	Kansas	3,676
26	Minnesota	3,646
27	Mississippi	3,608
28	New Jersey	3,590
29	Nebraska	3,462
30	Arizona	3,310
31	West Virginia	3,108
32	Pennsylvania	3,080
33	New Hampshire	3,012
34	Nevada	3,002
35	North Carolina	2,991
36	Florida	2,660
37	Idaho	2,599
38	Missouri	2,241
39	Virginia	2,167
40	Maine	2,049
41	Rhode Island	2,013
42	Wyoming	2,002
43	Arkansas	1,973
44	New Mexico	1,813
45	Maryland	1,673
46	South Dakota	1,637
47	Colorado	1,464
48	Oklahoma	1,346
49	Montana	1,343
50	Hawaii	1,330
	District of Columbia	1,625

Source: CQ Press using data from U.S. Bureau of the Census
   "State Trade Data" (http://www.census.gov/foreign-trade/statistics/state/)
*Based on the state from which the merchandise starts its journey to the port of export; that is, the data reflect the transportation
origin of exports. National figure does not include population or exports from Puerto Rico, Virgin Islands, and exports with
unidentified origin.

State Imports in 2015

National Total = $2,241,663,710,000*

ALPHA ORDER

RANK	STATE	IMPORTS	% of USA
24	Alabama	$21,880,000,000	1.0%
47	Alaska	2,485,200,000	0.1%
25	Arizona	19,679,300,000	0.9%
38	Arkansas	7,914,550,000	0.4%
1	California	408,179,500,000	18.2%
29	Colorado	13,487,500,000	0.6%
21	Connecticut	25,956,590,000	1.2%
36	Delaware	9,194,390,000	0.4%
10	Florida	73,436,520,000	3.3%
7	Georgia	88,545,290,000	3.9%
44	Hawaii	3,759,730,000	0.2%
39	Idaho	5,166,160,000	0.2%
5	Illinois	121,251,740,000	5.4%
14	Indiana	48,978,910,000	2.2%
34	Iowa	9,443,880,000	0.4%
31	Kansas	11,665,970,000	0.5%
16	Kentucky	38,537,640,000	1.7%
17	Louisiana	35,225,930,000	1.6%
45	Maine	3,672,720,000	0.2%
19	Maryland	31,501,450,000	1.4%
18	Massachusetts	33,492,580,000	1.5%
4	Michigan	124,088,080,000	5.5%
20	Minnesota	28,576,190,000	1.3%
28	Mississippi	14,062,910,000	0.6%
26	Missouri	18,444,050,000	0.8%
41	Montana	4,066,990,000	0.2%
40	Nebraska	4,129,780,000	0.2%
33	Nevada	9,590,070,000	0.4%
35	New Hampshire	9,283,460,000	0.4%
6	New Jersey	119,490,450,000	5.3%
48	New Mexico	2,244,460,000	0.1%
3	New York	133,085,610,000	5.9%
13	North Carolina	50,880,030,000	2.3%
46	North Dakota	3,146,040,000	0.1%
11	Ohio	68,842,880,000	3.1%
32	Oklahoma	10,993,760,000	0.5%
27	Oregon	14,814,730,000	0.7%
8	Pennsylvania	79,674,880,000	3.6%
37	Rhode Island	8,224,450,000	0.4%
15	South Carolina	38,987,610,000	1.7%
50	South Dakota	1,139,870,000	0.1%
9	Tennessee	76,864,470,000	3.4%
2	Texas	251,491,700,000	11.2%
30	Utah	12,093,200,000	0.5%
42	Vermont	4,022,640,000	0.2%
22	Virginia	25,016,620,000	1.1%
12	Washington	51,271,230,000	2.3%
43	West Virginia	3,776,370,000	0.2%
23	Wisconsin	22,963,700,000	1.0%
49	Wyoming	1,143,630,000	0.1%

RANK ORDER

RANK	STATE	IMPORTS	% of USA
1	California	$408,179,500,000	18.2%
2	Texas	251,491,700,000	11.2%
3	New York	133,085,610,000	5.9%
4	Michigan	124,088,080,000	5.5%
5	Illinois	121,251,740,000	5.4%
6	New Jersey	119,490,450,000	5.3%
7	Georgia	88,545,290,000	3.9%
8	Pennsylvania	79,674,880,000	3.6%
9	Tennessee	76,864,470,000	3.4%
10	Florida	73,436,520,000	3.3%
11	Ohio	68,842,880,000	3.1%
12	Washington	51,271,230,000	2.3%
13	North Carolina	50,880,030,000	2.3%
14	Indiana	48,978,910,000	2.2%
15	South Carolina	38,987,610,000	1.7%
16	Kentucky	38,537,640,000	1.7%
17	Louisiana	35,225,930,000	1.6%
18	Massachusetts	33,492,580,000	1.5%
19	Maryland	31,501,450,000	1.4%
20	Minnesota	28,576,190,000	1.3%
21	Connecticut	25,956,590,000	1.2%
22	Virginia	25,016,620,000	1.1%
23	Wisconsin	22,963,700,000	1.0%
24	Alabama	21,880,000,000	1.0%
25	Arizona	19,679,300,000	0.9%
26	Missouri	18,444,050,000	0.8%
27	Oregon	14,814,730,000	0.7%
28	Mississippi	14,062,910,000	0.6%
29	Colorado	13,487,500,000	0.6%
30	Utah	12,093,200,000	0.5%
31	Kansas	11,665,970,000	0.5%
32	Oklahoma	10,993,760,000	0.5%
33	Nevada	9,590,070,000	0.4%
34	Iowa	9,443,880,000	0.4%
35	New Hampshire	9,283,460,000	0.4%
36	Delaware	9,194,390,000	0.4%
37	Rhode Island	8,224,450,000	0.4%
38	Arkansas	7,914,550,000	0.4%
39	Idaho	5,166,160,000	0.2%
40	Nebraska	4,129,780,000	0.2%
41	Montana	4,066,990,000	0.2%
42	Vermont	4,022,640,000	0.2%
43	West Virginia	3,776,370,000	0.2%
44	Hawaii	3,759,730,000	0.2%
45	Maine	3,672,720,000	0.2%
46	North Dakota	3,146,040,000	0.1%
47	Alaska	2,485,200,000	0.1%
48	New Mexico	2,244,460,000	0.1%
49	Wyoming	1,143,630,000	0.1%
50	South Dakota	1,139,870,000	0.1%
	District of Columbia	912,120,000	0.0%

Source: U.S. Bureau of the Census
    "State Trade Data" (http://www.census.gov/foreign-trade/statistics/state/)
*Based on where the merchandise is destined, as known at the time of entry summary filing. If the contents of the shipment are destined to more than one state, territory, or possession, or if the entry summary represents a consolidated shipment, the state of destination is that with the greatest aggregate value.

Per Capita State Imports in 2015

National Per Capita = $6,877*

ALPHA ORDER

RANK ORDER

RANK	STATE	PER CAPITA		RANK	STATE	PER CAPITA
26	Alabama	$4,508		1	New Jersey	$13,373
34	Alaska	3,369		2	Michigan	12,512
40	Arizona	2,887		3	Tennessee	11,655
43	Arkansas	2,658		4	California	10,468
4	California	10,468		5	Delaware	9,739
45	Colorado	2,475		6	Illinois	9,444
14	Connecticut	7,241		7	Texas	9,169
5	Delaware	9,739		8	Kentucky	8,710
33	Florida	3,627		9	Georgia	8,681
9	Georgia	8,681		10	South Carolina	7,965
44	Hawaii	2,638		11	Rhode Island	7,791
36	Idaho	3,126		12	Louisiana	7,545
6	Illinois	9,444		13	Indiana	7,407
13	Indiana	7,407		14	Connecticut	7,241
38	Iowa	3,025		15	Washington	7,160
29	Kansas	4,013		16	New Hampshire	6,979
8	Kentucky	8,710		17	New York	6,739
12	Louisiana	7,545		18	Vermont	6,425
42	Maine	2,763		19	Pennsylvania	6,229
21	Maryland	5,255		20	Ohio	5,932
24	Massachusetts	4,937		21	Maryland	5,255
2	Michigan	12,512		22	Minnesota	5,212
22	Minnesota	5,212		23	North Carolina	5,070
25	Mississippi	4,704		24	Massachusetts	4,937
37	Missouri	3,035		25	Mississippi	4,704
31	Montana	3,941		26	Alabama	4,508
46	Nebraska	2,181		27	North Dakota	4,157
35	Nevada	3,326		28	Utah	4,044
16	New Hampshire	6,979		29	Kansas	4,013
1	New Jersey	13,373		30	Wisconsin	3,981
50	New Mexico	1,079		31	Montana	3,941
17	New York	6,739		32	Oregon	3,681
23	North Carolina	5,070		33	Florida	3,627
27	North Dakota	4,157		34	Alaska	3,369
20	Ohio	5,932		35	Nevada	3,326
41	Oklahoma	2,814		36	Idaho	3,126
32	Oregon	3,681		37	Missouri	3,035
19	Pennsylvania	6,229		38	Iowa	3,025
11	Rhode Island	7,791		39	Virginia	2,990
10	South Carolina	7,965		40	Arizona	2,887
49	South Dakota	1,329		41	Oklahoma	2,814
3	Tennessee	11,655		42	Maine	2,763
7	Texas	9,169		43	Arkansas	2,658
28	Utah	4,044		44	Hawaii	2,638
18	Vermont	6,425		45	Colorado	2,475
39	Virginia	2,990		46	Nebraska	2,181
15	Washington	7,160		47	West Virginia	2,051
47	West Virginia	2,051		48	Wyoming	1,950
30	Wisconsin	3,981		49	South Dakota	1,329
48	Wyoming	1,950		50	New Mexico	1,079
					District of Columbia	1,361

Source: CQ Press using data from U.S. Bureau of the Census
  "State Trade Data" (http://www.census.gov/foreign-trade/statistics/state/)
*Based on where the merchandise is destined, as known at the time of entry summary filing. If the contents of the shipment are destined to more than one state, territory, or possession, or if the entry summary represents a consolidated shipment, the state of destination is that with the greatest aggregate value. National figure does not include population or imports from Puerto Rico, Virgin Islands, and imports with unidentified origin.

Personal Income in 2015

National Total = $15,463,981,000,000*

RANK	STATE	INCOME	% of USA
26	Alabama	$184,784,917,000	1.2%
47	Alaska	41,460,746,000	0.3%
20	Arizona	267,361,132,000	1.7%
34	Arkansas	113,923,539,000	0.7%
1	California	2,103,669,473,000	13.6%
18	Colorado	277,731,754,000	1.8%
23	Connecticut	246,709,339,000	1.6%
44	Delaware	45,057,962,000	0.3%
4	Florida	900,636,248,000	5.8%
12	Georgia	411,721,423,000	2.7%
39	Hawaii	69,129,101,000	0.4%
41	Idaho	63,535,406,000	0.4%
5	Illinois	646,789,116,000	4.2%
19	Indiana	277,628,668,000	1.8%
30	Iowa	143,393,977,000	0.9%
31	Kansas	137,316,497,000	0.9%
29	Kentucky	170,755,826,000	1.1%
24	Louisiana	200,594,438,000	1.3%
42	Maine	56,893,803,000	0.4%
15	Maryland	336,187,435,000	2.2%
10	Massachusetts	425,352,524,000	2.8%
11	Michigan	424,807,490,000	2.7%
16	Minnesota	279,262,704,000	1.8%
35	Mississippi	104,045,259,000	0.7%
22	Missouri	257,338,334,000	1.7%
45	Montana	43,186,928,000	0.3%
36	Nebraska	92,048,473,000	0.6%
32	Nevada	121,095,970,000	0.8%
38	New Hampshire	74,388,007,000	0.5%
7	New Jersey	537,026,391,000	3.5%
37	New Mexico	79,104,093,000	0.5%
3	New York	1,161,414,144,000	7.5%
13	North Carolina	409,338,338,000	2.6%
46	North Dakota	42,349,688,000	0.3%
8	Ohio	505,950,314,000	3.3%
27	Oklahoma	178,250,475,000	1.2%
28	Oregon	176,401,260,000	1.1%
6	Pennsylvania	636,857,158,000	4.1%
43	Rhode Island	52,833,501,000	0.3%
25	South Carolina	187,532,342,000	1.2%
48	South Dakota	41,104,237,000	0.3%
17	Tennessee	277,832,327,000	1.8%
2	Texas	1,289,603,627,000	8.3%
33	Utah	117,763,901,000	0.8%
50	Vermont	30,417,564,000	0.2%
9	Virginia	436,349,531,000	2.8%
14	Washington	372,125,338,000	2.4%
40	West Virginia	67,787,227,000	0.4%
21	Wisconsin	264,987,588,000	1.7%
49	Wyoming	32,869,550,000	0.2%

RANK	STATE	INCOME	% of USA
1	California	$2,103,669,473,000	13.6%
2	Texas	1,289,603,627,000	8.3%
3	New York	1,161,414,144,000	7.5%
4	Florida	900,636,248,000	5.8%
5	Illinois	646,789,116,000	4.2%
6	Pennsylvania	636,857,158,000	4.1%
7	New Jersey	537,026,391,000	3.5%
8	Ohio	505,950,314,000	3.3%
9	Virginia	436,349,531,000	2.8%
10	Massachusetts	425,352,524,000	2.8%
11	Michigan	424,807,490,000	2.7%
12	Georgia	411,721,423,000	2.7%
13	North Carolina	409,338,338,000	2.6%
14	Washington	372,125,338,000	2.4%
15	Maryland	336,187,435,000	2.2%
16	Minnesota	279,262,704,000	1.8%
17	Tennessee	277,832,327,000	1.8%
18	Colorado	277,731,754,000	1.8%
19	Indiana	277,628,668,000	1.8%
20	Arizona	267,361,132,000	1.7%
21	Wisconsin	264,987,588,000	1.7%
22	Missouri	257,338,334,000	1.7%
23	Connecticut	246,709,339,000	1.6%
24	Louisiana	200,594,438,000	1.3%
25	South Carolina	187,532,342,000	1.2%
26	Alabama	184,784,917,000	1.2%
27	Oklahoma	178,250,475,000	1.2%
28	Oregon	176,401,260,000	1.1%
29	Kentucky	170,755,826,000	1.1%
30	Iowa	143,393,977,000	0.9%
31	Kansas	137,316,497,000	0.9%
32	Nevada	121,095,970,000	0.8%
33	Utah	117,763,901,000	0.8%
34	Arkansas	113,923,539,000	0.7%
35	Mississippi	104,045,259,000	0.7%
36	Nebraska	92,048,473,000	0.6%
37	New Mexico	79,104,093,000	0.5%
38	New Hampshire	74,388,007,000	0.5%
39	Hawaii	69,129,101,000	0.4%
40	West Virginia	67,787,227,000	0.4%
41	Idaho	63,535,406,000	0.4%
42	Maine	56,893,803,000	0.4%
43	Rhode Island	52,833,501,000	0.3%
44	Delaware	45,057,962,000	0.3%
45	Montana	43,186,928,000	0.3%
46	North Dakota	42,349,688,000	0.3%
47	Alaska	41,460,746,000	0.3%
48	South Dakota	41,104,237,000	0.3%
49	Wyoming	32,869,550,000	0.2%
50	Vermont	30,417,564,000	0.2%
	District of Columbia	49,275,917,000	0.3%

Source: U.S. Department of Commerce, Bureau of Economic Analysis
"Annual State Personal Income" (http://www.bea.gov/iTable/index_regional.cfm)
*The national total shown here is the sum of the state estimates. It differs from the national income and product accounts (NIPA) estimate of personal income because it omits the earnings of federal civilian and military personnel stationed abroad and of U.S. residents employed abroad temporarily by private U.S. firms.

Percent Change in Personal Income: 2014 to 2015

National Percent Change = 4.5% Increase*

ALPHA ORDER				RANK ORDER		
RANK	STATE	PERCENT CHANGE		RANK	STATE	PERCENT CHANGE
37	Alabama	3.2		1	Oregon	6.5
40	Alaska	3.1		2	California	6.4
18	Arizona	4.5		3	Delaware	6.3
44	Arkansas	2.2		4	Utah	6.2
2	California	6.4		5	Massachusetts	5.6
23	Colorado	4.2		6	Florida	5.5
41	Connecticut	2.9		6	Tennessee	5.5
3	Delaware	6.3		8	Nevada	5.4
6	Florida	5.5		8	South Carolina	5.4
10	Georgia	5.0		10	Georgia	5.0
11	Hawaii	4.8		11	Hawaii	4.8
13	Idaho	4.6		11	South Dakota	4.8
34	Illinois	3.5		13	Idaho	4.6
27	Indiana	4.0		13	Michigan	4.6
29	Iowa	3.8		13	North Carolina	4.6
45	Kansas	2.0		13	Virginia	4.6
20	Kentucky	4.4		13	Washington	4.6
37	Louisiana	3.2		18	Arizona	4.5
32	Maine	3.7		18	Texas	4.5
25	Maryland	4.1		20	Kentucky	4.4
5	Massachusetts	5.6		20	New Hampshire	4.4
13	Michigan	4.6		22	Rhode Island	4.3
23	Minnesota	4.2		23	Colorado	4.2
46	Mississippi	1.8		23	Minnesota	4.2
37	Missouri	3.2		25	Maryland	4.1
27	Montana	4.0		25	New Jersey	4.1
48	Nebraska	1.2		27	Indiana	4.0
8	Nevada	5.4		27	Montana	4.0
20	New Hampshire	4.4		29	Iowa	3.8
25	New Jersey	4.1		29	New York	3.8
34	New Mexico	3.5		29	Pennsylvania	3.8
29	New York	3.8		32	Maine	3.7
13	North Carolina	4.6		33	Wisconsin	3.6
50	North Dakota	(1.2)		34	Illinois	3.5
34	Ohio	3.5		34	New Mexico	3.5
46	Oklahoma	1.8		34	Ohio	3.5
1	Oregon	6.5		37	Alabama	3.2
29	Pennsylvania	3.8		37	Louisiana	3.2
22	Rhode Island	4.3		37	Missouri	3.2
8	South Carolina	5.4		40	Alaska	3.1
11	South Dakota	4.8		41	Connecticut	2.9
6	Tennessee	5.5		41	Vermont	2.9
18	Texas	4.5		43	West Virginia	2.5
4	Utah	6.2		44	Arkansas	2.2
41	Vermont	2.9		45	Kansas	2.0
13	Virginia	4.6		46	Mississippi	1.8
13	Washington	4.6		46	Oklahoma	1.8
43	West Virginia	2.5		48	Nebraska	1.2
33	Wisconsin	3.6		49	Wyoming	0.4
49	Wyoming	0.4		50	North Dakota	(1.2)
					District of Columbia	6.1

Source: U.S. Department of Commerce, Bureau of Economic Analysis
"Annual State Personal Income" (http://www.bea.gov/iTable/index_regional.cfm)
*Based on revised 2014 figures.

Per Capita Personal Income in 2015

National Per Capita = $48,112*

ALPHA ORDER			RANK ORDER		
RANK	STATE	PER CAPITA	RANK	STATE	PER CAPITA
47	Alabama	$38,030	1	Connecticut	$68,704
5	Alaska	56,147	2	Massachusetts	62,603
42	Arizona	39,156	3	New Jersey	59,949
46	Arkansas	38,252	4	New York	58,670
10	California	53,741	5	Alaska	56,147
13	Colorado	50,899	6	Wyoming	56,081
1	Connecticut	68,704	7	Maryland	55,972
22	Delaware	47,633	8	North Dakota	55,950
28	Florida	44,429	9	New Hampshire	55,905
40	Georgia	40,306	10	California	53,741
20	Hawaii	48,288	11	Virginia	52,052
44	Idaho	38,392	12	Washington	51,898
15	Illinois	50,295	13	Colorado	50,899
36	Indiana	41,940	14	Minnesota	50,871
26	Iowa	45,902	15	Illinois	50,295
23	Kansas	47,161	16	Rhode Island	50,018
43	Kentucky	38,588	17	Pennsylvania	49,745
31	Louisiana	42,947	18	Vermont	48,587
33	Maine	42,799	19	Nebraska	48,544
7	Maryland	55,972	20	Hawaii	48,288
2	Massachusetts	62,603	21	South Dakota	47,881
32	Michigan	42,812	22	Delaware	47,633
14	Minnesota	50,871	23	Kansas	47,161
50	Mississippi	34,771	24	Texas	46,947
34	Missouri	42,300	25	Wisconsin	45,914
38	Montana	41,809	26	Iowa	45,902
19	Nebraska	48,544	27	Oklahoma	45,573
37	Nevada	41,889	28	Florida	44,429
9	New Hampshire	55,905	29	Oregon	43,783
3	New Jersey	59,949	30	Ohio	43,566
48	New Mexico	37,938	31	Louisiana	42,947
4	New York	58,670	32	Michigan	42,812
39	North Carolina	40,759	33	Maine	42,799
8	North Dakota	55,950	34	Missouri	42,300
30	Ohio	43,566	35	Tennessee	42,094
27	Oklahoma	45,573	36	Indiana	41,940
29	Oregon	43,783	37	Nevada	41,889
17	Pennsylvania	49,745	38	Montana	41,809
16	Rhode Island	50,018	39	North Carolina	40,759
45	South Carolina	38,302	40	Georgia	40,306
21	South Dakota	47,881	41	Utah	39,308
35	Tennessee	42,094	42	Arizona	39,156
24	Texas	46,947	43	Kentucky	38,588
41	Utah	39,308	44	Idaho	38,392
18	Vermont	48,587	45	South Carolina	38,302
11	Virginia	52,052	46	Arkansas	38,252
12	Washington	51,898	47	Alabama	38,030
49	West Virginia	36,758	48	New Mexico	37,938
25	Wisconsin	45,914	49	West Virginia	36,758
6	Wyoming	56,081	50	Mississippi	34,771

District of Columbia   73,302

Source: U.S. Department of Commerce, Bureau of Economic Analysis
   "Annual State Personal Income" (http://www.bea.gov/iTable/index_regional.cfm)
*The national figure is based on the sum of the state estimates. It differs from the national income and product accounts
(NIPA) estimate of personal income because it omits the earnings of federal civilian and military personnel stationed abroad and
of U.S. residents employed abroad temporarily by private U.S. firms.

Percent Change in Per Capita Personal Income: 2014 to 2015

National Percent Change = 3.7% Increase*

ALPHA ORDER

RANK	STATE	PERCENT CHANGE
34	Alabama	3.0
38	Alaska	2.9
34	Arizona	3.0
45	Arkansas	1.8
1	California	5.4
43	Colorado	2.3
34	Connecticut	3.0
2	Delaware	5.2
21	Florida	3.6
15	Georgia	3.8
12	Hawaii	3.9
29	Idaho	3.3
18	Illinois	3.7
18	Indiana	3.7
29	Iowa	3.3
46	Kansas	1.7
11	Kentucky	4.1
40	Louisiana	2.7
15	Maine	3.8
21	Maryland	3.6
3	Massachusetts	5.0
5	Michigan	4.6
23	Minnesota	3.5
44	Mississippi	1.9
38	Missouri	2.9
34	Montana	3.0
48	Nebraska	0.5
23	Nevada	3.5
8	New Hampshire	4.2
15	New Jersey	3.8
23	New Mexico	3.5
23	New York	3.5
23	North Carolina	3.5
50	North Dakota	(3.4)
29	Ohio	3.3
47	Oklahoma	1.0
3	Oregon	5.0
18	Pennsylvania	3.7
8	Rhode Island	4.2
12	South Carolina	3.9
8	South Dakota	4.2
5	Tennessee	4.6
42	Texas	2.6
7	Utah	4.4
32	Vermont	3.1
12	Virginia	3.9
32	Washington	3.1
40	West Virginia	2.7
28	Wisconsin	3.4
49	Wyoming	0.1

RANK ORDER

RANK	STATE	PERCENT CHANGE
1	California	5.4
2	Delaware	5.2
3	Massachusetts	5.0
3	Oregon	5.0
5	Michigan	4.6
5	Tennessee	4.6
7	Utah	4.4
8	New Hampshire	4.2
8	Rhode Island	4.2
8	South Dakota	4.2
11	Kentucky	4.1
12	Hawaii	3.9
12	South Carolina	3.9
12	Virginia	3.9
15	Georgia	3.8
15	Maine	3.8
15	New Jersey	3.8
18	Illinois	3.7
18	Indiana	3.7
18	Pennsylvania	3.7
21	Florida	3.6
21	Maryland	3.6
23	Minnesota	3.5
23	Nevada	3.5
23	New Mexico	3.5
23	New York	3.5
23	North Carolina	3.5
28	Wisconsin	3.4
29	Idaho	3.3
29	Iowa	3.3
29	Ohio	3.3
32	Vermont	3.1
32	Washington	3.1
34	Alabama	3.0
34	Arizona	3.0
34	Connecticut	3.0
34	Montana	3.0
38	Alaska	2.9
38	Missouri	2.9
40	Louisiana	2.7
40	West Virginia	2.7
42	Texas	2.6
43	Colorado	2.3
44	Mississippi	1.9
45	Arkansas	1.8
46	Kansas	1.7
47	Oklahoma	1.0
48	Nebraska	0.5
49	Wyoming	0.1
50	North Dakota	(3.4)
	District of Columbia	4.2

Source: U.S. Department of Commerce, Bureau of Economic Analysis
"Annual State Personal Income" (http://www.bea.gov/iTable/index_regional.cfm)
*Based on revised 2014 figures.

Disposable Personal Income in 2015

National Total = $13,526,970,000,000*

ALPHA ORDER

RANK	STATE	INCOME	% of USA
26	Alabama	$167,035,750,000	1.2%
46	Alaska	37,644,245,000	0.3%
19	Arizona	240,127,344,000	1.8%
34	Arkansas	102,353,058,000	0.8%
1	California	1,796,837,596,000	13.3%
18	Colorado	241,354,515,000	1.8%
23	Connecticut	206,181,546,000	1.5%
44	Delaware	39,954,973,000	0.3%
4	Florida	800,304,059,000	5.9%
11	Georgia	364,301,711,000	2.7%
39	Hawaii	61,722,766,000	0.5%
41	Idaho	57,188,448,000	0.4%
6	Illinois	559,788,852,000	4.1%
17	Indiana	248,317,570,000	1.8%
30	Iowa	127,886,188,000	0.9%
31	Kansas	122,587,854,000	0.9%
29	Kentucky	152,581,369,000	1.1%
24	Louisiana	180,766,335,000	1.3%
42	Maine	50,912,481,000	0.4%
15	Maryland	289,740,978,000	2.1%
13	Massachusetts	356,868,334,000	2.6%
10	Michigan	375,766,940,000	2.8%
20	Minnesota	239,947,579,000	1.8%
35	Mississippi	95,194,808,000	0.7%
22	Missouri	228,262,971,000	1.7%
45	Montana	38,102,911,000	0.3%
36	Nebraska	81,695,253,000	0.6%
32	Nevada	108,405,323,000	0.8%
38	New Hampshire	66,733,661,000	0.5%
7	New Jersey	461,387,656,000	3.4%
37	New Mexico	71,719,335,000	0.5%
3	New York	965,046,953,000	7.1%
12	North Carolina	363,003,568,000	2.7%
47	North Dakota	37,342,536,000	0.3%
8	Ohio	447,905,775,000	3.3%
27	Oklahoma	160,731,283,000	1.2%
28	Oregon	153,405,770,000	1.1%
5	Pennsylvania	560,641,952,000	4.1%
43	Rhode Island	46,636,165,000	0.3%
25	South Carolina	168,776,887,000	1.2%
48	South Dakota	37,223,428,000	0.3%
16	Tennessee	253,781,412,000	1.9%
2	Texas	1,151,614,713,000	8.5%
33	Utah	104,482,947,000	0.8%
50	Vermont	27,159,687,000	0.2%
9	Virginia	380,075,013,000	2.8%
14	Washington	331,395,077,000	2.4%
40	West Virginia	60,980,800,000	0.5%
21	Wisconsin	234,113,313,000	1.7%
49	Wyoming	29,161,869,000	0.2%

RANK ORDER

RANK	STATE	INCOME	% of USA
1	California	$1,796,837,596,000	13.3%
2	Texas	1,151,614,713,000	8.5%
3	New York	965,046,953,000	7.1%
4	Florida	800,304,059,000	5.9%
5	Pennsylvania	560,641,952,000	4.1%
6	Illinois	559,788,852,000	4.1%
7	New Jersey	461,387,656,000	3.4%
8	Ohio	447,905,775,000	3.3%
9	Virginia	380,075,013,000	2.8%
10	Michigan	375,766,940,000	2.8%
11	Georgia	364,301,711,000	2.7%
12	North Carolina	363,003,568,000	2.7%
13	Massachusetts	356,868,334,000	2.6%
14	Washington	331,395,077,000	2.4%
15	Maryland	289,740,978,000	2.1%
16	Tennessee	253,781,412,000	1.9%
17	Indiana	248,317,570,000	1.8%
18	Colorado	241,354,515,000	1.8%
19	Arizona	240,127,344,000	1.8%
20	Minnesota	239,947,579,000	1.8%
21	Wisconsin	234,113,313,000	1.7%
22	Missouri	228,262,971,000	1.7%
23	Connecticut	206,181,546,000	1.5%
24	Louisiana	180,766,335,000	1.3%
25	South Carolina	168,776,887,000	1.2%
26	Alabama	167,035,750,000	1.2%
27	Oklahoma	160,731,283,000	1.2%
28	Oregon	153,405,770,000	1.1%
29	Kentucky	152,581,369,000	1.1%
30	Iowa	127,886,188,000	0.9%
31	Kansas	122,587,854,000	0.9%
32	Nevada	108,405,323,000	0.8%
33	Utah	104,482,947,000	0.8%
34	Arkansas	102,353,058,000	0.8%
35	Mississippi	95,194,808,000	0.7%
36	Nebraska	81,695,253,000	0.6%
37	New Mexico	71,719,335,000	0.5%
38	New Hampshire	66,733,661,000	0.5%
39	Hawaii	61,722,766,000	0.5%
40	West Virginia	60,980,800,000	0.5%
41	Idaho	57,188,448,000	0.4%
42	Maine	50,912,481,000	0.4%
43	Rhode Island	46,636,165,000	0.3%
44	Delaware	39,954,973,000	0.3%
45	Montana	38,102,911,000	0.3%
46	Alaska	37,644,245,000	0.3%
47	North Dakota	37,342,536,000	0.3%
48	South Dakota	37,223,428,000	0.3%
49	Wyoming	29,161,869,000	0.2%
50	Vermont	27,159,687,000	0.2%
	District of Columbia	41,818,443,000	0.3%

Source: U.S. Department of Commerce, Bureau of Economic Analysis
"Annual State Personal Income" (http://www.bea.gov/iTable/index_regional.cfm)
*Disposable personal income is personal income less personal tax and nontax payments. It is the income available to persons for spending or saving.

Per Capita Disposable Personal Income in 2015

National Per Capita = $42,085*

ALPHA ORDER				RANK ORDER		
RANK	STATE	PER CAPITA		RANK	STATE	PER CAPITA
47	Alabama	$34,377		1	Connecticut	$57,418
4	Alaska	50,979		2	Massachusetts	52,524
41	Arizona	35,168		3	New Jersey	51,506
48	Arkansas	34,367		4	Alaska	50,979
11	California	45,902		5	New Hampshire	50,153
13	Colorado	44,232		6	Wyoming	49,755
1	Connecticut	57,418		7	North Dakota	49,334
22	Delaware	42,239		8	New York	48,750
28	Florida	39,480		9	Maryland	48,239
40	Georgia	35,664		10	Washington	46,217
20	Hawaii	43,114		11	California	45,902
43	Idaho	34,556		12	Virginia	45,339
17	Illinois	43,529		13	Colorado	44,232
36	Indiana	37,512		14	Rhode Island	44,151
26	Iowa	40,938		15	Pennsylvania	43,792
23	Kansas	42,103		16	Minnesota	43,710
44	Kentucky	34,481		17	Illinois	43,529
29	Louisiana	38,702		18	Vermont	43,383
32	Maine	38,299		19	South Dakota	43,360
9	Maryland	48,239		20	Hawaii	43,114
2	Massachusetts	52,524		21	Nebraska	43,084
34	Michigan	37,870		22	Delaware	42,239
16	Minnesota	43,710		23	Kansas	42,103
50	Mississippi	31,813		24	Texas	41,924
35	Missouri	37,521		25	Oklahoma	41,094
38	Montana	36,888		26	Iowa	40,938
21	Nebraska	43,084		27	Wisconsin	40,565
37	Nevada	37,500		28	Florida	39,480
5	New Hampshire	50,153		29	Louisiana	38,702
3	New Jersey	51,506		30	Ohio	38,568
46	New Mexico	34,396		31	Tennessee	38,450
8	New York	48,750		32	Maine	38,299
39	North Carolina	36,146		33	Oregon	38,076
7	North Dakota	49,334		34	Michigan	37,870
30	Ohio	38,568		35	Missouri	37,521
25	Oklahoma	41,094		36	Indiana	37,512
33	Oregon	38,076		37	Nevada	37,500
15	Pennsylvania	43,792		38	Montana	36,888
14	Rhode Island	44,151		39	North Carolina	36,146
45	South Carolina	34,471		40	Georgia	35,664
19	South Dakota	43,360		41	Arizona	35,168
31	Tennessee	38,450		42	Utah	34,875
24	Texas	41,924		43	Idaho	34,556
42	Utah	34,875		44	Kentucky	34,481
18	Vermont	43,383		45	South Carolina	34,471
12	Virginia	45,339		46	New Mexico	34,396
10	Washington	46,217		47	Alabama	34,377
49	West Virginia	33,068		48	Arkansas	34,367
27	Wisconsin	40,565		49	West Virginia	33,068
6	Wyoming	49,755		50	Mississippi	31,813
					District of Columbia	62,209

Source: U.S. Department of Commerce, Bureau of Economic Analysis
"Annual State Personal Income" (http://www.bea.gov/iTable/index_regional.cfm)
*Disposable personal income is personal income less personal tax and nontax payments. It is the income available to persons for spending or saving.

Median Household Income in 2015

National Median = $54,920*

ALPHA ORDER				RANK ORDER		
RANK	**STATE**	**INCOME**		**RANK**	**STATE**	**INCOME**
45	Alabama	$44,995		1	Maryland	$73,472
3	Alaska	72,187		2	New Hampshire	73,156
32	Arizona	51,697		3	Alaska	72,187
48	Arkansas	42,613		4	Connecticut	71,213
14	California	62,017		5	Minnesota	67,168
8	Colorado	65,570		6	Hawaii	67,060
4	Connecticut	71,213		7	New Jersey	66,182
21	Delaware	56,795		8	Colorado	65,570
40	Florida	48,134		9	Virginia	64,926
37	Georgia	49,399		10	Massachusetts	64,903
6	Hawaii	67,060		11	Utah	63,943
35	Idaho	51,480		12	Washington	63,807
22	Illinois	56,758		13	Vermont	62,311
36	Indiana	50,140		14	California	62,017
16	Iowa	59,981		15	Wyoming	61,768
31	Kansas	52,343		16	Iowa	59,981
47	Kentucky	43,629		17	North Dakota	59,468
43	Louisiana	45,206		18	Nebraska	58,681
30	Maine	52,815		19	Pennsylvania	57,249
1	Maryland	73,472		20	Rhode Island	57,237
10	Massachusetts	64,903		21	Delaware	56,795
25	Michigan	54,609		22	Illinois	56,758
5	Minnesota	67,168		23	Oregon	56,545
50	Mississippi	36,168		24	Wisconsin	55,402
27	Missouri	54,335		25	Michigan	54,609
38	Montana	48,838		26	New York	54,407
18	Nebraska	58,681		27	Missouri	54,335
33	Nevada	51,565		28	Texas	54,239
2	New Hampshire	73,156		29	South Dakota	54,176
7	New Jersey	66,182		30	Maine	52,815
46	New Mexico	44,243		31	Kansas	52,343
26	New York	54,407		32	Arizona	51,697
39	North Carolina	48,262		33	Nevada	51,565
17	North Dakota	59,468		34	Ohio	51,547
34	Ohio	51,547		35	Idaho	51,480
41	Oklahoma	47,101		36	Indiana	50,140
23	Oregon	56,545		37	Georgia	49,399
19	Pennsylvania	57,249		38	Montana	48,838
20	Rhode Island	57,237		39	North Carolina	48,262
42	South Carolina	45,222		40	Florida	48,134
29	South Dakota	54,176		41	Oklahoma	47,101
44	Tennessee	45,072		42	South Carolina	45,222
28	Texas	54,239		43	Louisiana	45,206
11	Utah	63,943		44	Tennessee	45,072
13	Vermont	62,311		45	Alabama	44,995
9	Virginia	64,926		46	New Mexico	44,243
12	Washington	63,807		47	Kentucky	43,629
49	West Virginia	42,082		48	Arkansas	42,613
24	Wisconsin	55,402		49	West Virginia	42,082
15	Wyoming	61,768		50	Mississippi	36,168
					District of Columbia	66,512

Source: U.S. Bureau of the Census
   "Historical Income Tables" (http://www.census.gov/topics/income-poverty/income/data/tables.html)
*This is a 3-year-average of inflation-adjusted single-year medians for the years 2013 through 2015.

Regional Price Parities in 2014

National Index = 100.0*

ALPHA ORDER			RANK ORDER		
RANK	STATE	RATIO	RANK	STATE	RATIO
48	Alabama	87.8	1	Hawaii	116.8
8	Alaska	105.7	2	New York	115.7
25	Arizona	96.4	3	New Jersey	114.5
49	Arkansas	87.5	4	California	112.4
4	California	112.4	5	Maryland	110.3
12	Colorado	102.0	6	Connecticut	108.8
6	Connecticut	108.8	7	Massachusetts	107.1
13	Delaware	101.9	8	Alaska	105.7
16	Florida	99.1	9	New Hampshire	105.2
32	Georgia	92.0	10	Washington	103.8
1	Hawaii	116.8	11	Virginia	102.6
30	Idaho	93.4	12	Colorado	102.0
15	Illinois	100.7	13	Delaware	101.9
35	Indiana	91.4	14	Vermont	101.2
40	Iowa	90.3	15	Illinois	100.7
37	Kansas	90.7	16	Florida	99.1
46	Kentucky	88.7	17	Oregon	99.0
35	Louisiana	91.4	18	Rhode Island	98.7
22	Maine	97.1	19	Pennsylvania	98.2
5	Maryland	110.3	20	Nevada	97.7
7	Massachusetts	107.1	21	Minnesota	97.6
29	Michigan	94.1	22	Maine	97.1
21	Minnesota	97.6	23	Utah	97.0
50	Mississippi	86.7	24	Texas	96.6
43	Missouri	89.4	25	Arizona	96.4
28	Montana	94.2	26	Wyoming	96.2
38	Nebraska	90.6	27	New Mexico	95.0
20	Nevada	97.7	28	Montana	94.2
9	New Hampshire	105.2	29	Michigan	94.1
3	New Jersey	114.5	30	Idaho	93.4
27	New Mexico	95.0	30	Wisconsin	93.4
2	New York	115.7	32	Georgia	92.0
33	North Carolina	91.7	33	North Carolina	91.7
34	North Dakota	91.5	34	North Dakota	91.5
44	Ohio	89.3	35	Indiana	91.4
42	Oklahoma	90.1	35	Louisiana	91.4
17	Oregon	99.0	37	Kansas	90.7
19	Pennsylvania	98.2	38	Nebraska	90.6
18	Rhode Island	98.7	39	South Carolina	90.5
39	South Carolina	90.5	40	Iowa	90.3
47	South Dakota	88.0	41	Tennessee	90.2
41	Tennessee	90.2	42	Oklahoma	90.1
24	Texas	96.6	43	Missouri	89.4
23	Utah	97.0	44	Ohio	89.3
14	Vermont	101.2	45	West Virginia	88.9
11	Virginia	102.6	46	Kentucky	88.7
10	Washington	103.8	47	South Dakota	88.0
45	West Virginia	88.9	48	Alabama	87.8
30	Wisconsin	93.4	49	Arkansas	87.5
26	Wyoming	96.2	50	Mississippi	86.7
				District of Columbia	118.1

Source: U.S. Department of Commerce, Bureau of Economic Analysis
  "Annual State Personal Income" (http://www.bea.gov/iTable/index_regional.cfm)
*Regional Price Parities (RPPs) are regional price levels expressed as a percentage of the overall national price level for a given year. The price levels are determined by the average prices paid by consumers for the mix of goods and services consumed in each region. Taking the ratio of RPPs shows the difference in price levels across regions.

Real Personal Income in 2014

National Total = $13,560,792,824,000*

ALPHA ORDER

RANK	STATE	INCOME	% of USA
25	Alabama	$187,124,870,000	1.4%
48	Alaska	34,924,729,000	0.3%
21	Arizona	243,465,879,000	1.8%
32	Arkansas	116,966,485,000	0.9%
1	California	1,614,619,890,000	11.9%
22	Colorado	239,880,777,000	1.8%
23	Connecticut	202,281,797,000	1.5%
47	Delaware	38,167,473,000	0.3%
4	Florida	789,771,508,000	5.8%
11	Georgia	391,047,808,000	2.9%
41	Hawaii	51,866,351,000	0.4%
40	Idaho	59,688,375,000	0.4%
6	Illinois	569,444,373,000	4.2%
16	Indiana	268,134,808,000	2.0%
30	Iowa	140,417,751,000	1.0%
31	Kansas	136,259,539,000	1.0%
28	Kentucky	169,176,251,000	1.2%
24	Louisiana	195,214,996,000	1.4%
42	Maine	51,864,256,000	0.4%
15	Maryland	268,510,248,000	2.0%
13	Massachusetts	345,034,368,000	2.5%
9	Michigan	395,973,261,000	2.9%
19	Minnesota	252,080,190,000	1.9%
33	Mississippi	108,151,500,000	0.8%
18	Missouri	255,759,996,000	1.9%
46	Montana	40,488,325,000	0.3%
36	Nebraska	92,145,598,000	0.7%
34	Nevada	107,909,561,000	0.8%
39	New Hampshire	62,101,789,000	0.5%
8	New Jersey	413,381,469,000	3.0%
37	New Mexico	73,829,979,000	0.5%
3	New York	888,152,041,000	6.5%
10	North Carolina	391,476,632,000	2.9%
44	North Dakota	42,980,188,000	0.3%
7	Ohio	502,238,390,000	3.7%
27	Oklahoma	178,309,838,000	1.3%
29	Oregon	153,503,338,000	1.1%
5	Pennsylvania	573,375,059,000	4.2%
43	Rhode Island	47,089,331,000	0.3%
26	South Carolina	180,551,490,000	1.3%
45	South Dakota	40,921,115,000	0.3%
17	Tennessee	267,976,348,000	2.0%
2	Texas	1,172,159,138,000	8.6%
35	Utah	104,893,699,000	0.8%
50	Vermont	26,796,362,000	0.2%
12	Virginia	373,178,757,000	2.8%
14	Washington	314,560,114,000	2.3%
38	West Virginia	68,286,073,000	0.5%
20	Wisconsin	251,350,366,000	1.9%
49	Wyoming	31,213,404,000	0.2%

RANK ORDER

RANK	STATE	INCOME	% of USA
1	California	$1,614,619,890,000	11.9%
2	Texas	1,172,159,138,000	8.6%
3	New York	888,152,041,000	6.5%
4	Florida	789,771,508,000	5.8%
5	Pennsylvania	573,375,059,000	4.2%
6	Illinois	569,444,373,000	4.2%
7	Ohio	502,238,390,000	3.7%
8	New Jersey	413,381,469,000	3.0%
9	Michigan	395,973,261,000	2.9%
10	North Carolina	391,476,632,000	2.9%
11	Georgia	391,047,808,000	2.9%
12	Virginia	373,178,757,000	2.8%
13	Massachusetts	345,034,368,000	2.5%
14	Washington	314,560,114,000	2.3%
15	Maryland	268,510,248,000	2.0%
16	Indiana	268,134,808,000	2.0%
17	Tennessee	267,976,348,000	2.0%
18	Missouri	255,759,996,000	1.9%
19	Minnesota	252,080,190,000	1.9%
20	Wisconsin	251,350,366,000	1.9%
21	Arizona	243,465,879,000	1.8%
22	Colorado	239,880,777,000	1.8%
23	Connecticut	202,281,797,000	1.5%
24	Louisiana	195,214,996,000	1.4%
25	Alabama	187,124,870,000	1.4%
26	South Carolina	180,551,490,000	1.3%
27	Oklahoma	178,309,838,000	1.3%
28	Kentucky	169,176,251,000	1.2%
29	Oregon	153,503,338,000	1.1%
30	Iowa	140,417,751,000	1.0%
31	Kansas	136,259,539,000	1.0%
32	Arkansas	116,966,485,000	0.9%
33	Mississippi	108,151,500,000	0.8%
34	Nevada	107,909,561,000	0.8%
35	Utah	104,893,699,000	0.8%
36	Nebraska	92,145,598,000	0.7%
37	New Mexico	73,829,979,000	0.5%
38	West Virginia	68,286,073,000	0.5%
39	New Hampshire	62,101,789,000	0.5%
40	Idaho	59,688,375,000	0.4%
41	Hawaii	51,866,351,000	0.4%
42	Maine	51,864,256,000	0.4%
43	Rhode Island	47,089,331,000	0.3%
44	North Dakota	42,980,188,000	0.3%
45	South Dakota	40,921,115,000	0.3%
46	Montana	40,488,325,000	0.3%
47	Delaware	38,167,473,000	0.3%
48	Alaska	34,924,729,000	0.3%
49	Wyoming	31,213,404,000	0.2%
50	Vermont	26,796,362,000	0.2%
	District of Columbia	36,096,940,000	0.3%

Source: U.S. Department of Commerce, Bureau of Economic Analysis
"Annual State Personal Income" (http://www.bea.gov/iTable/index_regional.cfm)
*Real personal income is personal income at Regional Price Parities (RPPs) divided by the national Personal Consumption Expenditure price index (a measure of U.S. inflation). RPPs are regional price levels expressed as a percentage of the overall national price level for a given year. The price levels are determined by the average prices paid by consumers for the mix of goods and services consumed in each region. Taking the ratio of RPPs shows the difference in price levels across regions.

Percent Change in Real Personal Income: 2013 to 2014

National Percent Change = 3.6% Increase*

ALPHA ORDER

RANK	STATE	PERCENT CHANGE
43	Alabama	2.0
18	Alaska	3.8
12	Arizona	4.3
21	Arkansas	3.4
4	California	4.9
1	Colorado	6.2
38	Connecticut	2.3
43	Delaware	2.0
3	Florida	5.1
16	Georgia	4.1
12	Hawaii	4.3
26	Idaho	3.2
34	Illinois	2.5
36	Indiana	2.4
41	Iowa	2.1
50	Kansas	0.3
21	Kentucky	3.4
28	Louisiana	3.0
20	Maine	3.5
46	Maryland	1.8
25	Massachusetts	3.3
21	Michigan	3.4
27	Minnesota	3.1
47	Mississippi	1.4
40	Missouri	2.2
41	Montana	2.1
10	Nebraska	4.6
4	Nevada	4.9
28	New Hampshire	3.0
33	New Jersey	2.6
17	New Mexico	3.9
32	New York	2.7
19	North Carolina	3.6
4	North Dakota	4.9
36	Ohio	2.4
9	Oklahoma	4.7
4	Oregon	4.9
28	Pennsylvania	3.0
43	Rhode Island	2.0
12	South Carolina	4.3
38	South Dakota	2.3
21	Tennessee	3.4
2	Texas	5.5
10	Utah	4.6
49	Vermont	1.0
31	Virginia	2.8
8	Washington	4.8
48	West Virginia	1.1
34	Wisconsin	2.5
15	Wyoming	4.2

RANK ORDER

RANK	STATE	PERCENT CHANGE
1	Colorado	6.2
2	Texas	5.5
3	Florida	5.1
4	California	4.9
4	Nevada	4.9
4	North Dakota	4.9
4	Oregon	4.9
8	Washington	4.8
9	Oklahoma	4.7
10	Nebraska	4.6
10	Utah	4.6
12	Arizona	4.3
12	Hawaii	4.3
12	South Carolina	4.3
15	Wyoming	4.2
16	Georgia	4.1
17	New Mexico	3.9
18	Alaska	3.8
19	North Carolina	3.6
20	Maine	3.5
21	Arkansas	3.4
21	Kentucky	3.4
21	Michigan	3.4
21	Tennessee	3.4
25	Massachusetts	3.3
26	Idaho	3.2
27	Minnesota	3.1
28	Louisiana	3.0
28	New Hampshire	3.0
28	Pennsylvania	3.0
31	Virginia	2.8
32	New York	2.7
33	New Jersey	2.6
34	Illinois	2.5
34	Wisconsin	2.5
36	Indiana	2.4
36	Ohio	2.4
38	Connecticut	2.3
38	South Dakota	2.3
40	Missouri	2.2
41	Iowa	2.1
41	Montana	2.1
43	Alabama	2.0
43	Delaware	2.0
43	Rhode Island	2.0
46	Maryland	1.8
47	Mississippi	1.4
48	West Virginia	1.1
49	Vermont	1.0
50	Kansas	0.3
	District of Columbia	5.5

Source: U.S. Department of Commerce, Bureau of Economic Analysis
"Annual State Personal Income" (http://www.bea.gov/iTable/index_regional.cfm)
*Real personal income is personal income at Regional Price Parities (RPPs) divided by the national Personal Consumption Expenditure price index (a measure of U.S. inflation). RPPs are regional price levels expressed as a percentage of the overall national price level for a given year. The price levels are determined by the average prices paid by consumers for the mix of goods and services consumed in each region. Taking the ratio of RPPs shows the difference in price levels across regions.

Per Capita Real Personal Income in 2014

National Per Capita = $42,523*

Source: U.S. Department of Commerce, Bureau of Economic Analysis

ALPHA ORDER

RANK	STATE	PER CAPITA
40	Alabama	$38,611
7	Alaska	47,385
47	Arizona	36,183
35	Arkansas	39,425
28	California	41,622
18	Colorado	44,791
2	Connecticut	56,271
30	Delaware	40,779
33	Florida	39,676
38	Georgia	38,729
45	Hawaii	36,519
46	Idaho	36,511
21	Illinois	44,204
31	Indiana	40,640
13	Iowa	45,158
8	Kansas	46,945
41	Kentucky	38,339
27	Louisiana	41,991
37	Maine	38,988
15	Maryland	44,936
4	Massachusetts	51,077
32	Michigan	39,932
11	Minnesota	46,193
48	Mississippi	36,129
26	Missouri	42,178
34	Montana	39,568
5	Nebraska	48,936
42	Nevada	38,019
9	New Hampshire	46,764
10	New Jersey	46,246
	New Mexico	35,400
14	New York	44,972
36	North Carolina	39,382
1	North Dakota	58,078
24	Ohio	43,308
12	Oklahoma	45,961
39	Oregon	38,654
16	Pennsylvania	44,817
19	Rhode Island	44,638
43	South Carolina	37,388
6	South Dakota	47,956
29	Tennessee	40,926
23	Texas	43,447
49	Utah	35,624
25	Vermont	42,753
17	Virginia	44,810
20	Washington	44,535
44	West Virginia	36,936
22	Wisconsin	43,642
3	Wyoming	53,420

RANK ORDER

RANK	STATE	PER CAPITA
1	North Dakota	$58,078
2	Connecticut	56,271
3	Wyoming	53,420
4	Massachusetts	51,077
5	Nebraska	48,936
6	South Dakota	47,956
7	Alaska	47,385
8	Kansas	46,945
9	New Hampshire	46,764
10	New Jersey	46,246
11	Minnesota	46,193
12	Oklahoma	45,961
13	Iowa	45,158
14	New York	44,972
15	Maryland	44,936
16	Pennsylvania	44,817
17	Virginia	44,810
18	Colorado	44,791
19	Rhode Island	44,638
20	Washington	44,535
21	Illinois	44,204
22	Wisconsin	43,642
23	Texas	43,447
24	Ohio	43,308
25	Vermont	42,753
26	Missouri	42,178
27	Louisiana	41,991
28	California	41,622
29	Tennessee	40,926
30	Delaware	40,779
31	Indiana	40,640
32	Michigan	39,932
33	Florida	39,676
34	Montana	39,568
35	Arkansas	39,425
36	North Carolina	39,382
37	Maine	38,988
38	Georgia	38,729
39	Oregon	38,654
40	Alabama	38,611
41	Kentucky	38,339
42	Nevada	38,019
43	South Carolina	37,388
44	West Virginia	36,936
45	Hawaii	36,519
46	Idaho	36,511
47	Arizona	36,183
48	Mississippi	36,129
49	Utah	35,624
50	New Mexico	35,400
	District of Columbia	54,706

Source: U.S. Department of Commerce, Bureau of Economic Analysis
    "Annual State Personal Income" (http://www.bea.gov/iTable/index_regional.cfm)
*Real personal income is personal income at Regional Price Parities (RPPs) divided by the national Personal Consumption Expenditure price index (a measure of U.S. inflation). RPPs are regional price levels expressed as a percentage of the overall national price level for a given year. The price levels are determined by the average prices paid by consumers for the mix of goods and services consumed in each region. Taking the ratio of RPPs shows the difference in price levels across regions.

Percent Change in Per Capita Real Personal Income: 2013 to 2014

National Percent Change = 2.8% Increase*

ALPHA ORDER

RANK	STATE	PERCENT CHANGE
41	Alabama	1.7
5	Alaska	3.9
22	Arizona	2.7
16	Arkansas	3.1
5	California	3.9
1	Colorado	4.6
30	Connecticut	2.4
49	Delaware	0.8
12	Florida	3.4
19	Georgia	3.0
10	Hawaii	3.5
39	Idaho	1.8
23	Illinois	2.6
37	Indiana	1.9
42	Iowa	1.6
50	Kansas	0.1
16	Kentucky	3.1
28	Louisiana	2.5
12	Maine	3.4
47	Maryland	1.1
23	Massachusetts	2.6
14	Michigan	3.2
30	Minnesota	2.4
43	Mississippi	1.3
37	Missouri	1.9
46	Montana	1.2
7	Nebraska	3.8
16	Nevada	3.1
23	New Hampshire	2.6
34	New Jersey	2.2
2	New Mexico	4.0
32	New York	2.3
23	North Carolina	2.6
28	North Dakota	2.5
34	Ohio	2.2
2	Oklahoma	4.0
7	Oregon	3.8
20	Pennsylvania	2.9
39	Rhode Island	1.8
20	South Carolina	2.9
43	South Dakota	1.3
23	Tennessee	2.6
9	Texas	3.6
14	Utah	3.2
47	Vermont	1.1
36	Virginia	2.1
10	Washington	3.5
43	West Virginia	1.3
32	Wisconsin	2.3
2	Wyoming	4.0

RANK ORDER

RANK	STATE	PERCENT CHANGE
1	Colorado	4.6
2	New Mexico	4.0
2	Oklahoma	4.0
2	Wyoming	4.0
5	Alaska	3.9
5	California	3.9
7	Nebraska	3.8
7	Oregon	3.8
9	Texas	3.6
10	Hawaii	3.5
10	Washington	3.5
12	Florida	3.4
12	Maine	3.4
14	Michigan	3.2
14	Utah	3.2
16	Arkansas	3.1
16	Kentucky	3.1
16	Nevada	3.1
19	Georgia	3.0
20	Pennsylvania	2.9
20	South Carolina	2.9
22	Arizona	2.7
23	Illinois	2.6
23	Massachusetts	2.6
23	New Hampshire	2.6
23	North Carolina	2.6
23	Tennessee	2.6
28	Louisiana	2.5
28	North Dakota	2.5
30	Connecticut	2.4
30	Minnesota	2.4
32	New York	2.3
32	Wisconsin	2.3
34	New Jersey	2.2
34	Ohio	2.2
36	Virginia	2.1
37	Indiana	1.9
37	Missouri	1.9
39	Idaho	1.8
39	Rhode Island	1.8
41	Alabama	1.7
42	Iowa	1.6
43	Mississippi	1.3
43	South Dakota	1.3
43	West Virginia	1.3
46	Montana	1.2
47	Maryland	1.1
47	Vermont	1.1
49	Delaware	0.8
50	Kansas	0.1

| | District of Columbia | 3.9 |

Source: U.S. Department of Commerce, Bureau of Economic Analysis
"Annual State Personal Income" (http://www.bea.gov/iTable/index_regional.cfm)
*Real personal income is personal income at Regional Price Parities (RPPs) divided by the national Personal Consumption Expenditure price index (a measure of U.S. inflation). RPPs are regional price levels expressed as a percentage of the overall national price level for a given year. The price levels are determined by the average prices paid by consumers for the mix of goods and services consumed in each region. Taking the ratio of RPPs shows the difference in price levels across regions.

Personal Consumption Expenditures in 2015

National Total = $12,278,861,000,000*

ALPHA ORDER

RANK	STATE	EXPENDITURES	% of USA
27	Alabama	$148,022,000,000	1.2%
47	Alaska	35,941,000,000	0.3%
16	Arizona	232,614,000,000	1.9%
34	Arkansas	88,737,000,000	0.7%
1	California	1,554,880,000,000	12.7%
19	Colorado	221,708,000,000	1.8%
23	Connecticut	168,787,000,000	1.4%
45	Delaware	39,819,000,000	0.3%
4	Florida	750,615,000,000	6.1%
10	Georgia	340,740,000,000	2.8%
40	Hawaii	61,250,000,000	0.5%
42	Idaho	53,340,000,000	0.4%
5	Illinois	512,654,000,000	4.2%
18	Indiana	225,744,000,000	1.8%
30	Iowa	111,289,000,000	0.9%
31	Kansas	101,455,000,000	0.8%
28	Kentucky	141,286,000,000	1.2%
24	Louisiana	157,031,000,000	1.3%
41	Maine	55,207,000,000	0.4%
15	Maryland	258,294,000,000	2.1%
11	Massachusetts	337,835,000,000	2.8%
9	Michigan	374,871,000,000	3.1%
17	Minnesota	230,798,000,000	1.9%
35	Mississippi	87,777,000,000	0.7%
20	Missouri	220,159,000,000	1.8%
44	Montana	41,034,000,000	0.3%
37	Nebraska	70,996,000,000	0.6%
32	Nevada	101,052,000,000	0.8%
38	New Hampshire	63,132,000,000	0.5%
8	New Jersey	423,383,000,000	3.4%
36	New Mexico	72,022,000,000	0.6%
3	New York	896,329,000,000	7.3%
13	North Carolina	326,451,000,000	2.7%
46	North Dakota	36,236,000,000	0.3%
7	Ohio	423,481,000,000	3.4%
29	Oklahoma	126,736,000,000	1.0%
26	Oregon	153,488,000,000	1.3%
6	Pennsylvania	505,738,000,000	4.1%
43	Rhode Island	43,486,000,000	0.4%
25	South Carolina	156,868,000,000	1.3%
48	South Dakota	32,699,000,000	0.3%
21	Tennessee	218,250,000,000	1.8%
2	Texas	976,073,000,000	7.9%
33	Utah	100,044,000,000	0.8%
49	Vermont	29,133,000,000	0.2%
12	Virginia	336,993,000,000	2.7%
14	Washington	296,800,000,000	2.4%
39	West Virginia	61,385,000,000	0.5%
22	Wisconsin	215,823,000,000	1.8%
50	Wyoming	23,345,000,000	0.2%

RANK ORDER

RANK	STATE	EXPENDITURES	% of USA
1	California	$1,554,880,000,000	12.7%
2	Texas	976,073,000,000	7.9%
3	New York	896,329,000,000	7.3%
4	Florida	750,615,000,000	6.1%
5	Illinois	512,654,000,000	4.2%
6	Pennsylvania	505,738,000,000	4.1%
7	Ohio	423,481,000,000	3.4%
8	New Jersey	423,383,000,000	3.4%
9	Michigan	374,871,000,000	3.1%
10	Georgia	340,740,000,000	2.8%
11	Massachusetts	337,835,000,000	2.8%
12	Virginia	336,993,000,000	2.7%
13	North Carolina	326,451,000,000	2.7%
14	Washington	296,800,000,000	2.4%
15	Maryland	258,294,000,000	2.1%
16	Arizona	232,614,000,000	1.9%
17	Minnesota	230,798,000,000	1.9%
18	Indiana	225,744,000,000	1.8%
19	Colorado	221,708,000,000	1.8%
20	Missouri	220,159,000,000	1.8%
21	Tennessee	218,250,000,000	1.8%
22	Wisconsin	215,823,000,000	1.8%
23	Connecticut	168,787,000,000	1.4%
24	Louisiana	157,031,000,000	1.3%
25	South Carolina	156,868,000,000	1.3%
26	Oregon	153,488,000,000	1.3%
27	Alabama	148,022,000,000	1.2%
28	Kentucky	141,286,000,000	1.2%
29	Oklahoma	126,736,000,000	1.0%
30	Iowa	111,289,000,000	0.9%
31	Kansas	101,455,000,000	0.8%
32	Nevada	101,052,000,000	0.8%
33	Utah	100,044,000,000	0.8%
34	Arkansas	88,737,000,000	0.7%
35	Mississippi	87,777,000,000	0.7%
36	New Mexico	72,022,000,000	0.6%
37	Nebraska	70,996,000,000	0.6%
38	New Hampshire	63,132,000,000	0.5%
39	West Virginia	61,385,000,000	0.5%
40	Hawaii	61,250,000,000	0.5%
41	Maine	55,207,000,000	0.4%
42	Idaho	53,340,000,000	0.4%
43	Rhode Island	43,486,000,000	0.4%
44	Montana	41,034,000,000	0.3%
45	Delaware	39,819,000,000	0.3%
46	North Dakota	36,236,000,000	0.3%
47	Alaska	35,941,000,000	0.3%
48	South Dakota	32,699,000,000	0.3%
49	Vermont	29,133,000,000	0.2%
50	Wyoming	23,345,000,000	0.2%
	District of Columbia	37,032,000,000	0.3%

Source: U.S. Department of Commerce, Bureau of Economic Analysis
   "Personal Consumption Expenditures by State" (http://www.bea.gov/iTable/index_regional.cfm)
*PCE by state is the state counterpart of the Nation's personal consumption expenditures (PCE). PCE represents the goods and services purchased by or on behalf of households, plus the purchases of nonprofit institutions serving households. For each state and for the District of Columbia, personal consumption expenditures are those expenditures made by or on behalf of residents. These expenditures include expenditures on activities outside of the state.

Per Capita Personal Consumption Expenditures in 2015

National Per Capita = $38,196*

ALPHA ORDER			RANK ORDER		
RANK	STATE	PER CAPITA	RANK	STATE	PER CAPITA
48	Alabama	$30,459	1	Massachusetts	$49,717
2	Alaska	48,666	2	Alaska	48,666
37	Arizona	34,061	3	North Dakota	47,864
49	Arkansas	29,791	4	New Hampshire	47,441
21	California	39,715	5	New Jersey	47,256
16	Colorado	40,625	6	Connecticut	46,998
6	Connecticut	46,998	7	Vermont	46,531
11	Delaware	42,088	8	New York	45,272
28	Florida	37,020	9	Maryland	42,997
40	Georgia	33,353	10	Hawaii	42,778
10	Hawaii	42,778	11	Delaware	42,088
45	Idaho	32,226	12	Minnesota	42,038
18	Illinois	39,859	13	Maine	41,525
36	Indiana	34,098	14	Washington	41,386
31	Iowa	35,621	15	Rhode Island	41,163
34	Kansas	34,840	16	Colorado	40,625
47	Kentucky	31,925	17	Virginia	40,195
38	Louisiana	33,616	18	Illinois	39,859
13	Maine	41,525	19	Wyoming	39,825
9	Maryland	42,997	20	Montana	39,718
1	Massachusetts	49,717	21	California	39,715
25	Michigan	37,775	22	Pennsylvania	39,498
12	Minnesota	42,038	23	Oregon	38,090
50	Mississippi	29,330	24	South Dakota	38,085
30	Missouri	36,184	25	Michigan	37,775
20	Montana	39,718	26	Nebraska	37,437
26	Nebraska	37,437	27	Wisconsin	37,391
33	Nevada	34,949	28	Florida	37,020
4	New Hampshire	47,441	29	Ohio	36,460
5	New Jersey	47,256	30	Missouri	36,184
35	New Mexico	34,535	31	Iowa	35,621
8	New York	45,272	32	Texas	35,527
43	North Carolina	32,501	33	Nevada	34,949
3	North Dakota	47,864	34	Kansas	34,840
29	Ohio	36,460	35	New Mexico	34,535
44	Oklahoma	32,397	36	Indiana	34,098
23	Oregon	38,090	37	Arizona	34,061
22	Pennsylvania	39,498	38	Louisiana	33,616
15	Rhode Island	41,163	39	Utah	33,389
46	South Carolina	32,033	40	Georgia	33,353
24	South Dakota	38,085	41	West Virginia	33,282
42	Tennessee	33,062	42	Tennessee	33,062
32	Texas	35,527	43	North Carolina	32,501
39	Utah	33,389	44	Oklahoma	32,397
7	Vermont	46,531	45	Idaho	32,226
17	Virginia	40,195	46	South Carolina	32,033
14	Washington	41,386	47	Kentucky	31,925
41	West Virginia	33,282	48	Alabama	30,459
27	Wisconsin	37,391	49	Arkansas	29,791
19	Wyoming	39,825	50	Mississippi	29,330
				District of Columbia	55,078

Source: U.S. Department of Commerce, Bureau of Economic Analysis
   "Personal Consumption Expenditures by State" (http://www.bea.gov/iTable/index_regional.cfm)
*PCE by state is the state counterpart of the Nation's personal consumption expenditures (PCE). PCE represents the goods and services purchased by or on behalf of households, plus the purchases of nonprofit institutions serving households. For each state and for the District of Columbia, personal consumption expenditures are those expenditures made by or on behalf of residents. These expenditures include expenditures on activities outside of the state.

Percent Change in Personal Consumption Expenditures: 2014 to 2015

National Percent Change = 3.6% Increase*

<table>
<tr><td colspan="3">ALPHA ORDER</td><td colspan="3">RANK ORDER</td></tr>
<tr><th>RANK</th><th>STATE</th><th>PERCENT CHANGE</th><th>RANK</th><th>STATE</th><th>PERCENT CHANGE</th></tr>
<tr><td>40</td><td>Alabama</td><td>2.3</td><td>1</td><td>Florida</td><td>5.0</td></tr>
<tr><td>13</td><td>Alaska</td><td>3.7</td><td>2</td><td>Colorado</td><td>4.9</td></tr>
<tr><td>16</td><td>Arizona</td><td>3.5</td><td>2</td><td>Oregon</td><td>4.9</td></tr>
<tr><td>45</td><td>Arkansas</td><td>2.1</td><td>4</td><td>Utah</td><td>4.7</td></tr>
<tr><td>6</td><td>California</td><td>4.5</td><td>5</td><td>Washington</td><td>4.6</td></tr>
<tr><td>2</td><td>Colorado</td><td>4.9</td><td>6</td><td>California</td><td>4.5</td></tr>
<tr><td>40</td><td>Connecticut</td><td>2.3</td><td>7</td><td>Hawaii</td><td>4.0</td></tr>
<tr><td>12</td><td>Delaware</td><td>3.8</td><td>8</td><td>Massachusetts</td><td>3.9</td></tr>
<tr><td>1</td><td>Florida</td><td>5.0</td><td>8</td><td>Montana</td><td>3.9</td></tr>
<tr><td>16</td><td>Georgia</td><td>3.5</td><td>8</td><td>Nevada</td><td>3.9</td></tr>
<tr><td>7</td><td>Hawaii</td><td>4.0</td><td>8</td><td>Texas</td><td>3.9</td></tr>
<tr><td>14</td><td>Idaho</td><td>3.6</td><td>12</td><td>Delaware</td><td>3.8</td></tr>
<tr><td>26</td><td>Illinois</td><td>3.0</td><td>13</td><td>Alaska</td><td>3.7</td></tr>
<tr><td>38</td><td>Indiana</td><td>2.4</td><td>14</td><td>Idaho</td><td>3.6</td></tr>
<tr><td>46</td><td>Iowa</td><td>2.0</td><td>14</td><td>New York</td><td>3.6</td></tr>
<tr><td>33</td><td>Kansas</td><td>2.8</td><td>16</td><td>Arizona</td><td>3.5</td></tr>
<tr><td>35</td><td>Kentucky</td><td>2.7</td><td>16</td><td>Georgia</td><td>3.5</td></tr>
<tr><td>26</td><td>Louisiana</td><td>3.0</td><td>16</td><td>Michigan</td><td>3.5</td></tr>
<tr><td>46</td><td>Maine</td><td>2.0</td><td>16</td><td>Minnesota</td><td>3.5</td></tr>
<tr><td>22</td><td>Maryland</td><td>3.4</td><td>16</td><td>Rhode Island</td><td>3.5</td></tr>
<tr><td>8</td><td>Massachusetts</td><td>3.9</td><td>16</td><td>Tennessee</td><td>3.5</td></tr>
<tr><td>16</td><td>Michigan</td><td>3.5</td><td>22</td><td>Maryland</td><td>3.4</td></tr>
<tr><td>16</td><td>Minnesota</td><td>3.5</td><td>22</td><td>North Carolina</td><td>3.4</td></tr>
<tr><td>48</td><td>Mississippi</td><td>1.9</td><td>24</td><td>New Jersey</td><td>3.1</td></tr>
<tr><td>36</td><td>Missouri</td><td>2.6</td><td>24</td><td>South Carolina</td><td>3.1</td></tr>
<tr><td>8</td><td>Montana</td><td>3.9</td><td>26</td><td>Illinois</td><td>3.0</td></tr>
<tr><td>29</td><td>Nebraska</td><td>2.9</td><td>26</td><td>Louisiana</td><td>3.0</td></tr>
<tr><td>8</td><td>Nevada</td><td>3.9</td><td>26</td><td>New Hampshire</td><td>3.0</td></tr>
<tr><td>26</td><td>New Hampshire</td><td>3.0</td><td>29</td><td>Nebraska</td><td>2.9</td></tr>
<tr><td>24</td><td>New Jersey</td><td>3.1</td><td>29</td><td>Ohio</td><td>2.9</td></tr>
<tr><td>40</td><td>New Mexico</td><td>2.3</td><td>29</td><td>Virginia</td><td>2.9</td></tr>
<tr><td>14</td><td>New York</td><td>3.6</td><td>29</td><td>Wisconsin</td><td>2.9</td></tr>
<tr><td>22</td><td>North Carolina</td><td>3.4</td><td>33</td><td>Kansas</td><td>2.8</td></tr>
<tr><td>48</td><td>North Dakota</td><td>1.9</td><td>33</td><td>Vermont</td><td>2.8</td></tr>
<tr><td>29</td><td>Ohio</td><td>2.9</td><td>35</td><td>Kentucky</td><td>2.7</td></tr>
<tr><td>38</td><td>Oklahoma</td><td>2.4</td><td>36</td><td>Missouri</td><td>2.6</td></tr>
<tr><td>2</td><td>Oregon</td><td>4.9</td><td>36</td><td>Pennsylvania</td><td>2.6</td></tr>
<tr><td>36</td><td>Pennsylvania</td><td>2.6</td><td>38</td><td>Indiana</td><td>2.4</td></tr>
<tr><td>16</td><td>Rhode Island</td><td>3.5</td><td>38</td><td>Oklahoma</td><td>2.4</td></tr>
<tr><td>24</td><td>South Carolina</td><td>3.1</td><td>40</td><td>Alabama</td><td>2.3</td></tr>
<tr><td>40</td><td>South Dakota</td><td>2.3</td><td>40</td><td>Connecticut</td><td>2.3</td></tr>
<tr><td>16</td><td>Tennessee</td><td>3.5</td><td>40</td><td>New Mexico</td><td>2.3</td></tr>
<tr><td>8</td><td>Texas</td><td>3.9</td><td>40</td><td>South Dakota</td><td>2.3</td></tr>
<tr><td>4</td><td>Utah</td><td>4.7</td><td>40</td><td>West Virginia</td><td>2.3</td></tr>
<tr><td>33</td><td>Vermont</td><td>2.8</td><td>45</td><td>Arkansas</td><td>2.1</td></tr>
<tr><td>29</td><td>Virginia</td><td>2.9</td><td>46</td><td>Iowa</td><td>2.0</td></tr>
<tr><td>5</td><td>Washington</td><td>4.6</td><td>46</td><td>Maine</td><td>2.0</td></tr>
<tr><td>40</td><td>West Virginia</td><td>2.3</td><td>48</td><td>Mississippi</td><td>1.9</td></tr>
<tr><td>29</td><td>Wisconsin</td><td>2.9</td><td>48</td><td>North Dakota</td><td>1.9</td></tr>
<tr><td>50</td><td>Wyoming</td><td>1.5</td><td>50</td><td>Wyoming</td><td>1.5</td></tr>
<tr><td></td><td></td><td></td><td></td><td>District of Columbia</td><td>5.2</td></tr>
</table>

Source: U.S. Department of Commerce, Bureau of Economic Analysis
  "Personal Consumption Expenditures by State" (http://www.bea.gov/iTable/index_regional.cfm)
*PCE by state is the state counterpart of the Nation's personal consumption expenditures (PCE). PCE represents the goods and services purchased by or on behalf of households, plus the purchases of nonprofit institutions serving households. For each state and for the District of Columbia, personal consumption expenditures are those expenditures made by or on behalf of residents. These expenditures include expenditures on activities outside of the state.

Percent Change in Per Capita
Personal Consumption Expenditures: 2014 to 2015
National Percent Change = 2.7% Increase*

ALPHA ORDER

RANK	STATE	PERCENT CHANGE
36	Alabama	2.1
2	Alaska	3.4
39	Arizona	2.0
46	Arkansas	1.6
1	California	3.6
13	Colorado	2.9
29	Connecticut	2.4
19	Delaware	2.7
10	Florida	3.0
31	Georgia	2.3
7	Hawaii	3.1
31	Idaho	2.3
7	Illinois	3.1
36	Indiana	2.1
47	Iowa	1.5
25	Kansas	2.5
25	Kentucky	2.5
25	Louisiana	2.5
39	Maine	2.0
13	Maryland	2.9
7	Massachusetts	3.1
2	Michigan	3.4
13	Minnesota	2.9
39	Mississippi	2.0
34	Missouri	2.2
10	Montana	3.0
36	Nebraska	2.1
39	Nevada	2.0
19	New Hampshire	2.7
13	New Jersey	2.9
31	New Mexico	2.3
5	New York	3.3
29	North Carolina	2.4
50	North Dakota	(0.4)
19	Ohio	2.7
47	Oklahoma	1.5
2	Oregon	3.4
25	Pennsylvania	2.5
5	Rhode Island	3.3
44	South Carolina	1.8
45	South Dakota	1.7
19	Tennessee	2.7
43	Texas	1.9
18	Utah	2.8
13	Vermont	2.9
34	Virginia	2.2
10	Washington	3.0
23	West Virginia	2.6
23	Wisconsin	2.6
49	Wyoming	1.2

RANK ORDER

RANK	STATE	PERCENT CHANGE
1	California	3.6
2	Alaska	3.4
2	Michigan	3.4
2	Oregon	3.4
5	New York	3.3
5	Rhode Island	3.3
7	Hawaii	3.1
7	Illinois	3.1
7	Massachusetts	3.1
10	Florida	3.0
10	Montana	3.0
10	Washington	3.0
13	Colorado	2.9
13	Maryland	2.9
13	Minnesota	2.9
13	New Jersey	2.9
13	Vermont	2.9
18	Utah	2.8
19	Delaware	2.7
19	New Hampshire	2.7
19	Ohio	2.7
19	Tennessee	2.7
23	West Virginia	2.6
23	Wisconsin	2.6
25	Kansas	2.5
25	Kentucky	2.5
25	Louisiana	2.5
25	Pennsylvania	2.5
29	Connecticut	2.4
29	North Carolina	2.4
31	Georgia	2.3
31	Idaho	2.3
31	New Mexico	2.3
34	Missouri	2.2
34	Virginia	2.2
36	Alabama	2.1
36	Indiana	2.1
36	Nebraska	2.1
39	Arizona	2.0
39	Maine	2.0
39	Mississippi	2.0
39	Nevada	2.0
43	Texas	1.9
44	South Carolina	1.8
45	South Dakota	1.7
46	Arkansas	1.6
47	Iowa	1.5
47	Oklahoma	1.5
49	Wyoming	1.2
50	North Dakota	(0.4)
	District of Columbia	3.1

Source: U.S. Department of Commerce, Bureau of Economic Analysis
"Personal Consumption Expenditures by State" (http://www.bea.gov/iTable/index_regional.cfm)
*PCE by state is the state counterpart of the Nation's personal consumption expenditures (PCE). PCE represents the goods and services purchased by or on behalf of households, plus the purchases of nonprofit institutions serving households. For each state and for the District of Columbia, personal consumption expenditures are those expenditures made by or on behalf of residents. These expenditures include expenditures on activities outside of the state.

Bankruptcy Filings in 2016

National Total = 805,580 Bankruptcies*

ALPHA ORDER

RANK	STATE	BANKRUPTCIES	% of USA
10	Alabama	26,091	3.2%
50	Alaska	434	0.1%
19	Arizona	15,895	2.0%
26	Arkansas	10,535	1.3%
1	California	76,623	9.5%
23	Colorado	13,191	1.6%
34	Connecticut	5,914	0.7%
40	Delaware	2,876	0.4%
4	Florida	47,718	5.9%
3	Georgia	48,092	6.0%
44	Hawaii	1,463	0.2%
37	Idaho	3,841	0.5%
2	Illinois	54,856	6.8%
12	Indiana	24,693	3.1%
35	Iowa	4,350	0.5%
33	Kansas	6,553	0.8%
20	Kentucky	15,310	1.9%
22	Louisiana	13,825	1.7%
43	Maine	1,613	0.2%
17	Maryland	17,212	2.1%
31	Massachusetts	8,873	1.1%
8	Michigan	31,367	3.9%
27	Minnesota	9,776	1.2%
25	Mississippi	11,277	1.4%
15	Missouri	18,573	2.3%
45	Montana	1,365	0.2%
36	Nebraska	4,114	0.5%
30	Nevada	9,063	1.1%
42	New Hampshire	1,878	0.2%
11	New Jersey	25,651	3.2%
39	New Mexico	3,315	0.4%
9	New York	29,908	3.7%
21	North Carolina	15,275	1.9%
48	North Dakota	666	0.1%
5	Ohio	37,315	4.6%
29	Oklahoma	9,161	1.1%
28	Oregon	9,488	1.2%
14	Pennsylvania	21,962	2.7%
41	Rhode Island	2,364	0.3%
32	South Carolina	6,731	0.8%
46	South Dakota	1,078	0.1%
6	Tennessee	35,998	4.5%
7	Texas	33,755	4.2%
24	Utah	11,667	1.4%
49	Vermont	604	0.1%
13	Virginia	22,971	2.9%
18	Washington	16,859	2.1%
38	West Virginia	3,338	0.4%
16	Wisconsin	17,314	2.1%
47	Wyoming	936	0.1%

RANK ORDER

RANK	STATE	BANKRUPTCIES	% of USA
1	California	76,623	9.5%
2	Illinois	54,856	6.8%
3	Georgia	48,092	6.0%
4	Florida	47,718	5.9%
5	Ohio	37,315	4.6%
6	Tennessee	35,998	4.5%
7	Texas	33,755	4.2%
8	Michigan	31,367	3.9%
9	New York	29,908	3.7%
10	Alabama	26,091	3.2%
11	New Jersey	25,651	3.2%
12	Indiana	24,693	3.1%
13	Virginia	22,971	2.9%
14	Pennsylvania	21,962	2.7%
15	Missouri	18,573	2.3%
16	Wisconsin	17,314	2.1%
17	Maryland	17,212	2.1%
18	Washington	16,859	2.1%
19	Arizona	15,895	2.0%
20	Kentucky	15,310	1.9%
21	North Carolina	15,275	1.9%
22	Louisiana	13,825	1.7%
23	Colorado	13,191	1.6%
24	Utah	11,667	1.4%
25	Mississippi	11,277	1.4%
26	Arkansas	10,535	1.3%
27	Minnesota	9,776	1.2%
28	Oregon	9,488	1.2%
29	Oklahoma	9,161	1.1%
30	Nevada	9,063	1.1%
31	Massachusetts	8,873	1.1%
32	South Carolina	6,731	0.8%
33	Kansas	6,553	0.8%
34	Connecticut	5,914	0.7%
35	Iowa	4,350	0.5%
36	Nebraska	4,114	0.5%
37	Idaho	3,841	0.5%
38	West Virginia	3,338	0.4%
39	New Mexico	3,315	0.4%
40	Delaware	2,876	0.4%
41	Rhode Island	2,364	0.3%
42	New Hampshire	1,878	0.2%
43	Maine	1,613	0.2%
44	Hawaii	1,463	0.2%
45	Montana	1,365	0.2%
46	South Dakota	1,078	0.1%
47	Wyoming	936	0.1%
48	North Dakota	666	0.1%
49	Vermont	604	0.1%
50	Alaska	434	0.1%
	District of Columbia	697	0.1%

Source: CQ Press using data from Administrative Office of the U.S. Courts
"Table F-2, U.S. Bankruptcy Courts" (http://www.uscourts.gov/Statistics/BankruptcyStatistics.aspx)
*For 12 months through September 2016. Includes business (24,457) and non-business (781,123) filings. Includes all chapters of bankruptcy. National total includes 11,156 bankruptcies in U.S. territories.

Personal Bankruptcy Rate in 2016

National Rate = 238 Personal Bankruptcies per 100,000 Population*

ALPHA ORDER			RANK ORDER		
RANK	STATE	RATE	RANK	STATE	RATE
2	Alabama	531	1	Tennessee	534
50	Alaska	52	2	Alabama	531
26	Arizona	221	3	Georgia	457
8	Arkansas	344	4	Illinois	421
30	California	187	5	Utah	375
19	Colorado	231	6	Mississippi	368
34	Connecticut	158	7	Indiana	366
23	Delaware	224	8	Arkansas	344
24	Florida	223	9	Kentucky	340
3	Georgia	457	10	Ohio	316
47	Hawaii	98	11	Michigan	310
24	Idaho	223	12	Nevada	298
4	Illinois	421	13	Missouri	296
7	Indiana	366	14	Wisconsin	293
39	Iowa	133	15	Louisiana	288
27	Kansas	217	16	Maryland	280
9	Kentucky	340	17	New Jersey	278
15	Louisiana	288	18	Virginia	268
45	Maine	114	19	Colorado	231
16	Maryland	280	20	Oklahoma	228
43	Massachusetts	124	21	Oregon	226
11	Michigan	310	22	Washington	225
32	Minnesota	171	23	Delaware	224
6	Mississippi	368	24	Florida	223
13	Missouri	296	24	Idaho	223
42	Montana	125	26	Arizona	221
29	Nebraska	210	27	Kansas	217
12	Nevada	298	28	Rhode Island	216
41	New Hampshire	128	29	Nebraska	210
17	New Jersey	278	30	California	187
35	New Mexico	154	31	West Virginia	175
38	New York	143	32	Minnesota	171
37	North Carolina	146	33	Pennsylvania	166
49	North Dakota	83	34	Connecticut	158
10	Ohio	316	35	New Mexico	154
20	Oklahoma	228	36	Wyoming	153
21	Oregon	226	37	North Carolina	146
33	Pennsylvania	166	38	New York	143
28	Rhode Island	216	39	Iowa	133
39	South Carolina	133	39	South Carolina	133
44	South Dakota	120	41	New Hampshire	128
1	Tennessee	534	42	Montana	125
46	Texas	113	43	Massachusetts	124
5	Utah	375	44	South Dakota	120
48	Vermont	89	45	Maine	114
18	Virginia	268	46	Texas	113
22	Washington	225	47	Hawaii	98
31	West Virginia	175	48	Vermont	89
14	Wisconsin	293	49	North Dakota	83
36	Wyoming	153	50	Alaska	52
				District of Columbia	96

Source: CQ Press using data from Administrative Office of the U.S. Courts
"Table F-2, U.S. Bankruptcy Courts" (http://www.uscourts.gov/Statistics/BankruptcyStatistics.aspx)
*For 12 months through September 2016. National rate does not include bankruptcies or population in U.S. territories. Includes all nonbusiness bankruptcies.

Percent Change in Personal Bankruptcy Rate: 2015 to 2016

National Percent Change = 18.5% Decrease*

RANK	STATE	PERCENT CHANGE
5	Alabama	2.3
8	Alaska	0.0
43	Arizona	(12.0)
6	Arkansas	1.8
44	California	(13.4)
47	Colorado	(17.2)
34	Connecticut	(9.2)
13	Delaware	(2.2)
50	Florida	(22.0)
32	Georgia	(8.2)
33	Hawaii	(8.4)
35	Idaho	(9.3)
19	Illinois	(4.3)
38	Indiana	(10.3)
24	Iowa	(5.7)
31	Kansas	(7.7)
15	Kentucky	(2.6)
12	Louisiana	(1.7)
46	Maine	(16.2)
30	Maryland	(7.3)
23	Massachusetts	(5.3)
25	Michigan	(5.8)
42	Minnesota	(11.9)
2	Mississippi	3.4
28	Missouri	(6.6)
4	Montana	2.5
21	Nebraska	(5.0)
40	Nevada	(11.0)
49	New Hampshire	(17.9)
9	New Jersey	(0.4)
19	New Mexico	(4.3)
16	New York	(2.7)
25	North Carolina	(5.8)
1	North Dakota	9.2
22	Ohio	(5.1)
11	Oklahoma	(1.3)
48	Oregon	(17.8)
14	Pennsylvania	(2.4)
36	Rhode Island	(9.6)
29	South Carolina	(7.0)
18	South Dakota	(4.0)
17	Tennessee	(3.4)
25	Texas	(5.8)
38	Utah	(10.3)
40	Vermont	(11.0)
10	Virginia	(0.7)
45	Washington	(14.4)
3	West Virginia	2.9
37	Wisconsin	(10.1)
7	Wyoming	0.7

RANK	STATE	PERCENT CHANGE
1	North Dakota	9.2
2	Mississippi	3.4
3	West Virginia	2.9
4	Montana	2.5
5	Alabama	2.3
6	Arkansas	1.8
7	Wyoming	0.7
8	Alaska	0.0
9	New Jersey	(0.4)
10	Virginia	(0.7)
11	Oklahoma	(1.3)
12	Louisiana	(1.7)
13	Delaware	(2.2)
14	Pennsylvania	(2.4)
15	Kentucky	(2.6)
16	New York	(2.7)
17	Tennessee	(3.4)
18	South Dakota	(4.0)
19	Illinois	(4.3)
19	New Mexico	(4.3)
21	Nebraska	(5.0)
22	Ohio	(5.1)
23	Massachusetts	(5.3)
24	Iowa	(5.7)
25	Michigan	(5.8)
25	North Carolina	(5.8)
25	Texas	(5.8)
28	Missouri	(6.6)
29	South Carolina	(7.0)
30	Maryland	(7.3)
31	Kansas	(7.7)
32	Georgia	(8.2)
33	Hawaii	(8.4)
34	Connecticut	(9.2)
35	Idaho	(9.3)
36	Rhode Island	(9.6)
37	Wisconsin	(10.1)
38	Indiana	(10.3)
38	Utah	(10.3)
40	Nevada	(11.0)
40	Vermont	(11.0)
42	Minnesota	(11.9)
43	Arizona	(12.0)
44	California	(13.4)
45	Washington	(14.4)
46	Maine	(16.2)
47	Colorado	(17.2)
48	Oregon	(17.8)
49	New Hampshire	(17.9)
50	Florida	(22.0)

District of Columbia (5.9)

Source: CQ Press using data from Administrative Office of the U.S. Courts
"Table F-2, U.S. Bankruptcy Courts" (http://www.uscourts.gov/Statistics/BankruptcyStatistics.aspx)
*Twelve months ending in September 2015 to 12 months ending in September 2016. National rate does not include bankruptcies or population in U.S. territories. Includes all nonbusiness bankruptcies.

2017 State Business Tax Climate Index

National Average Score = 5.18*

ALPHA ORDER		
RANK	STATE	SCORE
32	Alabama	4.91
3	Alaska	7.29
21	Arizona	5.21
38	Arkansas	4.60
48	California	3.76
16	Colorado	5.38
43	Connecticut	4.34
19	Delaware	5.32
4	Florida	6.86
36	Georgia	4.68
26	Hawaii	5.13
20	Idaho	5.22
23	Illinois	5.21
8	Indiana	5.96
40	Iowa	4.51
22	Kansas	5.21
34	Kentucky	4.88
41	Louisiana	4.39
30	Maine	4.96
42	Maryland	4.36
27	Massachusetts	5.13
12	Michigan	5.64
46	Minnesota	4.19
28	Mississippi	5.13
15	Missouri	5.45
6	Montana	6.27
25	Nebraska	5.14
5	Nevada	6.46
7	New Hampshire	6.11
50	New Jersey	3.41
35	New Mexico	4.85
49	New York	3.61
11	North Carolina	5.73
29	North Dakota	4.98
45	Ohio	4.27
31	Oklahoma	4.95
10	Oregon	5.78
24	Pennsylvania	5.18
44	Rhode Island	4.30
37	South Carolina	4.66
2	South Dakota	7.49
13	Tennessee	5.58
14	Texas	5.57
9	Utah	5.96
47	Vermont	4.13
33	Virginia	4.90
17	Washington	5.38
18	West Virginia	5.32
39	Wisconsin	4.57
1	Wyoming	7.76

RANK ORDER		
RANK	STATE	SCORE
1	Wyoming	7.76
2	South Dakota	7.49
3	Alaska	7.29
4	Florida	6.86
5	Nevada	6.46
6	Montana	6.27
7	New Hampshire	6.11
8	Indiana	5.96
9	Utah	5.96
10	Oregon	5.78
11	North Carolina	5.73
12	Michigan	5.64
13	Tennessee	5.58
14	Texas	5.57
15	Missouri	5.45
16	Colorado	5.38
17	Washington	5.38
18	West Virginia	5.32
19	Delaware	5.32
20	Idaho	5.22
21	Arizona	5.21
22	Kansas	5.21
23	Illinois	5.21
24	Pennsylvania	5.18
25	Nebraska	5.14
26	Hawaii	5.13
27	Massachusetts	5.13
28	Mississippi	5.13
29	North Dakota	4.98
30	Maine	4.96
31	Oklahoma	4.95
32	Alabama	4.91
33	Virginia	4.90
34	Kentucky	4.88
35	New Mexico	4.85
36	Georgia	4.68
37	South Carolina	4.66
38	Arkansas	4.60
39	Wisconsin	4.57
40	Iowa	4.51
41	Louisiana	4.39
42	Maryland	4.36
43	Connecticut	4.34
44	Rhode Island	4.30
45	Ohio	4.27
46	Minnesota	4.19
47	Vermont	4.13
48	California	3.76
49	New York	3.61
50	New Jersey	3.41
	District of Columbia	4.19

Source: The Tax Foundation
"State Business Tax Climate Index" (September 2016, https://taxfoundation.org/2017-state-business-tax-climate-index/)
*This index looks at levels of taxation and complexity of compliance to compare the states on how "business friendly" each state is compared to the others. The scale for each factor considered is one to ten, with ten being the "best." Rankings are based on unrounded scores and reflect those of The Tax Foundation.

Fortune 500 Companies in 2016

National Total = 500 Companies*

ALPHA ORDER

RANK	STATE	COMPANIES	% of USA
35	Alabama	1	0.2%
38	Alaska	0	0.0%
25	Arizona	4	0.8%
22	Arkansas	6	1.2%
2	California	51	10.2%
17	Colorado	10	2.0%
8	Connecticut	19	3.8%
32	Delaware	2	0.4%
12	Florida	17	3.4%
10	Georgia	18	3.6%
38	Hawaii	0	0.0%
35	Idaho	1	0.2%
4	Illinois	36	7.2%
21	Indiana	7	1.4%
29	Iowa	3	0.6%
29	Kansas	3	0.6%
25	Kentucky	4	0.8%
32	Louisiana	2	0.4%
38	Maine	0	0.0%
25	Maryland	4	0.8%
14	Massachusetts	12	2.4%
10	Michigan	18	3.6%
12	Minnesota	17	3.4%
38	Mississippi	0	0.0%
17	Missouri	10	2.0%
38	Montana	0	0.0%
23	Nebraska	5	1.0%
32	Nevada	2	0.4%
38	New Hampshire	0	0.0%
8	New Jersey	19	3.8%
38	New Mexico	0	0.0%
1	New York	55	11.0%
14	North Carolina	12	2.4%
38	North Dakota	0	0.0%
5	Ohio	24	4.8%
23	Oklahoma	5	1.0%
29	Oregon	3	0.6%
7	Pennsylvania	20	4.0%
25	Rhode Island	4	0.8%
35	South Carolina	1	0.2%
38	South Dakota	0	0.0%
16	Tennessee	11	2.2%
2	Texas	51	10.2%
38	Utah	0	0.0%
38	Vermont	0	0.0%
6	Virginia	21	4.2%
17	Washington	10	2.0%
38	West Virginia	0	0.0%
17	Wisconsin	10	2.0%
38	Wyoming	0	0.0%

RANK ORDER

RANK	STATE	COMPANIES	% of USA
1	New York	55	11.0%
2	California	51	10.2%
2	Texas	51	10.2%
4	Illinois	36	7.2%
5	Ohio	24	4.8%
6	Virginia	21	4.2%
7	Pennsylvania	20	4.0%
8	Connecticut	19	3.8%
8	New Jersey	19	3.8%
10	Georgia	18	3.6%
10	Michigan	18	3.6%
12	Florida	17	3.4%
12	Minnesota	17	3.4%
14	Massachusetts	12	2.4%
14	North Carolina	12	2.4%
16	Tennessee	11	2.2%
17	Colorado	10	2.0%
17	Missouri	10	2.0%
17	Washington	10	2.0%
17	Wisconsin	10	2.0%
21	Indiana	7	1.4%
22	Arkansas	6	1.2%
23	Nebraska	5	1.0%
23	Oklahoma	5	1.0%
25	Arizona	4	0.8%
25	Kentucky	4	0.8%
25	Maryland	4	0.8%
25	Rhode Island	4	0.8%
29	Iowa	3	0.6%
29	Kansas	3	0.6%
29	Oregon	3	0.6%
32	Delaware	2	0.4%
32	Louisiana	2	0.4%
32	Nevada	2	0.4%
35	Alabama	1	0.2%
35	Idaho	1	0.2%
35	South Carolina	1	0.2%
38	Alaska	0	0.0%
38	Hawaii	0	0.0%
38	Maine	0	0.0%
38	Mississippi	0	0.0%
38	Montana	0	0.0%
38	New Hampshire	0	0.0%
38	New Mexico	0	0.0%
38	North Dakota	0	0.0%
38	South Dakota	0	0.0%
38	Utah	0	0.0%
38	Vermont	0	0.0%
38	West Virginia	0	0.0%
38	Wyoming	0	0.0%
	District of Columbia	2	0.4%

Source: Fortune magazine
"Fortune 500" (June 15, 2016)
*By state where each company's headquarters is located.

V. Education

(Continued)

(Continued)

Estimated Percent of School-Age Population in Public Schools in 2015

National Percent = 93.6%*

ALPHA ORDER

RANK	STATE	PERCENT
32	Alabama	91.8
2	Alaska	100.3
26	Arizona	93.1
9	Arkansas	95.4
8	California	95.5
6	Colorado	96.5
19	Connecticut	94.1
40	Delaware	90.2
32	Florida	91.8
15	Georgia	94.6
50	Hawaii	83.5
37	Idaho	90.9
18	Illinois	94.3
40	Indiana	90.2
14	Iowa	95.0
11	Kansas	95.2
22	Kentucky	93.8
44	Louisiana	89.2
11	Maine	95.2
43	Maryland	89.3
23	Massachusetts	93.7
21	Michigan	94.0
32	Minnesota	91.8
30	Mississippi	91.9
40	Missouri	90.2
49	Montana	87.8
29	Nebraska	92.0
25	Nevada	93.2
27	New Hampshire	92.6
9	New Jersey	95.4
19	New Mexico	94.1
39	New York	90.6
30	North Carolina	91.9
47	North Dakota	88.2
45	Ohio	89.1
4	Oklahoma	99.3
13	Oregon	95.1
47	Pennsylvania	88.2
36	Rhode Island	91.0
17	South Carolina	94.4
46	South Dakota	88.6
37	Tennessee	90.9
3	Texas	100.1
7	Utah	96.0
5	Vermont	97.5
16	Virginia	94.5
28	Washington	92.2
1	West Virginia	101.5
35	Wisconsin	91.3
24	Wyoming	93.6

RANK ORDER

RANK	STATE	PERCENT
1	West Virginia	101.5
2	Alaska	100.3
3	Texas	100.1
4	Oklahoma	99.3
5	Vermont	97.5
6	Colorado	96.5
7	Utah	96.0
8	California	95.5
9	Arkansas	95.4
9	New Jersey	95.4
11	Kansas	95.2
11	Maine	95.2
13	Oregon	95.1
14	Iowa	95.0
15	Georgia	94.6
16	Virginia	94.5
17	South Carolina	94.4
18	Illinois	94.3
19	Connecticut	94.1
19	New Mexico	94.1
21	Michigan	94.0
22	Kentucky	93.8
23	Massachusetts	93.7
24	Wyoming	93.6
25	Nevada	93.2
26	Arizona	93.1
27	New Hampshire	92.6
28	Washington	92.2
29	Nebraska	92.0
30	Mississippi	91.9
30	North Carolina	91.9
32	Alabama	91.8
32	Florida	91.8
32	Minnesota	91.8
35	Wisconsin	91.3
36	Rhode Island	91.0
37	Idaho	90.9
37	Tennessee	90.9
39	New York	90.6
40	Delaware	90.2
40	Indiana	90.2
40	Missouri	90.2
43	Maryland	89.3
44	Louisiana	89.2
45	Ohio	89.1
46	South Dakota	88.6
47	North Dakota	88.2
47	Pennsylvania	88.2
49	Montana	87.8
50	Hawaii	83.5

District of Columbia 108.3

Source: CQ Press using data from U.S. Department of Education, National Center for Education Statistics
"Selected Statistics From the Public Elementary and Secondary Education Universe: School Year 2014-15"
*Estimate based on 2015 Census population estimates for 5- to 17-year-olds compared to estimated 2014-2015 school year public school student membership. Student membership figures include counts for pre-kindergarten programs. Figures higher than 100 percent reflect using different sources for population and for student membership.

Regular Public Elementary and Secondary School Districts in 2015

National Total = 13,601 Districts*

ALPHA ORDER

RANK	STATE	DISTRICTS	% of USA
34	Alabama	134	1.0%
43	Alaska	53	0.4%
23	Arizona	234	1.7%
22	Arkansas	235	1.7%
1	California	1,058	7.8%
27	Colorado	178	1.3%
30	Connecticut	169	1.2%
48	Delaware	19	0.1%
41	Florida	67	0.5%
24	Georgia	180	1.3%
50	Hawaii	1	0.0%
36	Idaho	115	0.8%
3	Illinois	859	6.3%
17	Indiana	295	2.2%
13	Iowa	338	2.5%
15	Kansas	307	2.3%
29	Kentucky	173	1.3%
40	Louisiana	69	0.5%
20	Maine	243	1.8%
47	Maryland	24	0.2%
21	Massachusetts	238	1.7%
7	Michigan	548	4.0%
14	Minnesota	332	2.4%
32	Mississippi	146	1.1%
8	Missouri	520	3.8%
12	Montana	406	3.0%
19	Nebraska	245	1.8%
49	Nevada	18	0.1%
26	New Hampshire	179	1.3%
6	New Jersey	602	4.4%
38	New Mexico	89	0.7%
4	New York	691	5.1%
36	North Carolina	115	0.8%
28	North Dakota	175	1.3%
5	Ohio	617	4.5%
9	Oklahoma	517	3.8%
24	Oregon	180	1.3%
10	Pennsylvania	500	3.7%
46	Rhode Island	32	0.2%
39	South Carolina	84	0.6%
31	South Dakota	151	1.1%
32	Tennessee	146	1.1%
2	Texas	1,026	7.5%
45	Utah	41	0.3%
18	Vermont	294	2.2%
35	Virginia	130	1.0%
16	Washington	302	2.2%
42	West Virginia	55	0.4%
11	Wisconsin	422	3.1%
44	Wyoming	48	0.4%

RANK ORDER

RANK	STATE	DISTRICTS	% of USA
1	California	1,058	7.8%
2	Texas	1,026	7.5%
3	Illinois	859	6.3%
4	New York	691	5.1%
5	Ohio	617	4.5%
6	New Jersey	602	4.4%
7	Michigan	548	4.0%
8	Missouri	520	3.8%
9	Oklahoma	517	3.8%
10	Pennsylvania	500	3.7%
11	Wisconsin	422	3.1%
12	Montana	406	3.0%
13	Iowa	338	2.5%
14	Minnesota	332	2.4%
15	Kansas	307	2.3%
16	Washington	302	2.2%
17	Indiana	295	2.2%
18	Vermont	294	2.2%
19	Nebraska	245	1.8%
20	Maine	243	1.8%
21	Massachusetts	238	1.7%
22	Arkansas	235	1.7%
23	Arizona	234	1.7%
24	Georgia	180	1.3%
24	Oregon	180	1.3%
26	New Hampshire	179	1.3%
27	Colorado	178	1.3%
28	North Dakota	175	1.3%
29	Kentucky	173	1.3%
30	Connecticut	169	1.2%
31	South Dakota	151	1.1%
32	Mississippi	146	1.1%
32	Tennessee	146	1.1%
34	Alabama	134	1.0%
35	Virginia	130	1.0%
36	Idaho	115	0.8%
36	North Carolina	115	0.8%
38	New Mexico	89	0.7%
39	South Carolina	84	0.6%
40	Louisiana	69	0.5%
41	Florida	67	0.5%
42	West Virginia	55	0.4%
43	Alaska	53	0.4%
44	Wyoming	48	0.4%
45	Utah	41	0.3%
46	Rhode Island	32	0.2%
47	Maryland	24	0.2%
48	Delaware	19	0.1%
49	Nevada	18	0.1%
50	Hawaii	1	0.0%
	District of Columbia	1	0.0%

Source: U.S. Department of Education, National Center for Education Statistics
"Digest of Education Statistics 2016" (http://nces.ed.gov/programs/digest/index.asp)
*For school year 2014-2015. Regular school districts are agencies responsible for providing free public education for school-age children residing within their jurisdiction. Included in these figures are districts that reported having no students. This can occur when a small district has no pupils or contracts with another district to educate the students under its jurisdiction.

Private Elementary and Secondary Schools in 2014

National Total = 33,619 Schools*

<table>
<tr><td colspan="4">ALPHA ORDER</td><td colspan="4">RANK ORDER</td></tr>
<tr><td>RANK</td><td>STATE</td><td>SCHOOLS</td><td>% of USA</td><td>RANK</td><td>STATE</td><td>SCHOOLS</td><td>% of USA</td></tr>
<tr><td>25</td><td>Alabama</td><td>404</td><td>1.2%</td><td>1</td><td>California</td><td>3,392</td><td>10.1%</td></tr>
<tr><td>46</td><td>Alaska</td><td>50</td><td>0.1%</td><td>2</td><td>Pennsylvania</td><td>2,316</td><td>6.9%</td></tr>
<tr><td>28</td><td>Arizona</td><td>341</td><td>1.0%</td><td>3</td><td>Florida</td><td>2,137</td><td>6.4%</td></tr>
<tr><td>33</td><td>Arkansas</td><td>190</td><td>0.6%</td><td>4</td><td>New York</td><td>1,875</td><td>5.6%</td></tr>
<tr><td>1</td><td>California</td><td>3,392</td><td>10.1%</td><td>5</td><td>Texas</td><td>1,738</td><td>5.2%</td></tr>
<tr><td>22</td><td>Colorado</td><td>430</td><td>1.3%</td><td>6</td><td>Illinois</td><td>1,552</td><td>4.6%</td></tr>
<tr><td>26</td><td>Connecticut</td><td>403</td><td>1.2%</td><td>7</td><td>New Jersey</td><td>1,267</td><td>3.8%</td></tr>
<tr><td>43</td><td>Delaware</td><td>120</td><td>0.4%</td><td>8</td><td>Ohio</td><td>1,160</td><td>3.5%</td></tr>
<tr><td>3</td><td>Florida</td><td>2,137</td><td>6.4%</td><td>9</td><td>Virginia</td><td>907</td><td>2.7%</td></tr>
<tr><td>16</td><td>Georgia</td><td>743</td><td>2.2%</td><td>10</td><td>Wisconsin</td><td>897</td><td>2.7%</td></tr>
<tr><td>41</td><td>Hawaii</td><td>127</td><td>0.4%</td><td>11</td><td>Indiana</td><td>867</td><td>2.6%</td></tr>
<tr><td>32</td><td>Idaho</td><td>195</td><td>0.6%</td><td>12</td><td>Massachusetts</td><td>797</td><td>2.4%</td></tr>
<tr><td>6</td><td>Illinois</td><td>1,552</td><td>4.6%</td><td>13</td><td>Washington</td><td>795</td><td>2.4%</td></tr>
<tr><td>11</td><td>Indiana</td><td>867</td><td>2.6%</td><td>14</td><td>Michigan</td><td>783</td><td>2.3%</td></tr>
<tr><td>NA</td><td>Iowa**</td><td>NA</td><td>NA</td><td>15</td><td>Maryland</td><td>773</td><td>2.3%</td></tr>
<tr><td>27</td><td>Kansas</td><td>358</td><td>1.1%</td><td>16</td><td>Georgia</td><td>743</td><td>2.2%</td></tr>
<tr><td>21</td><td>Kentucky</td><td>470</td><td>1.4%</td><td>17</td><td>North Carolina</td><td>688</td><td>2.0%</td></tr>
<tr><td>24</td><td>Louisiana</td><td>422</td><td>1.3%</td><td>18</td><td>Tennessee</td><td>563</td><td>1.7%</td></tr>
<tr><td>34</td><td>Maine</td><td>186</td><td>0.6%</td><td>19</td><td>Minnesota</td><td>501</td><td>1.5%</td></tr>
<tr><td>15</td><td>Maryland</td><td>773</td><td>2.3%</td><td>20</td><td>Oregon</td><td>483</td><td>1.4%</td></tr>
<tr><td>12</td><td>Massachusetts</td><td>797</td><td>2.4%</td><td>21</td><td>Kentucky</td><td>470</td><td>1.4%</td></tr>
<tr><td>14</td><td>Michigan</td><td>783</td><td>2.3%</td><td>22</td><td>Colorado</td><td>430</td><td>1.3%</td></tr>
<tr><td>19</td><td>Minnesota</td><td>501</td><td>1.5%</td><td>23</td><td>South Carolina</td><td>427</td><td>1.3%</td></tr>
<tr><td>29</td><td>Mississippi</td><td>308</td><td>0.9%</td><td>24</td><td>Louisiana</td><td>422</td><td>1.3%</td></tr>
<tr><td>NA</td><td>Missouri**</td><td>NA</td><td>NA</td><td>25</td><td>Alabama</td><td>404</td><td>1.2%</td></tr>
<tr><td>39</td><td>Montana</td><td>140</td><td>0.4%</td><td>26</td><td>Connecticut</td><td>403</td><td>1.2%</td></tr>
<tr><td>31</td><td>Nebraska</td><td>223</td><td>0.7%</td><td>27</td><td>Kansas</td><td>358</td><td>1.1%</td></tr>
<tr><td>38</td><td>Nevada</td><td>142</td><td>0.4%</td><td>28</td><td>Arizona</td><td>341</td><td>1.0%</td></tr>
<tr><td>30</td><td>New Hampshire</td><td>278</td><td>0.8%</td><td>29</td><td>Mississippi</td><td>308</td><td>0.9%</td></tr>
<tr><td>7</td><td>New Jersey</td><td>1,267</td><td>3.8%</td><td>30</td><td>New Hampshire</td><td>278</td><td>0.8%</td></tr>
<tr><td>35</td><td>New Mexico</td><td>168</td><td>0.5%</td><td>31</td><td>Nebraska</td><td>223</td><td>0.7%</td></tr>
<tr><td>4</td><td>New York</td><td>1,875</td><td>5.6%</td><td>32</td><td>Idaho</td><td>195</td><td>0.6%</td></tr>
<tr><td>17</td><td>North Carolina</td><td>688</td><td>2.0%</td><td>33</td><td>Arkansas</td><td>190</td><td>0.6%</td></tr>
<tr><td>46</td><td>North Dakota</td><td>50</td><td>0.1%</td><td>34</td><td>Maine</td><td>186</td><td>0.6%</td></tr>
<tr><td>8</td><td>Ohio</td><td>1,160</td><td>3.5%</td><td>35</td><td>New Mexico</td><td>168</td><td>0.5%</td></tr>
<tr><td>36</td><td>Oklahoma</td><td>166</td><td>0.5%</td><td>36</td><td>Oklahoma</td><td>166</td><td>0.5%</td></tr>
<tr><td>20</td><td>Oregon</td><td>483</td><td>1.4%</td><td>37</td><td>Utah</td><td>159</td><td>0.5%</td></tr>
<tr><td>2</td><td>Pennsylvania</td><td>2,316</td><td>6.9%</td><td>38</td><td>Nevada</td><td>142</td><td>0.4%</td></tr>
<tr><td>40</td><td>Rhode Island</td><td>134</td><td>0.4%</td><td>39</td><td>Montana</td><td>140</td><td>0.4%</td></tr>
<tr><td>23</td><td>South Carolina</td><td>427</td><td>1.3%</td><td>40</td><td>Rhode Island</td><td>134</td><td>0.4%</td></tr>
<tr><td>45</td><td>South Dakota</td><td>70</td><td>0.2%</td><td>41</td><td>Hawaii</td><td>127</td><td>0.4%</td></tr>
<tr><td>18</td><td>Tennessee</td><td>563</td><td>1.7%</td><td>42</td><td>West Virginia</td><td>125</td><td>0.4%</td></tr>
<tr><td>5</td><td>Texas</td><td>1,738</td><td>5.2%</td><td>43</td><td>Delaware</td><td>120</td><td>0.4%</td></tr>
<tr><td>37</td><td>Utah</td><td>159</td><td>0.5%</td><td>44</td><td>Vermont</td><td>109</td><td>0.3%</td></tr>
<tr><td>44</td><td>Vermont</td><td>109</td><td>0.3%</td><td>45</td><td>South Dakota</td><td>70</td><td>0.2%</td></tr>
<tr><td>9</td><td>Virginia</td><td>907</td><td>2.7%</td><td>46</td><td>Alaska</td><td>50</td><td>0.1%</td></tr>
<tr><td>13</td><td>Washington</td><td>795</td><td>2.4%</td><td>46</td><td>North Dakota</td><td>50</td><td>0.1%</td></tr>
<tr><td>42</td><td>West Virginia</td><td>125</td><td>0.4%</td><td>48</td><td>Wyoming</td><td>40</td><td>0.1%</td></tr>
<tr><td>10</td><td>Wisconsin</td><td>897</td><td>2.7%</td><td>NA</td><td>Iowa**</td><td>NA</td><td>NA</td></tr>
<tr><td>48</td><td>Wyoming</td><td>40</td><td>0.1%</td><td>NA</td><td>Missouri**</td><td>NA</td><td>NA</td></tr>
<tr><td></td><td></td><td></td><td></td><td></td><td>District of Columbia</td><td>90</td><td>0.3%</td></tr>
</table>

Source: U.S. Department of Education, National Center for Education Statistics
   "Characteristics of Private Schools in the United States" (https://nces.ed.gov/pubsearch/pubsinfo.asp?pubid=2016243)
*For school year 2013-2014. Includes private schools that provide instruction for one or more grades kindergarten through 12 (or comparable ungraded levels).
**Not available.

Private Elementary and Secondary School Enrollment in 2014

National Total = 4,576,410 Students*

ALPHA ORDER					RANK ORDER			
RANK	STATE	STUDENTS	% of USA		RANK	STATE	STUDENTS	% of USA
23	Alabama	64,757	1.4%		1	California	513,164	11.2%
49	Alaska	3,979	0.1%		2	New York	401,119	8.8%
28	Arizona	45,019	1.0%		3	Florida	312,227	6.8%
35	Arkansas	25,862	0.6%		4	Texas	245,915	5.4%
1	California	513,164	11.2%		5	Illinois	227,709	5.0%
30	Colorado	42,187	0.9%		6	Pennsylvania	220,526	4.8%
22	Connecticut	64,840	1.4%		7	Ohio	208,971	4.6%
37	Delaware	20,722	0.5%		8	New Jersey	165,503	3.6%
3	Florida	312,227	6.8%		9	Wisconsin	142,724	3.1%
10	Georgia	130,260	2.8%		10	Georgia	130,260	2.8%
33	Hawaii	30,827	0.7%		11	Missouri	125,618	2.7%
43	Idaho	13,344	0.3%		12	Michigan	123,726	2.7%
5	Illinois	227,709	5.0%		13	Maryland	122,496	2.7%
17	Indiana	104,874	2.3%		14	Massachusetts	117,151	2.6%
25	Iowa	49,013	1.1%		15	Louisiana	115,178	2.5%
32	Kansas	35,346	0.8%		16	North Carolina	104,978	2.3%
24	Kentucky	63,293	1.4%		17	Indiana	104,874	2.3%
15	Louisiana	115,178	2.5%		18	Virginia	101,606	2.2%
42	Maine	16,819	0.4%		19	Washington	98,503	2.2%
13	Maryland	122,496	2.7%		20	Tennessee	81,545	1.8%
14	Massachusetts	117,151	2.6%		21	Minnesota	72,680	1.6%
12	Michigan	123,726	2.7%		22	Connecticut	64,840	1.4%
21	Minnesota	72,680	1.6%		23	Alabama	64,757	1.4%
29	Mississippi	43,969	1.0%		24	Kentucky	63,293	1.4%
11	Missouri	125,618	2.7%		25	Iowa	49,013	1.1%
45	Montana	8,427	0.2%		26	South Carolina	48,152	1.1%
31	Nebraska	37,444	0.8%		27	Oregon	47,164	1.0%
41	Nevada	17,101	0.4%		28	Arizona	45,019	1.0%
36	New Hampshire	20,772	0.5%		29	Mississippi	43,969	1.0%
8	New Jersey	165,503	3.6%		30	Colorado	42,187	0.9%
40	New Mexico	18,714	0.4%		31	Nebraska	37,444	0.8%
2	New York	401,119	8.8%		32	Kansas	35,346	0.8%
16	North Carolina	104,978	2.3%		33	Hawaii	30,827	0.7%
48	North Dakota	6,791	0.1%		34	Oklahoma	27,585	0.6%
7	Ohio	208,971	4.6%		35	Arkansas	25,862	0.6%
34	Oklahoma	27,585	0.6%		36	New Hampshire	20,772	0.5%
27	Oregon	47,164	1.0%		37	Delaware	20,722	0.5%
6	Pennsylvania	220,526	4.8%		38	Rhode Island	19,552	0.4%
38	Rhode Island	19,552	0.4%		39	Utah	19,396	0.4%
26	South Carolina	48,152	1.1%		40	New Mexico	18,714	0.4%
47	South Dakota	7,787	0.2%		41	Nevada	17,101	0.4%
20	Tennessee	81,545	1.8%		42	Maine	16,819	0.4%
4	Texas	245,915	5.4%		43	Idaho	13,344	0.3%
39	Utah	19,396	0.4%		44	West Virginia	12,767	0.3%
46	Vermont	8,087	0.2%		45	Montana	8,427	0.2%
18	Virginia	101,606	2.2%		46	Vermont	8,087	0.2%
19	Washington	98,503	2.2%		47	South Dakota	7,787	0.2%
44	West Virginia	12,767	0.3%		48	North Dakota	6,791	0.1%
9	Wisconsin	142,724	3.1%		49	Alaska	3,979	0.1%
50	Wyoming	1,957	0.0%		50	Wyoming	1,957	0.0%
						District of Columbia	18,263	0.4%

Source: U.S. Department of Education, National Center for Education Statistics
"Characteristics of Private Schools in the United States" (https://nces.ed.gov/pubsearch/pubsinfo.asp?pubid=2016243)
*For school year 2013-2014. Includes private schools that provide instruction for one or more grades kindergarten through 12 (or comparable ungraded levels).

Public Elementary and Secondary Schools in 2015

National Total = 98,373 Schools*

ALPHA ORDER

RANK	STATE	SCHOOLS	% of USA
24	Alabama	1,519	1.5%
44	Alaska	507	0.5%
15	Arizona	2,281	2.3%
32	Arkansas	1,100	1.1%
1	California	10,303	10.5%
21	Colorado	1,843	1.9%
29	Connecticut	1,299	1.3%
50	Delaware	219	0.2%
4	Florida	4,319	4.4%
14	Georgia	2,329	2.4%
49	Hawaii	289	0.3%
39	Idaho	742	0.8%
5	Illinois	4,201	4.3%
18	Indiana	1,910	1.9%
27	Iowa	1,364	1.4%
28	Kansas	1,337	1.4%
23	Kentucky	1,548	1.6%
26	Louisiana	1,383	1.4%
42	Maine	616	0.6%
25	Maryland	1,438	1.5%
19	Massachusetts	1,866	1.9%
7	Michigan	3,496	3.6%
11	Minnesota	2,435	2.5%
34	Mississippi	1,071	1.1%
12	Missouri	2,414	2.5%
37	Montana	824	0.8%
33	Nebraska	1,092	1.1%
41	Nevada	665	0.7%
45	New Hampshire	488	0.5%
10	New Jersey	2,571	2.6%
36	New Mexico	885	0.9%
3	New York	4,826	4.9%
9	North Carolina	2,594	2.6%
43	North Dakota	513	0.5%
6	Ohio	3,631	3.7%
22	Oklahoma	1,796	1.8%
31	Oregon	1,242	1.3%
8	Pennsylvania	3,055	3.1%
48	Rhode Island	307	0.3%
30	South Carolina	1,244	1.3%
40	South Dakota	698	0.7%
20	Tennessee	1,851	1.9%
2	Texas	8,798	8.9%
35	Utah	1,020	1.0%
47	Vermont	316	0.3%
17	Virginia	2,134	2.2%
13	Washington	2,398	2.4%
38	West Virginia	745	0.8%
16	Wisconsin	2,255	2.3%
46	Wyoming	367	0.4%

RANK ORDER

RANK	STATE	SCHOOLS	% of USA
1	California	10,303	10.5%
2	Texas	8,798	8.9%
3	New York	4,826	4.9%
4	Florida	4,319	4.4%
5	Illinois	4,201	4.3%
6	Ohio	3,631	3.7%
7	Michigan	3,496	3.6%
8	Pennsylvania	3,055	3.1%
9	North Carolina	2,594	2.6%
10	New Jersey	2,571	2.6%
11	Minnesota	2,435	2.5%
12	Missouri	2,414	2.5%
13	Washington	2,398	2.4%
14	Georgia	2,329	2.4%
15	Arizona	2,281	2.3%
16	Wisconsin	2,255	2.3%
17	Virginia	2,134	2.2%
18	Indiana	1,910	1.9%
19	Massachusetts	1,866	1.9%
20	Tennessee	1,851	1.9%
21	Colorado	1,843	1.9%
22	Oklahoma	1,796	1.8%
23	Kentucky	1,548	1.6%
24	Alabama	1,519	1.5%
25	Maryland	1,438	1.5%
26	Louisiana	1,383	1.4%
27	Iowa	1,364	1.4%
28	Kansas	1,337	1.4%
29	Connecticut	1,299	1.3%
30	South Carolina	1,244	1.3%
31	Oregon	1,242	1.3%
32	Arkansas	1,100	1.1%
33	Nebraska	1,092	1.1%
34	Mississippi	1,071	1.1%
35	Utah	1,020	1.0%
36	New Mexico	885	0.9%
37	Montana	824	0.8%
38	West Virginia	745	0.8%
39	Idaho	742	0.8%
40	South Dakota	698	0.7%
41	Nevada	665	0.7%
42	Maine	616	0.6%
43	North Dakota	513	0.5%
44	Alaska	507	0.5%
45	New Hampshire	488	0.5%
46	Wyoming	367	0.4%
47	Vermont	316	0.3%
48	Rhode Island	307	0.3%
49	Hawaii	289	0.3%
50	Delaware	219	0.2%
	District of Columbia	229	0.2%

Source: U.S. Department of Education, National Center for Education Statistics
   "Selected Statistics From the Public Elementary and Secondary Education Universe: School Year 2014-15"
*For school year 2014-2015.

Enrollment in Public Elementary and Secondary Schools in 2015

National Total = 50,312,581 Students*

ALPHA ORDER

RANK	STATE	STUDENTS	% of USA
24	Alabama	744,164	1.5%
47	Alaska	131,176	0.3%
13	Arizona	1,111,695	2.2%
33	Arkansas	490,917	1.0%
1	California	6,312,161	12.5%
19	Colorado	889,006	1.8%
30	Connecticut	542,678	1.1%
45	Delaware	134,042	0.3%
3	Florida	2,756,944	5.5%
6	Georgia	1,744,437	3.5%
42	Hawaii	182,384	0.4%
38	Idaho	290,885	0.6%
5	Illinois	2,050,239	4.1%
15	Indiana	1,046,269	2.1%
31	Iowa	505,311	1.0%
32	Kansas	497,275	1.0%
26	Kentucky	688,640	1.4%
25	Louisiana	716,800	1.4%
41	Maine	182,470	0.4%
20	Maryland	874,514	1.7%
17	Massachusetts	955,844	1.9%
10	Michigan	1,537,922	3.1%
22	Minnesota	857,235	1.7%
33	Mississippi	490,917	1.0%
18	Missouri	917,785	1.8%
43	Montana	144,532	0.3%
37	Nebraska	312,635	0.6%
35	Nevada	459,189	0.9%
40	New Hampshire	184,670	0.4%
11	New Jersey	1,400,579	2.8%
36	New Mexico	340,365	0.7%
4	New York	2,741,185	5.4%
9	North Carolina	1,548,895	3.1%
48	North Dakota	106,586	0.2%
8	Ohio	1,724,810	3.4%
27	Oklahoma	688,511	1.4%
29	Oregon	601,318	1.2%
7	Pennsylvania	1,743,160	3.5%
44	Rhode Island	141,959	0.3%
23	South Carolina	756,523	1.5%
46	South Dakota	133,040	0.3%
16	Tennessee	995,475	2.0%
2	Texas	5,233,765	10.4%
28	Utah	635,577	1.3%
50	Vermont	87,311	0.2%
12	Virginia	1,280,381	2.5%
14	Washington	1,073,638	2.1%
39	West Virginia	280,310	0.6%
21	Wisconsin	871,432	1.7%
49	Wyoming	94,067	0.2%

RANK ORDER

RANK	STATE	STUDENTS	% of USA
1	California	6,312,161	12.5%
2	Texas	5,233,765	10.4%
3	Florida	2,756,944	5.5%
4	New York	2,741,185	5.4%
5	Illinois	2,050,239	4.1%
6	Georgia	1,744,437	3.5%
7	Pennsylvania	1,743,160	3.5%
8	Ohio	1,724,810	3.4%
9	North Carolina	1,548,895	3.1%
10	Michigan	1,537,922	3.1%
11	New Jersey	1,400,579	2.8%
12	Virginia	1,280,381	2.5%
13	Arizona	1,111,695	2.2%
14	Washington	1,073,638	2.1%
15	Indiana	1,046,269	2.1%
16	Tennessee	995,475	2.0%
17	Massachusetts	955,844	1.9%
18	Missouri	917,785	1.8%
19	Colorado	889,006	1.8%
20	Maryland	874,514	1.7%
21	Wisconsin	871,432	1.7%
22	Minnesota	857,235	1.7%
23	South Carolina	756,523	1.5%
24	Alabama	744,164	1.5%
25	Louisiana	716,800	1.4%
26	Kentucky	688,640	1.4%
27	Oklahoma	688,511	1.4%
28	Utah	635,577	1.3%
29	Oregon	601,318	1.2%
30	Connecticut	542,678	1.1%
31	Iowa	505,311	1.0%
32	Kansas	497,275	1.0%
33	Arkansas	490,917	1.0%
33	Mississippi	490,917	1.0%
35	Nevada	459,189	0.9%
36	New Mexico	340,365	0.7%
37	Nebraska	312,635	0.6%
38	Idaho	290,885	0.6%
39	West Virginia	280,310	0.6%
40	New Hampshire	184,670	0.4%
41	Maine	182,470	0.4%
42	Hawaii	182,384	0.4%
43	Montana	144,532	0.3%
44	Rhode Island	141,959	0.3%
45	Delaware	134,042	0.3%
46	South Dakota	133,040	0.3%
47	Alaska	131,176	0.3%
48	North Dakota	106,586	0.2%
49	Wyoming	94,067	0.2%
50	Vermont	87,311	0.2%
	District of Columbia	80,958	0.2%

Source: U.S. Department of Education, National Center for Education Statistics
    "Selected Statistics From the Public Elementary and Secondary Education Universe: School Year 2014-15"
*For school year 2014-2015.

Public Elementary and Secondary School Teachers in 2015

National Total = 3,132,351 Teachers*

RANK	STATE	TEACHERS	% of USA
25	Alabama	42,737	1.4%
49	Alaska	7,759	0.2%
23	Arizona	48,124	1.5%
31	Arkansas	35,430	1.1%
2	California	267,685	8.5%
21	Colorado	51,388	1.6%
27	Connecticut	42,062	1.3%
44	Delaware	9,649	0.3%
4	Florida	180,442	5.8%
8	Georgia	111,470	3.6%
42	Hawaii	11,663	0.4%
39	Idaho	15,609	0.5%
5	Illinois	132,456	4.2%
19	Indiana	56,547	1.8%
30	Iowa	35,684	1.1%
29	Kansas	37,659	1.2%
28	Kentucky	41,586	1.3%
24	Louisiana	46,340	1.5%
40	Maine	14,937	0.5%
17	Maryland	59,194	1.9%
13	Massachusetts	71,859	2.3%
12	Michigan	85,038	2.7%
20	Minnesota	55,690	1.8%
32	Mississippi	32,311	1.0%
14	Missouri	67,356	2.2%
43	Montana	10,234	0.3%
35	Nebraska	22,988	0.7%
37	Nevada	21,656	0.7%
41	New Hampshire	14,773	0.5%
7	New Jersey	115,067	3.7%
36	New Mexico	22,411	0.7%
3	New York	203,781	6.5%
10	North Carolina	99,320	3.2%
47	North Dakota	9,049	0.3%
9	Ohio	106,526	3.4%
26	Oklahoma	42,073	1.3%
33	Oregon	27,850	0.9%
6	Pennsylvania	122,030	3.9%
46	Rhode Island	9,471	0.3%
22	South Carolina	49,475	1.6%
45	South Dakota	9,618	0.3%
15	Tennessee	65,341	2.1%
1	Texas	342,257	10.9%
34	Utah	27,374	0.9%
48	Vermont	8,276	0.3%
11	Virginia	89,968	2.9%
16	Washington	59,555	1.9%
38	West Virginia	20,029	0.6%
18	Wisconsin	58,376	1.9%
50	Wyoming	7,615	0.2%

RANK	STATE	TEACHERS	% of USA
1	Texas	342,257	10.9%
2	California	267,685	8.5%
3	New York	203,781	6.5%
4	Florida	180,442	5.8%
5	Illinois	132,456	4.2%
6	Pennsylvania	122,030	3.9%
7	New Jersey	115,067	3.7%
8	Georgia	111,470	3.6%
9	Ohio	106,526	3.4%
10	North Carolina	99,320	3.2%
11	Virginia	89,968	2.9%
12	Michigan	85,038	2.7%
13	Massachusetts	71,859	2.3%
14	Missouri	67,356	2.2%
15	Tennessee	65,341	2.1%
16	Washington	59,555	1.9%
17	Maryland	59,194	1.9%
18	Wisconsin	58,376	1.9%
19	Indiana	56,547	1.8%
20	Minnesota	55,690	1.8%
21	Colorado	51,388	1.6%
22	South Carolina	49,475	1.6%
23	Arizona	48,124	1.5%
24	Louisiana	46,340	1.5%
25	Alabama	42,737	1.4%
26	Oklahoma	42,073	1.3%
27	Connecticut	42,062	1.3%
28	Kentucky	41,586	1.3%
29	Kansas	37,659	1.2%
30	Iowa	35,684	1.1%
31	Arkansas	35,430	1.1%
32	Mississippi	32,311	1.0%
33	Oregon	27,850	0.9%
34	Utah	27,374	0.9%
35	Nebraska	22,988	0.7%
36	New Mexico	22,411	0.7%
37	Nevada	21,656	0.7%
38	West Virginia	20,029	0.6%
39	Idaho	15,609	0.5%
40	Maine	14,937	0.5%
41	New Hampshire	14,773	0.5%
42	Hawaii	11,663	0.4%
43	Montana	10,234	0.3%
44	Delaware	9,649	0.3%
45	South Dakota	9,618	0.3%
46	Rhode Island	9,471	0.3%
47	North Dakota	9,049	0.3%
48	Vermont	8,276	0.3%
49	Alaska	7,759	0.2%
50	Wyoming	7,615	0.2%
	District of Columbia	6,565	0.2%

Source: U.S. Department of Education, National Center for Education Statistics
   "Selected Statistics From the Public Elementary and Secondary Education Universe: School Year 2014-15"
*For school year 2014-2015. Counts are full-time equivalent figures.

Pupil-Teacher Ratio in Public Elementary and Secondary Schools in 2015

National Ratio = 16.1 Pupils Per Teacher*

ALPHA ORDER				RANK ORDER		
RANK	STATE	RATIO		RANK	STATE	RATIO
10	Alabama	17.4		1	California	23.6
12	Alaska	16.9		2	Utah	23.2
3	Arizona	23.1		3	Arizona	23.1
36	Arkansas	13.9		4	Oregon	21.6
1	California	23.6		5	Nevada	21.2
11	Colorado	17.3		6	Idaho	18.6
44	Connecticut	12.9		7	Indiana	18.5
36	Delaware	13.9		8	Michigan	18.1
22	Florida	15.3		9	Washington	18.0
16	Georgia	15.6		10	Alabama	17.4
16	Hawaii	15.6		11	Colorado	17.3
6	Idaho	18.6		12	Alaska	16.9
19	Illinois	15.5		13	Kentucky	16.6
7	Indiana	18.5		14	Oklahoma	16.4
32	Iowa	14.2		15	Ohio	16.2
43	Kansas	13.2		16	Georgia	15.6
13	Kentucky	16.6		16	Hawaii	15.6
19	Louisiana	15.5		16	North Carolina	15.6
47	Maine	12.2		19	Illinois	15.5
30	Maryland	14.8		19	Louisiana	15.5
42	Massachusetts	13.3		21	Minnesota	15.4
8	Michigan	18.1		22	Florida	15.3
21	Minnesota	15.4		22	South Carolina	15.3
25	Mississippi	15.2		22	Texas	15.3
39	Missouri	13.6		25	Mississippi	15.2
34	Montana	14.1		25	New Mexico	15.2
39	Nebraska	13.6		25	Tennessee	15.2
5	Nevada	21.2		28	Rhode Island	15.0
45	New Hampshire	12.5		29	Wisconsin	14.9
47	New Jersey	12.2		30	Maryland	14.8
25	New Mexico	15.2		31	Pennsylvania	14.3
41	New York	13.5		32	Iowa	14.2
16	North Carolina	15.6		32	Virginia	14.2
49	North Dakota	11.8		34	Montana	14.1
15	Ohio	16.2		35	West Virginia	14.0
14	Oklahoma	16.4		36	Arkansas	13.9
4	Oregon	21.6		36	Delaware	13.9
31	Pennsylvania	14.3		38	South Dakota	13.8
28	Rhode Island	15.0		39	Missouri	13.6
22	South Carolina	15.3		39	Nebraska	13.6
38	South Dakota	13.8		41	New York	13.5
25	Tennessee	15.2		42	Massachusetts	13.3
22	Texas	15.3		43	Kansas	13.2
2	Utah	23.2		44	Connecticut	12.9
50	Vermont	10.6		45	New Hampshire	12.5
32	Virginia	14.2		46	Wyoming	12.4
9	Washington	18.0		47	Maine	12.2
35	West Virginia	14.0		47	New Jersey	12.2
29	Wisconsin	14.9		49	North Dakota	11.8
46	Wyoming	12.4		50	Vermont	10.6
					District of Columbia	12.3

Source: U.S. Department of Education, National Center for Education Statistics
"Selected Statistics From the Public Elementary and Secondary Education Universe: School Year 2014-15"
*For school year 2014-2015. Based on full-time equivalency counts of teachers.

Estimated Average Salary of Public School Teachers in 2016
(National Education Association)
National Average = $58,064*

ALPHA ORDER

RANK	STATE	SALARY
34	Alabama	$49,781
6	Alaska	67,443
46	Arizona	45,477
39	Arkansas	48,220
3	California	72,842
33	Colorado	50,039
4	Connecticut	72,013
13	Delaware	59,085
35	Florida	49,199
23	Georgia	54,190
17	Hawaii	57,431
47	Idaho	45,409
11	Illinois	61,342
30	Indiana	50,715
22	Iowa	54,416
36	Kansas	49,197
26	Kentucky	51,666
43	Louisiana	46,733
32	Maine	50,229
7	Maryland	66,482
2	Massachusetts	76,981
10	Michigan	63,878
19	Minnesota	56,910
49	Mississippi	42,744
41	Missouri	47,849
28	Montana	51,215
27	Nebraska	51,364
18	Nevada	56,943
15	New Hampshire	58,802
5	New Jersey	69,330
42	New Mexico	47,163
1	New York	77,957
40	North Carolina	47,985
31	North Dakota	50,237
20	Ohio	56,410
48	Oklahoma	44,921
12	Oregon	60,064
9	Pennsylvania	64,991
8	Rhode Island	66,197
38	South Carolina	48,542
50	South Dakota	42,025
37	Tennessee	48,708
25	Texas	51,758
44	Utah	46,042
14	Vermont	58,901
29	Virginia	50,834
24	Washington	52,539
45	West Virginia	45,977
21	Wisconsin	54,766
16	Wyoming	57,761

RANK ORDER

RANK	STATE	SALARY
1	New York	$77,957
2	Massachusetts	76,981
3	California	72,842
4	Connecticut	72,013
5	New Jersey	69,330
6	Alaska	67,443
7	Maryland	66,482
8	Rhode Island	66,197
9	Pennsylvania	64,991
10	Michigan	63,878
11	Illinois	61,342
12	Oregon	60,064
13	Delaware	59,085
14	Vermont	58,901
15	New Hampshire	58,802
16	Wyoming	57,761
17	Hawaii	57,431
18	Nevada	56,943
19	Minnesota	56,910
20	Ohio	56,410
21	Wisconsin	54,766
22	Iowa	54,416
23	Georgia	54,190
24	Washington	52,539
25	Texas	51,758
26	Kentucky	51,666
27	Nebraska	51,364
28	Montana	51,215
29	Virginia	50,834
30	Indiana	50,715
31	North Dakota	50,237
32	Maine	50,229
33	Colorado	50,039
34	Alabama	49,781
35	Florida	49,199
36	Kansas	49,197
37	Tennessee	48,708
38	South Carolina	48,542
39	Arkansas	48,220
40	North Carolina	47,985
41	Missouri	47,849
42	New Mexico	47,163
43	Louisiana	46,733
44	Utah	46,042
45	West Virginia	45,977
46	Arizona	45,477
47	Idaho	45,409
48	Oklahoma	44,921
49	Mississippi	42,744
50	South Dakota	42,025
	District of Columbia	75,810

Source: National Education Association, Washington, D.C.

"Rankings and Estimates" (Copyright © 2016, NEA, used with permission, http://www.nea.org/home/32073.htm)

*Estimates for school year 2015-2016 for classroom teachers.

Average Teacher's Salary as a Percent of Average Annual Pay in 2015

National Average = 109.1% of Average Annual Pay*

ALPHA ORDER

RANK	STATE	PERCENT
28	Alabama	111.1
9	Alaska	122.5
46	Arizona	94.8
18	Arkansas	117.4
17	California	117.8
50	Colorado	92.2
32	Connecticut	109.7
33	Delaware	109.5
36	Florida	106.1
35	Georgia	108.5
11	Hawaii	122.1
19	Idaho	116.6
34	Illinois	109.3
20	Indiana	115.7
10	Iowa	122.3
26	Kansas	111.9
16	Kentucky	118.6
42	Louisiana	103.0
13	Maine	119.9
22	Maryland	115.4
24	Massachusetts	114.2
3	Michigan	127.6
36	Minnesota	106.1
25	Mississippi	113.3
38	Missouri	104.5
4	Montana	127.2
15	Nebraska	118.9
6	Nevada	124.2
27	New Hampshire	111.7
29	New Jersey	110.9
30	New Mexico	110.0
23	New York	115.2
43	North Carolina	102.9
45	North Dakota	98.9
14	Ohio	119.4
44	Oklahoma	101.8
7	Oregon	124.0
7	Pennsylvania	124.0
2	Rhode Island	130.4
21	South Carolina	115.5
41	South Dakota	103.2
40	Tennessee	103.4
47	Texas	94.4
39	Utah	103.7
1	Vermont	131.7
48	Virginia	93.5
49	Washington	92.7
30	West Virginia	110.0
12	Wisconsin	120.5
5	Wyoming	124.4

RANK ORDER

RANK	STATE	PERCENT
1	Vermont	131.7
2	Rhode Island	130.4
3	Michigan	127.6
4	Montana	127.2
5	Wyoming	124.4
6	Nevada	124.2
7	Oregon	124.0
7	Pennsylvania	124.0
9	Alaska	122.5
10	Iowa	122.3
11	Hawaii	122.1
12	Wisconsin	120.5
13	Maine	119.9
14	Ohio	119.4
15	Nebraska	118.9
16	Kentucky	118.6
17	California	117.8
18	Arkansas	117.4
19	Idaho	116.6
20	Indiana	115.7
21	South Carolina	115.5
22	Maryland	115.4
23	New York	115.2
24	Massachusetts	114.2
25	Mississippi	113.3
26	Kansas	111.9
27	New Hampshire	111.7
28	Alabama	111.1
29	New Jersey	110.9
30	New Mexico	110.0
30	West Virginia	110.0
32	Connecticut	109.7
33	Delaware	109.5
34	Illinois	109.3
35	Georgia	108.5
36	Florida	106.1
36	Minnesota	106.1
38	Missouri	104.5
39	Utah	103.7
40	Tennessee	103.4
41	South Dakota	103.2
42	Louisiana	103.0
43	North Carolina	102.9
44	Oklahoma	101.8
45	North Dakota	98.9
46	Arizona	94.8
47	Texas	94.4
48	Virginia	93.5
49	Washington	92.7
50	Colorado	92.2

District of Columbia   85.8

Source: CQ Press using data from National Education Association, Washington, D.C.
   "Rankings and Estimates" (Copyright © 2016, NEA, used with permission, http://www.nea.org/home/32073.htm)
   "Quarterly Census of Employment and Wages" (http://www.bls.gov/cew/home.htm)
*Average of public elementary and secondary teacher salary for school years 2014-2015 and 2015-2016 compared to each state's 2015 average annual pay for all workers covered by federal unemployment.

Percent of Public School Fourth Graders
Proficient or Better in Reading in 2015
National Percent = 35%*

RANK	STATE	PERCENT
43	Alabama	29
40	Alaska	30
40	Arizona	30
38	Arkansas	32
48	California	28
15	Colorado	39
4	Connecticut	43
21	Delaware	37
15	Florida	39
33	Georgia	34
43	Hawaii	29
26	Idaho	36
30	Illinois	35
9	Indiana	40
18	Iowa	38
30	Kansas	35
9	Kentucky	40
43	Louisiana	29
26	Maine	36
21	Maryland	37
1	Massachusetts	50
43	Michigan	29
15	Minnesota	39
49	Mississippi	26
26	Missouri	36
21	Montana	37
9	Nebraska	40
43	Nevada	29
2	New Hampshire	46
4	New Jersey	43
50	New Mexico	23
26	New York	36
18	North Carolina	38
21	North Dakota	37
18	Ohio	38
35	Oklahoma	33
33	Oregon	34
7	Pennsylvania	41
9	Rhode Island	40
35	South Carolina	33
30	South Dakota	35
35	Tennessee	33
39	Texas	31
9	Utah	40
3	Vermont	45
4	Virginia	43
9	Washington	40
40	West Virginia	30
21	Wisconsin	37
7	Wyoming	41

RANK	STATE	PERCENT
1	Massachusetts	50
2	New Hampshire	46
3	Vermont	45
4	Connecticut	43
4	New Jersey	43
4	Virginia	43
7	Pennsylvania	41
7	Wyoming	41
9	Indiana	40
9	Kentucky	40
9	Nebraska	40
9	Rhode Island	40
9	Utah	40
9	Washington	40
15	Colorado	39
15	Florida	39
15	Minnesota	39
18	Iowa	38
18	North Carolina	38
18	Ohio	38
21	Delaware	37
21	Maryland	37
21	Montana	37
21	North Dakota	37
21	Wisconsin	37
26	Idaho	36
26	Maine	36
26	Missouri	36
26	New York	36
30	Illinois	35
30	Kansas	35
30	South Dakota	35
33	Georgia	34
33	Oregon	34
35	Oklahoma	33
35	South Carolina	33
35	Tennessee	33
38	Arkansas	32
39	Texas	31
40	Alaska	30
40	Arizona	30
40	West Virginia	30
43	Alabama	29
43	Hawaii	29
43	Louisiana	29
43	Michigan	29
43	Nevada	29
48	California	28
49	Mississippi	26
50	New Mexico	23

District of Columbia 27

Source: U.S. Department of Education, National Center for Education Statistics
"The Nation's Report Card: Reading 2015" (http://nces.ed.gov/nationsreportcard/)
*There are four achievement levels: Below Basic, Basic, Proficient, and Advanced. Proficient represents solid academic mastery for 4th graders. Students reaching this level have demonstrated competency over challenging subject matter, including subject matter knowledge, application of such knowledge to real-world situations, and analytical skills appropriate to the subject matter.

Percent of Public School Eighth Graders
Proficient or Better in Reading in 2015
National Percent = 33%*

ALPHA ORDER

RANK	STATE	PERCENT
46	Alabama	26
33	Alaska	31
33	Arizona	31
43	Arkansas	27
40	California	28
9	Colorado	38
4	Connecticut	43
33	Delaware	31
36	Florida	30
36	Georgia	30
46	Hawaii	26
12	Idaho	37
25	Illinois	35
12	Indiana	37
17	Iowa	36
25	Kansas	35
17	Kentucky	36
48	Louisiana	23
17	Maine	36
12	Maryland	37
1	Massachusetts	46
32	Michigan	32
6	Minnesota	40
49	Mississippi	20
17	Missouri	36
12	Montana	37
9	Nebraska	38
43	Nevada	27
2	New Hampshire	45
5	New Jersey	41
49	New Mexico	20
30	New York	33
36	North Carolina	30
28	North Dakota	34
17	Ohio	36
39	Oklahoma	29
17	Oregon	36
7	Pennsylvania	39
25	Rhode Island	35
40	South Carolina	28
28	South Dakota	34
30	Tennessee	33
40	Texas	28
9	Utah	38
3	Vermont	44
17	Virginia	36
12	Washington	37
43	West Virginia	27
7	Wisconsin	39
17	Wyoming	36

RANK ORDER

RANK	STATE	PERCENT
1	Massachusetts	46
2	New Hampshire	45
3	Vermont	44
4	Connecticut	43
5	New Jersey	41
6	Minnesota	40
7	Pennsylvania	39
7	Wisconsin	39
9	Colorado	38
9	Nebraska	38
9	Utah	38
12	Idaho	37
12	Indiana	37
12	Maryland	37
12	Montana	37
12	Washington	37
17	Iowa	36
17	Kentucky	36
17	Maine	36
17	Missouri	36
17	Ohio	36
17	Oregon	36
17	Virginia	36
17	Wyoming	36
25	Illinois	35
25	Kansas	35
25	Rhode Island	35
28	North Dakota	34
28	South Dakota	34
30	New York	33
30	Tennessee	33
32	Michigan	32
33	Alaska	31
33	Arizona	31
33	Delaware	31
36	Florida	30
36	Georgia	30
36	North Carolina	30
39	Oklahoma	29
40	California	28
40	South Carolina	28
40	Texas	28
43	Arkansas	27
43	Nevada	27
43	West Virginia	27
46	Alabama	26
46	Hawaii	26
48	Louisiana	23
49	Mississippi	20
49	New Mexico	20
	District of Columbia	19

Source: U.S. Department of Education, National Center for Education Statistics
"The Nation's Report Card: Reading 2015" (http://nces.ed.gov/nationsreportcard/)

*There are four achievement levels: Below Basic, Basic, Proficient, and Advanced. Proficient represents solid academic mastery for 8th graders. Students reaching this level have demonstrated competency over challenging subject matter, including subject matter knowledge, application of such knowledge to real-world situations, and analytical skills appropriate to the subject matter.

Percent of Public School Fourth Graders Proficient or Better in Mathematics in 2015
National Percent = 39%*

ALPHA ORDER

RANK	STATE	PERCENT
50	Alabama	26
39	Alaska	35
29	Arizona	38
44	Arkansas	32
48	California	29
18	Colorado	43
21	Connecticut	41
33	Delaware	37
20	Florida	42
39	Georgia	35
29	Hawaii	38
29	Idaho	38
33	Illinois	37
4	Indiana	50
14	Iowa	44
21	Kansas	41
25	Kentucky	40
46	Louisiana	30
21	Maine	41
25	Maryland	40
1	Massachusetts	54
42	Michigan	34
2	Minnesota	53
46	Mississippi	30
29	Missouri	38
21	Montana	41
9	Nebraska	46
44	Nevada	32
3	New Hampshire	51
6	New Jersey	47
49	New Mexico	27
39	New York	35
14	North Carolina	44
10	North Dakota	45
10	Ohio	45
33	Oklahoma	37
33	Oregon	37
10	Pennsylvania	45
33	Rhode Island	37
38	South Carolina	36
25	South Dakota	40
25	Tennessee	40
14	Texas	44
14	Utah	44
18	Vermont	43
6	Virginia	47
6	Washington	47
43	West Virginia	33
10	Wisconsin	45
5	Wyoming	48

RANK ORDER

RANK	STATE	PERCENT
1	Massachusetts	54
2	Minnesota	53
3	New Hampshire	51
4	Indiana	50
5	Wyoming	48
6	New Jersey	47
6	Virginia	47
6	Washington	47
9	Nebraska	46
10	North Dakota	45
10	Ohio	45
10	Pennsylvania	45
10	Wisconsin	45
14	Iowa	44
14	North Carolina	44
14	Texas	44
14	Utah	44
18	Colorado	43
18	Vermont	43
20	Florida	42
21	Connecticut	41
21	Kansas	41
21	Maine	41
21	Montana	41
25	Kentucky	40
25	Maryland	40
25	South Dakota	40
25	Tennessee	40
29	Arizona	38
29	Hawaii	38
29	Idaho	38
29	Missouri	38
33	Delaware	37
33	Illinois	37
33	Oklahoma	37
33	Oregon	37
33	Rhode Island	37
38	South Carolina	36
39	Alaska	35
39	Georgia	35
39	New York	35
42	Michigan	34
43	West Virginia	33
44	Arkansas	32
44	Nevada	32
46	Louisiana	30
46	Mississippi	30
48	California	29
49	New Mexico	27
50	Alabama	26

| | District of Columbia | 31 |

Source: U.S. Department of Education, National Center for Education Statistics
"The Nation's Report Card: Mathematics 2015" (http://nces.ed.gov/nationsreportcard/)
*There are four achievement levels: Below Basic, Basic, Proficient, and Advanced. Proficient represents solid academic mastery for 4th graders. Students reaching this level have demonstrated competency over challenging subject matter, including subject matter knowledge, application of such knowledge to real-world situations, and analytical skills appropriate to the subject matter.

Percent of Public School Eighth Graders Proficient or Better in Mathematics in 2015
National Percent = 32%*

RANK	STATE	PERCENT
50	Alabama	17
28	Alaska	32
18	Arizona	35
44	Arkansas	25
40	California	27
14	Colorado	37
16	Connecticut	36
34	Delaware	30
41	Florida	26
38	Georgia	28
34	Hawaii	30
23	Idaho	34
28	Illinois	32
7	Indiana	39
14	Iowa	37
26	Kansas	33
38	Kentucky	28
49	Louisiana	18
18	Maine	35
18	Maryland	35
1	Massachusetts	51
36	Michigan	29
2	Minnesota	48
46	Mississippi	22
32	Missouri	31
7	Montana	39
11	Nebraska	38
41	Nevada	26
3	New Hampshire	46
3	New Jersey	46
47	New Mexico	21
32	New York	31
26	North Carolina	33
7	North Dakota	39
18	Ohio	35
45	Oklahoma	23
23	Oregon	34
16	Pennsylvania	36
28	Rhode Island	32
41	South Carolina	26
23	South Dakota	34
36	Tennessee	29
28	Texas	32
11	Utah	38
5	Vermont	42
11	Virginia	38
7	Washington	39
47	West Virginia	21
6	Wisconsin	41
18	Wyoming	35

RANK	STATE	PERCENT
1	Massachusetts	51
2	Minnesota	48
3	New Hampshire	46
3	New Jersey	46
5	Vermont	42
6	Wisconsin	41
7	Indiana	39
7	Montana	39
7	North Dakota	39
7	Washington	39
11	Nebraska	38
11	Utah	38
11	Virginia	38
14	Colorado	37
14	Iowa	37
16	Connecticut	36
16	Pennsylvania	36
18	Arizona	35
18	Maine	35
18	Maryland	35
18	Ohio	35
18	Wyoming	35
23	Idaho	34
23	Oregon	34
23	South Dakota	34
26	Kansas	33
26	North Carolina	33
28	Alaska	32
28	Illinois	32
28	Rhode Island	32
28	Texas	32
32	Missouri	31
32	New York	31
34	Delaware	30
34	Hawaii	30
36	Michigan	29
36	Tennessee	29
38	Georgia	28
38	Kentucky	28
40	California	27
41	Florida	26
41	Nevada	26
41	South Carolina	26
44	Arkansas	25
45	Oklahoma	23
46	Mississippi	22
47	New Mexico	21
47	West Virginia	21
49	Louisiana	18
50	Alabama	17
	District of Columbia	19

Source: U.S. Department of Education, National Center for Education Statistics
"The Nation's Report Card: Mathematics 2015" (http://nces.ed.gov/nationsreportcard/)
*There are four achievement levels: Below Basic, Basic, Proficient, and Advanced. Proficient represents solid academic mastery for 8th graders. Students reaching this level have demonstrated competency over challenging subject matter, including subject matter knowledge, application of such knowledge to real-world situations, and analytical skills appropriate to the subject matter.

Percent of Population Graduated from High School in 2015

National Percent = 87.1%*

ALPHA ORDER

RANK	STATE	PERCENT
45	Alabama	84.9
4	Alaska	92.6
37	Arizona	86.1
43	Arkansas	85.4
50	California	82.2
12	Colorado	91.2
18	Connecticut	90.2
27	Delaware	88.9
33	Florida	87.6
37	Georgia	86.1
15	Hawaii	90.9
21	Idaho	90.0
30	Illinois	88.6
31	Indiana	88.2
7	Iowa	91.7
17	Kansas	90.3
44	Kentucky	85.1
46	Louisiana	84.6
7	Maine	91.7
25	Maryland	89.6
18	Massachusetts	90.2
20	Michigan	90.1
3	Minnesota	92.8
48	Mississippi	83.5
27	Missouri	88.9
1	Montana	93.5
14	Nebraska	91.0
42	Nevada	85.6
2	New Hampshire	93.1
26	New Jersey	89.1
46	New Mexico	84.6
40	New York	86.0
35	North Carolina	86.6
5	North Dakota	92.5
23	Ohio	89.7
34	Oklahoma	87.3
21	Oregon	90.0
23	Pennsylvania	89.7
32	Rhode Island	87.7
36	South Carolina	86.3
13	South Dakota	91.1
37	Tennessee	86.1
49	Texas	82.4
10	Utah	91.5
7	Vermont	91.7
27	Virginia	88.9
16	Washington	90.8
40	West Virginia	86.0
11	Wisconsin	91.4
6	Wyoming	92.2

RANK ORDER

RANK	STATE	PERCENT
1	Montana	93.5
2	New Hampshire	93.1
3	Minnesota	92.8
4	Alaska	92.6
5	North Dakota	92.5
6	Wyoming	92.2
7	Iowa	91.7
7	Maine	91.7
7	Vermont	91.7
10	Utah	91.5
11	Wisconsin	91.4
12	Colorado	91.2
13	South Dakota	91.1
14	Nebraska	91.0
15	Hawaii	90.9
16	Washington	90.8
17	Kansas	90.3
18	Connecticut	90.2
18	Massachusetts	90.2
20	Michigan	90.1
21	Idaho	90.0
21	Oregon	90.0
23	Ohio	89.7
23	Pennsylvania	89.7
25	Maryland	89.6
26	New Jersey	89.1
27	Delaware	88.9
27	Missouri	88.9
27	Virginia	88.9
30	Illinois	88.6
31	Indiana	88.2
32	Rhode Island	87.7
33	Florida	87.6
34	Oklahoma	87.3
35	North Carolina	86.6
36	South Carolina	86.3
37	Arizona	86.1
37	Georgia	86.1
37	Tennessee	86.1
40	New York	86.0
40	West Virginia	86.0
42	Nevada	85.6
43	Arkansas	85.4
44	Kentucky	85.1
45	Alabama	84.9
46	Louisiana	84.6
46	New Mexico	84.6
48	Mississippi	83.5
49	Texas	82.4
50	California	82.2
	District of Columbia	89.8

Source: U.S. Bureau of the Census
   "2015 American Community Survey-Table R1501" (http://www.census.gov/programs-surveys/acs/)
*Persons age 25 and older. Includes equivalency status.

Public High School Graduates in 2013

National Total = 3,169,257 Graduates*

ALPHA ORDER

RANK	STATE	GRADUATES	% of USA
23	Alabama	44,233	1.4%
47	Alaska	7,860	0.2%
16	Arizona	62,208	2.0%
33	Arkansas	28,928	0.9%
1	California	422,125	13.3%
22	Colorado	50,968	1.6%
26	Connecticut	38,722	1.2%
46	Delaware	8,070	0.3%
4	Florida	158,029	5.0%
11	Georgia	92,416	2.9%
42	Hawaii	10,790	0.3%
39	Idaho	17,198	0.5%
5	Illinois	139,228	4.4%
13	Indiana	66,595	2.1%
31	Iowa	32,548	1.0%
32	Kansas	31,922	1.0%
24	Kentucky	42,888	1.4%
27	Louisiana	37,508	1.2%
41	Maine	13,170	0.4%
20	Maryland	58,896	1.9%
14	Massachusetts	66,360	2.1%
8	Michigan	104,210	3.3%
21	Minnesota	58,255	1.8%
34	Mississippi	26,502	0.8%
18	Missouri	61,407	1.9%
44	Montana	9,369	0.3%
36	Nebraska	20,442	0.6%
35	Nevada	23,038	0.7%
40	New Hampshire	14,262	0.5%
9	New Jersey	96,490	3.0%
37	New Mexico	19,232	0.6%
3	New York	180,351	5.7%
10	North Carolina	94,339	3.0%
48	North Dakota	6,900	0.2%
7	Ohio	122,491	3.9%
28	Oklahoma	37,033	1.2%
29	Oregon	33,899	1.1%
6	Pennsylvania	129,777	4.1%
43	Rhode Island	9,579	0.3%
25	South Carolina	42,246	1.3%
45	South Dakota	8,239	0.3%
19	Tennessee	61,323	1.9%
2	Texas	301,390	9.5%
30	Utah	33,186	1.0%
49	Vermont	6,491	0.2%
12	Virginia	83,279	2.6%
15	Washington	66,066	2.1%
38	West Virginia	17,924	0.6%
17	Wisconsin	61,425	1.9%
50	Wyoming	5,489	0.2%

RANK ORDER

RANK	STATE	GRADUATES	% of USA
1	California	422,125	13.3%
2	Texas	301,390	9.5%
3	New York	180,351	5.7%
4	Florida	158,029	5.0%
5	Illinois	139,228	4.4%
6	Pennsylvania	129,777	4.1%
7	Ohio	122,491	3.9%
8	Michigan	104,210	3.3%
9	New Jersey	96,490	3.0%
10	North Carolina	94,339	3.0%
11	Georgia	92,416	2.9%
12	Virginia	83,279	2.6%
13	Indiana	66,595	2.1%
14	Massachusetts	66,360	2.1%
15	Washington	66,066	2.1%
16	Arizona	62,208	2.0%
17	Wisconsin	61,425	1.9%
18	Missouri	61,407	1.9%
19	Tennessee	61,323	1.9%
20	Maryland	58,896	1.9%
21	Minnesota	58,255	1.8%
22	Colorado	50,968	1.6%
23	Alabama	44,233	1.4%
24	Kentucky	42,888	1.4%
25	South Carolina	42,246	1.3%
26	Connecticut	38,722	1.2%
27	Louisiana	37,508	1.2%
28	Oklahoma	37,033	1.2%
29	Oregon	33,899	1.1%
30	Utah	33,186	1.0%
31	Iowa	32,548	1.0%
32	Kansas	31,922	1.0%
33	Arkansas	28,928	0.9%
34	Mississippi	26,502	0.8%
35	Nevada	23,038	0.7%
36	Nebraska	20,442	0.6%
37	New Mexico	19,232	0.6%
38	West Virginia	17,924	0.6%
39	Idaho	17,198	0.5%
40	New Hampshire	14,262	0.5%
41	Maine	13,170	0.4%
42	Hawaii	10,790	0.3%
43	Rhode Island	9,579	0.3%
44	Montana	9,369	0.3%
45	South Dakota	8,239	0.3%
46	Delaware	8,070	0.3%
47	Alaska	7,860	0.2%
48	North Dakota	6,900	0.2%
49	Vermont	6,491	0.2%
50	Wyoming	5,489	0.2%
	District of Columbia	3,961	0.1%

Source: U.S. Department of Education, National Center for Education Statistics
  "Digest of Education Statistics 2015" (http://nces.ed.gov/programs/digest/index.asp)
*Diploma recipients for school year 2012-2013. Excludes persons receiving high school equivalency certificates.

Adjusted Cohort Graduation Rate for Public High Schools in 2015

National Average = 83.2%*

ALPHA ORDER

RANK	STATE	RATE
3	Alabama	89.3
46	Alaska	75.6
44	Arizona	77.4
25	Arkansas	84.9
31	California	82.0
45	Colorado	77.3
14	Connecticut	87.2
22	Delaware	85.6
42	Florida	77.9
40	Georgia	78.8
33	Hawaii	81.6
39	Idaho	78.9
22	Illinois	85.6
15	Indiana	87.1
1	Iowa	90.8
20	Kansas	85.7
8	Kentucky	88.0
43	Louisiana	77.5
12	Maine	87.5
16	Maryland	87.0
13	Massachusetts	87.3
36	Michigan	79.8
32	Minnesota	81.9
47	Mississippi	75.4
10	Missouri	87.8
19	Montana	86.0
5	Nebraska	88.9
49	Nevada	71.3
7	New Hampshire	88.1
2	New Jersey	89.7
50	New Mexico	68.6
38	New York	79.2
22	North Carolina	85.6
17	North Dakota	86.6
34	Ohio	80.7
30	Oklahoma	82.5
48	Oregon	73.8
26	Pennsylvania	84.8
29	Rhode Island	83.2
35	South Carolina	80.3
28	South Dakota	83.9
9	Tennessee	87.9
4	Texas	89.0
26	Utah	84.8
11	Vermont	87.7
20	Virginia	85.7
41	Washington	78.2
18	West Virginia	86.5
6	Wisconsin	88.4
37	Wyoming	79.3

RANK ORDER

RANK	STATE	RATE
1	Iowa	90.8
2	New Jersey	89.7
3	Alabama	89.3
4	Texas	89.0
5	Nebraska	88.9
6	Wisconsin	88.4
7	New Hampshire	88.1
8	Kentucky	88.0
9	Tennessee	87.9
10	Missouri	87.8
11	Vermont	87.7
12	Maine	87.5
13	Massachusetts	87.3
14	Connecticut	87.2
15	Indiana	87.1
16	Maryland	87.0
17	North Dakota	86.6
18	West Virginia	86.5
19	Montana	86.0
20	Kansas	85.7
20	Virginia	85.7
22	Delaware	85.6
22	Illinois	85.6
22	North Carolina	85.6
25	Arkansas	84.9
26	Pennsylvania	84.8
26	Utah	84.8
28	South Dakota	83.9
29	Rhode Island	83.2
30	Oklahoma	82.5
31	California	82.0
32	Minnesota	81.9
33	Hawaii	81.6
34	Ohio	80.7
35	South Carolina	80.3
36	Michigan	79.8
37	Wyoming	79.3
38	New York	79.2
39	Idaho	78.9
40	Georgia	78.8
41	Washington	78.2
42	Florida	77.9
43	Louisiana	77.5
44	Arizona	77.4
45	Colorado	77.3
46	Alaska	75.6
47	Mississippi	75.4
48	Oregon	73.8
49	Nevada	71.3
50	New Mexico	68.6
	District of Columbia	68.5

Source: U.S. Department of Education, National Center for Education Statistics
"ED Data Express" (http://eddataexpress.ed.gov/index.cfm)
*The Adjusted Cohort Graduation Rate (ACGR) is the number of students who graduate in four years with a regular high school diploma divided by the number of students who form the adjusted cohort for the graduating class. From the beginning of 9th grade, students who are entering that grade for the first time form a cohort that is "adjusted" by adding any students who subsequently transfer into the cohort and subtracting any students who subsequently transfer out, emigrate to another country, or die.

Adjusted Cohort Graduation Rate for Public High School
Economically Disadvantaged Students in 2015
National Average = 76.1%*

ALPHA ORDER

RANK	STATE	RATE
4	Alabama	84.7
45	Alaska	66.6
33	Arizona	73.1
8	Arkansas	81.7
15	California	78.0
48	Colorado	65.5
25	Connecticut	75.9
24	Delaware	76.0
39	Florida	70.4
31	Georgia	74.5
25	Hawaii	75.9
34	Idaho	72.0
17	Illinois	77.9
5	Indiana	84.2
2	Iowa	84.8
19	Kansas	77.3
2	Kentucky	84.8
37	Louisiana	70.8
28	Maine	75.6
13	Maryland	78.6
14	Massachusetts	78.2
42	Michigan	67.5
43	Minnesota	67.2
38	Mississippi	70.5
11	Missouri	80.7
21	Montana	76.9
10	Nebraska	81.4
49	Nevada	63.7
22	New Hampshire	76.7
8	New Jersey	81.7
50	New Mexico	63.5
35	New York	71.0
12	North Carolina	79.6
35	North Dakota	71.0
40	Ohio	68.7
18	Oklahoma	77.5
46	Oregon	66.4
25	Pennsylvania	75.9
28	Rhode Island	75.6
32	South Carolina	73.7
44	South Dakota	67.0
6	Tennessee	83.5
1	Texas	85.6
22	Utah	76.7
15	Vermont	78.0
30	Virginia	75.4
41	Washington	68.1
7	West Virginia	82.9
19	Wisconsin	77.3
47	Wyoming	66.0

RANK ORDER

RANK	STATE	RATE
1	Texas	85.6
2	Iowa	84.8
2	Kentucky	84.8
4	Alabama	84.7
5	Indiana	84.2
6	Tennessee	83.5
7	West Virginia	82.9
8	Arkansas	81.7
8	New Jersey	81.7
10	Nebraska	81.4
11	Missouri	80.7
12	North Carolina	79.6
13	Maryland	78.6
14	Massachusetts	78.2
15	California	78.0
15	Vermont	78.0
17	Illinois	77.9
18	Oklahoma	77.5
19	Kansas	77.3
19	Wisconsin	77.3
21	Montana	76.9
22	New Hampshire	76.7
22	Utah	76.7
24	Delaware	76.0
25	Connecticut	75.9
25	Hawaii	75.9
25	Pennsylvania	75.9
28	Maine	75.6
28	Rhode Island	75.6
30	Virginia	75.4
31	Georgia	74.5
32	South Carolina	73.7
33	Arizona	73.1
34	Idaho	72.0
35	New York	71.0
35	North Dakota	71.0
37	Louisiana	70.8
38	Mississippi	70.5
39	Florida	70.4
40	Ohio	68.7
41	Washington	68.1
42	Michigan	67.5
43	Minnesota	67.2
44	South Dakota	67.0
45	Alaska	66.6
46	Oregon	66.4
47	Wyoming	66.0
48	Colorado	65.5
49	Nevada	63.7
50	New Mexico	63.5

District of Columbia   68.2

Source: U.S. Department of Education, National Center for Education Statistics
"ED Data Express" (http://eddataexpress.ed.gov/index.cfm)
*The Adjusted Cohort Graduation Rate (ACGR) is calculated based on the number of students who graduate in 4 years or less with a regular
adjusted cohort for the graduating class. In order to calculate and report the 4-year ACGR states must follow the progress of each individual 9
who enter or leave schools or districts within their state. From the beginning of ninth grade (or the earliest high school grade) students who ar
by adding any students who subsequently transfer into the cohort from another state and subtracting any students who subsequently transfer

Adjusted Cohort Graduation Rate for Public High School Students with Limited English Proficiency in 2015
National Average = 65.1%*

ALPHA ORDER

RANK	STATE	RATE
9	Alabama	75.0
37	Alaska	56.0
49	Arizona	34.0
1	Arkansas	86.0
18	California	69.0
32	Colorado	61.1
21	Connecticut	67.0
18	Delaware	69.0
34	Florida	59.5
36	Georgia	56.4
46	Hawaii	46.0
15	Idaho	72.0
15	Illinois	72.0
9	Indiana	75.0
3	Iowa	83.0
4	Kansas	77.0
21	Kentucky	67.0
43	Louisiana	50.0
4	Maine	77.0
45	Maryland	49.0
24	Massachusetts	64.0
14	Michigan	72.1
27	Minnesota	63.1
41	Mississippi	53.0
17	Missouri	71.0
29	Montana	62.0
40	Nebraska	55.0
50	Nevada	32.0
4	New Hampshire	77.0
12	New Jersey	74.0
24	New Mexico	64.0
48	New York	36.0
35	North Carolina	58.0
29	North Dakota	62.0
43	Ohio	50.0
33	Oklahoma	60.0
42	Oregon	51.0
28	Pennsylvania	62.6
4	Rhode Island	77.0
8	South Carolina	76.0
37	South Dakota	56.0
9	Tennessee	75.0
13	Texas	73.3
23	Utah	66.0
18	Vermont	69.0
47	Virginia	44.6
39	Washington	55.8
1	West Virginia	86.0
29	Wisconsin	62.0
24	Wyoming	64.0

RANK ORDER

RANK	STATE	RATE
1	Arkansas	86.0
1	West Virginia	86.0
3	Iowa	83.0
4	Kansas	77.0
4	Maine	77.0
4	New Hampshire	77.0
4	Rhode Island	77.0
8	South Carolina	76.0
9	Alabama	75.0
9	Indiana	75.0
9	Tennessee	75.0
12	New Jersey	74.0
13	Texas	73.3
14	Michigan	72.1
15	Idaho	72.0
15	Illinois	72.0
17	Missouri	71.0
18	California	69.0
18	Delaware	69.0
18	Vermont	69.0
21	Connecticut	67.0
21	Kentucky	67.0
23	Utah	66.0
24	Massachusetts	64.0
24	New Mexico	64.0
24	Wyoming	64.0
27	Minnesota	63.1
28	Pennsylvania	62.6
29	Montana	62.0
29	North Dakota	62.0
29	Wisconsin	62.0
32	Colorado	61.1
33	Oklahoma	60.0
34	Florida	59.5
35	North Carolina	58.0
36	Georgia	56.4
37	Alaska	56.0
37	South Dakota	56.0
39	Washington	55.8
40	Nebraska	55.0
41	Mississippi	53.0
42	Oregon	51.0
43	Louisiana	50.0
43	Ohio	50.0
45	Maryland	49.0
46	Hawaii	46.0
47	Virginia	44.6
48	New York	36.0
49	Arizona	34.0
50	Nevada	32.0
	District of Columbia	62.0

Source: U.S. Department of Education, National Center for Education Statistics
"ED Data Express" (http://eddataexpress.ed.gov/index.cfm)
*The Adjusted Cohort Graduation Rate (ACGR) is calculated based on the number of students who graduate in 4 years or less with a regular adjusted cohort for the graduating class. In order to calculate and report the 4-year ACGR states must follow the progress of each individual 9 who enter or leave schools or districts within their state. From the beginning of ninth grade (or the earliest high school grade) students who ar by adding any students who subsequently transfer into the cohort from another state and subtracting any students who subsequently transfer

Adjusted Cohort Graduation Rate for Public High School Students with Disabilities in 2015
National Average = 64.6%*

ALPHA ORDER

RANK	STATE	RATE
11	Alabama	72.4
40	Alaska	57.0
30	Arizona	64.4
1	Arkansas	81.9
29	California	65.0
43	Colorado	53.8
28	Connecticut	65.6
26	Delaware	66.0
41	Florida	56.8
42	Georgia	54.3
33	Hawaii	60.0
37	Idaho	58.0
16	Illinois	70.5
15	Indiana	70.9
5	Iowa	77.0
4	Kansas	77.3
26	Kentucky	66.0
48	Louisiana	44.3
9	Maine	74.0
31	Maryland	63.9
18	Massachusetts	69.9
39	Michigan	57.1
32	Minnesota	61.1
49	Mississippi	30.7
6	Missouri	76.6
8	Montana	75.0
14	Nebraska	71.0
50	Nevada	29.0
10	New Hampshire	73.0
3	New Jersey	78.0
35	New Mexico	59.3
44	New York	52.9
24	North Carolina	67.3
20	North Dakota	68.0
25	Ohio	67.0
7	Oklahoma	75.6
45	Oregon	52.7
13	Pennsylvania	71.5
20	Rhode Island	68.0
47	South Carolina	49.0
33	South Dakota	60.0
17	Tennessee	70.0
2	Texas	78.2
22	Utah	67.9
12	Vermont	72.0
46	Virginia	52.6
37	Washington	58.0
19	West Virginia	69.0
23	Wisconsin	67.5
36	Wyoming	59.0

RANK ORDER

RANK	STATE	RATE
1	Arkansas	81.9
2	Texas	78.2
3	New Jersey	78.0
4	Kansas	77.3
5	Iowa	77.0
6	Missouri	76.6
7	Oklahoma	75.6
8	Montana	75.0
9	Maine	74.0
10	New Hampshire	73.0
11	Alabama	72.4
12	Vermont	72.0
13	Pennsylvania	71.5
14	Nebraska	71.0
15	Indiana	70.9
16	Illinois	70.5
17	Tennessee	70.0
18	Massachusetts	69.9
19	West Virginia	69.0
20	North Dakota	68.0
20	Rhode Island	68.0
22	Utah	67.9
23	Wisconsin	67.5
24	North Carolina	67.3
25	Ohio	67.0
26	Delaware	66.0
26	Kentucky	66.0
28	Connecticut	65.6
29	California	65.0
30	Arizona	64.4
31	Maryland	63.9
32	Minnesota	61.1
33	Hawaii	60.0
33	South Dakota	60.0
35	New Mexico	59.3
36	Wyoming	59.0
37	Idaho	58.0
37	Washington	58.0
39	Michigan	57.1
40	Alaska	57.0
41	Florida	56.8
42	Georgia	54.3
43	Colorado	53.8
44	New York	52.9
45	Oregon	52.7
46	Virginia	52.6
47	South Carolina	49.0
48	Louisiana	44.3
49	Mississippi	30.7
50	Nevada	29.0

	District of Columbia	46.0

Source: U.S. Department of Education, National Center for Education Statistics
"ED Data Express" (http://eddataexpress.ed.gov/index.cfm)
*The Adjusted Cohort Graduation Rate (ACGR) is calculated based on the number of students who graduate in 4 years or less with a regular adjusted cohort for the graduating class. In order to calculate and report the 4-year ACGR states must follow the progress of each individual 9 who enter or leave schools or districts within their state. From the beginning of ninth grade (or the earliest high school grade) students who ar by adding any students who subsequently transfer into the cohort from another state and subtracting any students who subsequently transfer

ACT Average Composite Score in 2016

National Average = 20.8*

RANK	STATE	AVERAGE SCORE
45	Alabama	19.1
38	Alaska	20.0
37	Arizona	20.1
34	Arkansas	20.2
15	California	22.6
27	Colorado	20.6
2	Connecticut	24.5
5	Delaware	23.6
41	Florida	19.9
23	Georgia	21.1
47	Hawaii	18.7
14	Idaho	22.7
25	Illinois	20.8
16	Indiana	22.3
17	Iowa	22.1
19	Kansas	21.9
38	Kentucky	20.0
44	Louisiana	19.5
5	Maine	23.6
13	Maryland	23.0
1	Massachusetts	24.8
31	Michigan	20.3
23	Minnesota	21.1
49	Mississippi	18.4
34	Missouri	20.2
31	Montana	20.3
22	Nebraska	21.4
50	Nevada	17.7
2	New Hampshire	24.5
10	New Jersey	23.1
41	New Mexico	19.9
4	New York	23.9
45	North Carolina	19.1
31	North Dakota	20.3
18	Ohio	22.0
30	Oklahoma	20.4
21	Oregon	21.7
10	Pennsylvania	23.1
8	Rhode Island	23.3
48	South Carolina	18.5
19	South Dakota	21.9
41	Tennessee	19.9
27	Texas	20.6
34	Utah	20.2
7	Vermont	23.4
8	Virginia	23.3
10	Washington	23.1
26	West Virginia	20.7
29	Wisconsin	20.5
38	Wyoming	20.0

RANK	STATE	AVERAGE SCORE
1	Massachusetts	24.8
2	Connecticut	24.5
2	New Hampshire	24.5
4	New York	23.9
5	Delaware	23.6
5	Maine	23.6
7	Vermont	23.4
8	Rhode Island	23.3
8	Virginia	23.3
10	New Jersey	23.1
10	Pennsylvania	23.1
10	Washington	23.1
13	Maryland	23.0
14	Idaho	22.7
15	California	22.6
16	Indiana	22.3
17	Iowa	22.1
18	Ohio	22.0
19	Kansas	21.9
19	South Dakota	21.9
21	Oregon	21.7
22	Nebraska	21.4
23	Georgia	21.1
23	Minnesota	21.1
25	Illinois	20.8
26	West Virginia	20.7
27	Colorado	20.6
27	Texas	20.6
29	Wisconsin	20.5
30	Oklahoma	20.4
31	Michigan	20.3
31	Montana	20.3
31	North Dakota	20.3
34	Arkansas	20.2
34	Missouri	20.2
34	Utah	20.2
37	Arizona	20.1
38	Alaska	20.0
38	Kentucky	20.0
38	Wyoming	20.0
41	Florida	19.9
41	New Mexico	19.9
41	Tennessee	19.9
44	Louisiana	19.5
45	Alabama	19.1
45	North Carolina	19.1
47	Hawaii	18.7
48	South Carolina	18.5
49	Mississippi	18.4
50	Nevada	17.7
	District of Columbia	22.2

Source: The American College Testing Program (Copyright © 2016)
"Average ACT Scores by State" (http://www.act.org/newsroom/)

*The ACT score range is 1 to 36. Approximately 2.1 million 2016 U.S. high school students took the test. Caution should be used in using ACT scores to compare states. The percentage of high school students taking the test varies greatly from one state to another. For example, all 11th grade students are required to take the test in eighteen states but, in Maine, only 10 percent of 11th grade students took the test.

Education Expenditures by State and Local Governments in 2014

National Total = $904,309,998,000*

ALPHA ORDER

RANK	STATE	EXPENDITURES	% of USA
24	Alabama	$13,140,501,000	1.5%
40	Alaska	3,575,363,000	0.4%
19	Arizona	15,075,973,000	1.7%
33	Arkansas	8,136,344,000	0.9%
1	California	111,036,634,000	12.3%
21	Colorado	14,563,170,000	1.6%
25	Connecticut	12,568,089,000	1.4%
41	Delaware	3,517,098,000	0.4%
4	Florida	39,038,473,000	4.3%
10	Georgia	25,439,926,000	2.8%
42	Hawaii	3,388,604,000	0.4%
45	Idaho	3,144,039,000	0.3%
6	Illinois	37,260,664,000	4.1%
17	Indiana	16,572,228,000	1.8%
29	Iowa	10,432,391,000	1.2%
31	Kansas	8,777,812,000	1.0%
27	Kentucky	11,541,435,000	1.3%
26	Louisiana	12,241,671,000	1.4%
43	Maine	3,313,109,000	0.4%
15	Maryland	19,400,170,000	2.1%
13	Massachusetts	21,476,816,000	2.4%
9	Michigan	28,559,081,000	3.2%
18	Minnesota	16,497,183,000	1.8%
34	Mississippi	7,601,561,000	0.8%
20	Missouri	14,605,892,000	1.6%
46	Montana	2,737,661,000	0.3%
36	Nebraska	6,254,818,000	0.7%
37	Nevada	5,546,352,000	0.6%
39	New Hampshire	3,784,088,000	0.4%
7	New Jersey	34,205,186,000	3.8%
35	New Mexico	6,291,090,000	0.7%
3	New York	73,296,897,000	8.1%
12	North Carolina	23,521,898,000	2.6%
47	North Dakota	2,639,282,000	0.3%
8	Ohio	32,820,265,000	3.6%
30	Oklahoma	10,115,134,000	1.1%
28	Oregon	10,987,797,000	1.2%
5	Pennsylvania	37,900,000,000	4.2%
44	Rhode Island	3,229,965,000	0.4%
23	South Carolina	13,177,625,000	1.5%
50	South Dakota	2,115,070,000	0.2%
22	Tennessee	14,047,832,000	1.6%
2	Texas	76,677,613,000	8.5%
32	Utah	8,373,503,000	0.9%
49	Vermont	2,505,229,000	0.3%
11	Virginia	24,425,451,000	2.7%
14	Washington	20,621,874,000	2.3%
38	West Virginia	5,425,599,000	0.6%
16	Wisconsin	17,462,986,000	1.9%
48	Wyoming	2,618,929,000	0.3%

RANK ORDER

RANK	STATE	EXPENDITURES	% of USA
1	California	$111,036,634,000	12.3%
2	Texas	76,677,613,000	8.5%
3	New York	73,296,897,000	8.1%
4	Florida	39,038,473,000	4.3%
5	Pennsylvania	37,900,000,000	4.2%
6	Illinois	37,260,664,000	4.1%
7	New Jersey	34,205,186,000	3.8%
8	Ohio	32,820,265,000	3.6%
9	Michigan	28,559,081,000	3.2%
10	Georgia	25,439,926,000	2.8%
11	Virginia	24,425,451,000	2.7%
12	North Carolina	23,521,898,000	2.6%
13	Massachusetts	21,476,816,000	2.4%
14	Washington	20,621,874,000	2.3%
15	Maryland	19,400,170,000	2.1%
16	Wisconsin	17,462,986,000	1.9%
17	Indiana	16,572,228,000	1.8%
18	Minnesota	16,497,183,000	1.8%
19	Arizona	15,075,973,000	1.7%
20	Missouri	14,605,892,000	1.6%
21	Colorado	14,563,170,000	1.6%
22	Tennessee	14,047,832,000	1.6%
23	South Carolina	13,177,625,000	1.5%
24	Alabama	13,140,501,000	1.5%
25	Connecticut	12,568,089,000	1.4%
26	Louisiana	12,241,671,000	1.4%
27	Kentucky	11,541,435,000	1.3%
28	Oregon	10,987,797,000	1.2%
29	Iowa	10,432,391,000	1.2%
30	Oklahoma	10,115,134,000	1.1%
31	Kansas	8,777,812,000	1.0%
32	Utah	8,373,503,000	0.9%
33	Arkansas	8,136,344,000	0.9%
34	Mississippi	7,601,561,000	0.8%
35	New Mexico	6,291,090,000	0.7%
36	Nebraska	6,254,818,000	0.7%
37	Nevada	5,546,352,000	0.6%
38	West Virginia	5,425,599,000	0.6%
39	New Hampshire	3,784,088,000	0.4%
40	Alaska	3,575,363,000	0.4%
41	Delaware	3,517,098,000	0.4%
42	Hawaii	3,388,604,000	0.4%
43	Maine	3,313,109,000	0.4%
44	Rhode Island	3,229,965,000	0.4%
45	Idaho	3,144,039,000	0.3%
46	Montana	2,737,661,000	0.3%
47	North Dakota	2,639,282,000	0.3%
48	Wyoming	2,618,929,000	0.3%
49	Vermont	2,505,229,000	0.3%
50	South Dakota	2,115,070,000	0.2%
	District of Columbia	2,623,627,000	0.3%

Source: U.S. Bureau of the Census, Governments Division
"2014 State and Local Government Finances" (http://www.census.gov/govs/local/)
*Direct general expenditures for higher, secondary, elementary, and, "other" education. Includes capital outlays.

Per Capita State and Local Government Expenditures for Education in 2014

National Per Capita = $2,839*

ALPHA ORDER

ALPHA ORDER

RANK ORDER

RANK	STATE	PER CAPITA		RANK	STATE	PER CAPITA
33	Alabama	$2,713		1	Alaska	$4,853
1	Alaska	4,853		2	Wyoming	4,487
46	Arizona	2,243		3	Vermont	3,996
30	Arkansas	2,742		4	New Jersey	3,833
24	California	2,871		5	Delaware	3,762
32	Colorado	2,722		6	New York	3,717
8	Connecticut	3,499		7	North Dakota	3,567
5	Delaware	3,762		8	Connecticut	3,499
48	Florida	1,963		9	Iowa	3,357
39	Georgia	2,522		10	Nebraska	3,325
44	Hawaii	2,392		11	Maryland	3,251
50	Idaho	1,925		12	Massachusetts	3,182
22	Illinois	2,896		13	Rhode Island	3,063
40	Indiana	2,513		14	Wisconsin	3,033
9	Iowa	3,357		15	Kansas	3,027
15	Kansas	3,027		16	Minnesota	3,025
36	Kentucky	2,615		17	New Mexico	3,020
35	Louisiana	2,634		18	Pennsylvania	2,963
41	Maine	2,490		19	Virginia	2,937
11	Maryland	3,251		20	West Virginia	2,935
12	Massachusetts	3,182		21	Washington	2,923
23	Michigan	2,880		22	Illinois	2,896
16	Minnesota	3,025		23	Michigan	2,880
38	Mississippi	2,540		24	California	2,871
43	Missouri	2,410		25	New Hampshire	2,848
34	Montana	2,676		26	Texas	2,846
10	Nebraska	3,325		26	Utah	2,846
49	Nevada	1,958		28	Ohio	2,831
25	New Hampshire	2,848		29	Oregon	2,769
4	New Jersey	3,833		30	Arkansas	2,742
17	New Mexico	3,020		31	South Carolina	2,729
6	New York	3,717		32	Colorado	2,722
45	North Carolina	2,368		33	Alabama	2,713
7	North Dakota	3,567		34	Montana	2,676
28	Ohio	2,831		35	Louisiana	2,634
37	Oklahoma	2,609		36	Kentucky	2,615
29	Oregon	2,769		37	Oklahoma	2,609
18	Pennsylvania	2,963		38	Mississippi	2,540
13	Rhode Island	3,063		39	Georgia	2,522
31	South Carolina	2,729		40	Indiana	2,513
42	South Dakota	2,481		41	Maine	2,490
47	Tennessee	2,146		42	South Dakota	2,481
26	Texas	2,846		43	Missouri	2,410
26	Utah	2,846		44	Hawaii	2,392
3	Vermont	3,996		45	North Carolina	2,368
19	Virginia	2,937		46	Arizona	2,243
21	Washington	2,923		47	Tennessee	2,146
20	West Virginia	2,935		48	Florida	1,963
14	Wisconsin	3,033		49	Nevada	1,958
2	Wyoming	4,487		50	Idaho	1,925
					District of Columbia	3,981

Source: CQ Press using data from U.S. Bureau of the Census, Governments Division
"2014 State and Local Government Finances" (http://www.census.gov/govs/local/)
*Direct general expenditures for higher, secondary, elementary, and, "other" education. Includes capital outlays.

Expenditures for Education as a Percent of
All State and Local Government Expenditures in 2014
National Percent = 33.4%*

ALPHA ORDER

RANK	STATE	PERCENT
13	Alabama	36.3
50	Alaska	24.5
19	Arizona	35.2
11	Arkansas	36.6
44	California	29.9
30	Colorado	33.5
20	Connecticut	35.1
9	Delaware	36.7
48	Florida	28.2
4	Georgia	38.8
49	Hawaii	24.8
42	Idaho	30.4
26	Illinois	34.1
22	Indiana	34.7
15	Iowa	36.2
12	Kansas	36.5
23	Kentucky	34.5
46	Louisiana	29.6
47	Maine	28.7
21	Maryland	34.9
39	Massachusetts	31.7
6	Michigan	37.6
37	Minnesota	32.1
40	Mississippi	31.4
26	Missouri	34.1
37	Montana	32.1
2	Nebraska	39.9
43	Nevada	30.0
7	New Hampshire	37.5
4	New Jersey	38.8
29	New Mexico	33.6
45	New York	29.8
34	North Carolina	32.7
36	North Dakota	32.3
24	Ohio	34.3
17	Oklahoma	35.4
41	Oregon	31.3
25	Pennsylvania	34.2
31	Rhode Island	33.3
16	South Carolina	35.6
33	South Dakota	33.2
35	Tennessee	32.4
3	Texas	39.0
1	Utah	40.0
8	Vermont	37.2
13	Virginia	36.3
31	Washington	33.3
9	West Virginia	36.7
18	Wisconsin	35.3
26	Wyoming	34.1

RANK ORDER

RANK	STATE	PERCENT
1	Utah	40.0
2	Nebraska	39.9
3	Texas	39.0
4	Georgia	38.8
4	New Jersey	38.8
6	Michigan	37.6
7	New Hampshire	37.5
8	Vermont	37.2
9	Delaware	36.7
9	West Virginia	36.7
11	Arkansas	36.6
12	Kansas	36.5
13	Alabama	36.3
13	Virginia	36.3
15	Iowa	36.2
16	South Carolina	35.6
17	Oklahoma	35.4
18	Wisconsin	35.3
19	Arizona	35.2
20	Connecticut	35.1
21	Maryland	34.9
22	Indiana	34.7
23	Kentucky	34.5
24	Ohio	34.3
25	Pennsylvania	34.2
26	Illinois	34.1
26	Missouri	34.1
26	Wyoming	34.1
29	New Mexico	33.6
30	Colorado	33.5
31	Rhode Island	33.3
31	Washington	33.3
33	South Dakota	33.2
34	North Carolina	32.7
35	Tennessee	32.4
36	North Dakota	32.3
37	Minnesota	32.1
37	Montana	32.1
39	Massachusetts	31.7
40	Mississippi	31.4
41	Oregon	31.3
42	Idaho	30.4
43	Nevada	30.0
44	California	29.9
45	New York	29.8
46	Louisiana	29.6
47	Maine	28.7
48	Florida	28.2
49	Hawaii	24.8
50	Alaska	24.5

District of Columbia 21.9

Source: CQ Press using data from U.S. Bureau of the Census, Governments Division
"2014 State and Local Government Finances" (http://www.census.gov/govs/local/)
*Direct general expenditures for higher, secondary, elementary, and "other" education as a percent of all direct general expenditures. Includes capital outlays.

State and Local Government Expenditures for Elementary and Secondary Education in 2014
National Total = $586,106,729,000*

ALPHA ORDER					RANK ORDER			

RANK	STATE	EXPENDITURES	% of USA	RANK	STATE	EXPENDITURES	% of USA
26	Alabama	$7,532,718,000	1.3%	1	California	$68,769,130,000	11.7%
40	Alaska	2,493,063,000	0.4%	2	New York	57,745,303,000	9.9%
24	Arizona	7,961,489,000	1.4%	3	Texas	47,339,605,000	8.1%
32	Arkansas	4,877,237,000	0.8%	4	New Jersey	26,133,086,000	4.5%
1	California	68,769,130,000	11.7%	5	Pennsylvania	26,107,317,000	4.5%
22	Colorado	8,786,339,000	1.5%	6	Illinois	25,898,091,000	4.4%
21	Connecticut	8,906,378,000	1.5%	7	Florida	25,775,790,000	4.4%
45	Delaware	1,908,296,000	0.3%	8	Ohio	21,479,740,000	3.7%
7	Florida	25,775,790,000	4.4%	9	Georgia	17,409,071,000	3.0%
9	Georgia	17,409,071,000	3.0%	10	Michigan	16,343,304,000	2.8%
43	Hawaii	2,139,147,000	0.4%	11	Virginia	16,055,837,000	2.7%
44	Idaho	1,959,703,000	0.3%	12	Massachusetts	15,229,109,000	2.6%
6	Illinois	25,898,091,000	4.4%	13	North Carolina	12,892,259,000	2.2%
19	Indiana	9,621,500,000	1.6%	14	Maryland	12,549,993,000	2.1%
28	Iowa	6,181,679,000	1.1%	15	Washington	12,452,073,000	2.1%
31	Kansas	5,438,290,000	0.9%	16	Minnesota	10,753,158,000	1.8%
27	Kentucky	6,797,330,000	1.2%	17	Wisconsin	10,601,074,000	1.8%
25	Louisiana	7,834,620,000	1.3%	18	Missouri	9,930,461,000	1.7%
41	Maine	2,309,852,000	0.4%	19	Indiana	9,621,500,000	1.6%
14	Maryland	12,549,993,000	2.1%	20	Tennessee	9,227,239,000	1.6%
12	Massachusetts	15,229,109,000	2.6%	21	Connecticut	8,906,378,000	1.5%
10	Michigan	16,343,304,000	2.8%	22	Colorado	8,786,339,000	1.5%
16	Minnesota	10,753,158,000	1.8%	23	South Carolina	8,084,511,000	1.4%
33	Mississippi	4,393,960,000	0.7%	24	Arizona	7,961,489,000	1.4%
18	Missouri	9,930,461,000	1.7%	25	Louisiana	7,834,620,000	1.3%
47	Montana	1,721,563,000	0.3%	26	Alabama	7,532,718,000	1.3%
35	Nebraska	3,914,540,000	0.7%	27	Kentucky	6,797,330,000	1.2%
36	Nevada	3,850,524,000	0.7%	28	Iowa	6,181,679,000	1.1%
39	New Hampshire	2,758,727,000	0.5%	29	Oregon	6,143,475,000	1.0%
4	New Jersey	26,133,086,000	4.5%	30	Oklahoma	5,942,301,000	1.0%
37	New Mexico	3,507,457,000	0.6%	31	Kansas	5,438,290,000	0.9%
2	New York	57,745,303,000	9.9%	32	Arkansas	4,877,237,000	0.8%
13	North Carolina	12,892,259,000	2.2%	33	Mississippi	4,393,960,000	0.7%
49	North Dakota	1,522,033,000	0.3%	34	Utah	4,270,287,000	0.7%
8	Ohio	21,479,740,000	3.7%	35	Nebraska	3,914,540,000	0.7%
30	Oklahoma	5,942,301,000	1.0%	36	Nevada	3,850,524,000	0.7%
29	Oregon	6,143,475,000	1.0%	37	New Mexico	3,507,457,000	0.6%
5	Pennsylvania	26,107,317,000	4.5%	38	West Virginia	3,168,288,000	0.5%
42	Rhode Island	2,282,611,000	0.4%	39	New Hampshire	2,758,727,000	0.5%
23	South Carolina	8,084,511,000	1.4%	40	Alaska	2,493,063,000	0.4%
50	South Dakota	1,315,216,000	0.2%	41	Maine	2,309,852,000	0.4%
20	Tennessee	9,227,239,000	1.6%	42	Rhode Island	2,282,611,000	0.4%
3	Texas	47,339,605,000	8.1%	43	Hawaii	2,139,147,000	0.4%
34	Utah	4,270,287,000	0.7%	44	Idaho	1,959,703,000	0.3%
48	Vermont	1,558,941,000	0.3%	45	Delaware	1,908,296,000	0.3%
11	Virginia	16,055,837,000	2.7%	46	Wyoming	1,760,433,000	0.3%
15	Washington	12,452,073,000	2.1%	47	Montana	1,721,563,000	0.3%
38	West Virginia	3,168,288,000	0.5%	48	Vermont	1,558,941,000	0.3%
17	Wisconsin	10,601,074,000	1.8%	49	North Dakota	1,522,033,000	0.3%
46	Wyoming	1,760,433,000	0.3%	50	South Dakota	1,315,216,000	0.2%
					District of Columbia	2,472,581,000	0.4%

Source: U.S. Bureau of the Census, Governments Division
   "2014 State and Local Government Finances" (http://www.census.gov/govs/local/)
*Direct general expenditures. Includes capital outlays.

Per Capita State and Local Government Expenditures for Elementary and Secondary Education in 2014
National Per Capita = $1,840*

ALPHA ORDER

RANK	STATE	PER CAPITA
36	Alabama	$1,555
1	Alaska	3,384
50	Arizona	1,185
33	Arkansas	1,644
22	California	1,778
34	Colorado	1,642
6	Connecticut	2,480
13	Delaware	2,041
48	Florida	1,296
26	Georgia	1,726
41	Hawaii	1,510
49	Idaho	1,200
15	Illinois	2,013
43	Indiana	1,459
16	Iowa	1,989
19	Kansas	1,876
39	Kentucky	1,540
28	Louisiana	1,686
25	Maine	1,736
9	Maryland	2,103
7	Massachusetts	2,256
32	Michigan	1,648
17	Minnesota	1,972
42	Mississippi	1,468
35	Missouri	1,638
30	Montana	1,683
10	Nebraska	2,081
46	Nevada	1,359
11	New Hampshire	2,076
3	New Jersey	2,928
29	New Mexico	1,684
3	New York	2,928
47	North Carolina	1,298
12	North Dakota	2,057
20	Ohio	1,853
40	Oklahoma	1,533
37	Oregon	1,548
13	Pennsylvania	2,041
8	Rhode Island	2,165
31	South Carolina	1,674
38	South Dakota	1,543
45	Tennessee	1,410
24	Texas	1,757
44	Utah	1,452
5	Vermont	2,486
18	Virginia	1,930
23	Washington	1,765
27	West Virginia	1,714
21	Wisconsin	1,841
2	Wyoming	3,016

RANK ORDER

RANK	STATE	PER CAPITA
1	Alaska	$3,384
2	Wyoming	3,016
3	New Jersey	2,928
3	New York	2,928
5	Vermont	2,486
6	Connecticut	2,480
7	Massachusetts	2,256
8	Rhode Island	2,165
9	Maryland	2,103
10	Nebraska	2,081
11	New Hampshire	2,076
12	North Dakota	2,057
13	Delaware	2,041
13	Pennsylvania	2,041
15	Illinois	2,013
16	Iowa	1,989
17	Minnesota	1,972
18	Virginia	1,930
19	Kansas	1,876
20	Ohio	1,853
21	Wisconsin	1,841
22	California	1,778
23	Washington	1,765
24	Texas	1,757
25	Maine	1,736
26	Georgia	1,726
27	West Virginia	1,714
28	Louisiana	1,686
29	New Mexico	1,684
30	Montana	1,683
31	South Carolina	1,674
32	Michigan	1,648
33	Arkansas	1,644
34	Colorado	1,642
35	Missouri	1,638
36	Alabama	1,555
37	Oregon	1,548
38	South Dakota	1,543
39	Kentucky	1,540
40	Oklahoma	1,533
41	Hawaii	1,510
42	Mississippi	1,468
43	Indiana	1,459
44	Utah	1,452
45	Tennessee	1,410
46	Nevada	1,359
47	North Carolina	1,298
48	Florida	1,296
49	Idaho	1,200
50	Arizona	1,185
	District of Columbia	3,752

Source: CQ Press using data from U.S. Bureau of the Census, Governments Division
"2014 State and Local Government Finances" (http://www.census.gov/govs/local/)
*Direct general expenditures. Includes capital outlays.

Expenditures for Elementary and Secondary Education as a Percent of All State and Local Government Expenditures in 2014
National Percent = 21.7%*

ALPHA ORDER

RANK	STATE	PERCENT
28	Alabama	20.8
49	Alaska	17.1
42	Arizona	18.6
19	Arkansas	21.9
45	California	18.5
33	Colorado	20.2
5	Connecticut	24.8
38	Delaware	19.9
42	Florida	18.6
3	Georgia	26.6
50	Hawaii	15.6
40	Idaho	18.9
8	Illinois	23.7
35	Indiana	20.1
23	Iowa	21.4
15	Kansas	22.6
32	Kentucky	20.3
39	Louisiana	19.0
37	Maine	20.0
15	Maryland	22.6
17	Massachusetts	22.5
21	Michigan	21.5
26	Minnesota	20.9
46	Mississippi	18.2
12	Missouri	23.2
33	Montana	20.2
4	Nebraska	25.0
26	Nevada	20.9
2	New Hampshire	27.3
1	New Jersey	29.7
41	New Mexico	18.7
10	New York	23.5
47	North Carolina	17.9
42	North Dakota	18.6
18	Ohio	22.4
28	Oklahoma	20.8
48	Oregon	17.5
9	Pennsylvania	23.6
10	Rhode Island	23.5
20	South Carolina	21.8
30	South Dakota	20.6
25	Tennessee	21.3
6	Texas	24.1
31	Utah	20.4
12	Vermont	23.2
7	Virginia	23.9
35	Washington	20.1
23	West Virginia	21.4
21	Wisconsin	21.5
14	Wyoming	22.9

RANK ORDER

RANK	STATE	PERCENT
1	New Jersey	29.7
2	New Hampshire	27.3
3	Georgia	26.6
4	Nebraska	25.0
5	Connecticut	24.8
6	Texas	24.1
7	Virginia	23.9
8	Illinois	23.7
9	Pennsylvania	23.6
10	New York	23.5
10	Rhode Island	23.5
12	Missouri	23.2
12	Vermont	23.2
14	Wyoming	22.9
15	Kansas	22.6
15	Maryland	22.6
17	Massachusetts	22.5
18	Ohio	22.4
19	Arkansas	21.9
20	South Carolina	21.8
21	Michigan	21.5
21	Wisconsin	21.5
23	Iowa	21.4
23	West Virginia	21.4
25	Tennessee	21.3
26	Minnesota	20.9
26	Nevada	20.9
28	Alabama	20.8
28	Oklahoma	20.8
30	South Dakota	20.6
31	Utah	20.4
32	Kentucky	20.3
33	Colorado	20.2
33	Montana	20.2
35	Indiana	20.1
35	Washington	20.1
37	Maine	20.0
38	Delaware	19.9
39	Louisiana	19.0
40	Idaho	18.9
41	New Mexico	18.7
42	Arizona	18.6
42	Florida	18.6
42	North Dakota	18.6
45	California	18.5
46	Mississippi	18.2
47	North Carolina	17.9
48	Oregon	17.5
49	Alaska	17.1
50	Hawaii	15.6
	District of Columbia	20.7

Source: CQ Press using data from U.S. Bureau of the Census, Governments Division
"2014 State and Local Government Finances" (http://www.census.gov/govs/local/)
*Direct general expenditures as a percent of all direct general expenditures. Includes capital outlays.

Estimated Per Pupil Public Elementary and
Secondary School Current Expenditures in 2016
National Per Pupil = $11,943*

ALPHA ORDER

RANK	STATE	PER PUPIL
36	Alabama	$9,206
4	Alaska	20,843
49	Arizona	7,753
33	Arkansas	9,715
21	California	11,329
31	Colorado	10,013
6	Connecticut	18,496
11	Delaware	16,312
36	Florida	9,206
39	Georgia	9,085
18	Hawaii	11,800
38	Idaho	9,117
14	Illinois	14,394
50	Indiana	7,538
27	Iowa	10,675
32	Kansas	9,828
19	Kentucky	11,796
22	Louisiana	11,262
45	Maine	8,825
13	Maryland	14,645
8	Massachusetts	17,471
12	Michigan	15,425
17	Minnesota	11,816
44	Mississippi	8,842
26	Missouri	10,802
25	Montana	11,028
29	Nebraska	10,158
35	Nevada	9,321
7	New Hampshire	17,994
3	New Jersey	21,741
28	New Mexico	10,438
2	New York	22,333
43	North Carolina	8,898
46	North Dakota	8,337
16	Ohio	11,939
47	Oklahoma	8,085
23	Oregon	11,232
10	Pennsylvania	16,316
5	Rhode Island	20,547
34	South Carolina	9,708
41	South Dakota	8,977
40	Tennessee	9,058
42	Texas	8,935
48	Utah	7,905
1	Vermont	25,286
24	Virginia	11,042
30	Washington	10,073
15	West Virginia	13,293
20	Wisconsin	11,458
9	Wyoming	16,511

RANK ORDER

RANK	STATE	PER PUPIL
1	Vermont	$25,286
2	New York	22,333
3	New Jersey	21,741
4	Alaska	20,843
5	Rhode Island	20,547
6	Connecticut	18,496
7	New Hampshire	17,994
8	Massachusetts	17,471
9	Wyoming	16,511
10	Pennsylvania	16,316
11	Delaware	16,312
12	Michigan	15,425
13	Maryland	14,645
14	Illinois	14,394
15	West Virginia	13,293
16	Ohio	11,939
17	Minnesota	11,816
18	Hawaii	11,800
19	Kentucky	11,796
20	Wisconsin	11,458
21	California	11,329
22	Louisiana	11,262
23	Oregon	11,232
24	Virginia	11,042
25	Montana	11,028
26	Missouri	10,802
27	Iowa	10,675
28	New Mexico	10,438
29	Nebraska	10,158
30	Washington	10,073
31	Colorado	10,013
32	Kansas	9,828
33	Arkansas	9,715
34	South Carolina	9,708
35	Nevada	9,321
36	Alabama	9,206
36	Florida	9,206
38	Idaho	9,117
39	Georgia	9,085
40	Tennessee	9,058
41	South Dakota	8,977
42	Texas	8,935
43	North Carolina	8,898
44	Mississippi	8,842
45	Maine	8,825
46	North Dakota	8,337
47	Oklahoma	8,085
48	Utah	7,905
49	Arizona	7,753
50	Indiana	7,538
	District of Columbia	15,370

Source: National Education Association, Washington, D.C.
  "Rankings and Estimates" (Copyright © 2016, NEA, used with permission, http://www.nea.org/home/32073.htm)
*Estimates for school year 2015-2016. Based on student membership.

Higher Education Expenditures by State and Local Governments in 2014

National Total = $268,976,777,000*

ALPHA ORDER

RANK	STATE	EXPENDITURES	% of USA
20	Alabama	$4,706,215,000	1.7%
43	Alaska	929,611,000	0.3%
18	Arizona	5,064,607,000	1.9%
34	Arkansas	2,639,380,000	1.0%
1	California	36,858,809,000	13.7%
19	Colorado	5,056,574,000	1.9%
32	Connecticut	2,909,217,000	1.1%
39	Delaware	1,211,090,000	0.5%
5	Florida	9,934,658,000	3.7%
14	Georgia	6,120,589,000	2.3%
40	Hawaii	1,133,626,000	0.4%
41	Idaho	1,022,017,000	0.4%
7	Illinois	9,569,326,000	3.6%
16	Indiana	5,808,227,000	2.2%
25	Iowa	3,788,630,000	1.4%
31	Kansas	3,076,107,000	1.1%
27	Kentucky	3,717,313,000	1.4%
30	Louisiana	3,146,725,000	1.2%
46	Maine	807,547,000	0.3%
15	Maryland	6,109,886,000	2.3%
17	Massachusetts	5,168,377,000	1.9%
4	Michigan	11,015,556,000	4.1%
21	Minnesota	4,676,531,000	1.7%
33	Mississippi	2,745,394,000	1.0%
23	Missouri	3,907,051,000	1.5%
45	Montana	834,123,000	0.3%
36	Nebraska	2,045,282,000	0.8%
38	Nevada	1,326,029,000	0.5%
44	New Hampshire	853,730,000	0.3%
12	New Jersey	6,276,116,000	2.3%
35	New Mexico	2,400,305,000	0.9%
3	New York	13,683,874,000	5.1%
9	North Carolina	9,328,046,000	3.5%
42	North Dakota	1,014,465,000	0.4%
8	Ohio	9,456,359,000	3.5%
29	Oklahoma	3,599,350,000	1.3%
22	Oregon	4,398,077,000	1.6%
6	Pennsylvania	9,767,318,000	3.6%
50	Rhode Island	650,598,000	0.2%
24	South Carolina	3,788,791,000	1.4%
49	South Dakota	677,740,000	0.3%
26	Tennessee	3,782,771,000	1.4%
2	Texas	27,105,067,000	10.1%
28	Utah	3,706,721,000	1.4%
48	Vermont	765,706,000	0.3%
10	Virginia	7,410,545,000	2.8%
11	Washington	6,281,125,000	2.3%
37	West Virginia	1,653,965,000	0.6%
13	Wisconsin	6,123,991,000	2.3%
47	Wyoming	772,574,000	0.3%

RANK ORDER

RANK	STATE	EXPENDITURES	% of USA
1	California	$36,858,809,000	13.7%
2	Texas	27,105,067,000	10.1%
3	New York	13,683,874,000	5.1%
4	Michigan	11,015,556,000	4.1%
5	Florida	9,934,658,000	3.7%
6	Pennsylvania	9,767,318,000	3.6%
7	Illinois	9,569,326,000	3.6%
8	Ohio	9,456,359,000	3.5%
9	North Carolina	9,328,046,000	3.5%
10	Virginia	7,410,545,000	2.8%
11	Washington	6,281,125,000	2.3%
12	New Jersey	6,276,116,000	2.3%
13	Wisconsin	6,123,991,000	2.3%
14	Georgia	6,120,589,000	2.3%
15	Maryland	6,109,886,000	2.3%
16	Indiana	5,808,227,000	2.2%
17	Massachusetts	5,168,377,000	1.9%
18	Arizona	5,064,607,000	1.9%
19	Colorado	5,056,574,000	1.9%
20	Alabama	4,706,215,000	1.7%
21	Minnesota	4,676,531,000	1.7%
22	Oregon	4,398,077,000	1.6%
23	Missouri	3,907,051,000	1.5%
24	South Carolina	3,788,791,000	1.4%
25	Iowa	3,788,630,000	1.4%
26	Tennessee	3,782,771,000	1.4%
27	Kentucky	3,717,313,000	1.4%
28	Utah	3,706,721,000	1.4%
29	Oklahoma	3,599,350,000	1.3%
30	Louisiana	3,146,725,000	1.2%
31	Kansas	3,076,107,000	1.1%
32	Connecticut	2,909,217,000	1.1%
33	Mississippi	2,745,394,000	1.0%
34	Arkansas	2,639,380,000	1.0%
35	New Mexico	2,400,305,000	0.9%
36	Nebraska	2,045,282,000	0.8%
37	West Virginia	1,653,965,000	0.6%
38	Nevada	1,326,029,000	0.5%
39	Delaware	1,211,090,000	0.5%
40	Hawaii	1,133,626,000	0.4%
41	Idaho	1,022,017,000	0.4%
42	North Dakota	1,014,465,000	0.4%
43	Alaska	929,611,000	0.3%
44	New Hampshire	853,730,000	0.3%
45	Montana	834,123,000	0.3%
46	Maine	807,547,000	0.3%
47	Wyoming	772,574,000	0.3%
48	Vermont	765,706,000	0.3%
49	South Dakota	677,740,000	0.3%
50	Rhode Island	650,598,000	0.2%
	District of Columbia	151,046,000	0.1%

Source: U.S. Bureau of the Census, Governments Division
"2014 State and Local Government Finances" (http://www.census.gov/govs/local/)
*Direct general expenditures. Includes capital outlays.

Per Capita State and Local Government Expenditures for Higher Education in 2014
National Per Capita = $844*

ALPHA ORDER

RANK	STATE	PER CAPITA
16	Alabama	$972
4	Alaska	1,262
37	Arizona	754
24	Arkansas	890
17	California	953
18	Colorado	945
31	Connecticut	810
3	Delaware	1,295
49	Florida	500
46	Georgia	607
32	Hawaii	800
44	Idaho	626
38	Illinois	744
26	Indiana	881
7	Iowa	1,219
13	Kansas	1,061
28	Kentucky	842
41	Louisiana	677
46	Maine	607
14	Maryland	1,024
35	Massachusetts	766
9	Michigan	1,111
27	Minnesota	858
21	Mississippi	917
42	Missouri	645
30	Montana	815
11	Nebraska	1,087
50	Nevada	468
43	New Hampshire	643
39	New Jersey	703
8	New Mexico	1,152
40	New York	694
19	North Carolina	939
1	North Dakota	1,371
29	Ohio	816
20	Oklahoma	928
10	Oregon	1,108
36	Pennsylvania	764
45	Rhode Island	617
34	South Carolina	785
33	South Dakota	795
48	Tennessee	578
15	Texas	1,006
5	Utah	1,260
6	Vermont	1,221
23	Virginia	891
24	Washington	890
22	West Virginia	895
12	Wisconsin	1,063
2	Wyoming	1,324

RANK ORDER

RANK	STATE	PER CAPITA
1	North Dakota	$1,371
2	Wyoming	1,324
3	Delaware	1,295
4	Alaska	1,262
5	Utah	1,260
6	Vermont	1,221
7	Iowa	1,219
8	New Mexico	1,152
9	Michigan	1,111
10	Oregon	1,108
11	Nebraska	1,087
12	Wisconsin	1,063
13	Kansas	1,061
14	Maryland	1,024
15	Texas	1,006
16	Alabama	972
17	California	953
18	Colorado	945
19	North Carolina	939
20	Oklahoma	928
21	Mississippi	917
22	West Virginia	895
23	Virginia	891
24	Arkansas	890
24	Washington	890
26	Indiana	881
27	Minnesota	858
28	Kentucky	842
29	Ohio	816
30	Montana	815
31	Connecticut	810
32	Hawaii	800
33	South Dakota	795
34	South Carolina	785
35	Massachusetts	766
36	Pennsylvania	764
37	Arizona	754
38	Illinois	744
39	New Jersey	703
40	New York	694
41	Louisiana	677
42	Missouri	645
43	New Hampshire	643
44	Idaho	626
45	Rhode Island	617
46	Georgia	607
46	Maine	607
48	Tennessee	578
49	Florida	500
50	Nevada	468
	District of Columbia	229

Source: CQ Press using data from U.S. Bureau of the Census, Governments Division
"2014 State and Local Government Finances" (http://www.census.gov/govs/local/)
*Direct general expenditures. Includes capital outlays.

Expenditures for Higher Education as a Percent
of All State and Local Government Expenditures in 2014
National Percent = 9.9%*

ALPHA ORDER

RANK	STATE	PERCENT
5	Alabama	13.0
49	Alaska	6.4
17	Arizona	11.8
16	Arkansas	11.9
29	California	9.9
18	Colorado	11.6
41	Connecticut	8.1
10	Delaware	12.6
44	Florida	7.2
33	Georgia	9.3
40	Hawaii	8.3
29	Idaho	9.9
36	Illinois	8.8
15	Indiana	12.1
4	Iowa	13.1
8	Kansas	12.8
22	Kentucky	11.1
42	Louisiana	7.6
47	Maine	7.0
23	Maryland	11.0
42	Massachusetts	7.6
2	Michigan	14.5
34	Minnesota	9.1
19	Mississippi	11.4
34	Missouri	9.1
32	Montana	9.8
5	Nebraska	13.0
44	Nevada	7.2
39	New Hampshire	8.5
46	New Jersey	7.1
8	New Mexico	12.8
50	New York	5.6
5	North Carolina	13.0
13	North Dakota	12.4
29	Ohio	9.9
10	Oklahoma	12.6
12	Oregon	12.5
36	Pennsylvania	8.8
48	Rhode Island	6.7
26	South Carolina	10.2
25	South Dakota	10.6
38	Tennessee	8.7
3	Texas	13.8
1	Utah	17.7
19	Vermont	11.4
23	Virginia	11.0
27	Washington	10.1
21	West Virginia	11.2
13	Wisconsin	12.4
27	Wyoming	10.1

RANK ORDER

RANK	STATE	PERCENT
1	Utah	17.7
2	Michigan	14.5
3	Texas	13.8
4	Iowa	13.1
5	Alabama	13.0
5	Nebraska	13.0
5	North Carolina	13.0
8	Kansas	12.8
8	New Mexico	12.8
10	Delaware	12.6
10	Oklahoma	12.6
12	Oregon	12.5
13	North Dakota	12.4
13	Wisconsin	12.4
15	Indiana	12.1
16	Arkansas	11.9
17	Arizona	11.8
18	Colorado	11.6
19	Mississippi	11.4
19	Vermont	11.4
21	West Virginia	11.2
22	Kentucky	11.1
23	Maryland	11.0
23	Virginia	11.0
25	South Dakota	10.6
26	South Carolina	10.2
27	Washington	10.1
27	Wyoming	10.1
29	California	9.9
29	Idaho	9.9
29	Ohio	9.9
32	Montana	9.8
33	Georgia	9.3
34	Minnesota	9.1
34	Missouri	9.1
36	Illinois	8.8
36	Pennsylvania	8.8
38	Tennessee	8.7
39	New Hampshire	8.5
40	Hawaii	8.3
41	Connecticut	8.1
42	Louisiana	7.6
42	Massachusetts	7.6
44	Florida	7.2
44	Nevada	7.2
46	New Jersey	7.1
47	Maine	7.0
48	Rhode Island	6.7
49	Alaska	6.4
50	New York	5.6

District of Columbia — 1.3

Source: CQ Press using data from U.S. Bureau of the Census, Governments Division
"2014 State and Local Government Finances" (http://www.census.gov/govs/local/)
*Direct general expenditures for higher education as a percent of all direct general expenditures. Includes capital outlays.

Average Faculty Salary at Institutions of Higher Education in 2015

National Average = $80,203*

RANK	STATE	AVERAGE SALARY
37	Alabama	$68,645
16	Alaska	77,679
14	Arizona	81,138
50	Arkansas	58,886
5	California	94,099
20	Colorado	76,469
3	Connecticut	99,655
6	Delaware	94,034
21	Florida	75,397
30	Georgia	72,174
13	Hawaii	82,085
48	Idaho	61,190
11	Illinois	84,644
18	Indiana	77,163
26	Iowa	73,926
42	Kansas	65,541
44	Kentucky	64,467
43	Louisiana	65,488
19	Maine	76,590
15	Maryland	80,705
1	Massachusetts	101,455
10	Michigan	84,815
22	Minnesota	75,158
49	Mississippi	60,032
31	Missouri	72,164
46	Montana	62,092
33	Nebraska	71,189
12	Nevada	82,388
8	New Hampshire	90,149
2	New Jersey	99,818
41	New Mexico	65,704
7	New York	92,094
29	North Carolina	73,083
39	North Dakota	66,832
23	Ohio	75,089
38	Oklahoma	67,003
25	Oregon	74,060
9	Pennsylvania	86,531
4	Rhode Island	94,306
40	South Carolina	66,617
47	South Dakota	61,922
35	Tennessee	70,602
24	Texas	74,985
36	Utah	69,170
17	Vermont	77,274
28	Virginia	73,443
27	Washington	73,684
45	West Virginia	63,622
32	Wisconsin	71,756
34	Wyoming	70,883

RANK	STATE	AVERAGE SALARY
1	Massachusetts	$101,455
2	New Jersey	99,818
3	Connecticut	99,655
4	Rhode Island	94,306
5	California	94,099
6	Delaware	94,034
7	New York	92,094
8	New Hampshire	90,149
9	Pennsylvania	86,531
10	Michigan	84,815
11	Illinois	84,644
12	Nevada	82,388
13	Hawaii	82,085
14	Arizona	81,138
15	Maryland	80,705
16	Alaska	77,679
17	Vermont	77,274
18	Indiana	77,163
19	Maine	76,590
20	Colorado	76,469
21	Florida	75,397
22	Minnesota	75,158
23	Ohio	75,089
24	Texas	74,985
25	Oregon	74,060
26	Iowa	73,926
27	Washington	73,684
28	Virginia	73,443
29	North Carolina	73,083
30	Georgia	72,174
31	Missouri	72,164
32	Wisconsin	71,756
33	Nebraska	71,189
34	Wyoming	70,883
35	Tennessee	70,602
36	Utah	69,170
37	Alabama	68,645
38	Oklahoma	67,003
39	North Dakota	66,832
40	South Carolina	66,617
41	New Mexico	65,704
42	Kansas	65,541
43	Louisiana	65,488
44	Kentucky	64,467
45	West Virginia	63,622
46	Montana	62,092
47	South Dakota	61,922
48	Idaho	61,190
49	Mississippi	60,032
50	Arkansas	58,886

| | District of Columbia | 92,005 |

Source: U.S. Department of Education, National Center for Education Statistics
"Digest of Education Statistics" (http://nces.ed.gov/programs/digest/index.asp)
*For 2014-2015 school year. For full-time instructional faculty on 9-month contracts at four-year and two-year public and private degree-granting institutions.

Average Student Costs at Public Institutions of Higher Education in 2015

National Average = $18,632*

ALPHA ORDER

RANK	STATE	AVERAGE COSTS
25	Alabama	$17,859
30	Alaska	16,814
16	Arizona	19,839
40	Arkansas	15,320
10	California	21,749
17	Colorado	19,710
7	Connecticut	22,435
6	Delaware	23,161
44	Florida	14,677
32	Georgia	16,522
20	Hawaii	19,131
48	Idaho	13,644
4	Illinois	23,792
24	Indiana	18,393
31	Iowa	16,708
39	Kansas	15,584
26	Kentucky	17,530
34	Louisiana	16,045
21	Maine	18,914
19	Maryland	19,375
8	Massachusetts	22,214
12	Michigan	20,843
23	Minnesota	18,726
37	Mississippi	15,710
28	Missouri	17,143
45	Montana	14,448
33	Nebraska	16,199
41	Nevada	15,138
1	New Hampshire	25,821
3	New Jersey	24,825
43	New Mexico	14,778
13	New York	20,549
36	North Carolina	15,771
46	North Dakota	14,217
14	Ohio	20,537
47	Oklahoma	14,147
18	Oregon	19,654
5	Pennsylvania	23,519
9	Rhode Island	22,030
15	South Carolina	20,354
42	South Dakota	14,983
27	Tennessee	17,147
29	Texas	16,872
50	Utah	12,970
2	Vermont	24,986
11	Virginia	20,941
22	Washington	18,863
38	West Virginia	15,644
35	Wisconsin	15,938
49	Wyoming	13,457

RANK ORDER

RANK	STATE	AVERAGE COSTS
1	New Hampshire	$25,821
2	Vermont	24,986
3	New Jersey	24,825
4	Illinois	23,792
5	Pennsylvania	23,519
6	Delaware	23,161
7	Connecticut	22,435
8	Massachusetts	22,214
9	Rhode Island	22,030
10	California	21,749
11	Virginia	20,941
12	Michigan	20,843
13	New York	20,549
14	Ohio	20,537
15	South Carolina	20,354
16	Arizona	19,839
17	Colorado	19,710
18	Oregon	19,654
19	Maryland	19,375
20	Hawaii	19,131
21	Maine	18,914
22	Washington	18,863
23	Minnesota	18,726
24	Indiana	18,393
25	Alabama	17,859
26	Kentucky	17,530
27	Tennessee	17,147
28	Missouri	17,143
29	Texas	16,872
30	Alaska	16,814
31	Iowa	16,708
32	Georgia	16,522
33	Nebraska	16,199
34	Louisiana	16,045
35	Wisconsin	15,938
36	North Carolina	15,771
37	Mississippi	15,710
38	West Virginia	15,644
39	Kansas	15,584
40	Arkansas	15,320
41	Nevada	15,138
42	South Dakota	14,983
43	New Mexico	14,778
44	Florida	14,677
45	Montana	14,448
46	North Dakota	14,217
47	Oklahoma	14,147
48	Idaho	13,644
49	Wyoming	13,457
50	Utah	12,970
	District of Columbia**	NA

Source: U.S. Department of Education, National Center for Education Statistics
   "Digest of Education Statistics" (http://nces.ed.gov/programs/digest/index.asp)
*Data for 2014-2015 school year. Based on average in-state tuition, room and board, and fees for full-time students in public four-year institutions for an entire academic year.
**Not available.

Average Student Costs at Private Institutions of Higher Education in 2015

National Average = $37,990*

ALPHA ORDER				RANK ORDER		
RANK	STATE	AVERAGE COSTS		RANK	STATE	AVERAGE COSTS
43	Alabama	$23,883		1	Massachusetts	$53,172
40	Alaska	25,961		2	Connecticut	49,824
45	Arizona	20,928		3	Maryland	49,648
38	Arkansas	27,486		4	Vermont	49,211
17	California	38,468		5	Rhode Island	48,870
24	Colorado	32,916		6	New York	48,845
2	Connecticut	49,824		7	Pennsylvania	47,894
41	Delaware	24,904		8	New Jersey	45,434
27	Florida	32,418		9	New Hampshire	44,995
22	Georgia	36,107		10	Maine	44,991
39	Hawaii	27,483		11	Oregon	44,215
49	Idaho	13,009		12	Washington	43,285
14	Illinois	39,778		13	Louisiana	42,620
15	Indiana	39,129		14	Illinois	39,778
25	Iowa	32,610		15	Indiana	39,129
42	Kansas	24,655		16	North Carolina	38,918
28	Kentucky	31,594		17	California	38,468
13	Louisiana	42,620		18	Ohio	37,976
10	Maine	44,991		19	Texas	37,743
3	Maryland	49,648		20	Minnesota	37,684
1	Massachusetts	53,172		21	Wisconsin	37,416
34	Michigan	29,423		22	Georgia	36,107
20	Minnesota	37,684		23	Tennessee	33,183
44	Mississippi	22,844		24	Colorado	32,916
32	Missouri	30,402		25	Iowa	32,610
33	Montana	29,635		26	Virginia	32,501
35	Nebraska	28,930		27	Florida	32,418
31	Nevada	30,812		28	Kentucky	31,594
9	New Hampshire	44,995		29	Oklahoma	31,093
8	New Jersey	45,434		30	South Carolina	30,957
37	New Mexico	28,464		31	Nevada	30,812
6	New York	48,845		32	Missouri	30,402
16	North Carolina	38,918		33	Montana	29,635
47	North Dakota	19,502		34	Michigan	29,423
18	Ohio	37,976		35	Nebraska	28,930
29	Oklahoma	31,093		36	South Dakota	28,531
11	Oregon	44,215		37	New Mexico	28,464
7	Pennsylvania	47,894		38	Arkansas	27,486
5	Rhode Island	48,870		39	Hawaii	27,483
30	South Carolina	30,957		40	Alaska	25,961
36	South Dakota	28,531		41	Delaware	24,904
23	Tennessee	33,183		42	Kansas	24,655
19	Texas	37,743		43	Alabama	23,883
48	Utah	15,435		44	Mississippi	22,844
4	Vermont	49,211		45	Arizona	20,928
26	Virginia	32,501		46	West Virginia	19,681
12	Washington	43,285		47	North Dakota	19,502
46	West Virginia	19,681		48	Utah	15,435
21	Wisconsin	37,416		49	Idaho	13,009
NA	Wyoming**	NA		NA	Wyoming**	NA
					District of Columbia	51,857

Source: U.S. Department of Education, National Center for Education Statistics
"Digest of Education Statistics" (http://nces.ed.gov/programs/digest/index.asp)
*Data for 2014-2015 school year. Based on average in-state tuition, room and board, and fees for full-time students in private four-year institutions for an entire academic year.
**Not available.

Average College Graduate Debt: Class of 2015

National Average Debt = $30,100*

ALPHA ORDER

RANK	STATE	AVERAGE DEBT
19	Alabama	$29,153
35	Alaska	26,171
42	Arizona	23,780
37	Arkansas	26,082
47	California	22,191
38	Colorado	25,840
3	Connecticut	34,773
4	Delaware	33,849
45	Florida	23,379
23	Georgia	27,754
44	Hawaii	23,456
28	Idaho	27,639
18	Illinois	29,305
20	Indiana	29,022
14	Iowa	29,547
22	Kansas	28,008
31	Kentucky	27,225
32	Louisiana	26,865
13	Maine	29,644
27	Maryland	27,672
7	Massachusetts	31,466
11	Michigan	30,045
6	Minnesota	31,526
12	Mississippi	29,942
29	Missouri	27,480
33	Montana	26,280
34	Nebraska	26,235
43	Nevada	23,462
1	New Hampshire	36,101
10	New Jersey	30,104
48	New Mexico	20,193
17	New York	29,320
39	North Carolina	25,645
NA	North Dakota**	NA
9	Ohio	30,239
40	Oklahoma	24,849
26	Oregon	27,697
2	Pennsylvania	34,798
5	Rhode Island	32,920
8	South Carolina	30,564
16	South Dakota	29,364
36	Tennessee	26,083
30	Texas	27,324
49	Utah	18,873
21	Vermont	28,283
24	Virginia	27,717
41	Washington	24,600
25	West Virginia	27,713
15	Wisconsin	29,460
46	Wyoming	22,683

RANK ORDER

RANK	STATE	AVERAGE DEBT
1	New Hampshire	$36,101
2	Pennsylvania	34,798
3	Connecticut	34,773
4	Delaware	33,849
5	Rhode Island	32,920
6	Minnesota	31,526
7	Massachusetts	31,466
8	South Carolina	30,564
9	Ohio	30,239
10	New Jersey	30,104
11	Michigan	30,045
12	Mississippi	29,942
13	Maine	29,644
14	Iowa	29,547
15	Wisconsin	29,460
16	South Dakota	29,364
17	New York	29,320
18	Illinois	29,305
19	Alabama	29,153
20	Indiana	29,022
21	Vermont	28,283
22	Kansas	28,008
23	Georgia	27,754
24	Virginia	27,717
25	West Virginia	27,713
26	Oregon	27,697
27	Maryland	27,672
28	Idaho	27,639
29	Missouri	27,480
30	Texas	27,324
31	Kentucky	27,225
32	Louisiana	26,865
33	Montana	26,280
34	Nebraska	26,235
35	Alaska	26,171
36	Tennessee	26,083
37	Arkansas	26,082
38	Colorado	25,840
39	North Carolina	25,645
40	Oklahoma	24,849
41	Washington	24,600
42	Arizona	23,780
43	Nevada	23,462
44	Hawaii	23,456
45	Florida	23,379
46	Wyoming	22,683
47	California	22,191
48	New Mexico	20,193
49	Utah	18,873
NA	North Dakota**	NA
	District of Columbia	31,452

Source: The Project on Student Debt
   "Student Debt and The Class of 2015" (October 2016, http://ticas.org/posd/map-state-data)
*For students receiving a bachelor's degree in 2015.
**Not available.

Percent of College Graduates with Debt: Class of 2015

National Percent = 68%*

ALPHA ORDER

RANK	STATE	PERCENT
43	Alabama	52
40	Alaska	55
36	Arizona	56
34	Arkansas	57
41	California	54
36	Colorado	56
14	Connecticut	64
13	Delaware	65
42	Florida	53
23	Georgia	61
46	Hawaii	50
3	Idaho	71
8	Illinois	66
23	Indiana	61
8	Iowa	66
17	Kansas	63
14	Kentucky	64
45	Louisiana	51
17	Maine	63
36	Maryland	56
8	Massachusetts	66
17	Michigan	63
5	Minnesota	70
21	Mississippi	62
23	Missouri	61
27	Montana	60
27	Nebraska	60
47	Nevada	47
1	New Hampshire	76
8	New Jersey	66
33	New Mexico	58
31	New York	59
23	North Carolina	61
NA	North Dakota**	NA
8	Ohio	66
43	Oklahoma	52
17	Oregon	63
3	Pennsylvania	71
14	Rhode Island	64
27	South Carolina	60
2	South Dakota	73
27	Tennessee	60
36	Texas	56
49	Utah	41
21	Vermont	62
31	Virginia	59
34	Washington	57
7	West Virginia	68
5	Wisconsin	70
48	Wyoming	46

RANK ORDER

RANK	STATE	PERCENT
1	New Hampshire	76
2	South Dakota	73
3	Idaho	71
3	Pennsylvania	71
5	Minnesota	70
5	Wisconsin	70
7	West Virginia	68
8	Illinois	66
8	Iowa	66
8	Massachusetts	66
8	New Jersey	66
8	Ohio	66
13	Delaware	65
14	Connecticut	64
14	Kentucky	64
14	Rhode Island	64
17	Kansas	63
17	Maine	63
17	Michigan	63
17	Oregon	63
21	Mississippi	62
21	Vermont	62
23	Georgia	61
23	Indiana	61
23	Missouri	61
23	North Carolina	61
27	Montana	60
27	Nebraska	60
27	South Carolina	60
27	Tennessee	60
31	New York	59
31	Virginia	59
33	New Mexico	58
34	Arkansas	57
34	Washington	57
36	Arizona	56
36	Colorado	56
36	Maryland	56
36	Texas	56
40	Alaska	55
41	California	54
42	Florida	53
43	Alabama	52
43	Oklahoma	52
45	Louisiana	51
46	Hawaii	50
47	Nevada	47
48	Wyoming	46
49	Utah	41
NA	North Dakota**	NA
	District of Columbia	55

Source: The Project on Student Debt
   "Student Debt and The Class of 2015" (October 2016, http://ticas.org/posd/map-state-data)
*For students receiving a bachelor's degree in 2015.
**Not available.

Institutions of Higher Education in 2016

National Total = 4,583 Institutions*

ALPHA ORDER

RANK	STATE	INSTITUTIONS	% of USA
21	Alabama	77	1.7%
49	Alaska	9	0.2%
17	Arizona	86	1.9%
31	Arkansas	53	1.2%
1	California	448	9.8%
16	Colorado	87	1.9%
33	Connecticut	43	0.9%
49	Delaware	9	0.2%
5	Florida	229	5.0%
10	Georgia	130	2.8%
44	Hawaii	20	0.4%
46	Idaho	19	0.4%
7	Illinois	185	4.0%
19	Indiana	84	1.8%
27	Iowa	64	1.4%
23	Kansas	75	1.6%
24	Kentucky	72	1.6%
27	Louisiana	64	1.4%
38	Maine	31	0.7%
30	Maryland	58	1.3%
12	Massachusetts	124	2.7%
15	Michigan	103	2.2%
13	Minnesota	115	2.5%
36	Mississippi	41	0.9%
11	Missouri	125	2.7%
43	Montana	22	0.5%
35	Nebraska	42	0.9%
40	Nevada	26	0.6%
39	New Hampshire	27	0.6%
24	New Jersey	72	1.6%
33	New Mexico	43	0.9%
2	New York	304	6.6%
8	North Carolina	150	3.3%
44	North Dakota	20	0.4%
6	Ohio	208	4.5%
26	Oklahoma	67	1.5%
29	Oregon	63	1.4%
4	Pennsylvania	256	5.6%
47	Rhode Island	13	0.3%
21	South Carolina	77	1.7%
41	South Dakota	25	0.5%
14	Tennessee	105	2.3%
3	Texas	272	5.9%
37	Utah	36	0.8%
42	Vermont	24	0.5%
9	Virginia	131	2.9%
17	Washington	86	1.9%
32	West Virginia	44	1.0%
19	Wisconsin	84	1.8%
48	Wyoming	10	0.2%

RANK ORDER

RANK	STATE	INSTITUTIONS	% of USA
1	California	448	9.8%
2	New York	304	6.6%
3	Texas	272	5.9%
4	Pennsylvania	256	5.6%
5	Florida	229	5.0%
6	Ohio	208	4.5%
7	Illinois	185	4.0%
8	North Carolina	150	3.3%
9	Virginia	131	2.9%
10	Georgia	130	2.8%
11	Missouri	125	2.7%
12	Massachusetts	124	2.7%
13	Minnesota	115	2.5%
14	Tennessee	105	2.3%
15	Michigan	103	2.2%
16	Colorado	87	1.9%
17	Arizona	86	1.9%
17	Washington	86	1.9%
19	Indiana	84	1.8%
19	Wisconsin	84	1.8%
21	Alabama	77	1.7%
21	South Carolina	77	1.7%
23	Kansas	75	1.6%
24	Kentucky	72	1.6%
24	New Jersey	72	1.6%
26	Oklahoma	67	1.5%
27	Iowa	64	1.4%
27	Louisiana	64	1.4%
29	Oregon	63	1.4%
30	Maryland	58	1.3%
31	Arkansas	53	1.2%
32	West Virginia	44	1.0%
33	Connecticut	43	0.9%
33	New Mexico	43	0.9%
35	Nebraska	42	0.9%
36	Mississippi	41	0.9%
37	Utah	36	0.8%
38	Maine	31	0.7%
39	New Hampshire	27	0.6%
40	Nevada	26	0.6%
41	South Dakota	25	0.5%
42	Vermont	24	0.5%
43	Montana	22	0.5%
44	Hawaii	20	0.4%
44	North Dakota	20	0.4%
46	Idaho	19	0.4%
47	Rhode Island	13	0.3%
48	Wyoming	10	0.2%
49	Alaska	9	0.2%
49	Delaware	9	0.2%
	District of Columbia	20	0.4%

Source: U.S. Department of Education, National Center for Education Statistics
   "Digest of Education Statistics" (http://nces.ed.gov/programs/digest/index.asp)
*For 2015-2016 school year. Consists of 3,004 four-year and 1,579 two-year public and private (profit and not-for-profit)
degree-granting institutions. Includes five U.S. Service Schools not shown by state.

Enrollment in Institutions of Higher Education in 2014

National Total = 20,207,369 Students*

ALPHA ORDER

RANK	STATE	STUDENTS	% of USA
23	Alabama	305,028	1.5%
50	Alaska	34,331	0.2%
8	Arizona	674,746	3.3%
34	Arkansas	169,571	0.8%
1	California	2,696,415	13.3%
21	Colorado	353,827	1.8%
32	Connecticut	201,928	1.0%
44	Delaware	60,368	0.3%
4	Florida	1,111,018	5.5%
12	Georgia	531,004	2.6%
42	Hawaii	73,505	0.4%
39	Idaho	118,953	0.6%
5	Illinois	824,980	4.1%
14	Indiana	436,327	2.2%
24	Iowa	282,482	1.4%
30	Kansas	226,401	1.1%
26	Kentucky	264,197	1.3%
28	Louisiana	245,938	1.2%
43	Maine	72,246	0.4%
18	Maryland	365,597	1.8%
13	Massachusetts	510,912	2.5%
9	Michigan	619,438	3.1%
16	Minnesota	433,854	2.1%
33	Mississippi	170,728	0.8%
17	Missouri	419,900	2.1%
47	Montana	51,942	0.3%
37	Nebraska	135,825	0.7%
38	Nevada	119,205	0.6%
40	New Hampshire	106,984	0.5%
15	New Jersey	436,208	2.2%
36	New Mexico	146,246	0.7%
3	New York	1,299,055	6.4%
11	North Carolina	570,045	2.8%
45	North Dakota	54,048	0.3%
7	Ohio	680,238	3.4%
31	Oklahoma	215,349	1.1%
29	Oregon	245,547	1.2%
6	Pennsylvania	750,651	3.7%
41	Rhode Island	83,499	0.4%
27	South Carolina	254,629	1.3%
46	South Dakota	53,963	0.3%
22	Tennessee	326,575	1.6%
2	Texas	1,555,462	7.7%
25	Utah	274,926	1.4%
48	Vermont	43,983	0.2%
10	Virginia	577,908	2.9%
19	Washington	365,193	1.8%
35	West Virginia	157,052	0.8%
20	Wisconsin	358,894	1.8%
49	Wyoming	35,461	0.2%

RANK ORDER

RANK	STATE	STUDENTS	% of USA
1	California	2,696,415	13.3%
2	Texas	1,555,462	7.7%
3	New York	1,299,055	6.4%
4	Florida	1,111,018	5.5%
5	Illinois	824,980	4.1%
6	Pennsylvania	750,651	3.7%
7	Ohio	680,238	3.4%
8	Arizona	674,746	3.3%
9	Michigan	619,438	3.1%
10	Virginia	577,908	2.9%
11	North Carolina	570,045	2.8%
12	Georgia	531,004	2.6%
13	Massachusetts	510,912	2.5%
14	Indiana	436,327	2.2%
15	New Jersey	436,208	2.2%
16	Minnesota	433,854	2.1%
17	Missouri	419,900	2.1%
18	Maryland	365,597	1.8%
19	Washington	365,193	1.8%
20	Wisconsin	358,894	1.8%
21	Colorado	353,827	1.8%
22	Tennessee	326,575	1.6%
23	Alabama	305,028	1.5%
24	Iowa	282,482	1.4%
25	Utah	274,926	1.4%
26	Kentucky	264,197	1.3%
27	South Carolina	254,629	1.3%
28	Louisiana	245,938	1.2%
29	Oregon	245,547	1.2%
30	Kansas	226,401	1.1%
31	Oklahoma	215,349	1.1%
32	Connecticut	201,928	1.0%
33	Mississippi	170,728	0.8%
34	Arkansas	169,571	0.8%
35	West Virginia	157,052	0.8%
36	New Mexico	146,246	0.7%
37	Nebraska	135,825	0.7%
38	Nevada	119,205	0.6%
39	Idaho	118,953	0.6%
40	New Hampshire	106,984	0.5%
41	Rhode Island	83,499	0.4%
42	Hawaii	73,505	0.4%
43	Maine	72,246	0.4%
44	Delaware	60,368	0.3%
45	North Dakota	54,048	0.3%
46	South Dakota	53,963	0.3%
47	Montana	51,942	0.3%
48	Vermont	43,983	0.2%
49	Wyoming	35,461	0.2%
50	Alaska	34,331	0.2%
	District of Columbia	90,053	0.4%

Source: U.S. Department of Education, National Center for Education Statistics
  "Digest of Education Statistics" (http://nces.ed.gov/programs/digest/index.asp)
*Fall 2014 enrollment. Includes full-time and part-time students at Title IV eligible, degree-granting four-year and two-year institutions. National total includes 14,734 students at U.S. Service Schools not shown by state.

Enrollment Rate in Institutions of Higher Education in 2014

National Rate = 642 Students per 1,000 Population 18 to 24 Years Old*

ALPHA ORDER

RANK	STATE	RATE
26	Alabama	636
50	Alaska	420
1	Arizona	1,004
34	Arkansas	592
16	California	675
15	Colorado	676
35	Connecticut	577
17	Delaware	673
28	Florida	623
46	Georgia	520
43	Hawaii	532
7	Idaho	762
19	Illinois	659
21	Indiana	652
3	Iowa	882
8	Kansas	749
32	Kentucky	614
45	Louisiana	527
24	Maine	641
23	Maryland	650
9	Massachusetts	731
30	Michigan	617
4	Minnesota	855
39	Mississippi	549
12	Missouri	707
48	Montana	514
11	Nebraska	709
49	Nevada	468
5	New Hampshire	833
41	New Jersey	547
13	New Mexico	702
20	New York	658
35	North Carolina	577
37	North Dakota	575
29	Ohio	619
39	Oklahoma	549
17	Oregon	673
33	Pennsylvania	612
10	Rhode Island	713
44	South Carolina	528
27	South Dakota	630
47	Tennessee	517
38	Texas	566
6	Utah	825
22	Vermont	651
14	Virginia	697
42	Washington	546
2	West Virginia	921
25	Wisconsin	637
30	Wyoming	617

RANK ORDER

RANK	STATE	RATE
1	Arizona	1,004
2	West Virginia	921
3	Iowa	882
4	Minnesota	855
5	New Hampshire	833
6	Utah	825
7	Idaho	762
8	Kansas	749
9	Massachusetts	731
10	Rhode Island	713
11	Nebraska	709
12	Missouri	707
13	New Mexico	702
14	Virginia	697
15	Colorado	676
16	California	675
17	Delaware	673
17	Oregon	673
19	Illinois	659
20	New York	658
21	Indiana	652
22	Vermont	651
23	Maryland	650
24	Maine	641
25	Wisconsin	637
26	Alabama	636
27	South Dakota	630
28	Florida	623
29	Ohio	619
30	Michigan	617
30	Wyoming	617
32	Kentucky	614
33	Pennsylvania	612
34	Arkansas	592
35	Connecticut	577
35	North Carolina	577
37	North Dakota	575
38	Texas	566
39	Mississippi	549
39	Oklahoma	549
41	New Jersey	547
42	Washington	546
43	Hawaii	532
44	South Carolina	528
45	Louisiana	527
46	Georgia	520
47	Tennessee	517
48	Montana	514
49	Nevada	468
50	Alaska	420

District of Columbia   1,118

Source: CQ Press using data from U.S. Department of Education, National Center for Education Statistics
"Digest of Education Statistics" (http://nces.ed.gov/programs/digest/index.asp)
*Based on fall 2014 enrollment and population. National rate includes U.S. Service Schools. Includes students at four-year and two-year public and private degree-granting institutions. Enrollment based on location of institution. Population based on residence.

Enrollment in Public Institutions of Higher Education in 2014

National Total = 14,655,015 Students*

ALPHA ORDER

RANK	STATE	STUDENTS	% of USA
21	Alabama	246,989	1.7%
49	Alaska	29,892	0.2%
12	Arizona	354,997	2.4%
33	Arkansas	151,399	1.0%
1	California	2,167,444	14.8%
18	Colorado	268,041	1.8%
35	Connecticut	122,303	0.8%
47	Delaware	41,012	0.3%
3	Florida	795,628	5.4%
9	Georgia	413,752	2.8%
40	Hawaii	57,052	0.4%
39	Idaho	76,806	0.5%
5	Illinois	529,462	3.6%
14	Indiana	328,442	2.2%
30	Iowa	169,896	1.2%
28	Kansas	183,222	1.3%
24	Kentucky	213,043	1.5%
25	Louisiana	210,943	1.4%
41	Maine	48,852	0.3%
16	Maryland	305,156	2.1%
22	Massachusetts	226,158	1.5%
6	Michigan	514,712	3.5%
19	Minnesota	259,695	1.8%
32	Mississippi	152,096	1.0%
20	Missouri	252,980	1.7%
43	Montana	47,024	0.3%
37	Nebraska	99,821	0.7%
36	Nevada	106,028	0.7%
45	New Hampshire	43,298	0.3%
13	New Jersey	351,316	2.4%
34	New Mexico	138,311	0.9%
4	New York	721,847	4.9%
8	North Carolina	455,178	3.1%
42	North Dakota	48,292	0.3%
7	Ohio	510,244	3.5%
29	Oklahoma	182,449	1.2%
27	Oregon	201,645	1.4%
10	Pennsylvania	413,591	2.8%
46	Rhode Island	42,765	0.3%
26	South Carolina	205,756	1.4%
44	South Dakota	44,132	0.3%
23	Tennessee	224,033	1.5%
2	Texas	1,365,339	9.3%
31	Utah	167,716	1.1%
50	Vermont	25,643	0.2%
11	Virginia	399,359	2.7%
15	Washington	312,523	2.1%
38	West Virginia	87,842	0.6%
17	Wisconsin	286,726	2.0%
48	Wyoming	34,316	0.2%

RANK ORDER

RANK	STATE	STUDENTS	% of USA
1	California	2,167,444	14.8%
2	Texas	1,365,339	9.3%
3	Florida	795,628	5.4%
4	New York	721,847	4.9%
5	Illinois	529,462	3.6%
6	Michigan	514,712	3.5%
7	Ohio	510,244	3.5%
8	North Carolina	455,178	3.1%
9	Georgia	413,752	2.8%
10	Pennsylvania	413,591	2.8%
11	Virginia	399,359	2.7%
12	Arizona	354,997	2.4%
13	New Jersey	351,316	2.4%
14	Indiana	328,442	2.2%
15	Washington	312,523	2.1%
16	Maryland	305,156	2.1%
17	Wisconsin	286,726	2.0%
18	Colorado	268,041	1.8%
19	Minnesota	259,695	1.8%
20	Missouri	252,980	1.7%
21	Alabama	246,989	1.7%
22	Massachusetts	226,158	1.5%
23	Tennessee	224,033	1.5%
24	Kentucky	213,043	1.5%
25	Louisiana	210,943	1.4%
26	South Carolina	205,756	1.4%
27	Oregon	201,645	1.4%
28	Kansas	183,222	1.3%
29	Oklahoma	182,449	1.2%
30	Iowa	169,896	1.2%
31	Utah	167,716	1.1%
32	Mississippi	152,096	1.0%
33	Arkansas	151,399	1.0%
34	New Mexico	138,311	0.9%
35	Connecticut	122,303	0.8%
36	Nevada	106,028	0.7%
37	Nebraska	99,821	0.7%
38	West Virginia	87,842	0.6%
39	Idaho	76,806	0.5%
40	Hawaii	57,052	0.4%
41	Maine	48,852	0.3%
42	North Dakota	48,292	0.3%
43	Montana	47,024	0.3%
44	South Dakota	44,132	0.3%
45	New Hampshire	43,298	0.3%
46	Rhode Island	42,765	0.3%
47	Delaware	41,012	0.3%
48	Wyoming	34,316	0.2%
49	Alaska	29,892	0.2%
50	Vermont	25,643	0.2%
	District of Columbia	5,115	0.0%

Source: U.S. Department of Education, National Center for Education Statistics
   "Digest of Education Statistics" (http://nces.ed.gov/programs/digest/index.asp)
*Fall 2014 enrollment. Includes full-time and part-time students at Title IV eligible, degree-granting four-year and two-year institutions. National total includes 14,734 students at U.S. Service Schools not shown by state.

Enrollment in Private Institutions of Higher Education in 2014

National Total = 5,552,354 Students*

ALPHA ORDER

RANK	STATE	STUDENTS	% of USA
27	Alabama	58,039	1.0%
49	Alaska	4,439	0.1%
4	Arizona	319,749	5.8%
42	Arkansas	18,172	0.3%
2	California	528,971	9.5%
20	Colorado	85,786	1.5%
22	Connecticut	79,625	1.4%
39	Delaware	19,356	0.3%
5	Florida	315,390	5.7%
13	Georgia	117,252	2.1%
43	Hawaii	16,453	0.3%
33	Idaho	42,147	0.8%
6	Illinois	295,518	5.3%
16	Indiana	107,885	1.9%
15	Iowa	112,586	2.0%
32	Kansas	43,179	0.8%
29	Kentucky	51,154	0.9%
36	Louisiana	34,995	0.6%
38	Maine	23,394	0.4%
26	Maryland	60,441	1.1%
7	Massachusetts	284,754	5.1%
18	Michigan	104,726	1.9%
10	Minnesota	174,159	3.1%
40	Mississippi	18,632	0.3%
12	Missouri	166,920	3.0%
48	Montana	4,918	0.1%
35	Nebraska	36,004	0.6%
44	Nevada	13,177	0.2%
25	New Hampshire	63,686	1.1%
21	New Jersey	84,892	1.5%
46	New Mexico	7,935	0.1%
1	New York	577,208	10.4%
14	North Carolina	114,867	2.1%
47	North Dakota	5,756	0.1%
11	Ohio	169,994	3.1%
37	Oklahoma	32,900	0.6%
31	Oregon	43,902	0.8%
3	Pennsylvania	337,060	6.1%
34	Rhode Island	40,734	0.7%
30	South Carolina	48,873	0.9%
45	South Dakota	9,831	0.2%
19	Tennessee	102,542	1.8%
8	Texas	190,123	3.4%
17	Utah	107,210	1.9%
41	Vermont	18,340	0.3%
9	Virginia	178,549	3.2%
28	Washington	52,670	0.9%
24	West Virginia	69,210	1.2%
23	Wisconsin	72,168	1.3%
50	Wyoming	1,145	0.0%

RANK ORDER

RANK	STATE	STUDENTS	% of USA
1	New York	577,208	10.4%
2	California	528,971	9.5%
3	Pennsylvania	337,060	6.1%
4	Arizona	319,749	5.8%
5	Florida	315,390	5.7%
6	Illinois	295,518	5.3%
7	Massachusetts	284,754	5.1%
8	Texas	190,123	3.4%
9	Virginia	178,549	3.2%
10	Minnesota	174,159	3.1%
11	Ohio	169,994	3.1%
12	Missouri	166,920	3.0%
13	Georgia	117,252	2.1%
14	North Carolina	114,867	2.1%
15	Iowa	112,586	2.0%
16	Indiana	107,885	1.9%
17	Utah	107,210	1.9%
18	Michigan	104,726	1.9%
19	Tennessee	102,542	1.8%
20	Colorado	85,786	1.5%
21	New Jersey	84,892	1.5%
22	Connecticut	79,625	1.4%
23	Wisconsin	72,168	1.3%
24	West Virginia	69,210	1.2%
25	New Hampshire	63,686	1.1%
26	Maryland	60,441	1.1%
27	Alabama	58,039	1.0%
28	Washington	52,670	0.9%
29	Kentucky	51,154	0.9%
30	South Carolina	48,873	0.9%
31	Oregon	43,902	0.8%
32	Kansas	43,179	0.8%
33	Idaho	42,147	0.8%
34	Rhode Island	40,734	0.7%
35	Nebraska	36,004	0.6%
36	Louisiana	34,995	0.6%
37	Oklahoma	32,900	0.6%
38	Maine	23,394	0.4%
39	Delaware	19,356	0.3%
40	Mississippi	18,632	0.3%
41	Vermont	18,340	0.3%
42	Arkansas	18,172	0.3%
43	Hawaii	16,453	0.3%
44	Nevada	13,177	0.2%
45	South Dakota	9,831	0.2%
46	New Mexico	7,935	0.1%
47	North Dakota	5,756	0.1%
48	Montana	4,918	0.1%
49	Alaska	4,439	0.1%
50	Wyoming	1,145	0.0%
	District of Columbia	84,938	1.5%

Source: U.S. Department of Education, National Center for Education Statistics
"Digest of Education Statistics" (http://nces.ed.gov/programs/digest/index.asp)
*Fall 2014 enrollment. Includes full-time and part-time students at Title IV eligible, degree-granting four-year and two-year institutions.

Percent of Population with a Bachelor's Degree or More in 2015

National Percent = 30.6%*

RANK	STATE	PERCENT
44	Alabama	24.2
24	Alaska	29.7
33	Arizona	27.7
48	Arkansas	21.8
14	California	32.3
2	Colorado	39.2
4	Connecticut	38.3
19	Delaware	30.9
28	Florida	28.4
23	Georgia	29.9
18	Hawaii	31.4
40	Idaho	26.0
12	Illinois	32.9
42	Indiana	24.9
35	Iowa	26.8
17	Kansas	31.7
46	Kentucky	23.3
47	Louisiana	23.2
22	Maine	30.1
3	Maryland	38.8
1	Massachusetts	41.5
31	Michigan	27.8
10	Minnesota	34.7
49	Mississippi	20.8
31	Missouri	27.8
20	Montana	30.6
21	Nebraska	30.2
45	Nevada	23.6
8	New Hampshire	35.7
5	New Jersey	37.6
38	New Mexico	26.5
9	New York	35.0
26	North Carolina	29.4
27	North Dakota	29.1
35	Ohio	26.8
43	Oklahoma	24.6
15	Oregon	32.2
24	Pennsylvania	29.7
13	Rhode Island	32.7
35	South Carolina	26.8
34	South Dakota	27.5
41	Tennessee	25.7
28	Texas	28.4
16	Utah	31.8
7	Vermont	36.9
6	Virginia	37.0
11	Washington	34.2
50	West Virginia	19.6
28	Wisconsin	28.4
39	Wyoming	26.2

RANK	STATE	PERCENT
1	Massachusetts	41.5
2	Colorado	39.2
3	Maryland	38.8
4	Connecticut	38.3
5	New Jersey	37.6
6	Virginia	37.0
7	Vermont	36.9
8	New Hampshire	35.7
9	New York	35.0
10	Minnesota	34.7
11	Washington	34.2
12	Illinois	32.9
13	Rhode Island	32.7
14	California	32.3
15	Oregon	32.2
16	Utah	31.8
17	Kansas	31.7
18	Hawaii	31.4
19	Delaware	30.9
20	Montana	30.6
21	Nebraska	30.2
22	Maine	30.1
23	Georgia	29.9
24	Alaska	29.7
24	Pennsylvania	29.7
26	North Carolina	29.4
27	North Dakota	29.1
28	Florida	28.4
28	Texas	28.4
28	Wisconsin	28.4
31	Michigan	27.8
31	Missouri	27.8
33	Arizona	27.7
34	South Dakota	27.5
35	Iowa	26.8
35	Ohio	26.8
35	South Carolina	26.8
38	New Mexico	26.5
39	Wyoming	26.2
40	Idaho	26.0
41	Tennessee	25.7
42	Indiana	24.9
43	Oklahoma	24.6
44	Alabama	24.2
45	Nevada	23.6
46	Kentucky	23.3
47	Louisiana	23.2
48	Arkansas	21.8
49	Mississippi	20.8
50	West Virginia	19.6

	District of Columbia	56.7

Source: U.S. Bureau of the Census
"2015 American Community Survey-Table R1502" (http://www.census.gov/programs-surveys/acs/)
*Persons age 25 and older.

Percent of Population Who Have Completed an Advanced Degree in 2015

National Percent = 11.6%*

<table>
<tr><th colspan="3">ALPHA ORDER</th><th colspan="3">RANK ORDER</th></tr>
<tr><th>RANK</th><th>STATE</th><th>PERCENT</th><th>RANK</th><th>STATE</th><th>PERCENT</th></tr>
<tr><td>40</td><td>Alabama</td><td>8.8</td><td>1</td><td>Massachusetts</td><td>18.4</td></tr>
<tr><td>21</td><td>Alaska</td><td>11.0</td><td>2</td><td>Maryland</td><td>17.7</td></tr>
<tr><td>29</td><td>Arizona</td><td>10.3</td><td>3</td><td>Connecticut</td><td>16.7</td></tr>
<tr><td>49</td><td>Arkansas</td><td>7.8</td><td>4</td><td>Virginia</td><td>15.7</td></tr>
<tr><td>15</td><td>California</td><td>12.0</td><td>5</td><td>New York</td><td>15.0</td></tr>
<tr><td>7</td><td>Colorado</td><td>14.5</td><td>6</td><td>Vermont</td><td>14.6</td></tr>
<tr><td>3</td><td>Connecticut</td><td>16.7</td><td>7</td><td>Colorado</td><td>14.5</td></tr>
<tr><td>11</td><td>Delaware</td><td>12.9</td><td>8</td><td>New Jersey</td><td>14.3</td></tr>
<tr><td>30</td><td>Florida</td><td>10.2</td><td>9</td><td>New Hampshire</td><td>13.7</td></tr>
<tr><td>20</td><td>Georgia</td><td>11.3</td><td>10</td><td>Rhode Island</td><td>13.4</td></tr>
<tr><td>24</td><td>Hawaii</td><td>10.6</td><td>11</td><td>Delaware</td><td>12.9</td></tr>
<tr><td>42</td><td>Idaho</td><td>8.2</td><td>12</td><td>Illinois</td><td>12.7</td></tr>
<tr><td>12</td><td>Illinois</td><td>12.7</td><td>13</td><td>Washington</td><td>12.5</td></tr>
<tr><td>38</td><td>Indiana</td><td>9.0</td><td>14</td><td>New Mexico</td><td>12.1</td></tr>
<tr><td>41</td><td>Iowa</td><td>8.7</td><td>15</td><td>California</td><td>12.0</td></tr>
<tr><td>19</td><td>Kansas</td><td>11.4</td><td>15</td><td>Oregon</td><td>12.0</td></tr>
<tr><td>33</td><td>Kentucky</td><td>9.7</td><td>17</td><td>Minnesota</td><td>11.8</td></tr>
<tr><td>45</td><td>Louisiana</td><td>8.0</td><td>18</td><td>Pennsylvania</td><td>11.6</td></tr>
<tr><td>24</td><td>Maine</td><td>10.6</td><td>19</td><td>Kansas</td><td>11.4</td></tr>
<tr><td>2</td><td>Maryland</td><td>17.7</td><td>20</td><td>Georgia</td><td>11.3</td></tr>
<tr><td>1</td><td>Massachusetts</td><td>18.4</td><td>21</td><td>Alaska</td><td>11.0</td></tr>
<tr><td>22</td><td>Michigan</td><td>10.8</td><td>22</td><td>Michigan</td><td>10.8</td></tr>
<tr><td>17</td><td>Minnesota</td><td>11.8</td><td>23</td><td>Utah</td><td>10.7</td></tr>
<tr><td>46</td><td>Mississippi</td><td>7.9</td><td>24</td><td>Hawaii</td><td>10.6</td></tr>
<tr><td>24</td><td>Missouri</td><td>10.6</td><td>24</td><td>Maine</td><td>10.6</td></tr>
<tr><td>30</td><td>Montana</td><td>10.2</td><td>24</td><td>Missouri</td><td>10.6</td></tr>
<tr><td>28</td><td>Nebraska</td><td>10.4</td><td>24</td><td>North Carolina</td><td>10.6</td></tr>
<tr><td>43</td><td>Nevada</td><td>8.1</td><td>28</td><td>Nebraska</td><td>10.4</td></tr>
<tr><td>9</td><td>New Hampshire</td><td>13.7</td><td>29</td><td>Arizona</td><td>10.3</td></tr>
<tr><td>8</td><td>New Jersey</td><td>14.3</td><td>30</td><td>Florida</td><td>10.2</td></tr>
<tr><td>14</td><td>New Mexico</td><td>12.1</td><td>30</td><td>Montana</td><td>10.2</td></tr>
<tr><td>5</td><td>New York</td><td>15.0</td><td>32</td><td>Ohio</td><td>10.0</td></tr>
<tr><td>24</td><td>North Carolina</td><td>10.6</td><td>33</td><td>Kentucky</td><td>9.7</td></tr>
<tr><td>50</td><td>North Dakota</td><td>7.7</td><td>33</td><td>Texas</td><td>9.7</td></tr>
<tr><td>32</td><td>Ohio</td><td>10.0</td><td>35</td><td>Tennessee</td><td>9.6</td></tr>
<tr><td>43</td><td>Oklahoma</td><td>8.1</td><td>36</td><td>South Carolina</td><td>9.5</td></tr>
<tr><td>15</td><td>Oregon</td><td>12.0</td><td>37</td><td>Wisconsin</td><td>9.4</td></tr>
<tr><td>18</td><td>Pennsylvania</td><td>11.6</td><td>38</td><td>Indiana</td><td>9.0</td></tr>
<tr><td>10</td><td>Rhode Island</td><td>13.4</td><td>38</td><td>Wyoming</td><td>9.0</td></tr>
<tr><td>36</td><td>South Carolina</td><td>9.5</td><td>40</td><td>Alabama</td><td>8.8</td></tr>
<tr><td>46</td><td>South Dakota</td><td>7.9</td><td>41</td><td>Iowa</td><td>8.7</td></tr>
<tr><td>35</td><td>Tennessee</td><td>9.6</td><td>42</td><td>Idaho</td><td>8.2</td></tr>
<tr><td>33</td><td>Texas</td><td>9.7</td><td>43</td><td>Nevada</td><td>8.1</td></tr>
<tr><td>23</td><td>Utah</td><td>10.7</td><td>43</td><td>Oklahoma</td><td>8.1</td></tr>
<tr><td>6</td><td>Vermont</td><td>14.6</td><td>45</td><td>Louisiana</td><td>8.0</td></tr>
<tr><td>4</td><td>Virginia</td><td>15.7</td><td>46</td><td>Mississippi</td><td>7.9</td></tr>
<tr><td>13</td><td>Washington</td><td>12.5</td><td>46</td><td>South Dakota</td><td>7.9</td></tr>
<tr><td>46</td><td>West Virginia</td><td>7.9</td><td>46</td><td>West Virginia</td><td>7.9</td></tr>
<tr><td>37</td><td>Wisconsin</td><td>9.4</td><td>49</td><td>Arkansas</td><td>7.8</td></tr>
<tr><td>38</td><td>Wyoming</td><td>9.0</td><td>50</td><td>North Dakota</td><td>7.7</td></tr>
<tr><td></td><td></td><td></td><td></td><td>District of Columbia</td><td>32.9</td></tr>
</table>

Source: U.S. Bureau of the Census
    "2015 American Community Survey-Table R1503" (http://www.census.gov/programs-surveys/acs/)
*Persons age 25 and older who have earned a master's degree or higher.

Public Libraries and Branches in 2014

National Total = 16,559 Libraries and Branches*

RANK	STATE	LIBRARIES	% of USA
22	Alabama	292	1.8%
44	Alaska	95	0.6%
32	Arizona	220	1.3%
28	Arkansas	233	1.4%
1	California	1,117	6.7%
25	Colorado	258	1.6%
29	Connecticut	229	1.4%
50	Delaware	32	0.2%
9	Florida	531	3.2%
14	Georgia	395	2.4%
49	Hawaii	50	0.3%
40	Idaho	143	0.9%
4	Illinois	780	4.7%
12	Indiana	427	2.6%
8	Iowa	558	3.4%
16	Kansas	366	2.2%
34	Kentucky	206	1.2%
21	Louisiana	340	2.1%
27	Maine	234	1.4%
36	Maryland	187	1.1%
10	Massachusetts	462	2.8%
6	Michigan	643	3.9%
19	Minnesota	356	2.1%
26	Mississippi	235	1.4%
17	Missouri	361	2.2%
42	Montana	115	0.7%
24	Nebraska	282	1.7%
45	Nevada	85	0.5%
30	New Hampshire	224	1.4%
13	New Jersey	424	2.6%
43	New Mexico	114	0.7%
2	New York	1,065	6.4%
15	North Carolina	385	2.3%
46	North Dakota	76	0.5%
5	Ohio	709	4.3%
33	Oklahoma	212	1.3%
31	Oregon	221	1.3%
7	Pennsylvania	621	3.8%
48	Rhode Island	70	0.4%
35	South Carolina	192	1.2%
39	South Dakota	144	0.9%
23	Tennessee	286	1.7%
3	Texas	865	5.2%
41	Utah	126	0.8%
38	Vermont	157	0.9%
18	Virginia	357	2.2%
20	Washington	344	2.1%
37	West Virginia	173	1.0%
11	Wisconsin	460	2.8%
46	Wyoming	76	0.5%

RANK	STATE	LIBRARIES	% of USA
1	California	1,117	6.7%
2	New York	1,065	6.4%
3	Texas	865	5.2%
4	Illinois	780	4.7%
5	Ohio	709	4.3%
6	Michigan	643	3.9%
7	Pennsylvania	621	3.8%
8	Iowa	558	3.4%
9	Florida	531	3.2%
10	Massachusetts	462	2.8%
11	Wisconsin	460	2.8%
12	Indiana	427	2.6%
13	New Jersey	424	2.6%
14	Georgia	395	2.4%
15	North Carolina	385	2.3%
16	Kansas	366	2.2%
17	Missouri	361	2.2%
18	Virginia	357	2.2%
19	Minnesota	356	2.1%
20	Washington	344	2.1%
21	Louisiana	340	2.1%
22	Alabama	292	1.8%
23	Tennessee	286	1.7%
24	Nebraska	282	1.7%
25	Colorado	258	1.6%
26	Mississippi	235	1.4%
27	Maine	234	1.4%
28	Arkansas	233	1.4%
29	Connecticut	229	1.4%
30	New Hampshire	224	1.4%
31	Oregon	221	1.3%
32	Arizona	220	1.3%
33	Oklahoma	212	1.3%
34	Kentucky	206	1.2%
35	South Carolina	192	1.2%
36	Maryland	187	1.1%
37	West Virginia	173	1.0%
38	Vermont	157	0.9%
39	South Dakota	144	0.9%
40	Idaho	143	0.9%
41	Utah	126	0.8%
42	Montana	115	0.7%
43	New Mexico	114	0.7%
44	Alaska	95	0.6%
45	Nevada	85	0.5%
46	North Dakota	76	0.5%
46	Wyoming	76	0.5%
48	Rhode Island	70	0.4%
49	Hawaii	50	0.3%
50	Delaware	32	0.2%
	District of Columbia	26	0.2%

Source: Institute of Museum and Library Services
"Public Library Survey Fiscal Year 2014" (http://www.imls.gov/research/default.aspx)
*For fiscal year 2014. Total of central and branch outlets. Does not include bookmobiles. There are 9,070 public libraries.

Rate of Public Libraries and Branches in 2014

National Average = 19,238 Population per Library*

ALPHA ORDER

RANK	STATE	RATE
25	Alabama	16,586
43	Alaska	7,755
6	Arizona	30,545
35	Arkansas	12,734
2	California	34,629
17	Colorado	20,735
28	Connecticut	15,685
7	Delaware	29,217
1	Florida	37,455
10	Georgia	25,537
8	Hawaii	28,327
38	Idaho	11,423
26	Illinois	16,497
29	Indiana	15,446
49	Iowa	5,570
42	Kansas	7,922
15	Kentucky	21,423
34	Louisiana	13,670
48	Maine	5,687
4	Maryland	31,911
33	Massachusetts	14,610
30	Michigan	15,421
31	Minnesota	15,318
35	Mississippi	12,734
24	Missouri	16,789
41	Montana	8,894
45	Nebraska	6,671
3	Nevada	33,330
46	New Hampshire	5,932
16	New Jersey	21,050
22	New Mexico	18,272
20	New York	18,515
9	North Carolina	25,804
40	North Dakota	9,736
27	Ohio	16,353
21	Oklahoma	18,290
23	Oregon	17,956
18	Pennsylvania	20,597
32	Rhode Island	15,064
11	South Carolina	25,148
47	South Dakota	5,921
14	Tennessee	22,883
5	Texas	31,150
12	Utah	23,348
50	Vermont	3,994
13	Virginia	23,298
19	Washington	20,506
39	West Virginia	10,685
37	Wisconsin	12,518
44	Wyoming	7,680

RANK ORDER

RANK	STATE	RATE
1	Florida	37,455
2	California	34,629
3	Nevada	33,330
4	Maryland	31,911
5	Texas	31,150
6	Arizona	30,545
7	Delaware	29,217
8	Hawaii	28,327
9	North Carolina	25,804
10	Georgia	25,537
11	South Carolina	25,148
12	Utah	23,348
13	Virginia	23,298
14	Tennessee	22,883
15	Kentucky	21,423
16	New Jersey	21,050
17	Colorado	20,735
18	Pennsylvania	20,597
19	Washington	20,506
20	New York	18,515
21	Oklahoma	18,290
22	New Mexico	18,272
23	Oregon	17,956
24	Missouri	16,789
25	Alabama	16,586
26	Illinois	16,497
27	Ohio	16,353
28	Connecticut	15,685
29	Indiana	15,446
30	Michigan	15,421
31	Minnesota	15,318
32	Rhode Island	15,064
33	Massachusetts	14,610
34	Louisiana	13,670
35	Arkansas	12,734
35	Mississippi	12,734
37	Wisconsin	12,518
38	Idaho	11,423
39	West Virginia	10,685
40	North Dakota	9,736
41	Montana	8,894
42	Kansas	7,922
43	Alaska	7,755
44	Wyoming	7,680
45	Nebraska	6,671
46	New Hampshire	5,932
47	South Dakota	5,921
48	Maine	5,687
49	Iowa	5,570
50	Vermont	3,994
	District of Columbia	25,346

Source: CQ Press using data from Institute of Museum and Library Services
"Public Library Survey Fiscal Year 2014" (http://www.imls.gov/research/default.aspx)
*For fiscal year 2014. Based on total of central and branch outlets. Does not include bookmobiles.

Rate of Books in Public Libraries in 2014

National Rate = 2,403 Books per 1,000 Population*

ALPHA ORDER				RANK ORDER		
RANK	STATE	RATE		RANK	STATE	RATE
36	Alabama	1,928		1	Massachusetts	4,633
16	Alaska	3,247		2	Maine	4,505
50	Arizona	1,225		3	Vermont	4,357
31	Arkansas	2,125		4	New Hampshire	4,354
44	California	1,691		5	Wyoming	4,278
37	Colorado	1,927		6	Rhode Island	4,014
7	Connecticut	3,846		7	Connecticut	3,846
43	Delaware	1,757		8	Iowa	3,838
47	Florida	1,589		9	Indiana	3,695
46	Georgia	1,646		10	Ohio	3,690
28	Hawaii	2,339		11	New York	3,591
24	Idaho	2,641		12	Illinois	3,380
12	Illinois	3,380		13	South Dakota	3,292
9	Indiana	3,695		14	Michigan	3,282
8	Iowa	3,838		15	Wisconsin	3,264
17	Kansas	3,188		16	Alaska	3,247
33	Kentucky	2,047		17	Kansas	3,188
25	Louisiana	2,559		18	Nebraska	3,128
2	Maine	4,505		19	New Jersey	3,117
30	Maryland	2,134		20	North Dakota	3,044
1	Massachusetts	4,633		21	Missouri	2,766
14	Michigan	3,282		22	West Virginia	2,723
23	Minnesota	2,680		23	Minnesota	2,680
40	Mississippi	1,885		24	Idaho	2,641
21	Missouri	2,766		25	Louisiana	2,559
26	Montana	2,509		26	Montana	2,509
18	Nebraska	3,128		27	Oregon	2,486
48	Nevada	1,517		28	Hawaii	2,339
4	New Hampshire	4,354		29	Utah	2,256
19	New Jersey	3,117		30	Maryland	2,134
34	New Mexico	2,039		31	Arkansas	2,125
11	New York	3,591		32	Virginia	2,109
45	North Carolina	1,686		33	Kentucky	2,047
20	North Dakota	3,044		34	New Mexico	2,039
10	Ohio	3,690		35	Pennsylvania	2,016
41	Oklahoma	1,844		36	Alabama	1,928
27	Oregon	2,486		37	Colorado	1,927
35	Pennsylvania	2,016		38	Washington	1,904
6	Rhode Island	4,014		39	South Carolina	1,886
39	South Carolina	1,886		40	Mississippi	1,885
13	South Dakota	3,292		41	Oklahoma	1,844
42	Tennessee	1,797		42	Tennessee	1,797
49	Texas	1,496		43	Delaware	1,757
29	Utah	2,256		44	California	1,691
3	Vermont	4,357		45	North Carolina	1,686
32	Virginia	2,109		46	Georgia	1,646
38	Washington	1,904		47	Florida	1,589
22	West Virginia	2,723		48	Nevada	1,517
15	Wisconsin	3,264		49	Texas	1,496
5	Wyoming	4,278		50	Arizona	1,225
					District of Columbia	2,756

Source: CQ Press using data from Institute of Museum and Library Services
   "Public Library Survey Fiscal Year 2014" (http://www.imls.gov/research/default.aspx)
*For fiscal year 2014. Includes serial back files in print.

Rate of Electronic Books in Public Libraries in 2014

National Rate = 670 Electronic Books per 1,000 Population*

ALPHA ORDER

RANK	STATE	RATE
19	Alabama	544
21	Alaska	477
34	Arizona	203
37	Arkansas	179
45	California	77
31	Colorado	260
26	Connecticut	346
22	Delaware	444
44	Florida	90
48	Georgia	33
50	Hawaii	16
38	Idaho	148
18	Illinois	556
16	Indiana	641
7	Iowa	1,499
41	Kansas	104
6	Kentucky	1,567
35	Louisiana	189
14	Maine	871
28	Maryland	320
11	Massachusetts	1,108
30	Michigan	283
17	Minnesota	637
49	Mississippi	20
47	Missouri	45
13	Montana	932
8	Nebraska	1,434
46	Nevada	76
3	New Hampshire	3,166
25	New Jersey	348
43	New Mexico	95
15	New York	740
27	North Carolina	336
20	North Dakota	520
2	Ohio	3,482
23	Oklahoma	425
12	Oregon	982
24	Pennsylvania	415
9	Rhode Island	1,163
42	South Carolina	102
10	South Dakota	1,145
5	Tennessee	2,329
40	Texas	127
36	Utah	188
39	Vermont	131
33	Virginia	240
32	Washington	253
4	West Virginia	2,597
1	Wisconsin	8,181
29	Wyoming	294

RANK ORDER

RANK	STATE	RATE
1	Wisconsin	8,181
2	Ohio	3,482
3	New Hampshire	3,166
4	West Virginia	2,597
5	Tennessee	2,329
6	Kentucky	1,567
7	Iowa	1,499
8	Nebraska	1,434
9	Rhode Island	1,163
10	South Dakota	1,145
11	Massachusetts	1,108
12	Oregon	982
13	Montana	932
14	Maine	871
15	New York	740
16	Indiana	641
17	Minnesota	637
18	Illinois	556
19	Alabama	544
20	North Dakota	520
21	Alaska	477
22	Delaware	444
23	Oklahoma	425
24	Pennsylvania	415
25	New Jersey	348
26	Connecticut	346
27	North Carolina	336
28	Maryland	320
29	Wyoming	294
30	Michigan	283
31	Colorado	260
32	Washington	253
33	Virginia	240
34	Arizona	203
35	Louisiana	189
36	Utah	188
37	Arkansas	179
38	Idaho	148
39	Vermont	131
40	Texas	127
41	Kansas	104
42	South Carolina	102
43	New Mexico	95
44	Florida	90
45	California	77
46	Nevada	76
47	Missouri	45
48	Georgia	33
49	Mississippi	20
50	Hawaii	16

District of Columbia   269

Source: CQ Press using data from Institute of Museum and Library Services
   "Public Library Survey Fiscal Year 2014" (http://www.imls.gov/research/default.aspx)
*For fiscal year 2014.

Internet Terminals in Public Libraries in 2014

National Total = 285,395 Terminals*

ALPHA ORDER

RANK	STATE	TERMINALS	% of USA
21	Alabama	5,263	1.8%
46	Alaska	978	0.3%
19	Arizona	5,593	2.0%
34	Arkansas	2,596	0.9%
1	California	21,735	7.6%
16	Colorado	6,401	2.2%
28	Connecticut	4,172	1.5%
49	Delaware	772	0.3%
4	Florida	16,781	5.9%
9	Georgia	8,604	3.0%
50	Hawaii	524	0.2%
37	Idaho	1,791	0.6%
5	Illinois	15,861	5.6%
8	Indiana	8,759	3.1%
26	Iowa	4,707	1.6%
29	Kansas	3,725	1.3%
24	Kentucky	4,858	1.7%
20	Louisiana	5,359	1.9%
36	Maine	1,860	0.7%
24	Maryland	4,858	1.7%
15	Massachusetts	6,429	2.3%
7	Michigan	11,925	4.2%
18	Minnesota	5,630	2.0%
33	Mississippi	2,769	1.0%
23	Missouri	4,939	1.7%
43	Montana	1,282	0.4%
32	Nebraska	2,932	1.0%
42	Nevada	1,307	0.5%
39	New Hampshire	1,460	0.5%
11	New Jersey	7,887	2.8%
38	New Mexico	1,608	0.6%
2	New York	19,411	6.8%
12	North Carolina	7,671	2.7%
48	North Dakota	832	0.3%
6	Ohio	12,931	4.5%
31	Oklahoma	3,067	1.1%
30	Oregon	3,132	1.1%
10	Pennsylvania	8,050	2.8%
41	Rhode Island	1,397	0.5%
27	South Carolina	4,203	1.5%
44	South Dakota	1,105	0.4%
22	Tennessee	5,043	1.8%
3	Texas	19,008	6.7%
35	Utah	2,085	0.7%
45	Vermont	1,045	0.4%
13	Virginia	6,875	2.4%
14	Washington	6,573	2.3%
40	West Virginia	1,450	0.5%
17	Wisconsin	6,284	2.2%
47	Wyoming	868	0.3%

RANK ORDER

RANK	STATE	TERMINALS	% of USA
1	California	21,735	7.6%
2	New York	19,411	6.8%
3	Texas	19,008	6.7%
4	Florida	16,781	5.9%
5	Illinois	15,861	5.6%
6	Ohio	12,931	4.5%
7	Michigan	11,925	4.2%
8	Indiana	8,759	3.1%
9	Georgia	8,604	3.0%
10	Pennsylvania	8,050	2.8%
11	New Jersey	7,887	2.8%
12	North Carolina	7,671	2.7%
13	Virginia	6,875	2.4%
14	Washington	6,573	2.3%
15	Massachusetts	6,429	2.3%
16	Colorado	6,401	2.2%
17	Wisconsin	6,284	2.2%
18	Minnesota	5,630	2.0%
19	Arizona	5,593	2.0%
20	Louisiana	5,359	1.9%
21	Alabama	5,263	1.8%
22	Tennessee	5,043	1.8%
23	Missouri	4,939	1.7%
24	Kentucky	4,858	1.7%
24	Maryland	4,858	1.7%
26	Iowa	4,707	1.6%
27	South Carolina	4,203	1.5%
28	Connecticut	4,172	1.5%
29	Kansas	3,725	1.3%
30	Oregon	3,132	1.1%
31	Oklahoma	3,067	1.1%
32	Nebraska	2,932	1.0%
33	Mississippi	2,769	1.0%
34	Arkansas	2,596	0.9%
35	Utah	2,085	0.7%
36	Maine	1,860	0.7%
37	Idaho	1,791	0.6%
38	New Mexico	1,608	0.6%
39	New Hampshire	1,460	0.5%
40	West Virginia	1,450	0.5%
41	Rhode Island	1,397	0.5%
42	Nevada	1,307	0.5%
43	Montana	1,282	0.4%
44	South Dakota	1,105	0.4%
45	Vermont	1,045	0.4%
46	Alaska	978	0.3%
47	Wyoming	868	0.3%
48	North Dakota	832	0.3%
49	Delaware	772	0.3%
50	Hawaii	524	0.2%
	District of Columbia	1,000	0.4%

Source: Institute of Museum and Library Services
   "Public Library Survey Fiscal Year 2014" (http://www.imls.gov/research/default.aspx)
*For fiscal year 2014. Total of public-use Internet terminals in central and branch outlets.

Rate of Internet Terminals in Public Libraries in 2014

National Rate = 17.2 Terminals per Library*

ALPHA ORDER

RANK	STATE	RATE
22	Alabama	18.0
43	Alaska	10.3
3	Arizona	25.4
38	Arkansas	11.1
14	California	19.5
4	Colorado	24.8
19	Connecticut	18.2
5	Delaware	24.1
1	Florida	31.6
9	Georgia	21.8
41	Hawaii	10.5
35	Idaho	12.5
11	Illinois	20.3
10	Indiana	20.5
45	Iowa	8.4
44	Kansas	10.2
6	Kentucky	23.6
25	Louisiana	15.8
47	Maine	7.9
2	Maryland	26.0
31	Massachusetts	13.9
18	Michigan	18.5
25	Minnesota	15.8
36	Mississippi	11.8
32	Missouri	13.7
38	Montana	11.1
42	Nebraska	10.4
27	Nevada	15.4
50	New Hampshire	6.5
17	New Jersey	18.6
30	New Mexico	14.1
19	New York	18.2
13	North Carolina	19.9
40	North Dakota	10.9
19	Ohio	18.2
28	Oklahoma	14.5
29	Oregon	14.2
34	Pennsylvania	13.0
12	Rhode Island	20.0
8	South Carolina	21.9
48	South Dakota	7.7
23	Tennessee	17.6
7	Texas	22.0
24	Utah	16.5
49	Vermont	6.7
15	Virginia	19.3
16	Washington	19.1
45	West Virginia	8.4
32	Wisconsin	13.7
37	Wyoming	11.4

RANK ORDER

RANK	STATE	RATE
1	Florida	31.6
2	Maryland	26.0
3	Arizona	25.4
4	Colorado	24.8
5	Delaware	24.1
6	Kentucky	23.6
7	Texas	22.0
8	South Carolina	21.9
9	Georgia	21.8
10	Indiana	20.5
11	Illinois	20.3
12	Rhode Island	20.0
13	North Carolina	19.9
14	California	19.5
15	Virginia	19.3
16	Washington	19.1
17	New Jersey	18.6
18	Michigan	18.5
19	Connecticut	18.2
19	New York	18.2
19	Ohio	18.2
22	Alabama	18.0
23	Tennessee	17.6
24	Utah	16.5
25	Louisiana	15.8
25	Minnesota	15.8
27	Nevada	15.4
28	Oklahoma	14.5
29	Oregon	14.2
30	New Mexico	14.1
31	Massachusetts	13.9
32	Missouri	13.7
32	Wisconsin	13.7
34	Pennsylvania	13.0
35	Idaho	12.5
36	Mississippi	11.8
37	Wyoming	11.4
38	Arkansas	11.1
38	Montana	11.1
40	North Dakota	10.9
41	Hawaii	10.5
42	Nebraska	10.4
43	Alaska	10.3
44	Kansas	10.2
45	Iowa	8.4
45	West Virginia	8.4
47	Maine	7.9
48	South Dakota	7.7
49	Vermont	6.7
50	New Hampshire	6.5

District of Columbia   38.5

Source: CQ Press using data from Institute of Museum and Library Services
"Public Library Survey Fiscal Year 2014" (http://www.imls.gov/research/default.aspx)
*For fiscal year 2014. Total of public-use Internet terminals in central and branch outlets divided by the number of outlets.

Per Capita State Art Agencies' Legislative Appropriations in 2017

National Per Capita = $1.08*

RANK	STATE	PER CAPITA
19	Alabama	$0.97
20	Alaska	0.94
45	Arizona	0.22
32	Arkansas	0.56
38	California	0.45
42	Colorado	0.36
13	Connecticut	1.18
3	Delaware	3.58
7	Florida	2.12
48	Georgia	0.10
2	Hawaii	4.01
37	Idaho	0.47
NA	Illinois**	NA
34	Indiana	0.50
41	Iowa	0.39
49	Kansas	0.06
30	Kentucky	0.59
39	Louisiana	0.45
27	Maine	0.67
4	Maryland	3.39
8	Massachusetts	2.10
21	Michigan	0.91
1	Minnesota	7.04
31	Mississippi	0.58
12	Missouri	1.21
35	Montana	0.49
23	Nebraska	0.82
28	Nevada	0.66
44	New Hampshire	0.23
9	New Jersey	1.83
29	New Mexico	0.63
5	New York	2.29
22	North Carolina	0.83
17	North Dakota	1.05
11	Ohio	1.27
25	Oklahoma	0.75
33	Oregon	0.51
24	Pennsylvania	0.75
6	Rhode Island	2.13
26	South Carolina	0.71
18	South Dakota	0.98
15	Tennessee	1.06
43	Texas	0.30
16	Utah	1.05
14	Vermont	1.08
40	Virginia	0.41
46	Washington	0.16
36	West Virginia	0.47
47	Wisconsin	0.14
10	Wyoming	1.77

RANK	STATE	PER CAPITA
1	Minnesota	$7.04
2	Hawaii	4.01
3	Delaware	3.58
4	Maryland	3.39
5	New York	2.29
6	Rhode Island	2.13
7	Florida	2.12
8	Massachusetts	2.10
9	New Jersey	1.83
10	Wyoming	1.77
11	Ohio	1.27
12	Missouri	1.21
13	Connecticut	1.18
14	Vermont	1.08
15	Tennessee	1.06
16	Utah	1.05
17	North Dakota	1.05
18	South Dakota	0.98
19	Alabama	0.97
20	Alaska	0.94
21	Michigan	0.91
22	North Carolina	0.83
23	Nebraska	0.82
24	Pennsylvania	0.75
25	Oklahoma	0.75
26	South Carolina	0.71
27	Maine	0.67
28	Nevada	0.66
29	New Mexico	0.63
30	Kentucky	0.59
31	Mississippi	0.58
32	Arkansas	0.56
33	Oregon	0.51
34	Indiana	0.50
35	Montana	0.49
36	West Virginia	0.47
37	Idaho	0.47
38	California	0.45
39	Louisiana	0.45
40	Virginia	0.41
41	Iowa	0.39
42	Colorado	0.36
43	Texas	0.30
44	New Hampshire	0.23
45	Arizona	0.22
46	Washington	0.16
47	Wisconsin	0.14
48	Georgia	0.10
49	Kansas	0.06
NA	Illinois**	NA

District of Columbia   32.36

Source: National Assembly of State Arts Agencies
    "State Arts Agency Legislative Appropriations Preview Fiscal Year 2017" (http://www.nasaa-arts.org/Research/Funding/)
*Projected figures for fiscal year 2017. Includes line item appropriations. Line items are legislative appropriations that are not controlled by the state art agencies but are passed through their budgets directly to another entity. Calculated using 2016 Census population estimates.
**Not available.

Federal Allocations for Head Start Program in 2015

National Total = $8,598,095,000*

ALPHA ORDER

RANK	STATE	EXPENDITURES	% of USA
17	Alabama	$133,689,882	1.6%
49	Alaska	14,697,027	0.2%
18	Arizona	131,546,248	1.5%
29	Arkansas	81,496,636	0.9%
1	California	1,039,415,453	12.1%
28	Colorado	88,256,495	1.0%
31	Connecticut	67,254,862	0.8%
48	Delaware	16,305,939	0.2%
4	Florida	345,209,484	4.0%
9	Georgia	217,928,237	2.5%
42	Hawaii	27,260,269	0.3%
40	Idaho	27,906,313	0.3%
5	Illinois	336,043,938	3.9%
22	Indiana	123,000,650	1.4%
34	Iowa	62,633,575	0.7%
33	Kansas	62,945,976	0.7%
16	Kentucky	136,136,445	1.6%
12	Louisiana	174,153,534	2.0%
38	Maine	33,851,143	0.4%
26	Maryland	94,632,101	1.1%
19	Massachusetts	130,475,615	1.5%
8	Michigan	284,964,075	3.3%
27	Minnesota	91,473,725	1.1%
10	Mississippi	195,189,104	2.3%
14	Missouri	150,433,720	1.7%
43	Montana	26,537,570	0.3%
37	Nebraska	46,654,413	0.5%
39	Nevada	33,442,154	0.4%
47	New Hampshire	16,527,565	0.2%
13	New Jersey	156,887,641	1.8%
32	New Mexico	65,502,509	0.8%
3	New York	527,069,097	6.1%
11	North Carolina	190,807,543	2.2%
45	North Dakota	21,282,228	0.2%
6	Ohio	309,427,962	3.6%
25	Oklahoma	107,630,356	1.3%
30	Oregon	78,684,207	0.9%
7	Pennsylvania	286,559,676	3.3%
41	Rhode Island	27,335,605	0.3%
24	South Carolina	110,668,372	1.3%
44	South Dakota	22,844,310	0.3%
15	Tennessee	148,440,179	1.7%
2	Texas	604,774,593	7.0%
36	Utah	51,029,723	0.6%
46	Vermont	16,536,670	0.2%
21	Virginia	124,211,408	1.4%
20	Washington	129,467,147	1.5%
35	West Virginia	62,577,957	0.7%
23	Wisconsin	114,647,779	1.3%
50	Wyoming	14,479,234	0.2%

RANK ORDER

RANK	STATE	EXPENDITURES	% of USA
1	California	$1,039,415,453	12.1%
2	Texas	604,774,593	7.0%
3	New York	527,069,097	6.1%
4	Florida	345,209,484	4.0%
5	Illinois	336,043,938	3.9%
6	Ohio	309,427,962	3.6%
7	Pennsylvania	286,559,676	3.3%
8	Michigan	284,964,075	3.3%
9	Georgia	217,928,237	2.5%
10	Mississippi	195,189,104	2.3%
11	North Carolina	190,807,543	2.2%
12	Louisiana	174,153,534	2.0%
13	New Jersey	156,887,641	1.8%
14	Missouri	150,433,720	1.7%
15	Tennessee	148,440,179	1.7%
16	Kentucky	136,136,445	1.6%
17	Alabama	133,689,882	1.6%
18	Arizona	131,546,248	1.5%
19	Massachusetts	130,475,615	1.5%
20	Washington	129,467,147	1.5%
21	Virginia	124,211,408	1.4%
22	Indiana	123,000,650	1.4%
23	Wisconsin	114,647,779	1.3%
24	South Carolina	110,668,372	1.3%
25	Oklahoma	107,630,356	1.3%
26	Maryland	94,632,101	1.1%
27	Minnesota	91,473,725	1.1%
28	Colorado	88,256,495	1.0%
29	Arkansas	81,496,636	0.9%
30	Oregon	78,684,207	0.9%
31	Connecticut	67,254,862	0.8%
32	New Mexico	65,502,509	0.8%
33	Kansas	62,945,976	0.7%
34	Iowa	62,633,575	0.7%
35	West Virginia	62,577,957	0.7%
36	Utah	51,029,723	0.6%
37	Nebraska	46,654,413	0.5%
38	Maine	33,851,143	0.4%
39	Nevada	33,442,154	0.4%
40	Idaho	27,906,313	0.3%
41	Rhode Island	27,335,605	0.3%
42	Hawaii	27,260,269	0.3%
43	Montana	26,537,570	0.3%
44	South Dakota	22,844,310	0.3%
45	North Dakota	21,282,228	0.2%
46	Vermont	16,536,670	0.2%
47	New Hampshire	16,527,565	0.2%
48	Delaware	16,305,939	0.2%
49	Alaska	14,697,027	0.2%
50	Wyoming	14,479,234	0.2%
	District of Columbia	28,020,388	0.3%

Source: U.S. Department of Health and Human Services, Administration for Children and Families
"Head Start Fact Sheet Fiscal Year 2015" (http://eclkc.ohs.acf.hhs.gov/hslc/mr/factsheets)
*For fiscal year 2015. National total includes $591,059,734 to Migrant and Native American programs not included in state totals, $305,537,904 to U.S. territories, $309,671,000 in "support activities" expenditures, and $500,000,000 to expand access to high-quality early learning and development opportunities for infants and toddlers through Early Head Start-Child Care Partnerships.

Head Start Program Enrollment in 2015

National Total = 944,581 Children*

RANK	STATE	ENROLLMENT	% of USA
14	Alabama	17,532	1.9%
49	Alaska	1,593	0.2%
22	Arizona	14,413	1.5%
30	Arkansas	10,273	1.1%
1	California	102,728	10.9%
28	Colorado	10,945	1.2%
35	Connecticut	6,495	0.7%
46	Delaware	2,281	0.2%
5	Florida	39,668	4.2%
10	Georgia	25,205	2.7%
39	Hawaii	3,217	0.3%
41	Idaho	3,182	0.3%
4	Illinois	41,188	4.4%
18	Indiana	15,310	1.6%
34	Iowa	7,756	0.8%
31	Kansas	8,356	0.9%
15	Kentucky	16,961	1.8%
12	Louisiana	21,655	2.3%
38	Maine	3,243	0.3%
29	Maryland	10,426	1.1%
25	Massachusetts	12,627	1.3%
8	Michigan	32,662	3.5%
27	Minnesota	11,459	1.2%
9	Mississippi	26,474	2.8%
16	Missouri	16,919	1.8%
40	Montana	3,193	0.3%
37	Nebraska	5,334	0.6%
42	Nevada	3,128	0.3%
48	New Hampshire	1,686	0.2%
17	New Jersey	16,021	1.7%
33	New Mexico	7,851	0.8%
3	New York	50,987	5.4%
11	North Carolina	21,800	2.3%
45	North Dakota	2,442	0.3%
6	Ohio	37,128	3.9%
19	Oklahoma	14,641	1.5%
24	Oregon	13,149	1.4%
7	Pennsylvania	36,605	3.9%
44	Rhode Island	2,893	0.3%
23	South Carolina	13,464	1.4%
43	South Dakota	2,912	0.3%
13	Tennessee	17,750	1.9%
2	Texas	73,202	7.7%
36	Utah	6,343	0.7%
50	Vermont	1,503	0.2%
21	Virginia	14,427	1.5%
26	Washington	12,370	1.3%
32	West Virginia	8,138	0.9%
20	Wisconsin	14,557	1.5%
47	Wyoming	1,724	0.2%

RANK	STATE	ENROLLMENT	% of USA
1	California	102,728	10.9%
2	Texas	73,202	7.7%
3	New York	50,987	5.4%
4	Illinois	41,188	4.4%
5	Florida	39,668	4.2%
6	Ohio	37,128	3.9%
7	Pennsylvania	36,605	3.9%
8	Michigan	32,662	3.5%
9	Mississippi	26,474	2.8%
10	Georgia	25,205	2.7%
11	North Carolina	21,800	2.3%
12	Louisiana	21,655	2.3%
13	Tennessee	17,750	1.9%
14	Alabama	17,532	1.9%
15	Kentucky	16,961	1.8%
16	Missouri	16,919	1.8%
17	New Jersey	16,021	1.7%
18	Indiana	15,310	1.6%
19	Oklahoma	14,641	1.5%
20	Wisconsin	14,557	1.5%
21	Virginia	14,427	1.5%
22	Arizona	14,413	1.5%
23	South Carolina	13,464	1.4%
24	Oregon	13,149	1.4%
25	Massachusetts	12,627	1.3%
26	Washington	12,370	1.3%
27	Minnesota	11,459	1.2%
28	Colorado	10,945	1.2%
29	Maryland	10,426	1.1%
30	Arkansas	10,273	1.1%
31	Kansas	8,356	0.9%
32	West Virginia	8,138	0.9%
33	New Mexico	7,851	0.8%
34	Iowa	7,756	0.8%
35	Connecticut	6,495	0.7%
36	Utah	6,343	0.7%
37	Nebraska	5,334	0.6%
38	Maine	3,243	0.3%
39	Hawaii	3,217	0.3%
40	Montana	3,193	0.3%
41	Idaho	3,182	0.3%
42	Nevada	3,128	0.3%
43	South Dakota	2,912	0.3%
44	Rhode Island	2,893	0.3%
45	North Dakota	2,442	0.3%
46	Delaware	2,281	0.2%
47	Wyoming	1,724	0.2%
48	New Hampshire	1,686	0.2%
49	Alaska	1,593	0.2%
50	Vermont	1,503	0.2%
	District of Columbia	3,306	0.3%

Source: U.S. Department of Health and Human Services, Administration for Children and Families
"Head Start Fact Sheet Fiscal Year 2015" (http://eclkc.ohs.acf.hhs.gov/hslc/mr/factsheets)
*For fiscal year 2015. National total includes 54,861 enrollees not included in state totals enrolled in Migrant and Native American programs and 40,598 enrollees in U.S. territories.

VI. Employment and Labor

Average Annual Pay in 2015

National Average = $52,942*

ALPHA ORDER				RANK ORDER		
RANK	STATE	ANNUAL PAY		RANK	STATE	ANNUAL PAY
35	Alabama	$44,273		1	New York	$67,521
9	Alaska	54,755		2	Massachusetts	66,692
22	Arizona	47,933		3	Connecticut	65,530
46	Arkansas	40,895		4	New Jersey	62,365
5	California	61,698		5	California	61,698
12	Colorado	54,182		6	Maryland	57,176
3	Connecticut	65,530		7	Washington	56,661
13	Delaware	53,991		8	Illinois	55,989
28	Florida	46,260		9	Alaska	54,755
20	Georgia	49,551		10	Texas	54,281
24	Hawaii	46,919		11	Virginia	54,276
49	Idaho	38,857		12	Colorado	54,182
8	Illinois	55,989		13	Delaware	53,991
38	Indiana	43,903		14	Minnesota	53,527
37	Iowa	44,095		15	New Hampshire	52,553
39	Kansas	43,878		16	Pennsylvania	52,187
40	Kentucky	43,365		17	North Dakota	50,696
29	Louisiana	45,928		18	Rhode Island	50,651
44	Maine	41,791		19	Michigan	50,063
6	Maryland	57,176		20	Georgia	49,551
2	Massachusetts	66,692		21	Oregon	48,328
19	Michigan	50,063		22	Arizona	47,933
14	Minnesota	53,527		23	Ohio	47,146
50	Mississippi	37,642		24	Hawaii	46,919
31	Missouri	45,565		25	Tennessee	46,742
48	Montana	40,056		26	North Carolina	46,530
41	Nebraska	42,854		27	Wyoming	46,306
30	Nevada	45,739		28	Florida	46,260
15	New Hampshire	52,553		29	Louisiana	45,928
4	New Jersey	62,365		30	Nevada	45,739
42	New Mexico	42,555		31	Missouri	45,565
1	New York	67,521		32	Wisconsin	45,365
26	North Carolina	46,530		33	Utah	44,318
17	North Dakota	50,696		34	Oklahoma	44,306
23	Ohio	47,146		35	Alabama	44,273
34	Oklahoma	44,306		36	Vermont	44,234
21	Oregon	48,328		37	Iowa	44,095
16	Pennsylvania	52,187		38	Indiana	43,903
18	Rhode Island	50,651		39	Kansas	43,878
43	South Carolina	42,002		40	Kentucky	43,365
47	South Dakota	40,181		41	Nebraska	42,854
25	Tennessee	46,742		42	New Mexico	42,555
10	Texas	54,281		43	South Carolina	42,002
33	Utah	44,318		44	Maine	41,791
36	Vermont	44,234		45	West Virginia	41,727
11	Virginia	54,276		46	Arkansas	40,895
7	Washington	56,661		47	South Dakota	40,181
45	West Virginia	41,727		48	Montana	40,056
32	Wisconsin	45,365		49	Idaho	38,857
27	Wyoming	46,306		50	Mississippi	37,642
				District of Columbia		88,159

Source: U.S. Department of Labor, Bureau of Labor Statistics
   "Quarterly Census of Employment and Wages" (http://www.bls.gov/cew/data.htm)
*Computed by dividing total annual wages of employees covered by unemployment insurance programs by the average monthly number of these employees. Includes bonuses, cash value of meals and lodging, tips and, in many states, employer contributions to certain deferred compensation plans such as 401(k) plans.

Percent Change in Average Annual Pay: 2014 to 2015

National Percent Change = 3.1% Increase*

RANK	STATE	PERCENT CHANGE
37	Alabama	2.3
32	Alaska	2.5
41	Arizona	2.2
37	Arkansas	2.3
1	California	4.5
27	Colorado	2.8
32	Connecticut	2.5
43	Delaware	1.5
14	Florida	3.3
25	Georgia	2.9
6	Hawaii	3.8
37	Idaho	2.3
9	Illinois	3.5
17	Indiana	3.2
7	Iowa	3.7
29	Kansas	2.7
12	Kentucky	3.4
46	Louisiana	1.3
14	Maine	3.3
17	Maryland	3.2
3	Massachusetts	4.0
14	Michigan	3.3
7	Minnesota	3.7
45	Mississippi	1.4
21	Missouri	3.0
21	Montana	3.0
2	Nebraska	4.1
37	Nevada	2.3
29	New Hampshire	2.7
25	New Jersey	2.9
43	New Mexico	1.5
32	New York	2.5
9	North Carolina	3.5
49	North Dakota	(0.3)
32	Ohio	2.5
48	Oklahoma	1.2
4	Oregon	3.9
17	Pennsylvania	3.2
29	Rhode Island	2.7
21	South Carolina	3.0
4	South Dakota	3.9
12	Tennessee	3.4
42	Texas	2.0
17	Utah	3.2
27	Vermont	2.8
32	Virginia	2.5
21	Washington	3.0
46	West Virginia	1.3
9	Wisconsin	3.5
50	Wyoming	(0.4)

RANK	STATE	PERCENT CHANGE
1	California	4.5
2	Nebraska	4.1
3	Massachusetts	4.0
4	Oregon	3.9
4	South Dakota	3.9
6	Hawaii	3.8
7	Iowa	3.7
7	Minnesota	3.7
9	Illinois	3.5
9	North Carolina	3.5
9	Wisconsin	3.5
12	Kentucky	3.4
12	Tennessee	3.4
14	Florida	3.3
14	Maine	3.3
14	Michigan	3.3
17	Indiana	3.2
17	Maryland	3.2
17	Pennsylvania	3.2
17	Utah	3.2
21	Missouri	3.0
21	Montana	3.0
21	South Carolina	3.0
21	Washington	3.0
25	Georgia	2.9
25	New Jersey	2.9
27	Colorado	2.8
27	Vermont	2.8
29	Kansas	2.7
29	New Hampshire	2.7
29	Rhode Island	2.7
32	Alaska	2.5
32	Connecticut	2.5
32	New York	2.5
32	Ohio	2.5
32	Virginia	2.5
37	Alabama	2.3
37	Arkansas	2.3
37	Idaho	2.3
37	Nevada	2.3
41	Arizona	2.2
42	Texas	2.0
43	Delaware	1.5
43	New Mexico	1.5
45	Mississippi	1.4
46	Louisiana	1.3
46	West Virginia	1.3
48	Oklahoma	1.2
49	North Dakota	(0.3)
50	Wyoming	(0.4)

District of Columbia   2.7

Source: CQ Press using data from U.S. Department of Labor, Bureau of Labor Statistics
   "Quarterly Census of Employment and Wages" (http://www.bls.gov/cew/data.htm)
*Includes bonuses, cash value of meals and lodging, tips and, in many states, employer contributions to certain deferred compensation plans such as 401(k) plans.

Median Earnings of Male Full-Time Workers in 2015

National Median = $49,938

<table>
<tr><td colspan="3">ALPHA ORDER</td><td colspan="3">RANK ORDER</td></tr>
<tr><td>RANK</td><td>STATE</td><td>EARNINGS</td><td>RANK</td><td>STATE</td><td>EARNINGS</td></tr>
<tr><td>37</td><td>Alabama</td><td>$45,057</td><td>1</td><td>Massachusetts</td><td>$61,761</td></tr>
<tr><td>8</td><td>Alaska</td><td>55,752</td><td>2</td><td>Connecticut</td><td>61,666</td></tr>
<tr><td>38</td><td>Arizona</td><td>44,421</td><td>3</td><td>New Jersey</td><td>61,462</td></tr>
<tr><td>50</td><td>Arkansas</td><td>40,570</td><td>4</td><td>Maryland</td><td>60,591</td></tr>
<tr><td>19</td><td>California</td><td>50,562</td><td>5</td><td>New Hampshire</td><td>56,525</td></tr>
<tr><td>14</td><td>Colorado</td><td>51,628</td><td>6</td><td>Washington</td><td>56,215</td></tr>
<tr><td>2</td><td>Connecticut</td><td>61,666</td><td>7</td><td>Wyoming</td><td>55,965</td></tr>
<tr><td>16</td><td>Delaware</td><td>51,037</td><td>8</td><td>Alaska</td><td>55,752</td></tr>
<tr><td>48</td><td>Florida</td><td>41,105</td><td>9</td><td>Virginia</td><td>54,392</td></tr>
<tr><td>35</td><td>Georgia</td><td>45,396</td><td>10</td><td>Illinois</td><td>52,161</td></tr>
<tr><td>24</td><td>Hawaii</td><td>48,074</td><td>11</td><td>New York</td><td>52,124</td></tr>
<tr><td>41</td><td>Idaho</td><td>43,264</td><td>12</td><td>North Dakota</td><td>52,031</td></tr>
<tr><td>10</td><td>Illinois</td><td>52,161</td><td>13</td><td>Minnesota</td><td>51,979</td></tr>
<tr><td>29</td><td>Indiana</td><td>47,092</td><td>14</td><td>Colorado</td><td>51,628</td></tr>
<tr><td>28</td><td>Iowa</td><td>47,298</td><td>15</td><td>Rhode Island</td><td>51,368</td></tr>
<tr><td>27</td><td>Kansas</td><td>47,864</td><td>16</td><td>Delaware</td><td>51,037</td></tr>
<tr><td>42</td><td>Kentucky</td><td>43,037</td><td>17</td><td>Pennsylvania</td><td>50,976</td></tr>
<tr><td>22</td><td>Louisiana</td><td>49,730</td><td>18</td><td>Utah</td><td>50,741</td></tr>
<tr><td>30</td><td>Maine</td><td>46,934</td><td>19</td><td>California</td><td>50,562</td></tr>
<tr><td>4</td><td>Maryland</td><td>60,591</td><td>20</td><td>Michigan</td><td>50,479</td></tr>
<tr><td>1</td><td>Massachusetts</td><td>61,761</td><td>21</td><td>Ohio</td><td>50,051</td></tr>
<tr><td>20</td><td>Michigan</td><td>50,479</td><td>22</td><td>Louisiana</td><td>49,730</td></tr>
<tr><td>13</td><td>Minnesota</td><td>51,979</td><td>23</td><td>Wisconsin</td><td>49,306</td></tr>
<tr><td>49</td><td>Mississippi</td><td>41,092</td><td>24</td><td>Hawaii</td><td>48,074</td></tr>
<tr><td>34</td><td>Missouri</td><td>45,897</td><td>25</td><td>Oregon</td><td>48,001</td></tr>
<tr><td>33</td><td>Montana</td><td>46,123</td><td>26</td><td>Vermont</td><td>47,960</td></tr>
<tr><td>32</td><td>Nebraska</td><td>46,763</td><td>27</td><td>Kansas</td><td>47,864</td></tr>
<tr><td>40</td><td>Nevada</td><td>43,681</td><td>28</td><td>Iowa</td><td>47,298</td></tr>
<tr><td>5</td><td>New Hampshire</td><td>56,525</td><td>29</td><td>Indiana</td><td>47,092</td></tr>
<tr><td>3</td><td>New Jersey</td><td>61,462</td><td>30</td><td>Maine</td><td>46,934</td></tr>
<tr><td>47</td><td>New Mexico</td><td>41,440</td><td>31</td><td>Texas</td><td>46,791</td></tr>
<tr><td>11</td><td>New York</td><td>52,124</td><td>32</td><td>Nebraska</td><td>46,763</td></tr>
<tr><td>46</td><td>North Carolina</td><td>42,039</td><td>33</td><td>Montana</td><td>46,123</td></tr>
<tr><td>12</td><td>North Dakota</td><td>52,031</td><td>34</td><td>Missouri</td><td>45,897</td></tr>
<tr><td>21</td><td>Ohio</td><td>50,051</td><td>35</td><td>Georgia</td><td>45,396</td></tr>
<tr><td>39</td><td>Oklahoma</td><td>43,829</td><td>36</td><td>West Virginia</td><td>45,082</td></tr>
<tr><td>25</td><td>Oregon</td><td>48,001</td><td>37</td><td>Alabama</td><td>45,057</td></tr>
<tr><td>17</td><td>Pennsylvania</td><td>50,976</td><td>38</td><td>Arizona</td><td>44,421</td></tr>
<tr><td>15</td><td>Rhode Island</td><td>51,368</td><td>39</td><td>Oklahoma</td><td>43,829</td></tr>
<tr><td>45</td><td>South Carolina</td><td>42,238</td><td>40</td><td>Nevada</td><td>43,681</td></tr>
<tr><td>43</td><td>South Dakota</td><td>42,605</td><td>41</td><td>Idaho</td><td>43,264</td></tr>
<tr><td>44</td><td>Tennessee</td><td>42,525</td><td>42</td><td>Kentucky</td><td>43,037</td></tr>
<tr><td>31</td><td>Texas</td><td>46,791</td><td>43</td><td>South Dakota</td><td>42,605</td></tr>
<tr><td>18</td><td>Utah</td><td>50,741</td><td>44</td><td>Tennessee</td><td>42,525</td></tr>
<tr><td>26</td><td>Vermont</td><td>47,960</td><td>45</td><td>South Carolina</td><td>42,238</td></tr>
<tr><td>9</td><td>Virginia</td><td>54,392</td><td>46</td><td>North Carolina</td><td>42,039</td></tr>
<tr><td>6</td><td>Washington</td><td>56,215</td><td>47</td><td>New Mexico</td><td>41,440</td></tr>
<tr><td>36</td><td>West Virginia</td><td>45,082</td><td>48</td><td>Florida</td><td>41,105</td></tr>
<tr><td>23</td><td>Wisconsin</td><td>49,306</td><td>49</td><td>Mississippi</td><td>41,092</td></tr>
<tr><td>7</td><td>Wyoming</td><td>55,965</td><td>50</td><td>Arkansas</td><td>40,570</td></tr>
<tr><td></td><td></td><td></td><td></td><td>District of Columbia</td><td>72,230</td></tr>
</table>

Source: U.S. Bureau of the Census
"2015 American Community Survey-Table R2001" (http://www.census.gov/programs-surveys/acs/)

Median Earnings of Female Full-Time Workers in 2015

National Median = $39,940

ALPHA ORDER

RANK ORDER

RANK	STATE	EARNINGS		RANK	STATE	EARNINGS
41	Alabama	$34,310		1	Massachusetts	$51,343
9	Alaska	43,455		2	Connecticut	50,802
23	Arizona	37,084		3	Maryland	50,635
47	Arkansas	32,003		4	New Jersey	50,373
10	California	43,335		5	New York	46,208
14	Colorado	41,690		6	Delaware	45,192
2	Connecticut	50,802		7	Washington	44,422
6	Delaware	45,192		8	Rhode Island	44,050
37	Florida	35,604		9	Alaska	43,455
29	Georgia	36,650		10	California	43,335
16	Hawaii	40,434		11	New Hampshire	43,172
49	Idaho	31,808		12	Virginia	42,342
15	Illinois	41,327		13	Minnesota	42,137
36	Indiana	35,753		14	Colorado	41,690
31	Iowa	36,264		15	Illinois	41,327
28	Kansas	36,671		16	Hawaii	40,434
38	Kentucky	35,294		17	Pennsylvania	40,214
43	Louisiana	33,832		18	Vermont	40,173
26	Maine	36,841		19	Oregon	38,774
3	Maryland	50,635		20	Wisconsin	38,594
1	Massachusetts	51,343		21	Michigan	37,486
21	Michigan	37,486		22	Ohio	37,365
13	Minnesota	42,137		23	Arizona	37,084
50	Mississippi	31,110		24	North Dakota	37,016
35	Missouri	35,759		25	Texas	36,934
44	Montana	33,443		26	Maine	36,841
27	Nebraska	36,834		27	Nebraska	36,834
30	Nevada	36,565		28	Kansas	36,671
11	New Hampshire	43,172		29	Georgia	36,650
4	New Jersey	50,373		30	Nevada	36,565
39	New Mexico	35,070		31	Iowa	36,264
5	New York	46,208		32	North Carolina	36,113
32	North Carolina	36,113		33	Wyoming	36,064
24	North Dakota	37,016		34	Utah	36,060
22	Ohio	37,365		35	Missouri	35,759
46	Oklahoma	32,096		36	Indiana	35,753
19	Oregon	38,774		37	Florida	35,604
17	Pennsylvania	40,214		38	Kentucky	35,294
8	Rhode Island	44,050		39	New Mexico	35,070
42	South Carolina	34,182		40	Tennessee	34,427
45	South Dakota	33,268		41	Alabama	34,310
40	Tennessee	34,427		42	South Carolina	34,182
25	Texas	36,934		43	Louisiana	33,832
34	Utah	36,060		44	Montana	33,443
18	Vermont	40,173		45	South Dakota	33,268
12	Virginia	42,342		46	Oklahoma	32,096
7	Washington	44,422		47	Arkansas	32,003
48	West Virginia	31,824		48	West Virginia	31,824
20	Wisconsin	38,594		49	Idaho	31,808
33	Wyoming	36,064		50	Mississippi	31,110
					District of Columbia	62,191

Source: U.S. Bureau of the Census
"2015 American Community Survey-Table R2002" (http://www.census.gov/programs-surveys/acs/)

State Minimum Wage Rates in 2017

National Rate = $7.25 per Hour*

ALPHA ORDER

RANK	STATE	MINIMUM WAGE
NA	Alabama**	NA
7	Alaska	9.80
5	Arizona	10.00
20	Arkansas	8.50
3	California	10.50
12	Colorado	9.30
4	Connecticut	10.10
22	Delaware	8.25
27	Florida	8.10
44	Georgia	5.15
13	Hawaii	9.25
30	Idaho	7.25
22	Illinois	8.25
30	Indiana	7.25
30	Iowa	7.25
30	Kansas	7.25
30	Kentucky	7.25
NA	Louisiana**	NA
14	Maine	9.00
17	Maryland	8.75
1	Massachusetts	11.00
16	Michigan	8.90
11	Minnesota	9.50
NA	Mississippi**	NA
28	Missouri	7.70
25	Montana	8.15
14	Nebraska	9.00
22	Nevada	8.25
30	New Hampshire	7.25
21	New Jersey	8.44
29	New Mexico	7.50
9	New York	9.70
30	North Carolina	7.25
30	North Dakota	7.25
25	Ohio	8.15
30	Oklahoma	7.25
8	Oregon	9.75
30	Pennsylvania	7.25
10	Rhode Island	9.60
NA	South Carolina**	NA
19	South Dakota	8.65
NA	Tennessee**	NA
30	Texas	7.25
30	Utah	7.25
5	Vermont	10.00
30	Virginia	7.25
1	Washington	11.00
17	West Virginia	8.75
30	Wisconsin	7.25
44	Wyoming	5.15

RANK ORDER

RANK	STATE	MINIMUM WAGE
1	Massachusetts	$11.00
1	Washington	11.00
3	California	10.50
4	Connecticut	10.10
5	Arizona	10.00
5	Vermont	10.00
7	Alaska	9.80
8	Oregon	9.75
9	New York	9.70
10	Rhode Island	9.60
11	Minnesota	9.50
12	Colorado	9.30
13	Hawaii	9.25
14	Maine	9.00
14	Nebraska	9.00
16	Michigan	8.90
17	Maryland	8.75
17	West Virginia	8.75
19	South Dakota	8.65
20	Arkansas	8.50
21	New Jersey	8.44
22	Delaware	8.25
22	Illinois	8.25
22	Nevada	8.25
25	Montana	8.15
25	Ohio	8.15
27	Florida	8.10
28	Missouri	7.70
29	New Mexico	7.50
30	Idaho	7.25
30	Indiana	7.25
30	Iowa	7.25
30	Kansas	7.25
30	Kentucky	7.25
30	New Hampshire	7.25
30	North Carolina	7.25
30	North Dakota	7.25
30	Oklahoma	7.25
30	Pennsylvania	7.25
30	Texas	7.25
30	Utah	7.25
30	Virginia	7.25
30	Wisconsin	7.25
44	Georgia	5.15
44	Wyoming	5.15
NA	Alabama**	NA
NA	Louisiana**	NA
NA	Mississippi**	NA
NA	South Carolina**	NA
NA	Tennessee**	NA

District of Columbia   11.50

Source: U.S. Department of Labor, Employment Standards Administration
"Minimum Wage Laws in the States" (http://www.dol.gov/whd/minwage/america.htm)
*As of January 1, 2017. State minimum wage rates are for those employers and jobs not covered by the federal program.
**No separate state program.

Average Hourly Earnings of Production Workers on Manufacturing Payrolls in 2016
National Average = $26.37*

ALPHA ORDER

RANK	STATE	HOURLY EARNINGS
33	Alabama	$19.40
1	Alaska	31.69
47	Arizona	16.95
49	Arkansas	15.82
8	California	22.01
2	Colorado	29.41
4	Connecticut	24.91
46	Delaware	17.47
13	Florida	21.34
43	Georgia	18.26
12	Hawaii	21.38
39	Idaho	18.78
28	Illinois	19.98
36	Indiana	19.00
35	Iowa	19.09
37	Kansas	18.94
20	Kentucky	20.63
11	Louisiana	21.61
10	Maine	21.80
31	Maryland	19.76
6	Massachusetts	22.28
21	Michigan	20.62
25	Minnesota	20.24
15	Mississippi	21.20
14	Missouri	21.24
40	Montana	18.71
44	Nebraska	18.06
29	Nevada	19.86
9	New Hampshire	21.93
7	New Jersey	22.27
48	New Mexico	16.39
26	New York	20.04
45	North Carolina	17.78
23	North Dakota	20.45
16	Ohio	20.98
41	Oklahoma	18.64
24	Oregon	20.31
30	Pennsylvania	19.80
42	Rhode Island	18.55
32	South Carolina	19.43
34	South Dakota	19.10
27	Tennessee	19.99
5	Texas	23.21
19	Utah	20.74
17	Vermont	20.90
38	Virginia	18.86
3	Washington	27.17
18	West Virginia	20.89
22	Wisconsin	20.48
NA	Wyoming**	NA

RANK ORDER

RANK	STATE	HOURLY EARNINGS
1	Alaska	$31.69
2	Colorado	29.41
3	Washington	27.17
4	Connecticut	24.91
5	Texas	23.21
6	Massachusetts	22.28
7	New Jersey	22.27
8	California	22.01
9	New Hampshire	21.93
10	Maine	21.80
11	Louisiana	21.61
12	Hawaii	21.38
13	Florida	21.34
14	Missouri	21.24
15	Mississippi	21.20
16	Ohio	20.98
17	Vermont	20.90
18	West Virginia	20.89
19	Utah	20.74
20	Kentucky	20.63
21	Michigan	20.62
22	Wisconsin	20.48
23	North Dakota	20.45
24	Oregon	20.31
25	Minnesota	20.24
26	New York	20.04
27	Tennessee	19.99
28	Illinois	19.98
29	Nevada	19.86
30	Pennsylvania	19.80
31	Maryland	19.76
32	South Carolina	19.43
33	Alabama	19.40
34	South Dakota	19.10
35	Iowa	19.09
36	Indiana	19.00
37	Kansas	18.94
38	Virginia	18.86
39	Idaho	18.78
40	Montana	18.71
41	Oklahoma	18.64
42	Rhode Island	18.55
43	Georgia	18.26
44	Nebraska	18.06
45	North Carolina	17.78
46	Delaware	17.47
47	Arizona	16.95
48	New Mexico	16.39
49	Arkansas	15.82
NA	Wyoming**	NA
	District of Columbia**	NA

Source: U.S. Department of Labor, Bureau of Labor Statistics
   "State and Metro Area Employment, Hours and Earnings" (http://www.bls.gov/sae/home.htm)
*Preliminary data for December 2016. Not seasonally adjusted except for national figure.
**Not available.

Average Weekly Earnings of Production Workers
on Manufacturing Payrolls in 2016
National Average = $1,073.26*

Source: U.S. Department of Labor, Bureau of Labor Statistics
 "State and Metro Area Employment, Hours and Earnings" (http://www.bls.gov/sae/home.htm)
*Preliminary data for December 2016. Not seasonally adjusted except for national figure.
**Not available.

ALPHA ORDER

RANK	STATE	WEEKLY EARNINGS
22	Alabama	$838.08
44	Alaska	728.87
47	Arizona	678.00
49	Arkansas	631.22
10	California	911.21
1	Colorado	1,202.87
3	Connecticut	1,091.06
45	Delaware	718.02
12	Florida	898.41
30	Georgia	807.09
18	Hawaii	850.92
42	Idaho	743.69
21	Illinois	839.16
29	Indiana	811.30
33	Iowa	799.87
27	Kansas	818.21
8	Kentucky	920.10
7	Louisiana	924.91
16	Maine	867.64
38	Maryland	780.52
5	Massachusetts	940.22
14	Michigan	886.66
26	Minnesota	821.74
9	Mississippi	911.60
15	Missouri	885.71
46	Montana	699.75
39	Nebraska	760.33
32	Nevada	802.34
6	New Hampshire	929.83
11	New Jersey	906.39
48	New Mexico	635.93
34	New York	789.58
41	North Carolina	755.65
35	North Dakota	783.24
13	Ohio	893.75
40	Oklahoma	758.65
31	Oregon	806.31
25	Pennsylvania	829.62
36	Rhode Island	780.96
20	South Carolina	849.09
43	South Dakota	731.53
17	Tennessee	867.57
4	Texas	995.71
19	Utah	850.34
28	Vermont	815.10
37	Virginia	780.80
2	Washington	1,141.14
24	West Virginia	831.42
23	Wisconsin	835.58
NA	Wyoming**	NA

RANK ORDER

RANK	STATE	WEEKLY EARNINGS
1	Colorado	$1,202.87
2	Washington	1,141.14
3	Connecticut	1,091.06
4	Texas	995.71
5	Massachusetts	940.22
6	New Hampshire	929.83
7	Louisiana	924.91
8	Kentucky	920.10
9	Mississippi	911.60
10	California	911.21
11	New Jersey	906.39
12	Florida	898.41
13	Ohio	893.75
14	Michigan	886.66
15	Missouri	885.71
16	Maine	867.64
17	Tennessee	867.57
18	Hawaii	850.92
19	Utah	850.34
20	South Carolina	849.09
21	Illinois	839.16
22	Alabama	838.08
23	Wisconsin	835.58
24	West Virginia	831.42
25	Pennsylvania	829.62
26	Minnesota	821.74
27	Kansas	818.21
28	Vermont	815.10
29	Indiana	811.30
30	Georgia	807.09
31	Oregon	806.31
32	Nevada	802.34
33	Iowa	799.87
34	New York	789.58
35	North Dakota	783.24
36	Rhode Island	780.96
37	Virginia	780.80
38	Maryland	780.52
39	Nebraska	760.33
40	Oklahoma	758.65
41	North Carolina	755.65
42	Idaho	743.69
43	South Dakota	731.53
44	Alaska	728.87
45	Delaware	718.02
46	Montana	699.75
47	Arizona	678.00
48	New Mexico	635.93
49	Arkansas	631.22
NA	Wyoming**	NA
	District of Columbia**	NA

Average Work Week of Production Workers on Manufacturing Payrolls in 2016
National Average = 40.7 Hours per Week*

ALPHA ORDER

RANK	STATE	WEEKLY HOURS
6	Alabama	43.2
49	Alaska	23.0
35	Arizona	40.0
36	Arkansas	39.9
25	California	41.4
29	Colorado	40.9
3	Connecticut	43.8
27	Delaware	41.1
17	Florida	42.1
2	Georgia	44.2
37	Hawaii	39.8
41	Idaho	39.6
20	Illinois	42.0
12	Indiana	42.7
22	Iowa	41.9
6	Kansas	43.2
1	Kentucky	44.6
11	Louisiana	42.8
37	Maine	39.8
42	Maryland	39.5
16	Massachusetts	42.2
8	Michigan	43.0
33	Minnesota	40.6
8	Mississippi	43.0
24	Missouri	41.7
48	Montana	37.4
17	Nebraska	42.1
34	Nevada	40.4
15	New Hampshire	42.4
31	New Jersey	40.7
45	New Mexico	38.8
43	New York	39.4
14	North Carolina	42.5
46	North Dakota	38.3
13	Ohio	42.6
31	Oklahoma	40.7
40	Oregon	39.7
22	Pennsylvania	41.9
17	Rhode Island	42.1
4	South Carolina	43.7
46	South Dakota	38.3
5	Tennessee	43.4
10	Texas	42.9
28	Utah	41.0
44	Vermont	39.0
25	Virginia	41.4
20	Washington	42.0
37	West Virginia	39.8
30	Wisconsin	40.8
NA	Wyoming**	NA

RANK ORDER

RANK	STATE	WEEKLY HOURS
1	Kentucky	44.6
2	Georgia	44.2
3	Connecticut	43.8
4	South Carolina	43.7
5	Tennessee	43.4
6	Alabama	43.2
6	Kansas	43.2
8	Michigan	43.0
8	Mississippi	43.0
10	Texas	42.9
11	Louisiana	42.8
12	Indiana	42.7
13	Ohio	42.6
14	North Carolina	42.5
15	New Hampshire	42.4
16	Massachusetts	42.2
17	Florida	42.1
17	Nebraska	42.1
17	Rhode Island	42.1
20	Illinois	42.0
20	Washington	42.0
22	Iowa	41.9
22	Pennsylvania	41.9
24	Missouri	41.7
25	California	41.4
25	Virginia	41.4
27	Delaware	41.1
28	Utah	41.0
29	Colorado	40.9
30	Wisconsin	40.8
31	New Jersey	40.7
31	Oklahoma	40.7
33	Minnesota	40.6
34	Nevada	40.4
35	Arizona	40.0
36	Arkansas	39.9
37	Hawaii	39.8
37	Maine	39.8
37	West Virginia	39.8
40	Oregon	39.7
41	Idaho	39.6
42	Maryland	39.5
43	New York	39.4
44	Vermont	39.0
45	New Mexico	38.8
46	North Dakota	38.3
46	South Dakota	38.3
48	Montana	37.4
49	Alaska	23.0
NA	Wyoming**	NA
	District of Columbia**	NA

Source: U.S. Department of Labor, Bureau of Labor Statistics
   "State and Metro Area Employment, Hours and Earnings" (http://www.bls.gov/sae/home.htm)
*Preliminary data for December 2016. Not seasonally adjusted except for national figure.
**Not available.

Average Weekly Unemployment Benefit in 2016

National Average = $344.72 a Week

RANK	STATE	BENEFIT
49	Alabama	$220.86
38	Alaska	279.88
48	Arizona	224.10
40	Arkansas	269.52
28	California	315.66
7	Colorado	413.42
14	Connecticut	375.04
42	Delaware	257.52
46	Florida	239.23
37	Georgia	282.91
3	Hawaii	456.85
32	Idaho	311.28
17	Illinois	361.30
39	Indiana	274.46
12	Iowa	382.60
15	Kansas	370.43
26	Kentucky	320.69
47	Louisiana	231.54
29	Maine	314.76
22	Maryland	333.81
2	Massachusetts	489.00
36	Michigan	305.50
5	Minnesota	434.51
50	Mississippi	206.11
43	Missouri	253.68
23	Montana	331.73
27	Nebraska	316.10
24	Nevada	328.77
31	New Hampshire	313.66
6	New Jersey	425.77
21	New Mexico	338.36
25	New York	327.91
45	North Carolina	247.08
1	North Dakota	513.84
18	Ohio	353.98
13	Oklahoma	377.07
16	Oregon	367.89
10	Pennsylvania	391.25
19	Rhode Island	343.65
44	South Carolina	252.18
30	South Dakota	314.30
41	Tennessee	263.61
9	Texas	403.42
11	Utah	386.60
20	Vermont	340.30
35	Virginia	307.41
4	Washington	443.52
34	West Virginia	308.79
33	Wisconsin	310.35
8	Wyoming	411.52

RANK	STATE	BENEFIT
1	North Dakota	$513.84
2	Massachusetts	489.00
3	Hawaii	456.85
4	Washington	443.52
5	Minnesota	434.51
6	New Jersey	425.77
7	Colorado	413.42
8	Wyoming	411.52
9	Texas	403.42
10	Pennsylvania	391.25
11	Utah	386.60
12	Iowa	382.60
13	Oklahoma	377.07
14	Connecticut	375.04
15	Kansas	370.43
16	Oregon	367.89
17	Illinois	361.30
18	Ohio	353.98
19	Rhode Island	343.65
20	Vermont	340.30
21	New Mexico	338.36
22	Maryland	333.81
23	Montana	331.73
24	Nevada	328.77
25	New York	327.91
26	Kentucky	320.69
27	Nebraska	316.10
28	California	315.66
29	Maine	314.76
30	South Dakota	314.30
31	New Hampshire	313.66
32	Idaho	311.28
33	Wisconsin	310.35
34	West Virginia	308.79
35	Virginia	307.41
36	Michigan	305.50
37	Georgia	282.91
38	Alaska	279.88
39	Indiana	274.46
40	Arkansas	269.52
41	Tennessee	263.61
42	Delaware	257.52
43	Missouri	253.68
44	South Carolina	252.18
45	North Carolina	247.08
46	Florida	239.23
47	Louisiana	231.54
48	Arizona	224.10
49	Alabama	220.86
50	Mississippi	206.11

| | District of Columbia | 311.26 |

Source: CQ Press using data from U.S. Department of Labor, Bureau of Labor Statistics
"Unemployment Insurance Data Summary" (http://workforcesecurity.doleta.gov/unemploy/finance.asp)

Workers' Compensation Benefit Payments in 2014

National Total = $62,306,736,000*

ALPHA ORDER

RANK	STATE	PAYMENTS	% of USA
29	Alabama	$636,575,000	1.0%
43	Alaska	214,995,000	0.3%
23	Arizona	737,095,000	1.2%
44	Arkansas	211,633,000	0.3%
1	California	12,093,241,000	19.4%
21	Colorado	798,711,000	1.3%
19	Connecticut	886,015,000	1.4%
41	Delaware	249,385,000	0.4%
3	Florida	3,147,769,000	5.1%
10	Georgia	1,433,242,000	2.3%
37	Hawaii	270,720,000	0.4%
39	Idaho	254,050,000	0.4%
5	Illinois	2,752,343,000	4.4%
30	Indiana	589,225,000	0.9%
28	Iowa	649,719,000	1.0%
32	Kansas	379,413,000	0.6%
26	Kentucky	656,611,000	1.1%
22	Louisiana	795,499,000	1.3%
40	Maine	253,217,000	0.4%
16	Maryland	955,474,000	1.5%
13	Massachusetts	1,148,384,000	1.8%
15	Michigan	1,034,772,000	1.7%
14	Minnesota	1,079,263,000	1.7%
34	Mississippi	336,689,000	0.5%
20	Missouri	853,094,000	1.4%
42	Montana	245,909,000	0.4%
35	Nebraska	325,263,000	0.5%
33	Nevada	369,396,000	0.6%
45	New Hampshire	210,224,000	0.3%
7	New Jersey	2,269,156,000	3.6%
38	New Mexico	262,383,000	0.4%
2	New York	5,581,295,000	9.0%
11	North Carolina	1,311,126,000	2.1%
46	North Dakota	191,448,000	0.3%
8	Ohio	2,027,964,000	3.3%
24	Oklahoma	714,367,000	1.1%
27	Oregon	655,971,000	1.1%
4	Pennsylvania	3,010,790,000	4.8%
48	Rhode Island	164,084,000	0.3%
18	South Carolina	888,850,000	1.4%
50	South Dakota	98,266,000	0.2%
25	Tennessee	710,062,000	1.1%
9	Texas	1,548,645,000	2.5%
36	Utah	271,969,000	0.4%
49	Vermont	152,749,000	0.2%
17	Virginia	933,059,000	1.5%
6	Washington	2,392,919,000	3.8%
31	West Virginia	423,527,000	0.7%
12	Wisconsin	1,163,372,000	1.9%
47	Wyoming	184,398,000	0.3%

RANK ORDER

RANK	STATE	PAYMENTS	% of USA
1	California	$12,093,241,000	19.4%
2	New York	5,581,295,000	9.0%
3	Florida	3,147,769,000	5.1%
4	Pennsylvania	3,010,790,000	4.8%
5	Illinois	2,752,343,000	4.4%
6	Washington	2,392,919,000	3.8%
7	New Jersey	2,269,156,000	3.6%
8	Ohio	2,027,964,000	3.3%
9	Texas	1,548,645,000	2.5%
10	Georgia	1,433,242,000	2.3%
11	North Carolina	1,311,126,000	2.1%
12	Wisconsin	1,163,372,000	1.9%
13	Massachusetts	1,148,384,000	1.8%
14	Minnesota	1,079,263,000	1.7%
15	Michigan	1,034,772,000	1.7%
16	Maryland	955,474,000	1.5%
17	Virginia	933,059,000	1.5%
18	South Carolina	888,850,000	1.4%
19	Connecticut	886,015,000	1.4%
20	Missouri	853,094,000	1.4%
21	Colorado	798,711,000	1.3%
22	Louisiana	795,499,000	1.3%
23	Arizona	737,095,000	1.2%
24	Oklahoma	714,367,000	1.1%
25	Tennessee	710,062,000	1.1%
26	Kentucky	656,611,000	1.1%
27	Oregon	655,971,000	1.1%
28	Iowa	649,719,000	1.0%
29	Alabama	636,575,000	1.0%
30	Indiana	589,225,000	0.9%
31	West Virginia	423,527,000	0.7%
32	Kansas	379,413,000	0.6%
33	Nevada	369,396,000	0.6%
34	Mississippi	336,689,000	0.5%
35	Nebraska	325,263,000	0.5%
36	Utah	271,969,000	0.4%
37	Hawaii	270,720,000	0.4%
38	New Mexico	262,383,000	0.4%
39	Idaho	254,050,000	0.4%
40	Maine	253,217,000	0.4%
41	Delaware	249,385,000	0.4%
42	Montana	245,909,000	0.4%
43	Alaska	214,995,000	0.3%
44	Arkansas	211,633,000	0.3%
45	New Hampshire	210,224,000	0.3%
46	North Dakota	191,448,000	0.3%
47	Wyoming	184,398,000	0.3%
48	Rhode Island	164,084,000	0.3%
49	Vermont	152,749,000	0.2%
50	South Dakota	98,266,000	0.2%
	District of Columbia	101,207,000	0.2%

Source: National Academy of Social Insurance (Washington, DC)
"Workers' Compensation: Benefits, Coverage, and Costs, 2014" (http://www.nasi.org)
*Estimated payments from private insurance, state and federal funds, and self insurance. National total includes payments for federal civilian employee program, Black Lung Program, and other federal programs.

Workers' Compensation Benefit Payment per Covered Worker in 2014

National Average = $470*

ALPHA ORDER

RANK	STATE	AVERAGE
30	Alabama	$367
3	Alaska	683
41	Arizona	297
49	Arkansas	192
2	California	777
37	Colorado	339
11	Connecticut	542
7	Delaware	598
21	Florida	434
28	Georgia	374
16	Hawaii	457
24	Idaho	401
15	Illinois	486
48	Indiana	207
19	Iowa	438
42	Kansas	287
29	Kentucky	372
22	Louisiana	421
18	Maine	442
25	Maryland	397
34	Massachusetts	346
45	Michigan	264
23	Minnesota	402
39	Mississippi	328
35	Missouri	342
9	Montana	580
32	Nebraska	354
40	Nevada	313
36	New Hampshire	340
7	New Jersey	598
32	New Mexico	354
5	New York	641
38	North Carolina	338
17	North Dakota	443
25	Ohio	397
14	Oklahoma	490
27	Oregon	386
10	Pennsylvania	545
31	Rhode Island	363
13	South Carolina	494
46	South Dakota	249
44	Tennessee	273
50	Texas	174
47	Utah	217
12	Vermont	518
43	Virginia	274
1	Washington	825
6	West Virginia	640
19	Wisconsin	438
4	Wyoming	666

RANK ORDER

RANK	STATE	AVERAGE
1	Washington	$825
2	California	777
3	Alaska	683
4	Wyoming	666
5	New York	641
6	West Virginia	640
7	Delaware	598
7	New Jersey	598
9	Montana	580
10	Pennsylvania	545
11	Connecticut	542
12	Vermont	518
13	South Carolina	494
14	Oklahoma	490
15	Illinois	486
16	Hawaii	457
17	North Dakota	443
18	Maine	442
19	Iowa	438
19	Wisconsin	438
21	Florida	434
22	Louisiana	421
23	Minnesota	402
24	Idaho	401
25	Maryland	397
25	Ohio	397
27	Oregon	386
28	Georgia	374
29	Kentucky	372
30	Alabama	367
31	Rhode Island	363
32	Nebraska	354
32	New Mexico	354
34	Massachusetts	346
35	Missouri	342
36	New Hampshire	340
37	Colorado	339
38	North Carolina	338
39	Mississippi	328
40	Nevada	313
41	Arizona	297
42	Kansas	287
43	Virginia	274
44	Tennessee	273
45	Michigan	264
46	South Dakota	249
47	Utah	217
48	Indiana	207
49	Arkansas	192
50	Texas	174

District of Columbia — 190

Source: CQ Press using data from National Academy of Social Insurance (Washington, DC)
"Workers' Compensation: Benefits, Coverage, and Costs, 2014" (http://www.nasi.org)
*Estimated payments from private insurance, state and federal funds, and self insurance. National rate includes payments for federal civilian employee program, Black Lung Program, and other federal programs. Total divided by number of workers covered by workers' compensation.

Percent Change in Workers' Compensation Benefit Payments: 2013 to 2014

National Percent Change = 0.3% Decrease*

RANK	STATE	PERCENT CHANGE
27	Alabama	(0.4)
50	Alaska	(15.0)
8	Arizona	2.9
12	Arkansas	1.7
25	California	(0.3)
38	Colorado	(3.4)
38	Connecticut	(3.4)
6	Delaware	3.8
23	Florida	0.5
19	Georgia	1.1
4	Hawaii	4.0
9	Idaho	2.7
3	Illinois	4.9
47	Indiana	(8.6)
12	Iowa	1.7
29	Kansas	(1.1)
34	Kentucky	(2.9)
35	Louisiana	(3.2)
24	Maine	0.2
19	Maryland	1.1
1	Massachusetts	8.1
48	Michigan	(8.8)
16	Minnesota	1.4
17	Mississippi	1.2
11	Missouri	1.8
28	Montana	(0.9)
2	Nebraska	6.1
25	Nevada	(0.3)
44	New Hampshire	(5.1)
15	New Jersey	1.6
42	New Mexico	(4.0)
21	New York	0.7
46	North Carolina	(8.1)
30	North Dakota	(1.3)
33	Ohio	(2.0)
49	Oklahoma	(12.1)
32	Oregon	(1.9)
22	Pennsylvania	0.6
35	Rhode Island	(3.2)
17	South Carolina	1.2
31	South Dakota	(1.4)
45	Tennessee	(6.7)
43	Texas	(4.5)
40	Utah	(3.6)
12	Vermont	1.7
4	Virginia	4.0
10	Washington	2.6
37	West Virginia	(3.3)
7	Wisconsin	3.3
41	Wyoming	(3.9)

RANK	STATE	PERCENT CHANGE
1	Massachusetts	8.1
2	Nebraska	6.1
3	Illinois	4.9
4	Hawaii	4.0
4	Virginia	4.0
6	Delaware	3.8
7	Wisconsin	3.3
8	Arizona	2.9
9	Idaho	2.7
10	Washington	2.6
11	Missouri	1.8
12	Arkansas	1.7
12	Iowa	1.7
12	Vermont	1.7
15	New Jersey	1.6
16	Minnesota	1.4
17	Mississippi	1.2
17	South Carolina	1.2
19	Georgia	1.1
19	Maryland	1.1
21	New York	0.7
22	Pennsylvania	0.6
23	Florida	0.5
24	Maine	0.2
25	California	(0.3)
25	Nevada	(0.3)
27	Alabama	(0.4)
28	Montana	(0.9)
29	Kansas	(1.1)
30	North Dakota	(1.3)
31	South Dakota	(1.4)
32	Oregon	(1.9)
33	Ohio	(2.0)
34	Kentucky	(2.9)
35	Louisiana	(3.2)
35	Rhode Island	(3.2)
37	West Virginia	(3.3)
38	Colorado	(3.4)
38	Connecticut	(3.4)
40	Utah	(3.6)
41	Wyoming	(3.9)
42	New Mexico	(4.0)
43	Texas	(4.5)
44	New Hampshire	(5.1)
45	Tennessee	(6.7)
46	North Carolina	(8.1)
47	Indiana	(8.6)
48	Michigan	(8.8)
49	Oklahoma	(12.1)
50	Alaska	(15.0)

	District of Columbia	(8.2)

Source: CQ Press using data from National Academy of Social Insurance (Washington, DC)
"Workers' Compensation: Benefits, Coverage, and Costs, 2014" (http://www.nasi.org)
*Estimated payments from private insurance, state and federal funds, and self insurance. National rate includes payments for federal civilian employee program, Black Lung Program, and other federal programs.

Civilian Labor Force in 2016

National Total = 159,640,000 Workers*

ALPHA ORDER

RANK	STATE	LABOR FORCE	% of USA
24	Alabama	2,203,251	1.4%
48	Alaska	358,092	0.2%
16	Arizona	3,264,621	2.0%
34	Arkansas	1,343,243	0.8%
1	California	19,385,568	12.1%
22	Colorado	2,926,075	1.8%
28	Connecticut	1,898,141	1.2%
45	Delaware	471,305	0.3%
3	Florida	9,946,702	6.2%
8	Georgia	4,993,859	3.1%
41	Hawaii	699,902	0.4%
38	Idaho	814,231	0.5%
5	Illinois	6,561,687	4.1%
15	Indiana	3,328,953	2.1%
30	Iowa	1,712,051	1.1%
32	Kansas	1,484,858	0.9%
27	Kentucky	2,016,835	1.3%
25	Louisiana	2,112,592	1.3%
42	Maine	693,943	0.4%
17	Maryland	3,197,717	2.0%
14	Massachusetts	3,601,354	2.3%
10	Michigan	4,887,215	3.1%
21	Minnesota	2,986,041	1.9%
35	Mississippi	1,288,231	0.8%
19	Missouri	3,139,008	2.0%
44	Montana	525,053	0.3%
36	Nebraska	1,016,226	0.6%
33	Nevada	1,432,144	0.9%
40	New Hampshire	752,598	0.5%
11	New Jersey	4,538,105	2.8%
37	New Mexico	930,008	0.6%
4	New York	9,623,664	6.0%
9	North Carolina	4,919,346	3.1%
47	North Dakota	431,506	0.3%
7	Ohio	5,708,571	3.6%
29	Oklahoma	1,832,693	1.1%
26	Oregon	2,073,957	1.3%
6	Pennsylvania	6,510,151	4.1%
43	Rhode Island	553,301	0.3%
23	South Carolina	2,307,885	1.4%
46	South Dakota	455,490	0.3%
18	Tennessee	3,192,652	2.0%
2	Texas	13,434,978	8.4%
31	Utah	1,522,018	1.0%
49	Vermont	344,965	0.2%
12	Virginia	4,278,223	2.7%
13	Washington	3,690,024	2.3%
39	West Virginia	792,297	0.5%
20	Wisconsin	3,132,918	2.0%
50	Wyoming	303,420	0.2%

RANK ORDER

RANK	STATE	LABOR FORCE	% of USA
1	California	19,385,568	12.1%
2	Texas	13,434,978	8.4%
3	Florida	9,946,702	6.2%
4	New York	9,623,664	6.0%
5	Illinois	6,561,687	4.1%
6	Pennsylvania	6,510,151	4.1%
7	Ohio	5,708,571	3.6%
8	Georgia	4,993,859	3.1%
9	North Carolina	4,919,346	3.1%
10	Michigan	4,887,215	3.1%
11	New Jersey	4,538,105	2.8%
12	Virginia	4,278,223	2.7%
13	Washington	3,690,024	2.3%
14	Massachusetts	3,601,354	2.3%
15	Indiana	3,328,953	2.1%
16	Arizona	3,264,621	2.0%
17	Maryland	3,197,717	2.0%
18	Tennessee	3,192,652	2.0%
19	Missouri	3,139,008	2.0%
20	Wisconsin	3,132,918	2.0%
21	Minnesota	2,986,041	1.9%
22	Colorado	2,926,075	1.8%
23	South Carolina	2,307,885	1.4%
24	Alabama	2,203,251	1.4%
25	Louisiana	2,112,592	1.3%
26	Oregon	2,073,957	1.3%
27	Kentucky	2,016,835	1.3%
28	Connecticut	1,898,141	1.2%
29	Oklahoma	1,832,693	1.1%
30	Iowa	1,712,051	1.1%
31	Utah	1,522,018	1.0%
32	Kansas	1,484,858	0.9%
33	Nevada	1,432,144	0.9%
34	Arkansas	1,343,243	0.8%
35	Mississippi	1,288,231	0.8%
36	Nebraska	1,016,226	0.6%
37	New Mexico	930,008	0.6%
38	Idaho	814,231	0.5%
39	West Virginia	792,297	0.5%
40	New Hampshire	752,598	0.5%
41	Hawaii	699,902	0.4%
42	Maine	693,943	0.4%
43	Rhode Island	553,301	0.3%
44	Montana	525,053	0.3%
45	Delaware	471,305	0.3%
46	South Dakota	455,490	0.3%
47	North Dakota	431,506	0.3%
48	Alaska	358,092	0.2%
49	Vermont	344,965	0.2%
50	Wyoming	303,420	0.2%
	District of Columbia	397,723	0.2%

Source: U.S. Department of Labor, Bureau of Labor Statistics
"Regional and State Employment and Unemployment" (press release, January 24, 2017, www.bls.gov/bls/newsrels.htm)
*Seasonally adjusted preliminary data as of December 2016. National total calculated through a different formula.

Employed Civilian Labor Force in 2016

National Total = 152,111,000 Employed Workers*

ALPHA ORDER

RANK	STATE	EMPLOYED	% of USA
24	Alabama	2,066,842	1.4%
49	Alaska	334,110	0.2%
16	Arizona	3,106,693	2.0%
34	Arkansas	1,290,950	0.8%
1	California	18,376,599	12.1%
22	Colorado	2,838,545	1.9%
28	Connecticut	1,814,687	1.2%
45	Delaware	451,045	0.3%
3	Florida	9,456,079	6.2%
8	Georgia	4,722,965	3.1%
41	Hawaii	679,897	0.4%
38	Idaho	784,186	0.5%
5	Illinois	6,187,173	4.1%
15	Indiana	3,194,602	2.1%
30	Iowa	1,650,835	1.1%
32	Kansas	1,422,113	0.9%
27	Kentucky	1,919,658	1.3%
25	Louisiana	1,983,243	1.3%
42	Maine	667,784	0.4%
17	Maryland	3,064,316	2.0%
13	Massachusetts	3,500,009	2.3%
10	Michigan	4,642,307	3.1%
21	Minnesota	2,870,803	1.9%
35	Mississippi	1,216,024	0.8%
20	Missouri	2,999,742	2.0%
44	Montana	504,233	0.3%
36	Nebraska	982,180	0.6%
33	Nevada	1,359,652	0.9%
40	New Hampshire	733,024	0.5%
11	New Jersey	4,322,996	2.8%
37	New Mexico	868,377	0.6%
4	New York	9,149,813	6.0%
9	North Carolina	4,667,739	3.1%
47	North Dakota	418,647	0.3%
7	Ohio	5,426,672	3.6%
29	Oklahoma	1,741,152	1.1%
26	Oregon	1,978,057	1.3%
6	Pennsylvania	6,144,452	4.0%
43	Rhode Island	525,466	0.3%
23	South Carolina	2,208,923	1.5%
46	South Dakota	442,923	0.3%
18	Tennessee	3,035,021	2.0%
2	Texas	12,810,651	8.4%
31	Utah	1,474,795	1.0%
48	Vermont	334,386	0.2%
12	Virginia	4,100,968	2.7%
14	Washington	3,499,282	2.3%
39	West Virginia	745,459	0.5%
19	Wisconsin	3,007,898	2.0%
50	Wyoming	288,746	0.2%

RANK ORDER

RANK	STATE	EMPLOYED	% of USA
1	California	18,376,599	12.1%
2	Texas	12,810,651	8.4%
3	Florida	9,456,079	6.2%
4	New York	9,149,813	6.0%
5	Illinois	6,187,173	4.1%
6	Pennsylvania	6,144,452	4.0%
7	Ohio	5,426,672	3.6%
8	Georgia	4,722,965	3.1%
9	North Carolina	4,667,739	3.1%
10	Michigan	4,642,307	3.1%
11	New Jersey	4,322,996	2.8%
12	Virginia	4,100,968	2.7%
13	Massachusetts	3,500,009	2.3%
14	Washington	3,499,282	2.3%
15	Indiana	3,194,602	2.1%
16	Arizona	3,106,693	2.0%
17	Maryland	3,064,316	2.0%
18	Tennessee	3,035,021	2.0%
19	Wisconsin	3,007,898	2.0%
20	Missouri	2,999,742	2.0%
21	Minnesota	2,870,803	1.9%
22	Colorado	2,838,545	1.9%
23	South Carolina	2,208,923	1.5%
24	Alabama	2,066,842	1.4%
25	Louisiana	1,983,243	1.3%
26	Oregon	1,978,057	1.3%
27	Kentucky	1,919,658	1.3%
28	Connecticut	1,814,687	1.2%
29	Oklahoma	1,741,152	1.1%
30	Iowa	1,650,835	1.1%
31	Utah	1,474,795	1.0%
32	Kansas	1,422,113	0.9%
33	Nevada	1,359,652	0.9%
34	Arkansas	1,290,950	0.8%
35	Mississippi	1,216,024	0.8%
36	Nebraska	982,180	0.6%
37	New Mexico	868,377	0.6%
38	Idaho	784,186	0.5%
39	West Virginia	745,459	0.5%
40	New Hampshire	733,024	0.5%
41	Hawaii	679,897	0.4%
42	Maine	667,784	0.4%
43	Rhode Island	525,466	0.3%
44	Montana	504,233	0.3%
45	Delaware	451,045	0.3%
46	South Dakota	442,923	0.3%
47	North Dakota	418,647	0.3%
48	Vermont	334,386	0.2%
49	Alaska	334,110	0.2%
50	Wyoming	288,746	0.2%
	District of Columbia	374,628	0.2%

Source: CQ Press using data from U.S. Department of Labor, Bureau of Labor Statistics
"Regional and State Employment and Unemployment" (press release, January 24, 2017, www.bls.gov/bls/newsrels.htm)
*Seasonally adjusted preliminary data as of December 2016. National total calculated through a different formula.

Employment to Population Ratio in 2016

National Percent = 59.4% of Population 16 Years and Older Employed*

ALPHA ORDER

RANK	STATE	PERCENT
47	Alabama	53.2
34	Alaska	58.4
38	Arizona	57.7
44	Arkansas	54.9
28	California	59.2
8	Colorado	65.5
15	Connecticut	62.1
31	Delaware	59.0
42	Florida	56.8
30	Georgia	59.1
31	Hawaii	59.0
16	Idaho	61.8
24	Illinois	60.4
18	Indiana	61.2
3	Iowa	66.6
13	Kansas	62.6
45	Kentucky	54.4
46	Louisiana	53.9
24	Maine	60.4
11	Maryland	63.7
12	Massachusetts	62.8
37	Michigan	58.1
7	Minnesota	66.0
49	Mississippi	51.8
16	Missouri	61.8
22	Montana	60.6
5	Nebraska	66.5
28	Nevada	59.2
3	New Hampshire	66.6
27	New Jersey	60.1
48	New Mexico	52.8
41	New York	56.9
36	North Carolina	58.3
1	North Dakota	69.7
34	Ohio	58.4
40	Oklahoma	57.0
22	Oregon	60.6
33	Pennsylvania	58.9
26	Rhode Island	60.3
43	South Carolina	56.2
6	South Dakota	66.2
39	Tennessee	57.6
21	Texas	60.9
2	Utah	67.7
10	Vermont	64.1
19	Virginia	61.0
19	Washington	61.0
50	West Virginia	49.4
9	Wisconsin	65.0
14	Wyoming	62.5

RANK ORDER

RANK	STATE	PERCENT
1	North Dakota	69.7
2	Utah	67.7
3	Iowa	66.6
3	New Hampshire	66.6
5	Nebraska	66.5
6	South Dakota	66.2
7	Minnesota	66.0
8	Colorado	65.5
9	Wisconsin	65.0
10	Vermont	64.1
11	Maryland	63.7
12	Massachusetts	62.8
13	Kansas	62.6
14	Wyoming	62.5
15	Connecticut	62.1
16	Idaho	61.8
16	Missouri	61.8
18	Indiana	61.2
19	Virginia	61.0
19	Washington	61.0
21	Texas	60.9
22	Montana	60.6
22	Oregon	60.6
24	Illinois	60.4
24	Maine	60.4
26	Rhode Island	60.3
27	New Jersey	60.1
28	California	59.2
28	Nevada	59.2
30	Georgia	59.1
31	Delaware	59.0
31	Hawaii	59.0
33	Pennsylvania	58.9
34	Alaska	58.4
34	Ohio	58.4
36	North Carolina	58.3
37	Michigan	58.1
38	Arizona	57.7
39	Tennessee	57.6
40	Oklahoma	57.0
41	New York	56.9
42	Florida	56.8
43	South Carolina	56.2
44	Arkansas	54.9
45	Kentucky	54.4
46	Louisiana	53.9
47	Alabama	53.2
48	New Mexico	52.8
49	Mississippi	51.8
50	West Virginia	49.4

District of Columbia   66.4

Source: CQ Press using data from U.S. Department of Labor, Bureau of Labor Statistics
"Regional and State Employment and Unemployment" (press release, January 24, 2017, www.bls.gov/bls/newsrels.htm)
*Seasonally adjusted preliminary data as of December 2016. Calculated with 2015 population data.

Unemployed Civilian Labor Force in 2016

National Total = 7,529,000 Unemployed Workers*

ALPHA ORDER

RANK	STATE	UNEMPLOYED	% of USA
17	Alabama	136,409	1.8%
42	Alaska	23,982	0.3%
14	Arizona	157,928	2.1%
35	Arkansas	52,293	0.7%
1	California	1,008,969	13.4%
28	Colorado	87,530	1.2%
29	Connecticut	83,454	1.1%
44	Delaware	20,260	0.3%
3	Florida	490,623	6.5%
8	Georgia	270,894	3.6%
45	Hawaii	20,005	0.3%
39	Idaho	30,045	0.4%
5	Illinois	374,514	5.0%
18	Indiana	134,351	1.8%
34	Iowa	61,216	0.8%
32	Kansas	62,745	0.8%
25	Kentucky	97,177	1.3%
20	Louisiana	129,349	1.7%
41	Maine	26,159	0.3%
19	Maryland	133,401	1.8%
23	Massachusetts	101,345	1.3%
10	Michigan	244,908	3.3%
22	Minnesota	115,238	1.5%
31	Mississippi	72,207	1.0%
16	Missouri	139,266	1.8%
43	Montana	20,820	0.3%
38	Nebraska	34,046	0.5%
30	Nevada	72,492	1.0%
46	New Hampshire	19,574	0.3%
11	New Jersey	215,109	2.9%
33	New Mexico	61,631	0.8%
4	New York	473,851	6.3%
9	North Carolina	251,607	3.3%
48	North Dakota	12,859	0.2%
7	Ohio	281,899	3.7%
27	Oklahoma	91,541	1.2%
26	Oregon	95,900	1.3%
6	Pennsylvania	365,699	4.9%
40	Rhode Island	27,835	0.4%
24	South Carolina	98,962	1.3%
49	South Dakota	12,567	0.2%
15	Tennessee	157,631	2.1%
2	Texas	624,327	8.3%
36	Utah	47,223	0.6%
50	Vermont	10,579	0.1%
13	Virginia	177,255	2.4%
12	Washington	190,742	2.5%
37	West Virginia	46,838	0.6%
21	Wisconsin	125,020	1.7%
47	Wyoming	14,674	0.2%

RANK ORDER

RANK	STATE	UNEMPLOYED	% of USA
1	California	1,008,969	13.4%
2	Texas	624,327	8.3%
3	Florida	490,623	6.5%
4	New York	473,851	6.3%
5	Illinois	374,514	5.0%
6	Pennsylvania	365,699	4.9%
7	Ohio	281,899	3.7%
8	Georgia	270,894	3.6%
9	North Carolina	251,607	3.3%
10	Michigan	244,908	3.3%
11	New Jersey	215,109	2.9%
12	Washington	190,742	2.5%
13	Virginia	177,255	2.4%
14	Arizona	157,928	2.1%
15	Tennessee	157,631	2.1%
16	Missouri	139,266	1.8%
17	Alabama	136,409	1.8%
18	Indiana	134,351	1.8%
19	Maryland	133,401	1.8%
20	Louisiana	129,349	1.7%
21	Wisconsin	125,020	1.7%
22	Minnesota	115,238	1.5%
23	Massachusetts	101,345	1.3%
24	South Carolina	98,962	1.3%
25	Kentucky	97,177	1.3%
26	Oregon	95,900	1.3%
27	Oklahoma	91,541	1.2%
28	Colorado	87,530	1.2%
29	Connecticut	83,454	1.1%
30	Nevada	72,492	1.0%
31	Mississippi	72,207	1.0%
32	Kansas	62,745	0.8%
33	New Mexico	61,631	0.8%
34	Iowa	61,216	0.8%
35	Arkansas	52,293	0.7%
36	Utah	47,223	0.6%
37	West Virginia	46,838	0.6%
38	Nebraska	34,046	0.5%
39	Idaho	30,045	0.4%
40	Rhode Island	27,835	0.4%
41	Maine	26,159	0.3%
42	Alaska	23,982	0.3%
43	Montana	20,820	0.3%
44	Delaware	20,260	0.3%
45	Hawaii	20,005	0.3%
46	New Hampshire	19,574	0.3%
47	Wyoming	14,674	0.2%
48	North Dakota	12,859	0.2%
49	South Dakota	12,567	0.2%
50	Vermont	10,579	0.1%
	District of Columbia	23,095	0.3%

Source: U.S. Department of Labor, Bureau of Labor Statistics
"Regional and State Employment and Unemployment" (press release, January 24, 2017, www.bls.gov/bls/newsrels.htm)
*Seasonally adjusted preliminary data as of December 2016. National total calculated through a different formula.

Unemployment Rate in 2016

National Rate = 4.7% of Labor Force Unemployed*

ALPHA ORDER			RANK ORDER		
RANK	STATE	PERCENT	RANK	STATE	PERCENT
3	Alabama	6.2	1	Alaska	6.7
1	Alaska	6.7	2	New Mexico	6.6
21	Arizona	4.8	3	Alabama	6.2
37	Arkansas	3.9	4	Louisiana	6.1
10	California	5.2	5	West Virginia	5.9
45	Colorado	3.0	6	Illinois	5.7
27	Connecticut	4.4	7	Mississippi	5.6
29	Delaware	4.3	7	Pennsylvania	5.6
17	Florida	4.9	9	Georgia	5.4
9	Georgia	5.4	10	California	5.2
47	Hawaii	2.9	10	Washington	5.2
40	Idaho	3.7	12	Nevada	5.1
6	Illinois	5.7	12	North Carolina	5.1
34	Indiana	4.0	14	Michigan	5.0
41	Iowa	3.6	14	Oklahoma	5.0
31	Kansas	4.2	14	Rhode Island	5.0
21	Kentucky	4.8	17	Florida	4.9
4	Louisiana	6.1	17	New York	4.9
39	Maine	3.8	17	Ohio	4.9
31	Maryland	4.2	17	Tennessee	4.9
48	Massachusetts	2.8	21	Arizona	4.8
14	Michigan	5.0	21	Kentucky	4.8
37	Minnesota	3.9	21	Wyoming	4.8
7	Mississippi	5.6	24	New Jersey	4.7
27	Missouri	4.4	25	Oregon	4.6
34	Montana	4.0	25	Texas	4.6
42	Nebraska	3.4	27	Connecticut	4.4
12	Nevada	5.1	27	Missouri	4.4
50	New Hampshire	2.6	29	Delaware	4.3
24	New Jersey	4.7	29	South Carolina	4.3
2	New Mexico	6.6	31	Kansas	4.2
17	New York	4.9	31	Maryland	4.2
12	North Carolina	5.1	33	Virginia	4.1
45	North Dakota	3.0	34	Indiana	4.0
17	Ohio	4.9	34	Montana	4.0
14	Oklahoma	5.0	34	Wisconsin	4.0
25	Oregon	4.6	37	Arkansas	3.9
7	Pennsylvania	5.6	37	Minnesota	3.9
14	Rhode Island	5.0	39	Maine	3.8
29	South Carolina	4.3	40	Idaho	3.7
48	South Dakota	2.8	41	Iowa	3.6
17	Tennessee	4.9	42	Nebraska	3.4
25	Texas	4.6	43	Utah	3.1
43	Utah	3.1	43	Vermont	3.1
43	Vermont	3.1	45	Colorado	3.0
33	Virginia	4.1	45	North Dakota	3.0
10	Washington	5.2	47	Hawaii	2.9
5	West Virginia	5.9	48	Massachusetts	2.8
34	Wisconsin	4.0	48	South Dakota	2.8
21	Wyoming	4.8	50	New Hampshire	2.6
				District of Columbia	5.8

Source: U.S. Department of Labor, Bureau of Labor Statistics
  "Regional and State Employment and Unemployment" (press release, January 24, 2017, www.bls.gov/bls/newsrels.htm)
*Seasonally adjusted preliminary data as of December 2016. National figure calculated through a different formula.

Women in Civilian Labor Force in 2015

National Total = 73,510,000 Women*

ALPHA ORDER

RANK	STATE	WOMEN	% of USA
25	Alabama	1,022,000	1.4%
49	Alaska	165,000	0.2%
19	Arizona	1,459,000	2.0%
33	Arkansas	632,000	0.9%
1	California	8,595,000	11.7%
22	Colorado	1,284,000	1.7%
28	Connecticut	918,000	1.2%
45	Delaware	234,000	0.3%
4	Florida	4,517,000	6.1%
9	Georgia	2,274,000	3.1%
42	Hawaii	322,000	0.4%
39	Idaho	364,000	0.5%
6	Illinois	3,058,000	4.2%
15	Indiana	1,548,000	2.1%
30	Iowa	811,000	1.1%
31	Kansas	696,000	0.9%
27	Kentucky	921,000	1.3%
24	Louisiana	1,041,000	1.4%
41	Maine	324,000	0.4%
16	Maryland	1,543,000	2.1%
13	Massachusetts	1,748,000	2.4%
10	Michigan	2,249,000	3.1%
21	Minnesota	1,410,000	1.9%
35	Mississippi	620,000	0.8%
17	Missouri	1,492,000	2.0%
44	Montana	246,000	0.3%
36	Nebraska	471,000	0.6%
32	Nevada	651,000	0.9%
40	New Hampshire	352,000	0.5%
11	New Jersey	2,098,000	2.9%
37	New Mexico	434,000	0.6%
3	New York	4,565,000	6.2%
8	North Carolina	2,297,000	3.1%
47	North Dakota	186,000	0.3%
7	Ohio	2,705,000	3.7%
29	Oklahoma	851,000	1.2%
26	Oregon	926,000	1.3%
5	Pennsylvania	3,061,000	4.2%
43	Rhode Island	274,000	0.4%
23	South Carolina	1,108,000	1.5%
46	South Dakota	215,000	0.3%
20	Tennessee	1,427,000	1.9%
2	Texas	5,854,000	8.0%
34	Utah	626,000	0.9%
48	Vermont	168,000	0.2%
12	Virginia	1,988,000	2.7%
14	Washington	1,640,000	2.2%
38	West Virginia	365,000	0.5%
18	Wisconsin	1,479,000	2.0%
50	Wyoming	136,000	0.2%

RANK ORDER

RANK	STATE	WOMEN	% of USA
1	California	8,595,000	11.7%
2	Texas	5,854,000	8.0%
3	New York	4,565,000	6.2%
4	Florida	4,517,000	6.1%
5	Pennsylvania	3,061,000	4.2%
6	Illinois	3,058,000	4.2%
7	Ohio	2,705,000	3.7%
8	North Carolina	2,297,000	3.1%
9	Georgia	2,274,000	3.1%
10	Michigan	2,249,000	3.1%
11	New Jersey	2,098,000	2.9%
12	Virginia	1,988,000	2.7%
13	Massachusetts	1,748,000	2.4%
14	Washington	1,640,000	2.2%
15	Indiana	1,548,000	2.1%
16	Maryland	1,543,000	2.1%
17	Missouri	1,492,000	2.0%
18	Wisconsin	1,479,000	2.0%
19	Arizona	1,459,000	2.0%
20	Tennessee	1,427,000	1.9%
21	Minnesota	1,410,000	1.9%
22	Colorado	1,284,000	1.7%
23	South Carolina	1,108,000	1.5%
24	Louisiana	1,041,000	1.4%
25	Alabama	1,022,000	1.4%
26	Oregon	926,000	1.3%
27	Kentucky	921,000	1.3%
28	Connecticut	918,000	1.2%
29	Oklahoma	851,000	1.2%
30	Iowa	811,000	1.1%
31	Kansas	696,000	0.9%
32	Nevada	651,000	0.9%
33	Arkansas	632,000	0.9%
34	Utah	626,000	0.9%
35	Mississippi	620,000	0.8%
36	Nebraska	471,000	0.6%
37	New Mexico	434,000	0.6%
38	West Virginia	365,000	0.5%
39	Idaho	364,000	0.5%
40	New Hampshire	352,000	0.5%
41	Maine	324,000	0.4%
42	Hawaii	322,000	0.4%
43	Rhode Island	274,000	0.4%
44	Montana	246,000	0.3%
45	Delaware	234,000	0.3%
46	South Dakota	215,000	0.3%
47	North Dakota	186,000	0.3%
48	Vermont	168,000	0.2%
49	Alaska	165,000	0.2%
50	Wyoming	136,000	0.2%
	District of Columbia	198,000	0.3%

Source: U.S. Department of Labor, Bureau of Labor Statistics
  "Geographic Profiles of Employment and Unemployment, 2015" (http://www.bls.gov/gps/)
*Annual averages.

Percent of Women in the Civilian Labor Force in 2015

National Percent = 56.7% of Women*

ALPHA ORDER

RANK	STATE	PERCENT
49	Alabama	51.0
9	Alaska	62.3
42	Arizona	53.9
44	Arkansas	53.0
40	California	55.0
18	Colorado	59.9
12	Connecticut	61.4
19	Delaware	59.1
43	Florida	53.1
35	Georgia	55.4
25	Hawaii	57.6
25	Idaho	57.6
20	Illinois	58.8
22	Indiana	58.5
1	Iowa	65.7
11	Kansas	61.6
47	Kentucky	51.7
35	Louisiana	55.4
27	Maine	57.5
10	Maryland	62.2
15	Massachusetts	61.0
38	Michigan	55.3
4	Minnesota	64.8
48	Mississippi	51.3
16	Missouri	60.6
17	Montana	60.1
5	Nebraska	64.1
29	Nevada	57.2
7	New Hampshire	63.7
31	New Jersey	56.9
46	New Mexico	52.5
39	New York	55.1
32	North Carolina	56.0
3	North Dakota	64.9
29	Ohio	57.2
34	Oklahoma	55.5
32	Oregon	56.0
24	Pennsylvania	57.7
13	Rhode Island	61.2
40	South Carolina	55.0
2	South Dakota	65.5
45	Tennessee	52.9
35	Texas	55.4
23	Utah	57.8
6	Vermont	63.8
21	Virginia	58.7
28	Washington	57.4
50	West Virginia	48.0
7	Wisconsin	63.7
13	Wyoming	61.2

RANK ORDER

RANK	STATE	PERCENT
1	Iowa	65.7
2	South Dakota	65.5
3	North Dakota	64.9
4	Minnesota	64.8
5	Nebraska	64.1
6	Vermont	63.8
7	New Hampshire	63.7
7	Wisconsin	63.7
9	Alaska	62.3
10	Maryland	62.2
11	Kansas	61.6
12	Connecticut	61.4
13	Rhode Island	61.2
13	Wyoming	61.2
15	Massachusetts	61.0
16	Missouri	60.6
17	Montana	60.1
18	Colorado	59.9
19	Delaware	59.1
20	Illinois	58.8
21	Virginia	58.7
22	Indiana	58.5
23	Utah	57.8
24	Pennsylvania	57.7
25	Hawaii	57.6
25	Idaho	57.6
27	Maine	57.5
28	Washington	57.4
29	Nevada	57.2
29	Ohio	57.2
31	New Jersey	56.9
32	North Carolina	56.0
32	Oregon	56.0
34	Oklahoma	55.5
35	Georgia	55.4
35	Louisiana	55.4
35	Texas	55.4
38	Michigan	55.3
39	New York	55.1
40	California	55.0
40	South Carolina	55.0
42	Arizona	53.9
43	Florida	53.1
44	Arkansas	53.0
45	Tennessee	52.9
46	New Mexico	52.5
47	Kentucky	51.7
48	Mississippi	51.3
49	Alabama	51.0
50	West Virginia	48.0

District of Columbia 66.8

Source: U.S. Department of Labor, Bureau of Labor Statistics
   "Geographic Profiles of Employment and Unemployment, 2015" (http://www.bls.gov/gps/)
*Annual averages.

Percent of Civilian Labor Force Comprised of Women in 2015

National Percent = 46.8% of Civilian Labor Force*

ALPHA ORDER

RANK	STATE	PERCENT
19	Alabama	47.4
43	Alaska	45.5
39	Arizona	46.1
24	Arkansas	47.3
45	California	45.3
42	Colorado	45.6
5	Connecticut	48.5
1	Delaware	49.9
27	Florida	47.1
15	Georgia	47.7
18	Hawaii	47.5
45	Idaho	45.3
31	Illinois	47.0
19	Indiana	47.4
14	Iowa	47.8
35	Kansas	46.6
19	Kentucky	47.4
9	Louisiana	48.1
11	Maine	47.9
5	Maryland	48.5
4	Massachusetts	48.7
24	Michigan	47.3
34	Minnesota	46.7
7	Mississippi	48.4
9	Missouri	48.1
31	Montana	47.0
27	Nebraska	47.1
44	Nevada	45.4
19	New Hampshire	47.4
37	New Jersey	46.3
33	New Mexico	46.9
26	New York	47.2
11	North Carolina	47.9
47	North Dakota	44.9
16	Ohio	47.6
41	Oklahoma	45.7
27	Oregon	47.1
16	Pennsylvania	47.6
2	Rhode Island	49.1
8	South Carolina	48.3
19	South Dakota	47.4
38	Tennessee	46.2
47	Texas	44.9
50	Utah	42.8
3	Vermont	48.8
27	Virginia	47.1
39	Washington	46.1
36	West Virginia	46.5
11	Wisconsin	47.9
49	Wyoming	44.3

RANK ORDER

RANK	STATE	PERCENT
1	Delaware	49.9
2	Rhode Island	49.1
3	Vermont	48.8
4	Massachusetts	48.7
5	Connecticut	48.5
5	Maryland	48.5
7	Mississippi	48.4
8	South Carolina	48.3
9	Louisiana	48.1
9	Missouri	48.1
11	Maine	47.9
11	North Carolina	47.9
11	Wisconsin	47.9
14	Iowa	47.8
15	Georgia	47.7
16	Ohio	47.6
16	Pennsylvania	47.6
18	Hawaii	47.5
19	Alabama	47.4
19	Indiana	47.4
19	Kentucky	47.4
19	New Hampshire	47.4
19	South Dakota	47.4
24	Arkansas	47.3
24	Michigan	47.3
26	New York	47.2
27	Florida	47.1
27	Nebraska	47.1
27	Oregon	47.1
27	Virginia	47.1
31	Illinois	47.0
31	Montana	47.0
33	New Mexico	46.9
34	Minnesota	46.7
35	Kansas	46.6
36	West Virginia	46.5
37	New Jersey	46.3
38	Tennessee	46.2
39	Arizona	46.1
39	Washington	46.1
41	Oklahoma	45.7
42	Colorado	45.6
43	Alaska	45.5
44	Nevada	45.4
45	California	45.3
45	Idaho	45.3
47	North Dakota	44.9
47	Texas	44.9
49	Wyoming	44.3
50	Utah	42.8

District of Columbia	51.0

Source: CQ Press using data from U.S. Department of Labor, Bureau of Labor Statistics
"Geographic Profiles of Employment and Unemployment, 2015" (http://www.bls.gov/gps/)
*Annual averages.

Job Growth: 2015 to 2016

National Percent Change = 1.5% Increase*

ALPHA ORDER

RANK	STATE	PERCENT CHANGE
25	Alabama	1.0
48	Alaska	(1.4)
21	Arizona	1.3
38	Arkansas	0.4
10	California	2.0
12	Colorado	1.9
43	Connecticut	(0.1)
34	Delaware	0.5
2	Florida	3.1
6	Georgia	2.4
8	Hawaii	2.1
12	Idaho	1.9
34	Illinois	0.5
28	Indiana	0.8
34	Iowa	0.5
46	Kansas	(0.7)
33	Kentucky	0.6
44	Louisiana	(0.2)
42	Maine	0.0
24	Maryland	1.1
8	Massachusetts	2.1
15	Michigan	1.7
19	Minnesota	1.5
47	Mississippi	(1.0)
7	Missouri	2.3
27	Montana	0.9
30	Nebraska	0.7
3	Nevada	3.0
15	New Hampshire	1.7
39	New Jersey	0.3
39	New Mexico	0.3
23	New York	1.2
10	North Carolina	2.0
49	North Dakota	(1.8)
28	Ohio	0.8
45	Oklahoma	(0.3)
1	Oregon	3.3
34	Pennsylvania	0.5
30	Rhode Island	0.7
15	South Carolina	1.7
20	South Dakota	1.4
18	Tennessee	1.6
14	Texas	1.8
5	Utah	2.8
30	Vermont	0.7
21	Virginia	1.3
3	Washington	3.0
39	West Virginia	0.3
25	Wisconsin	1.0
50	Wyoming	(2.8)

RANK ORDER

RANK	STATE	PERCENT CHANGE
1	Oregon	3.3
2	Florida	3.1
3	Nevada	3.0
3	Washington	3.0
5	Utah	2.8
6	Georgia	2.4
7	Missouri	2.3
8	Hawaii	2.1
8	Massachusetts	2.1
10	California	2.0
10	North Carolina	2.0
12	Colorado	1.9
12	Idaho	1.9
14	Texas	1.8
15	Michigan	1.7
15	New Hampshire	1.7
15	South Carolina	1.7
18	Tennessee	1.6
19	Minnesota	1.5
20	South Dakota	1.4
21	Arizona	1.3
21	Virginia	1.3
23	New York	1.2
24	Maryland	1.1
25	Alabama	1.0
25	Wisconsin	1.0
27	Montana	0.9
28	Indiana	0.8
28	Ohio	0.8
30	Nebraska	0.7
30	Rhode Island	0.7
30	Vermont	0.7
33	Kentucky	0.6
34	Delaware	0.5
34	Illinois	0.5
34	Iowa	0.5
34	Pennsylvania	0.5
38	Arkansas	0.4
39	New Jersey	0.3
39	New Mexico	0.3
39	West Virginia	0.3
42	Maine	0.0
43	Connecticut	(0.1)
44	Louisiana	(0.2)
45	Oklahoma	(0.3)
46	Kansas	(0.7)
47	Mississippi	(1.0)
48	Alaska	(1.4)
49	North Dakota	(1.8)
50	Wyoming	(2.8)

District of Columbia — 2.3

Source: CQ Press using data from U.S. Department of Labor, Bureau of Labor Statistics
"Regional and State Employment and Unemployment" (press release, January 24, 2017, www.bls.gov/bls/newsrels.htm)
*Nonfarm jobs. December 2015 to December 2016, seasonally adjusted. National figure based on nonfarm employment from a different survey.

Employees on Nonfarm Payrolls in 2016

National Total = 145,303,000 Employees*

ALPHA ORDER

RANK	STATE	EMPLOYEES	% of USA
24	Alabama	1,976,200	1.4%
48	Alaska	334,600	0.2%
20	Arizona	2,717,000	1.9%
34	Arkansas	1,232,200	0.8%
1	California	16,606,600	11.4%
22	Colorado	2,627,400	1.8%
28	Connecticut	1,678,000	1.2%
45	Delaware	458,500	0.3%
4	Florida	8,462,900	5.8%
8	Georgia	4,433,400	3.1%
41	Hawaii	655,200	0.5%
39	Idaho	700,700	0.5%
5	Illinois	6,002,600	4.1%
15	Indiana	3,083,700	2.1%
30	Iowa	1,582,100	1.1%
32	Kansas	1,392,400	1.0%
26	Kentucky	1,919,400	1.3%
25	Louisiana	1,975,400	1.4%
42	Maine	610,900	0.4%
21	Maryland	2,713,400	1.9%
13	Massachusetts	3,590,400	2.5%
9	Michigan	4,363,600	3.0%
18	Minnesota	2,919,300	2.0%
35	Mississippi	1,133,600	0.8%
19	Missouri	2,847,800	2.0%
44	Montana	465,300	0.3%
36	Nebraska	1,021,300	0.7%
33	Nevada	1,306,000	0.9%
40	New Hampshire	672,600	0.5%
11	New Jersey	4,086,400	2.8%
37	New Mexico	830,500	0.6%
3	New York	9,413,100	6.5%
10	North Carolina	4,360,200	3.0%
47	North Dakota	436,900	0.3%
7	Ohio	5,517,200	3.8%
29	Oklahoma	1,657,500	1.1%
27	Oregon	1,863,100	1.3%
6	Pennsylvania	5,900,100	4.1%
43	Rhode Island	492,100	0.3%
23	South Carolina	2,070,100	1.4%
46	South Dakota	437,300	0.3%
16	Tennessee	2,989,500	2.1%
2	Texas	12,141,300	8.4%
31	Utah	1,437,100	1.0%
49	Vermont	315,800	0.2%
12	Virginia	3,951,700	2.7%
14	Washington	3,292,700	2.3%
38	West Virginia	763,700	0.5%
17	Wisconsin	2,932,800	2.0%
50	Wyoming	278,700	0.2%

RANK ORDER

RANK	STATE	EMPLOYEES	% of USA
1	California	16,606,600	11.4%
2	Texas	12,141,300	8.4%
3	New York	9,413,100	6.5%
4	Florida	8,462,900	5.8%
5	Illinois	6,002,600	4.1%
6	Pennsylvania	5,900,100	4.1%
7	Ohio	5,517,200	3.8%
8	Georgia	4,433,400	3.1%
9	Michigan	4,363,600	3.0%
10	North Carolina	4,360,200	3.0%
11	New Jersey	4,086,400	2.8%
12	Virginia	3,951,700	2.7%
13	Massachusetts	3,590,400	2.5%
14	Washington	3,292,700	2.3%
15	Indiana	3,083,700	2.1%
16	Tennessee	2,989,500	2.1%
17	Wisconsin	2,932,800	2.0%
18	Minnesota	2,919,300	2.0%
19	Missouri	2,847,800	2.0%
20	Arizona	2,717,000	1.9%
21	Maryland	2,713,400	1.9%
22	Colorado	2,627,400	1.8%
23	South Carolina	2,070,100	1.4%
24	Alabama	1,976,200	1.4%
25	Louisiana	1,975,400	1.4%
26	Kentucky	1,919,400	1.3%
27	Oregon	1,863,100	1.3%
28	Connecticut	1,678,000	1.2%
29	Oklahoma	1,657,500	1.1%
30	Iowa	1,582,100	1.1%
31	Utah	1,437,100	1.0%
32	Kansas	1,392,400	1.0%
33	Nevada	1,306,000	0.9%
34	Arkansas	1,232,200	0.8%
35	Mississippi	1,133,600	0.8%
36	Nebraska	1,021,300	0.7%
37	New Mexico	830,500	0.6%
38	West Virginia	763,700	0.5%
39	Idaho	700,700	0.5%
40	New Hampshire	672,600	0.5%
41	Hawaii	655,200	0.5%
42	Maine	610,900	0.4%
43	Rhode Island	492,100	0.3%
44	Montana	465,300	0.3%
45	Delaware	458,500	0.3%
46	South Dakota	437,300	0.3%
47	North Dakota	436,900	0.3%
48	Alaska	334,600	0.2%
49	Vermont	315,800	0.2%
50	Wyoming	278,700	0.2%
	District of Columbia	785,600	0.5%

Source: U.S. Department of Labor, Bureau of Labor Statistics
"Regional and State Employment and Unemployment" (press release, January 24, 2017, www.bls.gov/bls/newsrels.htm)
*Seasonally adjusted preliminary data as of December 2016. National total calculated through a different formula.

Employees in Construction in 2016

National Total = 6,699,000 Employees*

ALPHA ORDER

RANK	STATE	EMPLOYEES	% of USA
30	Alabama	75,800	1.1%
49	Alaska	16,600	0.2%
18	Arizona	138,400	2.1%
35	Arkansas	49,000	0.7%
1	California	769,400	11.5%
12	Colorado	167,200	2.5%
33	Connecticut	55,500	0.8%
47	Delaware**	20,800	0.3%
3	Florida	462,900	6.9%
11	Georgia	178,900	2.7%
39	Hawaii**	39,200	0.6%
38	Idaho	40,500	0.6%
7	Illinois	208,100	3.1%
19	Indiana	131,800	2.0%
27	Iowa	89,800	1.3%
32	Kansas	57,600	0.9%
31	Kentucky	73,300	1.1%
17	Louisiana	145,500	2.2%
43	Maine	26,200	0.4%
13	Maryland**	158,100	2.4%
16	Massachusetts	153,600	2.3%
14	Michigan	156,200	2.3%
21	Minnesota	125,100	1.9%
36	Mississippi	45,000	0.7%
22	Missouri	121,300	1.8%
44	Montana	25,900	0.4%
34	Nebraska**	49,100	0.7%
28	Nevada	83,000	1.2%
42	New Hampshire	26,400	0.4%
15	New Jersey	153,900	2.3%
37	New Mexico	44,800	0.7%
4	New York	365,700	5.5%
8	North Carolina	199,800	3.0%
41	North Dakota	29,900	0.4%
6	Ohio	208,500	3.1%
29	Oklahoma	80,100	1.2%
24	Oregon	91,700	1.4%
5	Pennsylvania	235,600	3.5%
48	Rhode Island	18,200	0.3%
25	South Carolina	91,300	1.4%
45	South Dakota**	24,200	0.4%
20	Tennessee**	128,300	1.9%
2	Texas	693,700	10.4%
26	Utah	90,300	1.3%
50	Vermont	16,000	0.2%
10	Virginia	188,400	2.8%
9	Washington	190,300	2.8%
40	West Virginia	33,400	0.5%
23	Wisconsin	116,700	1.7%
46	Wyoming	21,600	0.3%

RANK ORDER

RANK	STATE	EMPLOYEES	% of USA
1	California	769,400	11.5%
2	Texas	693,700	10.4%
3	Florida	462,900	6.9%
4	New York	365,700	5.5%
5	Pennsylvania	235,600	3.5%
6	Ohio	208,500	3.1%
7	Illinois	208,100	3.1%
8	North Carolina	199,800	3.0%
9	Washington	190,300	2.8%
10	Virginia	188,400	2.8%
11	Georgia	178,900	2.7%
12	Colorado	167,200	2.5%
13	Maryland**	158,100	2.4%
14	Michigan	156,200	2.3%
15	New Jersey	153,900	2.3%
16	Massachusetts	153,600	2.3%
17	Louisiana	145,500	2.2%
18	Arizona	138,400	2.1%
19	Indiana	131,800	2.0%
20	Tennessee**	128,300	1.9%
21	Minnesota	125,100	1.9%
22	Missouri	121,300	1.8%
23	Wisconsin	116,700	1.7%
24	Oregon	91,700	1.4%
25	South Carolina	91,300	1.4%
26	Utah	90,300	1.3%
27	Iowa	89,800	1.3%
28	Nevada	83,000	1.2%
29	Oklahoma	80,100	1.2%
30	Alabama	75,800	1.1%
31	Kentucky	73,300	1.1%
32	Kansas	57,600	0.9%
33	Connecticut	55,500	0.8%
34	Nebraska**	49,100	0.7%
35	Arkansas	49,000	0.7%
36	Mississippi	45,000	0.7%
37	New Mexico	44,800	0.7%
38	Idaho	40,500	0.6%
39	Hawaii**	39,200	0.6%
40	West Virginia	33,400	0.5%
41	North Dakota	29,900	0.4%
42	New Hampshire	26,400	0.4%
43	Maine	26,200	0.4%
44	Montana	25,900	0.4%
45	South Dakota**	24,200	0.4%
46	Wyoming	21,600	0.3%
47	Delaware**	20,800	0.3%
48	Rhode Island	18,200	0.3%
49	Alaska	16,600	0.2%
50	Vermont	16,000	0.2%
	District of Columbia**	14,400	0.2%

Source: U.S. Department of Labor, Bureau of Labor Statistics
  "Regional and State Employment and Unemployment" (press release, January 24, 2017, www.bls.gov/bls/newsrels.htm)
*Seasonally adjusted preliminary data as of December 2016. National total calculated through a different formula.
**Figures for these states include employees in mining and logging.

Percent of Nonfarm Employees in Construction in 2016

National Percent = 4.6% of Employees*

RANK	STATE	PERCENT
43	Alabama	3.8
19	Alaska	5.0
17	Arizona	5.1
36	Arkansas	4.0
24	California	4.6
4	Colorado	6.4
50	Connecticut	3.3
26	Delaware**	4.5
14	Florida	5.5
36	Georgia	4.0
7	Hawaii**	6.0
8	Idaho	5.8
49	Illinois	3.5
29	Indiana	4.3
11	Iowa	5.7
35	Kansas	4.1
43	Kentucky	3.8
2	Louisiana	7.4
29	Maine	4.3
8	Maryland**	5.8
29	Massachusetts	4.3
48	Michigan	3.6
29	Minnesota	4.3
36	Mississippi	4.0
29	Missouri	4.3
13	Montana	5.6
21	Nebraska**	4.8
4	Nevada	6.4
41	New Hampshire	3.9
43	New Jersey	3.8
16	New Mexico	5.4
41	New York	3.9
24	North Carolina	4.6
3	North Dakota	6.8
43	Ohio	3.8
21	Oklahoma	4.8
20	Oregon	4.9
36	Pennsylvania	4.0
47	Rhode Island	3.7
27	South Carolina	4.4
14	South Dakota**	5.5
29	Tennessee**	4.3
11	Texas	5.7
6	Utah	6.3
17	Vermont	5.1
21	Virginia	4.8
8	Washington	5.8
27	West Virginia	4.4
36	Wisconsin	4.0
1	Wyoming	7.8

RANK	STATE	PERCENT
1	Wyoming	7.8
2	Louisiana	7.4
3	North Dakota	6.8
4	Colorado	6.4
4	Nevada	6.4
6	Utah	6.3
7	Hawaii**	6.0
8	Idaho	5.8
8	Maryland**	5.8
8	Washington	5.8
11	Iowa	5.7
11	Texas	5.7
13	Montana	5.6
14	Florida	5.5
14	South Dakota**	5.5
16	New Mexico	5.4
17	Arizona	5.1
17	Vermont	5.1
19	Alaska	5.0
20	Oregon	4.9
21	Nebraska**	4.8
21	Oklahoma	4.8
21	Virginia	4.8
24	California	4.6
24	North Carolina	4.6
26	Delaware**	4.5
27	South Carolina	4.4
27	West Virginia	4.4
29	Indiana	4.3
29	Maine	4.3
29	Massachusetts	4.3
29	Minnesota	4.3
29	Missouri	4.3
29	Tennessee**	4.3
35	Kansas	4.1
36	Arkansas	4.0
36	Georgia	4.0
36	Mississippi	4.0
36	Pennsylvania	4.0
36	Wisconsin	4.0
41	New Hampshire	3.9
41	New York	3.9
43	Alabama	3.8
43	Kentucky	3.8
43	New Jersey	3.8
43	Ohio	3.8
47	Rhode Island	3.7
48	Michigan	3.6
49	Illinois	3.5
50	Connecticut	3.3

District of Columbia** 1.8

Source: CQ Press using data from U.S. Department of Labor, Bureau of Labor Statistics
    "Regional and State Employment and Unemployment" (press release, January 24, 2017, www.bls.gov/bls/newsrels.htm)
*Seasonally adjusted preliminary data as of December 2016. National figure calculated through a different formula.
**Figures for these states include employees in mining and logging.

Employees in Education and Health Services in 2016

National Total = 22,971,000 Employees*

ALPHA ORDER

RANK	STATE	EMPLOYEES	% of USA
29	Alabama	232,400	1.0%
49	Alaska	50,800	0.2%
21	Arizona	422,000	1.8%
33	Arkansas	184,300	0.8%
1	California	2,581,100	11.2%
22	Colorado	331,600	1.4%
23	Connecticut	329,900	1.4%
44	Delaware	78,100	0.3%
4	Florida	1,265,900	5.5%
12	Georgia	557,700	2.4%
43	Hawaii	85,000	0.4%
42	Idaho	100,300	0.4%
7	Illinois	910,300	4.0%
16	Indiana	469,800	2.0%
30	Iowa	230,500	1.0%
31	Kansas	195,000	0.8%
25	Kentucky	275,500	1.2%
24	Louisiana	316,100	1.4%
39	Maine	125,200	0.5%
18	Maryland	445,800	1.9%
8	Massachusetts	796,000	3.5%
10	Michigan	669,400	2.9%
13	Minnesota	535,200	2.3%
36	Mississippi	140,200	0.6%
17	Missouri	458,000	2.0%
45	Montana	74,800	0.3%
34	Nebraska	153,200	0.7%
38	Nevada	128,000	0.6%
40	New Hampshire	120,700	0.5%
9	New Jersey	677,200	2.9%
35	New Mexico	141,600	0.6%
2	New York	1,960,400	8.5%
11	North Carolina	584,800	2.5%
48	North Dakota	61,200	0.3%
6	Ohio	928,300	4.0%
28	Oklahoma	238,500	1.0%
26	Oregon	275,300	1.2%
5	Pennsylvania	1,229,700	5.4%
41	Rhode Island	104,800	0.5%
27	South Carolina	250,300	1.1%
46	South Dakota	71,000	0.3%
20	Tennessee	438,500	1.9%
3	Texas	1,679,700	7.3%
32	Utah	192,400	0.8%
47	Vermont	65,200	0.3%
14	Virginia	530,000	2.3%
15	Washington	479,500	2.1%
37	West Virginia	134,600	0.6%
19	Wisconsin	440,700	1.9%
50	Wyoming	27,700	0.1%

RANK ORDER

RANK	STATE	EMPLOYEES	% of USA
1	California	2,581,100	11.2%
2	New York	1,960,400	8.5%
3	Texas	1,679,700	7.3%
4	Florida	1,265,900	5.5%
5	Pennsylvania	1,229,700	5.4%
6	Ohio	928,300	4.0%
7	Illinois	910,300	4.0%
8	Massachusetts	796,000	3.5%
9	New Jersey	677,200	2.9%
10	Michigan	669,400	2.9%
11	North Carolina	584,800	2.5%
12	Georgia	557,700	2.4%
13	Minnesota	535,200	2.3%
14	Virginia	530,000	2.3%
15	Washington	479,500	2.1%
16	Indiana	469,800	2.0%
17	Missouri	458,000	2.0%
18	Maryland	445,800	1.9%
19	Wisconsin	440,700	1.9%
20	Tennessee	438,500	1.9%
21	Arizona	422,000	1.8%
22	Colorado	331,600	1.4%
23	Connecticut	329,900	1.4%
24	Louisiana	316,100	1.4%
25	Kentucky	275,500	1.2%
26	Oregon	275,300	1.2%
27	South Carolina	250,300	1.1%
28	Oklahoma	238,500	1.0%
29	Alabama	232,400	1.0%
30	Iowa	230,500	1.0%
31	Kansas	195,000	0.8%
32	Utah	192,400	0.8%
33	Arkansas	184,300	0.8%
34	Nebraska	153,200	0.7%
35	New Mexico	141,600	0.6%
36	Mississippi	140,200	0.6%
37	West Virginia	134,600	0.6%
38	Nevada	128,000	0.6%
39	Maine	125,200	0.5%
40	New Hampshire	120,700	0.5%
41	Rhode Island	104,800	0.5%
42	Idaho	100,300	0.4%
43	Hawaii	85,000	0.4%
44	Delaware	78,100	0.3%
45	Montana	74,800	0.3%
46	South Dakota	71,000	0.3%
47	Vermont	65,200	0.3%
48	North Dakota	61,200	0.3%
49	Alaska	50,800	0.2%
50	Wyoming	27,700	0.1%
	District of Columbia	129,600	0.6%

Source: U.S. Department of Labor, Bureau of Labor Statistics
"Regional and State Employment and Unemployment" (press release, January 24, 2017, www.bls.gov/bls/newsrels.htm)
*Seasonally adjusted preliminary data as of December 2016. National total calculated through a different formula.

Percent of Nonfarm Employees in Education and Health Services in 2016

National Percent = 15.8% of Employees*

ALPHA ORDER				RANK ORDER		
RANK	STATE	PERCENT		RANK	STATE	PERCENT
48	Alabama	11.8		1	Massachusetts	22.2
23	Alaska	15.2		2	Rhode Island	21.3
20	Arizona	15.5		3	New York	20.8
26	Arkansas	15.0		3	Pennsylvania	20.8
20	California	15.5		5	Vermont	20.6
44	Colorado	12.6		6	Maine	20.5
7	Connecticut	19.7		7	Connecticut	19.7
11	Delaware	17.0		8	Minnesota	18.3
26	Florida	15.0		9	New Hampshire	17.9
44	Georgia	12.6		10	West Virginia	17.6
43	Hawaii	13.0		11	Delaware	17.0
36	Idaho	14.3		11	New Mexico	17.0
23	Illinois	15.2		13	Ohio	16.8
23	Indiana	15.2		14	New Jersey	16.6
32	Iowa	14.6		15	Maryland	16.4
37	Kansas	14.0		16	South Dakota	16.2
34	Kentucky	14.4		17	Missouri	16.1
19	Louisiana	16.0		17	Montana	16.1
6	Maine	20.5		19	Louisiana	16.0
15	Maryland	16.4		20	Arizona	15.5
1	Massachusetts	22.2		20	California	15.5
22	Michigan	15.3		22	Michigan	15.3
8	Minnesota	18.3		23	Alaska	15.2
46	Mississippi	12.4		23	Illinois	15.2
17	Missouri	16.1		23	Indiana	15.2
17	Montana	16.1		26	Arkansas	15.0
26	Nebraska	15.0		26	Florida	15.0
50	Nevada	9.8		26	Nebraska	15.0
9	New Hampshire	17.9		26	Wisconsin	15.0
14	New Jersey	16.6		30	Oregon	14.8
11	New Mexico	17.0		31	Tennessee	14.7
3	New York	20.8		32	Iowa	14.6
40	North Carolina	13.4		32	Washington	14.6
37	North Dakota	14.0		34	Kentucky	14.4
13	Ohio	16.8		34	Oklahoma	14.4
34	Oklahoma	14.4		36	Idaho	14.3
30	Oregon	14.8		37	Kansas	14.0
3	Pennsylvania	20.8		37	North Dakota	14.0
2	Rhode Island	21.3		39	Texas	13.8
47	South Carolina	12.1		40	North Carolina	13.4
16	South Dakota	16.2		40	Utah	13.4
31	Tennessee	14.7		40	Virginia	13.4
39	Texas	13.8		43	Hawaii	13.0
40	Utah	13.4		44	Colorado	12.6
5	Vermont	20.6		44	Georgia	12.6
40	Virginia	13.4		46	Mississippi	12.4
32	Washington	14.6		47	South Carolina	12.1
10	West Virginia	17.6		48	Alabama	11.8
26	Wisconsin	15.0		49	Wyoming	9.9
49	Wyoming	9.9		50	Nevada	9.8
					District of Columbia	16.5

Source: CQ Press using data from U.S. Department of Labor, Bureau of Labor Statistics
    "Regional and State Employment and Unemployment" (press release, January 24, 2017, www.bls.gov/bls/newsrels.htm)
*Seasonally adjusted preliminary data as of December 2016. National figure calculated through a different formula.

Employees in Financial Activities in 2016

National Total = 8,349,000 Employees*

ALPHA ORDER

RANK	STATE	EMPLOYEES	% of USA
25	Alabama	100,200	1.2%
48	Alaska	12,200	0.1%
13	Arizona	203,500	2.4%
35	Arkansas	49,900	0.6%
1	California	816,900	9.8%
17	Colorado	160,400	1.9%
23	Connecticut	132,300	1.6%
36	Delaware	47,500	0.6%
4	Florida	559,800	6.7%
9	Georgia	242,200	2.9%
45	Hawaii	28,100	0.3%
39	Idaho	35,900	0.4%
5	Illinois	377,000	4.5%
22	Indiana	133,900	1.6%
24	Iowa	111,300	1.3%
32	Kansas	81,300	1.0%
26	Kentucky	100,000	1.2%
29	Louisiana	91,000	1.1%
43	Maine	30,800	0.4%
21	Maryland	146,600	1.8%
10	Massachusetts	225,600	2.7%
12	Michigan	218,900	2.6%
15	Minnesota	186,600	2.2%
37	Mississippi	41,600	0.5%
16	Missouri	172,900	2.1%
46	Montana	24,800	0.3%
33	Nebraska	72,700	0.9%
34	Nevada	60,700	0.7%
38	New Hampshire	37,300	0.4%
8	New Jersey	257,600	3.1%
41	New Mexico	33,200	0.4%
3	New York	707,700	8.5%
11	North Carolina	221,800	2.7%
47	North Dakota	23,400	0.3%
7	Ohio	302,200	3.6%
31	Oklahoma	82,100	1.0%
27	Oregon	99,600	1.2%
6	Pennsylvania	319,600	3.8%
42	Rhode Island	32,000	0.4%
28	South Carolina	98,600	1.2%
44	South Dakota	30,400	0.4%
19	Tennessee	153,500	1.8%
2	Texas	746,700	8.9%
30	Utah	86,400	1.0%
49	Vermont	11,900	0.1%
14	Virginia	201,800	2.4%
20	Washington	152,700	1.8%
40	West Virginia	34,500	0.4%
18	Wisconsin	154,300	1.8%
50	Wyoming	10,500	0.1%

RANK ORDER

RANK	STATE	EMPLOYEES	% of USA
1	California	816,900	9.8%
2	Texas	746,700	8.9%
3	New York	707,700	8.5%
4	Florida	559,800	6.7%
5	Illinois	377,000	4.5%
6	Pennsylvania	319,600	3.8%
7	Ohio	302,200	3.6%
8	New Jersey	257,600	3.1%
9	Georgia	242,200	2.9%
10	Massachusetts	225,600	2.7%
11	North Carolina	221,800	2.7%
12	Michigan	218,900	2.6%
13	Arizona	203,500	2.4%
14	Virginia	201,800	2.4%
15	Minnesota	186,600	2.2%
16	Missouri	172,900	2.1%
17	Colorado	160,400	1.9%
18	Wisconsin	154,300	1.8%
19	Tennessee	153,500	1.8%
20	Washington	152,700	1.8%
21	Maryland	146,600	1.8%
22	Indiana	133,900	1.6%
23	Connecticut	132,300	1.6%
24	Iowa	111,300	1.3%
25	Alabama	100,200	1.2%
26	Kentucky	100,000	1.2%
27	Oregon	99,600	1.2%
28	South Carolina	98,600	1.2%
29	Louisiana	91,000	1.1%
30	Utah	86,400	1.0%
31	Oklahoma	82,100	1.0%
32	Kansas	81,300	1.0%
33	Nebraska	72,700	0.9%
34	Nevada	60,700	0.7%
35	Arkansas	49,900	0.6%
36	Delaware	47,500	0.6%
37	Mississippi	41,600	0.5%
38	New Hampshire	37,300	0.4%
39	Idaho	35,900	0.4%
40	West Virginia	34,500	0.4%
41	New Mexico	33,200	0.4%
42	Rhode Island	32,000	0.4%
43	Maine	30,800	0.4%
44	South Dakota	30,400	0.4%
45	Hawaii	28,100	0.3%
46	Montana	24,800	0.3%
47	North Dakota	23,400	0.3%
48	Alaska	12,200	0.1%
49	Vermont	11,900	0.1%
50	Wyoming	10,500	0.1%
	District of Columbia	30,300	0.4%

Source: U.S. Department of Labor, Bureau of Labor Statistics
   "Regional and State Employment and Unemployment" (press release, January 24, 2017, www.bls.gov/bls/newsrels.htm)
*Seasonally adjusted preliminary data as of December 2016. National total calculated through a different formula. Financial activities include insurance and real estate.

Percent of Nonfarm Employees in Financial Activities in 2016

National Percent = 5.7% of Employees*

ALPHA ORDER				RANK ORDER		
RANK	STATE	PERCENT		RANK	STATE	PERCENT
29	Alabama	5.1		1	Delaware	10.4
50	Alaska	3.6		2	Connecticut	7.9
3	Arizona	7.5		3	Arizona	7.5
45	Arkansas	4.0		3	New York	7.5
37	California	4.9		5	Nebraska	7.1
15	Colorado	6.1		6	Iowa	7.0
2	Connecticut	7.9		6	South Dakota	7.0
1	Delaware	10.4		8	Florida	6.6
8	Florida	6.6		9	Rhode Island	6.5
19	Georgia	5.5		10	Minnesota	6.4
43	Hawaii	4.3		11	Illinois	6.3
29	Idaho	5.1		11	Massachusetts	6.3
11	Illinois	6.3		11	New Jersey	6.3
43	Indiana	4.3		14	Texas	6.2
6	Iowa	7.0		15	Colorado	6.1
18	Kansas	5.8		15	Missouri	6.1
28	Kentucky	5.2		17	Utah	6.0
39	Louisiana	4.6		18	Kansas	5.8
34	Maine	5.0		19	Georgia	5.5
22	Maryland	5.4		19	New Hampshire	5.5
11	Massachusetts	6.3		19	Ohio	5.5
34	Michigan	5.0		22	Maryland	5.4
10	Minnesota	6.4		22	North Dakota	5.4
49	Mississippi	3.7		22	Pennsylvania	5.4
15	Missouri	6.1		25	Montana	5.3
25	Montana	5.3		25	Oregon	5.3
5	Nebraska	7.1		25	Wisconsin	5.3
39	Nevada	4.6		28	Kentucky	5.2
19	New Hampshire	5.5		29	Alabama	5.1
11	New Jersey	6.3		29	Idaho	5.1
45	New Mexico	4.0		29	North Carolina	5.1
3	New York	7.5		29	Tennessee	5.1
29	North Carolina	5.1		29	Virginia	5.1
22	North Dakota	5.4		34	Maine	5.0
19	Ohio	5.5		34	Michigan	5.0
34	Oklahoma	5.0		34	Oklahoma	5.0
25	Oregon	5.3		37	California	4.9
22	Pennsylvania	5.4		38	South Carolina	4.8
9	Rhode Island	6.5		39	Louisiana	4.6
38	South Carolina	4.8		39	Nevada	4.6
6	South Dakota	7.0		39	Washington	4.6
29	Tennessee	5.1		42	West Virginia	4.5
14	Texas	6.2		43	Hawaii	4.3
17	Utah	6.0		43	Indiana	4.3
47	Vermont	3.8		45	Arkansas	4.0
29	Virginia	5.1		45	New Mexico	4.0
39	Washington	4.6		47	Vermont	3.8
42	West Virginia	4.5		47	Wyoming	3.8
25	Wisconsin	5.3		49	Mississippi	3.7
47	Wyoming	3.8		50	Alaska	3.6

	District of Columbia	3.9

Source: CQ Press using data from U.S. Department of Labor, Bureau of Labor Statistics
   "Regional and State Employment and Unemployment" (press release, January 24, 2017, www.bls.gov/bls/newsrels.htm)
*Seasonally adjusted preliminary data as of December 2016. National figure calculated through a different formula. Financial activities include insurance and real estate.

Employees in Government in 2016

National Total = 22,223,000 Employees*

ALPHA ORDER

RANK	STATE	EMPLOYEES	% of USA
23	Alabama	381,900	1.7%
45	Alaska	80,900	0.4%
22	Arizona	408,100	1.8%
34	Arkansas	213,500	1.0%
1	California	2,539,500	11.4%
20	Colorado	426,200	1.9%
33	Connecticut	236,500	1.1%
48	Delaware	64,900	0.3%
4	Florida	1,100,900	5.0%
10	Georgia	693,900	3.1%
39	Hawaii	127,200	0.6%
40	Idaho	122,000	0.5%
5	Illinois	834,300	3.8%
18	Indiana	427,700	1.9%
29	Iowa	256,300	1.2%
30	Kansas	256,000	1.2%
27	Kentucky	314,000	1.4%
26	Louisiana	322,500	1.5%
41	Maine	99,400	0.4%
14	Maryland	510,000	2.3%
15	Massachusetts	454,800	2.0%
12	Michigan	603,300	2.7%
19	Minnesota	427,200	1.9%
31	Mississippi	244,000	1.1%
16	Missouri	435,100	2.0%
42	Montana	90,000	0.4%
36	Nebraska	172,300	0.8%
37	Nevada	160,000	0.7%
43	New Hampshire	86,600	0.4%
11	New Jersey	613,400	2.8%
35	New Mexico	189,500	0.9%
3	New York	1,449,200	6.5%
7	North Carolina	724,300	3.3%
44	North Dakota	82,400	0.4%
6	Ohio	778,900	3.5%
25	Oklahoma	352,600	1.6%
28	Oregon	311,300	1.4%
9	Pennsylvania	702,200	3.2%
49	Rhode Island	60,900	0.3%
24	South Carolina	365,800	1.6%
46	South Dakota	79,500	0.4%
17	Tennessee	428,800	1.9%
2	Texas	1,904,600	8.6%
32	Utah	237,100	1.1%
50	Vermont	57,500	0.3%
8	Virginia	714,100	3.2%
13	Washington	579,200	2.6%
38	West Virginia	151,400	0.7%
21	Wisconsin	412,700	1.9%
47	Wyoming	71,100	0.3%

RANK ORDER

RANK	STATE	EMPLOYEES	% of USA
1	California	2,539,500	11.4%
2	Texas	1,904,600	8.6%
3	New York	1,449,200	6.5%
4	Florida	1,100,900	5.0%
5	Illinois	834,300	3.8%
6	Ohio	778,900	3.5%
7	North Carolina	724,300	3.3%
8	Virginia	714,100	3.2%
9	Pennsylvania	702,200	3.2%
10	Georgia	693,900	3.1%
11	New Jersey	613,400	2.8%
12	Michigan	603,300	2.7%
13	Washington	579,200	2.6%
14	Maryland	510,000	2.3%
15	Massachusetts	454,800	2.0%
16	Missouri	435,100	2.0%
17	Tennessee	428,800	1.9%
18	Indiana	427,700	1.9%
19	Minnesota	427,200	1.9%
20	Colorado	426,200	1.9%
21	Wisconsin	412,700	1.9%
22	Arizona	408,100	1.8%
23	Alabama	381,900	1.7%
24	South Carolina	365,800	1.6%
25	Oklahoma	352,600	1.6%
26	Louisiana	322,500	1.5%
27	Kentucky	314,000	1.4%
28	Oregon	311,300	1.4%
29	Iowa	256,300	1.2%
30	Kansas	256,000	1.2%
31	Mississippi	244,000	1.1%
32	Utah	237,100	1.1%
33	Connecticut	236,500	1.1%
34	Arkansas	213,500	1.0%
35	New Mexico	189,500	0.9%
36	Nebraska	172,300	0.8%
37	Nevada	160,000	0.7%
38	West Virginia	151,400	0.7%
39	Hawaii	127,200	0.6%
40	Idaho	122,000	0.5%
41	Maine	99,400	0.4%
42	Montana	90,000	0.4%
43	New Hampshire	86,600	0.4%
44	North Dakota	82,400	0.4%
45	Alaska	80,900	0.4%
46	South Dakota	79,500	0.4%
47	Wyoming	71,100	0.3%
48	Delaware	64,900	0.3%
49	Rhode Island	60,900	0.3%
50	Vermont	57,500	0.3%
	District of Columbia	244,800	1.1%

Source: U.S. Department of Labor, Bureau of Labor Statistics
   "Regional and State Employment and Unemployment" (press release, January 24, 2017, www.bls.gov/bls/newsrels.htm)
*Seasonally adjusted preliminary data as of December 2016. National total calculated through a different formula.

Percent of Nonfarm Employees in Government in 2016

National Percent = 15.3% of Employees*

RANK	STATE	PERCENT
8	Alabama	19.3
2	Alaska	24.2
34	Arizona	15.0
19	Arkansas	17.3
32	California	15.3
27	Colorado	16.2
39	Connecticut	14.1
38	Delaware	14.2
45	Florida	13.0
29	Georgia	15.7
7	Hawaii	19.4
18	Idaho	17.4
42	Illinois	13.9
42	Indiana	13.9
27	Iowa	16.2
12	Kansas	18.4
24	Kentucky	16.4
25	Louisiana	16.3
25	Maine	16.3
11	Maryland	18.8
47	Massachusetts	12.7
44	Michigan	13.8
36	Minnesota	14.6
4	Mississippi	21.5
32	Missouri	15.3
8	Montana	19.3
20	Nebraska	16.9
49	Nevada	12.3
46	New Hampshire	12.9
34	New Jersey	15.0
3	New Mexico	22.8
31	New York	15.4
22	North Carolina	16.6
10	North Dakota	18.9
39	Ohio	14.1
5	Oklahoma	21.3
21	Oregon	16.7
50	Pennsylvania	11.9
48	Rhode Island	12.4
16	South Carolina	17.7
13	South Dakota	18.2
37	Tennessee	14.3
29	Texas	15.7
23	Utah	16.5
13	Vermont	18.2
15	Virginia	18.1
17	Washington	17.6
6	West Virginia	19.8
39	Wisconsin	14.1
1	Wyoming	25.5

RANK	STATE	PERCENT
1	Wyoming	25.5
2	Alaska	24.2
3	New Mexico	22.8
4	Mississippi	21.5
5	Oklahoma	21.3
6	West Virginia	19.8
7	Hawaii	19.4
8	Alabama	19.3
8	Montana	19.3
10	North Dakota	18.9
11	Maryland	18.8
12	Kansas	18.4
13	South Dakota	18.2
13	Vermont	18.2
15	Virginia	18.1
16	South Carolina	17.7
17	Washington	17.6
18	Idaho	17.4
19	Arkansas	17.3
20	Nebraska	16.9
21	Oregon	16.7
22	North Carolina	16.6
23	Utah	16.5
24	Kentucky	16.4
25	Louisiana	16.3
25	Maine	16.3
27	Colorado	16.2
27	Iowa	16.2
29	Georgia	15.7
29	Texas	15.7
31	New York	15.4
32	California	15.3
32	Missouri	15.3
34	Arizona	15.0
34	New Jersey	15.0
36	Minnesota	14.6
37	Tennessee	14.3
38	Delaware	14.2
39	Connecticut	14.1
39	Ohio	14.1
39	Wisconsin	14.1
42	Illinois	13.9
42	Indiana	13.9
44	Michigan	13.8
45	Florida	13.0
46	New Hampshire	12.9
47	Massachusetts	12.7
48	Rhode Island	12.4
49	Nevada	12.3
50	Pennsylvania	11.9

| | District of Columbia | 31.2 |

Source: CQ Press using data from U.S. Department of Labor, Bureau of Labor Statistics
   "Regional and State Employment and Unemployment" (press release, January 24, 2017, www.bls.gov/bls/newsrels.htm)
*Seasonally adjusted preliminary data as of December 2016. National figure calculated through a different formula.

Employees in Leisure and Hospitality in 2016

National Total = 15,637,000 Employees*

ALPHA ORDER

RANK	STATE	EMPLOYEES	% of USA
27	Alabama	191,100	1.2%
49	Alaska	35,100	0.2%
18	Arizona	313,600	2.0%
36	Arkansas	116,100	0.7%
1	California	1,920,100	12.3%
15	Colorado	332,300	2.1%
30	Connecticut	153,300	1.0%
45	Delaware	52,100	0.3%
3	Florida	1,202,200	7.7%
8	Georgia	478,000	3.1%
35	Hawaii	120,800	0.8%
40	Idaho	73,000	0.5%
5	Illinois	595,700	3.8%
19	Indiana	308,500	2.0%
31	Iowa	141,900	0.9%
34	Kansas	126,000	0.8%
28	Kentucky	189,600	1.2%
25	Louisiana	226,000	1.4%
42	Maine	65,500	0.4%
21	Maryland	278,700	1.8%
13	Massachusetts	358,100	2.3%
10	Michigan	436,600	2.8%
23	Minnesota	257,000	1.6%
33	Mississippi	134,300	0.9%
20	Missouri	305,900	2.0%
43	Montana	63,100	0.4%
38	Nebraska	90,600	0.6%
14	Nevada	349,000	2.2%
41	New Hampshire	71,900	0.5%
12	New Jersey	364,800	2.3%
37	New Mexico	96,400	0.6%
4	New York	930,300	5.9%
9	North Carolina	474,300	3.0%
47	North Dakota	41,300	0.3%
6	Ohio	564,600	3.6%
29	Oklahoma	170,200	1.1%
26	Oregon	197,600	1.3%
7	Pennsylvania	563,900	3.6%
44	Rhode Island	60,400	0.4%
24	South Carolina	242,400	1.6%
46	South Dakota	48,500	0.3%
17	Tennessee	319,300	2.0%
2	Texas	1,320,500	8.4%
32	Utah	141,100	0.9%
48	Vermont	37,600	0.2%
11	Virginia	401,700	2.6%
16	Washington	325,500	2.1%
39	West Virginia	76,700	0.5%
22	Wisconsin	273,400	1.7%
50	Wyoming	34,900	0.2%

RANK ORDER

RANK	STATE	EMPLOYEES	% of USA
1	California	1,920,100	12.3%
2	Texas	1,320,500	8.4%
3	Florida	1,202,200	7.7%
4	New York	930,300	5.9%
5	Illinois	595,700	3.8%
6	Ohio	564,600	3.6%
7	Pennsylvania	563,900	3.6%
8	Georgia	478,000	3.1%
9	North Carolina	474,300	3.0%
10	Michigan	436,600	2.8%
11	Virginia	401,700	2.6%
12	New Jersey	364,800	2.3%
13	Massachusetts	358,100	2.3%
14	Nevada	349,000	2.2%
15	Colorado	332,300	2.1%
16	Washington	325,500	2.1%
17	Tennessee	319,300	2.0%
18	Arizona	313,600	2.0%
19	Indiana	308,500	2.0%
20	Missouri	305,900	2.0%
21	Maryland	278,700	1.8%
22	Wisconsin	273,400	1.7%
23	Minnesota	257,000	1.6%
24	South Carolina	242,400	1.6%
25	Louisiana	226,000	1.4%
26	Oregon	197,600	1.3%
27	Alabama	191,100	1.2%
28	Kentucky	189,600	1.2%
29	Oklahoma	170,200	1.1%
30	Connecticut	153,300	1.0%
31	Iowa	141,900	0.9%
32	Utah	141,100	0.9%
33	Mississippi	134,300	0.9%
34	Kansas	126,000	0.8%
35	Hawaii	120,800	0.8%
36	Arkansas	116,100	0.7%
37	New Mexico	96,400	0.6%
38	Nebraska	90,600	0.6%
39	West Virginia	76,700	0.5%
40	Idaho	73,000	0.5%
41	New Hampshire	71,900	0.5%
42	Maine	65,500	0.4%
43	Montana	63,100	0.4%
44	Rhode Island	60,400	0.4%
45	Delaware	52,100	0.3%
46	South Dakota	48,500	0.3%
47	North Dakota	41,300	0.3%
48	Vermont	37,600	0.2%
49	Alaska	35,100	0.2%
50	Wyoming	34,900	0.2%
	District of Columbia	77,500	0.5%

Source: U.S. Department of Labor, Bureau of Labor Statistics
"Regional and State Employment and Unemployment" (press release, January 24, 2017, www.bls.gov/bls/newsrels.htm)
*Seasonally adjusted preliminary data as of December 2016. National total calculated through a different formula.

Percent of Nonfarm Employees in Leisure and Hospitality in 2016

National Percent = 10.8% of Employees*

ALPHA ORDER

ALPHA ORDER

RANK	STATE	PERCENT		RANK	STATE	PERCENT
40	Alabama	9.7		1	Nevada	26.7
25	Alaska	10.5		2	Hawaii	18.4
13	Arizona	11.5		3	Florida	14.2
43	Arkansas	9.4		4	Montana	13.6
11	California	11.6		5	Colorado	12.6
5	Colorado	12.6		6	Wyoming	12.5
45	Connecticut	9.1		7	Rhode Island	12.3
14	Delaware	11.4		8	Vermont	11.9
3	Florida	14.2		9	Mississippi	11.8
19	Georgia	10.8		10	South Carolina	11.7
2	Hawaii	18.4		11	California	11.6
26	Idaho	10.4		11	New Mexico	11.6
35	Illinois	9.9		13	Arizona	11.5
31	Indiana	10.0		14	Delaware	11.4
46	Iowa	9.0		14	Louisiana	11.4
46	Kansas	9.0		16	South Dakota	11.1
35	Kentucky	9.9		17	North Carolina	10.9
14	Louisiana	11.4		17	Texas	10.9
20	Maine	10.7		19	Georgia	10.8
27	Maryland	10.3		20	Maine	10.7
31	Massachusetts	10.0		20	Missouri	10.7
31	Michigan	10.0		20	New Hampshire	10.7
50	Minnesota	8.8		20	Tennessee	10.7
9	Mississippi	11.8		24	Oregon	10.6
20	Missouri	10.7		25	Alaska	10.5
4	Montana	13.6		26	Idaho	10.4
48	Nebraska	8.9		27	Maryland	10.3
1	Nevada	26.7		27	Oklahoma	10.3
20	New Hampshire	10.7		29	Ohio	10.2
48	New Jersey	8.9		29	Virginia	10.2
11	New Mexico	11.6		31	Indiana	10.0
35	New York	9.9		31	Massachusetts	10.0
17	North Carolina	10.9		31	Michigan	10.0
42	North Dakota	9.5		31	West Virginia	10.0
29	Ohio	10.2		35	Illinois	9.9
27	Oklahoma	10.3		35	Kentucky	9.9
24	Oregon	10.6		35	New York	9.9
41	Pennsylvania	9.6		35	Washington	9.9
7	Rhode Island	12.3		39	Utah	9.8
10	South Carolina	11.7		40	Alabama	9.7
16	South Dakota	11.1		41	Pennsylvania	9.6
20	Tennessee	10.7		42	North Dakota	9.5
17	Texas	10.9		43	Arkansas	9.4
39	Utah	9.8		44	Wisconsin	9.3
8	Vermont	11.9		45	Connecticut	9.1
29	Virginia	10.2		46	Iowa	9.0
35	Washington	9.9		46	Kansas	9.0
31	West Virginia	10.0		48	Nebraska	8.9
44	Wisconsin	9.3		48	New Jersey	8.9
6	Wyoming	12.5		50	Minnesota	8.8

| | District of Columbia | 9.9 |

Source: CQ Press using data from U.S. Department of Labor, Bureau of Labor Statistics
    "Regional and State Employment and Unemployment" (press release, January 24, 2017, www.bls.gov/bls/newsrels.htm)
*Seasonally adjusted preliminary data as of December 2016. National figure calculated through a different formula.

Employees in Manufacturing in 2016

National Total = 12,275,000 Employees*

ALPHA ORDER

RANK	STATE	EMPLOYEES	% of USA
NA	Alabama**	NA	NA
47	Alaska	15,700	0.1%
25	Arizona	160,100	1.3%
27	Arkansas	152,400	1.2%
1	California	1,282,800	10.5%
29	Colorado	140,800	1.1%
26	Connecticut	159,500	1.3%
44	Delaware	26,400	0.2%
12	Florida	355,800	2.9%
11	Georgia	387,000	3.2%
48	Hawaii	13,700	0.1%
36	Idaho	65,400	0.5%
6	Illinois	565,400	4.6%
7	Indiana	519,000	4.2%
22	Iowa	208,700	1.7%
24	Kansas	160,700	1.3%
18	Kentucky	245,400	2.0%
30	Louisiana	132,900	1.1%
37	Maine	50,100	0.4%
33	Maryland	108,000	0.9%
17	Massachusetts	251,300	2.0%
4	Michigan	596,100	4.9%
14	Minnesota	316,100	2.6%
28	Mississippi	140,900	1.1%
16	Missouri	259,400	2.1%
46	Montana	20,000	0.2%
34	Nebraska	96,400	0.8%
39	Nevada	42,500	0.3%
35	New Hampshire	67,400	0.5%
20	New Jersey	241,400	2.0%
43	New Mexico	26,500	0.2%
10	New York	443,300	3.6%
9	North Carolina	463,000	3.8%
45	North Dakota	24,700	0.2%
3	Ohio	689,700	5.6%
32	Oklahoma	126,100	1.0%
23	Oregon	186,100	1.5%
5	Pennsylvania	567,100	4.6%
41	Rhode Island	40,700	0.3%
19	South Carolina	242,200	2.0%
40	South Dakota	40,900	0.3%
13	Tennessee	343,300	2.8%
2	Texas	844,000	6.9%
31	Utah	129,100	1.1%
42	Vermont	30,000	0.2%
21	Virginia	229,500	1.9%
15	Washington	283,600	2.3%
38	West Virginia	46,400	0.4%
8	Wisconsin	474,000	3.9%
49	Wyoming	9,800	0.1%

RANK ORDER

RANK	STATE	EMPLOYEES	% of USA
1	California	1,282,800	10.5%
2	Texas	844,000	6.9%
3	Ohio	689,700	5.6%
4	Michigan	596,100	4.9%
5	Pennsylvania	567,100	4.6%
6	Illinois	565,400	4.6%
7	Indiana	519,000	4.2%
8	Wisconsin	474,000	3.9%
9	North Carolina	463,000	3.8%
10	New York	443,300	3.6%
11	Georgia	387,000	3.2%
12	Florida	355,800	2.9%
13	Tennessee	343,300	2.8%
14	Minnesota	316,100	2.6%
15	Washington	283,600	2.3%
16	Missouri	259,400	2.1%
17	Massachusetts	251,300	2.0%
18	Kentucky	245,400	2.0%
19	South Carolina	242,200	2.0%
20	New Jersey	241,400	2.0%
21	Virginia	229,500	1.9%
22	Iowa	208,700	1.7%
23	Oregon	186,100	1.5%
24	Kansas	160,700	1.3%
25	Arizona	160,100	1.3%
26	Connecticut	159,500	1.3%
27	Arkansas	152,400	1.2%
28	Mississippi	140,900	1.1%
29	Colorado	140,800	1.1%
30	Louisiana	132,900	1.1%
31	Utah	129,100	1.1%
32	Oklahoma	126,100	1.0%
33	Maryland	108,000	0.9%
34	Nebraska	96,400	0.8%
35	New Hampshire	67,400	0.5%
36	Idaho	65,400	0.5%
37	Maine	50,100	0.4%
38	West Virginia	46,400	0.4%
39	Nevada	42,500	0.3%
40	South Dakota	40,900	0.3%
41	Rhode Island	40,700	0.3%
42	Vermont	30,000	0.2%
43	New Mexico	26,500	0.2%
44	Delaware	26,400	0.2%
45	North Dakota	24,700	0.2%
46	Montana	20,000	0.2%
47	Alaska	15,700	0.1%
48	Hawaii	13,700	0.1%
49	Wyoming	9,800	0.1%
NA	Alabama**	NA	NA
	District of Columbia**	NA	NA

Source: U.S. Department of Labor, Bureau of Labor Statistics
"Regional and State Employment and Unemployment" (press release, January 24, 2017, www.bls.gov/bls/newsrels.htm)
*Seasonally adjusted preliminary data as of December 2016. National total calculated through a different formula.
**The Bureau of Labor Statistics does not publish seasonally adjusted figures in this category for these states.

Percent of Nonfarm Employees in Manufacturing in 2016

National Percent = 8.4% of Employees*

ALPHA ORDER				RANK ORDER		
RANK	STATE	PERCENT		RANK	STATE	PERCENT
NA	Alabama**	NA		1	Indiana	16.8
41	Alaska	4.7		2	Wisconsin	16.2
35	Arizona	5.9		3	Michigan	13.7
7	Arkansas	12.4		4	Iowa	13.2
29	California	7.7		5	Kentucky	12.8
40	Colorado	5.4		6	Ohio	12.5
17	Connecticut	9.5		7	Arkansas	12.4
37	Delaware	5.8		7	Mississippi	12.4
44	Florida	4.2		9	South Carolina	11.7
25	Georgia	8.7		10	Kansas	11.5
49	Hawaii	2.1		10	Tennessee	11.5
22	Idaho	9.3		12	Minnesota	10.8
19	Illinois	9.4		13	North Carolina	10.6
1	Indiana	16.8		14	New Hampshire	10.0
4	Iowa	13.2		14	Oregon	10.0
10	Kansas	11.5		16	Pennsylvania	9.6
5	Kentucky	12.8		17	Connecticut	9.5
33	Louisiana	6.7		17	Vermont	9.5
28	Maine	8.2		19	Illinois	9.4
45	Maryland	4.0		19	Nebraska	9.4
31	Massachusetts	7.0		19	South Dakota	9.4
3	Michigan	13.7		22	Idaho	9.3
12	Minnesota	10.8		23	Missouri	9.1
7	Mississippi	12.4		24	Utah	9.0
23	Missouri	9.1		25	Georgia	8.7
43	Montana	4.3		26	Washington	8.6
19	Nebraska	9.4		27	Rhode Island	8.3
47	Nevada	3.3		28	Maine	8.2
14	New Hampshire	10.0		29	California	7.7
35	New Jersey	5.9		30	Oklahoma	7.6
48	New Mexico	3.2		31	Massachusetts	7.0
41	New York	4.7		31	Texas	7.0
13	North Carolina	10.6		33	Louisiana	6.7
39	North Dakota	5.7		34	West Virginia	6.1
6	Ohio	12.5		35	Arizona	5.9
30	Oklahoma	7.6		35	New Jersey	5.9
14	Oregon	10.0		37	Delaware	5.8
16	Pennsylvania	9.6		37	Virginia	5.8
27	Rhode Island	8.3		39	North Dakota	5.7
9	South Carolina	11.7		40	Colorado	5.4
19	South Dakota	9.4		41	Alaska	4.7
10	Tennessee	11.5		41	New York	4.7
31	Texas	7.0		43	Montana	4.3
24	Utah	9.0		44	Florida	4.2
17	Vermont	9.5		45	Maryland	4.0
37	Virginia	5.8		46	Wyoming	3.5
26	Washington	8.6		47	Nevada	3.3
34	West Virginia	6.1		48	New Mexico	3.2
2	Wisconsin	16.2		49	Hawaii	2.1
46	Wyoming	3.5		NA	Alabama**	NA
					District of Columbia**	NA

Source: CQ Press using data from U.S. Department of Labor, Bureau of Labor Statistics
"Regional and State Employment and Unemployment" (press release, January 24, 2017, www.bls.gov/bls/newsrels.htm)
*Seasonally adjusted preliminary data as of December 2016. National figure calculated through a different formula.
**The Bureau of Labor Statistics does not publish seasonally adjusted figures in this category for these states.

Employees in Mining and Logging in 2016

National Total = 686,000 Employees*

ALPHA ORDER

RANK	STATE	EMPLOYEES	% of USA
16	Alabama	10,300	1.5%
11	Alaska	14,400	2.1%
13	Arizona	11,800	1.7%
26	Arkansas	6,500	0.9%
5	California	24,500	3.6%
4	Colorado	25,300	3.7%
47	Connecticut	500	0.1%
NA	Delaware**	NA	NA
29	Florida	5,800	0.8%
19	Georgia	8,800	1.3%
NA	Hawaii**	NA	NA
37	Idaho	3,600	0.5%
17	Illinois	9,100	1.3%
27	Indiana	6,100	0.9%
39	Iowa	2,200	0.3%
21	Kansas	7,400	1.1%
14	Kentucky	11,200	1.6%
3	Louisiana	37,100	5.4%
38	Maine	2,500	0.4%
40	Maryland	1,500	0.2%
42	Massachusetts	1,100	0.2%
25	Michigan	6,700	1.0%
31	Minnesota	5,400	0.8%
24	Mississippi	7,300	1.1%
35	Missouri	4,200	0.6%
21	Montana	7,400	1.1%
43	Nebraska	1,000	0.1%
12	Nevada	13,100	1.9%
43	New Hampshire	1,000	0.1%
41	New Jersey	1,300	0.2%
9	New Mexico	17,700	2.6%
32	New York	4,800	0.7%
30	North Carolina	5,600	0.8%
10	North Dakota	17,100	2.5%
14	Ohio	11,200	1.6%
2	Oklahoma	43,200	6.3%
21	Oregon	7,400	1.1%
6	Pennsylvania	22,600	3.3%
48	Rhode Island	200	0.0%
34	South Carolina	4,300	0.6%
45	South Dakota	800	0.1%
33	Tennessee	4,400	0.6%
1	Texas	228,700	33.3%
17	Utah	9,100	1.3%
45	Vermont	800	0.1%
20	Virginia	8,100	1.2%
28	Washington	5,900	0.9%
7	West Virginia	21,300	3.1%
36	Wisconsin	3,800	0.6%
8	Wyoming	19,300	2.8%

RANK ORDER

RANK	STATE	EMPLOYEES	% of USA
1	Texas	228,700	33.3%
2	Oklahoma	43,200	6.3%
3	Louisiana	37,100	5.4%
4	Colorado	25,300	3.7%
5	California	24,500	3.6%
6	Pennsylvania	22,600	3.3%
7	West Virginia	21,300	3.1%
8	Wyoming	19,300	2.8%
9	New Mexico	17,700	2.6%
10	North Dakota	17,100	2.5%
11	Alaska	14,400	2.1%
12	Nevada	13,100	1.9%
13	Arizona	11,800	1.7%
14	Kentucky	11,200	1.6%
14	Ohio	11,200	1.6%
16	Alabama	10,300	1.5%
17	Illinois	9,100	1.3%
17	Utah	9,100	1.3%
19	Georgia	8,800	1.3%
20	Virginia	8,100	1.2%
21	Kansas	7,400	1.1%
21	Montana	7,400	1.1%
21	Oregon	7,400	1.1%
24	Mississippi	7,300	1.1%
25	Michigan	6,700	1.0%
26	Arkansas	6,500	0.9%
27	Indiana	6,100	0.9%
28	Washington	5,900	0.9%
29	Florida	5,800	0.8%
30	North Carolina	5,600	0.8%
31	Minnesota	5,400	0.8%
32	New York	4,800	0.7%
33	Tennessee	4,400	0.6%
34	South Carolina	4,300	0.6%
35	Missouri	4,200	0.6%
36	Wisconsin	3,800	0.6%
37	Idaho	3,600	0.5%
38	Maine	2,500	0.4%
39	Iowa	2,200	0.3%
40	Maryland	1,500	0.2%
41	New Jersey	1,300	0.2%
42	Massachusetts	1,100	0.2%
43	Nebraska	1,000	0.1%
43	New Hampshire	1,000	0.1%
45	South Dakota	800	0.1%
45	Vermont	800	0.1%
47	Connecticut	500	0.1%
48	Rhode Island	200	0.0%
NA	Delaware**	NA	NA
NA	Hawaii**	NA	NA
	District of Columbia**	NA	NA

Source: U.S. Department of Labor, Bureau of Labor Statistics
   "Regional and State Employment and Unemployment" (press release, January 24, 2017, www.bls.gov/bls/newsrels.htm)
*Not seasonally adjusted preliminary data as of December 2016. National total calculated through a different formula.
**The Bureau of Labor Statistics does not publish figures in this category for these states.

Percent of Nonfarm Employees in Mining and Logging in 2016

National Percent = 0.5% of Employees*

ALPHA ORDER

RANK	STATE	PERCENT
15	Alabama	0.5
2	Alaska	4.5
19	Arizona	0.4
15	Arkansas	0.5
34	California	0.1
10	Colorado	1.0
45	Connecticut	0.0
NA	Delaware**	NA
34	Florida	0.1
23	Georgia	0.2
NA	Hawaii**	NA
15	Idaho	0.5
23	Illinois	0.2
23	Indiana	0.2
34	Iowa	0.1
15	Kansas	0.5
12	Kentucky	0.6
7	Louisiana	1.9
19	Maine	0.4
34	Maryland	0.1
45	Massachusetts	0.0
23	Michigan	0.2
23	Minnesota	0.2
12	Mississippi	0.6
34	Missouri	0.1
9	Montana	1.6
34	Nebraska	0.1
10	Nevada	1.0
34	New Hampshire	0.1
45	New Jersey	0.0
6	New Mexico	2.1
34	New York	0.1
34	North Carolina	0.1
3	North Dakota	3.9
23	Ohio	0.2
5	Oklahoma	2.6
19	Oregon	0.4
19	Pennsylvania	0.4
45	Rhode Island	0.0
23	South Carolina	0.2
23	South Dakota	0.2
34	Tennessee	0.1
7	Texas	1.9
12	Utah	0.6
23	Vermont	0.2
23	Virginia	0.2
23	Washington	0.2
4	West Virginia	2.8
34	Wisconsin	0.1
1	Wyoming	7.0

RANK ORDER

RANK	STATE	PERCENT
1	Wyoming	7.0
2	Alaska	4.5
3	North Dakota	3.9
4	West Virginia	2.8
5	Oklahoma	2.6
6	New Mexico	2.1
7	Louisiana	1.9
7	Texas	1.9
9	Montana	1.6
10	Colorado	1.0
10	Nevada	1.0
12	Kentucky	0.6
12	Mississippi	0.6
12	Utah	0.6
15	Alabama	0.5
15	Arkansas	0.5
15	Idaho	0.5
15	Kansas	0.5
19	Arizona	0.4
19	Maine	0.4
19	Oregon	0.4
19	Pennsylvania	0.4
23	Georgia	0.2
23	Illinois	0.2
23	Indiana	0.2
23	Michigan	0.2
23	Minnesota	0.2
23	Ohio	0.2
23	South Carolina	0.2
23	South Dakota	0.2
23	Vermont	0.2
23	Virginia	0.2
23	Washington	0.2
34	California	0.1
34	Florida	0.1
34	Iowa	0.1
34	Maryland	0.1
34	Missouri	0.1
34	Nebraska	0.1
34	New Hampshire	0.1
34	New York	0.1
34	North Carolina	0.1
34	Tennessee	0.1
34	Wisconsin	0.1
45	Connecticut	0.0
45	Massachusetts	0.0
45	New Jersey	0.0
45	Rhode Island	0.0
NA	Delaware**	NA
NA	Hawaii**	NA
	District of Columbia**	NA

Source: CQ Press using data from U.S. Department of Labor, Bureau of Labor Statistics
   "Regional and State Employment and Unemployment" (press release, January 24, 2017, www.bls.gov/bls/newsrels.htm)
*Not seasonally adjusted preliminary data as of December 2016. National figure calculated through a different formula.
**The Bureau of Labor Statistics does not publish seasonally adjusted figures in this category for these states.

Employees in Professional and Business Services in 2016

National Total = 20,503,000 Employees*

RANK	STATE	EMPLOYEES	% of USA
25	Alabama	230,500	1.1%
49	Alaska	26,500	0.1%
15	Arizona	412,200	2.0%
33	Arkansas	146,300	0.7%
1	California	2,594,200	12.7%
16	Colorado	412,000	2.0%
27	Connecticut	214,900	1.0%
43	Delaware	65,000	0.3%
3	Florida	1,301,600	6.3%
9	Georgia	689,800	3.4%
39	Hawaii	85,400	0.4%
38	Idaho	86,200	0.4%
5	Illinois	947,300	4.6%
21	Indiana	328,800	1.6%
34	Iowa	138,700	0.7%
30	Kansas	176,800	0.9%
26	Kentucky	223,700	1.1%
28	Louisiana	211,400	1.0%
44	Maine	64,800	0.3%
14	Maryland	440,800	2.1%
13	Massachusetts	557,200	2.7%
10	Michigan	673,200	3.3%
20	Minnesota	365,600	1.8%
37	Mississippi	98,500	0.5%
19	Missouri	386,000	1.9%
45	Montana	41,400	0.2%
35	Nebraska	122,300	0.6%
32	Nevada	168,900	0.8%
40	New Hampshire	79,700	0.4%
11	New Jersey	663,700	3.2%
36	New Mexico	102,800	0.5%
4	New York	1,291,900	6.3%
12	North Carolina	627,000	3.1%
46	North Dakota	36,100	0.2%
8	Ohio	716,500	3.5%
31	Oklahoma	176,100	0.9%
24	Oregon	250,100	1.2%
6	Pennsylvania	789,000	3.8%
41	Rhode Island	66,500	0.3%
23	South Carolina	281,900	1.4%
47	South Dakota	31,900	0.2%
18	Tennessee	406,600	2.0%
2	Texas	1,634,800	8.0%
29	Utah	204,500	1.0%
48	Vermont	27,800	0.1%
7	Virginia	727,700	3.5%
17	Washington	408,100	2.0%
42	West Virginia	66,300	0.3%
22	Wisconsin	317,200	1.5%
50	Wyoming	18,300	0.1%

RANK	STATE	EMPLOYEES	% of USA
1	California	2,594,200	12.7%
2	Texas	1,634,800	8.0%
3	Florida	1,301,600	6.3%
4	New York	1,291,900	6.3%
5	Illinois	947,300	4.6%
6	Pennsylvania	789,000	3.8%
7	Virginia	727,700	3.5%
8	Ohio	716,500	3.5%
9	Georgia	689,800	3.4%
10	Michigan	673,200	3.3%
11	New Jersey	663,700	3.2%
12	North Carolina	627,000	3.1%
13	Massachusetts	557,200	2.7%
14	Maryland	440,800	2.1%
15	Arizona	412,200	2.0%
16	Colorado	412,000	2.0%
17	Washington	408,100	2.0%
18	Tennessee	406,600	2.0%
19	Missouri	386,000	1.9%
20	Minnesota	365,600	1.8%
21	Indiana	328,800	1.6%
22	Wisconsin	317,200	1.5%
23	South Carolina	281,900	1.4%
24	Oregon	250,100	1.2%
25	Alabama	230,500	1.1%
26	Kentucky	223,700	1.1%
27	Connecticut	214,900	1.0%
28	Louisiana	211,400	1.0%
29	Utah	204,500	1.0%
30	Kansas	176,800	0.9%
31	Oklahoma	176,100	0.9%
32	Nevada	168,900	0.8%
33	Arkansas	146,300	0.7%
34	Iowa	138,700	0.7%
35	Nebraska	122,300	0.6%
36	New Mexico	102,800	0.5%
37	Mississippi	98,500	0.5%
38	Idaho	86,200	0.4%
39	Hawaii	85,400	0.4%
40	New Hampshire	79,700	0.4%
41	Rhode Island	66,500	0.3%
42	West Virginia	66,300	0.3%
43	Delaware	65,000	0.3%
44	Maine	64,800	0.3%
45	Montana	41,400	0.2%
46	North Dakota	36,100	0.2%
47	South Dakota	31,900	0.2%
48	Vermont	27,800	0.1%
49	Alaska	26,500	0.1%
50	Wyoming	18,300	0.1%
	District of Columbia	167,800	0.8%

Source: U.S. Department of Labor, Bureau of Labor Statistics
"Regional and State Employment and Unemployment" (press release, January 24, 2017, www.bls.gov/bls/newsrels.htm)
*Seasonally adjusted preliminary data as of December 2016. National total calculated through a different formula.

Percent of Nonfarm Employees in Professional and Business Services in 2016

National Percent = 14.1% of Employees*

ALPHA ORDER				RANK ORDER		
RANK	STATE	PERCENT		RANK	STATE	PERCENT
35	Alabama	11.7		1	Virginia	18.4
48	Alaska	7.9		2	Maryland	16.2
11	Arizona	15.2		2	New Jersey	16.2
33	Arkansas	11.9		4	Illinois	15.8
6	California	15.6		5	Colorado	15.7
5	Colorado	15.7		6	California	15.6
26	Connecticut	12.8		6	Georgia	15.6
13	Delaware	14.2		8	Massachusetts	15.5
9	Florida	15.4		9	Florida	15.4
6	Georgia	15.6		9	Michigan	15.4
23	Hawaii	13.0		11	Arizona	15.2
31	Idaho	12.3		12	North Carolina	14.4
4	Illinois	15.8		13	Delaware	14.2
38	Indiana	10.7		13	Utah	14.2
43	Iowa	8.8		15	New York	13.7
27	Kansas	12.7		16	Missouri	13.6
35	Kentucky	11.7		16	South Carolina	13.6
38	Louisiana	10.7		16	Tennessee	13.6
40	Maine	10.6		19	Rhode Island	13.5
2	Maryland	16.2		19	Texas	13.5
8	Massachusetts	15.5		21	Oregon	13.4
9	Michigan	15.4		21	Pennsylvania	13.4
28	Minnesota	12.5		23	Hawaii	13.0
45	Mississippi	8.7		23	Ohio	13.0
16	Missouri	13.6		25	Nevada	12.9
42	Montana	8.9		26	Connecticut	12.8
32	Nebraska	12.0		27	Kansas	12.7
25	Nevada	12.9		28	Minnesota	12.5
34	New Hampshire	11.8		29	New Mexico	12.4
2	New Jersey	16.2		29	Washington	12.4
29	New Mexico	12.4		31	Idaho	12.3
15	New York	13.7		32	Nebraska	12.0
12	North Carolina	14.4		33	Arkansas	11.9
47	North Dakota	8.3		34	New Hampshire	11.8
23	Ohio	13.0		35	Alabama	11.7
40	Oklahoma	10.6		35	Kentucky	11.7
21	Oregon	13.4		37	Wisconsin	10.8
21	Pennsylvania	13.4		38	Indiana	10.7
19	Rhode Island	13.5		38	Louisiana	10.7
16	South Carolina	13.6		40	Maine	10.6
49	South Dakota	7.3		40	Oklahoma	10.6
16	Tennessee	13.6		42	Montana	8.9
19	Texas	13.5		43	Iowa	8.8
13	Utah	14.2		43	Vermont	8.8
43	Vermont	8.8		45	Mississippi	8.7
1	Virginia	18.4		45	West Virginia	8.7
29	Washington	12.4		47	North Dakota	8.3
45	West Virginia	8.7		48	Alaska	7.9
37	Wisconsin	10.8		49	South Dakota	7.3
50	Wyoming	6.6		50	Wyoming	6.6

	District of Columbia	21.4

Source: CQ Press using data from U.S. Department of Labor, Bureau of Labor Statistics
"Regional and State Employment and Unemployment" (press release, January 24, 2017, www.bls.gov/bls/newsrels.htm)
*Seasonally adjusted preliminary data as of December 2016. National figure calculated through a different formula.

Employees in Trade, Transportation, and Public Utilities in 2016

National Total = 27,487,000 Employees*

ALPHA ORDER

RANK	STATE	EMPLOYEES	% of USA
26	Alabama	384,500	1.4%
48	Alaska	64,100	0.2%
20	Arizona	514,700	1.9%
33	Arkansas	255,200	0.9%
1	California	3,030,500	11.0%
22	Colorado	457,300	1.7%
30	Connecticut	297,300	1.1%
46	Delaware	79,400	0.3%
3	Florida	1,731,600	6.3%
8	Georgia	939,600	3.4%
41	Hawaii	120,500	0.4%
38	Idaho	140,100	0.5%
5	Illinois	1,203,100	4.4%
15	Indiana	597,600	2.2%
28	Iowa	316,900	1.2%
32	Kansas	265,400	1.0%
23	Kentucky	398,200	1.4%
25	Louisiana	392,200	1.4%
42	Maine	118,100	0.4%
21	Maryland	468,100	1.7%
16	Massachusetts	567,600	2.1%
11	Michigan	770,700	2.8%
19	Minnesota	534,000	1.9%
35	Mississippi	230,000	0.8%
18	Missouri	538,200	2.0%
44	Montana	94,000	0.3%
36	Nebraska	210,100	0.8%
34	Nevada	248,900	0.9%
37	New Hampshire	141,500	0.5%
9	New Jersey	869,800	3.2%
39	New Mexico	135,700	0.5%
4	New York	1,580,600	5.8%
10	North Carolina	827,300	3.0%
43	North Dakota	96,100	0.3%
7	Ohio	1,028,000	3.7%
29	Oklahoma	307,000	1.1%
27	Oregon	343,800	1.3%
6	Pennsylvania	1,130,300	4.1%
47	Rhode Island	77,000	0.3%
24	South Carolina	393,300	1.4%
45	South Dakota	90,100	0.3%
14	Tennessee	617,300	2.2%
2	Texas	2,455,200	8.9%
31	Utah	273,600	1.0%
49	Vermont	54,400	0.2%
12	Virginia	679,800	2.5%
13	Washington	620,800	2.3%
40	West Virginia	135,500	0.5%
17	Wisconsin	539,700	2.0%
50	Wyoming	52,200	0.2%

RANK ORDER

RANK	STATE	EMPLOYEES	% of USA
1	California	3,030,500	11.0%
2	Texas	2,455,200	8.9%
3	Florida	1,731,600	6.3%
4	New York	1,580,600	5.8%
5	Illinois	1,203,100	4.4%
6	Pennsylvania	1,130,300	4.1%
7	Ohio	1,028,000	3.7%
8	Georgia	939,600	3.4%
9	New Jersey	869,800	3.2%
10	North Carolina	827,300	3.0%
11	Michigan	770,700	2.8%
12	Virginia	679,800	2.5%
13	Washington	620,800	2.3%
14	Tennessee	617,300	2.2%
15	Indiana	597,600	2.2%
16	Massachusetts	567,600	2.1%
17	Wisconsin	539,700	2.0%
18	Missouri	538,200	2.0%
19	Minnesota	534,000	1.9%
20	Arizona	514,700	1.9%
21	Maryland	468,100	1.7%
22	Colorado	457,300	1.7%
23	Kentucky	398,200	1.4%
24	South Carolina	393,300	1.4%
25	Louisiana	392,200	1.4%
26	Alabama	384,500	1.4%
27	Oregon	343,800	1.3%
28	Iowa	316,900	1.2%
29	Oklahoma	307,000	1.1%
30	Connecticut	297,300	1.1%
31	Utah	273,600	1.0%
32	Kansas	265,400	1.0%
33	Arkansas	255,200	0.9%
34	Nevada	248,900	0.9%
35	Mississippi	230,000	0.8%
36	Nebraska	210,100	0.8%
37	New Hampshire	141,500	0.5%
38	Idaho	140,100	0.5%
39	New Mexico	135,700	0.5%
40	West Virginia	135,500	0.5%
41	Hawaii	120,500	0.4%
42	Maine	118,100	0.4%
43	North Dakota	96,100	0.3%
44	Montana	94,000	0.3%
45	South Dakota	90,100	0.3%
46	Delaware	79,400	0.3%
47	Rhode Island	77,000	0.3%
48	Alaska	64,100	0.2%
49	Vermont	54,400	0.2%
50	Wyoming	52,200	0.2%
	District of Columbia	32,100	0.1%

Source: U.S. Department of Labor, Bureau of Labor Statistics
   "Regional and State Employment and Unemployment" (press release, January 24, 2017, www.bls.gov/bls/newsrels.htm)
*Seasonally adjusted preliminary data as of December 2016. National total calculated through a different formula.

Percent of Nonfarm Employees in Trade, Transportation, and Public Utilities in 2016
National Percent = 18.9% of Employees*

ALPHA ORDER

RANK	STATE	PERCENT
18	Alabama	19.5
21	Alaska	19.2
28	Arizona	18.9
5	Arkansas	20.7
38	California	18.2
42	Colorado	17.4
39	Connecticut	17.7
43	Delaware	17.3
10	Florida	20.5
3	Georgia	21.2
35	Hawaii	18.4
14	Idaho	20.0
14	Illinois	20.0
19	Indiana	19.4
14	Iowa	20.0
23	Kansas	19.1
5	Kentucky	20.7
17	Louisiana	19.9
20	Maine	19.3
43	Maryland	17.3
49	Massachusetts	15.8
39	Michigan	17.7
37	Minnesota	18.3
11	Mississippi	20.3
28	Missouri	18.9
12	Montana	20.2
7	Nebraska	20.6
23	Nevada	19.1
4	New Hampshire	21.0
2	New Jersey	21.3
48	New Mexico	16.3
47	New York	16.8
25	North Carolina	19.0
1	North Dakota	22.0
32	Ohio	18.6
33	Oklahoma	18.5
33	Oregon	18.5
21	Pennsylvania	19.2
50	Rhode Island	15.6
25	South Carolina	19.0
7	South Dakota	20.6
7	Tennessee	20.6
12	Texas	20.2
25	Utah	19.0
45	Vermont	17.2
45	Virginia	17.2
28	Washington	18.9
39	West Virginia	17.7
35	Wisconsin	18.4
31	Wyoming	18.7

RANK ORDER

RANK	STATE	PERCENT
1	North Dakota	22.0
2	New Jersey	21.3
3	Georgia	21.2
4	New Hampshire	21.0
5	Arkansas	20.7
5	Kentucky	20.7
7	Nebraska	20.6
7	South Dakota	20.6
7	Tennessee	20.6
10	Florida	20.5
11	Mississippi	20.3
12	Montana	20.2
12	Texas	20.2
14	Idaho	20.0
14	Illinois	20.0
14	Iowa	20.0
17	Louisiana	19.9
18	Alabama	19.5
19	Indiana	19.4
20	Maine	19.3
21	Alaska	19.2
21	Pennsylvania	19.2
23	Kansas	19.1
23	Nevada	19.1
25	North Carolina	19.0
25	South Carolina	19.0
25	Utah	19.0
28	Arizona	18.9
28	Missouri	18.9
28	Washington	18.9
31	Wyoming	18.7
32	Ohio	18.6
33	Oklahoma	18.5
33	Oregon	18.5
35	Hawaii	18.4
35	Wisconsin	18.4
37	Minnesota	18.3
38	California	18.2
39	Connecticut	17.7
39	Michigan	17.7
39	West Virginia	17.7
42	Colorado	17.4
43	Delaware	17.3
43	Maryland	17.3
45	Vermont	17.2
45	Virginia	17.2
47	New York	16.8
48	New Mexico	16.3
49	Massachusetts	15.8
50	Rhode Island	15.6

District of Columbia   4.1

Source: CQ Press using data from U.S. Department of Labor, Bureau of Labor Statistics
"Regional and State Employment and Unemployment" (press release, January 24, 2017, www.bls.gov/bls/newsrels.htm)
*Seasonally adjusted preliminary data as of December 2016. National figure calculated through a different formula.

VII. Energy and Environment

Energy Consumption in 2014

National Total = 98,385,200,000,000,000 BTUs*

ALPHA ORDER

RANK	STATE	BTUs	% of USA
17	Alabama	1,958,200,000,000,000	2.0%
40	Alaska	603,100,000,000,000	0.6%
27	Arizona	1,422,600,000,000,000	1.4%
31	Arkansas	1,114,400,000,000,000	1.1%
2	California	7,620,100,000,000,000	7.7%
25	Colorado	1,477,200,000,000,000	1.5%
36	Connecticut	750,000,000,000,000	0.8%
48	Delaware	274,000,000,000,000	0.3%
4	Florida	4,121,700,000,000,000	4.2%
11	Georgia	2,851,000,000,000,000	2.9%
47	Hawaii	281,200,000,000,000	0.3%
42	Idaho	519,900,000,000,000	0.5%
5	Illinois	4,042,300,000,000,000	4.1%
9	Indiana	2,931,600,000,000,000	3.0%
24	Iowa	1,541,900,000,000,000	1.6%
30	Kansas	1,132,400,000,000,000	1.2%
21	Kentucky	1,770,700,000,000,000	1.8%
3	Louisiana	4,279,400,000,000,000	4.3%
43	Maine	410,500,000,000,000	0.4%
28	Maryland	1,400,600,000,000,000	1.4%
26	Massachusetts	1,437,600,000,000,000	1.5%
10	Michigan	2,881,500,000,000,000	2.9%
18	Minnesota	1,912,100,000,000,000	1.9%
29	Mississippi	1,155,500,000,000,000	1.2%
19	Missouri	1,903,800,000,000,000	1.9%
44	Montana	403,400,000,000,000	0.4%
33	Nebraska	864,300,000,000,000	0.9%
38	Nevada	660,300,000,000,000	0.7%
46	New Hampshire	310,100,000,000,000	0.3%
14	New Jersey	2,340,200,000,000,000	2.4%
37	New Mexico	679,100,000,000,000	0.7%
8	New York	3,742,900,000,000,000	3.8%
12	North Carolina	2,554,800,000,000,000	2.6%
39	North Dakota	640,100,000,000,000	0.7%
7	Ohio	3,809,600,000,000,000	3.9%
22	Oklahoma	1,679,900,000,000,000	1.7%
32	Oregon	987,100,000,000,000	1.0%
6	Pennsylvania	3,902,400,000,000,000	4.0%
49	Rhode Island	204,500,000,000,000	0.2%
23	South Carolina	1,632,100,000,000,000	1.7%
45	South Dakota	391,900,000,000,000	0.4%
15	Tennessee	2,194,500,000,000,000	2.2%
1	Texas	12,899,500,000,000,000	13.1%
34	Utah	798,000,000,000,000	0.8%
50	Vermont	139,900,000,000,000	0.1%
13	Virginia	2,430,200,000,000,000	2.5%
16	Washington	2,011,900,000,000,000	2.0%
35	West Virginia	752,900,000,000,000	0.8%
20	Wisconsin	1,868,900,000,000,000	1.9%
41	Wyoming	535,600,000,000,000	0.5%

RANK ORDER

RANK	STATE	BTUs	% of USA
1	Texas	12,899,500,000,000,000	13.1%
2	California	7,620,100,000,000,000	7.7%
3	Louisiana	4,279,400,000,000,000	4.3%
4	Florida	4,121,700,000,000,000	4.2%
5	Illinois	4,042,300,000,000,000	4.1%
6	Pennsylvania	3,902,400,000,000,000	4.0%
7	Ohio	3,809,600,000,000,000	3.9%
8	New York	3,742,900,000,000,000	3.8%
9	Indiana	2,931,600,000,000,000	3.0%
10	Michigan	2,881,500,000,000,000	2.9%
11	Georgia	2,851,000,000,000,000	2.9%
12	North Carolina	2,554,800,000,000,000	2.6%
13	Virginia	2,430,200,000,000,000	2.5%
14	New Jersey	2,340,200,000,000,000	2.4%
15	Tennessee	2,194,500,000,000,000	2.2%
16	Washington	2,011,900,000,000,000	2.0%
17	Alabama	1,958,200,000,000,000	2.0%
18	Minnesota	1,912,100,000,000,000	1.9%
19	Missouri	1,903,800,000,000,000	1.9%
20	Wisconsin	1,868,900,000,000,000	1.9%
21	Kentucky	1,770,700,000,000,000	1.8%
22	Oklahoma	1,679,900,000,000,000	1.7%
23	South Carolina	1,632,100,000,000,000	1.7%
24	Iowa	1,541,900,000,000,000	1.6%
25	Colorado	1,477,200,000,000,000	1.5%
26	Massachusetts	1,437,600,000,000,000	1.5%
27	Arizona	1,422,600,000,000,000	1.4%
28	Maryland	1,400,600,000,000,000	1.4%
29	Mississippi	1,155,500,000,000,000	1.2%
30	Kansas	1,132,400,000,000,000	1.2%
31	Arkansas	1,114,400,000,000,000	1.1%
32	Oregon	987,100,000,000,000	1.0%
33	Nebraska	864,300,000,000,000	0.9%
34	Utah	798,000,000,000,000	0.8%
35	West Virginia	752,900,000,000,000	0.8%
36	Connecticut	750,000,000,000,000	0.8%
37	New Mexico	679,100,000,000,000	0.7%
38	Nevada	660,300,000,000,000	0.7%
39	North Dakota	640,100,000,000,000	0.7%
40	Alaska	603,100,000,000,000	0.6%
41	Wyoming	535,600,000,000,000	0.5%
42	Idaho	519,900,000,000,000	0.5%
43	Maine	410,500,000,000,000	0.4%
44	Montana	403,400,000,000,000	0.4%
45	South Dakota	391,900,000,000,000	0.4%
46	New Hampshire	310,100,000,000,000	0.3%
47	Hawaii	281,200,000,000,000	0.3%
48	Delaware	274,000,000,000,000	0.3%
49	Rhode Island	204,500,000,000,000	0.2%
50	Vermont	139,900,000,000,000	0.1%
	District of Columbia	178,900,000,000,000	0.2%

Source: U.S. Department of Energy, Energy Information Administration
  "State Energy Data 2014: Consumption" (http://www.eia.gov/state/seds/)
*British Thermal Units: The amount of heat required to raise the temperature of one pound of water one degree. National total includes 17.4 trillion Btu of net imports of coal coke that are not allocated to the states.

Per Capita Energy Consumption in 2014

National Per Capita = 308,840,195 BTUs*

ALPHA ORDER

RANK	STATE	PER CAPITA
12	Alabama	404,318,289
4	Alaska	818,645,184
44	Arizona	211,696,649
17	Arkansas	375,609,388
48	California	196,999,494
34	Colorado	276,130,317
45	Connecticut	208,804,710
29	Delaware	293,064,427
46	Florida	207,237,854
33	Georgia	282,634,551
47	Hawaii	198,538,637
24	Idaho	318,267,411
25	Illinois	314,146,973
9	Indiana	444,502,870
5	Iowa	496,102,032
15	Kansas	390,568,953
13	Kentucky	401,241,135
1	Louisiana	920,720,845
27	Maine	308,479,852
39	Maryland	234,712,713
43	Massachusetts	212,980,586
31	Michigan	290,597,792
18	Minnesota	350,644,009
16	Mississippi	386,144,900
26	Missouri	314,110,211
14	Montana	394,381,674
8	Nebraska	459,454,215
41	Nevada	233,073,410
40	New Hampshire	233,378,464
36	New Jersey	262,207,254
22	New Mexico	326,016,407
50	New York	189,816,525
37	North Carolina	257,167,042
3	North Dakota	865,112,231
21	Ohio	328,572,188
10	Oklahoma	433,243,181
38	Oregon	248,741,864
28	Pennsylvania	305,099,892
49	Rhode Island	193,934,451
19	South Carolina	338,018,776
7	South Dakota	459,673,853
20	Tennessee	335,311,383
6	Texas	478,738,883
35	Utah	271,259,173
42	Vermont	223,131,691
30	Virginia	292,183,637
32	Washington	285,206,138
11	West Virginia	407,300,134
23	Wisconsin	324,553,255
2	Wyoming	917,685,842

RANK ORDER

RANK	STATE	PER CAPITA
1	Louisiana	920,720,845
2	Wyoming	917,685,842
3	North Dakota	865,112,231
4	Alaska	818,645,184
5	Iowa	496,102,032
6	Texas	478,738,883
7	South Dakota	459,673,853
8	Nebraska	459,454,215
9	Indiana	444,502,870
10	Oklahoma	433,243,181
11	West Virginia	407,300,134
12	Alabama	404,318,289
13	Kentucky	401,241,135
14	Montana	394,381,674
15	Kansas	390,568,953
16	Mississippi	386,144,900
17	Arkansas	375,609,388
18	Minnesota	350,644,009
19	South Carolina	338,018,776
20	Tennessee	335,311,383
21	Ohio	328,572,188
22	New Mexico	326,016,407
23	Wisconsin	324,553,255
24	Idaho	318,267,411
25	Illinois	314,146,973
26	Missouri	314,110,211
27	Maine	308,479,852
28	Pennsylvania	305,099,892
29	Delaware	293,064,427
30	Virginia	292,183,637
31	Michigan	290,597,792
32	Washington	285,206,138
33	Georgia	282,634,551
34	Colorado	276,130,317
35	Utah	271,259,173
36	New Jersey	262,207,254
37	North Carolina	257,167,042
38	Oregon	248,741,864
39	Maryland	234,712,713
40	New Hampshire	233,378,464
41	Nevada	233,073,410
42	Vermont	223,131,691
43	Massachusetts	212,980,586
44	Arizona	211,696,649
45	Connecticut	208,804,710
46	Florida	207,237,854
47	Hawaii	198,538,637
48	California	196,999,494
49	Rhode Island	193,934,451
50	New York	189,816,525
	District of Columbia	271,469,867

Source: CQ Press using data from U.S. Department of Energy, Energy Information Administration
"State Energy Data 2014: Consumption" (http://www.eia.gov/state/seds/)
*British Thermal Units: The amount of heat required to raise the temperature of one pound of water one degree. National figure includes 17.4 trillion Btu of net imports of coal coke that are not allocated to the states.

Energy Prices in 2014

National Rate = $21.33 per Million BTUs*

ALPHA ORDER

RANK	STATE	RATE
46	Alabama	$18.64
12	Alaska	24.43
7	Arizona	25.94
44	Arkansas	18.87
8	California	25.31
27	Colorado	21.25
3	Connecticut	27.84
13	Delaware	23.77
10	Florida	24.91
29	Georgia	20.95
1	Hawaii	37.38
34	Idaho	20.43
43	Illinois	19.02
49	Indiana	17.94
48	Iowa	18.24
25	Kansas	21.46
31	Kentucky	20.75
50	Louisiana	15.49
18	Maine	22.62
9	Maryland	25.25
5	Massachusetts	26.36
36	Michigan	20.01
40	Minnesota	19.65
30	Mississippi	20.78
20	Missouri	21.94
22	Montana	21.72
41	Nebraska	19.26
14	Nevada	23.52
2	New Hampshire	27.86
17	New Jersey	22.78
15	New Mexico	23.37
11	New York	24.57
16	North Carolina	23.02
47	North Dakota	18.51
36	Ohio	20.01
38	Oklahoma	19.97
19	Oregon	22.29
26	Pennsylvania	21.44
6	Rhode Island	26.34
21	South Carolina	21.74
35	South Dakota	20.32
24	Tennessee	21.47
42	Texas	19.05
33	Utah	20.71
4	Vermont	27.60
23	Virginia	21.66
28	Washington	21.11
38	West Virginia	19.97
32	Wisconsin	20.74
45	Wyoming	18.70

RANK ORDER

RANK	STATE	RATE
1	Hawaii	$37.38
2	New Hampshire	27.86
3	Connecticut	27.84
4	Vermont	27.60
5	Massachusetts	26.36
6	Rhode Island	26.34
7	Arizona	25.94
8	California	25.31
9	Maryland	25.25
10	Florida	24.91
11	New York	24.57
12	Alaska	24.43
13	Delaware	23.77
14	Nevada	23.52
15	New Mexico	23.37
16	North Carolina	23.02
17	New Jersey	22.78
18	Maine	22.62
19	Oregon	22.29
20	Missouri	21.94
21	South Carolina	21.74
22	Montana	21.72
23	Virginia	21.66
24	Tennessee	21.47
25	Kansas	21.46
26	Pennsylvania	21.44
27	Colorado	21.25
28	Washington	21.11
29	Georgia	20.95
30	Mississippi	20.78
31	Kentucky	20.75
32	Wisconsin	20.74
33	Utah	20.71
34	Idaho	20.43
35	South Dakota	20.32
36	Michigan	20.01
36	Ohio	20.01
38	Oklahoma	19.97
38	West Virginia	19.97
40	Minnesota	19.65
41	Nebraska	19.26
42	Texas	19.05
43	Illinois	19.02
44	Arkansas	18.87
45	Wyoming	18.70
46	Alabama	18.64
47	North Dakota	18.51
48	Iowa	18.24
49	Indiana	17.94
50	Louisiana	15.49
	District of Columbia	24.96

Source: U.S. Department of Energy, Energy Information Administration
    "State Energy Data 2014: Prices and Expenditures" (http://www.eia.gov/state/seds/)
*British Thermal Units: The amount of heat required to raise the temperature of one pound of water one degree.

Energy Expenditures in 2014

National Total = $1,394,974,000,000*

RANK	STATE	EXPENDITURES	% of USA
21	Alabama	$24,146,500,000	1.7%
43	Alaska	6,890,600,000	0.5%
23	Arizona	22,609,600,000	1.6%
33	Arkansas	13,884,900,000	1.0%
2	California	137,719,800,000	9.9%
27	Colorado	19,994,400,000	1.4%
30	Connecticut	15,483,400,000	1.1%
49	Delaware	3,848,500,000	0.3%
4	Florida	66,413,600,000	4.8%
10	Georgia	39,727,800,000	2.8%
41	Hawaii	7,378,600,000	0.5%
42	Idaho	6,980,200,000	0.5%
6	Illinois	51,550,000,000	3.7%
13	Indiana	34,151,900,000	2.4%
28	Iowa	18,021,800,000	1.3%
32	Kansas	14,646,300,000	1.0%
24	Kentucky	22,467,000,000	1.6%
8	Louisiana	45,399,700,000	3.3%
40	Maine	7,557,600,000	0.5%
22	Maryland	22,951,300,000	1.6%
16	Massachusetts	27,574,400,000	2.0%
9	Michigan	40,740,100,000	2.9%
20	Minnesota	25,312,200,000	1.8%
29	Mississippi	15,948,500,000	1.1%
17	Missouri	26,719,000,000	1.9%
46	Montana	5,527,500,000	0.4%
36	Nebraska	10,330,100,000	0.7%
35	Nevada	10,513,000,000	0.8%
44	New Hampshire	6,360,800,000	0.5%
11	New Jersey	39,116,900,000	2.8%
37	New Mexico	9,019,700,000	0.6%
3	New York	68,056,200,000	4.9%
12	North Carolina	37,283,200,000	2.7%
39	North Dakota	8,209,600,000	0.6%
7	Ohio	51,385,500,000	3.7%
26	Oklahoma	20,496,900,000	1.5%
31	Oregon	14,866,200,000	1.1%
5	Pennsylvania	55,665,800,000	4.0%
48	Rhode Island	4,203,700,000	0.3%
25	South Carolina	21,875,700,000	1.6%
47	South Dakota	4,819,400,000	0.3%
15	Tennessee	29,614,600,000	2.1%
1	Texas	162,555,800,000	11.7%
34	Utah	10,755,300,000	0.8%
50	Vermont	3,274,900,000	0.2%
14	Virginia	33,979,600,000	2.4%
19	Washington	25,804,200,000	1.8%
38	West Virginia	8,756,300,000	0.6%
18	Wisconsin	26,448,100,000	1.9%
45	Wyoming	5,841,200,000	0.4%

RANK	STATE	EXPENDITURES	% of USA
1	Texas	$162,555,800,000	11.7%
2	California	137,719,800,000	9.9%
3	New York	68,056,200,000	4.9%
4	Florida	66,413,600,000	4.8%
5	Pennsylvania	55,665,800,000	4.0%
6	Illinois	51,550,000,000	3.7%
7	Ohio	51,385,500,000	3.7%
8	Louisiana	45,399,700,000	3.3%
9	Michigan	40,740,100,000	2.9%
10	Georgia	39,727,800,000	2.8%
11	New Jersey	39,116,900,000	2.8%
12	North Carolina	37,283,200,000	2.7%
13	Indiana	34,151,900,000	2.4%
14	Virginia	33,979,600,000	2.4%
15	Tennessee	29,614,600,000	2.1%
16	Massachusetts	27,574,400,000	2.0%
17	Missouri	26,719,000,000	1.9%
18	Wisconsin	26,448,100,000	1.9%
19	Washington	25,804,200,000	1.8%
20	Minnesota	25,312,200,000	1.8%
21	Alabama	24,146,500,000	1.7%
22	Maryland	22,951,300,000	1.6%
23	Arizona	22,609,600,000	1.6%
24	Kentucky	22,467,000,000	1.6%
25	South Carolina	21,875,700,000	1.6%
26	Oklahoma	20,496,900,000	1.5%
27	Colorado	19,994,400,000	1.4%
28	Iowa	18,021,800,000	1.3%
29	Mississippi	15,948,500,000	1.1%
30	Connecticut	15,483,400,000	1.1%
31	Oregon	14,866,200,000	1.1%
32	Kansas	14,646,300,000	1.0%
33	Arkansas	13,884,900,000	1.0%
34	Utah	10,755,300,000	0.8%
35	Nevada	10,513,000,000	0.8%
36	Nebraska	10,330,100,000	0.7%
37	New Mexico	9,019,700,000	0.6%
38	West Virginia	8,756,300,000	0.6%
39	North Dakota	8,209,600,000	0.6%
40	Maine	7,557,600,000	0.5%
41	Hawaii	7,378,600,000	0.5%
42	Idaho	6,980,200,000	0.5%
43	Alaska	6,890,600,000	0.5%
44	New Hampshire	6,360,800,000	0.5%
45	Wyoming	5,841,200,000	0.4%
46	Montana	5,527,500,000	0.4%
47	South Dakota	4,819,400,000	0.3%
48	Rhode Island	4,203,700,000	0.3%
49	Delaware	3,848,500,000	0.3%
50	Vermont	3,274,900,000	0.2%
	District of Columbia	2,320,300,000	0.2%

Source: U.S. Department of Energy, Energy Information Administration
    "State Energy Data 2014: Prices and Expenditures" (http://www.eia.gov/state/seds/)
*The national total includes a negative $224 million for coal coke net imports, which is not allocated to the states.

Per Capita Energy Expenditures in 2014

National Per Capita = $4,379

ALPHA ORDER				RANK ORDER		
RANK	STATE	PER CAPITA		RANK	STATE	PER CAPITA
18	Alabama	$4,986		1	North Dakota	$11,095
4	Alaska	9,353		2	Wyoming	10,008
49	Arizona	3,365		3	Louisiana	9,768
21	Arkansas	4,680		4	Alaska	9,353
47	California	3,560		5	Texas	6,033
43	Colorado	3,738		6	Iowa	5,798
31	Connecticut	4,311		7	Maine	5,679
33	Delaware	4,116		8	South Dakota	5,653
50	Florida	3,339		9	Nebraska	5,491
39	Georgia	3,938		10	Montana	5,404
14	Hawaii	5,210		11	Mississippi	5,330
32	Idaho	4,273		12	Oklahoma	5,286
37	Illinois	4,006		13	Vermont	5,223
15	Indiana	5,178		14	Hawaii	5,210
6	Iowa	5,798		15	Indiana	5,178
17	Kansas	5,052		16	Kentucky	5,091
16	Kentucky	5,091		17	Kansas	5,052
3	Louisiana	9,768		18	Alabama	4,986
7	Maine	5,679		19	New Hampshire	4,787
40	Maryland	3,846		20	West Virginia	4,737
35	Massachusetts	4,085		21	Arkansas	4,680
34	Michigan	4,109		22	Minnesota	4,642
22	Minnesota	4,642		23	Wisconsin	4,593
11	Mississippi	5,330		24	South Carolina	4,531
27	Missouri	4,408		25	Tennessee	4,525
10	Montana	5,404		26	Ohio	4,432
9	Nebraska	5,491		27	Missouri	4,408
44	Nevada	3,711		28	New Jersey	4,383
19	New Hampshire	4,787		29	Pennsylvania	4,352
28	New Jersey	4,383		30	New Mexico	4,330
30	New Mexico	4,330		31	Connecticut	4,311
48	New York	3,451		32	Idaho	4,273
41	North Carolina	3,753		33	Delaware	4,116
1	North Dakota	11,095		34	Michigan	4,109
26	Ohio	4,432		35	Massachusetts	4,085
12	Oklahoma	5,286		35	Virginia	4,085
42	Oregon	3,746		37	Illinois	4,006
29	Pennsylvania	4,352		38	Rhode Island	3,987
38	Rhode Island	3,987		39	Georgia	3,938
24	South Carolina	4,531		40	Maryland	3,846
8	South Dakota	5,653		41	North Carolina	3,753
25	Tennessee	4,525		42	Oregon	3,746
5	Texas	6,033		43	Colorado	3,738
46	Utah	3,656		44	Nevada	3,711
13	Vermont	5,223		45	Washington	3,658
35	Virginia	4,085		46	Utah	3,656
45	Washington	3,658		47	California	3,560
20	West Virginia	4,737		48	New York	3,451
23	Wisconsin	4,593		49	Arizona	3,365
2	Wyoming	10,008		50	Florida	3,339
					District of Columbia	3,521

Source: CQ Press using data from U.S. Department of Energy, Energy Information Administration
"State Energy Data 2014: Prices and Expenditures" (http://www.eia.gov/state/seds/)

Average Monthly Electric Bill for Industrial Customers in 2015

National Average = $6,799 per Month

ALPHA ORDER

RANK	STATE	MONTHLY BILL
9	Alabama	$23,221
18	Alaska	12,594
21	Arizona	10,017
47	Arkansas	2,320
42	California	3,599
31	Colorado	5,797
23	Connecticut	8,311
11	Delaware	19,545
30	Florida	5,945
27	Georgia	7,602
1	Hawaii	95,955
49	Idaho	1,745
4	Illinois	39,956
14	Indiana	15,076
16	Iowa	13,681
45	Kansas	2,947
12	Kentucky	18,724
25	Louisiana	8,063
24	Maine	8,084
44	Maryland	3,129
29	Massachusetts	6,318
6	Michigan	29,723
17	Minnesota	12,793
26	Mississippi	7,924
22	Missouri	8,942
48	Montana	2,049
50	Nebraska	1,113
10	Nevada	21,470
28	New Hampshire	6,417
35	New Jersey	5,325
41	New Mexico	4,277
19	New York	12,457
15	North Carolina	14,619
32	North Dakota	5,758
13	Ohio	15,442
40	Oklahoma	4,300
46	Oregon	2,552
20	Pennsylvania	11,981
37	Rhode Island	4,941
5	South Carolina	34,461
39	South Dakota	4,556
2	Tennessee	94,944
38	Texas	4,847
36	Utah	5,051
3	Vermont	52,677
8	Virginia	27,346
43	Washington	3,329
33	West Virginia	5,550
7	Wisconsin	27,372
34	Wyoming	5,505

RANK ORDER

RANK	STATE	MONTHLY BILL
1	Hawaii	$95,955
2	Tennessee	94,944
3	Vermont	52,677
4	Illinois	39,956
5	South Carolina	34,461
6	Michigan	29,723
7	Wisconsin	27,372
8	Virginia	27,346
9	Alabama	23,221
10	Nevada	21,470
11	Delaware	19,545
12	Kentucky	18,724
13	Ohio	15,442
14	Indiana	15,076
15	North Carolina	14,619
16	Iowa	13,681
17	Minnesota	12,793
18	Alaska	12,594
19	New York	12,457
20	Pennsylvania	11,981
21	Arizona	10,017
22	Missouri	8,942
23	Connecticut	8,311
24	Maine	8,084
25	Louisiana	8,063
26	Mississippi	7,924
27	Georgia	7,602
28	New Hampshire	6,417
29	Massachusetts	6,318
30	Florida	5,945
31	Colorado	5,797
32	North Dakota	5,758
33	West Virginia	5,550
34	Wyoming	5,505
35	New Jersey	5,325
36	Utah	5,051
37	Rhode Island	4,941
38	Texas	4,847
39	South Dakota	4,556
40	Oklahoma	4,300
41	New Mexico	4,277
42	California	3,599
43	Washington	3,329
44	Maryland	3,129
45	Kansas	2,947
46	Oregon	2,552
47	Arkansas	2,320
48	Montana	2,049
49	Idaho	1,745
50	Nebraska	1,113

District of Columbia	1,743,958

Source: U.S. Department of Energy, Energy Information Administration
"Electric Sales, Revenue and Average Price 2015" (http://www.eia.gov/electricity/sales_revenue_price/index.cfm)

Average Monthly Electric Bill for Commercial Customers in 2015

National Average = $671 per Month

ALPHA ORDER				RANK ORDER		
RANK	STATE	MONTHLY BILL		RANK	STATE	MONTHLY BILL
26	Alabama	$583		1	Hawaii	$1,175
10	Alaska	793		2	Connecticut	1,131
8	Arizona	806		3	Maryland	1,102
44	Arkansas	449		4	New York	931
5	California	921		5	California	921
42	Colorado	460		6	Massachusetts	847
2	Connecticut	1,131		7	Rhode Island	827
14	Delaware	683		8	Arizona	806
17	Florida	641		9	New Jersey	805
12	Georgia	693		10	Alaska	793
1	Hawaii	1,175		11	Virginia	772
50	Idaho	382		12	Georgia	693
21	Illinois	627		13	Utah	688
28	Indiana	559		14	Delaware	683
49	Iowa	394		15	Texas	650
27	Kansas	567		16	North Dakota	649
37	Kentucky	514		17	Florida	641
25	Louisiana	605		18	Ohio	637
46	Maine	430		19	Minnesota	636
3	Maryland	1,102		20	Michigan	635
6	Massachusetts	847		21	Illinois	627
20	Michigan	635		22	Missouri	624
19	Minnesota	636		23	Tennessee	622
30	Mississippi	547		24	Wisconsin	614
22	Missouri	624		25	Louisiana	605
47	Montana	400		26	Alabama	583
44	Nebraska	449		27	Kansas	567
41	Nevada	462		28	Indiana	559
32	New Hampshire	529		29	Washington	549
9	New Jersey	805		30	Mississippi	547
31	New Mexico	537		31	New Mexico	537
4	New York	931		32	New Hampshire	529
33	North Carolina	527		33	North Carolina	527
16	North Dakota	649		34	South Carolina	522
18	Ohio	637		35	South Dakota	519
40	Oklahoma	477		36	Wyoming	517
38	Oregon	513		37	Kentucky	514
39	Pennsylvania	507		38	Oregon	513
7	Rhode Island	827		39	Pennsylvania	507
34	South Carolina	522		40	Oklahoma	477
35	South Dakota	519		41	Nevada	462
23	Tennessee	622		42	Colorado	460
15	Texas	650		43	Vermont	454
13	Utah	688		44	Arkansas	449
43	Vermont	454		44	Nebraska	449
11	Virginia	772		46	Maine	430
29	Washington	549		47	Montana	400
48	West Virginia	395		48	West Virginia	395
24	Wisconsin	614		49	Iowa	394
36	Wyoming	517		50	Idaho	382

District of Columbia   3,234

Source: U.S. Department of Energy, Energy Information Administration
"Electric Sales, Revenue and Average Price 2015" (http://www.eia.gov/electricity/sales_revenue_price/index.cfm)

Average Monthly Electric Bill for Residential Customers in 2015

National Average = $114 per Month

RANK	STATE	MONTHLY BILL
4	Alabama	$142
15	Alaska	120
14	Arizona	125
30	Arkansas	110
37	California	95
48	Colorado	83
1	Connecticut	153
9	Delaware	131
8	Florida	132
11	Georgia	129
2	Hawaii	152
37	Idaho	95
44	Illinois	90
24	Indiana	112
35	Iowa	99
27	Kansas	111
21	Kentucky	115
15	Louisiana	120
47	Maine	87
5	Maryland	140
17	Massachusetts	119
40	Michigan	94
42	Minnesota	92
6	Mississippi	137
19	Missouri	116
45	Montana	89
34	Nebraska	102
19	Nevada	116
21	New Hampshire	115
30	New Jersey	110
50	New Mexico	79
27	New York	111
13	North Carolina	126
33	North Dakota	105
24	Ohio	112
27	Oklahoma	111
36	Oregon	96
18	Pennsylvania	117
21	Rhode Island	115
3	South Carolina	144
32	South Dakota	109
11	Tennessee	129
7	Texas	136
49	Utah	81
37	Vermont	95
9	Virginia	131
46	Washington	88
24	West Virginia	112
40	Wisconsin	94
43	Wyoming	91

RANK	STATE	MONTHLY BILL
1	Connecticut	$153
2	Hawaii	152
3	South Carolina	144
4	Alabama	142
5	Maryland	140
6	Mississippi	137
7	Texas	136
8	Florida	132
9	Delaware	131
9	Virginia	131
11	Georgia	129
11	Tennessee	129
13	North Carolina	126
14	Arizona	125
15	Alaska	120
15	Louisiana	120
17	Massachusetts	119
18	Pennsylvania	117
19	Missouri	116
19	Nevada	116
21	Kentucky	115
21	New Hampshire	115
21	Rhode Island	115
24	Indiana	112
24	Ohio	112
24	West Virginia	112
27	Kansas	111
27	New York	111
27	Oklahoma	111
30	Arkansas	110
30	New Jersey	110
32	South Dakota	109
33	North Dakota	105
34	Nebraska	102
35	Iowa	99
36	Oregon	96
37	California	95
37	Idaho	95
37	Vermont	95
40	Michigan	94
40	Wisconsin	94
42	Minnesota	92
43	Wyoming	91
44	Illinois	90
45	Montana	89
46	Washington	88
47	Maine	87
48	Colorado	83
49	Utah	81
50	New Mexico	79
	District of Columbia	109

Source: U.S. Department of Energy, Energy Information Administration
"Electric Sales, Revenue and Average Price 2015" (http://www.eia.gov/electricity/sales_revenue_price/index.cfm)

Electricity Generated through Renewable Sources in 2015

National Total = 544,240,990,000 Kilowatthours*

ALPHA ORDER					RANK ORDER			
RANK	STATE	KWH	% of USA		RANK	STATE	KWH	% of USA
8	Alabama	13,151,088,000	2.4%		1	Washington	82,472,293,000	15.2%
43	Alaska	1,783,515,000	0.3%		2	California	59,203,470,000	10.9%
15	Arizona	10,670,993,000	2.0%		3	Texas	47,630,759,000	8.8%
29	Arkansas	5,011,079,000	0.9%		4	Oregon	39,204,182,000	7.2%
2	California	59,203,470,000	10.9%		5	New York	32,333,071,000	5.9%
16	Colorado	9,427,367,000	1.7%		6	Iowa	19,090,920,000	3.5%
48	Connecticut	1,107,374,000	0.2%		7	Oklahoma	17,032,522,000	3.1%
50	Delaware	129,936,000	0.0%		8	Alabama	13,151,088,000	2.4%
27	Florida	5,387,722,000	1.0%		9	Minnesota	12,436,710,000	2.3%
21	Georgia	7,846,583,000	1.4%		10	Montana	11,873,736,000	2.2%
47	Hawaii	1,339,620,000	0.2%		11	Idaho	11,703,685,000	2.2%
11	Idaho	11,703,685,000	2.2%		12	Illinois	11,447,947,000	2.1%
12	Illinois	11,447,947,000	2.1%		13	Kansas	11,081,207,000	2.0%
26	Indiana	5,498,889,000	1.0%		14	Tennessee	10,707,051,000	2.0%
6	Iowa	19,090,920,000	3.5%		15	Arizona	10,670,993,000	2.0%
13	Kansas	11,081,207,000	2.0%		16	Colorado	9,427,367,000	1.7%
33	Kentucky	3,844,607,000	0.7%		17	Michigan	8,782,182,000	1.6%
34	Louisiana	3,703,779,000	0.7%		18	North Carolina	8,704,955,000	1.6%
22	Maine	7,809,182,000	1.4%		19	North Dakota	8,603,466,000	1.6%
39	Maryland	2,690,987,000	0.5%		20	Pennsylvania	8,424,230,000	1.5%
40	Massachusetts	2,660,088,000	0.5%		21	Georgia	7,846,583,000	1.4%
17	Michigan	8,782,182,000	1.6%		22	Maine	7,809,182,000	1.4%
9	Minnesota	12,436,710,000	2.3%		23	Nevada	7,367,464,000	1.4%
46	Mississippi	1,506,532,000	0.3%		24	South Dakota	7,347,998,000	1.4%
37	Missouri	2,773,896,000	0.5%		25	Wisconsin	5,502,399,000	1.0%
10	Montana	11,873,736,000	2.2%		26	Indiana	5,498,889,000	1.0%
30	Nebraska	4,936,396,000	0.9%		27	Florida	5,387,722,000	1.0%
23	Nevada	7,367,464,000	1.4%		28	Virginia	5,302,586,000	1.0%
35	New Hampshire	3,318,049,000	0.6%		29	Arkansas	5,011,079,000	0.9%
44	New Jersey	1,604,663,000	0.3%		30	Nebraska	4,936,396,000	0.9%
36	New Mexico	2,833,619,000	0.5%		31	South Carolina	4,857,959,000	0.9%
5	New York	32,333,071,000	5.9%		32	Wyoming	4,624,969,000	0.8%
18	North Carolina	8,704,955,000	1.6%		33	Kentucky	3,844,607,000	0.7%
19	North Dakota	8,603,466,000	1.6%		34	Louisiana	3,703,779,000	0.7%
41	Ohio	2,514,506,000	0.5%		35	New Hampshire	3,318,049,000	0.6%
7	Oklahoma	17,032,522,000	3.1%		36	New Mexico	2,833,619,000	0.5%
4	Oregon	39,204,182,000	7.2%		37	Missouri	2,773,896,000	0.5%
20	Pennsylvania	8,424,230,000	1.5%		38	West Virginia	2,766,255,000	0.5%
49	Rhode Island	668,321,000	0.1%		39	Maryland	2,690,987,000	0.5%
31	South Carolina	4,857,959,000	0.9%		40	Massachusetts	2,660,088,000	0.5%
24	South Dakota	7,347,998,000	1.4%		41	Ohio	2,514,506,000	0.5%
14	Tennessee	10,707,051,000	2.0%		42	Vermont	1,977,498,000	0.4%
3	Texas	47,630,759,000	8.8%		43	Alaska	1,783,515,000	0.3%
45	Utah	1,511,680,000	0.3%		44	New Jersey	1,604,663,000	0.3%
42	Vermont	1,977,498,000	0.4%		45	Utah	1,511,680,000	0.3%
28	Virginia	5,302,586,000	1.0%		46	Mississippi	1,506,532,000	0.3%
1	Washington	82,472,293,000	15.2%		47	Hawaii	1,339,620,000	0.2%
38	West Virginia	2,766,255,000	0.5%		48	Connecticut	1,107,374,000	0.2%
25	Wisconsin	5,502,399,000	1.0%		49	Rhode Island	668,321,000	0.1%
32	Wyoming	4,624,969,000	0.8%		50	Delaware	129,936,000	0.0%
						District of Columbia	30,999,000	0.0%

Source: U.S. Department of Energy, Energy Information Administration
"Electricity" (http://www.eia.gov/electricity/data/state/)
*Includes hydroelectric, geothermal, solar thermal and photovoltaic, wind, wood and wood-derived fuels, and other biomass.

Percent of Electricity Generated through Renewable Sources in 2015

National Percent = 13.3%*

ALPHA ORDER

RANK	STATE	PERCENT
28	Alabama	8.6
10	Alaska	28.4
24	Arizona	9.4
26	Arkansas	9.0
9	California	30.1
17	Colorado	18.0
45	Connecticut	3.0
50	Delaware	1.7
46	Florida	2.3
35	Georgia	6.1
20	Hawaii	13.2
4	Idaho	74.7
36	Illinois	5.9
37	Indiana	5.3
8	Iowa	33.7
11	Kansas	24.3
39	Kentucky	4.6
43	Louisiana	3.4
6	Maine	66.5
32	Maryland	7.4
29	Massachusetts	8.3
31	Michigan	7.8
15	Minnesota	21.8
46	Mississippi	2.3
44	Missouri	3.3
7	Montana	40.5
21	Nebraska	12.4
16	Nevada	18.9
18	New Hampshire	16.6
48	New Jersey	2.2
27	New Mexico	8.7
12	New York	23.3
33	North Carolina	6.8
13	North Dakota	23.2
49	Ohio	2.1
14	Oklahoma	22.4
5	Oregon	67.7
40	Pennsylvania	3.9
23	Rhode Island	9.6
38	South Carolina	5.0
2	South Dakota	76.3
19	Tennessee	14.2
22	Texas	10.6
42	Utah	3.6
1	Vermont	99.8
34	Virginia	6.3
3	Washington	75.5
41	West Virginia	3.8
29	Wisconsin	8.3
24	Wyoming	9.4

RANK ORDER

RANK	STATE	PERCENT
1	Vermont	99.8
2	South Dakota	76.3
3	Washington	75.5
4	Idaho	74.7
5	Oregon	67.7
6	Maine	66.5
7	Montana	40.5
8	Iowa	33.7
9	California	30.1
10	Alaska	28.4
11	Kansas	24.3
12	New York	23.3
13	North Dakota	23.2
14	Oklahoma	22.4
15	Minnesota	21.8
16	Nevada	18.9
17	Colorado	18.0
18	New Hampshire	16.6
19	Tennessee	14.2
20	Hawaii	13.2
21	Nebraska	12.4
22	Texas	10.6
23	Rhode Island	9.6
24	Arizona	9.4
24	Wyoming	9.4
26	Arkansas	9.0
27	New Mexico	8.7
28	Alabama	8.6
29	Massachusetts	8.3
29	Wisconsin	8.3
31	Michigan	7.8
32	Maryland	7.4
33	North Carolina	6.8
34	Virginia	6.3
35	Georgia	6.1
36	Illinois	5.9
37	Indiana	5.3
38	South Carolina	5.0
39	Kentucky	4.6
40	Pennsylvania	3.9
41	West Virginia	3.8
42	Utah	3.6
43	Louisiana	3.4
44	Missouri	3.3
45	Connecticut	3.0
46	Florida	2.3
46	Mississippi	2.3
48	New Jersey	2.2
49	Ohio	2.1
50	Delaware	1.7
	District of Columbia	57.7

Source: CQ Press using data from U.S. Department of Energy, Energy Information Administration
"Electricity" (http://www.eia.gov/electricity/data/state/)
*Includes hydroelectric, geothermal, solar thermal and photovoltaic, wind, wood and wood-derived fuels, and other biomass.

Average Price of Natural Gas Delivered to Industrial Customers in 2015

National Average = $3.91 per Thousand Cubic Feet

ALPHA ORDER

RANK	STATE	RATE
46	Alabama	$4.08
15	Alaska	6.86
16	Arizona	6.78
14	Arkansas	6.91
21	California	6.41
28	Colorado	5.74
23	Connecticut	6.35
3	Delaware	10.11
20	Florida	6.43
44	Georgia	4.42
1	Hawaii	19.03
27	Idaho	5.83
31	Illinois	5.47
22	Indiana	6.36
34	Iowa	5.28
45	Kansas	4.24
43	Kentucky	4.45
47	Louisiana	3.31
7	Maine	8.95
4	Maryland	9.70
6	Massachusetts	9.22
18	Michigan	6.60
38	Minnesota	4.87
39	Mississippi	4.75
12	Missouri	7.58
19	Montana	6.53
42	Nebraska	4.56
11	Nevada	8.07
2	New Hampshire	10.33
10	New Jersey	8.09
41	New Mexico	4.62
17	New York	6.62
24	North Carolina	6.34
49	North Dakota	3.13
32	Ohio	5.35
13	Oklahoma	7.51
25	Oregon	6.28
9	Pennsylvania	8.59
5	Rhode Island	9.26
40	South Carolina	4.64
33	South Dakota	5.34
36	Tennessee	5.06
50	Texas	2.89
26	Utah	5.93
30	Vermont	5.50
37	Virginia	5.02
8	Washington	8.91
48	West Virginia	3.17
29	Wisconsin	5.65
35	Wyoming	5.07

RANK ORDER

RANK	STATE	RATE
1	Hawaii	$19.03
2	New Hampshire	10.33
3	Delaware	10.11
4	Maryland	9.70
5	Rhode Island	9.26
6	Massachusetts	9.22
7	Maine	8.95
8	Washington	8.91
9	Pennsylvania	8.59
10	New Jersey	8.09
11	Nevada	8.07
12	Missouri	7.58
13	Oklahoma	7.51
14	Arkansas	6.91
15	Alaska	6.86
16	Arizona	6.78
17	New York	6.62
18	Michigan	6.60
19	Montana	6.53
20	Florida	6.43
21	California	6.41
22	Indiana	6.36
23	Connecticut	6.35
24	North Carolina	6.34
25	Oregon	6.28
26	Utah	5.93
27	Idaho	5.83
28	Colorado	5.74
29	Wisconsin	5.65
30	Vermont	5.50
31	Illinois	5.47
32	Ohio	5.35
33	South Dakota	5.34
34	Iowa	5.28
35	Wyoming	5.07
36	Tennessee	5.06
37	Virginia	5.02
38	Minnesota	4.87
39	Mississippi	4.75
40	South Carolina	4.64
41	New Mexico	4.62
42	Nebraska	4.56
43	Kentucky	4.45
44	Georgia	4.42
45	Kansas	4.24
46	Alabama	4.08
47	Louisiana	3.31
48	West Virginia	3.17
49	North Dakota	3.13
50	Texas	2.89
	District of Columbia*	NA

Source: U.S. Department of Energy, Energy Information Administration
   "Natural Gas" (http://www.eia.gov/naturalgas/annual/)
*Not available.

Average Price of Natural Gas Delivered to Commercial Customers in 2015

National Average = $7.91 per Thousand Cubic Feet

ALPHA ORDER

RANK	STATE	RATE
5	Alabama	$11.26
31	Alaska	8.01
9	Arizona	10.53
24	Arkansas	8.43
30	California	8.04
38	Colorado	7.47
19	Connecticut	8.60
8	Delaware	10.70
6	Florida	10.92
20	Georgia	8.58
1	Hawaii	31.17
36	Idaho	7.59
41	Illinois	7.29
35	Indiana	7.61
46	Iowa	6.50
16	Kansas	8.87
17	Kentucky	8.75
29	Louisiana	8.07
2	Maine	14.16
11	Maryland	9.80
7	Massachusetts	10.81
37	Michigan	7.51
40	Minnesota	7.31
34	Mississippi	7.86
14	Missouri	9.14
26	Montana	8.13
47	Nebraska	6.40
18	Nevada	8.66
3	New Hampshire	13.63
21	New Jersey	8.50
49	New Mexico	6.32
43	New York	6.85
25	North Carolina	8.27
45	North Dakota	6.62
48	Ohio	6.39
28	Oklahoma	8.12
10	Oregon	10.09
13	Pennsylvania	9.32
4	Rhode Island	11.99
22	South Carolina	8.49
50	South Dakota	6.22
23	Tennessee	8.46
42	Texas	6.95
32	Utah	7.97
33	Vermont	7.89
26	Virginia	8.13
12	Washington	9.77
14	West Virginia	9.14
44	Wisconsin	6.78
39	Wyoming	7.43

RANK ORDER

RANK	STATE	RATE
1	Hawaii	$31.17
2	Maine	14.16
3	New Hampshire	13.63
4	Rhode Island	11.99
5	Alabama	11.26
6	Florida	10.92
7	Massachusetts	10.81
8	Delaware	10.70
9	Arizona	10.53
10	Oregon	10.09
11	Maryland	9.80
12	Washington	9.77
13	Pennsylvania	9.32
14	Missouri	9.14
14	West Virginia	9.14
16	Kansas	8.87
17	Kentucky	8.75
18	Nevada	8.66
19	Connecticut	8.60
20	Georgia	8.58
21	New Jersey	8.50
22	South Carolina	8.49
23	Tennessee	8.46
24	Arkansas	8.43
25	North Carolina	8.27
26	Montana	8.13
26	Virginia	8.13
28	Oklahoma	8.12
29	Louisiana	8.07
30	California	8.04
31	Alaska	8.01
32	Utah	7.97
33	Vermont	7.89
34	Mississippi	7.86
35	Indiana	7.61
36	Idaho	7.59
37	Michigan	7.51
38	Colorado	7.47
39	Wyoming	7.43
40	Minnesota	7.31
41	Illinois	7.29
42	Texas	6.95
43	New York	6.85
44	Wisconsin	6.78
45	North Dakota	6.62
46	Iowa	6.50
47	Nebraska	6.40
48	Ohio	6.39
49	New Mexico	6.32
50	South Dakota	6.22

District of Columbia   11.07

Source: U.S. Department of Energy, Energy Information Administration
"Natural Gas" (http://www.eia.gov/naturalgas/annual/)

Average Price of Natural Gas Delivered to Residential Customers in 2015

National Average = $10.38 per Thousand Cubic Feet

ALPHA ORDER

RANK	STATE	RATE
9	Alabama	$14.13
33	Alaska	9.64
3	Arizona	17.04
20	Arkansas	11.58
22	California	11.39
47	Colorado	8.27
13	Connecticut	12.50
12	Delaware	12.62
2	Florida	19.55
6	Georgia	14.62
1	Hawaii	40.08
42	Idaho	8.59
50	Illinois	7.97
37	Indiana	8.92
44	Iowa	8.51
30	Kansas	10.17
26	Kentucky	10.87
25	Louisiana	10.91
4	Maine	16.79
15	Maryland	12.03
10	Massachusetts	13.02
39	Michigan	8.81
40	Minnesota	8.79
32	Mississippi	9.70
19	Missouri	11.60
48	Montana	8.26
38	Nebraska	8.86
16	Nevada	11.82
5	New Hampshire	16.18
45	New Jersey	8.32
41	New Mexico	8.63
23	New York	11.20
21	North Carolina	11.57
49	North Dakota	8.15
35	Ohio	9.51
29	Oklahoma	10.24
14	Oregon	12.43
24	Pennsylvania	11.04
8	Rhode Island	14.24
11	South Carolina	12.65
46	South Dakota	8.30
34	Tennessee	9.62
27	Texas	10.62
31	Utah	9.72
7	Vermont	14.56
18	Virginia	11.64
17	Washington	11.80
28	West Virginia	10.48
43	Wisconsin	8.54
36	Wyoming	9.33

RANK ORDER

RANK	STATE	RATE
1	Hawaii	$40.08
2	Florida	19.55
3	Arizona	17.04
4	Maine	16.79
5	New Hampshire	16.18
6	Georgia	14.62
7	Vermont	14.56
8	Rhode Island	14.24
9	Alabama	14.13
10	Massachusetts	13.02
11	South Carolina	12.65
12	Delaware	12.62
13	Connecticut	12.50
14	Oregon	12.43
15	Maryland	12.03
16	Nevada	11.82
17	Washington	11.80
18	Virginia	11.64
19	Missouri	11.60
20	Arkansas	11.58
21	North Carolina	11.57
22	California	11.39
23	New York	11.20
24	Pennsylvania	11.04
25	Louisiana	10.91
26	Kentucky	10.87
27	Texas	10.62
28	West Virginia	10.48
29	Oklahoma	10.24
30	Kansas	10.17
31	Utah	9.72
32	Mississippi	9.70
33	Alaska	9.64
34	Tennessee	9.62
35	Ohio	9.51
36	Wyoming	9.33
37	Indiana	8.92
38	Nebraska	8.86
39	Michigan	8.81
40	Minnesota	8.79
41	New Mexico	8.63
42	Idaho	8.59
43	Wisconsin	8.54
44	Iowa	8.51
45	New Jersey	8.32
46	South Dakota	8.30
47	Colorado	8.27
48	Montana	8.26
49	North Dakota	8.15
50	Illinois	7.97
	District of Columbia	11.98

Source: U.S. Department of Energy, Energy Information Administration
"Natural Gas" (http://www.eia.gov/naturalgas/annual/)

Natural Gas Consumption in 2015

National Total = 27,306,285,000,000 Cubic Feet*

ALPHA ORDER

RANK	STATE	CUBIC FEET	% of USA
14	Alabama	676,592,000,000	2.5%
23	Alaska	334,291,000,000	1.2%
22	Arizona	352,584,000,000	1.3%
28	Arkansas	290,125,000,000	1.1%
2	California	2,309,759,000,000	8.5%
18	Colorado	469,175,000,000	1.7%
32	Connecticut	253,469,000,000	0.9%
42	Delaware	101,968,000,000	0.4%
5	Florida	1,337,820,000,000	4.9%
12	Georgia	692,267,000,000	2.5%
50	Hawaii	2,922,000,000	0.0%
41	Idaho	104,823,000,000	0.4%
7	Illinois	992,985,000,000	3.6%
11	Indiana	718,019,000,000	2.6%
24	Iowa	319,247,000,000	1.2%
33	Kansas	253,018,000,000	0.9%
31	Kentucky	268,863,000,000	1.0%
3	Louisiana	1,465,495,000,000	5.4%
48	Maine	52,190,000,000	0.2%
37	Maryland	214,906,000,000	0.8%
20	Massachusetts	444,263,000,000	1.6%
9	Michigan	852,903,000,000	3.1%
21	Minnesota	432,270,000,000	1.6%
15	Mississippi	519,276,000,000	1.9%
30	Missouri	269,198,000,000	1.0%
46	Montana	74,016,000,000	0.3%
39	Nebraska	161,552,000,000	0.6%
27	Nevada	297,426,000,000	1.1%
47	New Hampshire	68,707,000,000	0.3%
10	New Jersey	753,153,000,000	2.8%
34	New Mexico	250,131,000,000	0.9%
4	New York	1,358,156,000,000	5.0%
17	North Carolina	498,141,000,000	1.8%
44	North Dakota	92,630,000,000	0.3%
8	Ohio	970,867,000,000	3.6%
13	Oklahoma	680,705,000,000	2.5%
35	Oregon	236,747,000,000	0.9%
6	Pennsylvania	1,285,649,000,000	4.7%
43	Rhode Island	93,997,000,000	0.3%
29	South Carolina	273,136,000,000	1.0%
45	South Dakota	79,992,000,000	0.3%
25	Tennessee	313,377,000,000	1.1%
1	Texas	4,139,551,000,000	15.2%
36	Utah	230,131,000,000	0.8%
49	Vermont	11,950,000,000	0.0%
16	Virginia	499,263,000,000	1.8%
26	Washington	308,378,000,000	1.1%
38	West Virginia	175,775,000,000	0.6%
19	Wisconsin	458,482,000,000	1.7%
40	Wyoming	138,139,000,000	0.5%

RANK ORDER

RANK	STATE	CUBIC FEET	% of USA
1	Texas	4,139,551,000,000	15.2%
2	California	2,309,759,000,000	8.5%
3	Louisiana	1,465,495,000,000	5.4%
4	New York	1,358,156,000,000	5.0%
5	Florida	1,337,820,000,000	4.9%
6	Pennsylvania	1,285,649,000,000	4.7%
7	Illinois	992,985,000,000	3.6%
8	Ohio	970,867,000,000	3.6%
9	Michigan	852,903,000,000	3.1%
10	New Jersey	753,153,000,000	2.8%
11	Indiana	718,019,000,000	2.6%
12	Georgia	692,267,000,000	2.5%
13	Oklahoma	680,705,000,000	2.5%
14	Alabama	676,592,000,000	2.5%
15	Mississippi	519,276,000,000	1.9%
16	Virginia	499,263,000,000	1.8%
17	North Carolina	498,141,000,000	1.8%
18	Colorado	469,175,000,000	1.7%
19	Wisconsin	458,482,000,000	1.7%
20	Massachusetts	444,263,000,000	1.6%
21	Minnesota	432,270,000,000	1.6%
22	Arizona	352,584,000,000	1.3%
23	Alaska	334,291,000,000	1.2%
24	Iowa	319,247,000,000	1.2%
25	Tennessee	313,377,000,000	1.1%
26	Washington	308,378,000,000	1.1%
27	Nevada	297,426,000,000	1.1%
28	Arkansas	290,125,000,000	1.1%
29	South Carolina	273,136,000,000	1.0%
30	Missouri	269,198,000,000	1.0%
31	Kentucky	268,863,000,000	1.0%
32	Connecticut	253,469,000,000	0.9%
33	Kansas	253,018,000,000	0.9%
34	New Mexico	250,131,000,000	0.9%
35	Oregon	236,747,000,000	0.9%
36	Utah	230,131,000,000	0.8%
37	Maryland	214,906,000,000	0.8%
38	West Virginia	175,775,000,000	0.6%
39	Nebraska	161,552,000,000	0.6%
40	Wyoming	138,139,000,000	0.5%
41	Idaho	104,823,000,000	0.4%
42	Delaware	101,968,000,000	0.4%
43	Rhode Island	93,997,000,000	0.3%
44	North Dakota	92,630,000,000	0.3%
45	South Dakota	79,992,000,000	0.3%
46	Montana	74,016,000,000	0.3%
47	New Hampshire	68,707,000,000	0.3%
48	Maine	52,190,000,000	0.2%
49	Vermont	11,950,000,000	0.0%
50	Hawaii	2,922,000,000	0.0%
	District of Columbia	32,320,000,000	0.1%

Source: U.S. Department of Energy, Energy Information Administration
   "Natural Gas" (http://www.eia.gov/naturalgas/annual/)
*National total includes 95,486,000,000 cubic feet of consumption in the Gulf of Mexico not shown by state.

Coal Mines in 2015

National Total = 853 Mines*

ALPHA ORDER

RANK	STATE	MINES	% of USA
5	Alabama	37	4.3%
22	Alaska	1	0.1%
22	Arizona	1	0.1%
19	Arkansas	2	0.2%
NA	California**	NA	NA
13	Colorado	9	1.1%
NA	Connecticut**	NA	NA
NA	Delaware**	NA	NA
NA	Florida**	NA	NA
NA	Georgia**	NA	NA
NA	Hawaii**	NA	NA
NA	Idaho**	NA	NA
8	Illinois	23	2.7%
7	Indiana	24	2.8%
NA	Iowa**	NA	NA
22	Kansas	1	0.1%
1	Kentucky	210	24.6%
19	Louisiana	2	0.2%
NA	Maine**	NA	NA
9	Maryland	18	2.1%
NA	Massachusetts**	NA	NA
NA	Michigan**	NA	NA
NA	Minnesota**	NA	NA
19	Mississippi	2	0.2%
22	Missouri	1	0.1%
15	Montana	6	0.7%
NA	Nebraska**	NA	NA
NA	Nevada**	NA	NA
NA	New Hampshire**	NA	NA
NA	New Jersey**	NA	NA
18	New Mexico	3	0.4%
NA	New York**	NA	NA
NA	North Carolina**	NA	NA
17	North Dakota	4	0.5%
6	Ohio	25	2.9%
16	Oklahoma	5	0.6%
NA	Oregon**	NA	NA
2	Pennsylvania	195	22.9%
NA	Rhode Island**	NA	NA
NA	South Carolina**	NA	NA
NA	South Dakota**	NA	NA
12	Tennessee	10	1.2%
11	Texas	14	1.6%
13	Utah	9	1.1%
NA	Vermont**	NA	NA
4	Virginia	65	7.6%
NA	Washington**	NA	NA
3	West Virginia	151	17.7%
NA	Wisconsin**	NA	NA
10	Wyoming	16	1.9%

RANK ORDER

RANK	STATE	MINES	% of USA
1	Kentucky	210	24.6%
2	Pennsylvania	195	22.9%
3	West Virginia	151	17.7%
4	Virginia	65	7.6%
5	Alabama	37	4.3%
6	Ohio	25	2.9%
7	Indiana	24	2.8%
8	Illinois	23	2.7%
9	Maryland	18	2.1%
10	Wyoming	16	1.9%
11	Texas	14	1.6%
12	Tennessee	10	1.2%
13	Colorado	9	1.1%
13	Utah	9	1.1%
15	Montana	6	0.7%
16	Oklahoma	5	0.6%
17	North Dakota	4	0.5%
18	New Mexico	3	0.4%
19	Arkansas	2	0.2%
19	Louisiana	2	0.2%
19	Mississippi	2	0.2%
22	Alaska	1	0.1%
22	Arizona	1	0.1%
22	Kansas	1	0.1%
22	Missouri	1	0.1%
NA	California**	NA	NA
NA	Connecticut**	NA	NA
NA	Delaware**	NA	NA
NA	Florida**	NA	NA
NA	Georgia**	NA	NA
NA	Hawaii**	NA	NA
NA	Idaho**	NA	NA
NA	Iowa**	NA	NA
NA	Maine**	NA	NA
NA	Massachusetts**	NA	NA
NA	Michigan**	NA	NA
NA	Minnesota**	NA	NA
NA	Nebraska**	NA	NA
NA	Nevada**	NA	NA
NA	New Hampshire**	NA	NA
NA	New Jersey**	NA	NA
NA	New York**	NA	NA
NA	North Carolina**	NA	NA
NA	Oregon**	NA	NA
NA	Rhode Island**	NA	NA
NA	South Carolina**	NA	NA
NA	South Dakota**	NA	NA
NA	Vermont**	NA	NA
NA	Washington**	NA	NA
NA	Wisconsin**	NA	NA
	District of Columbia**	NA	NA

Source: U.S. Department of Energy, Energy Information Administration
   "Annual Coal Report" (http://www.eia.gov/coal/annual/)
*National total includes 19 coal mines in refuse recovery not shown by state.
**Not available or no mines.

Coal Production in 2015

National Total = 896,941,000 Short Tons*

ALPHA ORDER

RANK	STATE	SHORT TONS	% of USA
15	Alabama	13,191,000	1.5%
20	Alaska	1,177,000	0.1%
16	Arizona	6,805,000	0.8%
25	Arkansas	91,000	0.0%
NA	California**	NA	NA
11	Colorado	18,879,000	2.1%
NA	Connecticut**	NA	NA
NA	Delaware**	NA	NA
NA	Florida**	NA	NA
NA	Georgia**	NA	NA
NA	Hawaii**	NA	NA
NA	Idaho**	NA	NA
4	Illinois	56,101,000	6.3%
8	Indiana	34,295,000	3.8%
NA	Iowa**	NA	NA
23	Kansas	199,000	0.0%
3	Kentucky	61,425,000	6.8%
17	Louisiana	3,439,000	0.4%
NA	Maine**	NA	NA
19	Maryland	1,922,000	0.2%
NA	Massachusetts**	NA	NA
NA	Michigan**	NA	NA
NA	Minnesota**	NA	NA
18	Mississippi	3,143,000	0.4%
24	Missouri	138,000	0.0%
6	Montana	41,864,000	4.7%
NA	Nebraska**	NA	NA
NA	Nevada**	NA	NA
NA	New Hampshire**	NA	NA
NA	New Jersey**	NA	NA
10	New Mexico	19,679,000	2.2%
NA	New York**	NA	NA
NA	North Carolina**	NA	NA
9	North Dakota	28,802,000	3.2%
12	Ohio	17,041,000	1.9%
22	Oklahoma	780,000	0.1%
NA	Oregon**	NA	NA
5	Pennsylvania	50,031,000	5.6%
NA	Rhode Island**	NA	NA
NA	South Carolina**	NA	NA
NA	South Dakota**	NA	NA
21	Tennessee	897,000	0.1%
7	Texas	35,918,000	4.0%
13	Utah	14,419,000	1.6%
NA	Vermont**	NA	NA
14	Virginia	13,914,000	1.6%
NA	Washington**	NA	NA
2	West Virginia	95,633,000	10.7%
NA	Wisconsin**	NA	NA
1	Wyoming	375,773,000	41.9%

RANK ORDER

RANK	STATE	SHORT TONS	% of USA
1	Wyoming	375,773,000	41.9%
2	West Virginia	95,633,000	10.7%
3	Kentucky	61,425,000	6.8%
4	Illinois	56,101,000	6.3%
5	Pennsylvania	50,031,000	5.6%
6	Montana	41,864,000	4.7%
7	Texas	35,918,000	4.0%
8	Indiana	34,295,000	3.8%
9	North Dakota	28,802,000	3.2%
10	New Mexico	19,679,000	2.2%
11	Colorado	18,879,000	2.1%
12	Ohio	17,041,000	1.9%
13	Utah	14,419,000	1.6%
14	Virginia	13,914,000	1.6%
15	Alabama	13,191,000	1.5%
16	Arizona	6,805,000	0.8%
17	Louisiana	3,439,000	0.4%
18	Mississippi	3,143,000	0.4%
19	Maryland	1,922,000	0.2%
20	Alaska	1,177,000	0.1%
21	Tennessee	897,000	0.1%
22	Oklahoma	780,000	0.1%
23	Kansas	199,000	0.0%
24	Missouri	138,000	0.0%
25	Arkansas	91,000	0.0%
NA	California**	NA	NA
NA	Connecticut**	NA	NA
NA	Delaware**	NA	NA
NA	Florida**	NA	NA
NA	Georgia**	NA	NA
NA	Hawaii**	NA	NA
NA	Idaho**	NA	NA
NA	Iowa**	NA	NA
NA	Maine**	NA	NA
NA	Massachusetts**	NA	NA
NA	Michigan**	NA	NA
NA	Minnesota**	NA	NA
NA	Nebraska**	NA	NA
NA	Nevada**	NA	NA
NA	New Hampshire**	NA	NA
NA	New Jersey**	NA	NA
NA	New York**	NA	NA
NA	North Carolina**	NA	NA
NA	Oregon**	NA	NA
NA	Rhode Island**	NA	NA
NA	South Carolina**	NA	NA
NA	South Dakota**	NA	NA
NA	Vermont**	NA	NA
NA	Washington**	NA	NA
NA	Wisconsin**	NA	NA
	District of Columbia**	NA	NA

Source: U.S. Department of Energy, Energy Information Administration
"Annual Coal Report" (http://www.eia.gov/coal/annual/)
*National total includes 1,384,000 short tons from refuse recovery not shown by state.
**Not available or no production.

Gasoline Used in 2015

National Total = 141,223,831,000 Gallons*

ALPHA ORDER

RANK	STATE	GALLONS	% of USA
21	Alabama	2,693,621,000	1.9%
50	Alaska	292,676,000	0.2%
17	Arizona	2,817,171,000	2.0%
32	Arkansas	1,449,145,000	1.0%
1	California	15,119,963,000	10.7%
25	Colorado	2,267,717,000	1.6%
31	Connecticut	1,483,597,000	1.1%
45	Delaware	469,581,000	0.3%
3	Florida	8,801,605,000	6.2%
7	Georgia	4,958,128,000	3.5%
46	Hawaii	461,423,000	0.3%
40	Idaho	750,158,000	0.5%
5	Illinois	5,107,398,000	3.6%
14	Indiana	3,155,186,000	2.2%
29	Iowa	1,665,151,000	1.2%
33	Kansas	1,284,413,000	0.9%
26	Kentucky	2,184,747,000	1.5%
24	Louisiana	2,340,903,000	1.7%
39	Maine	784,443,000	0.6%
16	Maryland	2,842,601,000	2.0%
20	Massachusetts	2,797,063,000	2.0%
9	Michigan	4,697,295,000	3.3%
23	Minnesota	2,563,490,000	1.8%
28	Mississippi	1,693,817,000	1.2%
15	Missouri	3,139,992,000	2.2%
42	Montana	539,982,000	0.4%
37	Nebraska	891,405,000	0.6%
34	Nevada	1,153,966,000	0.8%
41	New Hampshire	716,055,000	0.5%
11	New Jersey	4,116,723,000	2.9%
36	New Mexico	981,607,000	0.7%
4	New York	5,476,920,000	3.9%
10	North Carolina	4,520,357,000	3.2%
43	North Dakota	471,451,000	0.3%
6	Ohio	5,099,848,000	3.6%
27	Oklahoma	1,956,297,000	1.4%
30	Oregon	1,556,347,000	1.1%
8	Pennsylvania	4,910,701,000	3.5%
47	Rhode Island	380,918,000	0.3%
18	South Carolina	2,816,907,000	2.0%
44	South Dakota	471,443,000	0.3%
13	Tennessee	3,258,699,000	2.3%
2	Texas	13,879,235,000	9.8%
35	Utah	1,117,474,000	0.8%
49	Vermont	312,937,000	0.2%
12	Virginia	4,024,639,000	2.8%
19	Washington	2,798,481,000	2.0%
38	West Virginia	865,036,000	0.6%
22	Wisconsin	2,602,085,000	1.8%
48	Wyoming	369,150,000	0.3%

RANK ORDER

RANK	STATE	GALLONS	% of USA
1	California	15,119,963,000	10.7%
2	Texas	13,879,235,000	9.8%
3	Florida	8,801,605,000	6.2%
4	New York	5,476,920,000	3.9%
5	Illinois	5,107,398,000	3.6%
6	Ohio	5,099,848,000	3.6%
7	Georgia	4,958,128,000	3.5%
8	Pennsylvania	4,910,701,000	3.5%
9	Michigan	4,697,295,000	3.3%
10	North Carolina	4,520,357,000	3.2%
11	New Jersey	4,116,723,000	2.9%
12	Virginia	4,024,639,000	2.8%
13	Tennessee	3,258,699,000	2.3%
14	Indiana	3,155,186,000	2.2%
15	Missouri	3,139,992,000	2.2%
16	Maryland	2,842,601,000	2.0%
17	Arizona	2,817,171,000	2.0%
18	South Carolina	2,816,907,000	2.0%
19	Washington	2,798,481,000	2.0%
20	Massachusetts	2,797,063,000	2.0%
21	Alabama	2,693,621,000	1.9%
22	Wisconsin	2,602,085,000	1.8%
23	Minnesota	2,563,490,000	1.8%
24	Louisiana	2,340,903,000	1.7%
25	Colorado	2,267,717,000	1.6%
26	Kentucky	2,184,747,000	1.5%
27	Oklahoma	1,956,297,000	1.4%
28	Mississippi	1,693,817,000	1.2%
29	Iowa	1,665,151,000	1.2%
30	Oregon	1,556,347,000	1.1%
31	Connecticut	1,483,597,000	1.1%
32	Arkansas	1,449,145,000	1.0%
33	Kansas	1,284,413,000	0.9%
34	Nevada	1,153,966,000	0.8%
35	Utah	1,117,474,000	0.8%
36	New Mexico	981,607,000	0.7%
37	Nebraska	891,405,000	0.6%
38	West Virginia	865,036,000	0.6%
39	Maine	784,443,000	0.6%
40	Idaho	750,158,000	0.5%
41	New Hampshire	716,055,000	0.5%
42	Montana	539,982,000	0.4%
43	North Dakota	471,451,000	0.3%
44	South Dakota	471,443,000	0.3%
45	Delaware	469,581,000	0.3%
46	Hawaii	461,423,000	0.3%
47	Rhode Island	380,918,000	0.3%
48	Wyoming	369,150,000	0.3%
49	Vermont	312,937,000	0.2%
50	Alaska	292,676,000	0.2%
	District of Columbia	113,884,000	0.1%

Source: U.S. Department of Transportation, Federal Highway Administration
"Highway Statistics 2015" (Table MF-21, http://www.fhwa.dot.gov/policyinformation/statistics/2015/)
*Includes gasoline for highway and nonhighway uses as well as for losses allowed for evaporation and handling. "Gasoline" includes gasohol but excludes "special fuels" such as diesel.

Per Capita Gasoline Used in 2015

National Per Capita = 440 Gallons*

<table>
<tr><td colspan="3">ALPHA ORDER</td><td colspan="3">RANK ORDER</td></tr>
<tr><td>RANK</td><td>STATE</td><td>PER CAPITA</td><td>RANK</td><td>STATE</td><td>PER CAPITA</td></tr>
<tr><td>6</td><td>Alabama</td><td>555</td><td>1</td><td>Wyoming</td><td>629</td></tr>
<tr><td>42</td><td>Alaska</td><td>397</td><td>2</td><td>North Dakota</td><td>623</td></tr>
<tr><td>38</td><td>Arizona</td><td>413</td><td>3</td><td>Maine</td><td>590</td></tr>
<tr><td>19</td><td>Arkansas</td><td>487</td><td>4</td><td>South Carolina</td><td>575</td></tr>
<tr><td>44</td><td>California</td><td>388</td><td>5</td><td>Mississippi</td><td>567</td></tr>
<tr><td>36</td><td>Colorado</td><td>416</td><td>6</td><td>Alabama</td><td>555</td></tr>
<tr><td>37</td><td>Connecticut</td><td>414</td><td>7</td><td>South Dakota</td><td>550</td></tr>
<tr><td>16</td><td>Delaware</td><td>497</td><td>8</td><td>New Hampshire</td><td>538</td></tr>
<tr><td>35</td><td>Florida</td><td>435</td><td>9</td><td>Iowa</td><td>533</td></tr>
<tr><td>20</td><td>Georgia</td><td>486</td><td>10</td><td>Montana</td><td>523</td></tr>
<tr><td>49</td><td>Hawaii</td><td>324</td><td>11</td><td>Missouri</td><td>517</td></tr>
<tr><td>30</td><td>Idaho</td><td>454</td><td>12</td><td>Texas</td><td>506</td></tr>
<tr><td>41</td><td>Illinois</td><td>398</td><td>13</td><td>Louisiana</td><td>501</td></tr>
<tr><td>22</td><td>Indiana</td><td>477</td><td>13</td><td>Oklahoma</td><td>501</td></tr>
<tr><td>9</td><td>Iowa</td><td>533</td><td>15</td><td>Vermont</td><td>500</td></tr>
<tr><td>33</td><td>Kansas</td><td>442</td><td>16</td><td>Delaware</td><td>497</td></tr>
<tr><td>17</td><td>Kentucky</td><td>494</td><td>17</td><td>Kentucky</td><td>494</td></tr>
<tr><td>13</td><td>Louisiana</td><td>501</td><td>17</td><td>Tennessee</td><td>494</td></tr>
<tr><td>3</td><td>Maine</td><td>590</td><td>19</td><td>Arkansas</td><td>487</td></tr>
<tr><td>23</td><td>Maryland</td><td>474</td><td>20</td><td>Georgia</td><td>486</td></tr>
<tr><td>39</td><td>Massachusetts</td><td>412</td><td>21</td><td>Virginia</td><td>481</td></tr>
<tr><td>23</td><td>Michigan</td><td>474</td><td>22</td><td>Indiana</td><td>477</td></tr>
<tr><td>28</td><td>Minnesota</td><td>468</td><td>23</td><td>Maryland</td><td>474</td></tr>
<tr><td>5</td><td>Mississippi</td><td>567</td><td>23</td><td>Michigan</td><td>474</td></tr>
<tr><td>11</td><td>Missouri</td><td>517</td><td>25</td><td>New Mexico</td><td>472</td></tr>
<tr><td>10</td><td>Montana</td><td>523</td><td>26</td><td>Nebraska</td><td>471</td></tr>
<tr><td>26</td><td>Nebraska</td><td>471</td><td>27</td><td>West Virginia</td><td>470</td></tr>
<tr><td>40</td><td>Nevada</td><td>400</td><td>28</td><td>Minnesota</td><td>468</td></tr>
<tr><td>8</td><td>New Hampshire</td><td>538</td><td>29</td><td>New Jersey</td><td>461</td></tr>
<tr><td>29</td><td>New Jersey</td><td>461</td><td>30</td><td>Idaho</td><td>454</td></tr>
<tr><td>25</td><td>New Mexico</td><td>472</td><td>31</td><td>Wisconsin</td><td>451</td></tr>
<tr><td>50</td><td>New York</td><td>277</td><td>32</td><td>North Carolina</td><td>450</td></tr>
<tr><td>32</td><td>North Carolina</td><td>450</td><td>33</td><td>Kansas</td><td>442</td></tr>
<tr><td>2</td><td>North Dakota</td><td>623</td><td>34</td><td>Ohio</td><td>439</td></tr>
<tr><td>34</td><td>Ohio</td><td>439</td><td>35</td><td>Florida</td><td>435</td></tr>
<tr><td>13</td><td>Oklahoma</td><td>501</td><td>36</td><td>Colorado</td><td>416</td></tr>
<tr><td>45</td><td>Oregon</td><td>387</td><td>37</td><td>Connecticut</td><td>414</td></tr>
<tr><td>46</td><td>Pennsylvania</td><td>384</td><td>38</td><td>Arizona</td><td>413</td></tr>
<tr><td>48</td><td>Rhode Island</td><td>361</td><td>39</td><td>Massachusetts</td><td>412</td></tr>
<tr><td>4</td><td>South Carolina</td><td>575</td><td>40</td><td>Nevada</td><td>400</td></tr>
<tr><td>7</td><td>South Dakota</td><td>550</td><td>41</td><td>Illinois</td><td>398</td></tr>
<tr><td>17</td><td>Tennessee</td><td>494</td><td>42</td><td>Alaska</td><td>397</td></tr>
<tr><td>12</td><td>Texas</td><td>506</td><td>43</td><td>Washington</td><td>391</td></tr>
<tr><td>47</td><td>Utah</td><td>374</td><td>44</td><td>California</td><td>388</td></tr>
<tr><td>15</td><td>Vermont</td><td>500</td><td>45</td><td>Oregon</td><td>387</td></tr>
<tr><td>21</td><td>Virginia</td><td>481</td><td>46</td><td>Pennsylvania</td><td>384</td></tr>
<tr><td>43</td><td>Washington</td><td>391</td><td>47</td><td>Utah</td><td>374</td></tr>
<tr><td>27</td><td>West Virginia</td><td>470</td><td>48</td><td>Rhode Island</td><td>361</td></tr>
<tr><td>31</td><td>Wisconsin</td><td>451</td><td>49</td><td>Hawaii</td><td>324</td></tr>
<tr><td>1</td><td>Wyoming</td><td>629</td><td>50</td><td>New York</td><td>277</td></tr>
<tr><td></td><td></td><td></td><td></td><td>District of Columbia</td><td>170</td></tr>
</table>

Source: CQ Press using data from U.S. Department of Transportation, Federal Highway Administration
"Highway Statistics 2015" (Table MF-21, http://www.fhwa.dot.gov/policyinformation/statistics/2015/)
*Includes gasoline for highway and nonhighway uses as well as for losses allowed for evaporation and handling. "Gasoline" includes gasohol but excludes "special fuels" such as diesel.

Daily Production of Crude Oil in 2015

National Total = 9,415,110 Barrels a Day*

ALPHA ORDER

RANK	STATE	BARRELS	% of USA
15	Alabama	26,564	0.3%
4	Alaska	482,852	5.1%
30	Arizona	101	0.0%
20	Arkansas	16,890	0.2%
3	California	551,463	5.9%
7	Colorado	345,841	3.7%
NA	Connecticut**	NA	NA
NA	Delaware**	NA	NA
24	Florida	6,049	0.1%
NA	Georgia**	NA	NA
NA	Hawaii**	NA	NA
NA	Idaho**	NA	NA
16	Illinois	26,088	0.3%
23	Indiana	6,079	0.1%
NA	Iowa**	NA	NA
10	Kansas	124,605	1.3%
22	Kentucky	7,841	0.1%
9	Louisiana	172,277	1.8%
NA	Maine**	NA	NA
NA	Maryland**	NA	NA
NA	Massachusetts**	NA	NA
19	Michigan	17,600	0.2%
NA	Minnesota**	NA	NA
14	Mississippi	68,268	0.7%
29	Missouri	408	0.0%
12	Montana	78,249	0.8%
21	Nebraska	7,934	0.1%
27	Nevada	770	0.0%
NA	New Hampshire**	NA	NA
NA	New Jersey**	NA	NA
6	New Mexico	402,044	4.3%
28	New York	764	0.0%
NA	North Carolina**	NA	NA
2	North Dakota	1,176,567	12.5%
13	Ohio	70,962	0.8%
5	Oklahoma	432,247	4.6%
NA	Oregon**	NA	NA
18	Pennsylvania	19,159	0.2%
NA	Rhode Island**	NA	NA
NA	South Carolina**	NA	NA
25	South Dakota	4,564	0.0%
26	Tennessee	811	0.0%
1	Texas	3,461,877	36.8%
11	Utah	101,334	1.1%
NA	Vermont**	NA	NA
31	Virginia	30	0.0%
NA	Washington**	NA	NA
17	West Virginia	21,836	0.2%
NA	Wisconsin**	NA	NA
8	Wyoming	236,984	2.5%

RANK ORDER

RANK	STATE	BARRELS	% of USA
1	Texas	3,461,877	36.8%
2	North Dakota	1,176,567	12.5%
3	California	551,463	5.9%
4	Alaska	482,852	5.1%
5	Oklahoma	432,247	4.6%
6	New Mexico	402,044	4.3%
7	Colorado	345,841	3.7%
8	Wyoming	236,984	2.5%
9	Louisiana	172,277	1.8%
10	Kansas	124,605	1.3%
11	Utah	101,334	1.1%
12	Montana	78,249	0.8%
13	Ohio	70,962	0.8%
14	Mississippi	68,268	0.7%
15	Alabama	26,564	0.3%
16	Illinois	26,088	0.3%
17	West Virginia	21,836	0.2%
18	Pennsylvania	19,159	0.2%
19	Michigan	17,600	0.2%
20	Arkansas	16,890	0.2%
21	Nebraska	7,934	0.1%
22	Kentucky	7,841	0.1%
23	Indiana	6,079	0.1%
24	Florida	6,049	0.1%
25	South Dakota	4,564	0.0%
26	Tennessee	811	0.0%
27	Nevada	770	0.0%
28	New York	764	0.0%
29	Missouri	408	0.0%
30	Arizona	101	0.0%
31	Virginia	30	0.0%
NA	Connecticut**	NA	NA
NA	Delaware**	NA	NA
NA	Georgia**	NA	NA
NA	Hawaii**	NA	NA
NA	Idaho**	NA	NA
NA	Iowa**	NA	NA
NA	Maine**	NA	NA
NA	Maryland**	NA	NA
NA	Massachusetts**	NA	NA
NA	Minnesota**	NA	NA
NA	New Hampshire**	NA	NA
NA	New Jersey**	NA	NA
NA	North Carolina**	NA	NA
NA	Oregon**	NA	NA
NA	Rhode Island**	NA	NA
NA	South Carolina**	NA	NA
NA	Vermont**	NA	NA
NA	Washington**	NA	NA
NA	Wisconsin**	NA	NA
	District of Columbia**	NA	NA

Source: CQ Press using data from U.S. Department of Energy, Energy Information Administration
"Petroleum Supply Annual 2015, Volume 1" (http://tonto.eia.doe.gov/dnav/pet/pet_crd_crpdn_adc_mbbl_m.htm)
*National total includes 1,546,049 barrels a day in federal offshore production. Figures for Alaska, California, Louisiana, and Texas include state offshore production.
**No reported production.

Fossil Fuel Emissions in 2014

National Total = 5,208,200,000 Metric Tons of Carbon Dioxide (CO2)*

ALPHA ORDER

RANK	STATE	TONS OF CO2	% of USA
15	Alabama	121,491,810	2.3%
41	Alaska	34,753,239	0.7%
23	Arizona	92,805,856	1.8%
29	Arkansas	68,605,439	1.3%
2	California	359,127,968	6.9%
24	Colorado	90,801,793	1.7%
40	Connecticut	35,126,546	0.7%
48	Delaware	13,317,480	0.3%
6	Florida	227,042,928	4.4%
11	Georgia	138,904,577	2.7%
43	Hawaii	18,202,055	0.3%
45	Idaho	16,644,548	0.3%
4	Illinois	233,376,040	4.5%
8	Indiana	203,253,179	3.9%
25	Iowa	83,210,492	1.6%
28	Kansas	69,606,420	1.3%
12	Kentucky	137,638,978	2.6%
7	Louisiana	206,913,616	4.0%
44	Maine	16,647,897	0.3%
34	Maryland	62,061,075	1.2%
32	Massachusetts	64,000,946	1.2%
10	Michigan	161,456,896	3.1%
22	Minnesota	94,082,628	1.8%
33	Mississippi	63,705,726	1.2%
13	Missouri	131,351,275	2.5%
42	Montana	32,246,039	0.6%
36	Nebraska	51,755,395	1.0%
39	Nevada	36,974,933	0.7%
47	New Hampshire	14,927,001	0.3%
16	New Jersey	114,206,873	2.2%
37	New Mexico	50,209,832	1.0%
9	New York	169,932,078	3.3%
14	North Carolina	125,647,668	2.4%
35	North Dakota	55,318,033	1.1%
5	Ohio	229,042,928	4.4%
17	Oklahoma	104,393,890	2.0%
38	Oregon	37,942,207	0.7%
3	Pennsylvania	242,135,305	4.6%
49	Rhode Island	10,643,019	0.2%
26	South Carolina	74,388,716	1.4%
46	South Dakota	15,279,918	0.3%
19	Tennessee	102,779,455	2.0%
1	Texas	708,810,034	13.6%
31	Utah	64,442,977	1.2%
50	Vermont	5,876,899	0.1%
18	Virginia	103,412,774	2.0%
27	Washington	73,451,344	1.4%
21	West Virginia	97,090,279	1.9%
20	Wisconsin	100,573,299	1.9%
30	Wyoming	65,162,680	1.3%

RANK ORDER

RANK	STATE	TONS OF CO2	% of USA
1	Texas	708,810,034	13.6%
2	California	359,127,968	6.9%
3	Pennsylvania	242,135,305	4.6%
4	Illinois	233,376,040	4.5%
5	Ohio	229,042,928	4.4%
6	Florida	227,042,928	4.4%
7	Louisiana	206,913,616	4.0%
8	Indiana	203,253,179	3.9%
9	New York	169,932,078	3.3%
10	Michigan	161,456,896	3.1%
11	Georgia	138,904,577	2.7%
12	Kentucky	137,638,978	2.6%
13	Missouri	131,351,275	2.5%
14	North Carolina	125,647,668	2.4%
15	Alabama	121,491,810	2.3%
16	New Jersey	114,206,873	2.2%
17	Oklahoma	104,393,890	2.0%
18	Virginia	103,412,774	2.0%
19	Tennessee	102,779,455	2.0%
20	Wisconsin	100,573,299	1.9%
21	West Virginia	97,090,279	1.9%
22	Minnesota	94,082,628	1.8%
23	Arizona	92,805,856	1.8%
24	Colorado	90,801,793	1.7%
25	Iowa	83,210,492	1.6%
26	South Carolina	74,388,716	1.4%
27	Washington	73,451,344	1.4%
28	Kansas	69,606,420	1.3%
29	Arkansas	68,605,439	1.3%
30	Wyoming	65,162,680	1.3%
31	Utah	64,442,977	1.2%
32	Massachusetts	64,000,946	1.2%
33	Mississippi	63,705,726	1.2%
34	Maryland	62,061,075	1.2%
35	North Dakota	55,318,033	1.1%
36	Nebraska	51,755,395	1.0%
37	New Mexico	50,209,832	1.0%
38	Oregon	37,942,207	0.7%
39	Nevada	36,974,933	0.7%
40	Connecticut	35,126,546	0.7%
41	Alaska	34,753,239	0.7%
42	Montana	32,246,039	0.6%
43	Hawaii	18,202,055	0.3%
44	Maine	16,647,897	0.3%
45	Idaho	16,644,548	0.3%
46	South Dakota	15,279,918	0.3%
47	New Hampshire	14,927,001	0.3%
48	Delaware	13,317,480	0.3%
49	Rhode Island	10,643,019	0.2%
50	Vermont	5,876,899	0.1%
	District of Columbia	3,000,211	0.1%

Source: U.S. Environmental Protection Agency
"Energy CO2 Emissions by State" (https://www.epa.gov/statelocalclimate/state-energy-co2-emissions)
*Carbon dioxide (CO2) emissions from fossil fuel combustion. This represents the largest source (94%) of total CO2 emissions from all emission sources. Emissions are based on the location where fossil fuels are used. Fuels can be used in one state to generate electricity consumed in another. National figure no longer includes non-energy use of fuels.

Per Capita Fossil Fuel Emissions in 2014

National Per Capita = 16.3 Metric Tons of Carbon Dioxide (CO2)*

ALPHA ORDER				RANK ORDER		
RANK	STATE	PER CAPITA		RANK	STATE	PER CAPITA
13	Alabama	25.1		1	Wyoming	111.6
4	Alaska	47.2		2	North Dakota	74.8
31	Arizona	13.8		3	West Virginia	52.5
16	Arkansas	23.1		4	Alaska	47.2
49	California	9.3		5	Louisiana	44.5
26	Colorado	17.0		6	Montana	31.5
45	Connecticut	9.8		7	Kentucky	31.2
30	Delaware	14.2		8	Indiana	30.8
39	Florida	11.4		9	Nebraska	27.5
31	Georgia	13.8		10	Oklahoma	26.9
34	Hawaii	12.9		11	Iowa	26.8
43	Idaho	10.2		12	Texas	26.3
22	Illinois	18.1		13	Alabama	25.1
8	Indiana	30.8		14	New Mexico	24.1
11	Iowa	26.8		15	Kansas	24.0
15	Kansas	24.0		16	Arkansas	23.1
7	Kentucky	31.2		17	Utah	21.9
5	Louisiana	44.5		18	Missouri	21.7
37	Maine	12.5		19	Mississippi	21.3
41	Maryland	10.4		20	Ohio	19.8
47	Massachusetts	9.5		21	Pennsylvania	18.9
27	Michigan	16.3		22	Illinois	18.1
25	Minnesota	17.3		23	South Dakota	17.9
19	Mississippi	21.3		24	Wisconsin	17.5
18	Missouri	21.7		25	Minnesota	17.3
6	Montana	31.5		26	Colorado	17.0
9	Nebraska	27.5		27	Michigan	16.3
33	Nevada	13.1		28	Tennessee	15.7
40	New Hampshire	11.2		29	South Carolina	15.4
35	New Jersey	12.8		30	Delaware	14.2
14	New Mexico	24.1		31	Arizona	13.8
50	New York	8.6		31	Georgia	13.8
36	North Carolina	12.6		33	Nevada	13.1
2	North Dakota	74.8		34	Hawaii	12.9
20	Ohio	19.8		35	New Jersey	12.8
10	Oklahoma	26.9		36	North Carolina	12.6
46	Oregon	9.6		37	Maine	12.5
21	Pennsylvania	18.9		38	Virginia	12.4
44	Rhode Island	10.1		39	Florida	11.4
29	South Carolina	15.4		40	New Hampshire	11.2
23	South Dakota	17.9		41	Maryland	10.4
28	Tennessee	15.7		41	Washington	10.4
12	Texas	26.3		43	Idaho	10.2
17	Utah	21.9		44	Rhode Island	10.1
48	Vermont	9.4		45	Connecticut	9.8
38	Virginia	12.4		46	Oregon	9.6
41	Washington	10.4		47	Massachusetts	9.5
3	West Virginia	52.5		48	Vermont	9.4
24	Wisconsin	17.5		49	California	9.3
1	Wyoming	111.6		50	New York	8.6
					District of Columbia	4.6

Source: CQ Press using data from U.S. Environmental Protection Agency
   "Energy CO2 Emissions by State" (https://www.epa.gov/statelocalclimate/state-energy-co2-emissions)
*Carbon dioxide (CO2) emissions from fossil fuel combustion. This represents the largest source (94%) of total CO2 emissions from all emission sources. Emissions are based on the location where fossil fuels are used. Fuels can be used in one state to generate electricity consumed in another. National figure no longer includes non-energy use of fuels.

Percent Change in Fossil Fuel Emissions: 2010 to 2014

National Percent Change = 2.8% Decrease*

ALPHA ORDER

RANK	STATE	PERCENT CHANGE
39	Alabama	(7.1)
44	Alaska	(9.3)
20	Arizona	(2.2)
4	Arkansas	4.6
19	California	(1.9)
29	Colorado	(4.0)
25	Connecticut	(3.2)
2	Delaware	11.8
34	Florida	(5.6)
50	Georgia	(18.5)
24	Hawaii	(3.1)
6	Idaho	4.0
11	Illinois	1.3
33	Indiana	(5.4)
39	Iowa	(7.1)
28	Kansas	(3.9)
43	Kentucky	(8.0)
32	Louisiana	(4.8)
42	Maine	(7.9)
46	Maryland	(10.7)
47	Massachusetts	(10.9)
18	Michigan	(1.8)
8	Minnesota	2.4
21	Mississippi	(2.3)
21	Missouri	(2.3)
38	Montana	(6.7)
4	Nebraska	4.6
15	Nevada	(1.2)
45	New Hampshire	(9.6)
14	New Jersey	(0.7)
36	New Mexico	(5.8)
23	New York	(2.6)
47	North Carolina	(10.9)
1	North Dakota	14.3
41	Ohio	(7.2)
16	Oklahoma	(1.3)
37	Oregon	(6.6)
30	Pennsylvania	(4.2)
27	Rhode Island	(3.6)
49	South Carolina	(11.4)
10	South Dakota	1.7
34	Tennessee	(5.6)
3	Texas	9.2
9	Utah	2.2
13	Vermont	(0.5)
31	Virginia	(4.4)
26	Washington	(3.3)
16	West Virginia	(1.3)
7	Wisconsin	2.5
12	Wyoming	0.5

RANK ORDER

RANK	STATE	PERCENT CHANGE
1	North Dakota	14.3
2	Delaware	11.8
3	Texas	9.2
4	Arkansas	4.6
4	Nebraska	4.6
6	Idaho	4.0
7	Wisconsin	2.5
8	Minnesota	2.4
9	Utah	2.2
10	South Dakota	1.7
11	Illinois	1.3
12	Wyoming	0.5
13	Vermont	(0.5)
14	New Jersey	(0.7)
15	Nevada	(1.2)
16	Oklahoma	(1.3)
16	West Virginia	(1.3)
18	Michigan	(1.8)
19	California	(1.9)
20	Arizona	(2.2)
21	Mississippi	(2.3)
21	Missouri	(2.3)
23	New York	(2.6)
24	Hawaii	(3.1)
25	Connecticut	(3.2)
26	Washington	(3.3)
27	Rhode Island	(3.6)
28	Kansas	(3.9)
29	Colorado	(4.0)
30	Pennsylvania	(4.2)
31	Virginia	(4.4)
32	Louisiana	(4.8)
33	Indiana	(5.4)
34	Florida	(5.6)
34	Tennessee	(5.6)
36	New Mexico	(5.8)
37	Oregon	(6.6)
38	Montana	(6.7)
39	Alabama	(7.1)
39	Iowa	(7.1)
41	Ohio	(7.2)
42	Maine	(7.9)
43	Kentucky	(8.0)
44	Alaska	(9.3)
45	New Hampshire	(9.6)
46	Maryland	(10.7)
47	Massachusetts	(10.9)
47	North Carolina	(10.9)
49	South Carolina	(11.4)
50	Georgia	(18.5)

District of Columbia — (7.2)

Source: CQ Press using data from U.S. Environmental Protection Agency
"Energy CO2 Emissions by State" (https://www.epa.gov/statelocalclimate/state-energy-co2-emissions)
*Based on metric tons of carbon dioxide (CO2).

Toxic Releases: Total Pollution Released in 2015

National Total = 3,355,699,241 Pounds*

ALPHA ORDER

RANK	STATE	POUNDS	% of USA
11	Alabama	84,544,211	2.5%
1	Alaska	586,438,952	17.5%
10	Arizona	85,520,478	2.5%
27	Arkansas	32,820,421	1.0%
30	California	31,262,132	0.9%
31	Colorado	27,218,068	0.8%
47	Connecticut	1,512,947	0.0%
44	Delaware	6,180,298	0.2%
19	Florida	60,541,062	1.8%
20	Georgia	56,233,008	1.7%
46	Hawaii	2,569,578	0.1%
21	Idaho	46,978,782	1.4%
7	Illinois	115,508,200	3.4%
6	Indiana	136,060,812	4.1%
26	Iowa	35,315,577	1.1%
38	Kansas	18,543,811	0.6%
18	Kentucky	62,345,344	1.9%
5	Louisiana	140,492,352	4.2%
41	Maine	9,449,081	0.3%
42	Maryland	8,079,719	0.2%
45	Massachusetts	3,392,685	0.1%
14	Michigan	72,804,804	2.2%
33	Minnesota	26,085,661	0.8%
16	Mississippi	64,922,056	1.9%
12	Missouri	75,491,117	2.2%
25	Montana	38,385,552	1.1%
36	Nebraska	20,929,989	0.6%
2	Nevada	323,537,281	9.6%
48	New Hampshire	471,294	0.0%
13	New Jersey	74,564,230	2.2%
35	New Mexico	22,398,411	0.7%
39	New York	16,021,213	0.5%
17	North Carolina	62,348,568	1.9%
22	North Dakota	46,911,141	1.4%
8	Ohio	108,055,304	3.2%
32	Oklahoma	26,892,337	0.8%
40	Oregon	15,700,298	0.5%
15	Pennsylvania	65,926,516	2.0%
49	Rhode Island	460,542	0.0%
23	South Carolina	38,985,963	1.2%
43	South Dakota	6,439,620	0.2%
9	Tennessee	86,737,425	2.6%
3	Texas	232,325,571	6.9%
4	Utah	229,213,529	6.8%
50	Vermont	354,804	0.0%
24	Virginia	38,726,321	1.2%
34	Washington	25,942,341	0.8%
29	West Virginia	31,460,470	0.9%
28	Wisconsin	32,060,074	1.0%
37	Wyoming	20,517,132	0.6%

RANK ORDER

RANK	STATE	POUNDS	% of USA
1	Alaska	586,438,952	17.5%
2	Nevada	323,537,281	9.6%
3	Texas	232,325,571	6.9%
4	Utah	229,213,529	6.8%
5	Louisiana	140,492,352	4.2%
6	Indiana	136,060,812	4.1%
7	Illinois	115,508,200	3.4%
8	Ohio	108,055,304	3.2%
9	Tennessee	86,737,425	2.6%
10	Arizona	85,520,478	2.5%
11	Alabama	84,544,211	2.5%
12	Missouri	75,491,117	2.2%
13	New Jersey	74,564,230	2.2%
14	Michigan	72,804,804	2.2%
15	Pennsylvania	65,926,516	2.0%
16	Mississippi	64,922,056	1.9%
17	North Carolina	62,348,568	1.9%
18	Kentucky	62,345,344	1.9%
19	Florida	60,541,062	1.8%
20	Georgia	56,233,008	1.7%
21	Idaho	46,978,782	1.4%
22	North Dakota	46,911,141	1.4%
23	South Carolina	38,985,963	1.2%
24	Virginia	38,726,321	1.2%
25	Montana	38,385,552	1.1%
26	Iowa	35,315,577	1.1%
27	Arkansas	32,820,421	1.0%
28	Wisconsin	32,060,074	1.0%
29	West Virginia	31,460,470	0.9%
30	California	31,262,132	0.9%
31	Colorado	27,218,068	0.8%
32	Oklahoma	26,892,337	0.8%
33	Minnesota	26,085,661	0.8%
34	Washington	25,942,341	0.8%
35	New Mexico	22,398,411	0.7%
36	Nebraska	20,929,989	0.6%
37	Wyoming	20,517,132	0.6%
38	Kansas	18,543,811	0.6%
39	New York	16,021,213	0.5%
40	Oregon	15,700,298	0.5%
41	Maine	9,449,081	0.3%
42	Maryland	8,079,719	0.2%
43	South Dakota	6,439,620	0.2%
44	Delaware	6,180,298	0.2%
45	Massachusetts	3,392,685	0.1%
46	Hawaii	2,569,578	0.1%
47	Connecticut	1,512,947	0.0%
48	New Hampshire	471,294	0.0%
49	Rhode Island	460,542	0.0%
50	Vermont	354,804	0.0%
	District of Columbia	22,159	0.0%

Source: U.S. Environmental Protection Agency, Office of Pollution Prevention and Toxics Information Management
"2015 Toxics Release Inventory" (http://www.epa.gov/triexplorer/)
*National total does not include 2,631,303 pounds of toxins in U.S. territories. Includes discharges to air, surface water, underground injection, and surface land. Includes both original (or manufacturing) industries and those added by EPA since it began tracking releases.

Toxic Releases: Total Air Emissions in 2015

National Total = 687,468,115 Pounds*

ALPHA ORDER

RANK	STATE	POUNDS	% of USA
5	Alabama	35,617,477	5.2%
47	Alaska	493,365	0.1%
35	Arizona	2,278,195	0.3%
18	Arkansas	15,545,002	2.3%
28	California	7,905,352	1.1%
36	Colorado	2,161,242	0.3%
46	Connecticut	706,427	0.1%
44	Delaware	712,043	0.1%
14	Florida	21,375,507	3.1%
4	Georgia	37,215,786	5.4%
41	Hawaii	1,562,955	0.2%
33	Idaho	4,786,154	0.7%
9	Illinois	25,564,583	3.7%
6	Indiana	35,130,149	5.1%
16	Iowa	19,636,624	2.9%
26	Kansas	8,987,229	1.3%
7	Kentucky	32,349,013	4.7%
2	Louisiana	51,679,957	7.5%
34	Maine	3,265,089	0.5%
32	Maryland	4,942,892	0.7%
43	Massachusetts	1,366,740	0.2%
20	Michigan	14,381,975	2.1%
24	Minnesota	9,080,641	1.3%
17	Mississippi	18,782,115	2.7%
23	Missouri	10,302,809	1.5%
39	Montana	1,887,044	0.3%
31	Nebraska	5,481,052	0.8%
40	Nevada	1,601,517	0.2%
48	New Hampshire	322,928	0.0%
38	New Jersey	1,916,229	0.3%
45	New Mexico	708,793	0.1%
30	New York	6,155,631	0.9%
12	North Carolina	22,531,210	3.3%
11	North Dakota	22,839,621	3.3%
3	Ohio	37,392,689	5.4%
21	Oklahoma	13,972,973	2.0%
29	Oregon	6,666,684	1.0%
13	Pennsylvania	22,437,125	3.3%
49	Rhode Island	293,200	0.0%
10	South Carolina	23,329,869	3.4%
42	South Dakota	1,409,419	0.2%
8	Tennessee	29,225,268	4.3%
1	Texas	57,835,052	8.4%
27	Utah	8,381,188	1.2%
50	Vermont	28,734	0.0%
15	Virginia	20,058,861	2.9%
25	Washington	9,076,248	1.3%
19	West Virginia	14,902,446	2.2%
22	Wisconsin	11,200,422	1.6%
37	Wyoming	1,984,070	0.3%

RANK ORDER

RANK	STATE	POUNDS	% of USA
1	Texas	57,835,052	8.4%
2	Louisiana	51,679,957	7.5%
3	Ohio	37,392,689	5.4%
4	Georgia	37,215,786	5.4%
5	Alabama	35,617,477	5.2%
6	Indiana	35,130,149	5.1%
7	Kentucky	32,349,013	4.7%
8	Tennessee	29,225,268	4.3%
9	Illinois	25,564,583	3.7%
10	South Carolina	23,329,869	3.4%
11	North Dakota	22,839,621	3.3%
12	North Carolina	22,531,210	3.3%
13	Pennsylvania	22,437,125	3.3%
14	Florida	21,375,507	3.1%
15	Virginia	20,058,861	2.9%
16	Iowa	19,636,624	2.9%
17	Mississippi	18,782,115	2.7%
18	Arkansas	15,545,002	2.3%
19	West Virginia	14,902,446	2.2%
20	Michigan	14,381,975	2.1%
21	Oklahoma	13,972,973	2.0%
22	Wisconsin	11,200,422	1.6%
23	Missouri	10,302,809	1.5%
24	Minnesota	9,080,641	1.3%
25	Washington	9,076,248	1.3%
26	Kansas	8,987,229	1.3%
27	Utah	8,381,188	1.2%
28	California	7,905,352	1.1%
29	Oregon	6,666,684	1.0%
30	New York	6,155,631	0.9%
31	Nebraska	5,481,052	0.8%
32	Maryland	4,942,892	0.7%
33	Idaho	4,786,154	0.7%
34	Maine	3,265,089	0.5%
35	Arizona	2,278,195	0.3%
36	Colorado	2,161,242	0.3%
37	Wyoming	1,984,070	0.3%
38	New Jersey	1,916,229	0.3%
39	Montana	1,887,044	0.3%
40	Nevada	1,601,517	0.2%
41	Hawaii	1,562,955	0.2%
42	South Dakota	1,409,419	0.2%
43	Massachusetts	1,366,740	0.2%
44	Delaware	712,043	0.1%
45	New Mexico	708,793	0.1%
46	Connecticut	706,427	0.1%
47	Alaska	493,365	0.1%
48	New Hampshire	322,928	0.0%
49	Rhode Island	293,200	0.0%
50	Vermont	28,734	0.0%
	District of Columbia	521	0.0%

Source: U.S. Environmental Protection Agency, Office of Pollution Prevention and Toxics Information Management
"2015 Toxics Release Inventory" (http://www.epa.gov/triexplorer/)
*Includes fugitive and point source air emissions. National total does not include 2,135,911 pounds of emissions in U.S. territories. Includes both original (or manufacturing) industries and those added by EPA since it began tracking releases.

Toxic Releases: Total Surface Water Discharges in 2015

National Total = 190,887,156 Pounds*

ALPHA ORDER

RANK	STATE	POUNDS	% of USA
5	Alabama	9,986,696	5.2%
38	Alaska	525,101	0.3%
48	Arizona	740	0.0%
15	Arkansas	5,024,712	2.6%
27	California	2,382,114	1.2%
33	Colorado	1,157,865	0.6%
43	Connecticut	68,623	0.0%
19	Delaware	3,862,398	2.0%
31	Florida	1,680,370	0.9%
6	Georgia	8,824,809	4.6%
37	Hawaii	621,767	0.3%
26	Idaho	2,632,799	1.4%
14	Illinois	5,561,777	2.9%
1	Indiana	17,352,972	9.1%
21	Iowa	3,688,233	1.9%
35	Kansas	961,551	0.5%
12	Kentucky	6,281,684	3.3%
3	Louisiana	12,294,647	6.4%
25	Maine	2,715,935	1.4%
36	Maryland	865,244	0.5%
46	Massachusetts	12,888	0.0%
24	Michigan	2,727,151	1.4%
30	Minnesota	1,731,149	0.9%
11	Mississippi	6,315,222	3.3%
28	Missouri	2,280,694	1.2%
42	Montana	107,894	0.1%
9	Nebraska	7,300,412	3.8%
47	Nevada	3,173	0.0%
50	New Hampshire	547	0.0%
16	New Jersey	4,761,531	2.5%
44	New Mexico	35,555	0.0%
13	New York	5,879,223	3.1%
7	North Carolina	8,429,059	4.4%
40	North Dakota	134,074	0.1%
8	Ohio	7,445,496	3.9%
22	Oklahoma	3,423,683	1.8%
34	Oregon	993,816	0.5%
10	Pennsylvania	6,766,291	3.5%
49	Rhode Island	733	0.0%
18	South Carolina	4,025,381	2.1%
23	South Dakota	3,404,885	1.8%
17	Tennessee	4,586,158	2.4%
2	Texas	14,462,086	7.6%
41	Utah	110,061	0.1%
39	Vermont	153,581	0.1%
4	Virginia	11,589,493	6.1%
29	Washington	2,236,168	1.2%
32	West Virginia	1,670,850	0.9%
20	Wisconsin	3,792,429	2.0%
45	Wyoming	15,337	0.0%

RANK ORDER

RANK	STATE	POUNDS	% of USA
1	Indiana	17,352,972	9.1%
2	Texas	14,462,086	7.6%
3	Louisiana	12,294,647	6.4%
4	Virginia	11,589,493	6.1%
5	Alabama	9,986,696	5.2%
6	Georgia	8,824,809	4.6%
7	North Carolina	8,429,059	4.4%
8	Ohio	7,445,496	3.9%
9	Nebraska	7,300,412	3.8%
10	Pennsylvania	6,766,291	3.5%
11	Mississippi	6,315,222	3.3%
12	Kentucky	6,281,684	3.3%
13	New York	5,879,223	3.1%
14	Illinois	5,561,777	2.9%
15	Arkansas	5,024,712	2.6%
16	New Jersey	4,761,531	2.5%
17	Tennessee	4,586,158	2.4%
18	South Carolina	4,025,381	2.1%
19	Delaware	3,862,398	2.0%
20	Wisconsin	3,792,429	2.0%
21	Iowa	3,688,233	1.9%
22	Oklahoma	3,423,683	1.8%
23	South Dakota	3,404,885	1.8%
24	Michigan	2,727,151	1.4%
25	Maine	2,715,935	1.4%
26	Idaho	2,632,799	1.4%
27	California	2,382,114	1.2%
28	Missouri	2,280,694	1.2%
29	Washington	2,236,168	1.2%
30	Minnesota	1,731,149	0.9%
31	Florida	1,680,370	0.9%
32	West Virginia	1,670,850	0.9%
33	Colorado	1,157,865	0.6%
34	Oregon	993,816	0.5%
35	Kansas	961,551	0.5%
36	Maryland	865,244	0.5%
37	Hawaii	621,767	0.3%
38	Alaska	525,101	0.3%
39	Vermont	153,581	0.1%
40	North Dakota	134,074	0.1%
41	Utah	110,061	0.1%
42	Montana	107,894	0.1%
43	Connecticut	68,623	0.0%
44	New Mexico	35,555	0.0%
45	Wyoming	15,337	0.0%
46	Massachusetts	12,888	0.0%
47	Nevada	3,173	0.0%
48	Arizona	740	0.0%
49	Rhode Island	733	0.0%
50	New Hampshire	547	0.0%
	District of Columbia	2,099	0.0%

Source: U.S. Environmental Protection Agency, Office of Pollution Prevention and Toxics Information Management
    "2015 Toxics Release Inventory" (http://www.epa.gov/triexplorer/)
*National total does not include 274,772 pounds of discharges in U.S. territories. Includes both original (or manufacturing)
industries and those added by EPA since it began tracking releases.

Hazardous Waste Sites on the National Priority List in 2017

National Total = 1,390 Sites*

ALPHA ORDER

RANK	STATE	SITES	% of USA
28	Alabama	15	1.1%
45	Alaska	6	0.4%
40	Arizona	9	0.6%
40	Arkansas	9	0.6%
2	California	99	7.1%
19	Colorado	21	1.5%
28	Connecticut	15	1.1%
31	Delaware	14	1.0%
6	Florida	55	4.0%
25	Georgia	17	1.2%
46	Hawaii	3	0.2%
40	Idaho	9	0.6%
9	Illinois	49	3.5%
11	Indiana	40	2.9%
33	Iowa	13	0.9%
33	Kansas	13	0.9%
33	Kentucky	13	0.9%
28	Louisiana	15	1.1%
33	Maine	13	0.9%
19	Maryland	21	1.5%
14	Massachusetts	34	2.4%
5	Michigan	67	4.8%
17	Minnesota	25	1.8%
40	Mississippi	9	0.6%
15	Missouri	33	2.4%
22	Montana	19	1.4%
25	Nebraska	17	1.2%
47	Nevada	2	0.1%
19	New Hampshire	21	1.5%
1	New Jersey	115	8.3%
27	New Mexico	16	1.2%
4	New York	87	6.3%
12	North Carolina	39	2.8%
50	North Dakota	0	0.0%
10	Ohio	43	3.1%
44	Oklahoma	8	0.6%
31	Oregon	14	1.0%
3	Pennsylvania	97	7.0%
37	Rhode Island	12	0.9%
17	South Carolina	25	1.8%
47	South Dakota	2	0.1%
23	Tennessee	18	1.3%
7	Texas	54	3.9%
23	Utah	18	1.3%
37	Vermont	12	0.9%
16	Virginia	31	2.2%
8	Washington	51	3.7%
39	West Virginia	10	0.7%
13	Wisconsin	38	2.7%
47	Wyoming	2	0.1%

RANK ORDER

RANK	STATE	SITES	% of USA
1	New Jersey	115	8.3%
2	California	99	7.1%
3	Pennsylvania	97	7.0%
4	New York	87	6.3%
5	Michigan	67	4.8%
6	Florida	55	4.0%
7	Texas	54	3.9%
8	Washington	51	3.7%
9	Illinois	49	3.5%
10	Ohio	43	3.1%
11	Indiana	40	2.9%
12	North Carolina	39	2.8%
13	Wisconsin	38	2.7%
14	Massachusetts	34	2.4%
15	Missouri	33	2.4%
16	Virginia	31	2.2%
17	Minnesota	25	1.8%
17	South Carolina	25	1.8%
19	Colorado	21	1.5%
19	Maryland	21	1.5%
19	New Hampshire	21	1.5%
22	Montana	19	1.4%
23	Tennessee	18	1.3%
23	Utah	18	1.3%
25	Georgia	17	1.2%
25	Nebraska	17	1.2%
27	New Mexico	16	1.2%
28	Alabama	15	1.1%
28	Connecticut	15	1.1%
28	Louisiana	15	1.1%
31	Delaware	14	1.0%
31	Oregon	14	1.0%
33	Iowa	13	0.9%
33	Kansas	13	0.9%
33	Kentucky	13	0.9%
33	Maine	13	0.9%
37	Rhode Island	12	0.9%
37	Vermont	12	0.9%
39	West Virginia	10	0.7%
40	Arizona	9	0.6%
40	Arkansas	9	0.6%
40	Idaho	9	0.6%
40	Mississippi	9	0.6%
44	Oklahoma	8	0.6%
45	Alaska	6	0.4%
46	Hawaii	3	0.2%
47	Nevada	2	0.1%
47	South Dakota	2	0.1%
47	Wyoming	2	0.1%
50	North Dakota	0	0.0%
	District of Columbia	1	0.1%

Source: U.S. Environmental Protection Agency
"National Priorities List (NPL) Sites in the United States" (http://www.epa.gov/superfund/sites/npl/)
*As of November 29, 2016. Includes final and proposed General Superfund and Federal Facilities Sites. National total includes 17 sites in Puerto Rico, two in Guam, and one in the U.S. Virgin Islands.

Hazardous Waste Sites on the National Priority List per 10,000 Square Miles in 2017
National Rate = 3.6 Sites per 10,000 Square Miles*

RANK	STATE	RATE
27	Alabama	2.9
49	Alaska	0.1
45	Arizona	0.8
38	Arkansas	1.7
20	California	6.0
35	Colorado	2.0
5	Connecticut	27.1
3	Delaware	56.2
14	Florida	8.4
27	Georgia	2.9
31	Hawaii	2.7
43	Idaho	1.1
13	Illinois	8.5
11	Indiana	11.0
32	Iowa	2.3
39	Kansas	1.6
26	Kentucky	3.2
27	Louisiana	2.9
25	Maine	3.7
8	Maryland	16.9
4	Massachusetts	32.2
19	Michigan	6.9
27	Minnesota	2.9
37	Mississippi	1.9
22	Missouri	4.7
41	Montana	1.3
33	Nebraska	2.2
47	Nevada	0.2
6	New Hampshire	22.5
1	New Jersey	131.8
41	New Mexico	1.3
9	New York	15.9
16	North Carolina	7.2
50	North Dakota	0.0
12	Ohio	9.6
43	Oklahoma	1.1
40	Oregon	1.4
7	Pennsylvania	21.1
2	Rhode Island	77.7
15	South Carolina	7.8
46	South Dakota	0.3
23	Tennessee	4.3
35	Texas	2.0
34	Utah	2.1
10	Vermont	12.5
16	Virginia	7.2
16	Washington	7.2
24	West Virginia	4.1
21	Wisconsin	5.8
47	Wyoming	0.2

RANK	STATE	RATE
1	New Jersey	131.8
2	Rhode Island	77.7
3	Delaware	56.2
4	Massachusetts	32.2
5	Connecticut	27.1
6	New Hampshire	22.5
7	Pennsylvania	21.1
8	Maryland	16.9
9	New York	15.9
10	Vermont	12.5
11	Indiana	11.0
12	Ohio	9.6
13	Illinois	8.5
14	Florida	8.4
15	South Carolina	7.8
16	North Carolina	7.2
16	Virginia	7.2
16	Washington	7.2
19	Michigan	6.9
20	California	6.0
21	Wisconsin	5.8
22	Missouri	4.7
23	Tennessee	4.3
24	West Virginia	4.1
25	Maine	3.7
26	Kentucky	3.2
27	Alabama	2.9
27	Georgia	2.9
27	Louisiana	2.9
27	Minnesota	2.9
31	Hawaii	2.7
32	Iowa	2.3
33	Nebraska	2.2
34	Utah	2.1
35	Colorado	2.0
35	Texas	2.0
37	Mississippi	1.9
38	Arkansas	1.7
39	Kansas	1.6
40	Oregon	1.4
41	Montana	1.3
41	New Mexico	1.3
43	Idaho	1.1
43	Oklahoma	1.1
45	Arizona	0.8
46	South Dakota	0.3
47	Nevada	0.2
47	Wyoming	0.2
49	Alaska	0.1
50	North Dakota	0.0
	District of Columbia**	NA

Source: CQ Press using data from U.S. Environmental Protection Agency
"National Priorities List (NPL) Sites in the United States" (http://www.epa.gov/superfund/sites/npl/)
*As of November 29, 2016. Includes final and proposed General Superfund and Federal Facilities Sites. National rate excludes sites and square miles in Puerto Rico, Guam and the Virgin Islands. Based on land and water area of states.
**The District of Columbia has one site in its 68 square miles.

Hazardous Waste Sites Deleted from the National Priorities List as of 2017

National Total = 392 Sites*

ALPHA ORDER

RANK	STATE	SITES	% of USA
39	Alabama	2	0.5%
31	Alaska	3	0.8%
31	Arizona	3	0.8%
13	Arkansas	8	2.0%
8	California	13	3.3%
31	Colorado	3	0.8%
31	Connecticut	3	0.8%
14	Delaware	7	1.8%
4	Florida	26	6.6%
24	Georgia	5	1.3%
44	Hawaii	1	0.3%
31	Idaho	3	0.8%
19	Illinois	6	1.5%
11	Indiana	10	2.6%
11	Iowa	10	2.6%
24	Kansas	5	1.3%
14	Kentucky	7	1.8%
9	Louisiana	12	3.1%
31	Maine	3	0.8%
28	Maryland	4	1.0%
19	Massachusetts	6	1.5%
6	Michigan	20	5.1%
5	Minnesota	21	5.4%
31	Mississippi	3	0.8%
24	Missouri	5	1.3%
49	Montana	0	0.0%
44	Nebraska	1	0.3%
49	Nevada	0	0.0%
44	New Hampshire	1	0.3%
1	New Jersey	35	8.9%
28	New Mexico	4	1.0%
2	New York	32	8.2%
31	North Carolina	3	0.8%
39	North Dakota	2	0.5%
14	Ohio	7	1.8%
14	Oklahoma	7	1.8%
24	Oregon	5	1.3%
3	Pennsylvania	30	7.7%
44	Rhode Island	1	0.3%
19	South Carolina	6	1.5%
39	South Dakota	2	0.5%
19	Tennessee	6	1.5%
9	Texas	12	3.1%
19	Utah	6	1.5%
39	Vermont	2	0.5%
28	Virginia	4	1.0%
7	Washington	17	4.3%
39	West Virginia	2	0.5%
14	Wisconsin	7	1.8%
44	Wyoming	1	0.3%

RANK ORDER

RANK	STATE	SITES	% of USA
1	New Jersey	35	8.9%
2	New York	32	8.2%
3	Pennsylvania	30	7.7%
4	Florida	26	6.6%
5	Minnesota	21	5.4%
6	Michigan	20	5.1%
7	Washington	17	4.3%
8	California	13	3.3%
9	Louisiana	12	3.1%
9	Texas	12	3.1%
11	Indiana	10	2.6%
11	Iowa	10	2.6%
13	Arkansas	8	2.0%
14	Delaware	7	1.8%
14	Kentucky	7	1.8%
14	Ohio	7	1.8%
14	Oklahoma	7	1.8%
14	Wisconsin	7	1.8%
19	Illinois	6	1.5%
19	Massachusetts	6	1.5%
19	South Carolina	6	1.5%
19	Tennessee	6	1.5%
19	Utah	6	1.5%
24	Georgia	5	1.3%
24	Kansas	5	1.3%
24	Missouri	5	1.3%
24	Oregon	5	1.3%
28	Maryland	4	1.0%
28	New Mexico	4	1.0%
28	Virginia	4	1.0%
31	Alaska	3	0.8%
31	Arizona	3	0.8%
31	Colorado	3	0.8%
31	Connecticut	3	0.8%
31	Idaho	3	0.8%
31	Maine	3	0.8%
31	Mississippi	3	0.8%
31	North Carolina	3	0.8%
39	Alabama	2	0.5%
39	North Dakota	2	0.5%
39	South Dakota	2	0.5%
39	Vermont	2	0.5%
39	West Virginia	2	0.5%
44	Hawaii	1	0.3%
44	Nebraska	1	0.3%
44	New Hampshire	1	0.3%
44	Rhode Island	1	0.3%
44	Wyoming	1	0.3%
49	Montana	0	0.0%
49	Nevada	0	0.0%
	District of Columbia	0	0.0%

Source: U.S. Environmental Protection Agency
"National Priorities List (NPL) Sites in the United States" (http://www.epa.gov/superfund/sites/npl/)
*Cumulative total as of November 29, 2017. National total includes six sites in Puerto Rico and four in other U.S. territories.

VIII. Geography

Total Area of States in Square Miles in 2010

National Total = 3,796,742 Square Miles*

ALPHA ORDER

RANK	STATE	MILES	% of USA
30	Alabama	52,420	1.4%
1	Alaska	665,384	17.5%
6	Arizona	113,990	3.0%
29	Arkansas	53,179	1.4%
3	California	163,695	4.3%
8	Colorado	104,094	2.7%
48	Connecticut	5,543	0.1%
49	Delaware	2,489	0.1%
22	Florida	65,758	1.7%
24	Georgia	59,425	1.6%
43	Hawaii	10,932	0.3%
14	Idaho	83,569	2.2%
25	Illinois	57,914	1.5%
38	Indiana	36,420	1.0%
26	Iowa	56,273	1.5%
15	Kansas	82,278	2.2%
37	Kentucky	40,408	1.1%
31	Louisiana	52,378	1.4%
39	Maine	35,380	0.9%
42	Maryland	12,406	0.3%
44	Massachusetts	10,554	0.3%
11	Michigan	96,714	2.5%
12	Minnesota	86,936	2.3%
32	Mississippi	48,432	1.3%
21	Missouri	69,707	1.8%
4	Montana	147,040	3.9%
16	Nebraska	77,348	2.0%
7	Nevada	110,572	2.9%
46	New Hampshire	9,349	0.2%
47	New Jersey	8,723	0.2%
5	New Mexico	121,590	3.2%
27	New York	54,555	1.4%
28	North Carolina	53,819	1.4%
19	North Dakota	70,698	1.9%
34	Ohio	44,826	1.2%
20	Oklahoma	69,899	1.8%
9	Oregon	98,379	2.6%
33	Pennsylvania	46,054	1.2%
50	Rhode Island	1,545	0.0%
40	South Carolina	32,020	0.8%
17	South Dakota	77,116	2.0%
36	Tennessee	42,144	1.1%
2	Texas	268,596	7.1%
13	Utah	84,897	2.2%
45	Vermont	9,616	0.3%
35	Virginia	42,775	1.1%
18	Washington	71,298	1.9%
41	West Virginia	24,230	0.6%
23	Wisconsin	65,496	1.7%
10	Wyoming	97,813	2.6%

RANK ORDER

RANK	STATE	MILES	% of USA
1	Alaska	665,384	17.5%
2	Texas	268,596	7.1%
3	California	163,695	4.3%
4	Montana	147,040	3.9%
5	New Mexico	121,590	3.2%
6	Arizona	113,990	3.0%
7	Nevada	110,572	2.9%
8	Colorado	104,094	2.7%
9	Oregon	98,379	2.6%
10	Wyoming	97,813	2.6%
11	Michigan	96,714	2.5%
12	Minnesota	86,936	2.3%
13	Utah	84,897	2.2%
14	Idaho	83,569	2.2%
15	Kansas	82,278	2.2%
16	Nebraska	77,348	2.0%
17	South Dakota	77,116	2.0%
18	Washington	71,298	1.9%
19	North Dakota	70,698	1.9%
20	Oklahoma	69,899	1.8%
21	Missouri	69,707	1.8%
22	Florida	65,758	1.7%
23	Wisconsin	65,496	1.7%
24	Georgia	59,425	1.6%
25	Illinois	57,914	1.5%
26	Iowa	56,273	1.5%
27	New York	54,555	1.4%
28	North Carolina	53,819	1.4%
29	Arkansas	53,179	1.4%
30	Alabama	52,420	1.4%
31	Louisiana	52,378	1.4%
32	Mississippi	48,432	1.3%
33	Pennsylvania	46,054	1.2%
34	Ohio	44,826	1.2%
35	Virginia	42,775	1.1%
36	Tennessee	42,144	1.1%
37	Kentucky	40,408	1.1%
38	Indiana	36,420	1.0%
39	Maine	35,380	0.9%
40	South Carolina	32,020	0.8%
41	West Virginia	24,230	0.6%
42	Maryland	12,406	0.3%
43	Hawaii	10,932	0.3%
44	Massachusetts	10,554	0.3%
45	Vermont	9,616	0.3%
46	New Hampshire	9,349	0.2%
47	New Jersey	8,723	0.2%
48	Connecticut	5,543	0.1%
49	Delaware	2,489	0.1%
50	Rhode Island	1,545	0.0%
	District of Columbia	68	0.0%

Source: U.S. Bureau of the Census
"State Area Measurements" (http://www.census.gov/geo/reference/state-area.html)
*Total of land and water area. Revised figures as of January 1, 2010

Land Area of States in Square Miles in 2010

National Total = 3,531,905 Square Miles of Land Area*

ALPHA ORDER

RANK	STATE	MILES	% of USA
28	Alabama	50,645	1.4%
1	Alaska	570,641	16.2%
6	Arizona	113,594	3.2%
27	Arkansas	52,035	1.5%
3	California	155,779	4.4%
8	Colorado	103,642	2.9%
48	Connecticut	4,842	0.1%
49	Delaware	1,949	0.1%
26	Florida	53,625	1.5%
21	Georgia	57,513	1.6%
47	Hawaii	6,423	0.2%
11	Idaho	82,643	2.3%
24	Illinois	55,519	1.6%
38	Indiana	35,826	1.0%
23	Iowa	55,857	1.6%
13	Kansas	81,759	2.3%
37	Kentucky	39,486	1.1%
33	Louisiana	43,204	1.2%
39	Maine	30,843	0.9%
42	Maryland	9,707	0.3%
45	Massachusetts	7,800	0.2%
22	Michigan	56,539	1.6%
14	Minnesota	79,627	2.3%
31	Mississippi	46,923	1.3%
18	Missouri	68,742	1.9%
4	Montana	145,546	4.1%
15	Nebraska	76,824	2.2%
7	Nevada	109,781	3.1%
44	New Hampshire	8,953	0.3%
46	New Jersey	7,354	0.2%
5	New Mexico	121,298	3.4%
30	New York	47,126	1.3%
29	North Carolina	48,618	1.4%
17	North Dakota	69,001	2.0%
35	Ohio	40,861	1.2%
19	Oklahoma	68,595	1.9%
10	Oregon	95,988	2.7%
32	Pennsylvania	44,743	1.3%
50	Rhode Island	1,034	0.0%
40	South Carolina	30,061	0.9%
16	South Dakota	75,811	2.1%
34	Tennessee	41,235	1.2%
2	Texas	261,232	7.4%
12	Utah	82,170	2.3%
43	Vermont	9,217	0.3%
36	Virginia	39,490	1.1%
20	Washington	66,456	1.9%
41	West Virginia	24,038	0.7%
25	Wisconsin	54,158	1.5%
9	Wyoming	97,093	2.7%

RANK ORDER

RANK	STATE	MILES	% of USA
1	Alaska	570,641	16.2%
2	Texas	261,232	7.4%
3	California	155,779	4.4%
4	Montana	145,546	4.1%
5	New Mexico	121,298	3.4%
6	Arizona	113,594	3.2%
7	Nevada	109,781	3.1%
8	Colorado	103,642	2.9%
9	Wyoming	97,093	2.7%
10	Oregon	95,988	2.7%
11	Idaho	82,643	2.3%
12	Utah	82,170	2.3%
13	Kansas	81,759	2.3%
14	Minnesota	79,627	2.3%
15	Nebraska	76,824	2.2%
16	South Dakota	75,811	2.1%
17	North Dakota	69,001	2.0%
18	Missouri	68,742	1.9%
19	Oklahoma	68,595	1.9%
20	Washington	66,456	1.9%
21	Georgia	57,513	1.6%
22	Michigan	56,539	1.6%
23	Iowa	55,857	1.6%
24	Illinois	55,519	1.6%
25	Wisconsin	54,158	1.5%
26	Florida	53,625	1.5%
27	Arkansas	52,035	1.5%
28	Alabama	50,645	1.4%
29	North Carolina	48,618	1.4%
30	New York	47,126	1.3%
31	Mississippi	46,923	1.3%
32	Pennsylvania	44,743	1.3%
33	Louisiana	43,204	1.2%
34	Tennessee	41,235	1.2%
35	Ohio	40,861	1.2%
36	Virginia	39,490	1.1%
37	Kentucky	39,486	1.1%
38	Indiana	35,826	1.0%
39	Maine	30,843	0.9%
40	South Carolina	30,061	0.9%
41	West Virginia	24,038	0.7%
42	Maryland	9,707	0.3%
43	Vermont	9,217	0.3%
44	New Hampshire	8,953	0.3%
45	Massachusetts	7,800	0.2%
46	New Jersey	7,354	0.2%
47	Hawaii	6,423	0.2%
48	Connecticut	4,842	0.1%
49	Delaware	1,949	0.1%
50	Rhode Island	1,034	0.0%
	District of Columbia	61	0.0%

Source: U.S. Bureau of the Census
"State Area Measurements" (http://www.census.gov/geo/reference/state-area.html)
*Includes dry land temporarily or partially covered by water, such as marshland, swamps, etc.; streams and canals under one-eighth mile wide; and lakes, reservoirs, and ponds under 40 acres. Revised figures as of August 2010.

Water Area of States in Square Miles in 2010

National Total = 264,837 Square Miles of Water*

<table>
<tr><td colspan="4">ALPHA ORDER</td><td colspan="4">RANK ORDER</td></tr>
<tr><th>RANK</th><th>STATE</th><th>MILES</th><th>% of USA</th><th>RANK</th><th>STATE</th><th>MILES</th><th>% of USA</th></tr>
<tr><td>23</td><td>Alabama</td><td>1,775</td><td>0.7%</td><td>1</td><td>Alaska</td><td>94,743</td><td>35.8%</td></tr>
<tr><td>1</td><td>Alaska</td><td>94,743</td><td>35.8%</td><td>2</td><td>Michigan</td><td>40,175</td><td>15.2%</td></tr>
<tr><td>48</td><td>Arizona</td><td>396</td><td>0.1%</td><td>3</td><td>Florida</td><td>12,133</td><td>4.6%</td></tr>
<tr><td>31</td><td>Arkansas</td><td>1,143</td><td>0.4%</td><td>4</td><td>Wisconsin</td><td>11,339</td><td>4.3%</td></tr>
<tr><td>6</td><td>California</td><td>7,916</td><td>3.0%</td><td>5</td><td>Louisiana</td><td>9,174</td><td>3.5%</td></tr>
<tr><td>44</td><td>Colorado</td><td>452</td><td>0.2%</td><td>6</td><td>California</td><td>7,916</td><td>3.0%</td></tr>
<tr><td>38</td><td>Connecticut</td><td>701</td><td>0.3%</td><td>7</td><td>New York</td><td>7,429</td><td>2.8%</td></tr>
<tr><td>40</td><td>Delaware</td><td>540</td><td>0.2%</td><td>8</td><td>Texas</td><td>7,365</td><td>2.8%</td></tr>
<tr><td>3</td><td>Florida</td><td>12,133</td><td>4.6%</td><td>9</td><td>Minnesota</td><td>7,309</td><td>2.8%</td></tr>
<tr><td>22</td><td>Georgia</td><td>1,912</td><td>0.7%</td><td>10</td><td>North Carolina</td><td>5,201</td><td>2.0%</td></tr>
<tr><td>13</td><td>Hawaii</td><td>4,509</td><td>1.7%</td><td>11</td><td>Washington</td><td>4,842</td><td>1.8%</td></tr>
<tr><td>33</td><td>Idaho</td><td>926</td><td>0.3%</td><td>12</td><td>Maine</td><td>4,537</td><td>1.7%</td></tr>
<tr><td>19</td><td>Illinois</td><td>2,395</td><td>0.9%</td><td>13</td><td>Hawaii</td><td>4,509</td><td>1.7%</td></tr>
<tr><td>39</td><td>Indiana</td><td>593</td><td>0.2%</td><td>14</td><td>Ohio</td><td>3,965</td><td>1.5%</td></tr>
<tr><td>45</td><td>Iowa</td><td>416</td><td>0.2%</td><td>15</td><td>Virginia</td><td>3,285</td><td>1.2%</td></tr>
<tr><td>42</td><td>Kansas</td><td>520</td><td>0.2%</td><td>16</td><td>Massachusetts</td><td>2,754</td><td>1.0%</td></tr>
<tr><td>34</td><td>Kentucky</td><td>921</td><td>0.3%</td><td>17</td><td>Utah</td><td>2,727</td><td>1.0%</td></tr>
<tr><td>5</td><td>Louisiana</td><td>9,174</td><td>3.5%</td><td>18</td><td>Maryland</td><td>2,699</td><td>1.0%</td></tr>
<tr><td>12</td><td>Maine</td><td>4,537</td><td>1.7%</td><td>19</td><td>Illinois</td><td>2,395</td><td>0.9%</td></tr>
<tr><td>18</td><td>Maryland</td><td>2,699</td><td>1.0%</td><td>20</td><td>Oregon</td><td>2,391</td><td>0.9%</td></tr>
<tr><td>16</td><td>Massachusetts</td><td>2,754</td><td>1.0%</td><td>21</td><td>South Carolina</td><td>1,960</td><td>0.7%</td></tr>
<tr><td>2</td><td>Michigan</td><td>40,175</td><td>15.2%</td><td>22</td><td>Georgia</td><td>1,912</td><td>0.7%</td></tr>
<tr><td>9</td><td>Minnesota</td><td>7,309</td><td>2.8%</td><td>23</td><td>Alabama</td><td>1,775</td><td>0.7%</td></tr>
<tr><td>25</td><td>Mississippi</td><td>1,509</td><td>0.6%</td><td>24</td><td>North Dakota</td><td>1,698</td><td>0.6%</td></tr>
<tr><td>32</td><td>Missouri</td><td>965</td><td>0.4%</td><td>25</td><td>Mississippi</td><td>1,509</td><td>0.6%</td></tr>
<tr><td>26</td><td>Montana</td><td>1,494</td><td>0.6%</td><td>26</td><td>Montana</td><td>1,494</td><td>0.6%</td></tr>
<tr><td>41</td><td>Nebraska</td><td>524</td><td>0.2%</td><td>27</td><td>New Jersey</td><td>1,368</td><td>0.5%</td></tr>
<tr><td>36</td><td>Nevada</td><td>791</td><td>0.3%</td><td>28</td><td>Pennsylvania</td><td>1,312</td><td>0.5%</td></tr>
<tr><td>47</td><td>New Hampshire</td><td>397</td><td>0.1%</td><td>29</td><td>South Dakota</td><td>1,305</td><td>0.5%</td></tr>
<tr><td>27</td><td>New Jersey</td><td>1,368</td><td>0.5%</td><td>30</td><td>Oklahoma</td><td>1,304</td><td>0.5%</td></tr>
<tr><td>49</td><td>New Mexico</td><td>292</td><td>0.1%</td><td>31</td><td>Arkansas</td><td>1,143</td><td>0.4%</td></tr>
<tr><td>7</td><td>New York</td><td>7,429</td><td>2.8%</td><td>32</td><td>Missouri</td><td>965</td><td>0.4%</td></tr>
<tr><td>10</td><td>North Carolina</td><td>5,201</td><td>2.0%</td><td>33</td><td>Idaho</td><td>926</td><td>0.3%</td></tr>
<tr><td>24</td><td>North Dakota</td><td>1,698</td><td>0.6%</td><td>34</td><td>Kentucky</td><td>921</td><td>0.3%</td></tr>
<tr><td>14</td><td>Ohio</td><td>3,965</td><td>1.5%</td><td>35</td><td>Tennessee</td><td>909</td><td>0.3%</td></tr>
<tr><td>30</td><td>Oklahoma</td><td>1,304</td><td>0.5%</td><td>36</td><td>Nevada</td><td>791</td><td>0.3%</td></tr>
<tr><td>20</td><td>Oregon</td><td>2,391</td><td>0.9%</td><td>37</td><td>Wyoming</td><td>720</td><td>0.3%</td></tr>
<tr><td>28</td><td>Pennsylvania</td><td>1,312</td><td>0.5%</td><td>38</td><td>Connecticut</td><td>701</td><td>0.3%</td></tr>
<tr><td>43</td><td>Rhode Island</td><td>511</td><td>0.2%</td><td>39</td><td>Indiana</td><td>593</td><td>0.2%</td></tr>
<tr><td>21</td><td>South Carolina</td><td>1,960</td><td>0.7%</td><td>40</td><td>Delaware</td><td>540</td><td>0.2%</td></tr>
<tr><td>29</td><td>South Dakota</td><td>1,305</td><td>0.5%</td><td>41</td><td>Nebraska</td><td>524</td><td>0.2%</td></tr>
<tr><td>35</td><td>Tennessee</td><td>909</td><td>0.3%</td><td>42</td><td>Kansas</td><td>520</td><td>0.2%</td></tr>
<tr><td>8</td><td>Texas</td><td>7,365</td><td>2.8%</td><td>43</td><td>Rhode Island</td><td>511</td><td>0.2%</td></tr>
<tr><td>17</td><td>Utah</td><td>2,727</td><td>1.0%</td><td>44</td><td>Colorado</td><td>452</td><td>0.2%</td></tr>
<tr><td>46</td><td>Vermont</td><td>400</td><td>0.2%</td><td>45</td><td>Iowa</td><td>416</td><td>0.2%</td></tr>
<tr><td>15</td><td>Virginia</td><td>3,285</td><td>1.2%</td><td>46</td><td>Vermont</td><td>400</td><td>0.2%</td></tr>
<tr><td>11</td><td>Washington</td><td>4,842</td><td>1.8%</td><td>47</td><td>New Hampshire</td><td>397</td><td>0.1%</td></tr>
<tr><td>50</td><td>West Virginia</td><td>192</td><td>0.1%</td><td>48</td><td>Arizona</td><td>396</td><td>0.1%</td></tr>
<tr><td>4</td><td>Wisconsin</td><td>11,339</td><td>4.3%</td><td>49</td><td>New Mexico</td><td>292</td><td>0.1%</td></tr>
<tr><td>37</td><td>Wyoming</td><td>720</td><td>0.3%</td><td>50</td><td>West Virginia</td><td>192</td><td>0.1%</td></tr>
<tr><td></td><td></td><td></td><td></td><td></td><td>District of Columbia</td><td>7</td><td>0.0%</td></tr>
</table>

Source: U.S. Bureau of the Census
   "State Area Measurements" (http://www.census.gov/geo/reference/state-area.html)
*Includes permanent inland water surface, such as lakes, reservoirs, and ponds having an area of 40 acres or more, canals one-eighth mile or more in width; coastal waters behind or sheltered by headlands or islands separated by less than 1 nautical mile of water, and islands under 40 acres in area. Excludes areas of oceans, bays, etc., lying within U.S. jurisdiction but not defined as inland water. Revised figures as of August 2010.

Highest Point of Elevation in Feet

National High Point = 20,320 Feet Above Sea Level (Mt. McKinley, Alaska)

ALPHA ORDER

RANK	STATE	HIGHEST POINT
35	Alabama	2,407
1	Alaska	20,320
12	Arizona	12,633
34	Arkansas	2,753
2	California	14,494
3	Colorado	14,433
36	Connecticut	2,380
49	Delaware	448
50	Florida	345
25	Georgia	4,784
6	Hawaii	13,796
11	Idaho	12,662
45	Illinois	1,235
44	Indiana	1,257
42	Iowa	1,670
28	Kansas	4,039
27	Kentucky	4,145
48	Louisiana	535
22	Maine	5,268
32	Maryland	3,360
31	Massachusetts	3,491
38	Michigan	1,979
37	Minnesota	2,301
47	Mississippi	806
41	Missouri	1,772
10	Montana	12,799
20	Nebraska	5,424
9	Nevada	13,140
18	New Hampshire	6,288
40	New Jersey	1,803
8	New Mexico	13,161
21	New York	5,344
16	North Carolina	6,684
30	North Dakota	3,506
43	Ohio	1,550
23	Oklahoma	4,973
13	Oregon	11,239
33	Pennsylvania	3,213
46	Rhode Island	812
29	South Carolina	3,560
15	South Dakota	7,242
17	Tennessee	6,643
14	Texas	8,749
7	Utah	13,528
26	Vermont	4,393
19	Virginia	5,729
4	Washington	14,411
24	West Virginia	4,863
39	Wisconsin	1,951
5	Wyoming	13,804

RANK ORDER

RANK	STATE	HIGHEST POINT
1	Alaska	20,320
2	California	14,494
3	Colorado	14,433
4	Washington	14,411
5	Wyoming	13,804
6	Hawaii	13,796
7	Utah	13,528
8	New Mexico	13,161
9	Nevada	13,140
10	Montana	12,799
11	Idaho	12,662
12	Arizona	12,633
13	Oregon	11,239
14	Texas	8,749
15	South Dakota	7,242
16	North Carolina	6,684
17	Tennessee	6,643
18	New Hampshire	6,288
19	Virginia	5,729
20	Nebraska	5,424
21	New York	5,344
22	Maine	5,268
23	Oklahoma	4,973
24	West Virginia	4,863
25	Georgia	4,784
26	Vermont	4,393
27	Kentucky	4,145
28	Kansas	4,039
29	South Carolina	3,560
30	North Dakota	3,506
31	Massachusetts	3,491
32	Maryland	3,360
33	Pennsylvania	3,213
34	Arkansas	2,753
35	Alabama	2,407
36	Connecticut	2,380
37	Minnesota	2,301
38	Michigan	1,979
39	Wisconsin	1,951
40	New Jersey	1,803
41	Missouri	1,772
42	Iowa	1,670
43	Ohio	1,550
44	Indiana	1,257
45	Illinois	1,235
46	Rhode Island	812
47	Mississippi	806
48	Louisiana	535
49	Delaware	448
50	Florida	345

	District of Columbia	410

Source: U.S. Department of Interior, U.S. Geological Survey
"Elevations and Distances in the United States" (http://erg.usgs.gov/isb/pubs/booklets/elvadist/elvadist.html)

Lowest Point of Elevation in Feet

National Low Point = 282 Feet Below Sea Level (Death Valley, California)*

RANK	STATE	LOWEST POINT
3	Alabama	0
3	Alaska	0
26	Arizona	70
25	Arkansas	55
1	California	(282)
50	Colorado	3,315
3	Connecticut	0
3	Delaware	0
3	Florida	0
3	Georgia	0
3	Hawaii	0
42	Idaho	710
32	Illinois	279
34	Indiana	320
37	Iowa	480
41	Kansas	679
31	Kentucky	257
2	Louisiana	(8)
3	Maine	0
3	Maryland	0
3	Massachusetts	0
38	Michigan	571
40	Minnesota	601
3	Mississippi	0
29	Missouri	230
46	Montana	1,800
44	Nebraska	840
36	Nevada	479
3	New Hampshire	0
3	New Jersey	0
48	New Mexico	2,842
3	New York	0
3	North Carolina	0
43	North Dakota	750
35	Ohio	455
33	Oklahoma	289
3	Oregon	0
3	Pennsylvania	0
3	Rhode Island	0
3	South Carolina	0
45	South Dakota	966
28	Tennessee	178
3	Texas	0
47	Utah	2,000
27	Vermont	95
3	Virginia	0
3	Washington	0
30	West Virginia	240
39	Wisconsin	579
49	Wyoming	3,099

RANK	STATE	LOWEST POINT
1	California	(282)
2	Louisiana	(8)
3	Alabama*	0
3	Alaska	0
3	Connecticut	0
3	Delaware	0
3	Florida	0
3	Georgia	0
3	Hawaii	0
3	Maine	0
3	Maryland	0
3	Massachusetts	0
3	Mississippi	0
3	New Hampshire	0
3	New Jersey	0
3	New York	0
3	North Carolina	0
3	Oregon	0
3	Pennsylvania	0
3	Rhode Island	0
3	South Carolina	0
3	Texas	0
3	Virginia	0
3	Washington	0
25	Arkansas	55
26	Arizona	70
27	Vermont	95
28	Tennessee	178
29	Missouri	230
30	West Virginia	240
31	Kentucky	257
32	Illinois	279
33	Oklahoma	289
34	Indiana	320
35	Ohio	455
36	Nevada	479
37	Iowa	480
38	Michigan	571
39	Wisconsin	579
40	Minnesota	601
41	Kansas	679
42	Idaho	710
43	North Dakota	750
44	Nebraska	840
45	South Dakota	966
46	Montana	1,800
47	Utah	2,000
48	New Mexico	2,842
49	Wyoming	3,099
50	Colorado	3,315

District of Columbia 1

Source: U.S. Department of Interior, U.S. Geological Survey
"Elevations and Distances in the United States" (http://erg.usgs.gov/isb/pubs/booklets/elvadist/elvadist.html)
*States with "0" have sea level as lowest point.

Approximate Mean Elevation in Feet

Approximate National Mean Elevation = 2,500 Feet Above Sea Level

ALPHA ORDER

RANK	STATE	MEAN ELEVATION
40	Alabama	500
15	Alaska	1,900
7	Arizona	4,100
36	Arkansas	650
11	California	2,900
1	Colorado	6,800
40	Connecticut	500
50	Delaware	60
48	Florida	100
37	Georgia	600
10	Hawaii	3,030
6	Idaho	5,000
37	Illinois	600
34	Indiana	700
22	Iowa	1,100
14	Kansas	2,000
33	Kentucky	750
48	Louisiana	100
37	Maine	600
43	Maryland	350
40	Massachusetts	500
29	Michigan	900
21	Minnesota	1,200
45	Mississippi	300
32	Missouri	800
8	Montana	3,400
12	Nebraska	2,600
5	Nevada	5,500
25	New Hampshire	1,000
46	New Jersey	250
4	New Mexico	5,700
25	New York	1,000
34	North Carolina	700
15	North Dakota	1,900
31	Ohio	850
20	Oklahoma	1,300
9	Oregon	3,300
22	Pennsylvania	1,100
47	Rhode Island	200
43	South Carolina	350
13	South Dakota	2,200
29	Tennessee	900
17	Texas	1,700
3	Utah	6,100
25	Vermont	1,000
28	Virginia	950
17	Washington	1,700
19	West Virginia	1,500
24	Wisconsin	1,050
2	Wyoming	6,700

RANK ORDER

RANK	STATE	MEAN ELEVATION
1	Colorado	6,800
2	Wyoming	6,700
3	Utah	6,100
4	New Mexico	5,700
5	Nevada	5,500
6	Idaho	5,000
7	Arizona	4,100
8	Montana	3,400
9	Oregon	3,300
10	Hawaii	3,030
11	California	2,900
12	Nebraska	2,600
13	South Dakota	2,200
14	Kansas	2,000
15	Alaska	1,900
15	North Dakota	1,900
17	Texas	1,700
17	Washington	1,700
19	West Virginia	1,500
20	Oklahoma	1,300
21	Minnesota	1,200
22	Iowa	1,100
22	Pennsylvania	1,100
24	Wisconsin	1,050
25	New Hampshire	1,000
25	New York	1,000
25	Vermont	1,000
28	Virginia	950
29	Michigan	900
29	Tennessee	900
31	Ohio	850
32	Missouri	800
33	Kentucky	750
34	Indiana	700
34	North Carolina	700
36	Arkansas	650
37	Georgia	600
37	Illinois	600
37	Maine	600
40	Alabama	500
40	Connecticut	500
40	Massachusetts	500
43	Maryland	350
43	South Carolina	350
45	Mississippi	300
46	New Jersey	250
47	Rhode Island	200
48	Florida	100
48	Louisiana	100
50	Delaware	60
	District of Columbia	150

Source: U.S. Department of Interior, U.S. Geological Survey
"Elevations and Distances in the United States" (http://erg.usgs.gov/isb/pubs/booklets/elvadist/elvadist.html)

Normal Daily Mean Temperature*

ALPHA ORDER				RANK ORDER		
RANK	STATE	MEAN TEMPERATURE		RANK	STATE	MEAN TEMPERATURE
7	Alabama	63.7		1	Hawaii	75.7
50	Alaska	31.9		2	Florida	72.0
6	Arizona	63.9		3	Louisiana	67.4
10	Arkansas	62.0		4	Texas	66.8
12	California	60.3		5	South Carolina	64.0
38	Colorado	48.4		6	Arizona	63.9
27	Connecticut	51.2		7	Alabama	63.7
20	Delaware**	54.4		8	Georgia	63.6
2	Florida	72.0		9	Mississippi	63.4
8	Georgia	63.6		10	Arkansas	62.0
1	Hawaii	75.7		11	Oklahoma	60.5
31	Idaho	50.3		12	California	60.3
33	Illinois	50.1		13	North Carolina	60.1
24	Indiana	52.0		14	Tennessee	58.7
39	Iowa	48.1		15	Virginia	57.2
22	Kansas	54.0		16	New Mexico	57.0
17	Kentucky	55.8		17	Kentucky	55.8
3	Louisiana	67.4		18	Missouri	55.2
47	Maine	42.5		19	Maryland**	54.6
19	Maryland**	54.6		20	Delaware**	54.4
37	Massachusetts	49.3		20	New Jersey	54.4
45	Michigan	44.7		22	Kansas	54.0
48	Minnesota	41.4		23	West Virginia	52.7
9	Mississippi	63.4		24	Indiana	52.0
18	Missouri	55.2		24	Nevada	52.0
46	Montana	44.0		26	Pennsylvania	51.6
36	Nebraska	49.4		27	Connecticut	51.2
24	Nevada	52.0		28	Oregon	51.1
41	New Hampshire**	45.9		28	Rhode Island**	51.1
20	New Jersey	54.4		28	Utah	51.1
16	New Mexico	57.0		31	Idaho	50.3
32	New York	50.2		32	New York	50.2
13	North Carolina	60.1		33	Illinois	50.1
49	North Dakota	41.3		34	Ohio	50.0
34	Ohio	50.0		34	Washington	50.0
11	Oklahoma	60.5		36	Nebraska	49.4
28	Oregon	51.1		37	Massachusetts	49.3
26	Pennsylvania	51.6		38	Colorado	48.4
28	Rhode Island**	51.1		39	Iowa	48.1
5	South Carolina	64.0		40	Wisconsin	46.3
42	South Dakota	45.2		41	New Hampshire**	45.9
14	Tennessee	58.7		42	South Dakota	45.2
4	Texas	66.8		42	Vermont**	45.2
28	Utah	51.1		44	Wyoming	44.8
42	Vermont**	45.2		45	Michigan	44.7
15	Virginia	57.2		46	Montana	44.0
34	Washington	50.0		47	Maine	42.5
23	West Virginia	52.7		48	Minnesota	41.4
40	Wisconsin	46.3		49	North Dakota	41.3
44	Wyoming	44.8		50	Alaska	31.9
					District of Columbia	55.9

Source: CQ Press using data from U.S. Department of Commerce, National Oceanic and Atmospheric Administration "Comparative Climatic Data Through 2012" (ftp://ftp.ncdc.noaa.gov/pub/data/ccd-data/CCD-2012.pdf)

*Based on 30-year averages, 1971-2000.

**Percentages from these states are from a single location. All other states are from two or more reporting cities within each state, which were averaged to determine each state's average.

Percent of Days That Are Sunny*

ALPHA ORDER

RANK	STATE	PERCENT OF DAYS SUNNY
26	Alabama	58
50	Alaska	38
1	Arizona	85
8	Arkansas	66
4	California	72
4	Colorado	72
34	Connecticut**	56
36	Delaware**	55
7	Florida	67
16	Georgia	63
8	Hawaii	66
14	Idaho	64
31	Illinois	57
26	Indiana	58
22	Iowa	60
8	Kansas	66
36	Kentucky	55
14	Louisiana	64
31	Maine**	57
31	Maryland**	57
36	Massachusetts	55
44	Michigan	49
36	Minnesota	55
16	Mississippi	63
26	Missouri	58
24	Montana	59
16	Nebraska	63
2	Nevada	76
48	New Hampshire	44
34	New Jersey**	56
3	New Mexico	75
42	New York	51
22	North Carolina	60
24	North Dakota	59
42	Ohio	51
12	Oklahoma	65
46	Oregon**	48
41	Pennsylvania	53
26	Rhode Island**	58
20	South Carolina	62
16	South Dakota	63
26	Tennessee	58
12	Texas	65
6	Utah	68
44	Vermont**	49
21	Virginia	61
47	Washington	45
49	West Virginia**	40
40	Wisconsin	54
8	Wyoming	66

RANK ORDER

RANK	STATE	PERCENT OF DAYS SUNNY
1	Arizona	85
2	Nevada	76
3	New Mexico	75
4	California	72
4	Colorado	72
6	Utah	68
7	Florida	67
8	Arkansas	66
8	Hawaii	66
8	Kansas	66
8	Wyoming	66
12	Oklahoma	65
12	Texas	65
14	Idaho	64
14	Louisiana	64
16	Georgia	63
16	Mississippi	63
16	Nebraska	63
16	South Dakota	63
20	South Carolina	62
21	Virginia	61
22	Iowa	60
22	North Carolina	60
24	Montana	59
24	North Dakota	59
26	Alabama	58
26	Indiana	58
26	Missouri	58
26	Rhode Island**	58
26	Tennessee	58
31	Illinois	57
31	Maine**	57
31	Maryland**	57
34	Connecticut**	56
34	New Jersey**	56
36	Delaware**	55
36	Kentucky	55
36	Massachusetts	55
36	Minnesota	55
40	Wisconsin	54
41	Pennsylvania	53
42	New York	51
42	Ohio	51
44	Michigan	49
44	Vermont**	49
46	Oregon**	48
47	Washington	45
48	New Hampshire	44
49	West Virginia**	40
50	Alaska	38
	District of Columbia**	56

Source: CQ Press using data from U.S. Department of Commerce, National Oceanic and Atmospheric Administration "Comparative Climatic Data Through 2012" (ftp://ftp.ncdc.noaa.gov/pub/data/ccd-data/CCD-2012.pdf)

*As a percent of possible sunshine updated through 2012.

**Percentages from these states are from a single location. All other states are from two or more reporting cities within each state, which were averaged to determine each state's average.

Average Wind Speed (MPH)*

ALPHA ORDER

RANK	STATE	MILES PER HOUR
41	Alabama	7.6
24	Alaska	9.3
42	Arizona	7.5
40	Arkansas	7.7
46	California	6.9
32	Colorado	8.5
19	Connecticut	9.6
26	Delaware**	9.0
33	Florida	8.3
45	Georgia	7.4
5	Hawaii	10.9
22	Idaho	9.4
18	Illinois	9.8
22	Indiana	9.4
6	Iowa	10.7
2	Kansas	12.0
39	Kentucky	7.8
36	Louisiana	8.1
27	Maine	8.9
30	Maryland**	8.6
1	Massachusetts	12.5
21	Michigan	9.5
11	Minnesota	10.2
48	Mississippi	6.5
13	Missouri	10.1
25	Montana	9.2
9	Nebraska	10.3
37	Nevada	8.0
47	New Hampshire**	6.7
15	New Jersey	10.0
16	New Mexico	9.9
11	New York	10.2
34	North Carolina	8.2
7	North Dakota	10.6
19	Ohio	9.6
3	Oklahoma	11.2
38	Oregon	7.9
30	Pennsylvania	8.6
8	Rhode Island	10.5
42	South Carolina	7.5
4	South Dakota	11.1
48	Tennessee	6.5
9	Texas	10.3
29	Utah**	8.8
27	Vermont**	8.9
34	Virginia	8.2
42	Washington	7.5
48	West Virginia	6.5
16	Wisconsin	9.9
13	Wyoming	10.1

RANK ORDER

RANK	STATE	MILES PER HOUR
1	Massachusetts	12.5
2	Kansas	12.0
3	Oklahoma	11.2
4	South Dakota	11.1
5	Hawaii	10.9
6	Iowa	10.7
7	North Dakota	10.6
8	Rhode Island	10.5
9	Nebraska	10.3
9	Texas	10.3
11	Minnesota	10.2
11	New York	10.2
13	Missouri	10.1
13	Wyoming	10.1
15	New Jersey	10.0
16	New Mexico	9.9
16	Wisconsin	9.9
18	Illinois	9.8
19	Connecticut	9.6
19	Ohio	9.6
21	Michigan	9.5
22	Idaho	9.4
22	Indiana	9.4
24	Alaska	9.3
25	Montana	9.2
26	Delaware**	9.0
27	Maine	8.9
27	Vermont**	8.9
29	Utah**	8.8
30	Maryland**	8.6
30	Pennsylvania	8.6
32	Colorado	8.5
33	Florida	8.3
34	North Carolina	8.2
34	Virginia	8.2
36	Louisiana	8.1
37	Nevada	8.0
38	Oregon	7.9
39	Kentucky	7.8
40	Arkansas	7.7
41	Alabama	7.6
42	Arizona	7.5
42	South Carolina	7.5
42	Washington	7.5
45	Georgia	7.4
46	California	6.9
47	New Hampshire**	6.7
48	Mississippi	6.5
48	Tennessee	6.5
48	West Virginia	6.5

	District of Columbia	8.4

Source: CQ Press using data from U.S. Department of Commerce, National Oceanic and Atmospheric Administration
"Comparative Climatic Data Through 2012" (ftp://ftp.ncdc.noaa.gov/pub/data/ccd-data/CCD-2012.pdf)
*Updated through 2012.
**Averages from these states are from a single location. All other states are from two or more reporting cities within each state,
which were averaged to determine each state's average.

Hazardous Weather Fatalities in 2015

National Total = 478 Fatalities*

RANK	STATE	FATALITIES	% of USA
11	Alabama	13	2.7%
20	Alaska	7	1.5%
17	Arizona	8	1.7%
14	Arkansas	10	2.1%
13	California	12	2.5%
34	Colorado	3	0.6%
37	Connecticut	2	0.4%
44	Delaware	0	0.0%
3	Florida	28	5.9%
25	Georgia	5	1.0%
28	Hawaii	4	0.8%
20	Idaho	7	1.5%
2	Illinois	32	6.7%
17	Indiana	8	1.7%
28	Iowa	4	0.8%
34	Kansas	3	0.6%
7	Kentucky	22	4.6%
28	Louisiana	4	0.8%
44	Maine	0	0.0%
28	Maryland	4	0.8%
44	Massachusetts	0	0.0%
44	Michigan	0	0.0%
42	Minnesota	1	0.2%
11	Mississippi	13	2.7%
4	Missouri	26	5.4%
42	Montana	1	0.2%
37	Nebraska	2	0.4%
5	Nevada	25	5.2%
37	New Hampshire	2	0.4%
22	New Jersey	6	1.3%
16	New Mexico	9	1.9%
25	New York	5	1.0%
25	North Carolina	5	1.0%
44	North Dakota	0	0.0%
22	Ohio	6	1.3%
9	Oklahoma	18	3.8%
22	Oregon	6	1.3%
10	Pennsylvania	15	3.1%
44	Rhode Island	0	0.0%
14	South Carolina	10	2.1%
34	South Dakota	3	0.6%
8	Tennessee	19	4.0%
1	Texas	86	18.0%
6	Utah	24	5.0%
44	Vermont	0	0.0%
37	Virginia	2	0.4%
17	Washington	8	1.7%
28	West Virginia	4	0.8%
28	Wisconsin	4	0.8%
37	Wyoming	2	0.4%

RANK	STATE	FATALITIES	% of USA
1	Texas	86	18.0%
2	Illinois	32	6.7%
3	Florida	28	5.9%
4	Missouri	26	5.4%
5	Nevada	25	5.2%
6	Utah	24	5.0%
7	Kentucky	22	4.6%
8	Tennessee	19	4.0%
9	Oklahoma	18	3.8%
10	Pennsylvania	15	3.1%
11	Alabama	13	2.7%
11	Mississippi	13	2.7%
13	California	12	2.5%
14	Arkansas	10	2.1%
14	South Carolina	10	2.1%
16	New Mexico	9	1.9%
17	Arizona	8	1.7%
17	Indiana	8	1.7%
17	Washington	8	1.7%
20	Alaska	7	1.5%
20	Idaho	7	1.5%
22	New Jersey	6	1.3%
22	Ohio	6	1.3%
22	Oregon	6	1.3%
25	Georgia	5	1.0%
25	New York	5	1.0%
25	North Carolina	5	1.0%
28	Hawaii	4	0.8%
28	Iowa	4	0.8%
28	Louisiana	4	0.8%
28	Maryland	4	0.8%
28	West Virginia	4	0.8%
28	Wisconsin	4	0.8%
34	Colorado	3	0.6%
34	Kansas	3	0.6%
34	South Dakota	3	0.6%
37	Connecticut	2	0.4%
37	Nebraska	2	0.4%
37	New Hampshire	2	0.4%
37	Virginia	2	0.4%
37	Wyoming	2	0.4%
42	Minnesota	1	0.2%
42	Montana	1	0.2%
44	Delaware	0	0.0%
44	Maine	0	0.0%
44	Massachusetts	0	0.0%
44	Michigan	0	0.0%
44	North Dakota	0	0.0%
44	Rhode Island	0	0.0%
44	Vermont	0	0.0%
	District of Columbia	0	0.0%

Source: National Weather Service, Water and Weather Services
   "2015 Summary of Hazardous Weather Fatalities" (http://www.nws.noaa.gov/om/hazstats.shtml)
*Includes lightning, tornado, thunderstorm, extreme temperature, flood, coastal storm, rip current, hurricane, winter storm, fog, avalanche, and other weather events. National total does not include 44 fatalities in U.S. waters or territories.

Tornadoes in 2016

National Total = 1,059 Tornadoes*

ALPHA ORDER

RANK	STATE	TORNADOES	% of USA
3	Alabama	87	8.2%
44	Alaska	0	0.0%
32	Arizona	3	0.3%
18	Arkansas	23	2.2%
27	California	7	0.7%
10	Colorado	45	4.2%
44	Connecticut	0	0.0%
44	Delaware	0	0.0%
7	Florida	48	4.5%
17	Georgia	27	2.5%
44	Hawaii	0	0.0%
41	Idaho	1	0.1%
6	Illinois	50	4.7%
12	Indiana	40	3.8%
9	Iowa	46	4.3%
1	Kansas	99	9.3%
13	Kentucky	32	3.0%
15	Louisiana	31	2.9%
36	Maine	2	0.2%
36	Maryland	2	0.2%
36	Massachusetts	2	0.2%
22	Michigan	15	1.4%
11	Minnesota	44	4.2%
4	Mississippi	67	6.3%
18	Missouri	23	2.2%
30	Montana	4	0.4%
8	Nebraska	47	4.4%
44	Nevada	0	0.0%
36	New Hampshire	2	0.2%
36	New Jersey	2	0.2%
32	New Mexico	3	0.3%
41	New York	1	0.1%
20	North Carolina	16	1.5%
13	North Dakota	32	3.0%
15	Ohio	31	2.9%
5	Oklahoma	55	5.2%
30	Oregon	4	0.4%
26	Pennsylvania	9	0.8%
44	Rhode Island	0	0.0%
32	South Carolina	3	0.3%
20	South Dakota	16	1.5%
24	Tennessee	11	1.0%
2	Texas	90	8.5%
32	Utah	3	0.3%
44	Vermont	0	0.0%
23	Virginia	12	1.1%
28	Washington	6	0.6%
28	West Virginia	6	0.6%
24	Wisconsin	11	1.0%
41	Wyoming	1	0.1%

RANK ORDER

RANK	STATE	TORNADOES	% of USA
1	Kansas	99	9.3%
2	Texas	90	8.5%
3	Alabama	87	8.2%
4	Mississippi	67	6.3%
5	Oklahoma	55	5.2%
6	Illinois	50	4.7%
7	Florida	48	4.5%
8	Nebraska	47	4.4%
9	Iowa	46	4.3%
10	Colorado	45	4.2%
11	Minnesota	44	4.2%
12	Indiana	40	3.8%
13	Kentucky	32	3.0%
13	North Dakota	32	3.0%
15	Louisiana	31	2.9%
15	Ohio	31	2.9%
17	Georgia	27	2.5%
18	Arkansas	23	2.2%
18	Missouri	23	2.2%
20	North Carolina	16	1.5%
20	South Dakota	16	1.5%
22	Michigan	15	1.4%
23	Virginia	12	1.1%
24	Tennessee	11	1.0%
24	Wisconsin	11	1.0%
26	Pennsylvania	9	0.8%
27	California	7	0.7%
28	Washington	6	0.6%
28	West Virginia	6	0.6%
30	Montana	4	0.4%
30	Oregon	4	0.4%
32	Arizona	3	0.3%
32	New Mexico	3	0.3%
32	South Carolina	3	0.3%
32	Utah	3	0.3%
36	Maine	2	0.2%
36	Maryland	2	0.2%
36	Massachusetts	2	0.2%
36	New Hampshire	2	0.2%
36	New Jersey	2	0.2%
41	Idaho	1	0.1%
41	New York	1	0.1%
41	Wyoming	1	0.1%
44	Alaska	0	0.0%
44	Connecticut	0	0.0%
44	Delaware	0	0.0%
44	Hawaii	0	0.0%
44	Nevada	0	0.0%
44	Rhode Island	0	0.0%
44	Vermont	0	0.0%
	District of Columbia	0	0.0%

Source: National Weather Service, Storm Prediction Center
"Annual Severe Weather Report Summary - 2016" (http://www.spc.noaa.gov/climo/online/monthly/newm.html)
*Preliminary figures. Tornadoes striking more than one state are counted in each state.

Fatalities Caused by Tornadoes: 2008 to 2016

National Total = 968 Fatalities

RANK	STATE	FATALITIES	% of USA
1	Alabama	260	26.9%
31	Alaska	0	0.0%
31	Arizona	0	0.0%
6	Arkansas	63	6.5%
31	California	0	0.0%
25	Colorado	1	0.1%
31	Connecticut	0	0.0%
31	Delaware	0	0.0%
20	Florida	4	0.4%
10	Georgia	23	2.4%
31	Hawaii	0	0.0%
31	Idaho	0	0.0%
11	Illinois	20	2.1%
12	Indiana	17	1.8%
13	Iowa	16	1.7%
16	Kansas	8	0.8%
7	Kentucky	31	3.2%
17	Louisiana	6	0.6%
31	Maine	0	0.0%
31	Maryland	0	0.0%
21	Massachusetts	3	0.3%
25	Michigan	1	0.1%
18	Minnesota	5	0.5%
3	Mississippi	76	7.9%
2	Missouri	191	19.7%
23	Montana	2	0.2%
23	Nebraska	2	0.2%
31	Nevada	0	0.0%
25	New Hampshire	1	0.1%
31	New Jersey	0	0.0%
31	New Mexico	0	0.0%
18	New York	5	0.5%
8	North Carolina	30	3.1%
25	North Dakota	1	0.1%
14	Ohio	11	1.1%
3	Oklahoma	76	7.9%
31	Oregon	0	0.0%
31	Pennsylvania	0	0.0%
31	Rhode Island	0	0.0%
21	South Carolina	3	0.3%
31	South Dakota	0	0.0%
5	Tennessee	75	7.7%
9	Texas	25	2.6%
31	Utah	0	0.0%
31	Vermont	0	0.0%
15	Virginia	10	1.0%
31	Washington	0	0.0%
25	West Virginia	1	0.1%
25	Wisconsin	1	0.1%
31	Wyoming	0	0.0%

RANK	STATE	FATALITIES	% of USA
1	Alabama	260	26.9%
2	Missouri	191	19.7%
3	Mississippi	76	7.9%
3	Oklahoma	76	7.9%
5	Tennessee	75	7.7%
6	Arkansas	63	6.5%
7	Kentucky	31	3.2%
8	North Carolina	30	3.1%
9	Texas	25	2.6%
10	Georgia	23	2.4%
11	Illinois	20	2.1%
12	Indiana	17	1.8%
13	Iowa	16	1.7%
14	Ohio	11	1.1%
15	Virginia	10	1.0%
16	Kansas	8	0.8%
17	Louisiana	6	0.6%
18	Minnesota	5	0.5%
18	New York	5	0.5%
20	Florida	4	0.4%
21	Massachusetts	3	0.3%
21	South Carolina	3	0.3%
23	Montana	2	0.2%
23	Nebraska	2	0.2%
25	Colorado	1	0.1%
25	Michigan	1	0.1%
25	New Hampshire	1	0.1%
25	North Dakota	1	0.1%
25	West Virginia	1	0.1%
25	Wisconsin	1	0.1%
31	Alaska	0	0.0%
31	Arizona	0	0.0%
31	California	0	0.0%
31	Connecticut	0	0.0%
31	Delaware	0	0.0%
31	Hawaii	0	0.0%
31	Idaho	0	0.0%
31	Maine	0	0.0%
31	Maryland	0	0.0%
31	Nevada	0	0.0%
31	New Jersey	0	0.0%
31	New Mexico	0	0.0%
31	Oregon	0	0.0%
31	Pennsylvania	0	0.0%
31	Rhode Island	0	0.0%
31	South Dakota	0	0.0%
31	Utah	0	0.0%
31	Vermont	0	0.0%
31	Washington	0	0.0%
31	Wyoming	0	0.0%
	District of Columbia	0	0.0%

Source: CQ Press using data from National Weather Service, Storm Prediction Center
"Annual U.S. Killer Tornado Statistics" (http://www.spc.noaa.gov/climo/torn/fatalmap.php)

Cost of Damage from Hazardous Weather in 2015

National Total = $4,781,220,000*

ALPHA ORDER

RANK	STATE	DAMAGE	% of USA
29	Alabama	$14,790,000	0.3%
22	Alaska	25,000,000	0.5%
30	Arizona	10,790,000	0.2%
13	Arkansas	45,510,000	1.0%
6	California	108,710,000	2.3%
33	Colorado	10,030,000	0.2%
45	Connecticut	1,500,000	0.0%
47	Delaware	550,000	0.0%
20	Florida	27,000,000	0.6%
16	Georgia	33,530,000	0.7%
50	Hawaii	120,000	0.0%
34	Idaho	8,740,000	0.2%
11	Illinois	73,610,000	1.5%
39	Indiana	5,350,000	0.1%
7	Iowa	105,710,000	2.2%
15	Kansas	34,860,000	0.7%
28	Kentucky	17,330,000	0.4%
24	Louisiana	22,690,000	0.5%
46	Maine	1,040,000	0.0%
44	Maryland	1,690,000	0.0%
38	Massachusetts	5,500,000	0.1%
10	Michigan	79,920,000	1.7%
37	Minnesota	7,120,000	0.1%
18	Mississippi	29,070,000	0.6%
8	Missouri	87,040,000	1.8%
41	Montana	4,420,000	0.1%
3	Nebraska	307,660,000	6.4%
40	Nevada	4,650,000	0.1%
49	New Hampshire	370,000	0.0%
12	New Jersey	65,600,000	1.4%
2	New Mexico	410,930,000	8.6%
17	New York	32,510,000	0.7%
21	North Carolina	25,630,000	0.5%
32	North Dakota	10,290,000	0.2%
14	Ohio	38,400,000	0.8%
5	Oklahoma	122,720,000	2.6%
23	Oregon	23,720,000	0.5%
26	Pennsylvania	20,540,000	0.4%
48	Rhode Island	510,000	0.0%
4	South Carolina	177,530,000	3.7%
36	South Dakota	7,870,000	0.2%
9	Tennessee	80,800,000	1.7%
1	Texas	2,594,980,000	54.3%
43	Utah	2,770,000	0.1%
42	Vermont	3,550,000	0.1%
27	Virginia	19,530,000	0.4%
19	Washington	28,960,000	0.6%
25	West Virginia	20,730,000	0.4%
34	Wisconsin	8,740,000	0.2%
31	Wyoming	10,600,000	0.2%

RANK ORDER

RANK	STATE	DAMAGE	% of USA
1	Texas	$2,594,980,000	54.3%
2	New Mexico	410,930,000	8.6%
3	Nebraska	307,660,000	6.4%
4	South Carolina	177,530,000	3.7%
5	Oklahoma	122,720,000	2.6%
6	California	108,710,000	2.3%
7	Iowa	105,710,000	2.2%
8	Missouri	87,040,000	1.8%
9	Tennessee	80,800,000	1.7%
10	Michigan	79,920,000	1.7%
11	Illinois	73,610,000	1.5%
12	New Jersey	65,600,000	1.4%
13	Arkansas	45,510,000	1.0%
14	Ohio	38,400,000	0.8%
15	Kansas	34,860,000	0.7%
16	Georgia	33,530,000	0.7%
17	New York	32,510,000	0.7%
18	Mississippi	29,070,000	0.6%
19	Washington	28,960,000	0.6%
20	Florida	27,000,000	0.6%
21	North Carolina	25,630,000	0.5%
22	Alaska	25,000,000	0.5%
23	Oregon	23,720,000	0.5%
24	Louisiana	22,690,000	0.5%
25	West Virginia	20,730,000	0.4%
26	Pennsylvania	20,540,000	0.4%
27	Virginia	19,530,000	0.4%
28	Kentucky	17,330,000	0.4%
29	Alabama	14,790,000	0.3%
30	Arizona	10,790,000	0.2%
31	Wyoming	10,600,000	0.2%
32	North Dakota	10,290,000	0.2%
33	Colorado	10,030,000	0.2%
34	Idaho	8,740,000	0.2%
34	Wisconsin	8,740,000	0.2%
36	South Dakota	7,870,000	0.2%
37	Minnesota	7,120,000	0.1%
38	Massachusetts	5,500,000	0.1%
39	Indiana	5,350,000	0.1%
40	Nevada	4,650,000	0.1%
41	Montana	4,420,000	0.1%
42	Vermont	3,550,000	0.1%
43	Utah	2,770,000	0.1%
44	Maryland	1,690,000	0.0%
45	Connecticut	1,500,000	0.0%
46	Maine	1,040,000	0.0%
47	Delaware	550,000	0.0%
48	Rhode Island	510,000	0.0%
49	New Hampshire	370,000	0.0%
50	Hawaii	120,000	0.0%
	District of Columbia	10,000	0.0%

Source: National Weather Service, Water and Weather Services
    "2015 Summary of Hazardous Weather Fatalities" (http://www.nws.noaa.gov/om/hazstats.shtml)
*Includes property and crop damage from lightning, tornado, thunderstorm, extreme temperature, flood, coastal storm, rip current, hurricane, winter storm, fog, avalanche, and other weather events. National total does not include damage costs in U.S. territories.

National Park Service Land in 2014

National Total = 84,479,064 Acres*

RANK	STATE	ACRES	% of USA
41	Alabama	22,737	0.0%
1	Alaska	54,654,154	64.7%
3	Arizona	2,947,312	3.5%
25	Arkansas	104,977	0.1%
2	California	8,144,518	9.6%
11	Colorado	737,812	0.9%
46	Connecticut	7,782	0.0%
48	Delaware	900	0.0%
4	Florida	2,638,658	3.1%
34	Georgia	63,338	0.1%
17	Hawaii	369,166	0.4%
13	Idaho	518,224	0.6%
49	Illinois	115	0.0%
43	Indiana	15,540	0.0%
47	Iowa	2,713	0.0%
44	Kansas	11,636	0.0%
27	Kentucky	95,942	0.1%
39	Louisiana	23,545	0.0%
29	Maine	91,826	0.1%
31	Maryland	73,893	0.1%
35	Massachusetts	57,962	0.1%
12	Michigan	718,148	0.9%
20	Minnesota	301,330	0.4%
24	Mississippi	118,587	0.1%
30	Missouri	83,476	0.1%
8	Montana	1,274,364	1.5%
36	Nebraska	45,735	0.1%
10	Nevada	778,512	0.9%
42	New Hampshire	21,015	0.0%
26	New Jersey	99,313	0.1%
15	New Mexico	391,078	0.5%
32	New York	72,992	0.1%
14	North Carolina	407,225	0.5%
33	North Dakota	72,568	0.1%
37	Ohio	34,544	0.0%
45	Oklahoma	10,241	0.0%
21	Oregon	199,319	0.2%
22	Pennsylvania	138,683	0.2%
50	Rhode Island	5	0.0%
38	South Carolina	32,348	0.0%
19	South Dakota	302,998	0.4%
16	Tennessee	384,978	0.5%
9	Texas	1,247,918	1.5%
6	Utah	2,117,683	2.5%
40	Vermont	23,265	0.0%
18	Virginia	364,371	0.4%
7	Washington	1,967,532	2.3%
28	West Virginia	92,721	0.1%
23	Wisconsin	133,755	0.2%
5	Wyoming	2,396,424	2.8%

RANK ORDER

RANK	STATE	ACRES	% of USA
1	Alaska	54,654,154	64.7%
2	California	8,144,518	9.6%
3	Arizona	2,947,312	3.5%
4	Florida	2,638,658	3.1%
5	Wyoming	2,396,424	2.8%
6	Utah	2,117,683	2.5%
7	Washington	1,967,532	2.3%
8	Montana	1,274,364	1.5%
9	Texas	1,247,918	1.5%
10	Nevada	778,512	0.9%
11	Colorado	737,812	0.9%
12	Michigan	718,148	0.9%
13	Idaho	518,224	0.6%
14	North Carolina	407,225	0.5%
15	New Mexico	391,078	0.5%
16	Tennessee	384,978	0.5%
17	Hawaii	369,166	0.4%
18	Virginia	364,371	0.4%
19	South Dakota	302,998	0.4%
20	Minnesota	301,330	0.4%
21	Oregon	199,319	0.2%
22	Pennsylvania	138,683	0.2%
23	Wisconsin	133,755	0.2%
24	Mississippi	118,587	0.1%
25	Arkansas	104,977	0.1%
26	New Jersey	99,313	0.1%
27	Kentucky	95,942	0.1%
28	West Virginia	92,721	0.1%
29	Maine	91,826	0.1%
30	Missouri	83,476	0.1%
31	Maryland	73,893	0.1%
32	New York	72,992	0.1%
33	North Dakota	72,568	0.1%
34	Georgia	63,338	0.1%
35	Massachusetts	57,962	0.1%
36	Nebraska	45,735	0.1%
37	Ohio	34,544	0.0%
38	South Carolina	32,348	0.0%
39	Louisiana	23,545	0.0%
40	Vermont	23,265	0.0%
41	Alabama	22,737	0.0%
42	New Hampshire	21,015	0.0%
43	Indiana	15,540	0.0%
44	Kansas	11,636	0.0%
45	Oklahoma	10,241	0.0%
46	Connecticut	7,782	0.0%
47	Iowa	2,713	0.0%
48	Delaware	900	0.0%
49	Illinois	115	0.0%
50	Rhode Island	5	0.0%
	District of Columbia	7,131	0.0%

ALPHA ORDER

Source: National Park Service
  "Listing of Acreage by State" (unpublished data)
*As of December 31, 2014. Includes federal and nonfederal land in national parks, monuments, historic sites, recreation areas, preserves, battlefields, grasslands, seashores, parkways, trails, and rivers. Does not include land in national forest or wildlife areas. Includes 58,057 acres in U.S. territories.

Recreation Visits to National Park Service Areas in 2014

National Total = 292,800,082 Visits*

ALPHA ORDER

RANK	STATE	VISITS	% of USA
37	Alabama	753,178	0.3%
25	Alaska	2,684,693	0.9%
5	Arizona	10,747,219	3.7%
24	Arkansas	3,132,898	1.1%
1	California	37,363,392	12.8%
16	Colorado	6,031,874	2.1%
49	Connecticut	34,082	0.0%
50	Delaware	0	0.0%
6	Florida	10,667,459	3.6%
12	Georgia	7,491,109	2.6%
18	Hawaii	5,213,817	1.8%
40	Idaho	553,739	0.2%
43	Illinois	218,132	0.1%
30	Indiana	1,778,385	0.6%
44	Iowa	216,898	0.1%
45	Kansas	98,591	0.0%
29	Kentucky	1,828,192	0.6%
41	Louisiana	510,522	0.2%
26	Maine	2,574,717	0.9%
13	Maryland	6,815,195	2.3%
8	Massachusetts	9,850,586	3.4%
28	Michigan	1,993,139	0.7%
36	Minnesota	811,616	0.3%
14	Mississippi	6,557,120	2.2%
23	Missouri	3,385,772	1.2%
20	Montana	4,590,398	1.6%
42	Nebraska	254,198	0.1%
17	Nevada	5,314,681	1.8%
48	New Hampshire	37,785	0.0%
21	New Jersey	4,389,637	1.5%
31	New Mexico	1,602,114	0.5%
4	New York	16,141,397	5.5%
3	North Carolina	16,710,759	5.7%
39	North Dakota	581,851	0.2%
27	Ohio	2,470,177	0.8%
34	Oklahoma	1,165,269	0.4%
35	Oregon	1,033,254	0.4%
9	Pennsylvania	9,005,244	3.1%
46	Rhode Island	51,523	0.0%
33	South Carolina	1,519,746	0.5%
22	South Dakota	3,861,090	1.3%
10	Tennessee	8,470,460	2.9%
19	Texas	4,680,387	1.6%
7	Utah	10,551,040	3.6%
47	Vermont	39,086	0.0%
2	Virginia	22,870,531	7.8%
11	Washington	7,652,073	2.6%
32	West Virginia	1,541,805	0.5%
38	Wisconsin	625,850	0.2%
15	Wyoming	6,387,455	2.2%

RANK ORDER

RANK	STATE	VISITS	% of USA
1	California	37,363,392	12.8%
2	Virginia	22,870,531	7.8%
3	North Carolina	16,710,759	5.7%
4	New York	16,141,397	5.5%
5	Arizona	10,747,219	3.7%
6	Florida	10,667,459	3.6%
7	Utah	10,551,040	3.6%
8	Massachusetts	9,850,586	3.4%
9	Pennsylvania	9,005,244	3.1%
10	Tennessee	8,470,460	2.9%
11	Washington	7,652,073	2.6%
12	Georgia	7,491,109	2.6%
13	Maryland	6,815,195	2.3%
14	Mississippi	6,557,120	2.2%
15	Wyoming	6,387,455	2.2%
16	Colorado	6,031,874	2.1%
17	Nevada	5,314,681	1.8%
18	Hawaii	5,213,817	1.8%
19	Texas	4,680,387	1.6%
20	Montana	4,590,398	1.6%
21	New Jersey	4,389,637	1.5%
22	South Dakota	3,861,090	1.3%
23	Missouri	3,385,772	1.2%
24	Arkansas	3,132,898	1.1%
25	Alaska	2,684,693	0.9%
26	Maine	2,574,717	0.9%
27	Ohio	2,470,177	0.8%
28	Michigan	1,993,139	0.7%
29	Kentucky	1,828,192	0.6%
30	Indiana	1,778,385	0.6%
31	New Mexico	1,602,114	0.5%
32	West Virginia	1,541,805	0.5%
33	South Carolina	1,519,746	0.5%
34	Oklahoma	1,165,269	0.4%
35	Oregon	1,033,254	0.4%
36	Minnesota	811,616	0.3%
37	Alabama	753,178	0.3%
38	Wisconsin	625,850	0.2%
39	North Dakota	581,851	0.2%
40	Idaho	553,739	0.2%
41	Louisiana	510,522	0.2%
42	Nebraska	254,198	0.1%
43	Illinois	218,132	0.1%
44	Iowa	216,898	0.1%
45	Kansas	98,591	0.0%
46	Rhode Island	51,523	0.0%
47	Vermont	39,086	0.0%
48	New Hampshire	37,785	0.0%
49	Connecticut	34,082	0.0%
50	Delaware	0	0.0%
	District of Columbia	37,701,216	12.9%

Source: National Park Service, Public Use Statistics Office
"National Park Service Statistical Abstract 2014" (https://irma.nps.gov/Stats/Reports/AbstractsandForecasts)
*National total includes 2,238,731 visits in U.S. territories.

Percent Change in National Park Service Recreation Visits: 2013 to 2014

National Percent Change = 7.0% Increase*

ALPHA ORDER

RANK	STATE	PERCENT CHANGE
37	Alabama	0.4
28	Alaska	3.8
17	Arizona	6.4
10	Arkansas	12.9
24	California	5.0
11	Colorado	11.8
2	Connecticut	49.1
NA	Delaware**	NA
30	Florida	3.7
19	Georgia	6.3
17	Hawaii	6.4
46	Idaho	(9.9)
26	Illinois	4.2
45	Indiana	(8.1)
13	Iowa	8.5
14	Kansas	7.3
8	Kentucky	13.9
49	Louisiana	(18.2)
9	Maine	13.6
32	Maryland	3.0
35	Massachusetts	1.8
38	Michigan	0.2
5	Minnesota	23.3
44	Mississippi	(3.4)
48	Missouri	(12.9)
15	Montana	7.2
41	Nebraska	(1.4)
12	Nevada	9.6
40	New Hampshire	(0.1)
47	New Jersey	(12.7)
20	New Mexico	5.9
3	New York	46.9
31	North Carolina	3.6
36	North Dakota	1.6
34	Ohio	2.7
22	Oklahoma	5.2
16	Oregon	6.6
43	Pennsylvania	(1.5)
20	Rhode Island	5.9
38	South Carolina	0.2
41	South Dakota	(1.4)
25	Tennessee	4.7
4	Texas	34.4
6	Utah	17.5
7	Vermont	14.6
28	Virginia	3.8
26	Washington	4.2
33	West Virginia	2.9
1	Wisconsin	95.6
23	Wyoming	5.1

RANK ORDER

RANK	STATE	PERCENT CHANGE
1	Wisconsin	95.6
2	Connecticut	49.1
3	New York	46.9
4	Texas	34.4
5	Minnesota	23.3
6	Utah	17.5
7	Vermont	14.6
8	Kentucky	13.9
9	Maine	13.6
10	Arkansas	12.9
11	Colorado	11.8
12	Nevada	9.6
13	Iowa	8.5
14	Kansas	7.3
15	Montana	7.2
16	Oregon	6.6
17	Arizona	6.4
17	Hawaii	6.4
19	Georgia	6.3
20	New Mexico	5.9
20	Rhode Island	5.9
22	Oklahoma	5.2
23	Wyoming	5.1
24	California	5.0
25	Tennessee	4.7
26	Illinois	4.2
26	Washington	4.2
28	Alaska	3.8
28	Virginia	3.8
30	Florida	3.7
31	North Carolina	3.6
32	Maryland	3.0
33	West Virginia	2.9
34	Ohio	2.7
35	Massachusetts	1.8
36	North Dakota	1.6
37	Alabama	0.4
38	Michigan	0.2
38	South Carolina	0.2
40	New Hampshire	(0.1)
41	Nebraska	(1.4)
41	South Dakota	(1.4)
43	Pennsylvania	(1.5)
44	Mississippi	(3.4)
45	Indiana	(8.1)
46	Idaho	(9.9)
47	New Jersey	(12.7)
48	Missouri	(12.9)
49	Louisiana	(18.2)
NA	Delaware**	NA

District of Columbia	10.2

Source: National Park Service, Public Use Statistics Office
"National Park Service Statistical Abstract 2014" (https://irma.nps.gov/Stats/Reports/AbstractsandForecasts)
*National percent change includes visits in U.S. territories.
**Not applicable.

IX. Government Finances: Federal

Internal Revenue Service Gross Collections in 2015

National Total = $3,302,677,258,000*

ALPHA ORDER

RANK	STATE	COLLECTIONS	% of USA
31	Alabama	$25,070,261,000	0.8%
48	Alaska	5,717,640,000	0.2%
23	Arizona	42,631,316,000	1.3%
27	Arkansas	32,508,761,000	1.0%
1	California	405,851,295,000	12.3%
22	Colorado	47,210,720,000	1.4%
19	Connecticut	59,174,581,000	1.8%
34	Delaware	22,640,853,000	0.7%
4	Florida	177,389,488,000	5.4%
11	Georgia	86,446,602,000	2.6%
42	Hawaii	8,221,290,000	0.2%
40	Idaho	9,785,027,000	0.3%
5	Illinois	158,042,273,000	4.8%
20	Indiana	57,972,825,000	1.8%
33	Iowa	23,969,391,000	0.7%
29	Kansas	27,019,291,000	0.8%
26	Kentucky	32,708,391,000	1.0%
24	Louisiana	42,628,150,000	1.3%
45	Maine	7,464,280,000	0.2%
17	Maryland	63,936,798,000	1.9%
9	Massachusetts	108,049,205,000	3.3%
14	Michigan	77,948,414,000	2.4%
10	Minnesota	106,927,808,000	3.2%
38	Mississippi	11,468,660,000	0.3%
16	Missouri	64,112,504,000	1.9%
47	Montana	5,805,098,000	0.2%
30	Nebraska	25,103,770,000	0.8%
36	Nevada	18,450,072,000	0.6%
39	New Hampshire	11,314,985,000	0.3%
6	New Jersey	153,917,572,000	4.7%
41	New Mexico	8,969,666,000	0.3%
3	New York	269,716,999,000	8.2%
13	North Carolina	78,736,401,000	2.4%
44	North Dakota	7,711,243,000	0.2%
7	Ohio	140,981,150,000	4.3%
25	Oklahoma	33,942,286,000	1.0%
28	Oregon	31,219,148,000	0.9%
8	Pennsylvania	136,108,810,000	4.1%
37	Rhode Island	14,373,318,000	0.4%
32	South Carolina	24,086,257,000	0.7%
43	South Dakota	7,732,138,000	0.2%
18	Tennessee	62,708,662,000	1.9%
2	Texas	279,904,425,000	8.5%
35	Utah	20,178,718,000	0.6%
50	Vermont	4,495,280,000	0.1%
12	Virginia	80,242,853,000	2.4%
15	Washington	73,334,437,000	2.2%
46	West Virginia	7,374,299,000	0.2%
21	Wisconsin	51,748,831,000	1.6%
49	Wyoming	5,284,146,000	0.2%

RANK ORDER

RANK	STATE	COLLECTIONS	% of USA
1	California	$405,851,295,000	12.3%
2	Texas	279,904,425,000	8.5%
3	New York	269,716,999,000	8.2%
4	Florida	177,389,488,000	5.4%
5	Illinois	158,042,273,000	4.8%
6	New Jersey	153,917,572,000	4.7%
7	Ohio	140,981,150,000	4.3%
8	Pennsylvania	136,108,810,000	4.1%
9	Massachusetts	108,049,205,000	3.3%
10	Minnesota	106,927,808,000	3.2%
11	Georgia	86,446,602,000	2.6%
12	Virginia	80,242,853,000	2.4%
13	North Carolina	78,736,401,000	2.4%
14	Michigan	77,948,414,000	2.4%
15	Washington	73,334,437,000	2.2%
16	Missouri	64,112,504,000	1.9%
17	Maryland	63,936,798,000	1.9%
18	Tennessee	62,708,662,000	1.9%
19	Connecticut	59,174,581,000	1.8%
20	Indiana	57,972,825,000	1.8%
21	Wisconsin	51,748,831,000	1.6%
22	Colorado	47,210,720,000	1.4%
23	Arizona	42,631,316,000	1.3%
24	Louisiana	42,628,150,000	1.3%
25	Oklahoma	33,942,286,000	1.0%
26	Kentucky	32,708,391,000	1.0%
27	Arkansas	32,508,761,000	1.0%
28	Oregon	31,219,148,000	0.9%
29	Kansas	27,019,291,000	0.8%
30	Nebraska	25,103,770,000	0.8%
31	Alabama	25,070,261,000	0.8%
32	South Carolina	24,086,257,000	0.7%
33	Iowa	23,969,391,000	0.7%
34	Delaware	22,640,853,000	0.7%
35	Utah	20,178,718,000	0.6%
36	Nevada	18,450,072,000	0.6%
37	Rhode Island	14,373,318,000	0.4%
38	Mississippi	11,468,660,000	0.3%
39	New Hampshire	11,314,985,000	0.3%
40	Idaho	9,785,027,000	0.3%
41	New Mexico	8,969,666,000	0.3%
42	Hawaii	8,221,290,000	0.2%
43	South Dakota	7,732,138,000	0.2%
44	North Dakota	7,711,243,000	0.2%
45	Maine	7,464,280,000	0.2%
46	West Virginia	7,374,299,000	0.2%
47	Montana	5,805,098,000	0.2%
48	Alaska	5,717,640,000	0.2%
49	Wyoming	5,284,146,000	0.2%
50	Vermont	4,495,280,000	0.1%
	District of Columbia	25,583,750,000	0.8%

Source: U.S. Department of the Treasury, Internal Revenue Service
"Fiscal Year 2015 IRS Data Book" (http://www.irs.gov/uac/SOI-Tax-Stats-IRS-Data-Book)
*Total includes $18,757,122,000 from U.S. citizens abroad and other miscellaneous returns not shown separately.

Per Capita Internal Revenue Service Gross Collections in 2015

National Per Capita = $10,234*

RANK	STATE	PER CAPITA
46	Alabama	$5,165
35	Alaska	7,751
41	Arizona	6,253
11	Arkansas	10,917
15	California	10,408
29	Colorado	8,664
4	Connecticut	16,507
1	Delaware	23,982
27	Florida	8,762
31	Georgia	8,476
43	Hawaii	5,769
42	Idaho	5,920
9	Illinois	12,310
26	Indiana	8,767
36	Iowa	7,678
21	Kansas	9,295
37	Kentucky	7,392
22	Louisiana	9,130
45	Maine	5,615
12	Maryland	10,665
5	Massachusetts	15,927
32	Michigan	7,860
2	Minnesota	19,504
50	Mississippi	3,836
14	Missouri	10,551
44	Montana	5,625
8	Nebraska	13,256
40	Nevada	6,398
30	New Hampshire	8,507
3	New Jersey	17,226
48	New Mexico	4,312
6	New York	13,659
33	North Carolina	7,846
18	North Dakota	10,189
10	Ohio	12,148
28	Oklahoma	8,687
34	Oregon	7,757
13	Pennsylvania	10,640
7	Rhode Island	13,616
47	South Carolina	4,921
23	South Dakota	9,013
20	Tennessee	9,508
17	Texas	10,204
39	Utah	6,747
38	Vermont	7,180
19	Virginia	9,590
16	Washington	10,242
49	West Virginia	4,005
25	Wisconsin	8,972
24	Wyoming	9,009

RANK	STATE	PER CAPITA
1	Delaware	$23,982
2	Minnesota	19,504
3	New Jersey	17,226
4	Connecticut	16,507
5	Massachusetts	15,927
6	New York	13,659
7	Rhode Island	13,616
8	Nebraska	13,256
9	Illinois	12,310
10	Ohio	12,148
11	Arkansas	10,917
12	Maryland	10,665
13	Pennsylvania	10,640
14	Missouri	10,551
15	California	10,408
16	Washington	10,242
17	Texas	10,204
18	North Dakota	10,189
19	Virginia	9,590
20	Tennessee	9,508
21	Kansas	9,295
22	Louisiana	9,130
23	South Dakota	9,013
24	Wyoming	9,009
25	Wisconsin	8,972
26	Indiana	8,767
27	Florida	8,762
28	Oklahoma	8,687
29	Colorado	8,664
30	New Hampshire	8,507
31	Georgia	8,476
32	Michigan	7,860
33	North Carolina	7,846
34	Oregon	7,757
35	Alaska	7,751
36	Iowa	7,678
37	Kentucky	7,392
38	Vermont	7,180
39	Utah	6,747
40	Nevada	6,398
41	Arizona	6,253
42	Idaho	5,920
43	Hawaii	5,769
44	Montana	5,625
45	Maine	5,615
46	Alabama	5,165
47	South Carolina	4,921
48	New Mexico	4,312
49	West Virginia	4,005
50	Mississippi	3,836
	District of Columbia	38,163

Source: CQ Press using data from U.S. Department of the Treasury, Internal Revenue Service
"Fiscal Year 2015 IRS Data Book" (http://www.irs.gov/uac/SOI-Tax-Stats-IRS-Data-Book)
*National per capita does not include collections from U.S. citizens abroad and other miscellaneous returns not shown separately.

Federal Individual Income Tax Collections in 2015

National Total = $2,815,544,615,000*

ALPHA ORDER

RANK	STATE	COLLECTIONS	% of USA
30	Alabama	$23,160,484,000	0.8%
48	Alaska	5,462,605,000	0.2%
24	Arizona	37,047,410,000	1.3%
28	Arkansas	23,959,297,000	0.9%
1	California	345,830,143,000	12.3%
21	Colorado	48,125,613,000	1.7%
20	Connecticut	49,189,122,000	1.7%
36	Delaware	13,196,278,000	0.5%
4	Florida	163,199,338,000	5.8%
12	Georgia	70,052,525,000	2.5%
42	Hawaii	7,468,136,000	0.3%
40	Idaho	9,389,727,000	0.3%
5	Illinois	132,643,232,000	4.7%
19	Indiana	50,811,098,000	1.8%
32	Iowa	21,556,743,000	0.8%
29	Kansas	23,284,508,000	0.8%
25	Kentucky	28,811,348,000	1.0%
23	Louisiana	40,681,260,000	1.4%
45	Maine	6,947,573,000	0.2%
16	Maryland	59,638,796,000	2.1%
9	Massachusetts	97,226,545,000	3.5%
11	Michigan	70,295,550,000	2.5%
10	Minnesota	79,347,688,000	2.8%
39	Mississippi	10,507,791,000	0.4%
18	Missouri	54,101,726,000	1.9%
47	Montana	5,538,068,000	0.2%
34	Nebraska	18,026,855,000	0.6%
35	Nevada	17,264,613,000	0.6%
37	New Hampshire	10,749,228,000	0.4%
8	New Jersey	114,834,184,000	4.1%
41	New Mexico	8,519,028,000	0.3%
2	New York	233,878,379,000	8.3%
14	North Carolina	67,278,363,000	2.4%
43	North Dakota	7,263,315,000	0.3%
6	Ohio	121,379,888,000	4.3%
27	Oklahoma	25,554,628,000	0.9%
26	Oregon	28,153,829,000	1.0%
7	Pennsylvania	115,272,208,000	4.1%
38	Rhode Island	10,672,687,000	0.4%
31	South Carolina	21,934,428,000	0.8%
44	South Dakota	7,118,323,000	0.3%
17	Tennessee	54,104,159,000	1.9%
3	Texas	226,945,577,000	8.1%
33	Utah	18,109,139,000	0.6%
50	Vermont	4,097,342,000	0.1%
13	Virginia	67,798,667,000	2.4%
15	Washington	65,551,576,000	2.3%
46	West Virginia	6,892,438,000	0.2%
22	Wisconsin	45,199,884,000	1.6%
49	Wyoming	4,855,460,000	0.2%

RANK ORDER

RANK	STATE	COLLECTIONS	% of USA
1	California	$345,830,143,000	12.3%
2	New York	233,878,379,000	8.3%
3	Texas	226,945,577,000	8.1%
4	Florida	163,199,338,000	5.8%
5	Illinois	132,643,232,000	4.7%
6	Ohio	121,379,888,000	4.3%
7	Pennsylvania	115,272,208,000	4.1%
8	New Jersey	114,834,184,000	4.1%
9	Massachusetts	97,226,545,000	3.5%
10	Minnesota	79,347,688,000	2.8%
11	Michigan	70,295,550,000	2.5%
12	Georgia	70,052,525,000	2.5%
13	Virginia	67,798,667,000	2.4%
14	North Carolina	67,278,363,000	2.4%
15	Washington	65,551,576,000	2.3%
16	Maryland	59,638,796,000	2.1%
17	Tennessee	54,104,159,000	1.9%
18	Missouri	54,101,726,000	1.9%
19	Indiana	50,811,098,000	1.8%
20	Connecticut	49,189,122,000	1.7%
21	Colorado	48,125,613,000	1.7%
22	Wisconsin	45,199,884,000	1.6%
23	Louisiana	40,681,260,000	1.4%
24	Arizona	37,047,410,000	1.3%
25	Kentucky	28,811,348,000	1.0%
26	Oregon	28,153,829,000	1.0%
27	Oklahoma	25,554,628,000	0.9%
28	Arkansas	23,959,297,000	0.9%
29	Kansas	23,284,508,000	0.8%
30	Alabama	23,160,484,000	0.8%
31	South Carolina	21,934,428,000	0.8%
32	Iowa	21,556,743,000	0.8%
33	Utah	18,109,139,000	0.6%
34	Nebraska	18,026,855,000	0.6%
35	Nevada	17,264,613,000	0.6%
36	Delaware	13,196,278,000	0.5%
37	New Hampshire	10,749,228,000	0.4%
38	Rhode Island	10,672,687,000	0.4%
39	Mississippi	10,507,791,000	0.4%
40	Idaho	9,389,727,000	0.3%
41	New Mexico	8,519,028,000	0.3%
42	Hawaii	7,468,136,000	0.3%
43	North Dakota	7,263,315,000	0.3%
44	South Dakota	7,118,323,000	0.3%
45	Maine	6,947,573,000	0.2%
46	West Virginia	6,892,438,000	0.2%
47	Montana	5,538,068,000	0.2%
48	Alaska	5,462,605,000	0.2%
49	Wyoming	4,855,460,000	0.2%
50	Vermont	4,097,342,000	0.1%
	District of Columbia	21,229,350,000	0.8%

Source: U.S. Department of the Treasury, Internal Revenue Service
"Fiscal Year 2015 IRS Data Book" (http://www.irs.gov/uac/SOI-Tax-Stats-IRS-Data-Book)
*Total includes $15,388,463,000 from U.S. citizens abroad and other miscellaneous returns not shown separately.

Average Revenue Collection per Federal Individual Income Tax Return in 2015

National Average = $18,917 per Return*

ALPHA ORDER				RANK ORDER		
RANK	STATE	PER RETURN		RANK	STATE	PER RETURN
43	Alabama	$11,301		1	Delaware	$29,691
34	Alaska	15,289		2	Minnesota	29,508
41	Arizona	13,016		3	Massachusetts	29,071
16	Arkansas	19,588		4	Connecticut	28,048
13	California	19,860		5	New Jersey	26,401
19	Colorado	18,881		6	New York	24,533
4	Connecticut	28,048		7	Ohio	21,816
1	Delaware	29,691		8	Illinois	21,617
24	Florida	17,342		9	Rhode Island	20,447
29	Georgia	15,964		10	Maryland	20,283
45	Hawaii	10,945		11	Nebraska	20,232
39	Idaho	13,387		12	Louisiana	20,218
8	Illinois	21,617		13	California	19,860
27	Indiana	16,515		14	Washington	19,628
37	Iowa	14,926		15	North Dakota	19,606
23	Kansas	17,427		16	Arkansas	19,588
35	Kentucky	15,207		17	Missouri	19,535
12	Louisiana	20,218		18	Texas	19,046
46	Maine	10,896		19	Colorado	18,881
10	Maryland	20,283		20	Pennsylvania	18,666
3	Massachusetts	29,071		21	Tennessee	18,463
36	Michigan	15,006		22	Virginia	17,500
2	Minnesota	29,508		23	Kansas	17,427
50	Mississippi	8,433		24	Florida	17,342
17	Missouri	19,535		25	Wyoming	17,272
44	Montana	11,266		26	South Dakota	17,266
11	Nebraska	20,232		27	Indiana	16,515
40	Nevada	13,038		28	Wisconsin	16,087
30	New Hampshire	15,697		29	Georgia	15,964
5	New Jersey	26,401		30	New Hampshire	15,697
48	New Mexico	9,341		31	Oklahoma	15,572
6	New York	24,533		32	Oregon	15,398
33	North Carolina	15,356		33	North Carolina	15,356
15	North Dakota	19,606		34	Alaska	15,289
7	Ohio	21,816		35	Kentucky	15,207
31	Oklahoma	15,572		36	Michigan	15,006
32	Oregon	15,398		37	Iowa	14,926
20	Pennsylvania	18,666		38	Utah	14,824
9	Rhode Island	20,447		39	Idaho	13,387
47	South Carolina	10,283		40	Nevada	13,038
26	South Dakota	17,266		41	Arizona	13,016
21	Tennessee	18,463		42	Vermont	12,700
18	Texas	19,046		43	Alabama	11,301
38	Utah	14,824		44	Montana	11,266
42	Vermont	12,700		45	Hawaii	10,945
22	Virginia	17,500		46	Maine	10,896
14	Washington	19,628		47	South Carolina	10,283
49	West Virginia	8,793		48	New Mexico	9,341
28	Wisconsin	16,087		49	West Virginia	8,793
25	Wyoming	17,272		50	Mississippi	8,433
					District of Columbia	62,859

Source: CQ Press using data from U.S. Department of the Treasury, Internal Revenue Service
"Fiscal Year 2015 IRS Data Book" (http://www.irs.gov/uac/SOI-Tax-Stats-IRS-Data-Book)
*National Rate includes collections and returns from U.S. citizens abroad and other miscellaneous returns not shown separately.

Adjusted Gross Income in 2014

National Total = $9,706,026,114,000*

ALPHA ORDER

RANK	STATE	A.G.I.	% of USA
27	Alabama	$107,936,740,000	1.1%
48	Alaska	24,272,390,000	0.3%
21	Arizona	161,928,643,000	1.7%
34	Arkansas	65,054,335,000	0.7%
1	California	1,287,368,304,000	13.3%
17	Colorado	179,600,634,000	1.9%
20	Connecticut	164,110,851,000	1.7%
44	Delaware	27,516,019,000	0.3%
4	Florida	570,292,720,000	5.9%
12	Georgia	253,487,684,000	2.6%
39	Hawaii	39,689,089,000	0.4%
41	Idaho	36,997,279,000	0.4%
5	Illinois	424,188,653,000	4.4%
19	Indiana	166,637,525,000	1.7%
30	Iowa	86,096,947,000	0.9%
31	Kansas	83,259,525,000	0.9%
28	Kentucky	98,331,729,000	1.0%
24	Louisiana	115,571,432,000	1.2%
42	Maine	34,159,794,000	0.4%
15	Maryland	213,549,098,000	2.2%
9	Massachusetts	285,581,083,000	2.9%
11	Michigan	266,767,393,000	2.7%
16	Minnesota	184,514,005,000	1.9%
35	Mississippi	57,992,430,000	0.6%
23	Missouri	156,727,536,000	1.6%
46	Montana	27,178,486,000	0.3%
36	Nebraska	54,867,033,000	0.6%
32	Nevada	77,642,876,000	0.8%
37	New Hampshire	47,606,625,000	0.5%
7	New Jersey	353,247,794,000	3.6%
38	New Mexico	46,264,952,000	0.5%
3	New York	754,932,479,000	7.8%
13	North Carolina	247,012,395,000	2.5%
45	North Dakota	27,236,634,000	0.3%
8	Ohio	313,149,940,000	3.2%
29	Oklahoma	97,488,903,000	1.0%
26	Oregon	109,310,786,000	1.1%
6	Pennsylvania	388,883,451,000	4.0%
43	Rhode Island	32,511,563,000	0.3%
25	South Carolina	111,386,099,000	1.1%
47	South Dakota	24,938,776,000	0.3%
22	Tennessee	161,050,478,000	1.7%
2	Texas	806,504,418,000	8.3%
33	Utah	74,268,005,000	0.8%
50	Vermont	18,588,007,000	0.2%
10	Virginia	279,345,572,000	2.9%
14	Washington	244,055,829,000	2.5%
40	West Virginia	39,461,888,000	0.4%
18	Wisconsin	167,540,416,000	1.7%
49	Wyoming	21,658,081,000	0.2%

RANK ORDER

RANK	STATE	A.G.I.	% of USA
1	California	$1,287,368,304,000	13.3%
2	Texas	806,504,418,000	8.3%
3	New York	754,932,479,000	7.8%
4	Florida	570,292,720,000	5.9%
5	Illinois	424,188,653,000	4.4%
6	Pennsylvania	388,883,451,000	4.0%
7	New Jersey	353,247,794,000	3.6%
8	Ohio	313,149,940,000	3.2%
9	Massachusetts	285,581,083,000	2.9%
10	Virginia	279,345,572,000	2.9%
11	Michigan	266,767,393,000	2.7%
12	Georgia	253,487,684,000	2.6%
13	North Carolina	247,012,395,000	2.5%
14	Washington	244,055,829,000	2.5%
15	Maryland	213,549,098,000	2.2%
16	Minnesota	184,514,005,000	1.9%
17	Colorado	179,600,634,000	1.9%
18	Wisconsin	167,540,416,000	1.7%
19	Indiana	166,637,525,000	1.7%
20	Connecticut	164,110,851,000	1.7%
21	Arizona	161,928,643,000	1.7%
22	Tennessee	161,050,478,000	1.7%
23	Missouri	156,727,536,000	1.6%
24	Louisiana	115,571,432,000	1.2%
25	South Carolina	111,386,099,000	1.1%
26	Oregon	109,310,786,000	1.1%
27	Alabama	107,936,740,000	1.1%
28	Kentucky	98,331,729,000	1.0%
29	Oklahoma	97,488,903,000	1.0%
30	Iowa	86,096,947,000	0.9%
31	Kansas	83,259,525,000	0.9%
32	Nevada	77,642,876,000	0.8%
33	Utah	74,268,005,000	0.8%
34	Arkansas	65,054,335,000	0.7%
35	Mississippi	57,992,430,000	0.6%
36	Nebraska	54,867,033,000	0.6%
37	New Hampshire	47,606,625,000	0.5%
38	New Mexico	46,264,952,000	0.5%
39	Hawaii	39,689,089,000	0.4%
40	West Virginia	39,461,888,000	0.4%
41	Idaho	36,997,279,000	0.4%
42	Maine	34,159,794,000	0.4%
43	Rhode Island	32,511,563,000	0.3%
44	Delaware	27,516,019,000	0.3%
45	North Dakota	27,236,634,000	0.3%
46	Montana	27,178,486,000	0.3%
47	South Dakota	24,938,776,000	0.3%
48	Alaska	24,272,390,000	0.3%
49	Wyoming	21,658,081,000	0.2%
50	Vermont	18,588,007,000	0.2%
	District of Columbia	29,796,594,000	0.3%

Source: U.S. Department of the Treasury, Internal Revenue Service
  "Individual Tax Statistics, State Income" (http://www.irs.gov/taxstats/index.html)
*Total includes $58,466,196,000 from U.S. citizens abroad and other miscellaneous returns not shown separately.

Per Capita Adjusted Gross Income in 2014

National Per Capita = $30,285*

ALPHA ORDER

RANK	STATE	PER CAPITA
45	Alabama	$22,286
15	Alaska	32,947
42	Arizona	24,097
48	Arkansas	21,927
13	California	33,282
12	Colorado	33,572
1	Connecticut	45,689
20	Delaware	29,431
25	Florida	28,674
38	Georgia	25,130
26	Hawaii	28,022
44	Idaho	22,649
14	Illinois	32,966
35	Indiana	25,266
27	Iowa	27,701
24	Kansas	28,717
46	Kentucky	22,282
39	Louisiana	24,865
34	Maine	25,670
8	Maryland	35,787
2	Massachusetts	42,309
31	Michigan	26,903
10	Minnesota	33,836
50	Mississippi	19,380
33	Missouri	25,859
32	Montana	26,571
22	Nebraska	29,167
29	Nevada	27,406
7	New Hampshire	35,828
3	New Jersey	39,580
47	New Mexico	22,210
4	New York	38,285
40	North Carolina	24,864
6	North Dakota	36,811
30	Ohio	27,009
37	Oklahoma	25,142
28	Oregon	27,546
17	Pennsylvania	30,404
16	Rhode Island	30,832
43	South Carolina	23,069
21	South Dakota	29,252
41	Tennessee	24,608
18	Texas	29,932
36	Utah	25,245
19	Vermont	29,647
11	Virginia	33,586
9	Washington	34,597
49	West Virginia	21,348
23	Wisconsin	29,095
5	Wyoming	37,109

RANK ORDER

RANK	STATE	PER CAPITA
1	Connecticut	$45,689
2	Massachusetts	42,309
3	New Jersey	39,580
4	New York	38,285
5	Wyoming	37,109
6	North Dakota	36,811
7	New Hampshire	35,828
8	Maryland	35,787
9	Washington	34,597
10	Minnesota	33,836
11	Virginia	33,586
12	Colorado	33,572
13	California	33,282
14	Illinois	32,966
15	Alaska	32,947
16	Rhode Island	30,832
17	Pennsylvania	30,404
18	Texas	29,932
19	Vermont	29,647
20	Delaware	29,431
21	South Dakota	29,252
22	Nebraska	29,167
23	Wisconsin	29,095
24	Kansas	28,717
25	Florida	28,674
26	Hawaii	28,022
27	Iowa	27,701
28	Oregon	27,546
29	Nevada	27,406
30	Ohio	27,009
31	Michigan	26,903
32	Montana	26,571
33	Missouri	25,859
34	Maine	25,670
35	Indiana	25,266
36	Utah	25,245
37	Oklahoma	25,142
38	Georgia	25,130
39	Louisiana	24,865
40	North Carolina	24,864
41	Tennessee	24,608
42	Arizona	24,097
43	South Carolina	23,069
44	Idaho	22,649
45	Alabama	22,286
46	Kentucky	22,282
47	New Mexico	22,210
48	Arkansas	21,927
49	West Virginia	21,348
50	Mississippi	19,380

	District of Columbia	45,215

Source: CQ Press using data from U.S. Department of the Treasury, Internal Revenue Service
"Individual Tax Statistics, State Income" (http://www.irs.gov/taxstats/index.html)
*National per capita does not include income from U.S. citizens abroad and other miscellaneous returns not shown separately.

Federal Business Income Tax Collections in 2015

National Total = $389,888,722,000*

ALPHA ORDER

RANK	STATE	COLLECTIONS	% of USA
33	Alabama	$1,465,831,000	0.4%
49	Alaska	194,313,000	0.0%
24	Arizona	3,862,387,000	1.0%
17	Arkansas	7,657,274,000	2.0%
1	California	51,290,979,000	13.2%
50	Colorado	(2,051,855,000)	
16	Connecticut	8,304,111,000	2.1%
13	Delaware	9,118,702,000	2.3%
12	Florida	10,623,903,000	2.7%
9	Georgia	12,764,920,000	3.3%
39	Hawaii	476,171,000	0.1%
45	Idaho	268,962,000	0.1%
6	Illinois	20,370,821,000	5.2%
23	Indiana	4,891,553,000	1.3%
30	Iowa	1,965,929,000	0.5%
31	Kansas	1,965,250,000	0.5%
28	Kentucky	2,629,863,000	0.7%
35	Louisiana	1,107,876,000	0.3%
43	Maine	305,706,000	0.1%
25	Maryland	3,616,792,000	0.9%
14	Massachusetts	8,786,713,000	2.3%
20	Michigan	6,312,321,000	1.6%
5	Minnesota	24,329,664,000	6.2%
37	Mississippi	747,840,000	0.2%
15	Missouri	8,473,144,000	2.2%
47	Montana	214,131,000	0.1%
19	Nebraska	6,870,025,000	1.8%
36	Nevada	867,208,000	0.2%
44	New Hampshire	296,413,000	0.1%
2	New Jersey	36,256,100,000	9.3%
46	New Mexico	248,014,000	0.1%
4	New York	30,839,677,000	7.9%
11	North Carolina	10,807,290,000	2.8%
41	North Dakota	353,450,000	0.1%
8	Ohio	14,649,198,000	3.8%
27	Oklahoma	3,330,908,000	0.9%
29	Oregon	1,989,938,000	0.5%
7	Pennsylvania	16,095,757,000	4.1%
26	Rhode Island	3,527,526,000	0.9%
32	South Carolina	1,731,619,000	0.4%
38	South Dakota	552,853,000	0.1%
18	Tennessee	7,004,232,000	1.8%
3	Texas	32,083,819,000	8.2%
34	Utah	1,312,427,000	0.3%
40	Vermont	359,193,000	0.1%
10	Virginia	11,776,145,000	3.0%
21	Washington	6,289,483,000	1.6%
42	West Virginia	349,649,000	0.1%
22	Wisconsin	5,724,903,000	1.5%
48	Wyoming	208,550,000	0.1%

RANK ORDER

RANK	STATE	COLLECTIONS	% of USA
1	California	$51,290,979,000	13.2%
2	New Jersey	36,256,100,000	9.3%
3	Texas	32,083,819,000	8.2%
4	New York	30,839,677,000	7.9%
5	Minnesota	24,329,664,000	6.2%
6	Illinois	20,370,821,000	5.2%
7	Pennsylvania	16,095,757,000	4.1%
8	Ohio	14,649,198,000	3.8%
9	Georgia	12,764,920,000	3.3%
10	Virginia	11,776,145,000	3.0%
11	North Carolina	10,807,290,000	2.8%
12	Florida	10,623,903,000	2.7%
13	Delaware	9,118,702,000	2.3%
14	Massachusetts	8,786,713,000	2.3%
15	Missouri	8,473,144,000	2.2%
16	Connecticut	8,304,111,000	2.1%
17	Arkansas	7,657,274,000	2.0%
18	Tennessee	7,004,232,000	1.8%
19	Nebraska	6,870,025,000	1.8%
20	Michigan	6,312,321,000	1.6%
21	Washington	6,289,483,000	1.6%
22	Wisconsin	5,724,903,000	1.5%
23	Indiana	4,891,553,000	1.3%
24	Arizona	3,862,387,000	1.0%
25	Maryland	3,616,792,000	0.9%
26	Rhode Island	3,527,526,000	0.9%
27	Oklahoma	3,330,908,000	0.9%
28	Kentucky	2,629,863,000	0.7%
29	Oregon	1,989,938,000	0.5%
30	Iowa	1,965,929,000	0.5%
31	Kansas	1,965,250,000	0.5%
32	South Carolina	1,731,619,000	0.4%
33	Alabama	1,465,831,000	0.4%
34	Utah	1,312,427,000	0.3%
35	Louisiana	1,107,876,000	0.3%
36	Nevada	867,208,000	0.2%
37	Mississippi	747,840,000	0.2%
38	South Dakota	552,853,000	0.1%
39	Hawaii	476,171,000	0.1%
40	Vermont	359,193,000	0.1%
41	North Dakota	353,450,000	0.1%
42	West Virginia	349,649,000	0.1%
43	Maine	305,706,000	0.1%
44	New Hampshire	296,413,000	0.1%
45	Idaho	268,962,000	0.1%
46	New Mexico	248,014,000	0.1%
47	Montana	214,131,000	0.1%
48	Wyoming	208,550,000	0.1%
49	Alaska	194,313,000	0.0%
50	Colorado	(2,051,855,000)	

District of Columbia		4,285,021,000	1.1%

Source: U.S. Department of the Treasury, Internal Revenue Service
"Fiscal Year 2015 IRS Data Book" (http://www.irs.gov/uac/SOI-Tax-Stats-IRS-Data-Book)
*Total includes collections and returns from international sources and others not distributed by state. Includes taxes on corporation income (Form 1120 series) and unrelated business income from tax-exempt organizations.

Average Revenue Collection per Federal Business Income Tax Return in 2015

National Average = $56,301 per Return*

ALPHA ORDER

RANK	STATE	PER CAPITA
34	Alabama	$21,512
40	Alaska	15,450
27	Arizona	32,378
7	Arkansas	144,439
15	California	62,261
50	Colorado	(13,191)
4	Connecticut	156,460
1	Delaware	369,702
42	Florida	12,954
18	Georgia	57,808
39	Hawaii	17,215
48	Idaho	7,662
17	Illinois	58,332
23	Indiana	44,253
28	Iowa	31,765
25	Kansas	38,380
24	Kentucky	40,020
43	Louisiana	12,939
46	Maine	10,273
29	Maryland	29,524
16	Massachusetts	60,724
26	Michigan	33,093
3	Minnesota	192,514
36	Mississippi	18,324
9	Missouri	85,975
49	Montana	6,138
5	Nebraska	155,663
44	Nevada	12,211
41	New Hampshire	13,752
2	New Jersey	192,726
47	New Mexico	8,348
20	New York	46,578
19	North Carolina	55,859
33	North Dakota	21,763
10	Ohio	84,540
22	Oklahoma	45,469
31	Oregon	26,449
11	Pennsylvania	74,430
6	Rhode Island	151,175
35	South Carolina	20,533
30	South Dakota	29,429
8	Tennessee	106,425
12	Texas	70,178
37	Utah	17,784
32	Vermont	22,886
13	Virginia	70,166
21	Washington	45,802
38	West Virginia	17,451
14	Wisconsin	62,794
45	Wyoming	11,271

RANK ORDER

RANK	STATE	PER CAPITA
1	Delaware	$369,702
2	New Jersey	192,726
3	Minnesota	192,514
4	Connecticut	156,460
5	Nebraska	155,663
6	Rhode Island	151,175
7	Arkansas	144,439
8	Tennessee	106,425
9	Missouri	85,975
10	Ohio	84,540
11	Pennsylvania	74,430
12	Texas	70,178
13	Virginia	70,166
14	Wisconsin	62,794
15	California	62,261
16	Massachusetts	60,724
17	Illinois	58,332
18	Georgia	57,808
19	North Carolina	55,859
20	New York	46,578
21	Washington	45,802
22	Oklahoma	45,469
23	Indiana	44,253
24	Kentucky	40,020
25	Kansas	38,380
26	Michigan	33,093
27	Arizona	32,378
28	Iowa	31,765
29	Maryland	29,524
30	South Dakota	29,429
31	Oregon	26,449
32	Vermont	22,886
33	North Dakota	21,763
34	Alabama	21,512
35	South Carolina	20,533
36	Mississippi	18,324
37	Utah	17,784
38	West Virginia	17,451
39	Hawaii	17,215
40	Alaska	15,450
41	New Hampshire	13,752
42	Florida	12,954
43	Louisiana	12,939
44	Nevada	12,211
45	Wyoming	11,271
46	Maine	10,273
47	New Mexico	8,348
48	Idaho	7,662
49	Montana	6,138
50	Colorado	(13,191)

District of Columbia 236,467

Source: CQ Press using data from U.S. Department of the Treasury, Internal Revenue Service
"Fiscal Year 2015 IRS Data Book" (http://www.irs.gov/uac/SOI-Tax-Stats-IRS-Data-Book)
*National average does not include income from U.S. citizens abroad and other miscellaneous returns not shown separately.
Includes taxes on corporation income (Form 1120 series) and unrelated business income from tax-exempt organizations.

Federal Tax Returns Filed in 2015

National Total = 243,249,108 Returns*

ALPHA ORDER

RANK ORDER

RANK	STATE	RETURNS	% of USA	RANK	STATE	RETURNS	% of USA
26	Alabama	3,090,023	1.3%	1	California	29,317,790	12.1%
48	Alaska	588,977	0.2%	2	Texas	18,958,807	7.8%
17	Arizona	4,561,056	1.9%	3	Florida	16,663,871	6.9%
34	Arkansas	1,948,158	0.8%	4	New York	16,045,517	6.6%
1	California	29,317,790	12.1%	5	Illinois	10,092,100	4.1%
19	Colorado	4,521,542	1.9%	6	Pennsylvania	9,794,427	4.0%
27	Connecticut	2,963,028	1.2%	7	Ohio	8,457,997	3.5%
45	Delaware	778,738	0.3%	8	New Jersey	7,391,663	3.0%
3	Florida	16,663,871	6.9%	9	Michigan	7,287,052	3.0%
10	Georgia	6,921,491	2.8%	10	Georgia	6,921,491	2.8%
40	Hawaii	1,123,626	0.5%	11	North Carolina	6,860,429	2.8%
38	Idaho	1,201,670	0.5%	12	Virginia	6,190,916	2.5%
5	Illinois	10,092,100	4.1%	13	Massachusetts	5,622,740	2.3%
16	Indiana	4,646,902	1.9%	14	Washington	5,592,705	2.3%
30	Iowa	2,419,357	1.0%	15	Maryland	4,701,897	1.9%
31	Kansas	2,226,908	0.9%	16	Indiana	4,646,902	1.9%
28	Kentucky	2,889,086	1.2%	17	Arizona	4,561,056	1.9%
24	Louisiana	3,211,608	1.3%	18	Missouri	4,544,187	1.9%
42	Maine	1,099,384	0.5%	19	Colorado	4,521,542	1.9%
15	Maryland	4,701,897	1.9%	20	Minnesota	4,469,301	1.8%
13	Massachusetts	5,622,740	2.3%	21	Wisconsin	4,457,166	1.8%
9	Michigan	7,287,052	3.0%	22	Tennessee	4,333,884	1.8%
20	Minnesota	4,469,301	1.8%	23	South Carolina	3,267,307	1.3%
35	Mississippi	1,852,241	0.8%	24	Louisiana	3,211,608	1.3%
18	Missouri	4,544,187	1.9%	25	Oregon	3,177,490	1.3%
43	Montana	946,995	0.4%	26	Alabama	3,090,023	1.3%
36	Nebraska	1,509,824	0.6%	27	Connecticut	2,963,028	1.2%
32	Nevada	2,103,071	0.9%	28	Kentucky	2,889,086	1.2%
41	New Hampshire	1,119,464	0.5%	29	Oklahoma	2,738,714	1.1%
8	New Jersey	7,391,663	3.0%	30	Iowa	2,419,357	1.0%
37	New Mexico	1,420,814	0.6%	31	Kansas	2,226,908	0.9%
4	New York	16,045,517	6.6%	32	Nevada	2,103,071	0.9%
11	North Carolina	6,860,429	2.8%	33	Utah	2,092,028	0.9%
47	North Dakota	683,037	0.3%	34	Arkansas	1,948,158	0.8%
7	Ohio	8,457,997	3.5%	35	Mississippi	1,852,241	0.8%
29	Oklahoma	2,738,714	1.1%	36	Nebraska	1,509,824	0.6%
25	Oregon	3,177,490	1.3%	37	New Mexico	1,420,814	0.6%
6	Pennsylvania	9,794,427	4.0%	38	Idaho	1,201,670	0.5%
44	Rhode Island	857,586	0.4%	39	West Virginia	1,157,957	0.5%
23	South Carolina	3,267,307	1.3%	40	Hawaii	1,123,626	0.5%
46	South Dakota	751,719	0.3%	41	New Hampshire	1,119,464	0.5%
22	Tennessee	4,333,884	1.8%	42	Maine	1,099,384	0.5%
2	Texas	18,958,807	7.8%	43	Montana	946,995	0.4%
33	Utah	2,092,028	0.9%	44	Rhode Island	857,586	0.4%
49	Vermont	577,268	0.2%	45	Delaware	778,738	0.3%
12	Virginia	6,190,916	2.5%	46	South Dakota	751,719	0.3%
14	Washington	5,592,705	2.3%	47	North Dakota	683,037	0.3%
39	West Virginia	1,157,957	0.5%	48	Alaska	588,977	0.2%
21	Wisconsin	4,457,166	1.8%	49	Vermont	577,268	0.2%
50	Wyoming	534,295	0.2%	50	Wyoming	534,295	0.2%
					District of Columbia	595,932	0.2%

Source: U.S. Department of the Treasury, Internal Revenue Service
  "Fiscal Year 2015 IRS Data Book" (http://www.irs.gov/uac/SOI-Tax-Stats-IRS-Data-Book)
*Total includes returns from international sources and other miscellaneous returns not shown separately.

Percent of Federal Returns Filed Electronically in 2015

National Percent = 67.2%*

ALPHA ORDER

RANK	STATE	PERCENT
7	Alabama	70.2
42	Alaska	64.3
22	Arizona	67.2
14	Arkansas	68.5
23	California	67.1
43	Colorado	64.1
26	Connecticut	66.8
28	Delaware	66.7
34	Florida	66.1
3	Georgia	71.0
50	Hawaii	58.8
39	Idaho	64.7
31	Illinois	66.4
12	Indiana	69.1
37	Iowa	65.3
20	Kansas	67.5
13	Kentucky	69.0
14	Louisiana	68.5
44	Maine	63.4
39	Maryland	64.7
8	Massachusetts	69.7
14	Michigan	68.5
26	Minnesota	66.8
5	Mississippi	70.3
28	Missouri	66.7
48	Montana	61.0
32	Nebraska	66.3
8	Nevada	69.7
36	New Hampshire	65.5
17	New Jersey	68.4
35	New Mexico	65.8
1	New York	72.1
21	North Carolina	67.3
49	North Dakota	59.9
11	Ohio	69.4
23	Oklahoma	67.1
41	Oregon	64.4
30	Pennsylvania	66.6
2	Rhode Island	71.4
10	South Carolina	69.5
45	South Dakota	62.1
4	Tennessee	70.5
17	Texas	68.4
5	Utah	70.3
47	Vermont	61.4
23	Virginia	67.1
38	Washington	64.9
32	West Virginia	66.3
19	Wisconsin	68.0
45	Wyoming	62.1

RANK ORDER

RANK	STATE	PERCENT
1	New York	72.1
2	Rhode Island	71.4
3	Georgia	71.0
4	Tennessee	70.5
5	Mississippi	70.3
5	Utah	70.3
7	Alabama	70.2
8	Massachusetts	69.7
8	Nevada	69.7
10	South Carolina	69.5
11	Ohio	69.4
12	Indiana	69.1
13	Kentucky	69.0
14	Arkansas	68.5
14	Louisiana	68.5
14	Michigan	68.5
17	New Jersey	68.4
17	Texas	68.4
19	Wisconsin	68.0
20	Kansas	67.5
21	North Carolina	67.3
22	Arizona	67.2
23	California	67.1
23	Oklahoma	67.1
23	Virginia	67.1
26	Connecticut	66.8
26	Minnesota	66.8
28	Delaware	66.7
28	Missouri	66.7
30	Pennsylvania	66.6
31	Illinois	66.4
32	Nebraska	66.3
32	West Virginia	66.3
34	Florida	66.1
35	New Mexico	65.8
36	New Hampshire	65.5
37	Iowa	65.3
38	Washington	64.9
39	Idaho	64.7
39	Maryland	64.7
41	Oregon	64.4
42	Alaska	64.3
43	Colorado	64.1
44	Maine	63.4
45	South Dakota	62.1
45	Wyoming	62.1
47	Vermont	61.4
48	Montana	61.0
49	North Dakota	59.9
50	Hawaii	58.8

District of Columbia   65.0

Source: CQ Press using data from U.S. Department of the Treasury, Internal Revenue Service
"Fiscal Year 2015 IRS Data Book" (http://www.irs.gov/uac/SOI-Tax-Stats-IRS-Data-Book)
*Total includes returns from international sources and other miscellaneous returns. Includes corporate, individual, partnership, estate, employment and other returns. Excludes returns that cannot be filed electronically including informational returns.

Federal Individual Income Tax Returns Filed in 2015

National Total = 148,840,642 Returns*

ALPHA ORDER					RANK ORDER			
RANK	STATE	RETURNS	% of USA		RANK	STATE	RETURNS	% of USA
24	Alabama	2,049,450	1.4%		1	California	17,413,557	11.7%
48	Alaska	357,296	0.2%		2	Texas	11,915,445	8.0%
18	Arizona	2,846,387	1.9%		3	New York	9,533,229	6.4%
34	Arkansas	1,223,188	0.8%		4	Florida	9,410,425	6.3%
1	California	17,413,557	11.7%		5	Pennsylvania	6,175,540	4.1%
22	Colorado	2,548,945	1.7%		6	Illinois	6,136,143	4.1%
28	Connecticut	1,753,774	1.2%		7	Ohio	5,563,760	3.7%
45	Delaware	444,459	0.3%		8	Michigan	4,684,599	3.1%
4	Florida	9,410,425	6.3%		9	Georgia	4,388,044	2.9%
9	Georgia	4,388,044	2.9%		10	North Carolina	4,381,105	2.9%
41	Hawaii	682,348	0.5%		11	New Jersey	4,349,614	2.9%
39	Idaho	701,416	0.5%		12	Virginia	3,874,174	2.6%
6	Illinois	6,136,143	4.1%		13	Massachusetts	3,344,477	2.2%
15	Indiana	3,076,743	2.1%		14	Washington	3,339,782	2.2%
30	Iowa	1,444,211	1.0%		15	Indiana	3,076,743	2.1%
31	Kansas	1,336,136	0.9%		16	Maryland	2,940,401	2.0%
26	Kentucky	1,894,598	1.3%		17	Tennessee	2,930,440	2.0%
25	Louisiana	2,012,095	1.4%		18	Arizona	2,846,387	1.9%
42	Maine	637,610	0.4%		19	Wisconsin	2,809,732	1.9%
16	Maryland	2,940,401	2.0%		20	Missouri	2,769,500	1.9%
13	Massachusetts	3,344,477	2.2%		21	Minnesota	2,689,044	1.8%
8	Michigan	4,684,599	3.1%		22	Colorado	2,548,945	1.7%
21	Minnesota	2,689,044	1.8%		23	South Carolina	2,133,141	1.4%
33	Mississippi	1,246,033	0.8%		24	Alabama	2,049,450	1.4%
20	Missouri	2,769,500	1.9%		25	Louisiana	2,012,095	1.4%
44	Montana	491,576	0.3%		26	Kentucky	1,894,598	1.3%
37	Nebraska	890,991	0.6%		27	Oregon	1,828,447	1.2%
32	Nevada	1,324,132	0.9%		28	Connecticut	1,753,774	1.2%
40	New Hampshire	684,794	0.5%		29	Oklahoma	1,641,080	1.1%
11	New Jersey	4,349,614	2.9%		30	Iowa	1,444,211	1.0%
36	New Mexico	911,996	0.6%		31	Kansas	1,336,136	0.9%
3	New York	9,533,229	6.4%		32	Nevada	1,324,132	0.9%
10	North Carolina	4,381,105	2.9%		33	Mississippi	1,246,033	0.8%
47	North Dakota	370,457	0.2%		34	Arkansas	1,223,188	0.8%
7	Ohio	5,563,760	3.7%		35	Utah	1,221,606	0.8%
29	Oklahoma	1,641,080	1.1%		36	New Mexico	911,996	0.6%
27	Oregon	1,828,447	1.2%		37	Nebraska	890,991	0.6%
5	Pennsylvania	6,175,540	4.1%		38	West Virginia	783,826	0.5%
43	Rhode Island	521,969	0.4%		39	Idaho	701,416	0.5%
23	South Carolina	2,133,141	1.4%		40	New Hampshire	684,794	0.5%
46	South Dakota	412,270	0.3%		41	Hawaii	682,348	0.5%
17	Tennessee	2,930,440	2.0%		42	Maine	637,610	0.4%
2	Texas	11,915,445	8.0%		43	Rhode Island	521,969	0.4%
35	Utah	1,221,606	0.8%		44	Montana	491,576	0.3%
49	Vermont	322,632	0.2%		45	Delaware	444,459	0.3%
12	Virginia	3,874,174	2.6%		46	South Dakota	412,270	0.3%
14	Washington	3,339,782	2.2%		47	North Dakota	370,457	0.2%
38	West Virginia	783,826	0.5%		48	Alaska	357,296	0.2%
19	Wisconsin	2,809,732	1.9%		49	Vermont	322,632	0.2%
50	Wyoming	281,111	0.2%		50	Wyoming	281,111	0.2%
						District of Columbia	337,730	0.2%

Source: U.S. Department of the Treasury, Internal Revenue Service
"Fiscal Year 2015 IRS Data Book" (http://www.irs.gov/uac/SOI-Tax-Stats-IRS-Data-Book)
*Total includes returns from international sources and other miscellaneous returns not shown separately.

Percent of Federal Individual Income Tax Returns Filed Electronically in 2015

National Percent = 85.8%*

ALPHA ORDER

RANK	STATE	PERCENT
19	Alabama	88.1
46	Alaska	84.9
47	Arizona	84.8
9	Arkansas	88.8
44	California	85.0
42	Colorado	85.2
31	Connecticut	85.9
38	Delaware	85.5
44	Florida	85.0
23	Georgia	87.3
50	Hawaii	80.4
14	Idaho	88.3
31	Illinois	85.9
8	Indiana	89.2
1	Iowa	91.9
3	Kansas	90.5
5	Kentucky	89.5
29	Louisiana	86.5
48	Maine	84.6
49	Maryland	81.6
30	Massachusetts	86.0
23	Michigan	87.3
18	Minnesota	88.2
10	Mississippi	88.7
26	Missouri	87.1
10	Montana	88.7
2	Nebraska	91.3
39	Nevada	85.4
33	New Hampshire	85.8
33	New Jersey	85.8
37	New Mexico	85.7
5	New York	89.5
22	North Carolina	87.4
7	North Dakota	89.4
23	Ohio	87.3
12	Oklahoma	88.5
41	Oregon	85.3
39	Pennsylvania	85.4
21	Rhode Island	87.6
19	South Carolina	88.1
4	South Dakota	90.2
13	Tennessee	88.4
42	Texas	85.2
14	Utah	88.3
28	Vermont	86.6
33	Virginia	85.8
33	Washington	85.8
27	West Virginia	87.0
14	Wisconsin	88.3
14	Wyoming	88.3

RANK ORDER

RANK	STATE	PERCENT
1	Iowa	91.9
2	Nebraska	91.3
3	Kansas	90.5
4	South Dakota	90.2
5	Kentucky	89.5
5	New York	89.5
7	North Dakota	89.4
8	Indiana	89.2
9	Arkansas	88.8
10	Mississippi	88.7
10	Montana	88.7
12	Oklahoma	88.5
13	Tennessee	88.4
14	Idaho	88.3
14	Utah	88.3
14	Wisconsin	88.3
14	Wyoming	88.3
18	Minnesota	88.2
19	Alabama	88.1
19	South Carolina	88.1
21	Rhode Island	87.6
22	North Carolina	87.4
23	Georgia	87.3
23	Michigan	87.3
23	Ohio	87.3
26	Missouri	87.1
27	West Virginia	87.0
28	Vermont	86.6
29	Louisiana	86.5
30	Massachusetts	86.0
31	Connecticut	85.9
31	Illinois	85.9
33	New Hampshire	85.8
33	New Jersey	85.8
33	Virginia	85.8
33	Washington	85.8
37	New Mexico	85.7
38	Delaware	85.5
39	Nevada	85.4
39	Pennsylvania	85.4
41	Oregon	85.3
42	Colorado	85.2
42	Texas	85.2
44	California	85.0
44	Florida	85.0
46	Alaska	84.9
47	Arizona	84.8
48	Maine	84.6
49	Maryland	81.6
50	Hawaii	80.4

District of Columbia   82.2

Source: CQ Press using data from U.S. Department of the Treasury, Internal Revenue Service
    "Fiscal Year 2015 IRS Data Book" (http://www.irs.gov/uac/SOI-Tax-Stats-IRS-Data-Book)
*Total includes returns from international sources and other miscellaneous returns. Includes returns filed electronically by practitioners.

Federal Business Income Tax Returns Filed in 2015

National Total = 6,933,424 Returns*

ALPHA ORDER

RANK ORDER

RANK	STATE	RETURNS	% of USA		RANK	STATE	RETURNS	% of USA
28	Alabama	68,139	1.0%		1	California	823,802	11.9%
50	Alaska	12,577	0.2%		2	Florida	820,149	11.8%
18	Arizona	119,289	1.7%		3	New York	662,113	9.5%
33	Arkansas	53,014	0.8%		4	Texas	457,175	6.6%
1	California	823,802	11.9%		5	Illinois	349,222	5.0%
13	Colorado	155,548	2.2%		6	Georgia	220,814	3.2%
32	Connecticut	53,075	0.8%		7	Pennsylvania	216,253	3.1%
42	Delaware	24,665	0.4%		8	North Carolina	193,476	2.8%
2	Florida	820,149	11.8%		9	Michigan	190,746	2.8%
6	Georgia	220,814	3.2%		10	New Jersey	188,123	2.7%
41	Hawaii	27,661	0.4%		11	Ohio	173,282	2.5%
37	Idaho	35,104	0.5%		12	Virginia	167,832	2.4%
5	Illinois	349,222	5.0%		13	Colorado	155,548	2.2%
19	Indiana	110,535	1.6%		14	Massachusetts	144,699	2.1%
31	Iowa	61,889	0.9%		15	Washington	137,318	2.0%
34	Kansas	51,205	0.7%		16	Minnesota	126,379	1.8%
30	Kentucky	65,713	0.9%		17	Maryland	122,504	1.8%
22	Louisiana	85,625	1.2%		18	Arizona	119,289	1.7%
39	Maine	29,759	0.4%		19	Indiana	110,535	1.6%
17	Maryland	122,504	1.8%		20	Missouri	98,554	1.4%
14	Massachusetts	144,699	2.1%		21	Wisconsin	91,170	1.3%
9	Michigan	190,746	2.8%		22	Louisiana	85,625	1.2%
16	Minnesota	126,379	1.8%		23	South Carolina	84,333	1.2%
36	Mississippi	40,812	0.6%		24	Oregon	75,236	1.1%
20	Missouri	98,554	1.4%		25	Utah	73,800	1.1%
38	Montana	34,887	0.5%		26	Oklahoma	73,256	1.1%
35	Nebraska	44,134	0.6%		27	Nevada	71,016	1.0%
27	Nevada	71,016	1.0%		28	Alabama	68,139	1.0%
44	New Hampshire	21,554	0.3%		29	Tennessee	65,814	0.9%
10	New Jersey	188,123	2.7%		30	Kentucky	65,713	0.9%
40	New Mexico	29,708	0.4%		31	Iowa	61,889	0.9%
3	New York	662,113	9.5%		32	Connecticut	53,075	0.8%
8	North Carolina	193,476	2.8%		33	Arkansas	53,014	0.8%
48	North Dakota	16,241	0.2%		34	Kansas	51,205	0.7%
11	Ohio	173,282	2.5%		35	Nebraska	44,134	0.6%
26	Oklahoma	73,256	1.1%		36	Mississippi	40,812	0.6%
24	Oregon	75,236	1.1%		37	Idaho	35,104	0.5%
7	Pennsylvania	216,253	3.1%		38	Montana	34,887	0.5%
43	Rhode Island	23,334	0.3%		39	Maine	29,759	0.4%
23	South Carolina	84,333	1.2%		40	New Mexico	29,708	0.4%
46	South Dakota	18,786	0.3%		41	Hawaii	27,661	0.4%
29	Tennessee	65,814	0.9%		42	Delaware	24,665	0.4%
4	Texas	457,175	6.6%		43	Rhode Island	23,334	0.3%
25	Utah	73,800	1.1%		44	New Hampshire	21,554	0.3%
49	Vermont	15,695	0.2%		45	West Virginia	20,036	0.3%
12	Virginia	167,832	2.4%		46	South Dakota	18,786	0.3%
15	Washington	137,318	2.0%		47	Wyoming	18,503	0.3%
45	West Virginia	20,036	0.3%		48	North Dakota	16,241	0.2%
21	Wisconsin	91,170	1.3%		49	Vermont	15,695	0.2%
47	Wyoming	18,503	0.3%		50	Alaska	12,577	0.2%
						District of Columbia	18,121	0.3%

Source: U.S. Department of the Treasury, Internal Revenue Service
  "Fiscal Year 2015 IRS Data Book" (http://www.irs.gov/uac/SOI-Tax-Stats-IRS-Data-Book)
*Total includes returns from international sources and other miscellaneous returns not shown separately.

Federal Tax Refunds in 2015

National Total = 119,020,846 Refunds*

ALPHA ORDER

RANK	STATE	REFUNDS	% of USA
24	Alabama	1,688,888	1.4%
48	Alaska	279,155	0.2%
20	Arizona	2,200,207	1.8%
35	Arkansas	1,004,632	0.8%
1	California	13,499,823	11.3%
22	Colorado	1,963,407	1.6%
28	Connecticut	1,376,855	1.2%
45	Delaware	357,104	0.3%
3	Florida	7,679,598	6.5%
9	Georgia	3,606,432	3.0%
41	Hawaii	541,056	0.5%
39	Idaho	550,280	0.5%
5	Illinois	5,090,973	4.3%
15	Indiana	2,579,102	2.2%
30	Iowa	1,149,875	1.0%
32	Kansas	1,056,793	0.9%
26	Kentucky	1,596,153	1.3%
25	Louisiana	1,664,436	1.4%
42	Maine	496,084	0.4%
17	Maryland	2,284,469	1.9%
14	Massachusetts	2,642,535	2.2%
8	Michigan	3,790,616	3.2%
21	Minnesota	2,085,879	1.8%
33	Mississippi	1,048,820	0.9%
18	Missouri	2,246,258	1.9%
44	Montana	373,971	0.3%
37	Nebraska	711,693	0.6%
31	Nevada	1,089,035	0.9%
40	New Hampshire	541,341	0.5%
11	New Jersey	3,445,981	2.9%
36	New Mexico	736,790	0.6%
4	New York	7,614,590	6.4%
10	North Carolina	3,501,232	2.9%
47	North Dakota	285,642	0.2%
7	Ohio	4,600,671	3.9%
29	Oklahoma	1,326,708	1.1%
27	Oregon	1,400,673	1.2%
6	Pennsylvania	4,982,628	4.2%
43	Rhode Island	430,732	0.4%
23	South Carolina	1,697,875	1.4%
46	South Dakota	323,534	0.3%
16	Tennessee	2,460,700	2.1%
2	Texas	9,993,614	8.4%
34	Utah	1,007,492	0.8%
49	Vermont	250,937	0.2%
12	Virginia	3,050,798	2.6%
13	Washington	2,680,439	2.3%
38	West Virginia	671,303	0.6%
19	Wisconsin	2,236,477	1.9%
50	Wyoming	229,270	0.2%

RANK ORDER

RANK	STATE	REFUNDS	% of USA
1	California	13,499,823	11.3%
2	Texas	9,993,614	8.4%
3	Florida	7,679,598	6.5%
4	New York	7,614,590	6.4%
5	Illinois	5,090,973	4.3%
6	Pennsylvania	4,982,628	4.2%
7	Ohio	4,600,671	3.9%
8	Michigan	3,790,616	3.2%
9	Georgia	3,606,432	3.0%
10	North Carolina	3,501,232	2.9%
11	New Jersey	3,445,981	2.9%
12	Virginia	3,050,798	2.6%
13	Washington	2,680,439	2.3%
14	Massachusetts	2,642,535	2.2%
15	Indiana	2,579,102	2.2%
16	Tennessee	2,460,700	2.1%
17	Maryland	2,284,469	1.9%
18	Missouri	2,246,258	1.9%
19	Wisconsin	2,236,477	1.9%
20	Arizona	2,200,207	1.8%
21	Minnesota	2,085,879	1.8%
22	Colorado	1,963,407	1.6%
23	South Carolina	1,697,875	1.4%
24	Alabama	1,688,888	1.4%
25	Louisiana	1,664,436	1.4%
26	Kentucky	1,596,153	1.3%
27	Oregon	1,400,673	1.2%
28	Connecticut	1,376,855	1.2%
29	Oklahoma	1,326,708	1.1%
30	Iowa	1,149,875	1.0%
31	Nevada	1,089,035	0.9%
32	Kansas	1,056,793	0.9%
33	Mississippi	1,048,820	0.9%
34	Utah	1,007,492	0.8%
35	Arkansas	1,004,632	0.8%
36	New Mexico	736,790	0.6%
37	Nebraska	711,693	0.6%
38	West Virginia	671,303	0.6%
39	Idaho	550,280	0.5%
40	New Hampshire	541,341	0.5%
41	Hawaii	541,056	0.5%
42	Maine	496,084	0.4%
43	Rhode Island	430,732	0.4%
44	Montana	373,971	0.3%
45	Delaware	357,104	0.3%
46	South Dakota	323,534	0.3%
47	North Dakota	285,642	0.2%
48	Alaska	279,155	0.2%
49	Vermont	250,937	0.2%
50	Wyoming	229,270	0.2%
	District of Columbia	266,006	0.2%

Source: U.S. Department of the Treasury, Internal Revenue Service
   "Fiscal Year 2015 IRS Data Book" (http://www.irs.gov/uac/SOI-Tax-Stats-IRS-Data-Book)
*Total includes refunds to international sources and other miscellaneous refunds not shown separately.

Value of Federal Tax Refunds in 2015

National Total = $403,272,691,000*

ALPHA ORDER

RANK	STATE	REFUNDS	% of USA
26	Alabama	$4,969,648,000	1.2%
48	Alaska	749,065,000	0.2%
20	Arizona	6,130,543,000	1.5%
36	Arkansas	2,751,699,000	0.7%
1	California	43,669,519,000	10.8%
23	Colorado	5,763,261,000	1.4%
21	Connecticut	5,809,336,000	1.4%
37	Delaware	2,088,389,000	0.5%
4	Florida	22,363,062,000	5.5%
9	Georgia	11,343,579,000	2.8%
41	Hawaii	1,443,955,000	0.4%
40	Idaho	1,462,684,000	0.4%
5	Illinois	16,223,435,000	4.0%
17	Indiana	7,038,056,000	1.7%
31	Iowa	3,274,327,000	0.8%
29	Kansas	3,414,268,000	0.8%
28	Kentucky	4,379,807,000	1.1%
25	Louisiana	5,061,648,000	1.3%
43	Maine	1,158,516,000	0.3%
19	Maryland	6,466,529,000	1.6%
13	Massachusetts	8,448,902,000	2.1%
10	Michigan	10,196,359,000	2.5%
14	Minnesota	8,129,131,000	2.0%
33	Mississippi	3,149,548,000	0.8%
18	Missouri	6,493,700,000	1.6%
45	Montana	876,398,000	0.2%
35	Nebraska	2,841,171,000	0.7%
32	Nevada	3,176,504,000	0.8%
42	New Hampshire	1,398,374,000	0.3%
7	New Jersey	14,602,857,000	3.6%
38	New Mexico	1,922,248,000	0.5%
3	New York	26,819,319,000	6.7%
11	North Carolina	9,647,853,000	2.4%
47	North Dakota	770,237,000	0.2%
8	Ohio	12,405,742,000	3.1%
24	Oklahoma	5,555,502,000	1.4%
30	Oregon	3,338,492,000	0.8%
6	Pennsylvania	15,204,268,000	3.8%
44	Rhode Island	1,103,189,000	0.3%
27	South Carolina	4,491,464,000	1.1%
46	South Dakota	861,087,000	0.2%
15	Tennessee	7,586,728,000	1.9%
2	Texas	35,311,419,000	8.8%
34	Utah	3,070,355,000	0.8%
50	Vermont	624,873,000	0.2%
12	Virginia	9,023,289,000	2.2%
16	Washington	7,241,697,000	1.8%
39	West Virginia	1,737,365,000	0.4%
22	Wisconsin	5,767,090,000	1.4%
49	Wyoming	664,833,000	0.2%

RANK ORDER

RANK	STATE	REFUNDS	% of USA
1	California	$43,669,519,000	10.8%
2	Texas	35,311,419,000	8.8%
3	New York	26,819,319,000	6.7%
4	Florida	22,363,062,000	5.5%
5	Illinois	16,223,435,000	4.0%
6	Pennsylvania	15,204,268,000	3.8%
7	New Jersey	14,602,857,000	3.6%
8	Ohio	12,405,742,000	3.1%
9	Georgia	11,343,579,000	2.8%
10	Michigan	10,196,359,000	2.5%
11	North Carolina	9,647,853,000	2.4%
12	Virginia	9,023,289,000	2.2%
13	Massachusetts	8,448,902,000	2.1%
14	Minnesota	8,129,131,000	2.0%
15	Tennessee	7,586,728,000	1.9%
16	Washington	7,241,697,000	1.8%
17	Indiana	7,038,056,000	1.7%
18	Missouri	6,493,700,000	1.6%
19	Maryland	6,466,529,000	1.6%
20	Arizona	6,130,543,000	1.5%
21	Connecticut	5,809,336,000	1.4%
22	Wisconsin	5,767,090,000	1.4%
23	Colorado	5,763,261,000	1.4%
24	Oklahoma	5,555,502,000	1.4%
25	Louisiana	5,061,648,000	1.3%
26	Alabama	4,969,648,000	1.2%
27	South Carolina	4,491,464,000	1.1%
28	Kentucky	4,379,807,000	1.1%
29	Kansas	3,414,268,000	0.8%
30	Oregon	3,338,492,000	0.8%
31	Iowa	3,274,327,000	0.8%
32	Nevada	3,176,504,000	0.8%
33	Mississippi	3,149,548,000	0.8%
34	Utah	3,070,355,000	0.8%
35	Nebraska	2,841,171,000	0.7%
36	Arkansas	2,751,699,000	0.7%
37	Delaware	2,088,389,000	0.5%
38	New Mexico	1,922,248,000	0.5%
39	West Virginia	1,737,365,000	0.4%
40	Idaho	1,462,684,000	0.4%
41	Hawaii	1,443,955,000	0.4%
42	New Hampshire	1,398,374,000	0.3%
43	Maine	1,158,516,000	0.3%
44	Rhode Island	1,103,189,000	0.3%
45	Montana	876,398,000	0.2%
46	South Dakota	861,087,000	0.2%
47	North Dakota	770,237,000	0.2%
48	Alaska	749,065,000	0.2%
49	Wyoming	664,833,000	0.2%
50	Vermont	624,873,000	0.2%
	District of Columbia	1,186,311,000	0.3%

Source: U.S. Department of the Treasury, Internal Revenue Service
"Fiscal Year 2015 IRS Data Book" (http://www.irs.gov/uac/SOI-Tax-Stats-IRS-Data-Book)
*Total includes refunds to international sources and other miscellaneous refunds not shown separately.

Average Value of Federal Tax Refunds in 2015

National Average = $3,388*

ALPHA ORDER

RANK	STATE	AVERAGE REFUND
20	Alabama	$2,943
37	Alaska	2,683
28	Arizona	2,786
31	Arkansas	2,739
9	California	3,235
21	Colorado	2,935
3	Connecticut	4,219
1	Delaware	5,848
23	Florida	2,912
13	Georgia	3,145
38	Hawaii	2,669
40	Idaho	2,658
12	Illinois	3,187
32	Indiana	2,729
26	Iowa	2,848
10	Kansas	3,231
30	Kentucky	2,744
17	Louisiana	3,041
50	Maine	2,335
27	Maryland	2,831
11	Massachusetts	3,197
36	Michigan	2,690
6	Minnesota	3,897
18	Mississippi	3,003
25	Missouri	2,891
49	Montana	2,343
5	Nebraska	3,992
22	Nevada	2,917
44	New Hampshire	2,583
2	New Jersey	4,238
42	New Mexico	2,609
8	New York	3,522
29	North Carolina	2,756
34	North Dakota	2,697
34	Ohio	2,697
4	Oklahoma	4,187
48	Oregon	2,383
15	Pennsylvania	3,051
46	Rhode Island	2,561
41	South Carolina	2,645
39	South Dakota	2,662
14	Tennessee	3,083
7	Texas	3,533
16	Utah	3,048
47	Vermont	2,490
19	Virginia	2,958
33	Washington	2,702
43	West Virginia	2,588
45	Wisconsin	2,579
24	Wyoming	2,900

RANK ORDER

RANK	STATE	AVERAGE REFUND
1	Delaware	$5,848
2	New Jersey	4,238
3	Connecticut	4,219
4	Oklahoma	4,187
5	Nebraska	3,992
6	Minnesota	3,897
7	Texas	3,533
8	New York	3,522
9	California	3,235
10	Kansas	3,231
11	Massachusetts	3,197
12	Illinois	3,187
13	Georgia	3,145
14	Tennessee	3,083
15	Pennsylvania	3,051
16	Utah	3,048
17	Louisiana	3,041
18	Mississippi	3,003
19	Virginia	2,958
20	Alabama	2,943
21	Colorado	2,935
22	Nevada	2,917
23	Florida	2,912
24	Wyoming	2,900
25	Missouri	2,891
26	Iowa	2,848
27	Maryland	2,831
28	Arizona	2,786
29	North Carolina	2,756
30	Kentucky	2,744
31	Arkansas	2,739
32	Indiana	2,729
33	Washington	2,702
34	North Dakota	2,697
34	Ohio	2,697
36	Michigan	2,690
37	Alaska	2,683
38	Hawaii	2,669
39	South Dakota	2,662
40	Idaho	2,658
41	South Carolina	2,645
42	New Mexico	2,609
43	West Virginia	2,588
44	New Hampshire	2,583
45	Wisconsin	2,579
46	Rhode Island	2,561
47	Vermont	2,490
48	Oregon	2,383
49	Montana	2,343
50	Maine	2,335
	District of Columbia	4,460

Source: CQ Press using data from U.S. Department of the Treasury, Internal Revenue Service
"Fiscal Year 2015 IRS Data Book" (http://www.irs.gov/uac/SOI-Tax-Stats-IRS-Data-Book)
*National average includes refunds to international sources and other miscellaneous refunds not shown separately.

Value of Federal Individual Income Tax Refunds in 2015

National Total = $346,394,376,000*

ALPHA ORDER

RANK	STATE	REFUNDS	% of USA
24	Alabama	$4,662,078,000	1.3%
48	Alaska	705,656,000	0.2%
18	Arizona	5,633,903,000	1.6%
35	Arkansas	2,618,477,000	0.8%
1	California	36,845,651,000	10.6%
21	Colorado	4,870,909,000	1.4%
27	Connecticut	3,906,818,000	1.1%
44	Delaware	867,929,000	0.3%
4	Florida	20,989,413,000	6.1%
9	Georgia	9,810,101,000	2.8%
39	Hawaii	1,316,682,000	0.4%
41	Idaho	1,282,415,000	0.4%
5	Illinois	14,048,816,000	4.1%
15	Indiana	6,511,762,000	1.9%
32	Iowa	2,850,790,000	0.8%
34	Kansas	2,619,713,000	0.8%
26	Kentucky	4,066,855,000	1.2%
23	Louisiana	4,808,521,000	1.4%
42	Maine	1,081,393,000	0.3%
17	Maryland	6,098,769,000	1.8%
13	Massachusetts	6,820,865,000	2.0%
10	Michigan	9,170,480,000	2.6%
22	Minnesota	4,826,504,000	1.4%
30	Mississippi	3,015,212,000	0.9%
19	Missouri	5,541,498,000	1.6%
45	Montana	829,607,000	0.2%
37	Nebraska	1,710,355,000	0.5%
31	Nevada	2,919,489,000	0.8%
40	New Hampshire	1,287,982,000	0.4%
8	New Jersey	9,818,252,000	2.8%
36	New Mexico	1,860,651,000	0.5%
3	New York	21,679,552,000	6.3%
11	North Carolina	8,771,645,000	2.5%
47	North Dakota	715,098,000	0.2%
7	Ohio	11,111,896,000	3.2%
28	Oklahoma	3,598,415,000	1.0%
29	Oregon	3,135,909,000	0.9%
6	Pennsylvania	12,378,832,000	3.6%
43	Rhode Island	1,052,892,000	0.3%
25	South Carolina	4,170,809,000	1.2%
46	South Dakota	790,758,000	0.2%
16	Tennessee	6,462,449,000	1.9%
2	Texas	29,523,396,000	8.5%
33	Utah	2,698,228,000	0.8%
50	Vermont	553,296,000	0.2%
12	Virginia	7,885,735,000	2.3%
14	Washington	6,645,034,000	1.9%
38	West Virginia	1,682,337,000	0.5%
20	Wisconsin	5,044,859,000	1.5%
49	Wyoming	632,121,000	0.2%

RANK ORDER

RANK	STATE	REFUNDS	% of USA
1	California	$36,845,651,000	10.6%
2	Texas	29,523,396,000	8.5%
3	New York	21,679,552,000	6.3%
4	Florida	20,989,413,000	6.1%
5	Illinois	14,048,816,000	4.1%
6	Pennsylvania	12,378,832,000	3.6%
7	Ohio	11,111,896,000	3.2%
8	New Jersey	9,818,252,000	2.8%
9	Georgia	9,810,101,000	2.8%
10	Michigan	9,170,480,000	2.6%
11	North Carolina	8,771,645,000	2.5%
12	Virginia	7,885,735,000	2.3%
13	Massachusetts	6,820,865,000	2.0%
14	Washington	6,645,034,000	1.9%
15	Indiana	6,511,762,000	1.9%
16	Tennessee	6,462,449,000	1.9%
17	Maryland	6,098,769,000	1.8%
18	Arizona	5,633,903,000	1.6%
19	Missouri	5,541,498,000	1.6%
20	Wisconsin	5,044,859,000	1.5%
21	Colorado	4,870,909,000	1.4%
22	Minnesota	4,826,504,000	1.4%
23	Louisiana	4,808,521,000	1.4%
24	Alabama	4,662,078,000	1.3%
25	South Carolina	4,170,809,000	1.2%
26	Kentucky	4,066,855,000	1.2%
27	Connecticut	3,906,818,000	1.1%
28	Oklahoma	3,598,415,000	1.0%
29	Oregon	3,135,909,000	0.9%
30	Mississippi	3,015,212,000	0.9%
31	Nevada	2,919,489,000	0.8%
32	Iowa	2,850,790,000	0.8%
33	Utah	2,698,228,000	0.8%
34	Kansas	2,619,713,000	0.8%
35	Arkansas	2,618,477,000	0.8%
36	New Mexico	1,860,651,000	0.5%
37	Nebraska	1,710,355,000	0.5%
38	West Virginia	1,682,337,000	0.5%
39	Hawaii	1,316,682,000	0.4%
40	New Hampshire	1,287,982,000	0.4%
41	Idaho	1,282,415,000	0.4%
42	Maine	1,081,393,000	0.3%
43	Rhode Island	1,052,892,000	0.3%
44	Delaware	867,929,000	0.3%
45	Montana	829,607,000	0.2%
46	South Dakota	790,758,000	0.2%
47	North Dakota	715,098,000	0.2%
48	Alaska	705,656,000	0.2%
49	Wyoming	632,121,000	0.2%
50	Vermont	553,296,000	0.2%
	District of Columbia	780,699,000	0.2%

Source: U.S. Department of the Treasury, Internal Revenue Service
"Fiscal Year 2015 IRS Data Book" (http://www.irs.gov/uac/SOI-Tax-Stats-IRS-Data-Book)
*Total includes refunds to international sources and other miscellaneous refunds not shown separately.

Average Value of Federal Individual Income Tax Refunds in 2015

National Average = $2,964*

<table>
<tr><td colspan="3">ALPHA ORDER</td><td colspan="3">RANK ORDER</td></tr>
<tr><th>RANK</th><th>STATE</th><th>AVERAGE REFUND</th><th>RANK</th><th>STATE</th><th>AVERAGE REFUND</th></tr>
<tr><td>9</td><td>Alabama</td><td>$2,805</td><td>1</td><td>Texas</td><td>$3,015</td></tr>
<tr><td>22</td><td>Alaska</td><td>2,594</td><td>2</td><td>Louisiana</td><td>2,946</td></tr>
<tr><td>21</td><td>Arizona</td><td>2,599</td><td>3</td><td>Mississippi</td><td>2,927</td></tr>
<tr><td>18</td><td>Arkansas</td><td>2,663</td><td>4</td><td>New York</td><td>2,906</td></tr>
<tr><td>11</td><td>California</td><td>2,779</td><td>5</td><td>New Jersey</td><td>2,904</td></tr>
<tr><td>31</td><td>Colorado</td><td>2,529</td><td>6</td><td>Connecticut</td><td>2,892</td></tr>
<tr><td>6</td><td>Connecticut</td><td>2,892</td><td>7</td><td>Wyoming</td><td>2,845</td></tr>
<tr><td>37</td><td>Delaware</td><td>2,497</td><td>8</td><td>Illinois</td><td>2,812</td></tr>
<tr><td>10</td><td>Florida</td><td>2,788</td><td>9</td><td>Alabama</td><td>2,805</td></tr>
<tr><td>13</td><td>Georgia</td><td>2,766</td><td>10</td><td>Florida</td><td>2,788</td></tr>
<tr><td>39</td><td>Hawaii</td><td>2,479</td><td>11</td><td>California</td><td>2,779</td></tr>
<tr><td>44</td><td>Idaho</td><td>2,386</td><td>12</td><td>Oklahoma</td><td>2,767</td></tr>
<tr><td>8</td><td>Illinois</td><td>2,812</td><td>13</td><td>Georgia</td><td>2,766</td></tr>
<tr><td>26</td><td>Indiana</td><td>2,559</td><td>14</td><td>Utah</td><td>2,728</td></tr>
<tr><td>31</td><td>Iowa</td><td>2,529</td><td>15</td><td>Nevada</td><td>2,725</td></tr>
<tr><td>29</td><td>Kansas</td><td>2,531</td><td>16</td><td>Maryland</td><td>2,711</td></tr>
<tr><td>23</td><td>Kentucky</td><td>2,584</td><td>17</td><td>Tennessee</td><td>2,670</td></tr>
<tr><td>2</td><td>Louisiana</td><td>2,946</td><td>18</td><td>Arkansas</td><td>2,663</td></tr>
<tr><td>50</td><td>Maine</td><td>2,221</td><td>19</td><td>Virginia</td><td>2,630</td></tr>
<tr><td>16</td><td>Maryland</td><td>2,711</td><td>20</td><td>Massachusetts</td><td>2,629</td></tr>
<tr><td>20</td><td>Massachusetts</td><td>2,629</td><td>21</td><td>Arizona</td><td>2,599</td></tr>
<tr><td>40</td><td>Michigan</td><td>2,461</td><td>22</td><td>Alaska</td><td>2,594</td></tr>
<tr><td>45</td><td>Minnesota</td><td>2,357</td><td>23</td><td>Kentucky</td><td>2,584</td></tr>
<tr><td>3</td><td>Mississippi</td><td>2,927</td><td>24</td><td>North Dakota</td><td>2,576</td></tr>
<tr><td>34</td><td>Missouri</td><td>2,516</td><td>25</td><td>New Mexico</td><td>2,570</td></tr>
<tr><td>47</td><td>Montana</td><td>2,288</td><td>26</td><td>Indiana</td><td>2,559</td></tr>
<tr><td>41</td><td>Nebraska</td><td>2,459</td><td>27</td><td>West Virginia</td><td>2,547</td></tr>
<tr><td>15</td><td>Nevada</td><td>2,725</td><td>28</td><td>North Carolina</td><td>2,545</td></tr>
<tr><td>43</td><td>New Hampshire</td><td>2,426</td><td>29</td><td>Kansas</td><td>2,531</td></tr>
<tr><td>5</td><td>New Jersey</td><td>2,904</td><td>29</td><td>Washington</td><td>2,531</td></tr>
<tr><td>25</td><td>New Mexico</td><td>2,570</td><td>31</td><td>Colorado</td><td>2,529</td></tr>
<tr><td>4</td><td>New York</td><td>2,906</td><td>31</td><td>Iowa</td><td>2,529</td></tr>
<tr><td>28</td><td>North Carolina</td><td>2,545</td><td>33</td><td>Pennsylvania</td><td>2,523</td></tr>
<tr><td>24</td><td>North Dakota</td><td>2,576</td><td>34</td><td>Missouri</td><td>2,516</td></tr>
<tr><td>42</td><td>Ohio</td><td>2,449</td><td>34</td><td>South Dakota</td><td>2,516</td></tr>
<tr><td>12</td><td>Oklahoma</td><td>2,767</td><td>36</td><td>Rhode Island</td><td>2,499</td></tr>
<tr><td>48</td><td>Oregon</td><td>2,283</td><td>37</td><td>Delaware</td><td>2,497</td></tr>
<tr><td>33</td><td>Pennsylvania</td><td>2,523</td><td>38</td><td>South Carolina</td><td>2,494</td></tr>
<tr><td>36</td><td>Rhode Island</td><td>2,499</td><td>39</td><td>Hawaii</td><td>2,479</td></tr>
<tr><td>38</td><td>South Carolina</td><td>2,494</td><td>40</td><td>Michigan</td><td>2,461</td></tr>
<tr><td>34</td><td>South Dakota</td><td>2,516</td><td>41</td><td>Nebraska</td><td>2,459</td></tr>
<tr><td>17</td><td>Tennessee</td><td>2,670</td><td>42</td><td>Ohio</td><td>2,449</td></tr>
<tr><td>1</td><td>Texas</td><td>3,015</td><td>43</td><td>New Hampshire</td><td>2,426</td></tr>
<tr><td>14</td><td>Utah</td><td>2,728</td><td>44</td><td>Idaho</td><td>2,386</td></tr>
<tr><td>49</td><td>Vermont</td><td>2,259</td><td>45</td><td>Minnesota</td><td>2,357</td></tr>
<tr><td>19</td><td>Virginia</td><td>2,630</td><td>46</td><td>Wisconsin</td><td>2,298</td></tr>
<tr><td>29</td><td>Washington</td><td>2,531</td><td>47</td><td>Montana</td><td>2,288</td></tr>
<tr><td>27</td><td>West Virginia</td><td>2,547</td><td>48</td><td>Oregon</td><td>2,283</td></tr>
<tr><td>46</td><td>Wisconsin</td><td>2,298</td><td>49</td><td>Vermont</td><td>2,259</td></tr>
<tr><td>7</td><td>Wyoming</td><td>2,845</td><td>50</td><td>Maine</td><td>2,221</td></tr>
<tr><td></td><td></td><td></td><td></td><td>District of Columbia</td><td>3,001</td></tr>
</table>

Source: CQ Press using data from U.S. Department of the Treasury, Internal Revenue Service
"Fiscal Year 2015 IRS Data Book" (http://www.irs.gov/uac/SOI-Tax-Stats-IRS-Data-Book)
*National average includes refunds to international sources and other miscellaneous refunds not shown separately.

Value of Federal Business Income Tax Refunds in 2015

National Total = $50,052,817,000*

ALPHA ORDER

RANK	STATE	REFUNDS	% of USA
30	Alabama	$268,009,000	0.5%
48	Alaska	30,430,000	0.1%
26	Arizona	408,292,000	0.8%
39	Arkansas	102,894,000	0.2%
1	California	6,020,462,000	12.0%
20	Colorado	810,668,000	1.6%
8	Connecticut	1,759,204,000	3.5%
12	Delaware	1,135,291,000	2.3%
16	Florida	994,054,000	2.0%
11	Georgia	1,370,898,000	2.7%
37	Hawaii	110,568,000	0.2%
35	Idaho	160,507,000	0.3%
9	Illinois	1,701,088,000	3.4%
25	Indiana	418,350,000	0.8%
27	Iowa	384,853,000	0.8%
21	Kansas	754,730,000	1.5%
31	Kentucky	264,666,000	0.5%
33	Louisiana	203,960,000	0.4%
42	Maine	60,423,000	0.1%
32	Maryland	241,970,000	0.5%
10	Massachusetts	1,411,766,000	2.8%
18	Michigan	885,429,000	1.8%
5	Minnesota	3,170,584,000	6.3%
38	Mississippi	109,459,000	0.2%
19	Missouri	856,446,000	1.7%
46	Montana	33,341,000	0.1%
14	Nebraska	1,106,152,000	2.2%
34	Nevada	168,332,000	0.3%
40	New Hampshire	82,499,000	0.2%
3	New Jersey	4,538,430,000	9.1%
43	New Mexico	42,223,000	0.1%
4	New York	4,440,837,000	8.9%
22	North Carolina	751,932,000	1.5%
44	North Dakota	41,986,000	0.1%
13	Ohio	1,124,009,000	2.2%
7	Oklahoma	1,814,093,000	3.6%
36	Oregon	156,420,000	0.3%
6	Pennsylvania	2,618,203,000	5.2%
49	Rhode Island	22,343,000	0.0%
29	South Carolina	274,495,000	0.5%
47	South Dakota	31,304,000	0.1%
17	Tennessee	965,894,000	1.9%
2	Texas	5,073,661,000	10.1%
28	Utah	318,427,000	0.6%
41	Vermont	64,421,000	0.1%
15	Virginia	1,003,939,000	2.0%
24	Washington	472,587,000	0.9%
45	West Virginia	41,012,000	0.1%
23	Wisconsin	604,902,000	1.2%
50	Wyoming	17,182,000	0.0%

RANK ORDER

RANK	STATE	REFUNDS	% of USA
1	California	$6,020,462,000	12.0%
2	Texas	5,073,661,000	10.1%
3	New Jersey	4,538,430,000	9.1%
4	New York	4,440,837,000	8.9%
5	Minnesota	3,170,584,000	6.3%
6	Pennsylvania	2,618,203,000	5.2%
7	Oklahoma	1,814,093,000	3.6%
8	Connecticut	1,759,204,000	3.5%
9	Illinois	1,701,088,000	3.4%
10	Massachusetts	1,411,766,000	2.8%
11	Georgia	1,370,898,000	2.7%
12	Delaware	1,135,291,000	2.3%
13	Ohio	1,124,009,000	2.2%
14	Nebraska	1,106,152,000	2.2%
15	Virginia	1,003,939,000	2.0%
16	Florida	994,054,000	2.0%
17	Tennessee	965,894,000	1.9%
18	Michigan	885,429,000	1.8%
19	Missouri	856,446,000	1.7%
20	Colorado	810,668,000	1.6%
21	Kansas	754,730,000	1.5%
22	North Carolina	751,932,000	1.5%
23	Wisconsin	604,902,000	1.2%
24	Washington	472,587,000	0.9%
25	Indiana	418,350,000	0.8%
26	Arizona	408,292,000	0.8%
27	Iowa	384,853,000	0.8%
28	Utah	318,427,000	0.6%
29	South Carolina	274,495,000	0.5%
30	Alabama	268,009,000	0.5%
31	Kentucky	264,666,000	0.5%
32	Maryland	241,970,000	0.5%
33	Louisiana	203,960,000	0.4%
34	Nevada	168,332,000	0.3%
35	Idaho	160,507,000	0.3%
36	Oregon	156,420,000	0.3%
37	Hawaii	110,568,000	0.2%
38	Mississippi	109,459,000	0.2%
39	Arkansas	102,894,000	0.2%
40	New Hampshire	82,499,000	0.2%
41	Vermont	64,421,000	0.1%
42	Maine	60,423,000	0.1%
43	New Mexico	42,223,000	0.1%
44	North Dakota	41,986,000	0.1%
45	West Virginia	41,012,000	0.1%
46	Montana	33,341,000	0.1%
47	South Dakota	31,304,000	0.1%
48	Alaska	30,430,000	0.1%
49	Rhode Island	22,343,000	0.0%
50	Wyoming	17,182,000	0.0%
	District of Columbia	367,921,000	0.7%

Source: U.S. Department of the Treasury, Internal Revenue Service
"Fiscal Year 2015 IRS Data Book" (http://www.irs.gov/uac/SOI-Tax-Stats-IRS-Data-Book)
*Total includes refunds to international sources and other miscellaneous refunds not shown separately. Includes taxes on corporation income (Form 1120 series) and unrelated business income from tax-exempt organizations.

Average Value of Federal Business Income Tax Refunds in 2015

National Average = $138,162*

ALPHA ORDER

RANK	STATE	AVERAGE REFUND
27	Alabama	$73,488
40	Alaska	35,591
24	Arizona	82,217
41	Arkansas	35,262
15	California	132,794
14	Colorado	134,976
3	Connecticut	440,351
1	Delaware	695,644
36	Florida	43,712
13	Georgia	153,895
33	Hawaii	50,673
21	Idaho	91,301
18	Illinois	114,590
28	Indiana	72,820
30	Iowa	63,246
12	Kansas	161,751
22	Kentucky	87,233
37	Louisiana	43,488
43	Maine	30,578
38	Maryland	39,654
8	Massachusetts	191,634
29	Michigan	72,398
5	Minnesota	371,785
39	Mississippi	39,247
16	Missouri	124,502
50	Montana	11,641
6	Nebraska	330,886
34	Nevada	48,330
35	New Hampshire	46,715
2	New Jersey	463,625
47	New Mexico	21,553
10	New York	176,126
23	North Carolina	82,766
45	North Dakota	26,258
20	Ohio	96,086
4	Oklahoma	422,472
42	Oregon	31,767
7	Pennsylvania	215,525
46	Rhode Island	24,181
25	South Carolina	76,653
48	South Dakota	17,878
9	Tennessee	191,077
11	Texas	173,702
17	Utah	118,023
32	Vermont	56,312
19	Virginia	112,954
31	Washington	58,919
44	West Virginia	27,488
26	Wisconsin	76,194
49	Wyoming	12,919

RANK ORDER

RANK	STATE	AVERAGE REFUND
1	Delaware	$695,644
2	New Jersey	463,625
3	Connecticut	440,351
4	Oklahoma	422,472
5	Minnesota	371,785
6	Nebraska	330,886
7	Pennsylvania	215,525
8	Massachusetts	191,634
9	Tennessee	191,077
10	New York	176,126
11	Texas	173,702
12	Kansas	161,751
13	Georgia	153,895
14	Colorado	134,976
15	California	132,794
16	Missouri	124,502
17	Utah	118,023
18	Illinois	114,590
19	Virginia	112,954
20	Ohio	96,086
21	Idaho	91,301
22	Kentucky	87,233
23	North Carolina	82,766
24	Arizona	82,217
25	South Carolina	76,653
26	Wisconsin	76,194
27	Alabama	73,488
28	Indiana	72,820
29	Michigan	72,398
30	Iowa	63,246
31	Washington	58,919
32	Vermont	56,312
33	Hawaii	50,673
34	Nevada	48,330
35	New Hampshire	46,715
36	Florida	43,712
37	Louisiana	43,488
38	Maryland	39,654
39	Mississippi	39,247
40	Alaska	35,591
41	Arkansas	35,262
42	Oregon	31,767
43	Maine	30,578
44	West Virginia	27,488
45	North Dakota	26,258
46	Rhode Island	24,181
47	New Mexico	21,553
48	South Dakota	17,878
49	Wyoming	12,919
50	Montana	11,641
	District of Columbia	351,405

Source: CQ Press using data from U.S. Department of the Treasury, Internal Revenue Service
"Fiscal Year 2015 IRS Data Book" (http://www.irs.gov/uac/SOI-Tax-Stats-IRS-Data-Book)
*National average includes refunds to international sources and other miscellaneous refunds not shown separately.

Federal Government Expenditures in 2015

National Total = $2,842,801,606,000*

ALPHA ORDER

RANK	STATE	EXPENDITURES	% of USA
19	Alabama	$61,679,811,710	2.2%
45	Alaska	7,988,540,901	0.3%
17	Arizona	62,859,902,581	2.2%
32	Arkansas	22,112,503,081	0.8%
1	California	261,070,877,920	9.2%
27	Colorado	35,811,456,596	1.3%
15	Connecticut	66,159,847,240	2.3%
47	Delaware	6,344,129,711	0.2%
4	Florida	154,814,880,155	5.4%
24	Georgia	54,061,806,670	1.9%
42	Hawaii	10,377,873,101	0.4%
40	Idaho	11,194,833,791	0.4%
13	Illinois	70,450,980,564	2.5%
6	Indiana	121,526,618,906	4.3%
34	Iowa	21,019,639,119	0.7%
35	Kansas	17,628,698,337	0.6%
9	Kentucky	76,864,081,910	2.7%
29	Louisiana	29,248,998,182	1.0%
41	Maine	10,832,939,096	0.4%
18	Maryland	61,972,970,681	2.2%
23	Massachusetts	58,548,869,385	2.1%
16	Michigan	65,118,303,378	2.3%
14	Minnesota	66,413,466,706	2.3%
33	Mississippi	21,667,102,607	0.8%
26	Missouri	46,534,929,982	1.6%
46	Montana	7,769,875,871	0.3%
39	Nebraska	11,243,586,182	0.4%
36	Nevada	17,486,305,035	0.6%
43	New Hampshire	9,183,660,400	0.3%
22	New Jersey	58,676,771,864	2.1%
31	New Mexico	22,130,879,669	0.8%
5	New York	150,628,375,223	5.3%
20	North Carolina	60,890,168,333	2.1%
21	North Dakota	60,098,466,286	2.1%
11	Ohio	72,926,588,903	2.6%
30	Oklahoma	26,321,688,025	0.9%
28	Oregon	31,847,399,269	1.1%
2	Pennsylvania	189,767,094,529	6.7%
44	Rhode Island	8,890,127,293	0.3%
10	South Carolina	73,927,515,782	2.6%
48	South Dakota	5,984,935,356	0.2%
12	Tennessee	72,063,344,155	2.5%
3	Texas	160,334,915,457	5.6%
38	Utah	13,683,680,602	0.5%
49	Vermont	5,021,268,579	0.2%
7	Virginia	91,150,225,191	3.2%
25	Washington	53,324,847,245	1.9%
37	West Virginia	15,608,878,940	0.5%
8	Wisconsin	83,085,641,882	2.9%
50	Wyoming	3,691,040,425	0.1%

RANK ORDER

RANK	STATE	EXPENDITURES	% of USA
1	California	$261,070,877,920	9.2%
2	Pennsylvania	189,767,094,529	6.7%
3	Texas	160,334,915,457	5.6%
4	Florida	154,814,880,155	5.4%
5	New York	150,628,375,223	5.3%
6	Indiana	121,526,618,906	4.3%
7	Virginia	91,150,225,191	3.2%
8	Wisconsin	83,085,641,882	2.9%
9	Kentucky	76,864,081,910	2.7%
10	South Carolina	73,927,515,782	2.6%
11	Ohio	72,926,588,903	2.6%
12	Tennessee	72,063,344,155	2.5%
13	Illinois	70,450,980,564	2.5%
14	Minnesota	66,413,466,706	2.3%
15	Connecticut	66,159,847,240	2.3%
16	Michigan	65,118,303,378	2.3%
17	Arizona	62,859,902,581	2.2%
18	Maryland	61,972,970,681	2.2%
19	Alabama	61,679,811,710	2.2%
20	North Carolina	60,890,168,333	2.1%
21	North Dakota	60,098,466,286	2.1%
22	New Jersey	58,676,771,864	2.1%
23	Massachusetts	58,548,869,385	2.1%
24	Georgia	54,061,806,670	1.9%
25	Washington	53,324,847,245	1.9%
26	Missouri	46,534,929,982	1.6%
27	Colorado	35,811,456,596	1.3%
28	Oregon	31,847,399,269	1.1%
29	Louisiana	29,248,998,182	1.0%
30	Oklahoma	26,321,688,025	0.9%
31	New Mexico	22,130,879,669	0.8%
32	Arkansas	22,112,503,081	0.8%
33	Mississippi	21,667,102,607	0.8%
34	Iowa	21,019,639,119	0.7%
35	Kansas	17,628,698,337	0.6%
36	Nevada	17,486,305,035	0.6%
37	West Virginia	15,608,878,940	0.5%
38	Utah	13,683,680,602	0.5%
39	Nebraska	11,243,586,182	0.4%
40	Idaho	11,194,833,791	0.4%
41	Maine	10,832,939,096	0.4%
42	Hawaii	10,377,873,101	0.4%
43	New Hampshire	9,183,660,400	0.3%
44	Rhode Island	8,890,127,293	0.3%
45	Alaska	7,988,540,901	0.3%
46	Montana	7,769,875,871	0.3%
47	Delaware	6,344,129,711	0.2%
48	South Dakota	5,984,935,356	0.2%
49	Vermont	5,021,268,579	0.2%
50	Wyoming	3,691,040,425	0.1%
	District of Columbia	30,122,976,519	1.1%

Source: U.S. Office of Management and Budget, USAspending.gov

"Prime Award Spending Data Summary" (https://www.usaspending.gov/, as of February 16, 2017)

*Total includes $84,637,287,000 in U.S. territories and internationally as well as expenditures not distributed by state. Expenditures allocated based on place of performance of a contract. Includes Contracts, Grants, Loans, and "Other Financial Assistance."

Per Capita Federal Government Expenditures in 2015

National Per Capita = $8,595*

RANK	STATE	PER CAPITA		RANK	STATE	PER CAPITA
8	Alabama	$12,707		1	North Dakota	$79,408
12	Alaska	10,829		2	Connecticut	18,456
15	Arizona	9,220		3	Indiana	18,378
27	Arkansas	7,426		4	Kentucky	17,372
36	California	6,695		5	South Carolina	15,103
37	Colorado	6,572		6	Pennsylvania	14,835
2	Connecticut	18,456		7	Wisconsin	14,405
35	Delaware	6,720		8	Alabama	12,707
23	Florida	7,647		9	Minnesota	12,114
49	Georgia	5,300		10	Tennessee	10,927
28	Hawaii	7,282		11	Virginia	10,893
32	Idaho	6,773		12	Alaska	10,829
48	Illinois	5,487		13	New Mexico	10,638
3	Indiana	18,378		14	Maryland	10,337
34	Iowa	6,733		15	Arizona	9,220
44	Kansas	6,065		16	Massachusetts	8,630
4	Kentucky	17,372		17	West Virginia	8,478
42	Louisiana	6,265		18	Rhode Island	8,422
19	Maine	8,148		19	Maine	8,148
14	Maryland	10,337		20	Vermont	8,020
16	Massachusetts	8,630		21	Oregon	7,913
39	Michigan	6,566		22	Missouri	7,659
9	Minnesota	12,114		23	Florida	7,647
29	Mississippi	7,248		24	New York	7,628
22	Missouri	7,659		25	Montana	7,528
25	Montana	7,528		26	Washington	7,447
46	Nebraska	5,937		27	Arkansas	7,426
45	Nevada	6,064		28	Hawaii	7,282
31	New Hampshire	6,904		29	Mississippi	7,248
38	New Jersey	6,567		30	South Dakota	6,976
13	New Mexico	10,638		31	New Hampshire	6,904
24	New York	7,628		32	Idaho	6,773
43	North Carolina	6,068		33	Oklahoma	6,736
1	North Dakota	79,408		34	Iowa	6,733
41	Ohio	6,284		35	Delaware	6,720
33	Oklahoma	6,736		36	California	6,695
21	Oregon	7,913		37	Colorado	6,572
6	Pennsylvania	14,835		38	New Jersey	6,567
18	Rhode Island	8,422		39	Michigan	6,566
5	South Carolina	15,103		40	Wyoming	6,293
30	South Dakota	6,976		41	Ohio	6,284
10	Tennessee	10,927		42	Louisiana	6,265
47	Texas	5,845		43	North Carolina	6,068
50	Utah	4,576		44	Kansas	6,065
20	Vermont	8,020		45	Nevada	6,064
11	Virginia	10,893		46	Nebraska	5,937
26	Washington	7,447		47	Texas	5,845
17	West Virginia	8,478		48	Illinois	5,487
7	Wisconsin	14,405		49	Georgia	5,300
40	Wyoming	6,293		50	Utah	4,576

District of Columbia 44,934

Source: CQ Press using data from U.S. Office of Management and Budget, USAspending.gov
"Prime Award Spending Data Summary" (https://www.usaspending.gov/, as of February 16, 2017)
*National per capita excludes expenditures and population for territories and undistributed amounts. Expenditures allocated based on place of performance of a contract. Includes Contracts, Grants, Loans, and "Other Financial Assistance."

Federal Government Contract Awards in 2015

National Total = $437,779,019,000*

ALPHA ORDER				RANK ORDER			
RANK	STATE	EXPENDITURES	% of USA	RANK	STATE	EXPENDITURES	% of USA
9	Alabama	$10,372,708,366	2.4%	1	Virginia	$48,687,775,946	11.1%
36	Alaska	1,872,545,544	0.4%	2	California	47,399,563,701	10.8%
12	Arizona	9,344,463,798	2.1%	3	Texas	35,368,401,137	8.1%
43	Arkansas	1,058,604,940	0.2%	4	Maryland	28,676,785,074	6.6%
2	California	47,399,563,701	10.8%	5	Pennsylvania	14,925,248,265	3.4%
13	Colorado	8,846,863,890	2.0%	6	Florida	13,581,880,418	3.1%
8	Connecticut	12,490,196,538	2.9%	7	Massachusetts	13,276,179,870	3.0%
48	Delaware	317,993,826	0.1%	8	Connecticut	12,490,196,538	2.9%
6	Florida	13,581,880,418	3.1%	9	Alabama	10,372,708,366	2.4%
16	Georgia	7,714,907,253	1.8%	10	Washington	10,056,285,421	2.3%
35	Hawaii	1,982,594,639	0.5%	11	New York	9,453,257,153	2.2%
32	Idaho	2,156,520,317	0.5%	12	Arizona	9,344,463,798	2.1%
15	Illinois	8,456,630,277	1.9%	13	Colorado	8,846,863,890	2.0%
26	Indiana	3,978,387,417	0.9%	14	Missouri	8,672,101,912	2.0%
37	Iowa	1,830,506,591	0.4%	15	Illinois	8,456,630,277	1.9%
34	Kansas	2,085,126,448	0.5%	16	Georgia	7,714,907,253	1.8%
18	Kentucky	6,513,016,501	1.5%	17	New Mexico	7,070,497,854	1.6%
30	Louisiana	2,762,571,373	0.6%	18	Kentucky	6,513,016,501	1.5%
38	Maine	1,503,929,135	0.3%	19	New Jersey	6,281,400,501	1.4%
4	Maryland	28,676,785,074	6.6%	20	Ohio	5,412,952,738	1.2%
7	Massachusetts	13,276,179,870	3.0%	21	South Carolina	5,070,325,974	1.2%
25	Michigan	4,214,494,699	1.0%	22	Tennessee	5,023,374,524	1.1%
24	Minnesota	4,712,224,274	1.1%	23	North Carolina	4,926,813,742	1.1%
27	Mississippi	3,845,529,250	0.9%	24	Minnesota	4,712,224,274	1.1%
14	Missouri	8,672,101,912	2.0%	25	Michigan	4,214,494,699	1.0%
45	Montana	510,984,725	0.1%	26	Indiana	3,978,387,417	0.9%
42	Nebraska	1,117,087,195	0.3%	27	Mississippi	3,845,529,250	0.9%
31	Nevada	2,466,999,421	0.6%	28	Wisconsin	2,900,696,337	0.7%
39	New Hampshire	1,460,633,137	0.3%	29	Oklahoma	2,818,574,937	0.6%
19	New Jersey	6,281,400,501	1.4%	30	Louisiana	2,762,571,373	0.6%
17	New Mexico	7,070,497,854	1.6%	31	Nevada	2,466,999,421	0.6%
11	New York	9,453,257,153	2.2%	32	Idaho	2,156,520,317	0.5%
23	North Carolina	4,926,813,742	1.1%	33	Utah	2,105,047,873	0.5%
46	North Dakota	500,221,846	0.1%	34	Kansas	2,085,126,448	0.5%
20	Ohio	5,412,952,738	1.2%	35	Hawaii	1,982,594,639	0.5%
29	Oklahoma	2,818,574,937	0.6%	36	Alaska	1,872,545,544	0.4%
40	Oregon	1,430,829,124	0.3%	37	Iowa	1,830,506,591	0.4%
5	Pennsylvania	14,925,248,265	3.4%	38	Maine	1,503,929,135	0.3%
44	Rhode Island	697,246,806	0.2%	39	New Hampshire	1,460,633,137	0.3%
21	South Carolina	5,070,325,974	1.2%	40	Oregon	1,430,829,124	0.3%
47	South Dakota	415,100,969	0.1%	41	West Virginia	1,283,764,161	0.3%
22	Tennessee	5,023,374,524	1.1%	42	Nebraska	1,117,087,195	0.3%
3	Texas	35,368,401,137	8.1%	43	Arkansas	1,058,604,940	0.2%
33	Utah	2,105,047,873	0.5%	44	Rhode Island	697,246,806	0.2%
49	Vermont	297,115,327	0.1%	45	Montana	510,984,725	0.1%
1	Virginia	48,687,775,946	11.1%	46	North Dakota	500,221,846	0.1%
10	Washington	10,056,285,421	2.3%	47	South Dakota	415,100,969	0.1%
41	West Virginia	1,283,764,161	0.3%	48	Delaware	317,993,826	0.1%
28	Wisconsin	2,900,696,337	0.7%	49	Vermont	297,115,327	0.1%
50	Wyoming	219,541,071	0.1%	50	Wyoming	219,541,071	0.1%
					District of Columbia	19,419,891,426	4.4%

Source: U.S. Office of Management and Budget, USAspending.gov
   "Prime Award Spending Data Summary" (https://www.usaspending.gov/, as of February 16, 2017)
*Total includes $40,192,625,000 in U.S. territories and internationally as well as expenditures not distributed by state.
Expenditures allocated based on place of performance of a contract. Does not include grants, co-operative agreements, or contracts under grants.

Per Capita Expenditures for Federal Government Contract Awards in 2015
National Per Capita = $1,239*

ALPHA ORDER

ALPHA ORDER

RANK ORDER

RANK	STATE	PER CAPITA
6	Alabama	$2,137
5	Alaska	2,538
13	Arizona	1,371
49	Arkansas	355
17	California	1,216
8	Colorado	1,624
3	Connecticut	3,484
50	Delaware	337
31	Florida	671
25	Georgia	756
12	Hawaii	1,391
14	Idaho	1,305
34	Illinois	659
35	Indiana	602
38	Iowa	586
27	Kansas	717
9	Kentucky	1,472
36	Louisiana	592
19	Maine	1,131
2	Maryland	4,783
7	Massachusetts	1,957
46	Michigan	425
22	Minnesota	860
16	Mississippi	1,286
10	Missouri	1,427
40	Montana	495
37	Nebraska	590
23	Nevada	855
20	New Hampshire	1,098
29	New Jersey	703
4	New Mexico	3,399
43	New York	479
41	North Carolina	491
32	North Dakota	661
45	Ohio	466
26	Oklahoma	721
48	Oregon	356
18	Pennsylvania	1,167
32	Rhode Island	661
21	South Carolina	1,036
42	South Dakota	484
24	Tennessee	762
15	Texas	1,289
28	Utah	704
44	Vermont	475
1	Virginia	5,819
11	Washington	1,404
30	West Virginia	697
39	Wisconsin	503
47	Wyoming	374

RANK	STATE	PER CAPITA
1	Virginia	$5,819
2	Maryland	4,783
3	Connecticut	3,484
4	New Mexico	3,399
5	Alaska	2,538
6	Alabama	2,137
7	Massachusetts	1,957
8	Colorado	1,624
9	Kentucky	1,472
10	Missouri	1,427
11	Washington	1,404
12	Hawaii	1,391
13	Arizona	1,371
14	Idaho	1,305
15	Texas	1,289
16	Mississippi	1,286
17	California	1,216
18	Pennsylvania	1,167
19	Maine	1,131
20	New Hampshire	1,098
21	South Carolina	1,036
22	Minnesota	860
23	Nevada	855
24	Tennessee	762
25	Georgia	756
26	Oklahoma	721
27	Kansas	717
28	Utah	704
29	New Jersey	703
30	West Virginia	697
31	Florida	671
32	North Dakota	661
32	Rhode Island	661
34	Illinois	659
35	Indiana	602
36	Louisiana	592
37	Nebraska	590
38	Iowa	586
39	Wisconsin	503
40	Montana	495
41	North Carolina	491
42	South Dakota	484
43	New York	479
44	Vermont	475
45	Ohio	466
46	Michigan	425
47	Wyoming	374
48	Oregon	356
49	Arkansas	355
50	Delaware	337

District of Columbia   28,969

Source: CQ Press using data from U.S. Office of Management and Budget, USAspending.gov
"Prime Award Spending Data Summary" (https://www.usaspending.gov/, as of February 16, 2017)
*National per capita excludes expenditures and population for territories and undistributed amounts. Expenditures allocated based on place of performance of a contract. Does not include grants, co-operative agreements, or contracts under grants.

Federal Government Assistance in 2015

National Total = $2,405,022,588,000*

ALPHA ORDER

RANK	STATE	EXPENDITURES	% of USA
20	Alabama	$51,307,103,344	2.1%
46	Alaska	6,115,995,357	0.3%
18	Arizona	53,515,438,783	2.2%
31	Arkansas	21,053,898,141	0.9%
1	California	213,671,314,219	8.9%
28	Colorado	26,964,592,706	1.1%
17	Connecticut	53,669,650,702	2.2%
47	Delaware	6,026,135,885	0.3%
3	Florida	141,232,999,737	5.9%
21	Georgia	46,346,899,417	1.9%
42	Hawaii	8,395,278,462	0.3%
41	Idaho	9,038,313,474	0.4%
12	Illinois	61,994,350,287	2.6%
6	Indiana	117,548,231,489	4.9%
32	Iowa	19,189,132,528	0.8%
34	Kansas	15,543,571,889	0.6%
8	Kentucky	70,351,065,409	2.9%
29	Louisiana	26,486,426,809	1.1%
40	Maine	9,329,009,961	0.4%
26	Maryland	33,296,185,607	1.4%
22	Massachusetts	45,272,689,515	1.9%
14	Michigan	60,903,808,679	2.5%
13	Minnesota	61,701,242,432	2.6%
33	Mississippi	17,821,573,357	0.7%
25	Missouri	37,862,828,070	1.6%
45	Montana	7,258,891,146	0.3%
39	Nebraska	10,126,498,987	0.4%
36	Nevada	15,019,305,614	0.6%
44	New Hampshire	7,723,027,263	0.3%
19	New Jersey	52,395,371,363	2.2%
35	New Mexico	15,060,381,815	0.6%
4	New York	141,175,118,070	5.9%
16	North Carolina	55,963,354,591	2.3%
15	North Dakota	59,598,244,440	2.5%
10	Ohio	67,513,636,165	2.8%
30	Oklahoma	23,503,113,088	1.0%
27	Oregon	30,416,570,145	1.3%
2	Pennsylvania	174,841,846,264	7.3%
43	Rhode Island	8,192,880,487	0.3%
9	South Carolina	68,857,189,808	2.9%
48	South Dakota	5,569,834,387	0.2%
11	Tennessee	67,039,969,631	2.8%
5	Texas	124,966,514,320	5.2%
38	Utah	11,578,632,729	0.5%
49	Vermont	4,724,153,252	0.2%
24	Virginia	42,462,449,245	1.8%
23	Washington	43,268,561,824	1.8%
37	West Virginia	14,325,114,779	0.6%
7	Wisconsin	80,184,945,545	3.3%
50	Wyoming	3,471,499,354	0.1%

RANK ORDER

RANK	STATE	EXPENDITURES	% of USA
1	California	$213,671,314,219	8.9%
2	Pennsylvania	174,841,846,264	7.3%
3	Florida	141,232,999,737	5.9%
4	New York	141,175,118,070	5.9%
5	Texas	124,966,514,320	5.2%
6	Indiana	117,548,231,489	4.9%
7	Wisconsin	80,184,945,545	3.3%
8	Kentucky	70,351,065,409	2.9%
9	South Carolina	68,857,189,808	2.9%
10	Ohio	67,513,636,165	2.8%
11	Tennessee	67,039,969,631	2.8%
12	Illinois	61,994,350,287	2.6%
13	Minnesota	61,701,242,432	2.6%
14	Michigan	60,903,808,679	2.5%
15	North Dakota	59,598,244,440	2.5%
16	North Carolina	55,963,354,591	2.3%
17	Connecticut	53,669,650,702	2.2%
18	Arizona	53,515,438,783	2.2%
19	New Jersey	52,395,371,363	2.2%
20	Alabama	51,307,103,344	2.1%
21	Georgia	46,346,899,417	1.9%
22	Massachusetts	45,272,689,515	1.9%
23	Washington	43,268,561,824	1.8%
24	Virginia	42,462,449,245	1.8%
25	Missouri	37,862,828,070	1.6%
26	Maryland	33,296,185,607	1.4%
27	Oregon	30,416,570,145	1.3%
28	Colorado	26,964,592,706	1.1%
29	Louisiana	26,486,426,809	1.1%
30	Oklahoma	23,503,113,088	1.0%
31	Arkansas	21,053,898,141	0.9%
32	Iowa	19,189,132,528	0.8%
33	Mississippi	17,821,573,357	0.7%
34	Kansas	15,543,571,889	0.6%
35	New Mexico	15,060,381,815	0.6%
36	Nevada	15,019,305,614	0.6%
37	West Virginia	14,325,114,779	0.6%
38	Utah	11,578,632,729	0.5%
39	Nebraska	10,126,498,987	0.4%
40	Maine	9,329,009,961	0.4%
41	Idaho	9,038,313,474	0.4%
42	Hawaii	8,395,278,462	0.3%
43	Rhode Island	8,192,880,487	0.3%
44	New Hampshire	7,723,027,263	0.3%
45	Montana	7,258,891,146	0.3%
46	Alaska	6,115,995,357	0.3%
47	Delaware	6,026,135,885	0.3%
48	South Dakota	5,569,834,387	0.2%
49	Vermont	4,724,153,252	0.2%
50	Wyoming	3,471,499,354	0.1%
	District of Columbia	10,703,085,093	0.4%

Source: CQ Press using data from U.S. Office of Management and Budget, USAspending.gov
"Prime Award Spending Data Summary" (https://www.usaspending.gov/, as of February 16, 2017)
*Total includes $44,444,662,000 in U.S. territories and internationally as well as expenditures not distributed by state.
Expenditures allocated based on place of performance of a contract. Includes grants, loans, and other financial assistance.

Per Capita Federal Government Assistance in 2015

National Per Capita = $7,356*

ALPHA ORDER				RANK ORDER		
RANK	STATE	PER CAPITA		RANK	STATE	PER CAPITA
9	Alabama	$10,570		1	North Dakota	$78,747
11	Alaska	8,291		2	Indiana	17,776
12	Arizona	7,850		3	Kentucky	15,900
19	Arkansas	7,070		4	Connecticut	14,972
40	California	5,480		5	South Carolina	14,067
46	Colorado	4,949		6	Wisconsin	13,902
4	Connecticut	14,972		7	Pennsylvania	13,668
25	Delaware	6,383		8	Minnesota	11,254
22	Florida	6,976		9	Alabama	10,570
49	Georgia	4,544		10	Tennessee	10,165
33	Hawaii	5,891		11	Alaska	8,291
41	Idaho	5,468		12	Arizona	7,850
47	Illinois	4,829		13	West Virginia	7,781
2	Indiana	17,776		14	Rhode Island	7,761
27	Iowa	6,146		15	Oregon	7,558
42	Kansas	5,347		16	Vermont	7,546
3	Kentucky	15,900		17	New Mexico	7,239
37	Louisiana	5,673		18	New York	7,149
21	Maine	7,017		19	Arkansas	7,070
39	Maryland	5,554		20	Montana	7,033
23	Massachusetts	6,673		21	Maine	7,017
28	Michigan	6,141		22	Florida	6,976
8	Minnesota	11,254		23	Massachusetts	6,673
31	Mississippi	5,962		24	South Dakota	6,492
26	Missouri	6,231		25	Delaware	6,383
20	Montana	7,033		26	Missouri	6,231
42	Nebraska	5,347		27	Iowa	6,146
44	Nevada	5,208		28	Michigan	6,141
36	New Hampshire	5,806		29	Washington	6,043
34	New Jersey	5,864		30	Oklahoma	6,015
17	New Mexico	7,239		31	Mississippi	5,962
18	New York	7,149		32	Wyoming	5,918
38	North Carolina	5,577		33	Hawaii	5,891
1	North Dakota	78,747		34	New Jersey	5,864
35	Ohio	5,818		35	Ohio	5,818
30	Oklahoma	6,015		36	New Hampshire	5,806
15	Oregon	7,558		37	Louisiana	5,673
7	Pennsylvania	13,668		38	North Carolina	5,577
14	Rhode Island	7,761		39	Maryland	5,554
5	South Carolina	14,067		40	California	5,480
24	South Dakota	6,492		41	Idaho	5,468
10	Tennessee	10,165		42	Kansas	5,347
48	Texas	4,556		42	Nebraska	5,347
50	Utah	3,872		44	Nevada	5,208
16	Vermont	7,546		45	Virginia	5,075
45	Virginia	5,075		46	Colorado	4,949
29	Washington	6,043		47	Illinois	4,829
13	West Virginia	7,781		48	Texas	4,556
6	Wisconsin	13,902		49	Georgia	4,544
32	Wyoming	5,918		50	Utah	3,872
					District of Columbia	15,966

Source: CQ Press using data from U.S. Office of Management and Budget, USAspending.gov
"Prime Award Spending Data Summary" (https://www.usaspending.gov/, as of February 16, 2017)
*National per capita excludes expenditures and population for territories and undistributed amounts. Expenditures allocated based on place of performance of a contract. Includes grants, loans and other financial assistance.

Federal Government Grants in 2015

National Total = $616,767,713,000*

ALPHA ORDER

RANK	STATE	EXPENDITURES	% of USA
29	Alabama	$6,702,957,552	1.1%
38	Alaska	3,320,993,825	0.5%
13	Arizona	13,283,921,811	2.2%
27	Arkansas	7,418,878,577	1.2%
1	California	80,898,273,148	13.1%
25	Colorado	9,122,470,579	1.5%
26	Connecticut	8,122,680,023	1.3%
46	Delaware	2,210,972,508	0.4%
5	Florida	22,817,150,697	3.7%
15	Georgia	12,050,689,527	2.0%
42	Hawaii	2,746,165,526	0.4%
43	Idaho	2,669,256,555	0.4%
9	Illinois	17,041,851,813	2.8%
19	Indiana	10,035,314,259	1.6%
32	Iowa	5,522,808,024	0.9%
36	Kansas	4,562,436,883	0.7%
22	Kentucky	9,640,129,202	1.6%
24	Louisiana	9,269,271,596	1.5%
39	Maine	3,031,435,770	0.5%
16	Maryland	11,732,269,588	1.9%
8	Massachusetts	17,657,848,690	2.9%
12	Michigan	14,189,819,711	2.3%
20	Minnesota	9,962,425,174	1.6%
33	Mississippi	5,469,159,834	0.9%
17	Missouri	10,949,841,891	1.8%
44	Montana	2,500,837,304	0.4%
41	Nebraska	2,803,344,029	0.5%
34	Nevada	5,072,375,445	0.8%
45	New Hampshire	2,238,407,163	0.4%
7	New Jersey	18,064,687,610	2.9%
31	New Mexico	6,464,651,719	1.0%
2	New York	60,883,060,505	9.9%
10	North Carolina	15,875,098,108	2.6%
48	North Dakota	1,752,649,293	0.3%
6	Ohio	20,181,122,660	3.3%
28	Oklahoma	6,863,529,204	1.1%
18	Oregon	10,570,785,868	1.7%
4	Pennsylvania	26,909,613,958	4.4%
40	Rhode Island	2,997,348,957	0.5%
30	South Carolina	6,589,508,645	1.1%
49	South Dakota	1,662,544,223	0.3%
14	Tennessee	12,100,359,770	2.0%
3	Texas	41,077,461,934	6.7%
37	Utah	3,607,293,435	0.6%
47	Vermont	2,064,702,629	0.3%
21	Virginia	9,874,297,638	1.6%
11	Washington	14,848,345,665	2.4%
35	West Virginia	5,047,265,165	0.8%
23	Wisconsin	9,483,858,366	1.5%
50	Wyoming	1,190,554,494	0.2%

RANK ORDER

RANK	STATE	EXPENDITURES	% of USA
1	California	$80,898,273,148	13.1%
2	New York	60,883,060,505	9.9%
3	Texas	41,077,461,934	6.7%
4	Pennsylvania	26,909,613,958	4.4%
5	Florida	22,817,150,697	3.7%
6	Ohio	20,181,122,660	3.3%
7	New Jersey	18,064,687,610	2.9%
8	Massachusetts	17,657,848,690	2.9%
9	Illinois	17,041,851,813	2.8%
10	North Carolina	15,875,098,108	2.6%
11	Washington	14,848,345,665	2.4%
12	Michigan	14,189,819,711	2.3%
13	Arizona	13,283,921,811	2.2%
14	Tennessee	12,100,359,770	2.0%
15	Georgia	12,050,689,527	2.0%
16	Maryland	11,732,269,588	1.9%
17	Missouri	10,949,841,891	1.8%
18	Oregon	10,570,785,868	1.7%
19	Indiana	10,035,314,259	1.6%
20	Minnesota	9,962,425,174	1.6%
21	Virginia	9,874,297,638	1.6%
22	Kentucky	9,640,129,202	1.6%
23	Wisconsin	9,483,858,366	1.5%
24	Louisiana	9,269,271,596	1.5%
25	Colorado	9,122,470,579	1.5%
26	Connecticut	8,122,680,023	1.3%
27	Arkansas	7,418,878,577	1.2%
28	Oklahoma	6,863,529,204	1.1%
29	Alabama	6,702,957,552	1.1%
30	South Carolina	6,589,508,645	1.1%
31	New Mexico	6,464,651,719	1.0%
32	Iowa	5,522,808,024	0.9%
33	Mississippi	5,469,159,834	0.9%
34	Nevada	5,072,375,445	0.8%
35	West Virginia	5,047,265,165	0.8%
36	Kansas	4,562,436,883	0.7%
37	Utah	3,607,293,435	0.6%
38	Alaska	3,320,993,825	0.5%
39	Maine	3,031,435,770	0.5%
40	Rhode Island	2,997,348,957	0.5%
41	Nebraska	2,803,344,029	0.5%
42	Hawaii	2,746,165,526	0.4%
43	Idaho	2,669,256,555	0.4%
44	Montana	2,500,837,304	0.4%
45	New Hampshire	2,238,407,163	0.4%
46	Delaware	2,210,972,508	0.4%
47	Vermont	2,064,702,629	0.3%
48	North Dakota	1,752,649,293	0.3%
49	South Dakota	1,662,544,223	0.3%
50	Wyoming	1,190,554,494	0.2%
	District of Columbia	8,491,889,850	1.4%

Source: U.S. Office of Management and Budget, USAspending.gov
"Prime Award Spending Data Summary" (https://www.usaspending.gov/, as of February 16, 2017)
*Total includes $17,123,097,000 in U.S. territories and internationally as well as expenditures not distributed by state.
Expenditures allocated based on place of performance of a contract. Includes funds awarded to a non-federal entity for a defined public or private purpose in which services are not rendered to the federal government.

Per Capita Expenditures for Federal Government Grants in 2015

National Per Capita = $1,869*

<table>
<tr><td colspan="3">ALPHA ORDER</td><td colspan="3">RANK ORDER</td></tr>
<tr><th>RANK</th><th>STATE</th><th>PER CAPITA</th><th>RANK</th><th>STATE</th><th>PER CAPITA</th></tr>
<tr><td>44</td><td>Alabama</td><td>$1,381</td><td>1</td><td>Alaska</td><td>$4,502</td></tr>
<tr><td>1</td><td>Alaska</td><td>4,502</td><td>2</td><td>Vermont</td><td>3,298</td></tr>
<tr><td>23</td><td>Arizona</td><td>1,948</td><td>3</td><td>New Mexico</td><td>3,108</td></tr>
<tr><td>9</td><td>Arkansas</td><td>2,491</td><td>4</td><td>New York</td><td>3,083</td></tr>
<tr><td>17</td><td>California</td><td>2,075</td><td>5</td><td>Rhode Island</td><td>2,839</td></tr>
<tr><td>35</td><td>Colorado</td><td>1,674</td><td>6</td><td>West Virginia</td><td>2,742</td></tr>
<tr><td>14</td><td>Connecticut</td><td>2,266</td><td>7</td><td>Oregon</td><td>2,627</td></tr>
<tr><td>11</td><td>Delaware</td><td>2,342</td><td>8</td><td>Massachusetts</td><td>2,603</td></tr>
<tr><td>50</td><td>Florida</td><td>1,127</td><td>9</td><td>Arkansas</td><td>2,491</td></tr>
<tr><td>48</td><td>Georgia</td><td>1,182</td><td>10</td><td>Montana</td><td>2,423</td></tr>
<tr><td>25</td><td>Hawaii</td><td>1,927</td><td>11</td><td>Delaware</td><td>2,342</td></tr>
<tr><td>37</td><td>Idaho</td><td>1,615</td><td>12</td><td>North Dakota</td><td>2,316</td></tr>
<tr><td>46</td><td>Illinois</td><td>1,327</td><td>13</td><td>Maine</td><td>2,280</td></tr>
<tr><td>40</td><td>Indiana</td><td>1,518</td><td>14</td><td>Connecticut</td><td>2,266</td></tr>
<tr><td>30</td><td>Iowa</td><td>1,769</td><td>15</td><td>Kentucky</td><td>2,179</td></tr>
<tr><td>39</td><td>Kansas</td><td>1,570</td><td>16</td><td>Pennsylvania</td><td>2,104</td></tr>
<tr><td>15</td><td>Kentucky</td><td>2,179</td><td>17</td><td>California</td><td>2,075</td></tr>
<tr><td>21</td><td>Louisiana</td><td>1,985</td><td>18</td><td>Washington</td><td>2,074</td></tr>
<tr><td>13</td><td>Maine</td><td>2,280</td><td>19</td><td>Wyoming</td><td>2,030</td></tr>
<tr><td>22</td><td>Maryland</td><td>1,957</td><td>20</td><td>New Jersey</td><td>2,022</td></tr>
<tr><td>8</td><td>Massachusetts</td><td>2,603</td><td>21</td><td>Louisiana</td><td>1,985</td></tr>
<tr><td>43</td><td>Michigan</td><td>1,431</td><td>22</td><td>Maryland</td><td>1,957</td></tr>
<tr><td>28</td><td>Minnesota</td><td>1,817</td><td>23</td><td>Arizona</td><td>1,948</td></tr>
<tr><td>27</td><td>Mississippi</td><td>1,830</td><td>24</td><td>South Dakota</td><td>1,938</td></tr>
<tr><td>29</td><td>Missouri</td><td>1,802</td><td>25</td><td>Hawaii</td><td>1,927</td></tr>
<tr><td>10</td><td>Montana</td><td>2,423</td><td>26</td><td>Tennessee</td><td>1,835</td></tr>
<tr><td>42</td><td>Nebraska</td><td>1,480</td><td>27</td><td>Mississippi</td><td>1,830</td></tr>
<tr><td>31</td><td>Nevada</td><td>1,759</td><td>28</td><td>Minnesota</td><td>1,817</td></tr>
<tr><td>34</td><td>New Hampshire</td><td>1,683</td><td>29</td><td>Missouri</td><td>1,802</td></tr>
<tr><td>20</td><td>New Jersey</td><td>2,022</td><td>30</td><td>Iowa</td><td>1,769</td></tr>
<tr><td>3</td><td>New Mexico</td><td>3,108</td><td>31</td><td>Nevada</td><td>1,759</td></tr>
<tr><td>4</td><td>New York</td><td>3,083</td><td>32</td><td>Oklahoma</td><td>1,757</td></tr>
<tr><td>38</td><td>North Carolina</td><td>1,582</td><td>33</td><td>Ohio</td><td>1,739</td></tr>
<tr><td>12</td><td>North Dakota</td><td>2,316</td><td>34</td><td>New Hampshire</td><td>1,683</td></tr>
<tr><td>33</td><td>Ohio</td><td>1,739</td><td>35</td><td>Colorado</td><td>1,674</td></tr>
<tr><td>32</td><td>Oklahoma</td><td>1,757</td><td>36</td><td>Wisconsin</td><td>1,644</td></tr>
<tr><td>7</td><td>Oregon</td><td>2,627</td><td>37</td><td>Idaho</td><td>1,615</td></tr>
<tr><td>16</td><td>Pennsylvania</td><td>2,104</td><td>38</td><td>North Carolina</td><td>1,582</td></tr>
<tr><td>5</td><td>Rhode Island</td><td>2,839</td><td>39</td><td>Kansas</td><td>1,570</td></tr>
<tr><td>45</td><td>South Carolina</td><td>1,346</td><td>40</td><td>Indiana</td><td>1,518</td></tr>
<tr><td>24</td><td>South Dakota</td><td>1,938</td><td>41</td><td>Texas</td><td>1,498</td></tr>
<tr><td>26</td><td>Tennessee</td><td>1,835</td><td>42</td><td>Nebraska</td><td>1,480</td></tr>
<tr><td>41</td><td>Texas</td><td>1,498</td><td>43</td><td>Michigan</td><td>1,431</td></tr>
<tr><td>47</td><td>Utah</td><td>1,206</td><td>44</td><td>Alabama</td><td>1,381</td></tr>
<tr><td>2</td><td>Vermont</td><td>3,298</td><td>45</td><td>South Carolina</td><td>1,346</td></tr>
<tr><td>49</td><td>Virginia</td><td>1,180</td><td>46</td><td>Illinois</td><td>1,327</td></tr>
<tr><td>18</td><td>Washington</td><td>2,074</td><td>47</td><td>Utah</td><td>1,206</td></tr>
<tr><td>6</td><td>West Virginia</td><td>2,742</td><td>48</td><td>Georgia</td><td>1,182</td></tr>
<tr><td>36</td><td>Wisconsin</td><td>1,644</td><td>49</td><td>Virginia</td><td>1,180</td></tr>
<tr><td>19</td><td>Wyoming</td><td>2,030</td><td>50</td><td>Florida</td><td>1,127</td></tr>
<tr><td></td><td></td><td></td><td></td><td>District of Columbia</td><td>12,667</td></tr>
</table>

Source: CQ Press using data from U.S. Office of Management and Budget, USAspending.gov
"Prime Award Spending Data Summary" (https://www.usaspending.gov/, as of February 16, 2017)
*National per capita excludes expenditures and population for territories and undistributed amounts. Expenditures allocated based on place of performance of a contract. Includes funds awarded to a non-federal entity for a defined public or private purpose in which services are not rendered to the federal government.

Federal Government Loans in 2015

National Total = $4,658,288,000*

<table>
<tr><td colspan="4">ALPHA ORDER</td><td colspan="4">RANK ORDER</td></tr>
<tr><td>RANK</td><td>STATE</td><td>EXPENDITURES</td><td>% of USA</td><td>RANK</td><td>STATE</td><td>EXPENDITURES</td><td>% of USA</td></tr>
<tr><td>30</td><td>Alabama</td><td>$15,929,715</td><td>0.3%</td><td>1</td><td>Washington</td><td>$1,349,952,564</td><td>29.0%</td></tr>
<tr><td>22</td><td>Alaska</td><td>25,598,021</td><td>0.5%</td><td>2</td><td>New York</td><td>1,016,769,069</td><td>21.8%</td></tr>
<tr><td>28</td><td>Arizona</td><td>18,364,305</td><td>0.4%</td><td>3</td><td>Virginia</td><td>645,194,957</td><td>13.9%</td></tr>
<tr><td>29</td><td>Arkansas</td><td>15,955,860</td><td>0.3%</td><td>4</td><td>North Carolina</td><td>243,769,752</td><td>5.2%</td></tr>
<tr><td>8</td><td>California</td><td>150,152,397</td><td>3.2%</td><td>5</td><td>Florida</td><td>239,022,997</td><td>5.1%</td></tr>
<tr><td>16</td><td>Colorado</td><td>31,351,980</td><td>0.7%</td><td>6</td><td>Ohio</td><td>232,447,924</td><td>5.0%</td></tr>
<tr><td>42</td><td>Connecticut</td><td>6,861,341</td><td>0.1%</td><td>7</td><td>Indiana</td><td>172,021,365</td><td>3.7%</td></tr>
<tr><td>45</td><td>Delaware</td><td>5,353,789</td><td>0.1%</td><td>8</td><td>California</td><td>150,152,397</td><td>3.2%</td></tr>
<tr><td>5</td><td>Florida</td><td>239,022,997</td><td>5.1%</td><td>9</td><td>Illinois</td><td>134,509,169</td><td>2.9%</td></tr>
<tr><td>12</td><td>Georgia</td><td>37,947,890</td><td>0.8%</td><td>10</td><td>Kentucky</td><td>85,775,596</td><td>1.8%</td></tr>
<tr><td>40</td><td>Hawaii</td><td>7,189,126</td><td>0.2%</td><td>11</td><td>Texas</td><td>41,434,793</td><td>0.9%</td></tr>
<tr><td>34</td><td>Idaho</td><td>8,718,137</td><td>0.2%</td><td>12</td><td>Georgia</td><td>37,947,890</td><td>0.8%</td></tr>
<tr><td>9</td><td>Illinois</td><td>134,509,169</td><td>2.9%</td><td>13</td><td>Nevada</td><td>35,436,556</td><td>0.8%</td></tr>
<tr><td>7</td><td>Indiana</td><td>172,021,365</td><td>3.7%</td><td>14</td><td>Pennsylvania</td><td>34,670,261</td><td>0.7%</td></tr>
<tr><td>17</td><td>Iowa</td><td>30,515,786</td><td>0.7%</td><td>15</td><td>New Jersey</td><td>32,171,909</td><td>0.7%</td></tr>
<tr><td>37</td><td>Kansas</td><td>7,855,571</td><td>0.2%</td><td>16</td><td>Colorado</td><td>31,351,980</td><td>0.7%</td></tr>
<tr><td>10</td><td>Kentucky</td><td>85,775,596</td><td>1.8%</td><td>17</td><td>Iowa</td><td>30,515,786</td><td>0.7%</td></tr>
<tr><td>20</td><td>Louisiana</td><td>29,421,043</td><td>0.6%</td><td>18</td><td>Missouri</td><td>30,345,124</td><td>0.7%</td></tr>
<tr><td>47</td><td>Maine</td><td>3,643,764</td><td>0.1%</td><td>19</td><td>Minnesota</td><td>29,576,453</td><td>0.6%</td></tr>
<tr><td>27</td><td>Maryland</td><td>18,529,247</td><td>0.4%</td><td>20</td><td>Louisiana</td><td>29,421,043</td><td>0.6%</td></tr>
<tr><td>35</td><td>Massachusetts</td><td>8,492,022</td><td>0.2%</td><td>21</td><td>South Carolina</td><td>27,884,851</td><td>0.6%</td></tr>
<tr><td>23</td><td>Michigan</td><td>25,273,644</td><td>0.5%</td><td>22</td><td>Alaska</td><td>25,598,021</td><td>0.5%</td></tr>
<tr><td>19</td><td>Minnesota</td><td>29,576,453</td><td>0.6%</td><td>23</td><td>Michigan</td><td>25,273,644</td><td>0.5%</td></tr>
<tr><td>33</td><td>Mississippi</td><td>9,134,770</td><td>0.2%</td><td>24</td><td>Wisconsin</td><td>25,164,916</td><td>0.5%</td></tr>
<tr><td>18</td><td>Missouri</td><td>30,345,124</td><td>0.7%</td><td>25</td><td>Tennessee</td><td>24,585,989</td><td>0.5%</td></tr>
<tr><td>39</td><td>Montana</td><td>7,238,609</td><td>0.2%</td><td>26</td><td>Oklahoma</td><td>18,984,067</td><td>0.4%</td></tr>
<tr><td>36</td><td>Nebraska</td><td>8,491,868</td><td>0.2%</td><td>27</td><td>Maryland</td><td>18,529,247</td><td>0.4%</td></tr>
<tr><td>13</td><td>Nevada</td><td>35,436,556</td><td>0.8%</td><td>28</td><td>Arizona</td><td>18,364,305</td><td>0.4%</td></tr>
<tr><td>46</td><td>New Hampshire</td><td>5,296,735</td><td>0.1%</td><td>29</td><td>Arkansas</td><td>15,955,860</td><td>0.3%</td></tr>
<tr><td>15</td><td>New Jersey</td><td>32,171,909</td><td>0.7%</td><td>30</td><td>Alabama</td><td>15,929,715</td><td>0.3%</td></tr>
<tr><td>41</td><td>New Mexico</td><td>6,881,025</td><td>0.1%</td><td>31</td><td>Oregon</td><td>15,857,967</td><td>0.3%</td></tr>
<tr><td>2</td><td>New York</td><td>1,016,769,069</td><td>21.8%</td><td>32</td><td>North Dakota</td><td>13,795,536</td><td>0.3%</td></tr>
<tr><td>4</td><td>North Carolina</td><td>243,769,752</td><td>5.2%</td><td>33</td><td>Mississippi</td><td>9,134,770</td><td>0.2%</td></tr>
<tr><td>32</td><td>North Dakota</td><td>13,795,536</td><td>0.3%</td><td>34</td><td>Idaho</td><td>8,718,137</td><td>0.2%</td></tr>
<tr><td>6</td><td>Ohio</td><td>232,447,924</td><td>5.0%</td><td>35</td><td>Massachusetts</td><td>8,492,022</td><td>0.2%</td></tr>
<tr><td>26</td><td>Oklahoma</td><td>18,984,067</td><td>0.4%</td><td>36</td><td>Nebraska</td><td>8,491,868</td><td>0.2%</td></tr>
<tr><td>31</td><td>Oregon</td><td>15,857,967</td><td>0.3%</td><td>37</td><td>Kansas</td><td>7,855,571</td><td>0.2%</td></tr>
<tr><td>14</td><td>Pennsylvania</td><td>34,670,261</td><td>0.7%</td><td>38</td><td>Utah</td><td>7,443,540</td><td>0.2%</td></tr>
<tr><td>50</td><td>Rhode Island</td><td>1,462,752</td><td>0.0%</td><td>39</td><td>Montana</td><td>7,238,609</td><td>0.2%</td></tr>
<tr><td>21</td><td>South Carolina</td><td>27,884,851</td><td>0.6%</td><td>40</td><td>Hawaii</td><td>7,189,126</td><td>0.2%</td></tr>
<tr><td>43</td><td>South Dakota</td><td>6,632,404</td><td>0.1%</td><td>41</td><td>New Mexico</td><td>6,881,025</td><td>0.1%</td></tr>
<tr><td>25</td><td>Tennessee</td><td>24,585,989</td><td>0.5%</td><td>42</td><td>Connecticut</td><td>6,861,341</td><td>0.1%</td></tr>
<tr><td>11</td><td>Texas</td><td>41,434,793</td><td>0.9%</td><td>43</td><td>South Dakota</td><td>6,632,404</td><td>0.1%</td></tr>
<tr><td>38</td><td>Utah</td><td>7,443,540</td><td>0.2%</td><td>44</td><td>Vermont</td><td>5,504,273</td><td>0.1%</td></tr>
<tr><td>44</td><td>Vermont</td><td>5,504,273</td><td>0.1%</td><td>45</td><td>Delaware</td><td>5,353,789</td><td>0.1%</td></tr>
<tr><td>3</td><td>Virginia</td><td>645,194,957</td><td>13.9%</td><td>46</td><td>New Hampshire</td><td>5,296,735</td><td>0.1%</td></tr>
<tr><td>1</td><td>Washington</td><td>1,349,952,564</td><td>29.0%</td><td>47</td><td>Maine</td><td>3,643,764</td><td>0.1%</td></tr>
<tr><td>49</td><td>West Virginia</td><td>3,414,095</td><td>0.1%</td><td>48</td><td>Wyoming</td><td>3,567,099</td><td>0.1%</td></tr>
<tr><td>24</td><td>Wisconsin</td><td>25,164,916</td><td>0.5%</td><td>49</td><td>West Virginia</td><td>3,414,095</td><td>0.1%</td></tr>
<tr><td>48</td><td>Wyoming</td><td>3,567,099</td><td>0.1%</td><td>50</td><td>Rhode Island</td><td>1,462,752</td><td>0.0%</td></tr>
<tr><td></td><td></td><td></td><td></td><td></td><td>District of Columbia</td><td>1,226,971</td><td>0.0%</td></tr>
</table>

Source: U.S. Office of Management and Budget, USAspending.gov
"Prime Award Spending Data Summary" (https://www.usaspending.gov/, as of February 16, 2017)
*Total includes a negative $304,532,000 in U.S. territories and internationally as well as expenditures not distributed by state. Expenditures allocated based on place of performance of a contract. Includes federal awards that the borrowers will eventually pay back to the government. Guaranteed loans require the federal government to pay the bank and take over the loan if the borrower defaults.

Per Capita Federal Government Loans in 2015

National Per Capita = $15.47*

<table>
<tr><td colspan="3">ALPHA ORDER</td><td colspan="3">RANK ORDER</td></tr>
<tr><td>RANK</td><td>STATE</td><td>PER CAPITA</td><td>RANK</td><td>STATE</td><td>PER CAPITA</td></tr>
<tr><td>37</td><td>Alabama</td><td>$3.28</td><td>1</td><td>Washington</td><td>$188.53</td></tr>
<tr><td>4</td><td>Alaska</td><td>34.70</td><td>2</td><td>Virginia</td><td>77.11</td></tr>
<tr><td>43</td><td>Arizona</td><td>2.69</td><td>3</td><td>New York</td><td>51.49</td></tr>
<tr><td>23</td><td>Arkansas</td><td>5.36</td><td>4</td><td>Alaska</td><td>34.70</td></tr>
<tr><td>32</td><td>California</td><td>3.85</td><td>5</td><td>Indiana</td><td>26.01</td></tr>
<tr><td>19</td><td>Colorado</td><td>5.75</td><td>6</td><td>North Carolina</td><td>24.29</td></tr>
<tr><td>46</td><td>Connecticut</td><td>1.91</td><td>7</td><td>Ohio</td><td>20.03</td></tr>
<tr><td>21</td><td>Delaware</td><td>5.67</td><td>8</td><td>Kentucky</td><td>19.39</td></tr>
<tr><td>11</td><td>Florida</td><td>11.81</td><td>9</td><td>North Dakota</td><td>18.23</td></tr>
<tr><td>34</td><td>Georgia</td><td>3.72</td><td>10</td><td>Nevada</td><td>12.29</td></tr>
<tr><td>25</td><td>Hawaii</td><td>5.04</td><td>11</td><td>Florida</td><td>11.81</td></tr>
<tr><td>24</td><td>Idaho</td><td>5.27</td><td>12</td><td>Illinois</td><td>10.48</td></tr>
<tr><td>12</td><td>Illinois</td><td>10.48</td><td>13</td><td>Iowa</td><td>9.77</td></tr>
<tr><td>5</td><td>Indiana</td><td>26.01</td><td>14</td><td>Vermont</td><td>8.79</td></tr>
<tr><td>13</td><td>Iowa</td><td>9.77</td><td>15</td><td>South Dakota</td><td>7.73</td></tr>
<tr><td>42</td><td>Kansas</td><td>2.70</td><td>16</td><td>Montana</td><td>7.01</td></tr>
<tr><td>8</td><td>Kentucky</td><td>19.39</td><td>17</td><td>Louisiana</td><td>6.30</td></tr>
<tr><td>17</td><td>Louisiana</td><td>6.30</td><td>18</td><td>Wyoming</td><td>6.08</td></tr>
<tr><td>40</td><td>Maine</td><td>2.74</td><td>19</td><td>Colorado</td><td>5.75</td></tr>
<tr><td>38</td><td>Maryland</td><td>3.09</td><td>20</td><td>South Carolina</td><td>5.70</td></tr>
<tr><td>50</td><td>Massachusetts</td><td>1.25</td><td>21</td><td>Delaware</td><td>5.67</td></tr>
<tr><td>44</td><td>Michigan</td><td>2.55</td><td>22</td><td>Minnesota</td><td>5.39</td></tr>
<tr><td>22</td><td>Minnesota</td><td>5.39</td><td>23</td><td>Arkansas</td><td>5.36</td></tr>
<tr><td>39</td><td>Mississippi</td><td>3.06</td><td>24</td><td>Idaho</td><td>5.27</td></tr>
<tr><td>26</td><td>Missouri</td><td>4.99</td><td>25</td><td>Hawaii</td><td>5.04</td></tr>
<tr><td>16</td><td>Montana</td><td>7.01</td><td>26</td><td>Missouri</td><td>4.99</td></tr>
<tr><td>28</td><td>Nebraska</td><td>4.48</td><td>27</td><td>Oklahoma</td><td>4.86</td></tr>
<tr><td>10</td><td>Nevada</td><td>12.29</td><td>28</td><td>Nebraska</td><td>4.48</td></tr>
<tr><td>30</td><td>New Hampshire</td><td>3.98</td><td>29</td><td>Wisconsin</td><td>4.36</td></tr>
<tr><td>35</td><td>New Jersey</td><td>3.60</td><td>30</td><td>New Hampshire</td><td>3.98</td></tr>
<tr><td>36</td><td>New Mexico</td><td>3.31</td><td>31</td><td>Oregon</td><td>3.94</td></tr>
<tr><td>3</td><td>New York</td><td>51.49</td><td>32</td><td>California</td><td>3.85</td></tr>
<tr><td>6</td><td>North Carolina</td><td>24.29</td><td>33</td><td>Tennessee</td><td>3.73</td></tr>
<tr><td>9</td><td>North Dakota</td><td>18.23</td><td>34</td><td>Georgia</td><td>3.72</td></tr>
<tr><td>7</td><td>Ohio</td><td>20.03</td><td>35</td><td>New Jersey</td><td>3.60</td></tr>
<tr><td>27</td><td>Oklahoma</td><td>4.86</td><td>36</td><td>New Mexico</td><td>3.31</td></tr>
<tr><td>31</td><td>Oregon</td><td>3.94</td><td>37</td><td>Alabama</td><td>3.28</td></tr>
<tr><td>41</td><td>Pennsylvania</td><td>2.71</td><td>38</td><td>Maryland</td><td>3.09</td></tr>
<tr><td>49</td><td>Rhode Island</td><td>1.39</td><td>39</td><td>Mississippi</td><td>3.06</td></tr>
<tr><td>20</td><td>South Carolina</td><td>5.70</td><td>40</td><td>Maine</td><td>2.74</td></tr>
<tr><td>15</td><td>South Dakota</td><td>7.73</td><td>41</td><td>Pennsylvania</td><td>2.71</td></tr>
<tr><td>33</td><td>Tennessee</td><td>3.73</td><td>42</td><td>Kansas</td><td>2.70</td></tr>
<tr><td>48</td><td>Texas</td><td>1.51</td><td>43</td><td>Arizona</td><td>2.69</td></tr>
<tr><td>45</td><td>Utah</td><td>2.49</td><td>44</td><td>Michigan</td><td>2.55</td></tr>
<tr><td>14</td><td>Vermont</td><td>8.79</td><td>45</td><td>Utah</td><td>2.49</td></tr>
<tr><td>2</td><td>Virginia</td><td>77.11</td><td>46</td><td>Connecticut</td><td>1.91</td></tr>
<tr><td>1</td><td>Washington</td><td>188.53</td><td>47</td><td>West Virginia</td><td>1.85</td></tr>
<tr><td>47</td><td>West Virginia</td><td>1.85</td><td>48</td><td>Texas</td><td>1.51</td></tr>
<tr><td>29</td><td>Wisconsin</td><td>4.36</td><td>49</td><td>Rhode Island</td><td>1.39</td></tr>
<tr><td>18</td><td>Wyoming</td><td>6.08</td><td>50</td><td>Massachusetts</td><td>1.25</td></tr>
<tr><td></td><td></td><td></td><td></td><td>District of Columbia</td><td>1.83</td></tr>
</table>

Source: CQ Press using data from U.S. Office of Management and Budget, USAspending.gov
"Prime Award Spending Data Summary" (https://www.usaspending.gov/, as of February 16, 2017)
*National per capita excludes expenditures and population for territories and undistributed amounts. Expenditures allocated based on place of performance of a contract. Includes Federal awards that the borrowers will eventually pay back to the government. Guaranteed loans require the federal government to pay the bank and take over the loan if the borrower defaults.

Federal Government "Other Financial Assistance" in 2015

National Total = $1,783,596,586,000*

ALPHA ORDER

ALPHA ORDER

RANK	STATE	EXPENDITURES	% of USA
17	Alabama	$44,588,216,077	2.5%
48	Alaska	2,769,403,511	0.2%
18	Arizona	40,213,152,667	2.3%
32	Arkansas	13,619,063,704	0.8%
2	California	132,622,888,674	7.4%
28	Colorado	17,810,770,147	1.0%
15	Connecticut	45,540,109,338	2.6%
47	Delaware	3,809,809,588	0.2%
3	Florida	118,176,826,043	6.6%
21	Georgia	34,258,262,000	1.9%
42	Hawaii	5,641,923,810	0.3%
40	Idaho	6,360,338,782	0.4%
16	Illinois	44,817,989,305	2.5%
4	Indiana	107,340,895,865	6.0%
31	Iowa	13,635,808,718	0.8%
34	Kansas	10,973,279,435	0.6%
9	Kentucky	60,625,160,611	3.4%
29	Louisiana	17,187,734,170	1.0%
41	Maine	6,293,930,427	0.4%
26	Maryland	21,545,386,772	1.2%
23	Massachusetts	27,606,348,803	1.5%
14	Michigan	46,688,715,324	2.6%
12	Minnesota	51,709,240,805	2.9%
33	Mississippi	12,343,278,753	0.7%
25	Missouri	26,882,641,055	1.5%
45	Montana	4,750,815,233	0.3%
39	Nebraska	7,314,663,090	0.4%
35	Nevada	9,911,493,613	0.6%
43	New Hampshire	5,479,323,365	0.3%
20	New Jersey	34,298,511,844	1.9%
37	New Mexico	8,588,849,071	0.5%
6	New York	79,275,288,496	4.4%
19	North Carolina	39,844,486,731	2.2%
10	North Dakota	57,831,799,611	3.2%
13	Ohio	47,100,065,581	2.6%
30	Oklahoma	16,620,599,817	0.9%
27	Oregon	19,829,926,310	1.1%
1	Pennsylvania	147,897,562,045	8.3%
44	Rhode Island	5,194,068,778	0.3%
8	South Carolina	62,239,796,312	3.5%
46	South Dakota	3,900,657,760	0.2%
11	Tennessee	54,915,023,872	3.1%
5	Texas	83,847,617,593	4.7%
38	Utah	7,963,895,754	0.4%
49	Vermont	2,653,946,350	0.1%
22	Virginia	31,942,956,650	1.8%
24	Washington	27,070,263,595	1.5%
36	West Virginia	9,274,435,519	0.5%
7	Wisconsin	70,675,922,263	4.0%
50	Wyoming	2,277,377,761	0.1%

RANK ORDER

RANK	STATE	EXPENDITURES	% of USA
1	Pennsylvania	$147,897,562,045	8.3%
2	California	132,622,888,674	7.4%
3	Florida	118,176,826,043	6.6%
4	Indiana	107,340,895,865	6.0%
5	Texas	83,847,617,593	4.7%
6	New York	79,275,288,496	4.4%
7	Wisconsin	70,675,922,263	4.0%
8	South Carolina	62,239,796,312	3.5%
9	Kentucky	60,625,160,611	3.4%
10	North Dakota	57,831,799,611	3.2%
11	Tennessee	54,915,023,872	3.1%
12	Minnesota	51,709,240,805	2.9%
13	Ohio	47,100,065,581	2.6%
14	Michigan	46,688,715,324	2.6%
15	Connecticut	45,540,109,338	2.6%
16	Illinois	44,817,989,305	2.5%
17	Alabama	44,588,216,077	2.5%
18	Arizona	40,213,152,667	2.3%
19	North Carolina	39,844,486,731	2.2%
20	New Jersey	34,298,511,844	1.9%
21	Georgia	34,258,262,000	1.9%
22	Virginia	31,942,956,650	1.8%
23	Massachusetts	27,606,348,803	1.5%
24	Washington	27,070,263,595	1.5%
25	Missouri	26,882,641,055	1.5%
26	Maryland	21,545,386,772	1.2%
27	Oregon	19,829,926,310	1.1%
28	Colorado	17,810,770,147	1.0%
29	Louisiana	17,187,734,170	1.0%
30	Oklahoma	16,620,599,817	0.9%
31	Iowa	13,635,808,718	0.8%
32	Arkansas	13,619,063,704	0.8%
33	Mississippi	12,343,278,753	0.7%
34	Kansas	10,973,279,435	0.6%
35	Nevada	9,911,493,613	0.6%
36	West Virginia	9,274,435,519	0.5%
37	New Mexico	8,588,849,071	0.5%
38	Utah	7,963,895,754	0.4%
39	Nebraska	7,314,663,090	0.4%
40	Idaho	6,360,338,782	0.4%
41	Maine	6,293,930,427	0.4%
42	Hawaii	5,641,923,810	0.3%
43	New Hampshire	5,479,323,365	0.3%
44	Rhode Island	5,194,068,778	0.3%
45	Montana	4,750,815,233	0.3%
46	South Dakota	3,900,657,760	0.2%
47	Delaware	3,809,809,588	0.2%
48	Alaska	2,769,403,511	0.2%
49	Vermont	2,653,946,350	0.1%
50	Wyoming	2,277,377,761	0.1%
	District of Columbia	2,209,968,272	0.1%

Source: CQ Press using data from U.S. Office of Management and Budget, USAspending.gov
"Prime Award Spending Data Summary" (https://www.usaspending.gov/, as of February 16, 2017)
*Total includes $27,626,097,000 in U.S. territories and internationally as well as expenditures not distributed by state.
Expenditures allocated based on place of performance of a contract. Includes direct payments to individuals (such as Medicare and food stamps), insurance payments (such as, unemployment benefits, flood insurance), and other types of assistance payments (such as, reimbursements for prescriptions for veterans).

Per Capita Federal Government "Other Financial Assistance" in 2015

National Per Capita = $5,472*

ALPHA ORDER			RANK ORDER		
RANK	STATE	PER CAPITA	RANK	STATE	PER CAPITA
9	Alabama	$9,186	1	North Dakota	$76,413
41	Alaska	3,754	2	Indiana	16,232
11	Arizona	5,898	3	Kentucky	13,702
19	Arkansas	4,573	4	South Carolina	12,715
46	California	3,401	5	Connecticut	12,704
48	Colorado	3,269	6	Wisconsin	12,253
5	Connecticut	12,704	7	Pennsylvania	11,562
30	Delaware	4,035	8	Minnesota	9,432
12	Florida	5,837	9	Alabama	9,186
47	Georgia	3,359	10	Tennessee	8,327
33	Hawaii	3,959	11	Arizona	5,898
36	Idaho	3,848	12	Florida	5,837
44	Illinois	3,491	13	West Virginia	5,038
2	Indiana	16,232	14	Oregon	4,927
22	Iowa	4,368	15	Rhode Island	4,920
40	Kansas	3,775	16	Maine	4,734
3	Kentucky	13,702	17	Michigan	4,708
42	Louisiana	3,681	18	Montana	4,603
16	Maine	4,734	19	Arkansas	4,573
43	Maryland	3,594	20	South Dakota	4,547
28	Massachusetts	4,069	21	Missouri	4,424
17	Michigan	4,708	22	Iowa	4,368
8	Minnesota	9,432	23	Oklahoma	4,254
25	Mississippi	4,129	24	Vermont	4,239
21	Missouri	4,424	25	Mississippi	4,129
18	Montana	4,603	25	New Mexico	4,129
35	Nebraska	3,862	27	New Hampshire	4,119
45	Nevada	3,437	28	Massachusetts	4,069
27	New Hampshire	4,119	29	Ohio	4,059
37	New Jersey	3,838	30	Delaware	4,035
25	New Mexico	4,129	31	New York	4,015
31	New York	4,015	32	North Carolina	3,970
32	North Carolina	3,970	33	Hawaii	3,959
1	North Dakota	76,413	34	Wyoming	3,883
29	Ohio	4,059	35	Nebraska	3,862
23	Oklahoma	4,254	36	Idaho	3,848
14	Oregon	4,927	37	New Jersey	3,838
7	Pennsylvania	11,562	38	Virginia	3,817
15	Rhode Island	4,920	39	Washington	3,781
4	South Carolina	12,715	40	Kansas	3,775
20	South Dakota	4,547	41	Alaska	3,754
10	Tennessee	8,327	42	Louisiana	3,681
49	Texas	3,057	43	Maryland	3,594
50	Utah	2,663	44	Illinois	3,491
24	Vermont	4,239	45	Nevada	3,437
38	Virginia	3,817	46	California	3,401
39	Washington	3,781	47	Georgia	3,359
13	West Virginia	5,038	48	Colorado	3,269
6	Wisconsin	12,253	49	Texas	3,057
34	Wyoming	3,883	50	Utah	2,663
				District of Columbia	3,297

Source: CQ Press using data from U.S. Office of Management and Budget, USAspending.gov
"Prime Award Spending Data Summary" (https://www.usaspending.gov/, as of February 16, 2017)
*National per capita excludes expenditures and population for territories and undistributed amounts. Expenditures allocated based on place of performance of a contract. Includes direct payments to individuals (such as Medicare and food stamps), insurance payments (such as, unemployment benefits, flood insurance), and other types of assistance payments (such as, reimbursements for prescriptions for veterans).

Federal Civilian Employees in 2015

National Total = 1,838,352 Employees*

ALPHA ORDER

RANK	STATE	EMPLOYEES	% of USA
13	Alabama	37,516	2.0%
38	Alaska	10,463	0.6%
14	Arizona	36,934	2.0%
35	Arkansas	12,744	0.7%
1	California	150,576	8.2%
15	Colorado	36,478	2.0%
42	Connecticut	7,942	0.4%
50	Delaware	3,024	0.2%
5	Florida	86,806	4.7%
6	Georgia	70,436	3.8%
23	Hawaii	23,018	1.3%
43	Idaho	7,521	0.4%
11	Illinois	44,892	2.4%
25	Indiana	21,944	1.2%
41	Iowa	8,001	0.4%
33	Kansas	15,550	0.8%
24	Kentucky	22,460	1.2%
28	Louisiana	18,884	1.0%
37	Maine	10,789	0.6%
4	Maryland	119,595	6.5%
21	Massachusetts	25,037	1.4%
18	Michigan	27,329	1.5%
32	Minnesota	16,272	0.9%
30	Mississippi	17,304	0.9%
17	Missouri	33,252	1.8%
40	Montana	8,462	0.5%
39	Nebraska	10,186	0.6%
36	Nevada	11,684	0.6%
49	New Hampshire	3,920	0.2%
22	New Jersey	24,466	1.3%
26	New Mexico	21,862	1.2%
8	New York	60,870	3.3%
12	North Carolina	41,940	2.3%
46	North Dakota	5,402	0.3%
10	Ohio	48,195	2.6%
16	Oklahoma	36,328	2.0%
31	Oregon	16,928	0.9%
7	Pennsylvania	61,880	3.4%
45	Rhode Island	6,577	0.4%
27	South Carolina	20,193	1.1%
44	South Dakota	7,227	0.4%
20	Tennessee	25,375	1.4%
3	Texas	131,212	7.1%
19	Utah	25,575	1.4%
48	Vermont	4,611	0.3%
2	Virginia	143,456	7.8%
9	Washington	51,969	2.8%
29	West Virginia	18,282	1.0%
34	Wisconsin	13,829	0.8%
47	Wyoming	4,788	0.3%

RANK ORDER

RANK	STATE	EMPLOYEES	% of USA
1	California	150,576	8.2%
2	Virginia	143,456	7.8%
3	Texas	131,212	7.1%
4	Maryland	119,595	6.5%
5	Florida	86,806	4.7%
6	Georgia	70,436	3.8%
7	Pennsylvania	61,880	3.4%
8	New York	60,870	3.3%
9	Washington	51,969	2.8%
10	Ohio	48,195	2.6%
11	Illinois	44,892	2.4%
12	North Carolina	41,940	2.3%
13	Alabama	37,516	2.0%
14	Arizona	36,934	2.0%
15	Colorado	36,478	2.0%
16	Oklahoma	36,328	2.0%
17	Missouri	33,252	1.8%
18	Michigan	27,329	1.5%
19	Utah	25,575	1.4%
20	Tennessee	25,375	1.4%
21	Massachusetts	25,037	1.4%
22	New Jersey	24,466	1.3%
23	Hawaii	23,018	1.3%
24	Kentucky	22,460	1.2%
25	Indiana	21,944	1.2%
26	New Mexico	21,862	1.2%
27	South Carolina	20,193	1.1%
28	Louisiana	18,884	1.0%
29	West Virginia	18,282	1.0%
30	Mississippi	17,304	0.9%
31	Oregon	16,928	0.9%
32	Minnesota	16,272	0.9%
33	Kansas	15,550	0.8%
34	Wisconsin	13,829	0.8%
35	Arkansas	12,744	0.7%
36	Nevada	11,684	0.6%
37	Maine	10,789	0.6%
38	Alaska	10,463	0.6%
39	Nebraska	10,186	0.6%
40	Montana	8,462	0.5%
41	Iowa	8,001	0.4%
42	Connecticut	7,942	0.4%
43	Idaho	7,521	0.4%
44	South Dakota	7,227	0.4%
45	Rhode Island	6,577	0.4%
46	North Dakota	5,402	0.3%
47	Wyoming	4,788	0.3%
48	Vermont	4,611	0.3%
49	New Hampshire	3,920	0.2%
50	Delaware	3,024	0.2%
	District of Columbia	132,982	7.2%

Source: U.S. Office of Personnel Management
   "Common Characteristics of the Government" (http://www.opm.gov/feddata/)
*Non-seasonal, full-time, permanent employees as of September. Head count based on place of employment. There were an estimated 2,058,924 federal civilian employees including seasonal and non permanent employees. Total includes 35,386 employees either outside the U.S. or unspecified. Excludes Central Intelligence Agency, Defense Intelligence Agency, and National Security Agency.

Rate of Federal Civilian Employees in 2015

National Rate = 57 Employees per 10,000 Population*

ALPHA ORDER

RANK	STATE	RATE
13	Alabama	77
4	Alaska	142
22	Arizona	54
29	Arkansas	43
37	California	39
18	Colorado	67
50	Connecticut	22
42	Delaware	32
29	Florida	43
17	Georgia	69
3	Hawaii	162
28	Idaho	46
40	Illinois	35
41	Indiana	33
48	Iowa	26
24	Kansas	53
25	Kentucky	51
36	Louisiana	40
12	Maine	81
1	Maryland	199
39	Massachusetts	37
46	Michigan	28
44	Minnesota	30
20	Mississippi	58
21	Missouri	55
10	Montana	82
22	Nebraska	54
34	Nevada	41
45	New Hampshire	29
47	New Jersey	27
5	New Mexico	105
43	New York	31
31	North Carolina	42
16	North Dakota	71
31	Ohio	42
7	Oklahoma	93
31	Oregon	42
26	Pennsylvania	48
19	Rhode Island	62
34	South Carolina	41
9	South Dakota	84
38	Tennessee	38
26	Texas	48
8	Utah	86
14	Vermont	74
2	Virginia	171
15	Washington	73
6	West Virginia	99
49	Wisconsin	24
10	Wyoming	82

RANK ORDER

RANK	STATE	RATE
1	Maryland	199
2	Virginia	171
3	Hawaii	162
4	Alaska	142
5	New Mexico	105
6	West Virginia	99
7	Oklahoma	93
8	Utah	86
9	South Dakota	84
10	Montana	82
10	Wyoming	82
12	Maine	81
13	Alabama	77
14	Vermont	74
15	Washington	73
16	North Dakota	71
17	Georgia	69
18	Colorado	67
19	Rhode Island	62
20	Mississippi	58
21	Missouri	55
22	Arizona	54
22	Nebraska	54
24	Kansas	53
25	Kentucky	51
26	Pennsylvania	48
26	Texas	48
28	Idaho	46
29	Arkansas	43
29	Florida	43
31	North Carolina	42
31	Ohio	42
31	Oregon	42
34	Nevada	41
34	South Carolina	41
36	Louisiana	40
37	California	39
38	Tennessee	38
39	Massachusetts	37
40	Illinois	35
41	Indiana	33
42	Delaware	32
43	New York	31
44	Minnesota	30
45	New Hampshire	29
46	Michigan	28
47	New Jersey	27
48	Iowa	26
49	Wisconsin	24
50	Connecticut	22

| | District of Columbia | 1,984 |

Source: CQ Press using data from U.S. Office of Personnel Management
"Common Characteristics of the Government" (http://www.opm.gov/feddata/)

*Non-seasonal, full-time, permanent employees as of September. Head count based on place of employment. There were an estimated 2,058,924 federal civilian employees including seasonal and non permanent employees. National rate excludes employees either outside the U.S. or unspecified. Excludes Central Intelligence Agency, Defense Intelligence Agency, and National Security Agency.

X. Government Finances: State and Local

(Continued)

(Continued)

State and Local Government Total Revenue in 2014

National Total = $3,633,773,979,000*

ALPHA ORDER

RANK	STATE	REVENUE	% of USA
27	Alabama	$43,222,447,000	1.2%
40	Alaska	17,147,596,000	0.5%
18	Arizona	59,743,647,000	1.6%
33	Arkansas	28,599,485,000	0.8%
1	California	552,479,863,000	15.2%
21	Colorado	57,555,580,000	1.6%
26	Connecticut	45,562,119,000	1.3%
47	Delaware	11,385,306,000	0.3%
4	Florida	179,241,826,000	4.9%
12	Georgia	87,383,680,000	2.4%
39	Hawaii	18,637,812,000	0.5%
42	Idaho	13,970,311,000	0.4%
5	Illinois	148,450,606,000	4.1%
20	Indiana	58,166,448,000	1.6%
30	Iowa	36,182,745,000	1.0%
32	Kansas	29,575,001,000	0.8%
28	Kentucky	41,252,195,000	1.1%
24	Louisiana	48,711,091,000	1.3%
41	Maine	13,996,162,000	0.4%
16	Maryland	67,902,232,000	1.9%
11	Massachusetts	88,328,466,000	2.4%
9	Michigan	99,461,634,000	2.7%
15	Minnesota	68,055,538,000	1.9%
31	Mississippi	31,218,067,000	0.9%
19	Missouri	58,176,511,000	1.6%
46	Montana	11,408,896,000	0.3%
37	Nebraska	23,919,573,000	0.7%
35	Nevada	27,424,781,000	0.8%
43	New Hampshire	12,488,815,000	0.3%
8	New Jersey	101,860,688,000	2.8%
36	New Mexico	25,064,070,000	0.7%
2	New York	364,432,918,000	10.0%
10	North Carolina	94,286,557,000	2.6%
45	North Dakota	12,294,021,000	0.3%
7	Ohio	134,167,215,000	3.7%
29	Oklahoma	38,227,311,000	1.1%
23	Oregon	50,782,806,000	1.4%
6	Pennsylvania	135,042,935,000	3.7%
44	Rhode Island	12,480,502,000	0.3%
25	South Carolina	46,895,232,000	1.3%
49	South Dakota	8,873,443,000	0.2%
22	Tennessee	57,297,096,000	1.6%
3	Texas	259,268,222,000	7.1%
34	Utah	28,206,557,000	0.8%
50	Vermont	7,722,876,000	0.2%
14	Virginia	81,666,250,000	2.2%
13	Washington	86,258,348,000	2.4%
38	West Virginia	19,013,060,000	0.5%
17	Wisconsin	65,258,927,000	1.8%
48	Wyoming	10,313,771,000	0.3%

RANK ORDER

RANK	STATE	REVENUE	% of USA
1	California	$552,479,863,000	15.2%
2	New York	364,432,918,000	10.0%
3	Texas	259,268,222,000	7.1%
4	Florida	179,241,826,000	4.9%
5	Illinois	148,450,606,000	4.1%
6	Pennsylvania	135,042,935,000	3.7%
7	Ohio	134,167,215,000	3.7%
8	New Jersey	101,860,688,000	2.8%
9	Michigan	99,461,634,000	2.7%
10	North Carolina	94,286,557,000	2.6%
11	Massachusetts	88,328,466,000	2.4%
12	Georgia	87,383,680,000	2.4%
13	Washington	86,258,348,000	2.4%
14	Virginia	81,666,250,000	2.2%
15	Minnesota	68,055,538,000	1.9%
16	Maryland	67,902,232,000	1.9%
17	Wisconsin	65,258,927,000	1.8%
18	Arizona	59,743,647,000	1.6%
19	Missouri	58,176,511,000	1.6%
20	Indiana	58,166,448,000	1.6%
21	Colorado	57,555,580,000	1.6%
22	Tennessee	57,297,096,000	1.6%
23	Oregon	50,782,806,000	1.4%
24	Louisiana	48,711,091,000	1.3%
25	South Carolina	46,895,232,000	1.3%
26	Connecticut	45,562,119,000	1.3%
27	Alabama	43,222,447,000	1.2%
28	Kentucky	41,252,195,000	1.1%
29	Oklahoma	38,227,311,000	1.1%
30	Iowa	36,182,745,000	1.0%
31	Mississippi	31,218,067,000	0.9%
32	Kansas	29,575,001,000	0.8%
33	Arkansas	28,599,485,000	0.8%
34	Utah	28,206,557,000	0.8%
35	Nevada	27,424,781,000	0.8%
36	New Mexico	25,064,070,000	0.7%
37	Nebraska	23,919,573,000	0.7%
38	West Virginia	19,013,060,000	0.5%
39	Hawaii	18,637,812,000	0.5%
40	Alaska	17,147,596,000	0.5%
41	Maine	13,996,162,000	0.4%
42	Idaho	13,970,311,000	0.4%
43	New Hampshire	12,488,815,000	0.3%
44	Rhode Island	12,480,502,000	0.3%
45	North Dakota	12,294,021,000	0.3%
46	Montana	11,408,896,000	0.3%
47	Delaware	11,385,306,000	0.3%
48	Wyoming	10,313,771,000	0.3%
49	South Dakota	8,873,443,000	0.2%
50	Vermont	7,722,876,000	0.2%
	District of Columbia	14,712,741,000	0.4%

Source: U.S. Bureau of the Census, Governments Division
    "2014 State and Local Government Finances" (http://www.census.gov/govs/local/)
*Total revenue includes all money received from external sources. This includes taxes, intergovernmental transfers and
insurance trust revenue, and revenue from government owned utilities and other commercial or auxiliary enterprise.

Per Capita State and Local Government Revenue in 2014

National Per Capita = $11,407*

<table>
<tr><td colspan="3">ALPHA ORDER</td><td colspan="3">RANK ORDER</td></tr>
<tr><td>RANK</td><td>STATE</td><td>PER CAPITA</td><td>RANK</td><td>STATE</td><td>PER CAPITA</td></tr>
<tr><td>45</td><td>Alabama</td><td>$8,924</td><td>1</td><td>Alaska</td><td>$23,276</td></tr>
<tr><td>1</td><td>Alaska</td><td>23,276</td><td>2</td><td>New York</td><td>18,482</td></tr>
<tr><td>46</td><td>Arizona</td><td>8,890</td><td>3</td><td>Wyoming</td><td>17,671</td></tr>
<tr><td>37</td><td>Arkansas</td><td>9,639</td><td>4</td><td>North Dakota</td><td>16,616</td></tr>
<tr><td>5</td><td>California</td><td>14,283</td><td>5</td><td>California</td><td>14,283</td></tr>
<tr><td>24</td><td>Colorado</td><td>10,759</td><td>6</td><td>Hawaii</td><td>13,159</td></tr>
<tr><td>10</td><td>Connecticut</td><td>12,685</td><td>7</td><td>Massachusetts</td><td>13,086</td></tr>
<tr><td>14</td><td>Delaware</td><td>12,177</td><td>8</td><td>Oregon</td><td>12,797</td></tr>
<tr><td>44</td><td>Florida</td><td>9,012</td><td>9</td><td>Nebraska</td><td>12,715</td></tr>
<tr><td>49</td><td>Georgia</td><td>8,663</td><td>10</td><td>Connecticut</td><td>12,685</td></tr>
<tr><td>6</td><td>Hawaii</td><td>13,159</td><td>11</td><td>Minnesota</td><td>12,480</td></tr>
<tr><td>50</td><td>Idaho</td><td>8,552</td><td>12</td><td>Vermont</td><td>12,318</td></tr>
<tr><td>19</td><td>Illinois</td><td>11,537</td><td>13</td><td>Washington</td><td>12,228</td></tr>
<tr><td>47</td><td>Indiana</td><td>8,819</td><td>14</td><td>Delaware</td><td>12,177</td></tr>
<tr><td>17</td><td>Iowa</td><td>11,642</td><td>15</td><td>New Mexico</td><td>12,033</td></tr>
<tr><td>31</td><td>Kansas</td><td>10,201</td><td>16</td><td>Rhode Island</td><td>11,836</td></tr>
<tr><td>43</td><td>Kentucky</td><td>9,348</td><td>17</td><td>Iowa</td><td>11,642</td></tr>
<tr><td>27</td><td>Louisiana</td><td>10,480</td><td>18</td><td>Ohio</td><td>11,572</td></tr>
<tr><td>26</td><td>Maine</td><td>10,518</td><td>19</td><td>Illinois</td><td>11,537</td></tr>
<tr><td>21</td><td>Maryland</td><td>11,379</td><td>20</td><td>New Jersey</td><td>11,413</td></tr>
<tr><td>7</td><td>Massachusetts</td><td>13,086</td><td>21</td><td>Maryland</td><td>11,379</td></tr>
<tr><td>32</td><td>Michigan</td><td>10,031</td><td>22</td><td>Wisconsin</td><td>11,333</td></tr>
<tr><td>11</td><td>Minnesota</td><td>12,480</td><td>23</td><td>Montana</td><td>11,154</td></tr>
<tr><td>28</td><td>Mississippi</td><td>10,432</td><td>24</td><td>Colorado</td><td>10,759</td></tr>
<tr><td>39</td><td>Missouri</td><td>9,599</td><td>25</td><td>Pennsylvania</td><td>10,558</td></tr>
<tr><td>23</td><td>Montana</td><td>11,154</td><td>26</td><td>Maine</td><td>10,518</td></tr>
<tr><td>9</td><td>Nebraska</td><td>12,715</td><td>27</td><td>Louisiana</td><td>10,480</td></tr>
<tr><td>36</td><td>Nevada</td><td>9,680</td><td>28</td><td>Mississippi</td><td>10,432</td></tr>
<tr><td>42</td><td>New Hampshire</td><td>9,399</td><td>29</td><td>South Dakota</td><td>10,408</td></tr>
<tr><td>20</td><td>New Jersey</td><td>11,413</td><td>30</td><td>West Virginia</td><td>10,286</td></tr>
<tr><td>15</td><td>New Mexico</td><td>12,033</td><td>31</td><td>Kansas</td><td>10,201</td></tr>
<tr><td>2</td><td>New York</td><td>18,482</td><td>32</td><td>Michigan</td><td>10,031</td></tr>
<tr><td>41</td><td>North Carolina</td><td>9,491</td><td>33</td><td>Oklahoma</td><td>9,859</td></tr>
<tr><td>4</td><td>North Dakota</td><td>16,616</td><td>34</td><td>Virginia</td><td>9,819</td></tr>
<tr><td>18</td><td>Ohio</td><td>11,572</td><td>35</td><td>South Carolina</td><td>9,712</td></tr>
<tr><td>33</td><td>Oklahoma</td><td>9,859</td><td>36</td><td>Nevada</td><td>9,680</td></tr>
<tr><td>8</td><td>Oregon</td><td>12,797</td><td>37</td><td>Arkansas</td><td>9,639</td></tr>
<tr><td>25</td><td>Pennsylvania</td><td>10,558</td><td>38</td><td>Texas</td><td>9,622</td></tr>
<tr><td>16</td><td>Rhode Island</td><td>11,836</td><td>39</td><td>Missouri</td><td>9,599</td></tr>
<tr><td>35</td><td>South Carolina</td><td>9,712</td><td>40</td><td>Utah</td><td>9,588</td></tr>
<tr><td>29</td><td>South Dakota</td><td>10,408</td><td>41</td><td>North Carolina</td><td>9,491</td></tr>
<tr><td>48</td><td>Tennessee</td><td>8,755</td><td>42</td><td>New Hampshire</td><td>9,399</td></tr>
<tr><td>38</td><td>Texas</td><td>9,622</td><td>43</td><td>Kentucky</td><td>9,348</td></tr>
<tr><td>40</td><td>Utah</td><td>9,588</td><td>44</td><td>Florida</td><td>9,012</td></tr>
<tr><td>12</td><td>Vermont</td><td>12,318</td><td>45</td><td>Alabama</td><td>8,924</td></tr>
<tr><td>34</td><td>Virginia</td><td>9,819</td><td>46</td><td>Arizona</td><td>8,890</td></tr>
<tr><td>13</td><td>Washington</td><td>12,228</td><td>47</td><td>Indiana</td><td>8,819</td></tr>
<tr><td>30</td><td>West Virginia</td><td>10,286</td><td>48</td><td>Tennessee</td><td>8,755</td></tr>
<tr><td>22</td><td>Wisconsin</td><td>11,333</td><td>49</td><td>Georgia</td><td>8,663</td></tr>
<tr><td>3</td><td>Wyoming</td><td>17,671</td><td>50</td><td>Idaho</td><td>8,552</td></tr>
<tr><td></td><td></td><td></td><td></td><td>District of Columbia</td><td>22,326</td></tr>
</table>

Source: CQ Press using data from U.S. Bureau of the Census, Governments Division
"2014 State and Local Government Finances" (http://www.census.gov/govs/local/)
*Total revenue includes all money received from external sources. This includes taxes, intergovernmental transfers and insurance trust revenue, and revenue from government owned utilities and other commercial or auxiliary enterprise.

State and Local Government Revenue from the Federal Government in 2014

National Total = $602,230,223,000

ALPHA ORDER					RANK ORDER			
RANK	STATE	REVENUE	% of USA		RANK	STATE	REVENUE	% of USA
25	Alabama	$8,974,721,000	1.5%		1	California	$71,593,541,000	11.9%
41	Alaska	3,094,110,000	0.5%		2	New York	54,612,354,000	9.1%
15	Arizona	11,589,002,000	1.9%		3	Texas	42,935,627,000	7.1%
32	Arkansas	6,353,955,000	1.1%		4	Florida	29,634,114,000	4.9%
1	California	71,593,541,000	11.9%		5	Pennsylvania	24,080,142,000	4.0%
26	Colorado	8,377,125,000	1.4%		6	Ohio	23,865,038,000	4.0%
30	Connecticut	6,914,369,000	1.1%		7	Illinois	21,334,005,000	3.5%
46	Delaware	2,094,937,000	0.3%		8	Michigan	19,289,308,000	3.2%
4	Florida	29,634,114,000	4.9%		9	North Carolina	17,652,536,000	2.9%
11	Georgia	15,501,052,000	2.6%		10	New Jersey	16,439,554,000	2.7%
39	Hawaii	3,127,142,000	0.5%		11	Georgia	15,501,052,000	2.6%
42	Idaho	2,662,121,000	0.4%		12	Massachusetts	15,098,338,000	2.5%
7	Illinois	21,334,005,000	3.5%		13	Washington	12,864,683,000	2.1%
16	Indiana	11,383,858,000	1.9%		14	Maryland	11,997,428,000	2.0%
31	Iowa	6,681,682,000	1.1%		15	Arizona	11,589,002,000	1.9%
36	Kansas	4,206,983,000	0.7%		16	Indiana	11,383,858,000	1.9%
21	Kentucky	10,210,337,000	1.7%		17	Virginia	11,297,406,000	1.9%
19	Louisiana	11,064,146,000	1.8%		18	Tennessee	11,295,371,000	1.9%
40	Maine	3,123,288,000	0.5%		19	Louisiana	11,064,146,000	1.8%
14	Maryland	11,997,428,000	2.0%		20	Missouri	10,925,235,000	1.8%
12	Massachusetts	15,098,338,000	2.5%		21	Kentucky	10,210,337,000	1.7%
8	Michigan	19,289,308,000	3.2%		22	Minnesota	9,773,901,000	1.6%
22	Minnesota	9,773,901,000	1.6%		23	Oregon	9,673,251,000	1.6%
28	Mississippi	7,621,741,000	1.3%		24	Wisconsin	9,607,728,000	1.6%
20	Missouri	10,925,235,000	1.8%		25	Alabama	8,974,721,000	1.5%
44	Montana	2,565,091,000	0.4%		26	Colorado	8,377,125,000	1.4%
37	Nebraska	3,381,385,000	0.6%		27	Oklahoma	7,700,837,000	1.3%
38	Nevada	3,362,714,000	0.6%		28	Mississippi	7,621,741,000	1.3%
48	New Hampshire	1,805,570,000	0.3%		29	South Carolina	7,486,144,000	1.2%
10	New Jersey	16,439,554,000	2.7%		30	Connecticut	6,914,369,000	1.1%
33	New Mexico	5,740,699,000	1.0%		31	Iowa	6,681,682,000	1.1%
2	New York	54,612,354,000	9.1%		32	Arkansas	6,353,955,000	1.1%
9	North Carolina	17,652,536,000	2.9%		33	New Mexico	5,740,699,000	1.0%
49	North Dakota	1,718,543,000	0.3%		34	Utah	4,742,163,000	0.8%
6	Ohio	23,865,038,000	4.0%		35	West Virginia	4,449,340,000	0.7%
27	Oklahoma	7,700,837,000	1.3%		36	Kansas	4,206,983,000	0.7%
23	Oregon	9,673,251,000	1.6%		37	Nebraska	3,381,385,000	0.6%
5	Pennsylvania	24,080,142,000	4.0%		38	Nevada	3,362,714,000	0.6%
43	Rhode Island	2,627,851,000	0.4%		39	Hawaii	3,127,142,000	0.5%
29	South Carolina	7,486,144,000	1.2%		40	Maine	3,123,288,000	0.5%
50	South Dakota	1,712,391,000	0.3%		41	Alaska	3,094,110,000	0.5%
18	Tennessee	11,295,371,000	1.9%		42	Idaho	2,662,121,000	0.4%
3	Texas	42,935,627,000	7.1%		43	Rhode Island	2,627,851,000	0.4%
34	Utah	4,742,163,000	0.8%		44	Montana	2,565,091,000	0.4%
47	Vermont	2,013,466,000	0.3%		45	Wyoming	2,184,134,000	0.4%
17	Virginia	11,297,406,000	1.9%		46	Delaware	2,094,937,000	0.3%
13	Washington	12,864,683,000	2.1%		47	Vermont	2,013,466,000	0.3%
35	West Virginia	4,449,340,000	0.7%		48	New Hampshire	1,805,570,000	0.3%
24	Wisconsin	9,607,728,000	1.6%		49	North Dakota	1,718,543,000	0.3%
45	Wyoming	2,184,134,000	0.4%		50	South Dakota	1,712,391,000	0.3%
						District of Columbia	3,789,766,000	0.6%

Source: U.S. Bureau of the Census, Governments Division
"2014 State and Local Government Finances" (http://www.census.gov/govs/local/)

Per Capita State and Local Government Revenue
from the Federal Government in 2014
National Per Capita = $1,890

ALPHA ORDER

RANK	STATE	PER CAPITA
27	Alabama	$1,853
1	Alaska	4,200
37	Arizona	1,725
19	Arkansas	2,142
28	California	1,851
43	Colorado	1,566
25	Connecticut	1,925
15	Delaware	2,241
46	Florida	1,490
45	Georgia	1,537
17	Hawaii	2,208
40	Idaho	1,630
39	Illinois	1,658
35	Indiana	1,726
18	Iowa	2,150
47	Kansas	1,451
14	Kentucky	2,314
11	Louisiana	2,380
12	Maine	2,347
21	Maryland	2,011
16	Massachusetts	2,237
24	Michigan	1,945
33	Minnesota	1,792
6	Mississippi	2,547
31	Missouri	1,803
7	Montana	2,508
32	Nebraska	1,798
50	Nevada	1,187
48	New Hampshire	1,359
29	New Jersey	1,842
5	New Mexico	2,756
4	New York	2,770
34	North Carolina	1,777
13	North Dakota	2,323
20	Ohio	2,058
23	Oklahoma	1,986
9	Oregon	2,438
26	Pennsylvania	1,883
8	Rhode Island	2,492
44	South Carolina	1,550
22	South Dakota	2,009
35	Tennessee	1,726
42	Texas	1,593
41	Utah	1,612
3	Vermont	3,211
49	Virginia	1,358
30	Washington	1,824
10	West Virginia	2,407
38	Wisconsin	1,668
2	Wyoming	3,742

RANK ORDER

RANK	STATE	PER CAPITA
1	Alaska	$4,200
2	Wyoming	3,742
3	Vermont	3,211
4	New York	2,770
5	New Mexico	2,756
6	Mississippi	2,547
7	Montana	2,508
8	Rhode Island	2,492
9	Oregon	2,438
10	West Virginia	2,407
11	Louisiana	2,380
12	Maine	2,347
13	North Dakota	2,323
14	Kentucky	2,314
15	Delaware	2,241
16	Massachusetts	2,237
17	Hawaii	2,208
18	Iowa	2,150
19	Arkansas	2,142
20	Ohio	2,058
21	Maryland	2,011
22	South Dakota	2,009
23	Oklahoma	1,986
24	Michigan	1,945
25	Connecticut	1,925
26	Pennsylvania	1,883
27	Alabama	1,853
28	California	1,851
29	New Jersey	1,842
30	Washington	1,824
31	Missouri	1,803
32	Nebraska	1,798
33	Minnesota	1,792
34	North Carolina	1,777
35	Indiana	1,726
35	Tennessee	1,726
37	Arizona	1,725
38	Wisconsin	1,668
39	Illinois	1,658
40	Idaho	1,630
41	Utah	1,612
42	Texas	1,593
43	Colorado	1,566
44	South Carolina	1,550
45	Georgia	1,537
46	Florida	1,490
47	Kansas	1,451
48	New Hampshire	1,359
49	Virginia	1,358
50	Nevada	1,187

| | District of Columbia | 5,751 |

Source: CQ Press using data from U.S. Bureau of the Census, Governments Division
"2014 State and Local Government Finances" (http://www.census.gov/govs/local/)

Percent of State and Local Government Revenue
from the Federal Government in 2014
National Percent = 16.6%*

ALPHA ORDER

RANK	STATE	PERCENT
12	Alabama	20.8
25	Alaska	18.0
16	Arizona	19.4
9	Arkansas	22.2
49	California	13.0
41	Colorado	14.6
37	Connecticut	15.2
24	Delaware	18.4
34	Florida	16.5
28	Georgia	17.7
31	Hawaii	16.8
19	Idaho	19.1
43	Illinois	14.4
15	Indiana	19.6
23	Iowa	18.5
45	Kansas	14.2
2	Kentucky	24.8
6	Louisiana	22.7
8	Maine	22.3
28	Maryland	17.7
30	Massachusetts	17.1
16	Michigan	19.4
43	Minnesota	14.4
3	Mississippi	24.4
21	Missouri	18.8
7	Montana	22.5
46	Nebraska	14.1
50	Nevada	12.3
42	New Hampshire	14.5
35	New Jersey	16.1
5	New Mexico	22.9
38	New York	15.0
22	North Carolina	18.7
47	North Dakota	14.0
26	Ohio	17.8
13	Oklahoma	20.1
20	Oregon	19.0
26	Pennsylvania	17.8
11	Rhode Island	21.1
36	South Carolina	16.0
18	South Dakota	19.3
14	Tennessee	19.7
33	Texas	16.6
31	Utah	16.8
1	Vermont	26.1
48	Virginia	13.8
39	Washington	14.9
4	West Virginia	23.4
40	Wisconsin	14.7
10	Wyoming	21.2

RANK ORDER

RANK	STATE	PERCENT
1	Vermont	26.1
2	Kentucky	24.8
3	Mississippi	24.4
4	West Virginia	23.4
5	New Mexico	22.9
6	Louisiana	22.7
7	Montana	22.5
8	Maine	22.3
9	Arkansas	22.2
10	Wyoming	21.2
11	Rhode Island	21.1
12	Alabama	20.8
13	Oklahoma	20.1
14	Tennessee	19.7
15	Indiana	19.6
16	Arizona	19.4
16	Michigan	19.4
18	South Dakota	19.3
19	Idaho	19.1
20	Oregon	19.0
21	Missouri	18.8
22	North Carolina	18.7
23	Iowa	18.5
24	Delaware	18.4
25	Alaska	18.0
26	Ohio	17.8
26	Pennsylvania	17.8
28	Georgia	17.7
28	Maryland	17.7
30	Massachusetts	17.1
31	Hawaii	16.8
31	Utah	16.8
33	Texas	16.6
34	Florida	16.5
35	New Jersey	16.1
36	South Carolina	16.0
37	Connecticut	15.2
38	New York	15.0
39	Washington	14.9
40	Wisconsin	14.7
41	Colorado	14.6
42	New Hampshire	14.5
43	Illinois	14.4
43	Minnesota	14.4
45	Kansas	14.2
46	Nebraska	14.1
47	North Dakota	14.0
48	Virginia	13.8
49	California	13.0
50	Nevada	12.3

District of Columbia 25.8

Source: CQ Press using data from U.S. Bureau of the Census, Governments Division
"2014 State and Local Government Finances" (http://www.census.gov/govs/local/)
*As a percent of total revenue.

State and Local Government Own Source Revenue in 2014

National Total = $2,155,884,617,000*

ALPHA ORDER

RANK	STATE	REVENUE	% of USA
27	Alabama	$25,661,790,000	1.2%
39	Alaska	11,173,127,000	0.5%
20	Arizona	33,182,581,000	1.5%
34	Arkansas	15,818,614,000	0.7%
1	California	299,196,226,000	13.9%
19	Colorado	36,242,452,000	1.7%
22	Connecticut	31,155,746,000	1.4%
46	Delaware	7,016,928,000	0.3%
4	Florida	108,862,065,000	5.0%
13	Georgia	50,376,740,000	2.3%
38	Hawaii	11,371,252,000	0.5%
44	Idaho	7,999,170,000	0.4%
5	Illinois	90,840,841,000	4.2%
17	Indiana	37,851,308,000	1.8%
29	Iowa	22,027,613,000	1.0%
31	Kansas	20,024,044,000	0.9%
28	Kentucky	22,968,567,000	1.1%
25	Louisiana	28,240,459,000	1.3%
42	Maine	8,404,553,000	0.4%
15	Maryland	44,015,727,000	2.0%
11	Massachusetts	54,085,767,000	2.5%
9	Michigan	59,082,931,000	2.7%
16	Minnesota	42,518,016,000	2.0%
33	Mississippi	16,946,608,000	0.8%
21	Missouri	31,800,690,000	1.5%
48	Montana	5,745,893,000	0.3%
37	Nebraska	13,300,576,000	0.6%
35	Nevada	15,544,377,000	0.7%
43	New Hampshire	8,174,037,000	0.4%
7	New Jersey	75,218,744,000	3.5%
36	New Mexico	13,883,346,000	0.6%
2	New York	215,403,604,000	10.0%
10	North Carolina	56,384,893,000	2.6%
41	North Dakota	9,215,405,000	0.4%
8	Ohio	72,679,347,000	3.4%
30	Oklahoma	21,977,211,000	1.0%
26	Oregon	26,255,196,000	1.2%
6	Pennsylvania	85,101,398,000	3.9%
45	Rhode Island	7,627,364,000	0.4%
24	South Carolina	28,914,061,000	1.3%
49	South Dakota	4,724,987,000	0.2%
23	Tennessee	30,752,871,000	1.4%
3	Texas	159,964,975,000	7.4%
32	Utah	16,948,833,000	0.8%
50	Vermont	4,662,563,000	0.2%
12	Virginia	54,001,036,000	2.5%
14	Washington	49,452,267,000	2.3%
40	West Virginia	11,122,930,000	0.5%
18	Wisconsin	37,587,588,000	1.7%
47	Wyoming	6,236,448,000	0.3%

RANK ORDER

RANK	STATE	REVENUE	% of USA
1	California	$299,196,226,000	13.9%
2	New York	215,403,604,000	10.0%
3	Texas	159,964,975,000	7.4%
4	Florida	108,862,065,000	5.0%
5	Illinois	90,840,841,000	4.2%
6	Pennsylvania	85,101,398,000	3.9%
7	New Jersey	75,218,744,000	3.5%
8	Ohio	72,679,347,000	3.4%
9	Michigan	59,082,931,000	2.7%
10	North Carolina	56,384,893,000	2.6%
11	Massachusetts	54,085,767,000	2.5%
12	Virginia	54,001,036,000	2.5%
13	Georgia	50,376,740,000	2.3%
14	Washington	49,452,267,000	2.3%
15	Maryland	44,015,727,000	2.0%
16	Minnesota	42,518,016,000	2.0%
17	Indiana	37,851,308,000	1.8%
18	Wisconsin	37,587,588,000	1.7%
19	Colorado	36,242,452,000	1.7%
20	Arizona	33,182,581,000	1.5%
21	Missouri	31,800,690,000	1.5%
22	Connecticut	31,155,746,000	1.4%
23	Tennessee	30,752,871,000	1.4%
24	South Carolina	28,914,061,000	1.3%
25	Louisiana	28,240,459,000	1.3%
26	Oregon	26,255,196,000	1.2%
27	Alabama	25,661,790,000	1.2%
28	Kentucky	22,968,567,000	1.1%
29	Iowa	22,027,613,000	1.0%
30	Oklahoma	21,977,211,000	1.0%
31	Kansas	20,024,044,000	0.9%
32	Utah	16,948,833,000	0.8%
33	Mississippi	16,946,608,000	0.8%
34	Arkansas	15,818,614,000	0.7%
35	Nevada	15,544,377,000	0.7%
36	New Mexico	13,883,346,000	0.6%
37	Nebraska	13,300,576,000	0.6%
38	Hawaii	11,371,252,000	0.5%
39	Alaska	11,173,127,000	0.5%
40	West Virginia	11,122,930,000	0.5%
41	North Dakota	9,215,405,000	0.4%
42	Maine	8,404,553,000	0.4%
43	New Hampshire	8,174,037,000	0.4%
44	Idaho	7,999,170,000	0.4%
45	Rhode Island	7,627,364,000	0.4%
46	Delaware	7,016,928,000	0.3%
47	Wyoming	6,236,448,000	0.3%
48	Montana	5,745,893,000	0.3%
49	South Dakota	4,724,987,000	0.2%
50	Vermont	4,662,563,000	0.2%
	District of Columbia	8,140,852,000	0.4%

Source: U.S. Bureau of the Census, Governments Division
    "2014 State and Local Government Finances" (http://www.census.gov/govs/local/)
*Own source revenue includes taxes, current charges, and miscellaneous general revenue. Excluded are intergovernmental transfers, insurance trust revenue, and revenue from government owned utilities and other commercial or auxiliary enterprise.

Per Capita State and Local Government Own Source Revenue in 2014

National Per Capita = $6,768*

<table>
<tr><th colspan="3">ALPHA ORDER</th><th colspan="3">RANK ORDER</th></tr>
<tr><th>RANK</th><th>STATE</th><th>PER CAPITA</th><th>RANK</th><th>STATE</th><th>PER CAPITA</th></tr>
<tr><td>44</td><td>Alabama</td><td>$5,299</td><td>1</td><td>Alaska</td><td>$15,166</td></tr>
<tr><td>1</td><td>Alaska</td><td>15,166</td><td>2</td><td>North Dakota</td><td>12,455</td></tr>
<tr><td>48</td><td>Arizona</td><td>4,938</td><td>3</td><td>New York</td><td>10,924</td></tr>
<tr><td>43</td><td>Arkansas</td><td>5,332</td><td>4</td><td>Wyoming</td><td>10,685</td></tr>
<tr><td>10</td><td>California</td><td>7,735</td><td>5</td><td>Connecticut</td><td>8,674</td></tr>
<tr><td>20</td><td>Colorado</td><td>6,775</td><td>6</td><td>New Jersey</td><td>8,428</td></tr>
<tr><td>5</td><td>Connecticut</td><td>8,674</td><td>7</td><td>Hawaii</td><td>8,029</td></tr>
<tr><td>11</td><td>Delaware</td><td>7,505</td><td>8</td><td>Massachusetts</td><td>8,013</td></tr>
<tr><td>42</td><td>Florida</td><td>5,474</td><td>9</td><td>Minnesota</td><td>7,797</td></tr>
<tr><td>47</td><td>Georgia</td><td>4,994</td><td>10</td><td>California</td><td>7,735</td></tr>
<tr><td>7</td><td>Hawaii</td><td>8,029</td><td>11</td><td>Delaware</td><td>7,505</td></tr>
<tr><td>49</td><td>Idaho</td><td>4,897</td><td>12</td><td>Vermont</td><td>7,436</td></tr>
<tr><td>17</td><td>Illinois</td><td>7,060</td><td>13</td><td>Maryland</td><td>7,376</td></tr>
<tr><td>35</td><td>Indiana</td><td>5,739</td><td>14</td><td>Rhode Island</td><td>7,233</td></tr>
<tr><td>15</td><td>Iowa</td><td>7,087</td><td>15</td><td>Iowa</td><td>7,087</td></tr>
<tr><td>19</td><td>Kansas</td><td>6,906</td><td>16</td><td>Nebraska</td><td>7,070</td></tr>
<tr><td>46</td><td>Kentucky</td><td>5,205</td><td>17</td><td>Illinois</td><td>7,060</td></tr>
<tr><td>29</td><td>Louisiana</td><td>6,076</td><td>18</td><td>Washington</td><td>7,010</td></tr>
<tr><td>26</td><td>Maine</td><td>6,316</td><td>19</td><td>Kansas</td><td>6,906</td></tr>
<tr><td>13</td><td>Maryland</td><td>7,376</td><td>20</td><td>Colorado</td><td>6,775</td></tr>
<tr><td>8</td><td>Massachusetts</td><td>8,013</td><td>21</td><td>New Mexico</td><td>6,665</td></tr>
<tr><td>32</td><td>Michigan</td><td>5,958</td><td>22</td><td>Pennsylvania</td><td>6,653</td></tr>
<tr><td>9</td><td>Minnesota</td><td>7,797</td><td>23</td><td>Oregon</td><td>6,616</td></tr>
<tr><td>38</td><td>Mississippi</td><td>5,663</td><td>24</td><td>Wisconsin</td><td>6,527</td></tr>
<tr><td>45</td><td>Missouri</td><td>5,247</td><td>25</td><td>Virginia</td><td>6,493</td></tr>
<tr><td>39</td><td>Montana</td><td>5,617</td><td>26</td><td>Maine</td><td>6,316</td></tr>
<tr><td>16</td><td>Nebraska</td><td>7,070</td><td>27</td><td>Ohio</td><td>6,268</td></tr>
<tr><td>41</td><td>Nevada</td><td>5,487</td><td>28</td><td>New Hampshire</td><td>6,152</td></tr>
<tr><td>28</td><td>New Hampshire</td><td>6,152</td><td>29</td><td>Louisiana</td><td>6,076</td></tr>
<tr><td>6</td><td>New Jersey</td><td>8,428</td><td>30</td><td>West Virginia</td><td>6,017</td></tr>
<tr><td>21</td><td>New Mexico</td><td>6,665</td><td>31</td><td>South Carolina</td><td>5,988</td></tr>
<tr><td>3</td><td>New York</td><td>10,924</td><td>32</td><td>Michigan</td><td>5,958</td></tr>
<tr><td>36</td><td>North Carolina</td><td>5,676</td><td>33</td><td>Texas</td><td>5,937</td></tr>
<tr><td>2</td><td>North Dakota</td><td>12,455</td><td>34</td><td>Utah</td><td>5,761</td></tr>
<tr><td>27</td><td>Ohio</td><td>6,268</td><td>35</td><td>Indiana</td><td>5,739</td></tr>
<tr><td>37</td><td>Oklahoma</td><td>5,668</td><td>36</td><td>North Carolina</td><td>5,676</td></tr>
<tr><td>23</td><td>Oregon</td><td>6,616</td><td>37</td><td>Oklahoma</td><td>5,668</td></tr>
<tr><td>22</td><td>Pennsylvania</td><td>6,653</td><td>38</td><td>Mississippi</td><td>5,663</td></tr>
<tr><td>14</td><td>Rhode Island</td><td>7,233</td><td>39</td><td>Montana</td><td>5,617</td></tr>
<tr><td>31</td><td>South Carolina</td><td>5,988</td><td>40</td><td>South Dakota</td><td>5,542</td></tr>
<tr><td>40</td><td>South Dakota</td><td>5,542</td><td>41</td><td>Nevada</td><td>5,487</td></tr>
<tr><td>50</td><td>Tennessee</td><td>4,699</td><td>42</td><td>Florida</td><td>5,474</td></tr>
<tr><td>33</td><td>Texas</td><td>5,937</td><td>43</td><td>Arkansas</td><td>5,332</td></tr>
<tr><td>34</td><td>Utah</td><td>5,761</td><td>44</td><td>Alabama</td><td>5,299</td></tr>
<tr><td>12</td><td>Vermont</td><td>7,436</td><td>45</td><td>Missouri</td><td>5,247</td></tr>
<tr><td>25</td><td>Virginia</td><td>6,493</td><td>46</td><td>Kentucky</td><td>5,205</td></tr>
<tr><td>18</td><td>Washington</td><td>7,010</td><td>47</td><td>Georgia</td><td>4,994</td></tr>
<tr><td>30</td><td>West Virginia</td><td>6,017</td><td>48</td><td>Arizona</td><td>4,938</td></tr>
<tr><td>24</td><td>Wisconsin</td><td>6,527</td><td>49</td><td>Idaho</td><td>4,897</td></tr>
<tr><td>4</td><td>Wyoming</td><td>10,685</td><td>50</td><td>Tennessee</td><td>4,699</td></tr>
<tr><td></td><td></td><td></td><td></td><td>District of Columbia</td><td>12,353</td></tr>
</table>

Source: CQ Press using data from U.S. Bureau of the Census, Governments Division
"2014 State and Local Government Finances" (http://www.census.gov/govs/local/)
*Own source revenue includes taxes, current charges, and miscellaneous general revenue. Excluded are intergovernmental transfers, insurance trust revenue, and revenue from government owned utilities and other commercial or auxiliary enterprise.

State and Local Government Tax Revenue in 2014

National Total = $1,490,815,697,000

ALPHA ORDER

RANK	STATE	REVENUE	% of USA
28	Alabama	$14,548,034,000	1.0%
43	Alaska	5,568,495,000	0.4%
21	Arizona	22,511,629,000	1.5%
32	Arkansas	11,142,975,000	0.7%
1	California	211,364,653,000	14.2%
20	Colorado	23,378,852,000	1.6%
18	Connecticut	26,057,957,000	1.7%
46	Delaware	4,124,541,000	0.3%
5	Florida	66,132,006,000	4.4%
13	Georgia	34,095,629,000	2.3%
38	Hawaii	8,102,950,000	0.5%
45	Idaho	5,288,315,000	0.4%
4	Illinois	70,820,964,000	4.8%
19	Indiana	24,726,965,000	1.7%
30	Iowa	13,756,096,000	0.9%
31	Kansas	12,706,184,000	0.9%
26	Kentucky	15,917,452,000	1.1%
24	Louisiana	18,078,599,000	1.2%
41	Maine	6,394,542,000	0.4%
14	Maryland	33,469,798,000	2.2%
9	Massachusetts	40,622,833,000	2.7%
10	Michigan	37,425,533,000	2.5%
16	Minnesota	30,780,731,000	2.1%
34	Mississippi	10,482,155,000	0.7%
22	Missouri	21,060,699,000	1.4%
47	Montana	3,929,013,000	0.3%
36	Nebraska	9,185,340,000	0.6%
33	Nevada	10,997,963,000	0.7%
42	New Hampshire	5,746,858,000	0.4%
7	New Jersey	57,637,527,000	3.9%
37	New Mexico	8,274,457,000	0.6%
2	New York	166,086,991,000	11.1%
11	North Carolina	36,007,944,000	2.4%
40	North Dakota	7,212,083,000	0.5%
8	Ohio	48,789,111,000	3.3%
29	Oklahoma	13,831,663,000	0.9%
25	Oregon	16,281,084,000	1.1%
6	Pennsylvania	60,217,207,000	4.0%
44	Rhode Island	5,454,286,000	0.4%
27	South Carolina	15,550,319,000	1.0%
50	South Dakota	3,143,170,000	0.2%
23	Tennessee	20,243,184,000	1.4%
3	Texas	109,121,168,000	7.3%
35	Utah	10,315,191,000	0.7%
48	Vermont	3,473,260,000	0.2%
12	Virginia	35,009,056,000	2.3%
15	Washington	32,186,993,000	2.2%
39	West Virginia	7,314,436,000	0.5%
17	Wisconsin	26,397,795,000	1.8%
49	Wyoming	3,472,604,000	0.2%

RANK ORDER

RANK	STATE	REVENUE	% of USA
1	California	$211,364,653,000	14.2%
2	New York	166,086,991,000	11.1%
3	Texas	109,121,168,000	7.3%
4	Illinois	70,820,964,000	4.8%
5	Florida	66,132,006,000	4.4%
6	Pennsylvania	60,217,207,000	4.0%
7	New Jersey	57,637,527,000	3.9%
8	Ohio	48,789,111,000	3.3%
9	Massachusetts	40,622,833,000	2.7%
10	Michigan	37,425,533,000	2.5%
11	North Carolina	36,007,944,000	2.4%
12	Virginia	35,009,056,000	2.3%
13	Georgia	34,095,629,000	2.3%
14	Maryland	33,469,798,000	2.2%
15	Washington	32,186,993,000	2.2%
16	Minnesota	30,780,731,000	2.1%
17	Wisconsin	26,397,795,000	1.8%
18	Connecticut	26,057,957,000	1.7%
19	Indiana	24,726,965,000	1.7%
20	Colorado	23,378,852,000	1.6%
21	Arizona	22,511,629,000	1.5%
22	Missouri	21,060,699,000	1.4%
23	Tennessee	20,243,184,000	1.4%
24	Louisiana	18,078,599,000	1.2%
25	Oregon	16,281,084,000	1.1%
26	Kentucky	15,917,452,000	1.1%
27	South Carolina	15,550,319,000	1.0%
28	Alabama	14,548,034,000	1.0%
29	Oklahoma	13,831,663,000	0.9%
30	Iowa	13,756,096,000	0.9%
31	Kansas	12,706,184,000	0.9%
32	Arkansas	11,142,975,000	0.7%
33	Nevada	10,997,963,000	0.7%
34	Mississippi	10,482,155,000	0.7%
35	Utah	10,315,191,000	0.7%
36	Nebraska	9,185,340,000	0.6%
37	New Mexico	8,274,457,000	0.6%
38	Hawaii	8,102,950,000	0.5%
39	West Virginia	7,314,436,000	0.5%
40	North Dakota	7,212,083,000	0.5%
41	Maine	6,394,542,000	0.4%
42	New Hampshire	5,746,858,000	0.4%
43	Alaska	5,568,495,000	0.4%
44	Rhode Island	5,454,286,000	0.4%
45	Idaho	5,288,315,000	0.4%
46	Delaware	4,124,541,000	0.3%
47	Montana	3,929,013,000	0.3%
48	Vermont	3,473,260,000	0.2%
49	Wyoming	3,472,604,000	0.2%
50	South Dakota	3,143,170,000	0.2%
	District of Columbia	6,378,407,000	0.4%

Source: U.S. Bureau of the Census, Governments Division
"2014 State and Local Government Finances" (http://www.census.gov/govs/local/)

Per Capita State and Local Government Tax Revenue in 2014

National Per Capita = $4,680

ALPHA ORDER

RANK	STATE	PER CAPITA
50	Alabama	$3,004
3	Alaska	7,559
45	Arizona	3,350
35	Arkansas	3,756
13	California	5,464
23	Colorado	4,370
4	Connecticut	7,255
21	Delaware	4,412
46	Florida	3,325
44	Georgia	3,380
8	Hawaii	5,721
47	Idaho	3,237
12	Illinois	5,504
36	Indiana	3,749
20	Iowa	4,426
22	Kansas	4,382
39	Kentucky	3,607
31	Louisiana	3,890
16	Maine	4,805
10	Maryland	5,609
6	Massachusetts	6,018
34	Michigan	3,774
9	Minnesota	5,645
42	Mississippi	3,503
43	Missouri	3,475
33	Montana	3,841
15	Nebraska	4,883
32	Nevada	3,882
24	New Hampshire	4,325
5	New Jersey	6,458
29	New Mexico	3,972
2	New York	8,423
38	North Carolina	3,625
1	North Dakota	9,747
26	Ohio	4,208
40	Oklahoma	3,567
27	Oregon	4,103
17	Pennsylvania	4,708
14	Rhode Island	5,172
48	South Carolina	3,221
37	South Dakota	3,687
49	Tennessee	3,093
28	Texas	4,050
41	Utah	3,506
11	Vermont	5,540
25	Virginia	4,209
19	Washington	4,563
30	West Virginia	3,957
18	Wisconsin	4,584
7	Wyoming	5,950

RANK ORDER

RANK	STATE	PER CAPITA
1	North Dakota	$9,747
2	New York	8,423
3	Alaska	7,559
4	Connecticut	7,255
5	New Jersey	6,458
6	Massachusetts	6,018
7	Wyoming	5,950
8	Hawaii	5,721
9	Minnesota	5,645
10	Maryland	5,609
11	Vermont	5,540
12	Illinois	5,504
13	California	5,464
14	Rhode Island	5,172
15	Nebraska	4,883
16	Maine	4,805
17	Pennsylvania	4,708
18	Wisconsin	4,584
19	Washington	4,563
20	Iowa	4,426
21	Delaware	4,412
22	Kansas	4,382
23	Colorado	4,370
24	New Hampshire	4,325
25	Virginia	4,209
26	Ohio	4,208
27	Oregon	4,103
28	Texas	4,050
29	New Mexico	3,972
30	West Virginia	3,957
31	Louisiana	3,890
32	Nevada	3,882
33	Montana	3,841
34	Michigan	3,774
35	Arkansas	3,756
36	Indiana	3,749
37	South Dakota	3,687
38	North Carolina	3,625
39	Kentucky	3,607
40	Oklahoma	3,567
41	Utah	3,506
42	Mississippi	3,503
43	Missouri	3,475
44	Georgia	3,380
45	Arizona	3,350
46	Florida	3,325
47	Idaho	3,237
48	South Carolina	3,221
49	Tennessee	3,093
50	Alabama	3,004
	District of Columbia	9,679

Source: CQ Press using data from U.S. Bureau of the Census, Governments Division
"2014 State and Local Government Finances" (http://www.census.gov/govs/local/)

Percent of State and Local Government Revenue from Taxes in 2014

National Percent = 41.0%

<table>
<tr><td colspan="3">ALPHA ORDER</td><td colspan="3">RANK ORDER</td></tr>
<tr><td>RANK</td><td>STATE</td><td>PERCENT</td><td>RANK</td><td>STATE</td><td>PERCENT</td></tr>
<tr><td>44</td><td>Alabama</td><td>33.7</td><td>1</td><td>North Dakota</td><td>58.7</td></tr>
<tr><td>49</td><td>Alaska</td><td>32.5</td><td>2</td><td>Connecticut</td><td>57.2</td></tr>
<tr><td>31</td><td>Arizona</td><td>37.7</td><td>3</td><td>New Jersey</td><td>56.6</td></tr>
<tr><td>22</td><td>Arkansas</td><td>39.0</td><td>4</td><td>Maryland</td><td>49.3</td></tr>
<tr><td>27</td><td>California</td><td>38.3</td><td>5</td><td>Illinois</td><td>47.7</td></tr>
<tr><td>19</td><td>Colorado</td><td>40.6</td><td>6</td><td>Massachusetts</td><td>46.0</td></tr>
<tr><td>2</td><td>Connecticut</td><td>57.2</td><td>6</td><td>New Hampshire</td><td>46.0</td></tr>
<tr><td>38</td><td>Delaware</td><td>36.2</td><td>8</td><td>Maine</td><td>45.7</td></tr>
<tr><td>35</td><td>Florida</td><td>36.9</td><td>9</td><td>New York</td><td>45.6</td></tr>
<tr><td>22</td><td>Georgia</td><td>39.0</td><td>10</td><td>Minnesota</td><td>45.2</td></tr>
<tr><td>14</td><td>Hawaii</td><td>43.5</td><td>11</td><td>Vermont</td><td>45.0</td></tr>
<tr><td>30</td><td>Idaho</td><td>37.9</td><td>12</td><td>Pennsylvania</td><td>44.6</td></tr>
<tr><td>5</td><td>Illinois</td><td>47.7</td><td>13</td><td>Rhode Island</td><td>43.7</td></tr>
<tr><td>17</td><td>Indiana</td><td>42.5</td><td>14</td><td>Hawaii</td><td>43.5</td></tr>
<tr><td>29</td><td>Iowa</td><td>38.0</td><td>15</td><td>Kansas</td><td>43.0</td></tr>
<tr><td>15</td><td>Kansas</td><td>43.0</td><td>16</td><td>Virginia</td><td>42.9</td></tr>
<tr><td>24</td><td>Kentucky</td><td>38.6</td><td>17</td><td>Indiana</td><td>42.5</td></tr>
<tr><td>34</td><td>Louisiana</td><td>37.1</td><td>18</td><td>Texas</td><td>42.1</td></tr>
<tr><td>8</td><td>Maine</td><td>45.7</td><td>19</td><td>Colorado</td><td>40.6</td></tr>
<tr><td>4</td><td>Maryland</td><td>49.3</td><td>20</td><td>Wisconsin</td><td>40.5</td></tr>
<tr><td>6</td><td>Massachusetts</td><td>46.0</td><td>21</td><td>Nevada</td><td>40.1</td></tr>
<tr><td>32</td><td>Michigan</td><td>37.6</td><td>22</td><td>Arkansas</td><td>39.0</td></tr>
<tr><td>10</td><td>Minnesota</td><td>45.2</td><td>22</td><td>Georgia</td><td>39.0</td></tr>
<tr><td>46</td><td>Mississippi</td><td>33.6</td><td>24</td><td>Kentucky</td><td>38.6</td></tr>
<tr><td>38</td><td>Missouri</td><td>36.2</td><td>25</td><td>West Virginia</td><td>38.5</td></tr>
<tr><td>43</td><td>Montana</td><td>34.4</td><td>26</td><td>Nebraska</td><td>38.4</td></tr>
<tr><td>26</td><td>Nebraska</td><td>38.4</td><td>27</td><td>California</td><td>38.3</td></tr>
<tr><td>21</td><td>Nevada</td><td>40.1</td><td>28</td><td>North Carolina</td><td>38.2</td></tr>
<tr><td>6</td><td>New Hampshire</td><td>46.0</td><td>29</td><td>Iowa</td><td>38.0</td></tr>
<tr><td>3</td><td>New Jersey</td><td>56.6</td><td>30</td><td>Idaho</td><td>37.9</td></tr>
<tr><td>48</td><td>New Mexico</td><td>33.0</td><td>31</td><td>Arizona</td><td>37.7</td></tr>
<tr><td>9</td><td>New York</td><td>45.6</td><td>32</td><td>Michigan</td><td>37.6</td></tr>
<tr><td>28</td><td>North Carolina</td><td>38.2</td><td>33</td><td>Washington</td><td>37.3</td></tr>
<tr><td>1</td><td>North Dakota</td><td>58.7</td><td>34</td><td>Louisiana</td><td>37.1</td></tr>
<tr><td>37</td><td>Ohio</td><td>36.4</td><td>35</td><td>Florida</td><td>36.9</td></tr>
<tr><td>38</td><td>Oklahoma</td><td>36.2</td><td>36</td><td>Utah</td><td>36.6</td></tr>
<tr><td>50</td><td>Oregon</td><td>32.1</td><td>37</td><td>Ohio</td><td>36.4</td></tr>
<tr><td>12</td><td>Pennsylvania</td><td>44.6</td><td>38</td><td>Delaware</td><td>36.2</td></tr>
<tr><td>13</td><td>Rhode Island</td><td>43.7</td><td>38</td><td>Missouri</td><td>36.2</td></tr>
<tr><td>47</td><td>South Carolina</td><td>33.2</td><td>38</td><td>Oklahoma</td><td>36.2</td></tr>
<tr><td>41</td><td>South Dakota</td><td>35.4</td><td>41</td><td>South Dakota</td><td>35.4</td></tr>
<tr><td>42</td><td>Tennessee</td><td>35.3</td><td>42</td><td>Tennessee</td><td>35.3</td></tr>
<tr><td>18</td><td>Texas</td><td>42.1</td><td>43</td><td>Montana</td><td>34.4</td></tr>
<tr><td>36</td><td>Utah</td><td>36.6</td><td>44</td><td>Alabama</td><td>33.7</td></tr>
<tr><td>11</td><td>Vermont</td><td>45.0</td><td>44</td><td>Wyoming</td><td>33.7</td></tr>
<tr><td>16</td><td>Virginia</td><td>42.9</td><td>46</td><td>Mississippi</td><td>33.6</td></tr>
<tr><td>33</td><td>Washington</td><td>37.3</td><td>47</td><td>South Carolina</td><td>33.2</td></tr>
<tr><td>25</td><td>West Virginia</td><td>38.5</td><td>48</td><td>New Mexico</td><td>33.0</td></tr>
<tr><td>20</td><td>Wisconsin</td><td>40.5</td><td>49</td><td>Alaska</td><td>32.5</td></tr>
<tr><td>44</td><td>Wyoming</td><td>33.7</td><td>50</td><td>Oregon</td><td>32.1</td></tr>
<tr><td></td><td></td><td></td><td></td><td>District of Columbia</td><td>43.4</td></tr>
</table>

Source: CQ Press using data from U.S. Bureau of the Census, Governments Division
"2014 State and Local Government Finances" (http://www.census.gov/govs/local/)

State and Local Government Tax Revenue
as a Percent of Personal Income in 2014
National Percent = 10.1% of Personal Income*

ALPHA ORDER

RANK	STATE	PERCENT
45	Alabama	8.1
3	Alaska	13.8
37	Arizona	8.8
21	Arkansas	10.0
14	California	10.7
37	Colorado	8.8
11	Connecticut	10.9
26	Delaware	9.7
49	Florida	7.7
40	Georgia	8.7
4	Hawaii	12.3
40	Idaho	8.7
8	Illinois	11.3
31	Indiana	9.3
21	Iowa	10.0
30	Kansas	9.4
26	Kentucky	9.7
31	Louisiana	9.3
6	Maine	11.7
16	Maryland	10.4
19	Massachusetts	10.1
34	Michigan	9.2
7	Minnesota	11.5
17	Mississippi	10.3
43	Missouri	8.4
29	Montana	9.5
19	Nebraska	10.1
28	Nevada	9.6
45	New Hampshire	8.1
9	New Jersey	11.2
12	New Mexico	10.8
2	New York	14.8
34	North Carolina	9.2
1	North Dakota	16.8
21	Ohio	10.0
48	Oklahoma	7.9
24	Oregon	9.8
24	Pennsylvania	9.8
12	Rhode Island	10.8
40	South Carolina	8.7
47	South Dakota	8.0
49	Tennessee	7.7
37	Texas	8.8
31	Utah	9.3
5	Vermont	11.8
43	Virginia	8.4
36	Washington	9.0
10	West Virginia	11.1
17	Wisconsin	10.3
15	Wyoming	10.6

RANK ORDER

RANK	STATE	PERCENT
1	North Dakota	16.8
2	New York	14.8
3	Alaska	13.8
4	Hawaii	12.3
5	Vermont	11.8
6	Maine	11.7
7	Minnesota	11.5
8	Illinois	11.3
9	New Jersey	11.2
10	West Virginia	11.1
11	Connecticut	10.9
12	New Mexico	10.8
12	Rhode Island	10.8
14	California	10.7
15	Wyoming	10.6
16	Maryland	10.4
17	Mississippi	10.3
17	Wisconsin	10.3
19	Massachusetts	10.1
19	Nebraska	10.1
21	Arkansas	10.0
21	Iowa	10.0
21	Ohio	10.0
24	Oregon	9.8
24	Pennsylvania	9.8
26	Delaware	9.7
26	Kentucky	9.7
28	Nevada	9.6
29	Montana	9.5
30	Kansas	9.4
31	Indiana	9.3
31	Louisiana	9.3
31	Utah	9.3
34	Michigan	9.2
34	North Carolina	9.2
36	Washington	9.0
37	Arizona	8.8
37	Colorado	8.8
37	Texas	8.8
40	Georgia	8.7
40	Idaho	8.7
40	South Carolina	8.7
43	Missouri	8.4
43	Virginia	8.4
45	Alabama	8.1
45	New Hampshire	8.1
47	South Dakota	8.0
48	Oklahoma	7.9
49	Florida	7.7
49	Tennessee	7.7

District of Columbia	13.7

Source: CQ Press using data from U.S. Bureau of the Census, Governments Division
"Annual State Personal Income" (http://www.bea.gov/iTable/index_regional.cfm) and
"2014 State and Local Government Finances" (http://www.census.gov/govs/local/)
*The personal income total used for this table is the sum of state estimates. This total differs from the national income and product accounts (NIPA) estimate of personal income because it omits the earnings of federal civilian and military personnel stationed abroad and of U.S. residents employed abroad temporarily by private U.S. firms.

State and Local Government General Sales Tax Revenue in 2014

National Total = $347,183,136,000*

ALPHA ORDER

RANK	STATE	REVENUE	% of USA
24	Alabama	$4,321,180,000	1.2%
46	Alaska	218,187,000	0.1%
9	Arizona	8,918,242,000	2.6%
27	Arkansas	4,174,892,000	1.2%
1	California	48,393,555,000	13.9%
17	Colorado	6,030,654,000	1.7%
28	Connecticut	3,981,362,000	1.1%
47	Delaware	0	0.0%
4	Florida	23,332,609,000	6.7%
11	Georgia	8,867,712,000	2.6%
34	Hawaii	3,043,432,000	0.9%
39	Idaho	1,374,224,000	0.4%
8	Illinois	10,047,181,000	2.9%
15	Indiana	7,003,426,000	2.0%
35	Iowa	2,958,955,000	0.9%
29	Kansas	3,900,138,000	1.1%
32	Kentucky	3,131,157,000	0.9%
16	Louisiana	6,930,614,000	2.0%
42	Maine	1,194,552,000	0.3%
25	Maryland	4,195,996,000	1.2%
20	Massachusetts	5,518,580,000	1.6%
12	Michigan	8,715,827,000	2.5%
18	Minnesota	5,638,700,000	1.6%
31	Mississippi	3,304,632,000	1.0%
19	Missouri	5,563,693,000	1.6%
47	Montana	0	0.0%
37	Nebraska	2,109,847,000	0.6%
26	Nevada	4,195,169,000	1.2%
47	New Hampshire	0	0.0%
10	New Jersey	8,885,847,000	2.6%
33	New Mexico	3,046,746,000	0.9%
3	New York	27,454,581,000	7.9%
14	North Carolina	8,171,871,000	2.4%
38	North Dakota	1,518,708,000	0.4%
6	Ohio	12,194,832,000	3.5%
23	Oklahoma	4,603,155,000	1.3%
47	Oregon	0	0.0%
7	Pennsylvania	10,180,794,000	2.9%
44	Rhode Island	915,468,000	0.3%
30	South Carolina	3,749,363,000	1.1%
40	South Dakota	1,271,045,000	0.4%
13	Tennessee	8,277,225,000	2.4%
2	Texas	39,246,418,000	11.3%
36	Utah	2,506,473,000	0.7%
45	Vermont	365,808,000	0.1%
22	Virginia	4,812,538,000	1.4%
5	Washington	14,628,195,000	4.2%
41	West Virginia	1,221,966,000	0.4%
21	Wisconsin	4,980,431,000	1.4%
43	Wyoming	952,119,000	0.3%

RANK ORDER

RANK	STATE	REVENUE	% of USA
1	California	$48,393,555,000	13.9%
2	Texas	39,246,418,000	11.3%
3	New York	27,454,581,000	7.9%
4	Florida	23,332,609,000	6.7%
5	Washington	14,628,195,000	4.2%
6	Ohio	12,194,832,000	3.5%
7	Pennsylvania	10,180,794,000	2.9%
8	Illinois	10,047,181,000	2.9%
9	Arizona	8,918,242,000	2.6%
10	New Jersey	8,885,847,000	2.6%
11	Georgia	8,867,712,000	2.6%
12	Michigan	8,715,827,000	2.5%
13	Tennessee	8,277,225,000	2.4%
14	North Carolina	8,171,871,000	2.4%
15	Indiana	7,003,426,000	2.0%
16	Louisiana	6,930,614,000	2.0%
17	Colorado	6,030,654,000	1.7%
18	Minnesota	5,638,700,000	1.6%
19	Missouri	5,563,693,000	1.6%
20	Massachusetts	5,518,580,000	1.6%
21	Wisconsin	4,980,431,000	1.4%
22	Virginia	4,812,538,000	1.4%
23	Oklahoma	4,603,155,000	1.3%
24	Alabama	4,321,180,000	1.2%
25	Maryland	4,195,996,000	1.2%
26	Nevada	4,195,169,000	1.2%
27	Arkansas	4,174,892,000	1.2%
28	Connecticut	3,981,362,000	1.1%
29	Kansas	3,900,138,000	1.1%
30	South Carolina	3,749,363,000	1.1%
31	Mississippi	3,304,632,000	1.0%
32	Kentucky	3,131,157,000	0.9%
33	New Mexico	3,046,746,000	0.9%
34	Hawaii	3,043,432,000	0.9%
35	Iowa	2,958,955,000	0.9%
36	Utah	2,506,473,000	0.7%
37	Nebraska	2,109,847,000	0.6%
38	North Dakota	1,518,708,000	0.4%
39	Idaho	1,374,224,000	0.4%
40	South Dakota	1,271,045,000	0.4%
41	West Virginia	1,221,966,000	0.4%
42	Maine	1,194,552,000	0.3%
43	Wyoming	952,119,000	0.3%
44	Rhode Island	915,468,000	0.3%
45	Vermont	365,808,000	0.1%
46	Alaska	218,187,000	0.1%
47	Delaware	0	0.0%
47	Montana	0	0.0%
47	New Hampshire	0	0.0%
47	Oregon	0	0.0%
	District of Columbia	1,135,037,000	0.3%

Source: U.S. Bureau of the Census, Governments Division
  "2014 State and Local Government Finances" (http://www.census.gov/govs/local/)
*Does not include special sales taxes such as those on sale of alcohol, gasoline, or tobacco.

Per Capita State and Local Government General Sales Tax Revenue in 2014

National Per Capita = $1,090*

ALPHA ORDER

RANK	STATE	PER CAPITA
29	Alabama	$892
46	Alaska	296
13	Arizona	1,327
10	Arkansas	1,407
15	California	1,251
18	Colorado	1,127
20	Connecticut	1,108
47	Delaware	0
17	Florida	1,173
30	Georgia	879
1	Hawaii	2,149
35	Idaho	841
39	Illinois	781
22	Indiana	1,062
26	Iowa	952
12	Kansas	1,345
41	Kentucky	710
5	Louisiana	1,491
28	Maine	898
42	Maryland	703
37	Massachusetts	818
30	Michigan	879
24	Minnesota	1,034
21	Mississippi	1,104
27	Missouri	918
47	Montana	0
19	Nebraska	1,122
7	Nevada	1,481
47	New Hampshire	0
25	New Jersey	996
8	New Mexico	1,463
11	New York	1,392
36	North Carolina	823
3	North Dakota	2,053
23	Ohio	1,052
16	Oklahoma	1,187
47	Oregon	0
38	Pennsylvania	796
32	Rhode Island	868
40	South Carolina	777
5	South Dakota	1,491
14	Tennessee	1,265
9	Texas	1,457
34	Utah	852
44	Vermont	583
45	Virginia	579
2	Washington	2,074
43	West Virginia	661
33	Wisconsin	865
4	Wyoming	1,631

RANK ORDER

RANK	STATE	PER CAPITA
1	Hawaii	$2,149
2	Washington	2,074
3	North Dakota	2,053
4	Wyoming	1,631
5	Louisiana	1,491
5	South Dakota	1,491
7	Nevada	1,481
8	New Mexico	1,463
9	Texas	1,457
10	Arkansas	1,407
11	New York	1,392
12	Kansas	1,345
13	Arizona	1,327
14	Tennessee	1,265
15	California	1,251
16	Oklahoma	1,187
17	Florida	1,173
18	Colorado	1,127
19	Nebraska	1,122
20	Connecticut	1,108
21	Mississippi	1,104
22	Indiana	1,062
23	Ohio	1,052
24	Minnesota	1,034
25	New Jersey	996
26	Iowa	952
27	Missouri	918
28	Maine	898
29	Alabama	892
30	Georgia	879
30	Michigan	879
32	Rhode Island	868
33	Wisconsin	865
34	Utah	852
35	Idaho	841
36	North Carolina	823
37	Massachusetts	818
38	Pennsylvania	796
39	Illinois	781
40	South Carolina	777
41	Kentucky	710
42	Maryland	703
43	West Virginia	661
44	Vermont	583
45	Virginia	579
46	Alaska	296
47	Delaware	0
47	Montana	0
47	New Hampshire	0
47	Oregon	0
	District of Columbia	1,722

Source: CQ Press using data from U.S. Bureau of the Census, Governments Division
  "2014 State and Local Government Finances" (http://www.census.gov/govs/local/)
*Does not include special sales taxes such as those on sale of alcohol, gasoline, or tobacco.

State and Local Government General Retail Sales Tax Rates in 2017

National Median = 6.85 Percent*

ALPHA ORDER				RANK ORDER		
RANK	STATE	PERCENT		RANK	STATE	PERCENT
4	Alabama	9.01		1	Louisiana	9.98
46	Alaska	1.76		2	Tennessee	9.46
10	Arizona	8.25		3	Arkansas	9.30
3	Arkansas	9.30		4	Alabama	9.01
10	California	8.25		5	Washington	8.92
16	Colorado	7.50		6	Oklahoma	8.86
32	Connecticut	6.35		7	Illinois	8.64
47	Delaware	0.00		8	Kansas	8.62
27	Florida	6.80		9	New York	8.49
21	Georgia	7.00		10	Arizona	8.25
45	Hawaii	4.35		10	California	8.25
37	Idaho	6.03		12	Texas	8.19
7	Illinois	8.64		13	Nevada	7.98
21	Indiana	7.00		14	Missouri	7.89
27	Iowa	6.80		15	New Mexico	7.55
8	Kansas	8.62		16	Colorado	7.50
38	Kentucky	6.00		17	Minnesota	7.30
1	Louisiana	9.98		18	South Carolina	7.22
42	Maine	5.50		19	Ohio	7.14
38	Maryland	6.00		20	Mississippi	7.07
35	Massachusetts	6.25		21	Georgia	7.00
38	Michigan	6.00		21	Indiana	7.00
17	Minnesota	7.30		21	Rhode Island	7.00
20	Mississippi	7.07		24	North Carolina	6.90
14	Missouri	7.89		25	Nebraska	6.89
47	Montana	0.00		26	New Jersey	6.85
25	Nebraska	6.89		27	Florida	6.80
13	Nevada	7.98		27	Iowa	6.80
47	New Hampshire	0.00		29	North Dakota	6.78
26	New Jersey	6.85		30	Utah	6.76
15	New Mexico	7.55		31	South Dakota	6.39
9	New York	8.49		32	Connecticut	6.35
24	North Carolina	6.90		33	Pennsylvania	6.34
29	North Dakota	6.78		34	West Virginia	6.29
19	Ohio	7.14		35	Massachusetts	6.25
6	Oklahoma	8.86		36	Vermont	6.18
47	Oregon	0.00		37	Idaho	6.03
33	Pennsylvania	6.34		38	Kentucky	6.00
21	Rhode Island	7.00		38	Maryland	6.00
18	South Carolina	7.22		38	Michigan	6.00
31	South Dakota	6.39		41	Virginia	5.63
2	Tennessee	9.46		42	Maine	5.50
12	Texas	8.19		43	Wisconsin	5.42
30	Utah	6.76		44	Wyoming	5.40
36	Vermont	6.18		45	Hawaii	4.35
41	Virginia	5.63		46	Alaska	1.76
5	Washington	8.92		47	Delaware	0.00
34	West Virginia	6.29		47	Montana	0.00
43	Wisconsin	5.42		47	New Hampshire	0.00
44	Wyoming	5.40		47	Oregon	0.00
					District of Columbia	5.75

Source: The Tax Foundation
"State and Local Sales Tax Rates in 2017" (https://taxfoundation.org/state-and-local-sales-tax-rates-in-2017/)
*As of January 1, 2017. There are great differences on what states exempt from sales taxes. These rates are based on average local rates where local governments can set different tax rates.

State and Local Government Property Tax Revenue in 2014

National Total = $466,391,582,000

ALPHA ORDER

RANK	STATE	REVENUE	% of USA
36	Alabama	$2,529,891,000	0.5%
40	Alaska	1,945,407,000	0.4%
20	Arizona	6,635,169,000	1.4%
39	Arkansas	2,001,147,000	0.4%
1	California	53,731,027,000	11.5%
19	Colorado	7,310,674,000	1.6%
13	Connecticut	9,970,863,000	2.1%
50	Delaware	775,062,000	0.2%
6	Florida	23,577,987,000	5.1%
12	Georgia	10,980,226,000	2.4%
46	Hawaii	1,391,717,000	0.3%
43	Idaho	1,516,715,000	0.3%
5	Illinois	25,851,113,000	5.5%
21	Indiana	6,401,317,000	1.4%
26	Iowa	4,743,125,000	1.0%
27	Kansas	4,165,885,000	0.9%
31	Kentucky	3,253,092,000	0.7%
28	Louisiana	3,898,282,000	0.8%
35	Maine	2,551,889,000	0.5%
17	Maryland	8,911,048,000	1.9%
8	Massachusetts	14,732,296,000	3.2%
10	Michigan	13,241,325,000	2.8%
18	Minnesota	7,699,536,000	1.7%
33	Mississippi	2,743,182,000	0.6%
22	Missouri	5,822,222,000	1.2%
44	Montana	1,499,299,000	0.3%
30	Nebraska	3,308,337,000	0.7%
34	Nevada	2,703,774,000	0.6%
29	New Hampshire	3,798,843,000	0.8%
4	New Jersey	27,394,531,000	5.9%
42	New Mexico	1,525,273,000	0.3%
2	New York	50,981,214,000	10.9%
16	North Carolina	9,457,263,000	2.0%
49	North Dakota	829,738,000	0.2%
9	Ohio	13,954,377,000	3.0%
38	Oklahoma	2,418,249,000	0.5%
24	Oregon	5,359,978,000	1.1%
7	Pennsylvania	17,971,292,000	3.9%
37	Rhode Island	2,433,767,000	0.5%
25	South Carolina	5,215,064,000	1.1%
48	South Dakota	1,110,503,000	0.2%
23	Tennessee	5,432,791,000	1.2%
3	Texas	44,108,867,000	9.5%
32	Utah	2,853,123,000	0.6%
45	Vermont	1,465,891,000	0.3%
11	Virginia	12,132,829,000	2.6%
14	Washington	9,633,480,000	2.1%
41	West Virginia	1,575,658,000	0.3%
15	Wisconsin	9,544,083,000	2.0%
47	Wyoming	1,232,157,000	0.3%

RANK ORDER

RANK	STATE	REVENUE	% of USA
1	California	$53,731,027,000	11.5%
2	New York	50,981,214,000	10.9%
3	Texas	44,108,867,000	9.5%
4	New Jersey	27,394,531,000	5.9%
5	Illinois	25,851,113,000	5.5%
6	Florida	23,577,987,000	5.1%
7	Pennsylvania	17,971,292,000	3.9%
8	Massachusetts	14,732,296,000	3.2%
9	Ohio	13,954,377,000	3.0%
10	Michigan	13,241,325,000	2.8%
11	Virginia	12,132,829,000	2.6%
12	Georgia	10,980,226,000	2.4%
13	Connecticut	9,970,863,000	2.1%
14	Washington	9,633,480,000	2.1%
15	Wisconsin	9,544,083,000	2.0%
16	North Carolina	9,457,263,000	2.0%
17	Maryland	8,911,048,000	1.9%
18	Minnesota	7,699,536,000	1.7%
19	Colorado	7,310,674,000	1.6%
20	Arizona	6,635,169,000	1.4%
21	Indiana	6,401,317,000	1.4%
22	Missouri	5,822,222,000	1.2%
23	Tennessee	5,432,791,000	1.2%
24	Oregon	5,359,978,000	1.1%
25	South Carolina	5,215,064,000	1.1%
26	Iowa	4,743,125,000	1.0%
27	Kansas	4,165,885,000	0.9%
28	Louisiana	3,898,282,000	0.8%
29	New Hampshire	3,798,843,000	0.8%
30	Nebraska	3,308,337,000	0.7%
31	Kentucky	3,253,092,000	0.7%
32	Utah	2,853,123,000	0.6%
33	Mississippi	2,743,182,000	0.6%
34	Nevada	2,703,774,000	0.6%
35	Maine	2,551,889,000	0.5%
36	Alabama	2,529,891,000	0.5%
37	Rhode Island	2,433,767,000	0.5%
38	Oklahoma	2,418,249,000	0.5%
39	Arkansas	2,001,147,000	0.4%
40	Alaska	1,945,407,000	0.4%
41	West Virginia	1,575,658,000	0.3%
42	New Mexico	1,525,273,000	0.3%
43	Idaho	1,516,715,000	0.3%
44	Montana	1,499,299,000	0.3%
45	Vermont	1,465,891,000	0.3%
46	Hawaii	1,391,717,000	0.3%
47	Wyoming	1,232,157,000	0.3%
48	South Dakota	1,110,503,000	0.2%
49	North Dakota	829,738,000	0.2%
50	Delaware	775,062,000	0.2%
	District of Columbia	2,070,974,000	0.4%

Source: U.S. Bureau of the Census, Governments Division
"2014 State and Local Government Finances" (http://www.census.gov/govs/local/)

Per Capita State and Local Government Property Tax Revenue in 2014

National Per Capita = $1,464

<table>
<tr><td colspan="3">ALPHA ORDER</td><td colspan="3">RANK ORDER</td></tr>
<tr><th>RANK</th><th>STATE</th><th>PER CAPITA</th><th>RANK</th><th>STATE</th><th>PER CAPITA</th></tr>
<tr><td>50</td><td>Alabama</td><td>$522</td><td>1</td><td>New Jersey</td><td>$3,069</td></tr>
<tr><td>4</td><td>Alaska</td><td>2,641</td><td>2</td><td>New Hampshire</td><td>2,859</td></tr>
<tr><td>33</td><td>Arizona</td><td>987</td><td>3</td><td>Connecticut</td><td>2,776</td></tr>
<tr><td>48</td><td>Arkansas</td><td>674</td><td>4</td><td>Alaska</td><td>2,641</td></tr>
<tr><td>22</td><td>California</td><td>1,389</td><td>5</td><td>New York</td><td>2,585</td></tr>
<tr><td>23</td><td>Colorado</td><td>1,367</td><td>6</td><td>Vermont</td><td>2,338</td></tr>
<tr><td>3</td><td>Connecticut</td><td>2,776</td><td>7</td><td>Rhode Island</td><td>2,308</td></tr>
<tr><td>45</td><td>Delaware</td><td>829</td><td>8</td><td>Massachusetts</td><td>2,183</td></tr>
<tr><td>29</td><td>Florida</td><td>1,185</td><td>9</td><td>Wyoming</td><td>2,111</td></tr>
<tr><td>31</td><td>Georgia</td><td>1,089</td><td>10</td><td>Illinois</td><td>2,009</td></tr>
<tr><td>34</td><td>Hawaii</td><td>983</td><td>11</td><td>Maine</td><td>1,918</td></tr>
<tr><td>40</td><td>Idaho</td><td>928</td><td>12</td><td>Nebraska</td><td>1,759</td></tr>
<tr><td>10</td><td>Illinois</td><td>2,009</td><td>13</td><td>Wisconsin</td><td>1,657</td></tr>
<tr><td>35</td><td>Indiana</td><td>971</td><td>14</td><td>Texas</td><td>1,637</td></tr>
<tr><td>15</td><td>Iowa</td><td>1,526</td><td>15</td><td>Iowa</td><td>1,526</td></tr>
<tr><td>19</td><td>Kansas</td><td>1,437</td><td>16</td><td>Maryland</td><td>1,493</td></tr>
<tr><td>46</td><td>Kentucky</td><td>737</td><td>17</td><td>Montana</td><td>1,466</td></tr>
<tr><td>43</td><td>Louisiana</td><td>839</td><td>18</td><td>Virginia</td><td>1,459</td></tr>
<tr><td>11</td><td>Maine</td><td>1,918</td><td>19</td><td>Kansas</td><td>1,437</td></tr>
<tr><td>16</td><td>Maryland</td><td>1,493</td><td>20</td><td>Minnesota</td><td>1,412</td></tr>
<tr><td>8</td><td>Massachusetts</td><td>2,183</td><td>21</td><td>Pennsylvania</td><td>1,405</td></tr>
<tr><td>26</td><td>Michigan</td><td>1,335</td><td>22</td><td>California</td><td>1,389</td></tr>
<tr><td>20</td><td>Minnesota</td><td>1,412</td><td>23</td><td>Colorado</td><td>1,367</td></tr>
<tr><td>41</td><td>Mississippi</td><td>917</td><td>24</td><td>Washington</td><td>1,366</td></tr>
<tr><td>37</td><td>Missouri</td><td>961</td><td>25</td><td>Oregon</td><td>1,351</td></tr>
<tr><td>17</td><td>Montana</td><td>1,466</td><td>26</td><td>Michigan</td><td>1,335</td></tr>
<tr><td>12</td><td>Nebraska</td><td>1,759</td><td>27</td><td>South Dakota</td><td>1,303</td></tr>
<tr><td>38</td><td>Nevada</td><td>954</td><td>28</td><td>Ohio</td><td>1,204</td></tr>
<tr><td>2</td><td>New Hampshire</td><td>2,859</td><td>29</td><td>Florida</td><td>1,185</td></tr>
<tr><td>1</td><td>New Jersey</td><td>3,069</td><td>30</td><td>North Dakota</td><td>1,121</td></tr>
<tr><td>47</td><td>New Mexico</td><td>732</td><td>31</td><td>Georgia</td><td>1,089</td></tr>
<tr><td>5</td><td>New York</td><td>2,585</td><td>32</td><td>South Carolina</td><td>1,080</td></tr>
<tr><td>39</td><td>North Carolina</td><td>952</td><td>33</td><td>Arizona</td><td>987</td></tr>
<tr><td>30</td><td>North Dakota</td><td>1,121</td><td>34</td><td>Hawaii</td><td>983</td></tr>
<tr><td>28</td><td>Ohio</td><td>1,204</td><td>35</td><td>Indiana</td><td>971</td></tr>
<tr><td>49</td><td>Oklahoma</td><td>624</td><td>36</td><td>Utah</td><td>970</td></tr>
<tr><td>25</td><td>Oregon</td><td>1,351</td><td>37</td><td>Missouri</td><td>961</td></tr>
<tr><td>21</td><td>Pennsylvania</td><td>1,405</td><td>38</td><td>Nevada</td><td>954</td></tr>
<tr><td>7</td><td>Rhode Island</td><td>2,308</td><td>39</td><td>North Carolina</td><td>952</td></tr>
<tr><td>32</td><td>South Carolina</td><td>1,080</td><td>40</td><td>Idaho</td><td>928</td></tr>
<tr><td>27</td><td>South Dakota</td><td>1,303</td><td>41</td><td>Mississippi</td><td>917</td></tr>
<tr><td>44</td><td>Tennessee</td><td>830</td><td>42</td><td>West Virginia</td><td>852</td></tr>
<tr><td>14</td><td>Texas</td><td>1,637</td><td>43</td><td>Louisiana</td><td>839</td></tr>
<tr><td>36</td><td>Utah</td><td>970</td><td>44</td><td>Tennessee</td><td>830</td></tr>
<tr><td>6</td><td>Vermont</td><td>2,338</td><td>45</td><td>Delaware</td><td>829</td></tr>
<tr><td>18</td><td>Virginia</td><td>1,459</td><td>46</td><td>Kentucky</td><td>737</td></tr>
<tr><td>24</td><td>Washington</td><td>1,366</td><td>47</td><td>New Mexico</td><td>732</td></tr>
<tr><td>42</td><td>West Virginia</td><td>852</td><td>48</td><td>Arkansas</td><td>674</td></tr>
<tr><td>13</td><td>Wisconsin</td><td>1,657</td><td>49</td><td>Oklahoma</td><td>624</td></tr>
<tr><td>9</td><td>Wyoming</td><td>2,111</td><td>50</td><td>Alabama</td><td>522</td></tr>
<tr><td></td><td></td><td></td><td></td><td>District of Columbia</td><td>3,143</td></tr>
</table>

Source: CQ Press using data from U.S. Bureau of the Census, Governments Division
   "2014 State and Local Government Finances" (http://www.census.gov/govs/local/)

State and Local Government Property Tax as a Percent of State and Local Government Total Revenue in 2014

National Percent = 12.8%

ALPHA ORDER

RANK	STATE	PERCENT
50	Alabama	5.9
25	Alaska	11.3
28	Arizona	11.1
45	Arkansas	7.0
38	California	9.7
21	Colorado	12.7
3	Connecticut	21.9
46	Delaware	6.8
17	Florida	13.2
22	Georgia	12.6
44	Hawaii	7.5
31	Idaho	10.9
7	Illinois	17.4
30	Indiana	11.0
18	Iowa	13.1
12	Kansas	14.1
43	Kentucky	7.9
42	Louisiana	8.0
6	Maine	18.2
18	Maryland	13.1
9	Massachusetts	16.7
15	Michigan	13.3
25	Minnesota	11.3
40	Mississippi	8.8
35	Missouri	10.0
18	Montana	13.1
14	Nebraska	13.8
37	Nevada	9.9
1	New Hampshire	30.4
2	New Jersey	26.9
49	New Mexico	6.1
13	New York	14.0
35	North Carolina	10.0
47	North Dakota	6.7
33	Ohio	10.4
48	Oklahoma	6.3
32	Oregon	10.6
15	Pennsylvania	13.3
4	Rhode Island	19.5
28	South Carolina	11.1
23	South Dakota	12.5
39	Tennessee	9.5
8	Texas	17.0
34	Utah	10.1
5	Vermont	19.0
10	Virginia	14.9
27	Washington	11.2
41	West Virginia	8.3
11	Wisconsin	14.6
24	Wyoming	11.9

RANK ORDER

RANK	STATE	PERCENT
1	New Hampshire	30.4
2	New Jersey	26.9
3	Connecticut	21.9
4	Rhode Island	19.5
5	Vermont	19.0
6	Maine	18.2
7	Illinois	17.4
8	Texas	17.0
9	Massachusetts	16.7
10	Virginia	14.9
11	Wisconsin	14.6
12	Kansas	14.1
13	New York	14.0
14	Nebraska	13.8
15	Michigan	13.3
15	Pennsylvania	13.3
17	Florida	13.2
18	Iowa	13.1
18	Maryland	13.1
18	Montana	13.1
21	Colorado	12.7
22	Georgia	12.6
23	South Dakota	12.5
24	Wyoming	11.9
25	Alaska	11.3
25	Minnesota	11.3
27	Washington	11.2
28	Arizona	11.1
28	South Carolina	11.1
30	Indiana	11.0
31	Idaho	10.9
32	Oregon	10.6
33	Ohio	10.4
34	Utah	10.1
35	Missouri	10.0
35	North Carolina	10.0
37	Nevada	9.9
38	California	9.7
39	Tennessee	9.5
40	Mississippi	8.8
41	West Virginia	8.3
42	Louisiana	8.0
43	Kentucky	7.9
44	Hawaii	7.5
45	Arkansas	7.0
46	Delaware	6.8
47	North Dakota	6.7
48	Oklahoma	6.3
49	New Mexico	6.1
50	Alabama	5.9

District of Columbia 14.1

Source: CQ Press using data from U.S. Bureau of the Census, Governments Division
"2014 State and Local Government Finances" (http://www.census.gov/govs/local/)

State and Local Government Property Tax Revenue as a Percent of State and Local Government Own Source Revenue in 2014
National Percent = 21.6%*

ALPHA ORDER

RANK	STATE	PERCENT
49	Alabama	9.9
35	Alaska	17.4
25	Arizona	20.0
44	Arkansas	12.7
32	California	18.0
23	Colorado	20.2
3	Connecticut	32.0
46	Delaware	11.0
18	Florida	21.7
17	Georgia	21.8
45	Hawaii	12.2
29	Idaho	19.0
7	Illinois	28.5
37	Indiana	16.9
19	Iowa	21.5
21	Kansas	20.8
41	Kentucky	14.2
43	Louisiana	13.8
6	Maine	30.4
23	Maryland	20.2
9	Massachusetts	27.2
16	Michigan	22.4
31	Minnesota	18.1
40	Mississippi	16.2
30	Missouri	18.3
10	Montana	26.1
12	Nebraska	24.9
35	Nevada	17.4
1	New Hampshire	46.5
2	New Jersey	36.4
46	New Mexico	11.0
13	New York	23.7
38	North Carolina	16.8
50	North Dakota	9.0
28	Ohio	19.2
46	Oklahoma	11.0
22	Oregon	20.4
20	Pennsylvania	21.1
4	Rhode Island	31.9
32	South Carolina	18.0
14	South Dakota	23.5
34	Tennessee	17.7
8	Texas	27.6
38	Utah	16.8
5	Vermont	31.4
15	Virginia	22.5
27	Washington	19.5
41	West Virginia	14.2
11	Wisconsin	25.4
26	Wyoming	19.8

RANK ORDER

RANK	STATE	PERCENT
1	New Hampshire	46.5
2	New Jersey	36.4
3	Connecticut	32.0
4	Rhode Island	31.9
5	Vermont	31.4
6	Maine	30.4
7	Illinois	28.5
8	Texas	27.6
9	Massachusetts	27.2
10	Montana	26.1
11	Wisconsin	25.4
12	Nebraska	24.9
13	New York	23.7
14	South Dakota	23.5
15	Virginia	22.5
16	Michigan	22.4
17	Georgia	21.8
18	Florida	21.7
19	Iowa	21.5
20	Pennsylvania	21.1
21	Kansas	20.8
22	Oregon	20.4
23	Colorado	20.2
23	Maryland	20.2
25	Arizona	20.0
26	Wyoming	19.8
27	Washington	19.5
28	Ohio	19.2
29	Idaho	19.0
30	Missouri	18.3
31	Minnesota	18.1
32	California	18.0
32	South Carolina	18.0
34	Tennessee	17.7
35	Alaska	17.4
35	Nevada	17.4
37	Indiana	16.9
38	North Carolina	16.8
38	Utah	16.8
40	Mississippi	16.2
41	Kentucky	14.2
41	West Virginia	14.2
43	Louisiana	13.8
44	Arkansas	12.7
45	Hawaii	12.2
46	Delaware	11.0
46	New Mexico	11.0
46	Oklahoma	11.0
49	Alabama	9.9
50	North Dakota	9.0

District of Columbia   25.4

Source: CQ Press using data from U.S. Bureau of the Census, Governments Division
    "2014 State and Local Government Finances" (http://www.census.gov/govs/local/)
*Own source revenue includes taxes, current charges, and miscellaneous general revenue. Excluded are intergovernmental transfers, insurance trust revenue, and revenue from government owned utilities and other commercial or auxiliary enterprise.

State and Local Tax Burden as a Percent of Income in 2012

National Percent = 9.8% of Income*

ALPHA ORDER				RANK ORDER		
RANK	STATE	PERCENT		RANK	STATE	PERCENT
37	Alabama	8.7		1	New York	12.7
50	Alaska	6.5		2	Connecticut	12.6
36	Arizona	8.8		3	New Jersey	12.2
17	Arkansas	10.1		4	California	11.0
4	California	11.0		4	Illinois	11.0
34	Colorado	8.9		4	Wisconsin	11.0
2	Connecticut	12.6		7	Maryland	10.9
13	Delaware	10.2		8	Minnesota	10.8
34	Florida	8.9		8	Rhode Island	10.8
32	Georgia	9.1		10	Massachusetts	10.3
13	Hawaii	10.2		10	Oregon	10.3
26	Idaho	9.3		10	Vermont	10.3
4	Illinois	11.0		13	Delaware	10.2
22	Indiana	9.5		13	Hawaii	10.2
30	Iowa	9.2		13	Maine	10.2
22	Kansas	9.5		13	Pennsylvania	10.2
22	Kentucky	9.5		17	Arkansas	10.1
45	Louisiana	7.6		18	North Carolina	9.8
13	Maine	10.2		18	Ohio	9.8
7	Maryland	10.9		18	West Virginia	9.8
10	Massachusetts	10.3		21	Utah	9.6
25	Michigan	9.4		22	Indiana	9.5
8	Minnesota	10.8		22	Kansas	9.5
40	Mississippi	8.6		22	Kentucky	9.5
26	Missouri	9.3		25	Michigan	9.4
37	Montana	8.7		26	Idaho	9.3
30	Nebraska	9.2		26	Missouri	9.3
43	Nevada	8.1		26	Virginia	9.3
44	New Hampshire	7.9		26	Washington	9.3
3	New Jersey	12.2		30	Iowa	9.2
37	New Mexico	8.7		30	Nebraska	9.2
1	New York	12.7		32	Georgia	9.1
18	North Carolina	9.8		33	North Dakota	9.0
33	North Dakota	9.0		34	Colorado	8.9
18	Ohio	9.8		34	Florida	8.9
40	Oklahoma	8.6		36	Arizona	8.8
10	Oregon	10.3		37	Alabama	8.7
13	Pennsylvania	10.2		37	Montana	8.7
8	Rhode Island	10.8		37	New Mexico	8.7
42	South Carolina	8.4		40	Mississippi	8.6
48	South Dakota	7.1		40	Oklahoma	8.6
47	Tennessee	7.3		42	South Carolina	8.4
45	Texas	7.6		43	Nevada	8.1
21	Utah	9.6		44	New Hampshire	7.9
10	Vermont	10.3		45	Louisiana	7.6
26	Virginia	9.3		45	Texas	7.6
26	Washington	9.3		47	Tennessee	7.3
18	West Virginia	9.8		48	South Dakota	7.1
4	Wisconsin	11.0		48	Wyoming	7.1
48	Wyoming	7.1		50	Alaska	6.5
				District of Columbia		10.6

Source: The Tax Foundation
"State and Local Tax Burdens: All States, One Year, 1977-2012"
(http://taxfoundation.org/article/state-and-local-tax-burdens-1977-2012)
*All state and local taxes.

State and Local Government Total Expenditures in 2014

National Total = $3,261,579,586,000*

ALPHA ORDER

RANK	STATE	EXPENDITURES	% of USA
26	Alabama	$42,869,408,000	1.3%
38	Alaska	16,773,713,000	0.5%
21	Arizona	52,969,802,000	1.6%
34	Arkansas	25,137,369,000	0.8%
1	California	473,515,694,000	14.5%
20	Colorado	53,459,785,000	1.6%
27	Connecticut	42,673,529,000	1.3%
45	Delaware	10,905,635,000	0.3%
4	Florida	159,918,989,000	4.9%
12	Georgia	78,805,741,000	2.4%
40	Hawaii	15,929,566,000	0.5%
42	Idaho	11,699,292,000	0.4%
5	Illinois	137,446,107,000	4.2%
19	Indiana	53,625,320,000	1.6%
30	Iowa	32,741,280,000	1.0%
32	Kansas	27,300,292,000	0.8%
28	Kentucky	39,630,707,000	1.2%
23	Louisiana	47,216,752,000	1.4%
41	Maine	12,760,354,000	0.4%
15	Maryland	63,622,217,000	2.0%
11	Massachusetts	82,164,376,000	2.5%
9	Michigan	89,217,627,000	2.7%
16	Minnesota	59,993,853,000	1.8%
31	Mississippi	27,841,610,000	0.9%
22	Missouri	50,587,347,000	1.6%
46	Montana	9,687,716,000	0.3%
37	Nebraska	20,900,603,000	0.6%
35	Nevada	22,247,082,000	0.7%
44	New Hampshire	11,461,915,000	0.4%
8	New Jersey	105,424,502,000	3.2%
36	New Mexico	21,710,145,000	0.7%
2	New York	308,860,808,000	9.5%
10	North Carolina	83,435,442,000	2.6%
47	North Dakota	9,107,358,000	0.3%
7	Ohio	117,213,881,000	3.6%
29	Oklahoma	33,210,365,000	1.0%
25	Oregon	42,974,229,000	1.3%
6	Pennsylvania	131,870,456,000	4.0%
43	Rhode Island	11,570,934,000	0.4%
24	South Carolina	43,891,697,000	1.3%
50	South Dakota	7,261,303,000	0.2%
18	Tennessee	56,125,069,000	1.7%
3	Texas	231,603,961,000	7.1%
33	Utah	25,202,134,000	0.8%
49	Vermont	7,441,876,000	0.2%
14	Virginia	75,615,115,000	2.3%
13	Washington	77,626,574,000	2.4%
39	West Virginia	16,757,409,000	0.5%
17	Wisconsin	57,429,497,000	1.8%
48	Wyoming	8,793,881,000	0.3%

RANK ORDER

RANK	STATE	EXPENDITURES	% of USA
1	California	$473,515,694,000	14.5%
2	New York	308,860,808,000	9.5%
3	Texas	231,603,961,000	7.1%
4	Florida	159,918,989,000	4.9%
5	Illinois	137,446,107,000	4.2%
6	Pennsylvania	131,870,456,000	4.0%
7	Ohio	117,213,881,000	3.6%
8	New Jersey	105,424,502,000	3.2%
9	Michigan	89,217,627,000	2.7%
10	North Carolina	83,435,442,000	2.6%
11	Massachusetts	82,164,376,000	2.5%
12	Georgia	78,805,741,000	2.4%
13	Washington	77,626,574,000	2.4%
14	Virginia	75,615,115,000	2.3%
15	Maryland	63,622,217,000	2.0%
16	Minnesota	59,993,853,000	1.8%
17	Wisconsin	57,429,497,000	1.8%
18	Tennessee	56,125,069,000	1.7%
19	Indiana	53,625,320,000	1.6%
20	Colorado	53,459,785,000	1.6%
21	Arizona	52,969,802,000	1.6%
22	Missouri	50,587,347,000	1.6%
23	Louisiana	47,216,752,000	1.4%
24	South Carolina	43,891,697,000	1.3%
25	Oregon	42,974,229,000	1.3%
26	Alabama	42,869,408,000	1.3%
27	Connecticut	42,673,529,000	1.3%
28	Kentucky	39,630,707,000	1.2%
29	Oklahoma	33,210,365,000	1.0%
30	Iowa	32,741,280,000	1.0%
31	Mississippi	27,841,610,000	0.9%
32	Kansas	27,300,292,000	0.8%
33	Utah	25,202,134,000	0.8%
34	Arkansas	25,137,369,000	0.8%
35	Nevada	22,247,082,000	0.7%
36	New Mexico	21,710,145,000	0.7%
37	Nebraska	20,900,603,000	0.6%
38	Alaska	16,773,713,000	0.5%
39	West Virginia	16,757,409,000	0.5%
40	Hawaii	15,929,566,000	0.5%
41	Maine	12,760,354,000	0.4%
42	Idaho	11,699,292,000	0.4%
43	Rhode Island	11,570,934,000	0.4%
44	New Hampshire	11,461,915,000	0.4%
45	Delaware	10,905,635,000	0.3%
46	Montana	9,687,716,000	0.3%
47	North Dakota	9,107,358,000	0.3%
48	Wyoming	8,793,881,000	0.3%
49	Vermont	7,441,876,000	0.2%
50	South Dakota	7,261,303,000	0.2%
	District of Columbia	15,349,269,000	0.5%

Source: U.S. Bureau of the Census, Governments Division
"2014 State and Local Government Finances" (http://www.census.gov/govs/local/)
*Total expenditures includes all money paid other than for retirement of debt and extension of loans. Includes payments from all sources of funds including current revenues and proceeds from borrowing and prior year fund balances. Includes intergovernmental transfers and expenditures for government owned utilities and other commercial or auxiliary enterprise, and insurance trust expenditures.

Per Capita State and Local Government Total Expenditures in 2014

National Per Capita = $10,238*

ALPHA ORDER

RANK	STATE	PER CAPITA
35	Alabama	$8,851
1	Alaska	22,769
47	Arizona	7,882
42	Arkansas	8,473
5	California	12,242
24	Colorado	9,993
7	Connecticut	11,881
10	Delaware	11,664
46	Florida	8,041
49	Georgia	7,812
11	Hawaii	11,247
50	Idaho	7,162
17	Illinois	10,682
45	Indiana	8,131
19	Iowa	10,534
28	Kansas	9,416
34	Kentucky	8,980
22	Louisiana	10,159
26	Maine	9,589
18	Maryland	10,662
6	Massachusetts	12,173
33	Michigan	8,998
14	Minnesota	11,002
29	Mississippi	9,304
44	Missouri	8,346
27	Montana	9,471
12	Nebraska	11,111
48	Nevada	7,853
36	New Hampshire	8,626
9	New Jersey	11,812
20	New Mexico	10,422
2	New York	15,663
43	North Carolina	8,399
4	North Dakota	12,309
23	Ohio	10,110
40	Oklahoma	8,565
16	Oregon	10,829
21	Pennsylvania	10,310
15	Rhode Island	10,973
31	South Carolina	9,090
41	South Dakota	8,517
38	Tennessee	8,576
37	Texas	8,596
39	Utah	8,567
8	Vermont	11,869
30	Virginia	9,091
13	Washington	11,004
32	West Virginia	9,065
25	Wisconsin	9,973
3	Wyoming	15,067

RANK ORDER

RANK	STATE	PER CAPITA
1	Alaska	$22,769
2	New York	15,663
3	Wyoming	15,067
4	North Dakota	12,309
5	California	12,242
6	Massachusetts	12,173
7	Connecticut	11,881
8	Vermont	11,869
9	New Jersey	11,812
10	Delaware	11,664
11	Hawaii	11,247
12	Nebraska	11,111
13	Washington	11,004
14	Minnesota	11,002
15	Rhode Island	10,973
16	Oregon	10,829
17	Illinois	10,682
18	Maryland	10,662
19	Iowa	10,534
20	New Mexico	10,422
21	Pennsylvania	10,310
22	Louisiana	10,159
23	Ohio	10,110
24	Colorado	9,993
25	Wisconsin	9,973
26	Maine	9,589
27	Montana	9,471
28	Kansas	9,416
29	Mississippi	9,304
30	Virginia	9,091
31	South Carolina	9,090
32	West Virginia	9,065
33	Michigan	8,998
34	Kentucky	8,980
35	Alabama	8,851
36	New Hampshire	8,626
37	Texas	8,596
38	Tennessee	8,576
39	Utah	8,567
40	Oklahoma	8,565
41	South Dakota	8,517
42	Arkansas	8,473
43	North Carolina	8,399
44	Missouri	8,346
45	Indiana	8,131
46	Florida	8,041
47	Arizona	7,882
48	Nevada	7,853
49	Georgia	7,812
50	Idaho	7,162

District of Columbia	23,292

Source: CQ Press using data from U.S. Bureau of the Census, Governments Division
"2014 State and Local Government Finances" (http://www.census.gov/govs/local/)
*Total expenditures includes all money paid other than for retirement of debt and extension of loans. Includes payments from all sources of funds including current revenues and proceeds from borrowing and prior year fund balances. Includes intergovernmental transfers and expenditures for government owned utilities and other commercial or auxiliary enterprise, and insurance trust expenditures.

State and Local Government Direct General Expenditures in 2014

National Total = $2,706,935,286,000*

ALPHA ORDER

RANK	STATE	EXPENDITURES	% of USA
25	Alabama	$36,170,448,000	1.3%
39	Alaska	14,587,029,000	0.5%
21	Arizona	42,844,737,000	1.6%
33	Arkansas	22,240,729,000	0.8%
1	California	371,051,142,000	13.7%
19	Colorado	43,527,450,000	1.6%
26	Connecticut	35,851,965,000	1.3%
45	Delaware	9,581,835,000	0.4%
4	Florida	138,466,880,000	5.1%
13	Georgia	65,498,531,000	2.4%
40	Hawaii	13,681,594,000	0.5%
42	Idaho	10,354,289,000	0.4%
6	Illinois	109,220,364,000	4.0%
18	Indiana	47,816,259,000	1.8%
29	Iowa	28,849,323,000	1.1%
32	Kansas	24,019,434,000	0.9%
28	Kentucky	33,418,364,000	1.2%
23	Louisiana	41,308,161,000	1.5%
41	Maine	11,544,830,000	0.4%
15	Maryland	55,581,241,000	2.1%
11	Massachusetts	67,713,490,000	2.5%
9	Michigan	76,011,922,000	2.8%
16	Minnesota	51,381,537,000	1.9%
31	Mississippi	24,183,924,000	0.9%
22	Missouri	42,803,239,000	1.6%
46	Montana	8,521,679,000	0.3%
37	Nebraska	15,683,151,000	0.6%
36	Nevada	18,464,365,000	0.7%
43	New Hampshire	10,099,685,000	0.4%
8	New Jersey	88,115,029,000	3.3%
35	New Mexico	18,749,197,000	0.7%
2	New York	245,641,610,000	9.1%
10	North Carolina	71,858,464,000	2.7%
47	North Dakota	8,177,818,000	0.3%
7	Ohio	95,743,714,000	3.5%
30	Oklahoma	28,552,574,000	1.1%
27	Oregon	35,054,570,000	1.3%
5	Pennsylvania	110,813,517,000	4.1%
44	Rhode Island	9,697,339,000	0.4%
24	South Carolina	37,017,220,000	1.4%
50	South Dakota	6,370,829,000	0.2%
20	Tennessee	43,379,825,000	1.6%
3	Texas	196,492,733,000	7.3%
34	Utah	20,958,980,000	0.8%
49	Vermont	6,732,917,000	0.2%
12	Virginia	67,311,845,000	2.5%
14	Washington	61,954,839,000	2.3%
38	West Virginia	14,795,176,000	0.5%
17	Wisconsin	49,402,895,000	1.8%
48	Wyoming	7,676,581,000	0.3%

RANK ORDER

RANK	STATE	EXPENDITURES	% of USA
1	California	$371,051,142,000	13.7%
2	New York	245,641,610,000	9.1%
3	Texas	196,492,733,000	7.3%
4	Florida	138,466,880,000	5.1%
5	Pennsylvania	110,813,517,000	4.1%
6	Illinois	109,220,364,000	4.0%
7	Ohio	95,743,714,000	3.5%
8	New Jersey	88,115,029,000	3.3%
9	Michigan	76,011,922,000	2.8%
10	North Carolina	71,858,464,000	2.7%
11	Massachusetts	67,713,490,000	2.5%
12	Virginia	67,311,845,000	2.5%
13	Georgia	65,498,531,000	2.4%
14	Washington	61,954,839,000	2.3%
15	Maryland	55,581,241,000	2.1%
16	Minnesota	51,381,537,000	1.9%
17	Wisconsin	49,402,895,000	1.8%
18	Indiana	47,816,259,000	1.8%
19	Colorado	43,527,450,000	1.6%
20	Tennessee	43,379,825,000	1.6%
21	Arizona	42,844,737,000	1.6%
22	Missouri	42,803,239,000	1.6%
23	Louisiana	41,308,161,000	1.5%
24	South Carolina	37,017,220,000	1.4%
25	Alabama	36,170,448,000	1.3%
26	Connecticut	35,851,965,000	1.3%
27	Oregon	35,054,570,000	1.3%
28	Kentucky	33,418,364,000	1.2%
29	Iowa	28,849,323,000	1.1%
30	Oklahoma	28,552,574,000	1.1%
31	Mississippi	24,183,924,000	0.9%
32	Kansas	24,019,434,000	0.9%
33	Arkansas	22,240,729,000	0.8%
34	Utah	20,958,980,000	0.8%
35	New Mexico	18,749,197,000	0.7%
36	Nevada	18,464,365,000	0.7%
37	Nebraska	15,683,151,000	0.6%
38	West Virginia	14,795,176,000	0.5%
39	Alaska	14,587,029,000	0.5%
40	Hawaii	13,681,594,000	0.5%
41	Maine	11,544,830,000	0.4%
42	Idaho	10,354,289,000	0.4%
43	New Hampshire	10,099,685,000	0.4%
44	Rhode Island	9,697,339,000	0.4%
45	Delaware	9,581,835,000	0.4%
46	Montana	8,521,679,000	0.3%
47	North Dakota	8,177,818,000	0.3%
48	Wyoming	7,676,581,000	0.3%
49	Vermont	6,732,917,000	0.2%
50	South Dakota	6,370,829,000	0.2%
	District of Columbia	11,960,017,000	0.4%

Source: U.S. Bureau of the Census, Governments Division
    "2014 State and Local Government Finances" (http://www.census.gov/govs/local/)
*Direct general expenditures include expenditures for current operations, assistance and subsidies, interest on debt, and capital outlay. Excludes intergovernmental transfers, expenditures for government owned utilities and other commercial or auxiliary enterprise, and insurance trust expenditures.

Per Capita State and Local Government Direct General Expenditures in 2014

National Per Capita = $8,497*

ALPHA ORDER

RANK	STATE	PER CAPITA
38	Alabama	$7,468
1	Alaska	19,800
49	Arizona	6,376
36	Arkansas	7,496
11	California	9,593
28	Colorado	8,137
8	Connecticut	9,981
6	Delaware	10,249
45	Florida	6,962
48	Georgia	6,493
10	Hawaii	9,660
50	Idaho	6,339
23	Illinois	8,488
41	Indiana	7,250
14	Iowa	9,282
26	Kansas	8,284
35	Kentucky	7,573
17	Louisiana	8,888
20	Maine	8,676
13	Maryland	9,314
7	Massachusetts	10,032
33	Michigan	7,666
12	Minnesota	9,422
30	Mississippi	8,082
44	Missouri	7,062
25	Montana	8,331
24	Nebraska	8,337
47	Nevada	6,518
34	New Hampshire	7,601
9	New Jersey	9,873
16	New Mexico	9,001
3	New York	12,457
42	North Carolina	7,233
4	North Dakota	11,053
27	Ohio	8,258
39	Oklahoma	7,364
18	Oregon	8,833
21	Pennsylvania	8,664
15	Rhode Island	9,196
32	South Carolina	7,667
37	South Dakota	7,473
46	Tennessee	6,628
40	Texas	7,292
43	Utah	7,124
5	Vermont	10,739
29	Virginia	8,093
19	Washington	8,783
31	West Virginia	8,004
22	Wisconsin	8,579
2	Wyoming	13,153

RANK ORDER

RANK	STATE	PER CAPITA
1	Alaska	$19,800
2	Wyoming	13,153
3	New York	12,457
4	North Dakota	11,053
5	Vermont	10,739
6	Delaware	10,249
7	Massachusetts	10,032
8	Connecticut	9,981
9	New Jersey	9,873
10	Hawaii	9,660
11	California	9,593
12	Minnesota	9,422
13	Maryland	9,314
14	Iowa	9,282
15	Rhode Island	9,196
16	New Mexico	9,001
17	Louisiana	8,888
18	Oregon	8,833
19	Washington	8,783
20	Maine	8,676
21	Pennsylvania	8,664
22	Wisconsin	8,579
23	Illinois	8,488
24	Nebraska	8,337
25	Montana	8,331
26	Kansas	8,284
27	Ohio	8,258
28	Colorado	8,137
29	Virginia	8,093
30	Mississippi	8,082
31	West Virginia	8,004
32	South Carolina	7,667
33	Michigan	7,666
34	New Hampshire	7,601
35	Kentucky	7,573
36	Arkansas	7,496
37	South Dakota	7,473
38	Alabama	7,468
39	Oklahoma	7,364
40	Texas	7,292
41	Indiana	7,250
42	North Carolina	7,233
43	Utah	7,124
44	Missouri	7,062
45	Florida	6,962
46	Tennessee	6,628
47	Nevada	6,518
48	Georgia	6,493
49	Arizona	6,376
50	Idaho	6,339

District of Columbia	18,149

Source: CQ Press using data from U.S. Bureau of the Census, Governments Division
"2014 State and Local Government Finances" (http://www.census.gov/govs/local/)
*Direct general expenditures include expenditures for current operations, assistance and subsidies, interest on debt, and capital outlay. Excludes intergovernmental transfers, expenditures for government owned utilities and other commercial or auxiliary enterprise, and insurance trust expenditures.

State and Local Government Debt Outstanding in 2014

National Total = $2,974,441,429,000*

ALPHA ORDER

RANK	STATE	DEBT	% of USA
28	Alabama	$31,076,160,000	1.0%
42	Alaska	9,051,396,000	0.3%
19	Arizona	48,736,629,000	1.6%
34	Arkansas	15,996,580,000	0.5%
1	California	425,877,580,000	14.3%
14	Colorado	54,071,718,000	1.8%
21	Connecticut	44,623,483,000	1.5%
44	Delaware	7,870,074,000	0.3%
4	Florida	155,141,747,000	5.2%
13	Georgia	56,865,443,000	1.9%
37	Hawaii	14,296,400,000	0.5%
45	Idaho	6,230,001,000	0.2%
5	Illinois	149,255,626,000	5.0%
17	Indiana	49,082,458,000	1.7%
32	Iowa	18,831,965,000	0.6%
30	Kansas	25,948,008,000	0.9%
24	Kentucky	40,200,564,000	1.4%
25	Louisiana	39,908,315,000	1.3%
43	Maine	8,448,135,000	0.3%
16	Maryland	49,971,623,000	1.7%
8	Massachusetts	91,397,851,000	3.1%
11	Michigan	76,671,294,000	2.6%
18	Minnesota	48,996,269,000	1.6%
38	Mississippi	14,243,954,000	0.5%
20	Missouri	46,433,292,000	1.6%
47	Montana	5,348,998,000	0.2%
36	Nebraska	15,123,936,000	0.5%
29	Nevada	26,213,861,000	0.9%
41	New Hampshire	10,727,405,000	0.4%
7	New Jersey	99,305,627,000	3.3%
35	New Mexico	15,706,476,000	0.5%
2	New York	344,923,293,000	11.6%
15	North Carolina	50,072,160,000	1.7%
48	North Dakota	5,289,221,000	0.2%
9	Ohio	85,865,285,000	2.9%
33	Oklahoma	18,646,070,000	0.6%
26	Oregon	35,739,451,000	1.2%
6	Pennsylvania	127,847,142,000	4.3%
39	Rhode Island	12,065,412,000	0.4%
23	South Carolina	42,914,604,000	1.4%
46	South Dakota	5,692,867,000	0.2%
27	Tennessee	34,770,742,000	1.2%
3	Texas	268,792,946,000	9.0%
31	Utah	20,274,150,000	0.7%
49	Vermont	4,559,103,000	0.2%
12	Virginia	65,490,932,000	2.2%
10	Washington	80,188,901,000	2.7%
40	West Virginia	11,488,588,000	0.4%
22	Wisconsin	43,102,641,000	1.4%
50	Wyoming	1,977,818,000	0.1%

RANK ORDER

RANK	STATE	DEBT	% of USA
1	California	$425,877,580,000	14.3%
2	New York	344,923,293,000	11.6%
3	Texas	268,792,946,000	9.0%
4	Florida	155,141,747,000	5.2%
5	Illinois	149,255,626,000	5.0%
6	Pennsylvania	127,847,142,000	4.3%
7	New Jersey	99,305,627,000	3.3%
8	Massachusetts	91,397,851,000	3.1%
9	Ohio	85,865,285,000	2.9%
10	Washington	80,188,901,000	2.7%
11	Michigan	76,671,294,000	2.6%
12	Virginia	65,490,932,000	2.2%
13	Georgia	56,865,443,000	1.9%
14	Colorado	54,071,718,000	1.8%
15	North Carolina	50,072,160,000	1.7%
16	Maryland	49,971,623,000	1.7%
17	Indiana	49,082,458,000	1.7%
18	Minnesota	48,996,269,000	1.6%
19	Arizona	48,736,629,000	1.6%
20	Missouri	46,433,292,000	1.6%
21	Connecticut	44,623,483,000	1.5%
22	Wisconsin	43,102,641,000	1.4%
23	South Carolina	42,914,604,000	1.4%
24	Kentucky	40,200,564,000	1.4%
25	Louisiana	39,908,315,000	1.3%
26	Oregon	35,739,451,000	1.2%
27	Tennessee	34,770,742,000	1.2%
28	Alabama	31,076,160,000	1.0%
29	Nevada	26,213,861,000	0.9%
30	Kansas	25,948,008,000	0.9%
31	Utah	20,274,150,000	0.7%
32	Iowa	18,831,965,000	0.6%
33	Oklahoma	18,646,070,000	0.6%
34	Arkansas	15,996,580,000	0.5%
35	New Mexico	15,706,476,000	0.5%
36	Nebraska	15,123,936,000	0.5%
37	Hawaii	14,296,400,000	0.5%
38	Mississippi	14,243,954,000	0.5%
39	Rhode Island	12,065,412,000	0.4%
40	West Virginia	11,488,588,000	0.4%
41	New Hampshire	10,727,405,000	0.4%
42	Alaska	9,051,396,000	0.3%
43	Maine	8,448,135,000	0.3%
44	Delaware	7,870,074,000	0.3%
45	Idaho	6,230,001,000	0.2%
46	South Dakota	5,692,867,000	0.2%
47	Montana	5,348,998,000	0.2%
48	North Dakota	5,289,221,000	0.2%
49	Vermont	4,559,103,000	0.2%
50	Wyoming	1,977,818,000	0.1%
	District of Columbia	13,087,235,000	0.4%

Source: U.S. Bureau of the Census, Governments Division
"2014 State and Local Government Finances" (http://www.census.gov/govs/local/)
*Includes short-term, long-term, full faith and credit, nonguaranteed, and public debt for private purposes.

Per Capita State and Local Government Debt Outstanding in 2014

National Per Capita = $9,337*

ALPHA ORDER

RANK	STATE	PER CAPITA
38	Alabama	$6,416
4	Alaska	12,286
34	Arizona	7,252
43	Arkansas	5,392
9	California	11,010
10	Colorado	10,108
3	Connecticut	12,423
21	Delaware	8,418
26	Florida	7,800
42	Georgia	5,637
11	Hawaii	10,094
49	Idaho	3,814
5	Illinois	11,599
31	Indiana	7,442
41	Iowa	6,059
18	Kansas	8,950
15	Kentucky	9,109
20	Louisiana	8,586
39	Maine	6,349
22	Maryland	8,374
2	Massachusetts	13,541
27	Michigan	7,732
17	Minnesota	8,985
48	Mississippi	4,760
28	Missouri	7,661
45	Montana	5,229
24	Nebraska	8,040
14	Nevada	9,253
23	New Hampshire	8,073
8	New Jersey	11,127
29	New Mexico	7,540
1	New York	17,492
46	North Carolina	5,040
35	North Dakota	7,149
32	Ohio	7,406
47	Oklahoma	4,809
16	Oregon	9,006
12	Pennsylvania	9,995
6	Rhode Island	11,442
19	South Carolina	8,888
37	South Dakota	6,677
44	Tennessee	5,313
13	Texas	9,976
36	Utah	6,892
33	Vermont	7,271
25	Virginia	7,874
7	Washington	11,368
40	West Virginia	6,215
30	Wisconsin	7,485
50	Wyoming	3,389

RANK ORDER

RANK	STATE	PER CAPITA
1	New York	$17,492
2	Massachusetts	13,541
3	Connecticut	12,423
4	Alaska	12,286
5	Illinois	11,599
6	Rhode Island	11,442
7	Washington	11,368
8	New Jersey	11,127
9	California	11,010
10	Colorado	10,108
11	Hawaii	10,094
12	Pennsylvania	9,995
13	Texas	9,976
14	Nevada	9,253
15	Kentucky	9,109
16	Oregon	9,006
17	Minnesota	8,985
18	Kansas	8,950
19	South Carolina	8,888
20	Louisiana	8,586
21	Delaware	8,418
22	Maryland	8,374
23	New Hampshire	8,073
24	Nebraska	8,040
25	Virginia	7,874
26	Florida	7,800
27	Michigan	7,732
28	Missouri	7,661
29	New Mexico	7,540
30	Wisconsin	7,485
31	Indiana	7,442
32	Ohio	7,406
33	Vermont	7,271
34	Arizona	7,252
35	North Dakota	7,149
36	Utah	6,892
37	South Dakota	6,677
38	Alabama	6,416
39	Maine	6,349
40	West Virginia	6,215
41	Iowa	6,059
42	Georgia	5,637
43	Arkansas	5,392
44	Tennessee	5,313
45	Montana	5,229
46	North Carolina	5,040
47	Oklahoma	4,809
48	Mississippi	4,760
49	Idaho	3,814
50	Wyoming	3,389
	District of Columbia	19,859

Source: CQ Press using data from U.S. Bureau of the Census, Governments Division
"2014 State and Local Government Finances" (http://www.census.gov/govs/local/)
*Includes short-term, long-term, full faith and credit, nonguaranteed, and public debt for private purposes.

State and Local Government Full-Time Equivalent Employees in 2015

National Total = 16,279,298 FTE Employees*

ALPHA ORDER

RANK	STATE	EMPLOYEES	% of USA
23	Alabama	282,274	1.7%
44	Alaska	53,897	0.3%
20	Arizona	285,532	1.8%
33	Arkansas	170,067	1.0%
1	California	1,775,061	10.9%
22	Colorado	282,690	1.7%
30	Connecticut	191,937	1.2%
46	Delaware	49,433	0.3%
4	Florida	876,388	5.4%
9	Georgia	506,306	3.1%
40	Hawaii	75,085	0.5%
39	Idaho	80,319	0.5%
5	Illinois	627,906	3.9%
16	Indiana	321,097	2.0%
32	Iowa	182,325	1.1%
28	Kansas	195,021	1.2%
26	Kentucky	243,219	1.5%
25	Louisiana	259,287	1.6%
42	Maine	70,346	0.4%
18	Maryland	303,422	1.9%
14	Massachusetts	337,809	2.1%
12	Michigan	436,699	2.7%
21	Minnesota	285,000	1.8%
31	Mississippi	190,861	1.2%
17	Missouri	316,803	1.9%
43	Montana	58,130	0.4%
36	Nebraska	118,405	0.7%
37	Nevada	108,112	0.7%
41	New Hampshire	71,216	0.4%
10	New Jersey	477,647	2.9%
35	New Mexico	125,206	0.8%
3	New York	1,173,582	7.2%
8	North Carolina	540,654	3.3%
48	North Dakota	47,432	0.3%
6	Ohio	584,108	3.6%
27	Oklahoma	217,629	1.3%
29	Oregon	192,235	1.2%
7	Pennsylvania	567,668	3.5%
47	Rhode Island	48,054	0.3%
24	South Carolina	261,929	1.6%
49	South Dakota	46,638	0.3%
15	Tennessee	324,357	2.0%
2	Texas	1,458,259	9.0%
34	Utah	142,465	0.9%
50	Vermont	40,502	0.2%
11	Virginia	446,165	2.7%
13	Washington	343,164	2.1%
38	West Virginia	102,541	0.6%
19	Wisconsin	286,345	1.8%
45	Wyoming	50,688	0.3%

RANK ORDER

RANK	STATE	EMPLOYEES	% of USA
1	California	1,775,061	10.9%
2	Texas	1,458,259	9.0%
3	New York	1,173,582	7.2%
4	Florida	876,388	5.4%
5	Illinois	627,906	3.9%
6	Ohio	584,108	3.6%
7	Pennsylvania	567,668	3.5%
8	North Carolina	540,654	3.3%
9	Georgia	506,306	3.1%
10	New Jersey	477,647	2.9%
11	Virginia	446,165	2.7%
12	Michigan	436,699	2.7%
13	Washington	343,164	2.1%
14	Massachusetts	337,809	2.1%
15	Tennessee	324,357	2.0%
16	Indiana	321,097	2.0%
17	Missouri	316,803	1.9%
18	Maryland	303,422	1.9%
19	Wisconsin	286,345	1.8%
20	Arizona	285,532	1.8%
21	Minnesota	285,000	1.8%
22	Colorado	282,690	1.7%
23	Alabama	282,274	1.7%
24	South Carolina	261,929	1.6%
25	Louisiana	259,287	1.6%
26	Kentucky	243,219	1.5%
27	Oklahoma	217,629	1.3%
28	Kansas	195,021	1.2%
29	Oregon	192,235	1.2%
30	Connecticut	191,937	1.2%
31	Mississippi	190,861	1.2%
32	Iowa	182,325	1.1%
33	Arkansas	170,067	1.0%
34	Utah	142,465	0.9%
35	New Mexico	125,206	0.8%
36	Nebraska	118,405	0.7%
37	Nevada	108,112	0.7%
38	West Virginia	102,541	0.6%
39	Idaho	80,319	0.5%
40	Hawaii	75,085	0.5%
41	New Hampshire	71,216	0.4%
42	Maine	70,346	0.4%
43	Montana	58,130	0.4%
44	Alaska	53,897	0.3%
45	Wyoming	50,688	0.3%
46	Delaware	49,433	0.3%
47	Rhode Island	48,054	0.3%
48	North Dakota	47,432	0.3%
49	South Dakota	46,638	0.3%
50	Vermont	40,502	0.2%
	District of Columbia	47,383	0.3%

Source: U.S. Bureau of the Census, Governments Division
   "Government Employment and Payroll" (http://www.census.gov/govs/apes/index.html)
*Full-time equivalent as of March 2015.

Rate of State and Local Government Full-Time Equivalent Employees in 2015

National Rate = 507 FTE Employees per 10,000 Population*

ALPHA ORDER

RANK	STATE	RATE
11	Alabama	582
2	Alaska	731
49	Arizona	419
12	Arkansas	571
44	California	455
31	Colorado	519
20	Connecticut	535
28	Delaware	524
48	Florida	433
35	Georgia	496
27	Hawaii	527
39	Idaho	486
38	Illinois	489
39	Indiana	486
10	Iowa	584
3	Kansas	671
17	Kentucky	550
16	Louisiana	555
26	Maine	529
32	Maryland	506
34	Massachusetts	498
47	Michigan	440
30	Minnesota	520
5	Mississippi	638
29	Missouri	521
13	Montana	563
7	Nebraska	625
50	Nevada	375
20	New Hampshire	535
20	New Jersey	535
8	New Mexico	602
9	New York	594
19	North Carolina	539
6	North Dakota	627
33	Ohio	503
14	Oklahoma	557
42	Oregon	478
46	Pennsylvania	444
44	Rhode Island	455
20	South Carolina	535
18	South Dakota	544
37	Tennessee	492
25	Texas	532
43	Utah	476
4	Vermont	647
24	Virginia	533
41	Washington	479
14	West Virginia	557
35	Wisconsin	496
1	Wyoming	864

RANK ORDER

RANK	STATE	RATE
1	Wyoming	864
2	Alaska	731
3	Kansas	671
4	Vermont	647
5	Mississippi	638
6	North Dakota	627
7	Nebraska	625
8	New Mexico	602
9	New York	594
10	Iowa	584
11	Alabama	582
12	Arkansas	571
13	Montana	563
14	Oklahoma	557
14	West Virginia	557
16	Louisiana	555
17	Kentucky	550
18	South Dakota	544
19	North Carolina	539
20	Connecticut	535
20	New Hampshire	535
20	New Jersey	535
20	South Carolina	535
24	Virginia	533
25	Texas	532
26	Maine	529
27	Hawaii	527
28	Delaware	524
29	Missouri	521
30	Minnesota	520
31	Colorado	519
32	Maryland	506
33	Ohio	503
34	Massachusetts	498
35	Georgia	496
35	Wisconsin	496
37	Tennessee	492
38	Illinois	489
39	Idaho	486
39	Indiana	486
41	Washington	479
42	Oregon	478
43	Utah	476
44	California	455
44	Rhode Island	455
46	Pennsylvania	444
47	Michigan	440
48	Florida	433
49	Arizona	419
50	Nevada	375

District of Columbia 707

Source: CQ Press using data from U.S. Bureau of the Census, Governments Division
"Government Employment and Payroll" (http://www.census.gov/govs/apes/index.html)
*Full-time equivalent as of March 2015.

Average Annual Earnings of Full-Time State and Local Government Employees in 2015
National Average = $57,356*

ALPHA ORDER

RANK	STATE	SALARY
40	Alabama	$45,831
6	Alaska	66,333
25	Arizona	53,357
49	Arkansas	41,503
1	California	77,285
16	Colorado	58,065
5	Connecticut	67,796
19	Delaware	56,964
30	Florida	50,191
44	Georgia	44,751
18	Hawaii	57,041
38	Idaho	46,629
11	Illinois	63,321
36	Indiana	47,362
17	Iowa	57,649
37	Kansas	46,744
46	Kentucky	44,474
41	Louisiana	45,306
35	Maine	47,450
10	Maryland	64,123
8	Massachusetts	64,620
14	Michigan	59,787
12	Minnesota	61,093
50	Mississippi	40,296
45	Missouri	44,479
33	Montana	48,468
29	Nebraska	52,181
9	Nevada	64,248
22	New Hampshire	54,145
2	New Jersey	72,957
34	New Mexico	48,239
3	New York	71,331
32	North Carolina	49,468
27	North Dakota	52,674
23	Ohio	53,962
47	Oklahoma	42,882
13	Oregon	59,790
15	Pennsylvania	58,496
7	Rhode Island	66,020
39	South Carolina	46,061
43	South Dakota	44,918
42	Tennessee	44,944
31	Texas	49,576
28	Utah	52,589
24	Vermont	53,383
26	Virginia	52,825
4	Washington	68,802
48	West Virginia	42,588
20	Wisconsin	56,379
21	Wyoming	55,289

RANK ORDER

RANK	STATE	SALARY
1	California	$77,285
2	New Jersey	72,957
3	New York	71,331
4	Washington	68,802
5	Connecticut	67,796
6	Alaska	66,333
7	Rhode Island	66,020
8	Massachusetts	64,620
9	Nevada	64,248
10	Maryland	64,123
11	Illinois	63,321
12	Minnesota	61,093
13	Oregon	59,790
14	Michigan	59,787
15	Pennsylvania	58,496
16	Colorado	58,065
17	Iowa	57,649
18	Hawaii	57,041
19	Delaware	56,964
20	Wisconsin	56,379
21	Wyoming	55,289
22	New Hampshire	54,145
23	Ohio	53,962
24	Vermont	53,383
25	Arizona	53,357
26	Virginia	52,825
27	North Dakota	52,674
28	Utah	52,589
29	Nebraska	52,181
30	Florida	50,191
31	Texas	49,576
32	North Carolina	49,468
33	Montana	48,468
34	New Mexico	48,239
35	Maine	47,450
36	Indiana	47,362
37	Kansas	46,744
38	Idaho	46,629
39	South Carolina	46,061
40	Alabama	45,831
41	Louisiana	45,306
42	Tennessee	44,944
43	South Dakota	44,918
44	Georgia	44,751
45	Missouri	44,479
46	Kentucky	44,474
47	Oklahoma	42,882
48	West Virginia	42,588
49	Arkansas	41,503
50	Mississippi	40,296

District of Columbia 82,067

Source: CQ Press using data from U.S. Bureau of the Census, Governments Division
"Government Employment and Payroll" (http://www.census.gov/govs/apes/index.html)
*March 2015 full-time payroll (multiplied by 12) divided by full-time employees.

State Government Total Revenue in 2014

National Total = $2,361,473,724,000*

<table>
<tr><td colspan="4">ALPHA ORDER</td><td colspan="4">RANK ORDER</td></tr>
<tr><th>RANK</th><th>STATE</th><th>REVENUE</th><th>% of USA</th><th>RANK</th><th>STATE</th><th>REVENUE</th><th>% of USA</th></tr>
<tr><td>29</td><td>Alabama</td><td>$28,280,058,000</td><td>1.2%</td><td>1</td><td>California</td><td>$353,368,448,000</td><td>15.0%</td></tr>
<tr><td>39</td><td>Alaska</td><td>12,871,274,000</td><td>0.5%</td><td>2</td><td>New York</td><td>205,805,610,000</td><td>8.7%</td></tr>
<tr><td>19</td><td>Arizona</td><td>39,393,637,000</td><td>1.7%</td><td>3</td><td>Texas</td><td>160,029,654,000</td><td>6.8%</td></tr>
<tr><td>31</td><td>Arkansas</td><td>23,448,309,000</td><td>1.0%</td><td>4</td><td>Florida</td><td>104,127,723,000</td><td>4.4%</td></tr>
<tr><td>1</td><td>California</td><td>353,368,448,000</td><td>15.0%</td><td>5</td><td>Ohio</td><td>96,424,844,000</td><td>4.1%</td></tr>
<tr><td>22</td><td>Colorado</td><td>34,387,619,000</td><td>1.5%</td><td>6</td><td>Illinois</td><td>91,273,714,000</td><td>3.9%</td></tr>
<tr><td>26</td><td>Connecticut</td><td>31,300,691,000</td><td>1.3%</td><td>7</td><td>Pennsylvania</td><td>89,542,347,000</td><td>3.8%</td></tr>
<tr><td>44</td><td>Delaware</td><td>9,298,130,000</td><td>0.4%</td><td>8</td><td>Michigan</td><td>69,430,950,000</td><td>2.9%</td></tr>
<tr><td>4</td><td>Florida</td><td>104,127,723,000</td><td>4.4%</td><td>9</td><td>New Jersey</td><td>65,657,635,000</td><td>2.8%</td></tr>
<tr><td>13</td><td>Georgia</td><td>54,207,370,000</td><td>2.3%</td><td>10</td><td>North Carolina</td><td>61,823,209,000</td><td>2.6%</td></tr>
<tr><td>38</td><td>Hawaii</td><td>15,055,561,000</td><td>0.6%</td><td>11</td><td>Massachusetts</td><td>61,749,738,000</td><td>2.6%</td></tr>
<tr><td>42</td><td>Idaho</td><td>10,508,580,000</td><td>0.4%</td><td>12</td><td>Washington</td><td>55,071,735,000</td><td>2.3%</td></tr>
<tr><td>6</td><td>Illinois</td><td>91,273,714,000</td><td>3.9%</td><td>13</td><td>Georgia</td><td>54,207,370,000</td><td>2.3%</td></tr>
<tr><td>18</td><td>Indiana</td><td>39,529,468,000</td><td>1.7%</td><td>14</td><td>Virginia</td><td>53,731,192,000</td><td>2.3%</td></tr>
<tr><td>30</td><td>Iowa</td><td>25,196,625,000</td><td>1.1%</td><td>15</td><td>Minnesota</td><td>49,809,320,000</td><td>2.1%</td></tr>
<tr><td>36</td><td>Kansas</td><td>19,012,887,000</td><td>0.8%</td><td>16</td><td>Wisconsin</td><td>47,214,125,000</td><td>2.0%</td></tr>
<tr><td>25</td><td>Kentucky</td><td>31,507,525,000</td><td>1.3%</td><td>17</td><td>Maryland</td><td>44,699,507,000</td><td>1.9%</td></tr>
<tr><td>23</td><td>Louisiana</td><td>33,275,548,000</td><td>1.4%</td><td>18</td><td>Indiana</td><td>39,529,468,000</td><td>1.7%</td></tr>
<tr><td>41</td><td>Maine</td><td>10,528,889,000</td><td>0.4%</td><td>19</td><td>Arizona</td><td>39,393,637,000</td><td>1.7%</td></tr>
<tr><td>17</td><td>Maryland</td><td>44,699,507,000</td><td>1.9%</td><td>20</td><td>Missouri</td><td>38,507,982,000</td><td>1.6%</td></tr>
<tr><td>11</td><td>Massachusetts</td><td>61,749,738,000</td><td>2.6%</td><td>21</td><td>Oregon</td><td>37,665,178,000</td><td>1.6%</td></tr>
<tr><td>8</td><td>Michigan</td><td>69,430,950,000</td><td>2.9%</td><td>22</td><td>Colorado</td><td>34,387,619,000</td><td>1.5%</td></tr>
<tr><td>15</td><td>Minnesota</td><td>49,809,320,000</td><td>2.1%</td><td>23</td><td>Louisiana</td><td>33,275,548,000</td><td>1.4%</td></tr>
<tr><td>32</td><td>Mississippi</td><td>23,346,924,000</td><td>1.0%</td><td>24</td><td>South Carolina</td><td>31,870,556,000</td><td>1.3%</td></tr>
<tr><td>20</td><td>Missouri</td><td>38,507,982,000</td><td>1.6%</td><td>25</td><td>Kentucky</td><td>31,507,525,000</td><td>1.3%</td></tr>
<tr><td>46</td><td>Montana</td><td>8,946,019,000</td><td>0.4%</td><td>26</td><td>Connecticut</td><td>31,300,691,000</td><td>1.3%</td></tr>
<tr><td>40</td><td>Nebraska</td><td>12,122,749,000</td><td>0.5%</td><td>27</td><td>Tennessee</td><td>31,290,576,000</td><td>1.3%</td></tr>
<tr><td>35</td><td>Nevada</td><td>19,049,438,000</td><td>0.8%</td><td>28</td><td>Oklahoma</td><td>28,534,050,000</td><td>1.2%</td></tr>
<tr><td>47</td><td>New Hampshire</td><td>8,265,021,000</td><td>0.3%</td><td>29</td><td>Alabama</td><td>28,280,058,000</td><td>1.2%</td></tr>
<tr><td>9</td><td>New Jersey</td><td>65,657,635,000</td><td>2.8%</td><td>30</td><td>Iowa</td><td>25,196,625,000</td><td>1.1%</td></tr>
<tr><td>33</td><td>New Mexico</td><td>20,423,333,000</td><td>0.9%</td><td>31</td><td>Arkansas</td><td>23,448,309,000</td><td>1.0%</td></tr>
<tr><td>2</td><td>New York</td><td>205,805,610,000</td><td>8.7%</td><td>32</td><td>Mississippi</td><td>23,346,924,000</td><td>1.0%</td></tr>
<tr><td>10</td><td>North Carolina</td><td>61,823,209,000</td><td>2.6%</td><td>33</td><td>New Mexico</td><td>20,423,333,000</td><td>0.9%</td></tr>
<tr><td>43</td><td>North Dakota</td><td>9,966,662,000</td><td>0.4%</td><td>34</td><td>Utah</td><td>19,418,534,000</td><td>0.8%</td></tr>
<tr><td>5</td><td>Ohio</td><td>96,424,844,000</td><td>4.1%</td><td>35</td><td>Nevada</td><td>19,049,438,000</td><td>0.8%</td></tr>
<tr><td>28</td><td>Oklahoma</td><td>28,534,050,000</td><td>1.2%</td><td>36</td><td>Kansas</td><td>19,012,887,000</td><td>0.8%</td></tr>
<tr><td>21</td><td>Oregon</td><td>37,665,178,000</td><td>1.6%</td><td>37</td><td>West Virginia</td><td>15,388,267,000</td><td>0.7%</td></tr>
<tr><td>7</td><td>Pennsylvania</td><td>89,542,347,000</td><td>3.8%</td><td>38</td><td>Hawaii</td><td>15,055,561,000</td><td>0.6%</td></tr>
<tr><td>45</td><td>Rhode Island</td><td>8,995,798,000</td><td>0.4%</td><td>39</td><td>Alaska</td><td>12,871,274,000</td><td>0.5%</td></tr>
<tr><td>24</td><td>South Carolina</td><td>31,870,556,000</td><td>1.3%</td><td>40</td><td>Nebraska</td><td>12,122,749,000</td><td>0.5%</td></tr>
<tr><td>50</td><td>South Dakota</td><td>6,124,116,000</td><td>0.3%</td><td>41</td><td>Maine</td><td>10,528,889,000</td><td>0.4%</td></tr>
<tr><td>27</td><td>Tennessee</td><td>31,290,576,000</td><td>1.3%</td><td>42</td><td>Idaho</td><td>10,508,580,000</td><td>0.4%</td></tr>
<tr><td>3</td><td>Texas</td><td>160,029,654,000</td><td>6.8%</td><td>43</td><td>North Dakota</td><td>9,966,662,000</td><td>0.4%</td></tr>
<tr><td>34</td><td>Utah</td><td>19,418,534,000</td><td>0.8%</td><td>44</td><td>Delaware</td><td>9,298,130,000</td><td>0.4%</td></tr>
<tr><td>49</td><td>Vermont</td><td>6,545,351,000</td><td>0.3%</td><td>45</td><td>Rhode Island</td><td>8,995,798,000</td><td>0.4%</td></tr>
<tr><td>14</td><td>Virginia</td><td>53,731,192,000</td><td>2.3%</td><td>46</td><td>Montana</td><td>8,946,019,000</td><td>0.4%</td></tr>
<tr><td>12</td><td>Washington</td><td>55,071,735,000</td><td>2.3%</td><td>47</td><td>New Hampshire</td><td>8,265,021,000</td><td>0.3%</td></tr>
<tr><td>37</td><td>West Virginia</td><td>15,388,267,000</td><td>0.7%</td><td>48</td><td>Wyoming</td><td>7,451,248,000</td><td>0.3%</td></tr>
<tr><td>16</td><td>Wisconsin</td><td>47,214,125,000</td><td>2.0%</td><td>49</td><td>Vermont</td><td>6,545,351,000</td><td>0.3%</td></tr>
<tr><td>48</td><td>Wyoming</td><td>7,451,248,000</td><td>0.3%</td><td>50</td><td>South Dakota</td><td>6,124,116,000</td><td>0.3%</td></tr>
<tr><td></td><td></td><td></td><td></td><td colspan="2">District of Columbia**</td><td>NA</td><td>NA</td></tr>
</table>

Source: U.S. Bureau of the Census, Governments Division
  "2014 State and Local Government Finances" (http://www.census.gov/govs/local/)
*Total revenue includes all money received from external sources. This includes taxes, intergovernmental transfers and insurance trust revenue, and revenue from government owned utilities and other commercial or auxiliary enterprise.
**Not applicable.

Per Capita State Government Total Revenue in 2014

National Per Capita = $7,428*

ALPHA ORDER				RANK ORDER		
RANK	STATE	PER CAPITA		RANK	STATE	PER CAPITA
47	Alabama	$5,839		1	Alaska	$17,471
1	Alaska	17,471		2	North Dakota	13,470
46	Arizona	5,862		3	Wyoming	12,767
21	Arkansas	7,903		4	Hawaii	10,630
11	California	9,135		5	Vermont	10,439
40	Colorado	6,428		6	New York	10,437
14	Connecticut	8,714		7	Delaware	9,945
7	Delaware	9,945		8	New Mexico	9,805
49	Florida	5,236		9	Oregon	9,491
48	Georgia	5,374		10	Massachusetts	9,148
4	Hawaii	10,630		11	California	9,135
39	Idaho	6,433		12	Minnesota	9,134
30	Illinois	7,093		13	Montana	8,746
44	Indiana	5,994		14	Connecticut	8,714
19	Iowa	8,107		15	Rhode Island	8,531
36	Kansas	6,558		16	West Virginia	8,325
29	Kentucky	7,140		17	Ohio	8,316
28	Louisiana	7,159		18	Wisconsin	8,199
20	Maine	7,912		19	Iowa	8,107
24	Maryland	7,491		20	Maine	7,912
10	Massachusetts	9,148		21	Arkansas	7,903
31	Michigan	7,002		22	Washington	7,807
12	Minnesota	9,134		23	Mississippi	7,802
23	Mississippi	7,802		24	Maryland	7,491
41	Missouri	6,353		25	Oklahoma	7,359
13	Montana	8,746		26	New Jersey	7,357
38	Nebraska	6,444		27	South Dakota	7,183
33	Nevada	6,724		28	Louisiana	7,159
43	New Hampshire	6,220		29	Kentucky	7,140
26	New Jersey	7,357		30	Illinois	7,093
8	New Mexico	9,805		31	Michigan	7,002
6	New York	10,437		32	Pennsylvania	7,001
42	North Carolina	6,223		33	Nevada	6,724
2	North Dakota	13,470		34	South Carolina	6,601
17	Ohio	8,316		34	Utah	6,601
25	Oklahoma	7,359		36	Kansas	6,558
9	Oregon	9,491		37	Virginia	6,460
32	Pennsylvania	7,001		38	Nebraska	6,444
15	Rhode Island	8,531		39	Idaho	6,433
34	South Carolina	6,601		40	Colorado	6,428
27	South Dakota	7,183		41	Missouri	6,353
50	Tennessee	4,781		42	North Carolina	6,223
45	Texas	5,939		43	New Hampshire	6,220
34	Utah	6,601		44	Indiana	5,994
5	Vermont	10,439		45	Texas	5,939
37	Virginia	6,460		46	Arizona	5,862
22	Washington	7,807		47	Alabama	5,839
16	West Virginia	8,325		48	Georgia	5,374
18	Wisconsin	8,199		49	Florida	5,236
3	Wyoming	12,767		50	Tennessee	4,781
				District of Columbia**		NA

Source: CQ Press using data from U.S. Bureau of the Census, Governments Division
"2014 State and Local Government Finances" (http://www.census.gov/govs/local/)
*Total revenue includes all money received from external sources. This includes taxes, intergovernmental transfers and insurance trust revenue, and revenue from government owned utilities and other commercial or auxiliary enterprise.
**Not applicable.

State Government Intergovernmental Revenue in 2014

National Total = $550,560,842,000*

<table>
<tr><td colspan="4">ALPHA ORDER</td><td colspan="4">RANK ORDER</td></tr>
<tr><td>RANK</td><td>STATE</td><td>REVENUE</td><td>% of USA</td><td>RANK</td><td>STATE</td><td>REVENUE</td><td>% of USA</td></tr>
<tr><td>25</td><td>Alabama</td><td>$8,135,043,000</td><td>1.5%</td><td>1</td><td>California</td><td>$63,516,604,000</td><td>11.5%</td></tr>
<tr><td>41</td><td>Alaska</td><td>2,810,194,000</td><td>0.5%</td><td>2</td><td>New York</td><td>49,128,275,000</td><td>8.9%</td></tr>
<tr><td>16</td><td>Arizona</td><td>10,951,041,000</td><td>2.0%</td><td>3</td><td>Texas</td><td>40,561,370,000</td><td>7.4%</td></tr>
<tr><td>32</td><td>Arkansas</td><td>6,096,896,000</td><td>1.1%</td><td>4</td><td>Florida</td><td>25,801,529,000</td><td>4.7%</td></tr>
<tr><td>1</td><td>California</td><td>63,516,604,000</td><td>11.5%</td><td>5</td><td>Ohio</td><td>22,350,068,000</td><td>4.1%</td></tr>
<tr><td>29</td><td>Colorado</td><td>7,277,716,000</td><td>1.3%</td><td>6</td><td>Pennsylvania</td><td>21,868,995,000</td><td>4.0%</td></tr>
<tr><td>30</td><td>Connecticut</td><td>6,364,610,000</td><td>1.2%</td><td>7</td><td>Illinois</td><td>18,227,252,000</td><td>3.3%</td></tr>
<tr><td>46</td><td>Delaware</td><td>2,101,677,000</td><td>0.4%</td><td>8</td><td>Michigan</td><td>17,929,672,000</td><td>3.3%</td></tr>
<tr><td>4</td><td>Florida</td><td>25,801,529,000</td><td>4.7%</td><td>9</td><td>New Jersey</td><td>16,049,091,000</td><td>2.9%</td></tr>
<tr><td>11</td><td>Georgia</td><td>14,611,862,000</td><td>2.7%</td><td>10</td><td>North Carolina</td><td>15,643,257,000</td><td>2.8%</td></tr>
<tr><td>40</td><td>Hawaii</td><td>2,810,537,000</td><td>0.5%</td><td>11</td><td>Georgia</td><td>14,611,862,000</td><td>2.7%</td></tr>
<tr><td>42</td><td>Idaho</td><td>2,531,469,000</td><td>0.5%</td><td>12</td><td>Massachusetts</td><td>14,165,615,000</td><td>2.6%</td></tr>
<tr><td>7</td><td>Illinois</td><td>18,227,252,000</td><td>3.3%</td><td>13</td><td>Washington</td><td>11,474,963,000</td><td>2.1%</td></tr>
<tr><td>14</td><td>Indiana</td><td>11,055,684,000</td><td>2.0%</td><td>14</td><td>Indiana</td><td>11,055,684,000</td><td>2.0%</td></tr>
<tr><td>31</td><td>Iowa</td><td>6,218,631,000</td><td>1.1%</td><td>15</td><td>Maryland</td><td>11,038,357,000</td><td>2.0%</td></tr>
<tr><td>36</td><td>Kansas</td><td>3,975,772,000</td><td>0.7%</td><td>16</td><td>Arizona</td><td>10,951,041,000</td><td>2.0%</td></tr>
<tr><td>21</td><td>Kentucky</td><td>9,768,931,000</td><td>1.8%</td><td>17</td><td>Tennessee</td><td>10,645,251,000</td><td>1.9%</td></tr>
<tr><td>19</td><td>Louisiana</td><td>10,214,940,000</td><td>1.9%</td><td>18</td><td>Missouri</td><td>10,394,689,000</td><td>1.9%</td></tr>
<tr><td>38</td><td>Maine</td><td>3,028,373,000</td><td>0.6%</td><td>19</td><td>Louisiana</td><td>10,214,940,000</td><td>1.9%</td></tr>
<tr><td>15</td><td>Maryland</td><td>11,038,357,000</td><td>2.0%</td><td>20</td><td>Virginia</td><td>10,027,820,000</td><td>1.8%</td></tr>
<tr><td>12</td><td>Massachusetts</td><td>14,165,615,000</td><td>2.6%</td><td>21</td><td>Kentucky</td><td>9,768,931,000</td><td>1.8%</td></tr>
<tr><td>8</td><td>Michigan</td><td>17,929,672,000</td><td>3.3%</td><td>22</td><td>Wisconsin</td><td>9,255,939,000</td><td>1.7%</td></tr>
<tr><td>23</td><td>Minnesota</td><td>9,111,060,000</td><td>1.7%</td><td>23</td><td>Minnesota</td><td>9,111,060,000</td><td>1.7%</td></tr>
<tr><td>28</td><td>Mississippi</td><td>7,377,669,000</td><td>1.3%</td><td>24</td><td>Oregon</td><td>8,791,134,000</td><td>1.6%</td></tr>
<tr><td>18</td><td>Missouri</td><td>10,394,689,000</td><td>1.9%</td><td>25</td><td>Alabama</td><td>8,135,043,000</td><td>1.5%</td></tr>
<tr><td>44</td><td>Montana</td><td>2,341,686,000</td><td>0.4%</td><td>26</td><td>South Carolina</td><td>7,639,636,000</td><td>1.4%</td></tr>
<tr><td>37</td><td>Nebraska</td><td>3,094,850,000</td><td>0.6%</td><td>27</td><td>Oklahoma</td><td>7,409,652,000</td><td>1.3%</td></tr>
<tr><td>39</td><td>Nevada</td><td>3,021,228,000</td><td>0.5%</td><td>28</td><td>Mississippi</td><td>7,377,669,000</td><td>1.3%</td></tr>
<tr><td>48</td><td>New Hampshire</td><td>1,853,129,000</td><td>0.3%</td><td>29</td><td>Colorado</td><td>7,277,716,000</td><td>1.3%</td></tr>
<tr><td>9</td><td>New Jersey</td><td>16,049,091,000</td><td>2.9%</td><td>30</td><td>Connecticut</td><td>6,364,610,000</td><td>1.2%</td></tr>
<tr><td>33</td><td>New Mexico</td><td>5,558,490,000</td><td>1.0%</td><td>31</td><td>Iowa</td><td>6,218,631,000</td><td>1.1%</td></tr>
<tr><td>2</td><td>New York</td><td>49,128,275,000</td><td>8.9%</td><td>32</td><td>Arkansas</td><td>6,096,896,000</td><td>1.1%</td></tr>
<tr><td>10</td><td>North Carolina</td><td>15,643,257,000</td><td>2.8%</td><td>33</td><td>New Mexico</td><td>5,558,490,000</td><td>1.0%</td></tr>
<tr><td>50</td><td>North Dakota</td><td>1,534,035,000</td><td>0.3%</td><td>34</td><td>West Virginia</td><td>4,350,205,000</td><td>0.8%</td></tr>
<tr><td>5</td><td>Ohio</td><td>22,350,068,000</td><td>4.1%</td><td>35</td><td>Utah</td><td>4,211,310,000</td><td>0.8%</td></tr>
<tr><td>27</td><td>Oklahoma</td><td>7,409,652,000</td><td>1.3%</td><td>36</td><td>Kansas</td><td>3,975,772,000</td><td>0.7%</td></tr>
<tr><td>24</td><td>Oregon</td><td>8,791,134,000</td><td>1.6%</td><td>37</td><td>Nebraska</td><td>3,094,850,000</td><td>0.6%</td></tr>
<tr><td>6</td><td>Pennsylvania</td><td>21,868,995,000</td><td>4.0%</td><td>38</td><td>Maine</td><td>3,028,373,000</td><td>0.6%</td></tr>
<tr><td>43</td><td>Rhode Island</td><td>2,509,818,000</td><td>0.5%</td><td>39</td><td>Nevada</td><td>3,021,228,000</td><td>0.5%</td></tr>
<tr><td>26</td><td>South Carolina</td><td>7,639,636,000</td><td>1.4%</td><td>40</td><td>Hawaii</td><td>2,810,537,000</td><td>0.5%</td></tr>
<tr><td>49</td><td>South Dakota</td><td>1,573,610,000</td><td>0.3%</td><td>41</td><td>Alaska</td><td>2,810,194,000</td><td>0.5%</td></tr>
<tr><td>17</td><td>Tennessee</td><td>10,645,251,000</td><td>1.9%</td><td>42</td><td>Idaho</td><td>2,531,469,000</td><td>0.5%</td></tr>
<tr><td>3</td><td>Texas</td><td>40,561,370,000</td><td>7.4%</td><td>43</td><td>Rhode Island</td><td>2,509,818,000</td><td>0.5%</td></tr>
<tr><td>35</td><td>Utah</td><td>4,211,310,000</td><td>0.8%</td><td>44</td><td>Montana</td><td>2,341,686,000</td><td>0.4%</td></tr>
<tr><td>47</td><td>Vermont</td><td>1,943,173,000</td><td>0.4%</td><td>45</td><td>Wyoming</td><td>2,208,034,000</td><td>0.4%</td></tr>
<tr><td>20</td><td>Virginia</td><td>10,027,820,000</td><td>1.8%</td><td>46</td><td>Delaware</td><td>2,101,677,000</td><td>0.4%</td></tr>
<tr><td>13</td><td>Washington</td><td>11,474,963,000</td><td>2.1%</td><td>47</td><td>Vermont</td><td>1,943,173,000</td><td>0.4%</td></tr>
<tr><td>34</td><td>West Virginia</td><td>4,350,205,000</td><td>0.8%</td><td>48</td><td>New Hampshire</td><td>1,853,129,000</td><td>0.3%</td></tr>
<tr><td>22</td><td>Wisconsin</td><td>9,255,939,000</td><td>1.7%</td><td>49</td><td>South Dakota</td><td>1,573,610,000</td><td>0.3%</td></tr>
<tr><td>45</td><td>Wyoming</td><td>2,208,034,000</td><td>0.4%</td><td>50</td><td>North Dakota</td><td>1,534,035,000</td><td>0.3%</td></tr>
<tr><td colspan="4"></td><td colspan="2">District of Columbia**</td><td>NA</td><td>NA</td></tr>
</table>

Source: U.S. Bureau of the Census, Governments Division
    "2014 State and Local Government Finances" (http://www.census.gov/govs/local/)
*Includes revenue from federal and local government sources.
**Not applicable.

Per Capita State Government Intergovernmental Revenue in 2014

National Per Capita = $1,732*

ALPHA ORDER

RANK	STATE	PER CAPITA
29	Alabama	$1,680
1	Alaska	3,815
34	Arizona	1,630
17	Arkansas	2,055
33	California	1,642
47	Colorado	1,360
26	Connecticut	1,772
11	Delaware	2,248
48	Florida	1,297
42	Georgia	1,449
19	Hawaii	1,984
40	Idaho	1,550
44	Illinois	1,417
30	Indiana	1,676
18	Iowa	2,001
46	Kansas	1,371
13	Kentucky	2,214
14	Louisiana	2,198
10	Maine	2,276
22	Maryland	1,850
15	Massachusetts	2,099
24	Michigan	1,808
31	Minnesota	1,671
6	Mississippi	2,465
27	Missouri	1,715
9	Montana	2,289
32	Nebraska	1,645
50	Nevada	1,066
45	New Hampshire	1,395
25	New Jersey	1,798
4	New Mexico	2,668
5	New York	2,491
39	North Carolina	1,575
16	North Dakota	2,073
20	Ohio	1,928
21	Oklahoma	1,911
12	Oregon	2,215
28	Pennsylvania	1,710
7	Rhode Island	2,380
38	South Carolina	1,582
23	South Dakota	1,846
35	Tennessee	1,627
41	Texas	1,505
43	Utah	1,432
3	Vermont	3,099
49	Virginia	1,206
35	Washington	1,627
8	West Virginia	2,353
37	Wisconsin	1,607
2	Wyoming	3,783

RANK ORDER

RANK	STATE	PER CAPITA
1	Alaska	$3,815
2	Wyoming	3,783
3	Vermont	3,099
4	New Mexico	2,668
5	New York	2,491
6	Mississippi	2,465
7	Rhode Island	2,380
8	West Virginia	2,353
9	Montana	2,289
10	Maine	2,276
11	Delaware	2,248
12	Oregon	2,215
13	Kentucky	2,214
14	Louisiana	2,198
15	Massachusetts	2,099
16	North Dakota	2,073
17	Arkansas	2,055
18	Iowa	2,001
19	Hawaii	1,984
20	Ohio	1,928
21	Oklahoma	1,911
22	Maryland	1,850
23	South Dakota	1,846
24	Michigan	1,808
25	New Jersey	1,798
26	Connecticut	1,772
27	Missouri	1,715
28	Pennsylvania	1,710
29	Alabama	1,680
30	Indiana	1,676
31	Minnesota	1,671
32	Nebraska	1,645
33	California	1,642
34	Arizona	1,630
35	Tennessee	1,627
35	Washington	1,627
37	Wisconsin	1,607
38	South Carolina	1,582
39	North Carolina	1,575
40	Idaho	1,550
41	Texas	1,505
42	Georgia	1,449
43	Utah	1,432
44	Illinois	1,417
45	New Hampshire	1,395
46	Kansas	1,371
47	Colorado	1,360
48	Florida	1,297
49	Virginia	1,206
50	Nevada	1,066

District of Columbia**   NA

Source: CQ Press using data from U.S. Bureau of the Census, Governments Division
    "2014 State and Local Government Finances" (http://www.census.gov/govs/local/)
*Includes revenue from federal and local government sources.
**Not applicable.

State Government Own Source Revenue in 2014

National Total = $1,189,180,885,000*

ALPHA ORDER

RANK	STATE	REVENUE	% of USA
28	Alabama	$14,813,338,000	1.2%
39	Alaska	7,626,168,000	0.6%
20	Arizona	18,738,967,000	1.6%
31	Arkansas	11,961,308,000	1.0%
1	California	167,224,905,000	14.1%
21	Colorado	17,461,557,000	1.5%
19	Connecticut	19,480,580,000	1.6%
42	Delaware	5,503,599,000	0.5%
4	Florida	51,025,555,000	4.3%
16	Georgia	24,395,323,000	2.1%
36	Hawaii	8,493,887,000	0.7%
44	Idaho	4,901,753,000	0.4%
5	Illinois	49,149,029,000	4.1%
18	Indiana	22,204,265,000	1.9%
30	Iowa	12,670,470,000	1.1%
32	Kansas	11,415,673,000	1.0%
25	Kentucky	15,499,360,000	1.3%
27	Louisiana	15,136,999,000	1.3%
43	Maine	5,164,225,000	0.4%
15	Maryland	25,242,387,000	2.1%
10	Massachusetts	34,881,948,000	2.9%
9	Michigan	37,201,336,000	3.1%
13	Minnesota	27,924,523,000	2.3%
34	Mississippi	10,198,540,000	0.9%
22	Missouri	16,282,248,000	1.4%
48	Montana	3,635,477,000	0.3%
41	Nebraska	6,694,308,000	0.6%
37	Nevada	8,458,578,000	0.7%
46	New Hampshire	4,062,813,000	0.3%
7	New Jersey	40,509,905,000	3.4%
35	New Mexico	10,032,301,000	0.8%
2	New York	97,740,710,000	8.2%
12	North Carolina	31,339,517,000	2.6%
40	North Dakota	7,315,858,000	0.6%
8	Ohio	39,751,073,000	3.3%
29	Oklahoma	14,031,683,000	1.2%
24	Oregon	15,564,758,000	1.3%
6	Pennsylvania	48,490,736,000	4.1%
45	Rhode Island	4,607,029,000	0.4%
26	South Carolina	15,436,370,000	1.3%
50	South Dakota	2,588,267,000	0.2%
23	Tennessee	15,847,770,000	1.3%
3	Texas	81,003,659,000	6.8%
33	Utah	10,767,744,000	0.9%
47	Vermont	3,828,571,000	0.3%
11	Virginia	31,440,745,000	2.6%
14	Washington	26,820,651,000	2.3%
38	West Virginia	7,903,104,000	0.7%
17	Wisconsin	23,139,208,000	1.9%
49	Wyoming	3,572,107,000	0.3%

RANK ORDER

RANK	STATE	REVENUE	% of USA
1	California	$167,224,905,000	14.1%
2	New York	97,740,710,000	8.2%
3	Texas	81,003,659,000	6.8%
4	Florida	51,025,555,000	4.3%
5	Illinois	49,149,029,000	4.1%
6	Pennsylvania	48,490,736,000	4.1%
7	New Jersey	40,509,905,000	3.4%
8	Ohio	39,751,073,000	3.3%
9	Michigan	37,201,336,000	3.1%
10	Massachusetts	34,881,948,000	2.9%
11	Virginia	31,440,745,000	2.6%
12	North Carolina	31,339,517,000	2.6%
13	Minnesota	27,924,523,000	2.3%
14	Washington	26,820,651,000	2.3%
15	Maryland	25,242,387,000	2.1%
16	Georgia	24,395,323,000	2.1%
17	Wisconsin	23,139,208,000	1.9%
18	Indiana	22,204,265,000	1.9%
19	Connecticut	19,480,580,000	1.6%
20	Arizona	18,738,967,000	1.6%
21	Colorado	17,461,557,000	1.5%
22	Missouri	16,282,248,000	1.4%
23	Tennessee	15,847,770,000	1.3%
24	Oregon	15,564,758,000	1.3%
25	Kentucky	15,499,360,000	1.3%
26	South Carolina	15,436,370,000	1.3%
27	Louisiana	15,136,999,000	1.3%
28	Alabama	14,813,338,000	1.2%
29	Oklahoma	14,031,683,000	1.2%
30	Iowa	12,670,470,000	1.1%
31	Arkansas	11,961,308,000	1.0%
32	Kansas	11,415,673,000	1.0%
33	Utah	10,767,744,000	0.9%
34	Mississippi	10,198,540,000	0.9%
35	New Mexico	10,032,301,000	0.8%
36	Hawaii	8,493,887,000	0.7%
37	Nevada	8,458,578,000	0.7%
38	West Virginia	7,903,104,000	0.7%
39	Alaska	7,626,168,000	0.6%
40	North Dakota	7,315,858,000	0.6%
41	Nebraska	6,694,308,000	0.6%
42	Delaware	5,503,599,000	0.5%
43	Maine	5,164,225,000	0.4%
44	Idaho	4,901,753,000	0.4%
45	Rhode Island	4,607,029,000	0.4%
46	New Hampshire	4,062,813,000	0.3%
47	Vermont	3,828,571,000	0.3%
48	Montana	3,635,477,000	0.3%
49	Wyoming	3,572,107,000	0.3%
50	South Dakota	2,588,267,000	0.2%
	District of Columbia**	NA	NA

Source: U.S. Bureau of the Census, Governments Division
  "2014 State and Local Government Finances" (http://www.census.gov/govs/local/)
*Own source revenue includes taxes, current charges, and miscellaneous general revenue. Excluded are intergovernmental transfers, insurance trust revenue, and revenue from government owned utilities and other commercial or auxiliary enterprise.
**Not applicable.

Per Capita State Government Own Source Revenue in 2014

National Per Capita = $3,741*

<table>
<tr><td colspan="3">ALPHA ORDER</td></tr>
<tr><th>RANK</th><th>STATE</th><th>PER CAPITA</th></tr>
<tr><td>40</td><td>Alabama</td><td>$3,059</td></tr>
<tr><td>1</td><td>Alaska</td><td>10,352</td></tr>
<tr><td>46</td><td>Arizona</td><td>2,789</td></tr>
<tr><td>18</td><td>Arkansas</td><td>4,032</td></tr>
<tr><td>14</td><td>California</td><td>4,323</td></tr>
<tr><td>36</td><td>Colorado</td><td>3,264</td></tr>
<tr><td>7</td><td>Connecticut</td><td>5,424</td></tr>
<tr><td>6</td><td>Delaware</td><td>5,887</td></tr>
<tr><td>48</td><td>Florida</td><td>2,566</td></tr>
<tr><td>50</td><td>Georgia</td><td>2,418</td></tr>
<tr><td>5</td><td>Hawaii</td><td>5,997</td></tr>
<tr><td>44</td><td>Idaho</td><td>3,001</td></tr>
<tr><td>23</td><td>Illinois</td><td>3,820</td></tr>
<tr><td>35</td><td>Indiana</td><td>3,367</td></tr>
<tr><td>17</td><td>Iowa</td><td>4,077</td></tr>
<tr><td>20</td><td>Kansas</td><td>3,937</td></tr>
<tr><td>32</td><td>Kentucky</td><td>3,512</td></tr>
<tr><td>37</td><td>Louisiana</td><td>3,257</td></tr>
<tr><td>22</td><td>Maine</td><td>3,881</td></tr>
<tr><td>16</td><td>Maryland</td><td>4,230</td></tr>
<tr><td>8</td><td>Massachusetts</td><td>5,168</td></tr>
<tr><td>27</td><td>Michigan</td><td>3,752</td></tr>
<tr><td>9</td><td>Minnesota</td><td>5,121</td></tr>
<tr><td>34</td><td>Mississippi</td><td>3,408</td></tr>
<tr><td>47</td><td>Missouri</td><td>2,686</td></tr>
<tr><td>31</td><td>Montana</td><td>3,554</td></tr>
<tr><td>30</td><td>Nebraska</td><td>3,559</td></tr>
<tr><td>45</td><td>Nevada</td><td>2,986</td></tr>
<tr><td>41</td><td>New Hampshire</td><td>3,058</td></tr>
<tr><td>12</td><td>New Jersey</td><td>4,539</td></tr>
<tr><td>11</td><td>New Mexico</td><td>4,816</td></tr>
<tr><td>10</td><td>New York</td><td>4,957</td></tr>
<tr><td>39</td><td>North Carolina</td><td>3,155</td></tr>
<tr><td>2</td><td>North Dakota</td><td>9,888</td></tr>
<tr><td>33</td><td>Ohio</td><td>3,428</td></tr>
<tr><td>29</td><td>Oklahoma</td><td>3,619</td></tr>
<tr><td>21</td><td>Oregon</td><td>3,922</td></tr>
<tr><td>25</td><td>Pennsylvania</td><td>3,791</td></tr>
<tr><td>13</td><td>Rhode Island</td><td>4,369</td></tr>
<tr><td>38</td><td>South Carolina</td><td>3,197</td></tr>
<tr><td>42</td><td>South Dakota</td><td>3,036</td></tr>
<tr><td>49</td><td>Tennessee</td><td>2,421</td></tr>
<tr><td>43</td><td>Texas</td><td>3,006</td></tr>
<tr><td>28</td><td>Utah</td><td>3,660</td></tr>
<tr><td>4</td><td>Vermont</td><td>6,106</td></tr>
<tr><td>26</td><td>Virginia</td><td>3,780</td></tr>
<tr><td>24</td><td>Washington</td><td>3,802</td></tr>
<tr><td>15</td><td>West Virginia</td><td>4,275</td></tr>
<tr><td>19</td><td>Wisconsin</td><td>4,018</td></tr>
<tr><td>3</td><td>Wyoming</td><td>6,120</td></tr>
</table>

<table>
<tr><td colspan="3">RANK ORDER</td></tr>
<tr><th>RANK</th><th>STATE</th><th>PER CAPITA</th></tr>
<tr><td>1</td><td>Alaska</td><td>$10,352</td></tr>
<tr><td>2</td><td>North Dakota</td><td>9,888</td></tr>
<tr><td>3</td><td>Wyoming</td><td>6,120</td></tr>
<tr><td>4</td><td>Vermont</td><td>6,106</td></tr>
<tr><td>5</td><td>Hawaii</td><td>5,997</td></tr>
<tr><td>6</td><td>Delaware</td><td>5,887</td></tr>
<tr><td>7</td><td>Connecticut</td><td>5,424</td></tr>
<tr><td>8</td><td>Massachusetts</td><td>5,168</td></tr>
<tr><td>9</td><td>Minnesota</td><td>5,121</td></tr>
<tr><td>10</td><td>New York</td><td>4,957</td></tr>
<tr><td>11</td><td>New Mexico</td><td>4,816</td></tr>
<tr><td>12</td><td>New Jersey</td><td>4,539</td></tr>
<tr><td>13</td><td>Rhode Island</td><td>4,369</td></tr>
<tr><td>14</td><td>California</td><td>4,323</td></tr>
<tr><td>15</td><td>West Virginia</td><td>4,275</td></tr>
<tr><td>16</td><td>Maryland</td><td>4,230</td></tr>
<tr><td>17</td><td>Iowa</td><td>4,077</td></tr>
<tr><td>18</td><td>Arkansas</td><td>4,032</td></tr>
<tr><td>19</td><td>Wisconsin</td><td>4,018</td></tr>
<tr><td>20</td><td>Kansas</td><td>3,937</td></tr>
<tr><td>21</td><td>Oregon</td><td>3,922</td></tr>
<tr><td>22</td><td>Maine</td><td>3,881</td></tr>
<tr><td>23</td><td>Illinois</td><td>3,820</td></tr>
<tr><td>24</td><td>Washington</td><td>3,802</td></tr>
<tr><td>25</td><td>Pennsylvania</td><td>3,791</td></tr>
<tr><td>26</td><td>Virginia</td><td>3,780</td></tr>
<tr><td>27</td><td>Michigan</td><td>3,752</td></tr>
<tr><td>28</td><td>Utah</td><td>3,660</td></tr>
<tr><td>29</td><td>Oklahoma</td><td>3,619</td></tr>
<tr><td>30</td><td>Nebraska</td><td>3,559</td></tr>
<tr><td>31</td><td>Montana</td><td>3,554</td></tr>
<tr><td>32</td><td>Kentucky</td><td>3,512</td></tr>
<tr><td>33</td><td>Ohio</td><td>3,428</td></tr>
<tr><td>34</td><td>Mississippi</td><td>3,408</td></tr>
<tr><td>35</td><td>Indiana</td><td>3,367</td></tr>
<tr><td>36</td><td>Colorado</td><td>3,264</td></tr>
<tr><td>37</td><td>Louisiana</td><td>3,257</td></tr>
<tr><td>38</td><td>South Carolina</td><td>3,197</td></tr>
<tr><td>39</td><td>North Carolina</td><td>3,155</td></tr>
<tr><td>40</td><td>Alabama</td><td>3,059</td></tr>
<tr><td>41</td><td>New Hampshire</td><td>3,058</td></tr>
<tr><td>42</td><td>South Dakota</td><td>3,036</td></tr>
<tr><td>43</td><td>Texas</td><td>3,006</td></tr>
<tr><td>44</td><td>Idaho</td><td>3,001</td></tr>
<tr><td>45</td><td>Nevada</td><td>2,986</td></tr>
<tr><td>46</td><td>Arizona</td><td>2,789</td></tr>
<tr><td>47</td><td>Missouri</td><td>2,686</td></tr>
<tr><td>48</td><td>Florida</td><td>2,566</td></tr>
<tr><td>49</td><td>Tennessee</td><td>2,421</td></tr>
<tr><td>50</td><td>Georgia</td><td>2,418</td></tr>
</table>

District of Columbia**   NA

Source: CQ Press using data from U.S. Bureau of the Census, Governments Division
   "2014 State and Local Government Finances" (http://www.census.gov/govs/local/)
*Own source revenue includes taxes, current charges, and miscellaneous general revenue. Excluded are intergovernmental transfers, insurance trust revenue, and revenue from government owned utilities and other commercial or auxiliary enterprise.
**Not applicable.

Projected vs. Actual State Tax Collections in 2016

National Percent = 99.7% of Projected Taxes*

ALPHA ORDER

RANK	STATE	PERCENT
15	Alabama	101.0
50	Alaska	40.0
6	Arizona	104.0
19	Arkansas	100.3
13	California	101.8
38	Colorado	97.2
41	Connecticut	95.9
29	Delaware	98.6
23	Florida	99.8
9	Georgia	102.6
4	Hawaii	104.3
15	Idaho	101.0
18	Illinois	100.8
29	Indiana	98.6
36	Iowa	97.7
35	Kansas	98.0
3	Kentucky	106.2
12	Louisiana	101.9
5	Maine	104.2
32	Maryland	98.2
24	Massachusetts	99.3
33	Michigan	98.1
20	Minnesota	100.2
41	Mississippi	95.9
17	Missouri	100.9
46	Montana	92.6
43	Nebraska	95.6
33	Nevada	98.1
1	New Hampshire	110.7
39	New Jersey	97.1
47	New Mexico	90.3
24	New York	99.3
11	North Carolina	102.0
49	North Dakota	71.2
29	Ohio	98.6
45	Oklahoma	94.2
14	Oregon	101.7
26	Pennsylvania	99.1
22	Rhode Island	100.1
8	South Carolina	102.7
26	South Dakota	99.1
2	Tennessee	107.7
40	Texas	96.5
20	Utah	100.2
7	Vermont	102.9
37	Virginia	97.3
10	Washington	102.4
44	West Virginia	94.4
28	Wisconsin	99.0
48	Wyoming	87.5

RANK ORDER

RANK	STATE	PERCENT
1	New Hampshire	110.7
2	Tennessee	107.7
3	Kentucky	106.2
4	Hawaii	104.3
5	Maine	104.2
6	Arizona	104.0
7	Vermont	102.9
8	South Carolina	102.7
9	Georgia	102.6
10	Washington	102.4
11	North Carolina	102.0
12	Louisiana	101.9
13	California	101.8
14	Oregon	101.7
15	Alabama	101.0
15	Idaho	101.0
17	Missouri	100.9
18	Illinois	100.8
19	Arkansas	100.3
20	Minnesota	100.2
20	Utah	100.2
22	Rhode Island	100.1
23	Florida	99.8
24	Massachusetts	99.3
24	New York	99.3
26	Pennsylvania	99.1
26	South Dakota	99.1
28	Wisconsin	99.0
29	Delaware	98.6
29	Indiana	98.6
29	Ohio	98.6
32	Maryland	98.2
33	Michigan	98.1
33	Nevada	98.1
35	Kansas	98.0
36	Iowa	97.7
37	Virginia	97.3
38	Colorado	97.2
39	New Jersey	97.1
40	Texas	96.5
41	Connecticut	95.9
41	Mississippi	95.9
43	Nebraska	95.6
44	West Virginia	94.4
45	Oklahoma	94.2
46	Montana	92.6
47	New Mexico	90.3
48	Wyoming	87.5
49	North Dakota	71.2
50	Alaska	40.0
	District of Columbia**	NA

Source: CQ Press using data from National Association of State Budget Officers
    "The Fiscal Survey of States" (Fall 2016, http://www.nasbo.org)
*For fiscal year 2016. This table compares sales, personal, and corporate income tax collections projected in adopting budgets
with the amount collected.
**Not available.

State Government Tax Revenue in 2015

National Total = $916,488,050,000

RANK	STATE	REVENUE	% of USA
26	Alabama	$9,755,439,000	1.1%
50	Alaska	863,723,000	0.1%
20	Arizona	14,082,100,000	1.5%
30	Arkansas	9,190,212,000	1.0%
1	California	151,172,643,000	16.5%
21	Colorado	12,810,632,000	1.4%
19	Connecticut	16,231,958,000	1.8%
43	Delaware	3,513,916,000	0.4%
5	Florida	37,217,759,000	4.1%
16	Georgia	19,723,730,000	2.2%
36	Hawaii	6,485,563,000	0.7%
42	Idaho	3,975,445,000	0.4%
4	Illinois	39,283,051,000	4.3%
17	Indiana	17,399,650,000	1.9%
31	Iowa	9,189,255,000	1.0%
33	Kansas	7,883,960,000	0.9%
24	Kentucky	11,597,983,000	1.3%
27	Louisiana	9,718,755,000	1.1%
41	Maine	4,064,075,000	0.4%
15	Maryland	19,849,988,000	2.2%
9	Massachusetts	27,012,206,000	2.9%
10	Michigan	26,957,337,000	2.9%
12	Minnesota	24,439,253,000	2.7%
32	Mississippi	7,906,514,000	0.9%
23	Missouri	11,956,143,000	1.3%
46	Montana	2,843,465,000	0.3%
40	Nebraska	5,086,759,000	0.6%
34	Nevada	7,532,989,000	0.8%
47	New Hampshire	2,487,737,000	0.3%
7	New Jersey	31,567,654,000	3.4%
37	New Mexico	6,009,443,000	0.7%
2	New York	78,242,729,000	8.5%
11	North Carolina	25,061,592,000	2.7%
38	North Dakota	5,739,843,000	0.6%
8	Ohio	28,297,156,000	3.1%
29	Oklahoma	9,407,393,000	1.0%
25	Oregon	10,575,165,000	1.2%
6	Pennsylvania	36,110,295,000	3.9%
44	Rhode Island	3,196,673,000	0.3%
28	South Carolina	9,633,031,000	1.1%
49	South Dakota	1,674,108,000	0.2%
22	Tennessee	12,697,655,000	1.4%
3	Texas	55,086,438,000	6.0%
35	Utah	6,703,356,000	0.7%
45	Vermont	3,043,152,000	0.3%
14	Virginia	20,536,885,000	2.2%
13	Washington	20,644,454,000	2.3%
39	West Virginia	5,565,984,000	0.6%
18	Wisconsin	17,019,026,000	1.9%
48	Wyoming	2,356,323,000	0.3%

RANK	STATE	REVENUE	% of USA
1	California	$151,172,643,000	16.5%
2	New York	78,242,729,000	8.5%
3	Texas	55,086,438,000	6.0%
4	Illinois	39,283,051,000	4.3%
5	Florida	37,217,759,000	4.1%
6	Pennsylvania	36,110,295,000	3.9%
7	New Jersey	31,567,654,000	3.4%
8	Ohio	28,297,156,000	3.1%
9	Massachusetts	27,012,206,000	2.9%
10	Michigan	26,957,337,000	2.9%
11	North Carolina	25,061,592,000	2.7%
12	Minnesota	24,439,253,000	2.7%
13	Washington	20,644,454,000	2.3%
14	Virginia	20,536,885,000	2.2%
15	Maryland	19,849,988,000	2.2%
16	Georgia	19,723,730,000	2.2%
17	Indiana	17,399,650,000	1.9%
18	Wisconsin	17,019,026,000	1.9%
19	Connecticut	16,231,958,000	1.8%
20	Arizona	14,082,100,000	1.5%
21	Colorado	12,810,632,000	1.4%
22	Tennessee	12,697,655,000	1.4%
23	Missouri	11,956,143,000	1.3%
24	Kentucky	11,597,983,000	1.3%
25	Oregon	10,575,165,000	1.2%
26	Alabama	9,755,439,000	1.1%
27	Louisiana	9,718,755,000	1.1%
28	South Carolina	9,633,031,000	1.1%
29	Oklahoma	9,407,393,000	1.0%
30	Arkansas	9,190,212,000	1.0%
31	Iowa	9,189,255,000	1.0%
32	Mississippi	7,906,514,000	0.9%
33	Kansas	7,883,960,000	0.9%
34	Nevada	7,532,989,000	0.8%
35	Utah	6,703,356,000	0.7%
36	Hawaii	6,485,563,000	0.7%
37	New Mexico	6,009,443,000	0.7%
38	North Dakota	5,739,843,000	0.6%
39	West Virginia	5,565,984,000	0.6%
40	Nebraska	5,086,759,000	0.6%
41	Maine	4,064,075,000	0.4%
42	Idaho	3,975,445,000	0.4%
43	Delaware	3,513,916,000	0.4%
44	Rhode Island	3,196,673,000	0.3%
45	Vermont	3,043,152,000	0.3%
46	Montana	2,843,465,000	0.3%
47	New Hampshire	2,487,737,000	0.3%
48	Wyoming	2,356,323,000	0.3%
49	South Dakota	1,674,108,000	0.2%
50	Alaska	863,723,000	0.1%
	District of Columbia	7,087,455,000	0.8%

Source: U.S. Bureau of the Census, Governments Division
"2015 State Government Tax Collections" (http://www.census.gov/govs/statetax/)

Per Capita State Government Tax Revenue in 2015

National Per Capita = $2,856

ALPHA ORDER

ALPHA ORDER

RANK	STATE	PER CAPITA
41	Alabama	$2,010
50	Alaska	1,171
40	Arizona	2,066
13	Arkansas	3,086
9	California	3,877
37	Colorado	2,351
4	Connecticut	4,528
10	Delaware	3,722
49	Florida	1,838
46	Georgia	1,934
3	Hawaii	4,551
36	Idaho	2,405
14	Illinois	3,060
28	Indiana	2,631
19	Iowa	2,943
25	Kansas	2,712
30	Kentucky	2,621
39	Louisiana	2,082
15	Maine	3,057
12	Maryland	3,311
7	Massachusetts	3,982
24	Michigan	2,718
5	Minnesota	4,458
27	Mississippi	2,645
43	Missouri	1,968
23	Montana	2,755
26	Nebraska	2,686
31	Nevada	2,612
48	New Hampshire	1,870
11	New Jersey	3,533
20	New Mexico	2,889
8	New York	3,962
32	North Carolina	2,497
1	North Dakota	7,584
34	Ohio	2,438
35	Oklahoma	2,408
29	Oregon	2,628
22	Pennsylvania	2,823
16	Rhode Island	3,028
43	South Carolina	1,968
45	South Dakota	1,951
47	Tennessee	1,925
42	Texas	2,008
38	Utah	2,241
2	Vermont	4,861
33	Virginia	2,454
21	Washington	2,883
17	West Virginia	3,023
18	Wisconsin	2,951
6	Wyoming	4,017

RANK ORDER

RANK	STATE	PER CAPITA
1	North Dakota	$7,584
2	Vermont	4,861
3	Hawaii	4,551
4	Connecticut	4,528
5	Minnesota	4,458
6	Wyoming	4,017
7	Massachusetts	3,982
8	New York	3,962
9	California	3,877
10	Delaware	3,722
11	New Jersey	3,533
12	Maryland	3,311
13	Arkansas	3,086
14	Illinois	3,060
15	Maine	3,057
16	Rhode Island	3,028
17	West Virginia	3,023
18	Wisconsin	2,951
19	Iowa	2,943
20	New Mexico	2,889
21	Washington	2,883
22	Pennsylvania	2,823
23	Montana	2,755
24	Michigan	2,718
25	Kansas	2,712
26	Nebraska	2,686
27	Mississippi	2,645
28	Indiana	2,631
29	Oregon	2,628
30	Kentucky	2,621
31	Nevada	2,612
32	North Carolina	2,497
33	Virginia	2,454
34	Ohio	2,438
35	Oklahoma	2,408
36	Idaho	2,405
37	Colorado	2,351
38	Utah	2,241
39	Louisiana	2,082
40	Arizona	2,066
41	Alabama	2,010
42	Texas	2,008
43	Missouri	1,968
43	South Carolina	1,968
45	South Dakota	1,951
46	Georgia	1,934
47	Tennessee	1,925
48	New Hampshire	1,870
49	Florida	1,838
50	Alaska	1,171
	District of Columbia	10,572

Source: CQ Press using data from U.S. Bureau of the Census, Governments Division
"2015 State Government Tax Collections" (http://www.census.gov/govs/statetax/)

State Government Tax Revenue as a Percent of Personal Income in 2015

National Percent = 5.9% of Personal Income

ALPHA ORDER

RANK	STATE	PERCENT
36	Alabama	5.3
50	Alaska	2.1
36	Arizona	5.3
6	Arkansas	8.1
10	California	7.2
43	Colorado	4.6
15	Connecticut	6.6
7	Delaware	7.8
47	Florida	4.1
40	Georgia	4.8
3	Hawaii	9.4
20	Idaho	6.3
24	Illinois	6.1
20	Indiana	6.3
17	Iowa	6.4
30	Kansas	5.7
13	Kentucky	6.8
40	Louisiana	4.8
12	Maine	7.1
28	Maryland	5.9
17	Massachusetts	6.4
20	Michigan	6.3
4	Minnesota	8.8
8	Mississippi	7.6
43	Missouri	4.6
15	Montana	6.6
34	Nebraska	5.5
23	Nevada	6.2
49	New Hampshire	3.3
28	New Jersey	5.9
8	New Mexico	7.6
14	New York	6.7
24	North Carolina	6.1
1	North Dakota	13.6
33	Ohio	5.6
36	Oklahoma	5.3
27	Oregon	6.0
30	Pennsylvania	5.7
24	Rhode Island	6.1
39	South Carolina	5.1
47	South Dakota	4.1
43	Tennessee	4.6
46	Texas	4.3
30	Utah	5.7
2	Vermont	10.0
42	Virginia	4.7
34	Washington	5.5
5	West Virginia	8.2
17	Wisconsin	6.4
10	Wyoming	7.2

RANK ORDER

RANK	STATE	PERCENT
1	North Dakota	13.6
2	Vermont	10.0
3	Hawaii	9.4
4	Minnesota	8.8
5	West Virginia	8.2
6	Arkansas	8.1
7	Delaware	7.8
8	Mississippi	7.6
8	New Mexico	7.6
10	California	7.2
10	Wyoming	7.2
12	Maine	7.1
13	Kentucky	6.8
14	New York	6.7
15	Connecticut	6.6
15	Montana	6.6
17	Iowa	6.4
17	Massachusetts	6.4
17	Wisconsin	6.4
20	Idaho	6.3
20	Indiana	6.3
20	Michigan	6.3
23	Nevada	6.2
24	Illinois	6.1
24	North Carolina	6.1
24	Rhode Island	6.1
27	Oregon	6.0
28	Maryland	5.9
28	New Jersey	5.9
30	Kansas	5.7
30	Pennsylvania	5.7
30	Utah	5.7
33	Ohio	5.6
34	Nebraska	5.5
34	Washington	5.5
36	Alabama	5.3
36	Arizona	5.3
36	Oklahoma	5.3
39	South Carolina	5.1
40	Georgia	4.8
40	Louisiana	4.8
42	Virginia	4.7
43	Colorado	4.6
43	Missouri	4.6
43	Tennessee	4.6
46	Texas	4.3
47	Florida	4.1
47	South Dakota	4.1
49	New Hampshire	3.3
50	Alaska	2.1

District of Columbia 14.4

Source: CQ Press using data from U.S. Bureau of the Census, Governments Division
"2015 State Government Tax Collections" (http://www.census.gov/govs/statetax/)
U.S. Department of Commerce, Bureau of Economic Analysis
"Annual State Personal Income" (http://www.bea.gov/iTable/index_regional.cfm)

State Government Individual Income Tax Revenue in 2015

National Total = $338,102,651,000

ALPHA ORDER

RANK	STATE	REVENUE	% of USA
24	Alabama	$3,336,587,000	1.0%
44	Alaska	0	0.0%
21	Arizona	3,760,883,000	1.1%
28	Arkansas	2,664,153,000	0.8%
1	California	77,929,551,000	23.0%
17	Colorado	6,375,248,000	1.9%
14	Connecticut	8,182,071,000	2.4%
39	Delaware	1,140,248,000	0.3%
44	Florida	0	0.0%
10	Georgia	9,678,524,000	2.9%
31	Hawaii	1,987,915,000	0.6%
35	Idaho	1,478,368,000	0.4%
3	Illinois	15,913,816,000	4.7%
19	Indiana	5,232,976,000	1.5%
23	Iowa	3,471,617,000	1.0%
29	Kansas	2,262,951,000	0.7%
20	Kentucky	4,069,501,000	1.2%
27	Louisiana	2,983,104,000	0.9%
34	Maine	1,533,130,000	0.5%
13	Maryland	8,346,145,000	2.5%
4	Massachusetts	14,491,903,000	4.3%
12	Michigan	8,825,375,000	2.6%
9	Minnesota	10,370,047,000	3.1%
33	Mississippi	1,783,438,000	0.5%
18	Missouri	5,856,131,000	1.7%
38	Montana	1,180,478,000	0.3%
30	Nebraska	2,239,582,000	0.7%
44	Nevada	0	0.0%
43	New Hampshire	96,038,000	0.0%
5	New Jersey	13,250,002,000	3.9%
36	New Mexico	1,381,254,000	0.4%
2	New York	43,713,484,000	12.9%
8	North Carolina	11,197,650,000	3.3%
41	North Dakota	536,619,000	0.2%
11	Ohio	8,882,973,000	2.6%
25	Oklahoma	3,252,290,000	1.0%
15	Oregon	7,309,115,000	2.2%
7	Pennsylvania	11,488,974,000	3.4%
37	Rhode Island	1,215,368,000	0.4%
22	South Carolina	3,741,800,000	1.1%
44	South Dakota	0	0.0%
42	Tennessee	302,196,000	0.1%
44	Texas	0	0.0%
26	Utah	3,157,718,000	0.9%
40	Vermont	709,310,000	0.2%
6	Virginia	11,903,945,000	3.5%
44	Washington	0	0.0%
32	West Virginia	1,932,457,000	0.6%
16	Wisconsin	7,069,248,000	2.1%
44	Wyoming	0	0.0%

RANK ORDER

RANK	STATE	REVENUE	% of USA
1	California	$77,929,551,000	23.0%
2	New York	43,713,484,000	12.9%
3	Illinois	15,913,816,000	4.7%
4	Massachusetts	14,491,903,000	4.3%
5	New Jersey	13,250,002,000	3.9%
6	Virginia	11,903,945,000	3.5%
7	Pennsylvania	11,488,974,000	3.4%
8	North Carolina	11,197,650,000	3.3%
9	Minnesota	10,370,047,000	3.1%
10	Georgia	9,678,524,000	2.9%
11	Ohio	8,882,973,000	2.6%
12	Michigan	8,825,375,000	2.6%
13	Maryland	8,346,145,000	2.5%
14	Connecticut	8,182,071,000	2.4%
15	Oregon	7,309,115,000	2.2%
16	Wisconsin	7,069,248,000	2.1%
17	Colorado	6,375,248,000	1.9%
18	Missouri	5,856,131,000	1.7%
19	Indiana	5,232,976,000	1.5%
20	Kentucky	4,069,501,000	1.2%
21	Arizona	3,760,883,000	1.1%
22	South Carolina	3,741,800,000	1.1%
23	Iowa	3,471,617,000	1.0%
24	Alabama	3,336,587,000	1.0%
25	Oklahoma	3,252,290,000	1.0%
26	Utah	3,157,718,000	0.9%
27	Louisiana	2,983,104,000	0.9%
28	Arkansas	2,664,153,000	0.8%
29	Kansas	2,262,951,000	0.7%
30	Nebraska	2,239,582,000	0.7%
31	Hawaii	1,987,915,000	0.6%
32	West Virginia	1,932,457,000	0.6%
33	Mississippi	1,783,438,000	0.5%
34	Maine	1,533,130,000	0.5%
35	Idaho	1,478,368,000	0.4%
36	New Mexico	1,381,254,000	0.4%
37	Rhode Island	1,215,368,000	0.4%
38	Montana	1,180,478,000	0.3%
39	Delaware	1,140,248,000	0.3%
40	Vermont	709,310,000	0.2%
41	North Dakota	536,619,000	0.2%
42	Tennessee	302,196,000	0.1%
43	New Hampshire	96,038,000	0.0%
44	Alaska	0	0.0%
44	Florida	0	0.0%
44	Nevada	0	0.0%
44	South Dakota	0	0.0%
44	Texas	0	0.0%
44	Washington	0	0.0%
44	Wyoming	0	0.0%

District of Columbia	1,868,468,000	0.6%

Source: U.S. Bureau of the Census, Governments Division
"2015 State Government Tax Collections" (http://www.census.gov/govs/statetax/)

Per Capita State Government Individual Income Tax Revenue in 2015

National Per Capita = $1,054

<table>
<tr><td colspan="3">ALPHA ORDER</td><td colspan="3">RANK ORDER</td></tr>
<tr><td>RANK</td><td>STATE</td><td>PER CAPITA</td><td>RANK</td><td>STATE</td><td>PER CAPITA</td></tr>
<tr><td>37</td><td>Alabama</td><td>$687</td><td>1</td><td>Connecticut</td><td>$2,282</td></tr>
<tr><td>44</td><td>Alaska</td><td>0</td><td>2</td><td>New York</td><td>2,214</td></tr>
<tr><td>41</td><td>Arizona</td><td>552</td><td>3</td><td>Massachusetts</td><td>2,136</td></tr>
<tr><td>28</td><td>Arkansas</td><td>895</td><td>4</td><td>California</td><td>1,999</td></tr>
<tr><td>4</td><td>California</td><td>1,999</td><td>5</td><td>Minnesota</td><td>1,892</td></tr>
<tr><td>15</td><td>Colorado</td><td>1,170</td><td>6</td><td>Oregon</td><td>1,816</td></tr>
<tr><td>1</td><td>Connecticut</td><td>2,282</td><td>7</td><td>New Jersey</td><td>1,483</td></tr>
<tr><td>13</td><td>Delaware</td><td>1,208</td><td>8</td><td>Virginia</td><td>1,423</td></tr>
<tr><td>44</td><td>Florida</td><td>0</td><td>9</td><td>Hawaii</td><td>1,395</td></tr>
<tr><td>25</td><td>Georgia</td><td>949</td><td>10</td><td>Maryland</td><td>1,392</td></tr>
<tr><td>9</td><td>Hawaii</td><td>1,395</td><td>11</td><td>Illinois</td><td>1,239</td></tr>
<tr><td>29</td><td>Idaho</td><td>894</td><td>12</td><td>Wisconsin</td><td>1,226</td></tr>
<tr><td>11</td><td>Illinois</td><td>1,239</td><td>13</td><td>Delaware</td><td>1,208</td></tr>
<tr><td>32</td><td>Indiana</td><td>791</td><td>14</td><td>Nebraska</td><td>1,183</td></tr>
<tr><td>21</td><td>Iowa</td><td>1,112</td><td>15</td><td>Colorado</td><td>1,170</td></tr>
<tr><td>33</td><td>Kansas</td><td>779</td><td>16</td><td>Maine</td><td>1,153</td></tr>
<tr><td>26</td><td>Kentucky</td><td>920</td><td>17</td><td>Rhode Island</td><td>1,151</td></tr>
<tr><td>39</td><td>Louisiana</td><td>639</td><td>18</td><td>Montana</td><td>1,144</td></tr>
<tr><td>16</td><td>Maine</td><td>1,153</td><td>19</td><td>Vermont</td><td>1,133</td></tr>
<tr><td>10</td><td>Maryland</td><td>1,392</td><td>20</td><td>North Carolina</td><td>1,116</td></tr>
<tr><td>3</td><td>Massachusetts</td><td>2,136</td><td>21</td><td>Iowa</td><td>1,112</td></tr>
<tr><td>30</td><td>Michigan</td><td>890</td><td>22</td><td>Utah</td><td>1,056</td></tr>
<tr><td>5</td><td>Minnesota</td><td>1,892</td><td>23</td><td>West Virginia</td><td>1,050</td></tr>
<tr><td>40</td><td>Mississippi</td><td>597</td><td>24</td><td>Missouri</td><td>964</td></tr>
<tr><td>24</td><td>Missouri</td><td>964</td><td>25</td><td>Georgia</td><td>949</td></tr>
<tr><td>18</td><td>Montana</td><td>1,144</td><td>26</td><td>Kentucky</td><td>920</td></tr>
<tr><td>14</td><td>Nebraska</td><td>1,183</td><td>27</td><td>Pennsylvania</td><td>898</td></tr>
<tr><td>44</td><td>Nevada</td><td>0</td><td>28</td><td>Arkansas</td><td>895</td></tr>
<tr><td>42</td><td>New Hampshire</td><td>72</td><td>29</td><td>Idaho</td><td>894</td></tr>
<tr><td>7</td><td>New Jersey</td><td>1,483</td><td>30</td><td>Michigan</td><td>890</td></tr>
<tr><td>38</td><td>New Mexico</td><td>664</td><td>31</td><td>Oklahoma</td><td>832</td></tr>
<tr><td>2</td><td>New York</td><td>2,214</td><td>32</td><td>Indiana</td><td>791</td></tr>
<tr><td>20</td><td>North Carolina</td><td>1,116</td><td>33</td><td>Kansas</td><td>779</td></tr>
<tr><td>36</td><td>North Dakota</td><td>709</td><td>34</td><td>Ohio</td><td>765</td></tr>
<tr><td>34</td><td>Ohio</td><td>765</td><td>35</td><td>South Carolina</td><td>764</td></tr>
<tr><td>31</td><td>Oklahoma</td><td>832</td><td>36</td><td>North Dakota</td><td>709</td></tr>
<tr><td>6</td><td>Oregon</td><td>1,816</td><td>37</td><td>Alabama</td><td>687</td></tr>
<tr><td>27</td><td>Pennsylvania</td><td>898</td><td>38</td><td>New Mexico</td><td>664</td></tr>
<tr><td>17</td><td>Rhode Island</td><td>1,151</td><td>39</td><td>Louisiana</td><td>639</td></tr>
<tr><td>35</td><td>South Carolina</td><td>764</td><td>40</td><td>Mississippi</td><td>597</td></tr>
<tr><td>44</td><td>South Dakota</td><td>0</td><td>41</td><td>Arizona</td><td>552</td></tr>
<tr><td>43</td><td>Tennessee</td><td>46</td><td>42</td><td>New Hampshire</td><td>72</td></tr>
<tr><td>44</td><td>Texas</td><td>0</td><td>43</td><td>Tennessee</td><td>46</td></tr>
<tr><td>22</td><td>Utah</td><td>1,056</td><td>44</td><td>Alaska</td><td>0</td></tr>
<tr><td>19</td><td>Vermont</td><td>1,133</td><td>44</td><td>Florida</td><td>0</td></tr>
<tr><td>8</td><td>Virginia</td><td>1,423</td><td>44</td><td>Nevada</td><td>0</td></tr>
<tr><td>44</td><td>Washington</td><td>0</td><td>44</td><td>South Dakota</td><td>0</td></tr>
<tr><td>23</td><td>West Virginia</td><td>1,050</td><td>44</td><td>Texas</td><td>0</td></tr>
<tr><td>12</td><td>Wisconsin</td><td>1,226</td><td>44</td><td>Washington</td><td>0</td></tr>
<tr><td>44</td><td>Wyoming</td><td>0</td><td>44</td><td>Wyoming</td><td>0</td></tr>
<tr><td></td><td></td><td></td><td></td><td>District of Columbia</td><td>2,787</td></tr>
</table>

Source: CQ Press using data from U.S. Bureau of the Census, Governments Division
"2015 State Government Tax Collections" (http://www.census.gov/govs/statetax/)

State Government Corporation Net Income Tax Revenue in 2015

National Total = $49,104,094,000

ALPHA ORDER

RANK	STATE	REVENUE	% of USA
24	Alabama	$533,586,000	1.1%
36	Alaska	227,852,000	0.5%
18	Arizona	690,960,000	1.4%
25	Arkansas	476,553,000	1.0%
1	California	9,007,182,000	18.3%
20	Colorado	673,230,000	1.4%
19	Connecticut	689,685,000	1.4%
29	Delaware	400,746,000	0.8%
6	Florida	2,237,500,000	4.6%
14	Georgia	1,000,536,000	2.0%
44	Hawaii	72,249,000	0.1%
37	Idaho	217,082,000	0.4%
3	Illinois	4,054,267,000	8.3%
15	Indiana	903,572,000	1.8%
26	Iowa	463,238,000	0.9%
27	Kansas	458,306,000	0.9%
17	Kentucky	751,910,000	1.5%
34	Louisiana	253,650,000	0.5%
41	Maine	168,966,000	0.3%
13	Maryland	1,003,588,000	2.0%
7	Massachusetts	2,227,381,000	4.5%
11	Michigan	1,185,568,000	2.4%
8	Minnesota	1,476,629,000	3.0%
23	Mississippi	534,547,000	1.1%
28	Missouri	425,776,000	0.9%
42	Montana	168,039,000	0.3%
33	Nebraska	344,477,000	0.7%
47	Nevada	0	0.0%
22	New Hampshire	576,679,000	1.2%
4	New Jersey	2,579,391,000	5.3%
35	New Mexico	249,947,000	0.5%
2	New York	5,084,187,000	10.4%
10	North Carolina	1,330,223,000	2.7%
39	North Dakota	186,039,000	0.4%
46	Ohio	2,586,000	0.0%
30	Oklahoma	388,530,000	0.8%
21	Oregon	621,727,000	1.3%
5	Pennsylvania	2,510,135,000	5.1%
40	Rhode Island	176,336,000	0.4%
31	South Carolina	377,329,000	0.8%
45	South Dakota	4,334,000	0.0%
9	Tennessee	1,400,973,000	2.9%
47	Texas	0	0.0%
32	Utah	368,681,000	0.8%
43	Vermont	112,643,000	0.2%
16	Virginia	817,851,000	1.7%
47	Washington	0	0.0%
38	West Virginia	188,758,000	0.4%
12	Wisconsin	1,032,411,000	2.1%
47	Wyoming	0	0.0%

RANK ORDER

RANK	STATE	REVENUE	% of USA
1	California	$9,007,182,000	18.3%
2	New York	5,084,187,000	10.4%
3	Illinois	4,054,267,000	8.3%
4	New Jersey	2,579,391,000	5.3%
5	Pennsylvania	2,510,135,000	5.1%
6	Florida	2,237,500,000	4.6%
7	Massachusetts	2,227,381,000	4.5%
8	Minnesota	1,476,629,000	3.0%
9	Tennessee	1,400,973,000	2.9%
10	North Carolina	1,330,223,000	2.7%
11	Michigan	1,185,568,000	2.4%
12	Wisconsin	1,032,411,000	2.1%
13	Maryland	1,003,588,000	2.0%
14	Georgia	1,000,536,000	2.0%
15	Indiana	903,572,000	1.8%
16	Virginia	817,851,000	1.7%
17	Kentucky	751,910,000	1.5%
18	Arizona	690,960,000	1.4%
19	Connecticut	689,685,000	1.4%
20	Colorado	673,230,000	1.4%
21	Oregon	621,727,000	1.3%
22	New Hampshire	576,679,000	1.2%
23	Mississippi	534,547,000	1.1%
24	Alabama	533,586,000	1.1%
25	Arkansas	476,553,000	1.0%
26	Iowa	463,238,000	0.9%
27	Kansas	458,306,000	0.9%
28	Missouri	425,776,000	0.9%
29	Delaware	400,746,000	0.8%
30	Oklahoma	388,530,000	0.8%
31	South Carolina	377,329,000	0.8%
32	Utah	368,681,000	0.8%
33	Nebraska	344,477,000	0.7%
34	Louisiana	253,650,000	0.5%
35	New Mexico	249,947,000	0.5%
36	Alaska	227,852,000	0.5%
37	Idaho	217,082,000	0.4%
38	West Virginia	188,758,000	0.4%
39	North Dakota	186,039,000	0.4%
40	Rhode Island	176,336,000	0.4%
41	Maine	168,966,000	0.3%
42	Montana	168,039,000	0.3%
43	Vermont	112,643,000	0.2%
44	Hawaii	72,249,000	0.1%
45	South Dakota	4,334,000	0.0%
46	Ohio	2,586,000	0.0%
47	Nevada	0	0.0%
47	Texas	0	0.0%
47	Washington	0	0.0%
47	Wyoming	0	0.0%
	District of Columbia	448,259,000	0.9%

Source: U.S. Bureau of the Census, Governments Division
"2015 State Government Tax Collections" (http://www.census.gov/govs/statetax/)

Per Capita State Government Corporation Net Income Tax Revenue in 2015

National Per Capita = $153

ALPHA ORDER

RANK	STATE	PER CAPITA
35	Alabama	$110
5	Alaska	309
37	Arizona	101
22	Arkansas	160
10	California	231
30	Colorado	124
13	Connecticut	192
2	Delaware	424
34	Florida	111
39	Georgia	98
44	Hawaii	51
28	Idaho	131
4	Illinois	316
26	Indiana	137
25	Iowa	148
23	Kansas	158
18	Kentucky	170
43	Louisiana	54
29	Maine	127
19	Maryland	167
3	Massachusetts	328
32	Michigan	120
7	Minnesota	269
16	Mississippi	179
42	Missouri	70
21	Montana	163
14	Nebraska	182
46	Nevada	0
1	New Hampshire	434
6	New Jersey	289
32	New Mexico	120
8	New York	257
27	North Carolina	133
9	North Dakota	246
46	Ohio	0
38	Oklahoma	99
24	Oregon	154
12	Pennsylvania	196
19	Rhode Island	167
41	South Carolina	77
45	South Dakota	5
11	Tennessee	212
46	Texas	0
31	Utah	123
15	Vermont	180
39	Virginia	98
46	Washington	0
36	West Virginia	103
16	Wisconsin	179
46	Wyoming	0

RANK ORDER

RANK	STATE	PER CAPITA
1	New Hampshire	$434
2	Delaware	424
3	Massachusetts	328
4	Illinois	316
5	Alaska	309
6	New Jersey	289
7	Minnesota	269
8	New York	257
9	North Dakota	246
10	California	231
11	Tennessee	212
12	Pennsylvania	196
13	Connecticut	192
14	Nebraska	182
15	Vermont	180
16	Mississippi	179
16	Wisconsin	179
18	Kentucky	170
19	Maryland	167
19	Rhode Island	167
21	Montana	163
22	Arkansas	160
23	Kansas	158
24	Oregon	154
25	Iowa	148
26	Indiana	137
27	North Carolina	133
28	Idaho	131
29	Maine	127
30	Colorado	124
31	Utah	123
32	Michigan	120
32	New Mexico	120
34	Florida	111
35	Alabama	110
36	West Virginia	103
37	Arizona	101
38	Oklahoma	99
39	Georgia	98
39	Virginia	98
41	South Carolina	77
42	Missouri	70
43	Louisiana	54
44	Hawaii	51
45	South Dakota	5
46	Nevada	0
46	Ohio	0
46	Texas	0
46	Washington	0
46	Wyoming	0

District of Columbia — 669

Source: CQ Press using data from U.S. Bureau of the Census, Governments Division
"2015 State Government Tax Collections" (http://www.census.gov/govs/statetax/)

State Government General Sales Tax Revenue in 2015

National Total = $286,154,392,000*

ALPHA ORDER

RANK	STATE	REVENUE	% of USA
34	Alabama	$2,463,912,000	0.9%
46	Alaska	0	0.0%
14	Arizona	6,466,167,000	2.3%
27	Arkansas	3,182,211,000	1.1%
1	California	38,464,704,000	13.4%
32	Colorado	2,817,773,000	1.0%
20	Connecticut	4,082,787,000	1.4%
46	Delaware	0	0.0%
3	Florida	21,800,895,000	7.6%
17	Georgia	5,256,592,000	1.8%
30	Hawaii	2,992,707,000	1.0%
38	Idaho	1,463,802,000	0.5%
10	Illinois	8,950,818,000	3.1%
11	Indiana	7,279,604,000	2.5%
29	Iowa	3,040,627,000	1.1%
28	Kansas	3,052,986,000	1.1%
26	Kentucky	3,267,331,000	1.1%
31	Louisiana	2,926,783,000	1.0%
41	Maine	1,280,298,000	0.4%
19	Maryland	4,409,919,000	1.5%
15	Massachusetts	5,803,934,000	2.0%
8	Michigan	9,211,783,000	3.2%
16	Minnesota	5,483,791,000	1.9%
24	Mississippi	3,422,774,000	1.2%
25	Missouri	3,380,034,000	1.2%
46	Montana	0	0.0%
37	Nebraska	1,787,880,000	0.6%
21	Nevada	4,080,507,000	1.4%
46	New Hampshire	0	0.0%
9	New Jersey	9,146,025,000	3.2%
35	New Mexico	2,256,088,000	0.8%
4	New York	13,104,421,000	4.6%
12	North Carolina	6,862,578,000	2.4%
39	North Dakota	1,389,083,000	0.5%
6	Ohio	11,900,176,000	4.2%
33	Oklahoma	2,682,008,000	0.9%
46	Oregon	0	0.0%
7	Pennsylvania	9,865,270,000	3.4%
43	Rhode Island	959,513,000	0.3%
23	South Carolina	3,568,788,000	1.2%
42	South Dakota	970,784,000	0.3%
13	Tennessee	6,547,191,000	2.3%
2	Texas	33,664,187,000	11.8%
36	Utah	1,882,901,000	0.7%
45	Vermont	366,667,000	0.1%
22	Virginia	3,793,215,000	1.3%
5	Washington	12,517,831,000	4.4%
40	West Virginia	1,293,327,000	0.5%
18	Wisconsin	4,892,126,000	1.7%
44	Wyoming	811,105,000	0.3%

RANK ORDER

RANK	STATE	REVENUE	% of USA
1	California	$38,464,704,000	13.4%
2	Texas	33,664,187,000	11.8%
3	Florida	21,800,895,000	7.6%
4	New York	13,104,421,000	4.6%
5	Washington	12,517,831,000	4.4%
6	Ohio	11,900,176,000	4.2%
7	Pennsylvania	9,865,270,000	3.4%
8	Michigan	9,211,783,000	3.2%
9	New Jersey	9,146,025,000	3.2%
10	Illinois	8,950,818,000	3.1%
11	Indiana	7,279,604,000	2.5%
12	North Carolina	6,862,578,000	2.4%
13	Tennessee	6,547,191,000	2.3%
14	Arizona	6,466,167,000	2.3%
15	Massachusetts	5,803,934,000	2.0%
16	Minnesota	5,483,791,000	1.9%
17	Georgia	5,256,592,000	1.8%
18	Wisconsin	4,892,126,000	1.7%
19	Maryland	4,409,919,000	1.5%
20	Connecticut	4,082,787,000	1.4%
21	Nevada	4,080,507,000	1.4%
22	Virginia	3,793,215,000	1.3%
23	South Carolina	3,568,788,000	1.2%
24	Mississippi	3,422,774,000	1.2%
25	Missouri	3,380,034,000	1.2%
26	Kentucky	3,267,331,000	1.1%
27	Arkansas	3,182,211,000	1.1%
28	Kansas	3,052,986,000	1.1%
29	Iowa	3,040,627,000	1.1%
30	Hawaii	2,992,707,000	1.0%
31	Louisiana	2,926,783,000	1.0%
32	Colorado	2,817,773,000	1.0%
33	Oklahoma	2,682,008,000	0.9%
34	Alabama	2,463,912,000	0.9%
35	New Mexico	2,256,088,000	0.8%
36	Utah	1,882,901,000	0.7%
37	Nebraska	1,787,880,000	0.6%
38	Idaho	1,463,802,000	0.5%
39	North Dakota	1,389,083,000	0.5%
40	West Virginia	1,293,327,000	0.5%
41	Maine	1,280,298,000	0.4%
42	South Dakota	970,784,000	0.3%
43	Rhode Island	959,513,000	0.3%
44	Wyoming	811,105,000	0.3%
45	Vermont	366,667,000	0.1%
46	Alaska	0	0.0%
46	Delaware	0	0.0%
46	Montana	0	0.0%
46	New Hampshire	0	0.0%
46	Oregon	0	0.0%
	District of Columbia	1,310,489,000	0.5%

Source: U.S. Bureau of the Census, Governments Division
  "2015 State Government Tax Collections" (http://www.census.gov/govs/statetax/)
*Does not include special sales taxes such as those on sale of alcohol, gasoline, or tobacco.

Per Capita State Government General Sales Tax Revenue in 2015

National Per Capita = $892*

ALPHA ORDER

RANK	STATE	PER CAPITA
44	Alabama	$508
46	Alaska	0
22	Arizona	948
13	Arkansas	1,069
19	California	986
42	Colorado	517
8	Connecticut	1,139
46	Delaware	0
12	Florida	1,077
43	Georgia	515
1	Hawaii	2,100
26	Idaho	886
34	Illinois	697
10	Indiana	1,101
20	Iowa	974
14	Kansas	1,050
30	Kentucky	738
39	Louisiana	627
21	Maine	963
31	Maryland	736
27	Massachusetts	856
24	Michigan	929
17	Minnesota	1,000
7	Mississippi	1,145
41	Missouri	556
46	Montana	0
23	Nebraska	944
4	Nevada	1,415
46	New Hampshire	0
16	New Jersey	1,024
11	New Mexico	1,084
37	New York	664
36	North Carolina	684
2	North Dakota	1,835
15	Ohio	1,025
35	Oklahoma	686
46	Oregon	0
29	Pennsylvania	771
25	Rhode Island	909
32	South Carolina	729
9	South Dakota	1,132
18	Tennessee	993
6	Texas	1,227
38	Utah	630
40	Vermont	586
45	Virginia	453
3	Washington	1,748
33	West Virginia	702
28	Wisconsin	848
5	Wyoming	1,383

RANK ORDER

RANK	STATE	PER CAPITA
1	Hawaii	$2,100
2	North Dakota	1,835
3	Washington	1,748
4	Nevada	1,415
5	Wyoming	1,383
6	Texas	1,227
7	Mississippi	1,145
8	Connecticut	1,139
9	South Dakota	1,132
10	Indiana	1,101
11	New Mexico	1,084
12	Florida	1,077
13	Arkansas	1,069
14	Kansas	1,050
15	Ohio	1,025
16	New Jersey	1,024
17	Minnesota	1,000
18	Tennessee	993
19	California	986
20	Iowa	974
21	Maine	963
22	Arizona	948
23	Nebraska	944
24	Michigan	929
25	Rhode Island	909
26	Idaho	886
27	Massachusetts	856
28	Wisconsin	848
29	Pennsylvania	771
30	Kentucky	738
31	Maryland	736
32	South Carolina	729
33	West Virginia	702
34	Illinois	697
35	Oklahoma	686
36	North Carolina	684
37	New York	664
38	Utah	630
39	Louisiana	627
40	Vermont	586
41	Missouri	556
42	Colorado	517
43	Georgia	515
44	Alabama	508
45	Virginia	453
46	Alaska	0
46	Delaware	0
46	Montana	0
46	New Hampshire	0
46	Oregon	0

District of Columbia   1,955

Source: CQ Press using data from U.S. Bureau of the Census, Governments Division
"2015 State Government Tax Collections" (http://www.census.gov/govs/statetax/)
*Does not include special sales taxes such as those on sale of alcohol, gasoline, or tobacco.

State Government Motor Fuels Sales Tax Revenue in 2015

National Total = $42,525,219,000

ALPHA ORDER

RANK	STATE	REVENUE	% of USA
24	Alabama	$560,188,000	1.3%
50	Alaska	42,003,000	0.1%
20	Arizona	753,814,000	1.8%
30	Arkansas	461,731,000	1.1%
1	California	5,711,160,000	13.4%
22	Colorado	667,948,000	1.6%
29	Connecticut	481,825,000	1.1%
46	Delaware	117,401,000	0.3%
4	Florida	2,481,760,000	5.8%
10	Georgia	1,025,819,000	2.4%
47	Hawaii	93,066,000	0.2%
38	Idaho	258,993,000	0.6%
8	Illinois	1,293,272,000	3.0%
17	Indiana	832,006,000	2.0%
26	Iowa	541,813,000	1.3%
32	Kansas	439,045,000	1.0%
16	Kentucky	850,276,000	2.0%
23	Louisiana	606,410,000	1.4%
39	Maine	243,891,000	0.6%
13	Maryland	923,483,000	2.2%
18	Massachusetts	756,121,000	1.8%
12	Michigan	1,010,395,000	2.4%
14	Minnesota	884,596,000	2.1%
34	Mississippi	428,013,000	1.0%
21	Missouri	695,145,000	1.6%
42	Montana	226,806,000	0.5%
36	Nebraska	327,665,000	0.8%
37	Nevada	304,364,000	0.7%
44	New Hampshire	146,796,000	0.3%
27	New Jersey	535,550,000	1.3%
40	New Mexico	240,177,000	0.6%
7	New York	1,648,106,000	3.9%
5	North Carolina	1,924,089,000	4.5%
41	North Dakota	232,296,000	0.5%
6	Ohio	1,907,996,000	4.5%
31	Oklahoma	455,288,000	1.1%
28	Oregon	524,665,000	1.2%
3	Pennsylvania	2,731,605,000	6.4%
48	Rhode Island	85,801,000	0.2%
25	South Carolina	545,955,000	1.3%
43	South Dakota	148,170,000	0.3%
15	Tennessee	857,605,000	2.0%
2	Texas	3,462,288,000	8.1%
35	Utah	377,390,000	0.9%
49	Vermont	85,619,000	0.2%
19	Virginia	755,681,000	1.8%
9	Washington	1,247,817,000	2.9%
33	West Virginia	433,877,000	1.0%
11	Wisconsin	1,014,656,000	2.4%
45	Wyoming	118,639,000	0.3%

RANK ORDER

RANK	STATE	REVENUE	% of USA
1	California	$5,711,160,000	13.4%
2	Texas	3,462,288,000	8.1%
3	Pennsylvania	2,731,605,000	6.4%
4	Florida	2,481,760,000	5.8%
5	North Carolina	1,924,089,000	4.5%
6	Ohio	1,907,996,000	4.5%
7	New York	1,648,106,000	3.9%
8	Illinois	1,293,272,000	3.0%
9	Washington	1,247,817,000	2.9%
10	Georgia	1,025,819,000	2.4%
11	Wisconsin	1,014,656,000	2.4%
12	Michigan	1,010,395,000	2.4%
13	Maryland	923,483,000	2.2%
14	Minnesota	884,596,000	2.1%
15	Tennessee	857,605,000	2.0%
16	Kentucky	850,276,000	2.0%
17	Indiana	832,006,000	2.0%
18	Massachusetts	756,121,000	1.8%
19	Virginia	755,681,000	1.8%
20	Arizona	753,814,000	1.8%
21	Missouri	695,145,000	1.6%
22	Colorado	667,948,000	1.6%
23	Louisiana	606,410,000	1.4%
24	Alabama	560,188,000	1.3%
25	South Carolina	545,955,000	1.3%
26	Iowa	541,813,000	1.3%
27	New Jersey	535,550,000	1.3%
28	Oregon	524,665,000	1.2%
29	Connecticut	481,825,000	1.1%
30	Arkansas	461,731,000	1.1%
31	Oklahoma	455,288,000	1.1%
32	Kansas	439,045,000	1.0%
33	West Virginia	433,877,000	1.0%
34	Mississippi	428,013,000	1.0%
35	Utah	377,390,000	0.9%
36	Nebraska	327,665,000	0.8%
37	Nevada	304,364,000	0.7%
38	Idaho	258,993,000	0.6%
39	Maine	243,891,000	0.6%
40	New Mexico	240,177,000	0.6%
41	North Dakota	232,296,000	0.5%
42	Montana	226,806,000	0.5%
43	South Dakota	148,170,000	0.3%
44	New Hampshire	146,796,000	0.3%
45	Wyoming	118,639,000	0.3%
46	Delaware	117,401,000	0.3%
47	Hawaii	93,066,000	0.2%
48	Rhode Island	85,801,000	0.2%
49	Vermont	85,619,000	0.2%
50	Alaska	42,003,000	0.1%
	District of Columbia	26,144,000	0.1%

Source: U.S. Bureau of the Census, Governments Division
"2015 State Government Tax Collections" (http://www.census.gov/govs/statetax/)

Per Capita State Government Motor Fuel Sales Tax Revenue in 2015

National Per Capita = $133

RANK	STATE	PER CAPITA
34	Alabama	$115
50	Alaska	57
38	Arizona	111
17	Arkansas	155
20	California	146
31	Colorado	123
23	Connecticut	134
30	Delaware	124
31	Florida	123
43	Georgia	101
48	Hawaii	65
16	Idaho	157
43	Illinois	101
27	Indiana	126
10	Iowa	174
19	Kansas	151
6	Kentucky	192
24	Louisiana	130
8	Maine	183
18	Maryland	154
38	Massachusetts	111
42	Michigan	102
15	Minnesota	161
21	Mississippi	143
36	Missouri	114
3	Montana	220
12	Nebraska	173
41	Nevada	106
40	New Hampshire	110
49	New Jersey	60
34	New Mexico	115
46	New York	83
6	North Carolina	192
1	North Dakota	307
14	Ohio	164
33	Oklahoma	117
24	Oregon	130
4	Pennsylvania	214
47	Rhode Island	81
37	South Carolina	112
12	South Dakota	173
24	Tennessee	130
27	Texas	126
27	Utah	126
22	Vermont	137
45	Virginia	90
10	Washington	174
2	West Virginia	236
9	Wisconsin	176
5	Wyoming	202

RANK	STATE	PER CAPITA
1	North Dakota	$307
2	West Virginia	236
3	Montana	220
4	Pennsylvania	214
5	Wyoming	202
6	Kentucky	192
6	North Carolina	192
8	Maine	183
9	Wisconsin	176
10	Iowa	174
10	Washington	174
12	Nebraska	173
12	South Dakota	173
14	Ohio	164
15	Minnesota	161
16	Idaho	157
17	Arkansas	155
18	Maryland	154
19	Kansas	151
20	California	146
21	Mississippi	143
22	Vermont	137
23	Connecticut	134
24	Louisiana	130
24	Oregon	130
24	Tennessee	130
27	Indiana	126
27	Texas	126
27	Utah	126
30	Delaware	124
31	Colorado	123
31	Florida	123
33	Oklahoma	117
34	Alabama	115
34	New Mexico	115
36	Missouri	114
37	South Carolina	112
38	Arizona	111
38	Massachusetts	111
40	New Hampshire	110
41	Nevada	106
42	Michigan	102
43	Georgia	101
43	Illinois	101
45	Virginia	90
46	New York	83
47	Rhode Island	81
48	Hawaii	65
49	New Jersey	60
50	Alaska	57

	District of Columbia	39

Source: CQ Press using data from U.S. Bureau of the Census, Governments Division
"2015 State Government Tax Collections" (http://www.census.gov/govs/statetax/)

State Tax Rates on Gasoline in 2017

National Median = 25.00 Cents per Gallon*

ALPHA ORDER

RANK	STATE	CENTS PER GALLON
43	Alabama	18.00
50	Alaska	8.95
40	Arizona	19.00
35	Arkansas	21.80
9	California	32.80
34	Colorado	22.00
26	Connecticut	25.00
32	Delaware	23.00
11	Florida	30.93
22	Georgia	26.30
49	Hawaii	16.00
7	Idaho	33.00
38	Illinois	20.10
43	Indiana	18.00
12	Iowa	30.70
25	Kansas	25.03
24	Kentucky	26.00
37	Louisiana	20.13
14	Maine	30.00
6	Maryland	33.50
29	Massachusetts	24.00
22	Michigan	26.30
18	Minnesota	28.60
42	Mississippi	18.40
45	Missouri	17.30
21	Montana	27.00
19	Nebraska	28.20
27	Nevada	24.81
31	New Hampshire	23.83
3	New Jersey	37.10
41	New Mexico	18.88
28	New York	24.20
4	North Carolina	34.55
32	North Dakota	23.00
20	Ohio	28.00
46	Oklahoma	17.00
14	Oregon	30.00
1	Pennsylvania	58.20
5	Rhode Island	34.00
47	South Carolina	16.75
14	South Dakota	30.00
36	Tennessee	21.40
39	Texas	20.00
17	Utah	29.40
13	Vermont	30.46
48	Virginia	16.20
2	Washington	49.40
10	West Virginia	32.20
8	Wisconsin	32.90
29	Wyoming	24.00

RANK ORDER

RANK	STATE	CENTS PER GALLON
1	Pennsylvania	58.20
2	Washington	49.40
3	New Jersey	37.10
4	North Carolina	34.55
5	Rhode Island	34.00
6	Maryland	33.50
7	Idaho	33.00
8	Wisconsin	32.90
9	California	32.80
10	West Virginia	32.20
11	Florida	30.93
12	Iowa	30.70
13	Vermont	30.46
14	Maine	30.00
14	Oregon	30.00
14	South Dakota	30.00
17	Utah	29.40
18	Minnesota	28.60
19	Nebraska	28.20
20	Ohio	28.00
21	Montana	27.00
22	Georgia	26.30
22	Michigan	26.30
24	Kentucky	26.00
25	Kansas	25.03
26	Connecticut	25.00
27	Nevada	24.81
28	New York	24.20
29	Massachusetts	24.00
29	Wyoming	24.00
31	New Hampshire	23.83
32	Delaware	23.00
32	North Dakota	23.00
34	Colorado	22.00
35	Arkansas	21.80
36	Tennessee	21.40
37	Louisiana	20.13
38	Illinois	20.10
39	Texas	20.00
40	Arizona	19.00
41	New Mexico	18.88
42	Mississippi	18.40
43	Alabama	18.00
43	Indiana	18.00
45	Missouri	17.30
46	Oklahoma	17.00
47	South Carolina	16.75
48	Virginia	16.20
49	Hawaii	16.00
50	Alaska	8.95
	District of Columbia	23.50

Source: Federation of Tax Administrators
  "Motor Fuel Excise Tax Rates" (http://www.taxadmin.org/current-tax-rates)
*As of January 1, 2017. Federal gasoline tax rate is an additional 18.4 cents per gallon. Many states also allow additional local
option taxes on gasoline.

State Government Motor Vehicle and Operators' License Tax Revenue in 2015

National Total = $27,138,871,000

ALPHA ORDER

RANK	STATE	REVENUE	% of USA
28	Alabama	$237,486,000	0.9%
48	Alaska	60,460,000	0.2%
26	Arizona	238,353,000	0.9%
36	Arkansas	175,805,000	0.6%
1	California	4,168,892,000	15.4%
17	Colorado	523,230,000	1.9%
25	Connecticut	269,159,000	1.0%
49	Delaware	60,344,000	0.2%
4	Florida	1,537,391,000	5.7%
22	Georgia	453,460,000	1.7%
35	Hawaii	178,935,000	0.7%
38	Idaho	153,550,000	0.6%
3	Illinois	1,794,068,000	6.6%
21	Indiana	479,088,000	1.8%
14	Iowa	614,951,000	2.3%
27	Kansas	238,151,000	0.9%
30	Kentucky	219,091,000	0.8%
44	Louisiana	87,086,000	0.3%
41	Maine	116,476,000	0.4%
18	Maryland	521,106,000	1.9%
16	Massachusetts	550,344,000	2.0%
6	Michigan	1,074,988,000	4.0%
9	Minnesota	773,098,000	2.8%
31	Mississippi	208,675,000	0.8%
24	Missouri	296,343,000	1.1%
37	Montana	167,559,000	0.6%
42	Nebraska	112,203,000	0.4%
32	Nevada	203,469,000	0.7%
39	New Hampshire	134,859,000	0.5%
12	New Jersey	692,472,000	2.6%
34	New Mexico	185,118,000	0.7%
5	New York	1,497,802,000	5.5%
11	North Carolina	723,917,000	2.7%
40	North Dakota	128,128,000	0.5%
8	Ohio	826,208,000	3.0%
10	Oklahoma	754,180,000	2.8%
15	Oregon	582,427,000	2.1%
7	Pennsylvania	969,484,000	3.6%
50	Rhode Island	60,003,000	0.2%
29	South Carolina	233,211,000	0.9%
45	South Dakota	84,533,000	0.3%
23	Tennessee	326,522,000	1.2%
2	Texas	2,245,272,000	8.3%
33	Utah	192,741,000	0.7%
47	Vermont	78,940,000	0.3%
20	Virginia	489,634,000	1.8%
13	Washington	680,636,000	2.5%
43	West Virginia	107,707,000	0.4%
19	Wisconsin	509,595,000	1.9%
46	Wyoming	79,709,000	0.3%

RANK ORDER

RANK	STATE	REVENUE	% of USA
1	California	$4,168,892,000	15.4%
2	Texas	2,245,272,000	8.3%
3	Illinois	1,794,068,000	6.6%
4	Florida	1,537,391,000	5.7%
5	New York	1,497,802,000	5.5%
6	Michigan	1,074,988,000	4.0%
7	Pennsylvania	969,484,000	3.6%
8	Ohio	826,208,000	3.0%
9	Minnesota	773,098,000	2.8%
10	Oklahoma	754,180,000	2.8%
11	North Carolina	723,917,000	2.7%
12	New Jersey	692,472,000	2.6%
13	Washington	680,636,000	2.5%
14	Iowa	614,951,000	2.3%
15	Oregon	582,427,000	2.1%
16	Massachusetts	550,344,000	2.0%
17	Colorado	523,230,000	1.9%
18	Maryland	521,106,000	1.9%
19	Wisconsin	509,595,000	1.9%
20	Virginia	489,634,000	1.8%
21	Indiana	479,088,000	1.8%
22	Georgia	453,460,000	1.7%
23	Tennessee	326,522,000	1.2%
24	Missouri	296,343,000	1.1%
25	Connecticut	269,159,000	1.0%
26	Arizona	238,353,000	0.9%
27	Kansas	238,151,000	0.9%
28	Alabama	237,486,000	0.9%
29	South Carolina	233,211,000	0.9%
30	Kentucky	219,091,000	0.8%
31	Mississippi	208,675,000	0.8%
32	Nevada	203,469,000	0.7%
33	Utah	192,741,000	0.7%
34	New Mexico	185,118,000	0.7%
35	Hawaii	178,935,000	0.7%
36	Arkansas	175,805,000	0.6%
37	Montana	167,559,000	0.6%
38	Idaho	153,550,000	0.6%
39	New Hampshire	134,859,000	0.5%
40	North Dakota	128,128,000	0.5%
41	Maine	116,476,000	0.4%
42	Nebraska	112,203,000	0.4%
43	West Virginia	107,707,000	0.4%
44	Louisiana	87,086,000	0.3%
45	South Dakota	84,533,000	0.3%
46	Wyoming	79,709,000	0.3%
47	Vermont	78,940,000	0.3%
48	Alaska	60,460,000	0.2%
49	Delaware	60,344,000	0.2%
50	Rhode Island	60,003,000	0.2%
	District of Columbia	42,012,000	0.2%

Source: U.S. Bureau of the Census, Governments Division
"2015 State Government Tax Collections" (http://www.census.gov/govs/statetax/)

Per Capita State Government Motor Vehicle and Operators' License Tax Revenue in 2015
National Per Capita = $85

ALPHA ORDER

RANK	STATE	PER CAPITA
45	Alabama	$49
22	Alaska	82
49	Arizona	35
38	Arkansas	59
12	California	107
15	Colorado	96
30	Connecticut	75
36	Delaware	64
27	Florida	76
48	Georgia	44
9	Hawaii	126
17	Idaho	93
7	Illinois	140
31	Indiana	72
1	Iowa	197
22	Kansas	82
43	Kentucky	50
50	Louisiana	19
19	Maine	88
21	Maryland	87
25	Massachusetts	81
11	Michigan	108
6	Minnesota	141
35	Mississippi	70
45	Missouri	49
4	Montana	162
38	Nebraska	59
33	Nevada	71
13	New Hampshire	101
26	New Jersey	77
18	New Mexico	89
27	New York	76
31	North Carolina	72
3	North Dakota	169
33	Ohio	71
2	Oklahoma	193
5	Oregon	145
27	Pennsylvania	76
42	Rhode Island	57
47	South Carolina	48
14	South Dakota	99
43	Tennessee	50
22	Texas	82
36	Utah	64
9	Vermont	126
38	Virginia	59
16	Washington	95
38	West Virginia	59
19	Wisconsin	88
8	Wyoming	136

RANK ORDER

RANK	STATE	PER CAPITA
1	Iowa	$197
2	Oklahoma	193
3	North Dakota	169
4	Montana	162
5	Oregon	145
6	Minnesota	141
7	Illinois	140
8	Wyoming	136
9	Hawaii	126
9	Vermont	126
11	Michigan	108
12	California	107
13	New Hampshire	101
14	South Dakota	99
15	Colorado	96
16	Washington	95
17	Idaho	93
18	New Mexico	89
19	Maine	88
19	Wisconsin	88
21	Maryland	87
22	Alaska	82
22	Kansas	82
22	Texas	82
25	Massachusetts	81
26	New Jersey	77
27	Florida	76
27	New York	76
27	Pennsylvania	76
30	Connecticut	75
31	Indiana	72
31	North Carolina	72
33	Nevada	71
33	Ohio	71
35	Mississippi	70
36	Delaware	64
36	Utah	64
38	Arkansas	59
38	Nebraska	59
38	Virginia	59
38	West Virginia	59
42	Rhode Island	57
43	Kentucky	50
43	Tennessee	50
45	Alabama	49
45	Missouri	49
47	South Carolina	48
48	Georgia	44
49	Arizona	35
50	Louisiana	19

District of Columbia		63

Source: CQ Press using data from U.S. Bureau of the Census, Governments Division
"2015 State Government Tax Collections" (http://www.census.gov/govs/statetax/)

State Government Tobacco Product Sales Tax Revenue in 2015

National Total = $17,741,659,000

ALPHA ORDER

RANK	STATE	REVENUE	% of USA
35	Alabama	$116,414,000	0.7%
44	Alaska	65,823,000	0.4%
17	Arizona	314,239,000	1.8%
24	Arkansas	225,097,000	1.3%
7	California	832,379,000	4.7%
27	Colorado	197,017,000	1.1%
16	Connecticut	357,944,000	2.0%
37	Delaware	102,695,000	0.6%
3	Florida	1,192,906,000	6.7%
26	Georgia	215,055,000	1.2%
33	Hawaii	129,659,000	0.7%
47	Idaho	48,408,000	0.3%
6	Illinois	861,954,000	4.9%
14	Indiana	439,264,000	2.5%
25	Iowa	223,069,000	1.3%
40	Kansas	96,303,000	0.5%
22	Kentucky	242,232,000	1.4%
30	Louisiana	138,400,000	0.8%
32	Maine	136,913,000	0.8%
15	Maryland	391,451,000	2.2%
11	Massachusetts	647,101,000	3.6%
5	Michigan	959,852,000	5.4%
10	Minnesota	652,046,000	3.7%
29	Mississippi	148,302,000	0.8%
39	Missouri	99,436,000	0.6%
41	Montana	85,042,000	0.5%
45	Nebraska	63,585,000	0.4%
34	Nevada	116,840,000	0.7%
23	New Hampshire	236,380,000	1.3%
9	New Jersey	715,556,000	4.0%
42	New Mexico	79,956,000	0.5%
2	New York	1,306,696,000	7.4%
19	North Carolina	276,458,000	1.6%
48	North Dakota	35,518,000	0.2%
8	Ohio	809,640,000	4.6%
18	Oklahoma	313,852,000	1.8%
20	Oregon	266,247,000	1.5%
4	Pennsylvania	978,006,000	5.5%
31	Rhode Island	137,980,000	0.8%
49	South Carolina	25,482,000	0.1%
46	South Dakota	61,004,000	0.3%
21	Tennessee	263,566,000	1.5%
1	Texas	1,491,765,000	8.4%
36	Utah	115,761,000	0.7%
43	Vermont	76,755,000	0.4%
28	Virginia	177,588,000	1.0%
13	Washington	474,183,000	2.7%
38	West Virginia	102,188,000	0.6%
12	Wisconsin	641,464,000	3.6%
50	Wyoming	24,696,000	0.1%

RANK ORDER

RANK	STATE	REVENUE	% of USA
1	Texas	$1,491,765,000	8.4%
2	New York	1,306,696,000	7.4%
3	Florida	1,192,906,000	6.7%
4	Pennsylvania	978,006,000	5.5%
5	Michigan	959,852,000	5.4%
6	Illinois	861,954,000	4.9%
7	California	832,379,000	4.7%
8	Ohio	809,640,000	4.6%
9	New Jersey	715,556,000	4.0%
10	Minnesota	652,046,000	3.7%
11	Massachusetts	647,101,000	3.6%
12	Wisconsin	641,464,000	3.6%
13	Washington	474,183,000	2.7%
14	Indiana	439,264,000	2.5%
15	Maryland	391,451,000	2.2%
16	Connecticut	357,944,000	2.0%
17	Arizona	314,239,000	1.8%
18	Oklahoma	313,852,000	1.8%
19	North Carolina	276,458,000	1.6%
20	Oregon	266,247,000	1.5%
21	Tennessee	263,566,000	1.5%
22	Kentucky	242,232,000	1.4%
23	New Hampshire	236,380,000	1.3%
24	Arkansas	225,097,000	1.3%
25	Iowa	223,069,000	1.3%
26	Georgia	215,055,000	1.2%
27	Colorado	197,017,000	1.1%
28	Virginia	177,588,000	1.0%
29	Mississippi	148,302,000	0.8%
30	Louisiana	138,400,000	0.8%
31	Rhode Island	137,980,000	0.8%
32	Maine	136,913,000	0.8%
33	Hawaii	129,659,000	0.7%
34	Nevada	116,840,000	0.7%
35	Alabama	116,414,000	0.7%
36	Utah	115,761,000	0.7%
37	Delaware	102,695,000	0.6%
38	West Virginia	102,188,000	0.6%
39	Missouri	99,436,000	0.6%
40	Kansas	96,303,000	0.5%
41	Montana	85,042,000	0.5%
42	New Mexico	79,956,000	0.5%
43	Vermont	76,755,000	0.4%
44	Alaska	65,823,000	0.4%
45	Nebraska	63,585,000	0.4%
46	South Dakota	61,004,000	0.3%
47	Idaho	48,408,000	0.3%
48	North Dakota	35,518,000	0.2%
49	South Carolina	25,482,000	0.1%
50	Wyoming	24,696,000	0.1%
	District of Columbia	31,492,000	0.2%

Source: U.S. Bureau of the Census, Governments Division
"2015 State Government Tax Collections" (http://www.census.gov/govs/statetax/)

Per Capita State Government Tobacco Sales Tax Revenue in 2015

National Per Capita = $55

ALPHA ORDER

RANK	STATE	PER CAPITA
45	Alabama	$24
12	Alaska	89
33	Arizona	46
16	Arkansas	76
46	California	21
39	Colorado	36
8	Connecticut	100
6	Delaware	109
27	Florida	59
46	Georgia	21
11	Hawaii	91
43	Idaho	29
21	Illinois	67
22	Indiana	66
18	Iowa	71
41	Kansas	33
29	Kentucky	55
42	Louisiana	30
7	Maine	103
26	Maryland	65
10	Massachusetts	95
9	Michigan	97
4	Minnesota	119
31	Mississippi	50
49	Missouri	16
13	Montana	82
40	Nebraska	34
35	Nevada	41
1	New Hampshire	178
14	New Jersey	80
38	New Mexico	38
22	New York	66
44	North Carolina	28
32	North Dakota	47
20	Ohio	70
14	Oklahoma	80
22	Oregon	66
16	Pennsylvania	76
2	Rhode Island	131
50	South Carolina	5
18	South Dakota	71
36	Tennessee	40
30	Texas	54
37	Utah	39
3	Vermont	123
46	Virginia	21
22	Washington	66
28	West Virginia	56
5	Wisconsin	111
34	Wyoming	42

RANK ORDER

RANK	STATE	PER CAPITA
1	New Hampshire	$178
2	Rhode Island	131
3	Vermont	123
4	Minnesota	119
5	Wisconsin	111
6	Delaware	109
7	Maine	103
8	Connecticut	100
9	Michigan	97
10	Massachusetts	95
11	Hawaii	91
12	Alaska	89
13	Montana	82
14	New Jersey	80
14	Oklahoma	80
16	Arkansas	76
16	Pennsylvania	76
18	Iowa	71
18	South Dakota	71
20	Ohio	70
21	Illinois	67
22	Indiana	66
22	New York	66
22	Oregon	66
22	Washington	66
26	Maryland	65
27	Florida	59
28	West Virginia	56
29	Kentucky	55
30	Texas	54
31	Mississippi	50
32	North Dakota	47
33	Arizona	46
34	Wyoming	42
35	Nevada	41
36	Tennessee	40
37	Utah	39
38	New Mexico	38
39	Colorado	36
40	Nebraska	34
41	Kansas	33
42	Louisiana	30
43	Idaho	29
44	North Carolina	28
45	Alabama	24
46	California	21
46	Georgia	21
46	Virginia	21
49	Missouri	16
50	South Carolina	5
	District of Columbia	47

Source: CQ Press using data from U.S. Bureau of the Census, Governments Division
"2015 State Government Tax Collections" (http://www.census.gov/govs/statetax/)

State Tax on a Pack of Cigarettes in 2017

National Median = $1.53 per Pack*

ALPHA ORDER

RANK	STATE	TAX PER PACK
38	Alabama	$0.68
12	Alaska	2.00
12	Arizona	2.00
32	Arkansas	1.15
36	California	0.87
37	Colorado	0.84
2	Connecticut	3.90
23	Delaware	1.60
28	Florida	1.34
48	Georgia	0.37
5	Hawaii	3.20
44	Idaho	0.57
17	Illinois	1.98
35	Indiana	1.00
27	Iowa	1.36
30	Kansas	1.29
42	Kentucky	0.60
33	Louisiana	1.08
12	Maine	2.00
12	Maryland	2.00
4	Massachusetts	3.51
12	Michigan	2.00
7	Minnesota	3.04
38	Mississippi	0.68
50	Missouri	0.17
20	Montana	1.70
40	Nebraska	0.64
18	Nevada	1.80
19	New Hampshire	1.78
9	New Jersey	2.70
22	New Mexico	1.66
1	New York	4.35
46	North Carolina	0.45
47	North Dakota	0.44
23	Ohio	1.60
34	Oklahoma	1.03
29	Oregon	1.32
10	Pennsylvania	2.60
3	Rhode Island	3.75
44	South Carolina	0.57
25	South Dakota	1.53
41	Tennessee	0.62
26	Texas	1.41
20	Utah	1.70
6	Vermont	3.08
49	Virginia	0.30
8	Washington	3.03
31	West Virginia	1.20
11	Wisconsin	2.52
42	Wyoming	0.60

RANK ORDER

RANK	STATE	TAX PER PACK
1	New York	$4.35
2	Connecticut	3.90
3	Rhode Island	3.75
4	Massachusetts	3.51
5	Hawaii	3.20
6	Vermont	3.08
7	Minnesota	3.04
8	Washington	3.03
9	New Jersey	2.70
10	Pennsylvania	2.60
11	Wisconsin	2.52
12	Alaska	2.00
12	Arizona	2.00
12	Maine	2.00
12	Maryland	2.00
12	Michigan	2.00
17	Illinois	1.98
18	Nevada	1.80
19	New Hampshire	1.78
20	Montana	1.70
20	Utah	1.70
22	New Mexico	1.66
23	Delaware	1.60
23	Ohio	1.60
25	South Dakota	1.53
26	Texas	1.41
27	Iowa	1.36
28	Florida	1.34
29	Oregon	1.32
30	Kansas	1.29
31	West Virginia	1.20
32	Arkansas	1.15
33	Louisiana	1.08
34	Oklahoma	1.03
35	Indiana	1.00
36	California	0.87
37	Colorado	0.84
38	Alabama	0.68
38	Mississippi	0.68
40	Nebraska	0.64
41	Tennessee	0.62
42	Kentucky	0.60
42	Wyoming	0.60
44	Idaho	0.57
44	South Carolina	0.57
46	North Carolina	0.45
47	North Dakota	0.44
48	Georgia	0.37
49	Virginia	0.30
50	Missouri	0.17

District of Columbia   2.50

Source: Federation of Tax Administrators
  "State Excise Tax Rates on Cigarettes" (http://www.taxadmin.org/current-tax-rates)
*As of January 1, 2017. Many states also allow additional local option taxes on cigarettes.

State Government Alcoholic Beverage Sales Tax Revenue in 2015

National Total = $6,430,879,000

ALPHA ORDER

RANK	STATE	REVENUE	% of USA
10	Alabama	$192,490,000	3.0%
34	Alaska	39,836,000	0.6%
22	Arizona	71,270,000	1.1%
26	Arkansas	53,256,000	0.8%
5	California	357,373,000	5.6%
33	Colorado	41,308,000	0.6%
23	Connecticut	61,612,000	1.0%
41	Delaware	20,708,000	0.3%
2	Florida	459,019,000	7.1%
11	Georgia	184,374,000	2.9%
28	Hawaii	50,281,000	0.8%
49	Idaho	8,937,000	0.1%
7	Illinois	283,177,000	4.4%
29	Indiana	46,064,000	0.7%
40	Iowa	22,686,000	0.4%
16	Kansas	132,589,000	2.1%
17	Kentucky	131,951,000	2.1%
25	Louisiana	57,416,000	0.9%
43	Maine	18,312,000	0.3%
37	Maryland	30,956,000	0.5%
21	Massachusetts	80,815,000	1.3%
14	Michigan	145,399,000	2.3%
20	Minnesota	85,142,000	1.3%
32	Mississippi	42,094,000	0.7%
35	Missouri	36,208,000	0.6%
36	Montana	33,860,000	0.5%
38	Nebraska	29,873,000	0.5%
31	Nevada	43,799,000	0.7%
47	New Hampshire	12,328,000	0.2%
15	New Jersey	138,548,000	2.2%
30	New Mexico	45,735,000	0.7%
9	New York	250,899,000	3.9%
3	North Carolina	359,880,000	5.6%
48	North Dakota	9,485,000	0.1%
19	Ohio	101,090,000	1.6%
18	Oklahoma	116,772,000	1.8%
45	Oregon	17,811,000	0.3%
4	Pennsylvania	358,886,000	5.6%
42	Rhode Island	19,538,000	0.3%
12	South Carolina	166,501,000	2.6%
46	South Dakota	16,690,000	0.3%
13	Tennessee	159,768,000	2.5%
1	Texas	1,147,565,000	17.8%
27	Utah	51,221,000	0.8%
39	Vermont	24,839,000	0.4%
8	Virginia	257,229,000	4.0%
6	Washington	331,405,000	5.2%
44	West Virginia	18,159,000	0.3%
24	Wisconsin	57,596,000	0.9%
50	Wyoming	1,885,000	0.0%

RANK ORDER

RANK	STATE	REVENUE	% of USA
1	Texas	$1,147,565,000	17.8%
2	Florida	459,019,000	7.1%
3	North Carolina	359,880,000	5.6%
4	Pennsylvania	358,886,000	5.6%
5	California	357,373,000	5.6%
6	Washington	331,405,000	5.2%
7	Illinois	283,177,000	4.4%
8	Virginia	257,229,000	4.0%
9	New York	250,899,000	3.9%
10	Alabama	192,490,000	3.0%
11	Georgia	184,374,000	2.9%
12	South Carolina	166,501,000	2.6%
13	Tennessee	159,768,000	2.5%
14	Michigan	145,399,000	2.3%
15	New Jersey	138,548,000	2.2%
16	Kansas	132,589,000	2.1%
17	Kentucky	131,951,000	2.1%
18	Oklahoma	116,772,000	1.8%
19	Ohio	101,090,000	1.6%
20	Minnesota	85,142,000	1.3%
21	Massachusetts	80,815,000	1.3%
22	Arizona	71,270,000	1.1%
23	Connecticut	61,612,000	1.0%
24	Wisconsin	57,596,000	0.9%
25	Louisiana	57,416,000	0.9%
26	Arkansas	53,256,000	0.8%
27	Utah	51,221,000	0.8%
28	Hawaii	50,281,000	0.8%
29	Indiana	46,064,000	0.7%
30	New Mexico	45,735,000	0.7%
31	Nevada	43,799,000	0.7%
32	Mississippi	42,094,000	0.7%
33	Colorado	41,308,000	0.6%
34	Alaska	39,836,000	0.6%
35	Missouri	36,208,000	0.6%
36	Montana	33,860,000	0.5%
37	Maryland	30,956,000	0.5%
38	Nebraska	29,873,000	0.5%
39	Vermont	24,839,000	0.4%
40	Iowa	22,686,000	0.4%
41	Delaware	20,708,000	0.3%
42	Rhode Island	19,538,000	0.3%
43	Maine	18,312,000	0.3%
44	West Virginia	18,159,000	0.3%
45	Oregon	17,811,000	0.3%
46	South Dakota	16,690,000	0.3%
47	New Hampshire	12,328,000	0.2%
48	North Dakota	9,485,000	0.1%
49	Idaho	8,937,000	0.1%
50	Wyoming	1,885,000	0.0%
	District of Columbia	6,244,000	0.1%

Source: U.S. Bureau of the Census, Governments Division
"2015 State Government Tax Collections" (http://www.census.gov/govs/statetax/)

Per Capita State Government Alcoholic Beverage Sales Tax Revenue in 2015

National Per Capita = $20

ALPHA ORDER

ALPHA ORDER

RANK ORDER

RANK	STATE	PER CAPITA
5	Alabama	$40
1	Alaska	54
37	Arizona	10
22	Arkansas	18
40	California	9
43	Colorado	8
24	Connecticut	17
17	Delaware	22
16	Florida	23
22	Georgia	18
8	Hawaii	35
47	Idaho	5
17	Illinois	22
44	Indiana	7
44	Iowa	7
2	Kansas	46
12	Kentucky	30
35	Louisiana	12
31	Maine	14
47	Maryland	5
35	Massachusetts	12
29	Michigan	15
26	Minnesota	16
31	Mississippi	14
46	Missouri	6
10	Montana	33
26	Nebraska	16
29	Nevada	15
40	New Hampshire	9
26	New Jersey	16
17	New Mexico	22
33	New York	13
7	North Carolina	36
33	North Dakota	13
40	Ohio	9
12	Oklahoma	30
49	Oregon	4
14	Pennsylvania	28
20	Rhode Island	19
9	South Carolina	34
20	South Dakota	19
15	Tennessee	24
4	Texas	42
24	Utah	17
5	Vermont	40
11	Virginia	31
2	Washington	46
37	West Virginia	10
37	Wisconsin	10
50	Wyoming	3

RANK	STATE	PER CAPITA
1	Alaska	$54
2	Kansas	46
2	Washington	46
4	Texas	42
5	Alabama	40
5	Vermont	40
7	North Carolina	36
8	Hawaii	35
9	South Carolina	34
10	Montana	33
11	Virginia	31
12	Kentucky	30
12	Oklahoma	30
14	Pennsylvania	28
15	Tennessee	24
16	Florida	23
17	Delaware	22
17	Illinois	22
17	New Mexico	22
20	Rhode Island	19
20	South Dakota	19
22	Arkansas	18
22	Georgia	18
24	Connecticut	17
24	Utah	17
26	Minnesota	16
26	Nebraska	16
26	New Jersey	16
29	Michigan	15
29	Nevada	15
31	Maine	14
31	Mississippi	14
33	New York	13
33	North Dakota	13
35	Louisiana	12
35	Massachusetts	12
37	Arizona	10
37	West Virginia	10
37	Wisconsin	10
40	California	9
40	New Hampshire	9
40	Ohio	9
43	Colorado	8
44	Indiana	7
44	Iowa	7
46	Missouri	6
47	Idaho	5
47	Maryland	5
49	Oregon	4
50	Wyoming	3

District of Columbia — 9

Source: CQ Press using data from U.S. Bureau of the Census, Governments Division
"2015 State Government Tax Collections" (http://www.census.gov/govs/statetax/)

State Government Total Expenditures in 2014

National Total = $2,048,405,642,000*

ALPHA ORDER

RANK	STATE	EXPENDITURES	% of USA
28	Alabama	$28,416,987,000	1.4%
38	Alaska	13,043,237,000	0.6%
19	Arizona	33,433,440,000	1.6%
31	Arkansas	20,476,493,000	1.0%
1	California	285,492,890,000	13.9%
21	Colorado	30,832,158,000	1.5%
25	Connecticut	29,658,168,000	1.4%
42	Delaware	8,871,454,000	0.4%
5	Florida	83,572,497,000	4.1%
14	Georgia	45,679,846,000	2.2%
39	Hawaii	12,548,539,000	0.6%
43	Idaho	8,523,206,000	0.4%
7	Illinois	77,579,925,000	3.8%
18	Indiana	36,141,456,000	1.8%
30	Iowa	21,385,336,000	1.0%
35	Kansas	17,030,164,000	0.8%
24	Kentucky	30,117,392,000	1.5%
20	Louisiana	32,077,901,000	1.6%
41	Maine	9,315,918,000	0.5%
16	Maryland	41,435,785,000	2.0%
10	Massachusetts	58,517,229,000	2.9%
9	Michigan	64,209,217,000	3.1%
15	Minnesota	42,140,750,000	2.1%
32	Mississippi	20,114,533,000	1.0%
23	Missouri	30,650,264,000	1.5%
47	Montana	7,276,481,000	0.4%
40	Nebraska	10,121,365,000	0.5%
37	Nevada	13,305,803,000	0.6%
46	New Hampshire	7,402,186,000	0.4%
8	New Jersey	70,030,056,000	3.4%
33	New Mexico	17,804,718,000	0.9%
2	New York	179,741,140,000	8.8%
11	North Carolina	51,447,701,000	2.5%
45	North Dakota	7,540,916,000	0.4%
6	Ohio	79,625,053,000	3.9%
29	Oklahoma	23,632,322,000	1.2%
26	Oregon	29,615,962,000	1.4%
4	Pennsylvania	87,463,890,000	4.3%
44	Rhode Island	8,366,774,000	0.4%
27	South Carolina	29,013,168,000	1.4%
50	South Dakota	4,566,813,000	0.2%
22	Tennessee	30,674,985,000	1.5%
3	Texas	131,322,259,000	6.4%
34	Utah	17,250,463,000	0.8%
48	Vermont	6,325,218,000	0.3%
12	Virginia	48,702,926,000	2.4%
13	Washington	47,858,031,000	2.3%
36	West Virginia	13,310,897,000	0.6%
17	Wisconsin	38,826,150,000	1.9%
49	Wyoming	5,915,580,000	0.3%

RANK ORDER

RANK	STATE	EXPENDITURES	% of USA
1	California	$285,492,890,000	13.9%
2	New York	179,741,140,000	8.8%
3	Texas	131,322,259,000	6.4%
4	Pennsylvania	87,463,890,000	4.3%
5	Florida	83,572,497,000	4.1%
6	Ohio	79,625,053,000	3.9%
7	Illinois	77,579,925,000	3.8%
8	New Jersey	70,030,056,000	3.4%
9	Michigan	64,209,217,000	3.1%
10	Massachusetts	58,517,229,000	2.9%
11	North Carolina	51,447,701,000	2.5%
12	Virginia	48,702,926,000	2.4%
13	Washington	47,858,031,000	2.3%
14	Georgia	45,679,846,000	2.2%
15	Minnesota	42,140,750,000	2.1%
16	Maryland	41,435,785,000	2.0%
17	Wisconsin	38,826,150,000	1.9%
18	Indiana	36,141,456,000	1.8%
19	Arizona	33,433,440,000	1.6%
20	Louisiana	32,077,901,000	1.6%
21	Colorado	30,832,158,000	1.5%
22	Tennessee	30,674,985,000	1.5%
23	Missouri	30,650,264,000	1.5%
24	Kentucky	30,117,392,000	1.5%
25	Connecticut	29,658,168,000	1.4%
26	Oregon	29,615,962,000	1.4%
27	South Carolina	29,013,168,000	1.4%
28	Alabama	28,416,987,000	1.4%
29	Oklahoma	23,632,322,000	1.2%
30	Iowa	21,385,336,000	1.0%
31	Arkansas	20,476,493,000	1.0%
32	Mississippi	20,114,533,000	1.0%
33	New Mexico	17,804,718,000	0.9%
34	Utah	17,250,463,000	0.8%
35	Kansas	17,030,164,000	0.8%
36	West Virginia	13,310,897,000	0.6%
37	Nevada	13,305,803,000	0.6%
38	Alaska	13,043,237,000	0.6%
39	Hawaii	12,548,539,000	0.6%
40	Nebraska	10,121,365,000	0.5%
41	Maine	9,315,918,000	0.5%
42	Delaware	8,871,454,000	0.4%
43	Idaho	8,523,206,000	0.4%
44	Rhode Island	8,366,774,000	0.4%
45	North Dakota	7,540,916,000	0.4%
46	New Hampshire	7,402,186,000	0.4%
47	Montana	7,276,481,000	0.4%
48	Vermont	6,325,218,000	0.3%
49	Wyoming	5,915,580,000	0.3%
50	South Dakota	4,566,813,000	0.2%

District of Columbia**   NA   NA

Source: U.S. Bureau of the Census, Governments Division
   "2014 State and Local Government Finances" (http://www.census.gov/govs/local/)
*Total expenditures includes all money paid other than for retirement of debt and extension of loans. Includes payments from all sources of funds including current revenues and proceeds from borrowing and prior year fund balances. Includes intergovernmental transfers and expenditures for government owned utilities and other commercial or auxiliary enterprise, and insurance trust expenditures. **Not applicable.

Per Capita State Government Total Expenditures in 2014

National Per Capita = $6,443*

RANK	STATE	PER CAPITA
34	Alabama	$5,867
1	Alaska	17,705
45	Arizona	4,975
20	Arkansas	6,902
15	California	7,381
37	Colorado	5,763
10	Connecticut	8,257
5	Delaware	9,489
50	Florida	4,202
49	Georgia	4,528
7	Hawaii	8,860
42	Idaho	5,218
31	Illinois	6,029
39	Indiana	5,480
22	Iowa	6,881
33	Kansas	5,874
25	Kentucky	6,825
20	Louisiana	6,902
18	Maine	7,001
19	Maryland	6,944
8	Massachusetts	8,669
29	Michigan	6,475
13	Minnesota	7,728
28	Mississippi	6,722
44	Missouri	5,057
17	Montana	7,114
40	Nebraska	5,380
47	Nevada	4,697
38	New Hampshire	5,571
12	New Jersey	7,847
9	New Mexico	8,548
6	New York	9,115
43	North Carolina	5,179
2	North Dakota	10,192
23	Ohio	6,868
30	Oklahoma	6,095
14	Oregon	7,463
24	Pennsylvania	6,838
11	Rhode Island	7,935
32	South Carolina	6,009
41	South Dakota	5,357
48	Tennessee	4,687
46	Texas	4,874
35	Utah	5,864
4	Vermont	10,088
36	Virginia	5,856
26	Washington	6,784
16	West Virginia	7,201
27	Wisconsin	6,743
3	Wyoming	10,136

RANK	STATE	PER CAPITA
1	Alaska	$17,705
2	North Dakota	10,192
3	Wyoming	10,136
4	Vermont	10,088
5	Delaware	9,489
6	New York	9,115
7	Hawaii	8,860
8	Massachusetts	8,669
9	New Mexico	8,548
10	Connecticut	8,257
11	Rhode Island	7,935
12	New Jersey	7,847
13	Minnesota	7,728
14	Oregon	7,463
15	California	7,381
16	West Virginia	7,201
17	Montana	7,114
18	Maine	7,001
19	Maryland	6,944
20	Arkansas	6,902
20	Louisiana	6,902
22	Iowa	6,881
23	Ohio	6,868
24	Pennsylvania	6,838
25	Kentucky	6,825
26	Washington	6,784
27	Wisconsin	6,743
28	Mississippi	6,722
29	Michigan	6,475
30	Oklahoma	6,095
31	Illinois	6,029
32	South Carolina	6,009
33	Kansas	5,874
34	Alabama	5,867
35	Utah	5,864
36	Virginia	5,856
37	Colorado	5,763
38	New Hampshire	5,571
39	Indiana	5,480
40	Nebraska	5,380
41	South Dakota	5,357
42	Idaho	5,218
43	North Carolina	5,179
44	Missouri	5,057
45	Arizona	4,975
46	Texas	4,874
47	Nevada	4,697
48	Tennessee	4,687
49	Georgia	4,528
50	Florida	4,202

District of Columbia**   NA

Source: CQ Press using data from U.S. Bureau of the Census, Governments Division
"2014 State and Local Government Finances" (http://www.census.gov/govs/local/)
*Total expenditures includes all money paid other than for retirement of debt and extension of loans. Includes payments from all sources of funds including current revenues and proceeds from borrowing and prior year fund balances. Includes intergovernmental transfers and expenditures for government owned utilities and other commercial or auxiliary enterprise, and insurance trust expenditures. **Not applicable.

State Government Direct General Expenditures in 2014

National Total = $1,241,212,643,000*

ALPHA ORDER

RANK	STATE	EXPENDITURES	% of USA
27	Alabama	$18,314,566,000	1.5%
37	Alaska	9,489,164,000	0.8%
19	Arizona	21,847,462,000	1.8%
31	Arkansas	13,424,964,000	1.1%
1	California	143,899,034,000	11.6%
25	Colorado	18,635,755,000	1.5%
24	Connecticut	19,471,166,000	1.6%
42	Delaware	6,641,097,000	0.5%
4	Florida	56,065,102,000	4.5%
14	Georgia	28,715,367,000	2.3%
36	Hawaii	10,958,915,000	0.9%
44	Idaho	5,387,740,000	0.4%
6	Illinois	46,716,433,000	3.8%
17	Indiana	23,854,009,000	1.9%
30	Iowa	13,804,904,000	1.1%
34	Kansas	11,076,755,000	0.9%
21	Kentucky	21,240,924,000	1.7%
20	Louisiana	21,709,111,000	1.7%
40	Maine	7,005,977,000	0.6%
15	Maryland	27,429,421,000	2.2%
9	Massachusetts	38,705,173,000	3.1%
10	Michigan	35,856,186,000	2.9%
16	Minnesota	24,123,943,000	1.9%
32	Mississippi	12,454,229,000	1.0%
23	Missouri	20,558,629,000	1.7%
46	Montana	4,880,990,000	0.4%
39	Nebraska	7,225,497,000	0.6%
41	Nevada	6,698,601,000	0.5%
45	New Hampshire	4,912,807,000	0.4%
8	New Jersey	41,708,576,000	3.4%
35	New Mexico	10,973,739,000	0.9%
2	New York	87,027,429,000	7.0%
11	North Carolina	32,278,153,000	2.6%
47	North Dakota	4,607,296,000	0.4%
7	Ohio	45,356,042,000	3.7%
29	Oklahoma	16,102,464,000	1.3%
26	Oregon	18,336,986,000	1.5%
5	Pennsylvania	54,520,628,000	4.4%
43	Rhode Island	5,674,506,000	0.5%
28	South Carolina	18,174,758,000	1.5%
49	South Dakota	3,339,023,000	0.3%
22	Tennessee	21,017,182,000	1.7%
3	Texas	86,200,501,000	6.9%
33	Utah	12,091,805,000	1.0%
48	Vermont	4,314,555,000	0.3%
12	Virginia	31,917,051,000	2.6%
13	Washington	30,373,087,000	2.4%
38	West Virginia	9,334,829,000	0.8%
18	Wisconsin	23,586,823,000	1.9%
50	Wyoming	3,173,289,000	0.3%

RANK ORDER

RANK	STATE	EXPENDITURES	% of USA
1	California	$143,899,034,000	11.6%
2	New York	87,027,429,000	7.0%
3	Texas	86,200,501,000	6.9%
4	Florida	56,065,102,000	4.5%
5	Pennsylvania	54,520,628,000	4.4%
6	Illinois	46,716,433,000	3.8%
7	Ohio	45,356,042,000	3.7%
8	New Jersey	41,708,576,000	3.4%
9	Massachusetts	38,705,173,000	3.1%
10	Michigan	35,856,186,000	2.9%
11	North Carolina	32,278,153,000	2.6%
12	Virginia	31,917,051,000	2.6%
13	Washington	30,373,087,000	2.4%
14	Georgia	28,715,367,000	2.3%
15	Maryland	27,429,421,000	2.2%
16	Minnesota	24,123,943,000	1.9%
17	Indiana	23,854,009,000	1.9%
18	Wisconsin	23,586,823,000	1.9%
19	Arizona	21,847,462,000	1.8%
20	Louisiana	21,709,111,000	1.7%
21	Kentucky	21,240,924,000	1.7%
22	Tennessee	21,017,182,000	1.7%
23	Missouri	20,558,629,000	1.7%
24	Connecticut	19,471,166,000	1.6%
25	Colorado	18,635,755,000	1.5%
26	Oregon	18,336,986,000	1.5%
27	Alabama	18,314,566,000	1.5%
28	South Carolina	18,174,758,000	1.5%
29	Oklahoma	16,102,464,000	1.3%
30	Iowa	13,804,904,000	1.1%
31	Arkansas	13,424,964,000	1.1%
32	Mississippi	12,454,229,000	1.0%
33	Utah	12,091,805,000	1.0%
34	Kansas	11,076,755,000	0.9%
35	New Mexico	10,973,739,000	0.9%
36	Hawaii	10,958,915,000	0.9%
37	Alaska	9,489,164,000	0.8%
38	West Virginia	9,334,829,000	0.8%
39	Nebraska	7,225,497,000	0.6%
40	Maine	7,005,977,000	0.6%
41	Nevada	6,698,601,000	0.5%
42	Delaware	6,641,097,000	0.5%
43	Rhode Island	5,674,506,000	0.5%
44	Idaho	5,387,740,000	0.4%
45	New Hampshire	4,912,807,000	0.4%
46	Montana	4,880,990,000	0.4%
47	North Dakota	4,607,296,000	0.4%
48	Vermont	4,314,555,000	0.3%
49	South Dakota	3,339,023,000	0.3%
50	Wyoming	3,173,289,000	0.3%
	District of Columbia**	NA	NA

Source: U.S. Bureau of the Census, Governments Division
"2014 State and Local Government Finances" (http://www.census.gov/govs/local/)
*Direct general expenditures include expenditures for current operations, assistance and subsidies, interest on debt, and capital outlay. Excludes intergovernmental transfers, expenditures for government owned utilities and other commercial or auxiliary enterprise, and insurance trust expenditures.
**Not applicable.

Per Capita State Government Direct General Expenditures in 2014

National Per Capita = $3,904*

<table>
<tr><td colspan="3">ALPHA ORDER</td><td colspan="3">RANK ORDER</td></tr>
<tr><th>RANK</th><th>STATE</th><th>PER CAPITA</th><th>RANK</th><th>STATE</th><th>PER CAPITA</th></tr>
<tr><td>34</td><td>Alabama</td><td>$3,781</td><td>1</td><td>Alaska</td><td>$12,881</td></tr>
<tr><td>1</td><td>Alaska</td><td>12,881</td><td>2</td><td>Hawaii</td><td>7,737</td></tr>
<tr><td>44</td><td>Arizona</td><td>3,251</td><td>3</td><td>Delaware</td><td>7,103</td></tr>
<tr><td>19</td><td>Arkansas</td><td>4,525</td><td>4</td><td>Vermont</td><td>6,881</td></tr>
<tr><td>36</td><td>California</td><td>3,720</td><td>5</td><td>North Dakota</td><td>6,227</td></tr>
<tr><td>41</td><td>Colorado</td><td>3,484</td><td>6</td><td>Massachusetts</td><td>5,734</td></tr>
<tr><td>8</td><td>Connecticut</td><td>5,421</td><td>7</td><td>Wyoming</td><td>5,437</td></tr>
<tr><td>3</td><td>Delaware</td><td>7,103</td><td>8</td><td>Connecticut</td><td>5,421</td></tr>
<tr><td>49</td><td>Florida</td><td>2,819</td><td>9</td><td>Rhode Island</td><td>5,381</td></tr>
<tr><td>48</td><td>Georgia</td><td>2,847</td><td>10</td><td>New Mexico</td><td>5,268</td></tr>
<tr><td>2</td><td>Hawaii</td><td>7,737</td><td>11</td><td>Maine</td><td>5,265</td></tr>
<tr><td>43</td><td>Idaho</td><td>3,298</td><td>12</td><td>West Virginia</td><td>5,050</td></tr>
<tr><td>38</td><td>Illinois</td><td>3,631</td><td>13</td><td>Kentucky</td><td>4,813</td></tr>
<tr><td>39</td><td>Indiana</td><td>3,617</td><td>14</td><td>Montana</td><td>4,772</td></tr>
<tr><td>20</td><td>Iowa</td><td>4,442</td><td>15</td><td>New Jersey</td><td>4,673</td></tr>
<tr><td>33</td><td>Kansas</td><td>3,820</td><td>16</td><td>Louisiana</td><td>4,671</td></tr>
<tr><td>13</td><td>Kentucky</td><td>4,813</td><td>17</td><td>Oregon</td><td>4,621</td></tr>
<tr><td>16</td><td>Louisiana</td><td>4,671</td><td>18</td><td>Maryland</td><td>4,597</td></tr>
<tr><td>11</td><td>Maine</td><td>5,265</td><td>19</td><td>Arkansas</td><td>4,525</td></tr>
<tr><td>18</td><td>Maryland</td><td>4,597</td><td>20</td><td>Iowa</td><td>4,442</td></tr>
<tr><td>6</td><td>Massachusetts</td><td>5,734</td><td>21</td><td>Minnesota</td><td>4,424</td></tr>
<tr><td>40</td><td>Michigan</td><td>3,616</td><td>22</td><td>New York</td><td>4,413</td></tr>
<tr><td>21</td><td>Minnesota</td><td>4,424</td><td>23</td><td>Washington</td><td>4,306</td></tr>
<tr><td>25</td><td>Mississippi</td><td>4,162</td><td>24</td><td>Pennsylvania</td><td>4,263</td></tr>
<tr><td>42</td><td>Missouri</td><td>3,392</td><td>25</td><td>Mississippi</td><td>4,162</td></tr>
<tr><td>14</td><td>Montana</td><td>4,772</td><td>26</td><td>Oklahoma</td><td>4,153</td></tr>
<tr><td>31</td><td>Nebraska</td><td>3,841</td><td>27</td><td>Utah</td><td>4,110</td></tr>
<tr><td>50</td><td>Nevada</td><td>2,364</td><td>28</td><td>Wisconsin</td><td>4,096</td></tr>
<tr><td>37</td><td>New Hampshire</td><td>3,697</td><td>29</td><td>South Dakota</td><td>3,916</td></tr>
<tr><td>15</td><td>New Jersey</td><td>4,673</td><td>30</td><td>Ohio</td><td>3,912</td></tr>
<tr><td>10</td><td>New Mexico</td><td>5,268</td><td>31</td><td>Nebraska</td><td>3,841</td></tr>
<tr><td>22</td><td>New York</td><td>4,413</td><td>32</td><td>Virginia</td><td>3,837</td></tr>
<tr><td>45</td><td>North Carolina</td><td>3,249</td><td>33</td><td>Kansas</td><td>3,820</td></tr>
<tr><td>5</td><td>North Dakota</td><td>6,227</td><td>34</td><td>Alabama</td><td>3,781</td></tr>
<tr><td>30</td><td>Ohio</td><td>3,912</td><td>35</td><td>South Carolina</td><td>3,764</td></tr>
<tr><td>26</td><td>Oklahoma</td><td>4,153</td><td>36</td><td>California</td><td>3,720</td></tr>
<tr><td>17</td><td>Oregon</td><td>4,621</td><td>37</td><td>New Hampshire</td><td>3,697</td></tr>
<tr><td>24</td><td>Pennsylvania</td><td>4,263</td><td>38</td><td>Illinois</td><td>3,631</td></tr>
<tr><td>9</td><td>Rhode Island</td><td>5,381</td><td>39</td><td>Indiana</td><td>3,617</td></tr>
<tr><td>35</td><td>South Carolina</td><td>3,764</td><td>40</td><td>Michigan</td><td>3,616</td></tr>
<tr><td>29</td><td>South Dakota</td><td>3,916</td><td>41</td><td>Colorado</td><td>3,484</td></tr>
<tr><td>46</td><td>Tennessee</td><td>3,211</td><td>42</td><td>Missouri</td><td>3,392</td></tr>
<tr><td>47</td><td>Texas</td><td>3,199</td><td>43</td><td>Idaho</td><td>3,298</td></tr>
<tr><td>27</td><td>Utah</td><td>4,110</td><td>44</td><td>Arizona</td><td>3,251</td></tr>
<tr><td>4</td><td>Vermont</td><td>6,881</td><td>45</td><td>North Carolina</td><td>3,249</td></tr>
<tr><td>32</td><td>Virginia</td><td>3,837</td><td>46</td><td>Tennessee</td><td>3,211</td></tr>
<tr><td>23</td><td>Washington</td><td>4,306</td><td>47</td><td>Texas</td><td>3,199</td></tr>
<tr><td>12</td><td>West Virginia</td><td>5,050</td><td>48</td><td>Georgia</td><td>2,847</td></tr>
<tr><td>28</td><td>Wisconsin</td><td>4,096</td><td>49</td><td>Florida</td><td>2,819</td></tr>
<tr><td>7</td><td>Wyoming</td><td>5,437</td><td>50</td><td>Nevada</td><td>2,364</td></tr>
</table>

District of Columbia**   NA

Source: CQ Press using data from U.S. Bureau of the Census, Governments Division
"2014 State and Local Government Finances" (http://www.census.gov/govs/local/)
*Direct general expenditures include expenditures for current operations, assistance and subsidies, interest on debt, and capital outlay. Excludes intergovernmental transfers, expenditures for government owned utilities and other commercial or auxiliary enterprise, and insurance trust expenditures.
**Not applicable.

State Government Debt Outstanding in 2014

National Total = $1,149,147,779,000*

ALPHA ORDER					RANK ORDER			

RANK	STATE	DEBT	% of USA		RANK	STATE	DEBT	% of USA
29	Alabama	$8,907,686,000	0.8%		1	California	$156,807,868,000	13.6%
39	Alaska	6,048,619,000	0.5%		2	New York	136,440,657,000	11.9%
25	Arizona	14,315,828,000	1.2%		3	Massachusetts	74,234,582,000	6.5%
42	Arkansas	4,533,255,000	0.4%		4	New Jersey	66,089,959,000	5.8%
1	California	156,807,868,000	13.6%		5	Illinois	65,831,516,000	5.7%
20	Colorado	16,929,327,000	1.5%		6	Pennsylvania	47,572,612,000	4.1%
10	Connecticut	33,229,567,000	2.9%		7	Texas	41,855,106,000	3.6%
41	Delaware	5,354,253,000	0.5%		8	Florida	36,348,245,000	3.2%
8	Florida	36,348,245,000	3.2%		9	Ohio	33,662,042,000	2.9%
26	Georgia	13,380,184,000	1.2%		10	Connecticut	33,229,567,000	2.9%
30	Hawaii	8,426,573,000	0.7%		11	Washington	31,601,016,000	2.7%
43	Idaho	3,606,305,000	0.3%		12	Michigan	31,528,074,000	2.7%
5	Illinois	65,831,516,000	5.7%		13	Virginia	27,739,117,000	2.4%
16	Indiana	21,120,303,000	1.8%		14	Maryland	26,378,595,000	2.3%
37	Iowa	6,343,482,000	0.6%		15	Wisconsin	22,367,764,000	1.9%
36	Kansas	6,742,696,000	0.6%		16	Indiana	21,120,303,000	1.8%
23	Kentucky	14,829,986,000	1.3%		17	Missouri	19,041,613,000	1.7%
18	Louisiana	18,996,129,000	1.7%		18	Louisiana	18,996,129,000	1.7%
40	Maine	5,473,870,000	0.5%		19	North Carolina	17,853,232,000	1.6%
14	Maryland	26,378,595,000	2.3%		20	Colorado	16,929,327,000	1.5%
3	Massachusetts	74,234,582,000	6.5%		21	Minnesota	15,818,353,000	1.4%
12	Michigan	31,528,074,000	2.7%		22	South Carolina	15,089,289,000	1.3%
21	Minnesota	15,818,353,000	1.4%		23	Kentucky	14,829,986,000	1.3%
34	Mississippi	7,104,085,000	0.6%		24	Oregon	14,583,105,000	1.3%
17	Missouri	19,041,613,000	1.7%		25	Arizona	14,315,828,000	1.2%
45	Montana	3,402,199,000	0.3%		26	Georgia	13,380,184,000	1.2%
48	Nebraska	1,908,707,000	0.2%		27	Rhode Island	9,388,127,000	0.8%
44	Nevada	3,520,774,000	0.3%		28	Oklahoma	9,047,456,000	0.8%
31	New Hampshire	8,098,921,000	0.7%		29	Alabama	8,907,686,000	0.8%
4	New Jersey	66,089,959,000	5.8%		30	Hawaii	8,426,573,000	0.7%
35	New Mexico	6,887,017,000	0.6%		31	New Hampshire	8,098,921,000	0.7%
2	New York	136,440,657,000	11.9%		32	West Virginia	7,986,591,000	0.7%
19	North Carolina	17,853,232,000	1.6%		33	Utah	7,327,147,000	0.6%
49	North Dakota	1,886,865,000	0.2%		34	Mississippi	7,104,085,000	0.6%
9	Ohio	33,662,042,000	2.9%		35	New Mexico	6,887,017,000	0.6%
28	Oklahoma	9,047,456,000	0.8%		36	Kansas	6,742,696,000	0.6%
24	Oregon	14,583,105,000	1.3%		37	Iowa	6,343,482,000	0.6%
6	Pennsylvania	47,572,612,000	4.1%		38	Tennessee	6,049,178,000	0.5%
27	Rhode Island	9,388,127,000	0.8%		39	Alaska	6,048,619,000	0.5%
22	South Carolina	15,089,289,000	1.3%		40	Maine	5,473,870,000	0.5%
47	South Dakota	3,239,167,000	0.3%		41	Delaware	5,354,253,000	0.5%
38	Tennessee	6,049,178,000	0.5%		42	Arkansas	4,533,255,000	0.4%
7	Texas	41,855,106,000	3.6%		43	Idaho	3,606,305,000	0.3%
33	Utah	7,327,147,000	0.6%		44	Nevada	3,520,774,000	0.3%
46	Vermont	3,291,205,000	0.3%		45	Montana	3,402,199,000	0.3%
13	Virginia	27,739,117,000	2.4%		46	Vermont	3,291,205,000	0.3%
11	Washington	31,601,016,000	2.7%		47	South Dakota	3,239,167,000	0.3%
32	West Virginia	7,986,591,000	0.7%		48	Nebraska	1,908,707,000	0.2%
15	Wisconsin	22,367,764,000	1.9%		49	North Dakota	1,886,865,000	0.2%
50	Wyoming	929,532,000	0.1%		50	Wyoming	929,532,000	0.1%
						District of Columbia**	NA	NA

Source: U.S. Bureau of the Census, Governments Division
"2014 State and Local Government Finances" (http://www.census.gov/govs/local/)
*Includes short-term, long-term, full faith and credit, nonguaranteed, and public debt for private purposes.
**Not applicable.

Per Capita State Government Debt Outstanding in 2014

National Per Capita = $3,615*

ALPHA ORDER

RANK ORDER

RANK	STATE	PER CAPITA	RANK	STATE	PER CAPITA
41	Alabama	$1,839	1	Massachusetts	$10,998
4	Alaska	8,210	2	Connecticut	9,251
39	Arizona	2,130	3	Rhode Island	8,903
46	Arkansas	1,528	4	Alaska	8,210
17	California	4,054	5	New Jersey	7,405
28	Colorado	3,165	6	New York	6,919
2	Connecticut	9,251	7	New Hampshire	6,095
9	Delaware	5,727	8	Hawaii	5,950
42	Florida	1,828	9	Delaware	5,727
47	Georgia	1,326	10	Vermont	5,249
8	Hawaii	5,950	11	Illinois	5,116
38	Idaho	2,208	12	Washington	4,480
11	Illinois	5,116	13	Maryland	4,421
26	Indiana	3,202	14	West Virginia	4,321
40	Iowa	2,041	15	Maine	4,113
37	Kansas	2,326	16	Louisiana	4,087
22	Kentucky	3,360	17	California	4,054
16	Louisiana	4,087	18	Wisconsin	3,884
15	Maine	4,113	19	South Dakota	3,799
13	Maryland	4,421	20	Pennsylvania	3,719
1	Massachusetts	10,998	21	Oregon	3,675
27	Michigan	3,180	22	Kentucky	3,360
32	Minnesota	2,901	23	Virginia	3,335
35	Mississippi	2,374	24	Montana	3,326
29	Missouri	3,142	25	New Mexico	3,306
24	Montana	3,326	26	Indiana	3,202
49	Nebraska	1,015	27	Michigan	3,180
48	Nevada	1,243	28	Colorado	3,165
7	New Hampshire	6,095	29	Missouri	3,142
5	New Jersey	7,405	30	South Carolina	3,125
25	New Mexico	3,306	31	Ohio	2,903
6	New York	6,919	32	Minnesota	2,901
43	North Carolina	1,797	33	North Dakota	2,550
33	North Dakota	2,550	34	Utah	2,491
31	Ohio	2,903	35	Mississippi	2,374
36	Oklahoma	2,333	36	Oklahoma	2,333
21	Oregon	3,675	37	Kansas	2,326
20	Pennsylvania	3,719	38	Idaho	2,208
3	Rhode Island	8,903	39	Arizona	2,130
30	South Carolina	3,125	40	Iowa	2,041
19	South Dakota	3,799	41	Alabama	1,839
50	Tennessee	924	42	Florida	1,828
45	Texas	1,553	43	North Carolina	1,797
34	Utah	2,491	44	Wyoming	1,593
10	Vermont	5,249	45	Texas	1,553
23	Virginia	3,335	46	Arkansas	1,528
12	Washington	4,480	47	Georgia	1,326
14	West Virginia	4,321	48	Nevada	1,243
18	Wisconsin	3,884	49	Nebraska	1,015
44	Wyoming	1,593	50	Tennessee	924

District of Columbia**   NA

Source: CQ Press using data from U.S. Bureau of the Census, Governments Division
   "2014 State and Local Government Finances" (http://www.census.gov/govs/local/)
*Includes short-term, long-term, full faith and credit, nonguaranteed, and public debt for private purposes.
**Not applicable.

State Government Full-Time Equivalent Employees in 2015

National Total = 4,341,978 FTE Employees*

	ALPHA ORDER					RANK ORDER		
RANK	STATE	EMPLOYEES	% of USA		RANK	STATE	EMPLOYEES	% of USA
15	Alabama	89,469	2.1%		1	California	404,069	9.3%
40	Alaska	26,201	0.6%		2	Texas	304,337	7.0%
23	Arizona	78,789	1.8%		3	New York	242,861	5.6%
30	Arkansas	63,297	1.5%		4	Florida	178,754	4.1%
1	California	404,069	9.3%		5	Pennsylvania	163,446	3.8%
21	Colorado	80,650	1.9%		6	Michigan	141,957	3.3%
29	Connecticut	63,528	1.5%		7	New Jersey	140,977	3.2%
41	Delaware	26,144	0.6%		8	North Carolina	140,242	3.2%
4	Florida	178,754	4.1%		9	Ohio	138,032	3.2%
10	Georgia	127,892	2.9%		10	Georgia	127,892	2.9%
31	Hawaii	58,478	1.3%		11	Virginia	127,181	2.9%
42	Idaho	23,430	0.5%		12	Illinois	123,953	2.9%
12	Illinois	123,953	2.9%		13	Washington	122,216	2.8%
16	Indiana	88,251	2.0%		14	Massachusetts	101,856	2.3%
34	Iowa	50,303	1.2%		15	Alabama	89,469	2.1%
35	Kansas	50,155	1.2%		16	Indiana	88,251	2.0%
19	Kentucky	85,734	2.0%		17	Maryland	87,591	2.0%
26	Louisiana	74,118	1.7%		18	Missouri	87,578	2.0%
43	Maine	21,005	0.5%		19	Kentucky	85,734	2.0%
17	Maryland	87,591	2.0%		20	Minnesota	82,277	1.9%
14	Massachusetts	101,856	2.3%		21	Colorado	80,650	1.9%
6	Michigan	141,957	3.3%		22	South Carolina	80,171	1.8%
20	Minnesota	82,277	1.9%		23	Arizona	78,789	1.8%
32	Mississippi	56,711	1.3%		24	Tennessee	78,383	1.8%
18	Missouri	87,578	2.0%		25	Wisconsin	74,383	1.7%
44	Montana	20,877	0.5%		26	Louisiana	74,118	1.7%
38	Nebraska	32,122	0.7%		27	Oklahoma	68,922	1.6%
39	Nevada	28,377	0.7%		28	Oregon	66,775	1.5%
46	New Hampshire	18,905	0.4%		29	Connecticut	63,528	1.5%
7	New Jersey	140,977	3.2%		30	Arkansas	63,297	1.5%
36	New Mexico	45,909	1.1%		31	Hawaii	58,478	1.3%
3	New York	242,861	5.6%		32	Mississippi	56,711	1.3%
8	North Carolina	140,242	3.2%		33	Utah	55,355	1.3%
45	North Dakota	19,339	0.4%		34	Iowa	50,303	1.2%
9	Ohio	138,032	3.2%		35	Kansas	50,155	1.2%
27	Oklahoma	68,922	1.6%		36	New Mexico	45,909	1.1%
28	Oregon	66,775	1.5%		37	West Virginia	40,131	0.9%
5	Pennsylvania	163,446	3.8%		38	Nebraska	32,122	0.7%
47	Rhode Island	18,370	0.4%		39	Nevada	28,377	0.7%
22	South Carolina	80,171	1.8%		40	Alaska	26,201	0.6%
49	South Dakota	14,475	0.3%		41	Delaware	26,144	0.6%
24	Tennessee	78,383	1.8%		42	Idaho	23,430	0.5%
2	Texas	304,337	7.0%		43	Maine	21,005	0.5%
33	Utah	55,355	1.3%		44	Montana	20,877	0.5%
48	Vermont	14,564	0.3%		45	North Dakota	19,339	0.4%
11	Virginia	127,181	2.9%		46	New Hampshire	18,905	0.4%
13	Washington	122,216	2.8%		47	Rhode Island	18,370	0.4%
37	West Virginia	40,131	0.9%		48	Vermont	14,564	0.3%
25	Wisconsin	74,383	1.7%		49	South Dakota	14,475	0.3%
50	Wyoming	13,438	0.3%		50	Wyoming	13,438	0.3%
						District of Columbia**	NA	NA

Source: U.S. Bureau of the Census, Governments Division
   "Government Employment and Payroll" (http://www.census.gov/govs/apes/index.html)
*Full-time equivalent as of March 2015.
**Not applicable.

Rate of State Government Full-Time Equivalent Employees in 2015

National Rate = 136 FTE Employees per 10,000 Population*

ALPHA ORDER

RANK	STATE	RATE
14	Alabama	184
2	Alaska	355
45	Arizona	116
9	Arkansas	213
47	California	104
31	Colorado	148
15	Connecticut	177
3	Delaware	277
50	Florida	88
41	Georgia	125
1	Hawaii	410
35	Idaho	142
49	Illinois	97
38	Indiana	133
24	Iowa	161
18	Kansas	173
11	Kentucky	194
25	Louisiana	159
26	Maine	158
32	Maryland	146
29	Massachusetts	150
34	Michigan	143
29	Minnesota	150
12	Mississippi	190
33	Missouri	144
10	Montana	202
20	Nebraska	170
48	Nevada	98
35	New Hampshire	142
26	New Jersey	158
7	New Mexico	221
42	New York	123
37	North Carolina	140
4	North Dakota	256
43	Ohio	119
16	Oklahoma	176
22	Oregon	166
40	Pennsylvania	128
17	Rhode Island	174
23	South Carolina	164
21	South Dakota	169
43	Tennessee	119
46	Texas	111
13	Utah	185
5	Vermont	233
28	Virginia	152
19	Washington	171
8	West Virginia	218
39	Wisconsin	129
6	Wyoming	229

RANK ORDER

RANK	STATE	RATE
1	Hawaii	410
2	Alaska	355
3	Delaware	277
4	North Dakota	256
5	Vermont	233
6	Wyoming	229
7	New Mexico	221
8	West Virginia	218
9	Arkansas	213
10	Montana	202
11	Kentucky	194
12	Mississippi	190
13	Utah	185
14	Alabama	184
15	Connecticut	177
16	Oklahoma	176
17	Rhode Island	174
18	Kansas	173
19	Washington	171
20	Nebraska	170
21	South Dakota	169
22	Oregon	166
23	South Carolina	164
24	Iowa	161
25	Louisiana	159
26	Maine	158
26	New Jersey	158
28	Virginia	152
29	Massachusetts	150
29	Minnesota	150
31	Colorado	148
32	Maryland	146
33	Missouri	144
34	Michigan	143
35	Idaho	142
35	New Hampshire	142
37	North Carolina	140
38	Indiana	133
39	Wisconsin	129
40	Pennsylvania	128
41	Georgia	125
42	New York	123
43	Ohio	119
43	Tennessee	119
45	Arizona	116
46	Texas	111
47	California	104
48	Nevada	98
49	Illinois	97
50	Florida	88
	District of Columbia**	NA

Source: CQ Press using data from U.S. Bureau of the Census, Governments Division
"Government Employment and Payroll" (http://www.census.gov/govs/apes/index.html)
*Full-time equivalent as of March 2015.
**Not applicable.

Average Annual Earnings of Full-Time State Government Employees in 2015

National Average = $61,910*

ALPHA ORDER

RANK	STATE	SALARY
34	Alabama	$53,976
11	Alaska	68,506
24	Arizona	58,221
47	Arkansas	48,012
1	California	82,524
12	Colorado	65,872
2	Connecticut	75,451
31	Delaware	55,119
39	Florida	52,046
46	Georgia	49,248
29	Hawaii	55,570
23	Idaho	58,526
7	Illinois	69,171
37	Indiana	52,956
3	Iowa	75,121
35	Kansas	53,868
41	Kentucky	51,760
32	Louisiana	55,109
40	Maine	51,867
15	Maryland	62,555
8	Massachusetts	69,145
9	Michigan	69,036
10	Minnesota	68,798
50	Mississippi	45,458
48	Missouri	46,015
33	Montana	54,504
43	Nebraska	50,975
25	Nevada	57,810
17	New Hampshire	61,210
4	New Jersey	74,914
30	New Mexico	55,120
5	New York	73,633
28	North Carolina	56,971
27	North Dakota	57,038
13	Ohio	63,021
44	Oklahoma	50,239
21	Oregon	59,093
18	Pennsylvania	60,483
6	Rhode Island	69,247
45	South Carolina	49,943
38	South Dakota	52,630
42	Tennessee	50,992
20	Texas	59,428
26	Utah	57,699
19	Vermont	60,175
22	Virginia	58,888
16	Washington	62,553
49	West Virginia	45,466
14	Wisconsin	62,623
36	Wyoming	53,706

RANK ORDER

RANK	STATE	SALARY
1	California	$82,524
2	Connecticut	75,451
3	Iowa	75,121
4	New Jersey	74,914
5	New York	73,633
6	Rhode Island	69,247
7	Illinois	69,171
8	Massachusetts	69,145
9	Michigan	69,036
10	Minnesota	68,798
11	Alaska	68,506
12	Colorado	65,872
13	Ohio	63,021
14	Wisconsin	62,623
15	Maryland	62,555
16	Washington	62,553
17	New Hampshire	61,210
18	Pennsylvania	60,483
19	Vermont	60,175
20	Texas	59,428
21	Oregon	59,093
22	Virginia	58,888
23	Idaho	58,526
24	Arizona	58,221
25	Nevada	57,810
26	Utah	57,699
27	North Dakota	57,038
28	North Carolina	56,971
29	Hawaii	55,570
30	New Mexico	55,120
31	Delaware	55,119
32	Louisiana	55,109
33	Montana	54,504
34	Alabama	53,976
35	Kansas	53,868
36	Wyoming	53,706
37	Indiana	52,956
38	South Dakota	52,630
39	Florida	52,046
40	Maine	51,867
41	Kentucky	51,760
42	Tennessee	50,992
43	Nebraska	50,975
44	Oklahoma	50,239
45	South Carolina	49,943
46	Georgia	49,248
47	Arkansas	48,012
48	Missouri	46,015
49	West Virginia	45,466
50	Mississippi	45,458

District of Columbia** — NA

Source: CQ Press using data from U.S. Bureau of the Census, Governments Division
    "Government Employment and Payroll" (http://www.census.gov/govs/apes/index.html)
*March 2015 full-time payroll (multiplied by 12) divided by full-time employees.
**Not applicable.

Local Government Total Revenue in 2014

National Total = $1,772,052,516,000*

ALPHA ORDER

RANK	STATE	REVENUE	% of USA
24	Alabama	$20,747,030,000	1.2%
38	Alaska	6,303,729,000	0.4%
21	Arizona	28,530,944,000	1.6%
36	Arkansas	9,964,608,000	0.6%
1	California	294,216,659,000	16.6%
18	Colorado	29,417,680,000	1.7%
27	Connecticut	18,726,524,000	1.1%
49	Delaware	3,501,274,000	0.2%
4	Florida	94,686,120,000	5.3%
11	Georgia	44,052,906,000	2.5%
46	Hawaii	3,812,189,000	0.2%
41	Idaho	5,468,764,000	0.3%
5	Illinois	76,279,992,000	4.3%
20	Indiana	28,821,403,000	1.6%
28	Iowa	16,037,323,000	0.9%
29	Kansas	14,619,449,000	0.8%
30	Kentucky	14,172,568,000	0.8%
23	Louisiana	21,222,421,000	1.2%
42	Maine	4,805,168,000	0.3%
16	Maryland	31,252,592,000	1.8%
14	Massachusetts	35,851,360,000	2.0%
8	Michigan	49,296,362,000	2.8%
17	Minnesota	29,955,459,000	1.7%
34	Mississippi	12,372,680,000	0.7%
22	Missouri	25,928,603,000	1.5%
47	Montana	3,777,487,000	0.2%
31	Nebraska	14,060,118,000	0.8%
33	Nevada	13,472,596,000	0.8%
39	New Hampshire	5,909,935,000	0.3%
9	New Jersey	49,002,608,000	2.8%
37	New Mexico	8,637,427,000	0.5%
2	New York	209,512,759,000	11.8%
10	North Carolina	45,610,681,000	2.6%
45	North Dakota	4,092,258,000	0.2%
7	Ohio	55,240,295,000	3.1%
32	Oklahoma	13,764,247,000	0.8%
26	Oregon	19,047,905,000	1.1%
6	Pennsylvania	65,963,783,000	3.7%
44	Rhode Island	4,652,848,000	0.3%
25	South Carolina	20,661,837,000	1.2%
48	South Dakota	3,511,548,000	0.2%
15	Tennessee	33,010,892,000	1.9%
3	Texas	131,245,545,000	7.4%
35	Utah	11,816,902,000	0.7%
50	Vermont	2,823,828,000	0.2%
13	Virginia	39,688,987,000	2.2%
12	Washington	42,463,940,000	2.4%
40	West Virginia	5,540,529,000	0.3%
19	Wisconsin	29,022,973,000	1.6%
43	Wyoming	4,764,040,000	0.3%

RANK ORDER

RANK	STATE	REVENUE	% of USA
1	California	$294,216,659,000	16.6%
2	New York	209,512,759,000	11.8%
3	Texas	131,245,545,000	7.4%
4	Florida	94,686,120,000	5.3%
5	Illinois	76,279,992,000	4.3%
6	Pennsylvania	65,963,783,000	3.7%
7	Ohio	55,240,295,000	3.1%
8	Michigan	49,296,362,000	2.8%
9	New Jersey	49,002,608,000	2.8%
10	North Carolina	45,610,681,000	2.6%
11	Georgia	44,052,906,000	2.5%
12	Washington	42,463,940,000	2.4%
13	Virginia	39,688,987,000	2.2%
14	Massachusetts	35,851,360,000	2.0%
15	Tennessee	33,010,892,000	1.9%
16	Maryland	31,252,592,000	1.8%
17	Minnesota	29,955,459,000	1.7%
18	Colorado	29,417,680,000	1.7%
19	Wisconsin	29,022,973,000	1.6%
20	Indiana	28,821,403,000	1.6%
21	Arizona	28,530,944,000	1.6%
22	Missouri	25,928,603,000	1.5%
23	Louisiana	21,222,421,000	1.2%
24	Alabama	20,747,030,000	1.2%
25	South Carolina	20,661,837,000	1.2%
26	Oregon	19,047,905,000	1.1%
27	Connecticut	18,726,524,000	1.1%
28	Iowa	16,037,323,000	0.9%
29	Kansas	14,619,449,000	0.8%
30	Kentucky	14,172,568,000	0.8%
31	Nebraska	14,060,118,000	0.8%
32	Oklahoma	13,764,247,000	0.8%
33	Nevada	13,472,596,000	0.8%
34	Mississippi	12,372,680,000	0.7%
35	Utah	11,816,902,000	0.7%
36	Arkansas	9,964,608,000	0.6%
37	New Mexico	8,637,427,000	0.5%
38	Alaska	6,303,729,000	0.4%
39	New Hampshire	5,909,935,000	0.3%
40	West Virginia	5,540,529,000	0.3%
41	Idaho	5,468,764,000	0.3%
42	Maine	4,805,168,000	0.3%
43	Wyoming	4,764,040,000	0.3%
44	Rhode Island	4,652,848,000	0.3%
45	North Dakota	4,092,258,000	0.2%
46	Hawaii	3,812,189,000	0.2%
47	Montana	3,777,487,000	0.2%
48	South Dakota	3,511,548,000	0.2%
49	Delaware	3,501,274,000	0.2%
50	Vermont	2,823,828,000	0.2%
	District of Columbia	14,712,741,000	0.8%

Source: U.S. Bureau of the Census, Governments Division
"2014 State and Local Government Finances" (http://www.census.gov/govs/local/)
*Total revenue includes all money received from external sources. This includes taxes, intergovernmental transfers and insurance trust revenue, and revenue from government owned utilities and other commercial or auxiliary enterprise.

Per Capita Local Government Total Revenue in 2014

National Per Capita = $5,563*

ALPHA ORDER

RANK	STATE	PER CAPITA
34	Alabama	$4,284
2	Alaska	8,557
37	Arizona	4,246
46	Arkansas	3,359
4	California	7,606
9	Colorado	5,499
14	Connecticut	5,214
42	Delaware	3,745
25	Florida	4,761
33	Georgia	4,367
50	Hawaii	2,692
47	Idaho	3,348
7	Illinois	5,928
32	Indiana	4,370
15	Iowa	5,160
18	Kansas	5,042
48	Kentucky	3,212
28	Louisiana	4,566
44	Maine	3,611
13	Maryland	5,237
12	Massachusetts	5,311
20	Michigan	4,972
10	Minnesota	5,493
39	Mississippi	4,135
36	Missouri	4,278
43	Montana	3,693
5	Nebraska	7,474
26	Nevada	4,756
30	New Hampshire	4,448
11	New Jersey	5,490
38	New Mexico	4,147
1	New York	10,625
27	North Carolina	4,591
8	North Dakota	5,531
24	Ohio	4,764
45	Oklahoma	3,550
22	Oregon	4,800
16	Pennsylvania	5,157
31	Rhode Island	4,412
35	South Carolina	4,279
40	South Dakota	4,119
17	Tennessee	5,044
21	Texas	4,871
41	Utah	4,017
29	Vermont	4,504
23	Virginia	4,772
6	Washington	6,020
49	West Virginia	2,997
19	Wisconsin	5,040
3	Wyoming	8,163

RANK ORDER

RANK	STATE	PER CAPITA
1	New York	$10,625
2	Alaska	8,557
3	Wyoming	8,163
4	California	7,606
5	Nebraska	7,474
6	Washington	6,020
7	Illinois	5,928
8	North Dakota	5,531
9	Colorado	5,499
10	Minnesota	5,493
11	New Jersey	5,490
12	Massachusetts	5,311
13	Maryland	5,237
14	Connecticut	5,214
15	Iowa	5,160
16	Pennsylvania	5,157
17	Tennessee	5,044
18	Kansas	5,042
19	Wisconsin	5,040
20	Michigan	4,972
21	Texas	4,871
22	Oregon	4,800
23	Virginia	4,772
24	Ohio	4,764
25	Florida	4,761
26	Nevada	4,756
27	North Carolina	4,591
28	Louisiana	4,566
29	Vermont	4,504
30	New Hampshire	4,448
31	Rhode Island	4,412
32	Indiana	4,370
33	Georgia	4,367
34	Alabama	4,284
35	South Carolina	4,279
36	Missouri	4,278
37	Arizona	4,246
38	New Mexico	4,147
39	Mississippi	4,135
40	South Dakota	4,119
41	Utah	4,017
42	Delaware	3,745
43	Montana	3,693
44	Maine	3,611
45	Oklahoma	3,550
46	Arkansas	3,359
47	Idaho	3,348
48	Kentucky	3,212
49	West Virginia	2,997
50	Hawaii	2,692

District of Columbia 22,326

Source: U.S. Bureau of the Census, Governments Division
   "2014 State and Local Government Finances" (http://www.census.gov/govs/local/)
*Total revenue includes all money received from external sources. This includes taxes, intergovernmental transfers and insurance trust revenue, and revenue from government owned utilities and other commercial or auxiliary enterprise.

Local Government Revenue from the Federal Government in 2014

National Total = $66,551,753,000

ALPHA ORDER

RANK	STATE	REVENUE	% of USA
18	Alabama	$969,666,000	1.5%
38	Alaska	290,986,000	0.4%
16	Arizona	1,039,901,000	1.6%
37	Arkansas	298,487,000	0.4%
1	California	11,667,891,000	17.5%
14	Colorado	1,189,558,000	1.8%
25	Connecticut	564,427,000	0.8%
50	Delaware	63,715,000	0.1%
4	Florida	4,165,314,000	6.3%
15	Georgia	1,173,577,000	1.8%
36	Hawaii	323,125,000	0.5%
46	Idaho	145,627,000	0.2%
5	Illinois	3,482,179,000	5.2%
32	Indiana	409,137,000	0.6%
28	Iowa	516,553,000	0.8%
39	Kansas	283,985,000	0.4%
29	Kentucky	478,394,000	0.7%
21	Louisiana	894,007,000	1.3%
48	Maine	126,156,000	0.2%
13	Maryland	1,326,827,000	2.0%
12	Massachusetts	1,439,502,000	2.2%
11	Michigan	1,566,692,000	2.4%
20	Minnesota	896,802,000	1.3%
30	Mississippi	427,902,000	0.6%
22	Missouri	796,752,000	1.2%
41	Montana	229,520,000	0.3%
35	Nebraska	347,354,000	0.5%
27	Nevada	520,637,000	0.8%
45	New Hampshire	146,857,000	0.2%
17	New Jersey	1,000,733,000	1.5%
34	New Mexico	369,309,000	0.6%
2	New York	6,443,777,000	9.7%
7	North Carolina	2,296,438,000	3.5%
40	North Dakota	234,916,000	0.4%
8	Ohio	2,104,366,000	3.2%
31	Oklahoma	410,798,000	0.6%
19	Oregon	897,614,000	1.3%
6	Pennsylvania	2,432,814,000	3.7%
44	Rhode Island	159,380,000	0.2%
33	South Carolina	396,919,000	0.6%
43	South Dakota	165,181,000	0.2%
23	Tennessee	733,986,000	1.1%
3	Texas	4,298,323,000	6.5%
26	Utah	535,877,000	0.8%
49	Vermont	75,318,000	0.1%
9	Virginia	1,836,228,000	2.8%
10	Washington	1,673,561,000	2.5%
42	West Virginia	188,702,000	0.3%
24	Wisconsin	592,325,000	0.9%
47	Wyoming	133,892,000	0.2%

RANK ORDER

RANK	STATE	REVENUE	% of USA
1	California	$11,667,891,000	17.5%
2	New York	6,443,777,000	9.7%
3	Texas	4,298,323,000	6.5%
4	Florida	4,165,314,000	6.3%
5	Illinois	3,482,179,000	5.2%
6	Pennsylvania	2,432,814,000	3.7%
7	North Carolina	2,296,438,000	3.5%
8	Ohio	2,104,366,000	3.2%
9	Virginia	1,836,228,000	2.8%
10	Washington	1,673,561,000	2.5%
11	Michigan	1,566,692,000	2.4%
12	Massachusetts	1,439,502,000	2.2%
13	Maryland	1,326,827,000	2.0%
14	Colorado	1,189,558,000	1.8%
15	Georgia	1,173,577,000	1.8%
16	Arizona	1,039,901,000	1.6%
17	New Jersey	1,000,733,000	1.5%
18	Alabama	969,666,000	1.5%
19	Oregon	897,614,000	1.3%
20	Minnesota	896,802,000	1.3%
21	Louisiana	894,007,000	1.3%
22	Missouri	796,752,000	1.2%
23	Tennessee	733,986,000	1.1%
24	Wisconsin	592,325,000	0.9%
25	Connecticut	564,427,000	0.8%
26	Utah	535,877,000	0.8%
27	Nevada	520,637,000	0.8%
28	Iowa	516,553,000	0.8%
29	Kentucky	478,394,000	0.7%
30	Mississippi	427,902,000	0.6%
31	Oklahoma	410,798,000	0.6%
32	Indiana	409,137,000	0.6%
33	South Carolina	396,919,000	0.6%
34	New Mexico	369,309,000	0.6%
35	Nebraska	347,354,000	0.5%
36	Hawaii	323,125,000	0.5%
37	Arkansas	298,487,000	0.4%
38	Alaska	290,986,000	0.4%
39	Kansas	283,985,000	0.4%
40	North Dakota	234,916,000	0.4%
41	Montana	229,520,000	0.3%
42	West Virginia	188,702,000	0.3%
43	South Dakota	165,181,000	0.2%
44	Rhode Island	159,380,000	0.2%
45	New Hampshire	146,857,000	0.2%
46	Idaho	145,627,000	0.2%
47	Wyoming	133,892,000	0.2%
48	Maine	126,156,000	0.2%
49	Vermont	75,318,000	0.1%
50	Delaware	63,715,000	0.1%
	District of Columbia	3,789,766,000	5.7%

Source: U.S. Bureau of the Census, Governments Division
"2014 State and Local Government Finances" (http://www.census.gov/govs/local/)

Per Capita Local Government Revenue from the Federal Government in 2014

National Per Capita = $209

ALPHA ORDER

RANK	STATE	PER CAPITA
17	Alabama	$200
1	Alaska	395
31	Arizona	155
44	Arkansas	101
4	California	302
12	Colorado	222
30	Connecticut	157
49	Delaware	68
16	Florida	209
36	Georgia	116
9	Hawaii	228
47	Idaho	89
5	Illinois	271
50	Indiana	62
26	Iowa	166
45	Kansas	98
40	Kentucky	108
19	Louisiana	192
46	Maine	95
12	Maryland	222
15	Massachusetts	213
29	Michigan	158
27	Minnesota	164
33	Mississippi	143
34	Missouri	131
11	Montana	224
21	Nebraska	185
22	Nevada	184
39	New Hampshire	111
37	New Jersey	112
25	New Mexico	177
2	New York	327
7	North Carolina	231
3	North Dakota	317
24	Ohio	181
41	Oklahoma	106
10	Oregon	226
20	Pennsylvania	190
32	Rhode Island	151
48	South Carolina	82
18	South Dakota	194
37	Tennessee	112
28	Texas	160
23	Utah	182
35	Vermont	120
14	Virginia	221
6	Washington	237
43	West Virginia	102
42	Wisconsin	103
8	Wyoming	229

RANK ORDER

RANK	STATE	PER CAPITA
1	Alaska	$395
2	New York	327
3	North Dakota	317
4	California	302
5	Illinois	271
6	Washington	237
7	North Carolina	231
8	Wyoming	229
9	Hawaii	228
10	Oregon	226
11	Montana	224
12	Colorado	222
12	Maryland	222
14	Virginia	221
15	Massachusetts	213
16	Florida	209
17	Alabama	200
18	South Dakota	194
19	Louisiana	192
20	Pennsylvania	190
21	Nebraska	185
22	Nevada	184
23	Utah	182
24	Ohio	181
25	New Mexico	177
26	Iowa	166
27	Minnesota	164
28	Texas	160
29	Michigan	158
30	Connecticut	157
31	Arizona	155
32	Rhode Island	151
33	Mississippi	143
34	Missouri	131
35	Vermont	120
36	Georgia	116
37	New Jersey	112
37	Tennessee	112
39	New Hampshire	111
40	Kentucky	108
41	Oklahoma	106
42	Wisconsin	103
43	West Virginia	102
44	Arkansas	101
45	Kansas	98
46	Maine	95
47	Idaho	89
48	South Carolina	82
49	Delaware	68
50	Indiana	62
	District of Columbia	5,751

Source: CQ Press using data from U.S. Bureau of the Census, Governments Division
"2014 State and Local Government Finances" (http://www.census.gov/govs/local/)

Local Government Own Source Revenue in 2014

National Total = $966,703,732,000*

ALPHA ORDER

RANK	STATE	REVENUE	% of USA
26	Alabama	$10,848,452,000	1.1%
39	Alaska	3,546,959,000	0.4%
22	Arizona	14,443,614,000	1.5%
37	Arkansas	3,857,306,000	0.4%
1	California	131,971,321,000	13.7%
15	Colorado	18,780,895,000	1.9%
25	Connecticut	11,675,166,000	1.2%
49	Delaware	1,513,329,000	0.2%
4	Florida	57,836,510,000	6.0%
9	Georgia	25,981,417,000	2.7%
44	Hawaii	2,877,365,000	0.3%
42	Idaho	3,097,417,000	0.3%
5	Illinois	41,691,812,000	4.3%
17	Indiana	15,647,043,000	1.6%
28	Iowa	9,357,143,000	1.0%
29	Kansas	8,608,371,000	0.9%
31	Kentucky	7,469,207,000	0.8%
24	Louisiana	13,103,460,000	1.4%
40	Maine	3,240,328,000	0.3%
16	Maryland	18,773,340,000	1.9%
14	Massachusetts	19,203,819,000	2.0%
13	Michigan	21,881,595,000	2.3%
20	Minnesota	14,593,493,000	1.5%
33	Mississippi	6,748,068,000	0.7%
18	Missouri	15,518,442,000	1.6%
47	Montana	2,110,416,000	0.2%
34	Nebraska	6,606,268,000	0.7%
32	Nevada	7,085,799,000	0.7%
36	New Hampshire	4,111,224,000	0.4%
7	New Jersey	34,708,839,000	3.6%
38	New Mexico	3,851,045,000	0.4%
2	New York	117,662,894,000	12.2%
10	North Carolina	25,045,376,000	2.6%
48	North Dakota	1,899,547,000	0.2%
8	Ohio	32,928,274,000	3.4%
30	Oklahoma	7,945,528,000	0.8%
27	Oregon	10,690,438,000	1.1%
6	Pennsylvania	36,610,662,000	3.8%
43	Rhode Island	3,020,335,000	0.3%
23	South Carolina	13,477,691,000	1.4%
46	South Dakota	2,136,720,000	0.2%
19	Tennessee	14,905,101,000	1.5%
3	Texas	78,961,316,000	8.2%
35	Utah	6,181,089,000	0.6%
50	Vermont	833,992,000	0.1%
12	Virginia	22,560,291,000	2.3%
11	Washington	22,631,616,000	2.3%
41	West Virginia	3,219,826,000	0.3%
21	Wisconsin	14,448,380,000	1.5%
45	Wyoming	2,664,341,000	0.3%

RANK ORDER

RANK	STATE	REVENUE	% of USA
1	California	$131,971,321,000	13.7%
2	New York	117,662,894,000	12.2%
3	Texas	78,961,316,000	8.2%
4	Florida	57,836,510,000	6.0%
5	Illinois	41,691,812,000	4.3%
6	Pennsylvania	36,610,662,000	3.8%
7	New Jersey	34,708,839,000	3.6%
8	Ohio	32,928,274,000	3.4%
9	Georgia	25,981,417,000	2.7%
10	North Carolina	25,045,376,000	2.6%
11	Washington	22,631,616,000	2.3%
12	Virginia	22,560,291,000	2.3%
13	Michigan	21,881,595,000	2.3%
14	Massachusetts	19,203,819,000	2.0%
15	Colorado	18,780,895,000	1.9%
16	Maryland	18,773,340,000	1.9%
17	Indiana	15,647,043,000	1.6%
18	Missouri	15,518,442,000	1.6%
19	Tennessee	14,905,101,000	1.5%
20	Minnesota	14,593,493,000	1.5%
21	Wisconsin	14,448,380,000	1.5%
22	Arizona	14,443,614,000	1.5%
23	South Carolina	13,477,691,000	1.4%
24	Louisiana	13,103,460,000	1.4%
25	Connecticut	11,675,166,000	1.2%
26	Alabama	10,848,452,000	1.1%
27	Oregon	10,690,438,000	1.1%
28	Iowa	9,357,143,000	1.0%
29	Kansas	8,608,371,000	0.9%
30	Oklahoma	7,945,528,000	0.8%
31	Kentucky	7,469,207,000	0.8%
32	Nevada	7,085,799,000	0.7%
33	Mississippi	6,748,068,000	0.7%
34	Nebraska	6,606,268,000	0.7%
35	Utah	6,181,089,000	0.6%
36	New Hampshire	4,111,224,000	0.4%
37	Arkansas	3,857,306,000	0.4%
38	New Mexico	3,851,045,000	0.4%
39	Alaska	3,546,959,000	0.4%
40	Maine	3,240,328,000	0.3%
41	West Virginia	3,219,826,000	0.3%
42	Idaho	3,097,417,000	0.3%
43	Rhode Island	3,020,335,000	0.3%
44	Hawaii	2,877,365,000	0.3%
45	Wyoming	2,664,341,000	0.3%
46	South Dakota	2,136,720,000	0.2%
47	Montana	2,110,416,000	0.2%
48	North Dakota	1,899,547,000	0.2%
49	Delaware	1,513,329,000	0.2%
50	Vermont	833,992,000	0.1%
	District of Columbia	8,140,852,000	0.8%

Source: U.S. Bureau of the Census, Governments Division
"2014 State and Local Government Finances" (http://www.census.gov/govs/local/)
*Own source revenue includes taxes, current charges, and miscellaneous general revenue. Excluded are intergovernmental transfers, insurance trust revenue, and revenue from government owned utilities and other commercial or auxiliary enterprise.

Per Capita Local Government Own Source Revenue in 2014

National Per Capita = $3,035*

ALPHA ORDER

RANK	STATE	PER CAPITA
37	Alabama	$2,240
2	Alaska	4,815
39	Arizona	2,149
50	Arkansas	1,300
7	California	3,412
6	Colorado	3,511
8	Connecticut	3,250
48	Delaware	1,619
16	Florida	2,908
26	Georgia	2,576
43	Hawaii	2,032
44	Idaho	1,896
9	Illinois	3,240
34	Indiana	2,372
13	Iowa	3,011
14	Kansas	2,969
47	Kentucky	1,693
21	Louisiana	2,819
33	Maine	2,435
11	Maryland	3,146
19	Massachusetts	2,845
38	Michigan	2,207
25	Minnesota	2,676
36	Mississippi	2,255
28	Missouri	2,560
41	Montana	2,063
5	Nebraska	3,512
32	Nevada	2,501
12	New Hampshire	3,094
4	New Jersey	3,889
45	New Mexico	1,849
1	New York	5,967
29	North Carolina	2,521
27	North Dakota	2,567
20	Ohio	2,840
42	Oklahoma	2,049
24	Oregon	2,694
18	Pennsylvania	2,862
17	Rhode Island	2,864
22	South Carolina	2,791
31	South Dakota	2,506
35	Tennessee	2,277
15	Texas	2,930
40	Utah	2,101
49	Vermont	1,330
23	Virginia	2,712
10	Washington	3,208
46	West Virginia	1,742
30	Wisconsin	2,509
3	Wyoming	4,565

RANK ORDER

RANK	STATE	PER CAPITA
1	New York	$5,967
2	Alaska	4,815
3	Wyoming	4,565
4	New Jersey	3,889
5	Nebraska	3,512
6	Colorado	3,511
7	California	3,412
8	Connecticut	3,250
9	Illinois	3,240
10	Washington	3,208
11	Maryland	3,146
12	New Hampshire	3,094
13	Iowa	3,011
14	Kansas	2,969
15	Texas	2,930
16	Florida	2,908
17	Rhode Island	2,864
18	Pennsylvania	2,862
19	Massachusetts	2,845
20	Ohio	2,840
21	Louisiana	2,819
22	South Carolina	2,791
23	Virginia	2,712
24	Oregon	2,694
25	Minnesota	2,676
26	Georgia	2,576
27	North Dakota	2,567
28	Missouri	2,560
29	North Carolina	2,521
30	Wisconsin	2,509
31	South Dakota	2,506
32	Nevada	2,501
33	Maine	2,435
34	Indiana	2,372
35	Tennessee	2,277
36	Mississippi	2,255
37	Alabama	2,240
38	Michigan	2,207
39	Arizona	2,149
40	Utah	2,101
41	Montana	2,063
42	Oklahoma	2,049
43	Hawaii	2,032
44	Idaho	1,896
45	New Mexico	1,849
46	West Virginia	1,742
47	Kentucky	1,693
48	Delaware	1,619
49	Vermont	1,330
50	Arkansas	1,300
	District of Columbia	12,353

Source: CQ Press using data from U.S. Bureau of the Census, Governments Division
"2014 State and Local Government Finances" (http://www.census.gov/govs/local/)
*Own source revenue includes taxes, current charges, and miscellaneous general revenue. Excluded are intergovernmental transfers, insurance trust revenue, and revenue from government owned utilities and other commercial or auxiliary enterprise.

Local Government Tax Revenue in 2014

National Total = $623,638,201,000

ALPHA ORDER

RANK	STATE	REVENUE	% of USA
29	Alabama	$5,254,280,000	0.8%
41	Alaska	2,175,626,000	0.3%
20	Arizona	9,087,358,000	1.5%
40	Arkansas	2,206,194,000	0.4%
2	California	73,294,783,000	11.8%
16	Colorado	11,623,458,000	1.9%
17	Connecticut	10,120,215,000	1.6%
49	Delaware	948,372,000	0.2%
5	Florida	30,747,656,000	4.9%
10	Georgia	15,467,127,000	2.5%
42	Hawaii	2,069,619,000	0.3%
44	Idaho	1,619,093,000	0.3%
4	Illinois	30,898,426,000	5.0%
23	Indiana	7,880,004,000	1.3%
27	Iowa	5,484,257,000	0.9%
28	Kansas	5,371,703,000	0.9%
30	Kentucky	4,813,907,000	0.8%
22	Louisiana	8,383,318,000	1.3%
37	Maine	2,547,361,000	0.4%
12	Maryland	14,540,729,000	2.3%
11	Massachusetts	15,385,830,000	2.5%
15	Michigan	12,324,928,000	2.0%
24	Minnesota	7,534,904,000	1.2%
36	Mississippi	2,907,640,000	0.5%
19	Missouri	9,820,042,000	1.6%
46	Montana	1,273,460,000	0.2%
32	Nebraska	4,297,587,000	0.7%
34	Nevada	3,854,794,000	0.6%
35	New Hampshire	3,461,141,000	0.6%
6	New Jersey	27,958,301,000	4.5%
38	New Mexico	2,517,025,000	0.4%
1	New York	89,108,009,000	14.3%
14	North Carolina	12,537,650,000	2.0%
48	North Dakota	1,091,648,000	0.2%
8	Ohio	21,768,486,000	3.5%
31	Oklahoma	4,728,361,000	0.8%
26	Oregon	6,597,444,000	1.1%
7	Pennsylvania	26,024,338,000	4.2%
39	Rhode Island	2,488,311,000	0.4%
25	South Carolina	6,617,755,000	1.1%
45	South Dakota	1,534,674,000	0.2%
21	Tennessee	8,436,855,000	1.4%
3	Texas	53,974,549,000	8.7%
33	Utah	4,002,702,000	0.6%
50	Vermont	510,729,000	0.1%
9	Virginia	16,059,784,000	2.6%
13	Washington	12,739,094,000	2.0%
43	West Virginia	1,927,848,000	0.3%
18	Wisconsin	10,033,202,000	1.6%
47	Wyoming	1,209,217,000	0.2%

RANK ORDER

RANK	STATE	REVENUE	% of USA
1	New York	$89,108,009,000	14.3%
2	California	73,294,783,000	11.8%
3	Texas	53,974,549,000	8.7%
4	Illinois	30,898,426,000	5.0%
5	Florida	30,747,656,000	4.9%
6	New Jersey	27,958,301,000	4.5%
7	Pennsylvania	26,024,338,000	4.2%
8	Ohio	21,768,486,000	3.5%
9	Virginia	16,059,784,000	2.6%
10	Georgia	15,467,127,000	2.5%
11	Massachusetts	15,385,830,000	2.5%
12	Maryland	14,540,729,000	2.3%
13	Washington	12,739,094,000	2.0%
14	North Carolina	12,537,650,000	2.0%
15	Michigan	12,324,928,000	2.0%
16	Colorado	11,623,458,000	1.9%
17	Connecticut	10,120,215,000	1.6%
18	Wisconsin	10,033,202,000	1.6%
19	Missouri	9,820,042,000	1.6%
20	Arizona	9,087,358,000	1.5%
21	Tennessee	8,436,855,000	1.4%
22	Louisiana	8,383,318,000	1.3%
23	Indiana	7,880,004,000	1.3%
24	Minnesota	7,534,904,000	1.2%
25	South Carolina	6,617,755,000	1.1%
26	Oregon	6,597,444,000	1.1%
27	Iowa	5,484,257,000	0.9%
28	Kansas	5,371,703,000	0.9%
29	Alabama	5,254,280,000	0.8%
30	Kentucky	4,813,907,000	0.8%
31	Oklahoma	4,728,361,000	0.8%
32	Nebraska	4,297,587,000	0.7%
33	Utah	4,002,702,000	0.6%
34	Nevada	3,854,794,000	0.6%
35	New Hampshire	3,461,141,000	0.6%
36	Mississippi	2,907,640,000	0.5%
37	Maine	2,547,361,000	0.4%
38	New Mexico	2,517,025,000	0.4%
39	Rhode Island	2,488,311,000	0.4%
40	Arkansas	2,206,194,000	0.4%
41	Alaska	2,175,626,000	0.3%
42	Hawaii	2,069,619,000	0.3%
43	West Virginia	1,927,848,000	0.3%
44	Idaho	1,619,093,000	0.3%
45	South Dakota	1,534,674,000	0.2%
46	Montana	1,273,460,000	0.2%
47	Wyoming	1,209,217,000	0.2%
48	North Dakota	1,091,648,000	0.2%
49	Delaware	948,372,000	0.2%
50	Vermont	510,729,000	0.1%
	District of Columbia	6,378,407,000	1.0%

Source: U.S. Bureau of the Census, Governments Division
"2014 State and Local Government Finances" (http://www.census.gov/govs/local/)

Per Capita Local Government Tax Revenue in 2014

National Per Capita = $1,958

ALPHA ORDER

RANK	STATE	PER CAPITA
44	Alabama	$1,085
3	Alaska	2,953
35	Arizona	1,352
50	Arkansas	744
17	California	1,895
11	Colorado	2,173
4	Connecticut	2,818
46	Delaware	1,014
27	Florida	1,546
28	Georgia	1,533
30	Hawaii	1,461
47	Idaho	991
7	Illinois	2,401
42	Indiana	1,195
23	Iowa	1,765
19	Kansas	1,853
43	Kentucky	1,091
21	Louisiana	1,804
16	Maine	1,914
6	Maryland	2,437
10	Massachusetts	2,279
39	Michigan	1,243
31	Minnesota	1,382
48	Mississippi	972
26	Missouri	1,620
38	Montana	1,245
9	Nebraska	2,285
33	Nevada	1,361
5	New Hampshire	2,605
2	New Jersey	3,133
41	New Mexico	1,208
1	New York	4,519
37	North Carolina	1,262
29	North Dakota	1,475
18	Ohio	1,877
40	Oklahoma	1,219
25	Oregon	1,663
13	Pennsylvania	2,035
8	Rhode Island	2,360
32	South Carolina	1,371
22	South Dakota	1,800
36	Tennessee	1,289
14	Texas	2,003
33	Utah	1,361
49	Vermont	815
15	Virginia	1,931
20	Washington	1,806
45	West Virginia	1,043
24	Wisconsin	1,742
12	Wyoming	2,072

RANK ORDER

RANK	STATE	PER CAPITA
1	New York	$4,519
2	New Jersey	3,133
3	Alaska	2,953
4	Connecticut	2,818
5	New Hampshire	2,605
6	Maryland	2,437
7	Illinois	2,401
8	Rhode Island	2,360
9	Nebraska	2,285
10	Massachusetts	2,279
11	Colorado	2,173
12	Wyoming	2,072
13	Pennsylvania	2,035
14	Texas	2,003
15	Virginia	1,931
16	Maine	1,914
17	California	1,895
18	Ohio	1,877
19	Kansas	1,853
20	Washington	1,806
21	Louisiana	1,804
22	South Dakota	1,800
23	Iowa	1,765
24	Wisconsin	1,742
25	Oregon	1,663
26	Missouri	1,620
27	Florida	1,546
28	Georgia	1,533
29	North Dakota	1,475
30	Hawaii	1,461
31	Minnesota	1,382
32	South Carolina	1,371
33	Nevada	1,361
33	Utah	1,361
35	Arizona	1,352
36	Tennessee	1,289
37	North Carolina	1,262
38	Montana	1,245
39	Michigan	1,243
40	Oklahoma	1,219
41	New Mexico	1,208
42	Indiana	1,195
43	Kentucky	1,091
44	Alabama	1,085
45	West Virginia	1,043
46	Delaware	1,014
47	Idaho	991
48	Mississippi	972
49	Vermont	815
50	Arkansas	744
	District of Columbia	9,679

Source: CQ Press using data from U.S. Bureau of the Census, Governments Division
"2014 State and Local Government Finances" (http://www.census.gov/govs/local/)

Local Government Total Expenditures in 2014

National Total = $1,722,749,379,000*

ALPHA ORDER

RANK	STATE	EXPENDITURES	% of USA
24	Alabama	$20,947,556,000	1.2%
39	Alaska	5,790,244,000	0.3%
20	Arizona	27,157,778,000	1.6%
36	Arkansas	9,878,688,000	0.6%
1	California	277,318,057,000	16.1%
18	Colorado	29,407,403,000	1.7%
27	Connecticut	17,919,935,000	1.0%
49	Delaware	3,425,629,000	0.2%
4	Florida	95,327,742,000	5.5%
11	Georgia	43,725,995,000	2.5%
47	Hawaii	3,636,526,000	0.2%
41	Idaho	5,193,297,000	0.3%
5	Illinois	76,782,425,000	4.5%
21	Indiana	26,811,104,000	1.6%
28	Iowa	16,361,630,000	0.9%
29	Kansas	14,384,010,000	0.8%
30	Kentucky	14,171,019,000	0.8%
23	Louisiana	21,218,123,000	1.2%
43	Maine	4,725,880,000	0.3%
16	Maryland	31,024,323,000	1.8%
14	Massachusetts	34,036,639,000	2.0%
10	Michigan	45,034,885,000	2.6%
17	Minnesota	30,540,155,000	1.8%
34	Mississippi	12,648,727,000	0.7%
22	Missouri	25,659,491,000	1.5%
46	Montana	3,798,965,000	0.2%
33	Nebraska	12,940,692,000	0.8%
32	Nevada	13,116,824,000	0.8%
40	New Hampshire	5,398,653,000	0.3%
8	New Jersey	47,924,882,000	2.8%
37	New Mexico	8,525,871,000	0.5%
2	New York	198,547,217,000	11.5%
9	North Carolina	45,311,764,000	2.6%
45	North Dakota	3,837,523,000	0.2%
7	Ohio	54,746,871,000	3.2%
31	Oklahoma	13,804,734,000	0.8%
26	Oregon	19,368,378,000	1.1%
6	Pennsylvania	63,116,030,000	3.7%
44	Rhode Island	4,384,078,000	0.3%
25	South Carolina	20,504,289,000	1.2%
48	South Dakota	3,441,055,000	0.2%
15	Tennessee	32,673,015,000	1.9%
3	Texas	130,720,181,000	7.6%
35	Utah	11,226,568,000	0.7%
50	Vermont	2,688,468,000	0.2%
13	Virginia	38,722,641,000	2.2%
12	Washington	40,281,316,000	2.3%
38	West Virginia	5,864,251,000	0.3%
19	Wisconsin	28,539,499,000	1.7%
42	Wyoming	4,789,084,000	0.3%

RANK ORDER

RANK	STATE	EXPENDITURES	% of USA
1	California	$277,318,057,000	16.1%
2	New York	198,547,217,000	11.5%
3	Texas	130,720,181,000	7.6%
4	Florida	95,327,742,000	5.5%
5	Illinois	76,782,425,000	4.5%
6	Pennsylvania	63,116,030,000	3.7%
7	Ohio	54,746,871,000	3.2%
8	New Jersey	47,924,882,000	2.8%
9	North Carolina	45,311,764,000	2.6%
10	Michigan	45,034,885,000	2.6%
11	Georgia	43,725,995,000	2.5%
12	Washington	40,281,316,000	2.3%
13	Virginia	38,722,641,000	2.2%
14	Massachusetts	34,036,639,000	2.0%
15	Tennessee	32,673,015,000	1.9%
16	Maryland	31,024,323,000	1.8%
17	Minnesota	30,540,155,000	1.8%
18	Colorado	29,407,403,000	1.7%
19	Wisconsin	28,539,499,000	1.7%
20	Arizona	27,157,778,000	1.6%
21	Indiana	26,811,104,000	1.6%
22	Missouri	25,659,491,000	1.5%
23	Louisiana	21,218,123,000	1.2%
24	Alabama	20,947,556,000	1.2%
25	South Carolina	20,504,289,000	1.2%
26	Oregon	19,368,378,000	1.1%
27	Connecticut	17,919,935,000	1.0%
28	Iowa	16,361,630,000	0.9%
29	Kansas	14,384,010,000	0.8%
30	Kentucky	14,171,019,000	0.8%
31	Oklahoma	13,804,734,000	0.8%
32	Nevada	13,116,824,000	0.8%
33	Nebraska	12,940,692,000	0.8%
34	Mississippi	12,648,727,000	0.7%
35	Utah	11,226,568,000	0.7%
36	Arkansas	9,878,688,000	0.6%
37	New Mexico	8,525,871,000	0.5%
38	West Virginia	5,864,251,000	0.3%
39	Alaska	5,790,244,000	0.3%
40	New Hampshire	5,398,653,000	0.3%
41	Idaho	5,193,297,000	0.3%
42	Wyoming	4,789,084,000	0.3%
43	Maine	4,725,880,000	0.3%
44	Rhode Island	4,384,078,000	0.3%
45	North Dakota	3,837,523,000	0.2%
46	Montana	3,798,965,000	0.2%
47	Hawaii	3,636,526,000	0.2%
48	South Dakota	3,441,055,000	0.2%
49	Delaware	3,425,629,000	0.2%
50	Vermont	2,688,468,000	0.2%
	District of Columbia	15,349,269,000	0.9%

Source: U.S. Bureau of the Census, Governments Division
"2014 State and Local Government Finances" (http://www.census.gov/govs/local/)
*Total expenditures includes all money paid other than for retirement of debt and extension of loans. Includes payments from all sources of funds including current revenues and proceeds from borrowing and prior year fund balances. Includes intergovernmental transfers and expenditures for government owned utilities and other commercial or auxiliary enterprise and insurance trust expenditures.

Per Capita Local Government Total Expenditures in 2014

National Per Capita = $5,408*

ALPHA ORDER

RANK	STATE	PER CAPITA
30	Alabama	$4,325
3	Alaska	7,860
39	Arizona	4,041
46	Arkansas	3,330
4	California	7,169
9	Colorado	5,497
16	Connecticut	4,989
43	Delaware	3,664
22	Florida	4,793
29	Georgia	4,335
50	Hawaii	2,568
48	Idaho	3,179
6	Illinois	5,967
37	Indiana	4,065
11	Iowa	5,264
17	Kansas	4,961
47	Kentucky	3,211
26	Louisiana	4,565
45	Maine	3,551
12	Maryland	5,199
14	Massachusetts	5,043
28	Michigan	4,542
8	Minnesota	5,601
34	Mississippi	4,227
33	Missouri	4,234
42	Montana	3,714
5	Nebraska	6,879
25	Nevada	4,630
38	New Hampshire	4,063
10	New Jersey	5,370
36	New Mexico	4,093
1	New York	10,069
27	North Carolina	4,561
13	North Dakota	5,187
23	Ohio	4,722
44	Oklahoma	3,560
20	Oregon	4,881
19	Pennsylvania	4,935
35	Rhode Island	4,158
32	South Carolina	4,247
40	South Dakota	4,036
15	Tennessee	4,992
21	Texas	4,851
41	Utah	3,816
31	Vermont	4,288
24	Virginia	4,656
7	Washington	5,710
49	West Virginia	3,172
18	Wisconsin	4,956
2	Wyoming	8,206

RANK ORDER

RANK	STATE	PER CAPITA
1	New York	$10,069
2	Wyoming	8,206
3	Alaska	7,860
4	California	7,169
5	Nebraska	6,879
6	Illinois	5,967
7	Washington	5,710
8	Minnesota	5,601
9	Colorado	5,497
10	New Jersey	5,370
11	Iowa	5,264
12	Maryland	5,199
13	North Dakota	5,187
14	Massachusetts	5,043
15	Tennessee	4,992
16	Connecticut	4,989
17	Kansas	4,961
18	Wisconsin	4,956
19	Pennsylvania	4,935
20	Oregon	4,881
21	Texas	4,851
22	Florida	4,793
23	Ohio	4,722
24	Virginia	4,656
25	Nevada	4,630
26	Louisiana	4,565
27	North Carolina	4,561
28	Michigan	4,542
29	Georgia	4,335
30	Alabama	4,325
31	Vermont	4,288
32	South Carolina	4,247
33	Missouri	4,234
34	Mississippi	4,227
35	Rhode Island	4,158
36	New Mexico	4,093
37	Indiana	4,065
38	New Hampshire	4,063
39	Arizona	4,041
40	South Dakota	4,036
41	Utah	3,816
42	Montana	3,714
43	Delaware	3,664
44	Oklahoma	3,560
45	Maine	3,551
46	Arkansas	3,330
47	Kentucky	3,211
48	Idaho	3,179
49	West Virginia	3,172
50	Hawaii	2,568

District of Columbia 23,292

Source: CQ Press using data from U.S. Bureau of the Census, Governments Division
"2014 State and Local Government Finances" (http://www.census.gov/govs/local/)
*Total expenditures includes all money paid other than for retirement of debt and extension of loans. Includes payments from all sources of funds including current revenues and proceeds from borrowing and prior year fund balances. Includes intergovernmental transfers and expenditures for government owned utilities and other commercial or auxiliary enterprise and insurance trust expenditures.

Local Government Direct General Expenditures in 2014

National Total = $1,465,722,643,000*

ALPHA ORDER

RANK	STATE	EXPENDITURES	% of USA
25	Alabama	$17,855,882,000	1.2%
40	Alaska	5,097,865,000	0.3%
22	Arizona	20,997,275,000	1.4%
35	Arkansas	8,815,765,000	0.6%
1	California	227,152,108,000	15.5%
18	Colorado	24,891,695,000	1.7%
27	Connecticut	16,380,799,000	1.1%
48	Delaware	2,940,738,000	0.2%
4	Florida	82,401,778,000	5.6%
11	Georgia	36,783,164,000	2.5%
49	Hawaii	2,722,679,000	0.2%
41	Idaho	4,966,549,000	0.3%
5	Illinois	62,503,931,000	4.3%
19	Indiana	23,962,250,000	1.6%
28	Iowa	15,044,419,000	1.0%
29	Kansas	12,942,679,000	0.9%
31	Kentucky	12,177,440,000	0.8%
23	Louisiana	19,599,050,000	1.3%
42	Maine	4,538,853,000	0.3%
15	Maryland	28,151,820,000	1.9%
14	Massachusetts	29,008,317,000	2.0%
9	Michigan	40,155,736,000	2.7%
16	Minnesota	27,257,594,000	1.9%
33	Mississippi	11,729,695,000	0.8%
21	Missouri	22,244,610,000	1.5%
45	Montana	3,640,689,000	0.2%
36	Nebraska	8,457,654,000	0.6%
32	Nevada	11,765,764,000	0.8%
39	New Hampshire	5,186,878,000	0.4%
8	New Jersey	46,406,453,000	3.2%
37	New Mexico	7,775,458,000	0.5%
2	New York	158,614,181,000	10.8%
10	North Carolina	39,580,311,000	2.7%
46	North Dakota	3,570,522,000	0.2%
7	Ohio	50,387,672,000	3.4%
30	Oklahoma	12,450,110,000	0.8%
26	Oregon	16,717,584,000	1.1%
6	Pennsylvania	56,292,889,000	3.8%
44	Rhode Island	4,022,833,000	0.3%
24	South Carolina	18,842,462,000	1.3%
47	South Dakota	3,031,806,000	0.2%
20	Tennessee	22,362,643,000	1.5%
3	Texas	110,292,232,000	7.5%
34	Utah	8,867,175,000	0.6%
50	Vermont	2,418,362,000	0.2%
12	Virginia	35,394,794,000	2.4%
13	Washington	31,581,752,000	2.2%
38	West Virginia	5,460,347,000	0.4%
17	Wisconsin	25,816,072,000	1.8%
43	Wyoming	4,503,292,000	0.3%

RANK ORDER

RANK	STATE	EXPENDITURES	% of USA
1	California	$227,152,108,000	15.5%
2	New York	158,614,181,000	10.8%
3	Texas	110,292,232,000	7.5%
4	Florida	82,401,778,000	5.6%
5	Illinois	62,503,931,000	4.3%
6	Pennsylvania	56,292,889,000	3.8%
7	Ohio	50,387,672,000	3.4%
8	New Jersey	46,406,453,000	3.2%
9	Michigan	40,155,736,000	2.7%
10	North Carolina	39,580,311,000	2.7%
11	Georgia	36,783,164,000	2.5%
12	Virginia	35,394,794,000	2.4%
13	Washington	31,581,752,000	2.2%
14	Massachusetts	29,008,317,000	2.0%
15	Maryland	28,151,820,000	1.9%
16	Minnesota	27,257,594,000	1.9%
17	Wisconsin	25,816,072,000	1.8%
18	Colorado	24,891,695,000	1.7%
19	Indiana	23,962,250,000	1.6%
20	Tennessee	22,362,643,000	1.5%
21	Missouri	22,244,610,000	1.5%
22	Arizona	20,997,275,000	1.4%
23	Louisiana	19,599,050,000	1.3%
24	South Carolina	18,842,462,000	1.3%
25	Alabama	17,855,882,000	1.2%
26	Oregon	16,717,584,000	1.1%
27	Connecticut	16,380,799,000	1.1%
28	Iowa	15,044,419,000	1.0%
29	Kansas	12,942,679,000	0.9%
30	Oklahoma	12,450,110,000	0.8%
31	Kentucky	12,177,440,000	0.8%
32	Nevada	11,765,764,000	0.8%
33	Mississippi	11,729,695,000	0.8%
34	Utah	8,867,175,000	0.6%
35	Arkansas	8,815,765,000	0.6%
36	Nebraska	8,457,654,000	0.6%
37	New Mexico	7,775,458,000	0.5%
38	West Virginia	5,460,347,000	0.4%
39	New Hampshire	5,186,878,000	0.4%
40	Alaska	5,097,865,000	0.3%
41	Idaho	4,966,549,000	0.3%
42	Maine	4,538,853,000	0.3%
43	Wyoming	4,503,292,000	0.3%
44	Rhode Island	4,022,833,000	0.3%
45	Montana	3,640,689,000	0.2%
46	North Dakota	3,570,522,000	0.2%
47	South Dakota	3,031,806,000	0.2%
48	Delaware	2,940,738,000	0.2%
49	Hawaii	2,722,679,000	0.2%
50	Vermont	2,418,362,000	0.2%
	District of Columbia	11,960,017,000	0.8%

Source: U.S. Bureau of the Census, Governments Division
"2014 State and Local Government Finances" (http://www.census.gov/govs/local/)
*Direct general expenditures include expenditures for current operations, assistance and subsidies, interest on debt, and capital outlay. Excludes intergovernmental transfers, expenditures for government owned utilities and other commercial or auxiliary enterprise, and insurance trust expenditures.

Per Capita Local Government Direct General Expenditures in 2014

National Per Capita = $4,601*

ALPHA ORDER

ALPHA ORDER

RANK	STATE	PER CAPITA
34	Alabama	$3,687
3	Alaska	6,920
44	Arizona	3,125
47	Arkansas	2,971
4	California	5,872
11	Colorado	4,653
12	Connecticut	4,561
43	Delaware	3,145
24	Florida	4,143
36	Georgia	3,647
50	Hawaii	1,922
45	Idaho	3,040
7	Illinois	4,857
37	Indiana	3,633
8	Iowa	4,840
16	Kansas	4,464
49	Kentucky	2,759
21	Louisiana	4,217
41	Maine	3,411
10	Maryland	4,718
19	Massachusetts	4,298
26	Michigan	4,050
6	Minnesota	4,999
28	Mississippi	3,920
35	Missouri	3,670
38	Montana	3,559
13	Nebraska	4,496
23	Nevada	4,153
29	New Hampshire	3,904
5	New Jersey	5,200
33	New Mexico	3,733
1	New York	8,044
27	North Carolina	3,984
9	North Dakota	4,826
18	Ohio	4,346
42	Oklahoma	3,211
22	Oregon	4,213
17	Pennsylvania	4,401
32	Rhode Island	3,815
30	South Carolina	3,902
39	South Dakota	3,556
40	Tennessee	3,417
25	Texas	4,093
46	Utah	3,014
31	Vermont	3,857
20	Virginia	4,256
15	Washington	4,477
48	West Virginia	2,954
14	Wisconsin	4,483
2	Wyoming	7,716

RANK ORDER

RANK	STATE	PER CAPITA
1	New York	$8,044
2	Wyoming	7,716
3	Alaska	6,920
4	California	5,872
5	New Jersey	5,200
6	Minnesota	4,999
7	Illinois	4,857
8	Iowa	4,840
9	North Dakota	4,826
10	Maryland	4,718
11	Colorado	4,653
12	Connecticut	4,561
13	Nebraska	4,496
14	Wisconsin	4,483
15	Washington	4,477
16	Kansas	4,464
17	Pennsylvania	4,401
18	Ohio	4,346
19	Massachusetts	4,298
20	Virginia	4,256
21	Louisiana	4,217
22	Oregon	4,213
23	Nevada	4,153
24	Florida	4,143
25	Texas	4,093
26	Michigan	4,050
27	North Carolina	3,984
28	Mississippi	3,920
29	New Hampshire	3,904
30	South Carolina	3,902
31	Vermont	3,857
32	Rhode Island	3,815
33	New Mexico	3,733
34	Alabama	3,687
35	Missouri	3,670
36	Georgia	3,647
37	Indiana	3,633
38	Montana	3,559
39	South Dakota	3,556
40	Tennessee	3,417
41	Maine	3,411
42	Oklahoma	3,211
43	Delaware	3,145
44	Arizona	3,125
45	Idaho	3,040
46	Utah	3,014
47	Arkansas	2,971
48	West Virginia	2,954
49	Kentucky	2,759
50	Hawaii	1,922
	District of Columbia	18,149

Source: CQ Press using data from U.S. Bureau of the Census, Governments Division
    "2014 State and Local Government Finances" (http://www.census.gov/govs/local/)
*Direct general expenditures include expenditures for current operations, assistance and subsidies, interest on debt, and capital outlay. Excludes intergovernmental transfers, expenditures for government owned utilities and other commercial or auxiliary enterprise, and insurance trust expenditures.

Local Government Debt Outstanding in 2014

National Total = $1,825,293,650,000*

ALPHA ORDER

RANK	STATE	DEBT	% of USA
24	Alabama	$22,168,474,000	1.2%
41	Alaska	3,002,777,000	0.2%
13	Arizona	34,420,801,000	1.9%
33	Arkansas	11,463,325,000	0.6%
1	California	269,069,712,000	14.7%
12	Colorado	37,142,391,000	2.0%
34	Connecticut	11,393,916,000	0.6%
46	Delaware	2,515,821,000	0.1%
4	Florida	118,793,502,000	6.5%
10	Georgia	43,485,259,000	2.4%
38	Hawaii	5,869,827,000	0.3%
45	Idaho	2,623,696,000	0.1%
5	Illinois	83,424,110,000	4.6%
18	Indiana	27,962,155,000	1.5%
32	Iowa	12,488,483,000	0.7%
28	Kansas	19,205,312,000	1.1%
21	Kentucky	25,370,578,000	1.4%
26	Louisiana	20,912,186,000	1.1%
42	Maine	2,974,265,000	0.2%
22	Maryland	23,593,028,000	1.3%
29	Massachusetts	17,163,269,000	0.9%
9	Michigan	45,143,220,000	2.5%
15	Minnesota	33,177,916,000	1.8%
37	Mississippi	7,139,869,000	0.4%
20	Missouri	27,391,679,000	1.5%
48	Montana	1,946,799,000	0.1%
30	Nebraska	13,215,229,000	0.7%
23	Nevada	22,693,087,000	1.2%
44	New Hampshire	2,628,484,000	0.1%
14	New Jersey	33,215,668,000	1.8%
36	New Mexico	8,819,459,000	0.5%
3	New York	208,482,636,000	11.4%
16	North Carolina	32,218,928,000	1.8%
40	North Dakota	3,402,356,000	0.2%
7	Ohio	52,203,243,000	2.9%
35	Oklahoma	9,598,614,000	0.5%
25	Oregon	21,156,346,000	1.2%
6	Pennsylvania	80,274,530,000	4.4%
43	Rhode Island	2,677,285,000	0.1%
19	South Carolina	27,825,315,000	1.5%
47	South Dakota	2,453,700,000	0.1%
17	Tennessee	28,721,564,000	1.6%
2	Texas	226,937,840,000	12.4%
31	Utah	12,947,003,000	0.7%
49	Vermont	1,267,898,000	0.1%
11	Virginia	37,751,815,000	2.1%
8	Washington	48,587,885,000	2.7%
39	West Virginia	3,501,997,000	0.2%
27	Wisconsin	20,734,877,000	1.1%
50	Wyoming	1,048,286,000	0.1%

RANK ORDER

RANK	STATE	DEBT	% of USA
1	California	$269,069,712,000	14.7%
2	Texas	226,937,840,000	12.4%
3	New York	208,482,636,000	11.4%
4	Florida	118,793,502,000	6.5%
5	Illinois	83,424,110,000	4.6%
6	Pennsylvania	80,274,530,000	4.4%
7	Ohio	52,203,243,000	2.9%
8	Washington	48,587,885,000	2.7%
9	Michigan	45,143,220,000	2.5%
10	Georgia	43,485,259,000	2.4%
11	Virginia	37,751,815,000	2.1%
12	Colorado	37,142,391,000	2.0%
13	Arizona	34,420,801,000	1.9%
14	New Jersey	33,215,668,000	1.8%
15	Minnesota	33,177,916,000	1.8%
16	North Carolina	32,218,928,000	1.8%
17	Tennessee	28,721,564,000	1.6%
18	Indiana	27,962,155,000	1.5%
19	South Carolina	27,825,315,000	1.5%
20	Missouri	27,391,679,000	1.5%
21	Kentucky	25,370,578,000	1.4%
22	Maryland	23,593,028,000	1.3%
23	Nevada	22,693,087,000	1.2%
24	Alabama	22,168,474,000	1.2%
25	Oregon	21,156,346,000	1.2%
26	Louisiana	20,912,186,000	1.1%
27	Wisconsin	20,734,877,000	1.1%
28	Kansas	19,205,312,000	1.1%
29	Massachusetts	17,163,269,000	0.9%
30	Nebraska	13,215,229,000	0.7%
31	Utah	12,947,003,000	0.7%
32	Iowa	12,488,483,000	0.7%
33	Arkansas	11,463,325,000	0.6%
34	Connecticut	11,393,916,000	0.6%
35	Oklahoma	9,598,614,000	0.5%
36	New Mexico	8,819,459,000	0.5%
37	Mississippi	7,139,869,000	0.4%
38	Hawaii	5,869,827,000	0.3%
39	West Virginia	3,501,997,000	0.2%
40	North Dakota	3,402,356,000	0.2%
41	Alaska	3,002,777,000	0.2%
42	Maine	2,974,265,000	0.2%
43	Rhode Island	2,677,285,000	0.1%
44	New Hampshire	2,628,484,000	0.1%
45	Idaho	2,623,696,000	0.1%
46	Delaware	2,515,821,000	0.1%
47	South Dakota	2,453,700,000	0.1%
48	Montana	1,946,799,000	0.1%
49	Vermont	1,267,898,000	0.1%
50	Wyoming	1,048,286,000	0.1%
	District of Columbia	13,087,235,000	0.7%

Source: U.S. Bureau of the Census, Governments Division
"2014 State and Local Government Finances" (http://www.census.gov/govs/local/)
*Includes short-term, long-term, full faith and credit, nonguaranteed, and public debt for private purposes.

Per Capita Local Government Debt Outstanding in 2014

National Per Capita = $5,730*

ALPHA ORDER

RANK	STATE	PER CAPITA
18	Alabama	$4,577
30	Alaska	4,076
16	Arizona	5,122
33	Arkansas	3,864
5	California	6,956
6	Colorado	6,943
37	Connecticut	3,172
39	Delaware	2,691
12	Florida	5,973
26	Georgia	4,311
29	Hawaii	4,144
50	Idaho	1,606
9	Illinois	6,483
27	Indiana	4,240
31	Iowa	4,018
8	Kansas	6,624
14	Kentucky	5,749
23	Louisiana	4,499
44	Maine	2,235
32	Maryland	3,954
40	Massachusetts	2,543
19	Michigan	4,553
11	Minnesota	6,084
43	Mississippi	2,386
21	Missouri	4,519
47	Montana	1,903
4	Nebraska	7,025
3	Nevada	8,010
46	New Hampshire	1,978
34	New Jersey	3,722
28	New Mexico	4,234
1	New York	10,573
36	North Carolina	3,243
17	North Dakota	4,598
22	Ohio	4,502
42	Oklahoma	2,475
15	Oregon	5,331
10	Pennsylvania	6,276
41	Rhode Island	2,539
13	South Carolina	5,763
38	South Dakota	2,878
25	Tennessee	4,389
2	Texas	8,422
24	Utah	4,401
45	Vermont	2,022
20	Virginia	4,539
7	Washington	6,888
48	West Virginia	1,894
35	Wisconsin	3,601
49	Wyoming	1,796

RANK ORDER

RANK	STATE	PER CAPITA
1	New York	$10,573
2	Texas	8,422
3	Nevada	8,010
4	Nebraska	7,025
5	California	6,956
6	Colorado	6,943
7	Washington	6,888
8	Kansas	6,624
9	Illinois	6,483
10	Pennsylvania	6,276
11	Minnesota	6,084
12	Florida	5,973
13	South Carolina	5,763
14	Kentucky	5,749
15	Oregon	5,331
16	Arizona	5,122
17	North Dakota	4,598
18	Alabama	4,577
19	Michigan	4,553
20	Virginia	4,539
21	Missouri	4,519
22	Ohio	4,502
23	Louisiana	4,499
24	Utah	4,401
25	Tennessee	4,389
26	Georgia	4,311
27	Indiana	4,240
28	New Mexico	4,234
29	Hawaii	4,144
30	Alaska	4,076
31	Iowa	4,018
32	Maryland	3,954
33	Arkansas	3,864
34	New Jersey	3,722
35	Wisconsin	3,601
36	North Carolina	3,243
37	Connecticut	3,172
38	South Dakota	2,878
39	Delaware	2,691
40	Massachusetts	2,543
41	Rhode Island	2,539
42	Oklahoma	2,475
43	Mississippi	2,386
44	Maine	2,235
45	Vermont	2,022
46	New Hampshire	1,978
47	Montana	1,903
48	West Virginia	1,894
49	Wyoming	1,796
50	Idaho	1,606

District of Columbia	19,859

Source: CQ Press using data from U.S. Bureau of the Census, Governments Division
"2014 State and Local Government Finances" (http://www.census.gov/govs/local/)
*Includes short-term, long-term, full faith and credit, nonguaranteed, and public debt for private purposes.

Local Government Full-Time Equivalent Employees in 2015

National Total = 11,937,320 FTE Employees*

ALPHA ORDER					RANK ORDER			
RANK	STATE	EMPLOYEES	% of USA		RANK	STATE	EMPLOYEES	% of USA
23	Alabama	192,805	1.6%		1	California	1,370,992	11.5%
47	Alaska	27,696	0.2%		2	Texas	1,153,922	9.7%
20	Arizona	206,743	1.7%		3	New York	930,721	7.8%
33	Arkansas	106,770	0.9%		4	Florida	697,634	5.8%
1	California	1,370,992	11.5%		5	Illinois	503,953	4.2%
22	Colorado	202,040	1.7%		6	Ohio	446,076	3.7%
31	Connecticut	128,409	1.1%		7	Pennsylvania	404,222	3.4%
49	Delaware	23,289	0.2%		8	North Carolina	400,412	3.4%
4	Florida	697,634	5.8%		9	Georgia	378,414	3.2%
9	Georgia	378,414	3.2%		10	New Jersey	336,670	2.8%
50	Hawaii	16,607	0.1%		11	Virginia	318,984	2.7%
39	Idaho	56,889	0.5%		12	Michigan	294,742	2.5%
5	Illinois	503,953	4.2%		13	Tennessee	245,974	2.1%
15	Indiana	232,846	2.0%		14	Massachusetts	235,953	2.0%
30	Iowa	132,022	1.1%		15	Indiana	232,846	2.0%
28	Kansas	144,866	1.2%		16	Missouri	229,225	1.9%
26	Kentucky	157,485	1.3%		17	Washington	220,948	1.9%
24	Louisiana	185,169	1.6%		18	Maryland	215,831	1.8%
41	Maine	49,341	0.4%		19	Wisconsin	211,962	1.8%
18	Maryland	215,831	1.8%		20	Arizona	206,743	1.7%
14	Massachusetts	235,953	2.0%		21	Minnesota	202,723	1.7%
12	Michigan	294,742	2.5%		22	Colorado	202,040	1.7%
21	Minnesota	202,723	1.7%		23	Alabama	192,805	1.6%
29	Mississippi	134,150	1.1%		24	Louisiana	185,169	1.6%
16	Missouri	229,225	1.9%		25	South Carolina	181,758	1.5%
42	Montana	37,253	0.3%		26	Kentucky	157,485	1.3%
35	Nebraska	86,283	0.7%		27	Oklahoma	148,707	1.2%
36	Nevada	79,735	0.7%		28	Kansas	144,866	1.2%
40	New Hampshire	52,311	0.4%		29	Mississippi	134,150	1.1%
10	New Jersey	336,670	2.8%		30	Iowa	132,022	1.1%
37	New Mexico	79,297	0.7%		31	Connecticut	128,409	1.1%
3	New York	930,721	7.8%		32	Oregon	125,460	1.1%
8	North Carolina	400,412	3.4%		33	Arkansas	106,770	0.9%
46	North Dakota	28,093	0.2%		34	Utah	87,110	0.7%
6	Ohio	446,076	3.7%		35	Nebraska	86,283	0.7%
27	Oklahoma	148,707	1.2%		36	Nevada	79,735	0.7%
32	Oregon	125,460	1.1%		37	New Mexico	79,297	0.7%
7	Pennsylvania	404,222	3.4%		38	West Virginia	62,410	0.5%
45	Rhode Island	29,684	0.2%		39	Idaho	56,889	0.5%
25	South Carolina	181,758	1.5%		40	New Hampshire	52,311	0.4%
44	South Dakota	32,163	0.3%		41	Maine	49,341	0.4%
13	Tennessee	245,974	2.1%		42	Montana	37,253	0.3%
2	Texas	1,153,922	9.7%		43	Wyoming	37,250	0.3%
34	Utah	87,110	0.7%		44	South Dakota	32,163	0.3%
48	Vermont	25,938	0.2%		45	Rhode Island	29,684	0.2%
11	Virginia	318,984	2.7%		46	North Dakota	28,093	0.2%
17	Washington	220,948	1.9%		47	Alaska	27,696	0.2%
38	West Virginia	62,410	0.5%		48	Vermont	25,938	0.2%
19	Wisconsin	211,962	1.8%		49	Delaware	23,289	0.2%
43	Wyoming	37,250	0.3%		50	Hawaii	16,607	0.1%
						District of Columbia	47,383	0.4%

Source: U.S. Bureau of the Census, Governments Division
"Government Employment and Payroll" (http://www.census.gov/govs/apes/index.html)
*As of March 2015.

Rate of Local Government Full-Time Equivalent Employees in 2015

National Rate = 372 FTE Employees per 10,000 Population*

ALPHA ORDER

RANK	STATE	RATE
10	Alabama	397
20	Alaska	375
44	Arizona	303
32	Arkansas	359
35	California	352
23	Colorado	371
33	Connecticut	358
49	Delaware	247
38	Florida	345
23	Georgia	371
50	Hawaii	117
39	Idaho	344
12	Illinois	393
35	Indiana	352
6	Iowa	423
2	Kansas	498
34	Kentucky	356
10	Louisiana	397
23	Maine	371
31	Maryland	360
37	Massachusetts	348
45	Michigan	297
28	Minnesota	370
5	Mississippi	449
18	Missouri	377
30	Montana	361
4	Nebraska	456
48	Nevada	276
12	New Hampshire	393
18	New Jersey	377
15	New Mexico	381
3	New York	471
9	North Carolina	399
23	North Dakota	371
14	Ohio	384
15	Oklahoma	381
42	Oregon	312
41	Pennsylvania	316
47	Rhode Island	281
23	South Carolina	371
20	South Dakota	375
22	Tennessee	373
7	Texas	421
46	Utah	291
8	Vermont	414
15	Virginia	381
43	Washington	309
40	West Virginia	339
29	Wisconsin	367
1	Wyoming	635

RANK ORDER

RANK	STATE	RATE
1	Wyoming	635
2	Kansas	498
3	New York	471
4	Nebraska	456
5	Mississippi	449
6	Iowa	423
7	Texas	421
8	Vermont	414
9	North Carolina	399
10	Alabama	397
10	Louisiana	397
12	Illinois	393
12	New Hampshire	393
14	Ohio	384
15	New Mexico	381
15	Oklahoma	381
15	Virginia	381
18	Missouri	377
18	New Jersey	377
20	Alaska	375
20	South Dakota	375
22	Tennessee	373
23	Colorado	371
23	Georgia	371
23	Maine	371
23	North Dakota	371
23	South Carolina	371
28	Minnesota	370
29	Wisconsin	367
30	Montana	361
31	Maryland	360
32	Arkansas	359
33	Connecticut	358
34	Kentucky	356
35	California	352
35	Indiana	352
37	Massachusetts	348
38	Florida	345
39	Idaho	344
40	West Virginia	339
41	Pennsylvania	316
42	Oregon	312
43	Washington	309
44	Arizona	303
45	Michigan	297
46	Utah	291
47	Rhode Island	281
48	Nevada	276
49	Delaware	247
50	Hawaii	117
	District of Columbia	707

Source: CQ Press using data from U.S. Bureau of the Census, Governments Division
"Government Employment and Payroll" (http://www.census.gov/govs/apes/index.html)
*Full-time equivalent as of March 2015.

Average Annual Earnings of Full-Time Local Government Employees in 2015

National Average = $55,754*

ALPHA ORDER

RANK	STATE	SALARY
42	Alabama	$42,272
7	Alaska	64,222
23	Arizona	51,596
50	Arkansas	37,779
1	California	75,765
19	Colorado	55,467
8	Connecticut	64,144
14	Delaware	59,026
27	Florida	49,731
40	Georgia	43,323
12	Hawaii	61,813
43	Idaho	41,852
11	Illinois	61,941
34	Indiana	45,298
25	Iowa	51,196
38	Kansas	44,305
47	Kentucky	40,747
44	Louisiana	41,524
33	Maine	45,549
6	Maryland	64,776
10	Massachusetts	62,715
18	Michigan	55,534
15	Minnesota	57,941
49	Mississippi	38,167
39	Missouri	43,908
35	Montana	45,171
21	Nebraska	52,605
5	Nevada	66,621
22	New Hampshire	51,750
3	New Jersey	72,133
36	New Mexico	44,429
4	New York	70,721
32	North Carolina	46,959
28	North Dakota	49,702
24	Ohio	51,483
48	Oklahoma	39,710
13	Oregon	60,190
16	Pennsylvania	57,702
9	Rhode Island	64,014
37	South Carolina	44,427
45	South Dakota	41,491
41	Tennessee	43,085
31	Texas	47,127
30	Utah	49,179
29	Vermont	49,256
26	Virginia	50,598
2	Washington	72,382
46	West Virginia	40,766
20	Wisconsin	54,319
17	Wyoming	55,900

RANK ORDER

RANK	STATE	SALARY
1	California	$75,765
2	Washington	72,382
3	New Jersey	72,133
4	New York	70,721
5	Nevada	66,621
6	Maryland	64,776
7	Alaska	64,222
8	Connecticut	64,144
9	Rhode Island	64,014
10	Massachusetts	62,715
11	Illinois	61,941
12	Hawaii	61,813
13	Oregon	60,190
14	Delaware	59,026
15	Minnesota	57,941
16	Pennsylvania	57,702
17	Wyoming	55,900
18	Michigan	55,534
19	Colorado	55,467
20	Wisconsin	54,319
21	Nebraska	52,605
22	New Hampshire	51,750
23	Arizona	51,596
24	Ohio	51,483
25	Iowa	51,196
26	Virginia	50,598
27	Florida	49,731
28	North Dakota	49,702
29	Vermont	49,256
30	Utah	49,179
31	Texas	47,127
32	North Carolina	46,959
33	Maine	45,549
34	Indiana	45,298
35	Montana	45,171
36	New Mexico	44,429
37	South Carolina	44,427
38	Kansas	44,305
39	Missouri	43,908
40	Georgia	43,323
41	Tennessee	43,085
42	Alabama	42,272
43	Idaho	41,852
44	Louisiana	41,524
45	South Dakota	41,491
46	West Virginia	40,766
47	Kentucky	40,747
48	Oklahoma	39,710
49	Mississippi	38,167
50	Arkansas	37,779
	District of Columbia	82,067

Source: CQ Press using data from U.S. Bureau of the Census, Governments Division
"Government Employment and Payroll" (http://www.census.gov/govs/apes/index.html)
*March 2015 full-time payroll (multiplied by 12) divided by full-time employees.

XI. Health

Average Annual Single Coverage Health Insurance Premium per Enrolled Employee in 2015
National Average = $5,963*

ALPHA ORDER

RANK	STATE	PREMIUM
39	Alabama	$5,733
1	Alaska	7,807
41	Arizona	5,668
50	Arkansas	5,119
21	California	5,938
34	Colorado	5,794
6	Connecticut	6,478
8	Delaware	6,288
28	Florida	5,839
45	Georgia	5,565
47	Hawaii	5,522
30	Idaho	5,820
13	Illinois	6,055
25	Indiana	5,868
44	Iowa	5,571
46	Kansas	5,558
16	Kentucky	5,984
19	Louisiana	5,973
17	Maine	5,979
11	Maryland	6,229
4	Massachusetts	6,519
37	Michigan	5,771
42	Minnesota	5,651
48	Mississippi	5,420
40	Missouri	5,726
22	Montana	5,932
35	Nebraska	5,788
32	Nevada	5,800
3	New Hampshire	6,573
10	New Jersey	6,248
38	New Mexico	5,759
2	New York	6,801
36	North Carolina	5,774
23	North Dakota	5,920
20	Ohio	5,939
43	Oklahoma	5,608
29	Oregon	5,822
9	Pennsylvania	6,286
5	Rhode Island	6,509
24	South Carolina	5,880
31	South Dakota	5,816
49	Tennessee	5,329
27	Texas	5,847
33	Utah	5,796
26	Vermont	5,861
18	Virginia	5,978
14	Washington	6,053
12	West Virginia	6,081
15	Wisconsin	6,011
7	Wyoming	6,420

RANK ORDER

RANK	STATE	PREMIUM
1	Alaska	$7,807
2	New York	6,801
3	New Hampshire	6,573
4	Massachusetts	6,519
5	Rhode Island	6,509
6	Connecticut	6,478
7	Wyoming	6,420
8	Delaware	6,288
9	Pennsylvania	6,286
10	New Jersey	6,248
11	Maryland	6,229
12	West Virginia	6,081
13	Illinois	6,055
14	Washington	6,053
15	Wisconsin	6,011
16	Kentucky	5,984
17	Maine	5,979
18	Virginia	5,978
19	Louisiana	5,973
20	Ohio	5,939
21	California	5,938
22	Montana	5,932
23	North Dakota	5,920
24	South Carolina	5,880
25	Indiana	5,868
26	Vermont	5,861
27	Texas	5,847
28	Florida	5,839
29	Oregon	5,822
30	Idaho	5,820
31	South Dakota	5,816
32	Nevada	5,800
33	Utah	5,796
34	Colorado	5,794
35	Nebraska	5,788
36	North Carolina	5,774
37	Michigan	5,771
38	New Mexico	5,759
39	Alabama	5,733
40	Missouri	5,726
41	Arizona	5,668
42	Minnesota	5,651
43	Oklahoma	5,608
44	Iowa	5,571
45	Georgia	5,565
46	Kansas	5,558
47	Hawaii	5,522
48	Mississippi	5,420
49	Tennessee	5,329
50	Arkansas	5,119
	District of Columbia	6,409

Source: U.S. Department of Health and Human Services, Agency for Healthcare Research and Quality
"Private-Sector Data by Firm Size and State" (Table II Series, Medical Expenditures Panel Survey)
(http://www.meps.ahrq.gov/mepsweb/survey_comp/Insurance.jsp)
*Enrolled employees at private-sector establishments that offer health insurance coverage.

Average Annual Family Coverage Health Insurance Premium per Enrolled Employee in 2015
National Average = $17,322*

ALPHA ORDER

RANK	STATE	PREMIUM
47	Alabama	$15,953
1	Alaska	21,089
27	Arizona	16,999
50	Arkansas	14,218
9	California	18,045
28	Colorado	16,940
8	Connecticut	18,269
4	Delaware	18,920
44	Florida	16,009
19	Georgia	17,307
46	Hawaii	15,959
35	Idaho	16,691
21	Illinois	17,227
25	Indiana	17,121
38	Iowa	16,257
34	Kansas	16,740
37	Kentucky	16,622
20	Louisiana	17,242
41	Maine	16,117
10	Maryland	17,961
5	Massachusetts	18,454
49	Michigan	15,628
29	Minnesota	16,925
42	Mississippi	16,081
31	Missouri	16,849
18	Montana	17,317
39	Nebraska	16,201
15	Nevada	17,434
3	New Hampshire	19,208
7	New Jersey	18,280
16	New Mexico	17,349
2	New York	19,630
23	North Carolina	17,141
43	North Dakota	16,020
30	Ohio	16,900
32	Oklahoma	16,811
23	Oregon	17,141
17	Pennsylvania	17,344
13	Rhode Island	17,590
33	South Carolina	16,764
40	South Dakota	16,194
48	Tennessee	15,635
22	Texas	17,216
45	Utah	15,998
11	Vermont	17,835
14	Virginia	17,566
36	Washington	16,627
6	West Virginia	18,322
12	Wisconsin	17,662
26	Wyoming	17,015

RANK ORDER

RANK	STATE	PREMIUM
1	Alaska	$21,089
2	New York	19,630
3	New Hampshire	19,208
4	Delaware	18,920
5	Massachusetts	18,454
6	West Virginia	18,322
7	New Jersey	18,280
8	Connecticut	18,269
9	California	18,045
10	Maryland	17,961
11	Vermont	17,835
12	Wisconsin	17,662
13	Rhode Island	17,590
14	Virginia	17,566
15	Nevada	17,434
16	New Mexico	17,349
17	Pennsylvania	17,344
18	Montana	17,317
19	Georgia	17,307
20	Louisiana	17,242
21	Illinois	17,227
22	Texas	17,216
23	North Carolina	17,141
23	Oregon	17,141
25	Indiana	17,121
26	Wyoming	17,015
27	Arizona	16,999
28	Colorado	16,940
29	Minnesota	16,925
30	Ohio	16,900
31	Missouri	16,849
32	Oklahoma	16,811
33	South Carolina	16,764
34	Kansas	16,740
35	Idaho	16,691
36	Washington	16,627
37	Kentucky	16,622
38	Iowa	16,257
39	Nebraska	16,201
40	South Dakota	16,194
41	Maine	16,117
42	Mississippi	16,081
43	North Dakota	16,020
44	Florida	16,009
45	Utah	15,998
46	Hawaii	15,959
47	Alabama	15,953
48	Tennessee	15,635
49	Michigan	15,628
50	Arkansas	14,218
	District of Columbia	19,104

Source: U.S. Department of Health and Human Services, Agency for Healthcare Research and Quality
"Private-Sector Data by Firm Size and State" (Table II Series, Medical Expenditures Panel Survey)
(http://www.meps.ahrq.gov/mepsweb/survey_comp/Insurance.jsp)
*Enrolled employees at private-sector establishments that offer health insurance coverage.

Percent of Private-Sector Establishments That Offer Health Insurance: 2015

National Percent = 45.7%

ALPHA ORDER			RANK ORDER		
RANK	STATE	PERCENT	RANK	STATE	PERCENT
5	Alabama	52.1	1	Hawaii	85.1
41	Alaska	41.7	2	New Jersey	53.4
33	Arizona	43.2	3	Nevada	52.7
11	Arkansas	49.7	4	Massachusetts	52.4
29	California	44.7	5	Alabama	52.1
35	Colorado	43.0	6	Rhode Island	51.0
15	Connecticut	48.6	7	Ohio	50.6
17	Delaware	47.9	8	West Virginia	50.2
46	Florida	38.2	9	Maryland	50.1
45	Georgia	39.9	10	Kansas	49.8
1	Hawaii	85.1	11	Arkansas	49.7
50	Idaho	33.9	11	Pennsylvania	49.7
31	Illinois	44.1	13	New Hampshire	48.9
32	Indiana	43.3	13	New York	48.9
25	Iowa	45.3	15	Connecticut	48.6
10	Kansas	49.8	16	Michigan	48.4
18	Kentucky	47.8	17	Delaware	47.9
36	Louisiana	42.7	18	Kentucky	47.8
42	Maine	41.6	19	Virginia	47.2
9	Maryland	50.1	20	Tennessee	47.0
4	Massachusetts	52.4	21	Missouri	46.2
16	Michigan	48.4	22	Oregon	45.9
30	Minnesota	44.3	23	Texas	45.8
38	Mississippi	42.3	24	Oklahoma	45.5
21	Missouri	46.2	25	Iowa	45.3
49	Montana	34.3	26	Wisconsin	45.2
48	Nebraska	35.4	27	South Carolina	45.0
3	Nevada	52.7	28	North Dakota	44.9
13	New Hampshire	48.9	29	California	44.7
2	New Jersey	53.4	30	Minnesota	44.3
33	New Mexico	43.2	31	Illinois	44.1
13	New York	48.9	32	Indiana	43.3
36	North Carolina	42.7	33	Arizona	43.2
28	North Dakota	44.9	33	New Mexico	43.2
7	Ohio	50.6	35	Colorado	43.0
24	Oklahoma	45.5	36	Louisiana	42.7
22	Oregon	45.9	36	North Carolina	42.7
11	Pennsylvania	49.7	38	Mississippi	42.3
6	Rhode Island	51.0	38	South Dakota	42.3
27	South Carolina	45.0	40	Washington	41.8
38	South Dakota	42.3	41	Alaska	41.7
20	Tennessee	47.0	42	Maine	41.6
23	Texas	45.8	43	Utah	40.7
43	Utah	40.7	44	Vermont	40.6
44	Vermont	40.6	45	Georgia	39.9
19	Virginia	47.2	46	Florida	38.2
40	Washington	41.8	47	Wyoming	38.0
8	West Virginia	50.2	48	Nebraska	35.4
26	Wisconsin	45.2	49	Montana	34.3
47	Wyoming	38.0	50	Idaho	33.9
				District of Columbia	69.6

Source: U.S. Department of Health and Human Services, Agency for Healthcare Research and Quality
"Private-Sector Data by Firm Size and State" (Table II Series, Medical Expenditures Panel Survey)
(http://www.meps.ahrq.gov/mepsweb/survey_comp/Insurance.jsp)

Persons Not Covered by Health Insurance in 2015

National Total = 29,757,544 Uninsured

ALPHA ORDER

RANK	STATE	UNINSURED	% of USA
20	Alabama	484,271	1.6%
42	Alaska	105,966	0.4%
12	Arizona	727,976	2.4%
29	Arkansas	277,547	0.9%
2	California	3,317,265	11.1%
22	Colorado	432,622	1.5%
34	Connecticut	210,522	0.7%
49	Delaware	54,498	0.2%
3	Florida	2,661,549	8.9%
4	Georgia	1,388,400	4.7%
48	Hawaii	54,531	0.2%
36	Idaho	180,345	0.6%
7	Illinois	900,289	3.0%
14	Indiana	627,761	2.1%
37	Iowa	154,970	0.5%
31	Kansas	260,508	0.9%
30	Kentucky	261,468	0.9%
17	Louisiana	545,631	1.8%
40	Maine	110,508	0.4%
23	Maryland	389,199	1.3%
35	Massachusetts	189,273	0.6%
15	Michigan	596,642	2.0%
32	Minnesota	245,108	0.8%
24	Mississippi	371,585	1.2%
16	Missouri	583,108	2.0%
39	Montana	118,509	0.4%
38	Nebraska	153,789	0.5%
25	Nevada	350,684	1.2%
44	New Hampshire	83,388	0.3%
9	New Jersey	771,196	2.6%
33	New Mexico	224,031	0.8%
5	New York	1,380,548	4.6%
6	North Carolina	1,102,787	3.7%
47	North Dakota	57,451	0.2%
11	Ohio	746,276	2.5%
18	Oklahoma	532,509	1.8%
28	Oregon	280,263	0.9%
8	Pennsylvania	801,927	2.7%
46	Rhode Island	59,410	0.2%
19	South Carolina	523,228	1.8%
43	South Dakota	85,915	0.3%
13	Tennessee	667,417	2.2%
1	Texas	4,615,225	15.5%
27	Utah	311,341	1.0%
50	Vermont	23,676	0.1%
10	Virginia	746,293	2.5%
21	Washington	467,967	1.6%
41	West Virginia	108,082	0.4%
26	Wisconsin	322,616	1.1%
45	Wyoming	66,494	0.2%

RANK ORDER

RANK	STATE	UNINSURED	% of USA
1	Texas	4,615,225	15.5%
2	California	3,317,265	11.1%
3	Florida	2,661,549	8.9%
4	Georgia	1,388,400	4.7%
5	New York	1,380,548	4.6%
6	North Carolina	1,102,787	3.7%
7	Illinois	900,289	3.0%
8	Pennsylvania	801,927	2.7%
9	New Jersey	771,196	2.6%
10	Virginia	746,293	2.5%
11	Ohio	746,276	2.5%
12	Arizona	727,976	2.4%
13	Tennessee	667,417	2.2%
14	Indiana	627,761	2.1%
15	Michigan	596,642	2.0%
16	Missouri	583,108	2.0%
17	Louisiana	545,631	1.8%
18	Oklahoma	532,509	1.8%
19	South Carolina	523,228	1.8%
20	Alabama	484,271	1.6%
21	Washington	467,967	1.6%
22	Colorado	432,622	1.5%
23	Maryland	389,199	1.3%
24	Mississippi	371,585	1.2%
25	Nevada	350,684	1.2%
26	Wisconsin	322,616	1.1%
27	Utah	311,341	1.0%
28	Oregon	280,263	0.9%
29	Arkansas	277,547	0.9%
30	Kentucky	261,468	0.9%
31	Kansas	260,508	0.9%
32	Minnesota	245,108	0.8%
33	New Mexico	224,031	0.8%
34	Connecticut	210,522	0.7%
35	Massachusetts	189,273	0.6%
36	Idaho	180,345	0.6%
37	Iowa	154,970	0.5%
38	Nebraska	153,789	0.5%
39	Montana	118,509	0.4%
40	Maine	110,508	0.4%
41	West Virginia	108,082	0.4%
42	Alaska	105,966	0.4%
43	South Dakota	85,915	0.3%
44	New Hampshire	83,388	0.3%
45	Wyoming	66,494	0.2%
46	Rhode Island	59,410	0.2%
47	North Dakota	57,451	0.2%
48	Hawaii	54,531	0.2%
49	Delaware	54,498	0.2%
50	Vermont	23,676	0.1%
	District of Columbia	24,980	0.1%

Source: U.S. Bureau of the Census
"2015 American Community Survey-Table S2701" (http://www.census.gov/programs-surveys/acs/)

Percent of Population Not Covered by Health Insurance in 2015

National Percent = 9.4% of Population*

ALPHA ORDER

RANK	STATE	PERCENT
19	Alabama	10.1
2	Alaska	14.9
15	Arizona	10.8
22	Arkansas	9.5
26	California	8.6
29	Colorado	8.1
40	Connecticut	6.0
43	Delaware	5.9
5	Florida	13.3
3	Georgia	13.9
48	Hawaii	4.0
12	Idaho	11.0
31	Illinois	7.1
21	Indiana	9.6
46	Iowa	5.0
23	Kansas	9.1
40	Kentucky	6.0
8	Louisiana	11.9
27	Maine	8.4
34	Maryland	6.6
50	Massachusetts	2.8
39	Michigan	6.1
47	Minnesota	4.5
6	Mississippi	12.7
20	Missouri	9.8
9	Montana	11.6
28	Nebraska	8.2
7	Nevada	12.3
38	New Hampshire	6.3
25	New Jersey	8.7
13	New Mexico	10.9
31	New York	7.1
11	North Carolina	11.2
30	North Dakota	7.8
36	Ohio	6.5
3	Oklahoma	13.9
33	Oregon	7.0
37	Pennsylvania	6.4
44	Rhode Island	5.7
13	South Carolina	10.9
18	South Dakota	10.2
17	Tennessee	10.3
1	Texas	17.1
16	Utah	10.5
49	Vermont	3.8
23	Virginia	9.1
34	Washington	6.6
40	West Virginia	6.0
44	Wisconsin	5.7
10	Wyoming	11.5

RANK ORDER

RANK	STATE	PERCENT
1	Texas	17.1
2	Alaska	14.9
3	Georgia	13.9
3	Oklahoma	13.9
5	Florida	13.3
6	Mississippi	12.7
7	Nevada	12.3
8	Louisiana	11.9
9	Montana	11.6
10	Wyoming	11.5
11	North Carolina	11.2
12	Idaho	11.0
13	New Mexico	10.9
13	South Carolina	10.9
15	Arizona	10.8
16	Utah	10.5
17	Tennessee	10.3
18	South Dakota	10.2
19	Alabama	10.1
20	Missouri	9.8
21	Indiana	9.6
22	Arkansas	9.5
23	Kansas	9.1
23	Virginia	9.1
25	New Jersey	8.7
26	California	8.6
27	Maine	8.4
28	Nebraska	8.2
29	Colorado	8.1
30	North Dakota	7.8
31	Illinois	7.1
31	New York	7.1
33	Oregon	7.0
34	Maryland	6.6
34	Washington	6.6
36	Ohio	6.5
37	Pennsylvania	6.4
38	New Hampshire	6.3
39	Michigan	6.1
40	Connecticut	6.0
40	Kentucky	6.0
40	West Virginia	6.0
43	Delaware	5.9
44	Rhode Island	5.7
44	Wisconsin	5.7
46	Iowa	5.0
47	Minnesota	4.5
48	Hawaii	4.0
49	Vermont	3.8
50	Massachusetts	2.8
	District of Columbia	3.8

Source: U.S. Bureau of the Census
"2015 American Community Survey-Table S2701" (http://www.census.gov/programs-surveys/acs/)
*This is a one-year figure. Census has discontinued three-year averages that had been used previously.

Percent of Population Lacking Access to Primary Care in 2017

National Percent = 11.4% of Population*

RANK	STATE	PERCENT
3	Alabama	27.1
40	Alaska	5.0
4	Arizona	21.4
30	Arkansas	9.5
26	California	10.6
33	Colorado	8.6
47	Connecticut	1.4
7	Delaware	20.1
27	Florida	10.1
20	Georgia	13.1
39	Hawaii	5.1
9	Idaho	17.7
14	Illinois	15.8
6	Indiana	20.8
17	Iowa	13.5
16	Kansas	14.6
15	Kentucky	15.2
2	Louisiana	32.2
45	Maine	3.2
32	Maryland	9.0
41	Massachusetts	4.7
17	Michigan	13.5
43	Minnesota	4.2
1	Mississippi	33.9
34	Missouri	8.2
22	Montana	13.0
49	Nebraska	0.6
27	Nevada	10.1
44	New Hampshire	3.4
50	New Jersey	0.2
12	New Mexico	16.6
37	New York	7.8
38	North Carolina	7.7
31	North Dakota	9.1
35	Ohio	8.1
11	Oklahoma	16.8
19	Oregon	13.3
45	Pennsylvania	3.2
41	Rhode Island	4.7
5	South Carolina	21.2
29	South Dakota	10.0
13	Tennessee	15.9
23	Texas	12.9
20	Utah	13.1
48	Vermont	1.0
25	Virginia	10.8
36	Washington	8.0
8	West Virginia	19.4
24	Wisconsin	11.8
10	Wyoming	17.3

RANK	STATE	PERCENT
1	Mississippi	33.9
2	Louisiana	32.2
3	Alabama	27.1
4	Arizona	21.4
5	South Carolina	21.2
6	Indiana	20.8
7	Delaware	20.1
8	West Virginia	19.4
9	Idaho	17.7
10	Wyoming	17.3
11	Oklahoma	16.8
12	New Mexico	16.6
13	Tennessee	15.9
14	Illinois	15.8
15	Kentucky	15.2
16	Kansas	14.6
17	Iowa	13.5
17	Michigan	13.5
19	Oregon	13.3
20	Georgia	13.1
20	Utah	13.1
22	Montana	13.0
23	Texas	12.9
24	Wisconsin	11.8
25	Virginia	10.8
26	California	10.6
27	Florida	10.1
27	Nevada	10.1
29	South Dakota	10.0
30	Arkansas	9.5
31	North Dakota	9.1
32	Maryland	9.0
33	Colorado	8.6
34	Missouri	8.2
35	Ohio	8.1
36	Washington	8.0
37	New York	7.8
38	North Carolina	7.7
39	Hawaii	5.1
40	Alaska	5.0
41	Massachusetts	4.7
41	Rhode Island	4.7
43	Minnesota	4.2
44	New Hampshire	3.4
45	Maine	3.2
45	Pennsylvania	3.2
47	Connecticut	1.4
48	Vermont	1.0
49	Nebraska	0.6
50	New Jersey	0.2

	District of Columbia	17.9

Source: CQ Press using data from U.S. Department of Health and Human Services, Division of Shortage Designation
   "State Population and HPSA Designation Population Statistics" (as of February 14, 2017)
   (https://datawarehouse.hrsa.gov/tools/hdwreports/Reports.aspx)
*Percent of population considered under-served by primary medical practitioners (Family and General Practice doctors, Internists, Ob/Gyns, and Pediatricians). An under-served population does not have primary medical care within reasonable economic and geographic bounds.

Physicians in 2013

National Total = 1,032,056 Physicians*

ALPHA ORDER					RANK ORDER			

RANK	STATE	PHYSICIANS	% of USA		RANK	STATE	PHYSICIANS	% of USA
27	Alabama	12,209	1.2%		1	California	126,034	12.2%
49	Alaska	1,924	0.2%		2	New York	91,188	8.8%
18	Arizona	18,313	1.8%		3	Texas	66,659	6.5%
32	Arkansas	7,188	0.7%		4	Florida	62,290	6.0%
1	California	126,034	12.2%		5	Pennsylvania	46,647	4.5%
21	Colorado	17,065	1.7%		6	Illinois	44,055	4.3%
23	Connecticut	16,138	1.6%		7	Ohio	38,265	3.7%
46	Delaware	2,722	0.3%		8	Massachusetts	37,205	3.6%
4	Florida	62,290	6.0%		9	New Jersey	32,455	3.1%
14	Georgia	26,434	2.6%		10	Michigan	30,913	3.0%
38	Hawaii	5,184	0.5%		11	North Carolina	29,840	2.9%
43	Idaho	3,350	0.3%		12	Maryland	28,869	2.8%
6	Illinois	44,055	4.3%		13	Virginia	27,130	2.6%
22	Indiana	16,793	1.6%		14	Georgia	26,434	2.6%
33	Iowa	7,047	0.7%		15	Washington	23,143	2.2%
30	Kansas	7,941	0.8%		16	Tennessee	20,234	2.0%
28	Kentucky	11,865	1.1%		17	Minnesota	19,398	1.9%
24	Louisiana	14,528	1.4%		18	Arizona	18,313	1.8%
42	Maine	4,638	0.4%		19	Wisconsin	17,986	1.7%
12	Maryland	28,869	2.8%		20	Missouri	17,693	1.7%
8	Massachusetts	37,205	3.6%		21	Colorado	17,065	1.7%
10	Michigan	30,913	3.0%		22	Indiana	16,793	1.6%
17	Minnesota	19,398	1.9%		23	Connecticut	16,138	1.6%
34	Mississippi	6,491	0.6%		24	Louisiana	14,528	1.4%
20	Missouri	17,693	1.7%		25	Oregon	14,030	1.4%
45	Montana	2,824	0.3%		26	South Carolina	13,093	1.3%
37	Nebraska	5,421	0.5%		27	Alabama	12,209	1.2%
35	Nevada	6,299	0.6%		28	Kentucky	11,865	1.1%
40	New Hampshire	4,815	0.5%		29	Oklahoma	8,060	0.8%
9	New Jersey	32,455	3.1%		30	Kansas	7,941	0.8%
36	New Mexico	6,159	0.6%		31	Utah	7,236	0.7%
2	New York	91,188	8.8%		32	Arkansas	7,188	0.7%
11	North Carolina	29,840	2.9%		33	Iowa	7,047	0.7%
48	North Dakota	2,060	0.2%		34	Mississippi	6,491	0.6%
7	Ohio	38,265	3.7%		35	Nevada	6,299	0.6%
29	Oklahoma	8,060	0.8%		36	New Mexico	6,159	0.6%
25	Oregon	14,030	1.4%		37	Nebraska	5,421	0.5%
5	Pennsylvania	46,647	4.5%		38	Hawaii	5,184	0.5%
41	Rhode Island	4,806	0.5%		39	West Virginia	5,083	0.5%
26	South Carolina	13,093	1.3%		40	New Hampshire	4,815	0.5%
47	South Dakota	2,310	0.2%		41	Rhode Island	4,806	0.5%
16	Tennessee	20,234	2.0%		42	Maine	4,638	0.4%
3	Texas	66,659	6.5%		43	Idaho	3,350	0.3%
31	Utah	7,236	0.7%		44	Vermont	2,886	0.3%
44	Vermont	2,886	0.3%		45	Montana	2,824	0.3%
13	Virginia	27,130	2.6%		46	Delaware	2,722	0.3%
15	Washington	23,143	2.2%		47	South Dakota	2,310	0.2%
39	West Virginia	5,083	0.5%		48	North Dakota	2,060	0.2%
19	Wisconsin	17,986	1.7%		49	Alaska	1,924	0.2%
50	Wyoming	1,287	0.1%		50	Wyoming	1,287	0.1%
						District of Columbia	5,853	0.6%

Source: American Medical Association (Chicago, Illinois)
   "Physician Characteristics and Distribution in the U.S." (2015 Edition)
*As of December 31, 2013. Total does not include 13,854 physicians in the U.S. territories and possessions, at APOs and FPOs, or whose addresses are unknown.

Rate of Physicians in 2013

National Rate = 326 Physicians per 100,000 Population*

ALPHA ORDER

RANK	STATE	RATE
41	Alabama	253
39	Alaska	262
32	Arizona	276
44	Arkansas	243
17	California	329
19	Colorado	324
6	Connecticut	449
27	Delaware	294
20	Florida	319
38	Georgia	265
7	Hawaii	369
50	Idaho	208
14	Illinois	342
40	Indiana	256
45	Iowa	228
33	Kansas	274
37	Kentucky	270
21	Louisiana	314
13	Maine	349
2	Maryland	487
1	Massachusetts	556
23	Michigan	312
11	Minnesota	358
48	Mississippi	217
28	Missouri	293
31	Montana	278
29	Nebraska	290
46	Nevada	226
10	New Hampshire	364
8	New Jersey	365
26	New Mexico	295
3	New York	464
25	North Carolina	303
30	North Dakota	285
16	Ohio	331
49	Oklahoma	209
12	Oregon	357
8	Pennsylvania	365
5	Rhode Island	457
33	South Carolina	274
36	South Dakota	273
24	Tennessee	311
42	Texas	252
43	Utah	249
4	Vermont	461
18	Virginia	328
15	Washington	332
33	West Virginia	274
22	Wisconsin	313
47	Wyoming	221

RANK ORDER

RANK	STATE	RATE
1	Massachusetts	556
2	Maryland	487
3	New York	464
4	Vermont	461
5	Rhode Island	457
6	Connecticut	449
7	Hawaii	369
8	New Jersey	365
8	Pennsylvania	365
10	New Hampshire	364
11	Minnesota	358
12	Oregon	357
13	Maine	349
14	Illinois	342
15	Washington	332
16	Ohio	331
17	California	329
18	Virginia	328
19	Colorado	324
20	Florida	319
21	Louisiana	314
22	Wisconsin	313
23	Michigan	312
24	Tennessee	311
25	North Carolina	303
26	New Mexico	295
27	Delaware	294
28	Missouri	293
29	Nebraska	290
30	North Dakota	285
31	Montana	278
32	Arizona	276
33	Kansas	274
33	South Carolina	274
33	West Virginia	274
36	South Dakota	273
37	Kentucky	270
38	Georgia	265
39	Alaska	262
40	Indiana	256
41	Alabama	253
42	Texas	252
43	Utah	249
44	Arkansas	243
45	Iowa	228
46	Nevada	226
47	Wyoming	221
48	Mississippi	217
49	Oklahoma	209
50	Idaho	208

District of Columbia	905

Source: CQ Press using data from American Medical Association (Chicago, Illinois)
"Physician Characteristics and Distribution in the U.S." (2015 Edition)
*As of December 31, 2013. National rate does not include physicians in the U.S. territories and possessions, at APOs and FPOs, or whose addresses are unknown.

Rate of Registered Nurses in 2015

National Rate = 856 Nurses per 100,000 Population*

ALPHA ORDER				RANK ORDER		
RANK	**STATE**	**RATE**		**RANK**	**STATE**	**RATE**
24	Alabama	906		1	South Dakota	1,393
37	Alaska	801		2	Massachusetts	1,235
43	Arizona	730		3	Rhode Island	1,132
40	Arkansas	755		4	North Dakota	1,106
50	California	654		5	Delaware	1,098
33	Colorado	840		6	Minnesota	1,088
25	Connecticut	905		6	Nebraska	1,088
5	Delaware	1,098		6	Ohio	1,088
35	Florida	834		9	West Virginia	1,087
46	Georgia	676		10	Missouri	1,084
38	Hawaii	771		11	Maine	1,069
42	Idaho	734		12	Pennsylvania	1,064
27	Illinois	880		13	Vermont	1,016
22	Indiana	921		14	Iowa	1,013
14	Iowa	1,013		15	Kentucky	986
19	Kansas	936		16	Wisconsin	962
15	Kentucky	986		17	New Hampshire	956
25	Louisiana	905		18	North Carolina	953
11	Maine	1,069		19	Kansas	936
31	Maryland	852		20	Montana	934
2	Massachusetts	1,235		21	Mississippi	930
23	Michigan	919		22	Indiana	921
6	Minnesota	1,088		23	Michigan	919
21	Mississippi	930		24	Alabama	906
10	Missouri	1,084		25	Connecticut	905
20	Montana	934		25	Louisiana	905
6	Nebraska	1,088		27	Illinois	880
47	Nevada	675		28	New Jersey	878
17	New Hampshire	956		29	New York	870
28	New Jersey	878		30	South Carolina	867
44	New Mexico	726		31	Maryland	852
29	New York	870		32	Tennessee	845
18	North Carolina	953		33	Colorado	840
4	North Dakota	1,106		34	Wyoming	837
6	Ohio	1,088		35	Florida	834
48	Oklahoma	667		36	Oregon	807
36	Oregon	807		37	Alaska	801
12	Pennsylvania	1,064		38	Hawaii	771
3	Rhode Island	1,132		39	Virginia	757
30	South Carolina	867		40	Arkansas	755
1	South Dakota	1,393		41	Washington	739
32	Tennessee	845		42	Idaho	734
45	Texas	724		43	Arizona	730
49	Utah	666		44	New Mexico	726
13	Vermont	1,016		45	Texas	724
39	Virginia	757		46	Georgia	676
41	Washington	739		47	Nevada	675
9	West Virginia	1,087		48	Oklahoma	667
16	Wisconsin	962		49	Utah	666
34	Wyoming	837		50	California	654
					District of Columbia	1,571

Source: CQ Press using data from U.S. Department of Labor, Bureau of Labor Statistics
"Occupational Employment and Wages, 2015" (http://www.bls.gov/oes/)
*Does not include self-employed.

Rate of Dentists in 2016

National Rate = 65 Dentists per 100,000 Population*

ALPHA ORDER

RANK	STATE	RATE
46	Alabama	47
5	Alaska	82
21	Arizona	59
50	Arkansas	43
3	California	85
10	Colorado	75
6	Connecticut	81
46	Delaware	47
23	Florida	57
42	Georgia	50
7	Hawaii	79
42	Idaho	50
11	Illinois	71
42	Indiana	50
25	Iowa	56
31	Kansas	54
20	Kentucky	62
40	Louisiana	51
34	Maine	53
7	Maryland	79
1	Massachusetts	93
17	Michigan	64
18	Minnesota	63
49	Mississippi	45
38	Missouri	52
18	Montana	63
12	Nebraska	69
25	Nevada	56
15	New Hampshire	67
2	New Jersey	87
31	New Mexico	54
4	New York	83
34	North Carolina	53
23	North Dakota	57
25	Ohio	56
38	Oklahoma	52
46	Oregon	47
13	Pennsylvania	68
28	Rhode Island	55
40	South Carolina	51
34	South Dakota	53
31	Tennessee	54
28	Texas	55
16	Utah	65
45	Vermont	48
13	Virginia	68
9	Washington	77
34	West Virginia	53
21	Wisconsin	59
28	Wyoming	55

RANK ORDER

RANK	STATE	RATE
1	Massachusetts	93
2	New Jersey	87
3	California	85
4	New York	83
5	Alaska	82
6	Connecticut	81
7	Hawaii	79
7	Maryland	79
9	Washington	77
10	Colorado	75
11	Illinois	71
12	Nebraska	69
13	Pennsylvania	68
13	Virginia	68
15	New Hampshire	67
16	Utah	65
17	Michigan	64
18	Minnesota	63
18	Montana	63
20	Kentucky	62
21	Arizona	59
21	Wisconsin	59
23	Florida	57
23	North Dakota	57
25	Iowa	56
25	Nevada	56
25	Ohio	56
28	Rhode Island	55
28	Texas	55
28	Wyoming	55
31	Kansas	54
31	New Mexico	54
31	Tennessee	54
34	Maine	53
34	North Carolina	53
34	South Dakota	53
34	West Virginia	53
38	Missouri	52
38	Oklahoma	52
40	Louisiana	51
40	South Carolina	51
42	Georgia	50
42	Idaho	50
42	Indiana	50
45	Vermont	48
46	Alabama	47
46	Delaware	47
46	Oregon	47
49	Mississippi	45
50	Arkansas	43

	District of Columbia	110

Source: CQ Press using data from American Dental Association as reported by The Henry J. Kaiser Family Foundation "Professionally Active Dentists" (http://kff.org/other/state-indicator/total-dentists/)

*Professionally active dentists. Rates calculated using 2015 Census population estimates.

Community Hospitals in 2015

National Total = 4,862 Hospitals*

ALPHA ORDER					RANK ORDER			
RANK	STATE		HOSPITALS	% of USA	RANK	STATE	HOSPITALS	% of USA
21	Alabama		95	2.0%	1	Texas	404	8.3%
47	Alaska		21	0.4%	2	California	342	7.0%
30	Arizona		71	1.5%	3	Florida	210	4.3%
27	Arkansas		80	1.6%	4	Illinois	188	3.9%
2	California		342	7.0%	5	Pennsylvania	186	3.8%
26	Colorado		81	1.7%	6	Ohio	179	3.7%
43	Connecticut		32	0.7%	7	New York	170	3.5%
50	Delaware		7	0.1%	8	Michigan	147	3.0%
3	Florida		210	4.3%	9	Georgia	141	2.9%
9	Georgia		141	2.9%	10	Kansas	131	2.7%
45	Hawaii		24	0.5%	11	Minnesota	130	2.7%
38	Idaho		40	0.8%	12	Wisconsin	127	2.6%
4	Illinois		188	3.9%	13	Missouri	121	2.5%
15	Indiana		120	2.5%	13	Tennessee	121	2.5%
17	Iowa		118	2.4%	15	Indiana	120	2.5%
10	Kansas		131	2.7%	15	Louisiana	120	2.5%
20	Kentucky		103	2.1%	17	Iowa	118	2.4%
15	Louisiana		120	2.5%	18	North Carolina	113	2.3%
42	Maine		34	0.7%	19	Oklahoma	110	2.3%
35	Maryland		50	1.0%	20	Kentucky	103	2.1%
28	Massachusetts		76	1.6%	21	Alabama	95	2.0%
8	Michigan		147	3.0%	21	Mississippi	95	2.0%
11	Minnesota		130	2.7%	23	Virginia	92	1.9%
21	Mississippi		95	2.0%	24	Washington	90	1.9%
13	Missouri		121	2.5%	25	Nebraska	88	1.8%
35	Montana		50	1.0%	26	Colorado	81	1.7%
25	Nebraska		88	1.8%	27	Arkansas	80	1.6%
40	Nevada		36	0.7%	28	Massachusetts	76	1.6%
44	New Hampshire		28	0.6%	29	New Jersey	75	1.5%
29	New Jersey		75	1.5%	30	Arizona	71	1.5%
40	New Mexico		36	0.7%	31	South Carolina	68	1.4%
7	New York		170	3.5%	32	Oregon	59	1.2%
18	North Carolina		113	2.3%	33	West Virginia	54	1.1%
38	North Dakota		40	0.8%	34	South Dakota	53	1.1%
6	Ohio		179	3.7%	35	Maryland	50	1.0%
19	Oklahoma		110	2.3%	35	Montana	50	1.0%
32	Oregon		59	1.2%	37	Utah	47	1.0%
5	Pennsylvania		186	3.8%	38	Idaho	40	0.8%
49	Rhode Island		11	0.2%	38	North Dakota	40	0.8%
31	South Carolina		68	1.4%	40	Nevada	36	0.7%
34	South Dakota		53	1.1%	40	New Mexico	36	0.7%
13	Tennessee		121	2.5%	42	Maine	34	0.7%
1	Texas		404	8.3%	43	Connecticut	32	0.7%
37	Utah		47	1.0%	44	New Hampshire	28	0.6%
48	Vermont		14	0.3%	45	Hawaii	24	0.5%
23	Virginia		92	1.9%	46	Wyoming	23	0.5%
24	Washington		90	1.9%	47	Alaska	21	0.4%
33	West Virginia		54	1.1%	48	Vermont	14	0.3%
12	Wisconsin		127	2.6%	49	Rhode Island	11	0.2%
46	Wyoming		23	0.5%	50	Delaware	7	0.1%
						District of Columbia	11	0.2%

Source: American Hospital Association (Chicago, IL)
   "Hospital Statistics" (2017 edition)
*Community hospitals are all nonfederal, short-term general, and special hospitals whose facilities and services are available to the public.

Rate of Community Hospitals in 2015

National Rate = 1.5 Community Hospitals per 100,000 Population*

ALPHA ORDER

RANK	STATE	RATE
21	Alabama	2.0
10	Alaska	2.8
42	Arizona	1.0
12	Arkansas	2.7
45	California	0.9
28	Colorado	1.5
45	Connecticut	0.9
50	Delaware	0.7
42	Florida	1.0
35	Georgia	1.4
25	Hawaii	1.7
15	Idaho	2.4
28	Illinois	1.5
23	Indiana	1.8
7	Iowa	3.8
5	Kansas	4.5
17	Kentucky	2.3
13	Louisiana	2.6
13	Maine	2.6
48	Maryland	0.8
39	Massachusetts	1.1
28	Michigan	1.5
15	Minnesota	2.4
8	Mississippi	3.2
21	Missouri	2.0
3	Montana	4.8
4	Nebraska	4.6
38	Nevada	1.2
20	New Hampshire	2.1
48	New Jersey	0.8
25	New Mexico	1.7
45	New York	0.9
39	North Carolina	1.1
2	North Dakota	5.3
28	Ohio	1.5
10	Oklahoma	2.8
28	Oregon	1.5
28	Pennsylvania	1.5
42	Rhode Island	1.0
35	South Carolina	1.4
1	South Dakota	6.2
23	Tennessee	1.8
28	Texas	1.5
27	Utah	1.6
18	Vermont	2.2
39	Virginia	1.1
37	Washington	1.3
9	West Virginia	2.9
18	Wisconsin	2.2
6	Wyoming	3.9

RANK ORDER

RANK	STATE	RATE
1	South Dakota	6.2
2	North Dakota	5.3
3	Montana	4.8
4	Nebraska	4.6
5	Kansas	4.5
6	Wyoming	3.9
7	Iowa	3.8
8	Mississippi	3.2
9	West Virginia	2.9
10	Alaska	2.8
10	Oklahoma	2.8
12	Arkansas	2.7
13	Louisiana	2.6
13	Maine	2.6
15	Idaho	2.4
15	Minnesota	2.4
17	Kentucky	2.3
18	Vermont	2.2
18	Wisconsin	2.2
20	New Hampshire	2.1
21	Alabama	2.0
21	Missouri	2.0
23	Indiana	1.8
23	Tennessee	1.8
25	Hawaii	1.7
25	New Mexico	1.7
27	Utah	1.6
28	Colorado	1.5
28	Illinois	1.5
28	Michigan	1.5
28	Ohio	1.5
28	Oregon	1.5
28	Pennsylvania	1.5
28	Texas	1.5
35	Georgia	1.4
35	South Carolina	1.4
37	Washington	1.3
38	Nevada	1.2
39	Massachusetts	1.1
39	North Carolina	1.1
39	Virginia	1.1
42	Arizona	1.0
42	Florida	1.0
42	Rhode Island	1.0
45	California	0.9
45	Connecticut	0.9
45	New York	0.9
48	Maryland	0.8
48	New Jersey	0.8
50	Delaware	0.7

District of Columbia — 1.6

Source: CQ Press using data from American Hospital Association (Chicago, IL)
"Hospital Statistics" (2017 edition)

*Community hospitals are all nonfederal, short-term general, and special hospitals whose facilities and services are available to the public.

Births in 2015

National Total = 3,978,497 Live Births*

ALPHA ORDER

RANK	STATE	BIRTHS	% of USA
24	Alabama	59,657	1.5%
46	Alaska	11,282	0.3%
14	Arizona	85,351	2.1%
32	Arkansas	38,886	1.0%
1	California	491,748	12.4%
22	Colorado	66,581	1.7%
35	Connecticut	35,746	0.9%
47	Delaware	11,166	0.3%
4	Florida	224,269	5.6%
8	Georgia	131,404	3.3%
40	Hawaii	18,420	0.5%
38	Idaho	22,827	0.6%
5	Illinois	158,116	4.0%
15	Indiana	84,040	2.1%
30	Iowa	39,482	1.0%
31	Kansas	39,154	1.0%
26	Kentucky	55,971	1.4%
23	Louisiana	64,692	1.6%
41	Maine	12,607	0.3%
18	Maryland	73,616	1.9%
19	Massachusetts	71,492	1.8%
10	Michigan	113,312	2.8%
20	Minnesota	69,834	1.8%
33	Mississippi	38,394	1.0%
17	Missouri	75,061	1.9%
42	Montana	12,583	0.3%
36	Nebraska	26,679	0.7%
34	Nevada	36,298	0.9%
43	New Hampshire	12,433	0.3%
12	New Jersey	103,127	2.6%
37	New Mexico	25,816	0.6%
3	New York	237,274	6.0%
9	North Carolina	120,843	3.0%
45	North Dakota	11,314	0.3%
7	Ohio	139,264	3.5%
27	Oklahoma	53,122	1.3%
29	Oregon	45,655	1.1%
6	Pennsylvania	141,047	3.5%
48	Rhode Island	10,993	0.3%
25	South Carolina	58,139	1.5%
44	South Dakota	12,336	0.3%
16	Tennessee	81,685	2.1%
2	Texas	403,618	10.1%
28	Utah	50,778	1.3%
50	Vermont	5,903	0.1%
11	Virginia	103,303	2.6%
13	Washington	88,990	2.2%
39	West Virginia	19,805	0.5%
21	Wisconsin	67,041	1.7%
49	Wyoming	7,765	0.2%

RANK ORDER

RANK	STATE	BIRTHS	% of USA
1	California	491,748	12.4%
2	Texas	403,618	10.1%
3	New York	237,274	6.0%
4	Florida	224,269	5.6%
5	Illinois	158,116	4.0%
6	Pennsylvania	141,047	3.5%
7	Ohio	139,264	3.5%
8	Georgia	131,404	3.3%
9	North Carolina	120,843	3.0%
10	Michigan	113,312	2.8%
11	Virginia	103,303	2.6%
12	New Jersey	103,127	2.6%
13	Washington	88,990	2.2%
14	Arizona	85,351	2.1%
15	Indiana	84,040	2.1%
16	Tennessee	81,685	2.1%
17	Missouri	75,061	1.9%
18	Maryland	73,616	1.9%
19	Massachusetts	71,492	1.8%
20	Minnesota	69,834	1.8%
21	Wisconsin	67,041	1.7%
22	Colorado	66,581	1.7%
23	Louisiana	64,692	1.6%
24	Alabama	59,657	1.5%
25	South Carolina	58,139	1.5%
26	Kentucky	55,971	1.4%
27	Oklahoma	53,122	1.3%
28	Utah	50,778	1.3%
29	Oregon	45,655	1.1%
30	Iowa	39,482	1.0%
31	Kansas	39,154	1.0%
32	Arkansas	38,886	1.0%
33	Mississippi	38,394	1.0%
34	Nevada	36,298	0.9%
35	Connecticut	35,746	0.9%
36	Nebraska	26,679	0.7%
37	New Mexico	25,816	0.6%
38	Idaho	22,827	0.6%
39	West Virginia	19,805	0.5%
40	Hawaii	18,420	0.5%
41	Maine	12,607	0.3%
42	Montana	12,583	0.3%
43	New Hampshire	12,433	0.3%
44	South Dakota	12,336	0.3%
45	North Dakota	11,314	0.3%
46	Alaska	11,282	0.3%
47	Delaware	11,166	0.3%
48	Rhode Island	10,993	0.3%
49	Wyoming	7,765	0.2%
50	Vermont	5,903	0.1%
	District of Columbia	9,578	0.2%

Source: U.S. Department of Health and Human Services, National Center for Health Statistics
  "National Vital Statistics Reports" (Vol. 66, No. 1, January 5, 2017, http://www.cdc.gov/nchs/births.htm)
*Final data by state of residence.

Birth Rate in 2015

National Rate = 12.4 Live Births per 1,000 Population*

ALPHA ORDER

RANK	STATE	RATE
26	Alabama	12.3
2	Alaska	15.3
22	Arizona	12.5
12	Arkansas	13.1
18	California	12.6
31	Colorado	12.2
47	Connecticut	10.0
37	Delaware	11.8
42	Florida	11.1
13	Georgia	12.9
13	Hawaii	12.9
8	Idaho	13.8
26	Illinois	12.3
16	Indiana	12.7
18	Iowa	12.6
10	Kansas	13.4
18	Kentucky	12.6
7	Louisiana	13.9
48	Maine	9.5
26	Maryland	12.3
45	Massachusetts	10.5
40	Michigan	11.4
16	Minnesota	12.7
15	Mississippi	12.8
26	Missouri	12.3
31	Montana	12.2
6	Nebraska	14.1
18	Nevada	12.6
50	New Hampshire	9.3
39	New Jersey	11.5
23	New Mexico	12.4
33	New York	12.0
33	North Carolina	12.0
3	North Dakota	14.9
33	Ohio	12.0
9	Oklahoma	13.6
41	Oregon	11.3
43	Pennsylvania	11.0
46	Rhode Island	10.4
36	South Carolina	11.9
5	South Dakota	14.4
23	Tennessee	12.4
4	Texas	14.7
1	Utah	16.9
49	Vermont	9.4
26	Virginia	12.3
23	Washington	12.4
44	West Virginia	10.7
38	Wisconsin	11.6
11	Wyoming	13.2

RANK ORDER

RANK	STATE	RATE
1	Utah	16.9
2	Alaska	15.3
3	North Dakota	14.9
4	Texas	14.7
5	South Dakota	14.4
6	Nebraska	14.1
7	Louisiana	13.9
8	Idaho	13.8
9	Oklahoma	13.6
10	Kansas	13.4
11	Wyoming	13.2
12	Arkansas	13.1
13	Georgia	12.9
13	Hawaii	12.9
15	Mississippi	12.8
16	Indiana	12.7
16	Minnesota	12.7
18	California	12.6
18	Iowa	12.6
18	Kentucky	12.6
18	Nevada	12.6
22	Arizona	12.5
23	New Mexico	12.4
23	Tennessee	12.4
23	Washington	12.4
26	Alabama	12.3
26	Illinois	12.3
26	Maryland	12.3
26	Missouri	12.3
26	Virginia	12.3
31	Colorado	12.2
31	Montana	12.2
33	New York	12.0
33	North Carolina	12.0
33	Ohio	12.0
36	South Carolina	11.9
37	Delaware	11.8
38	Wisconsin	11.6
39	New Jersey	11.5
40	Michigan	11.4
41	Oregon	11.3
42	Florida	11.1
43	Pennsylvania	11.0
44	West Virginia	10.7
45	Massachusetts	10.5
46	Rhode Island	10.4
47	Connecticut	10.0
48	Maine	9.5
49	Vermont	9.4
50	New Hampshire	9.3

	District of Columbia	14.2

Source: U.S. Department of Health and Human Services, National Center for Health Statistics
   "National Vital Statistics Reports" (Vol. 66, No. 1, January 5, 2017, http://www.cdc.gov/nchs/births.htm)
*Final data by state of residence.

Births of Low Birthweight as a Percent of All Births in 2015

National Percent = 8.1% of Live Births*

ALPHA ORDER			RANK ORDER		
RANK	STATE	PERCENT	RANK	STATE	PERCENT
3	Alabama	10.4	1	Mississippi	11.4
50	Alaska	5.8	2	Louisiana	10.6
34	Arizona	7.2	3	Alabama	10.4
8	Arkansas	9.2	4	West Virginia	9.6
40	California	6.8	5	Georgia	9.5
11	Colorado	9.0	5	South Carolina	9.5
27	Connecticut	7.9	7	Delaware	9.3
7	Delaware	9.3	8	Arkansas	9.2
14	Florida	8.6	8	Tennessee	9.2
5	Georgia	9.5	10	North Carolina	9.1
20	Hawaii	8.3	11	Colorado	9.0
43	Idaho	6.6	12	Kentucky	8.7
20	Illinois	8.3	12	New Mexico	8.7
26	Indiana	8.0	14	Florida	8.6
42	Iowa	6.7	14	Maryland	8.6
40	Kansas	6.8	14	Wyoming	8.6
12	Kentucky	8.7	17	Michigan	8.5
2	Louisiana	10.6	17	Nevada	8.5
38	Maine	6.9	17	Ohio	8.5
14	Maryland	8.6	20	Hawaii	8.3
32	Massachusetts	7.5	20	Illinois	8.3
17	Michigan	8.5	20	Missouri	8.3
45	Minnesota	6.4	23	Pennsylvania	8.2
1	Mississippi	11.4	23	Texas	8.2
20	Missouri	8.3	25	New Jersey	8.1
35	Montana	7.1	26	Indiana	8.0
35	Nebraska	7.1	27	Connecticut	7.9
17	Nevada	8.5	27	Oklahoma	7.9
38	New Hampshire	6.9	27	Virginia	7.9
25	New Jersey	8.1	30	New York	7.8
12	New Mexico	8.7	31	Rhode Island	7.6
30	New York	7.8	32	Massachusetts	7.5
10	North Carolina	9.1	33	Wisconsin	7.3
48	North Dakota	6.2	34	Arizona	7.2
17	Ohio	8.5	35	Montana	7.1
27	Oklahoma	7.9	35	Nebraska	7.1
45	Oregon	6.4	37	Utah	7.0
23	Pennsylvania	8.2	38	Maine	6.9
31	Rhode Island	7.6	38	New Hampshire	6.9
5	South Carolina	9.5	40	California	6.8
49	South Dakota	6.1	40	Kansas	6.8
8	Tennessee	9.2	42	Iowa	6.7
23	Texas	8.2	43	Idaho	6.6
37	Utah	7.0	43	Vermont	6.6
43	Vermont	6.6	45	Minnesota	6.4
27	Virginia	7.9	45	Oregon	6.4
45	Washington	6.4	45	Washington	6.4
4	West Virginia	9.6	48	North Dakota	6.2
33	Wisconsin	7.3	49	South Dakota	6.1
14	Wyoming	8.6	50	Alaska	5.8
				District of Columbia	10.0

Source: U.S. Department of Health and Human Services, National Center for Health Statistics
"National Vital Statistics Reports" (Vol. 66, No. 1, January 5, 2017, http://www.cdc.gov/nchs/births.htm)
*Final data by state of residence. Births of less than 2,500 grams (5 pounds 8 ounces).

Births to Teenage Mothers as a Percent of All Births in 2014

National Percent = 6.2% of Live Births*

ALPHA ORDER				RANK ORDER		
RANK	STATE	PERCENT		RANK	STATE	PERCENT
8	Alabama	8.4		1	Mississippi	9.9
26	Alaska	5.7		2	Arkansas	9.8
11	Arizona	7.6		2	New Mexico	9.8
2	Arkansas	9.8		4	West Virginia	9.7
31	California	5.4		5	Oklahoma	9.0
36	Colorado	5.1		6	Texas	8.8
46	Connecticut	3.9		7	Kentucky	8.7
28	Delaware	5.6		8	Alabama	8.4
25	Florida	5.8		9	Tennessee	8.3
13	Georgia	7.4		10	Louisiana	8.2
40	Hawaii	4.8		11	Arizona	7.6
26	Idaho	5.7		12	South Carolina	7.5
23	Illinois	6.0		13	Georgia	7.4
13	Indiana	7.4		13	Indiana	7.4
32	Iowa	5.2		15	Wyoming	7.1
17	Kansas	6.8		16	Missouri	6.9
7	Kentucky	8.7		17	Kansas	6.8
10	Louisiana	8.2		17	Nevada	6.8
32	Maine	5.2		17	North Carolina	6.8
42	Maryland	4.6		17	Ohio	6.8
50	Massachusetts	3.3		21	Montana	6.5
22	Michigan	6.1		22	Michigan	6.1
46	Minnesota	3.9		23	Illinois	6.0
1	Mississippi	9.9		23	South Dakota	6.0
16	Missouri	6.9		25	Florida	5.8
21	Montana	6.5		26	Alaska	5.7
32	Nebraska	5.2		26	Idaho	5.7
17	Nevada	6.8		28	Delaware	5.6
46	New Hampshire	3.9		29	Pennsylvania	5.5
49	New Jersey	3.6		29	Rhode Island	5.5
2	New Mexico	9.8		31	California	5.4
44	New York	4.2		32	Iowa	5.2
17	North Carolina	6.8		32	Maine	5.2
37	North Dakota	5.0		32	Nebraska	5.2
17	Ohio	6.8		32	Oregon	5.2
5	Oklahoma	9.0		36	Colorado	5.1
32	Oregon	5.2		37	North Dakota	5.0
29	Pennsylvania	5.5		37	Vermont	5.0
29	Rhode Island	5.5		37	Wisconsin	5.0
12	South Carolina	7.5		40	Hawaii	4.8
23	South Dakota	6.0		41	Virginia	4.7
9	Tennessee	8.3		42	Maryland	4.6
6	Texas	8.8		42	Washington	4.6
44	Utah	4.2		44	New York	4.2
37	Vermont	5.0		44	Utah	4.2
41	Virginia	4.7		46	Connecticut	3.9
42	Washington	4.6		46	Minnesota	3.9
4	West Virginia	9.7		46	New Hampshire	3.9
37	Wisconsin	5.0		49	New Jersey	3.6
15	Wyoming	7.1		50	Massachusetts	3.3
					District of Columbia	5.9

Source: CQ Press using data from U.S. Department of Health and Human Services, Centers for Disease Control and Prevention "CDC Wonder" (http://wonder.cdc.gov)
*Final data. Live births to women 15 to 19 years old by state of residence.

Births to Unmarried Women as a Percent of All Births in 2015

National Percent = 40.3% of Live Births*

ALPHA ORDER				RANK ORDER		
RANK	STATE	PERCENT		RANK	STATE	PERCENT
12	Alabama	43.9		1	Mississippi	53.5
35	Alaska	36.1		2	Louisiana	52.9
8	Arizona	45.5		3	New Mexico	52.1
11	Arkansas	45.0		4	Florida	47.8
29	California	38.8		5	Nevada	46.7
49	Colorado	22.7		6	South Carolina	46.5
30	Connecticut	37.5		7	Delaware	46.3
7	Delaware	46.3		8	Arizona	45.5
4	Florida	47.8		9	Georgia	45.2
9	Georgia	45.2		10	Rhode Island	45.1
33	Hawaii	37.1		11	Arkansas	45.0
48	Idaho	27.7		12	Alabama	43.9
24	Illinois	40.4		12	Tennessee	43.9
15	Indiana	43.3		14	West Virginia	43.8
38	Iowa	35.3		15	Indiana	43.3
36	Kansas	36.0		15	Ohio	43.3
19	Kentucky	41.6		17	Michigan	41.9
2	Louisiana	52.9		18	Oklahoma	41.8
23	Maine	40.5		19	Kentucky	41.6
27	Maryland	40.1		20	Texas	41.5
43	Massachusetts	33.4		21	Pennsylvania	41.2
17	Michigan	41.9		22	North Carolina	41.0
45	Minnesota	32.2		23	Maine	40.5
1	Mississippi	53.5		24	Illinois	40.4
24	Missouri	40.4		24	Missouri	40.4
34	Montana	36.3		26	Vermont	40.2
44	Nebraska	32.9		27	Maryland	40.1
5	Nevada	46.7		28	New York	39.5
41	New Hampshire	34.0		29	California	38.8
39	New Jersey	35.1		30	Connecticut	37.5
3	New Mexico	52.1		30	Wisconsin	37.5
28	New York	39.5		32	South Dakota	37.2
22	North Carolina	41.0		33	Hawaii	37.1
47	North Dakota	31.6		34	Montana	36.3
15	Ohio	43.3		35	Alaska	36.1
18	Oklahoma	41.8		36	Kansas	36.0
36	Oregon	36.0		36	Oregon	36.0
21	Pennsylvania	41.2		38	Iowa	35.3
10	Rhode Island	45.1		39	New Jersey	35.1
6	South Carolina	46.5		40	Virginia	34.4
32	South Dakota	37.2		41	New Hampshire	34.0
12	Tennessee	43.9		42	Wyoming	33.9
20	Texas	41.5		43	Massachusetts	33.4
50	Utah	18.8		44	Nebraska	32.9
26	Vermont	40.2		45	Minnesota	32.2
40	Virginia	34.4		46	Washington	32.1
46	Washington	32.1		47	North Dakota	31.6
14	West Virginia	43.8		48	Idaho	27.7
30	Wisconsin	37.5		49	Colorado	22.7
42	Wyoming	33.9		50	Utah	18.8
					District of Columbia	49.3

Source: U.S. Department of Health and Human Services, National Center for Health Statistics
   "National Vital Statistics Reports" (Vol. 66, No. 1, January 5, 2017, http://www.cdc.gov/nchs/births.htm)
*Final data by state of residence.

Percent of Women Receiving Late or No Prenatal Care in 2014

National Percent = 6.0% of Women*

<table>
<tr><td colspan="3">ALPHA ORDER</td><td colspan="3">RANK ORDER</td></tr>
<tr><td>RANK</td><td>STATE</td><td>PERCENT</td><td>RANK</td><td>STATE</td><td>PERCENT</td></tr>
<tr><td>10</td><td>Alabama</td><td>7.1</td><td>1</td><td>Texas</td><td>9.9</td></tr>
<tr><td>14</td><td>Alaska</td><td>6.7</td><td>2</td><td>Arkansas</td><td>9.2</td></tr>
<tr><td>6</td><td>Arizona</td><td>7.8</td><td>3</td><td>Nevada</td><td>8.7</td></tr>
<tr><td>2</td><td>Arkansas</td><td>9.2</td><td>4</td><td>Maryland</td><td>8.5</td></tr>
<tr><td>41</td><td>California</td><td>3.6</td><td>4</td><td>New Mexico</td><td>8.5</td></tr>
<tr><td>12</td><td>Colorado</td><td>6.8</td><td>6</td><td>Arizona</td><td>7.8</td></tr>
<tr><td>NA</td><td>Connecticut**</td><td>NA</td><td>6</td><td>Georgia</td><td>7.8</td></tr>
<tr><td>24</td><td>Delaware</td><td>5.8</td><td>8</td><td>Oklahoma</td><td>7.6</td></tr>
<tr><td>21</td><td>Florida</td><td>6.0</td><td>9</td><td>Wyoming</td><td>7.2</td></tr>
<tr><td>6</td><td>Georgia</td><td>7.8</td><td>10</td><td>Alabama</td><td>7.1</td></tr>
<tr><td>21</td><td>Hawaii</td><td>6.0</td><td>11</td><td>Ohio</td><td>7.0</td></tr>
<tr><td>32</td><td>Idaho</td><td>4.9</td><td>12</td><td>Colorado</td><td>6.8</td></tr>
<tr><td>34</td><td>Illinois</td><td>4.6</td><td>12</td><td>Louisiana</td><td>6.8</td></tr>
<tr><td>20</td><td>Indiana</td><td>6.3</td><td>14</td><td>Alaska</td><td>6.7</td></tr>
<tr><td>39</td><td>Iowa</td><td>3.9</td><td>14</td><td>South Carolina</td><td>6.7</td></tr>
<tr><td>41</td><td>Kansas</td><td>3.6</td><td>16</td><td>North Dakota</td><td>6.6</td></tr>
<tr><td>31</td><td>Kentucky</td><td>5.0</td><td>16</td><td>Pennsylvania</td><td>6.6</td></tr>
<tr><td>12</td><td>Louisiana</td><td>6.8</td><td>18</td><td>Montana</td><td>6.4</td></tr>
<tr><td>46</td><td>Maine</td><td>2.8</td><td>18</td><td>North Carolina</td><td>6.4</td></tr>
<tr><td>4</td><td>Maryland</td><td>8.5</td><td>20</td><td>Indiana</td><td>6.3</td></tr>
<tr><td>38</td><td>Massachusetts</td><td>4.1</td><td>21</td><td>Florida</td><td>6.0</td></tr>
<tr><td>33</td><td>Michigan</td><td>4.8</td><td>21</td><td>Hawaii</td><td>6.0</td></tr>
<tr><td>41</td><td>Minnesota</td><td>3.6</td><td>21</td><td>Tennessee</td><td>6.0</td></tr>
<tr><td>36</td><td>Mississippi</td><td>4.3</td><td>24</td><td>Delaware</td><td>5.8</td></tr>
<tr><td>28</td><td>Missouri</td><td>5.6</td><td>24</td><td>South Dakota</td><td>5.8</td></tr>
<tr><td>18</td><td>Montana</td><td>6.4</td><td>24</td><td>Washington</td><td>5.8</td></tr>
<tr><td>29</td><td>Nebraska</td><td>5.2</td><td>24</td><td>West Virginia</td><td>5.8</td></tr>
<tr><td>3</td><td>Nevada</td><td>8.7</td><td>28</td><td>Missouri</td><td>5.6</td></tr>
<tr><td>44</td><td>New Hampshire</td><td>3.3</td><td>29</td><td>Nebraska</td><td>5.2</td></tr>
<tr><td>NA</td><td>New Jersey**</td><td>NA</td><td>30</td><td>New York</td><td>5.1</td></tr>
<tr><td>4</td><td>New Mexico</td><td>8.5</td><td>31</td><td>Kentucky</td><td>5.0</td></tr>
<tr><td>30</td><td>New York</td><td>5.1</td><td>32</td><td>Idaho</td><td>4.9</td></tr>
<tr><td>18</td><td>North Carolina</td><td>6.4</td><td>33</td><td>Michigan</td><td>4.8</td></tr>
<tr><td>16</td><td>North Dakota</td><td>6.6</td><td>34</td><td>Illinois</td><td>4.6</td></tr>
<tr><td>11</td><td>Ohio</td><td>7.0</td><td>35</td><td>Oregon</td><td>4.4</td></tr>
<tr><td>8</td><td>Oklahoma</td><td>7.6</td><td>36</td><td>Mississippi</td><td>4.3</td></tr>
<tr><td>35</td><td>Oregon</td><td>4.4</td><td>36</td><td>Virginia</td><td>4.3</td></tr>
<tr><td>16</td><td>Pennsylvania</td><td>6.6</td><td>38</td><td>Massachusetts</td><td>4.1</td></tr>
<tr><td>NA</td><td>Rhode Island**</td><td>NA</td><td>39</td><td>Iowa</td><td>3.9</td></tr>
<tr><td>14</td><td>South Carolina</td><td>6.7</td><td>39</td><td>Wisconsin</td><td>3.9</td></tr>
<tr><td>24</td><td>South Dakota</td><td>5.8</td><td>41</td><td>California</td><td>3.6</td></tr>
<tr><td>21</td><td>Tennessee</td><td>6.0</td><td>41</td><td>Kansas</td><td>3.6</td></tr>
<tr><td>1</td><td>Texas</td><td>9.9</td><td>41</td><td>Minnesota</td><td>3.6</td></tr>
<tr><td>45</td><td>Utah</td><td>3.0</td><td>44</td><td>New Hampshire</td><td>3.3</td></tr>
<tr><td>47</td><td>Vermont</td><td>1.9</td><td>45</td><td>Utah</td><td>3.0</td></tr>
<tr><td>36</td><td>Virginia</td><td>4.3</td><td>46</td><td>Maine</td><td>2.8</td></tr>
<tr><td>24</td><td>Washington</td><td>5.8</td><td>47</td><td>Vermont</td><td>1.9</td></tr>
<tr><td>24</td><td>West Virginia</td><td>5.8</td><td>NA</td><td>Connecticut**</td><td>NA</td></tr>
<tr><td>39</td><td>Wisconsin</td><td>3.9</td><td>NA</td><td>New Jersey**</td><td>NA</td></tr>
<tr><td>9</td><td>Wyoming</td><td>7.2</td><td>NA</td><td>Rhode Island**</td><td>NA</td></tr>
</table>

District of Columbia   10.2

Source: CQ Press using data from U.S. Department of Health and Human Services, Centers for Disease Control and Prevention "CDC Wonder" (http://wonder.cdc.gov)

*Final data by state of residence. "Late" means care begun in third trimester. National figure is for reporting states only.

**Not available.

Reported Legal Abortions in 2013

Reporting States' Total = 664,435 Abortions*

ALPHA ORDER

RANK	STATE	ABORTIONS	% of USA
20	Alabama	8,485	1.3%
42	Alaska	1,450	0.2%
15	Arizona	13,401	2.0%
31	Arkansas	3,730	0.6%
NA	California**	NA	NA
17	Colorado	10,199	1.5%
16	Connecticut	10,560	1.6%
35	Delaware	3,042	0.5%
2	Florida	72,727	10.9%
6	Georgia	30,673	4.6%
38	Hawaii	1,967	0.3%
43	Idaho	1,375	0.2%
4	Illinois	40,750	6.1%
22	Indiana	8,179	1.2%
29	Iowa	4,423	0.7%
23	Kansas	7,422	1.1%
32	Kentucky	3,637	0.5%
18	Louisiana	9,977	1.5%
39	Maine	1,939	0.3%
NA	Maryland**	NA	NA
12	Massachusetts	19,448	2.9%
7	Michigan	26,120	3.9%
19	Minnesota	9,904	1.5%
37	Mississippi	2,170	0.3%
27	Missouri	5,416	0.8%
41	Montana	1,842	0.3%
36	Nebraska	2,177	0.3%
25	Nevada	6,056	0.9%
NA	New Hampshire**	NA	NA
10	New Jersey	21,720	3.3%
30	New Mexico	4,198	0.6%
1	New York	98,046	14.8%
9	North Carolina	22,820	3.4%
45	North Dakota	1,182	0.2%
8	Ohio	23,216	3.5%
28	Oklahoma	5,013	0.8%
21	Oregon	8,287	1.2%
5	Pennsylvania	32,108	4.8%
33	Rhode Island	3,251	0.5%
26	South Carolina	5,878	0.9%
46	South Dakota	601	0.1%
14	Tennessee	14,216	2.1%
3	Texas	63,168	9.5%
34	Utah	3,102	0.5%
44	Vermont	1,217	0.2%
11	Virginia	20,852	3.1%
13	Washington	17,592	2.6%
40	West Virginia	1,876	0.3%
24	Wisconsin	6,462	1.0%
NA	Wyoming**	NA	NA

RANK ORDER

RANK	STATE	ABORTIONS	% of USA
1	New York	98,046	14.8%
2	Florida	72,727	10.9%
3	Texas	63,168	9.5%
4	Illinois	40,750	6.1%
5	Pennsylvania	32,108	4.8%
6	Georgia	30,673	4.6%
7	Michigan	26,120	3.9%
8	Ohio	23,216	3.5%
9	North Carolina	22,820	3.4%
10	New Jersey	21,720	3.3%
11	Virginia	20,852	3.1%
12	Massachusetts	19,448	2.9%
13	Washington	17,592	2.6%
14	Tennessee	14,216	2.1%
15	Arizona	13,401	2.0%
16	Connecticut	10,560	1.6%
17	Colorado	10,199	1.5%
18	Louisiana	9,977	1.5%
19	Minnesota	9,904	1.5%
20	Alabama	8,485	1.3%
21	Oregon	8,287	1.2%
22	Indiana	8,179	1.2%
23	Kansas	7,422	1.1%
24	Wisconsin	6,462	1.0%
25	Nevada	6,056	0.9%
26	South Carolina	5,878	0.9%
27	Missouri	5,416	0.8%
28	Oklahoma	5,013	0.8%
29	Iowa	4,423	0.7%
30	New Mexico	4,198	0.6%
31	Arkansas	3,730	0.6%
32	Kentucky	3,637	0.5%
33	Rhode Island	3,251	0.5%
34	Utah	3,102	0.5%
35	Delaware	3,042	0.5%
36	Nebraska	2,177	0.3%
37	Mississippi	2,170	0.3%
38	Hawaii	1,967	0.3%
39	Maine	1,939	0.3%
40	West Virginia	1,876	0.3%
41	Montana	1,842	0.3%
42	Alaska	1,450	0.2%
43	Idaho	1,375	0.2%
44	Vermont	1,217	0.2%
45	North Dakota	1,182	0.2%
46	South Dakota	601	0.1%
NA	California**	NA	NA
NA	Maryland**	NA	NA
NA	New Hampshire**	NA	NA
NA	Wyoming**	NA	NA
	District of Columbia	2,561	0.4%

Source: U.S. Department of Health and Human Services, Centers for Disease Control and Prevention
"Abortion Surveillance-United States, 2013" (MMWR, Vol. 65, No. SS-12, 11/25/16, www.cdc.gov/mmwr/mmwr_ss/ss_pvol.html)
*By state of occurrence. Total is for reporting states only.
**Not reported.

Reported Legal Abortions per 1,000 Live Births in 2013

Reporting States' Ratio = 200 Abortions per 1,000 Live Births*

ALPHA ORDER

RANK	STATE	RATE
28	Alabama	146
30	Alaska	127
24	Arizona	157
35	Arkansas	99
NA	California**	NA
24	Colorado	157
4	Connecticut	293
5	Delaware	281
2	Florida	338
8	Georgia	238
33	Hawaii	104
43	Idaho	61
7	Illinois	260
36	Indiana	98
31	Iowa	113
16	Kansas	191
42	Kentucky	65
23	Louisiana	158
26	Maine	152
NA	Maryland**	NA
6	Massachusetts	271
9	Michigan	230
29	Minnesota	143
45	Mississippi	56
41	Missouri	72
27	Montana	149
40	Nebraska	83
19	Nevada	173
NA	New Hampshire**	NA
11	New Jersey	212
22	New Mexico	159
1	New York	414
15	North Carolina	192
32	North Dakota	112
20	Ohio	167
38	Oklahoma	94
17	Oregon	184
10	Pennsylvania	228
3	Rhode Island	301
34	South Carolina	103
46	South Dakota	49
18	Tennessee	178
21	Texas	163
43	Utah	61
12	Vermont	204
12	Virginia	204
14	Washington	203
39	West Virginia	90
37	Wisconsin	97
NA	Wyoming**	NA

RANK ORDER

RANK	STATE	RATE
1	New York	414
2	Florida	338
3	Rhode Island	301
4	Connecticut	293
5	Delaware	281
6	Massachusetts	271
7	Illinois	260
8	Georgia	238
9	Michigan	230
10	Pennsylvania	228
11	New Jersey	212
12	Vermont	204
12	Virginia	204
14	Washington	203
15	North Carolina	192
16	Kansas	191
17	Oregon	184
18	Tennessee	178
19	Nevada	173
20	Ohio	167
21	Texas	163
22	New Mexico	159
23	Louisiana	158
24	Arizona	157
24	Colorado	157
26	Maine	152
27	Montana	149
28	Alabama	146
29	Minnesota	143
30	Alaska	127
31	Iowa	113
32	North Dakota	112
33	Hawaii	104
34	South Carolina	103
35	Arkansas	99
36	Indiana	98
37	Wisconsin	97
38	Oklahoma	94
39	West Virginia	90
40	Nebraska	83
41	Missouri	72
42	Kentucky	65
43	Idaho	61
43	Utah	61
45	Mississippi	56
46	South Dakota	49
NA	California**	NA
NA	Maryland**	NA
NA	New Hampshire**	NA
NA	Wyoming**	NA

District of Columbia	276

Source: U.S. Department of Health and Human Services, Centers for Disease Control and Prevention
    "Abortion Surveillance-United States, 2013" (MMWR, Vol. 65, No. SS-12, 11/25/16, www.cdc.gov/mmwr/mmwr_ss/ss_pvol.html)
*By state of occurrence. National figure is for reporting states only.
**Not reported.

Infant Deaths in 2014

National Total = 23,215 Infant Deaths*

ALPHA ORDER

RANK	STATE	DEATHS	% of USA
15	Alabama	516	2.2%
42	Alaska	75	0.3%
14	Arizona	534	2.3%
29	Arkansas	290	1.2%
2	California	2,163	9.3%
27	Colorado	315	1.4%
35	Connecticut	176	0.8%
43	Delaware	74	0.3%
3	Florida	1,333	5.7%
6	Georgia	976	4.2%
41	Hawaii	83	0.4%
39	Idaho	125	0.5%
5	Illinois	1,045	4.5%
11	Indiana	595	2.6%
34	Iowa	191	0.8%
31	Kansas	247	1.1%
22	Kentucky	398	1.7%
16	Louisiana	483	2.1%
40	Maine	85	0.4%
17	Maryland	478	2.1%
27	Massachusetts	315	1.4%
10	Michigan	745	3.2%
25	Minnesota	352	1.5%
26	Mississippi	319	1.4%
18	Missouri	457	2.0%
45	Montana	68	0.3%
38	Nebraska	136	0.6%
33	Nevada	196	0.8%
47	New Hampshire	53	0.2%
19	New Jersey	454	2.0%
37	New Mexico	141	0.6%
4	New York	1,110	4.8%
8	North Carolina	857	3.7%
46	North Dakota	57	0.2%
7	Ohio	956	4.1%
20	Oklahoma	434	1.9%
32	Oregon	234	1.0%
9	Pennsylvania	838	3.6%
49	Rhode Island	48	0.2%
24	South Carolina	372	1.6%
44	South Dakota	72	0.3%
13	Tennessee	564	2.4%
1	Texas	2,337	10.1%
30	Utah	251	1.1%
50	Vermont	28	0.1%
11	Virginia	595	2.6%
21	Washington	402	1.7%
36	West Virginia	143	0.6%
23	Wisconsin	381	1.6%
48	Wyoming	49	0.2%

RANK ORDER

RANK	STATE	DEATHS	% of USA
1	Texas	2,337	10.1%
2	California	2,163	9.3%
3	Florida	1,333	5.7%
4	New York	1,110	4.8%
5	Illinois	1,045	4.5%
6	Georgia	976	4.2%
7	Ohio	956	4.1%
8	North Carolina	857	3.7%
9	Pennsylvania	838	3.6%
10	Michigan	745	3.2%
11	Indiana	595	2.6%
11	Virginia	595	2.6%
13	Tennessee	564	2.4%
14	Arizona	534	2.3%
15	Alabama	516	2.2%
16	Louisiana	483	2.1%
17	Maryland	478	2.1%
18	Missouri	457	2.0%
19	New Jersey	454	2.0%
20	Oklahoma	434	1.9%
21	Washington	402	1.7%
22	Kentucky	398	1.7%
23	Wisconsin	381	1.6%
24	South Carolina	372	1.6%
25	Minnesota	352	1.5%
26	Mississippi	319	1.4%
27	Colorado	315	1.4%
27	Massachusetts	315	1.4%
29	Arkansas	290	1.2%
30	Utah	251	1.1%
31	Kansas	247	1.1%
32	Oregon	234	1.0%
33	Nevada	196	0.8%
34	Iowa	191	0.8%
35	Connecticut	176	0.8%
36	West Virginia	143	0.6%
37	New Mexico	141	0.6%
38	Nebraska	136	0.6%
39	Idaho	125	0.5%
40	Maine	85	0.4%
41	Hawaii	83	0.4%
42	Alaska	75	0.3%
43	Delaware	74	0.3%
44	South Dakota	72	0.3%
45	Montana	68	0.3%
46	North Dakota	57	0.2%
47	New Hampshire	53	0.2%
48	Wyoming	49	0.2%
49	Rhode Island	48	0.2%
50	Vermont	28	0.1%
	District of Columbia	69	0.3%

Source: U.S. Department of Health and Human Services, National Center for Health Statistics
"National Vital Statistics Reports" (Vol. 65, No. 4, 2016, http://www.cdc.gov/nchs/deaths.htm)
*Final data. Deaths of infants under 1 year old by state of residence.

Infant Mortality Rate in 2014

National Rate = 5.8 Infant Deaths per 1,000 Live Births*

ALPHA ORDER

RANK	STATE	RATE
1	Alabama	8.7
15	Alaska	6.6
22	Arizona	6.2
4	Arkansas	7.5
49	California	4.3
40	Colorado	4.8
38	Connecticut	4.9
13	Delaware	6.7
23	Florida	6.1
4	Georgia	7.5
44	Hawaii	4.5
30	Idaho	5.5
15	Illinois	6.6
7	Indiana	7.1
40	Iowa	4.8
21	Kansas	6.3
7	Kentucky	7.1
4	Louisiana	7.5
13	Maine	6.7
17	Maryland	6.5
46	Massachusetts	4.4
17	Michigan	6.5
36	Minnesota	5.0
2	Mississippi	8.2
23	Missouri	6.1
30	Montana	5.5
34	Nebraska	5.1
30	Nevada	5.5
49	New Hampshire	4.3
46	New Jersey	4.4
33	New Mexico	5.4
42	New York	4.7
7	North Carolina	7.1
36	North Dakota	5.0
11	Ohio	6.9
3	Oklahoma	8.1
34	Oregon	5.1
25	Pennsylvania	5.9
46	Rhode Island	4.4
17	South Carolina	6.5
25	South Dakota	5.9
11	Tennessee	6.9
25	Texas	5.9
38	Utah	4.9
43	Vermont	4.6
28	Virginia	5.8
44	Washington	4.5
10	West Virginia	7.0
29	Wisconsin	5.7
20	Wyoming	6.4

RANK ORDER

RANK	STATE	RATE
1	Alabama	8.7
2	Mississippi	8.2
3	Oklahoma	8.1
4	Arkansas	7.5
4	Georgia	7.5
4	Louisiana	7.5
7	Indiana	7.1
7	Kentucky	7.1
7	North Carolina	7.1
10	West Virginia	7.0
11	Ohio	6.9
11	Tennessee	6.9
13	Delaware	6.7
13	Maine	6.7
15	Alaska	6.6
15	Illinois	6.6
17	Maryland	6.5
17	Michigan	6.5
17	South Carolina	6.5
20	Wyoming	6.4
21	Kansas	6.3
22	Arizona	6.2
23	Florida	6.1
23	Missouri	6.1
25	Pennsylvania	5.9
25	South Dakota	5.9
25	Texas	5.9
28	Virginia	5.8
29	Wisconsin	5.7
30	Idaho	5.5
30	Montana	5.5
30	Nevada	5.5
33	New Mexico	5.4
34	Nebraska	5.1
34	Oregon	5.1
36	Minnesota	5.0
36	North Dakota	5.0
38	Connecticut	4.9
38	Utah	4.9
40	Colorado	4.8
40	Iowa	4.8
42	New York	4.7
43	Vermont	4.6
44	Hawaii	4.5
44	Washington	4.5
46	Massachusetts	4.4
46	New Jersey	4.4
46	Rhode Island	4.4
49	California	4.3
49	New Hampshire	4.3
	District of Columbia	7.3

Source: U.S. Department of Health and Human Services, National Center for Health Statistics
"National Vital Statistics Reports" (Vol. 65, No. 4, 2016, http://www.cdc.gov/nchs/deaths.htm)
*Final data. Deaths of infants under 1 year old by state of residence.

Deaths in 2014

National Total = 2,626,418 Deaths*

ALPHA ORDER

RANK	STATE	DEATHS	% of USA
20	Alabama	50,215	1.9%
50	Alaska	4,128	0.2%
18	Arizona	51,538	2.0%
30	Arkansas	30,467	1.2%
1	California	245,929	9.4%
27	Colorado	35,237	1.3%
31	Connecticut	29,860	1.1%
45	Delaware	8,260	0.3%
2	Florida	185,956	7.1%
10	Georgia	76,887	2.9%
42	Hawaii	10,767	0.4%
40	Idaho	12,613	0.5%
7	Illinois	105,293	4.0%
14	Indiana	60,940	2.3%
32	Iowa	29,190	1.1%
33	Kansas	25,793	1.0%
23	Kentucky	44,838	1.7%
24	Louisiana	43,869	1.7%
39	Maine	13,510	0.5%
21	Maryland	45,867	1.7%
16	Massachusetts	55,200	2.1%
8	Michigan	93,914	3.6%
25	Minnesota	41,445	1.6%
29	Mississippi	30,557	1.2%
15	Missouri	58,320	2.2%
44	Montana	9,381	0.4%
38	Nebraska	15,978	0.6%
35	Nevada	21,793	0.8%
41	New Hampshire	11,516	0.4%
11	New Jersey	71,316	2.7%
36	New Mexico	17,579	0.7%
4	New York	149,944	5.7%
9	North Carolina	85,367	3.3%
47	North Dakota	6,184	0.2%
6	Ohio	114,509	4.4%
26	Oklahoma	38,464	1.5%
28	Oregon	34,151	1.3%
5	Pennsylvania	128,434	4.9%
43	Rhode Island	9,770	0.4%
22	South Carolina	45,454	1.7%
46	South Dakota	7,507	0.3%
12	Tennessee	64,661	2.5%
3	Texas	183,912	7.0%
37	Utah	16,719	0.6%
48	Vermont	5,623	0.2%
13	Virginia	63,598	2.4%
17	Washington	52,099	2.0%
34	West Virginia	22,186	0.8%
19	Wisconsin	50,291	1.9%
49	Wyoming	4,666	0.2%

RANK ORDER

RANK	STATE	DEATHS	% of USA
1	California	245,929	9.4%
2	Florida	185,956	7.1%
3	Texas	183,912	7.0%
4	New York	149,944	5.7%
5	Pennsylvania	128,434	4.9%
6	Ohio	114,509	4.4%
7	Illinois	105,293	4.0%
8	Michigan	93,914	3.6%
9	North Carolina	85,367	3.3%
10	Georgia	76,887	2.9%
11	New Jersey	71,316	2.7%
12	Tennessee	64,661	2.5%
13	Virginia	63,598	2.4%
14	Indiana	60,940	2.3%
15	Missouri	58,320	2.2%
16	Massachusetts	55,200	2.1%
17	Washington	52,099	2.0%
18	Arizona	51,538	2.0%
19	Wisconsin	50,291	1.9%
20	Alabama	50,215	1.9%
21	Maryland	45,867	1.7%
22	South Carolina	45,454	1.7%
23	Kentucky	44,838	1.7%
24	Louisiana	43,869	1.7%
25	Minnesota	41,445	1.6%
26	Oklahoma	38,464	1.5%
27	Colorado	35,237	1.3%
28	Oregon	34,151	1.3%
29	Mississippi	30,557	1.2%
30	Arkansas	30,467	1.2%
31	Connecticut	29,860	1.1%
32	Iowa	29,190	1.1%
33	Kansas	25,793	1.0%
34	West Virginia	22,186	0.8%
35	Nevada	21,793	0.8%
36	New Mexico	17,579	0.7%
37	Utah	16,719	0.6%
38	Nebraska	15,978	0.6%
39	Maine	13,510	0.5%
40	Idaho	12,613	0.5%
41	New Hampshire	11,516	0.4%
42	Hawaii	10,767	0.4%
43	Rhode Island	9,770	0.4%
44	Montana	9,381	0.4%
45	Delaware	8,260	0.3%
46	South Dakota	7,507	0.3%
47	North Dakota	6,184	0.2%
48	Vermont	5,623	0.2%
49	Wyoming	4,666	0.2%
50	Alaska	4,128	0.2%
	District of Columbia	4,723	0.2%

Source: U.S. Department of Health and Human Services, National Center for Health Statistics
"National Vital Statistics Reports" (Vol. 65, No. 4, 2016, http://www.cdc.gov/nchs/deaths.htm)
*Final data by state of residence.

Age-Adjusted Death Rate in 2014

National Rate = 724.6 Deaths per 100,000 Population*

ALPHA ORDER

RANK	STATE	RATE
3	Alabama	909.1
23	Alaska	736.8
45	Arizona	661.7
7	Arkansas	883.7
49	California	605.7
42	Colorado	664.4
47	Connecticut	646.5
24	Delaware	734.0
44	Florida	662.0
13	Georgia	801.9
50	Hawaii	588.7
27	Idaho	723.8
26	Illinois	726.0
10	Indiana	822.3
28	Iowa	722.9
16	Kansas	759.3
4	Kentucky	906.3
6	Louisiana	894.2
22	Maine	739.0
37	Maryland	699.5
43	Massachusetts	663.0
14	Michigan	783.7
46	Minnesota	647.0
1	Mississippi	937.6
12	Missouri	807.0
25	Montana	732.1
29	Nebraska	718.2
19	Nevada	749.2
35	New Hampshire	706.2
41	New Jersey	665.7
18	New Mexico	749.6
48	New York	636.5
15	North Carolina	775.9
39	North Dakota	692.7
11	Ohio	810.0
5	Oklahoma	897.5
34	Oregon	706.7
17	Pennsylvania	750.2
36	Rhode Island	700.9
9	South Carolina	829.1
32	South Dakota	710.4
8	Tennessee	880.0
20	Texas	745.3
33	Utah	709.6
38	Vermont	694.8
30	Virginia	717.5
40	Washington	672.9
2	West Virginia	929.1
31	Wisconsin	712.1
21	Wyoming	742.4

RANK ORDER

RANK	STATE	RATE
1	Mississippi	937.6
2	West Virginia	929.1
3	Alabama	909.1
4	Kentucky	906.3
5	Oklahoma	897.5
6	Louisiana	894.2
7	Arkansas	883.7
8	Tennessee	880.0
9	South Carolina	829.1
10	Indiana	822.3
11	Ohio	810.0
12	Missouri	807.0
13	Georgia	801.9
14	Michigan	783.7
15	North Carolina	775.9
16	Kansas	759.3
17	Pennsylvania	750.2
18	New Mexico	749.6
19	Nevada	749.2
20	Texas	745.3
21	Wyoming	742.4
22	Maine	739.0
23	Alaska	736.8
24	Delaware	734.0
25	Montana	732.1
26	Illinois	726.0
27	Idaho	723.8
28	Iowa	722.9
29	Nebraska	718.2
30	Virginia	717.5
31	Wisconsin	712.1
32	South Dakota	710.4
33	Utah	709.6
34	Oregon	706.7
35	New Hampshire	706.2
36	Rhode Island	700.9
37	Maryland	699.5
38	Vermont	694.8
39	North Dakota	692.7
40	Washington	672.9
41	New Jersey	665.7
42	Colorado	664.4
43	Massachusetts	663.0
44	Florida	662.0
45	Arizona	661.7
46	Minnesota	647.0
47	Connecticut	646.5
48	New York	636.5
49	California	605.7
50	Hawaii	588.7

| | District of Columbia | 743.8 |

Source: U.S. Department of Health and Human Services, National Center for Health Statistics
"National Vital Statistics Reports" (Vol. 65, No. 4, 2016, http://www.cdc.gov/nchs/deaths.htm)
*Final data by state of residence. Age-adjusted rates eliminate the distorting effects of the aging of the population. Rates based on the year 2000 standard population.

Estimated Deaths by Cancer in 2016

National Estimated Total = 595,690 Deaths

ALPHA ORDER

RANK	STATE	DEATHS	% of USA
20	Alabama	10,650	1.8%
49	Alaska	1,070	0.2%
18	Arizona	11,800	2.0%
29	Arkansas	6,830	1.1%
1	California	59,060	9.9%
28	Colorado	7,760	1.3%
30	Connecticut	6,780	1.1%
44	Delaware	2,050	0.3%
2	Florida	43,600	7.3%
10	Georgia	16,840	2.8%
42	Hawaii	2,480	0.4%
40	Idaho	2,810	0.5%
7	Illinois	24,080	4.0%
14	Indiana	13,510	2.3%
32	Iowa	6,470	1.1%
33	Kansas	5,540	0.9%
22	Kentucky	10,350	1.7%
25	Louisiana	9,110	1.5%
38	Maine	3,320	0.6%
21	Maryland	10,560	1.8%
17	Massachusetts	12,630	2.1%
8	Michigan	21,100	3.5%
24	Minnesota	9,850	1.7%
31	Mississippi	6,480	1.1%
15	Missouri	12,970	2.2%
45	Montana	2,020	0.3%
37	Nebraska	3,500	0.6%
34	Nevada	4,970	0.8%
41	New Hampshire	2,770	0.5%
11	New Jersey	16,150	2.7%
36	New Mexico	3,690	0.6%
4	New York	34,910	5.9%
9	North Carolina	19,620	3.3%
48	North Dakota	1,270	0.2%
6	Ohio	25,510	4.3%
26	Oklahoma	8,260	1.4%
27	Oregon	8,150	1.4%
5	Pennsylvania	28,700	4.8%
43	Rhode Island	2,090	0.4%
23	South Carolina	10,330	1.7%
46	South Dakota	1,640	0.3%
13	Tennessee	14,560	2.4%
3	Texas	39,450	6.6%
39	Utah	2,970	0.5%
47	Vermont	1,390	0.2%
12	Virginia	14,910	2.5%
16	Washington	12,770	2.1%
35	West Virginia	4,750	0.8%
19	Wisconsin	11,630	2.0%
50	Wyoming	1,000	0.2%

RANK ORDER

RANK	STATE	DEATHS	% of USA
1	California	59,060	9.9%
2	Florida	43,600	7.3%
3	Texas	39,450	6.6%
4	New York	34,910	5.9%
5	Pennsylvania	28,700	4.8%
6	Ohio	25,510	4.3%
7	Illinois	24,080	4.0%
8	Michigan	21,100	3.5%
9	North Carolina	19,620	3.3%
10	Georgia	16,840	2.8%
11	New Jersey	16,150	2.7%
12	Virginia	14,910	2.5%
13	Tennessee	14,560	2.4%
14	Indiana	13,510	2.3%
15	Missouri	12,970	2.2%
16	Washington	12,770	2.1%
17	Massachusetts	12,630	2.1%
18	Arizona	11,800	2.0%
19	Wisconsin	11,630	2.0%
20	Alabama	10,650	1.8%
21	Maryland	10,560	1.8%
22	Kentucky	10,350	1.7%
23	South Carolina	10,330	1.7%
24	Minnesota	9,850	1.7%
25	Louisiana	9,110	1.5%
26	Oklahoma	8,260	1.4%
27	Oregon	8,150	1.4%
28	Colorado	7,760	1.3%
29	Arkansas	6,830	1.1%
30	Connecticut	6,780	1.1%
31	Mississippi	6,480	1.1%
32	Iowa	6,470	1.1%
33	Kansas	5,540	0.9%
34	Nevada	4,970	0.8%
35	West Virginia	4,750	0.8%
36	New Mexico	3,690	0.6%
37	Nebraska	3,500	0.6%
38	Maine	3,320	0.6%
39	Utah	2,970	0.5%
40	Idaho	2,810	0.5%
41	New Hampshire	2,770	0.5%
42	Hawaii	2,480	0.4%
43	Rhode Island	2,090	0.4%
44	Delaware	2,050	0.3%
45	Montana	2,020	0.3%
46	South Dakota	1,640	0.3%
47	Vermont	1,390	0.2%
48	North Dakota	1,270	0.2%
49	Alaska	1,070	0.2%
50	Wyoming	1,000	0.2%
	District of Columbia	980	0.2%

Source: American Cancer Society
"Cancer Facts & Figures 2016" (Copyright 2016, American Cancer Society, www.cancer.org/research/cancer-facts-statistics.html)

Estimated Death Rate by Cancer in 2016

National Estimated Rate = 184.4 Deaths per 100,000 Population*

ALPHA ORDER

RANK	STATE	RATE
8	Alabama	219.0
47	Alaska	144.2
41	Arizona	170.2
4	Arkansas	228.6
46	California	150.5
49	Colorado	140.1
27	Connecticut	189.6
11	Delaware	215.3
14	Florida	211.5
45	Georgia	163.3
39	Hawaii	173.6
44	Idaho	166.9
29	Illinois	188.1
19	Indiana	203.7
18	Iowa	206.4
26	Kansas	190.6
3	Kentucky	233.3
23	Louisiana	194.6
2	Maine	249.3
37	Maryland	175.5
30	Massachusetts	185.4
13	Michigan	212.5
33	Minnesota	178.4
10	Mississippi	216.8
12	Missouri	212.9
24	Montana	193.8
31	Nebraska	183.5
42	Nevada	169.0
17	New Hampshire	207.5
32	New Jersey	180.6
34	New Mexico	177.3
36	New York	176.8
25	North Carolina	193.4
43	North Dakota	167.6
7	Ohio	219.6
15	Oklahoma	210.5
21	Oregon	199.1
5	Pennsylvania	224.5
22	Rhode Island	197.8
16	South Carolina	208.2
28	South Dakota	189.5
9	Tennessee	218.9
48	Texas	141.6
50	Utah	97.3
6	Vermont	222.5
34	Virginia	177.3
38	Washington	175.2
1	West Virginia	259.4
20	Wisconsin	201.3
40	Wyoming	170.8

RANK ORDER

RANK	STATE	RATE
1	West Virginia	259.4
2	Maine	249.3
3	Kentucky	233.3
4	Arkansas	228.6
5	Pennsylvania	224.5
6	Vermont	222.5
7	Ohio	219.6
8	Alabama	219.0
9	Tennessee	218.9
10	Mississippi	216.8
11	Delaware	215.3
12	Missouri	212.9
13	Michigan	212.5
14	Florida	211.5
15	Oklahoma	210.5
16	South Carolina	208.2
17	New Hampshire	207.5
18	Iowa	206.4
19	Indiana	203.7
20	Wisconsin	201.3
21	Oregon	199.1
22	Rhode Island	197.8
23	Louisiana	194.6
24	Montana	193.8
25	North Carolina	193.4
26	Kansas	190.6
27	Connecticut	189.6
28	South Dakota	189.5
29	Illinois	188.1
30	Massachusetts	185.4
31	Nebraska	183.5
32	New Jersey	180.6
33	Minnesota	178.4
34	New Mexico	177.3
34	Virginia	177.3
36	New York	176.8
37	Maryland	175.5
38	Washington	175.2
39	Hawaii	173.6
40	Wyoming	170.8
41	Arizona	170.2
42	Nevada	169.0
43	North Dakota	167.6
44	Idaho	166.9
45	Georgia	163.3
46	California	150.5
47	Alaska	144.2
48	Texas	141.6
49	Colorado	140.1
50	Utah	97.3

District of Columbia 143.9

Source: CQ Press using data from American Cancer Society
"Cancer Facts & Figures 2016" (Copyright 2016, American Cancer Society, www.cancer.org/research/cancer-facts-statistics.html)
*Rates calculated using 2016 Census resident population estimates. Not age-adjusted.

Estimated New Cancer Cases in 2016

National Estimated Total = 1,685,210 New Cases*

RANK	STATE	CASES	% of USA		RANK	STATE	CASES	% of USA
23	Alabama	27,020	1.6%		1	California	173,200	10.3%
49	Alaska	3,330	0.2%		2	Florida	121,240	7.2%
19	Arizona	32,510	1.9%		3	Texas	116,690	6.9%
32	Arkansas	16,460	1.0%		4	New York	110,280	6.5%
1	California	173,200	10.3%		5	Pennsylvania	83,560	5.0%
26	Colorado	24,730	1.5%		6	Ohio	66,020	3.9%
28	Connecticut	21,700	1.3%		7	Illinois	65,090	3.9%
45	Delaware	5,630	0.3%		8	Michigan	56,530	3.4%
2	Florida	121,240	7.2%		9	North Carolina	54,450	3.2%
11	Georgia	48,670	2.9%		10	New Jersey	49,750	3.0%
42	Hawaii	6,850	0.4%		11	Georgia	48,670	2.9%
41	Idaho	8,120	0.5%		12	Virginia	43,190	2.6%
7	Illinois	65,090	3.9%		13	Washington	37,770	2.2%
16	Indiana	35,180	2.1%		14	Tennessee	37,650	2.2%
30	Iowa	17,100	1.0%		15	Massachusetts	37,620	2.2%
33	Kansas	14,530	0.9%		16	Indiana	35,180	2.1%
24	Kentucky	25,720	1.5%		17	Missouri	34,270	2.0%
25	Louisiana	25,070	1.5%		18	Wisconsin	32,970	2.0%
39	Maine	9,270	0.6%		19	Arizona	32,510	1.9%
20	Maryland	30,990	1.8%		20	Maryland	30,990	1.8%
15	Massachusetts	37,620	2.2%		21	Minnesota	29,130	1.7%
8	Michigan	56,530	3.4%		22	South Carolina	27,980	1.7%
21	Minnesota	29,130	1.7%		23	Alabama	27,020	1.6%
31	Mississippi	16,680	1.0%		24	Kentucky	25,720	1.5%
17	Missouri	34,270	2.0%		25	Louisiana	25,070	1.5%
44	Montana	6,070	0.4%		26	Colorado	24,730	1.5%
38	Nebraska	9,740	0.6%		27	Oregon	22,510	1.3%
34	Nevada	14,390	0.9%		28	Connecticut	21,700	1.3%
40	New Hampshire	8,680	0.5%		29	Oklahoma	19,650	1.2%
10	New Jersey	49,750	3.0%		30	Iowa	17,100	1.0%
37	New Mexico	9,750	0.6%		31	Mississippi	16,680	1.0%
4	New York	110,280	6.5%		32	Arkansas	16,460	1.0%
9	North Carolina	54,450	3.2%		33	Kansas	14,530	0.9%
48	North Dakota	3,930	0.2%		34	Nevada	14,390	0.9%
6	Ohio	66,020	3.9%		35	West Virginia	11,770	0.7%
29	Oklahoma	19,650	1.2%		36	Utah	11,030	0.7%
27	Oregon	22,510	1.3%		37	New Mexico	9,750	0.6%
5	Pennsylvania	83,560	5.0%		38	Nebraska	9,740	0.6%
43	Rhode Island	6,190	0.4%		39	Maine	9,270	0.6%
22	South Carolina	27,980	1.7%		40	New Hampshire	8,680	0.5%
46	South Dakota	4,690	0.3%		41	Idaho	8,120	0.5%
14	Tennessee	37,650	2.2%		42	Hawaii	6,850	0.4%
3	Texas	116,690	6.9%		43	Rhode Island	6,190	0.4%
36	Utah	11,030	0.7%		44	Montana	6,070	0.4%
47	Vermont	4,050	0.2%		45	Delaware	5,630	0.3%
12	Virginia	43,190	2.6%		46	South Dakota	4,690	0.3%
13	Washington	37,770	2.2%		47	Vermont	4,050	0.2%
35	West Virginia	11,770	0.7%		48	North Dakota	3,930	0.2%
18	Wisconsin	32,970	2.0%		49	Alaska	3,330	0.2%
50	Wyoming	2,920	0.2%		50	Wyoming	2,920	0.2%
						District of Columbia	2,910	0.2%

ALPHA ORDER

RANK ORDER

Source: American Cancer Society

"Cancer Facts & Figures 2016" (Copyright 2016, American Cancer Society, www.cancer.org/research/cancer-facts-statistics.html)
*These estimates are offered as a rough guide and should not be regarded as definitive. They are calculated by the American Cancer Society using a model based on 1998-2012 incidence data. Totals do not include basal and squamous cell skin cancers or in situ carcinomas except urinary bladder.

Estimated Rate of New Cancer Cases in 2016

National Estimated Rate = 521.5 New Cases per 100,000 Population*

ALPHA ORDER				RANK ORDER		
RANK	STATE	RATE		RANK	STATE	RATE
21	Alabama	555.6		1	Maine	696.2
46	Alaska	448.9		2	Pennsylvania	653.6
44	Arizona	469.0		3	New Hampshire	650.3
23	Arkansas	550.8		4	Vermont	648.4
48	California	441.3		5	West Virginia	642.8
47	Colorado	446.3		6	Connecticut	606.7
6	Connecticut	606.7		7	Delaware	591.3
7	Delaware	591.3		8	Florida	588.2
8	Florida	588.2		9	Rhode Island	585.9
43	Georgia	472.0		10	Montana	582.2
42	Hawaii	479.5		11	Kentucky	579.7
41	Idaho	482.4		12	Wisconsin	570.5
36	Illinois	508.5		13	Michigan	569.4
29	Indiana	530.4		14	Ohio	568.4
25	Iowa	545.5		15	Tennessee	566.1
38	Kansas	499.8		16	South Carolina	564.0
11	Kentucky	579.7		17	Missouri	562.4
28	Louisiana	535.5		18	New York	558.5
1	Maine	696.2		19	Mississippi	558.1
33	Maryland	515.1		20	New Jersey	556.2
22	Massachusetts	552.3		21	Alabama	555.6
13	Michigan	569.4		22	Massachusetts	552.3
30	Minnesota	527.7		23	Arkansas	550.8
19	Mississippi	558.1		24	Oregon	549.9
17	Missouri	562.4		25	Iowa	545.5
10	Montana	582.2		26	South Dakota	541.9
35	Nebraska	510.7		27	North Carolina	536.6
40	Nevada	489.4		28	Louisiana	535.5
3	New Hampshire	650.3		29	Indiana	530.4
20	New Jersey	556.2		30	Minnesota	527.7
45	New Mexico	468.5		31	North Dakota	518.5
18	New York	558.5		32	Washington	518.2
27	North Carolina	536.6		33	Maryland	515.1
31	North Dakota	518.5		34	Virginia	513.4
14	Ohio	568.4		35	Nebraska	510.7
37	Oklahoma	500.8		36	Illinois	508.5
24	Oregon	549.9		37	Oklahoma	500.8
2	Pennsylvania	653.6		38	Kansas	499.8
9	Rhode Island	585.9		39	Wyoming	498.7
16	South Carolina	564.0		40	Nevada	489.4
26	South Dakota	541.9		41	Idaho	482.4
15	Tennessee	566.1		42	Hawaii	479.5
49	Texas	418.8		43	Georgia	472.0
50	Utah	361.5		44	Arizona	469.0
4	Vermont	648.4		45	New Mexico	468.5
34	Virginia	513.4		46	Alaska	448.9
32	Washington	518.2		47	Colorado	446.3
5	West Virginia	642.8		48	California	441.3
12	Wisconsin	570.5		49	Texas	418.8
39	Wyoming	498.7		50	Utah	361.5
					District of Columbia	427.2

Source: CQ Press using data from American Cancer Society
"Cancer Facts & Figures 2016" (Copyright 2016, American Cancer Society, www.cancer.org/research/cancer-facts-statistics.html)
*These estimates are offered as a rough guide and should not be regarded as definitive. They are calculated by the American Cancer Society using a model based on 1998-2012 incidence data. Totals do not include basal and squamous cell skin cancers or in situ carcinomas except urinary bladder. Rates calculated using 2016 Census resident population estimates.

Deaths by Accidents in 2014

National Total = 136,053 Deaths*

ALPHA ORDER

ALPHA ORDER / RANK ORDER

RANK	STATE	DEATHS	% of USA	RANK	STATE	DEATHS	% of USA
22	Alabama	2,463	1.8%	1	California	11,804	8.7%
47	Alaska	379	0.3%	2	Texas	9,723	7.1%
12	Arizona	3,322	2.4%	3	Florida	9,433	6.9%
33	Arkansas	1,458	1.1%	4	Pennsylvania	6,640	4.9%
1	California	11,804	8.7%	5	Ohio	6,178	4.5%
21	Colorado	2,517	1.9%	6	New York	5,945	4.4%
30	Connecticut	1,642	1.2%	7	Illinois	4,644	3.4%
46	Delaware	425	0.3%	8	North Carolina	4,558	3.4%
3	Florida	9,433	6.9%	9	Michigan	4,422	3.3%
10	Georgia	3,964	2.9%	10	Georgia	3,964	2.9%
44	Hawaii	476	0.3%	11	Tennessee	3,781	2.8%
39	Idaho	765	0.6%	12	Arizona	3,322	2.4%
7	Illinois	4,644	3.4%	13	Virginia	3,147	2.3%
17	Indiana	2,974	2.2%	14	Missouri	3,110	2.3%
32	Iowa	1,517	1.1%	15	Wisconsin	3,015	2.2%
35	Kansas	1,377	1.0%	16	Washington	2,997	2.2%
20	Kentucky	2,622	1.9%	17	Indiana	2,974	2.2%
26	Louisiana	2,344	1.7%	18	New Jersey	2,970	2.2%
41	Maine	690	0.5%	19	Massachusetts	2,692	2.0%
29	Maryland	1,674	1.2%	20	Kentucky	2,622	1.9%
19	Massachusetts	2,692	2.0%	21	Colorado	2,517	1.9%
9	Michigan	4,422	3.3%	22	Alabama	2,463	1.8%
25	Minnesota	2,385	1.8%	23	South Carolina	2,436	1.8%
28	Mississippi	1,712	1.3%	24	Oklahoma	2,421	1.8%
14	Missouri	3,110	2.3%	25	Minnesota	2,385	1.8%
43	Montana	581	0.4%	26	Louisiana	2,344	1.7%
38	Nebraska	781	0.6%	27	Oregon	1,803	1.3%
37	Nevada	1,166	0.9%	28	Mississippi	1,712	1.3%
40	New Hampshire	716	0.5%	29	Maryland	1,674	1.2%
18	New Jersey	2,970	2.2%	30	Connecticut	1,642	1.2%
31	New Mexico	1,534	1.1%	31	New Mexico	1,534	1.1%
6	New York	5,945	4.4%	32	Iowa	1,517	1.1%
8	North Carolina	4,558	3.4%	33	Arkansas	1,458	1.1%
49	North Dakota	349	0.3%	34	West Virginia	1,380	1.0%
5	Ohio	6,178	4.5%	35	Kansas	1,377	1.0%
24	Oklahoma	2,421	1.8%	36	Utah	1,167	0.9%
27	Oregon	1,803	1.3%	37	Nevada	1,166	0.9%
4	Pennsylvania	6,640	4.9%	38	Nebraska	781	0.6%
42	Rhode Island	592	0.4%	39	Idaho	765	0.6%
23	South Carolina	2,436	1.8%	40	New Hampshire	716	0.5%
45	South Dakota	462	0.3%	41	Maine	690	0.5%
11	Tennessee	3,781	2.8%	42	Rhode Island	592	0.4%
2	Texas	9,723	7.1%	43	Montana	581	0.4%
36	Utah	1,167	0.9%	44	Hawaii	476	0.3%
50	Vermont	322	0.2%	45	South Dakota	462	0.3%
13	Virginia	3,147	2.3%	46	Delaware	425	0.3%
16	Washington	2,997	2.2%	47	Alaska	379	0.3%
34	West Virginia	1,380	1.0%	48	Wyoming	361	0.3%
15	Wisconsin	3,015	2.2%	49	North Dakota	349	0.3%
48	Wyoming	361	0.3%	50	Vermont	322	0.2%
					District of Columbia	217	0.2%

Source: U.S. Department of Health and Human Services, National Center for Health Statistics
    "National Vital Statistics Reports" (Vol. 65, No. 4, 2016, http://www.cdc.gov/nchs/deaths.htm)
*Final data by state of residence. Includes motor vehicle deaths, poisoning, falls, drowning, and other accidents.

Age-Adjusted Death Rate by Accidents in 2014

National Rate = 40.5 Deaths per 100,000 Population*

ALPHA ORDER

RANK	STATE	RATE
13	Alabama	49.3
8	Alaska	55.0
20	Arizona	47.0
18	Arkansas	47.4
48	California	29.2
19	Colorado	47.1
35	Connecticut	41.0
30	Delaware	43.7
34	Florida	41.4
38	Georgia	40.1
47	Hawaii	30.1
23	Idaho	46.5
45	Illinois	34.4
29	Indiana	43.9
32	Iowa	42.1
28	Kansas	44.1
5	Kentucky	58.3
12	Louisiana	49.8
24	Maine	45.8
50	Maryland	26.6
43	Massachusetts	37.0
33	Michigan	41.7
40	Minnesota	39.4
6	Mississippi	56.2
16	Missouri	48.7
9	Montana	52.6
41	Nebraska	38.6
37	Nevada	40.2
11	New Hampshire	50.5
46	New Jersey	30.9
1	New Mexico	72.1
49	New York	27.6
26	North Carolina	44.4
31	North Dakota	43.3
10	Ohio	50.8
4	Oklahoma	60.4
35	Oregon	41.0
22	Pennsylvania	46.8
14	Rhode Island	49.2
17	South Carolina	48.2
14	South Dakota	49.2
7	Tennessee	55.6
42	Texas	37.3
25	Utah	45.5
26	Vermont	44.4
44	Virginia	36.8
38	Washington	40.1
2	West Virginia	71.0
21	Wisconsin	46.9
3	Wyoming	60.9

RANK ORDER

RANK	STATE	RATE
1	New Mexico	72.1
2	West Virginia	71.0
3	Wyoming	60.9
4	Oklahoma	60.4
5	Kentucky	58.3
6	Mississippi	56.2
7	Tennessee	55.6
8	Alaska	55.0
9	Montana	52.6
10	Ohio	50.8
11	New Hampshire	50.5
12	Louisiana	49.8
13	Alabama	49.3
14	Rhode Island	49.2
14	South Dakota	49.2
16	Missouri	48.7
17	South Carolina	48.2
18	Arkansas	47.4
19	Colorado	47.1
20	Arizona	47.0
21	Wisconsin	46.9
22	Pennsylvania	46.8
23	Idaho	46.5
24	Maine	45.8
25	Utah	45.5
26	North Carolina	44.4
26	Vermont	44.4
28	Kansas	44.1
29	Indiana	43.9
30	Delaware	43.7
31	North Dakota	43.3
32	Iowa	42.1
33	Michigan	41.7
34	Florida	41.4
35	Connecticut	41.0
35	Oregon	41.0
37	Nevada	40.2
38	Georgia	40.1
38	Washington	40.1
40	Minnesota	39.4
41	Nebraska	38.6
42	Texas	37.3
43	Massachusetts	37.0
44	Virginia	36.8
45	Illinois	34.4
46	New Jersey	30.9
47	Hawaii	30.1
48	California	29.2
49	New York	27.6
50	Maryland	26.6
	District of Columbia	33.1

Source: U.S. Department of Health and Human Services, National Center for Health Statistics
"National Vital Statistics Reports" (Vol. 65, No. 4, 2016, http://www.cdc.gov/nchs/deaths.htm)
*Final data by state of residence. Includes motor vehicle deaths, poisoning, falls, drowning, and other accidents. Age-adjusted rates based on the year 2000 standard population.

Deaths by Cerebrovascular Diseases in 2014

National Total = 133,103 Deaths*

RANK	STATE	DEATHS	% of USA
16	Alabama	2,663	2.0%
50	Alaska	157	0.1%
22	Arizona	2,235	1.7%
30	Arkansas	1,583	1.2%
1	California	13,731	10.3%
28	Colorado	1,714	1.3%
33	Connecticut	1,266	1.0%
44	Delaware	439	0.3%
3	Florida	9,770	7.3%
10	Georgia	3,948	3.0%
39	Hawaii	655	0.5%
40	Idaho	640	0.5%
7	Illinois	5,489	4.1%
14	Indiana	3,107	2.3%
31	Iowa	1,433	1.1%
32	Kansas	1,363	1.0%
25	Kentucky	2,050	1.5%
23	Louisiana	2,230	1.7%
41	Maine	628	0.5%
19	Maryland	2,469	1.9%
20	Massachusetts	2,460	1.8%
9	Michigan	4,596	3.5%
24	Minnesota	2,202	1.7%
29	Mississippi	1,584	1.2%
15	Missouri	3,030	2.3%
42	Montana	480	0.4%
38	Nebraska	798	0.6%
35	Nevada	948	0.7%
43	New Hampshire	474	0.4%
11	New Jersey	3,419	2.6%
37	New Mexico	822	0.6%
5	New York	6,212	4.7%
8	North Carolina	4,702	3.5%
47	North Dakota	325	0.2%
6	Ohio	5,791	4.4%
26	Oklahoma	1,847	1.4%
27	Oregon	1,821	1.4%
4	Pennsylvania	6,576	4.9%
46	Rhode Island	373	0.3%
21	South Carolina	2,393	1.8%
44	South Dakota	439	0.3%
12	Tennessee	3,326	2.5%
2	Texas	9,898	7.4%
36	Utah	856	0.6%
48	Vermont	266	0.2%
13	Virginia	3,229	2.4%
17	Washington	2,649	2.0%
34	West Virginia	1,103	0.8%
18	Wisconsin	2,511	1.9%
49	Wyoming	189	0.1%

RANK	STATE	DEATHS	% of USA
1	California	13,731	10.3%
2	Texas	9,898	7.4%
3	Florida	9,770	7.3%
4	Pennsylvania	6,576	4.9%
5	New York	6,212	4.7%
6	Ohio	5,791	4.4%
7	Illinois	5,489	4.1%
8	North Carolina	4,702	3.5%
9	Michigan	4,596	3.5%
10	Georgia	3,948	3.0%
11	New Jersey	3,419	2.6%
12	Tennessee	3,326	2.5%
13	Virginia	3,229	2.4%
14	Indiana	3,107	2.3%
15	Missouri	3,030	2.3%
16	Alabama	2,663	2.0%
17	Washington	2,649	2.0%
18	Wisconsin	2,511	1.9%
19	Maryland	2,469	1.9%
20	Massachusetts	2,460	1.8%
21	South Carolina	2,393	1.8%
22	Arizona	2,235	1.7%
23	Louisiana	2,230	1.7%
24	Minnesota	2,202	1.7%
25	Kentucky	2,050	1.5%
26	Oklahoma	1,847	1.4%
27	Oregon	1,821	1.4%
28	Colorado	1,714	1.3%
29	Mississippi	1,584	1.2%
30	Arkansas	1,583	1.2%
31	Iowa	1,433	1.1%
32	Kansas	1,363	1.0%
33	Connecticut	1,266	1.0%
34	West Virginia	1,103	0.8%
35	Nevada	948	0.7%
36	Utah	856	0.6%
37	New Mexico	822	0.6%
38	Nebraska	798	0.6%
39	Hawaii	655	0.5%
40	Idaho	640	0.5%
41	Maine	628	0.5%
42	Montana	480	0.4%
43	New Hampshire	474	0.4%
44	Delaware	439	0.3%
44	South Dakota	439	0.3%
46	Rhode Island	373	0.3%
47	North Dakota	325	0.2%
48	Vermont	266	0.2%
49	Wyoming	189	0.1%
50	Alaska	157	0.1%
	District of Columbia	214	0.2%

Source: U.S. Department of Health and Human Services, National Center for Health Statistics
"National Vital Statistics Reports" (Vol. 65, No. 4, 2016, http://www.cdc.gov/nchs/deaths.htm)
*Final data by state of residence. Cerebrovascular diseases include stroke and other disorders of the blood vessels of the brain.

Age-Adjusted Death Rate by Cerebrovascular Diseases in 2014

National Rate = 36.5 Deaths per 100,000 Population*

ALPHA ORDER

RANK	STATE	RATE
2	Alabama	48.3
41	Alaska	32.3
47	Arizona	28.3
5	Arkansas	45.4
36	California	33.9
38	Colorado	33.4
48	Connecticut	26.3
17	Delaware	38.8
40	Florida	33.0
10	Georgia	42.6
33	Hawaii	34.1
25	Idaho	36.8
22	Illinois	37.4
12	Indiana	41.7
34	Iowa	34.0
16	Kansas	39.0
11	Kentucky	41.8
4	Louisiana	45.6
39	Maine	33.2
19	Maryland	38.0
46	Massachusetts	28.7
20	Michigan	37.9
34	Minnesota	34.0
1	Mississippi	48.8
14	Missouri	41.0
27	Montana	36.4
29	Nebraska	34.7
37	Nevada	33.8
45	New Hampshire	28.9
43	New Jersey	31.4
29	New Mexico	34.7
49	New York	26.1
8	North Carolina	43.0
28	North Dakota	35.5
15	Ohio	40.0
8	Oklahoma	43.0
22	Oregon	37.4
26	Pennsylvania	36.7
50	Rhode Island	25.6
7	South Carolina	44.2
17	South Dakota	38.8
3	Tennessee	45.8
13	Texas	41.6
20	Utah	37.9
42	Vermont	31.7
24	Virginia	37.0
32	Washington	34.3
6	West Virginia	45.3
31	Wisconsin	34.6
44	Wyoming	30.2

RANK ORDER

RANK	STATE	RATE
1	Mississippi	48.8
2	Alabama	48.3
3	Tennessee	45.8
4	Louisiana	45.6
5	Arkansas	45.4
6	West Virginia	45.3
7	South Carolina	44.2
8	North Carolina	43.0
8	Oklahoma	43.0
10	Georgia	42.6
11	Kentucky	41.8
12	Indiana	41.7
13	Texas	41.6
14	Missouri	41.0
15	Ohio	40.0
16	Kansas	39.0
17	Delaware	38.8
17	South Dakota	38.8
19	Maryland	38.0
20	Michigan	37.9
20	Utah	37.9
22	Illinois	37.4
22	Oregon	37.4
24	Virginia	37.0
25	Idaho	36.8
26	Pennsylvania	36.7
27	Montana	36.4
28	North Dakota	35.5
29	Nebraska	34.7
29	New Mexico	34.7
31	Wisconsin	34.6
32	Washington	34.3
33	Hawaii	34.1
34	Iowa	34.0
34	Minnesota	34.0
36	California	33.9
37	Nevada	33.8
38	Colorado	33.4
39	Maine	33.2
40	Florida	33.0
41	Alaska	32.3
42	Vermont	31.7
43	New Jersey	31.4
44	Wyoming	30.2
45	New Hampshire	28.9
46	Massachusetts	28.7
47	Arizona	28.3
48	Connecticut	26.3
49	New York	26.1
50	Rhode Island	25.6
	District of Columbia	33.6

Source: U.S. Department of Health and Human Services, National Center for Health Statistics
"National Vital Statistics Reports" (Vol. 65, No. 4, 2016, http://www.cdc.gov/nchs/deaths.htm)
*Final data by state of residence. Cerebrovascular diseases include stroke and other disorders of the blood vessels of the brain. Age-adjusted rates based on the year 2000 standard population.

Deaths by Diseases of the Heart in 2014

National Total = 614,348 Deaths*

<table>
<tr><th colspan="4">ALPHA ORDER</th><th colspan="4">RANK ORDER</th></tr>
<tr><th>RANK</th><th>STATE</th><th>DEATHS</th><th>% of USA</th><th>RANK</th><th>STATE</th><th>DEATHS</th><th>% of USA</th></tr>
<tr><td>16</td><td>Alabama</td><td>12,461</td><td>2.0%</td><td>1</td><td>California</td><td>58,189</td><td>9.5%</td></tr>
<tr><td>50</td><td>Alaska</td><td>782</td><td>0.1%</td><td>2</td><td>Florida</td><td>44,511</td><td>7.2%</td></tr>
<tr><td>20</td><td>Arizona</td><td>10,805</td><td>1.8%</td><td>3</td><td>New York</td><td>43,116</td><td>7.0%</td></tr>
<tr><td>27</td><td>Arkansas</td><td>7,581</td><td>1.2%</td><td>4</td><td>Texas</td><td>41,479</td><td>6.8%</td></tr>
<tr><td>1</td><td>California</td><td>58,189</td><td>9.5%</td><td>5</td><td>Pennsylvania</td><td>31,353</td><td>5.1%</td></tr>
<tr><td>30</td><td>Colorado</td><td>6,900</td><td>1.1%</td><td>6</td><td>Ohio</td><td>27,000</td><td>4.4%</td></tr>
<tr><td>29</td><td>Connecticut</td><td>7,018</td><td>1.1%</td><td>7</td><td>Illinois</td><td>25,024</td><td>4.1%</td></tr>
<tr><td>45</td><td>Delaware</td><td>1,921</td><td>0.3%</td><td>8</td><td>Michigan</td><td>24,692</td><td>4.0%</td></tr>
<tr><td>2</td><td>Florida</td><td>44,511</td><td>7.2%</td><td>9</td><td>New Jersey</td><td>18,319</td><td>3.0%</td></tr>
<tr><td>11</td><td>Georgia</td><td>17,107</td><td>2.8%</td><td>10</td><td>North Carolina</td><td>17,592</td><td>2.9%</td></tr>
<tr><td>41</td><td>Hawaii</td><td>2,528</td><td>0.4%</td><td>11</td><td>Georgia</td><td>17,107</td><td>2.8%</td></tr>
<tr><td>40</td><td>Idaho</td><td>2,676</td><td>0.4%</td><td>12</td><td>Tennessee</td><td>15,223</td><td>2.5%</td></tr>
<tr><td>7</td><td>Illinois</td><td>25,024</td><td>4.1%</td><td>13</td><td>Missouri</td><td>14,338</td><td>2.3%</td></tr>
<tr><td>15</td><td>Indiana</td><td>13,764</td><td>2.2%</td><td>14</td><td>Virginia</td><td>13,874</td><td>2.3%</td></tr>
<tr><td>31</td><td>Iowa</td><td>6,615</td><td>1.1%</td><td>15</td><td>Indiana</td><td>13,764</td><td>2.2%</td></tr>
<tr><td>34</td><td>Kansas</td><td>5,479</td><td>0.9%</td><td>16</td><td>Alabama</td><td>12,461</td><td>2.0%</td></tr>
<tr><td>23</td><td>Kentucky</td><td>10,013</td><td>1.6%</td><td>17</td><td>Massachusetts</td><td>11,817</td><td>1.9%</td></tr>
<tr><td>22</td><td>Louisiana</td><td>10,647</td><td>1.7%</td><td>18</td><td>Wisconsin</td><td>11,229</td><td>1.8%</td></tr>
<tr><td>39</td><td>Maine</td><td>2,776</td><td>0.5%</td><td>19</td><td>Maryland</td><td>11,135</td><td>1.8%</td></tr>
<tr><td>19</td><td>Maryland</td><td>11,135</td><td>1.8%</td><td>20</td><td>Arizona</td><td>10,805</td><td>1.8%</td></tr>
<tr><td>17</td><td>Massachusetts</td><td>11,817</td><td>1.9%</td><td>21</td><td>Washington</td><td>10,710</td><td>1.7%</td></tr>
<tr><td>8</td><td>Michigan</td><td>24,692</td><td>4.0%</td><td>22</td><td>Louisiana</td><td>10,647</td><td>1.7%</td></tr>
<tr><td>26</td><td>Minnesota</td><td>7,659</td><td>1.2%</td><td>23</td><td>Kentucky</td><td>10,013</td><td>1.6%</td></tr>
<tr><td>28</td><td>Mississippi</td><td>7,538</td><td>1.2%</td><td>24</td><td>South Carolina</td><td>9,964</td><td>1.6%</td></tr>
<tr><td>13</td><td>Missouri</td><td>14,338</td><td>2.3%</td><td>25</td><td>Oklahoma</td><td>9,868</td><td>1.6%</td></tr>
<tr><td>44</td><td>Montana</td><td>1,957</td><td>0.3%</td><td>26</td><td>Minnesota</td><td>7,659</td><td>1.2%</td></tr>
<tr><td>38</td><td>Nebraska</td><td>3,296</td><td>0.5%</td><td>27</td><td>Arkansas</td><td>7,581</td><td>1.2%</td></tr>
<tr><td>33</td><td>Nevada</td><td>5,761</td><td>0.9%</td><td>28</td><td>Mississippi</td><td>7,538</td><td>1.2%</td></tr>
<tr><td>42</td><td>New Hampshire</td><td>2,464</td><td>0.4%</td><td>29</td><td>Connecticut</td><td>7,018</td><td>1.1%</td></tr>
<tr><td>9</td><td>New Jersey</td><td>18,319</td><td>3.0%</td><td>30</td><td>Colorado</td><td>6,900</td><td>1.1%</td></tr>
<tr><td>37</td><td>New Mexico</td><td>3,424</td><td>0.6%</td><td>31</td><td>Iowa</td><td>6,615</td><td>1.1%</td></tr>
<tr><td>3</td><td>New York</td><td>43,116</td><td>7.0%</td><td>32</td><td>Oregon</td><td>6,524</td><td>1.1%</td></tr>
<tr><td>10</td><td>North Carolina</td><td>17,592</td><td>2.9%</td><td>33</td><td>Nevada</td><td>5,761</td><td>0.9%</td></tr>
<tr><td>47</td><td>North Dakota</td><td>1,381</td><td>0.2%</td><td>34</td><td>Kansas</td><td>5,479</td><td>0.9%</td></tr>
<tr><td>6</td><td>Ohio</td><td>27,000</td><td>4.4%</td><td>35</td><td>West Virginia</td><td>4,692</td><td>0.8%</td></tr>
<tr><td>25</td><td>Oklahoma</td><td>9,868</td><td>1.6%</td><td>36</td><td>Utah</td><td>3,431</td><td>0.6%</td></tr>
<tr><td>32</td><td>Oregon</td><td>6,524</td><td>1.1%</td><td>37</td><td>New Mexico</td><td>3,424</td><td>0.6%</td></tr>
<tr><td>5</td><td>Pennsylvania</td><td>31,353</td><td>5.1%</td><td>38</td><td>Nebraska</td><td>3,296</td><td>0.5%</td></tr>
<tr><td>43</td><td>Rhode Island</td><td>2,341</td><td>0.4%</td><td>39</td><td>Maine</td><td>2,776</td><td>0.5%</td></tr>
<tr><td>24</td><td>South Carolina</td><td>9,964</td><td>1.6%</td><td>40</td><td>Idaho</td><td>2,676</td><td>0.4%</td></tr>
<tr><td>46</td><td>South Dakota</td><td>1,704</td><td>0.3%</td><td>41</td><td>Hawaii</td><td>2,528</td><td>0.4%</td></tr>
<tr><td>12</td><td>Tennessee</td><td>15,223</td><td>2.5%</td><td>42</td><td>New Hampshire</td><td>2,464</td><td>0.4%</td></tr>
<tr><td>4</td><td>Texas</td><td>41,479</td><td>6.8%</td><td>43</td><td>Rhode Island</td><td>2,341</td><td>0.4%</td></tr>
<tr><td>36</td><td>Utah</td><td>3,431</td><td>0.6%</td><td>44</td><td>Montana</td><td>1,957</td><td>0.3%</td></tr>
<tr><td>48</td><td>Vermont</td><td>1,311</td><td>0.2%</td><td>45</td><td>Delaware</td><td>1,921</td><td>0.3%</td></tr>
<tr><td>14</td><td>Virginia</td><td>13,874</td><td>2.3%</td><td>46</td><td>South Dakota</td><td>1,704</td><td>0.3%</td></tr>
<tr><td>21</td><td>Washington</td><td>10,710</td><td>1.7%</td><td>47</td><td>North Dakota</td><td>1,381</td><td>0.2%</td></tr>
<tr><td>35</td><td>West Virginia</td><td>4,692</td><td>0.8%</td><td>48</td><td>Vermont</td><td>1,311</td><td>0.2%</td></tr>
<tr><td>18</td><td>Wisconsin</td><td>11,229</td><td>1.8%</td><td>49</td><td>Wyoming</td><td>1,035</td><td>0.2%</td></tr>
<tr><td>49</td><td>Wyoming</td><td>1,035</td><td>0.2%</td><td>50</td><td>Alaska</td><td>782</td><td>0.1%</td></tr>
<tr><td></td><td></td><td></td><td></td><td></td><td>District of Columbia</td><td>1,324</td><td>0.2%</td></tr>
</table>

Source: U.S. Department of Health and Human Services, National Center for Health Statistics
"National Vital Statistics Reports" (Vol. 65, No. 4, 2016, http://www.cdc.gov/nchs/deaths.htm)
*Final data by state of residence.

Age-Adjusted Death Rate by Diseases of the Heart in 2014

National Rate = 167.0 Deaths per 100,000 Population*

ALPHA ORDER

RANK	STATE	RATE
3	Alabama	224.0
39	Alaska	146.6
47	Arizona	136.4
4	Arkansas	217.5
43	California	142.2
49	Colorado	130.3
40	Connecticut	145.6
20	Delaware	168.7
33	Florida	151.3
15	Georgia	179.7
46	Hawaii	136.7
32	Idaho	152.8
19	Illinois	169.7
13	Indiana	182.7
27	Iowa	157.3
26	Kansas	157.4
8	Kentucky	200.5
5	Louisiana	216.3
36	Maine	147.9
21	Maryland	167.8
45	Massachusetts	137.1
7	Michigan	200.9
50	Minnesota	116.5
1	Mississippi	229.9
10	Missouri	194.7
38	Montana	147.8
42	Nebraska	143.0
9	Nevada	197.2
36	New Hampshire	147.9
22	New Jersey	166.3
41	New Mexico	143.3
16	New York	178.3
25	North Carolina	158.7
35	North Dakota	149.2
12	Ohio	186.4
2	Oklahoma	228.1
48	Oregon	132.1
17	Pennsylvania	175.8
24	Rhode Island	160.8
14	South Carolina	181.1
31	South Dakota	154.6
6	Tennessee	205.6
18	Texas	169.9
34	Utah	151.0
28	Vermont	156.6
29	Virginia	156.1
44	Washington	137.2
11	West Virginia	192.9
30	Wisconsin	155.1
23	Wyoming	162.2

RANK ORDER

RANK	STATE	RATE
1	Mississippi	229.9
2	Oklahoma	228.1
3	Alabama	224.0
4	Arkansas	217.5
5	Louisiana	216.3
6	Tennessee	205.6
7	Michigan	200.9
8	Kentucky	200.5
9	Nevada	197.2
10	Missouri	194.7
11	West Virginia	192.9
12	Ohio	186.4
13	Indiana	182.7
14	South Carolina	181.1
15	Georgia	179.7
16	New York	178.3
17	Pennsylvania	175.8
18	Texas	169.9
19	Illinois	169.7
20	Delaware	168.7
21	Maryland	167.8
22	New Jersey	166.3
23	Wyoming	162.2
24	Rhode Island	160.8
25	North Carolina	158.7
26	Kansas	157.4
27	Iowa	157.3
28	Vermont	156.6
29	Virginia	156.1
30	Wisconsin	155.1
31	South Dakota	154.6
32	Idaho	152.8
33	Florida	151.3
34	Utah	151.0
35	North Dakota	149.2
36	Maine	147.9
36	New Hampshire	147.9
38	Montana	147.8
39	Alaska	146.6
40	Connecticut	145.6
41	New Mexico	143.3
42	Nebraska	143.0
43	California	142.2
44	Washington	137.2
45	Massachusetts	137.1
46	Hawaii	136.7
47	Arizona	136.4
48	Oregon	132.1
49	Colorado	130.3
50	Minnesota	116.5
	District of Columbia	207.8

Source: U.S. Department of Health and Human Services, National Center for Health Statistics
"National Vital Statistics Reports" (Vol. 65, No. 4, 2016, http://www.cdc.gov/nchs/deaths.htm)
*Final data by state of residence. Age-adjusted rates based on the year 2000 standard population.

Deaths by Suicide in 2014

National Total = 42,773 Suicides*

ALPHA ORDER

RANK ORDER

RANK	STATE	DEATHS	% of USA		RANK	STATE	DEATHS	% of USA
24	Alabama	715	1.7%		1	California	4,214	9.9%
44	Alaska	167	0.4%		2	Texas	3,254	7.6%
11	Arizona	1,244	2.9%		3	Florida	3,035	7.1%
31	Arkansas	515	1.2%		4	Pennsylvania	1,817	4.2%
1	California	4,214	9.9%		5	New York	1,700	4.0%
14	Colorado	1,083	2.5%		6	Ohio	1,491	3.5%
36	Connecticut	379	0.9%		7	Illinois	1,398	3.3%
47	Delaware	126	0.3%		8	Michigan	1,354	3.2%
3	Florida	3,035	7.1%		9	North Carolina	1,351	3.2%
10	Georgia	1,294	3.0%		10	Georgia	1,294	3.0%
43	Hawaii	204	0.5%		11	Arizona	1,244	2.9%
38	Idaho	320	0.7%		12	Virginia	1,122	2.6%
7	Illinois	1,398	3.3%		13	Washington	1,119	2.6%
16	Indiana	948	2.2%		14	Colorado	1,083	2.5%
34	Iowa	407	1.0%		15	Missouri	1,017	2.4%
32	Kansas	455	1.1%		16	Indiana	948	2.2%
23	Kentucky	727	1.7%		16	Tennessee	948	2.2%
26	Louisiana	679	1.6%		18	New Jersey	786	1.8%
42	Maine	220	0.5%		19	Oregon	782	1.8%
27	Maryland	606	1.4%		20	Wisconsin	769	1.8%
28	Massachusetts	596	1.4%		21	South Carolina	753	1.8%
8	Michigan	1,354	3.2%		22	Oklahoma	736	1.7%
25	Minnesota	686	1.6%		23	Kentucky	727	1.7%
35	Mississippi	380	0.9%		24	Alabama	715	1.7%
15	Missouri	1,017	2.4%		25	Minnesota	686	1.6%
39	Montana	251	0.6%		26	Louisiana	679	1.6%
39	Nebraska	251	0.6%		27	Maryland	606	1.4%
29	Nevada	573	1.3%		28	Massachusetts	596	1.4%
41	New Hampshire	247	0.6%		29	Nevada	573	1.3%
18	New Jersey	786	1.8%		30	Utah	559	1.3%
33	New Mexico	449	1.0%		31	Arkansas	515	1.2%
5	New York	1,700	4.0%		32	Kansas	455	1.1%
9	North Carolina	1,351	3.2%		33	New Mexico	449	1.0%
46	North Dakota	137	0.3%		34	Iowa	407	1.0%
6	Ohio	1,491	3.5%		35	Mississippi	380	0.9%
22	Oklahoma	736	1.7%		36	Connecticut	379	0.9%
19	Oregon	782	1.8%		37	West Virginia	359	0.8%
4	Pennsylvania	1,817	4.2%		38	Idaho	320	0.7%
50	Rhode Island	113	0.3%		39	Montana	251	0.6%
21	South Carolina	753	1.8%		39	Nebraska	251	0.6%
45	South Dakota	141	0.3%		41	New Hampshire	247	0.6%
16	Tennessee	948	2.2%		42	Maine	220	0.5%
2	Texas	3,254	7.6%		43	Hawaii	204	0.5%
30	Utah	559	1.3%		44	Alaska	167	0.4%
48	Vermont	124	0.3%		45	South Dakota	141	0.3%
12	Virginia	1,122	2.6%		46	North Dakota	137	0.3%
13	Washington	1,119	2.6%		47	Delaware	126	0.3%
37	West Virginia	359	0.8%		48	Vermont	124	0.3%
20	Wisconsin	769	1.8%		49	Wyoming	120	0.3%
49	Wyoming	120	0.3%		50	Rhode Island	113	0.3%
						District of Columbia	52	0.1%

Source: U.S. Department of Health and Human Services, National Center for Health Statistics
"National Vital Statistics Reports" (Vol. 65, No. 4, 2016, http://www.cdc.gov/nchs/deaths.htm)
*Final data by state of residence. Also referred to as "Intentional self-harm."

Age-Adjusted Death Rate by Suicide in 2014

National Rate = 13.0 Deaths per 100,000 Population*

ALPHA ORDER

RANK	STATE	RATE
24	Alabama	14.5
2	Alaska	22.1
13	Arizona	18.0
16	Arkansas	17.3
43	California	10.5
7	Colorado	19.9
46	Connecticut	9.8
33	Delaware	13.2
28	Florida	13.9
38	Georgia	12.6
29	Hawaii	13.8
6	Idaho	20.0
43	Illinois	10.5
25	Indiana	14.3
36	Iowa	12.9
20	Kansas	15.7
19	Kentucky	15.9
25	Louisiana	14.3
20	Maine	15.7
46	Maryland	9.8
49	Massachusetts	8.2
31	Michigan	13.3
41	Minnesota	12.2
40	Mississippi	12.5
18	Missouri	16.3
1	Montana	23.9
30	Nebraska	13.4
8	Nevada	19.6
14	New Hampshire	17.8
48	New Jersey	8.3
3	New Mexico	21.0
50	New York	8.1
35	North Carolina	13.0
14	North Dakota	17.8
38	Ohio	12.6
9	Oklahoma	19.1
11	Oregon	18.6
31	Pennsylvania	13.3
45	Rhode Island	10.1
22	South Carolina	15.2
17	South Dakota	17.1
27	Tennessee	14.1
41	Texas	12.2
5	Utah	20.5
10	Vermont	18.7
36	Virginia	12.9
22	Washington	15.2
12	West Virginia	18.1
34	Wisconsin	13.1
4	Wyoming	20.6

RANK ORDER

RANK	STATE	RATE
1	Montana	23.9
2	Alaska	22.1
3	New Mexico	21.0
4	Wyoming	20.6
5	Utah	20.5
6	Idaho	20.0
7	Colorado	19.9
8	Nevada	19.6
9	Oklahoma	19.1
10	Vermont	18.7
11	Oregon	18.6
12	West Virginia	18.1
13	Arizona	18.0
14	New Hampshire	17.8
14	North Dakota	17.8
16	Arkansas	17.3
17	South Dakota	17.1
18	Missouri	16.3
19	Kentucky	15.9
20	Kansas	15.7
20	Maine	15.7
22	South Carolina	15.2
22	Washington	15.2
24	Alabama	14.5
25	Indiana	14.3
25	Louisiana	14.3
27	Tennessee	14.1
28	Florida	13.9
29	Hawaii	13.8
30	Nebraska	13.4
31	Michigan	13.3
31	Pennsylvania	13.3
33	Delaware	13.2
34	Wisconsin	13.1
35	North Carolina	13.0
36	Iowa	12.9
36	Virginia	12.9
38	Georgia	12.6
38	Ohio	12.6
40	Mississippi	12.5
41	Minnesota	12.2
41	Texas	12.2
43	California	10.5
43	Illinois	10.5
45	Rhode Island	10.1
46	Connecticut	9.8
46	Maryland	9.8
48	New Jersey	8.3
49	Massachusetts	8.2
50	New York	8.1

District of Columbia	7.8

Source: U.S. Department of Health and Human Services, National Center for Health Statistics
"National Vital Statistics Reports" (Vol. 65, No. 4, 2016, http://www.cdc.gov/nchs/deaths.htm)
*Final data by state of residence. Also referred to as "Intentional self-harm." Age-adjusted rates based on the year 2000 standard population.

Deaths by AIDS in 2014

National Total = 6,721 Deaths*

ALPHA ORDER

RANK	STATE	DEATHS	% of USA
15	Alabama	127	1.9%
46	Alaska	3	0.0%
18	Arizona	112	1.7%
27	Arkansas	62	0.9%
2	California	730	10.9%
28	Colorado	53	0.8%
22	Connecticut	75	1.1%
32	Delaware	38	0.6%
1	Florida	890	13.2%
5	Georgia	376	5.6%
37	Hawaii	18	0.3%
40	Idaho	11	0.2%
11	Illinois	178	2.6%
20	Indiana	82	1.2%
35	Iowa	28	0.4%
36	Kansas	19	0.3%
29	Kentucky	50	0.7%
8	Louisiana	198	2.9%
42	Maine	7	0.1%
10	Maryland	195	2.9%
20	Massachusetts	82	1.2%
19	Michigan	100	1.5%
30	Minnesota	41	0.6%
16	Mississippi	126	1.9%
24	Missouri	71	1.1%
43	Montana	6	0.1%
37	Nebraska	18	0.3%
26	Nevada	65	1.0%
46	New Hampshire	3	0.0%
6	New Jersey	270	4.0%
34	New Mexico	29	0.4%
4	New York	635	9.4%
7	North Carolina	218	3.2%
46	North Dakota	3	0.0%
14	Ohio	152	2.3%
23	Oklahoma	72	1.1%
33	Oregon	34	0.5%
9	Pennsylvania	197	2.9%
41	Rhode Island	9	0.1%
12	South Carolina	175	2.6%
44	South Dakota	4	0.1%
13	Tennessee	165	2.5%
3	Texas	677	10.1%
44	Utah	4	0.1%
50	Vermont	1	0.0%
17	Virginia	113	1.7%
25	Washington	68	1.0%
39	West Virginia	14	0.2%
31	Wisconsin	40	0.6%
46	Wyoming	3	0.0%

RANK ORDER

RANK	STATE	DEATHS	% of USA
1	Florida	890	13.2%
2	California	730	10.9%
3	Texas	677	10.1%
4	New York	635	9.4%
5	Georgia	376	5.6%
6	New Jersey	270	4.0%
7	North Carolina	218	3.2%
8	Louisiana	198	2.9%
9	Pennsylvania	197	2.9%
10	Maryland	195	2.9%
11	Illinois	178	2.6%
12	South Carolina	175	2.6%
13	Tennessee	165	2.5%
14	Ohio	152	2.3%
15	Alabama	127	1.9%
16	Mississippi	126	1.9%
17	Virginia	113	1.7%
18	Arizona	112	1.7%
19	Michigan	100	1.5%
20	Indiana	82	1.2%
20	Massachusetts	82	1.2%
22	Connecticut	75	1.1%
23	Oklahoma	72	1.1%
24	Missouri	71	1.1%
25	Washington	68	1.0%
26	Nevada	65	1.0%
27	Arkansas	62	0.9%
28	Colorado	53	0.8%
29	Kentucky	50	0.7%
30	Minnesota	41	0.6%
31	Wisconsin	40	0.6%
32	Delaware	38	0.6%
33	Oregon	34	0.5%
34	New Mexico	29	0.4%
35	Iowa	28	0.4%
36	Kansas	19	0.3%
37	Hawaii	18	0.3%
37	Nebraska	18	0.3%
39	West Virginia	14	0.2%
40	Idaho	11	0.2%
41	Rhode Island	9	0.1%
42	Maine	7	0.1%
43	Montana	6	0.1%
44	South Dakota	4	0.1%
44	Utah	4	0.1%
46	Alaska	3	0.0%
46	New Hampshire	3	0.0%
46	North Dakota	3	0.0%
46	Wyoming	3	0.0%
50	Vermont	1	0.0%
	District of Columbia	74	1.1%

Source: U.S. Department of Health and Human Services, National Center for Health Statistics
"National Vital Statistics Reports" (Vol. 65, No. 4, 2016, http://www.cdc.gov/nchs/deaths.htm)
*Final data by state of residence. AIDS is Acquired Immunodeficiency Syndrome. It is a specific group of diseases or
conditions which are indicative of severe immunosuppression related to infection with the Human Immunodeficiency Virus (HIV).

Age-Adjusted Death Rate by AIDS in 2014

National Rate = 2.0 Deaths per 100,000 Population*

ALPHA ORDER

RANK	STATE	RATE
10	Alabama	2.5
NA	Alaska**	NA
19	Arizona	1.7
15	Arkansas	2.0
17	California	1.8
28	Colorado	1.0
17	Connecticut	1.8
4	Delaware	3.6
3	Florida	4.1
4	Georgia	3.6
NA	Hawaii**	NA
NA	Idaho**	NA
22	Illinois	1.3
24	Indiana	1.2
31	Iowa	0.9
NA	Kansas**	NA
27	Kentucky	1.1
1	Louisiana	4.2
NA	Maine**	NA
7	Maryland	2.9
28	Massachusetts	1.0
28	Michigan	1.0
34	Minnesota	0.7
1	Mississippi	4.2
24	Missouri	1.2
NA	Montana**	NA
NA	Nebraska**	NA
13	Nevada	2.2
NA	New Hampshire**	NA
9	New Jersey	2.6
20	New Mexico	1.4
7	New York	2.9
14	North Carolina	2.1
NA	North Dakota**	NA
22	Ohio	1.3
16	Oklahoma	1.9
33	Oregon	0.8
20	Pennsylvania	1.4
NA	Rhode Island**	NA
6	South Carolina	3.4
NA	South Dakota**	NA
12	Tennessee	2.4
10	Texas	2.5
NA	Utah**	NA
NA	Vermont**	NA
24	Virginia	1.2
31	Washington	0.9
NA	West Virginia**	NA
34	Wisconsin	0.7
NA	Wyoming**	NA

RANK ORDER

RANK	STATE	RATE
1	Louisiana	4.2
1	Mississippi	4.2
3	Florida	4.1
4	Delaware	3.6
4	Georgia	3.6
6	South Carolina	3.4
7	Maryland	2.9
7	New York	2.9
9	New Jersey	2.6
10	Alabama	2.5
10	Texas	2.5
12	Tennessee	2.4
13	Nevada	2.2
14	North Carolina	2.1
15	Arkansas	2.0
16	Oklahoma	1.9
17	California	1.8
17	Connecticut	1.8
19	Arizona	1.7
20	New Mexico	1.4
20	Pennsylvania	1.4
22	Illinois	1.3
22	Ohio	1.3
24	Indiana	1.2
24	Missouri	1.2
24	Virginia	1.2
27	Kentucky	1.1
28	Colorado	1.0
28	Massachusetts	1.0
28	Michigan	1.0
31	Iowa	0.9
31	Washington	0.9
33	Oregon	0.8
34	Minnesota	0.7
34	Wisconsin	0.7
NA	Alaska**	NA
NA	Hawaii**	NA
NA	Idaho**	NA
NA	Kansas**	NA
NA	Maine**	NA
NA	Montana**	NA
NA	Nebraska**	NA
NA	New Hampshire**	NA
NA	North Dakota**	NA
NA	Rhode Island**	NA
NA	South Dakota**	NA
NA	Utah**	NA
NA	Vermont**	NA
NA	West Virginia**	NA
NA	Wyoming**	NA

District of Columbia   11.2

Source: U.S. Department of Health and Human Services, National Center for Health Statistics
   "National Vital Statistics Reports" (Vol. 65, No. 4, 2016, http://www.cdc.gov/nchs/deaths.htm)
*Final data by state of residence. AIDS is Acquired Immunodeficiency Syndrome. It is a specific group of diseases or
conditions which are indicative of severe immunosuppression related to infection with the Human Immunodeficiency Virus (HIV).
Age-adjusted rates based on the year 2000 standard population.
**Insufficient data to determine a reliable rate.

Adult Per Capita Alcohol Consumption in 2014

National Per Capita = 2.6 Gallons Consumed per Adult 21 Years and Older*

ALPHA ORDER

RANK ORDER

RANK	STATE	GALLONS	RANK	STATE	GALLONS
42	Alabama	2.2	1	New Hampshire	5.1
8	Alaska	3.2	2	Delaware	4.0
20	Arizona	2.7	3	North Dakota	3.9
48	Arkansas	2.0	4	Nevada	3.8
27	California	2.6	5	Vermont	3.5
11	Colorado	3.1	6	Montana	3.4
20	Connecticut	2.7	6	Wisconsin	3.4
2	Delaware	4.0	8	Alaska	3.2
16	Florida	2.9	8	Idaho	3.2
42	Georgia	2.2	8	Minnesota	3.2
16	Hawaii	2.9	11	Colorado	3.1
8	Idaho	3.2	11	South Dakota	3.1
27	Illinois	2.6	11	Wyoming	3.1
42	Indiana	2.2	14	Maine	3.0
20	Iowa	2.7	14	Oregon	3.0
42	Kansas	2.2	16	Florida	2.9
47	Kentucky	2.1	16	Hawaii	2.9
16	Louisiana	2.9	16	Louisiana	2.9
14	Maine	3.0	16	Massachusetts	2.9
37	Maryland	2.4	20	Arizona	2.7
16	Massachusetts	2.9	20	Connecticut	2.7
27	Michigan	2.6	20	Iowa	2.7
8	Minnesota	3.2	20	Missouri	2.7
34	Mississippi	2.5	20	New Jersey	2.7
20	Missouri	2.7	20	New Mexico	2.7
6	Montana	3.4	20	Rhode Island	2.7
27	Nebraska	2.6	27	California	2.6
4	Nevada	3.8	27	Illinois	2.6
1	New Hampshire	5.1	27	Michigan	2.6
20	New Jersey	2.7	27	Nebraska	2.6
20	New Mexico	2.7	27	Pennsylvania	2.6
34	New York	2.5	27	South Carolina	2.6
39	North Carolina	2.3	27	Texas	2.6
3	North Dakota	3.9	34	Mississippi	2.5
39	Ohio	2.3	34	New York	2.5
42	Oklahoma	2.2	34	Washington	2.5
14	Oregon	3.0	37	Maryland	2.4
27	Pennsylvania	2.6	37	Virginia	2.4
20	Rhode Island	2.7	39	North Carolina	2.3
27	South Carolina	2.6	39	Ohio	2.3
11	South Dakota	3.1	39	Tennessee	2.3
39	Tennessee	2.3	42	Alabama	2.2
27	Texas	2.6	42	Georgia	2.2
50	Utah	1.6	42	Indiana	2.2
5	Vermont	3.5	42	Kansas	2.2
37	Virginia	2.4	42	Oklahoma	2.2
34	Washington	2.5	47	Kentucky	2.1
48	West Virginia	2.0	48	Arkansas	2.0
6	Wisconsin	3.4	48	West Virginia	2.0
11	Wyoming	3.1	50	Utah	1.6
				District of Columbia	4.3

Source: CQ Press using data from U.S. Dept of Health and Human Services, National Institute on Alcohol Abuse and Alcoholism "Apparent Per Capita Alcohol Consumption, 1977-2014" (https://pubs.niaaa.nih.gov/publications/surveillance.htm)
*This is apparent consumption of actual alcohol, not entire volume of an alcoholic beverage (for example, wine is roughly 11% absolute alcohol content). Apparent consumption is based on several sources which together approximate sales but do not actually measure consumption. Accordingly, figures for some states may be skewed by purchases by nonresidents.

Percent of Adults Who Smoke: 2015

National Median = 17.5% of Adults*

ALPHA ORDER

RANK ORDER

RANK	STATE	PERCENT
10	Alabama	21.4
16	Alaska	19.1
44	Arizona	14.0
3	Arkansas	24.9
49	California	11.7
36	Colorado	15.7
47	Connecticut	13.5
27	Delaware	17.4
35	Florida	15.8
23	Georgia	17.7
43	Hawaii	14.1
46	Idaho	13.8
40	Illinois	15.1
12	Indiana	20.6
21	Iowa	18.1
23	Kansas	17.7
1	Kentucky	26.0
7	Louisiana	21.9
15	Maine	19.5
40	Maryland	15.1
44	Massachusetts	14.0
11	Michigan	20.7
32	Minnesota	16.2
4	Mississippi	22.6
5	Missouri	22.3
19	Montana	18.9
29	Nebraska	17.1
25	Nevada	17.6
34	New Hampshire	15.9
47	New Jersey	13.5
26	New Mexico	17.5
38	New York	15.2
18	North Carolina	19.0
20	North Dakota	18.7
9	Ohio	21.6
6	Oklahoma	22.2
29	Oregon	17.1
21	Pennsylvania	18.1
37	Rhode Island	15.5
14	South Carolina	19.7
13	South Dakota	20.1
7	Tennessee	21.9
38	Texas	15.2
50	Utah	9.1
33	Vermont	16.0
31	Virginia	16.5
42	Washington	15.0
2	West Virginia	25.7
28	Wisconsin	17.3
16	Wyoming	19.1

RANK	STATE	PERCENT
1	Kentucky	26.0
2	West Virginia	25.7
3	Arkansas	24.9
4	Mississippi	22.6
5	Missouri	22.3
6	Oklahoma	22.2
7	Louisiana	21.9
7	Tennessee	21.9
9	Ohio	21.6
10	Alabama	21.4
11	Michigan	20.7
12	Indiana	20.6
13	South Dakota	20.1
14	South Carolina	19.7
15	Maine	19.5
16	Alaska	19.1
16	Wyoming	19.1
18	North Carolina	19.0
19	Montana	18.9
20	North Dakota	18.7
21	Iowa	18.1
21	Pennsylvania	18.1
23	Georgia	17.7
23	Kansas	17.7
25	Nevada	17.6
26	New Mexico	17.5
27	Delaware	17.4
28	Wisconsin	17.3
29	Nebraska	17.1
29	Oregon	17.1
31	Virginia	16.5
32	Minnesota	16.2
33	Vermont	16.0
34	New Hampshire	15.9
35	Florida	15.8
36	Colorado	15.7
37	Rhode Island	15.5
38	New York	15.2
38	Texas	15.2
40	Illinois	15.1
40	Maryland	15.1
42	Washington	15.0
43	Hawaii	14.1
44	Arizona	14.0
44	Massachusetts	14.0
46	Idaho	13.8
47	Connecticut	13.5
47	New Jersey	13.5
49	California	11.7
50	Utah	9.1
	District of Columbia	16.0

Source: U.S. Department of Health and Human Services, Centers for Disease Control and Prevention
"2015 Behavioral Risk Factor Surveillance Summary Prevalence Data" (https://www.cdc.gov/brfss/)
*Persons 18 and older who have smoked more than 100 cigarettes during their lifetime and who currently smoke every day or some days.

Percent of Adults Overweight or Obese: 2015

National Median = 65.3% of Adults*

ALPHA ORDER

RANK	STATE	PERCENT
8	Alabama	68.6
10	Alaska	67.2
28	Arizona	65.3
3	Arkansas	69.5
44	California	60.4
50	Colorado	56.6
42	Connecticut	61.7
14	Delaware	66.9
35	Florida	64.1
26	Georgia	65.5
49	Hawaii	57.0
29	Idaho	65.2
21	Illinois	66.2
16	Indiana	66.5
15	Iowa	66.6
9	Kansas	68.0
10	Kentucky	67.2
4	Louisiana	69.2
16	Maine	66.5
30	Maryland	65.0
46	Massachusetts	59.7
19	Michigan	66.3
39	Minnesota	62.8
2	Mississippi	70.1
19	Missouri	66.3
43	Montana	61.0
12	Nebraska	67.0
31	Nevada	64.7
37	New Hampshire	63.6
38	New Jersey	63.4
33	New Mexico	64.5
48	New York	59.5
25	North Carolina	65.9
12	North Dakota	67.0
16	Ohio	66.5
5	Oklahoma	69.0
32	Oregon	64.6
21	Pennsylvania	66.2
40	Rhode Island	62.7
21	South Carolina	66.2
33	South Dakota	64.5
6	Tennessee	68.7
6	Texas	68.7
46	Utah	59.7
45	Vermont	59.8
35	Virginia	64.1
41	Washington	62.5
1	West Virginia	71.1
24	Wisconsin	66.0
27	Wyoming	65.4

RANK ORDER

RANK	STATE	PERCENT
1	West Virginia	71.1
2	Mississippi	70.1
3	Arkansas	69.5
4	Louisiana	69.2
5	Oklahoma	69.0
6	Tennessee	68.7
6	Texas	68.7
8	Alabama	68.6
9	Kansas	68.0
10	Alaska	67.2
10	Kentucky	67.2
12	Nebraska	67.0
12	North Dakota	67.0
14	Delaware	66.9
15	Iowa	66.6
16	Indiana	66.5
16	Maine	66.5
16	Ohio	66.5
19	Michigan	66.3
19	Missouri	66.3
21	Illinois	66.2
21	Pennsylvania	66.2
21	South Carolina	66.2
24	Wisconsin	66.0
25	North Carolina	65.9
26	Georgia	65.5
27	Wyoming	65.4
28	Arizona	65.3
29	Idaho	65.2
30	Maryland	65.0
31	Nevada	64.7
32	Oregon	64.6
33	New Mexico	64.5
33	South Dakota	64.5
35	Florida	64.1
35	Virginia	64.1
37	New Hampshire	63.6
38	New Jersey	63.4
39	Minnesota	62.8
40	Rhode Island	62.7
41	Washington	62.5
42	Connecticut	61.7
43	Montana	61.0
44	California	60.4
45	Vermont	59.8
46	Massachusetts	59.7
46	Utah	59.7
48	New York	59.5
49	Hawaii	57.0
50	Colorado	56.6

District of Columbia   54.3

Source: CQ Press using data from U.S. Department of Health and Human Services, Centers for Disease Control and Prevention
"2015 Behavioral Risk Factor Surveillance Summary Prevalence Data" (https://www.cdc.gov/brfss/)
*Persons 18 and older. Overweight is defined as a Body Mass Index (BMI) of 25.0 to 29.9 regardless of sex. Obese is a BMI of 30.0 or greater. BMI is a ratio of height to weight. As an example, a person 5' 8" and weighing 165 pounds has a BMI of 25. The same height at 197 pounds has a BMI of 30. See http://www.cdc.gov/healthyweight/assessing/bmi/index.html.

Percent of Children Aged 19 to 35 Months Fully Immunized in 2015

National Percent = 72.2%*

ALPHA ORDER			RANK ORDER		
RANK	STATE	PERCENT	RANK	STATE	PERCENT
35	Alabama	70.6	1	Connecticut	80.6
48	Alaska	66.3	2	North Dakota	80.2
26	Arizona	72.3	3	Delaware	79.3
46	Arkansas	66.6	4	Massachusetts	78.5
17	California	75.0	5	Iowa	77.9
14	Colorado	75.4	6	Rhode Island	77.2
1	Connecticut	80.6	7	Washington	77.1
3	Delaware	79.3	8	Maryland	76.8
46	Florida	66.6	9	New Jersey	76.5
11	Georgia	75.6	10	North Carolina	76.4
20	Hawaii	73.8	11	Georgia	75.6
29	Idaho	71.6	11	South Dakota	75.6
33	Illinois	70.8	11	Vermont	75.6
18	Indiana	74.7	14	Colorado	75.4
5	Iowa	77.9	14	Oklahoma	75.4
16	Kansas	75.2	16	Kansas	75.2
24	Kentucky	73.0	17	California	75.0
33	Louisiana	70.8	18	Indiana	74.7
28	Maine	71.8	19	New Hampshire	74.1
8	Maryland	76.8	20	Hawaii	73.8
4	Massachusetts	78.5	20	Nebraska	73.8
44	Michigan	67.6	22	Wyoming	73.3
23	Minnesota	73.2	23	Minnesota	73.2
35	Mississippi	70.6	24	Kentucky	73.0
32	Missouri	71.0	25	Pennsylvania	72.8
42	Montana	68.1	26	Arizona	72.3
20	Nebraska	73.8	27	New York	71.9
30	Nevada	71.3	28	Maine	71.8
19	New Hampshire	74.1	29	Idaho	71.6
9	New Jersey	76.5	30	Nevada	71.3
37	New Mexico	70.1	31	Texas	71.2
27	New York	71.9	32	Missouri	71.0
10	North Carolina	76.4	33	Illinois	70.8
2	North Dakota	80.2	33	Louisiana	70.8
40	Ohio	68.3	35	Alabama	70.6
14	Oklahoma	75.4	35	Mississippi	70.6
45	Oregon	67.4	37	New Mexico	70.1
25	Pennsylvania	72.8	37	Tennessee	70.1
6	Rhode Island	77.2	39	Wisconsin	68.8
41	South Carolina	68.2	40	Ohio	68.3
11	South Dakota	75.6	41	South Carolina	68.2
37	Tennessee	70.1	42	Montana	68.1
31	Texas	71.2	42	Utah	68.1
42	Utah	68.1	44	Michigan	67.6
11	Vermont	75.6	45	Oregon	67.4
50	Virginia	64.4	46	Arkansas	66.6
7	Washington	77.1	46	Florida	66.6
49	West Virginia	64.9	48	Alaska	66.3
39	Wisconsin	68.8	49	West Virginia	64.9
22	Wyoming	73.3	50	Virginia	64.4
				District of Columbia	76.3

Source: U.S. Department of Health and Human Services, Centers for Disease Control and Prevention
"State Vaccination Coverage Levels" (MMWR, Vol. 65, No. 39, October 7, 2016, http://www.cdc.gov/mmwr/)
*Fully immunized (4:3:1:3:3:1:4 series) children received four doses of DTaP (Diphtheria, Tetanus Toxoids, Pertussis [Whooping Cough]), three doses of Poliovirus Vaccine, one dose of MCV (Measles-Containing Vaccine), full series (3 or 4 doses depending on product type) of Hib (Haemophilus influenzae type b), three doses of Hepatitis B vaccine, one dose of Varicella (chickenpox) vaccine, and four doses of PCV (pneumococcal conjugate vaccine). This differs from previous "fully" immunized tables.

XII. Households and Housing

Households in 2015

National Total = 118,208,250 Households*

ALPHA ORDER

RANK	STATE	HOUSEHOLDS	% of USA
24	Alabama	1,846,390	1.6%
49	Alaska	250,185	0.2%
17	Arizona	2,463,008	2.1%
31	Arkansas	1,144,663	1.0%
1	California	12,896,357	10.9%
22	Colorado	2,074,735	1.8%
29	Connecticut	1,343,703	1.1%
45	Delaware	352,595	0.3%
3	Florida	7,463,184	6.3%
10	Georgia	3,656,407	3.1%
42	Hawaii	445,936	0.4%
39	Idaho	597,421	0.5%
6	Illinois	4,794,523	4.1%
16	Indiana	2,515,143	2.1%
30	Iowa	1,247,249	1.1%
32	Kansas	1,111,582	0.9%
26	Kentucky	1,716,168	1.5%
25	Louisiana	1,737,908	1.5%
40	Maine	545,226	0.5%
20	Maryland	2,177,934	1.8%
14	Massachusetts	2,559,951	2.2%
8	Michigan	3,858,532	3.3%
21	Minnesota	2,147,262	1.8%
33	Mississippi	1,104,371	0.9%
18	Missouri	2,374,180	2.0%
43	Montana	414,804	0.4%
37	Nebraska	744,159	0.6%
34	Nevada	1,042,065	0.9%
41	New Hampshire	517,615	0.4%
11	New Jersey	3,187,963	2.7%
36	New Mexico	761,797	0.6%
4	New York	7,233,694	6.1%
9	North Carolina	3,843,745	3.3%
47	North Dakota	313,475	0.3%
7	Ohio	4,606,655	3.9%
28	Oklahoma	1,465,951	1.2%
27	Oregon	1,553,205	1.3%
5	Pennsylvania	4,956,037	4.2%
44	Rhode Island	407,484	0.3%
23	South Carolina	1,857,768	1.6%
46	South Dakota	339,437	0.3%
15	Tennessee	2,530,260	2.1%
2	Texas	9,421,412	8.0%
35	Utah	930,980	0.8%
48	Vermont	254,865	0.2%
12	Virginia	3,106,895	2.6%
13	Washington	2,728,573	2.3%
38	West Virginia	734,536	0.6%
19	Wisconsin	2,319,538	2.0%
50	Wyoming	228,937	0.2%

RANK ORDER

RANK	STATE	HOUSEHOLDS	% of USA
1	California	12,896,357	10.9%
2	Texas	9,421,412	8.0%
3	Florida	7,463,184	6.3%
4	New York	7,233,694	6.1%
5	Pennsylvania	4,956,037	4.2%
6	Illinois	4,794,523	4.1%
7	Ohio	4,606,655	3.9%
8	Michigan	3,858,532	3.3%
9	North Carolina	3,843,745	3.3%
10	Georgia	3,656,407	3.1%
11	New Jersey	3,187,963	2.7%
12	Virginia	3,106,895	2.6%
13	Washington	2,728,573	2.3%
14	Massachusetts	2,559,951	2.2%
15	Tennessee	2,530,260	2.1%
16	Indiana	2,515,143	2.1%
17	Arizona	2,463,008	2.1%
18	Missouri	2,374,180	2.0%
19	Wisconsin	2,319,538	2.0%
20	Maryland	2,177,934	1.8%
21	Minnesota	2,147,262	1.8%
22	Colorado	2,074,735	1.8%
23	South Carolina	1,857,768	1.6%
24	Alabama	1,846,390	1.6%
25	Louisiana	1,737,908	1.5%
26	Kentucky	1,716,168	1.5%
27	Oregon	1,553,205	1.3%
28	Oklahoma	1,465,951	1.2%
29	Connecticut	1,343,703	1.1%
30	Iowa	1,247,249	1.1%
31	Arkansas	1,144,663	1.0%
32	Kansas	1,111,582	0.9%
33	Mississippi	1,104,371	0.9%
34	Nevada	1,042,065	0.9%
35	Utah	930,980	0.8%
36	New Mexico	761,797	0.6%
37	Nebraska	744,159	0.6%
38	West Virginia	734,536	0.6%
39	Idaho	597,421	0.5%
40	Maine	545,226	0.5%
41	New Hampshire	517,615	0.4%
42	Hawaii	445,936	0.4%
43	Montana	414,804	0.4%
44	Rhode Island	407,484	0.3%
45	Delaware	352,595	0.3%
46	South Dakota	339,437	0.3%
47	North Dakota	313,475	0.3%
48	Vermont	254,865	0.2%
49	Alaska	250,185	0.2%
50	Wyoming	228,937	0.2%
	District of Columbia	281,787	0.2%

Source: U.S. Bureau of the Census
"2015 American Community Survey-Table CP02" (http://www.census.gov/programs-surveys/acs/)
*A household includes all persons who occupy a housing unit. A household consists of a single family, one person living alone, two or more families living together, or any other group of related or unrelated persons who share living arrangements.

Persons per Household in 2015

National Rate = 2.65 Persons per Household*

ALPHA ORDER

RANK	STATE	PERSONS
23	Alabama	2.57
5	Alaska	2.84
10	Arizona	2.71
32	Arkansas	2.53
3	California	2.97
23	Colorado	2.57
20	Connecticut	2.59
18	Delaware	2.61
13	Florida	2.66
8	Georgia	2.72
2	Hawaii	3.11
8	Idaho	2.72
15	Illinois	2.62
25	Indiana	2.56
45	Iowa	2.42
28	Kansas	2.55
34	Kentucky	2.50
18	Louisiana	2.61
48	Maine	2.37
11	Maryland	2.69
25	Massachusetts	2.56
33	Michigan	2.51
37	Minnesota	2.49
15	Mississippi	2.62
37	Missouri	2.49
45	Montana	2.42
41	Nebraska	2.48
7	Nevada	2.74
37	New Hampshire	2.49
6	New Jersey	2.75
12	New Mexico	2.68
13	New York	2.66
28	North Carolina	2.55
50	North Dakota	2.33
42	Ohio	2.45
20	Oklahoma	2.59
31	Oregon	2.54
34	Pennsylvania	2.50
37	Rhode Island	2.49
25	South Carolina	2.56
44	South Dakota	2.43
28	Tennessee	2.55
4	Texas	2.85
1	Utah	3.17
49	Vermont	2.36
15	Virginia	2.62
22	Washington	2.58
43	West Virginia	2.44
45	Wisconsin	2.42
34	Wyoming	2.50

RANK ORDER

RANK	STATE	PERSONS
1	Utah	3.17
2	Hawaii	3.11
3	California	2.97
4	Texas	2.85
5	Alaska	2.84
6	New Jersey	2.75
7	Nevada	2.74
8	Georgia	2.72
8	Idaho	2.72
10	Arizona	2.71
11	Maryland	2.69
12	New Mexico	2.68
13	Florida	2.66
13	New York	2.66
15	Illinois	2.62
15	Mississippi	2.62
15	Virginia	2.62
18	Delaware	2.61
18	Louisiana	2.61
20	Connecticut	2.59
20	Oklahoma	2.59
22	Washington	2.58
23	Alabama	2.57
23	Colorado	2.57
25	Indiana	2.56
25	Massachusetts	2.56
25	South Carolina	2.56
28	Kansas	2.55
28	North Carolina	2.55
28	Tennessee	2.55
31	Oregon	2.54
32	Arkansas	2.53
33	Michigan	2.51
34	Kentucky	2.50
34	Pennsylvania	2.50
34	Wyoming	2.50
37	Minnesota	2.49
37	Missouri	2.49
37	New Hampshire	2.49
37	Rhode Island	2.49
41	Nebraska	2.48
42	Ohio	2.45
43	West Virginia	2.44
44	South Dakota	2.43
45	Iowa	2.42
45	Montana	2.42
45	Wisconsin	2.42
48	Maine	2.37
49	Vermont	2.36
50	North Dakota	2.33
	District of Columbia	2.24

Source: U.S. Bureau of the Census
  "2015 American Community Survey-Table CP02" (http://www.census.gov/programs-surveys/acs/)
*A household includes all persons who occupy a housing unit. A household consists of a single family, one person living alone, two or more families living together, or any other group of related or unrelated persons who share living arrangements.

Percent of Households with One Person in 2015

National Percent = 27.9% of Households*

ALPHA ORDER

RANK	STATE	PERCENT
11	Alabama	29.9
43	Alaska	26.7
36	Arizona	27.6
30	Arkansas	28.4
48	California	24.0
37	Colorado	27.2
28	Connecticut	28.5
44	Delaware	26.6
23	Florida	28.9
42	Georgia	26.9
49	Hawaii	23.4
37	Idaho	27.2
18	Illinois	29.4
20	Indiana	29.1
20	Iowa	29.1
16	Kansas	29.5
28	Kentucky	28.5
3	Louisiana	30.7
14	Maine	29.6
40	Maryland	27.0
25	Massachusetts	28.8
16	Michigan	29.5
30	Minnesota	28.4
30	Mississippi	28.4
13	Missouri	29.7
2	Montana	31.5
10	Nebraska	30.0
27	Nevada	28.7
45	New Hampshire	26.2
46	New Jersey	25.9
4	New Mexico	30.6
9	New York	30.1
25	North Carolina	28.8
5	North Dakota	30.4
6	Ohio	30.3
33	Oklahoma	28.0
35	Oregon	27.9
19	Pennsylvania	29.2
1	Rhode Island	31.8
23	South Carolina	28.9
14	South Dakota	29.6
33	Tennessee	28.0
47	Texas	25.3
50	Utah	19.8
6	Vermont	30.3
39	Virginia	27.1
40	Washington	27.0
6	West Virginia	30.3
20	Wisconsin	29.1
11	Wyoming	29.9

RANK ORDER

RANK	STATE	PERCENT
1	Rhode Island	31.8
2	Montana	31.5
3	Louisiana	30.7
4	New Mexico	30.6
5	North Dakota	30.4
6	Ohio	30.3
6	Vermont	30.3
6	West Virginia	30.3
9	New York	30.1
10	Nebraska	30.0
11	Alabama	29.9
11	Wyoming	29.9
13	Missouri	29.7
14	Maine	29.6
14	South Dakota	29.6
16	Kansas	29.5
16	Michigan	29.5
18	Illinois	29.4
19	Pennsylvania	29.2
20	Indiana	29.1
20	Iowa	29.1
20	Wisconsin	29.1
23	Florida	28.9
23	South Carolina	28.9
25	Massachusetts	28.8
25	North Carolina	28.8
27	Nevada	28.7
28	Connecticut	28.5
28	Kentucky	28.5
30	Arkansas	28.4
30	Minnesota	28.4
30	Mississippi	28.4
33	Oklahoma	28.0
33	Tennessee	28.0
35	Oregon	27.9
36	Arizona	27.6
37	Colorado	27.2
37	Idaho	27.2
39	Virginia	27.1
40	Maryland	27.0
40	Washington	27.0
42	Georgia	26.9
43	Alaska	26.7
44	Delaware	26.6
45	New Hampshire	26.2
46	New Jersey	25.9
47	Texas	25.3
48	California	24.0
49	Hawaii	23.4
50	Utah	19.8

| | District of Columbia | 42.0 |

Source: U.S. Bureau of the Census
"2015 American Community Survey-Table CP02" (http://www.census.gov/programs-surveys/acs/)
*A household includes all persons who occupy a housing unit. A household consists of a single family, one person living alone, two or more families living together, or any other group of related or unrelated persons who share living arrangements.

Percent of Households Headed by Married Couples in 2015

National Percent = 48.0% of Households*

ALPHA ORDER

RANK	STATE	PERCENT
39	Alabama	46.8
28	Alaska	48.1
39	Arizona	46.8
17	Arkansas	49.0
16	California	49.2
11	Colorado	50.0
27	Connecticut	48.2
23	Delaware	48.3
43	Florida	46.2
29	Georgia	47.9
3	Hawaii	52.1
2	Idaho	53.7
36	Illinois	47.7
23	Indiana	48.3
8	Iowa	50.4
8	Kansas	50.4
23	Kentucky	48.3
49	Louisiana	43.0
21	Maine	48.5
29	Maryland	47.9
42	Massachusetts	46.4
38	Michigan	47.2
7	Minnesota	50.8
46	Mississippi	43.9
29	Missouri	47.9
19	Montana	48.9
15	Nebraska	49.6
47	Nevada	43.8
4	New Hampshire	52.0
5	New Jersey	51.2
45	New Mexico	44.9
48	New York	43.6
37	North Carolina	47.6
29	North Dakota	47.9
44	Ohio	46.1
20	Oklahoma	48.7
23	Oregon	48.3
34	Pennsylvania	47.8
50	Rhode Island	42.9
41	South Carolina	46.7
10	South Dakota	50.2
29	Tennessee	47.9
11	Texas	50.0
1	Utah	60.7
21	Vermont	48.5
14	Virginia	49.9
11	Washington	50.0
34	West Virginia	47.8
17	Wisconsin	49.0
5	Wyoming	51.2

RANK ORDER

RANK	STATE	PERCENT
1	Utah	60.7
2	Idaho	53.7
3	Hawaii	52.1
4	New Hampshire	52.0
5	New Jersey	51.2
5	Wyoming	51.2
7	Minnesota	50.8
8	Iowa	50.4
8	Kansas	50.4
10	South Dakota	50.2
11	Colorado	50.0
11	Texas	50.0
11	Washington	50.0
14	Virginia	49.9
15	Nebraska	49.6
16	California	49.2
17	Arkansas	49.0
17	Wisconsin	49.0
19	Montana	48.9
20	Oklahoma	48.7
21	Maine	48.5
21	Vermont	48.5
23	Delaware	48.3
23	Indiana	48.3
23	Kentucky	48.3
23	Oregon	48.3
27	Connecticut	48.2
28	Alaska	48.1
29	Georgia	47.9
29	Maryland	47.9
29	Missouri	47.9
29	North Dakota	47.9
29	Tennessee	47.9
34	Pennsylvania	47.8
34	West Virginia	47.8
36	Illinois	47.7
37	North Carolina	47.6
38	Michigan	47.2
39	Alabama	46.8
39	Arizona	46.8
41	South Carolina	46.7
42	Massachusetts	46.4
43	Florida	46.2
44	Ohio	46.1
45	New Mexico	44.9
46	Mississippi	43.9
47	Nevada	43.8
48	New York	43.6
49	Louisiana	43.0
50	Rhode Island	42.9

| | District of Columbia | 25.5 |

Source: U.S. Bureau of the Census
  "2015 American Community Survey-Table CP02" (http://www.census.gov/programs-surveys/acs/)
*A household includes all persons who occupy a housing unit. A household consists of a single family, one person living alone, two or more families living together, or any other group of related or unrelated persons who share living arrangements. Includes married same-sex couple households.

Percent of Households Headed by Single Mothers in 2015

National Percent = 6.8% of Households*

ALPHA ORDER

RANK	STATE	PERCENT
5	Alabama	7.9
8	Alaska	7.3
17	Arizona	6.9
17	Arkansas	6.9
26	California	6.6
43	Colorado	5.5
17	Connecticut	6.9
8	Delaware	7.3
22	Florida	6.7
3	Georgia	8.2
50	Hawaii	4.2
38	Idaho	5.8
22	Illinois	6.7
17	Indiana	6.9
38	Iowa	5.8
33	Kansas	6.1
22	Kentucky	6.7
2	Louisiana	8.7
38	Maine	5.8
17	Maryland	6.9
26	Massachusetts	6.6
22	Michigan	6.7
34	Minnesota	5.9
1	Mississippi	9.7
26	Missouri	6.6
47	Montana	4.8
34	Nebraska	5.9
10	Nevada	7.2
44	New Hampshire	5.3
26	New Jersey	6.6
10	New Mexico	7.2
15	New York	7.0
13	North Carolina	7.1
46	North Dakota	5.0
10	Ohio	7.2
15	Oklahoma	7.0
34	Oregon	5.9
30	Pennsylvania	6.4
6	Rhode Island	7.8
7	South Carolina	7.5
32	South Dakota	6.2
13	Tennessee	7.1
4	Texas	8.0
45	Utah	5.2
48	Vermont	4.5
30	Virginia	6.4
42	Washington	5.7
38	West Virginia	5.8
34	Wisconsin	5.9
48	Wyoming	4.5

RANK ORDER

RANK	STATE	PERCENT
1	Mississippi	9.7
2	Louisiana	8.7
3	Georgia	8.2
4	Texas	8.0
5	Alabama	7.9
6	Rhode Island	7.8
7	South Carolina	7.5
8	Alaska	7.3
8	Delaware	7.3
10	Nevada	7.2
10	New Mexico	7.2
10	Ohio	7.2
13	North Carolina	7.1
13	Tennessee	7.1
15	New York	7.0
15	Oklahoma	7.0
17	Arizona	6.9
17	Arkansas	6.9
17	Connecticut	6.9
17	Indiana	6.9
17	Maryland	6.9
22	Florida	6.7
22	Illinois	6.7
22	Kentucky	6.7
22	Michigan	6.7
26	California	6.6
26	Massachusetts	6.6
26	Missouri	6.6
26	New Jersey	6.6
30	Pennsylvania	6.4
30	Virginia	6.4
32	South Dakota	6.2
33	Kansas	6.1
34	Minnesota	5.9
34	Nebraska	5.9
34	Oregon	5.9
34	Wisconsin	5.9
38	Idaho	5.8
38	Iowa	5.8
38	Maine	5.8
38	West Virginia	5.8
42	Washington	5.7
43	Colorado	5.5
44	New Hampshire	5.3
45	Utah	5.2
46	North Dakota	5.0
47	Montana	4.8
48	Vermont	4.5
48	Wyoming	4.5
50	Hawaii	4.2

	District of Columbia	7.8

Source: U.S. Bureau of the Census
   "2015 American Community Survey-Table CP02" (http://www.census.gov/programs-surveys/acs/)
*No spouse present in household with children under 18 years old. A household includes all persons who occupy a housing unit.
A household consists of a single family, one person living alone, two or more families living together, or any other group of
related or unrelated persons who share living arrangements.

Percent of Households Headed by Single Fathers in 2015

National Percent = 2.3% of Households*

RANK	STATE	PERCENT
44	Alabama	1.9
1	Alaska	3.6
5	Arizona	2.8
24	Arkansas	2.3
8	California	2.6
16	Colorado	2.4
48	Connecticut	1.8
36	Delaware	2.1
29	Florida	2.2
29	Georgia	2.2
44	Hawaii	1.9
16	Idaho	2.4
40	Illinois	2.0
13	Indiana	2.5
8	Iowa	2.6
13	Kansas	2.5
16	Kentucky	2.4
16	Louisiana	2.4
6	Maine	2.7
24	Maryland	2.3
50	Massachusetts	1.6
24	Michigan	2.3
13	Minnesota	2.5
16	Mississippi	2.4
29	Missouri	2.2
29	Montana	2.2
29	Nebraska	2.2
3	Nevada	3.0
48	New Hampshire	1.8
40	New Jersey	2.0
4	New Mexico	2.9
36	New York	2.1
29	North Carolina	2.2
8	North Dakota	2.6
24	Ohio	2.3
6	Oklahoma	2.7
29	Oregon	2.2
36	Pennsylvania	2.1
44	Rhode Island	1.9
44	South Carolina	1.9
8	South Dakota	2.6
24	Tennessee	2.3
16	Texas	2.4
36	Utah	2.1
40	Vermont	2.0
40	Virginia	2.0
16	Washington	2.4
16	West Virginia	2.4
8	Wisconsin	2.6
2	Wyoming	3.4

RANK	STATE	PERCENT
1	Alaska	3.6
2	Wyoming	3.4
3	Nevada	3.0
4	New Mexico	2.9
5	Arizona	2.8
6	Maine	2.7
6	Oklahoma	2.7
8	California	2.6
8	Iowa	2.6
8	North Dakota	2.6
8	South Dakota	2.6
8	Wisconsin	2.6
13	Indiana	2.5
13	Kansas	2.5
13	Minnesota	2.5
16	Colorado	2.4
16	Idaho	2.4
16	Kentucky	2.4
16	Louisiana	2.4
16	Mississippi	2.4
16	Texas	2.4
16	Washington	2.4
16	West Virginia	2.4
24	Arkansas	2.3
24	Maryland	2.3
24	Michigan	2.3
24	Ohio	2.3
24	Tennessee	2.3
29	Florida	2.2
29	Georgia	2.2
29	Missouri	2.2
29	Montana	2.2
29	Nebraska	2.2
29	North Carolina	2.2
29	Oregon	2.2
36	Delaware	2.1
36	New York	2.1
36	Pennsylvania	2.1
36	Utah	2.1
40	Illinois	2.0
40	New Jersey	2.0
40	Vermont	2.0
40	Virginia	2.0
44	Alabama	1.9
44	Hawaii	1.9
44	Rhode Island	1.9
44	South Carolina	1.9
48	Connecticut	1.8
48	New Hampshire	1.8
50	Massachusetts	1.6
	District of Columbia	1.6

Source: U.S. Bureau of the Census
    "2015 American Community Survey-Table CP02" (http://www.census.gov/programs-surveys/acs/)
*No spouse present in household with children under 18 years old. A household includes all persons who occupy a housing unit.
A household consists of a single family, one person living alone, two or more families living together, or any other group of
related or unrelated persons who share living arrangements.

Same-Sex Couple Households in 2014

National Total = 783,100 Households*

RANK	STATE	HOUSEHOLDS	% of USA
32	Alabama	6,797	0.9%
46	Alaska	1,816	0.2%
15	Arizona	17,515	2.2%
35	Arkansas	5,399	0.7%
1	California	109,296	14.0%
17	Colorado	15,402	2.0%
25	Connecticut	9,701	1.2%
38	Delaware	3,850	0.5%
4	Florida	55,372	7.1%
8	Georgia	24,707	3.2%
39	Hawaii	3,831	0.5%
43	Idaho	2,599	0.3%
5	Illinois	29,115	3.7%
16	Indiana	15,431	2.0%
30	Iowa	7,080	0.9%
33	Kansas	5,674	0.7%
27	Kentucky	8,310	1.1%
26	Louisiana	8,906	1.1%
34	Maine	5,442	0.7%
18	Maryland	14,977	1.9%
9	Massachusetts	24,461	3.1%
14	Michigan	18,742	2.4%
19	Minnesota	14,539	1.9%
40	Mississippi	3,628	0.5%
23	Missouri	12,371	1.6%
47	Montana	1,235	0.2%
41	Nebraska	3,349	0.4%
28	Nevada	7,365	0.9%
37	New Hampshire	4,166	0.5%
12	New Jersey	20,061	2.6%
31	New Mexico	6,838	0.9%
2	New York	59,405	7.6%
10	North Carolina	23,127	3.0%
50	North Dakota	774	0.1%
7	Ohio	26,021	3.3%
29	Oklahoma	7,283	0.9%
20	Oregon	13,380	1.7%
6	Pennsylvania	28,654	3.7%
42	Rhode Island	2,917	0.4%
24	South Carolina	9,908	1.3%
48	South Dakota	1,094	0.1%
21	Tennessee	13,140	1.7%
3	Texas	58,654	7.5%
36	Utah	5,099	0.7%
44	Vermont	2,433	0.3%
13	Virginia	19,027	2.4%
11	Washington	22,981	2.9%
45	West Virginia	2,353	0.3%
22	Wisconsin	12,706	1.6%
49	Wyoming	945	0.1%

RANK	STATE	HOUSEHOLDS	% of USA
1	California	109,296	14.0%
2	New York	59,405	7.6%
3	Texas	58,654	7.5%
4	Florida	55,372	7.1%
5	Illinois	29,115	3.7%
6	Pennsylvania	28,654	3.7%
7	Ohio	26,021	3.3%
8	Georgia	24,707	3.2%
9	Massachusetts	24,461	3.1%
10	North Carolina	23,127	3.0%
11	Washington	22,981	2.9%
12	New Jersey	20,061	2.6%
13	Virginia	19,027	2.4%
14	Michigan	18,742	2.4%
15	Arizona	17,515	2.2%
16	Indiana	15,431	2.0%
17	Colorado	15,402	2.0%
18	Maryland	14,977	1.9%
19	Minnesota	14,539	1.9%
20	Oregon	13,380	1.7%
21	Tennessee	13,140	1.7%
22	Wisconsin	12,706	1.6%
23	Missouri	12,371	1.6%
24	South Carolina	9,908	1.3%
25	Connecticut	9,701	1.2%
26	Louisiana	8,906	1.1%
27	Kentucky	8,310	1.1%
28	Nevada	7,365	0.9%
29	Oklahoma	7,283	0.9%
30	Iowa	7,080	0.9%
31	New Mexico	6,838	0.9%
32	Alabama	6,797	0.9%
33	Kansas	5,674	0.7%
34	Maine	5,442	0.7%
35	Arkansas	5,399	0.7%
36	Utah	5,099	0.7%
37	New Hampshire	4,166	0.5%
38	Delaware	3,850	0.5%
39	Hawaii	3,831	0.5%
40	Mississippi	3,628	0.5%
41	Nebraska	3,349	0.4%
42	Rhode Island	2,917	0.4%
43	Idaho	2,599	0.3%
44	Vermont	2,433	0.3%
45	West Virginia	2,353	0.3%
46	Alaska	1,816	0.2%
47	Montana	1,235	0.2%
48	South Dakota	1,094	0.1%
49	Wyoming	945	0.1%
50	North Dakota	774	0.1%
	District of Columbia	5,224	0.7%

Source: U.S. Bureau of the Census
"Same Sex Couples Main" (http://www.census.gov/hhes/samesex/)
*The total is comprised of 334,829 married couples and 448,271 unmarried couples. Male couples are 377,903 of the households.
Female couples are 405,197 of the households.

Percent of Same-Sex Household Couples Who Are Married: 2014

National Percent = 42.8% of Same-Sex Households*

ALPHA ORDER

RANK	STATE	PERCENT
24	Alabama	43.2
50	Alaska	27.4
43	Arizona	33.9
17	Arkansas	45.6
12	California	48.8
35	Colorado	36.2
4	Connecticut	60.9
9	Delaware	52.3
44	Florida	33.2
47	Georgia	29.2
15	Hawaii	46.2
49	Idaho	28.2
21	Illinois	44.1
33	Indiana	36.9
3	Iowa	65.7
20	Kansas	44.8
42	Kentucky	34.2
37	Louisiana	35.8
18	Maine	45.5
6	Maryland	56.9
7	Massachusetts	56.5
39	Michigan	34.8
10	Minnesota	52.0
21	Mississippi	44.1
29	Missouri	39.9
23	Montana	43.7
48	Nebraska	28.7
45	Nevada	30.8
4	New Hampshire	60.9
14	New Jersey	47.9
38	New Mexico	35.3
11	New York	49.2
36	North Carolina	36.0
19	North Dakota	45.1
41	Ohio	34.5
13	Oklahoma	48.2
16	Oregon	46.0
28	Pennsylvania	40.7
31	Rhode Island	37.3
26	South Carolina	42.0
46	South Dakota	30.3
32	Tennessee	37.0
40	Texas	34.6
2	Utah	65.8
1	Vermont	66.8
27	Virginia	40.9
8	Washington	54.5
25	West Virginia	42.7
34	Wisconsin	36.5
30	Wyoming	39.4

RANK ORDER

RANK	STATE	PERCENT
1	Vermont	66.8
2	Utah	65.8
3	Iowa	65.7
4	Connecticut	60.9
4	New Hampshire	60.9
6	Maryland	56.9
7	Massachusetts	56.5
8	Washington	54.5
9	Delaware	52.3
10	Minnesota	52.0
11	New York	49.2
12	California	48.8
13	Oklahoma	48.2
14	New Jersey	47.9
15	Hawaii	46.2
16	Oregon	46.0
17	Arkansas	45.6
18	Maine	45.5
19	North Dakota	45.1
20	Kansas	44.8
21	Illinois	44.1
21	Mississippi	44.1
23	Montana	43.7
24	Alabama	43.2
25	West Virginia	42.7
26	South Carolina	42.0
27	Virginia	40.9
28	Pennsylvania	40.7
29	Missouri	39.9
30	Wyoming	39.4
31	Rhode Island	37.3
32	Tennessee	37.0
33	Indiana	36.9
34	Wisconsin	36.5
35	Colorado	36.2
36	North Carolina	36.0
37	Louisiana	35.8
38	New Mexico	35.3
39	Michigan	34.8
40	Texas	34.6
41	Ohio	34.5
42	Kentucky	34.2
43	Arizona	33.9
44	Florida	33.2
45	Nevada	30.8
46	South Dakota	30.3
47	Georgia	29.2
48	Nebraska	28.7
49	Idaho	28.2
50	Alaska	27.4
	District of Columbia	45.7

Source: U.S. Bureau of the Census
   "Same Sex Couples Main" (http://www.census.gov/hhes/samesex/)
*Male-couple households are 43.2 percent married. Female couple households are 42.3 percent married.

Housing Units in 2015

National Total = 134,793,665 Housing Units*

ALPHA ORDER					RANK ORDER			
RANK	STATE	HOUSING UNITS	% of USA		RANK	STATE	HOUSING UNITS	% of USA
23	Alabama	2,218,391	1.6%		1	California	13,988,399	10.4%
49	Alaska	309,453	0.2%		2	Texas	10,588,236	7.9%
14	Arizona	2,929,173	2.2%		3	Florida	9,210,287	6.8%
31	Arkansas	1,347,598	1.0%		4	New York	8,207,161	6.1%
1	California	13,988,399	10.4%		5	Pennsylvania	5,603,051	4.2%
22	Colorado	2,309,122	1.7%		6	Illinois	5,317,618	3.9%
29	Connecticut	1,496,056	1.1%		7	Ohio	5,156,546	3.8%
45	Delaware	421,734	0.3%		8	Michigan	4,550,324	3.4%
3	Florida	9,210,287	6.8%		9	North Carolina	4,491,090	3.3%
10	Georgia	4,182,228	3.1%		10	Georgia	4,182,228	3.1%
42	Hawaii	532,413	0.4%		11	New Jersey	3,593,722	2.7%
40	Idaho	692,482	0.5%		12	Virginia	3,468,952	2.6%
6	Illinois	5,317,618	3.9%		13	Washington	2,991,584	2.2%
17	Indiana	2,841,450	2.1%		14	Arizona	2,929,173	2.2%
30	Iowa	1,369,379	1.0%		15	Tennessee	2,892,407	2.1%
33	Kansas	1,253,889	0.9%		16	Massachusetts	2,845,805	2.1%
26	Kentucky	1,957,133	1.5%		17	Indiana	2,841,450	2.1%
25	Louisiana	2,024,737	1.5%		18	Missouri	2,746,644	2.0%
39	Maine	729,392	0.5%		19	Wisconsin	2,656,669	2.0%
20	Maryland	2,434,465	1.8%		20	Maryland	2,434,465	1.8%
16	Massachusetts	2,845,805	2.1%		21	Minnesota	2,397,081	1.8%
8	Michigan	4,550,324	3.4%		22	Colorado	2,309,122	1.7%
21	Minnesota	2,397,081	1.8%		23	Alabama	2,218,391	1.6%
32	Mississippi	1,300,932	1.0%		24	South Carolina	2,210,150	1.6%
18	Missouri	2,746,644	2.0%		25	Louisiana	2,024,737	1.5%
43	Montana	494,222	0.4%		26	Kentucky	1,957,133	1.5%
38	Nebraska	820,925	0.6%		27	Oregon	1,718,509	1.3%
34	Nevada	1,209,864	0.9%		28	Oklahoma	1,711,515	1.3%
41	New Hampshire	622,604	0.5%		29	Connecticut	1,496,056	1.1%
11	New Jersey	3,593,722	2.7%		30	Iowa	1,369,379	1.0%
36	New Mexico	914,979	0.7%		31	Arkansas	1,347,598	1.0%
4	New York	8,207,161	6.1%		32	Mississippi	1,300,932	1.0%
9	North Carolina	4,491,090	3.3%		33	Kansas	1,253,889	0.9%
47	North Dakota	362,889	0.3%		34	Nevada	1,209,864	0.9%
7	Ohio	5,156,546	3.8%		35	Utah	1,038,065	0.8%
28	Oklahoma	1,711,515	1.3%		36	New Mexico	914,979	0.7%
27	Oregon	1,718,509	1.3%		37	West Virginia	885,539	0.7%
5	Pennsylvania	5,603,051	4.2%		38	Nebraska	820,925	0.6%
44	Rhode Island	462,555	0.3%		39	Maine	729,392	0.5%
24	South Carolina	2,210,150	1.6%		40	Idaho	692,482	0.5%
46	South Dakota	380,307	0.3%		41	New Hampshire	622,604	0.5%
15	Tennessee	2,892,407	2.1%		42	Hawaii	532,413	0.4%
2	Texas	10,588,236	7.9%		43	Montana	494,222	0.4%
35	Utah	1,038,065	0.8%		44	Rhode Island	462,555	0.3%
48	Vermont	326,874	0.2%		45	Delaware	421,734	0.3%
12	Virginia	3,468,952	2.6%		46	South Dakota	380,307	0.3%
13	Washington	2,991,584	2.2%		47	North Dakota	362,889	0.3%
37	West Virginia	885,539	0.7%		48	Vermont	326,874	0.2%
19	Wisconsin	2,656,669	2.0%		49	Alaska	309,453	0.2%
50	Wyoming	269,469	0.2%		50	Wyoming	269,469	0.2%
						District of Columbia	309,596	0.2%

Source: U.S. Bureau of the Census
"2015 American Community Survey-Table B25001" (http://www.census.gov/programs-surveys/acs/)
*A housing unit is a house, an apartment, a mobile home, a group of rooms, or a single room that is occupied (or if vacant, is intended for occupancy) as separate living quarters. Separate living quarters are those in which the occupants live and eat separately from any other persons in the building and which have direct access from the outside of the building or through a common hall.

Housing Units per Square Mile in 2015

National Average = 38.1 Housing Units*

ALPHA ORDER

RANK	STATE	RATE
26	Alabama	43.7
50	Alaska	0.5
34	Arizona	25.8
33	Arkansas	25.9
13	California	89.7
38	Colorado	22.3
4	Connecticut	308.8
6	Delaware	215.8
8	Florida	170.8
19	Georgia	72.2
15	Hawaii	82.9
44	Idaho	8.4
11	Illinois	95.7
17	Indiana	79.2
36	Iowa	24.5
40	Kansas	15.3
22	Kentucky	49.3
24	Louisiana	46.5
37	Maine	23.6
5	Maryland	249.1
3	Massachusetts	363.0
16	Michigan	80.1
31	Minnesota	30.1
32	Mississippi	27.7
28	Missouri	39.9
48	Montana	3.4
43	Nebraska	10.7
42	Nevada	11.0
21	New Hampshire	69.4
1	New Jersey	484.5
45	New Mexico	7.5
7	New York	173.8
12	North Carolina	92.2
46	North Dakota	5.3
9	Ohio	125.9
35	Oklahoma	24.9
39	Oregon	17.9
10	Pennsylvania	125.0
2	Rhode Island	442.6
18	South Carolina	73.4
47	South Dakota	5.0
20	Tennessee	70.2
27	Texas	40.4
41	Utah	12.6
30	Vermont	35.3
14	Virginia	87.6
25	Washington	45.0
29	West Virginia	36.8
23	Wisconsin	48.9
49	Wyoming	2.8

RANK ORDER

RANK	STATE	RATE
1	New Jersey	484.5
2	Rhode Island	442.6
3	Massachusetts	363.0
4	Connecticut	308.8
5	Maryland	249.1
6	Delaware	215.8
7	New York	173.8
8	Florida	170.8
9	Ohio	125.9
10	Pennsylvania	125.0
11	Illinois	95.7
12	North Carolina	92.2
13	California	89.7
14	Virginia	87.6
15	Hawaii	82.9
16	Michigan	80.1
17	Indiana	79.2
18	South Carolina	73.4
19	Georgia	72.2
20	Tennessee	70.2
21	New Hampshire	69.4
22	Kentucky	49.3
23	Wisconsin	48.9
24	Louisiana	46.5
25	Washington	45.0
26	Alabama	43.7
27	Texas	40.4
28	Missouri	39.9
29	West Virginia	36.8
30	Vermont	35.3
31	Minnesota	30.1
32	Mississippi	27.7
33	Arkansas	25.9
34	Arizona	25.8
35	Oklahoma	24.9
36	Iowa	24.5
37	Maine	23.6
38	Colorado	22.3
39	Oregon	17.9
40	Kansas	15.3
41	Utah	12.6
42	Nevada	11.0
43	Nebraska	10.7
44	Idaho	8.4
45	New Mexico	7.5
46	North Dakota	5.3
47	South Dakota	5.0
48	Montana	3.4
49	Wyoming	2.8
50	Alaska	0.5

District of Columbia   5,075.3

Source: CQ Press using data from U.S. Bureau of the Census
"2015 American Community Survey-Table B25001" (http://www.census.gov/programs-surveys/acs/)
*Based on land area. A housing unit is a house, an apartment, a mobile home, a group of rooms, or a single room that is occupied (or if vacant, is intended for occupancy) as separate living quarters. Separate living quarters are those in which the occupants live and eat separately from any other persons in the building and which have direct access from the outside of the building or through a common hall.

Percent of Housing Units That Are Owner-Occupied in 2015

National Percent = 63.0% of Housing Units*

ALPHA ORDER

RANK	STATE	PERCENT
16	Alabama	67.9
34	Alaska	63.9
40	Arizona	61.9
31	Arkansas	65.2
49	California	53.6
37	Colorado	63.7
23	Connecticut	66.2
5	Delaware	70.8
36	Florida	63.8
41	Georgia	61.8
47	Hawaii	56.6
9	Idaho	69.0
29	Illinois	65.3
12	Indiana	68.2
6	Iowa	70.7
21	Kansas	66.4
22	Kentucky	66.3
33	Louisiana	64.6
2	Maine	71.0
25	Maryland	65.9
42	Massachusetts	61.7
8	Michigan	70.4
3	Minnesota	70.9
18	Mississippi	67.4
24	Missouri	66.1
20	Montana	66.7
25	Nebraska	65.9
48	Nevada	54.0
3	New Hampshire	70.9
38	New Jersey	63.0
17	New Mexico	67.5
50	New York	53.1
34	North Carolina	63.9
42	North Dakota	61.7
28	Ohio	65.4
29	Oklahoma	65.3
44	Oregon	61.1
11	Pennsylvania	68.7
46	Rhode Island	59.0
14	South Carolina	68.1
12	South Dakota	68.2
27	Tennessee	65.8
44	Texas	61.1
10	Utah	68.9
6	Vermont	70.7
32	Virginia	65.0
39	Washington	62.4
1	West Virginia	72.3
19	Wisconsin	66.8
15	Wyoming	68.0

RANK ORDER

RANK	STATE	PERCENT
1	West Virginia	72.3
2	Maine	71.0
3	Minnesota	70.9
3	New Hampshire	70.9
5	Delaware	70.8
6	Iowa	70.7
6	Vermont	70.7
8	Michigan	70.4
9	Idaho	69.0
10	Utah	68.9
11	Pennsylvania	68.7
12	Indiana	68.2
12	South Dakota	68.2
14	South Carolina	68.1
15	Wyoming	68.0
16	Alabama	67.9
17	New Mexico	67.5
18	Mississippi	67.4
19	Wisconsin	66.8
20	Montana	66.7
21	Kansas	66.4
22	Kentucky	66.3
23	Connecticut	66.2
24	Missouri	66.1
25	Maryland	65.9
25	Nebraska	65.9
27	Tennessee	65.8
28	Ohio	65.4
29	Illinois	65.3
29	Oklahoma	65.3
31	Arkansas	65.2
32	Virginia	65.0
33	Louisiana	64.6
34	Alaska	63.9
34	North Carolina	63.9
36	Florida	63.8
37	Colorado	63.7
38	New Jersey	63.0
39	Washington	62.4
40	Arizona	61.9
41	Georgia	61.8
42	Massachusetts	61.7
42	North Dakota	61.7
44	Oregon	61.1
44	Texas	61.1
46	Rhode Island	59.0
47	Hawaii	56.6
48	Nevada	54.0
49	California	53.6
50	New York	53.1
	District of Columbia	39.9

Source: U.S. Bureau of the Census
   "2015 American Community Survey-Table R2512" (http://www.census.gov/programs-surveys/acs/)
*For occupied housing units.

New Housing Units Authorized in 2016

National Total = 1,190,191 Units*

ALPHA ORDER

RANK	STATE	UNITS	% of USA
28	Alabama	14,471	1.2%
49	Alaska	1,503	0.1%
9	Arizona	35,900	3.0%
33	Arkansas	9,358	0.8%
3	California	100,265	8.4%
7	Colorado	38,393	3.2%
39	Connecticut	5,341	0.4%
37	Delaware	5,768	0.5%
2	Florida	113,912	9.6%
5	Georgia	51,052	4.3%
45	Hawaii	3,375	0.3%
32	Idaho	11,476	1.0%
16	Illinois	22,508	1.9%
23	Indiana	18,317	1.5%
29	Iowa	13,806	1.2%
34	Kansas	8,999	0.8%
30	Kentucky	12,798	1.1%
27	Louisiana	14,678	1.2%
41	Maine	4,164	0.3%
25	Maryland	16,925	1.4%
26	Massachusetts	15,407	1.3%
17	Michigan	22,426	1.9%
14	Minnesota	24,263	2.0%
36	Mississippi	6,900	0.6%
20	Missouri	19,004	1.6%
42	Montana	4,086	0.3%
35	Nebraska	8,108	0.7%
24	Nevada	17,951	1.5%
44	New Hampshire	3,607	0.3%
13	New Jersey	26,751	2.2%
40	New Mexico	4,856	0.4%
10	New York	34,387	2.9%
4	North Carolina	57,090	4.8%
43	North Dakota	3,968	0.3%
18	Ohio	22,269	1.9%
31	Oklahoma	12,521	1.1%
21	Oregon	18,969	1.6%
19	Pennsylvania	20,761	1.7%
50	Rhode Island	1,192	0.1%
11	South Carolina	31,356	2.6%
38	South Dakota	5,464	0.5%
8	Tennessee	36,864	3.1%
1	Texas	162,323	13.6%
15	Utah	22,935	1.9%
47	Vermont	1,832	0.2%
12	Virginia	31,067	2.6%
6	Washington	43,239	3.6%
46	West Virginia	2,525	0.2%
22	Wisconsin	18,706	1.6%
48	Wyoming	1,665	0.1%

RANK ORDER

RANK	STATE	UNITS	% of USA
1	Texas	162,323	13.6%
2	Florida	113,912	9.6%
3	California	100,265	8.4%
4	North Carolina	57,090	4.8%
5	Georgia	51,052	4.3%
6	Washington	43,239	3.6%
7	Colorado	38,393	3.2%
8	Tennessee	36,864	3.1%
9	Arizona	35,900	3.0%
10	New York	34,387	2.9%
11	South Carolina	31,356	2.6%
12	Virginia	31,067	2.6%
13	New Jersey	26,751	2.2%
14	Minnesota	24,263	2.0%
15	Utah	22,935	1.9%
16	Illinois	22,508	1.9%
17	Michigan	22,426	1.9%
18	Ohio	22,269	1.9%
19	Pennsylvania	20,761	1.7%
20	Missouri	19,004	1.6%
21	Oregon	18,969	1.6%
22	Wisconsin	18,706	1.6%
23	Indiana	18,317	1.5%
24	Nevada	17,951	1.5%
25	Maryland	16,925	1.4%
26	Massachusetts	15,407	1.3%
27	Louisiana	14,678	1.2%
28	Alabama	14,471	1.2%
29	Iowa	13,806	1.2%
30	Kentucky	12,798	1.1%
31	Oklahoma	12,521	1.1%
32	Idaho	11,476	1.0%
33	Arkansas	9,358	0.8%
34	Kansas	8,999	0.8%
35	Nebraska	8,108	0.7%
36	Mississippi	6,900	0.6%
37	Delaware	5,768	0.5%
38	South Dakota	5,464	0.5%
39	Connecticut	5,341	0.4%
40	New Mexico	4,856	0.4%
41	Maine	4,164	0.3%
42	Montana	4,086	0.3%
43	North Dakota	3,968	0.3%
44	New Hampshire	3,607	0.3%
45	Hawaii	3,375	0.3%
46	West Virginia	2,525	0.2%
47	Vermont	1,832	0.2%
48	Wyoming	1,665	0.1%
49	Alaska	1,503	0.1%
50	Rhode Island	1,192	0.1%
	District of Columbia	4,690	0.4%

Source: U.S. Bureau of the Census

"Building Permits Survey" (https://www.census.gov/construction/bps/stateannual.html)

*Preliminary and unadjusted year-to-date monthly data as of December 2016. Includes single and multifamily privately owned units. All places issuing building permits for privately owned residential structures. More than 98 percent of all privately owned residential buildings constructed are in permit-issuing places.

Value of New Housing Units Authorized in 2016

National Total = $232,748,132,000*

ALPHA ORDER RANK	STATE	VALUE	% of USA	RANK ORDER RANK	STATE	VALUE	% of USA
28	Alabama	$2,578,140,000	1.1%	1	Texas	$28,878,038,000	12.4%
49	Alaska	370,556,000	0.2%	2	Florida	25,149,880,000	10.8%
8	Arizona	7,830,227,000	3.4%	3	California	23,176,493,000	10.0%
34	Arkansas	1,582,651,000	0.7%	4	North Carolina	10,680,963,000	4.6%
3	California	23,176,493,000	10.0%	5	Georgia	9,132,348,000	3.9%
7	Colorado	8,682,599,000	3.7%	6	Washington	8,934,493,000	3.8%
38	Connecticut	1,176,302,000	0.5%	7	Colorado	8,682,599,000	3.7%
44	Delaware	718,630,000	0.3%	8	Arizona	7,830,227,000	3.4%
2	Florida	25,149,880,000	10.8%	9	Tennessee	6,432,702,000	2.8%
5	Georgia	9,132,348,000	3.9%	10	South Carolina	6,347,271,000	2.7%
36	Hawaii	1,261,126,000	0.5%	11	New York	6,116,612,000	2.6%
31	Idaho	2,123,733,000	0.9%	12	Virginia	5,312,198,000	2.3%
17	Illinois	4,448,540,000	1.9%	13	Utah	4,940,579,000	2.1%
21	Indiana	3,851,708,000	1.7%	14	Minnesota	4,916,760,000	2.1%
29	Iowa	2,535,030,000	1.1%	15	Ohio	4,580,404,000	2.0%
33	Kansas	1,642,286,000	0.7%	16	Michigan	4,515,776,000	1.9%
32	Kentucky	1,812,910,000	0.8%	17	Illinois	4,448,540,000	1.9%
27	Louisiana	2,754,368,000	1.2%	18	New Jersey	4,036,839,000	1.7%
41	Maine	813,050,000	0.3%	19	Oregon	3,946,373,000	1.7%
25	Maryland	3,215,527,000	1.4%	20	Pennsylvania	3,928,899,000	1.7%
23	Massachusetts	3,686,268,000	1.6%	21	Indiana	3,851,708,000	1.7%
16	Michigan	4,515,776,000	1.9%	22	Wisconsin	3,755,283,000	1.6%
14	Minnesota	4,916,760,000	2.1%	23	Massachusetts	3,686,268,000	1.6%
37	Mississippi	1,181,929,000	0.5%	24	Missouri	3,252,688,000	1.4%
24	Missouri	3,252,688,000	1.4%	25	Maryland	3,215,527,000	1.4%
42	Montana	752,026,000	0.3%	26	Nevada	2,872,037,000	1.2%
35	Nebraska	1,320,706,000	0.6%	27	Louisiana	2,754,368,000	1.2%
26	Nevada	2,872,037,000	1.2%	28	Alabama	2,578,140,000	1.1%
43	New Hampshire	734,658,000	0.3%	29	Iowa	2,535,030,000	1.1%
18	New Jersey	4,036,839,000	1.7%	30	Oklahoma	2,197,941,000	0.9%
39	New Mexico	905,096,000	0.4%	31	Idaho	2,123,733,000	0.9%
11	New York	6,116,612,000	2.6%	32	Kentucky	1,812,910,000	0.8%
4	North Carolina	10,680,963,000	4.6%	33	Kansas	1,642,286,000	0.7%
45	North Dakota	714,999,000	0.3%	34	Arkansas	1,582,651,000	0.7%
15	Ohio	4,580,404,000	2.0%	35	Nebraska	1,320,706,000	0.6%
30	Oklahoma	2,197,941,000	0.9%	36	Hawaii	1,261,126,000	0.5%
19	Oregon	3,946,373,000	1.7%	37	Mississippi	1,181,929,000	0.5%
20	Pennsylvania	3,928,899,000	1.7%	38	Connecticut	1,176,302,000	0.5%
50	Rhode Island	232,167,000	0.1%	39	New Mexico	905,096,000	0.4%
10	South Carolina	6,347,271,000	2.7%	40	South Dakota	858,207,000	0.4%
40	South Dakota	858,207,000	0.4%	41	Maine	813,050,000	0.3%
9	Tennessee	6,432,702,000	2.8%	42	Montana	752,026,000	0.3%
1	Texas	28,878,038,000	12.4%	43	New Hampshire	734,658,000	0.3%
13	Utah	4,940,579,000	2.1%	44	Delaware	718,630,000	0.3%
47	Vermont	403,110,000	0.2%	45	North Dakota	714,999,000	0.3%
12	Virginia	5,312,198,000	2.3%	46	Wyoming	552,953,000	0.2%
6	Washington	8,934,493,000	3.8%	47	Vermont	403,110,000	0.2%
48	West Virginia	393,534,000	0.2%	48	West Virginia	393,534,000	0.2%
22	Wisconsin	3,755,283,000	1.6%	49	Alaska	370,556,000	0.2%
46	Wyoming	552,953,000	0.2%	50	Rhode Island	232,167,000	0.1%
					District of Columbia	510,518,000	0.2%

Source: U.S. Bureau of the Census
    "Building Permits Survey" (https://www.census.gov/construction/bps/stateannual.html)
*Preliminary and unadjusted year-to-date monthly data as of December 2016. Includes single and multifamily privately owned units. All places issuing building permits for privately owned residential structures. More than 98 percent of all privately owned residential buildings constructed are in permit-issuing places.

Average Value of New Housing Units in 2016

National Average = $195,555 per Unit*

ALPHA ORDER

RANK	STATE	VALUE
35	Alabama	$178,159
3	Alaska	246,544
10	Arizona	218,112
43	Arkansas	169,123
5	California	231,152
6	Colorado	226,151
8	Connecticut	220,240
50	Delaware	124,589
7	Florida	220,783
34	Georgia	178,883
1	Hawaii	373,667
29	Idaho	185,059
21	Illinois	197,643
12	Indiana	210,281
31	Iowa	183,618
32	Kansas	182,496
49	Kentucky	141,656
26	Louisiana	187,653
22	Maine	195,257
24	Maryland	189,987
4	Massachusetts	239,259
19	Michigan	201,363
17	Minnesota	202,644
40	Mississippi	171,294
41	Missouri	171,158
30	Montana	184,049
44	Nebraska	162,889
45	Nevada	159,993
16	New Hampshire	203,676
48	New Jersey	150,904
28	New Mexico	186,387
37	New York	177,876
27	North Carolina	187,090
33	North Dakota	180,191
15	Ohio	205,685
38	Oklahoma	175,540
13	Oregon	208,043
25	Pennsylvania	189,244
23	Rhode Island	194,771
18	South Carolina	202,426
46	South Dakota	157,066
39	Tennessee	174,498
36	Texas	177,905
11	Utah	215,417
9	Vermont	220,038
42	Virginia	170,992
14	Washington	206,630
47	West Virginia	155,855
20	Wisconsin	200,753
2	Wyoming	332,104

RANK ORDER

RANK	STATE	VALUE
1	Hawaii	$373,667
2	Wyoming	332,104
3	Alaska	246,544
4	Massachusetts	239,259
5	California	231,152
6	Colorado	226,151
7	Florida	220,783
8	Connecticut	220,240
9	Vermont	220,038
10	Arizona	218,112
11	Utah	215,417
12	Indiana	210,281
13	Oregon	208,043
14	Washington	206,630
15	Ohio	205,685
16	New Hampshire	203,676
17	Minnesota	202,644
18	South Carolina	202,426
19	Michigan	201,363
20	Wisconsin	200,753
21	Illinois	197,643
22	Maine	195,257
23	Rhode Island	194,771
24	Maryland	189,987
25	Pennsylvania	189,244
26	Louisiana	187,653
27	North Carolina	187,090
28	New Mexico	186,387
29	Idaho	185,059
30	Montana	184,049
31	Iowa	183,618
32	Kansas	182,496
33	North Dakota	180,191
34	Georgia	178,883
35	Alabama	178,159
36	Texas	177,905
37	New York	177,876
38	Oklahoma	175,540
39	Tennessee	174,498
40	Mississippi	171,294
41	Missouri	171,158
42	Virginia	170,992
43	Arkansas	169,123
44	Nebraska	162,889
45	Nevada	159,993
46	South Dakota	157,066
47	West Virginia	155,855
48	New Jersey	150,904
49	Kentucky	141,656
50	Delaware	124,589
	District of Columbia	108,852

Source: CQ Press using data from U.S. Bureau of the Census
"Building Permits Survey" (https://www.census.gov/construction/bps/stateannual.html)
*Preliminary and unadjusted year-to-date monthly data as of December 2016. Includes single and multifamily privately owned units. All places issuing building permits for privately owned residential structures. More than 98 percent of all privately owned residential buildings constructed are in permit-issuing places.

Median Value of Owner-Occupied Housing in 2015

National Median = $194,500*

ALPHA ORDER				RANK ORDER		
RANK	STATE	MEDIAN		RANK	STATE	MEDIAN
44	Alabama	$134,100		1	Hawaii	$566,900
11	Alaska	259,600		2	California	449,100
22	Arizona	194,300		3	Massachusetts	352,100
48	Arkansas	120,700		4	New Jersey	322,600
2	California	449,100		5	Maryland	299,800
8	Colorado	283,800		6	New York	293,500
9	Connecticut	270,900		7	Washington	284,000
15	Delaware	240,200		8	Colorado	283,800
26	Florida	179,800		9	Connecticut	270,900
32	Georgia	159,300		10	Oregon	264,100
1	Hawaii	566,900		11	Alaska	259,600
27	Idaho	176,300		12	Virginia	257,800
24	Illinois	180,300		13	New Hampshire	244,500
45	Indiana	131,000		14	Rhode Island	241,000
43	Iowa	136,100		15	Delaware	240,200
40	Kansas	141,200		16	Utah	234,600
46	Kentucky	130,000		17	Vermont	223,700
33	Louisiana	155,600		18	Nevada	221,400
24	Maine	180,300		19	Wyoming	212,500
5	Maryland	299,800		20	Montana	209,500
3	Massachusetts	352,100		21	Minnesota	200,000
41	Michigan	137,500		22	Arizona	194,300
21	Minnesota	200,000		23	North Dakota	180,900
49	Mississippi	112,700		24	Illinois	180,300
38	Missouri	147,800		24	Maine	180,300
20	Montana	209,500		26	Florida	179,800
39	Nebraska	141,600		27	Idaho	176,300
18	Nevada	221,400		28	Pennsylvania	170,600
13	New Hampshire	244,500		29	Wisconsin	168,300
4	New Jersey	322,600		30	New Mexico	164,100
30	New Mexico	164,100		31	North Carolina	160,100
6	New York	293,500		32	Georgia	159,300
31	North Carolina	160,100		33	Louisiana	155,600
23	North Dakota	180,900		34	South Dakota	152,800
42	Ohio	136,400		35	Texas	152,000
47	Oklahoma	126,800		36	Tennessee	150,600
10	Oregon	264,100		37	South Carolina	148,600
28	Pennsylvania	170,600		38	Missouri	147,800
14	Rhode Island	241,000		39	Nebraska	141,600
37	South Carolina	148,600		40	Kansas	141,200
34	South Dakota	152,800		41	Michigan	137,500
36	Tennessee	150,600		42	Ohio	136,400
35	Texas	152,000		43	Iowa	136,100
16	Utah	234,600		44	Alabama	134,100
17	Vermont	223,700		45	Indiana	131,000
12	Virginia	257,800		46	Kentucky	130,000
7	Washington	284,000		47	Oklahoma	126,800
50	West Virginia	112,100		48	Arkansas	120,700
29	Wisconsin	168,300		49	Mississippi	112,700
19	Wyoming	212,500		50	West Virginia	112,100
					District of Columbia	551,300

Source: U.S. Bureau of the Census
  "2015 American Community Survey-Table R2510" (http://www.census.gov/programs-surveys/acs/)
*Housing units with a mortgage.

Percent Change in House Prices: 2015 to 2016

National Percent Change = 6.1% Increase*

ALPHA ORDER				RANK ORDER		
RANK	STATE	PERCENT CHANGE		RANK	STATE	PERCENT CHANGE
31	Alabama	4.5		1	Florida	10.7
44	Alaska	1.5		2	Oregon	10.5
12	Arizona	6.7		3	Washington	10.4
38	Arkansas	2.7		4	Colorado	10.0
10	California	7.2		5	Utah	9.5
4	Colorado	10.0		6	Idaho	8.9
46	Connecticut	0.8		7	Nevada	7.8
50	Delaware	(0.5)		7	Texas	7.8
1	Florida	10.7		9	Georgia	7.7
9	Georgia	7.7		10	California	7.2
48	Hawaii	0.7		11	Michigan	6.9
6	Idaho	8.9		12	Arizona	6.7
34	Illinois	3.8		13	Tennessee	6.5
15	Indiana	6.2		14	North Carolina	6.3
17	Iowa	6.1		15	Indiana	6.2
20	Kansas	5.8		15	Kentucky	6.2
15	Kentucky	6.2		17	Iowa	6.1
40	Louisiana	2.5		18	Minnesota	6.0
29	Maine	4.6		18	Wisconsin	6.0
40	Maryland	2.5		20	Kansas	5.8
26	Massachusetts	5.2		21	Missouri	5.7
11	Michigan	6.9		21	South Carolina	5.7
18	Minnesota	6.0		23	Ohio	5.6
32	Mississippi	4.2		23	Rhode Island	5.6
21	Missouri	5.7		25	Nebraska	5.3
29	Montana	4.6		26	Massachusetts	5.2
25	Nebraska	5.3		27	Virginia	5.0
7	Nevada	7.8		28	South Dakota	4.9
36	New Hampshire	3.5		29	Maine	4.6
37	New Jersey	2.8		29	Montana	4.6
46	New Mexico	0.8		31	Alabama	4.5
38	New York	2.7		32	Mississippi	4.2
14	North Carolina	6.3		33	Pennsylvania	4.0
40	North Dakota	2.5		34	Illinois	3.8
23	Ohio	5.6		35	Oklahoma	3.6
35	Oklahoma	3.6		36	New Hampshire	3.5
2	Oregon	10.5		37	New Jersey	2.8
33	Pennsylvania	4.0		38	Arkansas	2.7
23	Rhode Island	5.6		38	New York	2.7
21	South Carolina	5.7		40	Louisiana	2.5
28	South Dakota	4.9		40	Maryland	2.5
13	Tennessee	6.5		40	North Dakota	2.5
7	Texas	7.8		43	West Virginia	2.4
5	Utah	9.5		44	Alaska	1.5
49	Vermont	0.5		45	Wyoming	0.9
27	Virginia	5.0		46	Connecticut	0.8
3	Washington	10.4		46	New Mexico	0.8
43	West Virginia	2.4		48	Hawaii	0.7
18	Wisconsin	6.0		49	Vermont	0.5
45	Wyoming	0.9		50	Delaware	(0.5)
					District of Columbia	(2.7)

Source: Federal Housing Finance Agency
"State HPI Summary" (http://www.fhfa.gov/DataTools/Tools/Pages/House-Price-Index-%28HPI%29.aspx)
*Single-family house prices. As of September 30, 2016.

Percent Change in House Prices: 2012 to 2016

National Percent Change = 31.3% Increase*

ALPHA ORDER				RANK ORDER		
RANK	STATE	PERCENT CHANGE		RANK	STATE	PERCENT CHANGE
31	Alabama	18.8		1	Nevada	83.5
45	Alaska	11.9		2	Arizona	66.3
2	Arizona	66.3		3	California	61.8
37	Arkansas	15.8		4	Florida	57.6
3	California	61.8		5	Colorado	54.8
5	Colorado	54.8		6	Oregon	52.0
50	Connecticut	2.6		7	Washington	46.1
44	Delaware	12.0		8	Idaho	45.9
4	Florida	57.6		9	Georgia	44.6
9	Georgia	44.6		9	Utah	44.6
14	Hawaii	30.0		11	Michigan	41.4
8	Idaho	45.9		12	Texas	39.8
39	Illinois	15.0		13	North Dakota	35.1
26	Indiana	20.2		14	Hawaii	30.0
27	Iowa	19.7		15	Minnesota	29.8
28	Kansas	19.5		16	Tennessee	26.6
29	Kentucky	19.0		17	Montana	26.1
30	Louisiana	18.9		17	South Carolina	26.1
43	Maine	12.1		19	Nebraska	24.4
36	Maryland	16.0		20	North Carolina	24.0
23	Massachusetts	22.1		21	Ohio	22.5
11	Michigan	41.4		22	South Dakota	22.3
15	Minnesota	29.8		23	Massachusetts	22.1
40	Mississippi	14.4		24	Oklahoma	22.0
25	Missouri	21.7		25	Missouri	21.7
17	Montana	26.1		26	Indiana	20.2
19	Nebraska	24.4		27	Iowa	19.7
1	Nevada	83.5		28	Kansas	19.5
35	New Hampshire	17.8		29	Kentucky	19.0
48	New Jersey	9.2		30	Louisiana	18.9
47	New Mexico	9.8		31	Alabama	18.8
46	New York	11.1		32	Wisconsin	18.6
20	North Carolina	24.0		33	Rhode Island	18.4
13	North Dakota	35.1		34	Virginia	18.1
21	Ohio	22.5		35	New Hampshire	17.8
24	Oklahoma	22.0		36	Maryland	16.0
6	Oregon	52.0		37	Arkansas	15.8
41	Pennsylvania	14.0		38	Wyoming	15.4
33	Rhode Island	18.4		39	Illinois	15.0
17	South Carolina	26.1		40	Mississippi	14.4
22	South Dakota	22.3		41	Pennsylvania	14.0
16	Tennessee	26.6		42	West Virginia	13.9
12	Texas	39.8		43	Maine	12.1
9	Utah	44.6		44	Delaware	12.0
49	Vermont	8.6		45	Alaska	11.9
34	Virginia	18.1		46	New York	11.1
7	Washington	46.1		47	New Mexico	9.8
42	West Virginia	13.9		48	New Jersey	9.2
32	Wisconsin	18.6		49	Vermont	8.6
38	Wyoming	15.4		50	Connecticut	2.6
					District of Columbia	45.7

Source: Federal Housing Finance Agency
"State HPI Summary" (http://www.fhfa.gov/DataTools/Tools/Pages/House-Price-Index-%28HPI%29.aspx)
*Single-family house prices. As of September 30, 2016.

Percent of Owner-Occupied Housing Units with a Mortgage in 2015

National Percent = 63.3% with Mortgages

ALPHA ORDER

RANK	STATE	PERCENT
41	Alabama	56.8
20	Alaska	65.1
23	Arizona	64.2
46	Arkansas	54.8
3	California	71.2
2	Colorado	72.1
6	Connecticut	69.4
18	Delaware	65.4
40	Florida	57.1
15	Georgia	66.2
17	Hawaii	65.8
19	Idaho	65.3
22	Illinois	64.3
14	Indiana	66.3
34	Iowa	59.8
33	Kansas	60.2
39	Kentucky	57.9
47	Louisiana	52.4
28	Maine	62.2
1	Maryland	73.9
5	Massachusetts	70.0
31	Michigan	60.7
13	Minnesota	66.4
49	Mississippi	49.5
27	Missouri	62.3
42	Montana	56.7
30	Nebraska	61.7
10	Nevada	68.2
12	New Hampshire	67.0
11	New Jersey	67.5
43	New Mexico	55.9
29	New York	62.1
24	North Carolina	63.8
48	North Dakota	52.3
25	Ohio	63.7
44	Oklahoma	55.6
16	Oregon	66.0
32	Pennsylvania	60.6
7	Rhode Island	69.3
36	South Carolina	58.7
45	South Dakota	54.9
35	Tennessee	59.6
38	Texas	58.0
4	Utah	70.4
26	Vermont	62.9
8	Virginia	69.2
9	Washington	68.7
50	West Virginia	46.5
21	Wisconsin	64.8
37	Wyoming	58.3

RANK ORDER

RANK	STATE	PERCENT
1	Maryland	73.9
2	Colorado	72.1
3	California	71.2
4	Utah	70.4
5	Massachusetts	70.0
6	Connecticut	69.4
7	Rhode Island	69.3
8	Virginia	69.2
9	Washington	68.7
10	Nevada	68.2
11	New Jersey	67.5
12	New Hampshire	67.0
13	Minnesota	66.4
14	Indiana	66.3
15	Georgia	66.2
16	Oregon	66.0
17	Hawaii	65.8
18	Delaware	65.4
19	Idaho	65.3
20	Alaska	65.1
21	Wisconsin	64.8
22	Illinois	64.3
23	Arizona	64.2
24	North Carolina	63.8
25	Ohio	63.7
26	Vermont	62.9
27	Missouri	62.3
28	Maine	62.2
29	New York	62.1
30	Nebraska	61.7
31	Michigan	60.7
32	Pennsylvania	60.6
33	Kansas	60.2
34	Iowa	59.8
35	Tennessee	59.6
36	South Carolina	58.7
37	Wyoming	58.3
38	Texas	58.0
39	Kentucky	57.9
40	Florida	57.1
41	Alabama	56.8
42	Montana	56.7
43	New Mexico	55.9
44	Oklahoma	55.6
45	South Dakota	54.9
46	Arkansas	54.8
47	Louisiana	52.4
48	North Dakota	52.3
49	Mississippi	49.5
50	West Virginia	46.5

District of Columbia 76.1

Source: CQ Press using data from U.S. Bureau of the Census
"2015 American Community Survey-Table B25027" (http://www.census.gov/programs-surveys/acs/)

Median Monthly Mortgage Payment in 2015

National Median = $1,477*

RANK	STATE	MEDIAN
45	Alabama	$1,124
9	Alaska	1,817
27	Arizona	1,319
49	Arkansas	1,029
3	California	2,123
14	Colorado	1,558
5	Connecticut	2,020
17	Delaware	1,506
23	Florida	1,394
29	Georgia	1,299
2	Hawaii	2,248
40	Idaho	1,170
13	Illinois	1,588
46	Indiana	1,089
40	Iowa	1,170
31	Kansas	1,279
46	Kentucky	1,089
37	Louisiana	1,219
26	Maine	1,340
7	Maryland	1,909
4	Massachusetts	2,048
36	Michigan	1,220
18	Minnesota	1,459
48	Mississippi	1,083
39	Missouri	1,200
28	Montana	1,316
32	Nebraska	1,269
22	Nevada	1,396
8	New Hampshire	1,828
1	New Jersey	2,349
38	New Mexico	1,214
6	New York	2,009
33	North Carolina	1,234
30	North Dakota	1,297
34	Ohio	1,228
44	Oklahoma	1,159
15	Oregon	1,534
20	Pennsylvania	1,414
10	Rhode Island	1,730
42	South Carolina	1,168
35	South Dakota	1,225
43	Tennessee	1,167
19	Texas	1,453
21	Utah	1,408
16	Vermont	1,530
12	Virginia	1,692
11	Washington	1,704
50	West Virginia	972
25	Wisconsin	1,359
24	Wyoming	1,364

RANK	STATE	MEDIAN
1	New Jersey	$2,349
2	Hawaii	2,248
3	California	2,123
4	Massachusetts	2,048
5	Connecticut	2,020
6	New York	2,009
7	Maryland	1,909
8	New Hampshire	1,828
9	Alaska	1,817
10	Rhode Island	1,730
11	Washington	1,704
12	Virginia	1,692
13	Illinois	1,588
14	Colorado	1,558
15	Oregon	1,534
16	Vermont	1,530
17	Delaware	1,506
18	Minnesota	1,459
19	Texas	1,453
20	Pennsylvania	1,414
21	Utah	1,408
22	Nevada	1,396
23	Florida	1,394
24	Wyoming	1,364
25	Wisconsin	1,359
26	Maine	1,340
27	Arizona	1,319
28	Montana	1,316
29	Georgia	1,299
30	North Dakota	1,297
31	Kansas	1,279
32	Nebraska	1,269
33	North Carolina	1,234
34	Ohio	1,228
35	South Dakota	1,225
36	Michigan	1,220
37	Louisiana	1,219
38	New Mexico	1,214
39	Missouri	1,200
40	Idaho	1,170
40	Iowa	1,170
42	South Carolina	1,168
43	Tennessee	1,167
44	Oklahoma	1,159
45	Alabama	1,124
46	Indiana	1,089
46	Kentucky	1,089
48	Mississippi	1,083
49	Arkansas	1,029
50	West Virginia	972
	District of Columbia	2,312

Source: U.S. Bureau of the Census
   "2015 American Community Survey-Table R2511" (http://www.census.gov/programs-surveys/acs/)
*Monthly housing costs for owner-occupied housing.

Percent of Home Owners Spending 30% or More of Household Income on Housing Costs in 2015
National Percent = 29.4% of Home Owners*

ALPHA ORDER

RANK	STATE	PERCENT
33	Alabama	25.0
25	Alaska	27.9
15	Arizona	29.7
35	Arkansas	24.6
2	California	39.3
27	Colorado	27.6
7	Connecticut	33.2
12	Delaware	30.7
5	Florida	35.3
25	Georgia	27.9
1	Hawaii	39.8
22	Idaho	28.5
21	Illinois	29.1
47	Indiana	21.0
49	Iowa	19.9
45	Kansas	21.2
39	Kentucky	23.8
32	Louisiana	25.9
15	Maine	29.7
19	Maryland	29.4
8	Massachusetts	32.5
33	Michigan	25.0
42	Minnesota	23.1
13	Mississippi	30.1
41	Missouri	23.6
19	Montana	29.4
48	Nebraska	20.4
14	Nevada	29.8
17	New Hampshire	29.6
3	New Jersey	39.2
11	New Mexico	30.9
4	New York	35.9
28	North Carolina	27.3
50	North Dakota	16.3
40	Ohio	23.7
35	Oklahoma	24.6
9	Oregon	31.9
29	Pennsylvania	27.2
10	Rhode Island	31.8
24	South Carolina	28.0
44	South Dakota	21.8
31	Tennessee	26.3
30	Texas	26.7
38	Utah	24.1
6	Vermont	34.6
23	Virginia	28.1
18	Washington	29.5
46	West Virginia	21.1
35	Wisconsin	24.6
43	Wyoming	23.0

RANK ORDER

RANK	STATE	PERCENT
1	Hawaii	39.8
2	California	39.3
3	New Jersey	39.2
4	New York	35.9
5	Florida	35.3
6	Vermont	34.6
7	Connecticut	33.2
8	Massachusetts	32.5
9	Oregon	31.9
10	Rhode Island	31.8
11	New Mexico	30.9
12	Delaware	30.7
13	Mississippi	30.1
14	Nevada	29.8
15	Arizona	29.7
15	Maine	29.7
17	New Hampshire	29.6
18	Washington	29.5
19	Maryland	29.4
19	Montana	29.4
21	Illinois	29.1
22	Idaho	28.5
23	Virginia	28.1
24	South Carolina	28.0
25	Alaska	27.9
25	Georgia	27.9
27	Colorado	27.6
28	North Carolina	27.3
29	Pennsylvania	27.2
30	Texas	26.7
31	Tennessee	26.3
32	Louisiana	25.9
33	Alabama	25.0
33	Michigan	25.0
35	Arkansas	24.6
35	Oklahoma	24.6
35	Wisconsin	24.6
38	Utah	24.1
39	Kentucky	23.8
40	Ohio	23.7
41	Missouri	23.6
42	Minnesota	23.1
43	Wyoming	23.0
44	South Dakota	21.8
45	Kansas	21.2
46	West Virginia	21.1
47	Indiana	21.0
48	Nebraska	20.4
49	Iowa	19.9
50	North Dakota	16.3
	District of Columbia	26.6

Source: U.S. Bureau of the Census

"2015 American Community Survey-Table R2513" (http://www.census.gov/programs-surveys/acs/)

*For owner-occupied housing units with a mortgage.

Median Annual Real Estate Taxes in 2015

National Median = $2,259*

<table>
<tr><td colspan="3">ALPHA ORDER</td><td colspan="3">RANK ORDER</td></tr>
<tr><td>RANK</td><td>STATE</td><td>MEDIAN</td><td>RANK</td><td>STATE</td><td>MEDIAN</td></tr>
<tr><td>50</td><td>Alabama</td><td>$556</td><td>1</td><td>New Jersey</td><td>$7,777</td></tr>
<tr><td>12</td><td>Alaska</td><td>2,979</td><td>2</td><td>Connecticut</td><td>5,560</td></tr>
<tr><td>35</td><td>Arizona</td><td>1,393</td><td>3</td><td>New Hampshire</td><td>5,349</td></tr>
<tr><td>48</td><td>Arkansas</td><td>744</td><td>4</td><td>New York</td><td>4,868</td></tr>
<tr><td>9</td><td>California</td><td>3,395</td><td>5</td><td>Massachusetts</td><td>4,273</td></tr>
<tr><td>31</td><td>Colorado</td><td>1,513</td><td>6</td><td>Vermont</td><td>4,106</td></tr>
<tr><td>2</td><td>Connecticut</td><td>5,560</td><td>7</td><td>Illinois</td><td>4,101</td></tr>
<tr><td>37</td><td>Delaware</td><td>1,319</td><td>8</td><td>Rhode Island</td><td>3,965</td></tr>
<tr><td>27</td><td>Florida</td><td>1,733</td><td>9</td><td>California</td><td>3,395</td></tr>
<tr><td>34</td><td>Georgia</td><td>1,425</td><td>10</td><td>Wisconsin</td><td>3,227</td></tr>
<tr><td>32</td><td>Hawaii</td><td>1,482</td><td>11</td><td>Maryland</td><td>3,220</td></tr>
<tr><td>38</td><td>Idaho</td><td>1,315</td><td>12</td><td>Alaska</td><td>2,979</td></tr>
<tr><td>7</td><td>Illinois</td><td>4,101</td><td>13</td><td>Washington</td><td>2,895</td></tr>
<tr><td>41</td><td>Indiana</td><td>1,129</td><td>14</td><td>Texas</td><td>2,755</td></tr>
<tr><td>22</td><td>Iowa</td><td>2,043</td><td>15</td><td>Oregon</td><td>2,753</td></tr>
<tr><td>25</td><td>Kansas</td><td>1,949</td><td>16</td><td>Pennsylvania</td><td>2,671</td></tr>
<tr><td>44</td><td>Kentucky</td><td>1,093</td><td>17</td><td>Nebraska</td><td>2,528</td></tr>
<tr><td>47</td><td>Louisiana</td><td>800</td><td>18</td><td>Maine</td><td>2,435</td></tr>
<tr><td>18</td><td>Maine</td><td>2,435</td><td>19</td><td>Minnesota</td><td>2,240</td></tr>
<tr><td>11</td><td>Maryland</td><td>3,220</td><td>20</td><td>Michigan</td><td>2,211</td></tr>
<tr><td>5</td><td>Massachusetts</td><td>4,273</td><td>21</td><td>Ohio</td><td>2,121</td></tr>
<tr><td>20</td><td>Michigan</td><td>2,211</td><td>22</td><td>Iowa</td><td>2,043</td></tr>
<tr><td>19</td><td>Minnesota</td><td>2,240</td><td>23</td><td>Virginia</td><td>2,026</td></tr>
<tr><td>45</td><td>Mississippi</td><td>877</td><td>24</td><td>South Dakota</td><td>2,025</td></tr>
<tr><td>33</td><td>Missouri</td><td>1,445</td><td>25</td><td>Kansas</td><td>1,949</td></tr>
<tr><td>26</td><td>Montana</td><td>1,744</td><td>26</td><td>Montana</td><td>1,744</td></tr>
<tr><td>17</td><td>Nebraska</td><td>2,528</td><td>27</td><td>Florida</td><td>1,733</td></tr>
<tr><td>30</td><td>Nevada</td><td>1,529</td><td>28</td><td>North Dakota</td><td>1,724</td></tr>
<tr><td>3</td><td>New Hampshire</td><td>5,349</td><td>29</td><td>Utah</td><td>1,545</td></tr>
<tr><td>1</td><td>New Jersey</td><td>7,777</td><td>30</td><td>Nevada</td><td>1,529</td></tr>
<tr><td>39</td><td>New Mexico</td><td>1,273</td><td>31</td><td>Colorado</td><td>1,513</td></tr>
<tr><td>4</td><td>New York</td><td>4,868</td><td>32</td><td>Hawaii</td><td>1,482</td></tr>
<tr><td>36</td><td>North Carolina</td><td>1,365</td><td>33</td><td>Missouri</td><td>1,445</td></tr>
<tr><td>28</td><td>North Dakota</td><td>1,724</td><td>34</td><td>Georgia</td><td>1,425</td></tr>
<tr><td>21</td><td>Ohio</td><td>2,121</td><td>35</td><td>Arizona</td><td>1,393</td></tr>
<tr><td>42</td><td>Oklahoma</td><td>1,114</td><td>36</td><td>North Carolina</td><td>1,365</td></tr>
<tr><td>15</td><td>Oregon</td><td>2,753</td><td>37</td><td>Delaware</td><td>1,319</td></tr>
<tr><td>16</td><td>Pennsylvania</td><td>2,671</td><td>38</td><td>Idaho</td><td>1,315</td></tr>
<tr><td>8</td><td>Rhode Island</td><td>3,965</td><td>39</td><td>New Mexico</td><td>1,273</td></tr>
<tr><td>46</td><td>South Carolina</td><td>844</td><td>40</td><td>Wyoming</td><td>1,256</td></tr>
<tr><td>24</td><td>South Dakota</td><td>2,025</td><td>41</td><td>Indiana</td><td>1,129</td></tr>
<tr><td>43</td><td>Tennessee</td><td>1,099</td><td>42</td><td>Oklahoma</td><td>1,114</td></tr>
<tr><td>14</td><td>Texas</td><td>2,755</td><td>43</td><td>Tennessee</td><td>1,099</td></tr>
<tr><td>29</td><td>Utah</td><td>1,545</td><td>44</td><td>Kentucky</td><td>1,093</td></tr>
<tr><td>6</td><td>Vermont</td><td>4,106</td><td>45</td><td>Mississippi</td><td>877</td></tr>
<tr><td>23</td><td>Virginia</td><td>2,026</td><td>46</td><td>South Carolina</td><td>844</td></tr>
<tr><td>13</td><td>Washington</td><td>2,895</td><td>47</td><td>Louisiana</td><td>800</td></tr>
<tr><td>49</td><td>West Virginia</td><td>642</td><td>48</td><td>Arkansas</td><td>744</td></tr>
<tr><td>10</td><td>Wisconsin</td><td>3,227</td><td>49</td><td>West Virginia</td><td>642</td></tr>
<tr><td>40</td><td>Wyoming</td><td>1,256</td><td>50</td><td>Alabama</td><td>556</td></tr>
<tr><td></td><td></td><td></td><td></td><td>District of Columbia</td><td>2,843</td></tr>
</table>

Source: U.S. Bureau of the Census
   "2015 American Community Survey-Table B25103" (http://www.census.gov/programs-surveys/acs/)
*For owner-occupied housing units with or without mortgages.

Homeownership Rate in 2015

National Rate = 63.7%*

ALPHA ORDER

RANK	STATE	PERCENT
9	Alabama	70.0
40	Alaska	62.3
43	Arizona	61.7
21	Arkansas	67.1
49	California	54.3
36	Colorado	63.6
26	Connecticut	66.5
3	Delaware	73.3
34	Florida	64.8
38	Georgia	62.9
46	Hawaii	59.3
9	Idaho	70.0
31	Illinois	65.4
15	Indiana	69.4
16	Iowa	68.8
33	Kansas	64.9
19	Kentucky	67.9
37	Louisiana	63.3
11	Maine	69.9
21	Maryland	67.1
45	Massachusetts	60.5
2	Michigan	74.6
7	Minnesota	70.1
6	Mississippi	70.7
17	Missouri	68.5
29	Montana	66.4
18	Nebraska	68.1
48	Nevada	54.8
5	New Hampshire	71.6
35	New Jersey	64.0
26	New Mexico	66.5
50	New York	51.5
32	North Carolina	65.2
42	North Dakota	61.8
29	Ohio	66.4
20	Oklahoma	67.4
44	Oregon	61.1
14	Pennsylvania	69.6
47	Rhode Island	58.9
21	South Carolina	67.1
7	South Dakota	70.1
26	Tennessee	66.5
41	Texas	61.9
11	Utah	69.9
4	Vermont	71.8
21	Virginia	67.1
39	Washington	62.6
1	West Virginia	74.9
25	Wisconsin	66.6
11	Wyoming	69.9

RANK ORDER

RANK	STATE	PERCENT
1	West Virginia	74.9
2	Michigan	74.6
3	Delaware	73.3
4	Vermont	71.8
5	New Hampshire	71.6
6	Mississippi	70.7
7	Minnesota	70.1
7	South Dakota	70.1
9	Alabama	70.0
9	Idaho	70.0
11	Maine	69.9
11	Utah	69.9
11	Wyoming	69.9
14	Pennsylvania	69.6
15	Indiana	69.4
16	Iowa	68.8
17	Missouri	68.5
18	Nebraska	68.1
19	Kentucky	67.9
20	Oklahoma	67.4
21	Arkansas	67.1
21	Maryland	67.1
21	South Carolina	67.1
21	Virginia	67.1
25	Wisconsin	66.6
26	Connecticut	66.5
26	New Mexico	66.5
26	Tennessee	66.5
29	Montana	66.4
29	Ohio	66.4
31	Illinois	65.4
32	North Carolina	65.2
33	Kansas	64.9
34	Florida	64.8
35	New Jersey	64.0
36	Colorado	63.6
37	Louisiana	63.3
38	Georgia	62.9
39	Washington	62.6
40	Alaska	62.3
41	Texas	61.9
42	North Dakota	61.8
43	Arizona	61.7
44	Oregon	61.1
45	Massachusetts	60.5
46	Hawaii	59.3
47	Rhode Island	58.9
48	Nevada	54.8
49	California	54.3
50	New York	51.5

District of Columbia	40.4

Source: U.S. Bureau of the Census
  "Housing Vacancies and Homeownership, Annual Statistics: 2015" (http://www.census.gov/housing/hvs/data/ann14ind.html)
*Percent of households occupied by the owner.

Percent of Housing Units That Are Renter-Occupied in 2015

National Percent = 37.0% of Housing Units*

ALPHA ORDER

RANK	STATE	PERCENT
35	Alabama	32.1
16	Alaska	36.1
11	Arizona	38.1
20	Arkansas	34.8
2	California	46.4
14	Colorado	36.3
28	Connecticut	33.8
46	Delaware	29.2
15	Florida	36.2
10	Georgia	38.2
4	Hawaii	43.4
42	Idaho	31.0
21	Illinois	34.7
38	Indiana	31.8
44	Iowa	29.3
30	Kansas	33.6
29	Kentucky	33.7
18	Louisiana	35.4
49	Maine	29.0
25	Maryland	34.1
8	Massachusetts	38.3
43	Michigan	29.6
47	Minnesota	29.1
33	Mississippi	32.6
27	Missouri	33.9
31	Montana	33.3
25	Nebraska	34.1
3	Nevada	46.0
47	New Hampshire	29.1
13	New Jersey	37.0
34	New Mexico	32.5
1	New York	46.9
16	North Carolina	36.1
8	North Dakota	38.3
23	Ohio	34.6
21	Oklahoma	34.7
6	Oregon	38.9
40	Pennsylvania	31.3
5	Rhode Island	41.0
37	South Carolina	31.9
38	South Dakota	31.8
24	Tennessee	34.2
6	Texas	38.9
41	Utah	31.1
44	Vermont	29.3
19	Virginia	35.0
12	Washington	37.6
50	West Virginia	27.7
32	Wisconsin	33.2
36	Wyoming	32.0

RANK ORDER

RANK	STATE	PERCENT
1	New York	46.9
2	California	46.4
3	Nevada	46.0
4	Hawaii	43.4
5	Rhode Island	41.0
6	Oregon	38.9
6	Texas	38.9
8	Massachusetts	38.3
8	North Dakota	38.3
10	Georgia	38.2
11	Arizona	38.1
12	Washington	37.6
13	New Jersey	37.0
14	Colorado	36.3
15	Florida	36.2
16	Alaska	36.1
16	North Carolina	36.1
18	Louisiana	35.4
19	Virginia	35.0
20	Arkansas	34.8
21	Illinois	34.7
21	Oklahoma	34.7
23	Ohio	34.6
24	Tennessee	34.2
25	Maryland	34.1
25	Nebraska	34.1
27	Missouri	33.9
28	Connecticut	33.8
29	Kentucky	33.7
30	Kansas	33.6
31	Montana	33.3
32	Wisconsin	33.2
33	Mississippi	32.6
34	New Mexico	32.5
35	Alabama	32.1
36	Wyoming	32.0
37	South Carolina	31.9
38	Indiana	31.8
38	South Dakota	31.8
40	Pennsylvania	31.3
41	Utah	31.1
42	Idaho	31.0
43	Michigan	29.6
44	Iowa	29.3
44	Vermont	29.3
46	Delaware	29.2
47	Minnesota	29.1
47	New Hampshire	29.1
49	Maine	29.0
50	West Virginia	27.7

District of Columbia		60.1

Source: U.S. Bureau of the Census
  "2015 American Community Survey-Table R2512" (http://www.census.gov/programs-surveys/acs/)
*For occupied housing units.

Median Monthly Rental Payment in 2015

National Median = $959*

RANK	STATE	MEDIAN
44	Alabama	$729
7	Alaska	1,163
19	Arizona	933
48	Arkansas	695
2	California	1,311
9	Colorado	1,111
10	Connecticut	1,108
12	Delaware	1,049
13	Florida	1,046
23	Georgia	909
1	Hawaii	1,500
37	Idaho	770
18	Illinois	936
41	Indiana	758
46	Iowa	718
35	Kansas	782
47	Kentucky	702
30	Louisiana	800
31	Maine	792
3	Maryland	1,278
6	Massachusetts	1,164
29	Michigan	803
24	Minnesota	888
45	Mississippi	724
38	Missouri	763
38	Montana	763
42	Nebraska	750
15	Nevada	980
14	New Hampshire	1,017
4	New Jersey	1,214
34	New Mexico	783
5	New York	1,173
26	North Carolina	827
36	North Dakota	775
43	Ohio	746
40	Oklahoma	759
16	Oregon	943
25	Pennsylvania	868
17	Rhode Island	938
27	South Carolina	819
49	South Dakota	675
33	Tennessee	785
20	Texas	932
21	Utah	925
22	Vermont	923
8	Virginia	1,144
11	Washington	1,080
49	West Virginia	675
31	Wisconsin	792
28	Wyoming	815

RANK	STATE	MEDIAN
1	Hawaii	$1,500
2	California	1,311
3	Maryland	1,278
4	New Jersey	1,214
5	New York	1,173
6	Massachusetts	1,164
7	Alaska	1,163
8	Virginia	1,144
9	Colorado	1,111
10	Connecticut	1,108
11	Washington	1,080
12	Delaware	1,049
13	Florida	1,046
14	New Hampshire	1,017
15	Nevada	980
16	Oregon	943
17	Rhode Island	938
18	Illinois	936
19	Arizona	933
20	Texas	932
21	Utah	925
22	Vermont	923
23	Georgia	909
24	Minnesota	888
25	Pennsylvania	868
26	North Carolina	827
27	South Carolina	819
28	Wyoming	815
29	Michigan	803
30	Louisiana	800
31	Maine	792
31	Wisconsin	792
33	Tennessee	785
34	New Mexico	783
35	Kansas	782
36	North Dakota	775
37	Idaho	770
38	Missouri	763
38	Montana	763
40	Oklahoma	759
41	Indiana	758
42	Nebraska	750
43	Ohio	746
44	Alabama	729
45	Mississippi	724
46	Iowa	718
47	Kentucky	702
48	Arkansas	695
49	South Dakota	675
49	West Virginia	675

| | District of Columbia | 1,417 |

Source: U.S. Bureau of the Census
"2015 American Community Survey-Table R2514" (http://www.census.gov/programs-surveys/acs/)
*Monthly housing costs for renter-occupied housing.

Percent of Renters Spending 30% or More of Household Income on Rent and Utilities in 2015
National Percent = 46.8% of Renters

ALPHA ORDER

RANK	STATE	PERCENT
36	Alabama	42.7
28	Alaska	43.9
21	Arizona	44.9
39	Arkansas	41.8
1	California	52.9
9	Colorado	48.0
6	Connecticut	49.1
25	Delaware	44.0
1	Florida	52.9
16	Georgia	45.8
3	Hawaii	52.4
37	Idaho	42.5
17	Illinois	45.6
28	Indiana	43.9
43	Iowa	40.1
46	Kansas	38.9
41	Kentucky	40.6
14	Louisiana	46.0
23	Maine	44.8
10	Maryland	47.7
8	Massachusetts	48.1
13	Michigan	46.1
25	Minnesota	44.0
32	Mississippi	43.6
38	Missouri	41.9
42	Montana	40.5
44	Nebraska	39.7
11	Nevada	46.8
25	New Hampshire	44.0
4	New Jersey	50.5
19	New Mexico	45.3
5	New York	50.2
21	North Carolina	44.9
49	North Dakota	36.2
34	Ohio	43.3
44	Oklahoma	39.7
7	Oregon	48.2
20	Pennsylvania	45.2
24	Rhode Island	44.6
31	South Carolina	43.8
48	South Dakota	37.2
33	Tennessee	43.5
28	Texas	43.9
40	Utah	41.5
12	Vermont	46.3
14	Virginia	46.0
18	Washington	45.4
47	West Virginia	38.7
35	Wisconsin	43.0
50	Wyoming	35.9

RANK ORDER

RANK	STATE	PERCENT
1	California	52.9
1	Florida	52.9
3	Hawaii	52.4
4	New Jersey	50.5
5	New York	50.2
6	Connecticut	49.1
7	Oregon	48.2
8	Massachusetts	48.1
9	Colorado	48.0
10	Maryland	47.7
11	Nevada	46.8
12	Vermont	46.3
13	Michigan	46.1
14	Louisiana	46.0
14	Virginia	46.0
16	Georgia	45.8
17	Illinois	45.6
18	Washington	45.4
19	New Mexico	45.3
20	Pennsylvania	45.2
21	Arizona	44.9
21	North Carolina	44.9
23	Maine	44.8
24	Rhode Island	44.6
25	Delaware	44.0
25	Minnesota	44.0
25	New Hampshire	44.0
28	Alaska	43.9
28	Indiana	43.9
28	Texas	43.9
31	South Carolina	43.8
32	Mississippi	43.6
33	Tennessee	43.5
34	Ohio	43.3
35	Wisconsin	43.0
36	Alabama	42.7
37	Idaho	42.5
38	Missouri	41.9
39	Arkansas	41.8
40	Utah	41.5
41	Kentucky	40.6
42	Montana	40.5
43	Iowa	40.1
44	Nebraska	39.7
44	Oklahoma	39.7
46	Kansas	38.9
47	West Virginia	38.7
48	South Dakota	37.2
49	North Dakota	36.2
50	Wyoming	35.9
	District of Columbia	45.6

Source: U.S. Bureau of the Census
"2015 American Community Survey-Table R2515" (http://www.census.gov/programs-surveys/acs/)

State and Local Government Expenditures
for Housing and Community Development in 2014
National Total = $49,944,951,000*

ALPHA ORDER

RANK	STATE	EXPENDITURES	% of USA
26	Alabama	$467,397,000	0.9%
29	Alaska	390,734,000	0.8%
24	Arizona	528,021,000	1.1%
40	Arkansas	178,191,000	0.4%
1	California	8,182,504,000	16.4%
21	Colorado	795,067,000	1.6%
14	Connecticut	1,100,868,000	2.2%
44	Delaware	139,928,000	0.3%
4	Florida	2,375,390,000	4.8%
13	Georgia	1,264,421,000	2.5%
34	Hawaii	280,345,000	0.6%
46	Idaho	126,458,000	0.3%
6	Illinois	2,089,115,000	4.2%
20	Indiana	799,865,000	1.6%
39	Iowa	207,084,000	0.4%
35	Kansas	277,504,000	0.6%
28	Kentucky	399,401,000	0.8%
18	Louisiana	919,002,000	1.8%
33	Maine	295,991,000	0.6%
9	Maryland	1,480,741,000	3.0%
3	Massachusetts	2,769,214,000	5.5%
16	Michigan	1,066,380,000	2.1%
17	Minnesota	940,724,000	1.9%
36	Mississippi	276,353,000	0.6%
23	Missouri	610,665,000	1.2%
47	Montana	113,086,000	0.2%
41	Nebraska	165,486,000	0.3%
32	Nevada	303,663,000	0.6%
38	New Hampshire	207,289,000	0.4%
11	New Jersey	1,365,516,000	2.7%
42	New Mexico	154,999,000	0.3%
2	New York	5,459,897,000	10.9%
10	North Carolina	1,477,243,000	3.0%
49	North Dakota	75,881,000	0.2%
5	Ohio	2,162,182,000	4.3%
25	Oklahoma	492,226,000	1.0%
22	Oregon	632,600,000	1.3%
8	Pennsylvania	1,701,319,000	3.4%
37	Rhode Island	232,285,000	0.5%
27	South Carolina	456,185,000	0.9%
48	South Dakota	97,599,000	0.2%
19	Tennessee	873,366,000	1.7%
7	Texas	2,006,905,000	4.0%
31	Utah	311,819,000	0.6%
43	Vermont	149,598,000	0.3%
15	Virginia	1,084,185,000	2.2%
12	Washington	1,282,142,000	2.6%
45	West Virginia	132,571,000	0.3%
30	Wisconsin	338,498,000	0.7%
50	Wyoming	15,845,000	0.0%

RANK ORDER

RANK	STATE	EXPENDITURES	% of USA
1	California	$8,182,504,000	16.4%
2	New York	5,459,897,000	10.9%
3	Massachusetts	2,769,214,000	5.5%
4	Florida	2,375,390,000	4.8%
5	Ohio	2,162,182,000	4.3%
6	Illinois	2,089,115,000	4.2%
7	Texas	2,006,905,000	4.0%
8	Pennsylvania	1,701,319,000	3.4%
9	Maryland	1,480,741,000	3.0%
10	North Carolina	1,477,243,000	3.0%
11	New Jersey	1,365,516,000	2.7%
12	Washington	1,282,142,000	2.6%
13	Georgia	1,264,421,000	2.5%
14	Connecticut	1,100,868,000	2.2%
15	Virginia	1,084,185,000	2.2%
16	Michigan	1,066,380,000	2.1%
17	Minnesota	940,724,000	1.9%
18	Louisiana	919,002,000	1.8%
19	Tennessee	873,366,000	1.7%
20	Indiana	799,865,000	1.6%
21	Colorado	795,067,000	1.6%
22	Oregon	632,600,000	1.3%
23	Missouri	610,665,000	1.2%
24	Arizona	528,021,000	1.1%
25	Oklahoma	492,226,000	1.0%
26	Alabama	467,397,000	0.9%
27	South Carolina	456,185,000	0.9%
28	Kentucky	399,401,000	0.8%
29	Alaska	390,734,000	0.8%
30	Wisconsin	338,498,000	0.7%
31	Utah	311,819,000	0.6%
32	Nevada	303,663,000	0.6%
33	Maine	295,991,000	0.6%
34	Hawaii	280,345,000	0.6%
35	Kansas	277,504,000	0.6%
36	Mississippi	276,353,000	0.6%
37	Rhode Island	232,285,000	0.5%
38	New Hampshire	207,289,000	0.4%
39	Iowa	207,084,000	0.4%
40	Arkansas	178,191,000	0.4%
41	Nebraska	165,486,000	0.3%
42	New Mexico	154,999,000	0.3%
43	Vermont	149,598,000	0.3%
44	Delaware	139,928,000	0.3%
45	West Virginia	132,571,000	0.3%
46	Idaho	126,458,000	0.3%
47	Montana	113,086,000	0.2%
48	South Dakota	97,599,000	0.2%
49	North Dakota	75,881,000	0.2%
50	Wyoming	15,845,000	0.0%
	District of Columbia	691,203,000	1.4%

Source: U.S. Bureau of the Census, Governments Division
"2014 State and Local Government Finances" (http://www.census.gov/govs/local/)
*Direct general expenditures.

Per Capita State and Local Government Expenditures
for Housing and Community Development in 2014
National Per Capita = $157*

ALPHA ORDER

ALPHA ORDER

RANK	STATE	PER CAPITA
36	Alabama	$97
1	Alaska	530
42	Arizona	79
48	Arkansas	60
9	California	212
20	Colorado	149
3	Connecticut	306
19	Delaware	150
28	Florida	119
26	Georgia	125
10	Hawaii	198
43	Idaho	77
15	Illinois	162
27	Indiana	121
47	Iowa	67
37	Kansas	96
40	Kentucky	91
10	Louisiana	198
7	Maine	222
5	Maryland	248
2	Massachusetts	410
31	Michigan	108
14	Minnesota	173
39	Mississippi	92
35	Missouri	101
30	Montana	111
41	Nebraska	88
32	Nevada	107
17	New Hampshire	156
18	New Jersey	153
44	New Mexico	74
4	New York	277
20	North Carolina	149
34	North Dakota	103
12	Ohio	186
25	Oklahoma	127
16	Oregon	159
22	Pennsylvania	133
8	Rhode Island	220
38	South Carolina	94
29	South Dakota	114
22	Tennessee	133
44	Texas	74
33	Utah	106
6	Vermont	239
24	Virginia	130
13	Washington	182
46	West Virginia	72
49	Wisconsin	59
50	Wyoming	27

RANK ORDER

RANK	STATE	PER CAPITA
1	Alaska	$530
2	Massachusetts	410
3	Connecticut	306
4	New York	277
5	Maryland	248
6	Vermont	239
7	Maine	222
8	Rhode Island	220
9	California	212
10	Hawaii	198
10	Louisiana	198
12	Ohio	186
13	Washington	182
14	Minnesota	173
15	Illinois	162
16	Oregon	159
17	New Hampshire	156
18	New Jersey	153
19	Delaware	150
20	Colorado	149
20	North Carolina	149
22	Pennsylvania	133
22	Tennessee	133
24	Virginia	130
25	Oklahoma	127
26	Georgia	125
27	Indiana	121
28	Florida	119
29	South Dakota	114
30	Montana	111
31	Michigan	108
32	Nevada	107
33	Utah	106
34	North Dakota	103
35	Missouri	101
36	Alabama	97
37	Kansas	96
38	South Carolina	94
39	Mississippi	92
40	Kentucky	91
41	Nebraska	88
42	Arizona	79
43	Idaho	77
44	New Mexico	74
44	Texas	74
46	West Virginia	72
47	Iowa	67
48	Arkansas	60
49	Wisconsin	59
50	Wyoming	27
	District of Columbia	1,049

Source: CQ Press using data from U.S. Bureau of the Census, Governments Division
"2014 State and Local Government Finances" (http://www.census.gov/govs/local/)
*Direct general expenditures.

State & Local Government Spending for Housing and Community Development as a Percent of All State and Local Government Expenditures in 2014
National Percent = 1.8%*

ALPHA ORDER

RANK	STATE	PERCENT
34	Alabama	1.3
3	Alaska	2.7
36	Arizona	1.2
46	Arkansas	0.8
8	California	2.2
19	Colorado	1.8
2	Connecticut	3.1
27	Delaware	1.5
22	Florida	1.7
17	Georgia	1.9
15	Hawaii	2.0
36	Idaho	1.2
17	Illinois	1.9
22	Indiana	1.7
48	Iowa	0.7
36	Kansas	1.2
36	Kentucky	1.2
8	Louisiana	2.2
5	Maine	2.6
3	Maryland	2.7
1	Massachusetts	4.1
32	Michigan	1.4
19	Minnesota	1.8
41	Mississippi	1.1
32	Missouri	1.4
34	Montana	1.3
41	Nebraska	1.1
25	Nevada	1.6
12	New Hampshire	2.1
27	New Jersey	1.5
46	New Mexico	0.8
8	New York	2.2
12	North Carolina	2.1
44	North Dakota	0.9
7	Ohio	2.3
22	Oklahoma	1.7
19	Oregon	1.8
27	Pennsylvania	1.5
6	Rhode Island	2.4
36	South Carolina	1.2
27	South Dakota	1.5
15	Tennessee	2.0
43	Texas	1.0
27	Utah	1.5
8	Vermont	2.2
25	Virginia	1.6
12	Washington	2.1
44	West Virginia	0.9
48	Wisconsin	0.7
50	Wyoming	0.2

RANK ORDER

RANK	STATE	PERCENT
1	Massachusetts	4.1
2	Connecticut	3.1
3	Alaska	2.7
3	Maryland	2.7
5	Maine	2.6
6	Rhode Island	2.4
7	Ohio	2.3
8	California	2.2
8	Louisiana	2.2
8	New York	2.2
8	Vermont	2.2
12	New Hampshire	2.1
12	North Carolina	2.1
12	Washington	2.1
15	Hawaii	2.0
15	Tennessee	2.0
17	Georgia	1.9
17	Illinois	1.9
19	Colorado	1.8
19	Minnesota	1.8
19	Oregon	1.8
22	Florida	1.7
22	Indiana	1.7
22	Oklahoma	1.7
25	Nevada	1.6
25	Virginia	1.6
27	Delaware	1.5
27	New Jersey	1.5
27	Pennsylvania	1.5
27	South Dakota	1.5
27	Utah	1.5
32	Michigan	1.4
32	Missouri	1.4
34	Alabama	1.3
34	Montana	1.3
36	Arizona	1.2
36	Idaho	1.2
36	Kansas	1.2
36	Kentucky	1.2
36	South Carolina	1.2
41	Mississippi	1.1
41	Nebraska	1.1
43	Texas	1.0
44	North Dakota	0.9
44	West Virginia	0.9
46	Arkansas	0.8
46	New Mexico	0.8
48	Iowa	0.7
48	Wisconsin	0.7
50	Wyoming	0.2

District of Columbia	5.8

Source: CQ Press using data from U.S. Bureau of the Census, Governments Division
   "2014 State and Local Government Finances" (http://www.census.gov/govs/local/)
*As a percent of direct general expenditures.

XIII. Population

Population in 2016

National Total = 323,127,513*

ALPHA ORDER

ALPHA ORDER

RANK	STATE	POPULATION	% of USA
24	Alabama	4,863,300	1.5%
48	Alaska	741,894	0.2%
14	Arizona	6,931,071	2.1%
33	Arkansas	2,988,248	0.9%
1	California	39,250,017	12.1%
21	Colorado	5,540,545	1.7%
29	Connecticut	3,576,452	1.1%
45	Delaware	952,065	0.3%
3	Florida	20,612,439	6.4%
8	Georgia	10,310,371	3.2%
40	Hawaii	1,428,557	0.4%
39	Idaho	1,683,140	0.5%
5	Illinois	12,801,539	4.0%
17	Indiana	6,633,053	2.1%
30	Iowa	3,134,693	1.0%
35	Kansas	2,907,289	0.9%
26	Kentucky	4,436,974	1.4%
25	Louisiana	4,681,666	1.4%
42	Maine	1,331,479	0.4%
19	Maryland	6,016,447	1.9%
15	Massachusetts	6,811,779	2.1%
10	Michigan	9,928,300	3.1%
22	Minnesota	5,519,952	1.7%
32	Mississippi	2,988,726	0.9%
18	Missouri	6,093,000	1.9%
44	Montana	1,042,520	0.3%
37	Nebraska	1,907,116	0.6%
34	Nevada	2,940,058	0.9%
41	New Hampshire	1,334,795	0.4%
11	New Jersey	8,944,469	2.8%
36	New Mexico	2,081,015	0.6%
4	New York	19,745,289	6.1%
9	North Carolina	10,146,788	3.1%
47	North Dakota	757,952	0.2%
7	Ohio	11,614,373	3.6%
28	Oklahoma	3,923,561	1.2%
27	Oregon	4,093,465	1.3%
6	Pennsylvania	12,784,227	4.0%
43	Rhode Island	1,056,426	0.3%
23	South Carolina	4,961,119	1.5%
46	South Dakota	865,454	0.3%
16	Tennessee	6,651,194	2.1%
2	Texas	27,862,596	8.6%
31	Utah	3,051,217	0.9%
49	Vermont	624,594	0.2%
12	Virginia	8,411,808	2.6%
13	Washington	7,288,000	2.3%
38	West Virginia	1,831,102	0.6%
20	Wisconsin	5,778,708	1.8%
50	Wyoming	585,501	0.2%

RANK ORDER

RANK	STATE	POPULATION	% of USA
1	California	39,250,017	12.1%
2	Texas	27,862,596	8.6%
3	Florida	20,612,439	6.4%
4	New York	19,745,289	6.1%
5	Illinois	12,801,539	4.0%
6	Pennsylvania	12,784,227	4.0%
7	Ohio	11,614,373	3.6%
8	Georgia	10,310,371	3.2%
9	North Carolina	10,146,788	3.1%
10	Michigan	9,928,300	3.1%
11	New Jersey	8,944,469	2.8%
12	Virginia	8,411,808	2.6%
13	Washington	7,288,000	2.3%
14	Arizona	6,931,071	2.1%
15	Massachusetts	6,811,779	2.1%
16	Tennessee	6,651,194	2.1%
17	Indiana	6,633,053	2.1%
18	Missouri	6,093,000	1.9%
19	Maryland	6,016,447	1.9%
20	Wisconsin	5,778,708	1.8%
21	Colorado	5,540,545	1.7%
22	Minnesota	5,519,952	1.7%
23	South Carolina	4,961,119	1.5%
24	Alabama	4,863,300	1.5%
25	Louisiana	4,681,666	1.4%
26	Kentucky	4,436,974	1.4%
27	Oregon	4,093,465	1.3%
28	Oklahoma	3,923,561	1.2%
29	Connecticut	3,576,452	1.1%
30	Iowa	3,134,693	1.0%
31	Utah	3,051,217	0.9%
32	Mississippi	2,988,726	0.9%
33	Arkansas	2,988,248	0.9%
34	Nevada	2,940,058	0.9%
35	Kansas	2,907,289	0.9%
36	New Mexico	2,081,015	0.6%
37	Nebraska	1,907,116	0.6%
38	West Virginia	1,831,102	0.6%
39	Idaho	1,683,140	0.5%
40	Hawaii	1,428,557	0.4%
41	New Hampshire	1,334,795	0.4%
42	Maine	1,331,479	0.4%
43	Rhode Island	1,056,426	0.3%
44	Montana	1,042,520	0.3%
45	Delaware	952,065	0.3%
46	South Dakota	865,454	0.3%
47	North Dakota	757,952	0.2%
48	Alaska	741,894	0.2%
49	Vermont	624,594	0.2%
50	Wyoming	585,501	0.2%
	District of Columbia	681,170	0.2%

Source: U.S. Bureau of the Census
"Population Estimates" (December 2016, http://www.census.gov/programs-surveys/popest.html)
*Resident population estimate as of July 1, 2016.

Population in 2015

National Total = 320,896,618*

RANK	STATE	POPULATION	% of USA
24	Alabama	4,853,875	1.5%
48	Alaska	737,709	0.2%
14	Arizona	6,817,565	2.1%
33	Arkansas	2,977,853	0.9%
1	California	38,993,940	12.2%
22	Colorado	5,448,819	1.7%
29	Connecticut	3,584,730	1.1%
45	Delaware	944,076	0.3%
3	Florida	20,244,914	6.3%
8	Georgia	10,199,398	3.2%
40	Hawaii	1,425,157	0.4%
39	Idaho	1,652,828	0.5%
5	Illinois	12,839,047	4.0%
16	Indiana	6,612,768	2.1%
30	Iowa	3,121,997	1.0%
34	Kansas	2,906,721	0.9%
26	Kentucky	4,424,611	1.4%
25	Louisiana	4,668,960	1.5%
42	Maine	1,329,453	0.4%
19	Maryland	5,994,983	1.9%
15	Massachusetts	6,784,240	2.1%
10	Michigan	9,917,715	3.1%
21	Minnesota	5,482,435	1.7%
32	Mississippi	2,989,390	0.9%
18	Missouri	6,076,204	1.9%
44	Montana	1,032,073	0.3%
37	Nebraska	1,893,765	0.6%
35	Nevada	2,883,758	0.9%
41	New Hampshire	1,330,111	0.4%
11	New Jersey	8,935,421	2.8%
36	New Mexico	2,080,328	0.6%
4	New York	19,747,183	6.2%
9	North Carolina	10,035,186	3.1%
47	North Dakota	756,835	0.2%
7	Ohio	11,605,090	3.6%
28	Oklahoma	3,907,414	1.2%
27	Oregon	4,024,634	1.3%
6	Pennsylvania	12,791,904	4.0%
43	Rhode Island	1,055,607	0.3%
23	South Carolina	4,894,834	1.5%
46	South Dakota	857,919	0.3%
17	Tennessee	6,595,056	2.1%
2	Texas	27,429,639	8.5%
31	Utah	2,990,632	0.9%
49	Vermont	626,088	0.2%
12	Virginia	8,367,587	2.6%
13	Washington	7,160,290	2.2%
38	West Virginia	1,841,053	0.6%
20	Wisconsin	5,767,891	1.8%
50	Wyoming	586,555	0.2%

RANK	STATE	POPULATION	% of USA
1	California	38,993,940	12.2%
2	Texas	27,429,639	8.5%
3	Florida	20,244,914	6.3%
4	New York	19,747,183	6.2%
5	Illinois	12,839,047	4.0%
6	Pennsylvania	12,791,904	4.0%
7	Ohio	11,605,090	3.6%
8	Georgia	10,199,398	3.2%
9	North Carolina	10,035,186	3.1%
10	Michigan	9,917,715	3.1%
11	New Jersey	8,935,421	2.8%
12	Virginia	8,367,587	2.6%
13	Washington	7,160,290	2.2%
14	Arizona	6,817,565	2.1%
15	Massachusetts	6,784,240	2.1%
16	Indiana	6,612,768	2.1%
17	Tennessee	6,595,056	2.1%
18	Missouri	6,076,204	1.9%
19	Maryland	5,994,983	1.9%
20	Wisconsin	5,767,891	1.8%
21	Minnesota	5,482,435	1.7%
22	Colorado	5,448,819	1.7%
23	South Carolina	4,894,834	1.5%
24	Alabama	4,853,875	1.5%
25	Louisiana	4,668,960	1.5%
26	Kentucky	4,424,611	1.4%
27	Oregon	4,024,634	1.3%
28	Oklahoma	3,907,414	1.2%
29	Connecticut	3,584,730	1.1%
30	Iowa	3,121,997	1.0%
31	Utah	2,990,632	0.9%
32	Mississippi	2,989,390	0.9%
33	Arkansas	2,977,853	0.9%
34	Kansas	2,906,721	0.9%
35	Nevada	2,883,758	0.9%
36	New Mexico	2,080,328	0.6%
37	Nebraska	1,893,765	0.6%
38	West Virginia	1,841,053	0.6%
39	Idaho	1,652,828	0.5%
40	Hawaii	1,425,157	0.4%
41	New Hampshire	1,330,111	0.4%
42	Maine	1,329,453	0.4%
43	Rhode Island	1,055,607	0.3%
44	Montana	1,032,073	0.3%
45	Delaware	944,076	0.3%
46	South Dakota	857,919	0.3%
47	North Dakota	756,835	0.2%
48	Alaska	737,709	0.2%
49	Vermont	626,088	0.2%
50	Wyoming	586,555	0.2%
	District of Columbia	670,377	0.2%

Source: U.S. Bureau of the Census
"Population Estimates" (December 2016, http://www.census.gov/programs-surveys/popest.html)
*Resident population. Revised estimates of July 1, 2016.

Numerical Population Change: 2015 to 2016

National Total = 2,230,895 Increase*

ALPHA ORDER

RANK	STATE	GAIN/LOSS
30	Alabama	9,425
36	Alaska	4,185
5	Arizona	113,506
29	Arkansas	10,395
3	California	256,077
8	Colorado	91,726
48	Connecticut	(8,278)
33	Delaware	7,989
2	Florida	367,525
7	Georgia	110,973
37	Hawaii	3,400
16	Idaho	30,312
50	Illinois	(37,508)
19	Indiana	20,285
24	Iowa	12,696
42	Kansas	568
25	Kentucky	12,363
23	Louisiana	12,706
38	Maine	2,026
18	Maryland	21,464
17	Massachusetts	27,539
27	Michigan	10,585
15	Minnesota	37,517
43	Mississippi	(664)
20	Missouri	16,796
28	Montana	10,447
22	Nebraska	13,351
12	Nevada	56,300
35	New Hampshire	4,684
32	New Jersey	9,048
41	New Mexico	687
46	New York	(1,894)
6	North Carolina	111,602
39	North Dakota	1,117
31	Ohio	9,283
21	Oklahoma	16,147
9	Oregon	68,831
47	Pennsylvania	(7,677)
40	Rhode Island	819
10	South Carolina	66,285
34	South Dakota	7,535
13	Tennessee	56,138
1	Texas	432,957
11	Utah	60,585
45	Vermont	(1,494)
14	Virginia	44,221
4	Washington	127,710
49	West Virginia	(9,951)
26	Wisconsin	10,817
44	Wyoming	(1,054)

RANK ORDER

RANK	STATE	GAIN/LOSS
1	Texas	432,957
2	Florida	367,525
3	California	256,077
4	Washington	127,710
5	Arizona	113,506
6	North Carolina	111,602
7	Georgia	110,973
8	Colorado	91,726
9	Oregon	68,831
10	South Carolina	66,285
11	Utah	60,585
12	Nevada	56,300
13	Tennessee	56,138
14	Virginia	44,221
15	Minnesota	37,517
16	Idaho	30,312
17	Massachusetts	27,539
18	Maryland	21,464
19	Indiana	20,285
20	Missouri	16,796
21	Oklahoma	16,147
22	Nebraska	13,351
23	Louisiana	12,706
24	Iowa	12,696
25	Kentucky	12,363
26	Wisconsin	10,817
27	Michigan	10,585
28	Montana	10,447
29	Arkansas	10,395
30	Alabama	9,425
31	Ohio	9,283
32	New Jersey	9,048
33	Delaware	7,989
34	South Dakota	7,535
35	New Hampshire	4,684
36	Alaska	4,185
37	Hawaii	3,400
38	Maine	2,026
39	North Dakota	1,117
40	Rhode Island	819
41	New Mexico	687
42	Kansas	568
43	Mississippi	(664)
44	Wyoming	(1,054)
45	Vermont	(1,494)
46	New York	(1,894)
47	Pennsylvania	(7,677)
48	Connecticut	(8,278)
49	West Virginia	(9,951)
50	Illinois	(37,508)

District of Columbia — 10,793

Source: CQ Press using data from U.S. Bureau of the Census
"Population Estimates" (December 2016, http://www.census.gov/programs-surveys/popest.html)
*Resident population from July 1, 2015 to July 1, 2016.

Percent Change in Population: 2015 to 2016

National Percent Change = 0.7% Increase*

ALPHA ORDER				RANK ORDER		
RANK	STATE	PERCENT CHANGE		RANK	STATE	PERCENT CHANGE
32	Alabama	0.2		1	Nevada	2.0
20	Alaska	0.6		1	Utah	2.0
6	Arizona	1.7		3	Florida	1.8
27	Arkansas	0.3		3	Idaho	1.8
17	California	0.7		3	Washington	1.8
6	Colorado	1.7		6	Arizona	1.7
46	Connecticut	(0.2)		6	Colorado	1.7
16	Delaware	0.8		6	Oregon	1.7
3	Florida	1.8		9	Texas	1.6
11	Georgia	1.1		10	South Carolina	1.4
32	Hawaii	0.2		11	Georgia	1.1
3	Idaho	1.8		11	North Carolina	1.1
49	Illinois	(0.3)		13	Montana	1.0
27	Indiana	0.3		14	South Dakota	0.9
22	Iowa	0.4		14	Tennessee	0.9
41	Kansas	0.0		16	Delaware	0.8
27	Kentucky	0.3		17	California	0.7
27	Louisiana	0.3		17	Minnesota	0.7
32	Maine	0.2		17	Nebraska	0.7
22	Maryland	0.4		20	Alaska	0.6
22	Massachusetts	0.4		21	Virginia	0.5
36	Michigan	0.1		22	Iowa	0.4
17	Minnesota	0.7		22	Maryland	0.4
41	Mississippi	0.0		22	Massachusetts	0.4
27	Missouri	0.3		22	New Hampshire	0.4
13	Montana	1.0		22	Oklahoma	0.4
17	Nebraska	0.7		27	Arkansas	0.3
1	Nevada	2.0		27	Indiana	0.3
22	New Hampshire	0.4		27	Kentucky	0.3
36	New Jersey	0.1		27	Louisiana	0.3
41	New Mexico	0.0		27	Missouri	0.3
41	New York	0.0		32	Alabama	0.2
11	North Carolina	1.1		32	Hawaii	0.2
36	North Dakota	0.1		32	Maine	0.2
36	Ohio	0.1		32	Wisconsin	0.2
22	Oklahoma	0.4		36	Michigan	0.1
6	Oregon	1.7		36	New Jersey	0.1
45	Pennsylvania	(0.1)		36	North Dakota	0.1
36	Rhode Island	0.1		36	Ohio	0.1
10	South Carolina	1.4		36	Rhode Island	0.1
14	South Dakota	0.9		41	Kansas	0.0
14	Tennessee	0.9		41	Mississippi	0.0
9	Texas	1.6		41	New Mexico	0.0
1	Utah	2.0		41	New York	0.0
46	Vermont	(0.2)		45	Pennsylvania	(0.1)
21	Virginia	0.5		46	Connecticut	(0.2)
3	Washington	1.8		46	Vermont	(0.2)
50	West Virginia	(0.5)		46	Wyoming	(0.2)
32	Wisconsin	0.2		49	Illinois	(0.3)
46	Wyoming	(0.2)		50	West Virginia	(0.5)
					District of Columbia	1.6

Source: CQ Press using data from U.S. Bureau of the Census
"Population Estimates" (December 2016, http://www.census.gov/programs-surveys/popest.html)
*Resident population from July 1, 2015 to July 1, 2016.

Population per Square Mile in 2016

National Rate = 91.5 Persons per Square Mile*

RANK	STATE	RATE
27	Alabama	96.0
50	Alaska	1.3
33	Arizona	61.0
34	Arkansas	57.4
11	California	252.0
37	Colorado	53.5
4	Connecticut	738.6
6	Delaware	488.5
8	Florida	384.4
17	Georgia	179.3
13	Hawaii	222.4
44	Idaho	20.4
12	Illinois	230.6
16	Indiana	185.1
36	Iowa	56.1
41	Kansas	35.6
22	Kentucky	112.4
24	Louisiana	108.4
38	Maine	43.2
5	Maryland	619.8
3	Massachusetts	873.3
18	Michigan	175.6
30	Minnesota	69.3
32	Mississippi	63.7
28	Missouri	88.6
48	Montana	7.2
43	Nebraska	24.8
42	Nevada	26.8
21	New Hampshire	149.1
1	New Jersey	1,216.3
45	New Mexico	17.2
7	New York	419.0
15	North Carolina	208.7
47	North Dakota	11.0
10	Ohio	284.2
35	Oklahoma	57.2
39	Oregon	42.6
9	Pennsylvania	285.7
2	Rhode Island	1,021.7
19	South Carolina	165.0
46	South Dakota	11.4
20	Tennessee	161.3
25	Texas	106.7
40	Utah	37.1
31	Vermont	67.8
14	Virginia	213.0
23	Washington	109.7
29	West Virginia	76.2
25	Wisconsin	106.7
49	Wyoming	6.0

RANK	STATE	RATE
1	New Jersey	1,216.3
2	Rhode Island	1,021.7
3	Massachusetts	873.3
4	Connecticut	738.6
5	Maryland	619.8
6	Delaware	488.5
7	New York	419.0
8	Florida	384.4
9	Pennsylvania	285.7
10	Ohio	284.2
11	California	252.0
12	Illinois	230.6
13	Hawaii	222.4
14	Virginia	213.0
15	North Carolina	208.7
16	Indiana	185.1
17	Georgia	179.3
18	Michigan	175.6
19	South Carolina	165.0
20	Tennessee	161.3
21	New Hampshire	149.1
22	Kentucky	112.4
23	Washington	109.7
24	Louisiana	108.4
25	Texas	106.7
25	Wisconsin	106.7
27	Alabama	96.0
28	Missouri	88.6
29	West Virginia	76.2
30	Minnesota	69.3
31	Vermont	67.8
32	Mississippi	63.7
33	Arizona	61.0
34	Arkansas	57.4
35	Oklahoma	57.2
36	Iowa	56.1
37	Colorado	53.5
38	Maine	43.2
39	Oregon	42.6
40	Utah	37.1
41	Kansas	35.6
42	Nevada	26.8
43	Nebraska	24.8
44	Idaho	20.4
45	New Mexico	17.2
46	South Dakota	11.4
47	North Dakota	11.0
48	Montana	7.2
49	Wyoming	6.0
50	Alaska	1.3
	District of Columbia	11,166.7

Source: CQ Press using data from U.S. Bureau of the Census
"Population Estimates" (December 2016, http://www.census.gov/programs-surveys/popest.html)
*Resident population. Based on land area of states.

Male Population in 2015

National Total = 158,229,297 Males

ALPHA ORDER

RANK	STATE	MALES	% of USA
24	Alabama	2,353,184	1.5%
47	Alaska	389,025	0.2%
14	Arizona	3,391,490	2.1%
32	Arkansas	1,462,856	0.9%
1	California	19,443,068	12.3%
21	Colorado	2,743,763	1.7%
29	Connecticut	1,751,747	1.1%
45	Delaware	457,809	0.3%
3	Florida	9,902,539	6.3%
8	Georgia	4,979,882	3.1%
40	Hawaii	725,372	0.5%
39	Idaho	828,747	0.5%
5	Illinois	6,314,495	4.0%
16	Indiana	3,261,865	2.1%
30	Iowa	1,552,026	1.0%
33	Kansas	1,453,633	0.9%
26	Kentucky	2,179,094	1.4%
25	Louisiana	2,283,809	1.4%
42	Maine	651,257	0.4%
19	Maryland	2,911,085	1.8%
15	Massachusetts	3,296,118	2.1%
10	Michigan	4,878,148	3.1%
22	Minnesota	2,729,864	1.7%
34	Mississippi	1,451,850	0.9%
18	Missouri	2,985,045	1.9%
43	Montana	519,330	0.3%
37	Nebraska	945,168	0.6%
35	Nevada	1,450,551	0.9%
41	New Hampshire	657,656	0.4%
11	New Jersey	4,372,116	2.8%
36	New Mexico	1,033,421	0.7%
4	New York	9,611,513	6.1%
9	North Carolina	4,892,025	3.1%
48	North Dakota	388,853	0.2%
7	Ohio	5,686,530	3.6%
28	Oklahoma	1,937,124	1.2%
27	Oregon	1,993,170	1.3%
6	Pennsylvania	6,264,374	4.0%
44	Rhode Island	511,949	0.3%
23	South Carolina	2,378,968	1.5%
46	South Dakota	431,976	0.3%
17	Tennessee	3,217,461	2.0%
2	Texas	13,637,790	8.6%
31	Utah	1,507,100	1.0%
49	Vermont	308,526	0.2%
12	Virginia	4,124,765	2.6%
13	Washington	3,584,998	2.3%
38	West Virginia	911,060	0.6%
20	Wisconsin	2,867,600	1.8%
50	Wyoming	298,901	0.2%

RANK ORDER

RANK	STATE	MALES	% of USA
1	California	19,443,068	12.3%
2	Texas	13,637,790	8.6%
3	Florida	9,902,539	6.3%
4	New York	9,611,513	6.1%
5	Illinois	6,314,495	4.0%
6	Pennsylvania	6,264,374	4.0%
7	Ohio	5,686,530	3.6%
8	Georgia	4,979,882	3.1%
9	North Carolina	4,892,025	3.1%
10	Michigan	4,878,148	3.1%
11	New Jersey	4,372,116	2.8%
12	Virginia	4,124,765	2.6%
13	Washington	3,584,998	2.3%
14	Arizona	3,391,490	2.1%
15	Massachusetts	3,296,118	2.1%
16	Indiana	3,261,865	2.1%
17	Tennessee	3,217,461	2.0%
18	Missouri	2,985,045	1.9%
19	Maryland	2,911,085	1.8%
20	Wisconsin	2,867,600	1.8%
21	Colorado	2,743,763	1.7%
22	Minnesota	2,729,864	1.7%
23	South Carolina	2,378,968	1.5%
24	Alabama	2,353,184	1.5%
25	Louisiana	2,283,809	1.4%
26	Kentucky	2,179,094	1.4%
27	Oregon	1,993,170	1.3%
28	Oklahoma	1,937,124	1.2%
29	Connecticut	1,751,747	1.1%
30	Iowa	1,552,026	1.0%
31	Utah	1,507,100	1.0%
32	Arkansas	1,462,856	0.9%
33	Kansas	1,453,633	0.9%
34	Mississippi	1,451,850	0.9%
35	Nevada	1,450,551	0.9%
36	New Mexico	1,033,421	0.7%
37	Nebraska	945,168	0.6%
38	West Virginia	911,060	0.6%
39	Idaho	828,747	0.5%
40	Hawaii	725,372	0.5%
41	New Hampshire	657,656	0.4%
42	Maine	651,257	0.4%
43	Montana	519,330	0.3%
44	Rhode Island	511,949	0.3%
45	Delaware	457,809	0.3%
46	South Dakota	431,976	0.3%
47	Alaska	389,025	0.2%
48	North Dakota	388,853	0.2%
49	Vermont	308,526	0.2%
50	Wyoming	298,901	0.2%
	District of Columbia	318,601	0.2%

Source: U.S. Bureau of the Census

"State Characteristics: Vintage 2015" (http://www.census.gov/programs-surveys/popest/data/data-sets.html)

Female Population in 2015

National Total = 163,189,523 Females

RANK	STATE	FEMALES	% of USA
24	Alabama	2,505,795	1.5%
48	Alaska	349,407	0.2%
15	Arizona	3,436,575	2.1%
32	Arkansas	1,515,348	0.9%
1	California	19,701,750	12.1%
22	Colorado	2,712,811	1.7%
29	Connecticut	1,839,139	1.1%
45	Delaware	488,125	0.3%
3	Florida	10,368,733	6.4%
8	Georgia	5,234,978	3.2%
40	Hawaii	706,231	0.4%
39	Idaho	826,183	0.5%
5	Illinois	6,545,500	4.0%
17	Indiana	3,357,815	2.1%
30	Iowa	1,571,873	1.0%
34	Kansas	1,458,008	0.9%
26	Kentucky	2,245,998	1.4%
25	Louisiana	2,386,915	1.5%
41	Maine	678,071	0.4%
19	Maryland	3,095,316	1.9%
14	Massachusetts	3,498,304	2.1%
10	Michigan	5,044,428	3.1%
21	Minnesota	2,759,730	1.7%
31	Mississippi	1,540,483	0.9%
18	Missouri	3,098,627	1.9%
44	Montana	513,619	0.3%
37	Nebraska	951,022	0.6%
35	Nevada	1,440,294	0.9%
42	New Hampshire	672,952	0.4%
11	New Jersey	4,585,897	2.8%
36	New Mexico	1,051,688	0.6%
4	New York	10,184,278	6.2%
9	North Carolina	5,150,777	3.2%
47	North Dakota	368,074	0.2%
7	Ohio	5,926,893	3.6%
28	Oklahoma	1,974,214	1.2%
27	Oregon	2,035,807	1.2%
6	Pennsylvania	6,538,129	4.0%
43	Rhode Island	544,349	0.3%
23	South Carolina	2,517,178	1.5%
46	South Dakota	426,493	0.3%
16	Tennessee	3,382,838	2.1%
2	Texas	13,831,324	8.5%
33	Utah	1,488,819	0.9%
49	Vermont	317,516	0.2%
12	Virginia	4,258,228	2.6%
13	Washington	3,585,353	2.2%
38	West Virginia	933,068	0.6%
20	Wisconsin	2,903,737	1.8%
50	Wyoming	287,206	0.2%

RANK	STATE	FEMALES	% of USA
1	California	19,701,750	12.1%
2	Texas	13,831,324	8.5%
3	Florida	10,368,733	6.4%
4	New York	10,184,278	6.2%
5	Illinois	6,545,500	4.0%
6	Pennsylvania	6,538,129	4.0%
7	Ohio	5,926,893	3.6%
8	Georgia	5,234,978	3.2%
9	North Carolina	5,150,777	3.2%
10	Michigan	5,044,428	3.1%
11	New Jersey	4,585,897	2.8%
12	Virginia	4,258,228	2.6%
13	Washington	3,585,353	2.2%
14	Massachusetts	3,498,304	2.1%
15	Arizona	3,436,575	2.1%
16	Tennessee	3,382,838	2.1%
17	Indiana	3,357,815	2.1%
18	Missouri	3,098,627	1.9%
19	Maryland	3,095,316	1.9%
20	Wisconsin	2,903,737	1.8%
21	Minnesota	2,759,730	1.7%
22	Colorado	2,712,811	1.7%
23	South Carolina	2,517,178	1.5%
24	Alabama	2,505,795	1.5%
25	Louisiana	2,386,915	1.5%
26	Kentucky	2,245,998	1.4%
27	Oregon	2,035,807	1.2%
28	Oklahoma	1,974,214	1.2%
29	Connecticut	1,839,139	1.1%
30	Iowa	1,571,873	1.0%
31	Mississippi	1,540,483	0.9%
32	Arkansas	1,515,348	0.9%
33	Utah	1,488,819	0.9%
34	Kansas	1,458,008	0.9%
35	Nevada	1,440,294	0.9%
36	New Mexico	1,051,688	0.6%
37	Nebraska	951,022	0.6%
38	West Virginia	933,068	0.6%
39	Idaho	826,183	0.5%
40	Hawaii	706,231	0.4%
41	Maine	678,071	0.4%
42	New Hampshire	672,952	0.4%
43	Rhode Island	544,349	0.3%
44	Montana	513,619	0.3%
45	Delaware	488,125	0.3%
46	South Dakota	426,493	0.3%
47	North Dakota	368,074	0.2%
48	Alaska	349,407	0.2%
49	Vermont	317,516	0.2%
50	Wyoming	287,206	0.2%
	District of Columbia	353,627	0.2%

Source: U.S. Bureau of the Census
  "State Characteristics: Vintage 2015" (http://www.census.gov/programs-surveys/popest/data/data-sets.html)

Male to Female Ratio in 2015

National Ratio = 97.0 Males per 100 Females

<table>
<tr><td colspan="3">ALPHA ORDER</td><td colspan="3">RANK ORDER</td></tr>
<tr><td>RANK</td><td>STATE</td><td>RATIO</td><td>RANK</td><td>STATE</td><td>RATIO</td></tr>
<tr><td>49</td><td>Alabama</td><td>93.9</td><td>1</td><td>Alaska</td><td>111.3</td></tr>
<tr><td>1</td><td>Alaska</td><td>111.3</td><td>2</td><td>North Dakota</td><td>105.6</td></tr>
<tr><td>16</td><td>Arizona</td><td>98.7</td><td>3</td><td>Wyoming</td><td>104.1</td></tr>
<tr><td>30</td><td>Arkansas</td><td>96.5</td><td>4</td><td>Hawaii</td><td>102.7</td></tr>
<tr><td>16</td><td>California</td><td>98.7</td><td>5</td><td>South Dakota</td><td>101.3</td></tr>
<tr><td>7</td><td>Colorado</td><td>101.1</td><td>6</td><td>Utah</td><td>101.2</td></tr>
<tr><td>39</td><td>Connecticut</td><td>95.2</td><td>7</td><td>Colorado</td><td>101.1</td></tr>
<tr><td>50</td><td>Delaware</td><td>93.8</td><td>7</td><td>Montana</td><td>101.1</td></tr>
<tr><td>37</td><td>Florida</td><td>95.5</td><td>9</td><td>Nevada</td><td>100.7</td></tr>
<tr><td>40</td><td>Georgia</td><td>95.1</td><td>10</td><td>Idaho</td><td>100.3</td></tr>
<tr><td>4</td><td>Hawaii</td><td>102.7</td><td>11</td><td>Washington</td><td>100.0</td></tr>
<tr><td>10</td><td>Idaho</td><td>100.3</td><td>12</td><td>Kansas</td><td>99.7</td></tr>
<tr><td>30</td><td>Illinois</td><td>96.5</td><td>13</td><td>Nebraska</td><td>99.4</td></tr>
<tr><td>26</td><td>Indiana</td><td>97.1</td><td>14</td><td>Minnesota</td><td>98.9</td></tr>
<tr><td>16</td><td>Iowa</td><td>98.7</td><td>15</td><td>Wisconsin</td><td>98.8</td></tr>
<tr><td>12</td><td>Kansas</td><td>99.7</td><td>16</td><td>Arizona</td><td>98.7</td></tr>
<tr><td>27</td><td>Kentucky</td><td>97.0</td><td>16</td><td>California</td><td>98.7</td></tr>
<tr><td>36</td><td>Louisiana</td><td>95.7</td><td>16</td><td>Iowa</td><td>98.7</td></tr>
<tr><td>33</td><td>Maine</td><td>96.0</td><td>19</td><td>Texas</td><td>98.6</td></tr>
<tr><td>47</td><td>Maryland</td><td>94.0</td><td>20</td><td>New Mexico</td><td>98.3</td></tr>
<tr><td>45</td><td>Massachusetts</td><td>94.2</td><td>21</td><td>Oklahoma</td><td>98.1</td></tr>
<tr><td>29</td><td>Michigan</td><td>96.7</td><td>22</td><td>Oregon</td><td>97.9</td></tr>
<tr><td>14</td><td>Minnesota</td><td>98.9</td><td>23</td><td>New Hampshire</td><td>97.7</td></tr>
<tr><td>45</td><td>Mississippi</td><td>94.2</td><td>24</td><td>West Virginia</td><td>97.6</td></tr>
<tr><td>32</td><td>Missouri</td><td>96.3</td><td>25</td><td>Vermont</td><td>97.2</td></tr>
<tr><td>7</td><td>Montana</td><td>101.1</td><td>26</td><td>Indiana</td><td>97.1</td></tr>
<tr><td>13</td><td>Nebraska</td><td>99.4</td><td>27</td><td>Kentucky</td><td>97.0</td></tr>
<tr><td>9</td><td>Nevada</td><td>100.7</td><td>28</td><td>Virginia</td><td>96.9</td></tr>
<tr><td>23</td><td>New Hampshire</td><td>97.7</td><td>29</td><td>Michigan</td><td>96.7</td></tr>
<tr><td>38</td><td>New Jersey</td><td>95.3</td><td>30</td><td>Arkansas</td><td>96.5</td></tr>
<tr><td>20</td><td>New Mexico</td><td>98.3</td><td>30</td><td>Illinois</td><td>96.5</td></tr>
<tr><td>44</td><td>New York</td><td>94.4</td><td>32</td><td>Missouri</td><td>96.3</td></tr>
<tr><td>42</td><td>North Carolina</td><td>95.0</td><td>33</td><td>Maine</td><td>96.0</td></tr>
<tr><td>2</td><td>North Dakota</td><td>105.6</td><td>34</td><td>Ohio</td><td>95.9</td></tr>
<tr><td>34</td><td>Ohio</td><td>95.9</td><td>35</td><td>Pennsylvania</td><td>95.8</td></tr>
<tr><td>21</td><td>Oklahoma</td><td>98.1</td><td>36</td><td>Louisiana</td><td>95.7</td></tr>
<tr><td>22</td><td>Oregon</td><td>97.9</td><td>37</td><td>Florida</td><td>95.5</td></tr>
<tr><td>35</td><td>Pennsylvania</td><td>95.8</td><td>38</td><td>New Jersey</td><td>95.3</td></tr>
<tr><td>47</td><td>Rhode Island</td><td>94.0</td><td>39</td><td>Connecticut</td><td>95.2</td></tr>
<tr><td>43</td><td>South Carolina</td><td>94.5</td><td>40</td><td>Georgia</td><td>95.1</td></tr>
<tr><td>5</td><td>South Dakota</td><td>101.3</td><td>40</td><td>Tennessee</td><td>95.1</td></tr>
<tr><td>40</td><td>Tennessee</td><td>95.1</td><td>42</td><td>North Carolina</td><td>95.0</td></tr>
<tr><td>19</td><td>Texas</td><td>98.6</td><td>43</td><td>South Carolina</td><td>94.5</td></tr>
<tr><td>6</td><td>Utah</td><td>101.2</td><td>44</td><td>New York</td><td>94.4</td></tr>
<tr><td>25</td><td>Vermont</td><td>97.2</td><td>45</td><td>Massachusetts</td><td>94.2</td></tr>
<tr><td>28</td><td>Virginia</td><td>96.9</td><td>45</td><td>Mississippi</td><td>94.2</td></tr>
<tr><td>11</td><td>Washington</td><td>100.0</td><td>47</td><td>Maryland</td><td>94.0</td></tr>
<tr><td>24</td><td>West Virginia</td><td>97.6</td><td>47</td><td>Rhode Island</td><td>94.0</td></tr>
<tr><td>15</td><td>Wisconsin</td><td>98.8</td><td>49</td><td>Alabama</td><td>93.9</td></tr>
<tr><td>3</td><td>Wyoming</td><td>104.1</td><td>50</td><td>Delaware</td><td>93.8</td></tr>
<tr><td></td><td></td><td></td><td></td><td>District of Columbia</td><td>90.1</td></tr>
</table>

Source: CQ Press using data from U.S. Bureau of the Census
"State Characteristics: Vintage 2015" (http://www.census.gov/programs-surveys/popest/data/data-sets.html)

Median Age in 2015

National Median = 37.8 Years Old

<table>
<tr><td colspan="3">ALPHA ORDER</td><td colspan="3">RANK ORDER</td></tr>
<tr><th>RANK</th><th>STATE</th><th>MEDIAN AGE</th><th>RANK</th><th>STATE</th><th>MEDIAN AGE</th></tr>
<tr><td>18</td><td>Alabama</td><td>38.7</td><td>1</td><td>Maine</td><td>44.5</td></tr>
<tr><td>49</td><td>Alaska</td><td>33.3</td><td>2</td><td>New Hampshire</td><td>42.8</td></tr>
<tr><td>34</td><td>Arizona</td><td>37.3</td><td>2</td><td>Vermont</td><td>42.8</td></tr>
<tr><td>26</td><td>Arkansas</td><td>37.9</td><td>4</td><td>West Virginia</td><td>42.1</td></tr>
<tr><td>43</td><td>California</td><td>36.2</td><td>5</td><td>Florida</td><td>41.9</td></tr>
<tr><td>39</td><td>Colorado</td><td>36.5</td><td>6</td><td>Pennsylvania</td><td>40.7</td></tr>
<tr><td>7</td><td>Connecticut</td><td>40.6</td><td>7</td><td>Connecticut</td><td>40.6</td></tr>
<tr><td>8</td><td>Delaware</td><td>40.0</td><td>8</td><td>Delaware</td><td>40.0</td></tr>
<tr><td>5</td><td>Florida</td><td>41.9</td><td>9</td><td>Rhode Island</td><td>39.9</td></tr>
<tr><td>41</td><td>Georgia</td><td>36.3</td><td>10</td><td>Montana</td><td>39.8</td></tr>
<tr><td>28</td><td>Hawaii</td><td>37.8</td><td>11</td><td>Michigan</td><td>39.7</td></tr>
<tr><td>46</td><td>Idaho</td><td>35.9</td><td>12</td><td>New Jersey</td><td>39.6</td></tr>
<tr><td>30</td><td>Illinois</td><td>37.7</td><td>13</td><td>Massachusetts</td><td>39.4</td></tr>
<tr><td>33</td><td>Indiana</td><td>37.5</td><td>14</td><td>Ohio</td><td>39.3</td></tr>
<tr><td>25</td><td>Iowa</td><td>38.1</td><td>14</td><td>Oregon</td><td>39.3</td></tr>
<tr><td>45</td><td>Kansas</td><td>36.1</td><td>16</td><td>Wisconsin</td><td>39.2</td></tr>
<tr><td>18</td><td>Kentucky</td><td>38.7</td><td>17</td><td>South Carolina</td><td>39.0</td></tr>
<tr><td>40</td><td>Louisiana</td><td>36.4</td><td>18</td><td>Alabama</td><td>38.7</td></tr>
<tr><td>1</td><td>Maine</td><td>44.5</td><td>18</td><td>Kentucky</td><td>38.7</td></tr>
<tr><td>21</td><td>Maryland</td><td>38.4</td><td>20</td><td>Tennessee</td><td>38.6</td></tr>
<tr><td>13</td><td>Massachusetts</td><td>39.4</td><td>21</td><td>Maryland</td><td>38.4</td></tr>
<tr><td>11</td><td>Michigan</td><td>39.7</td><td>21</td><td>Missouri</td><td>38.4</td></tr>
<tr><td>26</td><td>Minnesota</td><td>37.9</td><td>21</td><td>North Carolina</td><td>38.4</td></tr>
<tr><td>36</td><td>Mississippi</td><td>36.9</td><td>24</td><td>New York</td><td>38.3</td></tr>
<tr><td>21</td><td>Missouri</td><td>38.4</td><td>25</td><td>Iowa</td><td>38.1</td></tr>
<tr><td>10</td><td>Montana</td><td>39.8</td><td>26</td><td>Arkansas</td><td>37.9</td></tr>
<tr><td>41</td><td>Nebraska</td><td>36.3</td><td>26</td><td>Minnesota</td><td>37.9</td></tr>
<tr><td>30</td><td>Nevada</td><td>37.7</td><td>28</td><td>Hawaii</td><td>37.8</td></tr>
<tr><td>2</td><td>New Hampshire</td><td>42.8</td><td>28</td><td>Virginia</td><td>37.8</td></tr>
<tr><td>12</td><td>New Jersey</td><td>39.6</td><td>30</td><td>Illinois</td><td>37.7</td></tr>
<tr><td>34</td><td>New Mexico</td><td>37.3</td><td>30</td><td>Nevada</td><td>37.7</td></tr>
<tr><td>24</td><td>New York</td><td>38.3</td><td>32</td><td>Washington</td><td>37.6</td></tr>
<tr><td>21</td><td>North Carolina</td><td>38.4</td><td>33</td><td>Indiana</td><td>37.5</td></tr>
<tr><td>47</td><td>North Dakota</td><td>34.6</td><td>34</td><td>Arizona</td><td>37.3</td></tr>
<tr><td>14</td><td>Ohio</td><td>39.3</td><td>34</td><td>New Mexico</td><td>37.3</td></tr>
<tr><td>43</td><td>Oklahoma</td><td>36.2</td><td>36</td><td>Mississippi</td><td>36.9</td></tr>
<tr><td>14</td><td>Oregon</td><td>39.3</td><td>36</td><td>South Dakota</td><td>36.9</td></tr>
<tr><td>6</td><td>Pennsylvania</td><td>40.7</td><td>36</td><td>Wyoming</td><td>36.9</td></tr>
<tr><td>9</td><td>Rhode Island</td><td>39.9</td><td>39</td><td>Colorado</td><td>36.5</td></tr>
<tr><td>17</td><td>South Carolina</td><td>39.0</td><td>40</td><td>Louisiana</td><td>36.4</td></tr>
<tr><td>36</td><td>South Dakota</td><td>36.9</td><td>41</td><td>Georgia</td><td>36.3</td></tr>
<tr><td>20</td><td>Tennessee</td><td>38.6</td><td>41</td><td>Nebraska</td><td>36.3</td></tr>
<tr><td>48</td><td>Texas</td><td>34.3</td><td>43</td><td>California</td><td>36.2</td></tr>
<tr><td>50</td><td>Utah</td><td>30.7</td><td>43</td><td>Oklahoma</td><td>36.2</td></tr>
<tr><td>2</td><td>Vermont</td><td>42.8</td><td>45</td><td>Kansas</td><td>36.1</td></tr>
<tr><td>28</td><td>Virginia</td><td>37.8</td><td>46</td><td>Idaho</td><td>35.9</td></tr>
<tr><td>32</td><td>Washington</td><td>37.6</td><td>47</td><td>North Dakota</td><td>34.6</td></tr>
<tr><td>4</td><td>West Virginia</td><td>42.1</td><td>48</td><td>Texas</td><td>34.3</td></tr>
<tr><td>16</td><td>Wisconsin</td><td>39.2</td><td>49</td><td>Alaska</td><td>33.3</td></tr>
<tr><td>36</td><td>Wyoming</td><td>36.9</td><td>50</td><td>Utah</td><td>30.7</td></tr>
<tr><td></td><td></td><td></td><td></td><td>District of Columbia</td><td>33.8</td></tr>
</table>

Source: U.S. Bureau of the Census
   "State Characteristics: Vintage 2015" (http://www.census.gov/programs-surveys/popest/data/data-sets.html)

Male Median Age in 2015

National Median = 36.5 Years Old

ALPHA ORDER

RANK	STATE	MEDIAN AGE
18	Alabama	37.3
49	Alaska	32.7
34	Arizona	36.0
28	Arkansas	36.6
43	California	35.1
38	Colorado	35.5
7	Connecticut	38.9
9	Delaware	38.3
5	Florida	40.3
45	Georgia	35.0
34	Hawaii	36.0
41	Idaho	35.2
30	Illinois	36.4
32	Indiana	36.3
25	Iowa	36.8
46	Kansas	34.9
18	Kentucky	37.3
41	Louisiana	35.2
1	Maine	43.2
25	Maryland	36.8
15	Massachusetts	37.9
9	Michigan	38.3
23	Minnesota	36.9
39	Mississippi	35.4
21	Missouri	37.0
8	Montana	38.7
40	Nebraska	35.3
21	Nevada	37.0
2	New Hampshire	41.7
14	New Jersey	38.0
36	New Mexico	35.9
25	New York	36.8
23	North Carolina	36.9
47	North Dakota	33.6
15	Ohio	37.9
43	Oklahoma	35.1
9	Oregon	38.3
6	Pennsylvania	39.0
13	Rhode Island	38.1
17	South Carolina	37.4
36	South Dakota	35.9
18	Tennessee	37.3
48	Texas	33.4
50	Utah	30.1
3	Vermont	41.3
30	Virginia	36.4
29	Washington	36.5
4	West Virginia	40.8
12	Wisconsin	38.2
33	Wyoming	36.2

RANK ORDER

RANK	STATE	MEDIAN AGE
1	Maine	43.2
2	New Hampshire	41.7
3	Vermont	41.3
4	West Virginia	40.8
5	Florida	40.3
6	Pennsylvania	39.0
7	Connecticut	38.9
8	Montana	38.7
9	Delaware	38.3
9	Michigan	38.3
9	Oregon	38.3
12	Wisconsin	38.2
13	Rhode Island	38.1
14	New Jersey	38.0
15	Massachusetts	37.9
15	Ohio	37.9
17	South Carolina	37.4
18	Alabama	37.3
18	Kentucky	37.3
18	Tennessee	37.3
21	Missouri	37.0
21	Nevada	37.0
23	Minnesota	36.9
23	North Carolina	36.9
25	Iowa	36.8
25	Maryland	36.8
25	New York	36.8
28	Arkansas	36.6
29	Washington	36.5
30	Illinois	36.4
30	Virginia	36.4
32	Indiana	36.3
33	Wyoming	36.2
34	Arizona	36.0
34	Hawaii	36.0
36	New Mexico	35.9
36	South Dakota	35.9
38	Colorado	35.5
39	Mississippi	35.4
40	Nebraska	35.3
41	Idaho	35.2
41	Louisiana	35.2
43	California	35.1
43	Oklahoma	35.1
45	Georgia	35.0
46	Kansas	34.9
47	North Dakota	33.6
48	Texas	33.4
49	Alaska	32.7
50	Utah	30.1
	District of Columbia	33.6

Source: U.S. Bureau of the Census
"State Characteristics: Vintage 2015" (http://www.census.gov/programs-surveys/popest/data/data-sets.html)

Female Median Age in 2015

National Median = 39.1 Years Old

<table>
<tr><td colspan="3">ALPHA ORDER</td><td colspan="3">RANK ORDER</td></tr>
<tr><th>RANK</th><th>STATE</th><th>MEDIAN AGE</th><th>RANK</th><th>STATE</th><th>MEDIAN AGE</th></tr>
<tr><td>18</td><td>Alabama</td><td>40.2</td><td>1</td><td>Maine</td><td>45.6</td></tr>
<tr><td>49</td><td>Alaska</td><td>34.1</td><td>2</td><td>Vermont</td><td>44.1</td></tr>
<tr><td>33</td><td>Arizona</td><td>38.7</td><td>3</td><td>New Hampshire</td><td>43.8</td></tr>
<tr><td>27</td><td>Arkansas</td><td>39.3</td><td>4</td><td>Florida</td><td>43.4</td></tr>
<tr><td>44</td><td>California</td><td>37.4</td><td>4</td><td>West Virginia</td><td>43.4</td></tr>
<tr><td>42</td><td>Colorado</td><td>37.5</td><td>6</td><td>Connecticut</td><td>42.3</td></tr>
<tr><td>6</td><td>Connecticut</td><td>42.3</td><td>6</td><td>Pennsylvania</td><td>42.3</td></tr>
<tr><td>9</td><td>Delaware</td><td>41.5</td><td>8</td><td>Rhode Island</td><td>41.7</td></tr>
<tr><td>4</td><td>Florida</td><td>43.4</td><td>9</td><td>Delaware</td><td>41.5</td></tr>
<tr><td>39</td><td>Georgia</td><td>37.6</td><td>10</td><td>New Jersey</td><td>41.2</td></tr>
<tr><td>24</td><td>Hawaii</td><td>39.8</td><td>11</td><td>Michigan</td><td>41.1</td></tr>
<tr><td>46</td><td>Idaho</td><td>36.7</td><td>12</td><td>Montana</td><td>40.9</td></tr>
<tr><td>29</td><td>Illinois</td><td>38.9</td><td>13</td><td>Massachusetts</td><td>40.8</td></tr>
<tr><td>31</td><td>Indiana</td><td>38.8</td><td>13</td><td>Ohio</td><td>40.8</td></tr>
<tr><td>26</td><td>Iowa</td><td>39.4</td><td>15</td><td>South Carolina</td><td>40.6</td></tr>
<tr><td>39</td><td>Kansas</td><td>37.6</td><td>16</td><td>Wisconsin</td><td>40.4</td></tr>
<tr><td>19</td><td>Kentucky</td><td>40.1</td><td>17</td><td>Oregon</td><td>40.3</td></tr>
<tr><td>38</td><td>Louisiana</td><td>37.7</td><td>18</td><td>Alabama</td><td>40.2</td></tr>
<tr><td>1</td><td>Maine</td><td>45.6</td><td>19</td><td>Kentucky</td><td>40.1</td></tr>
<tr><td>21</td><td>Maryland</td><td>39.9</td><td>20</td><td>Tennessee</td><td>40.0</td></tr>
<tr><td>13</td><td>Massachusetts</td><td>40.8</td><td>21</td><td>Maryland</td><td>39.9</td></tr>
<tr><td>11</td><td>Michigan</td><td>41.1</td><td>21</td><td>New York</td><td>39.9</td></tr>
<tr><td>31</td><td>Minnesota</td><td>38.8</td><td>21</td><td>North Carolina</td><td>39.9</td></tr>
<tr><td>35</td><td>Mississippi</td><td>38.4</td><td>24</td><td>Hawaii</td><td>39.8</td></tr>
<tr><td>24</td><td>Missouri</td><td>39.8</td><td>24</td><td>Missouri</td><td>39.8</td></tr>
<tr><td>12</td><td>Montana</td><td>40.9</td><td>26</td><td>Iowa</td><td>39.4</td></tr>
<tr><td>44</td><td>Nebraska</td><td>37.4</td><td>27</td><td>Arkansas</td><td>39.3</td></tr>
<tr><td>36</td><td>Nevada</td><td>38.3</td><td>28</td><td>Virginia</td><td>39.2</td></tr>
<tr><td>3</td><td>New Hampshire</td><td>43.8</td><td>29</td><td>Illinois</td><td>38.9</td></tr>
<tr><td>10</td><td>New Jersey</td><td>41.2</td><td>29</td><td>New Mexico</td><td>38.9</td></tr>
<tr><td>29</td><td>New Mexico</td><td>38.9</td><td>31</td><td>Indiana</td><td>38.8</td></tr>
<tr><td>21</td><td>New York</td><td>39.9</td><td>31</td><td>Minnesota</td><td>38.8</td></tr>
<tr><td>21</td><td>North Carolina</td><td>39.9</td><td>33</td><td>Arizona</td><td>38.7</td></tr>
<tr><td>47</td><td>North Dakota</td><td>35.8</td><td>33</td><td>Washington</td><td>38.7</td></tr>
<tr><td>13</td><td>Ohio</td><td>40.8</td><td>35</td><td>Mississippi</td><td>38.4</td></tr>
<tr><td>42</td><td>Oklahoma</td><td>37.5</td><td>36</td><td>Nevada</td><td>38.3</td></tr>
<tr><td>17</td><td>Oregon</td><td>40.3</td><td>37</td><td>South Dakota</td><td>38.1</td></tr>
<tr><td>6</td><td>Pennsylvania</td><td>42.3</td><td>38</td><td>Louisiana</td><td>37.7</td></tr>
<tr><td>8</td><td>Rhode Island</td><td>41.7</td><td>39</td><td>Georgia</td><td>37.6</td></tr>
<tr><td>15</td><td>South Carolina</td><td>40.6</td><td>39</td><td>Kansas</td><td>37.6</td></tr>
<tr><td>37</td><td>South Dakota</td><td>38.1</td><td>39</td><td>Wyoming</td><td>37.6</td></tr>
<tr><td>20</td><td>Tennessee</td><td>40.0</td><td>42</td><td>Colorado</td><td>37.5</td></tr>
<tr><td>48</td><td>Texas</td><td>35.3</td><td>42</td><td>Oklahoma</td><td>37.5</td></tr>
<tr><td>50</td><td>Utah</td><td>31.2</td><td>44</td><td>California</td><td>37.4</td></tr>
<tr><td>2</td><td>Vermont</td><td>44.1</td><td>44</td><td>Nebraska</td><td>37.4</td></tr>
<tr><td>28</td><td>Virginia</td><td>39.2</td><td>46</td><td>Idaho</td><td>36.7</td></tr>
<tr><td>33</td><td>Washington</td><td>38.7</td><td>47</td><td>North Dakota</td><td>35.8</td></tr>
<tr><td>4</td><td>West Virginia</td><td>43.4</td><td>48</td><td>Texas</td><td>35.3</td></tr>
<tr><td>16</td><td>Wisconsin</td><td>40.4</td><td>49</td><td>Alaska</td><td>34.1</td></tr>
<tr><td>39</td><td>Wyoming</td><td>37.6</td><td>50</td><td>Utah</td><td>31.2</td></tr>
<tr><td></td><td></td><td></td><td></td><td>District of Columbia</td><td>34.0</td></tr>
</table>

Source: U.S. Bureau of the Census
"State Characteristics: Vintage 2015" (http://www.census.gov/programs-surveys/popest/data/data-sets.html)

White Population in 2015

National Total = 247,784,609*

<table>
<tr><td colspan="4">ALPHA ORDER</td><td colspan="4">RANK ORDER</td></tr>
<tr><td>RANK</td><td>STATE</td><td>POPULATION</td><td>% of USA</td><td>RANK</td><td>STATE</td><td>POPULATION</td><td>% of USA</td></tr>
<tr><td>25</td><td>Alabama</td><td>3,374,569</td><td>1.4%</td><td>1</td><td>California</td><td>28,535,273</td><td>11.5%</td></tr>
<tr><td>49</td><td>Alaska</td><td>491,362</td><td>0.2%</td><td>2</td><td>Texas</td><td>21,889,275</td><td>8.8%</td></tr>
<tr><td>14</td><td>Arizona</td><td>5,698,416</td><td>2.3%</td><td>3</td><td>Florida</td><td>15,748,458</td><td>6.4%</td></tr>
<tr><td>33</td><td>Arkansas</td><td>2,367,701</td><td>1.0%</td><td>4</td><td>New York</td><td>13,874,048</td><td>5.6%</td></tr>
<tr><td>1</td><td>California</td><td>28,535,273</td><td>11.5%</td><td>5</td><td>Pennsylvania</td><td>10,573,536</td><td>4.3%</td></tr>
<tr><td>20</td><td>Colorado</td><td>4,776,848</td><td>1.9%</td><td>6</td><td>Illinois</td><td>9,939,733</td><td>4.0%</td></tr>
<tr><td>29</td><td>Connecticut</td><td>2,902,834</td><td>1.2%</td><td>7</td><td>Ohio</td><td>9,604,912</td><td>3.9%</td></tr>
<tr><td>46</td><td>Delaware</td><td>666,187</td><td>0.3%</td><td>8</td><td>Michigan</td><td>7,909,096</td><td>3.2%</td></tr>
<tr><td>3</td><td>Florida</td><td>15,748,458</td><td>6.4%</td><td>9</td><td>North Carolina</td><td>7,154,774</td><td>2.9%</td></tr>
<tr><td>11</td><td>Georgia</td><td>6,295,964</td><td>2.5%</td><td>10</td><td>New Jersey</td><td>6,506,870</td><td>2.6%</td></tr>
<tr><td>50</td><td>Hawaii</td><td>382,852</td><td>0.2%</td><td>11</td><td>Georgia</td><td>6,295,964</td><td>2.5%</td></tr>
<tr><td>39</td><td>Idaho</td><td>1,545,478</td><td>0.6%</td><td>12</td><td>Virginia</td><td>5,886,416</td><td>2.4%</td></tr>
<tr><td>6</td><td>Illinois</td><td>9,939,733</td><td>4.0%</td><td>13</td><td>Washington</td><td>5,756,587</td><td>2.3%</td></tr>
<tr><td>15</td><td>Indiana</td><td>5,681,607</td><td>2.3%</td><td>14</td><td>Arizona</td><td>5,698,416</td><td>2.3%</td></tr>
<tr><td>30</td><td>Iowa</td><td>2,866,320</td><td>1.2%</td><td>15</td><td>Indiana</td><td>5,681,607</td><td>2.3%</td></tr>
<tr><td>32</td><td>Kansas</td><td>2,523,011</td><td>1.0%</td><td>16</td><td>Massachusetts</td><td>5,580,385</td><td>2.3%</td></tr>
<tr><td>22</td><td>Kentucky</td><td>3,897,987</td><td>1.6%</td><td>17</td><td>Tennessee</td><td>5,199,238</td><td>2.1%</td></tr>
<tr><td>27</td><td>Louisiana</td><td>2,954,189</td><td>1.2%</td><td>18</td><td>Missouri</td><td>5,069,110</td><td>2.0%</td></tr>
<tr><td>40</td><td>Maine</td><td>1,261,773</td><td>0.5%</td><td>19</td><td>Wisconsin</td><td>5,057,594</td><td>2.0%</td></tr>
<tr><td>23</td><td>Maryland</td><td>3,581,757</td><td>1.4%</td><td>20</td><td>Colorado</td><td>4,776,848</td><td>1.9%</td></tr>
<tr><td>16</td><td>Massachusetts</td><td>5,580,385</td><td>2.3%</td><td>21</td><td>Minnesota</td><td>4,685,506</td><td>1.9%</td></tr>
<tr><td>8</td><td>Michigan</td><td>7,909,096</td><td>3.2%</td><td>22</td><td>Kentucky</td><td>3,897,987</td><td>1.6%</td></tr>
<tr><td>21</td><td>Minnesota</td><td>4,685,506</td><td>1.9%</td><td>23</td><td>Maryland</td><td>3,581,757</td><td>1.4%</td></tr>
<tr><td>35</td><td>Mississippi</td><td>1,779,783</td><td>0.7%</td><td>24</td><td>Oregon</td><td>3,529,686</td><td>1.4%</td></tr>
<tr><td>18</td><td>Missouri</td><td>5,069,110</td><td>2.0%</td><td>25</td><td>Alabama</td><td>3,374,569</td><td>1.4%</td></tr>
<tr><td>42</td><td>Montana</td><td>921,857</td><td>0.4%</td><td>26</td><td>South Carolina</td><td>3,347,647</td><td>1.4%</td></tr>
<tr><td>38</td><td>Nebraska</td><td>1,689,616</td><td>0.7%</td><td>27</td><td>Louisiana</td><td>2,954,189</td><td>1.2%</td></tr>
<tr><td>34</td><td>Nevada</td><td>2,187,769</td><td>0.9%</td><td>28</td><td>Oklahoma</td><td>2,925,858</td><td>1.2%</td></tr>
<tr><td>41</td><td>New Hampshire</td><td>1,249,686</td><td>0.5%</td><td>29</td><td>Connecticut</td><td>2,902,834</td><td>1.2%</td></tr>
<tr><td>10</td><td>New Jersey</td><td>6,506,870</td><td>2.6%</td><td>30</td><td>Iowa</td><td>2,866,320</td><td>1.2%</td></tr>
<tr><td>37</td><td>New Mexico</td><td>1,721,137</td><td>0.7%</td><td>31</td><td>Utah</td><td>2,732,481</td><td>1.1%</td></tr>
<tr><td>4</td><td>New York</td><td>13,874,048</td><td>5.6%</td><td>32</td><td>Kansas</td><td>2,523,011</td><td>1.0%</td></tr>
<tr><td>9</td><td>North Carolina</td><td>7,154,774</td><td>2.9%</td><td>33</td><td>Arkansas</td><td>2,367,701</td><td>1.0%</td></tr>
<tr><td>45</td><td>North Dakota</td><td>670,430</td><td>0.3%</td><td>34</td><td>Nevada</td><td>2,187,769</td><td>0.9%</td></tr>
<tr><td>7</td><td>Ohio</td><td>9,604,912</td><td>3.9%</td><td>35</td><td>Mississippi</td><td>1,779,783</td><td>0.7%</td></tr>
<tr><td>28</td><td>Oklahoma</td><td>2,925,858</td><td>1.2%</td><td>36</td><td>West Virginia</td><td>1,726,320</td><td>0.7%</td></tr>
<tr><td>24</td><td>Oregon</td><td>3,529,686</td><td>1.4%</td><td>37</td><td>New Mexico</td><td>1,721,137</td><td>0.7%</td></tr>
<tr><td>5</td><td>Pennsylvania</td><td>10,573,536</td><td>4.3%</td><td>38</td><td>Nebraska</td><td>1,689,616</td><td>0.7%</td></tr>
<tr><td>43</td><td>Rhode Island</td><td>895,343</td><td>0.4%</td><td>39</td><td>Idaho</td><td>1,545,478</td><td>0.6%</td></tr>
<tr><td>26</td><td>South Carolina</td><td>3,347,647</td><td>1.4%</td><td>40</td><td>Maine</td><td>1,261,773</td><td>0.5%</td></tr>
<tr><td>44</td><td>South Dakota</td><td>734,385</td><td>0.3%</td><td>41</td><td>New Hampshire</td><td>1,249,686</td><td>0.5%</td></tr>
<tr><td>17</td><td>Tennessee</td><td>5,199,238</td><td>2.1%</td><td>42</td><td>Montana</td><td>921,857</td><td>0.4%</td></tr>
<tr><td>2</td><td>Texas</td><td>21,889,275</td><td>8.8%</td><td>43</td><td>Rhode Island</td><td>895,343</td><td>0.4%</td></tr>
<tr><td>31</td><td>Utah</td><td>2,732,481</td><td>1.1%</td><td>44</td><td>South Dakota</td><td>734,385</td><td>0.3%</td></tr>
<tr><td>47</td><td>Vermont</td><td>593,361</td><td>0.2%</td><td>45</td><td>North Dakota</td><td>670,430</td><td>0.3%</td></tr>
<tr><td>12</td><td>Virginia</td><td>5,886,416</td><td>2.4%</td><td>46</td><td>Delaware</td><td>666,187</td><td>0.3%</td></tr>
<tr><td>13</td><td>Washington</td><td>5,756,587</td><td>2.3%</td><td>47</td><td>Vermont</td><td>593,361</td><td>0.2%</td></tr>
<tr><td>36</td><td>West Virginia</td><td>1,726,320</td><td>0.7%</td><td>48</td><td>Wyoming</td><td>543,292</td><td>0.2%</td></tr>
<tr><td>19</td><td>Wisconsin</td><td>5,057,594</td><td>2.0%</td><td>49</td><td>Alaska</td><td>491,362</td><td>0.2%</td></tr>
<tr><td>48</td><td>Wyoming</td><td>543,292</td><td>0.2%</td><td>50</td><td>Hawaii</td><td>382,852</td><td>0.2%</td></tr>
<tr><td></td><td></td><td></td><td></td><td></td><td>District of Columbia</td><td>296,292</td><td>0.1%</td></tr>
</table>

Source: U.S. Bureau of the Census
"State Characteristics: Vintage 2015" (http://www.census.gov/programs-surveys/popest/data/data-sets.html)
*Those who identified themselves as one race. "White" is defined by Census as a person having origins in any of the original peoples of Europe, North Africa, or the Middle East. There are 197,970,812 non-Hispanic whites. Census states "Race is a self-identification data item in which respondents choose the race or races with which they most closely identify."

Percent of Population White in 2015

National Percent = 77.1%*

ALPHA ORDER

RANK	STATE	PERCENT
43	Alabama	69.5
45	Alaska	66.5
21	Arizona	83.5
31	Arkansas	79.5
37	California	72.9
15	Colorado	87.5
27	Connecticut	80.8
40	Delaware	70.4
33	Florida	77.7
47	Georgia	61.6
50	Hawaii	26.7
5	Idaho	93.4
34	Illinois	77.3
17	Indiana	85.8
7	Iowa	91.8
16	Kansas	86.7
12	Kentucky	88.1
46	Louisiana	63.2
1	Maine	94.9
48	Maryland	59.6
26	Massachusetts	82.1
29	Michigan	79.7
19	Minnesota	85.4
49	Mississippi	59.5
22	Missouri	83.3
9	Montana	89.2
10	Nebraska	89.1
35	Nevada	75.7
3	New Hampshire	93.9
38	New Jersey	72.6
25	New Mexico	82.5
42	New York	70.1
39	North Carolina	71.2
11	North Dakota	88.6
23	Ohio	82.7
36	Oklahoma	74.8
13	Oregon	87.6
24	Pennsylvania	82.6
20	Rhode Island	84.8
44	South Carolina	68.4
18	South Dakota	85.5
32	Tennessee	78.8
29	Texas	79.7
8	Utah	91.2
2	Vermont	94.8
41	Virginia	70.2
28	Washington	80.3
4	West Virginia	93.6
13	Wisconsin	87.6
6	Wyoming	92.7

RANK ORDER

RANK	STATE	PERCENT
1	Maine	94.9
2	Vermont	94.8
3	New Hampshire	93.9
4	West Virginia	93.6
5	Idaho	93.4
6	Wyoming	92.7
7	Iowa	91.8
8	Utah	91.2
9	Montana	89.2
10	Nebraska	89.1
11	North Dakota	88.6
12	Kentucky	88.1
13	Oregon	87.6
13	Wisconsin	87.6
15	Colorado	87.5
16	Kansas	86.7
17	Indiana	85.8
18	South Dakota	85.5
19	Minnesota	85.4
20	Rhode Island	84.8
21	Arizona	83.5
22	Missouri	83.3
23	Ohio	82.7
24	Pennsylvania	82.6
25	New Mexico	82.5
26	Massachusetts	82.1
27	Connecticut	80.8
28	Washington	80.3
29	Michigan	79.7
29	Texas	79.7
31	Arkansas	79.5
32	Tennessee	78.8
33	Florida	77.7
34	Illinois	77.3
35	Nevada	75.7
36	Oklahoma	74.8
37	California	72.9
38	New Jersey	72.6
39	North Carolina	71.2
40	Delaware	70.4
41	Virginia	70.2
42	New York	70.1
43	Alabama	69.5
44	South Carolina	68.4
45	Alaska	66.5
46	Louisiana	63.2
47	Georgia	61.6
48	Maryland	59.6
49	Mississippi	59.5
50	Hawaii	26.7

District of Columbia	44.1

Source: CQ Press using data from U.S. Bureau of the Census

"State Characteristics: Vintage 2015" (http://www.census.gov/programs-surveys/popest/data/data-sets.html)

*Those who identified themselves as one race. "White" is defined by Census as a person having origins in any of the original peoples of Europe, North Africa, or the Middle East. Non-Hispanic whites comprise 61.6% of the total population. Census states "Race is a self-identification data item in which respondents choose the race or races with which they most closely identify."

Black Population in 2015

National Total = 42,632,530*

ALPHA ORDER

RANK	STATE	POPULATION	% of USA
16	Alabama	1,300,596	3.1%
42	Alaska	28,825	0.1%
26	Arizona	330,467	0.8%
22	Arkansas	466,112	1.1%
5	California	2,552,858	6.0%
31	Colorado	245,197	0.6%
23	Connecticut	418,185	1.0%
32	Delaware	211,859	0.5%
3	Florida	3,408,632	8.0%
4	Georgia	3,240,294	7.6%
41	Hawaii	37,413	0.1%
47	Idaho	13,932	0.0%
7	Illinois	1,888,404	4.4%
20	Indiana	636,646	1.5%
34	Iowa	110,050	0.3%
33	Kansas	182,881	0.4%
25	Kentucky	366,396	0.9%
10	Louisiana	1,517,482	3.6%
44	Maine	19,272	0.0%
8	Maryland	1,829,583	4.3%
21	Massachusetts	574,106	1.3%
13	Michigan	1,410,066	3.3%
27	Minnesota	328,815	0.8%
18	Mississippi	1,124,875	2.6%
19	Missouri	718,518	1.7%
50	Montana	6,250	0.0%
35	Nebraska	93,900	0.2%
30	Nevada	268,042	0.6%
43	New Hampshire	19,819	0.0%
15	New Jersey	1,329,948	3.1%
39	New Mexico	53,429	0.1%
1	New York	3,491,047	8.2%
6	North Carolina	2,223,003	5.2%
45	North Dakota	18,392	0.0%
12	Ohio	1,477,218	3.5%
28	Oklahoma	303,944	0.7%
36	Oregon	83,636	0.2%
11	Pennsylvania	1,497,476	3.5%
37	Rhode Island	83,101	0.2%
14	South Carolina	1,353,056	3.2%
46	South Dakota	15,760	0.0%
17	Tennessee	1,129,765	2.7%
2	Texas	3,444,190	8.1%
40	Utah	40,163	0.1%
49	Vermont	8,140	0.0%
9	Virginia	1,654,264	3.9%
29	Washington	294,992	0.7%
38	West Virginia	67,175	0.2%
24	Wisconsin	381,376	0.9%
48	Wyoming	8,286	0.0%

RANK ORDER

RANK	STATE	POPULATION	% of USA
1	New York	3,491,047	8.2%
2	Texas	3,444,190	8.1%
3	Florida	3,408,632	8.0%
4	Georgia	3,240,294	7.6%
5	California	2,552,858	6.0%
6	North Carolina	2,223,003	5.2%
7	Illinois	1,888,404	4.4%
8	Maryland	1,829,583	4.3%
9	Virginia	1,654,264	3.9%
10	Louisiana	1,517,482	3.6%
11	Pennsylvania	1,497,476	3.5%
12	Ohio	1,477,218	3.5%
13	Michigan	1,410,066	3.3%
14	South Carolina	1,353,056	3.2%
15	New Jersey	1,329,948	3.1%
16	Alabama	1,300,596	3.1%
17	Tennessee	1,129,765	2.7%
18	Mississippi	1,124,875	2.6%
19	Missouri	718,518	1.7%
20	Indiana	636,646	1.5%
21	Massachusetts	574,106	1.3%
22	Arkansas	466,112	1.1%
23	Connecticut	418,185	1.0%
24	Wisconsin	381,376	0.9%
25	Kentucky	366,396	0.9%
26	Arizona	330,467	0.8%
27	Minnesota	328,815	0.8%
28	Oklahoma	303,944	0.7%
29	Washington	294,992	0.7%
30	Nevada	268,042	0.6%
31	Colorado	245,197	0.6%
32	Delaware	211,859	0.5%
33	Kansas	182,881	0.4%
34	Iowa	110,050	0.3%
35	Nebraska	93,900	0.2%
36	Oregon	83,636	0.2%
37	Rhode Island	83,101	0.2%
38	West Virginia	67,175	0.2%
39	New Mexico	53,429	0.1%
40	Utah	40,163	0.1%
41	Hawaii	37,413	0.1%
42	Alaska	28,825	0.1%
43	New Hampshire	19,819	0.0%
44	Maine	19,272	0.0%
45	North Dakota	18,392	0.0%
46	South Dakota	15,760	0.0%
47	Idaho	13,932	0.0%
48	Wyoming	8,286	0.0%
49	Vermont	8,140	0.0%
50	Montana	6,250	0.0%
	District of Columbia	324,694	0.8%

Source: U.S. Bureau of the Census
"State Characteristics: Vintage 2015" (http://www.census.gov/programs-surveys/popest/data/data-sets.html)
*Those who identified themselves as one race. "Black" is defined by Census as a person having origins in any of the Black racial groups of Africa. Census states "Race is a self-identification data item in which respondents choose the race or races with which they most closely identify."

Percent of Population Black in 2015

National Percent = 13.3%*

ALPHA ORDER

RANK	STATE	PERCENT
6	Alabama	26.8
36	Alaska	3.9
33	Arizona	4.8
13	Arkansas	15.7
29	California	6.5
34	Colorado	4.5
21	Connecticut	11.6
7	Delaware	22.4
12	Florida	16.8
3	Georgia	31.7
39	Hawaii	2.6
49	Idaho	0.8
15	Illinois	14.7
22	Indiana	9.6
38	Iowa	3.5
30	Kansas	6.3
25	Kentucky	8.3
2	Louisiana	32.5
45	Maine	1.4
4	Maryland	30.5
24	Massachusetts	8.4
16	Michigan	14.2
31	Minnesota	6.0
1	Mississippi	37.6
19	Missouri	11.8
50	Montana	0.6
32	Nebraska	5.0
23	Nevada	9.3
44	New Hampshire	1.5
14	New Jersey	14.8
39	New Mexico	2.6
10	New York	17.6
8	North Carolina	22.1
41	North Dakota	2.4
17	Ohio	12.7
27	Oklahoma	7.8
42	Oregon	2.1
20	Pennsylvania	11.7
26	Rhode Island	7.9
5	South Carolina	27.6
43	South Dakota	1.8
11	Tennessee	17.1
18	Texas	12.5
47	Utah	1.3
47	Vermont	1.3
9	Virginia	19.7
35	Washington	4.1
37	West Virginia	3.6
28	Wisconsin	6.6
45	Wyoming	1.4

RANK ORDER

RANK	STATE	PERCENT
1	Mississippi	37.6
2	Louisiana	32.5
3	Georgia	31.7
4	Maryland	30.5
5	South Carolina	27.6
6	Alabama	26.8
7	Delaware	22.4
8	North Carolina	22.1
9	Virginia	19.7
10	New York	17.6
11	Tennessee	17.1
12	Florida	16.8
13	Arkansas	15.7
14	New Jersey	14.8
15	Illinois	14.7
16	Michigan	14.2
17	Ohio	12.7
18	Texas	12.5
19	Missouri	11.8
20	Pennsylvania	11.7
21	Connecticut	11.6
22	Indiana	9.6
23	Nevada	9.3
24	Massachusetts	8.4
25	Kentucky	8.3
26	Rhode Island	7.9
27	Oklahoma	7.8
28	Wisconsin	6.6
29	California	6.5
30	Kansas	6.3
31	Minnesota	6.0
32	Nebraska	5.0
33	Arizona	4.8
34	Colorado	4.5
35	Washington	4.1
36	Alaska	3.9
37	West Virginia	3.6
38	Iowa	3.5
39	Hawaii	2.6
39	New Mexico	2.6
41	North Dakota	2.4
42	Oregon	2.1
43	South Dakota	1.8
44	New Hampshire	1.5
45	Maine	1.4
45	Wyoming	1.4
47	Utah	1.3
47	Vermont	1.3
49	Idaho	0.8
50	Montana	0.6
	District of Columbia	48.3

Source: CQ Press using data from U.S. Bureau of the Census
   "State Characteristics: Vintage 2015" (http://www.census.gov/programs-surveys/popest/data/data-sets.html)
*Those who identified themselves as one race. "Black" is defined by Census as a person having origins in any of the Black racial groups of Africa. Census states "Race is a self-identification data item in which respondents choose the race or races with which they most closely identify."

Hispanic Population in 2015

National Total = 56,592,793*

ALPHA ORDER

ALPHA ORDER

RANK	STATE	POPULATION	% of USA
33	Alabama	203,325	0.4%
43	Alaska	51,826	0.1%
6	Arizona	2,098,410	3.7%
32	Arkansas	213,957	0.4%
1	California	15,184,548	26.8%
8	Colorado	1,164,274	2.1%
18	Connecticut	553,781	1.0%
41	Delaware	85,305	0.2%
3	Florida	4,964,077	8.8%
10	Georgia	955,434	1.7%
39	Hawaii	148,705	0.3%
34	Idaho	202,430	0.4%
5	Illinois	2,175,116	3.8%
21	Indiana	441,909	0.8%
36	Iowa	178,620	0.3%
27	Kansas	336,594	0.6%
37	Kentucky	152,224	0.3%
31	Louisiana	232,532	0.4%
49	Maine	20,924	0.0%
17	Maryland	572,373	1.0%
15	Massachusetts	759,194	1.3%
20	Michigan	485,974	0.9%
28	Minnesota	284,214	0.5%
40	Mississippi	91,564	0.2%
30	Missouri	247,567	0.4%
45	Montana	37,201	0.1%
35	Nebraska	197,416	0.3%
44	New Hampshire	45,619	0.1%
7	New Jersey	1,762,181	3.1%
9	New Mexico	1,001,258	1.8%
4	New York	3,726,804	6.6%
11	North Carolina	916,742	1.6%
48	North Dakota	26,814	0.0%
22	Ohio	414,641	0.7%
24	Oklahoma	396,459	0.7%
19	Oregon	511,901	0.9%
13	Pennsylvania	872,386	1.5%
38	Rhode Island	152,084	0.3%
29	South Carolina	268,352	0.5%
46	South Dakota	31,214	0.1%
26	Tennessee	340,508	0.6%
2	Texas	10,670,101	18.9%
23	Utah	411,143	0.7%
50	Vermont	11,525	0.0%
16	Virginia	754,737	1.3%
12	Washington	886,418	1.6%
47	West Virginia	27,809	0.0%
25	Wisconsin	381,877	0.7%
42	Wyoming	58,207	0.1%

RANK ORDER

RANK	STATE	POPULATION	% of USA
1	California	15,184,548	26.8%
2	Texas	10,670,101	18.9%
3	Florida	4,964,077	8.8%
4	New York	3,726,804	6.6%
5	Illinois	2,175,116	3.8%
6	Arizona	2,098,410	3.7%
7	New Jersey	1,762,181	3.1%
8	Colorado	1,164,274	2.1%
9	New Mexico	1,001,258	1.8%
10	Georgia	955,434	1.7%
11	North Carolina	916,742	1.6%
12	Washington	886,418	1.6%
13	Pennsylvania	872,386	1.5%
14	Nevada	813,391	1.4%
15	Massachusetts	759,194	1.3%
16	Virginia	754,737	1.3%
17	Maryland	572,373	1.0%
18	Connecticut	553,781	1.0%
19	Oregon	511,901	0.9%
20	Michigan	485,974	0.9%
21	Indiana	441,909	0.8%
22	Ohio	414,641	0.7%
23	Utah	411,143	0.7%
24	Oklahoma	396,459	0.7%
25	Wisconsin	381,877	0.7%
26	Tennessee	340,508	0.6%
27	Kansas	336,594	0.6%
28	Minnesota	284,214	0.5%
29	South Carolina	268,352	0.5%
30	Missouri	247,567	0.4%
31	Louisiana	232,532	0.4%
32	Arkansas	213,957	0.4%
33	Alabama	203,325	0.4%
34	Idaho	202,430	0.4%
35	Nebraska	197,416	0.3%
36	Iowa	178,620	0.3%
37	Kentucky	152,224	0.3%
38	Rhode Island	152,084	0.3%
39	Hawaii	148,705	0.3%
40	Mississippi	91,564	0.2%
41	Delaware	85,305	0.2%
42	Wyoming	58,207	0.1%
43	Alaska	51,826	0.1%
44	New Hampshire	45,619	0.1%
45	Montana	37,201	0.1%
46	South Dakota	31,214	0.1%
47	West Virginia	27,809	0.0%
48	North Dakota	26,814	0.0%
49	Maine	20,924	0.0%
50	Vermont	11,525	0.0%
	District of Columbia	71,128	0.1%

Source: U.S. Bureau of the Census
"State Characteristics: Vintage 2015" (http://www.census.gov/programs-surveys/popest/data/data-sets.html)
*Persons of Hispanic origin may be of any race. Census states "Race is a self-identification data item in which respondents choose the race or races with which they most closely identify."

Percent of Population Hispanic in 2015

National Percent = 17.6%*

ALPHA ORDER

RANK	STATE	PERCENT
39	Alabama	4.2
29	Alaska	7.0
4	Arizona	30.7
28	Arkansas	7.2
2	California	38.8
7	Colorado	21.3
11	Connecticut	15.4
26	Delaware	9.0
6	Florida	24.5
24	Georgia	9.4
19	Hawaii	10.4
16	Idaho	12.2
10	Illinois	16.9
31	Indiana	6.7
33	Iowa	5.7
17	Kansas	11.6
45	Kentucky	3.4
37	Louisiana	5.0
49	Maine	1.6
23	Maryland	9.5
18	Massachusetts	11.2
38	Michigan	4.9
35	Minnesota	5.2
47	Mississippi	3.1
40	Missouri	4.1
41	Montana	3.6
19	Nebraska	10.4
5	Nevada	28.1
45	New Hampshire	3.4
8	New Jersey	19.7
1	New Mexico	48.0
9	New York	18.8
25	North Carolina	9.1
44	North Dakota	3.5
41	Ohio	3.6
21	Oklahoma	10.1
14	Oregon	12.7
30	Pennsylvania	6.8
12	Rhode Island	14.4
34	South Carolina	5.5
41	South Dakota	3.6
35	Tennessee	5.2
2	Texas	38.8
13	Utah	13.7
48	Vermont	1.8
26	Virginia	9.0
15	Washington	12.4
50	West Virginia	1.5
32	Wisconsin	6.6
22	Wyoming	9.9

RANK ORDER

RANK	STATE	PERCENT
1	New Mexico	48.0
2	California	38.8
2	Texas	38.8
4	Arizona	30.7
5	Nevada	28.1
6	Florida	24.5
7	Colorado	21.3
8	New Jersey	19.7
9	New York	18.8
10	Illinois	16.9
11	Connecticut	15.4
12	Rhode Island	14.4
13	Utah	13.7
14	Oregon	12.7
15	Washington	12.4
16	Idaho	12.2
17	Kansas	11.6
18	Massachusetts	11.2
19	Hawaii	10.4
19	Nebraska	10.4
21	Oklahoma	10.1
22	Wyoming	9.9
23	Maryland	9.5
24	Georgia	9.4
25	North Carolina	9.1
26	Delaware	9.0
26	Virginia	9.0
28	Arkansas	7.2
29	Alaska	7.0
30	Pennsylvania	6.8
31	Indiana	6.7
32	Wisconsin	6.6
33	Iowa	5.7
34	South Carolina	5.5
35	Minnesota	5.2
35	Tennessee	5.2
37	Louisiana	5.0
38	Michigan	4.9
39	Alabama	4.2
40	Missouri	4.1
41	Montana	3.6
41	Ohio	3.6
41	South Dakota	3.6
44	North Dakota	3.5
45	Kentucky	3.4
45	New Hampshire	3.4
47	Mississippi	3.1
48	Vermont	1.8
49	Maine	1.6
50	West Virginia	1.5
	District of Columbia	10.6

Source: CQ Press using data from U.S. Bureau of the Census
"State Characteristics: Vintage 2015" (http://www.census.gov/programs-surveys/popest/data/data-sets.html)
*Persons of Hispanic origin may be of any race. Census states "Race is a self-identification data item in which respondents choose the race or races with which they most closely identify."

Asian Population in 2015

National Total = 17,982,195*

ALPHA ORDER

RANK	STATE	POPULATION	% of USA
33	Alabama	67,196	0.4%
36	Alaska	46,191	0.3%
19	Arizona	231,462	1.3%
35	Arkansas	46,911	0.3%
1	California	5,736,988	31.9%
21	Colorado	176,793	1.0%
22	Connecticut	166,341	0.9%
39	Delaware	36,972	0.2%
7	Florida	576,690	3.2%
12	Georgia	409,119	2.3%
9	Hawaii	533,402	3.0%
43	Idaho	24,609	0.1%
5	Illinois	707,192	3.9%
24	Indiana	141,740	0.8%
32	Iowa	73,564	0.4%
29	Kansas	84,577	0.5%
34	Kentucky	63,953	0.4%
27	Louisiana	85,870	0.5%
44	Maine	16,378	0.1%
13	Maryland	391,985	2.2%
10	Massachusetts	445,927	2.5%
14	Michigan	297,650	1.7%
16	Minnesota	268,042	1.5%
42	Mississippi	31,774	0.2%
25	Missouri	121,406	0.7%
49	Montana	8,582	0.0%
37	Nebraska	44,479	0.2%
17	Nevada	246,974	1.4%
41	New Hampshire	34,843	0.2%
4	New Jersey	868,800	4.8%
40	New Mexico	35,933	0.2%
2	New York	1,733,570	9.6%
15	North Carolina	284,153	1.6%
47	North Dakota	10,564	0.1%
18	Ohio	244,720	1.4%
28	Oklahoma	85,766	0.5%
20	Oregon	177,473	1.0%
11	Pennsylvania	435,121	2.4%
38	Rhode Island	37,871	0.2%
30	South Carolina	77,980	0.4%
46	South Dakota	11,813	0.1%
26	Tennessee	117,196	0.7%
3	Texas	1,299,874	7.2%
31	Utah	74,734	0.4%
48	Vermont	10,277	0.1%
8	Virginia	545,973	3.0%
6	Washington	603,214	3.4%
45	West Virginia	15,538	0.1%
23	Wisconsin	159,645	0.9%
50	Wyoming	6,072	0.0%

RANK ORDER

RANK	STATE	POPULATION	% of USA
1	California	5,736,988	31.9%
2	New York	1,733,570	9.6%
3	Texas	1,299,874	7.2%
4	New Jersey	868,800	4.8%
5	Illinois	707,192	3.9%
6	Washington	603,214	3.4%
7	Florida	576,690	3.2%
8	Virginia	545,973	3.0%
9	Hawaii	533,402	3.0%
10	Massachusetts	445,927	2.5%
11	Pennsylvania	435,121	2.4%
12	Georgia	409,119	2.3%
13	Maryland	391,985	2.2%
14	Michigan	297,650	1.7%
15	North Carolina	284,153	1.6%
16	Minnesota	268,042	1.5%
17	Nevada	246,974	1.4%
18	Ohio	244,720	1.4%
19	Arizona	231,462	1.3%
20	Oregon	177,473	1.0%
21	Colorado	176,793	1.0%
22	Connecticut	166,341	0.9%
23	Wisconsin	159,645	0.9%
24	Indiana	141,740	0.8%
25	Missouri	121,406	0.7%
26	Tennessee	117,196	0.7%
27	Louisiana	85,870	0.5%
28	Oklahoma	85,766	0.5%
29	Kansas	84,577	0.5%
30	South Carolina	77,980	0.4%
31	Utah	74,734	0.4%
32	Iowa	73,564	0.4%
33	Alabama	67,196	0.4%
34	Kentucky	63,953	0.4%
35	Arkansas	46,911	0.3%
36	Alaska	46,191	0.3%
37	Nebraska	44,479	0.2%
38	Rhode Island	37,871	0.2%
39	Delaware	36,972	0.2%
40	New Mexico	35,933	0.2%
41	New Hampshire	34,843	0.2%
42	Mississippi	31,774	0.2%
43	Idaho	24,609	0.1%
44	Maine	16,378	0.1%
45	West Virginia	15,538	0.1%
46	South Dakota	11,813	0.1%
47	North Dakota	10,564	0.1%
48	Vermont	10,277	0.1%
49	Montana	8,582	0.0%
50	Wyoming	6,072	0.0%
	District of Columbia	28,298	0.2%

Source: U.S. Bureau of the Census
   "State Characteristics: Vintage 2015" (http://www.census.gov/programs-surveys/popest/data/data-sets.html)
*Those who identified themselves as one race. Census states "Race is a self-identification data item in which respondents choose the race or races with which they most closely identify."

Percent of Population Asian in 2015

National Percent = 5.6%*

ALPHA ORDER

RANK	STATE	PERCENT
42	Alabama	1.4
10	Alaska	6.3
19	Arizona	3.4
38	Arkansas	1.6
2	California	14.7
21	Colorado	3.2
14	Connecticut	4.6
17	Delaware	3.9
24	Florida	2.8
16	Georgia	4.0
1	Hawaii	37.3
41	Idaho	1.5
11	Illinois	5.5
32	Indiana	2.1
29	Iowa	2.4
23	Kansas	2.9
42	Kentucky	1.4
35	Louisiana	1.8
46	Maine	1.2
8	Maryland	6.5
7	Massachusetts	6.6
22	Michigan	3.0
12	Minnesota	4.9
47	Mississippi	1.1
34	Missouri	2.0
49	Montana	0.8
30	Nebraska	2.3
5	Nevada	8.5
27	New Hampshire	2.6
3	New Jersey	9.7
37	New Mexico	1.7
4	New York	8.8
24	North Carolina	2.8
42	North Dakota	1.4
32	Ohio	2.1
31	Oklahoma	2.2
15	Oregon	4.4
19	Pennsylvania	3.4
18	Rhode Island	3.6
38	South Carolina	1.6
42	South Dakota	1.4
35	Tennessee	1.8
13	Texas	4.7
28	Utah	2.5
38	Vermont	1.6
8	Virginia	6.5
6	Washington	8.4
49	West Virginia	0.8
24	Wisconsin	2.8
48	Wyoming	1.0

RANK ORDER

RANK	STATE	PERCENT
1	Hawaii	37.3
2	California	14.7
3	New Jersey	9.7
4	New York	8.8
5	Nevada	8.5
6	Washington	8.4
7	Massachusetts	6.6
8	Maryland	6.5
8	Virginia	6.5
10	Alaska	6.3
11	Illinois	5.5
12	Minnesota	4.9
13	Texas	4.7
14	Connecticut	4.6
15	Oregon	4.4
16	Georgia	4.0
17	Delaware	3.9
18	Rhode Island	3.6
19	Arizona	3.4
19	Pennsylvania	3.4
21	Colorado	3.2
22	Michigan	3.0
23	Kansas	2.9
24	Florida	2.8
24	North Carolina	2.8
24	Wisconsin	2.8
27	New Hampshire	2.6
28	Utah	2.5
29	Iowa	2.4
30	Nebraska	2.3
31	Oklahoma	2.2
32	Indiana	2.1
32	Ohio	2.1
34	Missouri	2.0
35	Louisiana	1.8
35	Tennessee	1.8
37	New Mexico	1.7
38	Arkansas	1.6
38	South Carolina	1.6
38	Vermont	1.6
41	Idaho	1.5
42	Alabama	1.4
42	Kentucky	1.4
42	North Dakota	1.4
42	South Dakota	1.4
46	Maine	1.2
47	Mississippi	1.1
48	Wyoming	1.0
49	Montana	0.8
49	West Virginia	0.8
	District of Columbia	4.2

Source: CQ Press using data from U.S. Bureau of the Census
"State Characteristics: Vintage 2015" (http://www.census.gov/programs-surveys/popest/data/data-sets.html)
*Those who identified themselves as one race. Census states "Race is a self-identification data item in which respondents choose the race or races with which they most closely identify."

American Indian Population in 2015

National Total = 4,010,885*

ALPHA ORDER

RANK	STATE	POPULATION	% of USA
28	Alabama	33,980	0.8%
9	Alaska	109,515	2.7%
2	Arizona	362,968	9.0%
34	Arkansas	29,268	0.7%
1	California	648,172	16.2%
11	Colorado	86,567	2.2%
39	Connecticut	19,132	0.5%
47	Delaware	6,189	0.2%
10	Florida	101,060	2.5%
20	Georgia	51,405	1.3%
46	Hawaii	6,475	0.2%
35	Idaho	28,833	0.7%
13	Illinois	75,460	1.9%
36	Indiana	26,656	0.7%
42	Iowa	15,662	0.4%
27	Kansas	34,810	0.9%
43	Kentucky	13,012	0.3%
26	Louisiana	35,648	0.9%
45	Maine	9,194	0.2%
29	Maryland	33,792	0.8%
31	Massachusetts	32,751	0.8%
16	Michigan	71,545	1.8%
14	Minnesota	73,101	1.8%
40	Mississippi	17,810	0.4%
30	Missouri	33,499	0.8%
17	Montana	67,916	1.7%
37	Nebraska	26,492	0.7%
21	Nevada	47,610	1.2%
49	New Hampshire	3,885	0.1%
19	New Jersey	53,775	1.3%
5	New Mexico	219,237	5.5%
6	New York	190,539	4.8%
7	North Carolina	156,173	3.9%
25	North Dakota	41,315	1.0%
32	Ohio	31,847	0.8%
3	Oklahoma	355,795	8.9%
15	Oregon	72,327	1.8%
24	Pennsylvania	45,343	1.1%
44	Rhode Island	10,192	0.3%
38	South Carolina	26,412	0.7%
12	South Dakota	76,698	1.9%
33	Tennessee	29,480	0.7%
4	Texas	280,463	7.0%
22	Utah	46,023	1.1%
50	Vermont	2,381	0.1%
23	Virginia	45,483	1.1%
8	Washington	135,957	3.4%
48	West Virginia	4,459	0.1%
18	Wisconsin	65,072	1.6%
41	Wyoming	15,757	0.4%

RANK ORDER

RANK	STATE	POPULATION	% of USA
1	California	648,172	16.2%
2	Arizona	362,968	9.0%
3	Oklahoma	355,795	8.9%
4	Texas	280,463	7.0%
5	New Mexico	219,237	5.5%
6	New York	190,539	4.8%
7	North Carolina	156,173	3.9%
8	Washington	135,957	3.4%
9	Alaska	109,515	2.7%
10	Florida	101,060	2.5%
11	Colorado	86,567	2.2%
12	South Dakota	76,698	1.9%
13	Illinois	75,460	1.9%
14	Minnesota	73,101	1.8%
15	Oregon	72,327	1.8%
16	Michigan	71,545	1.8%
17	Montana	67,916	1.7%
18	Wisconsin	65,072	1.6%
19	New Jersey	53,775	1.3%
20	Georgia	51,405	1.3%
21	Nevada	47,610	1.2%
22	Utah	46,023	1.1%
23	Virginia	45,483	1.1%
24	Pennsylvania	45,343	1.1%
25	North Dakota	41,315	1.0%
26	Louisiana	35,648	0.9%
27	Kansas	34,810	0.9%
28	Alabama	33,980	0.8%
29	Maryland	33,792	0.8%
30	Missouri	33,499	0.8%
31	Massachusetts	32,751	0.8%
32	Ohio	31,847	0.8%
33	Tennessee	29,480	0.7%
34	Arkansas	29,268	0.7%
35	Idaho	28,833	0.7%
36	Indiana	26,656	0.7%
37	Nebraska	26,492	0.7%
38	South Carolina	26,412	0.7%
39	Connecticut	19,132	0.5%
40	Mississippi	17,810	0.4%
41	Wyoming	15,757	0.4%
42	Iowa	15,662	0.4%
43	Kentucky	13,012	0.3%
44	Rhode Island	10,192	0.3%
45	Maine	9,194	0.2%
46	Hawaii	6,475	0.2%
47	Delaware	6,189	0.2%
48	West Virginia	4,459	0.1%
49	New Hampshire	3,885	0.1%
50	Vermont	2,381	0.1%
	District of Columbia	3,750	0.1%

Source: U.S. Bureau of the Census

"State Characteristics: Vintage 2015" (http://www.census.gov/programs-surveys/popest/data/data-sets.html)

*Those who identified themselves as one race. Includes Alaska Native populations. Census states "Race is a self-identification data item in which respondents choose the race or races with which they most closely identify."

Percent of Population American Indian in 2015

National Percent = 1.2%*

RANK	STATE	PERCENT
26	Alabama	0.7
1	Alaska	14.8
7	Arizona	5.3
21	Arkansas	1.0
11	California	1.7
13	Colorado	1.6
35	Connecticut	0.5
26	Delaware	0.7
35	Florida	0.5
35	Georgia	0.5
35	Hawaii	0.5
11	Idaho	1.7
30	Illinois	0.6
43	Indiana	0.4
35	Iowa	0.5
19	Kansas	1.2
47	Kentucky	0.3
25	Louisiana	0.8
26	Maine	0.7
30	Maryland	0.6
35	Massachusetts	0.5
26	Michigan	0.7
18	Minnesota	1.3
30	Mississippi	0.6
30	Missouri	0.6
5	Montana	6.6
17	Nebraska	1.4
13	Nevada	1.6
47	New Hampshire	0.3
30	New Jersey	0.6
2	New Mexico	10.5
21	New York	1.0
13	North Carolina	1.6
6	North Dakota	5.5
47	Ohio	0.3
3	Oklahoma	9.1
10	Oregon	1.8
43	Pennsylvania	0.4
21	Rhode Island	1.0
35	South Carolina	0.5
4	South Dakota	8.9
43	Tennessee	0.4
21	Texas	1.0
16	Utah	1.5
43	Vermont	0.4
35	Virginia	0.5
9	Washington	1.9
50	West Virginia	0.2
20	Wisconsin	1.1
8	Wyoming	2.7

RANK	STATE	PERCENT
1	Alaska	14.8
2	New Mexico	10.5
3	Oklahoma	9.1
4	South Dakota	8.9
5	Montana	6.6
6	North Dakota	5.5
7	Arizona	5.3
8	Wyoming	2.7
9	Washington	1.9
10	Oregon	1.8
11	California	1.7
11	Idaho	1.7
13	Colorado	1.6
13	Nevada	1.6
13	North Carolina	1.6
16	Utah	1.5
17	Nebraska	1.4
18	Minnesota	1.3
19	Kansas	1.2
20	Wisconsin	1.1
21	Arkansas	1.0
21	New York	1.0
21	Rhode Island	1.0
21	Texas	1.0
25	Louisiana	0.8
26	Alabama	0.7
26	Delaware	0.7
26	Maine	0.7
26	Michigan	0.7
30	Illinois	0.6
30	Maryland	0.6
30	Mississippi	0.6
30	Missouri	0.6
30	New Jersey	0.6
35	Connecticut	0.5
35	Florida	0.5
35	Georgia	0.5
35	Hawaii	0.5
35	Iowa	0.5
35	Massachusetts	0.5
35	South Carolina	0.5
35	Virginia	0.5
43	Indiana	0.4
43	Pennsylvania	0.4
43	Tennessee	0.4
43	Vermont	0.4
47	Kentucky	0.3
47	New Hampshire	0.3
47	Ohio	0.3
50	West Virginia	0.2
	District of Columbia	0.6

Source: CQ Press using data from U.S. Bureau of the Census
"State Characteristics: Vintage 2015" (http://www.census.gov/programs-surveys/popest/data/data-sets.html)
*Those who identified themselves as one race. Includes Alaska Native populations. Census states "Race is a self-identification data item in which respondents choose the race or races with which they most closely identify."

Native Hawaiian or Other Pacific Islander Population in 2015

National Total = 760,190*

ALPHA ORDER

RANK	STATE	POPULATION	% of USA
26	Alabama	5,067	0.7%
15	Alaska	9,612	1.3%
9	Arizona	18,166	2.4%
19	Arkansas	8,757	1.2%
1	California	196,652	25.9%
13	Colorado	10,525	1.4%
30	Connecticut	3,942	0.5%
43	Delaware	866	0.1%
7	Florida	22,857	3.0%
12	Georgia	12,229	1.6%
2	Hawaii	142,260	18.7%
34	Idaho	3,383	0.4%
20	Illinois	8,317	1.1%
28	Indiana	4,149	0.5%
36	Iowa	3,209	0.4%
35	Kansas	3,300	0.4%
31	Kentucky	3,701	0.5%
37	Louisiana	3,131	0.4%
49	Maine	478	0.1%
23	Maryland	6,479	0.9%
21	Massachusetts	6,863	0.9%
29	Michigan	3,998	0.5%
32	Minnesota	3,567	0.5%
41	Mississippi	1,826	0.2%
17	Missouri	8,857	1.2%
42	Montana	922	0.1%
39	Nebraska	2,338	0.3%
8	Nevada	21,876	2.9%
46	New Hampshire	639	0.1%
16	New Jersey	9,202	1.2%
33	New Mexico	3,485	0.5%
6	New York	26,786	3.5%
11	North Carolina	12,395	1.6%
47	North Dakota	623	0.1%
25	Ohio	6,155	0.8%
22	Oklahoma	6,718	0.9%
10	Oregon	17,674	2.3%
18	Pennsylvania	8,799	1.2%
40	Rhode Island	1,882	0.2%
27	South Carolina	4,580	0.6%
45	South Dakota	662	0.1%
24	Tennessee	6,419	0.8%
4	Texas	38,217	5.0%
5	Utah	30,195	4.0%
50	Vermont	241	0.0%
14	Virginia	9,777	1.3%
3	Washington	53,195	7.0%
48	West Virginia	546	0.1%
38	Wisconsin	2,934	0.4%
44	Wyoming	676	0.1%

RANK ORDER

RANK	STATE	POPULATION	% of USA
1	California	196,652	25.9%
2	Hawaii	142,260	18.7%
3	Washington	53,195	7.0%
4	Texas	38,217	5.0%
5	Utah	30,195	4.0%
6	New York	26,786	3.5%
7	Florida	22,857	3.0%
8	Nevada	21,876	2.9%
9	Arizona	18,166	2.4%
10	Oregon	17,674	2.3%
11	North Carolina	12,395	1.6%
12	Georgia	12,229	1.6%
13	Colorado	10,525	1.4%
14	Virginia	9,777	1.3%
15	Alaska	9,612	1.3%
16	New Jersey	9,202	1.2%
17	Missouri	8,857	1.2%
18	Pennsylvania	8,799	1.2%
19	Arkansas	8,757	1.2%
20	Illinois	8,317	1.1%
21	Massachusetts	6,863	0.9%
22	Oklahoma	6,718	0.9%
23	Maryland	6,479	0.9%
24	Tennessee	6,419	0.8%
25	Ohio	6,155	0.8%
26	Alabama	5,067	0.7%
27	South Carolina	4,580	0.6%
28	Indiana	4,149	0.5%
29	Michigan	3,998	0.5%
30	Connecticut	3,942	0.5%
31	Kentucky	3,701	0.5%
32	Minnesota	3,567	0.5%
33	New Mexico	3,485	0.5%
34	Idaho	3,383	0.4%
35	Kansas	3,300	0.4%
36	Iowa	3,209	0.4%
37	Louisiana	3,131	0.4%
38	Wisconsin	2,934	0.4%
39	Nebraska	2,338	0.3%
40	Rhode Island	1,882	0.2%
41	Mississippi	1,826	0.2%
42	Montana	922	0.1%
43	Delaware	866	0.1%
44	Wyoming	676	0.1%
45	South Dakota	662	0.1%
46	New Hampshire	639	0.1%
47	North Dakota	623	0.1%
48	West Virginia	546	0.1%
49	Maine	478	0.1%
50	Vermont	241	0.0%
	District of Columbia	1,063	0.1%

Source: U.S. Bureau of the Census

"State Characteristics: Vintage 2015" (http://www.census.gov/programs-surveys/popest/data/data-sets.html)

*Those who identified themselves as one race. Census states "Race is a self-identification data item in which respondents choose the race or races with which they most closely identify."

Percent of Population Native Hawaiian or Other Pacific Islander in 2015

National Percent = 0.2%*

RANK	STATE	PERCENT
15	Alabama	0.1
2	Alaska	1.3
8	Arizona	0.3
8	Arkansas	0.3
6	California	0.5
10	Colorado	0.2
15	Connecticut	0.1
15	Delaware	0.1
15	Florida	0.1
15	Georgia	0.1
1	Hawaii	9.9
10	Idaho	0.2
15	Illinois	0.1
15	Indiana	0.1
15	Iowa	0.1
15	Kansas	0.1
15	Kentucky	0.1
15	Louisiana	0.1
46	Maine	0.0
15	Maryland	0.1
15	Massachusetts	0.1
46	Michigan	0.0
15	Minnesota	0.1
15	Mississippi	0.1
15	Missouri	0.1
15	Montana	0.1
15	Nebraska	0.1
4	Nevada	0.8
46	New Hampshire	0.0
15	New Jersey	0.1
10	New Mexico	0.2
15	New York	0.1
15	North Carolina	0.1
15	North Dakota	0.1
15	Ohio	0.1
10	Oklahoma	0.2
7	Oregon	0.4
15	Pennsylvania	0.1
10	Rhode Island	0.2
15	South Carolina	0.1
15	South Dakota	0.1
15	Tennessee	0.1
15	Texas	0.1
3	Utah	1.0
46	Vermont	0.0
15	Virginia	0.1
5	Washington	0.7
46	West Virginia	0.0
15	Wisconsin	0.1
15	Wyoming	0.1

RANK	STATE	PERCENT
1	Hawaii	9.9
2	Alaska	1.3
3	Utah	1.0
4	Nevada	0.8
5	Washington	0.7
6	California	0.5
7	Oregon	0.4
8	Arizona	0.3
8	Arkansas	0.3
10	Colorado	0.2
10	Idaho	0.2
10	New Mexico	0.2
10	Oklahoma	0.2
10	Rhode Island	0.2
15	Alabama	0.1
15	Connecticut	0.1
15	Delaware	0.1
15	Florida	0.1
15	Georgia	0.1
15	Illinois	0.1
15	Indiana	0.1
15	Iowa	0.1
15	Kansas	0.1
15	Kentucky	0.1
15	Louisiana	0.1
15	Maryland	0.1
15	Massachusetts	0.1
15	Minnesota	0.1
15	Mississippi	0.1
15	Missouri	0.1
15	Montana	0.1
15	Nebraska	0.1
15	New Jersey	0.1
15	New York	0.1
15	North Carolina	0.1
15	North Dakota	0.1
15	Ohio	0.1
15	Pennsylvania	0.1
15	South Carolina	0.1
15	South Dakota	0.1
15	Tennessee	0.1
15	Texas	0.1
15	Virginia	0.1
15	Wisconsin	0.1
15	Wyoming	0.1
46	Maine	0.0
46	Michigan	0.0
46	New Hampshire	0.0
46	Vermont	0.0
46	West Virginia	0.0
	District of Columbia	0.2

Source: CQ Press using data from U.S. Bureau of the Census
"State Characteristics: Vintage 2015" (http://www.census.gov/programs-surveys/popest/data/data-sets.html)
*Those who identified themselves as one race. Census states "Race is a self-identification data item in which respondents choose the race or races with which they most closely identify."

Non-Hispanic White Population in 2015

National Total = 197,970,812*

ALPHA ORDER

RANK	STATE	POPULATION	% of USA
23	Alabama	3,204,583	1.6%
49	Alaska	454,152	0.2%
20	Arizona	3,810,113	1.9%
33	Arkansas	2,175,903	1.1%
1	California	14,882,158	7.5%
22	Colorado	3,747,011	1.9%
30	Connecticut	2,448,089	1.2%
46	Delaware	598,243	0.3%
3	Florida	11,209,143	5.7%
10	Georgia	5,501,469	2.8%
50	Hawaii	327,577	0.2%
38	Idaho	1,365,111	0.7%
7	Illinois	7,957,165	4.0%
11	Indiana	5,292,562	2.7%
28	Iowa	2,707,637	1.4%
32	Kansas	2,223,682	1.1%
21	Kentucky	3,767,688	1.9%
27	Louisiana	2,760,773	1.4%
39	Maine	1,244,470	0.6%
24	Maryland	3,125,763	1.6%
15	Massachusetts	4,996,581	2.5%
8	Michigan	7,498,342	3.8%
19	Minnesota	4,446,535	2.2%
34	Mississippi	1,706,249	0.9%
17	Missouri	4,857,557	2.5%
41	Montana	893,712	0.5%
36	Nebraska	1,516,993	0.8%
37	Nevada	1,466,661	0.7%
40	New Hampshire	1,211,229	0.6%
13	New Jersey	5,037,715	2.5%
42	New Mexico	801,529	0.4%
4	New York	11,092,475	5.6%
9	North Carolina	6,404,363	3.2%
45	North Dakota	649,139	0.3%
6	Ohio	9,265,946	4.7%
29	Oklahoma	2,602,419	1.3%
26	Oregon	3,086,301	1.6%
5	Pennsylvania	9,908,594	5.0%
43	Rhode Island	780,981	0.4%
25	South Carolina	3,125,427	1.6%
44	South Dakota	711,352	0.4%
16	Tennessee	4,909,189	2.5%
2	Texas	11,821,951	6.0%
31	Utah	2,367,093	1.2%
47	Vermont	583,864	0.3%
12	Virginia	5,257,241	2.7%
14	Washington	5,004,916	2.5%
35	West Virginia	1,702,770	0.9%
18	Wisconsin	4,725,221	2.4%
48	Wyoming	492,194	0.2%

RANK ORDER

RANK	STATE	POPULATION	% of USA
1	California	14,882,158	7.5%
2	Texas	11,821,951	6.0%
3	Florida	11,209,143	5.7%
4	New York	11,092,475	5.6%
5	Pennsylvania	9,908,594	5.0%
6	Ohio	9,265,946	4.7%
7	Illinois	7,957,165	4.0%
8	Michigan	7,498,342	3.8%
9	North Carolina	6,404,363	3.2%
10	Georgia	5,501,469	2.8%
11	Indiana	5,292,562	2.7%
12	Virginia	5,257,241	2.7%
13	New Jersey	5,037,715	2.5%
14	Washington	5,004,916	2.5%
15	Massachusetts	4,996,581	2.5%
16	Tennessee	4,909,189	2.5%
17	Missouri	4,857,557	2.5%
18	Wisconsin	4,725,221	2.4%
19	Minnesota	4,446,535	2.2%
20	Arizona	3,810,113	1.9%
21	Kentucky	3,767,688	1.9%
22	Colorado	3,747,011	1.9%
23	Alabama	3,204,583	1.6%
24	Maryland	3,125,763	1.6%
25	South Carolina	3,125,427	1.6%
26	Oregon	3,086,301	1.6%
27	Louisiana	2,760,773	1.4%
28	Iowa	2,707,637	1.4%
29	Oklahoma	2,602,419	1.3%
30	Connecticut	2,448,089	1.2%
31	Utah	2,367,093	1.2%
32	Kansas	2,223,682	1.1%
33	Arkansas	2,175,903	1.1%
34	Mississippi	1,706,249	0.9%
35	West Virginia	1,702,770	0.9%
36	Nebraska	1,516,993	0.8%
37	Nevada	1,466,661	0.7%
38	Idaho	1,365,111	0.7%
39	Maine	1,244,470	0.6%
40	New Hampshire	1,211,229	0.6%
41	Montana	893,712	0.5%
42	New Mexico	801,529	0.4%
43	Rhode Island	780,981	0.4%
44	South Dakota	711,352	0.4%
45	North Dakota	649,139	0.3%
46	Delaware	598,243	0.3%
47	Vermont	583,864	0.3%
48	Wyoming	492,194	0.2%
49	Alaska	454,152	0.2%
50	Hawaii	327,577	0.2%
	District of Columbia	242,981	0.1%

Source: U.S. Bureau of the Census
    "State Characteristics: Vintage 2015" (http://www.census.gov/programs-surveys/popest/data/data-sets.html)
*Those who identified themselves as one race. "White" is defined by Census as a person having origins in any of the original peoples of Europe, North Africa, or the Middle East. This is a subset of the 247,784,609 white population. Persons of Hispanic origin may be of any race. Census states "Race is a self-identification data item in which respondents choose the race or races with which they most closely identify."

Percent of Population Non-Hispanic White in 2015

National Percent = 61.6%*

ALPHA ORDER

RANK	STATE	PERCENT
31	Alabama	66.0
37	Alaska	61.5
42	Arizona	55.8
26	Arkansas	73.1
49	California	38.0
28	Colorado	68.7
29	Connecticut	68.2
34	Delaware	63.2
43	Florida	55.3
44	Georgia	53.9
50	Hawaii	22.9
11	Idaho	82.5
36	Illinois	61.9
14	Indiana	80.0
5	Iowa	86.7
21	Kansas	76.4
8	Kentucky	85.1
38	Louisiana	59.1
1	Maine	93.6
45	Maryland	52.0
25	Massachusetts	73.5
22	Michigan	75.6
13	Minnesota	81.0
39	Mississippi	57.0
16	Missouri	79.8
6	Montana	86.5
14	Nebraska	80.0
46	Nevada	50.7
4	New Hampshire	91.0
40	New Jersey	56.2
48	New Mexico	38.4
41	New York	56.0
32	North Carolina	63.8
7	North Dakota	85.8
16	Ohio	79.8
30	Oklahoma	66.5
20	Oregon	76.6
19	Pennsylvania	77.4
24	Rhode Island	73.9
32	South Carolina	63.8
10	South Dakota	82.9
23	Tennessee	74.4
47	Texas	43.0
18	Utah	79.0
2	Vermont	93.3
35	Virginia	62.7
27	Washington	69.8
3	West Virginia	92.3
12	Wisconsin	81.9
9	Wyoming	84.0

RANK ORDER

RANK	STATE	PERCENT
1	Maine	93.6
2	Vermont	93.3
3	West Virginia	92.3
4	New Hampshire	91.0
5	Iowa	86.7
6	Montana	86.5
7	North Dakota	85.8
8	Kentucky	85.1
9	Wyoming	84.0
10	South Dakota	82.9
11	Idaho	82.5
12	Wisconsin	81.9
13	Minnesota	81.0
14	Indiana	80.0
14	Nebraska	80.0
16	Missouri	79.8
16	Ohio	79.8
18	Utah	79.0
19	Pennsylvania	77.4
20	Oregon	76.6
21	Kansas	76.4
22	Michigan	75.6
23	Tennessee	74.4
24	Rhode Island	73.9
25	Massachusetts	73.5
26	Arkansas	73.1
27	Washington	69.8
28	Colorado	68.7
29	Connecticut	68.2
30	Oklahoma	66.5
31	Alabama	66.0
32	North Carolina	63.8
32	South Carolina	63.8
34	Delaware	63.2
35	Virginia	62.7
36	Illinois	61.9
37	Alaska	61.5
38	Louisiana	59.1
39	Mississippi	57.0
40	New Jersey	56.2
41	New York	56.0
42	Arizona	55.8
43	Florida	55.3
44	Georgia	53.9
45	Maryland	52.0
46	Nevada	50.7
47	Texas	43.0
48	New Mexico	38.4
49	California	38.0
50	Hawaii	22.9

| | District of Columbia | 36.1 |

Source: CQ Press using data from U.S. Bureau of the Census
"State Characteristics: Vintage 2015" (http://www.census.gov/programs-surveys/popest/data/data-sets.html)
*Those who identified themselves as one race. "White" is defined by Census as a person having origins in any of the original peoples of Europe, North Africa, or the Middle East. This non-Hispanic white subset is 79.9% of the total white population. Persons of Hispanic origin may be of any race. Census states "Race is a self-identification data item in which respondents choose the race or races with which they most closely identify."

Multiple Race Population in 2015

National Total = 8,248,411*

ALPHA ORDER

RANK ORDER

RANK	STATE	POPULATION	% of USA
31	Alabama	77,571	0.9%
36	Alaska	52,927	0.6%
16	Arizona	186,586	2.3%
34	Arkansas	59,455	0.7%
1	California	1,474,875	17.9%
18	Colorado	160,644	1.9%
29	Connecticut	80,452	1.0%
44	Delaware	23,861	0.3%
4	Florida	413,575	5.0%
14	Georgia	205,849	2.5%
5	Hawaii	329,201	4.0%
39	Idaho	38,695	0.5%
10	Illinois	240,889	2.9%
23	Indiana	128,882	1.6%
35	Iowa	55,094	0.7%
28	Kansas	83,062	1.0%
30	Kentucky	80,043	1.0%
32	Louisiana	74,404	0.9%
45	Maine	22,233	0.3%
17	Maryland	162,805	2.0%
19	Massachusetts	154,390	1.9%
12	Michigan	230,221	2.8%
22	Minnesota	130,563	1.6%
40	Mississippi	36,265	0.4%
21	Missouri	132,282	1.6%
43	Montana	27,422	0.3%
38	Nebraska	39,365	0.5%
24	Nevada	118,574	1.4%
46	New Hampshire	21,736	0.3%
15	New Jersey	189,418	2.3%
37	New Mexico	51,888	0.6%
3	New York	479,801	5.8%
13	North Carolina	212,304	2.6%
48	North Dakota	15,603	0.2%
7	Ohio	248,571	3.0%
11	Oklahoma	233,257	2.8%
20	Oregon	148,181	1.8%
8	Pennsylvania	242,228	2.9%
42	Rhode Island	27,909	0.3%
27	South Carolina	86,471	1.0%
47	South Dakota	19,151	0.2%
25	Tennessee	118,201	1.4%
2	Texas	517,095	6.3%
33	Utah	72,323	0.9%
50	Vermont	11,642	0.1%
9	Virginia	241,080	2.9%
6	Washington	326,406	4.0%
41	West Virginia	30,090	0.4%
26	Wisconsin	104,716	1.3%
49	Wyoming	12,024	0.1%

RANK	STATE	POPULATION	% of USA
1	California	1,474,875	17.9%
2	Texas	517,095	6.3%
3	New York	479,801	5.8%
4	Florida	413,575	5.0%
5	Hawaii	329,201	4.0%
6	Washington	326,406	4.0%
7	Ohio	248,571	3.0%
8	Pennsylvania	242,228	2.9%
9	Virginia	241,080	2.9%
10	Illinois	240,889	2.9%
11	Oklahoma	233,257	2.8%
12	Michigan	230,221	2.8%
13	North Carolina	212,304	2.6%
14	Georgia	205,849	2.5%
15	New Jersey	189,418	2.3%
16	Arizona	186,586	2.3%
17	Maryland	162,805	2.0%
18	Colorado	160,644	1.9%
19	Massachusetts	154,390	1.9%
20	Oregon	148,181	1.8%
21	Missouri	132,282	1.6%
22	Minnesota	130,563	1.6%
23	Indiana	128,882	1.6%
24	Nevada	118,574	1.4%
25	Tennessee	118,201	1.4%
26	Wisconsin	104,716	1.3%
27	South Carolina	86,471	1.0%
28	Kansas	83,062	1.0%
29	Connecticut	80,452	1.0%
30	Kentucky	80,043	1.0%
31	Alabama	77,571	0.9%
32	Louisiana	74,404	0.9%
33	Utah	72,323	0.9%
34	Arkansas	59,455	0.7%
35	Iowa	55,094	0.7%
36	Alaska	52,927	0.6%
37	New Mexico	51,888	0.6%
38	Nebraska	39,365	0.5%
39	Idaho	38,695	0.5%
40	Mississippi	36,265	0.4%
41	West Virginia	30,090	0.4%
42	Rhode Island	27,909	0.3%
43	Montana	27,422	0.3%
44	Delaware	23,861	0.3%
45	Maine	22,233	0.3%
46	New Hampshire	21,736	0.3%
47	South Dakota	19,151	0.2%
48	North Dakota	15,603	0.2%
49	Wyoming	12,024	0.1%
50	Vermont	11,642	0.1%
	District of Columbia	18,131	0.2%

Source: U.S. Bureau of the Census

"State Characteristics: Vintage 2015" (http://www.census.gov/programs-surveys/popest/data/data-sets.html)
*This includes those who identified themselves as two or more races. This is the population who did not identify themselves as one race (White, Black, American Indian/Native Alaska Native, Asian, or Native Hawaiian or Other Pacific Islander) but as a member of multiple racial groups. Census states "Race is a self-identification data item in which respondents choose the race or races with which they most closely identify."

Percent of Population Multiple Races in 2015

National Percent = 2.6%*

ALPHA ORDER				RANK ORDER		

RANK	STATE	PERCENT		RANK	STATE	PERCENT
46	Alabama	1.6		1	Hawaii	23.0
2	Alaska	7.2		2	Alaska	7.2
11	Arizona	2.7		3	Oklahoma	6.0
32	Arkansas	2.0		4	Washington	4.6
6	California	3.8		5	Nevada	4.1
8	Colorado	2.9		6	California	3.8
23	Connecticut	2.2		7	Oregon	3.7
15	Delaware	2.5		8	Colorado	2.9
32	Florida	2.0		8	Kansas	2.9
32	Georgia	2.0		8	Virginia	2.9
1	Hawaii	23.0		11	Arizona	2.7
20	Idaho	2.3		11	Maryland	2.7
35	Illinois	1.9		11	Montana	2.7
35	Indiana	1.9		14	Rhode Island	2.6
40	Iowa	1.8		15	Delaware	2.5
8	Kansas	2.9		15	New Mexico	2.5
40	Kentucky	1.8		17	Minnesota	2.4
46	Louisiana	1.6		17	New York	2.4
45	Maine	1.7		17	Utah	2.4
11	Maryland	2.7		20	Idaho	2.3
20	Massachusetts	2.3		20	Massachusetts	2.3
20	Michigan	2.3		20	Michigan	2.3
17	Minnesota	2.4		23	Connecticut	2.2
50	Mississippi	1.2		23	Missouri	2.2
23	Missouri	2.2		23	South Dakota	2.2
11	Montana	2.7		26	Nebraska	2.1
26	Nebraska	2.1		26	New Jersey	2.1
5	Nevada	4.1		26	North Carolina	2.1
46	New Hampshire	1.6		26	North Dakota	2.1
26	New Jersey	2.1		26	Ohio	2.1
15	New Mexico	2.5		26	Wyoming	2.1
17	New York	2.4		32	Arkansas	2.0
26	North Carolina	2.1		32	Florida	2.0
26	North Dakota	2.1		32	Georgia	2.0
26	Ohio	2.1		35	Illinois	1.9
3	Oklahoma	6.0		35	Indiana	1.9
7	Oregon	3.7		35	Pennsylvania	1.9
35	Pennsylvania	1.9		35	Texas	1.9
14	Rhode Island	2.6		35	Vermont	1.9
40	South Carolina	1.8		40	Iowa	1.8
23	South Dakota	2.2		40	Kentucky	1.8
40	Tennessee	1.8		40	South Carolina	1.8
35	Texas	1.9		40	Tennessee	1.8
17	Utah	2.4		40	Wisconsin	1.8
35	Vermont	1.9		45	Maine	1.7
8	Virginia	2.9		46	Alabama	1.6
4	Washington	4.6		46	Louisiana	1.6
46	West Virginia	1.6		46	New Hampshire	1.6
40	Wisconsin	1.8		46	West Virginia	1.6
26	Wyoming	2.1		50	Mississippi	1.2
					District of Columbia	2.7

Source: CQ Press using data from U.S. Bureau of the Census
"State Characteristics: Vintage 2015" (http://www.census.gov/programs-surveys/popest/data/data-sets.html)
*This includes those who identified themselves as two or more races. This is the population who did not identify themselves as one race (White, Black, American Indian/Native Alaska Native, Asian, or Native Hawaiian or Other Pacific Islander) but as a member of multiple racial groups. Census states "Race is a self-identification data item in which respondents choose the race or races with which they most closely identify."

Population under 5 Years Old in 2015

National Total = 19,907,281

ALPHA ORDER

RANK	STATE	POPULATION	% of USA
24	Alabama	292,973	1.5%
46	Alaska	55,449	0.3%
14	Arizona	429,244	2.2%
33	Arkansas	190,858	1.0%
1	California	2,508,752	12.6%
22	Colorado	335,607	1.7%
34	Connecticut	187,620	0.9%
45	Delaware	55,838	0.3%
4	Florida	1,101,071	5.5%
8	Georgia	660,045	3.3%
40	Hawaii	92,412	0.5%
38	Idaho	112,923	0.6%
5	Illinois	783,662	3.9%
15	Indiana	419,490	2.1%
31	Iowa	196,781	1.0%
30	Kansas	197,480	1.0%
26	Kentucky	277,389	1.4%
23	Louisiana	310,817	1.6%
41	Maine	64,687	0.3%
18	Maryland	369,035	1.9%
19	Massachusetts	366,562	1.8%
10	Michigan	571,776	2.9%
20	Minnesota	350,534	1.8%
32	Mississippi	192,782	1.0%
17	Missouri	374,360	1.9%
43	Montana	61,886	0.3%
37	Nebraska	130,631	0.7%
35	Nevada	176,617	0.9%
42	New Hampshire	64,594	0.3%
11	New Jersey	530,134	2.7%
36	New Mexico	135,024	0.7%
3	New York	1,184,387	5.9%
9	North Carolina	604,711	3.0%
48	North Dakota	53,147	0.3%
7	Ohio	693,088	3.5%
27	Oklahoma	267,948	1.3%
29	Oregon	230,790	1.2%
6	Pennsylvania	714,919	3.6%
47	Rhode Island	55,128	0.3%
25	South Carolina	289,990	1.5%
44	South Dakota	61,244	0.3%
16	Tennessee	402,183	2.0%
2	Texas	1,983,640	10.0%
28	Utah	250,703	1.3%
50	Vermont	30,408	0.2%
12	Virginia	515,157	2.6%
13	Washington	447,922	2.3%
39	West Virginia	103,410	0.5%
21	Wisconsin	339,726	1.7%
49	Wyoming	38,395	0.2%

RANK ORDER

RANK	STATE	POPULATION	% of USA
1	California	2,508,752	12.6%
2	Texas	1,983,640	10.0%
3	New York	1,184,387	5.9%
4	Florida	1,101,071	5.5%
5	Illinois	783,662	3.9%
6	Pennsylvania	714,919	3.6%
7	Ohio	693,088	3.5%
8	Georgia	660,045	3.3%
9	North Carolina	604,711	3.0%
10	Michigan	571,776	2.9%
11	New Jersey	530,134	2.7%
12	Virginia	515,157	2.6%
13	Washington	447,922	2.3%
14	Arizona	429,244	2.2%
15	Indiana	419,490	2.1%
16	Tennessee	402,183	2.0%
17	Missouri	374,360	1.9%
18	Maryland	369,035	1.9%
19	Massachusetts	366,562	1.8%
20	Minnesota	350,534	1.8%
21	Wisconsin	339,726	1.7%
22	Colorado	335,607	1.7%
23	Louisiana	310,817	1.6%
24	Alabama	292,973	1.5%
25	South Carolina	289,990	1.5%
26	Kentucky	277,389	1.4%
27	Oklahoma	267,948	1.3%
28	Utah	250,703	1.3%
29	Oregon	230,790	1.2%
30	Kansas	197,480	1.0%
31	Iowa	196,781	1.0%
32	Mississippi	192,782	1.0%
33	Arkansas	190,858	1.0%
34	Connecticut	187,620	0.9%
35	Nevada	176,617	0.9%
36	New Mexico	135,024	0.7%
37	Nebraska	130,631	0.7%
38	Idaho	112,923	0.6%
39	West Virginia	103,410	0.5%
40	Hawaii	92,412	0.5%
41	Maine	64,687	0.3%
42	New Hampshire	64,594	0.3%
43	Montana	61,886	0.3%
44	South Dakota	61,244	0.3%
45	Delaware	55,838	0.3%
46	Alaska	55,449	0.3%
47	Rhode Island	55,128	0.3%
48	North Dakota	53,147	0.3%
49	Wyoming	38,395	0.2%
50	Vermont	30,408	0.2%
	District of Columbia	43,352	0.2%

Source: U.S. Bureau of the Census
"State Characteristics: Vintage 2015" (http://www.census.gov/programs-surveys/popest/data/data-sets.html)

Percent of Population under 5 Years Old in 2015

National Percent = 6.2% of Population

RANK	STATE	PERCENT
31	Alabama	6.0
2	Alaska	7.5
19	Arizona	6.3
15	Arkansas	6.4
15	California	6.4
23	Colorado	6.2
46	Connecticut	5.2
36	Delaware	5.9
44	Florida	5.4
12	Georgia	6.5
12	Hawaii	6.5
8	Idaho	6.8
26	Illinois	6.1
19	Indiana	6.3
19	Iowa	6.3
8	Kansas	6.8
19	Kentucky	6.3
10	Louisiana	6.7
48	Maine	4.9
26	Maryland	6.1
44	Massachusetts	5.4
40	Michigan	5.8
15	Minnesota	6.4
15	Mississippi	6.4
23	Missouri	6.2
31	Montana	6.0
6	Nebraska	6.9
26	Nevada	6.1
48	New Hampshire	4.9
36	New Jersey	5.9
12	New Mexico	6.5
31	New York	6.0
31	North Carolina	6.0
5	North Dakota	7.0
31	Ohio	6.0
6	Oklahoma	6.9
41	Oregon	5.7
42	Pennsylvania	5.6
46	Rhode Island	5.2
36	South Carolina	5.9
4	South Dakota	7.1
26	Tennessee	6.1
3	Texas	7.2
1	Utah	8.4
48	Vermont	4.9
26	Virginia	6.1
23	Washington	6.2
42	West Virginia	5.6
36	Wisconsin	5.9
11	Wyoming	6.6

RANK	STATE	PERCENT
1	Utah	8.4
2	Alaska	7.5
3	Texas	7.2
4	South Dakota	7.1
5	North Dakota	7.0
6	Nebraska	6.9
6	Oklahoma	6.9
8	Idaho	6.8
8	Kansas	6.8
10	Louisiana	6.7
11	Wyoming	6.6
12	Georgia	6.5
12	Hawaii	6.5
12	New Mexico	6.5
15	Arkansas	6.4
15	California	6.4
15	Minnesota	6.4
15	Mississippi	6.4
19	Arizona	6.3
19	Indiana	6.3
19	Iowa	6.3
19	Kentucky	6.3
23	Colorado	6.2
23	Missouri	6.2
23	Washington	6.2
26	Illinois	6.1
26	Maryland	6.1
26	Nevada	6.1
26	Tennessee	6.1
26	Virginia	6.1
31	Alabama	6.0
31	Montana	6.0
31	New York	6.0
31	North Carolina	6.0
31	Ohio	6.0
36	Delaware	5.9
36	New Jersey	5.9
36	South Carolina	5.9
36	Wisconsin	5.9
40	Michigan	5.8
41	Oregon	5.7
42	Pennsylvania	5.6
42	West Virginia	5.6
44	Florida	5.4
44	Massachusetts	5.4
46	Connecticut	5.2
46	Rhode Island	5.2
48	Maine	4.9
48	New Hampshire	4.9
48	Vermont	4.9
	District of Columbia	6.4

Source: CQ Press using data from U.S. Bureau of the Census
"State Characteristics: Vintage 2015" (http://www.census.gov/programs-surveys/popest/data/data-sets.html)

Population 5 to 17 Years Old in 2015

National Total = 53,737,830

<table>
<tr><td colspan="4">ALPHA ORDER</td><td colspan="4">RANK ORDER</td></tr>
<tr><td>RANK</td><td>STATE</td><td>POPULATION</td><td>% of USA</td><td>RANK</td><td>STATE</td><td>POPULATION</td><td>% of USA</td></tr>
<tr><td>23</td><td>Alabama</td><td>810,523</td><td>1.5%</td><td>1</td><td>California</td><td>6,612,164</td><td>12.3%</td></tr>
<tr><td>47</td><td>Alaska</td><td>130,817</td><td>0.2%</td><td>2</td><td>Texas</td><td>5,228,131</td><td>9.7%</td></tr>
<tr><td>13</td><td>Arizona</td><td>1,193,606</td><td>2.2%</td><td>3</td><td>New York</td><td>3,026,430</td><td>5.6%</td></tr>
<tr><td>34</td><td>Arkansas</td><td>514,442</td><td>1.0%</td><td>4</td><td>Florida</td><td>3,004,058</td><td>5.6%</td></tr>
<tr><td>1</td><td>California</td><td>6,612,164</td><td>12.3%</td><td>5</td><td>Illinois</td><td>2,175,011</td><td>4.0%</td></tr>
<tr><td>22</td><td>Colorado</td><td>921,458</td><td>1.7%</td><td>6</td><td>Pennsylvania</td><td>1,975,355</td><td>3.7%</td></tr>
<tr><td>30</td><td>Connecticut</td><td>576,439</td><td>1.1%</td><td>7</td><td>Ohio</td><td>1,935,389</td><td>3.6%</td></tr>
<tr><td>46</td><td>Delaware</td><td>148,548</td><td>0.3%</td><td>8</td><td>Georgia</td><td>1,844,127</td><td>3.4%</td></tr>
<tr><td>4</td><td>Florida</td><td>3,004,058</td><td>5.6%</td><td>9</td><td>North Carolina</td><td>1,685,857</td><td>3.1%</td></tr>
<tr><td>8</td><td>Georgia</td><td>1,844,127</td><td>3.4%</td><td>10</td><td>Michigan</td><td>1,635,528</td><td>3.0%</td></tr>
<tr><td>40</td><td>Hawaii</td><td>218,421</td><td>0.4%</td><td>11</td><td>New Jersey</td><td>1,468,687</td><td>2.7%</td></tr>
<tr><td>38</td><td>Idaho</td><td>319,914</td><td>0.6%</td><td>12</td><td>Virginia</td><td>1,355,265</td><td>2.5%</td></tr>
<tr><td>5</td><td>Illinois</td><td>2,175,011</td><td>4.0%</td><td>13</td><td>Arizona</td><td>1,193,606</td><td>2.2%</td></tr>
<tr><td>15</td><td>Indiana</td><td>1,159,966</td><td>2.2%</td><td>14</td><td>Washington</td><td>1,163,920</td><td>2.2%</td></tr>
<tr><td>32</td><td>Iowa</td><td>532,015</td><td>1.0%</td><td>15</td><td>Indiana</td><td>1,159,966</td><td>2.2%</td></tr>
<tr><td>33</td><td>Kansas</td><td>522,077</td><td>1.0%</td><td>16</td><td>Tennessee</td><td>1,095,428</td><td>2.0%</td></tr>
<tr><td>26</td><td>Kentucky</td><td>734,278</td><td>1.4%</td><td>17</td><td>Massachusetts</td><td>1,020,525</td><td>1.9%</td></tr>
<tr><td>24</td><td>Louisiana</td><td>803,996</td><td>1.5%</td><td>18</td><td>Missouri</td><td>1,017,116</td><td>1.9%</td></tr>
<tr><td>42</td><td>Maine</td><td>191,693</td><td>0.4%</td><td>19</td><td>Maryland</td><td>979,191</td><td>1.8%</td></tr>
<tr><td>19</td><td>Maryland</td><td>979,191</td><td>1.8%</td><td>20</td><td>Wisconsin</td><td>954,900</td><td>1.8%</td></tr>
<tr><td>17</td><td>Massachusetts</td><td>1,020,525</td><td>1.9%</td><td>21</td><td>Minnesota</td><td>933,853</td><td>1.7%</td></tr>
<tr><td>10</td><td>Michigan</td><td>1,635,528</td><td>3.0%</td><td>22</td><td>Colorado</td><td>921,458</td><td>1.7%</td></tr>
<tr><td>21</td><td>Minnesota</td><td>933,853</td><td>1.7%</td><td>23</td><td>Alabama</td><td>810,523</td><td>1.5%</td></tr>
<tr><td>31</td><td>Mississippi</td><td>534,066</td><td>1.0%</td><td>24</td><td>Louisiana</td><td>803,996</td><td>1.5%</td></tr>
<tr><td>18</td><td>Missouri</td><td>1,017,116</td><td>1.9%</td><td>25</td><td>South Carolina</td><td>801,598</td><td>1.5%</td></tr>
<tr><td>43</td><td>Montana</td><td>164,534</td><td>0.3%</td><td>26</td><td>Kentucky</td><td>734,278</td><td>1.4%</td></tr>
<tr><td>37</td><td>Nebraska</td><td>339,706</td><td>0.6%</td><td>27</td><td>Oklahoma</td><td>693,373</td><td>1.3%</td></tr>
<tr><td>35</td><td>Nevada</td><td>492,547</td><td>0.9%</td><td>28</td><td>Utah</td><td>661,793</td><td>1.2%</td></tr>
<tr><td>41</td><td>New Hampshire</td><td>199,404</td><td>0.4%</td><td>29</td><td>Oregon</td><td>632,066</td><td>1.2%</td></tr>
<tr><td>11</td><td>New Jersey</td><td>1,468,687</td><td>2.7%</td><td>30</td><td>Connecticut</td><td>576,439</td><td>1.1%</td></tr>
<tr><td>36</td><td>New Mexico</td><td>361,884</td><td>0.7%</td><td>31</td><td>Mississippi</td><td>534,066</td><td>1.0%</td></tr>
<tr><td>3</td><td>New York</td><td>3,026,430</td><td>5.6%</td><td>32</td><td>Iowa</td><td>532,015</td><td>1.0%</td></tr>
<tr><td>9</td><td>North Carolina</td><td>1,685,857</td><td>3.1%</td><td>33</td><td>Kansas</td><td>522,077</td><td>1.0%</td></tr>
<tr><td>48</td><td>North Dakota</td><td>120,779</td><td>0.2%</td><td>34</td><td>Arkansas</td><td>514,442</td><td>1.0%</td></tr>
<tr><td>7</td><td>Ohio</td><td>1,935,389</td><td>3.6%</td><td>35</td><td>Nevada</td><td>492,547</td><td>0.9%</td></tr>
<tr><td>27</td><td>Oklahoma</td><td>693,373</td><td>1.3%</td><td>36</td><td>New Mexico</td><td>361,884</td><td>0.7%</td></tr>
<tr><td>29</td><td>Oregon</td><td>632,066</td><td>1.2%</td><td>37</td><td>Nebraska</td><td>339,706</td><td>0.6%</td></tr>
<tr><td>6</td><td>Pennsylvania</td><td>1,975,355</td><td>3.7%</td><td>38</td><td>Idaho</td><td>319,914</td><td>0.6%</td></tr>
<tr><td>44</td><td>Rhode Island</td><td>155,916</td><td>0.3%</td><td>39</td><td>West Virginia</td><td>276,186</td><td>0.5%</td></tr>
<tr><td>25</td><td>South Carolina</td><td>801,598</td><td>1.5%</td><td>40</td><td>Hawaii</td><td>218,421</td><td>0.4%</td></tr>
<tr><td>45</td><td>South Dakota</td><td>150,080</td><td>0.3%</td><td>41</td><td>New Hampshire</td><td>199,404</td><td>0.4%</td></tr>
<tr><td>16</td><td>Tennessee</td><td>1,095,428</td><td>2.0%</td><td>42</td><td>Maine</td><td>191,693</td><td>0.4%</td></tr>
<tr><td>2</td><td>Texas</td><td>5,228,131</td><td>9.7%</td><td>43</td><td>Montana</td><td>164,534</td><td>0.3%</td></tr>
<tr><td>28</td><td>Utah</td><td>661,793</td><td>1.2%</td><td>44</td><td>Rhode Island</td><td>155,916</td><td>0.3%</td></tr>
<tr><td>50</td><td>Vermont</td><td>89,515</td><td>0.2%</td><td>45</td><td>South Dakota</td><td>150,080</td><td>0.3%</td></tr>
<tr><td>12</td><td>Virginia</td><td>1,355,265</td><td>2.5%</td><td>46</td><td>Delaware</td><td>148,548</td><td>0.3%</td></tr>
<tr><td>14</td><td>Washington</td><td>1,163,920</td><td>2.2%</td><td>47</td><td>Alaska</td><td>130,817</td><td>0.2%</td></tr>
<tr><td>39</td><td>West Virginia</td><td>276,186</td><td>0.5%</td><td>48</td><td>North Dakota</td><td>120,779</td><td>0.2%</td></tr>
<tr><td>20</td><td>Wisconsin</td><td>954,900</td><td>1.8%</td><td>49</td><td>Wyoming</td><td>100,500</td><td>0.2%</td></tr>
<tr><td>49</td><td>Wyoming</td><td>100,500</td><td>0.2%</td><td>50</td><td>Vermont</td><td>89,515</td><td>0.2%</td></tr>
<tr><td></td><td></td><td></td><td></td><td></td><td>District of Columbia</td><td>74,755</td><td>0.1%</td></tr>
</table>

Source: CQ Press using data from U.S. Bureau of the Census
"State Characteristics: Vintage 2015" (http://www.census.gov/programs-surveys/popest/data/data-sets.html)

Percent of Population 5 to 17 Years Old in 2015

National Percent = 16.7% of Population

ALPHA ORDER

RANK	STATE	PERCENT
24	Alabama	16.7
8	Alaska	17.7
10	Arizona	17.5
14	Arkansas	17.3
20	California	16.9
20	Colorado	16.9
36	Connecticut	16.1
39	Delaware	15.7
47	Florida	14.8
4	Georgia	18.1
42	Hawaii	15.3
2	Idaho	19.3
20	Illinois	16.9
10	Indiana	17.5
17	Iowa	17.0
5	Kansas	17.9
27	Kentucky	16.6
15	Louisiana	17.2
49	Maine	14.4
33	Maryland	16.3
44	Massachusetts	15.0
29	Michigan	16.5
17	Minnesota	17.0
7	Mississippi	17.8
24	Missouri	16.7
38	Montana	15.9
5	Nebraska	17.9
17	Nevada	17.0
44	New Hampshire	15.0
31	New Jersey	16.4
13	New Mexico	17.4
42	New York	15.3
23	North Carolina	16.8
37	North Dakota	16.0
24	Ohio	16.7
8	Oklahoma	17.7
39	Oregon	15.7
41	Pennsylvania	15.4
47	Rhode Island	14.8
31	South Carolina	16.4
10	South Dakota	17.5
27	Tennessee	16.6
3	Texas	19.0
1	Utah	22.1
50	Vermont	14.3
34	Virginia	16.2
34	Washington	16.2
44	West Virginia	15.0
29	Wisconsin	16.5
16	Wyoming	17.1

RANK ORDER

RANK	STATE	PERCENT
1	Utah	22.1
2	Idaho	19.3
3	Texas	19.0
4	Georgia	18.1
5	Kansas	17.9
5	Nebraska	17.9
7	Mississippi	17.8
8	Alaska	17.7
8	Oklahoma	17.7
10	Arizona	17.5
10	Indiana	17.5
10	South Dakota	17.5
13	New Mexico	17.4
14	Arkansas	17.3
15	Louisiana	17.2
16	Wyoming	17.1
17	Iowa	17.0
17	Minnesota	17.0
17	Nevada	17.0
20	California	16.9
20	Colorado	16.9
20	Illinois	16.9
23	North Carolina	16.8
24	Alabama	16.7
24	Missouri	16.7
24	Ohio	16.7
27	Kentucky	16.6
27	Tennessee	16.6
29	Michigan	16.5
29	Wisconsin	16.5
31	New Jersey	16.4
31	South Carolina	16.4
33	Maryland	16.3
34	Virginia	16.2
34	Washington	16.2
36	Connecticut	16.1
37	North Dakota	16.0
38	Montana	15.9
39	Delaware	15.7
39	Oregon	15.7
41	Pennsylvania	15.4
42	Hawaii	15.3
42	New York	15.3
44	Massachusetts	15.0
44	New Hampshire	15.0
44	West Virginia	15.0
47	Florida	14.8
47	Rhode Island	14.8
49	Maine	14.4
50	Vermont	14.3
	District of Columbia	11.1

Source: CQ Press using data from U.S. Bureau of the Census
"State Characteristics: Vintage 2015" (http://www.census.gov/programs-surveys/popest/data/data-sets.html)

Population 18 Years Old and Older in 2015

National Total = 247,773,709

RANK	STATE	POPULATION	% of USA
24	Alabama	3,755,483	1.5%
48	Alaska	552,166	0.2%
15	Arizona	5,205,215	2.1%
31	Arkansas	2,272,904	0.9%
1	California	30,023,902	12.1%
22	Colorado	4,199,509	1.7%
29	Connecticut	2,826,827	1.1%
45	Delaware	741,548	0.3%
3	Florida	16,166,143	6.5%
10	Georgia	7,710,688	3.1%
40	Hawaii	1,120,770	0.5%
39	Idaho	1,222,093	0.5%
6	Illinois	9,901,322	4.0%
17	Indiana	5,040,224	2.0%
30	Iowa	2,395,103	1.0%
34	Kansas	2,192,084	0.9%
26	Kentucky	3,413,425	1.4%
25	Louisiana	3,555,911	1.4%
41	Maine	1,072,948	0.4%
19	Maryland	4,658,175	1.9%
14	Massachusetts	5,407,335	2.2%
9	Michigan	7,715,272	3.1%
21	Minnesota	4,205,207	1.7%
32	Mississippi	2,265,485	0.9%
18	Missouri	4,692,196	1.9%
44	Montana	806,529	0.3%
38	Nebraska	1,425,853	0.6%
33	Nevada	2,221,681	0.9%
42	New Hampshire	1,066,610	0.4%
11	New Jersey	6,959,192	2.8%
36	New Mexico	1,588,201	0.6%
4	New York	15,584,974	6.3%
8	North Carolina	7,752,234	3.1%
47	North Dakota	583,001	0.2%
7	Ohio	8,984,946	3.6%
28	Oklahoma	2,950,017	1.2%
27	Oregon	3,166,121	1.3%
5	Pennsylvania	10,112,229	4.1%
43	Rhode Island	845,254	0.3%
23	South Carolina	3,804,558	1.5%
46	South Dakota	647,145	0.3%
16	Tennessee	5,102,688	2.1%
2	Texas	20,257,343	8.2%
35	Utah	2,083,423	0.8%
49	Vermont	506,119	0.2%
12	Virginia	6,512,571	2.6%
13	Washington	5,558,509	2.2%
37	West Virginia	1,464,532	0.6%
20	Wisconsin	4,476,711	1.8%
50	Wyoming	447,212	0.2%

RANK	STATE	POPULATION	% of USA
1	California	30,023,902	12.1%
2	Texas	20,257,343	8.2%
3	Florida	16,166,143	6.5%
4	New York	15,584,974	6.3%
5	Pennsylvania	10,112,229	4.1%
6	Illinois	9,901,322	4.0%
7	Ohio	8,984,946	3.6%
8	North Carolina	7,752,234	3.1%
9	Michigan	7,715,272	3.1%
10	Georgia	7,710,688	3.1%
11	New Jersey	6,959,192	2.8%
12	Virginia	6,512,571	2.6%
13	Washington	5,558,509	2.2%
14	Massachusetts	5,407,335	2.2%
15	Arizona	5,205,215	2.1%
16	Tennessee	5,102,688	2.1%
17	Indiana	5,040,224	2.0%
18	Missouri	4,692,196	1.9%
19	Maryland	4,658,175	1.9%
20	Wisconsin	4,476,711	1.8%
21	Minnesota	4,205,207	1.7%
22	Colorado	4,199,509	1.7%
23	South Carolina	3,804,558	1.5%
24	Alabama	3,755,483	1.5%
25	Louisiana	3,555,911	1.4%
26	Kentucky	3,413,425	1.4%
27	Oregon	3,166,121	1.3%
28	Oklahoma	2,950,017	1.2%
29	Connecticut	2,826,827	1.1%
30	Iowa	2,395,103	1.0%
31	Arkansas	2,272,904	0.9%
32	Mississippi	2,265,485	0.9%
33	Nevada	2,221,681	0.9%
34	Kansas	2,192,084	0.9%
35	Utah	2,083,423	0.8%
36	New Mexico	1,588,201	0.6%
37	West Virginia	1,464,532	0.6%
38	Nebraska	1,425,853	0.6%
39	Idaho	1,222,093	0.5%
40	Hawaii	1,120,770	0.5%
41	Maine	1,072,948	0.4%
42	New Hampshire	1,066,610	0.4%
43	Rhode Island	845,254	0.3%
44	Montana	806,529	0.3%
45	Delaware	741,548	0.3%
46	South Dakota	647,145	0.3%
47	North Dakota	583,001	0.2%
48	Alaska	552,166	0.2%
49	Vermont	506,119	0.2%
50	Wyoming	447,212	0.2%
	District of Columbia	554,121	0.2%

Source: U.S. Bureau of the Census

"State Characteristics: Vintage 2015" (http://www.census.gov/programs-surveys/popest/data/data-sets.html)

Percent of Population 18 Years Old and Older in 2015

National Percent = 77.1% of Population

ALPHA ORDER				RANK ORDER		
RANK	STATE	PERCENT		RANK	STATE	PERCENT
23	Alabama	77.3		1	Vermont	80.8
47	Alaska	74.8		2	Maine	80.7
37	Arizona	76.2		3	New Hampshire	80.2
35	Arkansas	76.3		4	Rhode Island	80.0
32	California	76.7		5	Florida	79.7
28	Colorado	77.0		6	Massachusetts	79.6
9	Connecticut	78.7		7	West Virginia	79.4
12	Delaware	78.4		8	Pennsylvania	79.0
5	Florida	79.7		9	Connecticut	78.7
42	Georgia	75.5		9	New York	78.7
13	Hawaii	78.3		11	Oregon	78.6
48	Idaho	73.8		12	Delaware	78.4
28	Illinois	77.0		13	Hawaii	78.3
39	Indiana	76.1		14	Montana	78.1
32	Iowa	76.7		15	Michigan	77.8
45	Kansas	75.3		16	New Jersey	77.7
26	Kentucky	77.1		16	South Carolina	77.7
39	Louisiana	76.1		16	Virginia	77.7
2	Maine	80.7		19	Maryland	77.6
19	Maryland	77.6		19	Wisconsin	77.6
6	Massachusetts	79.6		21	Washington	77.5
15	Michigan	77.8		22	Ohio	77.4
34	Minnesota	76.6		23	Alabama	77.3
41	Mississippi	75.7		23	Tennessee	77.3
26	Missouri	77.1		25	North Carolina	77.2
14	Montana	78.1		26	Kentucky	77.1
46	Nebraska	75.2		26	Missouri	77.1
31	Nevada	76.9		28	Colorado	77.0
3	New Hampshire	80.2		28	Illinois	77.0
16	New Jersey	77.7		28	North Dakota	77.0
37	New Mexico	76.2		31	Nevada	76.9
9	New York	78.7		32	California	76.7
25	North Carolina	77.2		32	Iowa	76.7
28	North Dakota	77.0		34	Minnesota	76.6
22	Ohio	77.4		35	Arkansas	76.3
43	Oklahoma	75.4		35	Wyoming	76.3
11	Oregon	78.6		37	Arizona	76.2
8	Pennsylvania	79.0		37	New Mexico	76.2
4	Rhode Island	80.0		39	Indiana	76.1
16	South Carolina	77.7		39	Louisiana	76.1
43	South Dakota	75.4		41	Mississippi	75.7
23	Tennessee	77.3		42	Georgia	75.5
49	Texas	73.7		43	Oklahoma	75.4
50	Utah	69.5		43	South Dakota	75.4
1	Vermont	80.8		45	Kansas	75.3
16	Virginia	77.7		46	Nebraska	75.2
21	Washington	77.5		47	Alaska	74.8
7	West Virginia	79.4		48	Idaho	73.8
19	Wisconsin	77.6		49	Texas	73.7
35	Wyoming	76.3		50	Utah	69.5
					District of Columbia	82.4

Source: CQ Press using data from U.S. Bureau of the Census
"State Characteristics: Vintage 2015" (http://www.census.gov/programs-surveys/popest/data/data-sets.html)

Population 18 to 24 Years Old in 2015

National Total = 31,219,892

<table>
<tr><td colspan="4">ALPHA ORDER</td></tr>
<tr><td>RANK</td><td>STATE</td><td>POPULATION</td><td>% of USA</td></tr>
<tr><td>24</td><td>Alabama</td><td>468,660</td><td>1.5%</td></tr>
<tr><td>48</td><td>Alaska</td><td>80,623</td><td>0.3%</td></tr>
<tr><td>14</td><td>Arizona</td><td>672,434</td><td>2.2%</td></tr>
<tr><td>34</td><td>Arkansas</td><td>284,141</td><td>0.9%</td></tr>
<tr><td>1</td><td>California</td><td>3,935,102</td><td>12.6%</td></tr>
<tr><td>21</td><td>Colorado</td><td>531,082</td><td>1.7%</td></tr>
<tr><td>29</td><td>Connecticut</td><td>352,215</td><td>1.1%</td></tr>
<tr><td>46</td><td>Delaware</td><td>87,900</td><td>0.3%</td></tr>
<tr><td>4</td><td>Florida</td><td>1,758,723</td><td>5.6%</td></tr>
<tr><td>8</td><td>Georgia</td><td>1,017,007</td><td>3.3%</td></tr>
<tr><td>40</td><td>Hawaii</td><td>136,178</td><td>0.4%</td></tr>
<tr><td>39</td><td>Idaho</td><td>155,924</td><td>0.5%</td></tr>
<tr><td>5</td><td>Illinois</td><td>1,235,848</td><td>4.0%</td></tr>
<tr><td>16</td><td>Indiana</td><td>665,744</td><td>2.1%</td></tr>
<tr><td>31</td><td>Iowa</td><td>322,179</td><td>1.0%</td></tr>
<tr><td>32</td><td>Kansas</td><td>304,237</td><td>1.0%</td></tr>
<tr><td>26</td><td>Kentucky</td><td>423,779</td><td>1.4%</td></tr>
<tr><td>25</td><td>Louisiana</td><td>455,796</td><td>1.5%</td></tr>
<tr><td>43</td><td>Maine</td><td>110,754</td><td>0.4%</td></tr>
<tr><td>20</td><td>Maryland</td><td>554,122</td><td>1.8%</td></tr>
<tr><td>13</td><td>Massachusetts</td><td>701,025</td><td>2.2%</td></tr>
<tr><td>10</td><td>Michigan</td><td>987,418</td><td>3.2%</td></tr>
<tr><td>22</td><td>Minnesota</td><td>506,298</td><td>1.6%</td></tr>
<tr><td>33</td><td>Mississippi</td><td>303,494</td><td>1.0%</td></tr>
<tr><td>18</td><td>Missouri</td><td>587,399</td><td>1.9%</td></tr>
<tr><td>44</td><td>Montana</td><td>100,810</td><td>0.3%</td></tr>
<tr><td>37</td><td>Nebraska</td><td>192,774</td><td>0.6%</td></tr>
<tr><td>35</td><td>Nevada</td><td>252,520</td><td>0.8%</td></tr>
<tr><td>41</td><td>New Hampshire</td><td>129,025</td><td>0.4%</td></tr>
<tr><td>12</td><td>New Jersey</td><td>792,745</td><td>2.5%</td></tr>
<tr><td>36</td><td>New Mexico</td><td>204,850</td><td>0.7%</td></tr>
<tr><td>3</td><td>New York</td><td>1,942,413</td><td>6.2%</td></tr>
<tr><td>9</td><td>North Carolina</td><td>988,097</td><td>3.2%</td></tr>
<tr><td>45</td><td>North Dakota</td><td>95,477</td><td>0.3%</td></tr>
<tr><td>7</td><td>Ohio</td><td>1,085,332</td><td>3.5%</td></tr>
<tr><td>27</td><td>Oklahoma</td><td>389,737</td><td>1.2%</td></tr>
<tr><td>28</td><td>Oregon</td><td>363,784</td><td>1.2%</td></tr>
<tr><td>6</td><td>Pennsylvania</td><td>1,204,533</td><td>3.9%</td></tr>
<tr><td>42</td><td>Rhode Island</td><td>114,978</td><td>0.4%</td></tr>
<tr><td>23</td><td>South Carolina</td><td>477,124</td><td>1.5%</td></tr>
<tr><td>47</td><td>South Dakota</td><td>84,674</td><td>0.3%</td></tr>
<tr><td>17</td><td>Tennessee</td><td>626,568</td><td>2.0%</td></tr>
<tr><td>2</td><td>Texas</td><td>2,771,653</td><td>8.9%</td></tr>
<tr><td>30</td><td>Utah</td><td>340,322</td><td>1.1%</td></tr>
<tr><td>49</td><td>Vermont</td><td>67,928</td><td>0.2%</td></tr>
<tr><td>11</td><td>Virginia</td><td>822,968</td><td>2.6%</td></tr>
<tr><td>15</td><td>Washington</td><td>666,370</td><td>2.1%</td></tr>
<tr><td>38</td><td>West Virginia</td><td>165,594</td><td>0.5%</td></tr>
<tr><td>19</td><td>Wisconsin</td><td>563,369</td><td>1.8%</td></tr>
<tr><td>50</td><td>Wyoming</td><td>56,514</td><td>0.2%</td></tr>
</table>

<table>
<tr><td colspan="4">RANK ORDER</td></tr>
<tr><td>RANK</td><td>STATE</td><td>POPULATION</td><td>% of USA</td></tr>
<tr><td>1</td><td>California</td><td>3,935,102</td><td>12.6%</td></tr>
<tr><td>2</td><td>Texas</td><td>2,771,653</td><td>8.9%</td></tr>
<tr><td>3</td><td>New York</td><td>1,942,413</td><td>6.2%</td></tr>
<tr><td>4</td><td>Florida</td><td>1,758,723</td><td>5.6%</td></tr>
<tr><td>5</td><td>Illinois</td><td>1,235,848</td><td>4.0%</td></tr>
<tr><td>6</td><td>Pennsylvania</td><td>1,204,533</td><td>3.9%</td></tr>
<tr><td>7</td><td>Ohio</td><td>1,085,332</td><td>3.5%</td></tr>
<tr><td>8</td><td>Georgia</td><td>1,017,007</td><td>3.3%</td></tr>
<tr><td>9</td><td>North Carolina</td><td>988,097</td><td>3.2%</td></tr>
<tr><td>10</td><td>Michigan</td><td>987,418</td><td>3.2%</td></tr>
<tr><td>11</td><td>Virginia</td><td>822,968</td><td>2.6%</td></tr>
<tr><td>12</td><td>New Jersey</td><td>792,745</td><td>2.5%</td></tr>
<tr><td>13</td><td>Massachusetts</td><td>701,025</td><td>2.2%</td></tr>
<tr><td>14</td><td>Arizona</td><td>672,434</td><td>2.2%</td></tr>
<tr><td>15</td><td>Washington</td><td>666,370</td><td>2.1%</td></tr>
<tr><td>16</td><td>Indiana</td><td>665,744</td><td>2.1%</td></tr>
<tr><td>17</td><td>Tennessee</td><td>626,568</td><td>2.0%</td></tr>
<tr><td>18</td><td>Missouri</td><td>587,399</td><td>1.9%</td></tr>
<tr><td>19</td><td>Wisconsin</td><td>563,369</td><td>1.8%</td></tr>
<tr><td>20</td><td>Maryland</td><td>554,122</td><td>1.8%</td></tr>
<tr><td>21</td><td>Colorado</td><td>531,082</td><td>1.7%</td></tr>
<tr><td>22</td><td>Minnesota</td><td>506,298</td><td>1.6%</td></tr>
<tr><td>23</td><td>South Carolina</td><td>477,124</td><td>1.5%</td></tr>
<tr><td>24</td><td>Alabama</td><td>468,660</td><td>1.5%</td></tr>
<tr><td>25</td><td>Louisiana</td><td>455,796</td><td>1.5%</td></tr>
<tr><td>26</td><td>Kentucky</td><td>423,779</td><td>1.4%</td></tr>
<tr><td>27</td><td>Oklahoma</td><td>389,737</td><td>1.2%</td></tr>
<tr><td>28</td><td>Oregon</td><td>363,784</td><td>1.2%</td></tr>
<tr><td>29</td><td>Connecticut</td><td>352,215</td><td>1.1%</td></tr>
<tr><td>30</td><td>Utah</td><td>340,322</td><td>1.1%</td></tr>
<tr><td>31</td><td>Iowa</td><td>322,179</td><td>1.0%</td></tr>
<tr><td>32</td><td>Kansas</td><td>304,237</td><td>1.0%</td></tr>
<tr><td>33</td><td>Mississippi</td><td>303,494</td><td>1.0%</td></tr>
<tr><td>34</td><td>Arkansas</td><td>284,141</td><td>0.9%</td></tr>
<tr><td>35</td><td>Nevada</td><td>252,520</td><td>0.8%</td></tr>
<tr><td>36</td><td>New Mexico</td><td>204,850</td><td>0.7%</td></tr>
<tr><td>37</td><td>Nebraska</td><td>192,774</td><td>0.6%</td></tr>
<tr><td>38</td><td>West Virginia</td><td>165,594</td><td>0.5%</td></tr>
<tr><td>39</td><td>Idaho</td><td>155,924</td><td>0.5%</td></tr>
<tr><td>40</td><td>Hawaii</td><td>136,178</td><td>0.4%</td></tr>
<tr><td>41</td><td>New Hampshire</td><td>129,025</td><td>0.4%</td></tr>
<tr><td>42</td><td>Rhode Island</td><td>114,978</td><td>0.4%</td></tr>
<tr><td>43</td><td>Maine</td><td>110,754</td><td>0.4%</td></tr>
<tr><td>44</td><td>Montana</td><td>100,810</td><td>0.3%</td></tr>
<tr><td>45</td><td>North Dakota</td><td>95,477</td><td>0.3%</td></tr>
<tr><td>46</td><td>Delaware</td><td>87,900</td><td>0.3%</td></tr>
<tr><td>47</td><td>South Dakota</td><td>84,674</td><td>0.3%</td></tr>
<tr><td>48</td><td>Alaska</td><td>80,623</td><td>0.3%</td></tr>
<tr><td>49</td><td>Vermont</td><td>67,928</td><td>0.2%</td></tr>
<tr><td>50</td><td>Wyoming</td><td>56,514</td><td>0.2%</td></tr>
<tr><td></td><td>District of Columbia</td><td>81,651</td><td>0.3%</td></tr>
</table>

Source: U.S. Bureau of the Census
"State Characteristics: Vintage 2015" (http://www.census.gov/programs-surveys/popest/data/data-sets.html)

Percent of Population 18 to 24 Years Old in 2015

National Percent = 9.7% of Population

<table>
<tr><td colspan="3">ALPHA ORDER</td><td colspan="3">RANK ORDER</td></tr>
<tr><td>RANK</td><td>STATE</td><td>PERCENT</td><td>RANK</td><td>STATE</td><td>PERCENT</td></tr>
<tr><td>31</td><td>Alabama</td><td>9.6</td><td>1</td><td>North Dakota</td><td>12.6</td></tr>
<tr><td>3</td><td>Alaska</td><td>10.9</td><td>2</td><td>Utah</td><td>11.4</td></tr>
<tr><td>18</td><td>Arizona</td><td>9.8</td><td>3</td><td>Alaska</td><td>10.9</td></tr>
<tr><td>35</td><td>Arkansas</td><td>9.5</td><td>3</td><td>Rhode Island</td><td>10.9</td></tr>
<tr><td>10</td><td>California</td><td>10.1</td><td>3</td><td>Vermont</td><td>10.9</td></tr>
<tr><td>27</td><td>Colorado</td><td>9.7</td><td>6</td><td>Kansas</td><td>10.4</td></tr>
<tr><td>18</td><td>Connecticut</td><td>9.8</td><td>7</td><td>Iowa</td><td>10.3</td></tr>
<tr><td>40</td><td>Delaware</td><td>9.3</td><td>7</td><td>Massachusetts</td><td>10.3</td></tr>
<tr><td>48</td><td>Florida</td><td>8.7</td><td>9</td><td>Nebraska</td><td>10.2</td></tr>
<tr><td>14</td><td>Georgia</td><td>10.0</td><td>10</td><td>California</td><td>10.1</td></tr>
<tr><td>35</td><td>Hawaii</td><td>9.5</td><td>10</td><td>Indiana</td><td>10.1</td></tr>
<tr><td>38</td><td>Idaho</td><td>9.4</td><td>10</td><td>Mississippi</td><td>10.1</td></tr>
<tr><td>31</td><td>Illinois</td><td>9.6</td><td>10</td><td>Texas</td><td>10.1</td></tr>
<tr><td>10</td><td>Indiana</td><td>10.1</td><td>14</td><td>Georgia</td><td>10.0</td></tr>
<tr><td>7</td><td>Iowa</td><td>10.3</td><td>14</td><td>Michigan</td><td>10.0</td></tr>
<tr><td>6</td><td>Kansas</td><td>10.4</td><td>14</td><td>Oklahoma</td><td>10.0</td></tr>
<tr><td>31</td><td>Kentucky</td><td>9.6</td><td>17</td><td>South Dakota</td><td>9.9</td></tr>
<tr><td>18</td><td>Louisiana</td><td>9.8</td><td>18</td><td>Arizona</td><td>9.8</td></tr>
<tr><td>50</td><td>Maine</td><td>8.3</td><td>18</td><td>Connecticut</td><td>9.8</td></tr>
<tr><td>43</td><td>Maryland</td><td>9.2</td><td>18</td><td>Louisiana</td><td>9.8</td></tr>
<tr><td>7</td><td>Massachusetts</td><td>10.3</td><td>18</td><td>Montana</td><td>9.8</td></tr>
<tr><td>14</td><td>Michigan</td><td>10.0</td><td>18</td><td>New Mexico</td><td>9.8</td></tr>
<tr><td>43</td><td>Minnesota</td><td>9.2</td><td>18</td><td>New York</td><td>9.8</td></tr>
<tr><td>10</td><td>Mississippi</td><td>10.1</td><td>18</td><td>North Carolina</td><td>9.8</td></tr>
<tr><td>27</td><td>Missouri</td><td>9.7</td><td>18</td><td>Virginia</td><td>9.8</td></tr>
<tr><td>18</td><td>Montana</td><td>9.8</td><td>18</td><td>Wisconsin</td><td>9.8</td></tr>
<tr><td>9</td><td>Nebraska</td><td>10.2</td><td>27</td><td>Colorado</td><td>9.7</td></tr>
<tr><td>48</td><td>Nevada</td><td>8.7</td><td>27</td><td>Missouri</td><td>9.7</td></tr>
<tr><td>27</td><td>New Hampshire</td><td>9.7</td><td>27</td><td>New Hampshire</td><td>9.7</td></tr>
<tr><td>47</td><td>New Jersey</td><td>8.8</td><td>27</td><td>South Carolina</td><td>9.7</td></tr>
<tr><td>18</td><td>New Mexico</td><td>9.8</td><td>31</td><td>Alabama</td><td>9.6</td></tr>
<tr><td>18</td><td>New York</td><td>9.8</td><td>31</td><td>Illinois</td><td>9.6</td></tr>
<tr><td>18</td><td>North Carolina</td><td>9.8</td><td>31</td><td>Kentucky</td><td>9.6</td></tr>
<tr><td>1</td><td>North Dakota</td><td>12.6</td><td>31</td><td>Wyoming</td><td>9.6</td></tr>
<tr><td>40</td><td>Ohio</td><td>9.3</td><td>35</td><td>Arkansas</td><td>9.5</td></tr>
<tr><td>14</td><td>Oklahoma</td><td>10.0</td><td>35</td><td>Hawaii</td><td>9.5</td></tr>
<tr><td>45</td><td>Oregon</td><td>9.0</td><td>35</td><td>Tennessee</td><td>9.5</td></tr>
<tr><td>38</td><td>Pennsylvania</td><td>9.4</td><td>38</td><td>Idaho</td><td>9.4</td></tr>
<tr><td>3</td><td>Rhode Island</td><td>10.9</td><td>38</td><td>Pennsylvania</td><td>9.4</td></tr>
<tr><td>27</td><td>South Carolina</td><td>9.7</td><td>40</td><td>Delaware</td><td>9.3</td></tr>
<tr><td>17</td><td>South Dakota</td><td>9.9</td><td>40</td><td>Ohio</td><td>9.3</td></tr>
<tr><td>35</td><td>Tennessee</td><td>9.5</td><td>40</td><td>Washington</td><td>9.3</td></tr>
<tr><td>10</td><td>Texas</td><td>10.1</td><td>43</td><td>Maryland</td><td>9.2</td></tr>
<tr><td>2</td><td>Utah</td><td>11.4</td><td>43</td><td>Minnesota</td><td>9.2</td></tr>
<tr><td>3</td><td>Vermont</td><td>10.9</td><td>45</td><td>Oregon</td><td>9.0</td></tr>
<tr><td>18</td><td>Virginia</td><td>9.8</td><td>45</td><td>West Virginia</td><td>9.0</td></tr>
<tr><td>40</td><td>Washington</td><td>9.3</td><td>47</td><td>New Jersey</td><td>8.8</td></tr>
<tr><td>45</td><td>West Virginia</td><td>9.0</td><td>48</td><td>Florida</td><td>8.7</td></tr>
<tr><td>18</td><td>Wisconsin</td><td>9.8</td><td>48</td><td>Nevada</td><td>8.7</td></tr>
<tr><td>31</td><td>Wyoming</td><td>9.6</td><td>50</td><td>Maine</td><td>8.3</td></tr>
<tr><td></td><td></td><td></td><td></td><td>District of Columbia</td><td>12.1</td></tr>
</table>

Source: CQ Press using data from U.S. Bureau of the Census
"State Characteristics: Vintage 2015" (http://www.census.gov/programs-surveys/popest/data/data-sets.html)

Population 25 to 44 Years Old in 2015

National Total = 84,726,985

RANK	STATE	POPULATION	% of USA
25	Alabama	1,235,222	1.5%
46	Alaska	210,642	0.2%
15	Arizona	1,755,258	2.1%
34	Arkansas	754,732	0.9%
1	California	11,023,370	13.0%
19	Colorado	1,556,878	1.8%
29	Connecticut	872,873	1.0%
45	Delaware	236,537	0.3%
4	Florida	5,062,786	6.0%
8	Georgia	2,772,876	3.3%
40	Hawaii	392,626	0.5%
39	Idaho	420,323	0.5%
5	Illinois	3,444,157	4.1%
17	Indiana	1,673,615	2.0%
33	Iowa	757,905	0.9%
35	Kansas	733,342	0.9%
26	Kentucky	1,127,424	1.3%
23	Louisiana	1,246,888	1.5%
42	Maine	307,297	0.4%
18	Maryland	1,604,442	1.9%
14	Massachusetts	1,777,941	2.1%
10	Michigan	2,398,869	2.8%
21	Minnesota	1,420,841	1.7%
32	Mississippi	760,829	0.9%
20	Missouri	1,539,442	1.8%
44	Montana	248,359	0.3%
37	Nebraska	481,176	0.6%
31	Nevada	803,651	0.9%
41	New Hampshire	311,207	0.4%
11	New Jersey	2,319,211	2.7%
36	New Mexico	523,652	0.6%
3	New York	5,375,357	6.3%
9	North Carolina	2,604,399	3.1%
48	North Dakota	197,791	0.2%
7	Ohio	2,884,127	3.4%
28	Oklahoma	1,016,531	1.2%
27	Oregon	1,081,083	1.3%
6	Pennsylvania	3,162,375	3.7%
43	Rhode Island	265,644	0.3%
24	South Carolina	1,238,763	1.5%
47	South Dakota	209,041	0.2%
16	Tennessee	1,709,475	2.0%
2	Texas	7,706,174	9.1%
30	Utah	840,860	1.0%
50	Vermont	142,298	0.2%
12	Virginia	2,273,157	2.7%
13	Washington	1,980,829	2.3%
38	West Virginia	446,032	0.5%
22	Wisconsin	1,416,753	1.7%
49	Wyoming	153,641	0.2%

RANK	STATE	POPULATION	% of USA
1	California	11,023,370	13.0%
2	Texas	7,706,174	9.1%
3	New York	5,375,357	6.3%
4	Florida	5,062,786	6.0%
5	Illinois	3,444,157	4.1%
6	Pennsylvania	3,162,375	3.7%
7	Ohio	2,884,127	3.4%
8	Georgia	2,772,876	3.3%
9	North Carolina	2,604,399	3.1%
10	Michigan	2,398,869	2.8%
11	New Jersey	2,319,211	2.7%
12	Virginia	2,273,157	2.7%
13	Washington	1,980,829	2.3%
14	Massachusetts	1,777,941	2.1%
15	Arizona	1,755,258	2.1%
16	Tennessee	1,709,475	2.0%
17	Indiana	1,673,615	2.0%
18	Maryland	1,604,442	1.9%
19	Colorado	1,556,878	1.8%
20	Missouri	1,539,442	1.8%
21	Minnesota	1,420,841	1.7%
22	Wisconsin	1,416,753	1.7%
23	Louisiana	1,246,888	1.5%
24	South Carolina	1,238,763	1.5%
25	Alabama	1,235,222	1.5%
26	Kentucky	1,127,424	1.3%
27	Oregon	1,081,083	1.3%
28	Oklahoma	1,016,531	1.2%
29	Connecticut	872,873	1.0%
30	Utah	840,860	1.0%
31	Nevada	803,651	0.9%
32	Mississippi	760,829	0.9%
33	Iowa	757,905	0.9%
34	Arkansas	754,732	0.9%
35	Kansas	733,342	0.9%
36	New Mexico	523,652	0.6%
37	Nebraska	481,176	0.6%
38	West Virginia	446,032	0.5%
39	Idaho	420,323	0.5%
40	Hawaii	392,626	0.5%
41	New Hampshire	311,207	0.4%
42	Maine	307,297	0.4%
43	Rhode Island	265,644	0.3%
44	Montana	248,359	0.3%
45	Delaware	236,537	0.3%
46	Alaska	210,642	0.2%
47	South Dakota	209,041	0.2%
48	North Dakota	197,791	0.2%
49	Wyoming	153,641	0.2%
50	Vermont	142,298	0.2%
	District of Columbia	248,284	0.3%

Source: U.S. Bureau of the Census
"State Characteristics: Vintage 2015" (http://www.census.gov/programs-surveys/popest/data/data-sets.html)

Percent of Population 25 to 44 Years Old in 2015

National Percent = 26.4% of Population

<table>
<tr><td colspan="3">ALPHA ORDER</td><td colspan="3">RANK ORDER</td></tr>
<tr><th>RANK</th><th>STATE</th><th>PERCENT</th><th>RANK</th><th>STATE</th><th>PERCENT</th></tr>
<tr><td>26</td><td>Alabama</td><td>25.4</td><td>1</td><td>Alaska</td><td>28.5</td></tr>
<tr><td>1</td><td>Alaska</td><td>28.5</td><td>1</td><td>Colorado</td><td>28.5</td></tr>
<tr><td>24</td><td>Arizona</td><td>25.7</td><td>3</td><td>California</td><td>28.2</td></tr>
<tr><td>30</td><td>Arkansas</td><td>25.3</td><td>4</td><td>Texas</td><td>28.1</td></tr>
<tr><td>3</td><td>California</td><td>28.2</td><td>4</td><td>Utah</td><td>28.1</td></tr>
<tr><td>1</td><td>Colorado</td><td>28.5</td><td>6</td><td>Nevada</td><td>27.8</td></tr>
<tr><td>43</td><td>Connecticut</td><td>24.3</td><td>7</td><td>Washington</td><td>27.6</td></tr>
<tr><td>37</td><td>Delaware</td><td>25.0</td><td>8</td><td>Hawaii</td><td>27.4</td></tr>
<tr><td>37</td><td>Florida</td><td>25.0</td><td>9</td><td>New York</td><td>27.2</td></tr>
<tr><td>10</td><td>Georgia</td><td>27.1</td><td>10</td><td>Georgia</td><td>27.1</td></tr>
<tr><td>8</td><td>Hawaii</td><td>27.4</td><td>10</td><td>Virginia</td><td>27.1</td></tr>
<tr><td>26</td><td>Idaho</td><td>25.4</td><td>12</td><td>Illinois</td><td>26.8</td></tr>
<tr><td>12</td><td>Illinois</td><td>26.8</td><td>12</td><td>Oregon</td><td>26.8</td></tr>
<tr><td>30</td><td>Indiana</td><td>25.3</td><td>14</td><td>Louisiana</td><td>26.7</td></tr>
<tr><td>43</td><td>Iowa</td><td>24.3</td><td>14</td><td>Maryland</td><td>26.7</td></tr>
<tr><td>34</td><td>Kansas</td><td>25.2</td><td>16</td><td>Massachusetts</td><td>26.2</td></tr>
<tr><td>25</td><td>Kentucky</td><td>25.5</td><td>16</td><td>Wyoming</td><td>26.2</td></tr>
<tr><td>14</td><td>Louisiana</td><td>26.7</td><td>18</td><td>North Dakota</td><td>26.1</td></tr>
<tr><td>49</td><td>Maine</td><td>23.1</td><td>19</td><td>Oklahoma</td><td>26.0</td></tr>
<tr><td>14</td><td>Maryland</td><td>26.7</td><td>20</td><td>Minnesota</td><td>25.9</td></tr>
<tr><td>16</td><td>Massachusetts</td><td>26.2</td><td>20</td><td>New Jersey</td><td>25.9</td></tr>
<tr><td>45</td><td>Michigan</td><td>24.2</td><td>20</td><td>North Carolina</td><td>25.9</td></tr>
<tr><td>20</td><td>Minnesota</td><td>25.9</td><td>20</td><td>Tennessee</td><td>25.9</td></tr>
<tr><td>26</td><td>Mississippi</td><td>25.4</td><td>24</td><td>Arizona</td><td>25.7</td></tr>
<tr><td>30</td><td>Missouri</td><td>25.3</td><td>25</td><td>Kentucky</td><td>25.5</td></tr>
<tr><td>47</td><td>Montana</td><td>24.0</td><td>26</td><td>Alabama</td><td>25.4</td></tr>
<tr><td>26</td><td>Nebraska</td><td>25.4</td><td>26</td><td>Idaho</td><td>25.4</td></tr>
<tr><td>6</td><td>Nevada</td><td>27.8</td><td>26</td><td>Mississippi</td><td>25.4</td></tr>
<tr><td>48</td><td>New Hampshire</td><td>23.4</td><td>26</td><td>Nebraska</td><td>25.4</td></tr>
<tr><td>20</td><td>New Jersey</td><td>25.9</td><td>30</td><td>Arkansas</td><td>25.3</td></tr>
<tr><td>35</td><td>New Mexico</td><td>25.1</td><td>30</td><td>Indiana</td><td>25.3</td></tr>
<tr><td>9</td><td>New York</td><td>27.2</td><td>30</td><td>Missouri</td><td>25.3</td></tr>
<tr><td>20</td><td>North Carolina</td><td>25.9</td><td>30</td><td>South Carolina</td><td>25.3</td></tr>
<tr><td>18</td><td>North Dakota</td><td>26.1</td><td>34</td><td>Kansas</td><td>25.2</td></tr>
<tr><td>39</td><td>Ohio</td><td>24.8</td><td>35</td><td>New Mexico</td><td>25.1</td></tr>
<tr><td>19</td><td>Oklahoma</td><td>26.0</td><td>35</td><td>Rhode Island</td><td>25.1</td></tr>
<tr><td>12</td><td>Oregon</td><td>26.8</td><td>37</td><td>Delaware</td><td>25.0</td></tr>
<tr><td>40</td><td>Pennsylvania</td><td>24.7</td><td>37</td><td>Florida</td><td>25.0</td></tr>
<tr><td>35</td><td>Rhode Island</td><td>25.1</td><td>39</td><td>Ohio</td><td>24.8</td></tr>
<tr><td>30</td><td>South Carolina</td><td>25.3</td><td>40</td><td>Pennsylvania</td><td>24.7</td></tr>
<tr><td>42</td><td>South Dakota</td><td>24.4</td><td>41</td><td>Wisconsin</td><td>24.5</td></tr>
<tr><td>20</td><td>Tennessee</td><td>25.9</td><td>42</td><td>South Dakota</td><td>24.4</td></tr>
<tr><td>4</td><td>Texas</td><td>28.1</td><td>43</td><td>Connecticut</td><td>24.3</td></tr>
<tr><td>4</td><td>Utah</td><td>28.1</td><td>43</td><td>Iowa</td><td>24.3</td></tr>
<tr><td>50</td><td>Vermont</td><td>22.7</td><td>45</td><td>Michigan</td><td>24.2</td></tr>
<tr><td>10</td><td>Virginia</td><td>27.1</td><td>45</td><td>West Virginia</td><td>24.2</td></tr>
<tr><td>7</td><td>Washington</td><td>27.6</td><td>47</td><td>Montana</td><td>24.0</td></tr>
<tr><td>45</td><td>West Virginia</td><td>24.2</td><td>48</td><td>New Hampshire</td><td>23.4</td></tr>
<tr><td>41</td><td>Wisconsin</td><td>24.5</td><td>49</td><td>Maine</td><td>23.1</td></tr>
<tr><td>16</td><td>Wyoming</td><td>26.2</td><td>50</td><td>Vermont</td><td>22.7</td></tr>
<tr><td></td><td></td><td></td><td></td><td>District of Columbia</td><td>36.9</td></tr>
</table>

Source: CQ Press using data from U.S. Bureau of the Census
"State Characteristics: Vintage 2015" (http://www.census.gov/programs-surveys/popest/data/data-sets.html)

Population 45 to 64 Years Old in 2015

National Total = 84,065,980

ALPHA ORDER

RANK	STATE	POPULATION	% of USA
24	Alabama	1,287,439	1.5%
47	Alaska	188,064	0.2%
17	Arizona	1,657,469	2.0%
32	Arkansas	756,882	0.9%
1	California	9,876,676	11.7%
22	Colorado	1,399,924	1.7%
28	Connecticut	1,034,933	1.2%
45	Delaware	256,596	0.3%
3	Florida	5,402,166	6.4%
10	Georgia	2,615,881	3.1%
42	Hawaii	355,052	0.4%
41	Idaho	402,352	0.5%
6	Illinois	3,391,040	4.0%
16	Indiana	1,734,738	2.1%
30	Iowa	812,142	1.0%
34	Kansas	728,095	0.9%
26	Kentucky	1,189,457	1.4%
25	Louisiana	1,200,133	1.4%
40	Maine	404,361	0.5%
18	Maryland	1,650,040	2.0%
13	Massachusetts	1,883,147	2.2%
8	Michigan	2,758,314	3.3%
21	Minnesota	1,472,425	1.8%
31	Mississippi	761,461	0.9%
19	Missouri	1,610,433	1.9%
44	Montana	279,349	0.3%
38	Nebraska	473,192	0.6%
33	Nevada	743,392	0.9%
39	New Hampshire	407,436	0.5%
11	New Jersey	2,503,610	3.0%
36	New Mexico	529,294	0.6%
4	New York	5,302,889	6.3%
9	North Carolina	2,642,914	3.1%
49	North Dakota	182,452	0.2%
7	Ohio	3,172,535	3.8%
29	Oklahoma	967,499	1.2%
27	Oregon	1,060,378	1.3%
5	Pennsylvania	3,565,533	4.2%
43	Rhode Island	294,656	0.4%
23	South Carolina	1,293,876	1.5%
46	South Dakota	219,010	0.3%
15	Tennessee	1,750,093	2.1%
2	Texas	6,554,348	7.8%
35	Utah	594,374	0.7%
48	Vermont	186,000	0.2%
12	Virginia	2,228,053	2.7%
14	Washington	1,875,264	2.2%
37	West Virginia	516,618	0.6%
20	Wisconsin	1,594,455	1.9%
50	Wyoming	152,358	0.2%

RANK ORDER

RANK	STATE	POPULATION	% of USA
1	California	9,876,676	11.7%
2	Texas	6,554,348	7.8%
3	Florida	5,402,166	6.4%
4	New York	5,302,889	6.3%
5	Pennsylvania	3,565,533	4.2%
6	Illinois	3,391,040	4.0%
7	Ohio	3,172,535	3.8%
8	Michigan	2,758,314	3.3%
9	North Carolina	2,642,914	3.1%
10	Georgia	2,615,881	3.1%
11	New Jersey	2,503,610	3.0%
12	Virginia	2,228,053	2.7%
13	Massachusetts	1,883,147	2.2%
14	Washington	1,875,264	2.2%
15	Tennessee	1,750,093	2.1%
16	Indiana	1,734,738	2.1%
17	Arizona	1,657,469	2.0%
18	Maryland	1,650,040	2.0%
19	Missouri	1,610,433	1.9%
20	Wisconsin	1,594,455	1.9%
21	Minnesota	1,472,425	1.8%
22	Colorado	1,399,924	1.7%
23	South Carolina	1,293,876	1.5%
24	Alabama	1,287,439	1.5%
25	Louisiana	1,200,133	1.4%
26	Kentucky	1,189,457	1.4%
27	Oregon	1,060,378	1.3%
28	Connecticut	1,034,933	1.2%
29	Oklahoma	967,499	1.2%
30	Iowa	812,142	1.0%
31	Mississippi	761,461	0.9%
32	Arkansas	756,882	0.9%
33	Nevada	743,392	0.9%
34	Kansas	728,095	0.9%
35	Utah	594,374	0.7%
36	New Mexico	529,294	0.6%
37	West Virginia	516,618	0.6%
38	Nebraska	473,192	0.6%
39	New Hampshire	407,436	0.5%
40	Maine	404,361	0.5%
41	Idaho	402,352	0.5%
42	Hawaii	355,052	0.4%
43	Rhode Island	294,656	0.4%
44	Montana	279,349	0.3%
45	Delaware	256,596	0.3%
46	South Dakota	219,010	0.3%
47	Alaska	188,064	0.2%
48	Vermont	186,000	0.2%
49	North Dakota	182,452	0.2%
50	Wyoming	152,358	0.2%
	District of Columbia	147,182	0.2%

Source: U.S. Bureau of the Census
"State Characteristics: Vintage 2015" (http://www.census.gov/programs-surveys/popest/data/data-sets.html)

Percent of Population 45 to 64 Years Old in 2015

National Percent = 26.2% of Population

ALPHA ORDER

RANK	STATE	PERCENT
21	Alabama	26.5
36	Alaska	25.5
46	Arizona	24.3
38	Arkansas	25.4
41	California	25.2
32	Colorado	25.7
4	Connecticut	28.8
14	Delaware	27.1
19	Florida	26.6
35	Georgia	25.6
44	Hawaii	24.8
46	Idaho	24.3
24	Illinois	26.4
28	Indiana	26.2
30	Iowa	26.0
42	Kansas	25.0
16	Kentucky	26.9
32	Louisiana	25.7
2	Maine	30.4
12	Maryland	27.5
10	Massachusetts	27.7
9	Michigan	27.8
17	Minnesota	26.8
38	Mississippi	25.4
21	Missouri	26.5
15	Montana	27.0
42	Nebraska	25.0
32	Nevada	25.7
1	New Hampshire	30.6
6	New Jersey	27.9
38	New Mexico	25.4
17	New York	26.8
26	North Carolina	26.3
48	North Dakota	24.1
13	Ohio	27.3
45	Oklahoma	24.7
26	Oregon	26.3
6	Pennsylvania	27.9
6	Rhode Island	27.9
24	South Carolina	26.4
36	South Dakota	25.5
21	Tennessee	26.5
49	Texas	23.9
50	Utah	19.8
3	Vermont	29.7
19	Virginia	26.6
28	Washington	26.2
5	West Virginia	28.0
11	Wisconsin	27.6
30	Wyoming	26.0

RANK ORDER

RANK	STATE	PERCENT
1	New Hampshire	30.6
2	Maine	30.4
3	Vermont	29.7
4	Connecticut	28.8
5	West Virginia	28.0
6	New Jersey	27.9
6	Pennsylvania	27.9
6	Rhode Island	27.9
9	Michigan	27.8
10	Massachusetts	27.7
11	Wisconsin	27.6
12	Maryland	27.5
13	Ohio	27.3
14	Delaware	27.1
15	Montana	27.0
16	Kentucky	26.9
17	Minnesota	26.8
17	New York	26.8
19	Florida	26.6
19	Virginia	26.6
21	Alabama	26.5
21	Missouri	26.5
21	Tennessee	26.5
24	Illinois	26.4
24	South Carolina	26.4
26	North Carolina	26.3
26	Oregon	26.3
28	Indiana	26.2
28	Washington	26.2
30	Iowa	26.0
30	Wyoming	26.0
32	Colorado	25.7
32	Louisiana	25.7
32	Nevada	25.7
35	Georgia	25.6
36	Alaska	25.5
36	South Dakota	25.5
38	Arkansas	25.4
38	Mississippi	25.4
38	New Mexico	25.4
41	California	25.2
42	Kansas	25.0
42	Nebraska	25.0
44	Hawaii	24.8
45	Oklahoma	24.7
46	Arizona	24.3
46	Idaho	24.3
48	North Dakota	24.1
49	Texas	23.9
50	Utah	19.8
	District of Columbia	21.9

Source: CQ Press using data from U.S. Bureau of the Census
"State Characteristics: Vintage 2015" (http://www.census.gov/programs-surveys/popest/data/data-sets.html)

Population 65 Years Old and Older in 2015

National Total = 47,760,852

ALPHA ORDER

RANK	STATE	POPULATION	% of USA
23	Alabama	764,162	1.6%
50	Alaska	72,837	0.2%
13	Arizona	1,120,054	2.3%
31	Arkansas	477,149	1.0%
1	California	5,188,754	10.9%
24	Colorado	711,625	1.5%
29	Connecticut	566,806	1.2%
45	Delaware	160,515	0.3%
2	Florida	3,942,468	8.3%
11	Georgia	1,304,924	2.7%
41	Hawaii	236,914	0.5%
40	Idaho	243,494	0.5%
7	Illinois	1,830,277	3.8%
17	Indiana	966,127	2.0%
30	Iowa	502,877	1.1%
33	Kansas	426,410	0.9%
25	Kentucky	672,765	1.4%
27	Louisiana	653,094	1.4%
39	Maine	250,536	0.5%
20	Maryland	849,571	1.8%
14	Massachusetts	1,045,222	2.2%
8	Michigan	1,570,671	3.3%
21	Minnesota	805,643	1.7%
32	Mississippi	439,701	0.9%
18	Missouri	954,922	2.0%
43	Montana	178,011	0.4%
38	Nebraska	278,711	0.6%
34	Nevada	422,118	0.9%
42	New Hampshire	218,942	0.5%
10	New Jersey	1,343,626	2.8%
36	New Mexico	330,405	0.7%
4	New York	2,964,315	6.2%
9	North Carolina	1,516,824	3.2%
48	North Dakota	107,281	0.2%
6	Ohio	1,842,952	3.9%
28	Oklahoma	576,250	1.2%
26	Oregon	660,876	1.4%
5	Pennsylvania	2,179,788	4.6%
44	Rhode Island	169,976	0.4%
22	South Carolina	794,795	1.7%
46	South Dakota	134,420	0.3%
16	Tennessee	1,016,552	2.1%
3	Texas	3,225,168	6.8%
37	Utah	307,867	0.6%
47	Vermont	109,893	0.2%
12	Virginia	1,188,393	2.5%
15	Washington	1,036,046	2.2%
35	West Virginia	336,288	0.7%
19	Wisconsin	902,134	1.9%
49	Wyoming	84,699	0.2%

RANK ORDER

RANK	STATE	POPULATION	% of USA
1	California	5,188,754	10.9%
2	Florida	3,942,468	8.3%
3	Texas	3,225,168	6.8%
4	New York	2,964,315	6.2%
5	Pennsylvania	2,179,788	4.6%
6	Ohio	1,842,952	3.9%
7	Illinois	1,830,277	3.8%
8	Michigan	1,570,671	3.3%
9	North Carolina	1,516,824	3.2%
10	New Jersey	1,343,626	2.8%
11	Georgia	1,304,924	2.7%
12	Virginia	1,188,393	2.5%
13	Arizona	1,120,054	2.3%
14	Massachusetts	1,045,222	2.2%
15	Washington	1,036,046	2.2%
16	Tennessee	1,016,552	2.1%
17	Indiana	966,127	2.0%
18	Missouri	954,922	2.0%
19	Wisconsin	902,134	1.9%
20	Maryland	849,571	1.8%
21	Minnesota	805,643	1.7%
22	South Carolina	794,795	1.7%
23	Alabama	764,162	1.6%
24	Colorado	711,625	1.5%
25	Kentucky	672,765	1.4%
26	Oregon	660,876	1.4%
27	Louisiana	653,094	1.4%
28	Oklahoma	576,250	1.2%
29	Connecticut	566,806	1.2%
30	Iowa	502,877	1.1%
31	Arkansas	477,149	1.0%
32	Mississippi	439,701	0.9%
33	Kansas	426,410	0.9%
34	Nevada	422,118	0.9%
35	West Virginia	336,288	0.7%
36	New Mexico	330,405	0.7%
37	Utah	307,867	0.6%
38	Nebraska	278,711	0.6%
39	Maine	250,536	0.5%
40	Idaho	243,494	0.5%
41	Hawaii	236,914	0.5%
42	New Hampshire	218,942	0.5%
43	Montana	178,011	0.4%
44	Rhode Island	169,976	0.4%
45	Delaware	160,515	0.3%
46	South Dakota	134,420	0.3%
47	Vermont	109,893	0.2%
48	North Dakota	107,281	0.2%
49	Wyoming	84,699	0.2%
50	Alaska	72,837	0.2%
	District of Columbia	77,004	0.2%

Source: U.S. Bureau of the Census
"State Characteristics: Vintage 2015" (http://www.census.gov/programs-surveys/popest/data/data-sets.html)

Percent of Population 65 Years Old and Older in 2015

National Percent = 14.9% of Population

ALPHA ORDER

RANK	STATE	PERCENT
20	Alabama	15.7
50	Alaska	9.9
10	Arizona	16.4
15	Arkansas	16.0
45	California	13.3
46	Colorado	13.0
17	Connecticut	15.8
6	Delaware	17.0
1	Florida	19.4
47	Georgia	12.8
8	Hawaii	16.5
30	Idaho	14.7
40	Illinois	14.2
35	Indiana	14.6
13	Iowa	16.1
35	Kansas	14.6
26	Kentucky	15.2
44	Louisiana	14.0
2	Maine	18.8
43	Maryland	14.1
24	Massachusetts	15.4
17	Michigan	15.8
30	Minnesota	14.7
30	Mississippi	14.7
20	Missouri	15.7
5	Montana	17.2
30	Nebraska	14.7
35	Nevada	14.6
8	New Hampshire	16.5
28	New Jersey	15.0
17	New Mexico	15.8
28	New York	15.0
27	North Carolina	15.1
40	North Dakota	14.2
16	Ohio	15.9
30	Oklahoma	14.7
10	Oregon	16.4
6	Pennsylvania	17.0
13	Rhode Island	16.1
12	South Carolina	16.2
20	South Dakota	15.7
24	Tennessee	15.4
48	Texas	11.7
49	Utah	10.3
4	Vermont	17.6
40	Virginia	14.2
39	Washington	14.4
3	West Virginia	18.2
23	Wisconsin	15.6
38	Wyoming	14.5

RANK ORDER

RANK	STATE	PERCENT
1	Florida	19.4
2	Maine	18.8
3	West Virginia	18.2
4	Vermont	17.6
5	Montana	17.2
6	Delaware	17.0
6	Pennsylvania	17.0
8	Hawaii	16.5
8	New Hampshire	16.5
10	Arizona	16.4
10	Oregon	16.4
12	South Carolina	16.2
13	Iowa	16.1
13	Rhode Island	16.1
15	Arkansas	16.0
16	Ohio	15.9
17	Connecticut	15.8
17	Michigan	15.8
17	New Mexico	15.8
20	Alabama	15.7
20	Missouri	15.7
20	South Dakota	15.7
23	Wisconsin	15.6
24	Massachusetts	15.4
24	Tennessee	15.4
26	Kentucky	15.2
27	North Carolina	15.1
28	New Jersey	15.0
28	New York	15.0
30	Idaho	14.7
30	Minnesota	14.7
30	Mississippi	14.7
30	Nebraska	14.7
30	Oklahoma	14.7
35	Indiana	14.6
35	Kansas	14.6
35	Nevada	14.6
38	Wyoming	14.5
39	Washington	14.4
40	Illinois	14.2
40	North Dakota	14.2
40	Virginia	14.2
43	Maryland	14.1
44	Louisiana	14.0
45	California	13.3
46	Colorado	13.0
47	Georgia	12.8
48	Texas	11.7
49	Utah	10.3
50	Alaska	9.9
	District of Columbia	11.5

Source: CQ Press using data from U.S. Bureau of the Census
"State Characteristics: Vintage 2015" (http://www.census.gov/programs-surveys/popest/data/data-sets.html)

Population 85 Years Old and Older in 2015

National Total = 6,287,161

ALPHA ORDER

RANK ORDER

RANK	STATE	POPULATION	% of USA
23	Alabama	85,439	1.4%
50	Alaska	6,137	0.1%
15	Arizona	130,789	2.1%
32	Arkansas	55,980	0.9%
1	California	707,777	11.3%
25	Colorado	83,979	1.3%
22	Connecticut	90,124	1.4%
46	Delaware	18,652	0.3%
2	Florida	540,276	8.6%
13	Georgia	135,947	2.2%
38	Hawaii	38,303	0.6%
43	Idaho	27,934	0.4%
6	Illinois	258,717	4.1%
17	Indiana	127,810	2.0%
27	Iowa	79,186	1.3%
31	Kansas	64,625	1.0%
28	Kentucky	77,361	1.2%
29	Louisiana	75,979	1.2%
40	Maine	32,025	0.5%
21	Maryland	113,214	1.8%
11	Massachusetts	158,558	2.5%
8	Michigan	212,912	3.4%
19	Minnesota	118,209	1.9%
33	Mississippi	50,296	0.8%
18	Missouri	126,730	2.0%
44	Montana	22,425	0.4%
34	Nebraska	42,224	0.7%
35	Nevada	39,648	0.6%
41	New Hampshire	28,944	0.5%
9	New Jersey	197,010	3.1%
37	New Mexico	38,702	0.6%
3	New York	433,471	6.9%
10	North Carolina	175,044	2.8%
47	North Dakota	18,086	0.3%
7	Ohio	253,020	4.0%
30	Oklahoma	69,449	1.1%
24	Oregon	84,329	1.3%
5	Pennsylvania	333,828	5.3%
42	Rhode Island	28,413	0.5%
26	South Carolina	82,256	1.3%
45	South Dakota	21,368	0.3%
20	Tennessee	113,736	1.8%
4	Texas	374,439	6.0%
39	Utah	35,708	0.6%
48	Vermont	14,374	0.2%
12	Virginia	142,512	2.3%
14	Washington	130,984	2.1%
36	West Virginia	39,264	0.6%
16	Wisconsin	129,257	2.1%
49	Wyoming	10,264	0.2%

RANK	STATE	POPULATION	% of USA
1	California	707,777	11.3%
2	Florida	540,276	8.6%
3	New York	433,471	6.9%
4	Texas	374,439	6.0%
5	Pennsylvania	333,828	5.3%
6	Illinois	258,717	4.1%
7	Ohio	253,020	4.0%
8	Michigan	212,912	3.4%
9	New Jersey	197,010	3.1%
10	North Carolina	175,044	2.8%
11	Massachusetts	158,558	2.5%
12	Virginia	142,512	2.3%
13	Georgia	135,947	2.2%
14	Washington	130,984	2.1%
15	Arizona	130,789	2.1%
16	Wisconsin	129,257	2.1%
17	Indiana	127,810	2.0%
18	Missouri	126,730	2.0%
19	Minnesota	118,209	1.9%
20	Tennessee	113,736	1.8%
21	Maryland	113,214	1.8%
22	Connecticut	90,124	1.4%
23	Alabama	85,439	1.4%
24	Oregon	84,329	1.3%
25	Colorado	83,979	1.3%
26	South Carolina	82,256	1.3%
27	Iowa	79,186	1.3%
28	Kentucky	77,361	1.2%
29	Louisiana	75,979	1.2%
30	Oklahoma	69,449	1.1%
31	Kansas	64,625	1.0%
32	Arkansas	55,980	0.9%
33	Mississippi	50,296	0.8%
34	Nebraska	42,224	0.7%
35	Nevada	39,648	0.6%
36	West Virginia	39,264	0.6%
37	New Mexico	38,702	0.6%
38	Hawaii	38,303	0.6%
39	Utah	35,708	0.6%
40	Maine	32,025	0.5%
41	New Hampshire	28,944	0.5%
42	Rhode Island	28,413	0.5%
43	Idaho	27,934	0.4%
44	Montana	22,425	0.4%
45	South Dakota	21,368	0.3%
46	Delaware	18,652	0.3%
47	North Dakota	18,086	0.3%
48	Vermont	14,374	0.2%
49	Wyoming	10,264	0.2%
50	Alaska	6,137	0.1%
	District of Columbia	11,447	0.2%

Source: U.S. Bureau of the Census
"State Characteristics: Vintage 2015" (http://www.census.gov/programs-surveys/popest/data/data-sets.html)

Percent of Population 85 Years Old and Older in 2015

National Percent = 2.0% of Population

<table>
<tr><td colspan="3">ALPHA ORDER</td><td colspan="3">RANK ORDER</td></tr>
<tr><td>RANK</td><td>STATE</td><td>PERCENT</td><td>RANK</td><td>STATE</td><td>PERCENT</td></tr>
<tr><td>32</td><td>Alabama</td><td>1.8</td><td>1</td><td>Florida</td><td>2.7</td></tr>
<tr><td>50</td><td>Alaska</td><td>0.8</td><td>1</td><td>Hawaii</td><td>2.7</td></tr>
<tr><td>27</td><td>Arizona</td><td>1.9</td><td>1</td><td>Rhode Island</td><td>2.7</td></tr>
<tr><td>27</td><td>Arkansas</td><td>1.9</td><td>4</td><td>Pennsylvania</td><td>2.6</td></tr>
<tr><td>32</td><td>California</td><td>1.8</td><td>5</td><td>Connecticut</td><td>2.5</td></tr>
<tr><td>45</td><td>Colorado</td><td>1.5</td><td>5</td><td>Iowa</td><td>2.5</td></tr>
<tr><td>5</td><td>Connecticut</td><td>2.5</td><td>5</td><td>South Dakota</td><td>2.5</td></tr>
<tr><td>25</td><td>Delaware</td><td>2.0</td><td>8</td><td>Maine</td><td>2.4</td></tr>
<tr><td>1</td><td>Florida</td><td>2.7</td><td>8</td><td>North Dakota</td><td>2.4</td></tr>
<tr><td>48</td><td>Georgia</td><td>1.3</td><td>10</td><td>Massachusetts</td><td>2.3</td></tr>
<tr><td>1</td><td>Hawaii</td><td>2.7</td><td>10</td><td>Vermont</td><td>2.3</td></tr>
<tr><td>37</td><td>Idaho</td><td>1.7</td><td>12</td><td>Kansas</td><td>2.2</td></tr>
<tr><td>25</td><td>Illinois</td><td>2.0</td><td>12</td><td>Minnesota</td><td>2.2</td></tr>
<tr><td>27</td><td>Indiana</td><td>1.9</td><td>12</td><td>Montana</td><td>2.2</td></tr>
<tr><td>5</td><td>Iowa</td><td>2.5</td><td>12</td><td>Nebraska</td><td>2.2</td></tr>
<tr><td>12</td><td>Kansas</td><td>2.2</td><td>12</td><td>New Hampshire</td><td>2.2</td></tr>
<tr><td>37</td><td>Kentucky</td><td>1.7</td><td>12</td><td>New Jersey</td><td>2.2</td></tr>
<tr><td>44</td><td>Louisiana</td><td>1.6</td><td>12</td><td>New York</td><td>2.2</td></tr>
<tr><td>8</td><td>Maine</td><td>2.4</td><td>12</td><td>Ohio</td><td>2.2</td></tr>
<tr><td>27</td><td>Maryland</td><td>1.9</td><td>12</td><td>Wisconsin</td><td>2.2</td></tr>
<tr><td>10</td><td>Massachusetts</td><td>2.3</td><td>21</td><td>Michigan</td><td>2.1</td></tr>
<tr><td>21</td><td>Michigan</td><td>2.1</td><td>21</td><td>Missouri</td><td>2.1</td></tr>
<tr><td>12</td><td>Minnesota</td><td>2.2</td><td>21</td><td>Oregon</td><td>2.1</td></tr>
<tr><td>37</td><td>Mississippi</td><td>1.7</td><td>21</td><td>West Virginia</td><td>2.1</td></tr>
<tr><td>21</td><td>Missouri</td><td>2.1</td><td>25</td><td>Delaware</td><td>2.0</td></tr>
<tr><td>12</td><td>Montana</td><td>2.2</td><td>25</td><td>Illinois</td><td>2.0</td></tr>
<tr><td>12</td><td>Nebraska</td><td>2.2</td><td>27</td><td>Arizona</td><td>1.9</td></tr>
<tr><td>46</td><td>Nevada</td><td>1.4</td><td>27</td><td>Arkansas</td><td>1.9</td></tr>
<tr><td>12</td><td>New Hampshire</td><td>2.2</td><td>27</td><td>Indiana</td><td>1.9</td></tr>
<tr><td>12</td><td>New Jersey</td><td>2.2</td><td>27</td><td>Maryland</td><td>1.9</td></tr>
<tr><td>27</td><td>New Mexico</td><td>1.9</td><td>27</td><td>New Mexico</td><td>1.9</td></tr>
<tr><td>12</td><td>New York</td><td>2.2</td><td>32</td><td>Alabama</td><td>1.8</td></tr>
<tr><td>37</td><td>North Carolina</td><td>1.7</td><td>32</td><td>California</td><td>1.8</td></tr>
<tr><td>8</td><td>North Dakota</td><td>2.4</td><td>32</td><td>Oklahoma</td><td>1.8</td></tr>
<tr><td>12</td><td>Ohio</td><td>2.2</td><td>32</td><td>Washington</td><td>1.8</td></tr>
<tr><td>32</td><td>Oklahoma</td><td>1.8</td><td>32</td><td>Wyoming</td><td>1.8</td></tr>
<tr><td>21</td><td>Oregon</td><td>2.1</td><td>37</td><td>Idaho</td><td>1.7</td></tr>
<tr><td>4</td><td>Pennsylvania</td><td>2.6</td><td>37</td><td>Kentucky</td><td>1.7</td></tr>
<tr><td>1</td><td>Rhode Island</td><td>2.7</td><td>37</td><td>Mississippi</td><td>1.7</td></tr>
<tr><td>37</td><td>South Carolina</td><td>1.7</td><td>37</td><td>North Carolina</td><td>1.7</td></tr>
<tr><td>5</td><td>South Dakota</td><td>2.5</td><td>37</td><td>South Carolina</td><td>1.7</td></tr>
<tr><td>37</td><td>Tennessee</td><td>1.7</td><td>37</td><td>Tennessee</td><td>1.7</td></tr>
<tr><td>46</td><td>Texas</td><td>1.4</td><td>37</td><td>Virginia</td><td>1.7</td></tr>
<tr><td>49</td><td>Utah</td><td>1.2</td><td>44</td><td>Louisiana</td><td>1.6</td></tr>
<tr><td>10</td><td>Vermont</td><td>2.3</td><td>45</td><td>Colorado</td><td>1.5</td></tr>
<tr><td>37</td><td>Virginia</td><td>1.7</td><td>46</td><td>Nevada</td><td>1.4</td></tr>
<tr><td>32</td><td>Washington</td><td>1.8</td><td>46</td><td>Texas</td><td>1.4</td></tr>
<tr><td>21</td><td>West Virginia</td><td>2.1</td><td>48</td><td>Georgia</td><td>1.3</td></tr>
<tr><td>12</td><td>Wisconsin</td><td>2.2</td><td>49</td><td>Utah</td><td>1.2</td></tr>
<tr><td>32</td><td>Wyoming</td><td>1.8</td><td>50</td><td>Alaska</td><td>0.8</td></tr>
<tr><td></td><td></td><td></td><td></td><td>District of Columbia</td><td>1.7</td></tr>
</table>

Source: CQ Press using data from U.S. Bureau of the Census
"State Characteristics: Vintage 2015" (http://www.census.gov/programs-surveys/popest/data/data-sets.html)

Percent of Native Population Born in Their State of Residence in 2015

National Percent = 67.6%

ALPHA ORDER

RANK	STATE	PERCENT
13	Alabama	72.6
45	Alaska	45.4
46	Arizona	45.3
26	Arkansas	64.8
7	California	75.4
44	Colorado	47.4
27	Connecticut	64.6
43	Delaware	50.2
47	Florida	45.0
33	Georgia	61.0
29	Hawaii	64.4
41	Idaho	50.9
5	Illinois	78.3
15	Indiana	71.9
9	Iowa	74.6
31	Kansas	63.0
14	Kentucky	72.1
3	Louisiana	81.6
23	Maine	66.3
37	Maryland	55.7
11	Massachusetts	73.5
1	Michigan	82.0
10	Minnesota	73.8
12	Mississippi	73.3
19	Missouri	68.9
38	Montana	55.4
18	Nebraska	69.7
50	Nevada	31.9
48	New Hampshire	44.8
21	New Jersey	67.4
35	New Mexico	58.8
2	New York	81.8
32	North Carolina	62.1
24	North Dakota	66.2
4	Ohio	78.6
28	Oklahoma	64.5
41	Oregon	50.9
6	Pennsylvania	78.0
25	Rhode Island	65.4
34	South Carolina	60.6
22	South Dakota	67.1
30	Tennessee	63.3
15	Texas	71.9
20	Utah	67.8
40	Vermont	52.2
36	Virginia	56.4
39	Washington	54.8
17	West Virginia	70.8
8	Wisconsin	75.0
49	Wyoming	42.2

RANK ORDER

RANK	STATE	PERCENT
1	Michigan	82.0
2	New York	81.8
3	Louisiana	81.6
4	Ohio	78.6
5	Illinois	78.3
6	Pennsylvania	78.0
7	California	75.4
8	Wisconsin	75.0
9	Iowa	74.6
10	Minnesota	73.8
11	Massachusetts	73.5
12	Mississippi	73.3
13	Alabama	72.6
14	Kentucky	72.1
15	Indiana	71.9
15	Texas	71.9
17	West Virginia	70.8
18	Nebraska	69.7
19	Missouri	68.9
20	Utah	67.8
21	New Jersey	67.4
22	South Dakota	67.1
23	Maine	66.3
24	North Dakota	66.2
25	Rhode Island	65.4
26	Arkansas	64.8
27	Connecticut	64.6
28	Oklahoma	64.5
29	Hawaii	64.4
30	Tennessee	63.3
31	Kansas	63.0
32	North Carolina	62.1
33	Georgia	61.0
34	South Carolina	60.6
35	New Mexico	58.8
36	Virginia	56.4
37	Maryland	55.7
38	Montana	55.4
39	Washington	54.8
40	Vermont	52.2
41	Idaho	50.9
41	Oregon	50.9
43	Delaware	50.2
44	Colorado	47.4
45	Alaska	45.4
46	Arizona	45.3
47	Florida	45.0
48	New Hampshire	44.8
49	Wyoming	42.2
50	Nevada	31.9
	District of Columbia	41.7

Source: U.S. Bureau of the Census
"2015 American Community Survey-Table R0601" (http://www.census.gov/programs-surveys/acs/)

Domestic Migration of Population: 2015 to 2016

National Net Migration = 0 People*

ALPHA ORDER				RANK ORDER		
RANK	STATE	NET MIGRATION		RANK	STATE	NET MIGRATION
20	Alabama	(864)		1	Florida	207,155
29	Alaska	(4,587)		2	Texas	125,703
4	Arizona	61,544		3	Washington	67,571
19	Arkansas	195		4	Arizona	61,544
48	California	(109,023)		5	North Carolina	59,584
6	Colorado	50,216		6	Colorado	50,216
45	Connecticut	(29,880)		7	Oregon	50,038
15	Delaware	3,027		8	South Carolina	47,084
1	Florida	207,155		9	Georgia	36,781
9	Georgia	36,781		10	Nevada	34,575
35	Hawaii	(10,021)		11	Tennessee	30,519
13	Idaho	17,143		12	Utah	19,778
49	Illinois	(114,144)		13	Idaho	17,143
36	Indiana	(12,135)		14	Montana	6,853
24	Iowa	(3,392)		15	Delaware	3,027
39	Kansas	(18,595)		16	New Hampshire	2,187
25	Kentucky	(3,429)		17	Maine	2,169
37	Louisiana	(12,243)		18	South Dakota	941
17	Maine	2,169		19	Arkansas	195
42	Maryland	(26,232)		20	Alabama	(864)
41	Massachusetts	(25,606)		21	Minnesota	(1,762)
44	Michigan	(27,839)		22	Nebraska	(2,144)
21	Minnesota	(1,762)		23	Vermont	(2,865)
33	Mississippi	(9,690)		24	Iowa	(3,392)
30	Missouri	(6,250)		25	Kentucky	(3,429)
14	Montana	6,853		26	Rhode Island	(3,784)
22	Nebraska	(2,144)		27	Oklahoma	(3,822)
10	Nevada	34,575		28	Wyoming	(4,347)
16	New Hampshire	2,187		29	Alaska	(4,587)
47	New Jersey	(66,791)		30	Missouri	(6,250)
34	New Mexico	(9,748)		31	North Dakota	(6,259)
50	New York	(191,367)		32	West Virginia	(7,659)
5	North Carolina	59,584		33	Mississippi	(9,690)
31	North Dakota	(6,259)		34	New Mexico	(9,748)
43	Ohio	(27,558)		35	Hawaii	(10,021)
27	Oklahoma	(3,822)		36	Indiana	(12,135)
7	Oregon	50,038		37	Louisiana	(12,243)
46	Pennsylvania	(45,565)		38	Wisconsin	(12,395)
26	Rhode Island	(3,784)		39	Kansas	(18,595)
8	South Carolina	47,084		40	Virginia	(25,343)
18	South Dakota	941		41	Massachusetts	(25,606)
11	Tennessee	30,519		42	Maryland	(26,232)
2	Texas	125,703		43	Ohio	(27,558)
12	Utah	19,778		44	Michigan	(27,839)
23	Vermont	(2,865)		45	Connecticut	(29,880)
40	Virginia	(25,343)		46	Pennsylvania	(45,565)
3	Washington	67,571		47	New Jersey	(66,791)
32	West Virginia	(7,659)		48	California	(109,023)
38	Wisconsin	(12,395)		49	Illinois	(114,144)
28	Wyoming	(4,347)		50	New York	(191,367)
					District of Columbia	2,276

Source: U.S. Bureau of the Census
  "State Population Totals Tables" (http://www.census.gov/programs-surveys/popest/data/data-sets.html)
*From July 1, 2015 to June 30, 2016. Includes armed forces residing in each state. Net Domestic Migration is the difference between domestic inmigration to an area and domestic outmigration from it during the period. Domestic inmigration and outmigration consist of moves where both the origins and destinations are within the United States (excluding Puerto Rico).

Net International Migration: 2015 to 2016

National Net = 999,163 Immigrants*

ALPHA ORDER

RANK	STATE	IMMIGRANTS	% of USA
34	Alabama	4,738	0.5%
42	Alaska	2,030	0.2%
17	Arizona	14,861	1.5%
37	Arkansas	3,335	0.3%
1	California	142,553	14.3%
20	Colorado	10,557	1.1%
16	Connecticut	17,058	1.7%
39	Delaware	2,556	0.3%
2	Florida	118,831	11.9%
12	Georgia	23,831	2.4%
24	Hawaii	7,438	0.7%
44	Idaho	1,726	0.2%
9	Illinois	30,934	3.1%
19	Indiana	11,052	1.1%
30	Iowa	6,336	0.6%
31	Kansas	5,851	0.6%
28	Kentucky	6,734	0.7%
26	Louisiana	7,223	0.7%
43	Maine	1,785	0.2%
10	Maryland	26,408	2.6%
6	Massachusetts	40,898	4.1%
13	Michigan	22,511	2.3%
18	Minnesota	13,644	1.4%
40	Mississippi	2,223	0.2%
22	Missouri	8,413	0.8%
49	Montana	569	0.1%
36	Nebraska	4,187	0.4%
25	Nevada	7,392	0.7%
41	New Hampshire	2,175	0.2%
5	New Jersey	50,087	5.0%
38	New Mexico	2,637	0.3%
3	New York	118,478	11.9%
14	North Carolina	20,494	2.1%
46	North Dakota	1,575	0.2%
15	Ohio	19,591	2.0%
29	Oklahoma	6,716	0.7%
27	Oregon	6,934	0.7%
7	Pennsylvania	34,678	3.5%
35	Rhode Island	4,203	0.4%
32	South Carolina	5,760	0.6%
45	South Dakota	1,632	0.2%
21	Tennessee	9,440	0.9%
4	Texas	91,839	9.2%
33	Utah	5,634	0.6%
48	Vermont	955	0.1%
8	Virginia	32,545	3.3%
11	Washington	24,410	2.4%
47	West Virginia	1,076	0.1%
23	Wisconsin	7,990	0.8%
50	Wyoming	524	0.1%

RANK ORDER

RANK	STATE	IMMIGRANTS	% of USA
1	California	142,553	14.3%
2	Florida	118,831	11.9%
3	New York	118,478	11.9%
4	Texas	91,839	9.2%
5	New Jersey	50,087	5.0%
6	Massachusetts	40,898	4.1%
7	Pennsylvania	34,678	3.5%
8	Virginia	32,545	3.3%
9	Illinois	30,934	3.1%
10	Maryland	26,408	2.6%
11	Washington	24,410	2.4%
12	Georgia	23,831	2.4%
13	Michigan	22,511	2.3%
14	North Carolina	20,494	2.1%
15	Ohio	19,591	2.0%
16	Connecticut	17,058	1.7%
17	Arizona	14,861	1.5%
18	Minnesota	13,644	1.4%
19	Indiana	11,052	1.1%
20	Colorado	10,557	1.1%
21	Tennessee	9,440	0.9%
22	Missouri	8,413	0.8%
23	Wisconsin	7,990	0.8%
24	Hawaii	7,438	0.7%
25	Nevada	7,392	0.7%
26	Louisiana	7,223	0.7%
27	Oregon	6,934	0.7%
28	Kentucky	6,734	0.7%
29	Oklahoma	6,716	0.7%
30	Iowa	6,336	0.6%
31	Kansas	5,851	0.6%
32	South Carolina	5,760	0.6%
33	Utah	5,634	0.6%
34	Alabama	4,738	0.5%
35	Rhode Island	4,203	0.4%
36	Nebraska	4,187	0.4%
37	Arkansas	3,335	0.3%
38	New Mexico	2,637	0.3%
39	Delaware	2,556	0.3%
40	Mississippi	2,223	0.2%
41	New Hampshire	2,175	0.2%
42	Alaska	2,030	0.2%
43	Maine	1,785	0.2%
44	Idaho	1,726	0.2%
45	South Dakota	1,632	0.2%
46	North Dakota	1,575	0.2%
47	West Virginia	1,076	0.1%
48	Vermont	955	0.1%
49	Montana	569	0.1%
50	Wyoming	524	0.1%
	District of Columbia	4,116	0.4%

Source: U.S. Bureau of the Census

"State Population Totals Tables" (http://www.census.gov/programs-surveys/popest/data/data-sets.html)

*From July 1, 2015 to June 30, 2016. Net International Migration is the difference between migration to an area from outside the United States (immigration) and migration from the area to outside the United States (emigration) during the period. Includes legal immigration and estimates of undocumented immigration.

Percent of Population Foreign Born in 2015

National Percent = 13.5% of Population*

ALPHA ORDER

RANK	STATE	PERCENT
45	Alabama	3.5
23	Alaska	7.9
14	Arizona	13.4
34	Arkansas	4.8
1	California	27.3
18	Colorado	9.8
10	Connecticut	14.5
20	Delaware	9.3
4	Florida	20.2
16	Georgia	10.0
6	Hawaii	17.7
31	Idaho	5.7
11	Illinois	14.2
33	Indiana	4.9
34	Iowa	4.8
25	Kansas	7.1
44	Kentucky	3.6
40	Louisiana	4.0
46	Maine	3.4
9	Maryland	15.2
8	Massachusetts	16.1
27	Michigan	6.6
21	Minnesota	8.3
48	Mississippi	2.4
40	Missouri	4.0
49	Montana	2.1
26	Nebraska	6.8
5	Nevada	19.3
29	New Hampshire	6.0
3	New Jersey	22.1
19	New Mexico	9.4
2	New York	22.9
23	North Carolina	7.9
42	North Dakota	3.8
39	Ohio	4.3
29	Oklahoma	6.0
17	Oregon	9.9
28	Pennsylvania	6.5
13	Rhode Island	13.5
34	South Carolina	4.8
47	South Dakota	3.2
32	Tennessee	5.0
7	Texas	17.0
22	Utah	8.2
38	Vermont	4.5
15	Virginia	12.2
12	Washington	13.7
50	West Virginia	1.6
34	Wisconsin	4.8
42	Wyoming	3.8

RANK ORDER

RANK	STATE	PERCENT
1	California	27.3
2	New York	22.9
3	New Jersey	22.1
4	Florida	20.2
5	Nevada	19.3
6	Hawaii	17.7
7	Texas	17.0
8	Massachusetts	16.1
9	Maryland	15.2
10	Connecticut	14.5
11	Illinois	14.2
12	Washington	13.7
13	Rhode Island	13.5
14	Arizona	13.4
15	Virginia	12.2
16	Georgia	10.0
17	Oregon	9.9
18	Colorado	9.8
19	New Mexico	9.4
20	Delaware	9.3
21	Minnesota	8.3
22	Utah	8.2
23	Alaska	7.9
23	North Carolina	7.9
25	Kansas	7.1
26	Nebraska	6.8
27	Michigan	6.6
28	Pennsylvania	6.5
29	New Hampshire	6.0
29	Oklahoma	6.0
31	Idaho	5.7
32	Tennessee	5.0
33	Indiana	4.9
34	Arkansas	4.8
34	Iowa	4.8
34	South Carolina	4.8
34	Wisconsin	4.8
38	Vermont	4.5
39	Ohio	4.3
40	Louisiana	4.0
40	Missouri	4.0
42	North Dakota	3.8
42	Wyoming	3.8
44	Kentucky	3.6
45	Alabama	3.5
46	Maine	3.4
47	South Dakota	3.2
48	Mississippi	2.4
49	Montana	2.1
50	West Virginia	1.6
	District of Columbia	14.1

Source: U.S. Bureau of the Census
"2015 American Community Survey-Table R0501" (http://www.census.gov/programs-surveys/acs/)
*"Foreign born" are persons not born in the United States, Puerto Rico, a U.S. Island Area, or abroad of American parent or parents.

Percent of Population Speaking a Language Other Than English at Home in 2015
National Percent = 21.5%*

ALPHA ORDER

RANK	STATE	PERCENT
47	Alabama	5.1
17	Alaska	16.2
8	Arizona	27.1
37	Arkansas	7.3
1	California	44.6
16	Colorado	17.2
12	Connecticut	22.4
22	Delaware	13.1
7	Florida	29.0
21	Georgia	14.0
9	Hawaii	26.1
28	Idaho	10.2
10	Illinois	23.0
32	Indiana	8.4
35	Iowa	7.7
23	Kansas	11.8
46	Kentucky	5.3
33	Louisiana	8.2
42	Maine	6.1
15	Maryland	18.5
10	Massachusetts	23.0
30	Michigan	9.5
24	Minnesota	11.5
49	Mississippi	3.9
44	Missouri	6.0
48	Montana	4.2
26	Nebraska	11.1
6	Nevada	30.2
34	New Hampshire	7.8
5	New Jersey	30.8
3	New Mexico	34.3
4	New York	30.9
24	North Carolina	11.5
45	North Dakota	5.9
38	Ohio	6.9
29	Oklahoma	10.1
19	Oregon	15.1
27	Pennsylvania	10.9
13	Rhode Island	22.2
40	South Carolina	6.8
41	South Dakota	6.6
38	Tennessee	6.9
2	Texas	35.4
20	Utah	14.8
42	Vermont	6.1
18	Virginia	15.9
14	Washington	19.3
50	West Virginia	2.6
31	Wisconsin	8.7
36	Wyoming	7.5

RANK ORDER

RANK	STATE	PERCENT
1	California	44.6
2	Texas	35.4
3	New Mexico	34.3
4	New York	30.9
5	New Jersey	30.8
6	Nevada	30.2
7	Florida	29.0
8	Arizona	27.1
9	Hawaii	26.1
10	Illinois	23.0
10	Massachusetts	23.0
12	Connecticut	22.4
13	Rhode Island	22.2
14	Washington	19.3
15	Maryland	18.5
16	Colorado	17.2
17	Alaska	16.2
18	Virginia	15.9
19	Oregon	15.1
20	Utah	14.8
21	Georgia	14.0
22	Delaware	13.1
23	Kansas	11.8
24	Minnesota	11.5
24	North Carolina	11.5
26	Nebraska	11.1
27	Pennsylvania	10.9
28	Idaho	10.2
29	Oklahoma	10.1
30	Michigan	9.5
31	Wisconsin	8.7
32	Indiana	8.4
33	Louisiana	8.2
34	New Hampshire	7.8
35	Iowa	7.7
36	Wyoming	7.5
37	Arkansas	7.3
38	Ohio	6.9
38	Tennessee	6.9
40	South Carolina	6.8
41	South Dakota	6.6
42	Maine	6.1
42	Vermont	6.1
44	Missouri	6.0
45	North Dakota	5.9
46	Kentucky	5.3
47	Alabama	5.1
48	Montana	4.2
49	Mississippi	3.9
50	West Virginia	2.6

District of Columbia   17.4

Source: U.S. Bureau of the Census
     "2015 American Community Survey-Table R1601" (http://www.census.gov/programs-surveys/acs/)
*Population five years old and older.

Percent of Population Speaking Spanish at Home in 2015

National Percent = 13.3%*

ALPHA ORDER			RANK ORDER		
RANK	STATE	PERCENT	RANK	STATE	PERCENT
37	Alabama	3.3	1	Texas	29.5
32	Alaska	4.0	2	California	29.1
6	Arizona	20.6	3	New Mexico	27.2
27	Arkansas	5.2	4	Florida	21.3
2	California	29.1	5	Nevada	21.2
10	Colorado	12.2	6	Arizona	20.6
12	Connecticut	11.8	7	New Jersey	15.9
23	Delaware	7.2	8	New York	15.2
4	Florida	21.3	9	Illinois	13.5
17	Georgia	8.0	10	Colorado	12.2
41	Hawaii	2.4	11	Rhode Island	11.9
20	Idaho	7.6	12	Connecticut	11.8
9	Illinois	13.5	13	Utah	10.2
29	Indiana	4.6	14	Oregon	9.2
32	Iowa	4.0	15	Washington	8.7
19	Kansas	7.7	16	Massachusetts	8.6
39	Kentucky	2.6	17	Georgia	8.0
36	Louisiana	3.5	18	Maryland	7.9
50	Maine	0.8	19	Kansas	7.7
18	Maryland	7.9	20	Idaho	7.6
16	Massachusetts	8.6	20	North Carolina	7.6
38	Michigan	2.9	22	Nebraska	7.4
35	Minnesota	3.8	23	Delaware	7.2
41	Mississippi	2.4	23	Oklahoma	7.2
39	Missouri	2.6	25	Virginia	7.0
46	Montana	1.5	26	Wyoming	5.5
22	Nebraska	7.4	27	Arkansas	5.2
5	Nevada	21.2	28	Wisconsin	4.7
44	New Hampshire	2.1	29	Indiana	4.6
7	New Jersey	15.9	29	Pennsylvania	4.6
3	New Mexico	27.2	31	South Carolina	4.3
8	New York	15.2	32	Alaska	4.0
20	North Carolina	7.6	32	Iowa	4.0
46	North Dakota	1.5	34	Tennessee	3.9
43	Ohio	2.3	35	Minnesota	3.8
23	Oklahoma	7.2	36	Louisiana	3.5
14	Oregon	9.2	37	Alabama	3.3
29	Pennsylvania	4.6	38	Michigan	2.9
11	Rhode Island	11.9	39	Kentucky	2.6
31	South Carolina	4.3	39	Missouri	2.6
44	South Dakota	2.1	41	Hawaii	2.4
34	Tennessee	3.9	41	Mississippi	2.4
1	Texas	29.5	43	Ohio	2.3
13	Utah	10.2	44	New Hampshire	2.1
48	Vermont	1.1	44	South Dakota	2.1
25	Virginia	7.0	46	Montana	1.5
15	Washington	8.7	46	North Dakota	1.5
48	West Virginia	1.1	48	Vermont	1.1
28	Wisconsin	4.7	48	West Virginia	1.1
26	Wyoming	5.5	50	Maine	0.8
				District of Columbia	8.9

Source: U.S. Bureau of the Census
   "2015 American Community Survey-Table R1602" (http://www.census.gov/programs-surveys/acs/)
*Population five years old and older.

Marriage Rate for Men in 2015

National Rate = 18.5 Marriages per 1,000 Men*

ALPHA ORDER

RANK	STATE	RATE
33	Alabama	17.5
2	Alaska	25.5
27	Arizona	18.2
11	Arkansas	20.7
26	California	18.4
17	Colorado	20.0
47	Connecticut	15.6
24	Delaware	18.5
30	Florida	18.1
13	Georgia	20.2
2	Hawaii	25.5
5	Idaho	22.8
40	Illinois	16.5
21	Indiana	18.6
10	Iowa	20.8
27	Kansas	18.2
7	Kentucky	21.8
21	Louisiana	18.6
41	Maine	16.3
38	Maryland	17.1
45	Massachusetts	16.0
47	Michigan	15.6
36	Minnesota	17.3
32	Mississippi	17.6
27	Missouri	18.2
31	Montana	18.0
21	Nebraska	18.6
9	Nevada	21.4
49	New Hampshire	15.1
50	New Jersey	14.4
33	New Mexico	17.5
41	New York	16.3
17	North Carolina	20.0
6	North Dakota	22.5
39	Ohio	16.9
12	Oklahoma	20.6
24	Oregon	18.5
37	Pennsylvania	17.2
46	Rhode Island	15.8
19	South Carolina	19.1
20	South Dakota	18.7
13	Tennessee	20.2
8	Texas	21.5
1	Utah	26.6
43	Vermont	16.2
13	Virginia	20.2
16	Washington	20.1
35	West Virginia	17.4
44	Wisconsin	16.1
4	Wyoming	23.4

RANK ORDER

RANK	STATE	RATE
1	Utah	26.6
2	Alaska	25.5
2	Hawaii	25.5
4	Wyoming	23.4
5	Idaho	22.8
6	North Dakota	22.5
7	Kentucky	21.8
8	Texas	21.5
9	Nevada	21.4
10	Iowa	20.8
11	Arkansas	20.7
12	Oklahoma	20.6
13	Georgia	20.2
13	Tennessee	20.2
13	Virginia	20.2
16	Washington	20.1
17	Colorado	20.0
17	North Carolina	20.0
19	South Carolina	19.1
20	South Dakota	18.7
21	Indiana	18.6
21	Louisiana	18.6
21	Nebraska	18.6
24	Delaware	18.5
24	Oregon	18.5
26	California	18.4
27	Arizona	18.2
27	Kansas	18.2
27	Missouri	18.2
30	Florida	18.1
31	Montana	18.0
32	Mississippi	17.6
33	Alabama	17.5
33	New Mexico	17.5
35	West Virginia	17.4
36	Minnesota	17.3
37	Pennsylvania	17.2
38	Maryland	17.1
39	Ohio	16.9
40	Illinois	16.5
41	Maine	16.3
41	New York	16.3
43	Vermont	16.2
44	Wisconsin	16.1
45	Massachusetts	16.0
46	Rhode Island	15.8
47	Connecticut	15.6
47	Michigan	15.6
49	New Hampshire	15.1
50	New Jersey	14.4
	District of Columbia	26.6

Source: U.S. Bureau of the Census
"2015 American Community Survey-Table GCT1252" (http://www.census.gov/programs-surveys/acs/)
*Men age 15 and older. Marriages in the last year.

Estimated Median Age of Men at First Marriage in 2015

National Median = 29.7 Years*

ALPHA ORDER

RANK	STATE	YEARS
36	Alabama	28.4
41	Alaska	28.0
16	Arizona	29.7
47	Arkansas	27.2
4	California	30.6
23	Colorado	29.3
4	Connecticut	30.6
15	Delaware	29.8
10	Florida	30.4
31	Georgia	28.8
29	Hawaii	28.9
48	Idaho	26.8
11	Illinois	30.3
29	Indiana	28.9
40	Iowa	28.2
43	Kansas	27.6
41	Kentucky	28.0
23	Louisiana	29.3
18	Maine	29.6
8	Maryland	30.5
1	Massachusetts	31.0
13	Michigan	30.1
26	Minnesota	29.2
33	Mississippi	28.6
37	Missouri	28.3
32	Montana	28.7
33	Nebraska	28.6
16	Nevada	29.7
8	New Hampshire	30.5
4	New Jersey	30.6
37	New Mexico	28.3
1	New York	31.0
28	North Carolina	29.1
46	North Dakota	27.4
19	Ohio	29.5
43	Oklahoma	27.6
12	Oregon	30.2
13	Pennsylvania	30.1
3	Rhode Island	30.7
23	South Carolina	29.3
49	South Dakota	26.4
37	Tennessee	28.3
33	Texas	28.6
49	Utah	26.4
4	Vermont	30.6
20	Virginia	29.4
26	Washington	29.2
20	West Virginia	29.4
20	Wisconsin	29.4
45	Wyoming	27.5

RANK ORDER

RANK	STATE	YEARS
1	Massachusetts	31.0
1	New York	31.0
3	Rhode Island	30.7
4	California	30.6
4	Connecticut	30.6
4	New Jersey	30.6
4	Vermont	30.6
8	Maryland	30.5
8	New Hampshire	30.5
10	Florida	30.4
11	Illinois	30.3
12	Oregon	30.2
13	Michigan	30.1
13	Pennsylvania	30.1
15	Delaware	29.8
16	Arizona	29.7
16	Nevada	29.7
18	Maine	29.6
19	Ohio	29.5
20	Virginia	29.4
20	West Virginia	29.4
20	Wisconsin	29.4
23	Colorado	29.3
23	Louisiana	29.3
23	South Carolina	29.3
26	Minnesota	29.2
26	Washington	29.2
28	North Carolina	29.1
29	Hawaii	28.9
29	Indiana	28.9
31	Georgia	28.8
32	Montana	28.7
33	Mississippi	28.6
33	Nebraska	28.6
33	Texas	28.6
36	Alabama	28.4
37	Missouri	28.3
37	New Mexico	28.3
37	Tennessee	28.3
40	Iowa	28.2
41	Alaska	28.0
41	Kentucky	28.0
43	Kansas	27.6
43	Oklahoma	27.6
45	Wyoming	27.5
46	North Dakota	27.4
47	Arkansas	27.2
48	Idaho	26.8
49	South Dakota	26.4
49	Utah	26.4
	District of Columbia	30.7

Source: U.S. Bureau of the Census
    "2015 American Community Survey-Table R1204" (http://www.census.gov/programs-surveys/acs/)
*The median age at first marriage is calculated indirectly by estimating the proportion of young people who will marry during their
lifetime, calculating one-half of this proportion, and determining the age (at the time of the survey) of people at this half-way
mark. It does not represent the actual median age of the population who married during the calendar year.

Marriage Rate for Women in 2015

National Rate = 17.2 Marriages per 1,000 Women*

RANK	STATE	RATE
34	Alabama	16.2
1	Alaska	30.7
27	Arizona	17.3
11	Arkansas	20.2
31	California	16.9
12	Colorado	20.0
48	Connecticut	13.2
22	Delaware	18.4
36	Florida	16.1
16	Georgia	19.1
4	Hawaii	21.8
8	Idaho	20.8
43	Illinois	15.2
23	Indiana	18.3
13	Iowa	19.9
18	Kansas	18.9
9	Kentucky	20.6
33	Louisiana	16.6
38	Maine	15.9
41	Maryland	15.5
47	Massachusetts	14.0
44	Michigan	14.5
27	Minnesota	17.3
34	Mississippi	16.2
29	Missouri	17.2
21	Montana	18.6
29	Nebraska	17.2
15	Nevada	19.4
46	New Hampshire	14.3
49	New Jersey	12.8
25	New Mexico	17.9
44	New York	14.5
25	North Carolina	17.9
3	North Dakota	22.4
38	Ohio	15.9
6	Oklahoma	21.5
24	Oregon	18.2
40	Pennsylvania	15.8
50	Rhode Island	12.5
31	South Carolina	16.9
7	South Dakota	21.1
19	Tennessee	18.7
10	Texas	20.4
2	Utah	28.3
42	Vermont	15.4
19	Virginia	18.7
16	Washington	19.1
14	West Virginia	19.5
37	Wisconsin	16.0
5	Wyoming	21.7

RANK	STATE	RATE
1	Alaska	30.7
2	Utah	28.3
3	North Dakota	22.4
4	Hawaii	21.8
5	Wyoming	21.7
6	Oklahoma	21.5
7	South Dakota	21.1
8	Idaho	20.8
9	Kentucky	20.6
10	Texas	20.4
11	Arkansas	20.2
12	Colorado	20.0
13	Iowa	19.9
14	West Virginia	19.5
15	Nevada	19.4
16	Georgia	19.1
16	Washington	19.1
18	Kansas	18.9
19	Tennessee	18.7
19	Virginia	18.7
21	Montana	18.6
22	Delaware	18.4
23	Indiana	18.3
24	Oregon	18.2
25	New Mexico	17.9
25	North Carolina	17.9
27	Arizona	17.3
27	Minnesota	17.3
29	Missouri	17.2
29	Nebraska	17.2
31	California	16.9
31	South Carolina	16.9
33	Louisiana	16.6
34	Alabama	16.2
34	Mississippi	16.2
36	Florida	16.1
37	Wisconsin	16.0
38	Maine	15.9
38	Ohio	15.9
40	Pennsylvania	15.8
41	Maryland	15.5
42	Vermont	15.4
43	Illinois	15.2
44	Michigan	14.5
44	New York	14.5
46	New Hampshire	14.3
47	Massachusetts	14.0
48	Connecticut	13.2
49	New Jersey	12.8
50	Rhode Island	12.5
	District of Columbia	20.9

Source: U.S. Bureau of the Census
    "2015 American Community Survey-Table GCT1251" (http://www.census.gov/programs-surveys/acs/)
*Women age 15 and older. Marriages in the last year.

Estimated Median Age of Women at First Marriage in 2015

National Median = 27.8 Years*

ALPHA ORDER

RANK	STATE	YEARS
32	Alabama	26.9
41	Alaska	26.2
26	Arizona	27.3
46	Arkansas	25.7
8	California	28.7
23	Colorado	27.4
5	Connecticut	29.2
11	Delaware	28.5
12	Florida	28.4
22	Georgia	27.5
14	Hawaii	28.2
49	Idaho	25.3
8	Illinois	28.7
36	Indiana	26.7
38	Iowa	26.4
45	Kansas	25.9
41	Kentucky	26.2
23	Louisiana	27.4
29	Maine	27.2
7	Maryland	29.0
2	Massachusetts	29.9
15	Michigan	27.9
26	Minnesota	27.3
31	Mississippi	27.0
38	Missouri	26.4
29	Montana	27.2
34	Nebraska	26.8
15	Nevada	27.9
13	New Hampshire	28.3
5	New Jersey	29.2
20	New Mexico	27.6
3	New York	29.7
26	North Carolina	27.3
48	North Dakota	25.4
18	Ohio	27.7
46	Oklahoma	25.7
15	Oregon	27.9
10	Pennsylvania	28.6
1	Rhode Island	30.1
18	South Carolina	27.7
41	South Dakota	26.2
38	Tennessee	26.4
37	Texas	26.6
50	Utah	24.3
4	Vermont	29.4
20	Virginia	27.6
32	Washington	26.9
34	West Virginia	26.8
23	Wisconsin	27.4
44	Wyoming	26.1

RANK ORDER

RANK	STATE	YEARS
1	Rhode Island	30.1
2	Massachusetts	29.9
3	New York	29.7
4	Vermont	29.4
5	Connecticut	29.2
5	New Jersey	29.2
7	Maryland	29.0
8	California	28.7
8	Illinois	28.7
10	Pennsylvania	28.6
11	Delaware	28.5
12	Florida	28.4
13	New Hampshire	28.3
14	Hawaii	28.2
15	Michigan	27.9
15	Nevada	27.9
15	Oregon	27.9
18	Ohio	27.7
18	South Carolina	27.7
20	New Mexico	27.6
20	Virginia	27.6
22	Georgia	27.5
23	Colorado	27.4
23	Louisiana	27.4
23	Wisconsin	27.4
26	Arizona	27.3
26	Minnesota	27.3
26	North Carolina	27.3
29	Maine	27.2
29	Montana	27.2
31	Mississippi	27.0
32	Alabama	26.9
32	Washington	26.9
34	Nebraska	26.8
34	West Virginia	26.8
36	Indiana	26.7
37	Texas	26.6
38	Iowa	26.4
38	Missouri	26.4
38	Tennessee	26.4
41	Alaska	26.2
41	Kentucky	26.2
41	South Dakota	26.2
44	Wyoming	26.1
45	Kansas	25.9
46	Arkansas	25.7
46	Oklahoma	25.7
48	North Dakota	25.4
49	Idaho	25.3
50	Utah	24.3
	District of Columbia	30.6

Source: U.S. Bureau of the Census
    "2015 American Community Survey-Table R1205" (http://www.census.gov/programs-surveys/acs/)
*The median age at first marriage is calculated indirectly by estimating the proportion of young people who will marry during their lifetime, calculating one-half of this proportion, and determining the age (at the time of the survey) of people at this half-way mark. It does not represent the actual median age of the population who married during the calendar year.

Ratio of Unmarried Men to Unmarried Women in 2015

National Ratio = 110.7 Unmarried Men for Every 100 Unmarried Women*

<table>
<tr><td colspan="3">ALPHA ORDER</td><td colspan="3">RANK ORDER</td></tr>
<tr><td>RANK</td><td>STATE</td><td>RATIO</td><td>RANK</td><td>STATE</td><td>RATIO</td></tr>
<tr><td>47</td><td>Alabama</td><td>104.4</td><td>1</td><td>Alaska</td><td>136.8</td></tr>
<tr><td>1</td><td>Alaska</td><td>136.8</td><td>2</td><td>North Dakota</td><td>134.3</td></tr>
<tr><td>13</td><td>Arizona</td><td>114.6</td><td>3</td><td>Hawaii</td><td>127.0</td></tr>
<tr><td>27</td><td>Arkansas</td><td>111.6</td><td>4</td><td>Montana</td><td>121.6</td></tr>
<tr><td>16</td><td>California</td><td>114.3</td><td>5</td><td>Colorado</td><td>119.8</td></tr>
<tr><td>5</td><td>Colorado</td><td>119.8</td><td>6</td><td>Kansas</td><td>119.0</td></tr>
<tr><td>39</td><td>Connecticut</td><td>108.3</td><td>7</td><td>South Dakota</td><td>117.7</td></tr>
<tr><td>49</td><td>Delaware</td><td>104.0</td><td>8</td><td>Washington</td><td>116.9</td></tr>
<tr><td>32</td><td>Florida</td><td>109.8</td><td>9</td><td>Utah</td><td>116.5</td></tr>
<tr><td>47</td><td>Georgia</td><td>104.4</td><td>10</td><td>Nebraska</td><td>116.4</td></tr>
<tr><td>3</td><td>Hawaii</td><td>127.0</td><td>11</td><td>West Virginia</td><td>116.3</td></tr>
<tr><td>25</td><td>Idaho</td><td>112.4</td><td>11</td><td>Wyoming</td><td>116.3</td></tr>
<tr><td>37</td><td>Illinois</td><td>108.6</td><td>13</td><td>Arizona</td><td>114.6</td></tr>
<tr><td>38</td><td>Indiana</td><td>108.4</td><td>14</td><td>Oklahoma</td><td>114.5</td></tr>
<tr><td>15</td><td>Iowa</td><td>114.4</td><td>15</td><td>Iowa</td><td>114.4</td></tr>
<tr><td>6</td><td>Kansas</td><td>119.0</td><td>16</td><td>California</td><td>114.3</td></tr>
<tr><td>18</td><td>Kentucky</td><td>113.7</td><td>17</td><td>New Mexico</td><td>114.2</td></tr>
<tr><td>42</td><td>Louisiana</td><td>106.3</td><td>18</td><td>Kentucky</td><td>113.7</td></tr>
<tr><td>36</td><td>Maine</td><td>108.8</td><td>19</td><td>New Hampshire</td><td>113.4</td></tr>
<tr><td>46</td><td>Maryland</td><td>104.5</td><td>20</td><td>Wisconsin</td><td>113.2</td></tr>
<tr><td>43</td><td>Massachusetts</td><td>105.8</td><td>21</td><td>Nevada</td><td>112.9</td></tr>
<tr><td>31</td><td>Michigan</td><td>109.9</td><td>22</td><td>Minnesota</td><td>112.7</td></tr>
<tr><td>22</td><td>Minnesota</td><td>112.7</td><td>22</td><td>Oregon</td><td>112.7</td></tr>
<tr><td>50</td><td>Mississippi</td><td>103.9</td><td>22</td><td>Texas</td><td>112.7</td></tr>
<tr><td>30</td><td>Missouri</td><td>110.2</td><td>25</td><td>Idaho</td><td>112.4</td></tr>
<tr><td>4</td><td>Montana</td><td>121.6</td><td>25</td><td>Vermont</td><td>112.4</td></tr>
<tr><td>10</td><td>Nebraska</td><td>116.4</td><td>27</td><td>Arkansas</td><td>111.6</td></tr>
<tr><td>21</td><td>Nevada</td><td>112.9</td><td>28</td><td>Virginia</td><td>110.7</td></tr>
<tr><td>19</td><td>New Hampshire</td><td>113.4</td><td>29</td><td>New Jersey</td><td>110.3</td></tr>
<tr><td>29</td><td>New Jersey</td><td>110.3</td><td>30</td><td>Missouri</td><td>110.2</td></tr>
<tr><td>17</td><td>New Mexico</td><td>114.2</td><td>31</td><td>Michigan</td><td>109.9</td></tr>
<tr><td>44</td><td>New York</td><td>105.3</td><td>32</td><td>Florida</td><td>109.8</td></tr>
<tr><td>40</td><td>North Carolina</td><td>108.1</td><td>33</td><td>Pennsylvania</td><td>109.6</td></tr>
<tr><td>2</td><td>North Dakota</td><td>134.3</td><td>34</td><td>South Carolina</td><td>109.1</td></tr>
<tr><td>35</td><td>Ohio</td><td>108.9</td><td>35</td><td>Ohio</td><td>108.9</td></tr>
<tr><td>14</td><td>Oklahoma</td><td>114.5</td><td>36</td><td>Maine</td><td>108.8</td></tr>
<tr><td>22</td><td>Oregon</td><td>112.7</td><td>37</td><td>Illinois</td><td>108.6</td></tr>
<tr><td>33</td><td>Pennsylvania</td><td>109.6</td><td>38</td><td>Indiana</td><td>108.4</td></tr>
<tr><td>45</td><td>Rhode Island</td><td>105.2</td><td>39</td><td>Connecticut</td><td>108.3</td></tr>
<tr><td>34</td><td>South Carolina</td><td>109.1</td><td>40</td><td>North Carolina</td><td>108.1</td></tr>
<tr><td>7</td><td>South Dakota</td><td>117.7</td><td>40</td><td>Tennessee</td><td>108.1</td></tr>
<tr><td>40</td><td>Tennessee</td><td>108.1</td><td>42</td><td>Louisiana</td><td>106.3</td></tr>
<tr><td>22</td><td>Texas</td><td>112.7</td><td>43</td><td>Massachusetts</td><td>105.8</td></tr>
<tr><td>9</td><td>Utah</td><td>116.5</td><td>44</td><td>New York</td><td>105.3</td></tr>
<tr><td>25</td><td>Vermont</td><td>112.4</td><td>45</td><td>Rhode Island</td><td>105.2</td></tr>
<tr><td>28</td><td>Virginia</td><td>110.7</td><td>46</td><td>Maryland</td><td>104.5</td></tr>
<tr><td>8</td><td>Washington</td><td>116.9</td><td>47</td><td>Alabama</td><td>104.4</td></tr>
<tr><td>11</td><td>West Virginia</td><td>116.3</td><td>47</td><td>Georgia</td><td>104.4</td></tr>
<tr><td>20</td><td>Wisconsin</td><td>113.2</td><td>49</td><td>Delaware</td><td>104.0</td></tr>
<tr><td>11</td><td>Wyoming</td><td>116.3</td><td>50</td><td>Mississippi</td><td>103.9</td></tr>
<tr><td></td><td></td><td></td><td></td><td>District of Columbia</td><td>90.9</td></tr>
</table>

Source: U.S. Bureau of the Census
  "2015 American Community Survey-Table R1203" (http://www.census.gov/programs-surveys/acs/)
*Population 15 to 44 years old.

Divorce Rate for Men in 2015

National Rate = 7.9 Divorces per 1,000 Men*

RANK	STATE	RATE
8	Alabama	10.7
15	Alaska	9.0
24	Arizona	8.3
8	Arkansas	10.7
45	California	6.1
25	Colorado	8.1
39	Connecticut	7.0
45	Delaware	6.1
25	Florida	8.1
12	Georgia	9.8
41	Hawaii	6.8
2	Idaho	12.2
41	Illinois	6.8
11	Indiana	10.0
35	Iowa	7.4
4	Kansas	11.7
7	Kentucky	10.8
19	Louisiana	8.8
6	Maine	11.4
34	Maryland	7.5
43	Massachusetts	6.4
32	Michigan	7.9
43	Minnesota	6.4
15	Mississippi	9.0
20	Missouri	8.7
37	Montana	7.1
25	Nebraska	8.1
1	Nevada	12.6
36	New Hampshire	7.2
47	New Jersey	6.0
30	New Mexico	8.0
48	New York	5.6
22	North Carolina	8.6
32	North Dakota	7.9
13	Ohio	9.3
4	Oklahoma	11.7
25	Oregon	8.1
40	Pennsylvania	6.9
50	Rhode Island	4.5
18	South Carolina	8.9
48	South Dakota	5.6
15	Tennessee	9.0
20	Texas	8.7
25	Utah	8.1
22	Vermont	8.6
30	Virginia	8.0
14	Washington	9.1
3	West Virginia	12.0
37	Wisconsin	7.1
10	Wyoming	10.2

RANK	STATE	RATE
1	Nevada	12.6
2	Idaho	12.2
3	West Virginia	12.0
4	Kansas	11.7
4	Oklahoma	11.7
6	Maine	11.4
7	Kentucky	10.8
8	Alabama	10.7
8	Arkansas	10.7
10	Wyoming	10.2
11	Indiana	10.0
12	Georgia	9.8
13	Ohio	9.3
14	Washington	9.1
15	Alaska	9.0
15	Mississippi	9.0
15	Tennessee	9.0
18	South Carolina	8.9
19	Louisiana	8.8
20	Missouri	8.7
20	Texas	8.7
22	North Carolina	8.6
22	Vermont	8.6
24	Arizona	8.3
25	Colorado	8.1
25	Florida	8.1
25	Nebraska	8.1
25	Oregon	8.1
25	Utah	8.1
30	New Mexico	8.0
30	Virginia	8.0
32	Michigan	7.9
32	North Dakota	7.9
34	Maryland	7.5
35	Iowa	7.4
36	New Hampshire	7.2
37	Montana	7.1
37	Wisconsin	7.1
39	Connecticut	7.0
40	Pennsylvania	6.9
41	Hawaii	6.8
41	Illinois	6.8
43	Massachusetts	6.4
43	Minnesota	6.4
45	California	6.1
45	Delaware	6.1
47	New Jersey	6.0
48	New York	5.6
48	South Dakota	5.6
50	Rhode Island	4.5
	District of Columbia	6.8

Source: U.S. Bureau of the Census
"2015 American Community Survey-Table GCT1254" (http://www.census.gov/programs-surveys/acs/)
*Men age 15 and older. Divorces in the last year.

Divorce Rate for Women in 2015

National Rate = 8.3 Divorces per 1,000 Women*

ALPHA ORDER

RANK	STATE	RATE
15	Alabama	9.4
4	Alaska	11.7
19	Arizona	9.3
2	Arkansas	13.2
44	California	6.9
24	Colorado	8.8
39	Connecticut	7.6
48	Delaware	6.1
26	Florida	8.7
30	Georgia	8.1
49	Hawaii	5.6
9	Idaho	10.4
42	Illinois	7.1
7	Indiana	10.6
34	Iowa	7.7
23	Kansas	9.0
6	Kentucky	11.0
34	Louisiana	7.7
34	Maine	7.7
40	Maryland	7.4
32	Massachusetts	7.8
34	Michigan	7.7
32	Minnesota	7.8
11	Mississippi	9.9
15	Missouri	9.4
15	Montana	9.4
13	Nebraska	9.6
3	Nevada	12.3
34	New Hampshire	7.7
46	New Jersey	6.4
19	New Mexico	9.3
45	New York	6.7
31	North Carolina	7.9
42	North Dakota	7.1
28	Ohio	8.4
5	Oklahoma	11.6
15	Oregon	9.4
41	Pennsylvania	7.3
50	Rhode Island	5.5
26	South Carolina	8.7
22	South Dakota	9.2
19	Tennessee	9.3
12	Texas	9.8
9	Utah	10.4
29	Vermont	8.2
24	Virginia	8.8
14	Washington	9.5
7	West Virginia	10.6
46	Wisconsin	6.4
1	Wyoming	15.5

RANK ORDER

RANK	STATE	RATE
1	Wyoming	15.5
2	Arkansas	13.2
3	Nevada	12.3
4	Alaska	11.7
5	Oklahoma	11.6
6	Kentucky	11.0
7	Indiana	10.6
7	West Virginia	10.6
9	Idaho	10.4
9	Utah	10.4
11	Mississippi	9.9
12	Texas	9.8
13	Nebraska	9.6
14	Washington	9.5
15	Alabama	9.4
15	Missouri	9.4
15	Montana	9.4
15	Oregon	9.4
19	Arizona	9.3
19	New Mexico	9.3
19	Tennessee	9.3
22	South Dakota	9.2
23	Kansas	9.0
24	Colorado	8.8
24	Virginia	8.8
26	Florida	8.7
26	South Carolina	8.7
28	Ohio	8.4
29	Vermont	8.2
30	Georgia	8.1
31	North Carolina	7.9
32	Massachusetts	7.8
32	Minnesota	7.8
34	Iowa	7.7
34	Louisiana	7.7
34	Maine	7.7
34	Michigan	7.7
34	New Hampshire	7.7
39	Connecticut	7.6
40	Maryland	7.4
41	Pennsylvania	7.3
42	Illinois	7.1
42	North Dakota	7.1
44	California	6.9
45	New York	6.7
46	New Jersey	6.4
46	Wisconsin	6.4
48	Delaware	6.1
49	Hawaii	5.6
50	Rhode Island	5.5
	District of Columbia	9.0

Source: U.S. Bureau of the Census

"2015 American Community Survey-Table GCT1253" (http://www.census.gov/programs-surveys/acs/)

*Women age 15 and older. Divorces in the last year.

Average Family Size in 2015

National Average = 3.26 Persons per Family

ALPHA ORDER

RANK	STATE	PERSONS
18	Alabama	3.20
4	Alaska	3.46
9	Arizona	3.34
35	Arkansas	3.10
3	California	3.56
27	Colorado	3.16
18	Connecticut	3.20
23	Delaware	3.17
14	Florida	3.29
11	Georgia	3.33
1	Hawaii	3.69
12	Idaho	3.31
14	Illinois	3.29
23	Indiana	3.17
47	Iowa	2.99
23	Kansas	3.17
39	Kentucky	3.07
13	Louisiana	3.30
50	Maine	2.89
16	Maryland	3.28
21	Massachusetts	3.18
32	Michigan	3.12
39	Minnesota	3.07
17	Mississippi	3.23
36	Missouri	3.09
42	Montana	3.05
33	Nebraska	3.11
6	Nevada	3.41
44	New Hampshire	3.01
9	New Jersey	3.34
7	New Mexico	3.40
8	New York	3.35
29	North Carolina	3.14
49	North Dakota	2.94
39	Ohio	3.07
21	Oklahoma	3.18
36	Oregon	3.09
36	Pennsylvania	3.09
23	Rhode Island	3.17
27	South Carolina	3.16
44	South Dakota	3.01
30	Tennessee	3.13
4	Texas	3.46
2	Utah	3.67
48	Vermont	2.95
20	Virginia	3.19
30	Washington	3.13
43	West Virginia	3.03
46	Wisconsin	3.00
33	Wyoming	3.11

RANK ORDER

RANK	STATE	PERSONS
1	Hawaii	3.69
2	Utah	3.67
3	California	3.56
4	Alaska	3.46
4	Texas	3.46
6	Nevada	3.41
7	New Mexico	3.40
8	New York	3.35
9	Arizona	3.34
9	New Jersey	3.34
11	Georgia	3.33
12	Idaho	3.31
13	Louisiana	3.30
14	Florida	3.29
14	Illinois	3.29
16	Maryland	3.28
17	Mississippi	3.23
18	Alabama	3.20
18	Connecticut	3.20
20	Virginia	3.19
21	Massachusetts	3.18
21	Oklahoma	3.18
23	Delaware	3.17
23	Indiana	3.17
23	Kansas	3.17
23	Rhode Island	3.17
27	Colorado	3.16
27	South Carolina	3.16
29	North Carolina	3.14
30	Tennessee	3.13
30	Washington	3.13
32	Michigan	3.12
33	Nebraska	3.11
33	Wyoming	3.11
35	Arkansas	3.10
36	Missouri	3.09
36	Oregon	3.09
36	Pennsylvania	3.09
39	Kentucky	3.07
39	Minnesota	3.07
39	Ohio	3.07
42	Montana	3.05
43	West Virginia	3.03
44	New Hampshire	3.01
44	South Dakota	3.01
46	Wisconsin	3.00
47	Iowa	2.99
48	Vermont	2.95
49	North Dakota	2.94
50	Maine	2.89
	District of Columbia	3.16

Source: U.S. Bureau of the Census
   "2015 American Community Survey-Table DP02" (http://www.census.gov/programs-surveys/acs/)

Seats in the U.S. House of Representatives in 2017

National Total = 435 Seats*

ALPHA ORDER

RANK	STATE	SEATS	% of USA
22	Alabama	7	1.6%
44	Alaska	1	0.2%
14	Arizona	9	2.1%
30	Arkansas	4	0.9%
1	California	53	12.2%
22	Colorado	7	1.6%
27	Connecticut	5	1.1%
44	Delaware	1	0.2%
3	Florida	27	6.2%
8	Georgia	14	3.2%
39	Hawaii	2	0.5%
39	Idaho	2	0.5%
5	Illinois	18	4.1%
14	Indiana	9	2.1%
30	Iowa	4	0.9%
30	Kansas	4	0.9%
25	Kentucky	6	1.4%
25	Louisiana	6	1.4%
39	Maine	2	0.5%
18	Maryland	8	1.8%
14	Massachusetts	9	2.1%
8	Michigan	14	3.2%
18	Minnesota	8	1.8%
30	Mississippi	4	0.9%
18	Missouri	8	1.8%
44	Montana	1	0.2%
36	Nebraska	3	0.7%
30	Nevada	4	0.9%
39	New Hampshire	2	0.5%
11	New Jersey	12	2.8%
36	New Mexico	3	0.7%
3	New York	27	6.2%
10	North Carolina	13	3.0%
44	North Dakota	1	0.2%
7	Ohio	16	3.7%
27	Oklahoma	5	1.1%
27	Oregon	5	1.1%
5	Pennsylvania	18	4.1%
39	Rhode Island	2	0.5%
22	South Carolina	7	1.6%
44	South Dakota	1	0.2%
14	Tennessee	9	2.1%
2	Texas	36	8.3%
30	Utah	4	0.9%
44	Vermont	1	0.2%
12	Virginia	11	2.5%
13	Washington	10	2.3%
36	West Virginia	3	0.7%
18	Wisconsin	8	1.8%
44	Wyoming	1	0.2%

RANK ORDER

RANK	STATE	SEATS	% of USA
1	California	53	12.2%
2	Texas	36	8.3%
3	Florida	27	6.2%
3	New York	27	6.2%
5	Illinois	18	4.1%
5	Pennsylvania	18	4.1%
7	Ohio	16	3.7%
8	Georgia	14	3.2%
8	Michigan	14	3.2%
10	North Carolina	13	3.0%
11	New Jersey	12	2.8%
12	Virginia	11	2.5%
13	Washington	10	2.3%
14	Arizona	9	2.1%
14	Indiana	9	2.1%
14	Massachusetts	9	2.1%
14	Tennessee	9	2.1%
18	Maryland	8	1.8%
18	Minnesota	8	1.8%
18	Missouri	8	1.8%
18	Wisconsin	8	1.8%
22	Alabama	7	1.6%
22	Colorado	7	1.6%
22	South Carolina	7	1.6%
25	Kentucky	6	1.4%
25	Louisiana	6	1.4%
27	Connecticut	5	1.1%
27	Oklahoma	5	1.1%
27	Oregon	5	1.1%
30	Arkansas	4	0.9%
30	Iowa	4	0.9%
30	Kansas	4	0.9%
30	Mississippi	4	0.9%
30	Nevada	4	0.9%
30	Utah	4	0.9%
36	Nebraska	3	0.7%
36	New Mexico	3	0.7%
36	West Virginia	3	0.7%
39	Hawaii	2	0.5%
39	Idaho	2	0.5%
39	Maine	2	0.5%
39	New Hampshire	2	0.5%
39	Rhode Island	2	0.5%
44	Alaska	1	0.2%
44	Delaware	1	0.2%
44	Montana	1	0.2%
44	North Dakota	1	0.2%
44	South Dakota	1	0.2%
44	Vermont	1	0.2%
44	Wyoming	1	0.2%
	District of Columbia**	0	0.0%

Source: U.S. Bureau of the Census
"Congressional Apportionment" (http://www.census.gov/topics/public-sector/congressional-apportionment.html)
*This table shows the number of seats after reapportionment of the 2010 Census. This apportionment became effective with the Congress elected in November 2012 and that took office in January 2013.
**The District of Columbia has one non-voting delegate. Each state has two members in the U.S. Senate.

Estimated Population per U.S. House Seat in 2017

National Rate = 741,256 Persons per House Member*

ALPHA ORDER				RANK ORDER		
RANK	STATE	RATE		RANK	STATE	RATE
41	Alabama	694,757		1	Montana	1,042,520
23	Alaska	741,894		2	Delaware	952,065
12	Arizona	770,119		3	South Dakota	865,454
21	Arkansas	747,062		4	Idaho	841,570
24	California	740,566		5	Oregon	818,693
6	Colorado	791,506		6	Colorado	791,506
35	Connecticut	715,290		7	Oklahoma	784,712
2	Delaware	952,065		8	Iowa	783,673
14	Florida	763,424		9	North Carolina	780,522
28	Georgia	736,455		10	Louisiana	780,278
36	Hawaii	714,279		11	Texas	773,961
4	Idaho	841,570		12	Arizona	770,119
37	Illinois	711,197		13	Virginia	764,710
27	Indiana	737,006		14	Florida	763,424
8	Iowa	783,673		15	Utah	762,804
32	Kansas	726,822		16	Missouri	761,625
25	Kentucky	739,496		17	North Dakota	757,952
10	Louisiana	780,278		18	Massachusetts	756,864
45	Maine	665,740		19	Maryland	752,056
19	Maryland	752,056		20	Mississippi	747,182
18	Massachusetts	756,864		21	Arkansas	747,062
39	Michigan	709,164		22	New Jersey	745,372
43	Minnesota	689,994		23	Alaska	741,894
20	Mississippi	747,182		24	California	740,566
16	Missouri	761,625		25	Kentucky	739,496
1	Montana	1,042,520		26	Tennessee	739,022
46	Nebraska	635,705		27	Indiana	737,006
29	Nevada	735,015		28	Georgia	736,455
44	New Hampshire	667,398		29	Nevada	735,015
22	New Jersey	745,372		30	New York	731,307
42	New Mexico	693,672		31	Washington	728,800
30	New York	731,307		32	Kansas	726,822
9	North Carolina	780,522		33	Ohio	725,898
17	North Dakota	757,952		34	Wisconsin	722,339
33	Ohio	725,898		35	Connecticut	715,290
7	Oklahoma	784,712		36	Hawaii	714,279
5	Oregon	818,693		37	Illinois	711,197
38	Pennsylvania	710,235		38	Pennsylvania	710,235
50	Rhode Island	528,213		39	Michigan	709,164
40	South Carolina	708,731		40	South Carolina	708,731
3	South Dakota	865,454		41	Alabama	694,757
26	Tennessee	739,022		42	New Mexico	693,672
11	Texas	773,961		43	Minnesota	689,994
15	Utah	762,804		44	New Hampshire	667,398
47	Vermont	624,594		45	Maine	665,740
13	Virginia	764,710		46	Nebraska	635,705
31	Washington	728,800		47	Vermont	624,594
48	West Virginia	610,367		48	West Virginia	610,367
34	Wisconsin	722,339		49	Wyoming	585,501
49	Wyoming	585,501		50	Rhode Island	528,213
				District of Columbia**		NA

Source: CQ Press using data from U.S. Bureau of the Census
"Congressional Apportionment" (http://www.census.gov/population/apportionment/)
*Rates calculated using 2016 population estimates and do not include population of the District of Columbia. The District has one non-voting delegate. Each state has two members in the U.S. Senate. This table is based only on U.S. Representatives and not U.S. Senate members. This table reflects reapportionment resulting from the 2010 census and taking effect after the 2012 election. **Not applicable.

State Legislators in 2016

National Total = 7,383 Legislators*

ALPHA ORDER

RANK ORDER

RANK	STATE	LEGISLATORS	% of USA		RANK	STATE	LEGISLATORS	% of USA
27	Alabama	140	1.9%		1	New Hampshire	424	5.7%
49	Alaska	60	0.8%		2	Pennsylvania	253	3.4%
43	Arizona	90	1.2%		3	Georgia	236	3.2%
30	Arkansas	135	1.8%		4	New York	213	2.9%
35	California	120	1.6%		5	Minnesota	201	2.7%
42	Colorado	100	1.4%		6	Massachusetts	200	2.7%
9	Connecticut	187	2.5%		7	Missouri	197	2.7%
48	Delaware	62	0.8%		8	Maryland	188	2.5%
18	Florida	160	2.2%		9	Connecticut	187	2.5%
3	Georgia	236	3.2%		10	Maine	186	2.5%
46	Hawaii	76	1.0%		11	Texas	181	2.5%
39	Idaho	105	1.4%		12	Vermont	180	2.4%
13	Illinois	177	2.4%		13	Illinois	177	2.4%
19	Indiana	150	2.0%		14	Mississippi	174	2.4%
19	Iowa	150	2.0%		15	North Carolina	170	2.3%
17	Kansas	165	2.2%		15	South Carolina	170	2.3%
29	Kentucky	138	1.9%		17	Kansas	165	2.2%
25	Louisiana	144	2.0%		18	Florida	160	2.2%
10	Maine	186	2.5%		19	Indiana	150	2.0%
8	Maryland	188	2.5%		19	Iowa	150	2.0%
6	Massachusetts	200	2.7%		19	Montana	150	2.0%
23	Michigan	148	2.0%		22	Oklahoma	149	2.0%
5	Minnesota	201	2.7%		23	Michigan	148	2.0%
14	Mississippi	174	2.4%		24	Washington	147	2.0%
7	Missouri	197	2.7%		25	Louisiana	144	2.0%
19	Montana	150	2.0%		26	North Dakota	141	1.9%
50	Nebraska	49	0.7%		27	Alabama	140	1.9%
47	Nevada	63	0.9%		27	Virginia	140	1.9%
1	New Hampshire	424	5.7%		29	Kentucky	138	1.9%
35	New Jersey	120	1.6%		30	Arkansas	135	1.8%
38	New Mexico	112	1.5%		31	West Virginia	134	1.8%
4	New York	213	2.9%		32	Ohio	132	1.8%
15	North Carolina	170	2.3%		32	Tennessee	132	1.8%
26	North Dakota	141	1.9%		32	Wisconsin	132	1.8%
32	Ohio	132	1.8%		35	California	120	1.6%
22	Oklahoma	149	2.0%		35	New Jersey	120	1.6%
43	Oregon	90	1.2%		37	Rhode Island	113	1.5%
2	Pennsylvania	253	3.4%		38	New Mexico	112	1.5%
37	Rhode Island	113	1.5%		39	Idaho	105	1.4%
15	South Carolina	170	2.3%		39	South Dakota	105	1.4%
39	South Dakota	105	1.4%		41	Utah	104	1.4%
32	Tennessee	132	1.8%		42	Colorado	100	1.4%
11	Texas	181	2.5%		43	Arizona	90	1.2%
41	Utah	104	1.4%		43	Oregon	90	1.2%
12	Vermont	180	2.4%		43	Wyoming	90	1.2%
27	Virginia	140	1.9%		46	Hawaii	76	1.0%
24	Washington	147	2.0%		47	Nevada	63	0.9%
31	West Virginia	134	1.8%		48	Delaware	62	0.8%
32	Wisconsin	132	1.8%		49	Alaska	60	0.8%
43	Wyoming	90	1.2%		50	Nebraska	49	0.7%
						District of Columbia**	NA	NA

Source: National Conference of State Legislatures (Denver, CO)
"2016 Partisan Composition" (http://www.ncsl.org/research/about-state-legislatures/partisan-composition.aspx)
*There are 1,972 state senators (including Nebraska's 49 unicameral seats) and 5,411 state house members.
**Not applicable.

Population per State Legislator in 2016

National Rate = 43,674 Population per Legislator*

ALPHA ORDER

RANK	STATE	RATE
22	Alabama	34,738
42	Alaska	12,365
6	Arizona	77,012
32	Arkansas	22,135
1	California	327,083
12	Colorado	55,405
34	Connecticut	19,125
40	Delaware	15,356
3	Florida	128,828
20	Georgia	43,688
35	Hawaii	18,797
39	Idaho	16,030
8	Illinois	72,325
18	Indiana	44,220
33	Iowa	20,898
37	Kansas	17,620
25	Kentucky	32,152
24	Louisiana	32,512
45	Maine	7,158
26	Maryland	32,002
23	Massachusetts	34,059
9	Michigan	67,083
30	Minnesota	27,462
38	Mississippi	17,177
27	Missouri	30,929
46	Montana	6,950
21	Nebraska	38,921
16	Nevada	46,668
50	New Hampshire	3,148
7	New Jersey	74,537
36	New Mexico	18,580
4	New York	92,701
11	North Carolina	59,687
48	North Dakota	5,376
5	Ohio	87,988
31	Oklahoma	26,333
17	Oregon	45,483
13	Pennsylvania	50,531
43	Rhode Island	9,349
29	South Carolina	29,183
44	South Dakota	8,242
14	Tennessee	50,388
2	Texas	153,937
28	Utah	29,339
49	Vermont	3,470
10	Virginia	60,084
15	Washington	49,578
41	West Virginia	13,665
19	Wisconsin	43,778
47	Wyoming	6,506

RANK ORDER

RANK	STATE	RATE
1	California	327,083
2	Texas	153,937
3	Florida	128,828
4	New York	92,701
5	Ohio	87,988
6	Arizona	77,012
7	New Jersey	74,537
8	Illinois	72,325
9	Michigan	67,083
10	Virginia	60,084
11	North Carolina	59,687
12	Colorado	55,405
13	Pennsylvania	50,531
14	Tennessee	50,388
15	Washington	49,578
16	Nevada	46,668
17	Oregon	45,483
18	Indiana	44,220
19	Wisconsin	43,778
20	Georgia	43,688
21	Nebraska	38,921
22	Alabama	34,738
23	Massachusetts	34,059
24	Louisiana	32,512
25	Kentucky	32,152
26	Maryland	32,002
27	Missouri	30,929
28	Utah	29,339
29	South Carolina	29,183
30	Minnesota	27,462
31	Oklahoma	26,333
32	Arkansas	22,135
33	Iowa	20,898
34	Connecticut	19,125
35	Hawaii	18,797
36	New Mexico	18,580
37	Kansas	17,620
38	Mississippi	17,177
39	Idaho	16,030
40	Delaware	15,356
41	West Virginia	13,665
42	Alaska	12,365
43	Rhode Island	9,349
44	South Dakota	8,242
45	Maine	7,158
46	Montana	6,950
47	Wyoming	6,506
48	North Dakota	5,376
49	Vermont	3,470
50	New Hampshire	3,148
	District of Columbia**	NA

Source: CQ Press using data from National Conference of State Legislatures (Denver, CO)
"2016 Partisan Composition" (http://www.ncsl.org/research/about-state-legislatures/partisan-composition.aspx)
*There are 1,972 state senators (including Nebraska's 49 unicameral seats) and 5,411 state house members. National rate does not include population for the District of Columbia. Calculated using 2016 population estimates.
**Not applicable.

Registered Voters in 2014

National Total = 142,166,000

ALPHA ORDER					RANK ORDER			

RANK	STATE	REGISTERED	% of USA		RANK	STATE	REGISTERED	% of USA
25	Alabama	2,366,000	1.7%		1	California	14,113,000	9.9%
48	Alaska	336,000	0.2%		2	Texas	9,946,000	7.0%
21	Arizona	2,738,000	1.9%		3	Florida	8,691,000	6.1%
33	Arkansas	1,292,000	0.9%		4	New York	8,078,000	5.7%
1	California	14,113,000	9.9%		5	Pennsylvania	6,121,000	4.3%
22	Colorado	2,654,000	1.9%		6	Illinois	5,716,000	4.0%
28	Connecticut	1,668,000	1.2%		7	Ohio	5,657,000	4.0%
45	Delaware	442,000	0.3%		8	Michigan	5,159,000	3.6%
3	Florida	8,691,000	6.1%		9	North Carolina	4,779,000	3.4%
10	Georgia	4,306,000	3.0%		10	Georgia	4,306,000	3.0%
43	Hawaii	490,000	0.3%		11	Virginia	3,924,000	2.8%
41	Idaho	671,000	0.5%		12	New Jersey	3,919,000	2.8%
6	Illinois	5,716,000	4.0%		13	Washington	3,281,000	2.3%
17	Indiana	3,048,000	2.1%		14	Massachusetts	3,250,000	2.3%
31	Iowa	1,584,000	1.1%		15	Missouri	3,194,000	2.2%
32	Kansas	1,353,000	1.0%		16	Tennessee	3,088,000	2.2%
26	Kentucky	2,298,000	1.6%		17	Indiana	3,048,000	2.1%
24	Louisiana	2,398,000	1.7%		18	Wisconsin	3,005,000	2.1%
39	Maine	799,000	0.6%		19	Maryland	2,995,000	2.1%
19	Maryland	2,995,000	2.1%		20	Minnesota	2,822,000	2.0%
14	Massachusetts	3,250,000	2.3%		21	Arizona	2,738,000	1.9%
8	Michigan	5,159,000	3.6%		22	Colorado	2,654,000	1.9%
20	Minnesota	2,822,000	2.0%		23	South Carolina	2,458,000	1.7%
30	Mississippi	1,628,000	1.1%		24	Louisiana	2,398,000	1.7%
15	Missouri	3,194,000	2.2%		25	Alabama	2,366,000	1.7%
42	Montana	506,000	0.4%		26	Kentucky	2,298,000	1.6%
38	Nebraska	873,000	0.6%		27	Oregon	2,008,000	1.4%
35	Nevada	1,088,000	0.8%		28	Connecticut	1,668,000	1.2%
40	New Hampshire	694,000	0.5%		29	Oklahoma	1,644,000	1.2%
12	New Jersey	3,919,000	2.8%		30	Mississippi	1,628,000	1.1%
36	New Mexico	919,000	0.6%		31	Iowa	1,584,000	1.1%
4	New York	8,078,000	5.7%		32	Kansas	1,353,000	1.0%
9	North Carolina	4,779,000	3.4%		33	Arkansas	1,292,000	0.9%
47	North Dakota	363,000	0.3%		34	Utah	1,101,000	0.8%
7	Ohio	5,657,000	4.0%		35	Nevada	1,088,000	0.8%
29	Oklahoma	1,644,000	1.2%		36	New Mexico	919,000	0.6%
27	Oregon	2,008,000	1.4%		37	West Virginia	896,000	0.6%
5	Pennsylvania	6,121,000	4.3%		38	Nebraska	873,000	0.6%
44	Rhode Island	486,000	0.3%		39	Maine	799,000	0.6%
23	South Carolina	2,458,000	1.7%		40	New Hampshire	694,000	0.5%
46	South Dakota	401,000	0.3%		41	Idaho	671,000	0.5%
16	Tennessee	3,088,000	2.2%		42	Montana	506,000	0.4%
2	Texas	9,946,000	7.0%		43	Hawaii	490,000	0.3%
34	Utah	1,101,000	0.8%		44	Rhode Island	486,000	0.3%
49	Vermont	324,000	0.2%		45	Delaware	442,000	0.3%
11	Virginia	3,924,000	2.8%		46	South Dakota	401,000	0.3%
13	Washington	3,281,000	2.3%		47	North Dakota	363,000	0.3%
37	West Virginia	896,000	0.6%		48	Alaska	336,000	0.2%
18	Wisconsin	3,005,000	2.1%		49	Vermont	324,000	0.2%
50	Wyoming	241,000	0.2%		50	Wyoming	241,000	0.2%
						District of Columbia	353,000	0.2%

Source: U.S. Bureau of the Census
"Voting and Registration" (Table 4a, http://www.census.gov/topics/public-sector/voting.htmll)

Percent of Eligible Voters Reported Registered in 2014

National Percent = 64.6%*

ALPHA ORDER

RANK	STATE	PERCENT
19	Alabama	67.2
22	Alaska	66.8
40	Arizona	62.3
38	Arkansas	62.8
47	California	57.7
9	Colorado	71.1
28	Connecticut	65.1
22	Delaware	66.8
39	Florida	62.6
36	Georgia	63.7
50	Hawaii	51.3
43	Idaho	60.7
35	Illinois	63.9
29	Indiana	64.9
13	Iowa	69.6
17	Kansas	67.9
7	Kentucky	71.6
6	Louisiana	71.7
1	Maine	76.5
3	Maryland	72.2
18	Massachusetts	67.5
8	Michigan	71.2
5	Minnesota	71.8
2	Mississippi	76.0
4	Missouri	72.1
32	Montana	64.8
21	Nebraska	66.9
46	Nevada	58.5
16	New Hampshire	68.3
27	New Jersey	66.3
29	New Mexico	64.9
44	New York	59.4
12	North Carolina	69.7
26	North Dakota	66.4
25	Ohio	66.5
42	Oklahoma	61.1
11	Oregon	70.0
33	Pennsylvania	64.4
37	Rhode Island	63.6
14	South Carolina	68.9
29	South Dakota	64.9
34	Tennessee	64.1
45	Texas	59.1
48	Utah	57.2
19	Vermont	67.2
24	Virginia	66.6
15	Washington	68.7
41	West Virginia	62.2
10	Wisconsin	71.0
49	Wyoming	56.5

RANK ORDER

RANK	STATE	PERCENT
1	Maine	76.5
2	Mississippi	76.0
3	Maryland	72.2
4	Missouri	72.1
5	Minnesota	71.8
6	Louisiana	71.7
7	Kentucky	71.6
8	Michigan	71.2
9	Colorado	71.1
10	Wisconsin	71.0
11	Oregon	70.0
12	North Carolina	69.7
13	Iowa	69.6
14	South Carolina	68.9
15	Washington	68.7
16	New Hampshire	68.3
17	Kansas	67.9
18	Massachusetts	67.5
19	Alabama	67.2
19	Vermont	67.2
21	Nebraska	66.9
22	Alaska	66.8
22	Delaware	66.8
24	Virginia	66.6
25	Ohio	66.5
26	North Dakota	66.4
27	New Jersey	66.3
28	Connecticut	65.1
29	Indiana	64.9
29	New Mexico	64.9
29	South Dakota	64.9
32	Montana	64.8
33	Pennsylvania	64.4
34	Tennessee	64.1
35	Illinois	63.9
36	Georgia	63.7
37	Rhode Island	63.6
38	Arkansas	62.8
39	Florida	62.6
40	Arizona	62.3
41	West Virginia	62.2
42	Oklahoma	61.1
43	Idaho	60.7
44	New York	59.4
45	Texas	59.1
46	Nevada	58.5
47	California	57.7
48	Utah	57.2
49	Wyoming	56.5
50	Hawaii	51.3
	District of Columbia	73.5

Source: U.S. Bureau of the Census
"Voting and Registration" (Table 4a, http://www.census.gov/topics/public-sector/voting.htmll)
*As a percent of citizen population 18 and older.

Persons Voting in 2014

National Total = 92,251,000

RANK	STATE	VOTERS	% of USA
27	Alabama	1,497,000	1.6%
48	Alaska	255,000	0.3%
19	Arizona	1,785,000	1.9%
33	Arkansas	798,000	0.9%
1	California	8,949,000	9.7%
15	Colorado	2,211,000	2.4%
29	Connecticut	1,195,000	1.3%
45	Delaware	299,000	0.3%
2	Florida	6,220,000	6.7%
10	Georgia	2,919,000	3.2%
42	Hawaii	399,000	0.4%
41	Idaho	462,000	0.5%
6	Illinois	3,734,000	4.0%
23	Indiana	1,646,000	1.8%
28	Iowa	1,203,000	1.3%
30	Kansas	962,000	1.0%
25	Kentucky	1,525,000	1.7%
22	Louisiana	1,677,000	1.8%
37	Maine	642,000	0.7%
18	Maryland	2,028,000	2.2%
14	Massachusetts	2,259,000	2.4%
7	Michigan	3,416,000	3.7%
17	Minnesota	2,047,000	2.2%
32	Mississippi	907,000	1.0%
21	Missouri	1,713,000	1.9%
43	Montana	391,000	0.4%
38	Nebraska	579,000	0.6%
35	Nevada	693,000	0.8%
39	New Hampshire	509,000	0.6%
16	New Jersey	2,151,000	2.3%
36	New Mexico	646,000	0.7%
4	New York	4,680,000	5.1%
9	North Carolina	3,170,000	3.4%
46	North Dakota	279,000	0.3%
8	Ohio	3,378,000	3.7%
31	Oklahoma	920,000	1.0%
24	Oregon	1,594,000	1.7%
5	Pennsylvania	3,803,000	4.1%
44	Rhode Island	331,000	0.4%
26	South Carolina	1,514,000	1.6%
47	South Dakota	273,000	0.3%
20	Tennessee	1,763,000	1.9%
3	Texas	5,836,000	6.3%
34	Utah	703,000	0.8%
49	Vermont	205,000	0.2%
11	Virginia	2,453,000	2.7%
12	Washington	2,390,000	2.6%
40	West Virginia	484,000	0.5%
13	Wisconsin	2,343,000	2.5%
50	Wyoming	172,000	0.2%

RANK	STATE	VOTERS	% of USA
1	California	8,949,000	9.7%
2	Florida	6,220,000	6.7%
3	Texas	5,836,000	6.3%
4	New York	4,680,000	5.1%
5	Pennsylvania	3,803,000	4.1%
6	Illinois	3,734,000	4.0%
7	Michigan	3,416,000	3.7%
8	Ohio	3,378,000	3.7%
9	North Carolina	3,170,000	3.4%
10	Georgia	2,919,000	3.2%
11	Virginia	2,453,000	2.7%
12	Washington	2,390,000	2.6%
13	Wisconsin	2,343,000	2.5%
14	Massachusetts	2,259,000	2.4%
15	Colorado	2,211,000	2.4%
16	New Jersey	2,151,000	2.3%
17	Minnesota	2,047,000	2.2%
18	Maryland	2,028,000	2.2%
19	Arizona	1,785,000	1.9%
20	Tennessee	1,763,000	1.9%
21	Missouri	1,713,000	1.9%
22	Louisiana	1,677,000	1.8%
23	Indiana	1,646,000	1.8%
24	Oregon	1,594,000	1.7%
25	Kentucky	1,525,000	1.7%
26	South Carolina	1,514,000	1.6%
27	Alabama	1,497,000	1.6%
28	Iowa	1,203,000	1.3%
29	Connecticut	1,195,000	1.3%
30	Kansas	962,000	1.0%
31	Oklahoma	920,000	1.0%
32	Mississippi	907,000	1.0%
33	Arkansas	798,000	0.9%
34	Utah	703,000	0.8%
35	Nevada	693,000	0.8%
36	New Mexico	646,000	0.7%
37	Maine	642,000	0.7%
38	Nebraska	579,000	0.6%
39	New Hampshire	509,000	0.6%
40	West Virginia	484,000	0.5%
41	Idaho	462,000	0.5%
42	Hawaii	399,000	0.4%
43	Montana	391,000	0.4%
44	Rhode Island	331,000	0.4%
45	Delaware	299,000	0.3%
46	North Dakota	279,000	0.3%
47	South Dakota	273,000	0.3%
48	Alaska	255,000	0.3%
49	Vermont	205,000	0.2%
50	Wyoming	172,000	0.2%
	District of Columbia	247,000	0.3%

Source: U.S. Bureau of the Census
"Voting and Registration" (Table 4a, http://www.census.gov/topics/public-sector/voting.htmll)

Percent of Eligible Population Reported Voting in 2014

National Percent = 41.9%*

ALPHA ORDER				RANK ORDER		
RANK	STATE	PERCENT		RANK	STATE	PERCENT
27	Alabama	42.5		1	Maine	61.5
8	Alaska	50.7		2	Colorado	59.3
35	Arizona	40.6		3	Oregon	55.5
39	Arkansas	38.8		4	Wisconsin	55.4
42	California	36.6		5	Iowa	52.9
2	Colorado	59.3		6	Minnesota	52.0
18	Connecticut	46.7		7	North Dakota	51.0
21	Delaware	45.2		8	Alaska	50.7
22	Florida	44.8		9	Louisiana	50.2
26	Georgia	43.2		9	New Hampshire	50.2
31	Hawaii	41.8		11	Montana	50.1
31	Idaho	41.8		12	Washington	50.0
33	Illinois	41.7		13	Maryland	48.9
46	Indiana	35.1		14	Kansas	48.3
5	Iowa	52.9		15	Kentucky	47.5
14	Kansas	48.3		16	Michigan	47.1
15	Kentucky	47.5		17	Massachusetts	46.9
9	Louisiana	50.2		18	Connecticut	46.7
1	Maine	61.5		19	North Carolina	46.2
13	Maryland	48.9		20	New Mexico	45.6
17	Massachusetts	46.9		21	Delaware	45.2
16	Michigan	47.1		22	Florida	44.8
6	Minnesota	52.0		23	Nebraska	44.3
30	Mississippi	42.3		24	South Dakota	44.1
40	Missouri	38.7		25	Rhode Island	43.3
11	Montana	50.1		26	Georgia	43.2
23	Nebraska	44.3		27	Alabama	42.5
41	Nevada	37.3		27	Vermont	42.5
9	New Hampshire	50.2		29	South Carolina	42.4
45	New Jersey	36.4		30	Mississippi	42.3
20	New Mexico	45.6		31	Hawaii	41.8
48	New York	34.4		31	Idaho	41.8
19	North Carolina	46.2		33	Illinois	41.7
7	North Dakota	51.0		33	Virginia	41.7
38	Ohio	39.7		35	Arizona	40.6
49	Oklahoma	34.2		36	Wyoming	40.3
3	Oregon	55.5		37	Pennsylvania	40.0
37	Pennsylvania	40.0		38	Ohio	39.7
25	Rhode Island	43.3		39	Arkansas	38.8
29	South Carolina	42.4		40	Missouri	38.7
24	South Dakota	44.1		41	Nevada	37.3
42	Tennessee	36.6		42	California	36.6
47	Texas	34.6		42	Tennessee	36.6
44	Utah	36.5		44	Utah	36.5
27	Vermont	42.5		45	New Jersey	36.4
33	Virginia	41.7		46	Indiana	35.1
12	Washington	50.0		47	Texas	34.6
50	West Virginia	33.6		48	New York	34.4
4	Wisconsin	55.4		49	Oklahoma	34.2
36	Wyoming	40.3		50	West Virginia	33.6
					District of Columbia	51.4

Source: U.S. Bureau of the Census
   "Voting and Registration" (Table 4a, http://www.census.gov/topics/public-sector/voting.htmll)
*As a percent of citizen population 18 and older.

Percent of Registered Population Reported Voting in 2014

National Percent = 64.9%*

RANK	STATE	PERCENT
35	Alabama	63.3
8	Alaska	75.9
31	Arizona	65.2
39	Arkansas	61.8
34	California	63.4
1	Colorado	83.3
13	Connecticut	71.6
25	Delaware	67.6
13	Florida	71.6
23	Georgia	67.8
2	Hawaii	81.4
20	Idaho	68.9
30	Illinois	65.3
48	Indiana	54.0
8	Iowa	75.9
16	Kansas	71.1
26	Kentucky	66.4
18	Louisiana	69.9
3	Maine	80.4
24	Maryland	67.7
19	Massachusetts	69.5
29	Michigan	66.2
12	Minnesota	72.5
46	Mississippi	55.7
50	Missouri	53.6
6	Montana	77.3
27	Nebraska	66.3
33	Nevada	63.7
10	New Hampshire	73.3
47	New Jersey	54.9
17	New Mexico	70.3
43	New York	57.9
27	North Carolina	66.3
7	North Dakota	76.9
41	Ohio	59.7
45	Oklahoma	56.0
4	Oregon	79.4
38	Pennsylvania	62.1
21	Rhode Island	68.1
40	South Carolina	61.6
21	South Dakota	68.1
44	Tennessee	57.1
42	Texas	58.7
32	Utah	63.9
35	Vermont	63.3
37	Virginia	62.5
11	Washington	72.8
48	West Virginia	54.0
5	Wisconsin	78.0
15	Wyoming	71.4

RANK	STATE	PERCENT
1	Colorado	83.3
2	Hawaii	81.4
3	Maine	80.4
4	Oregon	79.4
5	Wisconsin	78.0
6	Montana	77.3
7	North Dakota	76.9
8	Alaska	75.9
8	Iowa	75.9
10	New Hampshire	73.3
11	Washington	72.8
12	Minnesota	72.5
13	Connecticut	71.6
13	Florida	71.6
15	Wyoming	71.4
16	Kansas	71.1
17	New Mexico	70.3
18	Louisiana	69.9
19	Massachusetts	69.5
20	Idaho	68.9
21	Rhode Island	68.1
21	South Dakota	68.1
23	Georgia	67.8
24	Maryland	67.7
25	Delaware	67.6
26	Kentucky	66.4
27	Nebraska	66.3
27	North Carolina	66.3
29	Michigan	66.2
30	Illinois	65.3
31	Arizona	65.2
32	Utah	63.9
33	Nevada	63.7
34	California	63.4
35	Alabama	63.3
35	Vermont	63.3
37	Virginia	62.5
38	Pennsylvania	62.1
39	Arkansas	61.8
40	South Carolina	61.6
41	Ohio	59.7
42	Texas	58.7
43	New York	57.9
44	Tennessee	57.1
45	Oklahoma	56.0
46	Mississippi	55.7
47	New Jersey	54.9
48	Indiana	54.0
48	West Virginia	54.0
50	Missouri	53.6
	District of Columbia	70.0

Source: CQ Press using data from U.S. Bureau of the Census
"Voting and Registration" (Table 4a, http://www.census.gov/topics/public-sector/voting.htmll)
*As a percent of citizen population 18 and older registered to vote.

XIV. Social Welfare

Poverty Rate in 2015

National Rate = 14.7% of Population in Poverty*

ALPHA ORDER

RANK	STATE	PERCENT
5	Alabama	18.5
46	Alaska	10.3
8	Arizona	17.4
4	Arkansas	19.1
19	California	15.3
37	Colorado	11.5
45	Connecticut	10.5
33	Delaware	12.4
16	Florida	15.7
9	Georgia	17.0
44	Hawaii	10.6
20	Idaho	15.1
28	Illinois	13.6
25	Indiana	14.5
34	Iowa	12.2
31	Kansas	13.0
5	Kentucky	18.5
3	Louisiana	19.6
29	Maine	13.4
49	Maryland	9.7
37	Massachusetts	11.5
15	Michigan	15.8
47	Minnesota	10.2
1	Mississippi	22.0
21	Missouri	14.8
24	Montana	14.6
32	Nebraska	12.6
23	Nevada	14.7
50	New Hampshire	8.2
43	New Jersey	10.8
2	New Mexico	20.4
17	New York	15.4
12	North Carolina	16.4
42	North Dakota	11.0
21	Ohio	14.8
13	Oklahoma	16.1
17	Oregon	15.4
30	Pennsylvania	13.2
26	Rhode Island	13.9
11	South Carolina	16.6
27	South Dakota	13.7
10	Tennessee	16.7
14	Texas	15.9
39	Utah	11.3
47	Vermont	10.2
40	Virginia	11.2
34	Washington	12.2
7	West Virginia	17.9
36	Wisconsin	12.1
41	Wyoming	11.1

RANK ORDER

RANK	STATE	PERCENT
1	Mississippi	22.0
2	New Mexico	20.4
3	Louisiana	19.6
4	Arkansas	19.1
5	Alabama	18.5
5	Kentucky	18.5
7	West Virginia	17.9
8	Arizona	17.4
9	Georgia	17.0
10	Tennessee	16.7
11	South Carolina	16.6
12	North Carolina	16.4
13	Oklahoma	16.1
14	Texas	15.9
15	Michigan	15.8
16	Florida	15.7
17	New York	15.4
17	Oregon	15.4
19	California	15.3
20	Idaho	15.1
21	Missouri	14.8
21	Ohio	14.8
23	Nevada	14.7
24	Montana	14.6
25	Indiana	14.5
26	Rhode Island	13.9
27	South Dakota	13.7
28	Illinois	13.6
29	Maine	13.4
30	Pennsylvania	13.2
31	Kansas	13.0
32	Nebraska	12.6
33	Delaware	12.4
34	Iowa	12.2
34	Washington	12.2
36	Wisconsin	12.1
37	Colorado	11.5
37	Massachusetts	11.5
39	Utah	11.3
40	Virginia	11.2
41	Wyoming	11.1
42	North Dakota	11.0
43	New Jersey	10.8
44	Hawaii	10.6
45	Connecticut	10.5
46	Alaska	10.3
47	Minnesota	10.2
47	Vermont	10.2
49	Maryland	9.7
50	New Hampshire	8.2
	District of Columbia	17.3

Source: U.S. Bureau of the Census
   "2015 American Community Survey-Table DP03" (http://www.census.gov/programs-surveys/acs/)
*This is a one-year figure. Census has discontinued three-year averages that had been used previously. The poverty threshold for a family of four (two children) in 2015 was $24,250.

Percent of Senior Citizens Living in Poverty in 2015

National Percent = 9.0%*

RANK	STATE	PERCENT
10	Alabama	9.9
50	Alaska	4.5
17	Arizona	9.0
6	Arkansas	10.3
10	California	9.9
43	Colorado	7.0
40	Connecticut	7.2
48	Delaware	6.2
6	Florida	10.3
13	Georgia	9.7
29	Hawaii	7.8
20	Idaho	8.7
21	Illinois	8.5
40	Indiana	7.2
43	Iowa	7.0
36	Kansas	7.3
3	Kentucky	11.2
1	Louisiana	12.8
19	Maine	8.8
36	Maryland	7.3
15	Massachusetts	9.2
29	Michigan	7.8
45	Minnesota	6.9
2	Mississippi	12.5
21	Missouri	8.5
32	Montana	7.6
34	Nebraska	7.4
24	Nevada	8.4
49	New Hampshire	6.1
28	New Jersey	7.9
5	New Mexico	11.1
3	New York	11.2
15	North Carolina	9.2
18	North Dakota	8.9
32	Ohio	7.6
24	Oklahoma	8.4
36	Oregon	7.3
29	Pennsylvania	7.8
6	Rhode Island	10.3
14	South Carolina	9.3
26	South Dakota	8.3
12	Tennessee	9.8
6	Texas	10.3
46	Utah	6.8
47	Vermont	6.6
36	Virginia	7.3
34	Washington	7.4
21	West Virginia	8.5
42	Wisconsin	7.1
27	Wyoming	8.0

RANK	STATE	PERCENT
1	Louisiana	12.8
2	Mississippi	12.5
3	Kentucky	11.2
3	New York	11.2
5	New Mexico	11.1
6	Arkansas	10.3
6	Florida	10.3
6	Rhode Island	10.3
6	Texas	10.3
10	Alabama	9.9
10	California	9.9
12	Tennessee	9.8
13	Georgia	9.7
14	South Carolina	9.3
15	Massachusetts	9.2
15	North Carolina	9.2
17	Arizona	9.0
18	North Dakota	8.9
19	Maine	8.8
20	Idaho	8.7
21	Illinois	8.5
21	Missouri	8.5
21	West Virginia	8.5
24	Nevada	8.4
24	Oklahoma	8.4
26	South Dakota	8.3
27	Wyoming	8.0
28	New Jersey	7.9
29	Hawaii	7.8
29	Michigan	7.8
29	Pennsylvania	7.8
32	Montana	7.6
32	Ohio	7.6
34	Nebraska	7.4
34	Washington	7.4
36	Kansas	7.3
36	Maryland	7.3
36	Oregon	7.3
36	Virginia	7.3
40	Connecticut	7.2
40	Indiana	7.2
42	Wisconsin	7.1
43	Colorado	7.0
43	Iowa	7.0
45	Minnesota	6.9
46	Utah	6.8
47	Vermont	6.6
48	Delaware	6.2
49	New Hampshire	6.1
50	Alaska	4.5
	District of Columbia	15.2

Source: U.S. Bureau of the Census
  "2015 American Community Survey-Table DP03" (http://www.census.gov/programs-surveys/acs/)
*People 65 years and older living with incomes below the poverty level.

Percent of Children Living in Poverty in 2015

National Percent = 20.7%*

ALPHA ORDER

RANK	STATE	PERCENT
5	Alabama	26.6
37	Alaska	15.2
8	Arizona	24.7
4	Arkansas	27.2
19	California	21.2
41	Colorado	14.7
42	Connecticut	14.5
24	Delaware	19.4
13	Florida	23.1
9	Georgia	24.5
43	Hawaii	14.2
30	Idaho	17.8
28	Illinois	19.1
20	Indiana	20.9
38	Iowa	14.8
32	Kansas	17.2
6	Kentucky	25.9
3	Louisiana	28.4
31	Maine	17.4
45	Maryland	13.2
38	Massachusetts	14.8
15	Michigan	22.4
47	Minnesota	13.1
1	Mississippi	31.3
23	Missouri	20.2
24	Montana	19.4
33	Nebraska	16.8
20	Nevada	20.9
50	New Hampshire	10.7
35	New Jersey	15.6
2	New Mexico	28.6
17	New York	22.0
12	North Carolina	23.5
49	North Dakota	12.1
18	Ohio	21.3
16	Oklahoma	22.2
22	Oregon	20.3
24	Pennsylvania	19.4
24	Rhode Island	19.4
11	South Carolina	24.0
29	South Dakota	18.1
10	Tennessee	24.2
14	Texas	23.0
48	Utah	12.9
44	Vermont	13.3
38	Virginia	14.8
36	Washington	15.5
7	West Virginia	25.2
34	Wisconsin	16.4
45	Wyoming	13.2

RANK ORDER

RANK	STATE	PERCENT
1	Mississippi	31.3
2	New Mexico	28.6
3	Louisiana	28.4
4	Arkansas	27.2
5	Alabama	26.6
6	Kentucky	25.9
7	West Virginia	25.2
8	Arizona	24.7
9	Georgia	24.5
10	Tennessee	24.2
11	South Carolina	24.0
12	North Carolina	23.5
13	Florida	23.1
14	Texas	23.0
15	Michigan	22.4
16	Oklahoma	22.2
17	New York	22.0
18	Ohio	21.3
19	California	21.2
20	Indiana	20.9
20	Nevada	20.9
22	Oregon	20.3
23	Missouri	20.2
24	Delaware	19.4
24	Montana	19.4
24	Pennsylvania	19.4
24	Rhode Island	19.4
28	Illinois	19.1
29	South Dakota	18.1
30	Idaho	17.8
31	Maine	17.4
32	Kansas	17.2
33	Nebraska	16.8
34	Wisconsin	16.4
35	New Jersey	15.6
36	Washington	15.5
37	Alaska	15.2
38	Iowa	14.8
38	Massachusetts	14.8
38	Virginia	14.8
41	Colorado	14.7
42	Connecticut	14.5
43	Hawaii	14.2
44	Vermont	13.3
45	Maryland	13.2
45	Wyoming	13.2
47	Minnesota	13.1
48	Utah	12.9
49	North Dakota	12.1
50	New Hampshire	10.7
	District of Columbia	25.6

Source: U.S. Bureau of the Census
"2015 American Community Survey-Table DP03" (http://www.census.gov/programs-surveys/acs/)
*Children 17 and under living in families with incomes below the poverty level.

Percent of Families Living in Poverty in 2015

National Percent = 10.6%*

<table>
<tr><td colspan="3">ALPHA ORDER</td><td colspan="3">RANK ORDER</td></tr>
<tr><td>RANK</td><td>STATE</td><td>PERCENT</td><td>RANK</td><td>STATE</td><td>PERCENT</td></tr>
<tr><td>5</td><td>Alabama</td><td>13.7</td><td>1</td><td>Mississippi</td><td>17.0</td></tr>
<tr><td>43</td><td>Alaska</td><td>7.0</td><td>2</td><td>New Mexico</td><td>14.8</td></tr>
<tr><td>9</td><td>Arizona</td><td>12.5</td><td>3</td><td>Louisiana</td><td>14.7</td></tr>
<tr><td>5</td><td>Arkansas</td><td>13.7</td><td>4</td><td>Kentucky</td><td>14.0</td></tr>
<tr><td>16</td><td>California</td><td>11.3</td><td>5</td><td>Alabama</td><td>13.7</td></tr>
<tr><td>41</td><td>Colorado</td><td>7.6</td><td>5</td><td>Arkansas</td><td>13.7</td></tr>
<tr><td>42</td><td>Connecticut</td><td>7.4</td><td>7</td><td>West Virginia</td><td>13.5</td></tr>
<tr><td>30</td><td>Delaware</td><td>8.7</td><td>8</td><td>Georgia</td><td>13.0</td></tr>
<tr><td>16</td><td>Florida</td><td>11.3</td><td>9</td><td>Arizona</td><td>12.5</td></tr>
<tr><td>8</td><td>Georgia</td><td>13.0</td><td>10</td><td>Tennessee</td><td>12.3</td></tr>
<tr><td>44</td><td>Hawaii</td><td>6.9</td><td>11</td><td>Texas</td><td>12.2</td></tr>
<tr><td>19</td><td>Idaho</td><td>10.9</td><td>12</td><td>South Carolina</td><td>12.1</td></tr>
<tr><td>26</td><td>Illinois</td><td>9.8</td><td>13</td><td>North Carolina</td><td>11.8</td></tr>
<tr><td>22</td><td>Indiana</td><td>10.2</td><td>14</td><td>Oklahoma</td><td>11.7</td></tr>
<tr><td>40</td><td>Iowa</td><td>7.7</td><td>15</td><td>New York</td><td>11.6</td></tr>
<tr><td>32</td><td>Kansas</td><td>8.4</td><td>16</td><td>California</td><td>11.3</td></tr>
<tr><td>4</td><td>Kentucky</td><td>14.0</td><td>16</td><td>Florida</td><td>11.3</td></tr>
<tr><td>3</td><td>Louisiana</td><td>14.7</td><td>18</td><td>Michigan</td><td>11.1</td></tr>
<tr><td>29</td><td>Maine</td><td>8.9</td><td>19</td><td>Idaho</td><td>10.9</td></tr>
<tr><td>46</td><td>Maryland</td><td>6.7</td><td>19</td><td>Nevada</td><td>10.9</td></tr>
<tr><td>36</td><td>Massachusetts</td><td>7.9</td><td>21</td><td>Ohio</td><td>10.7</td></tr>
<tr><td>18</td><td>Michigan</td><td>11.1</td><td>22</td><td>Indiana</td><td>10.2</td></tr>
<tr><td>48</td><td>Minnesota</td><td>6.3</td><td>22</td><td>Missouri</td><td>10.2</td></tr>
<tr><td>1</td><td>Mississippi</td><td>17.0</td><td>24</td><td>Rhode Island</td><td>10.1</td></tr>
<tr><td>22</td><td>Missouri</td><td>10.2</td><td>25</td><td>Oregon</td><td>9.9</td></tr>
<tr><td>27</td><td>Montana</td><td>9.3</td><td>26</td><td>Illinois</td><td>9.8</td></tr>
<tr><td>31</td><td>Nebraska</td><td>8.5</td><td>27</td><td>Montana</td><td>9.3</td></tr>
<tr><td>19</td><td>Nevada</td><td>10.9</td><td>28</td><td>Pennsylvania</td><td>9.1</td></tr>
<tr><td>50</td><td>New Hampshire</td><td>5.0</td><td>29</td><td>Maine</td><td>8.9</td></tr>
<tr><td>35</td><td>New Jersey</td><td>8.1</td><td>30</td><td>Delaware</td><td>8.7</td></tr>
<tr><td>2</td><td>New Mexico</td><td>14.8</td><td>31</td><td>Nebraska</td><td>8.5</td></tr>
<tr><td>15</td><td>New York</td><td>11.6</td><td>32</td><td>Kansas</td><td>8.4</td></tr>
<tr><td>13</td><td>North Carolina</td><td>11.8</td><td>33</td><td>South Dakota</td><td>8.3</td></tr>
<tr><td>44</td><td>North Dakota</td><td>6.9</td><td>33</td><td>Utah</td><td>8.3</td></tr>
<tr><td>21</td><td>Ohio</td><td>10.7</td><td>35</td><td>New Jersey</td><td>8.1</td></tr>
<tr><td>14</td><td>Oklahoma</td><td>11.7</td><td>36</td><td>Massachusetts</td><td>7.9</td></tr>
<tr><td>25</td><td>Oregon</td><td>9.9</td><td>36</td><td>Washington</td><td>7.9</td></tr>
<tr><td>28</td><td>Pennsylvania</td><td>9.1</td><td>36</td><td>Wisconsin</td><td>7.9</td></tr>
<tr><td>24</td><td>Rhode Island</td><td>10.1</td><td>39</td><td>Virginia</td><td>7.8</td></tr>
<tr><td>12</td><td>South Carolina</td><td>12.1</td><td>40</td><td>Iowa</td><td>7.7</td></tr>
<tr><td>33</td><td>South Dakota</td><td>8.3</td><td>41</td><td>Colorado</td><td>7.6</td></tr>
<tr><td>10</td><td>Tennessee</td><td>12.3</td><td>42</td><td>Connecticut</td><td>7.4</td></tr>
<tr><td>11</td><td>Texas</td><td>12.2</td><td>43</td><td>Alaska</td><td>7.0</td></tr>
<tr><td>33</td><td>Utah</td><td>8.3</td><td>44</td><td>Hawaii</td><td>6.9</td></tr>
<tr><td>49</td><td>Vermont</td><td>5.8</td><td>44</td><td>North Dakota</td><td>6.9</td></tr>
<tr><td>39</td><td>Virginia</td><td>7.8</td><td>46</td><td>Maryland</td><td>6.7</td></tr>
<tr><td>36</td><td>Washington</td><td>7.9</td><td>46</td><td>Wyoming</td><td>6.7</td></tr>
<tr><td>7</td><td>West Virginia</td><td>13.5</td><td>48</td><td>Minnesota</td><td>6.3</td></tr>
<tr><td>36</td><td>Wisconsin</td><td>7.9</td><td>49</td><td>Vermont</td><td>5.8</td></tr>
<tr><td>46</td><td>Wyoming</td><td>6.7</td><td>50</td><td>New Hampshire</td><td>5.0</td></tr>
<tr><td></td><td></td><td></td><td></td><td>District of Columbia</td><td>14.0</td></tr>
</table>

Source: U.S. Bureau of the Census
  "2015 American Community Survey-Table DP03" (http://www.census.gov/programs-surveys/acs/)
*Families living with incomes below the poverty level.

Percent of Female-Headed Families with Children Living in Poverty in 2015

National Percent = 39.2%*

ALPHA ORDER

RANK	STATE	PERCENT
4	Alabama	47.7
49	Alaska	26.6
20	Arizona	40.1
6	Arkansas	46.2
29	California	37.0
39	Colorado	33.7
44	Connecticut	32.6
35	Delaware	34.2
27	Florida	37.1
14	Georgia	42.5
50	Hawaii	26.2
10	Idaho	43.4
23	Illinois	38.8
11	Indiana	43.2
30	Iowa	36.8
32	Kansas	36.5
5	Kentucky	47.0
1	Louisiana	49.8
27	Maine	37.1
48	Maryland	27.1
38	Massachusetts	33.8
8	Michigan	44.2
46	Minnesota	32.1
2	Mississippi	49.6
18	Missouri	41.3
7	Montana	45.3
26	Nebraska	38.0
33	Nevada	35.7
47	New Hampshire	30.3
40	New Jersey	33.6
9	New Mexico	43.9
25	New York	38.3
15	North Carolina	42.4
42	North Dakota	33.1
12	Ohio	43.1
16	Oklahoma	42.1
23	Oregon	38.8
22	Pennsylvania	39.2
19	Rhode Island	40.6
17	South Carolina	41.9
34	South Dakota	34.3
13	Tennessee	42.7
21	Texas	39.9
36	Utah	34.1
43	Vermont	32.8
41	Virginia	33.3
37	Washington	34.0
3	West Virginia	48.7
31	Wisconsin	36.7
45	Wyoming	32.2

RANK ORDER

RANK	STATE	PERCENT
1	Louisiana	49.8
2	Mississippi	49.6
3	West Virginia	48.7
4	Alabama	47.7
5	Kentucky	47.0
6	Arkansas	46.2
7	Montana	45.3
8	Michigan	44.2
9	New Mexico	43.9
10	Idaho	43.4
11	Indiana	43.2
12	Ohio	43.1
13	Tennessee	42.7
14	Georgia	42.5
15	North Carolina	42.4
16	Oklahoma	42.1
17	South Carolina	41.9
18	Missouri	41.3
19	Rhode Island	40.6
20	Arizona	40.1
21	Texas	39.9
22	Pennsylvania	39.2
23	Illinois	38.8
23	Oregon	38.8
25	New York	38.3
26	Nebraska	38.0
27	Florida	37.1
27	Maine	37.1
29	California	37.0
30	Iowa	36.8
31	Wisconsin	36.7
32	Kansas	36.5
33	Nevada	35.7
34	South Dakota	34.3
35	Delaware	34.2
36	Utah	34.1
37	Washington	34.0
38	Massachusetts	33.8
39	Colorado	33.7
40	New Jersey	33.6
41	Virginia	33.3
42	North Dakota	33.1
43	Vermont	32.8
44	Connecticut	32.6
45	Wyoming	32.2
46	Minnesota	32.1
47	New Hampshire	30.3
48	Maryland	27.1
49	Alaska	26.6
50	Hawaii	26.2
	District of Columbia	40.3

Source: U.S. Bureau of the Census
   "2015 American Community Survey-Table DP03" (http://www.census.gov/programs-surveys/acs/)
*Households headed by females with own children under 18 years living with them with incomes below the poverty level as a percent of all such female-headed households.

State and Local Government Expenditures for Public Welfare Programs in 2014

National Total = $542,569,109,000*

ALPHA ORDER

RANK	STATE	EXPENDITURES	% of USA
28	Alabama	$6,522,927,000	1.2%
44	Alaska	2,094,542,000	0.4%
20	Arizona	8,897,641,000	1.6%
30	Arkansas	5,730,027,000	1.1%
1	California	75,051,203,000	13.8%
26	Colorado	6,750,953,000	1.2%
25	Connecticut	6,982,566,000	1.3%
43	Delaware	2,132,984,000	0.4%
5	Florida	25,604,831,000	4.7%
13	Georgia	11,624,933,000	2.1%
40	Hawaii	2,619,061,000	0.5%
42	Idaho	2,260,612,000	0.4%
7	Illinois	19,422,277,000	3.6%
17	Indiana	10,614,671,000	2.0%
31	Iowa	5,522,364,000	1.0%
34	Kansas	3,822,474,000	0.7%
21	Kentucky	8,285,945,000	1.5%
23	Louisiana	8,000,477,000	1.5%
36	Maine	3,396,015,000	0.6%
16	Maryland	11,014,022,000	2.0%
8	Massachusetts	16,444,421,000	3.0%
10	Michigan	13,888,145,000	2.6%
11	Minnesota	13,368,605,000	2.5%
32	Mississippi	5,441,258,000	1.0%
22	Missouri	8,213,862,000	1.5%
47	Montana	1,523,666,000	0.3%
39	Nebraska	2,707,480,000	0.5%
38	Nevada	2,931,403,000	0.5%
45	New Hampshire	1,878,296,000	0.3%
9	New Jersey	15,263,099,000	2.8%
33	New Mexico	4,324,475,000	0.8%
2	New York	55,681,472,000	10.3%
12	North Carolina	12,786,380,000	2.4%
48	North Dakota	1,121,339,000	0.2%
6	Ohio	22,269,137,000	4.1%
29	Oklahoma	6,513,780,000	1.2%
24	Oregon	7,561,080,000	1.4%
4	Pennsylvania	26,512,667,000	4.9%
41	Rhode Island	2,474,947,000	0.5%
27	South Carolina	6,610,618,000	1.2%
49	South Dakota	993,541,000	0.2%
18	Tennessee	10,251,260,000	1.9%
3	Texas	32,513,562,000	6.0%
37	Utah	3,266,006,000	0.6%
46	Vermont	1,675,823,000	0.3%
15	Virginia	11,058,608,000	2.0%
19	Washington	9,959,197,000	1.8%
35	West Virginia	3,708,396,000	0.7%
14	Wisconsin	11,346,447,000	2.1%
50	Wyoming	818,690,000	0.2%

RANK ORDER

RANK	STATE	EXPENDITURES	% of USA
1	California	$75,051,203,000	13.8%
2	New York	55,681,472,000	10.3%
3	Texas	32,513,562,000	6.0%
4	Pennsylvania	26,512,667,000	4.9%
5	Florida	25,604,831,000	4.7%
6	Ohio	22,269,137,000	4.1%
7	Illinois	19,422,277,000	3.6%
8	Massachusetts	16,444,421,000	3.0%
9	New Jersey	15,263,099,000	2.8%
10	Michigan	13,888,145,000	2.6%
11	Minnesota	13,368,605,000	2.5%
12	North Carolina	12,786,380,000	2.4%
13	Georgia	11,624,933,000	2.1%
14	Wisconsin	11,346,447,000	2.1%
15	Virginia	11,058,608,000	2.0%
16	Maryland	11,014,022,000	2.0%
17	Indiana	10,614,671,000	2.0%
18	Tennessee	10,251,260,000	1.9%
19	Washington	9,959,197,000	1.8%
20	Arizona	8,897,641,000	1.6%
21	Kentucky	8,285,945,000	1.5%
22	Missouri	8,213,862,000	1.5%
23	Louisiana	8,000,477,000	1.5%
24	Oregon	7,561,080,000	1.4%
25	Connecticut	6,982,566,000	1.3%
26	Colorado	6,750,953,000	1.2%
27	South Carolina	6,610,618,000	1.2%
28	Alabama	6,522,927,000	1.2%
29	Oklahoma	6,513,780,000	1.2%
30	Arkansas	5,730,027,000	1.1%
31	Iowa	5,522,364,000	1.0%
32	Mississippi	5,441,258,000	1.0%
33	New Mexico	4,324,475,000	0.8%
34	Kansas	3,822,474,000	0.7%
35	West Virginia	3,708,396,000	0.7%
36	Maine	3,396,015,000	0.6%
37	Utah	3,266,006,000	0.6%
38	Nevada	2,931,403,000	0.5%
39	Nebraska	2,707,480,000	0.5%
40	Hawaii	2,619,061,000	0.5%
41	Rhode Island	2,474,947,000	0.5%
42	Idaho	2,260,612,000	0.4%
43	Delaware	2,132,984,000	0.4%
44	Alaska	2,094,542,000	0.4%
45	New Hampshire	1,878,296,000	0.3%
46	Vermont	1,675,823,000	0.3%
47	Montana	1,523,666,000	0.3%
48	North Dakota	1,121,339,000	0.2%
49	South Dakota	993,541,000	0.2%
50	Wyoming	818,690,000	0.2%
	District of Columbia	3,110,924,000	0.6%

Source: U.S. Bureau of the Census, Governments Division
"2014 State and Local Government Finances" (http://www.census.gov/govs/local/)
*Direct general expenditures. Includes funds for cash assistance programs, medical and other vendor payments, welfare institutions, and other public welfare programs.

Per Capita State and Local Government Expenditures for Public Welfare Programs in 2014
National Per Capita = $1,703*

ALPHA ORDER

RANK	STATE	PER CAPITA
39	Alabama	$1,347
1	Alaska	2,843
41	Arizona	1,324
15	Arkansas	1,931
14	California	1,940
45	Colorado	1,262
13	Connecticut	1,944
8	Delaware	2,281
43	Florida	1,287
48	Georgia	1,152
19	Hawaii	1,849
36	Idaho	1,384
29	Illinois	1,509
26	Indiana	1,609
22	Iowa	1,777
42	Kansas	1,318
18	Kentucky	1,878
23	Louisiana	1,721
4	Maine	2,552
20	Maryland	1,846
6	Massachusetts	2,436
35	Michigan	1,401
5	Minnesota	2,452
21	Mississippi	1,818
38	Missouri	1,355
30	Montana	1,490
31	Nebraska	1,439
50	Nevada	1,035
32	New Hampshire	1,414
24	New Jersey	1,710
9	New Mexico	2,076
2	New York	2,824
43	North Carolina	1,287
28	North Dakota	1,516
16	Ohio	1,921
25	Oklahoma	1,680
17	Oregon	1,905
10	Pennsylvania	2,073
7	Rhode Island	2,347
37	South Carolina	1,369
47	South Dakota	1,165
27	Tennessee	1,566
46	Texas	1,207
49	Utah	1,110
3	Vermont	2,673
40	Virginia	1,330
33	Washington	1,412
11	West Virginia	2,006
12	Wisconsin	1,970
34	Wyoming	1,403

RANK ORDER

RANK	STATE	PER CAPITA
1	Alaska	$2,843
2	New York	2,824
3	Vermont	2,673
4	Maine	2,552
5	Minnesota	2,452
6	Massachusetts	2,436
7	Rhode Island	2,347
8	Delaware	2,281
9	New Mexico	2,076
10	Pennsylvania	2,073
11	West Virginia	2,006
12	Wisconsin	1,970
13	Connecticut	1,944
14	California	1,940
15	Arkansas	1,931
16	Ohio	1,921
17	Oregon	1,905
18	Kentucky	1,878
19	Hawaii	1,849
20	Maryland	1,846
21	Mississippi	1,818
22	Iowa	1,777
23	Louisiana	1,721
24	New Jersey	1,710
25	Oklahoma	1,680
26	Indiana	1,609
27	Tennessee	1,566
28	North Dakota	1,516
29	Illinois	1,509
30	Montana	1,490
31	Nebraska	1,439
32	New Hampshire	1,414
33	Washington	1,412
34	Wyoming	1,403
35	Michigan	1,401
36	Idaho	1,384
37	South Carolina	1,369
38	Missouri	1,355
39	Alabama	1,347
40	Virginia	1,330
41	Arizona	1,324
42	Kansas	1,318
43	Florida	1,287
43	North Carolina	1,287
45	Colorado	1,262
46	Texas	1,207
47	South Dakota	1,165
48	Georgia	1,152
49	Utah	1,110
50	Nevada	1,035
	District of Columbia	4,721

Source: CQ Press using data from U.S. Bureau of the Census, Governments Division
"2014 State and Local Government Finances" (http://www.census.gov/govs/local/)
*Direct general expenditures. Includes funds for cash assistance programs, medical and other vendor payments, welfare institutions, and other public welfare programs.

State and Local Government Spending for Public Welfare Programs as a Percent of All State and Local Government Expenditures in 2014
National Percent = 20.0%*

ALPHA ORDER

RANK	STATE	PERCENT
32	Alabama	18.0
48	Alaska	14.4
21	Arizona	20.8
3	Arkansas	25.8
22	California	20.2
47	Colorado	15.5
24	Connecticut	19.5
17	Delaware	22.3
30	Florida	18.5
37	Georgia	17.7
27	Hawaii	19.1
19	Idaho	21.8
35	Illinois	17.8
18	Indiana	22.2
27	Iowa	19.1
43	Kansas	15.9
7	Kentucky	24.8
25	Louisiana	19.4
1	Maine	29.4
23	Maryland	19.8
8	Massachusetts	24.3
31	Michigan	18.3
2	Minnesota	26.0
16	Mississippi	22.5
26	Missouri	19.2
33	Montana	17.9
38	Nebraska	17.3
43	Nevada	15.9
29	New Hampshire	18.6
38	New Jersey	17.3
12	New Mexico	23.1
15	New York	22.7
35	North Carolina	17.8
49	North Dakota	13.7
11	Ohio	23.3
14	Oklahoma	22.8
20	Oregon	21.6
9	Pennsylvania	23.9
4	Rhode Island	25.5
33	South Carolina	17.9
45	South Dakota	15.6
10	Tennessee	23.6
40	Texas	16.5
45	Utah	15.6
6	Vermont	24.9
41	Virginia	16.4
42	Washington	16.1
5	West Virginia	25.1
13	Wisconsin	23.0
50	Wyoming	10.7

RANK ORDER

RANK	STATE	PERCENT
1	Maine	29.4
2	Minnesota	26.0
3	Arkansas	25.8
4	Rhode Island	25.5
5	West Virginia	25.1
6	Vermont	24.9
7	Kentucky	24.8
8	Massachusetts	24.3
9	Pennsylvania	23.9
10	Tennessee	23.6
11	Ohio	23.3
12	New Mexico	23.1
13	Wisconsin	23.0
14	Oklahoma	22.8
15	New York	22.7
16	Mississippi	22.5
17	Delaware	22.3
18	Indiana	22.2
19	Idaho	21.8
20	Oregon	21.6
21	Arizona	20.8
22	California	20.2
23	Maryland	19.8
24	Connecticut	19.5
25	Louisiana	19.4
26	Missouri	19.2
27	Hawaii	19.1
27	Iowa	19.1
29	New Hampshire	18.6
30	Florida	18.5
31	Michigan	18.3
32	Alabama	18.0
33	Montana	17.9
33	South Carolina	17.9
35	Illinois	17.8
35	North Carolina	17.8
37	Georgia	17.7
38	Nebraska	17.3
38	New Jersey	17.3
40	Texas	16.5
41	Virginia	16.4
42	Washington	16.1
43	Kansas	15.9
43	Nevada	15.9
45	South Dakota	15.6
45	Utah	15.6
47	Colorado	15.5
48	Alaska	14.4
49	North Dakota	13.7
50	Wyoming	10.7

District of Columbia 26.0

Source: CQ Press using data from U.S. Bureau of the Census, Governments Division
"2014 State and Local Government Finances" (http://www.census.gov/govs/local/)
*As a percent of direct general expenditures. Includes funds for cash assistance programs, medical and other vendor payments, welfare institutions, and other public welfare programs.

Social Security (OASDI) Payments in 2014

National Total = $843,243,000,000*

ALPHA ORDER					RANK ORDER			

RANK	STATE	PAYMENTS	% of USA	RANK	STATE	PAYMENTS	% of USA
20	Alabama	$15,314,000,000	1.8%	1	California	$78,795,000,000	9.3%
50	Alaska	1,215,000,000	0.1%	2	Florida	60,672,000,000	7.2%
18	Arizona	17,722,000,000	2.1%	3	Texas	53,527,000,000	6.3%
30	Arkansas	9,113,000,000	1.1%	4	New York	52,284,000,000	6.2%
1	California	78,795,000,000	9.3%	5	Pennsylvania	40,805,000,000	4.8%
27	Colorado	11,449,000,000	1.3%	6	Ohio	32,669,000,000	3.9%
29	Connecticut	10,417,000,000	1.2%	7	Michigan	32,591,000,000	3.8%
44	Delaware	2,973,000,000	0.4%	8	Illinois	32,186,000,000	3.8%
2	Florida	60,672,000,000	7.2%	9	North Carolina	27,935,000,000	3.3%
11	Georgia	23,702,000,000	2.8%	10	New Jersey	25,141,000,000	3.0%
42	Hawaii	3,613,000,000	0.4%	11	Georgia	23,702,000,000	2.8%
40	Idaho	4,285,000,000	0.5%	12	Virginia	20,679,000,000	2.4%
8	Illinois	32,186,000,000	3.8%	13	Tennessee	19,401,000,000	2.3%
14	Indiana	19,337,000,000	2.3%	14	Indiana	19,337,000,000	2.3%
31	Iowa	8,971,000,000	1.1%	15	Washington	18,391,000,000	2.2%
33	Kansas	7,741,000,000	0.9%	16	Massachusetts	17,908,000,000	2.1%
24	Kentucky	13,054,000,000	1.5%	17	Missouri	17,726,000,000	2.1%
26	Louisiana	11,499,000,000	1.4%	18	Arizona	17,722,000,000	2.1%
39	Maine	4,362,000,000	0.5%	19	Wisconsin	17,119,000,000	2.0%
23	Maryland	14,133,000,000	1.7%	20	Alabama	15,314,000,000	1.8%
16	Massachusetts	17,908,000,000	2.1%	21	South Carolina	14,961,000,000	1.8%
7	Michigan	32,591,000,000	3.8%	22	Minnesota	14,317,000,000	1.7%
22	Minnesota	14,317,000,000	1.7%	23	Maryland	14,133,000,000	1.7%
32	Mississippi	8,583,000,000	1.0%	24	Kentucky	13,054,000,000	1.5%
17	Missouri	17,726,000,000	2.1%	25	Oregon	11,595,000,000	1.4%
45	Montana	2,930,000,000	0.3%	26	Louisiana	11,499,000,000	1.4%
38	Nebraska	4,699,000,000	0.6%	27	Colorado	11,449,000,000	1.3%
34	Nevada	6,852,000,000	0.8%	28	Oklahoma	10,494,000,000	1.2%
41	New Hampshire	4,256,000,000	0.5%	29	Connecticut	10,417,000,000	1.2%
10	New Jersey	25,141,000,000	3.0%	30	Arkansas	9,113,000,000	1.1%
36	New Mexico	5,366,000,000	0.6%	31	Iowa	8,971,000,000	1.1%
4	New York	52,284,000,000	6.2%	32	Mississippi	8,583,000,000	1.0%
9	North Carolina	27,935,000,000	3.3%	33	Kansas	7,741,000,000	0.9%
48	North Dakota	1,726,000,000	0.2%	34	Nevada	6,852,000,000	0.8%
6	Ohio	32,669,000,000	3.9%	35	West Virginia	6,608,000,000	0.8%
28	Oklahoma	10,494,000,000	1.2%	36	New Mexico	5,366,000,000	0.6%
25	Oregon	11,595,000,000	1.4%	37	Utah	5,289,000,000	0.6%
5	Pennsylvania	40,805,000,000	4.8%	38	Nebraska	4,699,000,000	0.6%
43	Rhode Island	3,146,000,000	0.4%	39	Maine	4,362,000,000	0.5%
21	South Carolina	14,961,000,000	1.8%	40	Idaho	4,285,000,000	0.5%
46	South Dakota	2,265,000,000	0.3%	41	New Hampshire	4,256,000,000	0.5%
13	Tennessee	19,401,000,000	2.3%	42	Hawaii	3,613,000,000	0.4%
3	Texas	53,527,000,000	6.3%	43	Rhode Island	3,146,000,000	0.4%
37	Utah	5,289,000,000	0.6%	44	Delaware	2,973,000,000	0.4%
47	Vermont	2,009,000,000	0.2%	45	Montana	2,930,000,000	0.3%
12	Virginia	20,679,000,000	2.4%	46	South Dakota	2,265,000,000	0.3%
15	Washington	18,391,000,000	2.2%	47	Vermont	2,009,000,000	0.2%
35	West Virginia	6,608,000,000	0.8%	48	North Dakota	1,726,000,000	0.2%
19	Wisconsin	17,119,000,000	2.0%	49	Wyoming	1,481,000,000	0.2%
49	Wyoming	1,481,000,000	0.2%	50	Alaska	1,215,000,000	0.1%
					District of Columbia	1,058,000,000	0.1%

Source: U.S. Department of Health and Human Services, Social Security Administration
"Social Security Bulletin, Annual Statistical Supplement 2015" (https://www.ssa.gov/policy/docs/statcomps/supplement/)
*"OASDI" is Old Age, Survivors and Disability Insurance. National total includes $13,879,000,000 in payments to recipients in U.S. territories and foreign countries.

Per Capita Social Security (OASDI) Payments in 2014

National Per Capita = $2,619*

ALPHA ORDER

RANK	STATE	PER CAPITA
8	Alabama	$3,162
50	Alaska	1,649
31	Arizona	2,637
10	Arkansas	3,072
47	California	2,037
46	Colorado	2,140
19	Connecticut	2,900
7	Delaware	3,180
11	Florida	3,051
44	Georgia	2,350
36	Hawaii	2,551
33	Idaho	2,623
38	Illinois	2,501
16	Indiana	2,932
20	Iowa	2,886
27	Kansas	2,670
15	Kentucky	2,958
41	Louisiana	2,474
3	Maine	3,278
43	Maryland	2,368
29	Massachusetts	2,653
2	Michigan	3,287
32	Minnesota	2,625
21	Mississippi	2,868
17	Missouri	2,925
22	Montana	2,864
39	Nebraska	2,498
42	Nevada	2,419
5	New Hampshire	3,203
24	New Jersey	2,817
35	New Mexico	2,576
30	New York	2,652
25	North Carolina	2,812
45	North Dakota	2,333
23	Ohio	2,818
26	Oklahoma	2,706
18	Oregon	2,922
6	Pennsylvania	3,190
12	Rhode Island	2,983
9	South Carolina	3,099
28	South Dakota	2,657
14	Tennessee	2,964
48	Texas	1,987
49	Utah	1,798
4	Vermont	3,204
40	Virginia	2,486
34	Washington	2,607
1	West Virginia	3,575
13	Wisconsin	2,973
37	Wyoming	2,538

RANK ORDER

RANK	STATE	PER CAPITA
1	West Virginia	$3,575
2	Michigan	3,287
3	Maine	3,278
4	Vermont	3,204
5	New Hampshire	3,203
6	Pennsylvania	3,190
7	Delaware	3,180
8	Alabama	3,162
9	South Carolina	3,099
10	Arkansas	3,072
11	Florida	3,051
12	Rhode Island	2,983
13	Wisconsin	2,973
14	Tennessee	2,964
15	Kentucky	2,958
16	Indiana	2,932
17	Missouri	2,925
18	Oregon	2,922
19	Connecticut	2,900
20	Iowa	2,886
21	Mississippi	2,868
22	Montana	2,864
23	Ohio	2,818
24	New Jersey	2,817
25	North Carolina	2,812
26	Oklahoma	2,706
27	Kansas	2,670
28	South Dakota	2,657
29	Massachusetts	2,653
30	New York	2,652
31	Arizona	2,637
32	Minnesota	2,625
33	Idaho	2,623
34	Washington	2,607
35	New Mexico	2,576
36	Hawaii	2,551
37	Wyoming	2,538
38	Illinois	2,501
39	Nebraska	2,498
40	Virginia	2,486
41	Louisiana	2,474
42	Nevada	2,419
43	Maryland	2,368
44	Georgia	2,350
45	North Dakota	2,333
46	Colorado	2,140
47	California	2,037
48	Texas	1,987
49	Utah	1,798
50	Alaska	1,649

District of Columbia   1,605

Source: CQ Press using data from U.S. Department of Health and Human Services, Social Security Administration

"Social Security Bulletin, Annual Statistical Supplement 2015" (https://www.ssa.gov/policy/docs/statcomps/supplement/)

*"OASDI" is Old Age, Survivors and Disability Insurance. National per capita does not include payments or population in U.S. territories and foreign countries.

Social Security (OASDI) Monthly Payments in 2014

National Total = $71,693,353,000*

<table>
<tr><td colspan="4">ALPHA ORDER</td><td colspan="4">RANK ORDER</td></tr>
<tr><th>RANK</th><th>STATE</th><th>PAYMENTS</th><th>% of USA</th><th>RANK</th><th>STATE</th><th>PAYMENTS</th><th>% of USA</th></tr>
<tr><td>20</td><td>Alabama</td><td>$1,276,223,000</td><td>1.8%</td><td>1</td><td>California</td><td>$6,701,027,000</td><td>9.3%</td></tr>
<tr><td>50</td><td>Alaska</td><td>103,133,000</td><td>0.1%</td><td>2</td><td>Florida</td><td>5,190,945,000</td><td>7.2%</td></tr>
<tr><td>16</td><td>Arizona</td><td>1,517,597,000</td><td>2.1%</td><td>3</td><td>Texas</td><td>4,502,644,000</td><td>6.3%</td></tr>
<tr><td>30</td><td>Arkansas</td><td>761,036,000</td><td>1.1%</td><td>4</td><td>New York</td><td>4,421,858,000</td><td>6.2%</td></tr>
<tr><td>1</td><td>California</td><td>6,701,027,000</td><td>9.3%</td><td>5</td><td>Pennsylvania</td><td>3,432,758,000</td><td>4.8%</td></tr>
<tr><td>26</td><td>Colorado</td><td>977,802,000</td><td>1.4%</td><td>6</td><td>Michigan</td><td>2,736,513,000</td><td>3.8%</td></tr>
<tr><td>28</td><td>Connecticut</td><td>885,983,000</td><td>1.2%</td><td>7</td><td>Ohio</td><td>2,725,919,000</td><td>3.8%</td></tr>
<tr><td>44</td><td>Delaware</td><td>254,374,000</td><td>0.4%</td><td>8</td><td>Illinois</td><td>2,707,116,000</td><td>3.8%</td></tr>
<tr><td>2</td><td>Florida</td><td>5,190,945,000</td><td>7.2%</td><td>9</td><td>North Carolina</td><td>2,375,750,000</td><td>3.3%</td></tr>
<tr><td>11</td><td>Georgia</td><td>2,006,085,000</td><td>2.8%</td><td>10</td><td>New Jersey</td><td>2,134,807,000</td><td>3.0%</td></tr>
<tr><td>42</td><td>Hawaii</td><td>310,833,000</td><td>0.4%</td><td>11</td><td>Georgia</td><td>2,006,085,000</td><td>2.8%</td></tr>
<tr><td>40</td><td>Idaho</td><td>365,258,000</td><td>0.5%</td><td>12</td><td>Virginia</td><td>1,758,795,000</td><td>2.5%</td></tr>
<tr><td>8</td><td>Illinois</td><td>2,707,116,000</td><td>3.8%</td><td>13</td><td>Tennessee</td><td>1,633,490,000</td><td>2.3%</td></tr>
<tr><td>14</td><td>Indiana</td><td>1,626,829,000</td><td>2.3%</td><td>14</td><td>Indiana</td><td>1,626,829,000</td><td>2.3%</td></tr>
<tr><td>31</td><td>Iowa</td><td>758,169,000</td><td>1.1%</td><td>15</td><td>Washington</td><td>1,572,324,000</td><td>2.2%</td></tr>
<tr><td>33</td><td>Kansas</td><td>653,569,000</td><td>0.9%</td><td>16</td><td>Arizona</td><td>1,517,597,000</td><td>2.1%</td></tr>
<tr><td>24</td><td>Kentucky</td><td>1,081,642,000</td><td>1.5%</td><td>17</td><td>Massachusetts</td><td>1,517,385,000</td><td>2.1%</td></tr>
<tr><td>27</td><td>Louisiana</td><td>944,524,000</td><td>1.3%</td><td>18</td><td>Missouri</td><td>1,487,510,000</td><td>2.1%</td></tr>
<tr><td>39</td><td>Maine</td><td>368,682,000</td><td>0.5%</td><td>19</td><td>Wisconsin</td><td>1,454,566,000</td><td>2.0%</td></tr>
<tr><td>23</td><td>Maryland</td><td>1,203,106,000</td><td>1.7%</td><td>20</td><td>Alabama</td><td>1,276,223,000</td><td>1.8%</td></tr>
<tr><td>17</td><td>Massachusetts</td><td>1,517,385,000</td><td>2.1%</td><td>21</td><td>South Carolina</td><td>1,272,517,000</td><td>1.8%</td></tr>
<tr><td>6</td><td>Michigan</td><td>2,736,513,000</td><td>3.8%</td><td>22</td><td>Minnesota</td><td>1,220,801,000</td><td>1.7%</td></tr>
<tr><td>22</td><td>Minnesota</td><td>1,220,801,000</td><td>1.7%</td><td>23</td><td>Maryland</td><td>1,203,106,000</td><td>1.7%</td></tr>
<tr><td>32</td><td>Mississippi</td><td>714,962,000</td><td>1.0%</td><td>24</td><td>Kentucky</td><td>1,081,642,000</td><td>1.5%</td></tr>
<tr><td>18</td><td>Missouri</td><td>1,487,510,000</td><td>2.1%</td><td>25</td><td>Oregon</td><td>990,560,000</td><td>1.4%</td></tr>
<tr><td>45</td><td>Montana</td><td>248,665,000</td><td>0.3%</td><td>26</td><td>Colorado</td><td>977,802,000</td><td>1.4%</td></tr>
<tr><td>38</td><td>Nebraska</td><td>397,847,000</td><td>0.6%</td><td>27</td><td>Louisiana</td><td>944,524,000</td><td>1.3%</td></tr>
<tr><td>34</td><td>Nevada</td><td>588,318,000</td><td>0.8%</td><td>28</td><td>Connecticut</td><td>885,983,000</td><td>1.2%</td></tr>
<tr><td>41</td><td>New Hampshire</td><td>363,341,000</td><td>0.5%</td><td>29</td><td>Oklahoma</td><td>877,523,000</td><td>1.2%</td></tr>
<tr><td>10</td><td>New Jersey</td><td>2,134,807,000</td><td>3.0%</td><td>30</td><td>Arkansas</td><td>761,036,000</td><td>1.1%</td></tr>
<tr><td>36</td><td>New Mexico</td><td>453,482,000</td><td>0.6%</td><td>31</td><td>Iowa</td><td>758,169,000</td><td>1.1%</td></tr>
<tr><td>4</td><td>New York</td><td>4,421,858,000</td><td>6.2%</td><td>32</td><td>Mississippi</td><td>714,962,000</td><td>1.0%</td></tr>
<tr><td>9</td><td>North Carolina</td><td>2,375,750,000</td><td>3.3%</td><td>33</td><td>Kansas</td><td>653,569,000</td><td>0.9%</td></tr>
<tr><td>48</td><td>North Dakota</td><td>144,728,000</td><td>0.2%</td><td>34</td><td>Nevada</td><td>588,318,000</td><td>0.8%</td></tr>
<tr><td>7</td><td>Ohio</td><td>2,725,919,000</td><td>3.8%</td><td>35</td><td>West Virginia</td><td>544,609,000</td><td>0.8%</td></tr>
<tr><td>29</td><td>Oklahoma</td><td>877,523,000</td><td>1.2%</td><td>36</td><td>New Mexico</td><td>453,482,000</td><td>0.6%</td></tr>
<tr><td>25</td><td>Oregon</td><td>990,560,000</td><td>1.4%</td><td>37</td><td>Utah</td><td>449,903,000</td><td>0.6%</td></tr>
<tr><td>5</td><td>Pennsylvania</td><td>3,432,758,000</td><td>4.8%</td><td>38</td><td>Nebraska</td><td>397,847,000</td><td>0.6%</td></tr>
<tr><td>43</td><td>Rhode Island</td><td>266,541,000</td><td>0.4%</td><td>39</td><td>Maine</td><td>368,682,000</td><td>0.5%</td></tr>
<tr><td>21</td><td>South Carolina</td><td>1,272,517,000</td><td>1.8%</td><td>40</td><td>Idaho</td><td>365,258,000</td><td>0.5%</td></tr>
<tr><td>46</td><td>South Dakota</td><td>192,240,000</td><td>0.3%</td><td>41</td><td>New Hampshire</td><td>363,341,000</td><td>0.5%</td></tr>
<tr><td>13</td><td>Tennessee</td><td>1,633,490,000</td><td>2.3%</td><td>42</td><td>Hawaii</td><td>310,833,000</td><td>0.4%</td></tr>
<tr><td>3</td><td>Texas</td><td>4,502,644,000</td><td>6.3%</td><td>43</td><td>Rhode Island</td><td>266,541,000</td><td>0.4%</td></tr>
<tr><td>37</td><td>Utah</td><td>449,903,000</td><td>0.6%</td><td>44</td><td>Delaware</td><td>254,374,000</td><td>0.4%</td></tr>
<tr><td>47</td><td>Vermont</td><td>170,863,000</td><td>0.2%</td><td>45</td><td>Montana</td><td>248,665,000</td><td>0.3%</td></tr>
<tr><td>12</td><td>Virginia</td><td>1,758,795,000</td><td>2.5%</td><td>46</td><td>South Dakota</td><td>192,240,000</td><td>0.3%</td></tr>
<tr><td>15</td><td>Washington</td><td>1,572,324,000</td><td>2.2%</td><td>47</td><td>Vermont</td><td>170,863,000</td><td>0.2%</td></tr>
<tr><td>35</td><td>West Virginia</td><td>544,609,000</td><td>0.8%</td><td>48</td><td>North Dakota</td><td>144,728,000</td><td>0.2%</td></tr>
<tr><td>19</td><td>Wisconsin</td><td>1,454,566,000</td><td>2.0%</td><td>49</td><td>Wyoming</td><td>126,060,000</td><td>0.2%</td></tr>
<tr><td>49</td><td>Wyoming</td><td>126,060,000</td><td>0.2%</td><td>50</td><td>Alaska</td><td>103,133,000</td><td>0.1%</td></tr>
<tr><td></td><td></td><td></td><td></td><td></td><td>District of Columbia</td><td>89,987,000</td><td>0.1%</td></tr>
</table>

Source: U.S. Department of Health and Human Services, Social Security Administration
"Social Security Bulletin, Annual Statistical Supplement 2015" (https://www.ssa.gov/policy/docs/statcomps/supplement/)
*For December 2014. "OASDI" is Old Age, Survivors and Disability Insurance. National total includes $1,132,154,000 in payments to recipients in U.S. territories and foreign countries.

Social Security (OASDI) Beneficiaries in 2014

National Total = 59,007,158*

ALPHA ORDER

RANK	STATE	BENEFICIARIES	% of USA
20	Alabama	1,095,925	1.9%
50	Alaska	89,047	0.2%
18	Arizona	1,207,102	2.0%
29	Arkansas	673,193	1.1%
1	California	5,538,810	9.4%
27	Colorado	794,937	1.3%
30	Connecticut	654,533	1.1%
45	Delaware	192,187	0.3%
2	Florida	4,223,274	7.2%
10	Georgia	1,676,778	2.8%
42	Hawaii	251,591	0.4%
40	Idaho	306,264	0.5%
7	Illinois	2,155,290	3.7%
14	Indiana	1,286,099	2.2%
32	Iowa	616,301	1.0%
33	Kansas	521,955	0.9%
23	Kentucky	954,284	1.6%
25	Louisiana	854,211	1.4%
39	Maine	325,496	0.6%
24	Maryland	936,372	1.6%
17	Massachusetts	1,224,469	2.1%
8	Michigan	2,121,776	3.6%
22	Minnesota	965,018	1.6%
31	Mississippi	640,772	1.1%
15	Missouri	1,246,269	2.1%
44	Montana	212,535	0.4%
38	Nebraska	326,078	0.6%
34	Nevada	475,811	0.8%
41	New Hampshire	283,983	0.5%
11	New Jersey	1,568,016	2.7%
36	New Mexico	399,987	0.7%
4	New York	3,482,978	5.9%
9	North Carolina	1,948,531	3.3%
48	North Dakota	124,372	0.2%
6	Ohio	2,267,508	3.8%
28	Oklahoma	749,794	1.3%
26	Oregon	798,156	1.4%
5	Pennsylvania	2,722,892	4.6%
43	Rhode Island	216,029	0.4%
21	South Carolina	1,040,971	1.8%
46	South Dakota	165,499	0.3%
13	Tennessee	1,371,562	2.3%
3	Texas	3,842,249	6.5%
37	Utah	365,730	0.6%
47	Vermont	140,634	0.2%
12	Virginia	1,415,661	2.4%
16	Washington	1,230,039	2.1%
35	West Virginia	464,823	0.8%
19	Wisconsin	1,153,149	2.0%
49	Wyoming	101,296	0.2%

RANK ORDER

RANK	STATE	BENEFICIARIES	% of USA
1	California	5,538,810	9.4%
2	Florida	4,223,274	7.2%
3	Texas	3,842,249	6.5%
4	New York	3,482,978	5.9%
5	Pennsylvania	2,722,892	4.6%
6	Ohio	2,267,508	3.8%
7	Illinois	2,155,290	3.7%
8	Michigan	2,121,776	3.6%
9	North Carolina	1,948,531	3.3%
10	Georgia	1,676,778	2.8%
11	New Jersey	1,568,016	2.7%
12	Virginia	1,415,661	2.4%
13	Tennessee	1,371,562	2.3%
14	Indiana	1,286,099	2.2%
15	Missouri	1,246,269	2.1%
16	Washington	1,230,039	2.1%
17	Massachusetts	1,224,469	2.1%
18	Arizona	1,207,102	2.0%
19	Wisconsin	1,153,149	2.0%
20	Alabama	1,095,925	1.9%
21	South Carolina	1,040,971	1.8%
22	Minnesota	965,018	1.6%
23	Kentucky	954,284	1.6%
24	Maryland	936,372	1.6%
25	Louisiana	854,211	1.4%
26	Oregon	798,156	1.4%
27	Colorado	794,937	1.3%
28	Oklahoma	749,794	1.3%
29	Arkansas	673,193	1.1%
30	Connecticut	654,533	1.1%
31	Mississippi	640,772	1.1%
32	Iowa	616,301	1.0%
33	Kansas	521,955	0.9%
34	Nevada	475,811	0.8%
35	West Virginia	464,823	0.8%
36	New Mexico	399,987	0.7%
37	Utah	365,730	0.6%
38	Nebraska	326,078	0.6%
39	Maine	325,496	0.6%
40	Idaho	306,264	0.5%
41	New Hampshire	283,983	0.5%
42	Hawaii	251,591	0.4%
43	Rhode Island	216,029	0.4%
44	Montana	212,535	0.4%
45	Delaware	192,187	0.3%
46	South Dakota	165,499	0.3%
47	Vermont	140,634	0.2%
48	North Dakota	124,372	0.2%
49	Wyoming	101,296	0.2%
50	Alaska	89,047	0.2%
	District of Columbia	79,716	0.1%

Source: U.S. Department of Health and Human Services, Social Security Administration
"Social Security Bulletin, Annual Statistical Supplement 2015" (https://www.ssa.gov/policy/docs/statcomps/supplement/)
*For December 2014. "OASDI" is Old Age, Survivors and Disability Insurance. National total includes 1,507,206 beneficiaries in U.S. territories and foreign countries.

Average Monthly Social Security (OASDI) Payment in 2014

National Average = $1,227 Each Month per Beneficiary*

ALPHA ORDER				RANK ORDER		
RANK	STATE	PER BENEFICIARY		RANK	STATE	PER BENEFICIARY
41	Alabama	$1,165		1	New Jersey	$1,361
44	Alaska	1,158		2	Connecticut	1,354
13	Arizona	1,257		3	Delaware	1,324
48	Arkansas	1,130		4	Michigan	1,290
31	California	1,210		5	Maryland	1,285
23	Colorado	1,230		6	New Hampshire	1,279
2	Connecticut	1,354		7	Washington	1,278
3	Delaware	1,324		8	New York	1,270
26	Florida	1,229		9	Indiana	1,265
33	Georgia	1,196		9	Minnesota	1,265
21	Hawaii	1,235		11	Pennsylvania	1,261
35	Idaho	1,193		11	Wisconsin	1,261
14	Illinois	1,256		13	Arizona	1,257
9	Indiana	1,265		14	Illinois	1,256
23	Iowa	1,230		15	Kansas	1,252
15	Kansas	1,252		16	Wyoming	1,244
46	Kentucky	1,133		17	Virginia	1,242
50	Louisiana	1,106		18	Oregon	1,241
46	Maine	1,133		19	Massachusetts	1,239
5	Maryland	1,285		20	Nevada	1,236
19	Massachusetts	1,239		21	Hawaii	1,235
4	Michigan	1,290		22	Rhode Island	1,234
9	Minnesota	1,265		23	Colorado	1,230
49	Mississippi	1,116		23	Iowa	1,230
34	Missouri	1,194		23	Utah	1,230
39	Montana	1,170		26	Florida	1,229
28	Nebraska	1,220		27	South Carolina	1,222
20	Nevada	1,236		28	Nebraska	1,220
6	New Hampshire	1,279		29	North Carolina	1,219
1	New Jersey	1,361		30	Vermont	1,215
45	New Mexico	1,134		31	California	1,210
8	New York	1,270		32	Ohio	1,202
29	North Carolina	1,219		33	Georgia	1,196
42	North Dakota	1,164		34	Missouri	1,194
32	Ohio	1,202		35	Idaho	1,193
39	Oklahoma	1,170		36	Tennessee	1,191
18	Oregon	1,241		37	Texas	1,172
11	Pennsylvania	1,261		37	West Virginia	1,172
22	Rhode Island	1,234		39	Montana	1,170
27	South Carolina	1,222		39	Oklahoma	1,170
43	South Dakota	1,162		41	Alabama	1,165
36	Tennessee	1,191		42	North Dakota	1,164
37	Texas	1,172		43	South Dakota	1,162
23	Utah	1,230		44	Alaska	1,158
30	Vermont	1,215		45	New Mexico	1,134
17	Virginia	1,242		46	Kentucky	1,133
7	Washington	1,278		46	Maine	1,133
37	West Virginia	1,172		48	Arkansas	1,130
11	Wisconsin	1,261		49	Mississippi	1,116
16	Wyoming	1,244		50	Louisiana	1,106
					District of Columbia	1,129

Source: CQ Press using data from U.S. Department of Health and Human Services, Social Security Administration
"Social Security Bulletin, Annual Statistical Supplement 2015" (https://www.ssa.gov/policy/docs/statcomps/supplement/)
*As of December 2014. "OASDI" is Old Age, Survivors and Disability Insurance. National average does not include
beneficiaries or payments in U.S. territories or foreign countries.

Social Security Supplemental Security Income Beneficiaries in 2014

National Total = 8,335,704 Beneficiaries*

ALPHA ORDER

RANK	STATE	BENEFICIARIES	% of USA
16	Alabama	174,544	2.1%
48	Alaska	12,424	0.1%
22	Arizona	119,308	1.4%
26	Arkansas	111,464	1.3%
1	California	1,305,589	15.7%
31	Colorado	72,831	0.9%
33	Connecticut	63,244	0.8%
45	Delaware	16,655	0.2%
4	Florida	560,809	6.7%
9	Georgia	256,197	3.1%
42	Hawaii	25,215	0.3%
40	Idaho	30,451	0.4%
8	Illinois	275,772	3.3%
20	Indiana	127,944	1.5%
34	Iowa	51,223	0.6%
36	Kansas	48,870	0.6%
12	Kentucky	188,535	2.3%
15	Louisiana	181,261	2.2%
37	Maine	37,627	0.5%
24	Maryland	118,153	1.4%
11	Massachusetts	188,606	2.3%
7	Michigan	277,362	3.3%
28	Minnesota	94,215	1.1%
21	Mississippi	125,603	1.5%
19	Missouri	142,743	1.7%
44	Montana	18,249	0.2%
41	Nebraska	27,683	0.3%
35	Nevada	50,714	0.6%
43	New Hampshire	19,656	0.2%
14	New Jersey	181,864	2.2%
32	New Mexico	64,072	0.8%
3	New York	654,316	7.8%
10	North Carolina	235,256	2.8%
49	North Dakota	8,237	0.1%
6	Ohio	313,170	3.8%
27	Oklahoma	96,969	1.2%
29	Oregon	85,051	1.0%
5	Pennsylvania	373,914	4.5%
38	Rhode Island	33,345	0.4%
23	South Carolina	118,245	1.4%
47	South Dakota	14,880	0.2%
13	Tennessee	183,778	2.2%
2	Texas	665,989	8.0%
39	Utah	31,163	0.4%
46	Vermont	15,825	0.2%
17	Virginia	155,434	1.9%
18	Washington	151,180	1.8%
30	West Virginia	77,725	0.9%
25	Wisconsin	117,641	1.4%
50	Wyoming	6,807	0.1%

RANK ORDER

RANK	STATE	BENEFICIARIES	% of USA
1	California	1,305,589	15.7%
2	Texas	665,989	8.0%
3	New York	654,316	7.8%
4	Florida	560,809	6.7%
5	Pennsylvania	373,914	4.5%
6	Ohio	313,170	3.8%
7	Michigan	277,362	3.3%
8	Illinois	275,772	3.3%
9	Georgia	256,197	3.1%
10	North Carolina	235,256	2.8%
11	Massachusetts	188,606	2.3%
12	Kentucky	188,535	2.3%
13	Tennessee	183,778	2.2%
14	New Jersey	181,864	2.2%
15	Louisiana	181,261	2.2%
16	Alabama	174,544	2.1%
17	Virginia	155,434	1.9%
18	Washington	151,180	1.8%
19	Missouri	142,743	1.7%
20	Indiana	127,944	1.5%
21	Mississippi	125,603	1.5%
22	Arizona	119,308	1.4%
23	South Carolina	118,245	1.4%
24	Maryland	118,153	1.4%
25	Wisconsin	117,641	1.4%
26	Arkansas	111,464	1.3%
27	Oklahoma	96,969	1.2%
28	Minnesota	94,215	1.1%
29	Oregon	85,051	1.0%
30	West Virginia	77,725	0.9%
31	Colorado	72,831	0.9%
32	New Mexico	64,072	0.8%
33	Connecticut	63,244	0.8%
34	Iowa	51,223	0.6%
35	Nevada	50,714	0.6%
36	Kansas	48,870	0.6%
37	Maine	37,627	0.5%
38	Rhode Island	33,345	0.4%
39	Utah	31,163	0.4%
40	Idaho	30,451	0.4%
41	Nebraska	27,683	0.3%
42	Hawaii	25,215	0.3%
43	New Hampshire	19,656	0.2%
44	Montana	18,249	0.2%
45	Delaware	16,655	0.2%
46	Vermont	15,825	0.2%
47	South Dakota	14,880	0.2%
48	Alaska	12,424	0.1%
49	North Dakota	8,237	0.1%
50	Wyoming	6,807	0.1%
	District of Columbia	26,852	0.3%

Source: U.S. Department of Health and Human Services, Social Security Administration
"Social Security Bulletin, Annual Statistical Supplement 2015" (https://www.ssa.gov/policy/docs/statcomps/supplement/)
*For December 2014. National total includes1,044 beneficiaries in U.S. territories or otherwise not distributed by state. The SSI program provides income support to persons age 65 and older and blind or disabled adults and children.

Average Monthly Social Security
Supplemental Security Income Payment in 2014
National Average = $516.62 Each Month per Beneficiary*

ALPHA ORDER

RANK	STATE	AVERAGE BENEFIT
34	Alabama	$504.26
40	Alaska	494.94
11	Arizona	525.11
24	Arkansas	511.65
27	California	510.39
25	Colorado	511.17
13	Connecticut	521.61
12	Delaware	522.47
20	Florida	516.73
23	Georgia	511.93
21	Hawaii	516.46
30	Idaho	508.35
5	Illinois	538.39
8	Indiana	526.63
44	Iowa	492.35
28	Kansas	510.21
22	Kentucky	513.55
18	Louisiana	518.27
46	Maine	486.56
4	Maryland	539.54
19	Massachusetts	516.83
2	Michigan	541.53
7	Minnesota	528.03
39	Mississippi	497.61
32	Missouri	507.81
45	Montana	489.15
42	Nebraska	493.05
10	Nevada	525.21
41	New Hampshire	493.68
37	New Jersey	498.81
43	New Mexico	492.95
9	New York	525.97
36	North Carolina	499.47
50	North Dakota	464.15
6	Ohio	537.62
26	Oklahoma	510.82
15	Oregon	520.97
1	Pennsylvania	543.42
16	Rhode Island	518.82
35	South Carolina	501.46
49	South Dakota	481.83
33	Tennessee	506.89
38	Texas	497.92
29	Utah	509.83
48	Vermont	485.78
31	Virginia	508.13
3	Washington	541.42
17	West Virginia	518.49
14	Wisconsin	520.98
47	Wyoming	485.90

RANK ORDER

RANK	STATE	AVERAGE BENEFIT
1	Pennsylvania	$543.42
2	Michigan	541.53
3	Washington	541.42
4	Maryland	539.54
5	Illinois	538.39
6	Ohio	537.62
7	Minnesota	528.03
8	Indiana	526.63
9	New York	525.97
10	Nevada	525.21
11	Arizona	525.11
12	Delaware	522.47
13	Connecticut	521.61
14	Wisconsin	520.98
15	Oregon	520.97
16	Rhode Island	518.82
17	West Virginia	518.49
18	Louisiana	518.27
19	Massachusetts	516.83
20	Florida	516.73
21	Hawaii	516.46
22	Kentucky	513.55
23	Georgia	511.93
24	Arkansas	511.65
25	Colorado	511.17
26	Oklahoma	510.82
27	California	510.39
28	Kansas	510.21
29	Utah	509.83
30	Idaho	508.35
31	Virginia	508.13
32	Missouri	507.81
33	Tennessee	506.89
34	Alabama	504.26
35	South Carolina	501.46
36	North Carolina	499.47
37	New Jersey	498.81
38	Texas	497.92
39	Mississippi	497.61
40	Alaska	494.94
41	New Hampshire	493.68
42	Nebraska	493.05
43	New Mexico	492.95
44	Iowa	492.35
45	Montana	489.15
46	Maine	486.56
47	Wyoming	485.90
48	Vermont	485.78
49	South Dakota	481.83
50	North Dakota	464.15
	District of Columbia	560.99

Source: U.S. Department of Health and Human Services, Social Security Administration
"Social Security Bulletin, Annual Statistical Supplement 2015" (https://www.ssa.gov/policy/docs/statcomps/supplement/)
*As of December 2014. National average includes payments to beneficiaries in U.S. territories and foreign countries. The SSI program provides income support to persons age 65 and older and blind or disabled adults and children.

Medicare Enrollees in 2015

National Total = 55,584,149 Enrollees*

RANK	STATE	ENROLLEES	% of USA
20	Alabama	969,195	1.7%
50	Alaska	84,065	0.2%
18	Arizona	1,136,440	2.0%
30	Arkansas	595,242	1.1%
1	California	5,655,925	10.2%
26	Colorado	786,473	1.4%
29	Connecticut	631,287	1.1%
45	Delaware	180,731	0.3%
2	Florida	4,029,249	7.2%
10	Georgia	1,521,936	2.7%
42	Hawaii	244,786	0.4%
40	Idaho	282,322	0.5%
7	Illinois	2,069,252	3.7%
16	Indiana	1,151,972	2.1%
31	Iowa	572,457	1.0%
33	Kansas	487,578	0.9%
24	Kentucky	863,953	1.6%
25	Louisiana	794,082	1.4%
39	Maine	306,808	0.6%
22	Maryland	932,023	1.7%
14	Massachusetts	1,219,918	2.2%
8	Michigan	1,897,517	3.4%
23	Minnesota	913,362	1.6%
32	Mississippi	560,883	1.0%
17	Missouri	1,137,461	2.0%
44	Montana	201,533	0.4%
38	Nebraska	314,062	0.6%
34	Nevada	453,726	0.8%
41	New Hampshire	266,504	0.5%
11	New Jersey	1,494,408	2.7%
36	New Mexico	373,362	0.7%
4	New York	3,349,461	6.0%
9	North Carolina	1,771,186	3.2%
48	North Dakota	119,001	0.2%
6	Ohio	2,156,972	3.9%
28	Oklahoma	679,606	1.2%
27	Oregon	755,475	1.4%
5	Pennsylvania	2,536,760	4.6%
43	Rhode Island	203,515	0.4%
21	South Carolina	942,234	1.7%
46	South Dakota	156,252	0.3%
13	Tennessee	1,237,091	2.2%
3	Texas	3,638,829	6.5%
37	Utah	345,970	0.6%
47	Vermont	131,558	0.2%
12	Virginia	1,351,001	2.4%
15	Washington	1,191,991	2.1%
35	West Virginia	417,255	0.8%
19	Wisconsin	1,051,152	1.9%
49	Wyoming	95,167	0.2%

RANK	STATE	ENROLLEES	% of USA
1	California	5,655,925	10.2%
2	Florida	4,029,249	7.2%
3	Texas	3,638,829	6.5%
4	New York	3,349,461	6.0%
5	Pennsylvania	2,536,760	4.6%
6	Ohio	2,156,972	3.9%
7	Illinois	2,069,252	3.7%
8	Michigan	1,897,517	3.4%
9	North Carolina	1,771,186	3.2%
10	Georgia	1,521,936	2.7%
11	New Jersey	1,494,408	2.7%
12	Virginia	1,351,001	2.4%
13	Tennessee	1,237,091	2.2%
14	Massachusetts	1,219,918	2.2%
15	Washington	1,191,991	2.1%
16	Indiana	1,151,972	2.1%
17	Missouri	1,137,461	2.0%
18	Arizona	1,136,440	2.0%
19	Wisconsin	1,051,152	1.9%
20	Alabama	969,195	1.7%
21	South Carolina	942,234	1.7%
22	Maryland	932,023	1.7%
23	Minnesota	913,362	1.6%
24	Kentucky	863,953	1.6%
25	Louisiana	794,082	1.4%
26	Colorado	786,473	1.4%
27	Oregon	755,475	1.4%
28	Oklahoma	679,606	1.2%
29	Connecticut	631,287	1.1%
30	Arkansas	595,242	1.1%
31	Iowa	572,457	1.0%
32	Mississippi	560,883	1.0%
33	Kansas	487,578	0.9%
34	Nevada	453,726	0.8%
35	West Virginia	417,255	0.8%
36	New Mexico	373,362	0.7%
37	Utah	345,970	0.6%
38	Nebraska	314,062	0.6%
39	Maine	306,808	0.6%
40	Idaho	282,322	0.5%
41	New Hampshire	266,504	0.5%
42	Hawaii	244,786	0.4%
43	Rhode Island	203,515	0.4%
44	Montana	201,533	0.4%
45	Delaware	180,731	0.3%
46	South Dakota	156,252	0.3%
47	Vermont	131,558	0.2%
48	North Dakota	119,001	0.2%
49	Wyoming	95,167	0.2%
50	Alaska	84,065	0.2%
	District of Columbia	88,684	0.2%

Source: U.S. Department of Health and Human Services, Centers for Medicare and Medicaid Services
"Medicare Enrollment Dashboard"
(https://www.cms.gov/Research-Statistics-Data-and-Systems/Statistics-Trends-and-Reports/CMSProgramStatistics/Dashboard.html)
*Includes original Medicare, Medicare Advantage, and other Medicare health plans. Total includes 1,236,483 enrollees in Puerto Rico and other outlying areas, foreign countries, or whose address is unknown.

Percent of Population Enrolled in Medicare in 2015

National Percent = 16.9% of Population*

RANK	STATE	PERCENT
4	Alabama	20.0
50	Alaska	11.4
34	Arizona	16.7
4	Arkansas	20.0
46	California	14.5
47	Colorado	14.4
25	Connecticut	17.6
13	Delaware	19.1
7	Florida	19.9
45	Georgia	14.9
29	Hawaii	17.2
30	Idaho	17.1
40	Illinois	16.1
27	Indiana	17.4
20	Iowa	18.3
33	Kansas	16.8
9	Kentucky	19.5
31	Louisiana	17.0
1	Maine	23.1
44	Maryland	15.5
23	Massachusetts	18.0
13	Michigan	19.1
34	Minnesota	16.7
15	Mississippi	18.8
18	Missouri	18.7
9	Montana	19.5
37	Nebraska	16.6
42	Nevada	15.7
4	New Hampshire	20.0
34	New Jersey	16.7
24	New Mexico	17.9
31	New York	17.0
25	North Carolina	17.6
42	North Dakota	15.7
19	Ohio	18.6
27	Oklahoma	17.4
15	Oregon	18.8
8	Pennsylvania	19.8
11	Rhode Island	19.3
12	South Carolina	19.2
21	South Dakota	18.2
15	Tennessee	18.8
48	Texas	13.3
49	Utah	11.6
3	Vermont	21.0
40	Virginia	16.1
37	Washington	16.6
2	West Virginia	22.7
21	Wisconsin	18.2
39	Wyoming	16.2

RANK	STATE	PERCENT
1	Maine	23.1
2	West Virginia	22.7
3	Vermont	21.0
4	Alabama	20.0
4	Arkansas	20.0
4	New Hampshire	20.0
7	Florida	19.9
8	Pennsylvania	19.8
9	Kentucky	19.5
9	Montana	19.5
11	Rhode Island	19.3
12	South Carolina	19.2
13	Delaware	19.1
13	Michigan	19.1
15	Mississippi	18.8
15	Oregon	18.8
15	Tennessee	18.8
18	Missouri	18.7
19	Ohio	18.6
20	Iowa	18.3
21	South Dakota	18.2
21	Wisconsin	18.2
23	Massachusetts	18.0
24	New Mexico	17.9
25	Connecticut	17.6
25	North Carolina	17.6
27	Indiana	17.4
27	Oklahoma	17.4
29	Hawaii	17.2
30	Idaho	17.1
31	Louisiana	17.0
31	New York	17.0
33	Kansas	16.8
34	Arizona	16.7
34	Minnesota	16.7
34	New Jersey	16.7
37	Nebraska	16.6
37	Washington	16.6
39	Wyoming	16.2
40	Illinois	16.1
40	Virginia	16.1
42	Nevada	15.7
42	North Dakota	15.7
44	Maryland	15.5
45	Georgia	14.9
46	California	14.5
47	Colorado	14.4
48	Texas	13.3
49	Utah	11.6
50	Alaska	11.4

	District of Columbia	13.2

Source: CQ Press using data from U.S. Department of Health and Human Services, Centers for Medicare and Medicaid Services
    "Medicare Enrollment Dashboard"
    (https://www.cms.gov/Research-Statistics-Data-and-Systems/Statistics-Trends-and-Reports/CMSProgramStatistics/Dashboard.html)
*Includes original Medicare, Medicare Advantage, and other Medicare health plans. National rate does not include enrollees or
population in Puerto Rico and other outlying areas, foreign countries, or whose address is unknown.

Medicare Actual Costs in 2014

National Total = $323,949,765,345*

ALPHA ORDER

RANK	STATE	ACTUAL COSTS	% of USA
20	Alabama	$5,802,325,140	1.8%
50	Alaska	613,283,588	0.2%
22	Arizona	5,295,888,954	1.6%
29	Arkansas	3,643,000,340	1.1%
1	California	28,627,234,000	8.8%
30	Colorado	3,454,839,335	1.1%
26	Connecticut	4,661,395,514	1.4%
41	Delaware	1,521,814,949	0.5%
2	Florida	24,022,251,982	7.4%
12	Georgia	8,615,373,199	2.7%
48	Hawaii	724,044,531	0.2%
42	Idaho	1,342,920,225	0.4%
5	Illinois	14,427,405,413	4.5%
15	Indiana	7,706,209,605	2.4%
28	Iowa	3,667,784,157	1.1%
31	Kansas	3,425,975,531	1.1%
23	Kentucky	5,264,528,311	1.6%
21	Louisiana	5,319,216,431	1.6%
38	Maine	1,820,112,402	0.6%
13	Maryland	8,229,334,246	2.5%
11	Massachusetts	9,011,751,761	2.8%
8	Michigan	12,439,662,151	3.8%
32	Minnesota	3,227,949,433	1.0%
27	Mississippi	4,341,822,511	1.3%
16	Missouri	6,837,678,982	2.1%
43	Montana	1,097,189,888	0.3%
36	Nebraska	2,189,038,211	0.7%
34	Nevada	2,506,825,983	0.8%
37	New Hampshire	1,884,763,147	0.6%
7	New Jersey	12,598,629,473	3.9%
39	New Mexico	1,697,692,946	0.5%
4	New York	20,134,675,129	6.2%
10	North Carolina	10,182,275,189	3.1%
47	North Dakota	751,408,257	0.2%
9	Ohio	11,492,048,709	3.5%
25	Oklahoma	4,769,948,934	1.5%
33	Oregon	2,791,411,830	0.9%
6	Pennsylvania	13,236,775,808	4.1%
44	Rhode Island	1,078,135,801	0.3%
19	South Carolina	5,812,896,393	1.8%
45	South Dakota	947,297,116	0.3%
17	Tennessee	6,674,629,838	2.1%
3	Texas	24,005,829,572	7.4%
40	Utah	1,596,643,740	0.5%
46	Vermont	894,370,468	0.3%
14	Virginia	8,132,123,064	2.5%
18	Washington	5,923,324,680	1.8%
35	West Virginia	2,403,234,000	0.7%
24	Wisconsin	5,098,167,206	1.6%
49	Wyoming	669,185,375	0.2%

RANK ORDER

RANK	STATE	ACTUAL COSTS	% of USA
1	California	$28,627,234,000	8.8%
2	Florida	24,022,251,982	7.4%
3	Texas	24,005,829,572	7.4%
4	New York	20,134,675,129	6.2%
5	Illinois	14,427,405,413	4.5%
6	Pennsylvania	13,236,775,808	4.1%
7	New Jersey	12,598,629,473	3.9%
8	Michigan	12,439,662,151	3.8%
9	Ohio	11,492,048,709	3.5%
10	North Carolina	10,182,275,189	3.1%
11	Massachusetts	9,011,751,761	2.8%
12	Georgia	8,615,373,199	2.7%
13	Maryland	8,229,334,246	2.5%
14	Virginia	8,132,123,064	2.5%
15	Indiana	7,706,209,605	2.4%
16	Missouri	6,837,678,982	2.1%
17	Tennessee	6,674,629,838	2.1%
18	Washington	5,923,324,680	1.8%
19	South Carolina	5,812,896,393	1.8%
20	Alabama	5,802,325,140	1.8%
21	Louisiana	5,319,216,431	1.6%
22	Arizona	5,295,888,954	1.6%
23	Kentucky	5,264,528,311	1.6%
24	Wisconsin	5,098,167,206	1.6%
25	Oklahoma	4,769,948,934	1.5%
26	Connecticut	4,661,395,514	1.4%
27	Mississippi	4,341,822,511	1.3%
28	Iowa	3,667,784,157	1.1%
29	Arkansas	3,643,000,340	1.1%
30	Colorado	3,454,839,335	1.1%
31	Kansas	3,425,975,531	1.1%
32	Minnesota	3,227,949,433	1.0%
33	Oregon	2,791,411,830	0.9%
34	Nevada	2,506,825,983	0.8%
35	West Virginia	2,403,234,000	0.7%
36	Nebraska	2,189,038,211	0.7%
37	New Hampshire	1,884,763,147	0.6%
38	Maine	1,820,112,402	0.6%
39	New Mexico	1,697,692,946	0.5%
40	Utah	1,596,643,740	0.5%
41	Delaware	1,521,814,949	0.5%
42	Idaho	1,342,920,225	0.4%
43	Montana	1,097,189,888	0.3%
44	Rhode Island	1,078,135,801	0.3%
45	South Dakota	947,297,116	0.3%
46	Vermont	894,370,468	0.3%
47	North Dakota	751,408,257	0.2%
48	Hawaii	724,044,531	0.2%
49	Wyoming	669,185,375	0.2%
50	Alaska	613,283,588	0.2%
	District of Columbia	695,950,736	0.2%

Source: U.S. Department of Health and Human Services, Centers for Medicare and Medicaid Services
"Medicare Geographic Variation" (Public Use File)
(https://www.cms.gov/Research-Statistics-Data-and-Systems/Statistics-Trends-and-Reports/Medicare-Geographic-Variation/)
*Total actual costs not standardized for geographical variations. National figure includes payments to enrollees in Puerto Rico and other outlying areas.

Medicare Actual Costs per Beneficiary in 2014

National Rate = $6,275*

ALPHA ORDER

RANK	STATE	PER BENEFICIARY
30	Alabama	$6,238
4	Alaska	8,313
44	Arizona	5,044
26	Arkansas	6,324
39	California	5,601
47	Colorado	4,818
6	Connecticut	7,999
3	Delaware	8,994
28	Florida	6,282
32	Georgia	6,046
50	Hawaii	3,298
43	Idaho	5,045
9	Illinois	7,489
17	Indiana	6,964
20	Iowa	6,635
12	Kansas	7,379
25	Kentucky	6,359
16	Louisiana	7,066
29	Maine	6,259
1	Maryland	9,884
5	Massachusetts	8,060
18	Michigan	6,755
49	Minnesota	3,732
7	Mississippi	7,975
27	Missouri	6,287
36	Montana	5,762
11	Nebraska	7,399
31	Nevada	6,118
8	New Hampshire	7,765
2	New Jersey	9,189
46	New Mexico	4,948
22	New York	6,502
33	North Carolina	5,974
19	North Dakota	6,643
38	Ohio	5,614
13	Oklahoma	7,365
48	Oregon	3,950
40	Pennsylvania	5,505
35	Rhode Island	5,799
23	South Carolina	6,486
24	South Dakota	6,406
37	Tennessee	5,619
15	Texas	7,082
42	Utah	5,073
14	Vermont	7,230
21	Virginia	6,530
41	Washington	5,391
34	West Virginia	5,914
45	Wisconsin	5,043
10	Wyoming	7,460

RANK ORDER

RANK	STATE	PER BENEFICIARY
1	Maryland	$9,884
2	New Jersey	9,189
3	Delaware	8,994
4	Alaska	8,313
5	Massachusetts	8,060
6	Connecticut	7,999
7	Mississippi	7,975
8	New Hampshire	7,765
9	Illinois	7,489
10	Wyoming	7,460
11	Nebraska	7,399
12	Kansas	7,379
13	Oklahoma	7,365
14	Vermont	7,230
15	Texas	7,082
16	Louisiana	7,066
17	Indiana	6,964
18	Michigan	6,755
19	North Dakota	6,643
20	Iowa	6,635
21	Virginia	6,530
22	New York	6,502
23	South Carolina	6,486
24	South Dakota	6,406
25	Kentucky	6,359
26	Arkansas	6,324
27	Missouri	6,287
28	Florida	6,282
29	Maine	6,259
30	Alabama	6,238
31	Nevada	6,118
32	Georgia	6,046
33	North Carolina	5,974
34	West Virginia	5,914
35	Rhode Island	5,799
36	Montana	5,762
37	Tennessee	5,619
38	Ohio	5,614
39	California	5,601
40	Pennsylvania	5,505
41	Washington	5,391
42	Utah	5,073
43	Idaho	5,045
44	Arizona	5,044
45	Wisconsin	5,043
46	New Mexico	4,948
47	Colorado	4,818
48	Oregon	3,950
49	Minnesota	3,732
50	Hawaii	3,298

District of Columbia — 9,570

Source: CQ Press using data from U.S. Department of Health and Human Services, Centers for Medicare and Medicaid Services "Medicare Geographic Variation" (Public Use File)
(https://www.cms.gov/Research-Statistics-Data-and-Systems/Statistics-Trends-and-Reports/Medicare-Geographic-Variation/)
*Total actual costs not standardized for geographical variations. National figure includes payments and enrollees in Puerto Rico and other outlying areas.

Medicaid Enrollment in 2014

National Total = 71,705,460 Enrollees*

ALPHA ORDER

RANK	STATE	ENROLLEES	% of USA
24	Alabama	1,054,941	1.5%
46	Alaska	132,556	0.2%
12	Arizona	1,548,325	2.2%
32	Arkansas	595,807	0.8%
1	California	11,522,853	16.1%
23	Colorado	1,079,699	1.5%
30	Connecticut	724,741	1.0%
43	Delaware	227,554	0.3%
5	Florida	3,531,945	4.9%
9	Georgia	1,961,085	2.7%
37	Hawaii	321,027	0.4%
39	Idaho	266,172	0.4%
6	Illinois	3,249,835	4.5%
20	Indiana	1,176,447	1.6%
33	Iowa	593,572	0.8%
36	Kansas	399,299	0.6%
18	Kentucky	1,209,552	1.7%
15	Louisiana	1,305,671	1.8%
41	Maine	262,334	0.4%
14	Maryland	1,309,260	1.8%
10	Massachusetts	1,878,120	2.6%
4	Michigan	3,871,806	5.4%
21	Minnesota	1,112,174	1.6%
31	Mississippi	699,153	1.0%
28	Missouri	825,974	1.2%
47	Montana	131,923	0.2%
42	Nebraska	242,578	0.3%
34	Nevada	533,734	0.7%
45	New Hampshire	142,315	0.2%
13	New Jersey	1,542,022	2.2%
29	New Mexico	727,214	1.0%
2	New York	5,845,589	8.2%
11	North Carolina	1,717,658	2.4%
49	North Dakota	79,031	0.1%
7	Ohio	2,796,017	3.9%
27	Oklahoma	826,434	1.2%
25	Oregon	1,051,645	1.5%
8	Pennsylvania	2,152,846	3.0%
40	Rhode Island	263,574	0.4%
22	South Carolina	1,089,973	1.5%
48	South Dakota	122,352	0.2%
16	Tennessee	1,288,631	1.8%
3	Texas	4,137,121	5.8%
38	Utah	287,754	0.4%
44	Vermont	188,337	0.3%
26	Virginia	961,843	1.3%
17	Washington	1,245,322	1.7%
35	West Virginia	486,839	0.7%
19	Wisconsin	1,199,773	1.7%
50	Wyoming	68,320	0.1%

RANK ORDER

RANK	STATE	ENROLLEES	% of USA
1	California	11,522,853	16.1%
2	New York	5,845,589	8.2%
3	Texas	4,137,121	5.8%
4	Michigan	3,871,806	5.4%
5	Florida	3,531,945	4.9%
6	Illinois	3,249,835	4.5%
7	Ohio	2,796,017	3.9%
8	Pennsylvania	2,152,846	3.0%
9	Georgia	1,961,085	2.7%
10	Massachusetts	1,878,120	2.6%
11	North Carolina	1,717,658	2.4%
12	Arizona	1,548,325	2.2%
13	New Jersey	1,542,022	2.2%
14	Maryland	1,309,260	1.8%
15	Louisiana	1,305,671	1.8%
16	Tennessee	1,288,631	1.8%
17	Washington	1,245,322	1.7%
18	Kentucky	1,209,552	1.7%
19	Wisconsin	1,199,773	1.7%
20	Indiana	1,176,447	1.6%
21	Minnesota	1,112,174	1.6%
22	South Carolina	1,089,973	1.5%
23	Colorado	1,079,699	1.5%
24	Alabama	1,054,941	1.5%
25	Oregon	1,051,645	1.5%
26	Virginia	961,843	1.3%
27	Oklahoma	826,434	1.2%
28	Missouri	825,974	1.2%
29	New Mexico	727,214	1.0%
30	Connecticut	724,741	1.0%
31	Mississippi	699,153	1.0%
32	Arkansas	595,807	0.8%
33	Iowa	593,572	0.8%
34	Nevada	533,734	0.7%
35	West Virginia	486,839	0.7%
36	Kansas	399,299	0.6%
37	Hawaii	321,027	0.4%
38	Utah	287,754	0.4%
39	Idaho	266,172	0.4%
40	Rhode Island	263,574	0.4%
41	Maine	262,334	0.4%
42	Nebraska	242,578	0.3%
43	Delaware	227,554	0.3%
44	Vermont	188,337	0.3%
45	New Hampshire	142,315	0.2%
46	Alaska	132,556	0.2%
47	Montana	131,923	0.2%
48	South Dakota	122,352	0.2%
49	North Dakota	79,031	0.1%
50	Wyoming	68,320	0.1%
	District of Columbia	257,450	0.4%

Source: U.S. Department of Health and Human Services, Centers for Medicare and Medicaid Services
    "2014 Medicaid Managed Care Enrollment Report" (https://www.medicaid.gov/medicaid/managed-care/enrollment/index.html)
*Unduplicated enrollment as of July 1, 2014. National total includes 1,459,263 Medicaid enrollees in Puerto Rico.

Percent of Population Enrolled in Medicaid in 2014

National Percent = 22.1% of Population*

ALPHA ORDER

RANK	STATE	PERCENT
20	Alabama	21.8
32	Alaska	18.0
16	Arizona	23.0
26	Arkansas	20.1
4	California	29.8
24	Colorado	20.2
24	Connecticut	20.2
13	Delaware	24.3
33	Florida	17.8
29	Georgia	19.4
17	Hawaii	22.7
39	Idaho	16.3
11	Illinois	25.3
33	Indiana	17.8
30	Iowa	19.1
42	Kansas	13.8
8	Kentucky	27.4
6	Louisiana	28.1
27	Maine	19.7
19	Maryland	21.9
7	Massachusetts	27.8
1	Michigan	39.0
23	Minnesota	20.4
15	Mississippi	23.4
43	Missouri	13.6
44	Montana	12.9
44	Nebraska	12.9
31	Nevada	18.8
48	New Hampshire	10.7
36	New Jersey	17.3
2	New Mexico	34.9
5	New York	29.6
36	North Carolina	17.3
48	North Dakota	10.7
14	Ohio	24.1
21	Oklahoma	21.3
9	Oregon	26.5
38	Pennsylvania	16.8
12	Rhode Island	25.0
18	South Carolina	22.6
41	South Dakota	14.4
27	Tennessee	19.7
40	Texas	15.4
50	Utah	9.8
3	Vermont	30.0
47	Virginia	11.6
35	Washington	17.7
10	West Virginia	26.3
22	Wisconsin	20.8
46	Wyoming	11.7

RANK ORDER

RANK	STATE	PERCENT
1	Michigan	39.0
2	New Mexico	34.9
3	Vermont	30.0
4	California	29.8
5	New York	29.6
6	Louisiana	28.1
7	Massachusetts	27.8
8	Kentucky	27.4
9	Oregon	26.5
10	West Virginia	26.3
11	Illinois	25.3
12	Rhode Island	25.0
13	Delaware	24.3
14	Ohio	24.1
15	Mississippi	23.4
16	Arizona	23.0
17	Hawaii	22.7
18	South Carolina	22.6
19	Maryland	21.9
20	Alabama	21.8
21	Oklahoma	21.3
22	Wisconsin	20.8
23	Minnesota	20.4
24	Colorado	20.2
24	Connecticut	20.2
26	Arkansas	20.1
27	Maine	19.7
27	Tennessee	19.7
29	Georgia	19.4
30	Iowa	19.1
31	Nevada	18.8
32	Alaska	18.0
33	Florida	17.8
33	Indiana	17.8
35	Washington	17.7
36	New Jersey	17.3
36	North Carolina	17.3
38	Pennsylvania	16.8
39	Idaho	16.3
40	Texas	15.4
41	South Dakota	14.4
42	Kansas	13.8
43	Missouri	13.6
44	Montana	12.9
44	Nebraska	12.9
46	Wyoming	11.7
47	Virginia	11.6
48	New Hampshire	10.7
48	North Dakota	10.7
50	Utah	9.8
	District of Columbia	39.1

Source: CQ Press using data from U.S. Department of Health and Human Services, Centers for Medicare and Medicaid Services
"2014 Medicaid Managed Care Enrollment Report" (https://www.medicaid.gov/medicaid/managed-care/enrollment/index.html)
*Unduplicated enrollment as of July 1, 2013. National percent does not include recipients or population in U.S. territories.

Estimated Medicaid Expenditures in 2016

National Total = $558,298,000,000*

ALPHA ORDER

RANK	STATE	EXPENDITURES	% of USA
28	Alabama	$6,333,000,000	1.1%
46	Alaska	1,580,000,000	0.3%
12	Arizona	11,407,000,000	2.0%
27	Arkansas	6,505,000,000	1.2%
1	California	92,603,000,000	16.6%
21	Colorado	8,979,000,000	1.6%
26	Connecticut	7,216,000,000	1.3%
44	Delaware	1,852,000,000	0.3%
6	Florida	24,600,000,000	4.4%
17	Georgia	9,885,000,000	1.8%
40	Hawaii	2,149,000,000	0.4%
41	Idaho	2,097,000,000	0.4%
7	Illinois	19,272,000,000	3.5%
14	Indiana	11,271,000,000	2.0%
33	Iowa	5,123,000,000	0.9%
35	Kansas	3,494,000,000	0.6%
16	Kentucky	9,893,000,000	1.8%
24	Louisiana	7,951,000,000	1.4%
37	Maine	2,655,000,000	0.5%
18	Maryland	9,618,000,000	1.7%
9	Massachusetts	15,166,000,000	2.7%
8	Michigan	16,791,000,000	3.0%
13	Minnesota	11,358,000,000	2.0%
31	Mississippi	5,558,000,000	1.0%
19	Missouri	9,153,000,000	1.6%
47	Montana	1,295,000,000	0.2%
42	Nebraska	1,983,000,000	0.4%
36	Nevada	3,347,000,000	0.6%
43	New Hampshire	1,958,000,000	0.4%
10	New Jersey	14,303,000,000	2.6%
30	New Mexico	5,644,000,000	1.0%
2	New York	48,095,000,000	8.6%
11	North Carolina	13,699,000,000	2.5%
48	North Dakota	1,166,000,000	0.2%
5	Ohio	25,441,000,000	4.6%
32	Oklahoma	5,340,000,000	1.0%
20	Oregon	9,135,000,000	1.6%
4	Pennsylvania	28,986,000,000	5.2%
39	Rhode Island	2,502,000,000	0.4%
29	South Carolina	6,240,000,000	1.1%
49	South Dakota	856,000,000	0.2%
15	Tennessee	10,416,000,000	1.9%
3	Texas	42,090,000,000	7.5%
38	Utah	2,615,000,000	0.5%
45	Vermont	1,623,000,000	0.3%
22	Virginia	8,870,000,000	1.6%
25	Washington	7,574,000,000	1.4%
34	West Virginia	3,530,000,000	0.6%
23	Wisconsin	8,434,000,000	1.5%
50	Wyoming	647,000,000	0.1%

RANK ORDER

RANK	STATE	EXPENDITURES	% of USA
1	California	$92,603,000,000	16.6%
2	New York	48,095,000,000	8.6%
3	Texas	42,090,000,000	7.5%
4	Pennsylvania	28,986,000,000	5.2%
5	Ohio	25,441,000,000	4.6%
6	Florida	24,600,000,000	4.4%
7	Illinois	19,272,000,000	3.5%
8	Michigan	16,791,000,000	3.0%
9	Massachusetts	15,166,000,000	2.7%
10	New Jersey	14,303,000,000	2.6%
11	North Carolina	13,699,000,000	2.5%
12	Arizona	11,407,000,000	2.0%
13	Minnesota	11,358,000,000	2.0%
14	Indiana	11,271,000,000	2.0%
15	Tennessee	10,416,000,000	1.9%
16	Kentucky	9,893,000,000	1.8%
17	Georgia	9,885,000,000	1.8%
18	Maryland	9,618,000,000	1.7%
19	Missouri	9,153,000,000	1.6%
20	Oregon	9,135,000,000	1.6%
21	Colorado	8,979,000,000	1.6%
22	Virginia	8,870,000,000	1.6%
23	Wisconsin	8,434,000,000	1.5%
24	Louisiana	7,951,000,000	1.4%
25	Washington	7,574,000,000	1.4%
26	Connecticut	7,216,000,000	1.3%
27	Arkansas	6,505,000,000	1.2%
28	Alabama	6,333,000,000	1.1%
29	South Carolina	6,240,000,000	1.1%
30	New Mexico	5,644,000,000	1.0%
31	Mississippi	5,558,000,000	1.0%
32	Oklahoma	5,340,000,000	1.0%
33	Iowa	5,123,000,000	0.9%
34	West Virginia	3,530,000,000	0.6%
35	Kansas	3,494,000,000	0.6%
36	Nevada	3,347,000,000	0.6%
37	Maine	2,655,000,000	0.5%
38	Utah	2,615,000,000	0.5%
39	Rhode Island	2,502,000,000	0.4%
40	Hawaii	2,149,000,000	0.4%
41	Idaho	2,097,000,000	0.4%
42	Nebraska	1,983,000,000	0.4%
43	New Hampshire	1,958,000,000	0.4%
44	Delaware	1,852,000,000	0.3%
45	Vermont	1,623,000,000	0.3%
46	Alaska	1,580,000,000	0.3%
47	Montana	1,295,000,000	0.2%
48	North Dakota	1,166,000,000	0.2%
49	South Dakota	856,000,000	0.2%
50	Wyoming	647,000,000	0.1%
	District of Columbia**	NA	NA

Source: National Association of State Budget Officers
"State Expenditure Report" (http://www.nasbo.org)
*Estimates for fiscal year 2016.
**Not available.

Percent Change in Medicaid Expenditures: 2015 to 2016

National Percent Change = 6.9% Increase*

ALPHA ORDER			RANK ORDER		
RANK	STATE	PERCENT CHANGE	RANK	STATE	PERCENT CHANGE
30	Alabama	4.1	1	Indiana	23.0
40	Alaska	1.6	2	New Hampshire	21.1
49	Arizona	(3.1)	3	Montana	16.7
15	Arkansas	7.4	4	Colorado	15.9
10	California	10.4	5	Texas	15.2
4	Colorado	15.9	6	Mississippi	14.0
36	Connecticut	3.4	7	Nevada	12.5
47	Delaware	(1.2)	8	Illinois	12.0
11	Florida	9.1	9	Hawaii	10.5
41	Georgia	0.3	10	California	10.4
9	Hawaii	10.5	11	Florida	9.1
24	Idaho	5.0	11	Massachusetts	9.1
8	Illinois	12.0	11	New Mexico	9.1
1	Indiana	23.0	14	Virginia	7.7
37	Iowa	2.9	15	Arkansas	7.4
18	Kansas	6.5	16	Utah	7.2
31	Kentucky	3.9	17	Nebraska	6.9
31	Louisiana	3.9	18	Kansas	6.5
26	Maine	4.8	18	Pennsylvania	6.5
44	Maryland	(0.3)	20	Minnesota	6.0
11	Massachusetts	9.1	21	New York	5.3
29	Michigan	4.5	22	Missouri	5.1
20	Minnesota	6.0	22	Oregon	5.1
6	Mississippi	14.0	24	Idaho	5.0
22	Missouri	5.1	24	North Dakota	5.0
3	Montana	16.7	26	Maine	4.8
17	Nebraska	6.9	27	Ohio	4.6
7	Nevada	12.5	27	Vermont	4.6
2	New Hampshire	21.1	29	Michigan	4.5
33	New Jersey	3.8	30	Alabama	4.1
11	New Mexico	9.1	31	Kentucky	3.9
21	New York	5.3	31	Louisiana	3.9
46	North Carolina	(0.6)	33	New Jersey	3.8
24	North Dakota	5.0	34	Wyoming	3.7
27	Ohio	4.6	35	Tennessee	3.6
45	Oklahoma	(0.5)	36	Connecticut	3.4
22	Oregon	5.1	37	Iowa	2.9
18	Pennsylvania	6.5	38	Rhode Island	1.8
38	Rhode Island	1.8	38	South Dakota	1.8
41	South Carolina	0.3	40	Alaska	1.6
38	South Dakota	1.8	41	Georgia	0.3
35	Tennessee	3.6	41	South Carolina	0.3
5	Texas	15.2	43	West Virginia	0.0
16	Utah	7.2	44	Maryland	(0.3)
27	Vermont	4.6	45	Oklahoma	(0.5)
14	Virginia	7.7	46	North Carolina	(0.6)
48	Washington	(2.4)	47	Delaware	(1.2)
43	West Virginia	0.0	48	Washington	(2.4)
50	Wisconsin	(5.0)	49	Arizona	(3.1)
34	Wyoming	3.7	50	Wisconsin	(5.0)
				District of Columbia**	NA

Source: National Association of State Budget Officers
"State Expenditure Report" (http://www.nasbo.org)
*Estimates for fiscal year 2016.
**Not available.

Percent of Population Receiving Public Aid in 2014

National Percent = 3.6% of Population*

ALPHA ORDER

RANK	STATE	PERCENT
8	Alabama	4.3
28	Alaska	2.8
41	Arizona	2.2
11	Arkansas	4.2
1	California	6.3
41	Colorado	2.2
35	Connecticut	2.5
23	Delaware	3.2
21	Florida	3.3
28	Georgia	2.8
17	Hawaii	3.4
46	Idaho	2.0
35	Illinois	2.5
41	Indiana	2.2
33	Iowa	2.6
41	Kansas	2.2
2	Kentucky	5.5
11	Louisiana	4.2
15	Maine	3.6
28	Maryland	2.8
13	Massachusetts	3.8
17	Michigan	3.4
35	Minnesota	2.5
4	Mississippi	4.7
17	Missouri	3.4
35	Montana	2.5
45	Nebraska	2.1
26	Nevada	2.9
47	New Hampshire	1.9
32	New Jersey	2.7
4	New Mexico	4.7
6	New York	4.6
33	North Carolina	2.6
48	North Dakota	1.5
14	Ohio	3.7
26	Oklahoma	2.9
17	Oregon	3.4
8	Pennsylvania	4.3
7	Rhode Island	4.4
25	South Carolina	3.0
35	South Dakota	2.5
8	Tennessee	4.3
28	Texas	2.8
49	Utah	1.4
16	Vermont	3.5
35	Virginia	2.5
21	Washington	3.3
3	West Virginia	5.1
24	Wisconsin	3.1
50	Wyoming	1.3

RANK ORDER

RANK	STATE	PERCENT
1	California	6.3
2	Kentucky	5.5
3	West Virginia	5.1
4	Mississippi	4.7
4	New Mexico	4.7
6	New York	4.6
7	Rhode Island	4.4
8	Alabama	4.3
8	Pennsylvania	4.3
8	Tennessee	4.3
11	Arkansas	4.2
11	Louisiana	4.2
13	Massachusetts	3.8
14	Ohio	3.7
15	Maine	3.6
16	Vermont	3.5
17	Hawaii	3.4
17	Michigan	3.4
17	Missouri	3.4
17	Oregon	3.4
21	Florida	3.3
21	Washington	3.3
23	Delaware	3.2
24	Wisconsin	3.1
25	South Carolina	3.0
26	Nevada	2.9
26	Oklahoma	2.9
28	Alaska	2.8
28	Georgia	2.8
28	Maryland	2.8
28	Texas	2.8
32	New Jersey	2.7
33	Iowa	2.6
33	North Carolina	2.6
35	Connecticut	2.5
35	Illinois	2.5
35	Minnesota	2.5
35	Montana	2.5
35	South Dakota	2.5
35	Virginia	2.5
41	Arizona	2.2
41	Colorado	2.2
41	Indiana	2.2
41	Kansas	2.2
45	Nebraska	2.1
46	Idaho	2.0
47	New Hampshire	1.9
48	North Dakota	1.5
49	Utah	1.4
50	Wyoming	1.3

District of Columbia   6.4

Source: CQ Press using data from U.S. Department of Health and Human Services, Social Security Administration
"Social Security Bulletin, Annual Statistical Supplement 2015" (https://www.ssa.gov/policy/docs/statcomps/supplement/) and
U.S. Department of Health and Human Services, Administration for Children and Families
"TANF Caseload Data" (http://www.acf.hhs.gov/programs/ofa/programs/tanf/data-reports)
*As of December 2014. Includes recipients of Temporary Assistance to Needy Families (TANF) and/or Supplemental Security
Income payments.

Recipients of Temporary Assistance to Needy Families (TANF) Payments in 2016
National Total = 2,658,643 Monthly Recipients*

ALPHA ORDER

RANK	STATE	RECIPIENTS	% of USA
26	Alabama	23,557	0.9%
41	Alaska	8,466	0.3%
29	Arizona	20,048	0.8%
44	Arkansas	7,772	0.3%
1	California	959,956	36.1%
14	Colorado	43,003	1.6%
27	Connecticut	21,562	0.8%
36	Delaware	11,771	0.4%
5	Florida	76,021	2.9%
24	Georgia	23,764	0.9%
30	Hawaii	16,873	0.6%
48	Idaho	2,817	0.1%
19	Illinois	32,551	1.2%
32	Indiana	14,878	0.6%
23	Iowa	24,738	0.9%
35	Kansas	11,883	0.4%
11	Kentucky	45,512	1.7%
34	Louisiana	13,284	0.5%
42	Maine	7,904	0.3%
10	Maryland	51,255	1.9%
9	Massachusetts	56,969	2.1%
15	Michigan	39,018	1.5%
13	Minnesota	44,700	1.7%
37	Mississippi	11,086	0.4%
20	Missouri	29,974	1.1%
43	Montana	7,776	0.3%
38	Nebraska	10,579	0.4%
25	Nevada	23,564	0.9%
47	New Hampshire	4,639	0.2%
17	New Jersey	37,898	1.4%
21	New Mexico	28,925	1.1%
2	New York	238,021	9.0%
22	North Carolina	27,127	1.0%
49	North Dakota	2,594	0.1%
4	Ohio	105,525	4.0%
31	Oklahoma	15,590	0.6%
18	Oregon	36,377	1.4%
3	Pennsylvania	142,627	5.4%
39	Rhode Island	9,116	0.3%
28	South Carolina	20,508	0.8%
45	South Dakota	5,967	0.2%
6	Tennessee	66,162	2.5%
8	Texas	60,428	2.3%
40	Utah	9,107	0.3%
46	Vermont	5,788	0.2%
12	Virginia	44,714	1.7%
7	Washington	64,017	2.4%
33	West Virginia	14,527	0.5%
16	Wisconsin	37,978	1.4%
50	Wyoming	1,068	0.0%

RANK ORDER

RANK	STATE	RECIPIENTS	% of USA
1	California	959,956	36.1%
2	New York	238,021	9.0%
3	Pennsylvania	142,627	5.4%
4	Ohio	105,525	4.0%
5	Florida	76,021	2.9%
6	Tennessee	66,162	2.5%
7	Washington	64,017	2.4%
8	Texas	60,428	2.3%
9	Massachusetts	56,969	2.1%
10	Maryland	51,255	1.9%
11	Kentucky	45,512	1.7%
12	Virginia	44,714	1.7%
13	Minnesota	44,700	1.7%
14	Colorado	43,003	1.6%
15	Michigan	39,018	1.5%
16	Wisconsin	37,978	1.4%
17	New Jersey	37,898	1.4%
18	Oregon	36,377	1.4%
19	Illinois	32,551	1.2%
20	Missouri	29,974	1.1%
21	New Mexico	28,925	1.1%
22	North Carolina	27,127	1.0%
23	Iowa	24,738	0.9%
24	Georgia	23,764	0.9%
25	Nevada	23,564	0.9%
26	Alabama	23,557	0.9%
27	Connecticut	21,562	0.8%
28	South Carolina	20,508	0.8%
29	Arizona	20,048	0.8%
30	Hawaii	16,873	0.6%
31	Oklahoma	15,590	0.6%
32	Indiana	14,878	0.6%
33	West Virginia	14,527	0.5%
34	Louisiana	13,284	0.5%
35	Kansas	11,883	0.4%
36	Delaware	11,771	0.4%
37	Mississippi	11,086	0.4%
38	Nebraska	10,579	0.4%
39	Rhode Island	9,116	0.3%
40	Utah	9,107	0.3%
41	Alaska	8,466	0.3%
42	Maine	7,904	0.3%
43	Montana	7,776	0.3%
44	Arkansas	7,772	0.3%
45	South Dakota	5,967	0.2%
46	Vermont	5,788	0.2%
47	New Hampshire	4,639	0.2%
48	Idaho	2,817	0.1%
49	North Dakota	2,594	0.1%
50	Wyoming	1,068	0.0%
	District of Columbia	13,503	0.5%

Source: U.S. Department of Health and Human Services, Administration for Children and Families
"TANF Caseload Data" (http://www.acf.hhs.gov/programs/ofa/programs/tanf/data-reports)
*As of June 2016. National total includes 25,156 recipients in U.S. territories (22,429 in Puerto Rico).

Percent Change in TANF Recipients: 2015 to 2016

National Percent Change = 11.3% Decrease*

ALPHA ORDER				RANK ORDER		
RANK	STATE	PERCENT CHANGE		RANK	STATE	PERCENT CHANGE
43	Alabama	(20.2)		1	Wyoming	56.6
15	Alaska	(1.7)		2	Maryland	21.5
32	Arizona	(12.1)		3	Louisiana	16.9
47	Arkansas	(22.2)		4	Montana	11.0
34	California	(12.7)		5	Idaho	6.7
14	Colorado	(1.6)		6	Nebraska	6.4
37	Connecticut	(15.2)		7	Minnesota	5.3
20	Delaware	(6.2)		8	Utah	3.2
22	Florida	(7.4)		9	Oklahoma	2.6
18	Georgia	(4.7)		9	South Dakota	2.6
41	Hawaii	(18.7)		11	Vermont	2.2
5	Idaho	6.7		12	North Carolina	1.6
44	Illinois	(20.4)		13	New Mexico	0.0
30	Indiana	(11.4)		14	Colorado	(1.6)
24	Iowa	(8.5)		15	Alaska	(1.7)
32	Kansas	(12.1)		16	West Virginia	(3.8)
19	Kentucky	(6.1)		17	Ohio	(4.6)
3	Louisiana	16.9		18	Georgia	(4.7)
46	Maine	(20.6)		19	Kentucky	(6.1)
2	Maryland	21.5		20	Delaware	(6.2)
36	Massachusetts	(12.9)		21	New York	(6.3)
45	Michigan	(20.5)		22	Florida	(7.4)
7	Minnesota	5.3		23	North Dakota	(8.0)
35	Mississippi	(12.8)		24	Iowa	(8.5)
50	Missouri	(47.7)		25	Pennsylvania	(9.1)
4	Montana	11.0		26	Washington	(9.4)
6	Nebraska	6.4		27	Texas	(9.5)
30	Nevada	(11.4)		28	Virginia	(9.8)
39	New Hampshire	(16.3)		29	South Carolina	(10.7)
49	New Jersey	(28.7)		30	Indiana	(11.4)
13	New Mexico	0.0		30	Nevada	(11.4)
21	New York	(6.3)		32	Arizona	(12.1)
12	North Carolina	1.6		32	Kansas	(12.1)
23	North Dakota	(8.0)		34	California	(12.7)
17	Ohio	(4.6)		35	Mississippi	(12.8)
9	Oklahoma	2.6		36	Massachusetts	(12.9)
38	Oregon	(16.1)		37	Connecticut	(15.2)
25	Pennsylvania	(9.1)		38	Oregon	(16.1)
40	Rhode Island	(17.8)		39	New Hampshire	(16.3)
29	South Carolina	(10.7)		40	Rhode Island	(17.8)
9	South Dakota	2.6		41	Hawaii	(18.7)
42	Tennessee	(19.6)		42	Tennessee	(19.6)
27	Texas	(9.5)		43	Alabama	(20.2)
8	Utah	3.2		44	Illinois	(20.4)
11	Vermont	2.2		45	Michigan	(20.5)
28	Virginia	(9.8)		46	Maine	(20.6)
26	Washington	(9.4)		47	Arkansas	(22.2)
16	West Virginia	(3.8)		48	Wisconsin	(24.8)
48	Wisconsin	(24.8)		49	New Jersey	(28.7)
1	Wyoming	56.6		50	Missouri	(47.7)
					District of Columbia	(2.8)

Source: CQ Press using data from U.S. Department of Health and Human Services, Administration for Children and Families
  "TANF Caseload Data" (http://www.acf.hhs.gov/programs/ofa/programs/tanf/data-reports)
*June 2015 to June 2016. National percent includes recipients in U.S. territories.

TANF Work Participation Rates in 2014

National Rate = 45.3%*

	ALPHA ORDER				RANK ORDER	
RANK	STATE	PERCENT		RANK	STATE	PERCENT
25	Alabama	49.0		1	Illinois	94.7
31	Alaska	44.3		2	Idaho	91.5
48	Arizona	27.4		3	Maine	87.0
27	Arkansas	45.7		4	Wyoming	82.1
40	California	37.5		5	Ohio	76.2
39	Colorado	38.0		6	Wisconsin	72.5
19	Connecticut	53.1		7	New Hampshire	72.0
44	Delaware	36.1		8	Michigan	66.5
25	Florida	49.0		9	Nebraska	64.9
19	Georgia	53.1		10	South Dakota	62.8
23	Hawaii	51.7		11	Minnesota	60.1
2	Idaho	91.5		12	Oregon	59.9
1	Illinois	94.7		13	Massachusetts	59.0
42	Indiana	37.1		14	Kentucky	57.3
16	Iowa	55.7		15	North Dakota	56.6
32	Kansas	44.1		16	Iowa	55.7
14	Kentucky	57.3		17	Mississippi	54.4
41	Louisiana	37.4		18	North Carolina	53.4
3	Maine	87.0		19	Connecticut	53.1
24	Maryland	50.6		19	Georgia	53.1
13	Massachusetts	59.0		21	Oklahoma	52.3
8	Michigan	66.5		22	West Virginia	52.2
11	Minnesota	60.1		23	Hawaii	51.7
17	Mississippi	54.4		24	Maryland	50.6
50	Missouri	20.7		25	Alabama	49.0
35	Montana	42.5		25	Florida	49.0
9	Nebraska	64.9		27	Arkansas	45.7
33	Nevada	43.3		28	Vermont	45.2
7	New Hampshire	72.0		29	New York	44.9
46	New Jersey	35.7		30	Virginia	44.7
44	New Mexico	36.1		31	Alaska	44.3
29	New York	44.9		32	Kansas	44.1
18	North Carolina	53.4		33	Nevada	43.3
15	North Dakota	56.6		34	South Carolina	43.1
5	Ohio	76.2		35	Montana	42.5
21	Oklahoma	52.3		36	Utah	41.6
12	Oregon	59.9		37	Tennessee	41.2
43	Pennsylvania	36.8		38	Washington	39.2
47	Rhode Island	35.5		39	Colorado	38.0
34	South Carolina	43.1		40	California	37.5
10	South Dakota	62.8		41	Louisiana	37.4
37	Tennessee	41.2		42	Indiana	37.1
49	Texas	26.7		43	Pennsylvania	36.8
36	Utah	41.6		44	Delaware	36.1
28	Vermont	45.2		44	New Mexico	36.1
30	Virginia	44.7		46	New Jersey	35.7
38	Washington	39.2		47	Rhode Island	35.5
22	West Virginia	52.2		48	Arizona	27.4
6	Wisconsin	72.5		49	Texas	26.7
4	Wyoming	82.1		50	Missouri	20.7
					District of Columbia	39.8

Source: U.S. Department of Health and Human Services, Administration for Children and Families
"Work Participation Rates - Fiscal Year 2014" (Table 6C) (http://www.acf.hhs.gov/programs/ofa/resource/wpr2014)
*For fiscal year 2014. Work-eligible individuals with hours of participation in various work and training activities. National average includes recipients in U.S. territories.

Average Monthly TANF Assistance per Family in 2014

National Average = $389*

ALPHA ORDER

RANK	STATE	PER FAMILY
45	Alabama	$193
1	Alaska	602
42	Arizona	216
49	Arkansas	154
5	California	482
18	Colorado	375
9	Connecticut	451
36	Delaware	249
37	Florida	236
40	Georgia	218
3	Hawaii	553
27	Idaho	298
41	Illinois	217
45	Indiana	193
25	Iowa	315
33	Kansas	267
33	Kentucky	267
30	Louisiana	289
17	Maine	377
4	Maryland	505
8	Massachusetts	463
23	Michigan	334
21	Minnesota	349
50	Mississippi	140
38	Missouri	220
13	Montana	418
30	Nebraska	289
22	Nevada	338
6	New Hampshire	474
26	New Jersey	312
29	New Mexico	294
2	New York	573
43	North Carolina	213
28	North Dakota	297
20	Ohio	354
47	Oklahoma	188
10	Oregon	437
24	Pennsylvania	327
11	Rhode Island	428
44	South Carolina	196
14	South Dakota	410
48	Tennessee	167
38	Texas	220
16	Utah	383
7	Vermont	467
35	Virginia	253
19	Washington	366
32	West Virginia	283
12	Wisconsin	423
14	Wyoming	410

RANK ORDER

RANK	STATE	PER FAMILY
1	Alaska	$602
2	New York	573
3	Hawaii	553
4	Maryland	505
5	California	482
6	New Hampshire	474
7	Vermont	467
8	Massachusetts	463
9	Connecticut	451
10	Oregon	437
11	Rhode Island	428
12	Wisconsin	423
13	Montana	418
14	South Dakota	410
14	Wyoming	410
16	Utah	383
17	Maine	377
18	Colorado	375
19	Washington	366
20	Ohio	354
21	Minnesota	349
22	Nevada	338
23	Michigan	334
24	Pennsylvania	327
25	Iowa	315
26	New Jersey	312
27	Idaho	298
28	North Dakota	297
29	New Mexico	294
30	Louisiana	289
30	Nebraska	289
32	West Virginia	283
33	Kansas	267
33	Kentucky	267
35	Virginia	253
36	Delaware	249
37	Florida	236
38	Missouri	220
38	Texas	220
40	Georgia	218
41	Illinois	217
42	Arizona	216
43	North Carolina	213
44	South Carolina	196
45	Alabama	193
45	Indiana	193
47	Oklahoma	188
48	Tennessee	167
49	Arkansas	154
50	Mississippi	140

District of Columbia — 330

Source: U.S. Department of Health and Human Services, Administration for Children and Families
"Characteristics and Financial Circumstances of TANF Recipients, Fiscal Year 2014 " (Table 37)
(https://www.acf.hhs.gov/ofa/resource/characteristics-and-financial-circumstances-of-tanf-recipients-fiscal-year-2014)
*For fiscal year 2014. National average includes families in U.S. territories.

Percent of Households with Food Insecurity in 2015

National Percent = 13.7% of Households*

ALPHA ORDER

RANK	STATE	PERCENT
4	Alabama	17.6
25	Alaska	13.3
15	Arizona	14.9
2	Arkansas	19.2
31	California	12.6
34	Colorado	12.1
28	Connecticut	13.1
35	Delaware	11.9
30	Florida	12.7
15	Georgia	14.9
48	Hawaii	9.7
24	Idaho	13.8
41	Illinois	11.1
18	Indiana	14.8
44	Iowa	10.6
20	Kansas	14.6
4	Kentucky	17.6
3	Louisiana	18.4
9	Maine	15.8
43	Maryland	10.7
48	Massachusetts	9.7
15	Michigan	14.9
46	Minnesota	9.9
1	Mississippi	20.8
12	Missouri	15.2
33	Montana	12.2
18	Nebraska	14.8
22	Nevada	14.2
45	New Hampshire	10.1
41	New Jersey	11.1
21	New Mexico	14.4
23	New York	14.1
8	North Carolina	15.9
50	North Dakota	8.5
6	Ohio	16.1
10	Oklahoma	15.5
6	Oregon	16.1
32	Pennsylvania	12.4
37	Rhode Island	11.8
26	South Carolina	13.2
38	South Dakota	11.5
13	Tennessee	15.1
11	Texas	15.4
35	Utah	11.9
39	Vermont	11.4
47	Virginia	9.8
29	Washington	12.9
14	West Virginia	15.0
40	Wisconsin	11.3
26	Wyoming	13.2

RANK ORDER

RANK	STATE	PERCENT
1	Mississippi	20.8
2	Arkansas	19.2
3	Louisiana	18.4
4	Alabama	17.6
4	Kentucky	17.6
6	Ohio	16.1
6	Oregon	16.1
8	North Carolina	15.9
9	Maine	15.8
10	Oklahoma	15.5
11	Texas	15.4
12	Missouri	15.2
13	Tennessee	15.1
14	West Virginia	15.0
15	Arizona	14.9
15	Georgia	14.9
15	Michigan	14.9
18	Indiana	14.8
18	Nebraska	14.8
20	Kansas	14.6
21	New Mexico	14.4
22	Nevada	14.2
23	New York	14.1
24	Idaho	13.8
25	Alaska	13.3
26	South Carolina	13.2
26	Wyoming	13.2
28	Connecticut	13.1
29	Washington	12.9
30	Florida	12.7
31	California	12.6
32	Pennsylvania	12.4
33	Montana	12.2
34	Colorado	12.1
35	Delaware	11.9
35	Utah	11.9
37	Rhode Island	11.8
38	South Dakota	11.5
39	Vermont	11.4
40	Wisconsin	11.3
41	Illinois	11.1
41	New Jersey	11.1
43	Maryland	10.7
44	Iowa	10.6
45	New Hampshire	10.1
46	Minnesota	9.9
47	Virginia	9.8
48	Hawaii	9.7
48	Massachusetts	9.7
50	North Dakota	8.5

	District of Columbia	13.2

Source: U.S. Department of Agriculture, Economic Research Service
"Household Food Security in the United States, 2015" (www.ers.usda.gov/topics/food-nutrition-assistance/food-security-in-the-us/)
*Three-year average for 2013-2015. Refers to households for which access to enough food is limited by a lack of money and other resources. About one-third of food-insecure households have very low food security, meaning that at times the food intake of some household members is reduced and their normal eating patterns are disrupted.

Supplemental Nutrition Assistance Program Benefits in 2016

National Total = $66,596,773,104*

ALPHA ORDER

RANK	STATE	BENEFITS	% of USA
15	Alabama	$1,254,835,320	1.9%
44	Alaska	175,483,424	0.3%
14	Arizona	1,402,230,493	2.1%
33	Arkansas	577,775,082	0.9%
1	California	7,237,700,086	10.9%
28	Colorado	728,042,703	1.1%
30	Connecticut	685,510,011	1.0%
43	Delaware	220,683,314	0.3%
3	Florida	5,220,518,996	7.8%
7	Georgia	2,663,017,763	4.0%
36	Hawaii	484,225,008	0.7%
40	Idaho	255,423,930	0.4%
5	Illinois	3,040,976,772	4.6%
23	Indiana	1,068,458,926	1.6%
34	Iowa	507,597,206	0.8%
37	Kansas	342,324,968	0.5%
24	Kentucky	980,976,984	1.5%
12	Louisiana	1,547,434,119	2.3%
41	Maine	254,898,802	0.4%
21	Maryland	1,079,151,904	1.6%
18	Massachusetts	1,189,716,303	1.8%
10	Michigan	2,167,714,845	3.3%
32	Minnesota	602,563,639	0.9%
27	Mississippi	814,420,697	1.2%
19	Missouri	1,182,957,874	1.8%
45	Montana	166,365,465	0.2%
42	Nebraska	240,677,417	0.4%
31	Nevada	629,519,652	0.9%
47	New Hampshire	120,552,043	0.2%
16	New Jersey	1,223,052,433	1.8%
29	New Mexico	693,426,783	1.0%
4	New York	4,922,406,430	7.4%
9	North Carolina	2,248,946,897	3.4%
49	North Dakota	78,700,888	0.1%
8	Ohio	2,396,032,919	3.6%
26	Oklahoma	885,643,482	1.3%
22	Oregon	1,072,982,185	1.6%
6	Pennsylvania	2,729,024,683	4.1%
39	Rhode Island	272,677,781	0.4%
17	South Carolina	1,222,104,228	1.8%
46	South Dakota	144,590,242	0.2%
11	Tennessee	1,672,282,240	2.5%
2	Texas	5,308,544,560	8.0%
38	Utah	301,869,697	0.5%
48	Vermont	116,470,075	0.2%
20	Virginia	1,169,412,644	1.8%
13	Washington	1,452,893,518	2.2%
35	West Virginia	499,059,458	0.7%
25	Wisconsin	922,851,050	1.4%
50	Wyoming	48,510,210	0.1%

RANK ORDER

RANK	STATE	BENEFITS	% of USA
1	California	$7,237,700,086	10.9%
2	Texas	5,308,544,560	8.0%
3	Florida	5,220,518,996	7.8%
4	New York	4,922,406,430	7.4%
5	Illinois	3,040,976,772	4.6%
6	Pennsylvania	2,729,024,683	4.1%
7	Georgia	2,663,017,763	4.0%
8	Ohio	2,396,032,919	3.6%
9	North Carolina	2,248,946,897	3.4%
10	Michigan	2,167,714,845	3.3%
11	Tennessee	1,672,282,240	2.5%
12	Louisiana	1,547,434,119	2.3%
13	Washington	1,452,893,518	2.2%
14	Arizona	1,402,230,493	2.1%
15	Alabama	1,254,835,320	1.9%
16	New Jersey	1,223,052,433	1.8%
17	South Carolina	1,222,104,228	1.8%
18	Massachusetts	1,189,716,303	1.8%
19	Missouri	1,182,957,874	1.8%
20	Virginia	1,169,412,644	1.8%
21	Maryland	1,079,151,904	1.6%
22	Oregon	1,072,982,185	1.6%
23	Indiana	1,068,458,926	1.6%
24	Kentucky	980,976,984	1.5%
25	Wisconsin	922,851,050	1.4%
26	Oklahoma	885,643,482	1.3%
27	Mississippi	814,420,697	1.2%
28	Colorado	728,042,703	1.1%
29	New Mexico	693,426,783	1.0%
30	Connecticut	685,510,011	1.0%
31	Nevada	629,519,652	0.9%
32	Minnesota	602,563,639	0.9%
33	Arkansas	577,775,082	0.9%
34	Iowa	507,597,206	0.8%
35	West Virginia	499,059,458	0.7%
36	Hawaii	484,225,008	0.7%
37	Kansas	342,324,968	0.5%
38	Utah	301,869,697	0.5%
39	Rhode Island	272,677,781	0.4%
40	Idaho	255,423,930	0.4%
41	Maine	254,898,802	0.4%
42	Nebraska	240,677,417	0.4%
43	Delaware	220,683,314	0.3%
44	Alaska	175,483,424	0.3%
45	Montana	166,365,465	0.2%
46	South Dakota	144,590,242	0.2%
47	New Hampshire	120,552,043	0.2%
48	Vermont	116,470,075	0.2%
49	North Dakota	78,700,888	0.1%
50	Wyoming	48,510,210	0.1%
	District of Columbia	210,436,410	0.3%

Source: U.S. Department of Agriculture, Food, Nutrition and Consumer Services
"Supplemental Nutrition Assistance Program" (http://www.fns.usda.gov/pd/snapmain.htm)
*Preliminary data for fiscal year 2016. National total includes $163,100,545 to U.S. territories. Costs are for benefits only and exclude administrative expenditures. Program formerly called the Food Stamp Program.

Monthly Supplemental Nutrition Assistance Program Recipients in 2016

National Total = 44,219,363 Recipients*

ALPHA ORDER

RANK	STATE	RECIPIENTS	% of USA
16	Alabama	850,804	1.9%
47	Alaska	82,326	0.2%
13	Arizona	960,105	2.2%
33	Arkansas	426,069	1.0%
1	California	4,340,042	9.8%
29	Colorado	475,690	1.1%
32	Connecticut	431,597	1.0%
43	Delaware	147,559	0.3%
3	Florida	3,454,530	7.8%
7	Georgia	1,733,473	3.9%
40	Hawaii	176,729	0.4%
39	Idaho	185,303	0.4%
5	Illinois	1,914,393	4.3%
22	Indiana	741,610	1.7%
34	Iowa	380,705	0.9%
36	Kansas	253,833	0.6%
25	Kentucky	666,264	1.5%
14	Louisiana	927,168	2.1%
38	Maine	189,245	0.4%
21	Maryland	744,343	1.7%
20	Massachusetts	779,192	1.8%
10	Michigan	1,473,614	3.3%
28	Minnesota	478,783	1.1%
27	Mississippi	582,658	1.3%
18	Missouri	810,690	1.8%
44	Montana	116,626	0.3%
41	Nebraska	175,851	0.4%
31	Nevada	439,782	1.0%
45	New Hampshire	98,464	0.2%
15	New Jersey	879,987	2.0%
30	New Mexico	471,247	1.1%
4	New York	2,968,227	6.7%
9	North Carolina	1,568,387	3.5%
49	North Dakota	54,252	0.1%
8	Ohio	1,608,633	3.6%
26	Oklahoma	612,869	1.4%
23	Oregon	734,864	1.7%
6	Pennsylvania	1,863,836	4.2%
42	Rhode Island	171,055	0.4%
19	South Carolina	805,012	1.8%
46	South Dakota	95,983	0.2%
11	Tennessee	1,113,231	2.5%
2	Texas	3,768,472	8.5%
37	Utah	219,820	0.5%
48	Vermont	79,715	0.2%
17	Virginia	826,354	1.9%
12	Washington	1,011,412	2.3%
35	West Virginia	357,531	0.8%
24	Wisconsin	728,077	1.6%
50	Wyoming	33,853	0.1%

RANK ORDER

RANK	STATE	RECIPIENTS	% of USA
1	California	4,340,042	9.8%
2	Texas	3,768,472	8.5%
3	Florida	3,454,530	7.8%
4	New York	2,968,227	6.7%
5	Illinois	1,914,393	4.3%
6	Pennsylvania	1,863,836	4.2%
7	Georgia	1,733,473	3.9%
8	Ohio	1,608,633	3.6%
9	North Carolina	1,568,387	3.5%
10	Michigan	1,473,614	3.3%
11	Tennessee	1,113,231	2.5%
12	Washington	1,011,412	2.3%
13	Arizona	960,105	2.2%
14	Louisiana	927,168	2.1%
15	New Jersey	879,987	2.0%
16	Alabama	850,804	1.9%
17	Virginia	826,354	1.9%
18	Missouri	810,690	1.8%
19	South Carolina	805,012	1.8%
20	Massachusetts	779,192	1.8%
21	Maryland	744,343	1.7%
22	Indiana	741,610	1.7%
23	Oregon	734,864	1.7%
24	Wisconsin	728,077	1.6%
25	Kentucky	666,264	1.5%
26	Oklahoma	612,869	1.4%
27	Mississippi	582,658	1.3%
28	Minnesota	478,783	1.1%
29	Colorado	475,690	1.1%
30	New Mexico	471,247	1.1%
31	Nevada	439,782	1.0%
32	Connecticut	431,597	1.0%
33	Arkansas	426,069	1.0%
34	Iowa	380,705	0.9%
35	West Virginia	357,531	0.8%
36	Kansas	253,833	0.6%
37	Utah	219,820	0.5%
38	Maine	189,245	0.4%
39	Idaho	185,303	0.4%
40	Hawaii	176,729	0.4%
41	Nebraska	175,851	0.4%
42	Rhode Island	171,055	0.4%
43	Delaware	147,559	0.3%
44	Montana	116,626	0.3%
45	New Hampshire	98,464	0.2%
46	South Dakota	95,983	0.2%
47	Alaska	82,326	0.2%
48	Vermont	79,715	0.2%
49	North Dakota	54,252	0.1%
50	Wyoming	33,853	0.1%
	District of Columbia	134,625	0.3%

Source: U.S. Department of Agriculture, Food, Nutrition and Consumer Services
"Supplemental Nutrition Assistance Program" (http://www.fns.usda.gov/pd/snapmain.htm)
*Preliminary for fiscal year 2016. National total includes 74,473 recipients in U.S. territories. Program formerly called the Food Stamp Program.

Average Monthly Supplemental Nutrition Assistance Program Benefit per Recipient in 2016
National Average = $125.50 per Recipient*

ALPHA ORDER				RANK ORDER		
RANK	STATE	PER RECIPIENT		RANK	STATE	PER RECIPIENT
18	Alabama	$122.91		1	Hawaii	$228.33
2	Alaska	177.63		2	Alaska	177.63
24	Arizona	121.71		3	Louisiana	139.08
44	Arkansas	113.01		4	California	138.97
4	California	138.97		5	New York	138.20
10	Colorado	127.54		6	Rhode Island	132.84
8	Connecticut	132.36		7	Illinois	132.37
16	Delaware	124.63		8	Connecticut	132.36
13	Florida	125.93		9	Georgia	128.02
9	Georgia	128.02		10	Colorado	127.54
1	Hawaii	228.33		11	Massachusetts	127.24
41	Idaho	114.87		12	South Carolina	126.51
7	Illinois	132.37		13	Florida	125.93
30	Indiana	120.06		14	South Dakota	125.53
47	Iowa	111.11		15	Tennessee	125.18
45	Kansas	112.39		16	Delaware	124.63
19	Kentucky	122.70		17	Ohio	124.12
3	Louisiana	139.08		18	Alabama	122.91
46	Maine	112.24		19	Kentucky	122.70
28	Maryland	120.82		20	New Mexico	122.62
11	Massachusetts	127.24		21	Michigan	122.58
21	Michigan	122.58		22	Pennsylvania	122.02
49	Minnesota	104.88		23	Vermont	121.76
38	Mississippi	116.48		24	Arizona	121.71
26	Missouri	121.60		25	Oregon	121.68
35	Montana	118.87		26	Missouri	121.60
43	Nebraska	114.05		27	North Dakota	120.89
34	Nevada	119.29		28	Maryland	120.82
50	New Hampshire	102.03		29	Oklahoma	120.42
40	New Jersey	115.82		30	Indiana	120.06
20	New Mexico	122.62		31	Washington	119.71
5	New York	138.20		32	North Carolina	119.49
32	North Carolina	119.49		33	Wyoming	119.41
27	North Dakota	120.89		34	Nevada	119.29
17	Ohio	124.12		35	Montana	118.87
29	Oklahoma	120.42		36	Virginia	117.93
25	Oregon	121.68		37	Texas	117.39
22	Pennsylvania	122.02		38	Mississippi	116.48
6	Rhode Island	132.84		39	West Virginia	116.32
12	South Carolina	126.51		40	New Jersey	115.82
14	South Dakota	125.53		41	Idaho	114.87
15	Tennessee	125.18		42	Utah	114.44
37	Texas	117.39		43	Nebraska	114.05
42	Utah	114.44		44	Arkansas	113.01
23	Vermont	121.76		45	Kansas	112.39
36	Virginia	117.93		46	Maine	112.24
31	Washington	119.71		47	Iowa	111.11
39	West Virginia	116.32		48	Wisconsin	105.63
48	Wisconsin	105.63		49	Minnesota	104.88
33	Wyoming	119.41		50	New Hampshire	102.03
					District of Columbia	130.26

Source: U.S. Department of Agriculture, Food, Nutrition and Consumer Services
"Supplemental Nutrition Assistance Program" (http://www.fns.usda.gov/pd/snapmain.htm)
*Preliminary for fiscal year 2016. National average includes recipients in U.S. territories. Program formerly called the Food Stamp Program.

Percent of Population Receiving
Supplemental Nutrition Assistance Program Benefits in 2016
National Percent = 13.7%*

<table>
<tr><td colspan="3">ALPHA ORDER</td><td colspan="3">RANK ORDER</td></tr>
<tr><td>RANK</td><td>STATE</td><td>PERCENT</td><td>RANK</td><td>STATE</td><td>PERCENT</td></tr>
<tr><td>6</td><td>Alabama</td><td>17.5</td><td>1</td><td>New Mexico</td><td>22.6</td></tr>
<tr><td>37</td><td>Alaska</td><td>11.1</td><td>2</td><td>Louisiana</td><td>19.8</td></tr>
<tr><td>23</td><td>Arizona</td><td>13.9</td><td>3</td><td>Mississippi</td><td>19.5</td></tr>
<tr><td>21</td><td>Arkansas</td><td>14.3</td><td>3</td><td>West Virginia</td><td>19.5</td></tr>
<tr><td>37</td><td>California</td><td>11.1</td><td>5</td><td>Oregon</td><td>18.0</td></tr>
<tr><td>46</td><td>Colorado</td><td>8.6</td><td>6</td><td>Alabama</td><td>17.5</td></tr>
<tr><td>32</td><td>Connecticut</td><td>12.1</td><td>7</td><td>Florida</td><td>16.8</td></tr>
<tr><td>13</td><td>Delaware</td><td>15.5</td><td>7</td><td>Georgia</td><td>16.8</td></tr>
<tr><td>7</td><td>Florida</td><td>16.8</td><td>9</td><td>Tennessee</td><td>16.7</td></tr>
<tr><td>7</td><td>Georgia</td><td>16.8</td><td>10</td><td>Rhode Island</td><td>16.2</td></tr>
<tr><td>30</td><td>Hawaii</td><td>12.4</td><td>10</td><td>South Carolina</td><td>16.2</td></tr>
<tr><td>40</td><td>Idaho</td><td>11.0</td><td>12</td><td>Oklahoma</td><td>15.6</td></tr>
<tr><td>15</td><td>Illinois</td><td>15.0</td><td>13</td><td>Delaware</td><td>15.5</td></tr>
<tr><td>35</td><td>Indiana</td><td>11.2</td><td>13</td><td>North Carolina</td><td>15.5</td></tr>
<tr><td>32</td><td>Iowa</td><td>12.1</td><td>15</td><td>Illinois</td><td>15.0</td></tr>
<tr><td>44</td><td>Kansas</td><td>8.7</td><td>15</td><td>Kentucky</td><td>15.0</td></tr>
<tr><td>15</td><td>Kentucky</td><td>15.0</td><td>15</td><td>Nevada</td><td>15.0</td></tr>
<tr><td>2</td><td>Louisiana</td><td>19.8</td><td>15</td><td>New York</td><td>15.0</td></tr>
<tr><td>22</td><td>Maine</td><td>14.2</td><td>19</td><td>Michigan</td><td>14.8</td></tr>
<tr><td>30</td><td>Maryland</td><td>12.4</td><td>20</td><td>Pennsylvania</td><td>14.6</td></tr>
<tr><td>34</td><td>Massachusetts</td><td>11.4</td><td>21</td><td>Arkansas</td><td>14.3</td></tr>
<tr><td>19</td><td>Michigan</td><td>14.8</td><td>22</td><td>Maine</td><td>14.2</td></tr>
<tr><td>44</td><td>Minnesota</td><td>8.7</td><td>23</td><td>Arizona</td><td>13.9</td></tr>
<tr><td>3</td><td>Mississippi</td><td>19.5</td><td>23</td><td>Ohio</td><td>13.9</td></tr>
<tr><td>27</td><td>Missouri</td><td>13.3</td><td>23</td><td>Washington</td><td>13.9</td></tr>
<tr><td>35</td><td>Montana</td><td>11.2</td><td>26</td><td>Texas</td><td>13.5</td></tr>
<tr><td>43</td><td>Nebraska</td><td>9.2</td><td>27</td><td>Missouri</td><td>13.3</td></tr>
<tr><td>15</td><td>Nevada</td><td>15.0</td><td>28</td><td>Vermont</td><td>12.8</td></tr>
<tr><td>47</td><td>New Hampshire</td><td>7.4</td><td>29</td><td>Wisconsin</td><td>12.6</td></tr>
<tr><td>41</td><td>New Jersey</td><td>9.8</td><td>30</td><td>Hawaii</td><td>12.4</td></tr>
<tr><td>1</td><td>New Mexico</td><td>22.6</td><td>30</td><td>Maryland</td><td>12.4</td></tr>
<tr><td>15</td><td>New York</td><td>15.0</td><td>32</td><td>Connecticut</td><td>12.1</td></tr>
<tr><td>13</td><td>North Carolina</td><td>15.5</td><td>32</td><td>Iowa</td><td>12.1</td></tr>
<tr><td>48</td><td>North Dakota</td><td>7.2</td><td>34</td><td>Massachusetts</td><td>11.4</td></tr>
<tr><td>23</td><td>Ohio</td><td>13.9</td><td>35</td><td>Indiana</td><td>11.2</td></tr>
<tr><td>12</td><td>Oklahoma</td><td>15.6</td><td>35</td><td>Montana</td><td>11.2</td></tr>
<tr><td>5</td><td>Oregon</td><td>18.0</td><td>37</td><td>Alaska</td><td>11.1</td></tr>
<tr><td>20</td><td>Pennsylvania</td><td>14.6</td><td>37</td><td>California</td><td>11.1</td></tr>
<tr><td>10</td><td>Rhode Island</td><td>16.2</td><td>37</td><td>South Dakota</td><td>11.1</td></tr>
<tr><td>10</td><td>South Carolina</td><td>16.2</td><td>40</td><td>Idaho</td><td>11.0</td></tr>
<tr><td>37</td><td>South Dakota</td><td>11.1</td><td>41</td><td>New Jersey</td><td>9.8</td></tr>
<tr><td>9</td><td>Tennessee</td><td>16.7</td><td>41</td><td>Virginia</td><td>9.8</td></tr>
<tr><td>26</td><td>Texas</td><td>13.5</td><td>43</td><td>Nebraska</td><td>9.2</td></tr>
<tr><td>48</td><td>Utah</td><td>7.2</td><td>44</td><td>Kansas</td><td>8.7</td></tr>
<tr><td>28</td><td>Vermont</td><td>12.8</td><td>44</td><td>Minnesota</td><td>8.7</td></tr>
<tr><td>41</td><td>Virginia</td><td>9.8</td><td>46</td><td>Colorado</td><td>8.6</td></tr>
<tr><td>23</td><td>Washington</td><td>13.9</td><td>47</td><td>New Hampshire</td><td>7.4</td></tr>
<tr><td>3</td><td>West Virginia</td><td>19.5</td><td>48</td><td>North Dakota</td><td>7.2</td></tr>
<tr><td>29</td><td>Wisconsin</td><td>12.6</td><td>48</td><td>Utah</td><td>7.2</td></tr>
<tr><td>50</td><td>Wyoming</td><td>5.8</td><td>50</td><td>Wyoming</td><td>5.8</td></tr>
<tr><td></td><td></td><td></td><td></td><td>District of Columbia</td><td>19.8</td></tr>
</table>

Source: CQ Press using data from U.S. Department of Agriculture, Food, Nutrition and Consumer Services
    "Supplemental Nutrition Assistance Program" (http://www.fns.usda.gov/pd/snapmain.htm)
*Preliminary data for fiscal year 2016. National rate does not include recipients in U.S. territories. Program formerly called the
Food Stamp Program.

Percent of Households Receiving
Supplemental Nutrition Assistance Program Benefits in 2016
National Percent = 18.4% of Households*

ALPHA ORDER

RANK	STATE	PERCENT
11	Alabama	21.6
36	Alaska	13.8
27	Arizona	17.3
31	Arkansas	16.7
32	California	16.2
43	Colorado	10.9
23	Connecticut	18.2
15	Delaware	20.2
3	Florida	25.1
9	Georgia	21.9
17	Hawaii	20.0
38	Idaho	13.3
13	Illinois	20.8
40	Indiana	13.1
35	Iowa	14.3
46	Kansas	10.3
22	Kentucky	18.3
6	Louisiana	24.3
24	Maine	18.1
25	Maryland	17.9
26	Massachusetts	17.6
15	Michigan	20.2
44	Minnesota	10.8
5	Mississippi	24.4
33	Missouri	15.9
39	Montana	13.2
45	Nebraska	10.5
12	Nevada	21.3
47	New Hampshire	9.3
36	New Jersey	13.8
1	New Mexico	28.5
8	New York	22.6
19	North Carolina	19.8
49	North Dakota	8.1
28	Ohio	17.2
21	Oklahoma	18.8
2	Oregon	27.0
20	Pennsylvania	19.2
4	Rhode Island	24.6
14	South Carolina	20.4
42	South Dakota	12.4
10	Tennessee	21.7
29	Texas	16.9
47	Utah	9.3
29	Vermont	16.9
41	Virginia	12.5
17	Washington	20.0
6	West Virginia	24.3
34	Wisconsin	15.5
50	Wyoming	6.3

RANK ORDER

RANK	STATE	PERCENT
1	New Mexico	28.5
2	Oregon	27.0
3	Florida	25.1
4	Rhode Island	24.6
5	Mississippi	24.4
6	Louisiana	24.3
6	West Virginia	24.3
8	New York	22.6
9	Georgia	21.9
10	Tennessee	21.7
11	Alabama	21.6
12	Nevada	21.3
13	Illinois	20.8
14	South Carolina	20.4
15	Delaware	20.2
15	Michigan	20.2
17	Hawaii	20.0
17	Washington	20.0
19	North Carolina	19.8
20	Pennsylvania	19.2
21	Oklahoma	18.8
22	Kentucky	18.3
23	Connecticut	18.2
24	Maine	18.1
25	Maryland	17.9
26	Massachusetts	17.6
27	Arizona	17.3
28	Ohio	17.2
29	Texas	16.9
29	Vermont	16.9
31	Arkansas	16.7
32	California	16.2
33	Missouri	15.9
34	Wisconsin	15.5
35	Iowa	14.3
36	Alaska	13.8
36	New Jersey	13.8
38	Idaho	13.3
39	Montana	13.2
40	Indiana	13.1
41	Virginia	12.5
42	South Dakota	12.4
43	Colorado	10.9
44	Minnesota	10.8
45	Nebraska	10.5
46	Kansas	10.3
47	New Hampshire	9.3
47	Utah	9.3
49	North Dakota	8.1
50	Wyoming	6.3

District of Columbia   26.9

Source: CQ Press using data from U.S. Department of Agriculture, Food, Nutrition and Consumer Services "Supplemental Nutrition Assistance Program" (http://www.fns.usda.gov/pd/snapmain.htm)
*Preliminary data for fiscal year 2016. Percent calculated using 2015 estimated total households. National percent excludes households in U.S. territories. Program formerly called the Food Stamp Program.

Average Monthly Participants in Women, Infants, and Children (WIC) Special Nutrition Program in 2016
National Total = 7,696,692 Participants*

ALPHA ORDER

RANK	STATE	PARTICIPANTS	% of USA
18	Alabama	129,160	1.7%
44	Alaska	19,121	0.2%
12	Arizona	163,995	2.1%
30	Arkansas	80,555	1.0%
1	California	1,175,214	15.3%
28	Colorado	86,999	1.1%
36	Connecticut	49,155	0.6%
46	Delaware	18,062	0.2%
3	Florida	481,520	6.3%
5	Georgia	253,653	3.3%
40	Hawaii	30,117	0.4%
38	Idaho	39,010	0.5%
10	Illinois	225,159	2.9%
14	Indiana	147,906	1.9%
32	Iowa	61,163	0.8%
33	Kansas	58,955	0.8%
23	Kentucky	111,926	1.5%
20	Louisiana	127,387	1.7%
41	Maine	20,806	0.3%
16	Maryland	139,576	1.8%
22	Massachusetts	114,419	1.5%
9	Michigan	234,546	3.0%
21	Minnesota	116,031	1.5%
29	Mississippi	84,867	1.1%
19	Missouri	127,551	1.7%
45	Montana	18,296	0.2%
39	Nebraska	38,125	0.5%
31	Nevada	70,411	0.9%
47	New Hampshire	14,121	0.2%
13	New Jersey	155,285	2.0%
35	New Mexico	51,902	0.7%
4	New York	459,101	6.0%
6	North Carolina	241,286	3.1%
48	North Dakota	12,884	0.2%
8	Ohio	234,719	3.0%
24	Oklahoma	110,725	1.4%
27	Oregon	92,792	1.2%
7	Pennsylvania	237,211	3.1%
42	Rhode Island	20,375	0.3%
25	South Carolina	107,257	1.4%
43	South Dakota	19,123	0.2%
15	Tennessee	143,730	1.9%
2	Texas	859,819	11.2%
34	Utah	56,584	0.7%
49	Vermont	12,756	0.2%
17	Virginia	132,404	1.7%
11	Washington	168,878	2.2%
37	West Virginia	40,391	0.5%
26	Wisconsin	100,152	1.3%
50	Wyoming	10,783	0.1%

RANK ORDER

RANK	STATE	PARTICIPANTS	% of USA
1	California	1,175,214	15.3%
2	Texas	859,819	11.2%
3	Florida	481,520	6.3%
4	New York	459,101	6.0%
5	Georgia	253,653	3.3%
6	North Carolina	241,286	3.1%
7	Pennsylvania	237,211	3.1%
8	Ohio	234,719	3.0%
9	Michigan	234,546	3.0%
10	Illinois	225,159	2.9%
11	Washington	168,878	2.2%
12	Arizona	163,995	2.1%
13	New Jersey	155,285	2.0%
14	Indiana	147,906	1.9%
15	Tennessee	143,730	1.9%
16	Maryland	139,576	1.8%
17	Virginia	132,404	1.7%
18	Alabama	129,160	1.7%
19	Missouri	127,551	1.7%
20	Louisiana	127,387	1.7%
21	Minnesota	116,031	1.5%
22	Massachusetts	114,419	1.5%
23	Kentucky	111,926	1.5%
24	Oklahoma	110,725	1.4%
25	South Carolina	107,257	1.4%
26	Wisconsin	100,152	1.3%
27	Oregon	92,792	1.2%
28	Colorado	86,999	1.1%
29	Mississippi	84,867	1.1%
30	Arkansas	80,555	1.0%
31	Nevada	70,411	0.9%
32	Iowa	61,163	0.8%
33	Kansas	58,955	0.8%
34	Utah	56,584	0.7%
35	New Mexico	51,902	0.7%
36	Connecticut	49,155	0.6%
37	West Virginia	40,391	0.5%
38	Idaho	39,010	0.5%
39	Nebraska	38,125	0.5%
40	Hawaii	30,117	0.4%
41	Maine	20,806	0.3%
42	Rhode Island	20,375	0.3%
43	South Dakota	19,123	0.2%
44	Alaska	19,121	0.2%
45	Montana	18,296	0.2%
46	Delaware	18,062	0.2%
47	New Hampshire	14,121	0.2%
48	North Dakota	12,884	0.2%
49	Vermont	12,756	0.2%
50	Wyoming	10,783	0.1%
	District of Columbia	14,363	0.2%

Source: U.S. Department of Agriculture, Food, Nutrition and Consumer Services
   "WIC Program (http://www.fns.usda.gov/pd/wicmain.htm)
*Preliminary data for fiscal year 2016. National total includes 176,368 participants in outlying areas not shown separately (Puerto Rico has 155,746 participants).

Average Monthly Benefit per Participant in Women, Infants, and Children (WIC) Special Nutrition Program in 2016
National Average = $42.74*

ALPHA ORDER				RANK ORDER		
RANK	STATE	AVERAGE BENEFIT		RANK	STATE	AVERAGE BENEFIT
13	Alabama	$45.52		1	Mississippi	$54.94
5	Alaska	52.93		2	New Jersey	53.47
14	Arizona	44.93		3	Hawaii	53.08
18	Arkansas	44.25		4	New York	53.03
12	California	46.13		5	Alaska	52.93
28	Colorado	41.03		6	Illinois	52.03
19	Connecticut	43.65		7	Louisiana	47.25
29	Delaware	40.90		8	North Dakota	47.24
22	Florida	42.03		9	Vermont	47.17
31	Georgia	39.57		10	Pennsylvania	46.74
3	Hawaii	53.08		11	South Dakota	46.21
44	Idaho	34.74		12	California	46.13
6	Illinois	52.03		13	Alabama	45.52
39	Indiana	36.99		14	Arizona	44.93
48	Iowa	30.74		15	South Carolina	44.90
36	Kansas	37.92		16	Rhode Island	44.57
32	Kentucky	39.53		17	Maryland	44.37
7	Louisiana	47.25		18	Arkansas	44.25
30	Maine	39.70		19	Connecticut	43.65
17	Maryland	44.37		20	North Carolina	42.47
34	Massachusetts	39.02		21	Washington	42.06
35	Michigan	38.60		22	Florida	42.03
26	Minnesota	41.65		23	West Virginia	41.91
1	Mississippi	54.94		24	Tennessee	41.78
42	Missouri	35.87		25	Montana	41.70
25	Montana	41.70		26	Minnesota	41.65
27	Nebraska	41.48		27	Nebraska	41.48
45	Nevada	34.44		28	Colorado	41.03
47	New Hampshire	33.16		29	Delaware	40.90
2	New Jersey	53.47		30	Maine	39.70
41	New Mexico	36.00		31	Georgia	39.57
4	New York	53.03		32	Kentucky	39.53
20	North Carolina	42.47		33	Wisconsin	39.27
8	North Dakota	47.24		34	Massachusetts	39.02
49	Ohio	30.01		35	Michigan	38.60
40	Oklahoma	36.29		36	Kansas	37.92
38	Oregon	37.03		37	Utah	37.66
10	Pennsylvania	46.74		38	Oregon	37.03
16	Rhode Island	44.57		39	Indiana	36.99
15	South Carolina	44.90		40	Oklahoma	36.29
11	South Dakota	46.21		41	New Mexico	36.00
24	Tennessee	41.78		42	Missouri	35.87
50	Texas	29.82		43	Virginia	35.65
37	Utah	37.66		44	Idaho	34.74
9	Vermont	47.17		45	Nevada	34.44
43	Virginia	35.65		46	Wyoming	33.47
21	Washington	42.06		47	New Hampshire	33.16
23	West Virginia	41.91		48	Iowa	30.74
33	Wisconsin	39.27		49	Ohio	30.01
46	Wyoming	33.47		50	Texas	29.82
					District of Columbia	44.11

Source: U.S. Department of Agriculture, Food, Nutrition and Consumer Services
"WIC Program (http://www.fns.usda.gov/pd/wicmain.htm)
*Preliminary data for fiscal year 2016. National average includes outlying areas and Indian reservations not shown separately.

Percent of Public Elementary and Secondary School Students Eligible for Free or Reduced-Price Meals in 2015
National Percent = 51.6%*

ALPHA ORDER

RANK	STATE	PERCENT
16	Alabama	51.7
34	Alaska	43.1
42	Arizona	38.9
5	Arkansas	62.3
7	California	58.7
35	Colorado	41.6
44	Connecticut	37.7
46	Delaware	37.1
9	Florida	58.4
4	Georgia	62.4
20	Hawaii	50.1
23	Idaho	48.5
14	Illinois	54.1
22	Indiana	49.1
37	Iowa	40.7
21	Kansas	49.9
11	Kentucky	56.9
2	Louisiana	63.6
24	Maine	47.1
31	Maryland	45.0
39	Massachusetts	39.9
26	Michigan	46.6
43	Minnesota	38.3
1	Mississippi	73.7
17	Missouri	51.3
33	Montana	43.6
32	Nebraska	44.3
15	Nevada	52.2
50	New Hampshire	29.0
48	New Jersey	36.7
3	New Mexico	62.5
19	New York	50.9
10	North Carolina	57.2
49	North Dakota	30.4
30	Ohio	45.1
6	Oklahoma	60.1
18	Oregon	51.1
29	Pennsylvania	45.6
25	Rhode Island	46.8
13	South Carolina	55.7
40	South Dakota	39.5
12	Tennessee	55.9
7	Texas	58.7
47	Utah	36.9
41	Vermont	39.0
38	Virginia	40.2
28	Washington	45.9
27	West Virginia	46.1
36	Wisconsin	41.5
45	Wyoming	37.6

RANK ORDER

RANK	STATE	PERCENT
1	Mississippi	73.7
2	Louisiana	63.6
3	New Mexico	62.5
4	Georgia	62.4
5	Arkansas	62.3
6	Oklahoma	60.1
7	California	58.7
7	Texas	58.7
9	Florida	58.4
10	North Carolina	57.2
11	Kentucky	56.9
12	Tennessee	55.9
13	South Carolina	55.7
14	Illinois	54.1
15	Nevada	52.2
16	Alabama	51.7
17	Missouri	51.3
18	Oregon	51.1
19	New York	50.9
20	Hawaii	50.1
21	Kansas	49.9
22	Indiana	49.1
23	Idaho	48.5
24	Maine	47.1
25	Rhode Island	46.8
26	Michigan	46.6
27	West Virginia	46.1
28	Washington	45.9
29	Pennsylvania	45.6
30	Ohio	45.1
31	Maryland	45.0
32	Nebraska	44.3
33	Montana	43.6
34	Alaska	43.1
35	Colorado	41.6
36	Wisconsin	41.5
37	Iowa	40.7
38	Virginia	40.2
39	Massachusetts	39.9
40	South Dakota	39.5
41	Vermont	39.0
42	Arizona	38.9
43	Minnesota	38.3
44	Connecticut	37.7
45	Wyoming	37.6
46	Delaware	37.1
47	Utah	36.9
48	New Jersey	36.7
49	North Dakota	30.4
50	New Hampshire	29.0

District of Columbia   92.5

Source: CQ Press using data from U.S. Department of Education, National Center for Education Statistics
   "Common Core of Data (CCD) Database" (http://nces.ed.gov/ccd/)
*For school year 2014-2015.

Child Support Collections in 2015

National Total = $28,213,383,325*

<table>
<tr><td colspan="4">ALPHA ORDER</td><td colspan="4">RANK ORDER</td></tr>
<tr><th>RANK</th><th>STATE</th><th>COLLECTIONS</th><th>% of USA</th><th>RANK</th><th>STATE</th><th>COLLECTIONS</th><th>% of USA</th></tr>
<tr><td>26</td><td>Alabama</td><td>$320,480,355</td><td>1.1%</td><td>1</td><td>Texas</td><td>$3,869,737,092</td><td>13.7%</td></tr>
<tr><td>40</td><td>Alaska</td><td>99,574,780</td><td>0.4%</td><td>2</td><td>California</td><td>2,247,498,866</td><td>8.0%</td></tr>
<tr><td>28</td><td>Arizona</td><td>313,943,546</td><td>1.1%</td><td>3</td><td>New York</td><td>1,701,208,206</td><td>6.0%</td></tr>
<tr><td>32</td><td>Arkansas</td><td>234,810,293</td><td>0.8%</td><td>4</td><td>Ohio</td><td>1,662,243,146</td><td>5.9%</td></tr>
<tr><td>2</td><td>California</td><td>2,247,498,866</td><td>8.0%</td><td>5</td><td>Florida</td><td>1,443,751,002</td><td>5.1%</td></tr>
<tr><td>27</td><td>Colorado</td><td>318,996,217</td><td>1.1%</td><td>6</td><td>Michigan</td><td>1,324,213,639</td><td>4.7%</td></tr>
<tr><td>31</td><td>Connecticut</td><td>242,487,423</td><td>0.9%</td><td>7</td><td>Pennsylvania</td><td>1,247,383,434</td><td>4.4%</td></tr>
<tr><td>46</td><td>Delaware</td><td>75,417,449</td><td>0.3%</td><td>8</td><td>New Jersey</td><td>1,154,241,606</td><td>4.1%</td></tr>
<tr><td>5</td><td>Florida</td><td>1,443,751,002</td><td>5.1%</td><td>9</td><td>Illinois</td><td>807,772,022</td><td>2.9%</td></tr>
<tr><td>10</td><td>Georgia</td><td>678,646,491</td><td>2.4%</td><td>10</td><td>Georgia</td><td>678,646,491</td><td>2.4%</td></tr>
<tr><td>41</td><td>Hawaii</td><td>98,888,615</td><td>0.4%</td><td>11</td><td>North Carolina</td><td>661,805,785</td><td>2.3%</td></tr>
<tr><td>38</td><td>Idaho</td><td>169,281,382</td><td>0.6%</td><td>12</td><td>Wisconsin</td><td>639,018,256</td><td>2.3%</td></tr>
<tr><td>9</td><td>Illinois</td><td>807,772,022</td><td>2.9%</td><td>13</td><td>Washington</td><td>637,489,204</td><td>2.3%</td></tr>
<tr><td>19</td><td>Indiana</td><td>553,887,280</td><td>2.0%</td><td>14</td><td>Massachusetts</td><td>626,665,708</td><td>2.2%</td></tr>
<tr><td>29</td><td>Iowa</td><td>307,628,096</td><td>1.1%</td><td>15</td><td>Virginia</td><td>610,461,256</td><td>2.2%</td></tr>
<tr><td>36</td><td>Kansas</td><td>182,652,580</td><td>0.6%</td><td>16</td><td>Tennessee</td><td>601,662,972</td><td>2.1%</td></tr>
<tr><td>22</td><td>Kentucky</td><td>383,607,980</td><td>1.4%</td><td>17</td><td>Missouri</td><td>596,717,964</td><td>2.1%</td></tr>
<tr><td>21</td><td>Louisiana</td><td>406,865,602</td><td>1.4%</td><td>18</td><td>Minnesota</td><td>583,371,957</td><td>2.1%</td></tr>
<tr><td>42</td><td>Maine</td><td>98,680,730</td><td>0.3%</td><td>19</td><td>Indiana</td><td>553,887,280</td><td>2.0%</td></tr>
<tr><td>20</td><td>Maryland</td><td>533,041,437</td><td>1.9%</td><td>20</td><td>Maryland</td><td>533,041,437</td><td>1.9%</td></tr>
<tr><td>14</td><td>Massachusetts</td><td>626,665,708</td><td>2.2%</td><td>21</td><td>Louisiana</td><td>406,865,602</td><td>1.4%</td></tr>
<tr><td>6</td><td>Michigan</td><td>1,324,213,639</td><td>4.7%</td><td>22</td><td>Kentucky</td><td>383,607,980</td><td>1.4%</td></tr>
<tr><td>18</td><td>Minnesota</td><td>583,371,957</td><td>2.1%</td><td>23</td><td>Oregon</td><td>354,419,271</td><td>1.3%</td></tr>
<tr><td>25</td><td>Mississippi</td><td>322,142,959</td><td>1.1%</td><td>24</td><td>Oklahoma</td><td>348,822,105</td><td>1.2%</td></tr>
<tr><td>17</td><td>Missouri</td><td>596,717,964</td><td>2.1%</td><td>25</td><td>Mississippi</td><td>322,142,959</td><td>1.1%</td></tr>
<tr><td>49</td><td>Montana</td><td>62,718,670</td><td>0.2%</td><td>26</td><td>Alabama</td><td>320,480,355</td><td>1.1%</td></tr>
<tr><td>34</td><td>Nebraska</td><td>206,767,027</td><td>0.7%</td><td>27</td><td>Colorado</td><td>318,996,217</td><td>1.1%</td></tr>
<tr><td>37</td><td>Nevada</td><td>179,728,430</td><td>0.6%</td><td>28</td><td>Arizona</td><td>313,943,546</td><td>1.1%</td></tr>
<tr><td>45</td><td>New Hampshire</td><td>78,122,974</td><td>0.3%</td><td>29</td><td>Iowa</td><td>307,628,096</td><td>1.1%</td></tr>
<tr><td>8</td><td>New Jersey</td><td>1,154,241,606</td><td>4.1%</td><td>30</td><td>South Carolina</td><td>276,692,044</td><td>1.0%</td></tr>
<tr><td>39</td><td>New Mexico</td><td>121,805,960</td><td>0.4%</td><td>31</td><td>Connecticut</td><td>242,487,423</td><td>0.9%</td></tr>
<tr><td>3</td><td>New York</td><td>1,701,208,206</td><td>6.0%</td><td>32</td><td>Arkansas</td><td>234,810,293</td><td>0.8%</td></tr>
<tr><td>11</td><td>North Carolina</td><td>661,805,785</td><td>2.3%</td><td>33</td><td>Utah</td><td>208,930,091</td><td>0.7%</td></tr>
<tr><td>43</td><td>North Dakota</td><td>96,939,840</td><td>0.3%</td><td>34</td><td>Nebraska</td><td>206,767,027</td><td>0.7%</td></tr>
<tr><td>4</td><td>Ohio</td><td>1,662,243,146</td><td>5.9%</td><td>35</td><td>West Virginia</td><td>199,206,476</td><td>0.7%</td></tr>
<tr><td>24</td><td>Oklahoma</td><td>348,822,105</td><td>1.2%</td><td>36</td><td>Kansas</td><td>182,652,580</td><td>0.6%</td></tr>
<tr><td>23</td><td>Oregon</td><td>354,419,271</td><td>1.3%</td><td>37</td><td>Nevada</td><td>179,728,430</td><td>0.6%</td></tr>
<tr><td>7</td><td>Pennsylvania</td><td>1,247,383,434</td><td>4.4%</td><td>38</td><td>Idaho</td><td>169,281,382</td><td>0.6%</td></tr>
<tr><td>47</td><td>Rhode Island</td><td>73,768,669</td><td>0.3%</td><td>39</td><td>New Mexico</td><td>121,805,960</td><td>0.4%</td></tr>
<tr><td>30</td><td>South Carolina</td><td>276,692,044</td><td>1.0%</td><td>40</td><td>Alaska</td><td>99,574,780</td><td>0.4%</td></tr>
<tr><td>44</td><td>South Dakota</td><td>92,266,271</td><td>0.3%</td><td>41</td><td>Hawaii</td><td>98,888,615</td><td>0.4%</td></tr>
<tr><td>16</td><td>Tennessee</td><td>601,662,972</td><td>2.1%</td><td>42</td><td>Maine</td><td>98,680,730</td><td>0.3%</td></tr>
<tr><td>1</td><td>Texas</td><td>3,869,737,092</td><td>13.7%</td><td>43</td><td>North Dakota</td><td>96,939,840</td><td>0.3%</td></tr>
<tr><td>33</td><td>Utah</td><td>208,930,091</td><td>0.7%</td><td>44</td><td>South Dakota</td><td>92,266,271</td><td>0.3%</td></tr>
<tr><td>50</td><td>Vermont</td><td>44,091,884</td><td>0.2%</td><td>45</td><td>New Hampshire</td><td>78,122,974</td><td>0.3%</td></tr>
<tr><td>15</td><td>Virginia</td><td>610,461,256</td><td>2.2%</td><td>46</td><td>Delaware</td><td>75,417,449</td><td>0.3%</td></tr>
<tr><td>13</td><td>Washington</td><td>637,489,204</td><td>2.3%</td><td>47</td><td>Rhode Island</td><td>73,768,669</td><td>0.3%</td></tr>
<tr><td>35</td><td>West Virginia</td><td>199,206,476</td><td>0.7%</td><td>48</td><td>Wyoming</td><td>65,484,853</td><td>0.2%</td></tr>
<tr><td>12</td><td>Wisconsin</td><td>639,018,256</td><td>2.3%</td><td>49</td><td>Montana</td><td>62,718,670</td><td>0.2%</td></tr>
<tr><td>48</td><td>Wyoming</td><td>65,484,853</td><td>0.2%</td><td>50</td><td>Vermont</td><td>44,091,884</td><td>0.2%</td></tr>
<tr><td></td><td></td><td></td><td></td><td></td><td>District of Columbia</td><td>47,343,430</td><td>0.2%</td></tr>
</table>

Source: U.S. Department of Health and Human Services, Office of Child Support Enforcement
"Child Support Enforcement Annual Report to Congress" (https://www.acf.hhs.gov/css/data)
*Fiscal year 2015. Total does not include $345,750,850 collected in U.S. territories.

XV. Transportation

Federal Highway Funding in 2015

National Total = $37,798,000,000*

<table>
<tr><td colspan="4">ALPHA ORDER</td><td colspan="4">RANK ORDER</td></tr>
<tr><td>RANK</td><td>STATE</td><td>FUNDS</td><td>% of USA</td><td>RANK</td><td>STATE</td><td>FUNDS</td><td>% of USA</td></tr>
<tr><td>16</td><td>Alabama</td><td>$732,263,000</td><td>1.9%</td><td>1</td><td>California</td><td>$3,542,468,000</td><td>9.4%</td></tr>
<tr><td>30</td><td>Alaska</td><td>483,955,000</td><td>1.3%</td><td>2</td><td>Texas</td><td>3,331,597,000</td><td>8.8%</td></tr>
<tr><td>18</td><td>Arizona</td><td>706,182,000</td><td>1.9%</td><td>3</td><td>Florida</td><td>1,828,689,000</td><td>4.8%</td></tr>
<tr><td>28</td><td>Arkansas</td><td>499,714,000</td><td>1.3%</td><td>4</td><td>New York</td><td>1,620,088,000</td><td>4.3%</td></tr>
<tr><td>1</td><td>California</td><td>3,542,468,000</td><td>9.4%</td><td>5</td><td>Pennsylvania</td><td>1,583,603,000</td><td>4.2%</td></tr>
<tr><td>27</td><td>Colorado</td><td>516,113,000</td><td>1.4%</td><td>6</td><td>Illinois</td><td>1,372,231,000</td><td>3.6%</td></tr>
<tr><td>29</td><td>Connecticut</td><td>484,771,000</td><td>1.3%</td><td>7</td><td>Ohio</td><td>1,293,739,000</td><td>3.4%</td></tr>
<tr><td>48</td><td>Delaware</td><td>163,268,000</td><td>0.4%</td><td>8</td><td>Georgia</td><td>1,246,239,000</td><td>3.3%</td></tr>
<tr><td>3</td><td>Florida</td><td>1,828,689,000</td><td>4.8%</td><td>9</td><td>Michigan</td><td>1,016,208,000</td><td>2.7%</td></tr>
<tr><td>8</td><td>Georgia</td><td>1,246,239,000</td><td>3.3%</td><td>10</td><td>North Carolina</td><td>1,006,630,000</td><td>2.7%</td></tr>
<tr><td>49</td><td>Hawaii</td><td>163,244,000</td><td>0.4%</td><td>11</td><td>Virginia</td><td>982,180,000</td><td>2.6%</td></tr>
<tr><td>41</td><td>Idaho</td><td>276,061,000</td><td>0.7%</td><td>12</td><td>New Jersey</td><td>963,683,000</td><td>2.5%</td></tr>
<tr><td>6</td><td>Illinois</td><td>1,372,231,000</td><td>3.6%</td><td>13</td><td>Indiana</td><td>919,669,000</td><td>2.4%</td></tr>
<tr><td>13</td><td>Indiana</td><td>919,669,000</td><td>2.4%</td><td>14</td><td>Missouri</td><td>913,720,000</td><td>2.4%</td></tr>
<tr><td>32</td><td>Iowa</td><td>474,345,000</td><td>1.3%</td><td>15</td><td>Tennessee</td><td>815,605,000</td><td>2.2%</td></tr>
<tr><td>36</td><td>Kansas</td><td>364,737,000</td><td>1.0%</td><td>16</td><td>Alabama</td><td>732,263,000</td><td>1.9%</td></tr>
<tr><td>22</td><td>Kentucky</td><td>641,292,000</td><td>1.7%</td><td>17</td><td>Wisconsin</td><td>726,227,000</td><td>1.9%</td></tr>
<tr><td>19</td><td>Louisiana</td><td>677,413,000</td><td>1.8%</td><td>18</td><td>Arizona</td><td>706,182,000</td><td>1.9%</td></tr>
<tr><td>47</td><td>Maine</td><td>178,166,000</td><td>0.5%</td><td>19</td><td>Louisiana</td><td>677,413,000</td><td>1.8%</td></tr>
<tr><td>26</td><td>Maryland</td><td>580,007,000</td><td>1.5%</td><td>20</td><td>Washington</td><td>654,305,000</td><td>1.7%</td></tr>
<tr><td>25</td><td>Massachusetts</td><td>586,192,000</td><td>1.6%</td><td>21</td><td>South Carolina</td><td>646,307,000</td><td>1.7%</td></tr>
<tr><td>9</td><td>Michigan</td><td>1,016,208,000</td><td>2.7%</td><td>22</td><td>Kentucky</td><td>641,292,000</td><td>1.7%</td></tr>
<tr><td>23</td><td>Minnesota</td><td>629,373,000</td><td>1.7%</td><td>23</td><td>Minnesota</td><td>629,373,000</td><td>1.7%</td></tr>
<tr><td>33</td><td>Mississippi</td><td>466,804,000</td><td>1.2%</td><td>24</td><td>Oklahoma</td><td>612,128,000</td><td>1.6%</td></tr>
<tr><td>14</td><td>Missouri</td><td>913,720,000</td><td>2.4%</td><td>25</td><td>Massachusetts</td><td>586,192,000</td><td>1.6%</td></tr>
<tr><td>35</td><td>Montana</td><td>396,007,000</td><td>1.0%</td><td>26</td><td>Maryland</td><td>580,007,000</td><td>1.5%</td></tr>
<tr><td>40</td><td>Nebraska</td><td>278,977,000</td><td>0.7%</td><td>27</td><td>Colorado</td><td>516,113,000</td><td>1.4%</td></tr>
<tr><td>38</td><td>Nevada</td><td>350,473,000</td><td>0.9%</td><td>28</td><td>Arkansas</td><td>499,714,000</td><td>1.3%</td></tr>
<tr><td>50</td><td>New Hampshire</td><td>159,470,000</td><td>0.4%</td><td>29</td><td>Connecticut</td><td>484,771,000</td><td>1.3%</td></tr>
<tr><td>12</td><td>New Jersey</td><td>963,683,000</td><td>2.5%</td><td>30</td><td>Alaska</td><td>483,955,000</td><td>1.3%</td></tr>
<tr><td>37</td><td>New Mexico</td><td>354,440,000</td><td>0.9%</td><td>31</td><td>Oregon</td><td>482,423,000</td><td>1.3%</td></tr>
<tr><td>4</td><td>New York</td><td>1,620,088,000</td><td>4.3%</td><td>32</td><td>Iowa</td><td>474,345,000</td><td>1.3%</td></tr>
<tr><td>10</td><td>North Carolina</td><td>1,006,630,000</td><td>2.7%</td><td>33</td><td>Mississippi</td><td>466,804,000</td><td>1.2%</td></tr>
<tr><td>44</td><td>North Dakota</td><td>239,622,000</td><td>0.6%</td><td>34</td><td>West Virginia</td><td>421,798,000</td><td>1.1%</td></tr>
<tr><td>7</td><td>Ohio</td><td>1,293,739,000</td><td>3.4%</td><td>35</td><td>Montana</td><td>396,007,000</td><td>1.0%</td></tr>
<tr><td>24</td><td>Oklahoma</td><td>612,128,000</td><td>1.6%</td><td>36</td><td>Kansas</td><td>364,737,000</td><td>1.0%</td></tr>
<tr><td>31</td><td>Oregon</td><td>482,423,000</td><td>1.3%</td><td>37</td><td>New Mexico</td><td>354,440,000</td><td>0.9%</td></tr>
<tr><td>5</td><td>Pennsylvania</td><td>1,583,603,000</td><td>4.2%</td><td>38</td><td>Nevada</td><td>350,473,000</td><td>0.9%</td></tr>
<tr><td>45</td><td>Rhode Island</td><td>211,082,000</td><td>0.6%</td><td>39</td><td>Utah</td><td>335,149,000</td><td>0.9%</td></tr>
<tr><td>21</td><td>South Carolina</td><td>646,307,000</td><td>1.7%</td><td>40</td><td>Nebraska</td><td>278,977,000</td><td>0.7%</td></tr>
<tr><td>42</td><td>South Dakota</td><td>272,191,000</td><td>0.7%</td><td>41</td><td>Idaho</td><td>276,061,000</td><td>0.7%</td></tr>
<tr><td>15</td><td>Tennessee</td><td>815,605,000</td><td>2.2%</td><td>42</td><td>South Dakota</td><td>272,191,000</td><td>0.7%</td></tr>
<tr><td>2</td><td>Texas</td><td>3,331,597,000</td><td>8.8%</td><td>43</td><td>Wyoming</td><td>247,263,000</td><td>0.7%</td></tr>
<tr><td>39</td><td>Utah</td><td>335,149,000</td><td>0.9%</td><td>44</td><td>North Dakota</td><td>239,622,000</td><td>0.6%</td></tr>
<tr><td>46</td><td>Vermont</td><td>195,887,000</td><td>0.5%</td><td>45</td><td>Rhode Island</td><td>211,082,000</td><td>0.6%</td></tr>
<tr><td>11</td><td>Virginia</td><td>982,180,000</td><td>2.6%</td><td>46</td><td>Vermont</td><td>195,887,000</td><td>0.5%</td></tr>
<tr><td>20</td><td>Washington</td><td>654,305,000</td><td>1.7%</td><td>47</td><td>Maine</td><td>178,166,000</td><td>0.5%</td></tr>
<tr><td>34</td><td>West Virginia</td><td>421,798,000</td><td>1.1%</td><td>48</td><td>Delaware</td><td>163,268,000</td><td>0.4%</td></tr>
<tr><td>17</td><td>Wisconsin</td><td>726,227,000</td><td>1.9%</td><td>49</td><td>Hawaii</td><td>163,244,000</td><td>0.4%</td></tr>
<tr><td>43</td><td>Wyoming</td><td>247,263,000</td><td>0.7%</td><td>50</td><td>New Hampshire</td><td>159,470,000</td><td>0.4%</td></tr>
<tr><td></td><td></td><td></td><td></td><td></td><td>District of Columbia</td><td>154,003,000</td><td>0.4%</td></tr>
</table>

Source: U.S. Department of Transportation, Federal Highway Administration
"Federal-aid Highway Fund Apportionments" (Table FA-4, http://www.fhwa.dot.gov/policyinformation/statistics/2014/)
*Fiscal Year 2015. National total does not include federal funds for U.S. territories.

Per Capita Federal Highway Funding in 2015

National Per Capita = $118*

ALPHA ORDER

RANK	STATE	PER CAPITA
16	Alabama	$151
1	Alaska	656
41	Arizona	104
11	Arkansas	168
46	California	91
45	Colorado	95
22	Connecticut	135
9	Delaware	173
48	Florida	90
29	Georgia	122
35	Hawaii	115
12	Idaho	167
40	Illinois	107
21	Indiana	139
15	Iowa	152
26	Kansas	125
19	Kentucky	145
19	Louisiana	145
23	Maine	134
44	Maryland	97
49	Massachusetts	86
42	Michigan	102
35	Minnesota	115
14	Mississippi	156
17	Missouri	150
3	Montana	384
18	Nebraska	147
29	Nevada	122
32	New Hampshire	120
39	New Jersey	108
10	New Mexico	170
50	New York	82
43	North Carolina	100
4	North Dakota	317
38	Ohio	111
13	Oklahoma	157
32	Oregon	120
27	Pennsylvania	124
8	Rhode Island	200
24	South Carolina	132
4	South Dakota	317
27	Tennessee	124
31	Texas	121
37	Utah	112
6	Vermont	313
34	Virginia	117
46	Washington	91
7	West Virginia	229
25	Wisconsin	126
2	Wyoming	422

RANK ORDER

RANK	STATE	PER CAPITA
1	Alaska	$656
2	Wyoming	422
3	Montana	384
4	North Dakota	317
4	South Dakota	317
6	Vermont	313
7	West Virginia	229
8	Rhode Island	200
9	Delaware	173
10	New Mexico	170
11	Arkansas	168
12	Idaho	167
13	Oklahoma	157
14	Mississippi	156
15	Iowa	152
16	Alabama	151
17	Missouri	150
18	Nebraska	147
19	Kentucky	145
19	Louisiana	145
21	Indiana	139
22	Connecticut	135
23	Maine	134
24	South Carolina	132
25	Wisconsin	126
26	Kansas	125
27	Pennsylvania	124
27	Tennessee	124
29	Georgia	122
29	Nevada	122
31	Texas	121
32	New Hampshire	120
32	Oregon	120
34	Virginia	117
35	Hawaii	115
35	Minnesota	115
37	Utah	112
38	Ohio	111
39	New Jersey	108
40	Illinois	107
41	Arizona	104
42	Michigan	102
43	North Carolina	100
44	Maryland	97
45	Colorado	95
46	California	91
46	Washington	91
48	Florida	90
49	Massachusetts	86
50	New York	82

District of Columbia	230

Source: CQ Press using data from U.S. Department of Transportation, Federal Highway Administration
"Federal-aid Highway Fund Apportionments" (Table FA-4, http://www.fhwa.dot.gov/policyinformation/statistics/2014/)
*Fiscal Year 2015. National per capita does not include population or federal funds for U.S. territories.

Public Road and Street Mileage in 2015

National Total = 4,154,727 Miles*

ALPHA ORDER

RANK	STATE	MILES	% of USA
18	Alabama	102,019	2.5%
46	Alaska	16,129	0.4%
33	Arizona	66,122	1.6%
17	Arkansas	102,609	2.5%
2	California	195,834	4.7%
22	Colorado	88,740	2.1%
44	Connecticut	21,512	0.5%
48	Delaware	6,416	0.2%
9	Florida	122,659	3.0%
7	Georgia	128,134	3.1%
50	Hawaii	4,455	0.1%
35	Idaho	51,163	1.2%
3	Illinois	145,840	3.5%
19	Indiana	96,571	2.3%
13	Iowa	114,442	2.8%
4	Kansas	140,654	3.4%
26	Kentucky	79,857	1.9%
34	Louisiana	61,419	1.5%
43	Maine	22,911	0.6%
41	Maryland	32,037	0.8%
40	Massachusetts	36,423	0.9%
10	Michigan	122,286	2.9%
5	Minnesota	138,767	3.3%
27	Mississippi	76,777	1.8%
6	Missouri	131,549	3.2%
30	Montana	75,007	1.8%
21	Nebraska	94,481	2.3%
37	Nevada	43,900	1.1%
45	New Hampshire	16,138	0.4%
38	New Jersey	39,065	0.9%
32	New Mexico	69,069	1.7%
14	New York	114,365	2.8%
16	North Carolina	106,334	2.6%
23	North Dakota	87,128	2.1%
8	Ohio	122,926	3.0%
15	Oklahoma	112,711	2.7%
31	Oregon	73,544	1.8%
11	Pennsylvania	120,091	2.9%
49	Rhode Island	6,046	0.1%
28	South Carolina	76,250	1.8%
24	South Dakota	82,576	2.0%
20	Tennessee	95,637	2.3%
1	Texas	313,596	7.5%
36	Utah	46,299	1.1%
47	Vermont	14,252	0.3%
29	Virginia	75,061	1.8%
25	Washington	80,338	1.9%
39	West Virginia	38,770	0.9%
12	Wisconsin	115,372	2.8%
42	Wyoming	28,942	0.7%

RANK ORDER

RANK	STATE	MILES	% of USA
1	Texas	313,596	7.5%
2	California	195,834	4.7%
3	Illinois	145,840	3.5%
4	Kansas	140,654	3.4%
5	Minnesota	138,767	3.3%
6	Missouri	131,549	3.2%
7	Georgia	128,134	3.1%
8	Ohio	122,926	3.0%
9	Florida	122,659	3.0%
10	Michigan	122,286	2.9%
11	Pennsylvania	120,091	2.9%
12	Wisconsin	115,372	2.8%
13	Iowa	114,442	2.8%
14	New York	114,365	2.8%
15	Oklahoma	112,711	2.7%
16	North Carolina	106,334	2.6%
17	Arkansas	102,609	2.5%
18	Alabama	102,019	2.5%
19	Indiana	96,571	2.3%
20	Tennessee	95,637	2.3%
21	Nebraska	94,481	2.3%
22	Colorado	88,740	2.1%
23	North Dakota	87,128	2.1%
24	South Dakota	82,576	2.0%
25	Washington	80,338	1.9%
26	Kentucky	79,857	1.9%
27	Mississippi	76,777	1.8%
28	South Carolina	76,250	1.8%
29	Virginia	75,061	1.8%
30	Montana	75,007	1.8%
31	Oregon	73,544	1.8%
32	New Mexico	69,069	1.7%
33	Arizona	66,122	1.6%
34	Louisiana	61,419	1.5%
35	Idaho	51,163	1.2%
36	Utah	46,299	1.1%
37	Nevada	43,900	1.1%
38	New Jersey	39,065	0.9%
39	West Virginia	38,770	0.9%
40	Massachusetts	36,423	0.9%
41	Maryland	32,037	0.8%
42	Wyoming	28,942	0.7%
43	Maine	22,911	0.6%
44	Connecticut	21,512	0.5%
45	New Hampshire	16,138	0.4%
46	Alaska	16,129	0.4%
47	Vermont	14,252	0.3%
48	Delaware	6,416	0.2%
49	Rhode Island	6,046	0.1%
50	Hawaii	4,455	0.1%
	District of Columbia	1,507	0.0%

Source: U.S. Department of Transportation, Federal Highway Administration
   "Highway Statistics 2015" (Table HM-20, http://www.fhwa.dot.gov/policyinformation/statistics/2015/)
*Does not include 17,184 miles of roads and streets in Puerto Rico.

Percent of Public Road and Street Mileage Federally Funded in 2015

National Percent = 24.6% of Public Road and Street Mileage*

ALPHA ORDER

RANK	STATE	PERCENT
18	Alabama	26.2
4	Alaska	29.4
43	Arizona	20.8
39	Arkansas	22.0
7	California	29.0
45	Colorado	19.8
4	Connecticut	29.4
24	Delaware	24.6
37	Florida	22.5
22	Georgia	24.8
1	Hawaii	35.1
36	Idaho	22.8
27	Illinois	24.5
24	Indiana	24.6
34	Iowa	22.9
24	Kansas	24.6
48	Kentucky	17.9
34	Louisiana	22.9
14	Maine	27.6
21	Maryland	25.0
2	Massachusetts	31.0
3	Michigan	30.0
31	Minnesota	23.9
8	Mississippi	28.6
33	Missouri	23.4
47	Montana	19.6
41	Nebraska	21.8
50	Nevada	17.1
39	New Hampshire	22.0
12	New Jersey	28.0
49	New Mexico	17.8
29	New York	24.2
38	North Carolina	22.1
42	North Dakota	21.6
27	Ohio	24.5
10	Oklahoma	28.5
19	Oregon	25.3
32	Pennsylvania	23.8
6	Rhode Island	29.1
13	South Carolina	27.9
30	South Dakota	24.1
46	Tennessee	19.7
8	Texas	28.6
44	Utah	20.6
15	Vermont	27.3
11	Virginia	28.3
19	Washington	25.3
15	West Virginia	27.3
22	Wisconsin	24.8
17	Wyoming	27.2

RANK ORDER

RANK	STATE	PERCENT
1	Hawaii	35.1
2	Massachusetts	31.0
3	Michigan	30.0
4	Alaska	29.4
4	Connecticut	29.4
6	Rhode Island	29.1
7	California	29.0
8	Mississippi	28.6
8	Texas	28.6
10	Oklahoma	28.5
11	Virginia	28.3
12	New Jersey	28.0
13	South Carolina	27.9
14	Maine	27.6
15	Vermont	27.3
15	West Virginia	27.3
17	Wyoming	27.2
18	Alabama	26.2
19	Oregon	25.3
19	Washington	25.3
21	Maryland	25.0
22	Georgia	24.8
22	Wisconsin	24.8
24	Delaware	24.6
24	Indiana	24.6
24	Kansas	24.6
27	Illinois	24.5
27	Ohio	24.5
29	New York	24.2
30	South Dakota	24.1
31	Minnesota	23.9
32	Pennsylvania	23.8
33	Missouri	23.4
34	Iowa	22.9
34	Louisiana	22.9
36	Idaho	22.8
37	Florida	22.5
38	North Carolina	22.1
39	Arkansas	22.0
39	New Hampshire	22.0
41	Nebraska	21.8
42	North Dakota	21.6
43	Arizona	20.8
44	Utah	20.6
45	Colorado	19.8
46	Tennessee	19.7
47	Montana	19.6
48	Kentucky	17.9
49	New Mexico	17.8
50	Nevada	17.1

District of Columbia — 30.1

Source: CQ Press using data from U.S. Department of Transportation, Federal Highway Administration
"Highway Statistics 2015" (Table HM-15, http://www.fhwa.dot.gov/policyinformation/statistics/2015/)
*National percent does not include federally-funded highway miles in Puerto Rico.

Interstate Highway Mileage in 2015

National Total = 48,053 Miles*

ALPHA ORDER

RANK	STATE	MILES	% of USA
18	Alabama	1,001	2.1%
17	Alaska	1,081	2.2%
14	Arizona	1,169	2.4%
34	Arkansas	703	1.5%
2	California	2,451	5.1%
20	Colorado	952	2.0%
45	Connecticut	346	0.7%
50	Delaware	41	0.1%
7	Florida	1,495	3.1%
12	Georgia	1,247	2.6%
49	Hawaii	55	0.1%
36	Idaho	612	1.3%
3	Illinois	2,185	4.5%
10	Indiana	1,265	2.6%
31	Iowa	788	1.6%
27	Kansas	874	1.8%
29	Kentucky	842	1.8%
21	Louisiana	937	1.9%
44	Maine	365	0.8%
42	Maryland	480	1.0%
38	Massachusetts	575	1.2%
11	Michigan	1,252	2.6%
24	Minnesota	914	1.9%
30	Mississippi	807	1.7%
8	Missouri	1,380	2.9%
13	Montana	1,192	2.5%
41	Nebraska	482	1.0%
37	Nevada	597	1.2%
47	New Hampshire	225	0.5%
43	New Jersey	432	0.9%
19	New Mexico	1,000	2.1%
5	New York	1,744	3.6%
9	North Carolina	1,271	2.6%
39	North Dakota	571	1.2%
6	Ohio	1,574	3.3%
23	Oklahoma	933	1.9%
33	Oregon	730	1.5%
4	Pennsylvania	1,867	3.9%
48	Rhode Island	70	0.1%
28	South Carolina	851	1.8%
35	South Dakota	679	1.4%
16	Tennessee	1,104	2.3%
1	Texas	3,417	7.1%
21	Utah	937	1.9%
46	Vermont	320	0.7%
15	Virginia	1,122	2.3%
32	Washington	764	1.6%
40	West Virginia	554	1.2%
26	Wisconsin	876	1.8%
24	Wyoming	914	1.9%

RANK ORDER

RANK	STATE	MILES	% of USA
1	Texas	3,417	7.1%
2	California	2,451	5.1%
3	Illinois	2,185	4.5%
4	Pennsylvania	1,867	3.9%
5	New York	1,744	3.6%
6	Ohio	1,574	3.3%
7	Florida	1,495	3.1%
8	Missouri	1,380	2.9%
9	North Carolina	1,271	2.6%
10	Indiana	1,265	2.6%
11	Michigan	1,252	2.6%
12	Georgia	1,247	2.6%
13	Montana	1,192	2.5%
14	Arizona	1,169	2.4%
15	Virginia	1,122	2.3%
16	Tennessee	1,104	2.3%
17	Alaska	1,081	2.2%
18	Alabama	1,001	2.1%
19	New Mexico	1,000	2.1%
20	Colorado	952	2.0%
21	Louisiana	937	1.9%
21	Utah	937	1.9%
23	Oklahoma	933	1.9%
24	Minnesota	914	1.9%
24	Wyoming	914	1.9%
26	Wisconsin	876	1.8%
27	Kansas	874	1.8%
28	South Carolina	851	1.8%
29	Kentucky	842	1.8%
30	Mississippi	807	1.7%
31	Iowa	788	1.6%
32	Washington	764	1.6%
33	Oregon	730	1.5%
34	Arkansas	703	1.5%
35	South Dakota	679	1.4%
36	Idaho	612	1.3%
37	Nevada	597	1.2%
38	Massachusetts	575	1.2%
39	North Dakota	571	1.2%
40	West Virginia	554	1.2%
41	Nebraska	482	1.0%
42	Maryland	480	1.0%
43	New Jersey	432	0.9%
44	Maine	365	0.8%
45	Connecticut	346	0.7%
46	Vermont	320	0.7%
47	New Hampshire	225	0.5%
48	Rhode Island	70	0.1%
49	Hawaii	55	0.1%
50	Delaware	41	0.1%
	District of Columbia	12	0.0%

Source: U.S. Department of Transportation, Federal Highway Administration
"Highway Statistics 2015" (Table HM-15, http://www.fhwa.dot.gov/policyinformation/statistics/2015/)
*Does not include 282 miles of highway in Puerto Rico that are part of the interstate system.

Rural Road and Street Mileage in 2015

National Total = 2,945,513 Rural Miles*

ALPHA ORDER

RANK	STATE	MILES	% of USA
16	Alabama	75,788	2.6%
42	Alaska	13,296	0.5%
34	Arizona	39,800	1.4%
11	Arkansas	85,481	2.9%
10	California	86,349	2.9%
20	Colorado	68,271	2.3%
47	Connecticut	5,683	0.2%
48	Delaware	3,010	0.1%
35	Florida	36,489	1.2%
15	Georgia	77,788	2.6%
49	Hawaii	1,668	0.1%
32	Idaho	45,231	1.5%
6	Illinois	96,185	3.3%
21	Indiana	66,356	2.3%
5	Iowa	101,969	3.5%
2	Kansas	126,780	4.3%
23	Kentucky	64,822	2.2%
33	Louisiana	43,808	1.5%
40	Maine	19,910	0.7%
41	Maryland	13,461	0.5%
45	Massachusetts	6,369	0.2%
13	Michigan	84,322	2.9%
3	Minnesota	116,624	4.0%
26	Mississippi	63,912	2.2%
4	Missouri	107,165	3.6%
19	Montana	70,822	2.4%
9	Nebraska	87,335	3.0%
37	Nevada	34,263	1.2%
44	New Hampshire	11,083	0.4%
46	New Jersey	5,684	0.2%
27	New Mexico	60,712	2.1%
24	New York	64,398	2.2%
22	North Carolina	65,502	2.2%
12	North Dakota	85,003	2.9%
17	Ohio	75,492	2.6%
7	Oklahoma	94,790	3.2%
28	Oregon	58,641	2.0%
18	Pennsylvania	72,492	2.5%
50	Rhode Island	1,361	0.0%
29	South Carolina	57,681	2.0%
14	South Dakota	79,193	2.7%
25	Tennessee	64,336	2.2%
1	Texas	205,222	7.0%
36	Utah	35,246	1.2%
43	Vermont	12,791	0.4%
31	Virginia	47,273	1.6%
30	Washington	56,305	1.9%
38	West Virginia	31,627	1.1%
8	Wisconsin	91,716	3.1%
39	Wyoming	26,010	0.9%

RANK ORDER

RANK	STATE	MILES	% of USA
1	Texas	205,222	7.0%
2	Kansas	126,780	4.3%
3	Minnesota	116,624	4.0%
4	Missouri	107,165	3.6%
5	Iowa	101,969	3.5%
6	Illinois	96,185	3.3%
7	Oklahoma	94,790	3.2%
8	Wisconsin	91,716	3.1%
9	Nebraska	87,335	3.0%
10	California	86,349	2.9%
11	Arkansas	85,481	2.9%
12	North Dakota	85,003	2.9%
13	Michigan	84,322	2.9%
14	South Dakota	79,193	2.7%
15	Georgia	77,788	2.6%
16	Alabama	75,788	2.6%
17	Ohio	75,492	2.6%
18	Pennsylvania	72,492	2.5%
19	Montana	70,822	2.4%
20	Colorado	68,271	2.3%
21	Indiana	66,356	2.3%
22	North Carolina	65,502	2.2%
23	Kentucky	64,822	2.2%
24	New York	64,398	2.2%
25	Tennessee	64,336	2.2%
26	Mississippi	63,912	2.2%
27	New Mexico	60,712	2.1%
28	Oregon	58,641	2.0%
29	South Carolina	57,681	2.0%
30	Washington	56,305	1.9%
31	Virginia	47,273	1.6%
32	Idaho	45,231	1.5%
33	Louisiana	43,808	1.5%
34	Arizona	39,800	1.4%
35	Florida	36,489	1.2%
36	Utah	35,246	1.2%
37	Nevada	34,263	1.2%
38	West Virginia	31,627	1.1%
39	Wyoming	26,010	0.9%
40	Maine	19,910	0.7%
41	Maryland	13,461	0.5%
42	Alaska	13,296	0.5%
43	Vermont	12,791	0.4%
44	New Hampshire	11,083	0.4%
45	Massachusetts	6,369	0.2%
46	New Jersey	5,684	0.2%
47	Connecticut	5,683	0.2%
48	Delaware	3,010	0.1%
49	Hawaii	1,668	0.1%
50	Rhode Island	1,361	0.0%
	District of Columbia	0	0.0%

Source: U.S. Department of Transportation, Federal Highway Administration
    "Highway Statistics 2015" (Table HM-20, http://www.fhwa.dot.gov/policyinformation/statistics/2015/)
*Does not include 3,067 miles of rural roads and streets in Puerto Rico.

Urban Road and Street Mileage in 2015

National Total = 1,209,214 Urban Miles*

ALPHA ORDER				RANK ORDER			
RANK	STATE	MILES	% of USA	RANK	STATE	MILES	% of USA
17	Alabama	26,231	2.2%	1	California	109,485	9.1%
47	Alaska	2,833	0.2%	2	Texas	108,373	9.0%
16	Arizona	26,322	2.2%	3	Florida	86,170	7.1%
27	Arkansas	17,128	1.4%	4	Georgia	50,346	4.2%
1	California	109,485	9.1%	5	New York	49,967	4.1%
22	Colorado	20,469	1.7%	6	Illinois	49,655	4.1%
28	Connecticut	15,829	1.3%	7	Pennsylvania	47,599	3.9%
43	Delaware	3,406	0.3%	8	Ohio	47,434	3.9%
3	Florida	86,170	7.1%	9	North Carolina	40,832	3.4%
4	Georgia	50,346	4.2%	10	Michigan	37,964	3.1%
48	Hawaii	2,788	0.2%	11	New Jersey	33,381	2.8%
39	Idaho	5,932	0.5%	12	Tennessee	31,301	2.6%
6	Illinois	49,655	4.1%	13	Indiana	30,214	2.5%
13	Indiana	30,214	2.5%	14	Massachusetts	30,054	2.5%
33	Iowa	12,473	1.0%	15	Virginia	27,789	2.3%
31	Kansas	13,874	1.1%	16	Arizona	26,322	2.2%
29	Kentucky	15,035	1.2%	17	Alabama	26,231	2.2%
26	Louisiana	17,610	1.5%	18	Missouri	24,384	2.0%
45	Maine	3,001	0.2%	19	Washington	24,033	2.0%
23	Maryland	18,576	1.5%	20	Wisconsin	23,656	2.0%
14	Massachusetts	30,054	2.5%	21	Minnesota	22,144	1.8%
10	Michigan	37,964	3.1%	22	Colorado	20,469	1.7%
21	Minnesota	22,144	1.8%	23	Maryland	18,576	1.5%
32	Mississippi	12,865	1.1%	24	South Carolina	18,569	1.5%
18	Missouri	24,384	2.0%	25	Oklahoma	17,922	1.5%
42	Montana	4,186	0.3%	26	Louisiana	17,610	1.5%
37	Nebraska	7,146	0.6%	27	Arkansas	17,128	1.4%
35	Nevada	9,638	0.8%	28	Connecticut	15,829	1.3%
40	New Hampshire	5,056	0.4%	29	Kentucky	15,035	1.2%
11	New Jersey	33,381	2.8%	30	Oregon	14,902	1.2%
36	New Mexico	8,356	0.7%	31	Kansas	13,874	1.1%
5	New York	49,967	4.1%	32	Mississippi	12,865	1.1%
9	North Carolina	40,832	3.4%	33	Iowa	12,473	1.0%
49	North Dakota	2,125	0.2%	34	Utah	11,052	0.9%
8	Ohio	47,434	3.9%	35	Nevada	9,638	0.8%
25	Oklahoma	17,922	1.5%	36	New Mexico	8,356	0.7%
30	Oregon	14,902	1.2%	37	Nebraska	7,146	0.6%
7	Pennsylvania	47,599	3.9%	38	West Virginia	7,143	0.6%
41	Rhode Island	4,686	0.4%	39	Idaho	5,932	0.5%
24	South Carolina	18,569	1.5%	40	New Hampshire	5,056	0.4%
44	South Dakota	3,383	0.3%	41	Rhode Island	4,686	0.4%
12	Tennessee	31,301	2.6%	42	Montana	4,186	0.3%
2	Texas	108,373	9.0%	43	Delaware	3,406	0.3%
34	Utah	11,052	0.9%	44	South Dakota	3,383	0.3%
50	Vermont	1,462	0.1%	45	Maine	3,001	0.2%
15	Virginia	27,789	2.3%	46	Wyoming	2,931	0.2%
19	Washington	24,033	2.0%	47	Alaska	2,833	0.2%
38	West Virginia	7,143	0.6%	48	Hawaii	2,788	0.2%
20	Wisconsin	23,656	2.0%	49	North Dakota	2,125	0.2%
46	Wyoming	2,931	0.2%	50	Vermont	1,462	0.1%
					District of Columbia	1,507	0.1%

Source: U.S. Department of Transportation, Federal Highway Administration
   "Highway Statistics 2015" (Table HM-20, http://www.fhwa.dot.gov/policyinformation/statistics/2015/)
*Does not include 14,116 miles of urban roads and streets in Puerto Rico.

Percent of Roadways in Mediocre or Poor Condition in 2013

National Percent = 19.9%*

ALPHA ORDER				RANK ORDER		
RANK	STATE	PERCENT		RANK	STATE	PERCENT
39	Alabama	10.7		1	Hawaii	43.2
14	Alaska	25.4		2	Connecticut	42.3
41	Arizona	9.7		3	California	38.4
29	Arkansas	16.3		4	Rhode Island	38.0
3	California	38.4		5	New Jersey	37.8
21	Colorado	21.2		6	Michigan	35.8
2	Connecticut	42.3		7	Washington	33.0
28	Delaware	16.4		8	Oklahoma	30.2
47	Florida	7.0		9	West Virginia	29.7
34	Georgia	12.1		10	New York	28.3
1	Hawaii	43.2		11	Maine	27.0
25	Idaho	18.0		12	New Hampshire	26.1
22	Illinois	20.6		13	Wisconsin	25.6
26	Indiana	17.4		14	Alaska	25.4
30	Iowa	14.4		15	New Mexico	25.3
36	Kansas	11.0		16	Louisiana	24.9
44	Kentucky	9.0		16	Mississippi	24.9
16	Louisiana	24.9		18	Vermont	24.4
11	Maine	27.0		19	Maryland	24.2
19	Maryland	24.2		20	Pennsylvania	22.8
33	Massachusetts	12.8		21	Colorado	21.2
6	Michigan	35.8		22	Illinois	20.6
40	Minnesota	10.3		23	Missouri	20.2
16	Mississippi	24.9		24	Virginia	19.8
23	Missouri	20.2		25	Idaho	18.0
43	Montana	9.1		26	Indiana	17.4
49	Nebraska	4.7		27	Utah	17.3
50	Nevada	3.6		28	Delaware	16.4
12	New Hampshire	26.1		29	Arkansas	16.3
5	New Jersey	37.8		30	Iowa	14.4
15	New Mexico	25.3		31	Texas	14.2
10	New York	28.3		32	Ohio	13.5
37	North Carolina	10.9		33	Massachusetts	12.8
37	North Dakota	10.9		34	Georgia	12.1
32	Ohio	13.5		34	South Carolina	12.1
8	Oklahoma	30.2		36	Kansas	11.0
45	Oregon	8.8		37	North Carolina	10.9
20	Pennsylvania	22.8		37	North Dakota	10.9
4	Rhode Island	38.0		39	Alabama	10.7
34	South Carolina	12.1		40	Minnesota	10.3
42	South Dakota	9.2		41	Arizona	9.7
48	Tennessee	6.8		42	South Dakota	9.2
31	Texas	14.2		43	Montana	9.1
27	Utah	17.3		44	Kentucky	9.0
18	Vermont	24.4		45	Oregon	8.8
24	Virginia	19.8		46	Wyoming	8.3
7	Washington	33.0		47	Florida	7.0
9	West Virginia	29.7		48	Tennessee	6.8
13	Wisconsin	25.6		49	Nebraska	4.7
46	Wyoming	8.3		50	Nevada	3.6

District of Columbia 94.5

Source: CQ Press using data from U.S. Department of Transportation, Bureau of Transportation Statistics
"State Transportation Statistics 2015" (Table 1-4, https://www.rita.dot.gov/bts/publications/state_transportation_statistics)
*Does not include 14,062 miles for which the condition is not reported. Road condition ratings are derived from the International Roughness Index (IRI) and the Present Serviceability Rating (PSR). States are required to report to the Federal Highway Administration (FHWA) IRI data for the Interstate system, other principal arterials, rural minor arterials, and the National Highway System regardless of functional system.

Bridges in 2015

National Total = 609,539 Bridges*

Source: U.S. Department of Transportation, Federal Highway Administration
"Deficient Bridges by State and Highway System, 2015" (http://www.fhwa.dot.gov/bridge/deficient.htm)
*As of December 2015. Includes federal-aid and nonfederal-aid system bridges. National total does not include 2,306 bridges in Puerto Rico.

ALPHA ORDER

RANK	STATE	BRIDGES	% of USA
15	Alabama	16,095	2.6%
47	Alaska	1,493	0.2%
29	Arizona	8,056	1.3%
23	Arkansas	12,853	2.1%
4	California	25,318	4.2%
27	Colorado	8,624	1.4%
39	Connecticut	4,225	0.7%
49	Delaware	875	0.1%
24	Florida	12,198	2.0%
17	Georgia	14,790	2.4%
48	Hawaii	1,142	0.2%
38	Idaho	4,369	0.7%
3	Illinois	26,674	4.4%
11	Indiana	19,145	3.1%
7	Iowa	24,242	4.0%
5	Kansas	25,047	4.1%
18	Kentucky	14,261	2.3%
22	Louisiana	13,012	2.1%
45	Maine	2,431	0.4%
34	Maryland	5,313	0.9%
36	Massachusetts	5,167	0.8%
25	Michigan	11,086	1.8%
21	Minnesota	13,301	2.2%
14	Mississippi	17,057	2.8%
6	Missouri	24,398	4.0%
35	Montana	5,243	0.9%
16	Nebraska	15,341	2.5%
46	Nevada	1,919	0.3%
44	New Hampshire	2,470	0.4%
32	New Jersey	6,686	1.1%
40	New Mexico	3,960	0.6%
13	New York	17,461	2.9%
12	North Carolina	18,124	3.0%
37	North Dakota	4,401	0.7%
2	Ohio	27,104	4.4%
8	Oklahoma	23,049	3.8%
30	Oregon	8,037	1.3%
9	Pennsylvania	22,783	3.7%
50	Rhode Island	766	0.1%
26	South Carolina	9,344	1.5%
33	South Dakota	5,866	1.0%
10	Tennessee	20,106	3.3%
1	Texas	53,209	8.7%
42	Utah	3,019	0.5%
43	Vermont	2,749	0.5%
20	Virginia	13,884	2.3%
28	Washington	8,158	1.3%
31	West Virginia	7,215	1.2%
19	Wisconsin	14,134	2.3%
41	Wyoming	3,085	0.5%

RANK ORDER

RANK	STATE	BRIDGES	% of USA
1	Texas	53,209	8.7%
2	Ohio	27,104	4.4%
3	Illinois	26,674	4.4%
4	California	25,318	4.2%
5	Kansas	25,047	4.1%
6	Missouri	24,398	4.0%
7	Iowa	24,242	4.0%
8	Oklahoma	23,049	3.8%
9	Pennsylvania	22,783	3.7%
10	Tennessee	20,106	3.3%
11	Indiana	19,145	3.1%
12	North Carolina	18,124	3.0%
13	New York	17,461	2.9%
14	Mississippi	17,057	2.8%
15	Alabama	16,095	2.6%
16	Nebraska	15,341	2.5%
17	Georgia	14,790	2.4%
18	Kentucky	14,261	2.3%
19	Wisconsin	14,134	2.3%
20	Virginia	13,884	2.3%
21	Minnesota	13,301	2.2%
22	Louisiana	13,012	2.1%
23	Arkansas	12,853	2.1%
24	Florida	12,198	2.0%
25	Michigan	11,086	1.8%
26	South Carolina	9,344	1.5%
27	Colorado	8,624	1.4%
28	Washington	8,158	1.3%
29	Arizona	8,056	1.3%
30	Oregon	8,037	1.3%
31	West Virginia	7,215	1.2%
32	New Jersey	6,686	1.1%
33	South Dakota	5,866	1.0%
34	Maryland	5,313	0.9%
35	Montana	5,243	0.9%
36	Massachusetts	5,167	0.8%
37	North Dakota	4,401	0.7%
38	Idaho	4,369	0.7%
39	Connecticut	4,225	0.7%
40	New Mexico	3,960	0.6%
41	Wyoming	3,085	0.5%
42	Utah	3,019	0.5%
43	Vermont	2,749	0.5%
44	New Hampshire	2,470	0.4%
45	Maine	2,431	0.4%
46	Nevada	1,919	0.3%
47	Alaska	1,493	0.2%
48	Hawaii	1,142	0.2%
49	Delaware	875	0.1%
50	Rhode Island	766	0.1%
	District of Columbia	254	0.0%

Deficient Bridges in 2015

National Total = 141,651 Deficient Bridges*

RANK	STATE	BRIDGES	% of USA
17	Alabama	3,468	2.4%
45	Alaska	582	0.4%
36	Arizona	919	0.6%
21	Arkansas	2,857	2.0%
4	California	6,428	4.5%
34	Colorado	1,372	1.0%
31	Connecticut	1,444	1.0%
50	Delaware	177	0.1%
28	Florida	2,011	1.4%
24	Georgia	2,352	1.7%
46	Hawaii	495	0.3%
40	Idaho	835	0.6%
11	Illinois	4,203	3.0%
13	Indiana	4,027	2.8%
7	Iowa	6,096	4.3%
12	Kansas	4,094	2.9%
10	Kentucky	4,381	3.1%
14	Louisiana	3,797	2.7%
41	Maine	831	0.6%
33	Maryland	1,384	1.0%
22	Massachusetts	2,692	1.9%
20	Michigan	3,044	2.1%
35	Minnesota	1,185	0.8%
19	Mississippi	3,447	2.4%
5	Missouri	6,281	4.4%
38	Montana	914	0.6%
18	Nebraska	3,458	2.4%
49	Nevada	254	0.2%
42	New Hampshire	765	0.5%
25	New Jersey	2,310	1.6%
44	New Mexico	626	0.4%
3	New York	6,688	4.7%
9	North Carolina	5,174	3.7%
36	North Dakota	919	0.6%
6	Ohio	6,171	4.4%
8	Oklahoma	5,362	3.8%
29	Oregon	1,854	1.3%
2	Pennsylvania	9,102	6.4%
48	Rhode Island	429	0.3%
30	South Carolina	1,852	1.3%
32	South Dakota	1,388	1.0%
15	Tennessee	3,633	2.6%
1	Texas	9,936	7.0%
47	Utah	481	0.3%
39	Vermont	848	0.6%
16	Virginia	3,580	2.5%
26	Washington	2,104	1.5%
23	West Virginia	2,554	1.8%
27	Wisconsin	2,024	1.4%
43	Wyoming	649	0.5%

RANK	STATE	BRIDGES	% of USA
1	Texas	9,936	7.0%
2	Pennsylvania	9,102	6.4%
3	New York	6,688	4.7%
4	California	6,428	4.5%
5	Missouri	6,281	4.4%
6	Ohio	6,171	4.4%
7	Iowa	6,096	4.3%
8	Oklahoma	5,362	3.8%
9	North Carolina	5,174	3.7%
10	Kentucky	4,381	3.1%
11	Illinois	4,203	3.0%
12	Kansas	4,094	2.9%
13	Indiana	4,027	2.8%
14	Louisiana	3,797	2.7%
15	Tennessee	3,633	2.6%
16	Virginia	3,580	2.5%
17	Alabama	3,468	2.4%
18	Nebraska	3,458	2.4%
19	Mississippi	3,447	2.4%
20	Michigan	3,044	2.1%
21	Arkansas	2,857	2.0%
22	Massachusetts	2,692	1.9%
23	West Virginia	2,554	1.8%
24	Georgia	2,352	1.7%
25	New Jersey	2,310	1.6%
26	Washington	2,104	1.5%
27	Wisconsin	2,024	1.4%
28	Florida	2,011	1.4%
29	Oregon	1,854	1.3%
30	South Carolina	1,852	1.3%
31	Connecticut	1,444	1.0%
32	South Dakota	1,388	1.0%
33	Maryland	1,384	1.0%
34	Colorado	1,372	1.0%
35	Minnesota	1,185	0.8%
36	Arizona	919	0.6%
36	North Dakota	919	0.6%
38	Montana	914	0.6%
39	Vermont	848	0.6%
40	Idaho	835	0.6%
41	Maine	831	0.6%
42	New Hampshire	765	0.5%
43	Wyoming	649	0.5%
44	New Mexico	626	0.4%
45	Alaska	582	0.4%
46	Hawaii	495	0.3%
47	Utah	481	0.3%
48	Rhode Island	429	0.3%
49	Nevada	254	0.2%
50	Delaware	177	0.1%
	District of Columbia	174	0.1%

Source: U.S. Department of Transportation, Federal Highway Administration

"Deficient Bridges by State and Highway System, 2015" (http://www.fhwa.dot.gov/bridge/deficient.htm)

*As of December 2015. Includes federal-aid and nonfederal-aid system bridges. National total does not include 1,264 deficient bridges in Puerto Rico. Bridges classified as deficient are either functionally obsolete or structurally deficient and are not necessarily unsafe.

Deficient Bridges as a Percent of Total Bridges in 2015

National Percent = 23.2% of Bridges Are Deficient*

ALPHA ORDER			RANK ORDER		
RANK	STATE	PERCENT	RANK	STATE	PERCENT
29	Alabama	21.5	1	Rhode Island	56.0
5	Alaska	39.0	2	Massachusetts	52.1
49	Arizona	11.4	3	Hawaii	43.3
28	Arkansas	22.2	4	Pennsylvania	40.0
21	California	25.4	5	Alaska	39.0
42	Colorado	15.9	6	New York	38.3
9	Connecticut	34.2	7	West Virginia	35.4
33	Delaware	20.2	8	New Jersey	34.5
40	Florida	16.5	9	Connecticut	34.2
42	Georgia	15.9	9	Maine	34.2
3	Hawaii	43.3	11	New Hampshire	31.0
36	Idaho	19.1	12	Vermont	30.8
45	Illinois	15.8	13	Kentucky	30.7
30	Indiana	21.0	14	Louisiana	29.2
22	Iowa	25.1	15	North Carolina	28.5
41	Kansas	16.3	16	Michigan	27.5
13	Kentucky	30.7	17	Maryland	26.0
14	Louisiana	29.2	18	Virginia	25.8
9	Maine	34.2	18	Washington	25.8
17	Maryland	26.0	20	Missouri	25.7
2	Massachusetts	52.1	21	California	25.4
16	Michigan	27.5	22	Iowa	25.1
50	Minnesota	8.9	23	South Dakota	23.7
33	Mississippi	20.2	24	Oklahoma	23.3
20	Missouri	25.7	25	Oregon	23.1
39	Montana	17.4	26	Ohio	22.8
27	Nebraska	22.5	27	Nebraska	22.5
48	Nevada	13.2	28	Arkansas	22.2
11	New Hampshire	31.0	29	Alabama	21.5
8	New Jersey	34.5	30	Indiana	21.0
45	New Mexico	15.8	30	Wyoming	21.0
6	New York	38.3	32	North Dakota	20.9
15	North Carolina	28.5	33	Delaware	20.2
32	North Dakota	20.9	33	Mississippi	20.2
26	Ohio	22.8	35	South Carolina	19.8
24	Oklahoma	23.3	36	Idaho	19.1
25	Oregon	23.1	37	Texas	18.7
4	Pennsylvania	40.0	38	Tennessee	18.1
1	Rhode Island	56.0	39	Montana	17.4
35	South Carolina	19.8	40	Florida	16.5
23	South Dakota	23.7	41	Kansas	16.3
38	Tennessee	18.1	42	Colorado	15.9
37	Texas	18.7	42	Georgia	15.9
42	Utah	15.9	42	Utah	15.9
12	Vermont	30.8	45	Illinois	15.8
18	Virginia	25.8	45	New Mexico	15.8
18	Washington	25.8	47	Wisconsin	14.3
7	West Virginia	35.4	48	Nevada	13.2
47	Wisconsin	14.3	49	Arizona	11.4
30	Wyoming	21.0	50	Minnesota	8.9
				District of Columbia	68.5

Source: CQ Press using data from U.S. Department of Transportation, Federal Highway Administration
    "Deficient Bridges by State and Highway System, 2015" (http://www.fhwa.dot.gov/bridge/deficient.htm)
*As of December 2015. Includes federal-aid and nonfederal-aid system bridges. National percent does not include bridges in
Puerto Rico. Bridges classified as deficient are either functionally obsolete or structurally deficient and are not necessarily
unsafe.

Vehicle-Miles of Travel in 2015

National Total = 3,095,372,701,000 Miles

ALPHA ORDER

RANK	STATE	MILES	% of USA
16	Alabama	67,257,005,000	2.2%
50	Alaska	5,045,390,000	0.2%
17	Arizona	65,044,858,000	2.1%
30	Arkansas	34,897,334,000	1.1%
1	California	335,538,557,000	10.8%
24	Colorado	50,437,338,000	1.6%
32	Connecticut	31,591,794,000	1.0%
45	Delaware	9,930,610,000	0.3%
3	Florida	206,982,464,000	6.7%
5	Georgia	118,106,561,000	3.8%
43	Hawaii	10,300,530,000	0.3%
39	Idaho	16,661,950,000	0.5%
8	Illinois	105,223,406,000	3.4%
12	Indiana	78,818,673,000	2.5%
31	Iowa	33,160,976,000	1.1%
33	Kansas	31,379,125,000	1.0%
25	Kentucky	48,674,696,000	1.6%
26	Louisiana	48,180,253,000	1.6%
40	Maine	14,629,439,000	0.5%
21	Maryland	57,515,824,000	1.9%
20	Massachusetts	59,257,481,000	1.9%
10	Michigan	97,843,197,000	3.2%
22	Minnesota	57,394,872,000	1.9%
28	Mississippi	39,890,362,000	1.3%
15	Missouri	71,917,519,000	2.3%
42	Montana	12,345,071,000	0.4%
37	Nebraska	20,100,959,000	0.6%
36	Nevada	25,925,442,000	0.8%
41	New Hampshire	13,093,742,000	0.4%
14	New Jersey	75,393,419,000	2.4%
35	New Mexico	27,435,418,000	0.9%
4	New York	127,230,214,000	4.1%
7	North Carolina	111,878,569,000	3.6%
44	North Dakota	10,036,217,000	0.3%
6	Ohio	113,672,505,000	3.7%
27	Oklahoma	47,713,000,000	1.5%
29	Oregon	35,998,505,000	1.2%
9	Pennsylvania	100,945,060,000	3.3%
48	Rhode Island	7,832,561,000	0.3%
23	South Carolina	51,726,048,000	1.7%
47	South Dakota	9,324,353,000	0.3%
13	Tennessee	76,670,318,000	2.5%
2	Texas	258,122,309,000	8.3%
34	Utah	29,603,663,000	1.0%
49	Vermont	7,313,842,000	0.2%
11	Virginia	82,624,528,000	2.7%
19	Washington	59,652,504,000	1.9%
38	West Virginia	19,826,643,000	0.6%
18	Wisconsin	62,073,368,000	2.0%
46	Wyoming	9,597,036,000	0.3%

RANK ORDER

RANK	STATE	MILES	% of USA
1	California	335,538,557,000	10.8%
2	Texas	258,122,309,000	8.3%
3	Florida	206,982,464,000	6.7%
4	New York	127,230,214,000	4.1%
5	Georgia	118,106,561,000	3.8%
6	Ohio	113,672,505,000	3.7%
7	North Carolina	111,878,569,000	3.6%
8	Illinois	105,223,406,000	3.4%
9	Pennsylvania	100,945,060,000	3.3%
10	Michigan	97,843,197,000	3.2%
11	Virginia	82,624,528,000	2.7%
12	Indiana	78,818,673,000	2.5%
13	Tennessee	76,670,318,000	2.5%
14	New Jersey	75,393,419,000	2.4%
15	Missouri	71,917,519,000	2.3%
16	Alabama	67,257,005,000	2.2%
17	Arizona	65,044,858,000	2.1%
18	Wisconsin	62,073,368,000	2.0%
19	Washington	59,652,504,000	1.9%
20	Massachusetts	59,257,481,000	1.9%
21	Maryland	57,515,824,000	1.9%
22	Minnesota	57,394,872,000	1.9%
23	South Carolina	51,726,048,000	1.7%
24	Colorado	50,437,338,000	1.6%
25	Kentucky	48,674,696,000	1.6%
26	Louisiana	48,180,253,000	1.6%
27	Oklahoma	47,713,000,000	1.5%
28	Mississippi	39,890,362,000	1.3%
29	Oregon	35,998,505,000	1.2%
30	Arkansas	34,897,334,000	1.1%
31	Iowa	33,160,976,000	1.1%
32	Connecticut	31,591,794,000	1.0%
33	Kansas	31,379,125,000	1.0%
34	Utah	29,603,663,000	1.0%
35	New Mexico	27,435,418,000	0.9%
36	Nevada	25,925,442,000	0.8%
37	Nebraska	20,100,959,000	0.6%
38	West Virginia	19,826,643,000	0.6%
39	Idaho	16,661,950,000	0.5%
40	Maine	14,629,439,000	0.5%
41	New Hampshire	13,093,742,000	0.4%
42	Montana	12,345,071,000	0.4%
43	Hawaii	10,300,530,000	0.3%
44	North Dakota	10,036,217,000	0.3%
45	Delaware	9,930,610,000	0.3%
46	Wyoming	9,597,036,000	0.3%
47	South Dakota	9,324,353,000	0.3%
48	Rhode Island	7,832,561,000	0.3%
49	Vermont	7,313,842,000	0.2%
50	Alaska	5,045,390,000	0.2%
	District of Columbia	3,557,193,000	0.1%

Source: U.S. Department of Transportation, Federal Highway Administration
"Highway Statistics 2015" (Table VM-2, http://www.fhwa.dot.gov/policyinformation/statistics/2015/)

Highway Fatalities in 2014

National Total = 32,675 Fatalities

ALPHA ORDER

RANK	STATE	FATALITIES	% of USA
13	Alabama	820	2.5%
48	Alaska	73	0.2%
14	Arizona	770	2.4%
25	Arkansas	466	1.4%
2	California	3,074	9.4%
24	Colorado	488	1.5%
37	Connecticut	248	0.8%
45	Delaware	121	0.4%
3	Florida	2,494	7.6%
6	Georgia	1,164	3.6%
46	Hawaii	95	0.3%
40	Idaho	186	0.6%
10	Illinois	924	2.8%
16	Indiana	746	2.3%
33	Iowa	321	1.0%
28	Kansas	385	1.2%
19	Kentucky	672	2.1%
17	Louisiana	737	2.3%
44	Maine	131	0.4%
27	Maryland	442	1.4%
32	Massachusetts	328	1.0%
11	Michigan	901	2.8%
30	Minnesota	361	1.1%
21	Mississippi	607	1.9%
15	Missouri	766	2.3%
39	Montana	192	0.6%
38	Nebraska	225	0.7%
34	Nevada	290	0.9%
46	New Hampshire	95	0.3%
22	New Jersey	556	1.7%
29	New Mexico	383	1.2%
7	New York	1,039	3.2%
4	North Carolina	1,284	3.9%
43	North Dakota	135	0.4%
8	Ohio	1,006	3.1%
20	Oklahoma	669	2.0%
31	Oregon	357	1.1%
5	Pennsylvania	1,195	3.7%
49	Rhode Island	52	0.2%
12	South Carolina	824	2.5%
42	South Dakota	136	0.4%
9	Tennessee	962	2.9%
1	Texas	3,538	10.8%
36	Utah	256	0.8%
50	Vermont	44	0.1%
18	Virginia	703	2.2%
26	Washington	462	1.4%
35	West Virginia	272	0.8%
23	Wisconsin	507	1.6%
41	Wyoming	150	0.5%

RANK ORDER

RANK	STATE	FATALITIES	% of USA
1	Texas	3,538	10.8%
2	California	3,074	9.4%
3	Florida	2,494	7.6%
4	North Carolina	1,284	3.9%
5	Pennsylvania	1,195	3.7%
6	Georgia	1,164	3.6%
7	New York	1,039	3.2%
8	Ohio	1,006	3.1%
9	Tennessee	962	2.9%
10	Illinois	924	2.8%
11	Michigan	901	2.8%
12	South Carolina	824	2.5%
13	Alabama	820	2.5%
14	Arizona	770	2.4%
15	Missouri	766	2.3%
16	Indiana	746	2.3%
17	Louisiana	737	2.3%
18	Virginia	703	2.2%
19	Kentucky	672	2.1%
20	Oklahoma	669	2.0%
21	Mississippi	607	1.9%
22	New Jersey	556	1.7%
23	Wisconsin	507	1.6%
24	Colorado	488	1.5%
25	Arkansas	466	1.4%
26	Washington	462	1.4%
27	Maryland	442	1.4%
28	Kansas	385	1.2%
29	New Mexico	383	1.2%
30	Minnesota	361	1.1%
31	Oregon	357	1.1%
32	Massachusetts	328	1.0%
33	Iowa	321	1.0%
34	Nevada	290	0.9%
35	West Virginia	272	0.8%
36	Utah	256	0.8%
37	Connecticut	248	0.8%
38	Nebraska	225	0.7%
39	Montana	192	0.6%
40	Idaho	186	0.6%
41	Wyoming	150	0.5%
42	South Dakota	136	0.4%
43	North Dakota	135	0.4%
44	Maine	131	0.4%
45	Delaware	121	0.4%
46	Hawaii	95	0.3%
46	New Hampshire	95	0.3%
48	Alaska	73	0.2%
49	Rhode Island	52	0.2%
50	Vermont	44	0.1%
	District of Columbia	23	0.1%

Source: U.S. Department of Transportation, National Highway Traffic Safety Administration
   "Traffic Safety Facts 2014" (https://crashstats.nhtsa.dot.gov/)

Highway Fatality Rate in 2014

National Rate = 1.08 Fatalities per 100 Million Vehicle-Miles of Travel

ALPHA ORDER

RANK	STATE	RATE
17	Alabama	1.25
7	Alaska	1.50
20	Arizona	1.23
13	Arkansas	1.37
35	California	0.92
30	Colorado	1.00
41	Connecticut	0.80
16	Delaware	1.26
19	Florida	1.24
27	Georgia	1.04
32	Hawaii	0.93
23	Idaho	1.15
38	Illinois	0.88
31	Indiana	0.94
29	Iowa	1.02
17	Kansas	1.25
11	Kentucky	1.40
5	Louisiana	1.53
35	Maine	0.92
44	Maryland	0.78
50	Massachusetts	0.57
32	Michigan	0.93
48	Minnesota	0.63
4	Mississippi	1.54
26	Missouri	1.08
3	Montana	1.58
23	Nebraska	1.15
23	Nevada	1.15
46	New Hampshire	0.73
45	New Jersey	0.74
6	New Mexico	1.51
41	New York	0.80
22	North Carolina	1.19
15	North Dakota	1.28
37	Ohio	0.89
11	Oklahoma	1.40
28	Oregon	1.03
21	Pennsylvania	1.20
47	Rhode Island	0.68
1	South Carolina	1.65
8	South Dakota	1.47
14	Tennessee	1.33
9	Texas	1.46
32	Utah	0.93
49	Vermont	0.62
39	Virginia	0.87
41	Washington	0.80
10	West Virginia	1.42
40	Wisconsin	0.84
2	Wyoming	1.59

RANK ORDER

RANK	STATE	RATE
1	South Carolina	1.65
2	Wyoming	1.59
3	Montana	1.58
4	Mississippi	1.54
5	Louisiana	1.53
6	New Mexico	1.51
7	Alaska	1.50
8	South Dakota	1.47
9	Texas	1.46
10	West Virginia	1.42
11	Kentucky	1.40
11	Oklahoma	1.40
13	Arkansas	1.37
14	Tennessee	1.33
15	North Dakota	1.28
16	Delaware	1.26
17	Alabama	1.25
17	Kansas	1.25
19	Florida	1.24
20	Arizona	1.23
21	Pennsylvania	1.20
22	North Carolina	1.19
23	Idaho	1.15
23	Nebraska	1.15
23	Nevada	1.15
26	Missouri	1.08
27	Georgia	1.04
28	Oregon	1.03
29	Iowa	1.02
30	Colorado	1.00
31	Indiana	0.94
32	Hawaii	0.93
32	Michigan	0.93
32	Utah	0.93
35	California	0.92
35	Maine	0.92
37	Ohio	0.89
38	Illinois	0.88
39	Virginia	0.87
40	Wisconsin	0.84
41	Connecticut	0.80
41	New York	0.80
41	Washington	0.80
44	Maryland	0.78
45	New Jersey	0.74
46	New Hampshire	0.73
47	Rhode Island	0.68
48	Minnesota	0.63
49	Vermont	0.62
50	Massachusetts	0.57
	District of Columbia	0.65

Source: U.S. Department of Transportation, National Highway Traffic Safety Administration
"Traffic Safety Facts 2014" (https://crashstats.nhtsa.dot.gov/)

Percent of Traffic Fatalities That Were Speeding-Related in 2014

National Percent = 28.3%*

ALPHA ORDER

RANK	STATE	PERCENT	RANK	STATE	PERCENT
26	Alabama	28.9	1	New Hampshire	49.5
35	Alaska	24.7	2	Pennsylvania	42.6
18	Arizona	33.0	3	North Carolina	38.7
49	Arkansas	11.8	4	Illinois	37.7
19	California	32.2	5	North Dakota	37.0
13	Colorado	34.4	5	South Carolina	37.0
28	Connecticut	27.8	7	Delaware	36.4
7	Delaware	36.4	8	Texas	36.3
50	Florida	9.8	9	Hawaii	35.8
44	Georgia	18.3	10	Missouri	34.9
9	Hawaii	35.8	11	Utah	34.8
34	Idaho	25.8	12	Nevada	34.5
4	Illinois	37.7	13	Colorado	34.4
30	Indiana	27.3	13	Washington	34.4
48	Iowa	14.0	15	Vermont	34.1
27	Kansas	28.3	16	New Mexico	33.7
43	Kentucky	18.6	17	Wisconsin	33.1
29	Louisiana	27.7	18	Arizona	33.0
24	Maine	29.8	19	California	32.2
23	Maryland	30.3	20	Wyoming	32.0
37	Massachusetts	23.5	21	New York	31.0
33	Michigan	26.1	22	Minnesota	30.7
22	Minnesota	30.7	23	Maryland	30.3
46	Mississippi	15.8	24	Maine	29.8
10	Missouri	34.9	25	Oregon	29.4
32	Montana	27.1	26	Alabama	28.9
42	Nebraska	21.8	27	Kansas	28.3
12	Nevada	34.5	28	Connecticut	27.8
1	New Hampshire	49.5	29	Louisiana	27.7
45	New Jersey	17.8	30	Indiana	27.3
16	New Mexico	33.7	31	Ohio	27.2
21	New York	31.0	32	Montana	27.1
3	North Carolina	38.7	33	Michigan	26.1
5	North Dakota	37.0	34	Idaho	25.8
31	Ohio	27.2	35	Alaska	24.7
40	Oklahoma	22.7	36	West Virginia	24.3
25	Oregon	29.4	37	Massachusetts	23.5
2	Pennsylvania	42.6	38	Rhode Island	23.1
38	Rhode Island	23.1	39	Tennessee	22.9
5	South Carolina	37.0	40	Oklahoma	22.7
41	South Dakota	22.1	41	South Dakota	22.1
39	Tennessee	22.9	42	Nebraska	21.8
8	Texas	36.3	43	Kentucky	18.6
11	Utah	34.8	44	Georgia	18.3
15	Vermont	34.1	45	New Jersey	17.8
47	Virginia	14.1	46	Mississippi	15.8
13	Washington	34.4	47	Virginia	14.1
36	West Virginia	24.3	48	Iowa	14.0
17	Wisconsin	33.1	49	Arkansas	11.8
20	Wyoming	32.0	50	Florida	9.8
				District of Columbia	52.2

Note: Column header for the second half of the table reads "RANK ORDER".

Source: CQ Press using data from U.S. Department of Transportation, National Highway Traffic Safety Administration
"Traffic Safety Facts 2014" (https://crashstats.nhtsa.dot.gov/)
*A speeding-related crash is if the driver was charged with a speeding-related offense or if an officer indicated that racing, driving too fast for conditions, or exceeding the posted speed limit was a contributing factor in the crash.

Percent of Vehicles Involved in Fatal Crashes That Were Large Trucks in 2014

National Percent = 8.3%*

ALPHA ORDER

RANK	STATE	PERCENT
32	Alabama	7.1
46	Alaska	5.0
38	Arizona	5.9
9	Arkansas	11.2
35	California	6.6
24	Colorado	8.7
44	Connecticut	5.3
34	Delaware	6.8
45	Florida	5.1
25	Georgia	8.3
48	Hawaii	3.1
21	Idaho	9.0
21	Illinois	9.0
7	Indiana	12.4
10	Iowa	10.9
18	Kansas	9.1
28	Kentucky	7.5
23	Louisiana	8.9
39	Maine	5.8
27	Maryland	7.6
40	Massachusetts	5.6
33	Michigan	7.0
8	Minnesota	11.9
16	Mississippi	9.4
18	Missouri	9.1
48	Montana	3.1
3	Nebraska	14.7
47	Nevada	3.7
15	New Hampshire	9.5
13	New Jersey	10.3
4	New Mexico	13.9
30	New York	7.4
37	North Carolina	6.3
1	North Dakota	25.4
18	Ohio	9.1
6	Oklahoma	13.6
36	Oregon	6.5
14	Pennsylvania	9.8
48	Rhode Island	3.1
40	South Carolina	5.6
12	South Dakota	10.5
26	Tennessee	7.9
10	Texas	10.9
40	Utah	5.6
2	Vermont	14.8
16	Virginia	9.4
40	Washington	5.6
31	West Virginia	7.2
28	Wisconsin	7.5
5	Wyoming	13.8

RANK ORDER

RANK	STATE	PERCENT
1	North Dakota	25.4
2	Vermont	14.8
3	Nebraska	14.7
4	New Mexico	13.9
5	Wyoming	13.8
6	Oklahoma	13.6
7	Indiana	12.4
8	Minnesota	11.9
9	Arkansas	11.2
10	Iowa	10.9
10	Texas	10.9
12	South Dakota	10.5
13	New Jersey	10.3
14	Pennsylvania	9.8
15	New Hampshire	9.5
16	Mississippi	9.4
16	Virginia	9.4
18	Kansas	9.1
18	Missouri	9.1
18	Ohio	9.1
21	Idaho	9.0
21	Illinois	9.0
23	Louisiana	8.9
24	Colorado	8.7
25	Georgia	8.3
26	Tennessee	7.9
27	Maryland	7.6
28	Kentucky	7.5
28	Wisconsin	7.5
30	New York	7.4
31	West Virginia	7.2
32	Alabama	7.1
33	Michigan	7.0
34	Delaware	6.8
35	California	6.6
36	Oregon	6.5
37	North Carolina	6.3
38	Arizona	5.9
39	Maine	5.8
40	Massachusetts	5.6
40	South Carolina	5.6
40	Utah	5.6
40	Washington	5.6
44	Connecticut	5.3
45	Florida	5.1
46	Alaska	5.0
47	Nevada	3.7
48	Hawaii	3.1
48	Montana	3.1
48	Rhode Island	3.1

| | District of Columbia | 15.4 |

Source: U.S. Department of Transportation, National Highway Traffic Safety Administration
"Traffic Safety Facts: Large Trucks" (https://crashstats.nhtsa.dot.gov/)
*Large trucks are those with gross vehicle weight greater than 10,000 pounds. In 2014, 3,744 large trucks were involved in fatal crashes.

Lives Saved by Child Restraints, Seat Belts, Air Bags, and Motorcycle Helmets in 2015
National Total = 18,552 Lives

RANK	STATE	LIVES	% of USA
14	Alabama	435	2.3%
47	Alaska	36	0.2%
21	Arizona	331	1.8%
26	Arkansas	281	1.5%
2	California	1,800	9.7%
29	Colorado	262	1.4%
36	Connecticut	124	0.7%
44	Delaware	53	0.3%
3	Florida	1,339	7.2%
4	Georgia	874	4.7%
49	Hawaii	28	0.2%
39	Idaho	107	0.6%
11	Illinois	522	2.8%
13	Indiana	470	2.5%
30	Iowa	201	1.1%
31	Kansas	187	1.0%
18	Kentucky	377	2.0%
19	Louisiana	359	1.9%
41	Maine	75	0.4%
21	Maryland	331	1.8%
37	Massachusetts	119	0.6%
7	Michigan	565	3.0%
27	Minnesota	272	1.5%
17	Mississippi	382	2.1%
15	Missouri	415	2.2%
40	Montana	87	0.5%
38	Nebraska	110	0.6%
32	Nevada	177	1.0%
46	New Hampshire	46	0.2%
28	New Jersey	268	1.4%
35	New Mexico	130	0.7%
6	New York	602	3.2%
5	North Carolina	829	4.5%
42	North Dakota	62	0.3%
9	Ohio	526	2.8%
23	Oklahoma	328	1.8%
25	Oregon	284	1.5%
10	Pennsylvania	525	2.8%
50	Rhode Island	17	0.1%
12	South Carolina	479	2.6%
43	South Dakota	57	0.3%
8	Tennessee	531	2.9%
1	Texas	2,132	11.5%
34	Utah	136	0.7%
48	Vermont	30	0.2%
16	Virginia	401	2.2%
20	Washington	352	1.9%
33	West Virginia	139	0.7%
24	Wisconsin	294	1.6%
44	Wyoming	53	0.3%

RANK	STATE	LIVES	% of USA
1	Texas	2,132	11.5%
2	California	1,800	9.7%
3	Florida	1,339	7.2%
4	Georgia	874	4.7%
5	North Carolina	829	4.5%
6	New York	602	3.2%
7	Michigan	565	3.0%
8	Tennessee	531	2.9%
9	Ohio	526	2.8%
10	Pennsylvania	525	2.8%
11	Illinois	522	2.8%
12	South Carolina	479	2.6%
13	Indiana	470	2.5%
14	Alabama	435	2.3%
15	Missouri	415	2.2%
16	Virginia	401	2.2%
17	Mississippi	382	2.1%
18	Kentucky	377	2.0%
19	Louisiana	359	1.9%
20	Washington	352	1.9%
21	Arizona	331	1.8%
21	Maryland	331	1.8%
23	Oklahoma	328	1.8%
24	Wisconsin	294	1.6%
25	Oregon	284	1.5%
26	Arkansas	281	1.5%
27	Minnesota	272	1.5%
28	New Jersey	268	1.4%
29	Colorado	262	1.4%
30	Iowa	201	1.1%
31	Kansas	187	1.0%
32	Nevada	177	1.0%
33	West Virginia	139	0.7%
34	Utah	136	0.7%
35	New Mexico	130	0.7%
36	Connecticut	124	0.7%
37	Massachusetts	119	0.6%
38	Nebraska	110	0.6%
39	Idaho	107	0.6%
40	Montana	87	0.5%
41	Maine	75	0.4%
42	North Dakota	62	0.3%
43	South Dakota	57	0.3%
44	Delaware	53	0.3%
44	Wyoming	53	0.3%
46	New Hampshire	46	0.2%
47	Alaska	36	0.2%
48	Vermont	30	0.2%
49	Hawaii	28	0.2%
50	Rhode Island	17	0.1%
	District of Columbia	7	0.0%

Source: CQ Press using data from U.S. Department of Transportation, National Highway Traffic Safety Administration
"Traffic Safety Facts: Lives Saved in 2015" (https://crashstats.nhtsa.dot.gov/)

Safety Belt Usage Rate in 2015

National Rate = 88.5% Use Safety Belts

ALPHA ORDER

RANK	STATE	PERCENT
7	Alabama	93.3
22	Alaska	89.3
27	Arizona	86.6
46	Arkansas	77.7
1	California	97.3
34	Colorado	85.2
33	Connecticut	85.4
19	Delaware	90.4
21	Florida	89.4
1	Georgia	97.3
11	Hawaii	92.8
39	Idaho	81.1
4	Illinois	95.2
15	Indiana	91.9
9	Iowa	93.0
38	Kansas	82.1
25	Kentucky	86.7
30	Louisiana	85.9
32	Maine	85.5
10	Maryland	92.9
48	Massachusetts	74.1
11	Michigan	92.8
6	Minnesota	94.0
44	Mississippi	79.6
42	Missouri	79.9
47	Montana	77.0
44	Nebraska	79.6
14	Nevada	92.1
50	New Hampshire	69.5
17	New Jersey	91.4
7	New Mexico	93.3
13	New York	92.2
20	North Carolina	89.9
41	North Dakota	80.4
36	Ohio	83.9
35	Oklahoma	84.5
3	Oregon	95.5
37	Pennsylvania	82.7
25	Rhode Island	86.7
16	South Carolina	91.6
49	South Dakota	73.6
28	Tennessee	86.2
18	Texas	90.5
24	Utah	87.2
29	Vermont	86.0
40	Virginia	80.9
5	Washington	94.6
23	West Virginia	89.0
31	Wisconsin	85.8
43	Wyoming	79.8

RANK ORDER

RANK	STATE	PERCENT
1	California	97.3
1	Georgia	97.3
3	Oregon	95.5
4	Illinois	95.2
5	Washington	94.6
6	Minnesota	94.0
7	Alabama	93.3
7	New Mexico	93.3
9	Iowa	93.0
10	Maryland	92.9
11	Hawaii	92.8
11	Michigan	92.8
13	New York	92.2
14	Nevada	92.1
15	Indiana	91.9
16	South Carolina	91.6
17	New Jersey	91.4
18	Texas	90.5
19	Delaware	90.4
20	North Carolina	89.9
21	Florida	89.4
22	Alaska	89.3
23	West Virginia	89.0
24	Utah	87.2
25	Kentucky	86.7
25	Rhode Island	86.7
27	Arizona	86.6
28	Tennessee	86.2
29	Vermont	86.0
30	Louisiana	85.9
31	Wisconsin	85.8
32	Maine	85.5
33	Connecticut	85.4
34	Colorado	85.2
35	Oklahoma	84.5
36	Ohio	83.9
37	Pennsylvania	82.7
38	Kansas	82.1
39	Idaho	81.1
40	Virginia	80.9
41	North Dakota	80.4
42	Missouri	79.9
43	Wyoming	79.8
44	Mississippi	79.6
44	Nebraska	79.6
46	Arkansas	77.7
47	Montana	77.0
48	Massachusetts	74.1
49	South Dakota	73.6
50	New Hampshire	69.5
	District of Columbia	95.5

Source: U.S. Department of Transportation, National Highway Traffic Safety Administration
"Traffic Safety Facts: Seat Belt Use in 2015" (https://crashstats.nhtsa.dot.gov/)

Percent of Passenger Car Occupant Fatalities
Where Victim Used a Seat Belt in 2014
National Percent = 47% of Passenger Car Occupant Fatalities*

ALPHA ORDER

RANK	STATE	PERCENT
36	Alabama	39
46	Alaska	29
39	Arizona	36
27	Arkansas	43
2	California	61
25	Colorado	45
39	Connecticut	36
1	Delaware	65
10	Florida	53
19	Georgia	47
36	Hawaii	39
19	Idaho	47
14	Illinois	51
19	Indiana	47
17	Iowa	50
27	Kansas	43
27	Kentucky	43
43	Louisiana	34
2	Maine	61
10	Maryland	53
44	Massachusetts	33
13	Michigan	52
7	Minnesota	58
34	Mississippi	40
39	Missouri	36
47	Montana	28
45	Nebraska	31
18	Nevada	48
50	New Hampshire	22
10	New Jersey	53
24	New Mexico	46
2	New York	61
9	North Carolina	54
47	North Dakota	28
34	Ohio	40
30	Oklahoma	42
6	Oregon	59
38	Pennsylvania	38
5	Rhode Island	60
19	South Carolina	47
47	South Dakota	28
30	Tennessee	42
14	Texas	51
14	Utah	51
32	Vermont	41
19	Virginia	47
8	Washington	56
42	West Virginia	35
26	Wisconsin	44
32	Wyoming	41

RANK ORDER

RANK	STATE	PERCENT
1	Delaware	65
2	California	61
2	Maine	61
2	New York	61
5	Rhode Island	60
6	Oregon	59
7	Minnesota	58
8	Washington	56
9	North Carolina	54
10	Florida	53
10	Maryland	53
10	New Jersey	53
13	Michigan	52
14	Illinois	51
14	Texas	51
14	Utah	51
17	Iowa	50
18	Nevada	48
19	Georgia	47
19	Idaho	47
19	Indiana	47
19	South Carolina	47
19	Virginia	47
24	New Mexico	46
25	Colorado	45
26	Wisconsin	44
27	Arkansas	43
27	Kansas	43
27	Kentucky	43
30	Oklahoma	42
30	Tennessee	42
32	Vermont	41
32	Wyoming	41
34	Mississippi	40
34	Ohio	40
36	Alabama	39
36	Hawaii	39
38	Pennsylvania	38
39	Arizona	36
39	Connecticut	36
39	Missouri	36
42	West Virginia	35
43	Louisiana	34
44	Massachusetts	33
45	Nebraska	31
46	Alaska	29
47	Montana	28
47	North Dakota	28
47	South Dakota	28
50	New Hampshire	22

| | District of Columbia | 70 |

Source: U.S. Department of Transportation, National Highway Traffic Safety Administration
"Traffic Safety Facts: Occupant Protection" (https://crashstats.nhtsa.dot.gov/)
*Only those fatalities where seat belts are known to have been used are counted.

Fatalities in Alcohol-Related Crashes in 2014

National Total = 11,731 Fatalities*

RANK	STATE	FATALITIES	% of USA
11	Alabama	312	2.7%
48	Alaska	29	0.2%
17	Arizona	246	2.1%
26	Arkansas	162	1.4%
2	California	1,053	9.0%
23	Colorado	187	1.6%
33	Connecticut	113	1.0%
44	Delaware	51	0.4%
3	Florida	807	6.9%
10	Georgia	326	2.8%
46	Hawaii	35	0.3%
41	Idaho	59	0.5%
7	Illinois	369	3.1%
18	Indiana	239	2.0%
35	Iowa	105	0.9%
31	Kansas	121	1.0%
22	Kentucky	196	1.7%
13	Louisiana	300	2.6%
45	Maine	49	0.4%
27	Maryland	154	1.3%
27	Massachusetts	154	1.3%
14	Michigan	266	2.3%
31	Minnesota	121	1.0%
19	Mississippi	207	1.8%
16	Missouri	249	2.1%
37	Montana	85	0.7%
38	Nebraska	77	0.7%
34	Nevada	112	1.0%
47	New Hampshire	34	0.3%
21	New Jersey	201	1.7%
29	New Mexico	144	1.2%
6	New York	379	3.2%
4	North Carolina	427	3.6%
39	North Dakota	66	0.6%
8	Ohio	355	3.0%
24	Oklahoma	181	1.5%
30	Oregon	125	1.1%
5	Pennsylvania	396	3.4%
49	Rhode Island	18	0.2%
9	South Carolina	329	2.8%
43	South Dakota	52	0.4%
11	Tennessee	312	2.7%
1	Texas	1,671	14.2%
40	Utah	63	0.5%
50	Vermont	14	0.1%
15	Virginia	256	2.2%
25	Washington	168	1.4%
36	West Virginia	96	0.8%
20	Wisconsin	202	1.7%
42	Wyoming	53	0.5%

RANK	STATE	FATALITIES	% of USA
1	Texas	1,671	14.2%
2	California	1,053	9.0%
3	Florida	807	6.9%
4	North Carolina	427	3.6%
5	Pennsylvania	396	3.4%
6	New York	379	3.2%
7	Illinois	369	3.1%
8	Ohio	355	3.0%
9	South Carolina	329	2.8%
10	Georgia	326	2.8%
11	Alabama	312	2.7%
11	Tennessee	312	2.7%
13	Louisiana	300	2.6%
14	Michigan	266	2.3%
15	Virginia	256	2.2%
16	Missouri	249	2.1%
17	Arizona	246	2.1%
18	Indiana	239	2.0%
19	Mississippi	207	1.8%
20	Wisconsin	202	1.7%
21	New Jersey	201	1.7%
22	Kentucky	196	1.7%
23	Colorado	187	1.6%
24	Oklahoma	181	1.5%
25	Washington	168	1.4%
26	Arkansas	162	1.4%
27	Maryland	154	1.3%
27	Massachusetts	154	1.3%
29	New Mexico	144	1.2%
30	Oregon	125	1.1%
31	Kansas	121	1.0%
31	Minnesota	121	1.0%
33	Connecticut	113	1.0%
34	Nevada	112	1.0%
35	Iowa	105	0.9%
36	West Virginia	96	0.8%
37	Montana	85	0.7%
38	Nebraska	77	0.7%
39	North Dakota	66	0.6%
40	Utah	63	0.5%
41	Idaho	59	0.5%
42	Wyoming	53	0.5%
43	South Dakota	52	0.4%
44	Delaware	51	0.4%
45	Maine	49	0.4%
46	Hawaii	35	0.3%
47	New Hampshire	34	0.3%
48	Alaska	29	0.2%
49	Rhode Island	18	0.2%
50	Vermont	14	0.1%
	District of Columbia	6	0.1%

Source: U.S. Department of Transportation, National Highway Traffic Safety Administration
"Traffic Safety Facts: Alcohol-Impaired Driving" (https://crashstats.nhtsa.dot.gov/)
*Drivers with Blood Alcohol Content (BAC) of .01 or more. "Legally Drunk" BAC differs from state to state but is often .08 or higher.

Fatalities in Alcohol-Related Crashes
as a Percent of All Highway Fatalities in 2014
National Percent = 36% of Highway Fatalities*

RANK	STATE	PERCENT
13	Alabama	38
11	Alaska	39
39	Arizona	32
25	Arkansas	35
31	California	34
13	Colorado	38
4	Connecticut	46
6	Delaware	42
39	Florida	32
48	Georgia	28
18	Hawaii	37
39	Idaho	32
8	Illinois	40
39	Indiana	32
34	Iowa	33
45	Kansas	31
46	Kentucky	29
7	Louisiana	41
13	Maine	38
25	Maryland	35
2	Massachusetts	47
46	Michigan	29
34	Minnesota	33
31	Mississippi	34
34	Missouri	33
5	Montana	44
31	Nebraska	34
11	Nevada	39
19	New Hampshire	36
19	New Jersey	36
13	New Mexico	38
19	New York	36
34	North Carolina	33
1	North Dakota	49
25	Ohio	35
49	Oklahoma	27
25	Oregon	35
34	Pennsylvania	33
25	Rhode Island	35
8	South Carolina	40
13	South Dakota	38
39	Tennessee	32
2	Texas	47
50	Utah	24
39	Vermont	32
19	Virginia	36
19	Washington	36
25	West Virginia	35
8	Wisconsin	40
19	Wyoming	36

RANK	STATE	PERCENT
1	North Dakota	49
2	Massachusetts	47
2	Texas	47
4	Connecticut	46
5	Montana	44
6	Delaware	42
7	Louisiana	41
8	Illinois	40
8	South Carolina	40
8	Wisconsin	40
11	Alaska	39
11	Nevada	39
13	Alabama	38
13	Colorado	38
13	Maine	38
13	New Mexico	38
13	South Dakota	38
18	Hawaii	37
19	New Hampshire	36
19	New Jersey	36
19	New York	36
19	Virginia	36
19	Washington	36
19	Wyoming	36
25	Arkansas	35
25	Maryland	35
25	Ohio	35
25	Oregon	35
25	Rhode Island	35
25	West Virginia	35
31	California	34
31	Mississippi	34
31	Nebraska	34
34	Iowa	33
34	Minnesota	33
34	Missouri	33
34	North Carolina	33
34	Pennsylvania	33
39	Arizona	32
39	Florida	32
39	Idaho	32
39	Indiana	32
39	Tennessee	32
39	Vermont	32
45	Kansas	31
46	Kentucky	29
46	Michigan	29
48	Georgia	28
49	Oklahoma	27
50	Utah	24
	District of Columbia	26

Source: U.S. Department of Transportation, National Highway Traffic Safety Administration
   "Traffic Safety Facts: Alcohol-Impaired Driving" (https://crashstats.nhtsa.dot.gov/)
*Drivers with Blood Alcohol Content (BAC) of .01 or more. "Legally Drunk" BAC differs from state to state but is often .08 or higher.

Percent of Fatal Traffic Accidents Involving Older Drivers in 2014

National Percent = 13.4%*

ALPHA ORDER

RANK	STATE	PERCENT
31	Alabama	13.9
50	Alaska	5.9
33	Arizona	13.8
30	Arkansas	14.1
44	California	10.4
42	Colorado	11.4
37	Connecticut	12.8
4	Delaware	17.4
21	Florida	14.7
40	Georgia	11.9
19	Hawaii	14.8
2	Idaho	18.6
26	Illinois	14.4
38	Indiana	12.5
9	Iowa	16.5
12	Kansas	16.0
23	Kentucky	14.5
45	Louisiana	9.6
10	Maine	16.3
34	Maryland	13.5
41	Massachusetts	11.6
12	Michigan	16.0
11	Minnesota	16.2
35	Mississippi	13.2
17	Missouri	15.1
31	Montana	13.9
4	Nebraska	17.4
43	Nevada	10.9
27	New Hampshire	14.3
27	New Jersey	14.3
48	New Mexico	7.6
15	New York	15.7
23	North Carolina	14.5
49	North Dakota	6.8
23	Ohio	14.5
18	Oklahoma	15.0
4	Oregon	17.4
3	Pennsylvania	18.0
1	Rhode Island	27.7
38	South Carolina	12.5
7	South Dakota	16.8
14	Tennessee	15.9
47	Texas	9.3
36	Utah	12.9
8	Vermont	16.7
19	Virginia	14.8
29	Washington	14.2
16	West Virginia	15.6
22	Wisconsin	14.6
45	Wyoming	9.6

RANK ORDER

RANK	STATE	PERCENT
1	Rhode Island	27.7
2	Idaho	18.6
3	Pennsylvania	18.0
4	Delaware	17.4
4	Nebraska	17.4
4	Oregon	17.4
7	South Dakota	16.8
8	Vermont	16.7
9	Iowa	16.5
10	Maine	16.3
11	Minnesota	16.2
12	Kansas	16.0
12	Michigan	16.0
14	Tennessee	15.9
15	New York	15.7
16	West Virginia	15.6
17	Missouri	15.1
18	Oklahoma	15.0
19	Hawaii	14.8
19	Virginia	14.8
21	Florida	14.7
22	Wisconsin	14.6
23	Kentucky	14.5
23	North Carolina	14.5
23	Ohio	14.5
26	Illinois	14.4
27	New Hampshire	14.3
27	New Jersey	14.3
29	Washington	14.2
30	Arkansas	14.1
31	Alabama	13.9
31	Montana	13.9
33	Arizona	13.8
34	Maryland	13.5
35	Mississippi	13.2
36	Utah	12.9
37	Connecticut	12.8
38	Indiana	12.5
38	South Carolina	12.5
40	Georgia	11.9
41	Massachusetts	11.6
42	Colorado	11.4
43	Nevada	10.9
44	California	10.4
45	Louisiana	9.6
45	Wyoming	9.6
47	Texas	9.3
48	New Mexico	7.6
49	North Dakota	6.8
50	Alaska	5.9
	District of Columbia	0.0

Source: U.S. Department of Transportation, National Highway Traffic Safety Administration
"Traffic Safety Facts: Older Population" (https://crashstats.nhtsa.dot.gov/)
*Drivers 65 years old and older. People 65 or older make up 14 percent of the total U.S. population.

Percent of Highway Fatalities Who Were Young Drivers in 2014

National Percent = 5.3% of Fatalities*

<table>
<tr><td colspan="3">ALPHA ORDER</td><td colspan="3">RANK ORDER</td></tr>
<tr><th>RANK</th><th>STATE</th><th>PERCENT</th><th>RANK</th><th>STATE</th><th>PERCENT</th></tr>
<tr><td>32</td><td>Alabama</td><td>5.0</td><td>1</td><td>Montana</td><td>8.9</td></tr>
<tr><td>26</td><td>Alaska</td><td>5.5</td><td>2</td><td>Iowa</td><td>8.4</td></tr>
<tr><td>46</td><td>Arizona</td><td>3.6</td><td>3</td><td>Utah</td><td>7.8</td></tr>
<tr><td>33</td><td>Arkansas</td><td>4.9</td><td>4</td><td>Kansas</td><td>7.5</td></tr>
<tr><td>35</td><td>California</td><td>4.7</td><td>5</td><td>North Dakota</td><td>7.4</td></tr>
<tr><td>23</td><td>Colorado</td><td>5.7</td><td>6</td><td>Nebraska</td><td>7.1</td></tr>
<tr><td>44</td><td>Connecticut</td><td>4.0</td><td>7</td><td>Maine</td><td>6.9</td></tr>
<tr><td>50</td><td>Delaware</td><td>2.5</td><td>8</td><td>Vermont</td><td>6.8</td></tr>
<tr><td>41</td><td>Florida</td><td>4.1</td><td>9</td><td>South Carolina</td><td>6.7</td></tr>
<tr><td>28</td><td>Georgia</td><td>5.3</td><td>10</td><td>Mississippi</td><td>6.6</td></tr>
<tr><td>16</td><td>Hawaii</td><td>6.3</td><td>10</td><td>Nevada</td><td>6.6</td></tr>
<tr><td>12</td><td>Idaho</td><td>6.5</td><td>12</td><td>Idaho</td><td>6.5</td></tr>
<tr><td>37</td><td>Illinois</td><td>4.4</td><td>12</td><td>Ohio</td><td>6.5</td></tr>
<tr><td>36</td><td>Indiana</td><td>4.6</td><td>14</td><td>Kentucky</td><td>6.4</td></tr>
<tr><td>2</td><td>Iowa</td><td>8.4</td><td>14</td><td>North Carolina</td><td>6.4</td></tr>
<tr><td>4</td><td>Kansas</td><td>7.5</td><td>16</td><td>Hawaii</td><td>6.3</td></tr>
<tr><td>14</td><td>Kentucky</td><td>6.4</td><td>17</td><td>Oklahoma</td><td>6.1</td></tr>
<tr><td>33</td><td>Louisiana</td><td>4.9</td><td>17</td><td>Washington</td><td>6.1</td></tr>
<tr><td>7</td><td>Maine</td><td>6.9</td><td>19</td><td>Missouri</td><td>5.9</td></tr>
<tr><td>49</td><td>Maryland</td><td>2.7</td><td>19</td><td>South Dakota</td><td>5.9</td></tr>
<tr><td>48</td><td>Massachusetts</td><td>3.0</td><td>19</td><td>Wisconsin</td><td>5.9</td></tr>
<tr><td>28</td><td>Michigan</td><td>5.3</td><td>22</td><td>Rhode Island</td><td>5.8</td></tr>
<tr><td>37</td><td>Minnesota</td><td>4.4</td><td>23</td><td>Colorado</td><td>5.7</td></tr>
<tr><td>10</td><td>Mississippi</td><td>6.6</td><td>23</td><td>New Mexico</td><td>5.7</td></tr>
<tr><td>19</td><td>Missouri</td><td>5.9</td><td>23</td><td>Texas</td><td>5.7</td></tr>
<tr><td>1</td><td>Montana</td><td>8.9</td><td>26</td><td>Alaska</td><td>5.5</td></tr>
<tr><td>6</td><td>Nebraska</td><td>7.1</td><td>27</td><td>Virginia</td><td>5.4</td></tr>
<tr><td>10</td><td>Nevada</td><td>6.6</td><td>28</td><td>Georgia</td><td>5.3</td></tr>
<tr><td>28</td><td>New Hampshire</td><td>5.3</td><td>28</td><td>Michigan</td><td>5.3</td></tr>
<tr><td>41</td><td>New Jersey</td><td>4.1</td><td>28</td><td>New Hampshire</td><td>5.3</td></tr>
<tr><td>23</td><td>New Mexico</td><td>5.7</td><td>28</td><td>Oregon</td><td>5.3</td></tr>
<tr><td>41</td><td>New York</td><td>4.1</td><td>32</td><td>Alabama</td><td>5.0</td></tr>
<tr><td>14</td><td>North Carolina</td><td>6.4</td><td>33</td><td>Arkansas</td><td>4.9</td></tr>
<tr><td>5</td><td>North Dakota</td><td>7.4</td><td>33</td><td>Louisiana</td><td>4.9</td></tr>
<tr><td>12</td><td>Ohio</td><td>6.5</td><td>35</td><td>California</td><td>4.7</td></tr>
<tr><td>17</td><td>Oklahoma</td><td>6.1</td><td>36</td><td>Indiana</td><td>4.6</td></tr>
<tr><td>28</td><td>Oregon</td><td>5.3</td><td>37</td><td>Illinois</td><td>4.4</td></tr>
<tr><td>37</td><td>Pennsylvania</td><td>4.4</td><td>37</td><td>Minnesota</td><td>4.4</td></tr>
<tr><td>22</td><td>Rhode Island</td><td>5.8</td><td>37</td><td>Pennsylvania</td><td>4.4</td></tr>
<tr><td>9</td><td>South Carolina</td><td>6.7</td><td>37</td><td>Tennessee</td><td>4.4</td></tr>
<tr><td>19</td><td>South Dakota</td><td>5.9</td><td>41</td><td>Florida</td><td>4.1</td></tr>
<tr><td>37</td><td>Tennessee</td><td>4.4</td><td>41</td><td>New Jersey</td><td>4.1</td></tr>
<tr><td>23</td><td>Texas</td><td>5.7</td><td>41</td><td>New York</td><td>4.1</td></tr>
<tr><td>3</td><td>Utah</td><td>7.8</td><td>44</td><td>Connecticut</td><td>4.0</td></tr>
<tr><td>8</td><td>Vermont</td><td>6.8</td><td>44</td><td>West Virginia</td><td>4.0</td></tr>
<tr><td>27</td><td>Virginia</td><td>5.4</td><td>46</td><td>Arizona</td><td>3.6</td></tr>
<tr><td>17</td><td>Washington</td><td>6.1</td><td>47</td><td>Wyoming</td><td>3.3</td></tr>
<tr><td>44</td><td>West Virginia</td><td>4.0</td><td>48</td><td>Massachusetts</td><td>3.0</td></tr>
<tr><td>19</td><td>Wisconsin</td><td>5.9</td><td>49</td><td>Maryland</td><td>2.7</td></tr>
<tr><td>47</td><td>Wyoming</td><td>3.3</td><td>50</td><td>Delaware</td><td>2.5</td></tr>
<tr><td></td><td></td><td></td><td></td><td>District of Columbia</td><td>13.0</td></tr>
</table>

Source: CQ Press using data from U.S. Department of Transportation, National Highway Traffic Safety Administration
"Traffic Safety Facts: Young Drivers" (https://crashstats.nhtsa.dot.gov/)
*Drivers 15 to 20 years old. Based on 1,717 fatalities of young drivers. An additional 2,555 passengers and nonoccupants were killed in crashes involving young drivers. Young drivers accounted for 6 percent of all drivers.

Licensed Drivers in 2015

National Total = 218,084,465 Licensed Drivers

ALPHA ORDER

RANK	STATE	DRIVERS	% of USA
22	Alabama	3,907,038	1.8%
49	Alaska	533,227	0.2%
15	Arizona	4,978,762	2.3%
31	Arkansas	2,119,578	1.0%
1	California	25,532,920	11.7%
21	Colorado	3,974,521	1.8%
29	Connecticut	2,566,673	1.2%
45	Delaware	742,524	0.3%
3	Florida	14,262,715	6.5%
10	Georgia	6,906,191	3.2%
42	Hawaii	909,797	0.4%
39	Idaho	1,135,009	0.5%
6	Illinois	8,462,193	3.9%
17	Indiana	4,467,848	2.0%
30	Iowa	2,224,130	1.0%
32	Kansas	2,028,657	0.9%
26	Kentucky	3,021,266	1.4%
24	Louisiana	3,357,091	1.5%
41	Maine	1,019,879	0.5%
20	Maryland	4,185,752	1.9%
14	Massachusetts	5,040,662	2.3%
9	Michigan	7,104,484	3.3%
25	Minnesota	3,351,430	1.5%
33	Mississippi	1,988,396	0.9%
18	Missouri	4,213,302	1.9%
43	Montana	781,427	0.4%
37	Nebraska	1,394,301	0.6%
35	Nevada	1,835,511	0.8%
40	New Hampshire	1,074,766	0.5%
11	New Jersey	6,179,318	2.8%
36	New Mexico	1,467,782	0.7%
4	New York	11,689,839	5.4%
8	North Carolina	7,160,621	3.3%
48	North Dakota	545,027	0.2%
7	Ohio	7,923,439	3.6%
28	Oklahoma	2,621,733	1.2%
27	Oregon	2,808,548	1.3%
5	Pennsylvania	8,942,967	4.1%
44	Rhode Island	745,470	0.3%
23	South Carolina	3,683,824	1.7%
46	South Dakota	655,707	0.3%
16	Tennessee	4,621,401	2.1%
2	Texas	15,879,876	7.3%
34	Utah	1,913,564	0.9%
47	Vermont	548,799	0.3%
12	Virginia	5,820,209	2.7%
13	Washington	5,516,134	2.5%
38	West Virginia	1,167,346	0.5%
19	Wisconsin	4,194,759	1.9%
50	Wyoming	422,450	0.2%

RANK ORDER

RANK	STATE	DRIVERS	% of USA
1	California	25,532,920	11.7%
2	Texas	15,879,876	7.3%
3	Florida	14,262,715	6.5%
4	New York	11,689,839	5.4%
5	Pennsylvania	8,942,967	4.1%
6	Illinois	8,462,193	3.9%
7	Ohio	7,923,439	3.6%
8	North Carolina	7,160,621	3.3%
9	Michigan	7,104,484	3.3%
10	Georgia	6,906,191	3.2%
11	New Jersey	6,179,318	2.8%
12	Virginia	5,820,209	2.7%
13	Washington	5,516,134	2.5%
14	Massachusetts	5,040,662	2.3%
15	Arizona	4,978,762	2.3%
16	Tennessee	4,621,401	2.1%
17	Indiana	4,467,848	2.0%
18	Missouri	4,213,302	1.9%
19	Wisconsin	4,194,759	1.9%
20	Maryland	4,185,752	1.9%
21	Colorado	3,974,521	1.8%
22	Alabama	3,907,038	1.8%
23	South Carolina	3,683,824	1.7%
24	Louisiana	3,357,091	1.5%
25	Minnesota	3,351,430	1.5%
26	Kentucky	3,021,266	1.4%
27	Oregon	2,808,548	1.3%
28	Oklahoma	2,621,733	1.2%
29	Connecticut	2,566,673	1.2%
30	Iowa	2,224,130	1.0%
31	Arkansas	2,119,578	1.0%
32	Kansas	2,028,657	0.9%
33	Mississippi	1,988,396	0.9%
34	Utah	1,913,564	0.9%
35	Nevada	1,835,511	0.8%
36	New Mexico	1,467,782	0.7%
37	Nebraska	1,394,301	0.6%
38	West Virginia	1,167,346	0.5%
39	Idaho	1,135,009	0.5%
40	New Hampshire	1,074,766	0.5%
41	Maine	1,019,879	0.5%
42	Hawaii	909,797	0.4%
43	Montana	781,427	0.4%
44	Rhode Island	745,470	0.3%
45	Delaware	742,524	0.3%
46	South Dakota	655,707	0.3%
47	Vermont	548,799	0.3%
48	North Dakota	545,027	0.2%
49	Alaska	533,227	0.2%
50	Wyoming	422,450	0.2%
	District of Columbia	455,602	0.2%

Source: U.S. Department of Transportation, Federal Highway Administration
"Highway Statistics 2015" (Table DL-22, http://www.fhwa.dot.gov/policyinformation/statistics/2015/)

Licensed Drivers per 1,000 Driving Age Population in 2015

National Ratio = 851 Licensed Drivers

ALPHA ORDER

RANK	STATE	RATIO
2	Alabama	1,006
10	Alaska	933
11	Arizona	924
19	Arkansas	901
44	California	822
13	Colorado	917
26	Connecticut	878
5	Delaware	971
36	Florida	857
32	Georgia	864
46	Hawaii	789
21	Idaho	894
43	Illinois	826
40	Indiana	855
20	Iowa	898
23	Kansas	893
38	Kentucky	856
15	Louisiana	912
12	Maine	923
29	Maryland	870
18	Massachusetts	904
25	Michigan	890
48	Minnesota	771
42	Mississippi	847
30	Missouri	868
8	Montana	939
7	Nebraska	945
45	Nevada	800
4	New Hampshire	977
34	New Jersey	859
23	New Mexico	893
50	New York	727
21	North Carolina	894
16	North Dakota	907
41	Ohio	852
35	Oklahoma	858
33	Oregon	860
36	Pennsylvania	857
38	Rhode Island	856
9	South Carolina	938
3	South Dakota	980
28	Tennessee	876
49	Texas	755
26	Utah	878
1	Vermont	1,053
31	Virginia	866
6	Washington	961
47	West Virginia	774
16	Wisconsin	907
14	Wyoming	915

RANK ORDER

RANK	STATE	RATIO
1	Vermont	1,053
2	Alabama	1,006
3	South Dakota	980
4	New Hampshire	977
5	Delaware	971
6	Washington	961
7	Nebraska	945
8	Montana	939
9	South Carolina	938
10	Alaska	933
11	Arizona	924
12	Maine	923
13	Colorado	917
14	Wyoming	915
15	Louisiana	912
16	North Dakota	907
16	Wisconsin	907
18	Massachusetts	904
19	Arkansas	901
20	Iowa	898
21	Idaho	894
21	North Carolina	894
23	Kansas	893
23	New Mexico	893
25	Michigan	890
26	Connecticut	878
26	Utah	878
28	Tennessee	876
29	Maryland	870
30	Missouri	868
31	Virginia	866
32	Georgia	864
33	Oregon	860
34	New Jersey	859
35	Oklahoma	858
36	Florida	857
36	Pennsylvania	857
38	Kentucky	856
38	Rhode Island	856
40	Indiana	855
41	Ohio	852
42	Mississippi	847
43	Illinois	826
44	California	822
45	Nevada	800
46	Hawaii	789
47	West Virginia	774
48	Minnesota	771
49	Texas	755
50	New York	727

District of Columbia 807

Source: CQ Press using data from U.S. Department of Transportation, Federal Highway Administration
"Highway Statistics 2015" (Table DL-1C, http://www.fhwa.dot.gov/policyinformation/statistics/2015/)

Motor Vehicle Registrations in 2015

National Total = 263,610,219 Motor Vehicles*

RANK	STATE	VEHICLES	% of USA
19	Alabama	5,400,419	2.0%
48	Alaska	815,122	0.3%
15	Arizona	5,630,647	2.1%
31	Arkansas	2,772,214	1.1%
1	California	29,424,012	11.2%
22	Colorado	5,005,172	1.9%
30	Connecticut	2,841,764	1.1%
45	Delaware	964,316	0.4%
3	Florida	16,105,008	6.1%
9	Georgia	8,137,621	3.1%
42	Hawaii	1,242,319	0.5%
37	Idaho	1,854,019	0.7%
6	Illinois	10,595,254	4.0%
13	Indiana	6,045,114	2.3%
27	Iowa	3,636,898	1.4%
32	Kansas	2,634,856	1.0%
24	Kentucky	4,151,982	1.6%
26	Louisiana	3,901,432	1.5%
43	Maine	1,104,001	0.4%
25	Maryland	4,135,158	1.6%
21	Massachusetts	5,069,601	1.9%
8	Michigan	8,294,108	3.1%
20	Minnesota	5,281,269	2.0%
35	Mississippi	2,068,853	0.8%
16	Missouri	5,624,005	2.1%
39	Montana	1,645,227	0.6%
36	Nebraska	1,981,296	0.8%
33	Nevada	2,316,056	0.9%
41	New Hampshire	1,296,137	0.5%
14	New Jersey	5,938,585	2.3%
38	New Mexico	1,823,445	0.7%
4	New York	10,638,765	4.0%
10	North Carolina	7,928,973	3.0%
46	North Dakota	890,803	0.3%
7	Ohio	10,557,323	4.0%
29	Oklahoma	2,988,512	1.1%
28	Oregon	3,607,482	1.4%
5	Pennsylvania	10,598,694	4.0%
47	Rhode Island	875,097	0.3%
23	South Carolina	4,162,651	1.6%
44	South Dakota	1,082,289	0.4%
17	Tennessee	5,612,123	2.1%
2	Texas	21,864,841	8.3%
34	Utah	2,229,193	0.8%
50	Vermont	655,347	0.2%
11	Virginia	7,238,905	2.7%
12	Washington	6,725,467	2.6%
40	West Virginia	1,613,345	0.6%
18	Wisconsin	5,466,581	2.1%
49	Wyoming	814,989	0.3%

RANK	STATE	VEHICLES	% of USA
1	California	29,424,012	11.2%
2	Texas	21,864,841	8.3%
3	Florida	16,105,008	6.1%
4	New York	10,638,765	4.0%
5	Pennsylvania	10,598,694	4.0%
6	Illinois	10,595,254	4.0%
7	Ohio	10,557,323	4.0%
8	Michigan	8,294,108	3.1%
9	Georgia	8,137,621	3.1%
10	North Carolina	7,928,973	3.0%
11	Virginia	7,238,905	2.7%
12	Washington	6,725,467	2.6%
13	Indiana	6,045,114	2.3%
14	New Jersey	5,938,585	2.3%
15	Arizona	5,630,647	2.1%
16	Missouri	5,624,005	2.1%
17	Tennessee	5,612,123	2.1%
18	Wisconsin	5,466,581	2.1%
19	Alabama	5,400,419	2.0%
20	Minnesota	5,281,269	2.0%
21	Massachusetts	5,069,601	1.9%
22	Colorado	5,005,172	1.9%
23	South Carolina	4,162,651	1.6%
24	Kentucky	4,151,982	1.6%
25	Maryland	4,135,158	1.6%
26	Louisiana	3,901,432	1.5%
27	Iowa	3,636,898	1.4%
28	Oregon	3,607,482	1.4%
29	Oklahoma	2,988,512	1.1%
30	Connecticut	2,841,764	1.1%
31	Arkansas	2,772,214	1.1%
32	Kansas	2,634,856	1.0%
33	Nevada	2,316,056	0.9%
34	Utah	2,229,193	0.8%
35	Mississippi	2,068,853	0.8%
36	Nebraska	1,981,296	0.8%
37	Idaho	1,854,019	0.7%
38	New Mexico	1,823,445	0.7%
39	Montana	1,645,227	0.6%
40	West Virginia	1,613,345	0.6%
41	New Hampshire	1,296,137	0.5%
42	Hawaii	1,242,319	0.5%
43	Maine	1,104,001	0.4%
44	South Dakota	1,082,289	0.4%
45	Delaware	964,316	0.4%
46	North Dakota	890,803	0.3%
47	Rhode Island	875,097	0.3%
48	Alaska	815,122	0.3%
49	Wyoming	814,989	0.3%
50	Vermont	655,347	0.2%
	District of Columbia	322,929	0.1%

Source: U.S. Department of Transportation, Federal Highway Administration
"Highway Statistics 2015" (Table MV-1, http://www.fhwa.dot.gov/policyinformation/statistics/2015/)
*Includes automobiles, trucks and buses and motorcycles.

Motor Vehicles per Driving Age Population in 2015

National Rate = 1.05 Motor Vehicles*

ALPHA ORDER

RANK	STATE	RATE
8	Alabama	1.40
7	Alaska	1.44
27	Arizona	1.09
15	Arkansas	1.19
45	California	0.97
14	Colorado	1.20
44	Connecticut	0.98
10	Delaware	1.30
39	Florida	1.01
34	Georgia	1.05
25	Hawaii	1.10
5	Idaho	1.51
37	Illinois	1.04
19	Indiana	1.17
6	Iowa	1.49
19	Kansas	1.17
15	Kentucky	1.19
31	Louisiana	1.07
42	Maine	1.00
48	Maryland	0.87
46	Massachusetts	0.93
34	Michigan	1.05
12	Minnesota	1.23
47	Mississippi	0.89
19	Missouri	1.17
1	Montana	2.01
9	Nebraska	1.36
34	Nevada	1.05
15	New Hampshire	1.19
49	New Jersey	0.83
24	New Mexico	1.12
50	New York	0.67
39	North Carolina	1.01
4	North Dakota	1.54
22	Ohio	1.14
43	Oklahoma	0.99
22	Oregon	1.14
38	Pennsylvania	1.02
39	Rhode Island	1.01
27	South Carolina	1.09
3	South Dakota	1.64
27	Tennessee	1.09
30	Texas	1.08
32	Utah	1.06
11	Vermont	1.26
25	Virginia	1.10
13	Washington	1.21
32	West Virginia	1.06
15	Wisconsin	1.19
2	Wyoming	1.77

RANK ORDER

RANK	STATE	RATE
1	Montana	2.01
2	Wyoming	1.77
3	South Dakota	1.64
4	North Dakota	1.54
5	Idaho	1.51
6	Iowa	1.49
7	Alaska	1.44
8	Alabama	1.40
9	Nebraska	1.36
10	Delaware	1.30
11	Vermont	1.26
12	Minnesota	1.23
13	Washington	1.21
14	Colorado	1.20
15	Arkansas	1.19
15	Kentucky	1.19
15	New Hampshire	1.19
15	Wisconsin	1.19
19	Indiana	1.17
19	Kansas	1.17
19	Missouri	1.17
22	Ohio	1.14
22	Oregon	1.14
24	New Mexico	1.12
25	Hawaii	1.10
25	Virginia	1.10
27	Arizona	1.09
27	South Carolina	1.09
27	Tennessee	1.09
30	Texas	1.08
31	Louisiana	1.07
32	Utah	1.06
32	West Virginia	1.06
34	Georgia	1.05
34	Michigan	1.05
34	Nevada	1.05
37	Illinois	1.04
38	Pennsylvania	1.02
39	Florida	1.01
39	North Carolina	1.01
39	Rhode Island	1.01
42	Maine	1.00
43	Oklahoma	0.99
44	Connecticut	0.98
45	California	0.97
46	Massachusetts	0.93
47	Mississippi	0.89
48	Maryland	0.87
49	New Jersey	0.83
50	New York	0.67

District of Columbia	0.59

Source: CQ Press using data from U.S. Department of Transportation, Federal Highway Administration
"Highway Statistics 2015" (Table MV-1, http://www.fhwa.dot.gov/policyinformation/statistics/2015/)
*Persons age 16 and older. Motor Vehicles include automobiles, trucks, buses, and motorcycles.

Average Travel Time to Work in 2015

National Average = 26.4 Minutes*

RANK	STATE	MINUTES
23	Alabama	24.6
43	Alaska	19.2
20	Arizona	25.1
37	Arkansas	22.1
5	California	28.9
18	Colorado	25.4
14	Connecticut	26.4
16	Delaware	26.0
12	Florida	27.0
8	Georgia	28.0
10	Hawaii	27.4
42	Idaho	20.5
6	Illinois	28.8
34	Indiana	23.3
44	Iowa	19.0
44	Kansas	19.0
34	Kentucky	23.3
19	Louisiana	25.3
29	Maine	24.0
2	Maryland	32.6
4	Massachusetts	29.7
24	Michigan	24.4
32	Minnesota	23.4
25	Mississippi	24.3
30	Missouri	23.6
48	Montana	18.0
47	Nebraska	18.4
27	Nevada	24.2
9	New Hampshire	27.6
3	New Jersey	31.3
39	New Mexico	21.7
1	New York	33.1
25	North Carolina	24.3
50	North Dakota	16.6
32	Ohio	23.4
40	Oklahoma	21.4
30	Oregon	23.6
13	Pennsylvania	26.8
22	Rhode Island	24.7
27	South Carolina	24.2
49	South Dakota	16.9
21	Tennessee	24.8
15	Texas	26.3
41	Utah	21.3
36	Vermont	23.0
7	Virginia	28.2
11	Washington	27.1
17	West Virginia	25.5
38	Wisconsin	22.0
44	Wyoming	19.0

RANK	STATE	MINUTES
1	New York	33.1
2	Maryland	32.6
3	New Jersey	31.3
4	Massachusetts	29.7
5	California	28.9
6	Illinois	28.8
7	Virginia	28.2
8	Georgia	28.0
9	New Hampshire	27.6
10	Hawaii	27.4
11	Washington	27.1
12	Florida	27.0
13	Pennsylvania	26.8
14	Connecticut	26.4
15	Texas	26.3
16	Delaware	26.0
17	West Virginia	25.5
18	Colorado	25.4
19	Louisiana	25.3
20	Arizona	25.1
21	Tennessee	24.8
22	Rhode Island	24.7
23	Alabama	24.6
24	Michigan	24.4
25	Mississippi	24.3
25	North Carolina	24.3
27	Nevada	24.2
27	South Carolina	24.2
29	Maine	24.0
30	Missouri	23.6
30	Oregon	23.6
32	Minnesota	23.4
32	Ohio	23.4
34	Indiana	23.3
34	Kentucky	23.3
36	Vermont	23.0
37	Arkansas	22.1
38	Wisconsin	22.0
39	New Mexico	21.7
40	Oklahoma	21.4
41	Utah	21.3
42	Idaho	20.5
43	Alaska	19.2
44	Iowa	19.0
44	Kansas	19.0
44	Wyoming	19.0
47	Nebraska	18.4
48	Montana	18.0
49	South Dakota	16.9
50	North Dakota	16.6

District of Columbia	29.8

Source: U.S. Bureau of the Census
   "2015 American Community Survey-Table R0801" (http://www.census.gov/programs-surveys/acs/)
*Workers 16 and older not working at home.

Percent of Commuters Who Drive to Work Alone in 2015

National Percent = 76.6%*

ALPHA ORDER

RANK	STATE	PERCENT
1	Alabama	85.5
48	Alaska	67.9
34	Arizona	77.1
10	Arkansas	82.6
41	California	73.9
37	Colorado	76.5
29	Connecticut	78.4
17	Delaware	81.4
25	Florida	79.7
27	Georgia	79.6
49	Hawaii	67.4
34	Idaho	77.1
43	Illinois	73.6
5	Indiana	83.1
22	Iowa	81.0
10	Kansas	82.6
13	Kentucky	82.1
7	Louisiana	82.8
25	Maine	79.7
42	Maryland	73.8
47	Massachusetts	70.2
7	Michigan	82.8
30	Minnesota	78.1
2	Mississippi	85.4
16	Missouri	81.8
40	Montana	74.5
14	Nebraska	82.0
31	Nevada	77.8
21	New Hampshire	81.1
45	New Jersey	71.8
17	New Mexico	81.4
50	New York	52.7
17	North Carolina	81.4
14	North Dakota	82.0
4	Ohio	83.2
12	Oklahoma	82.5
46	Oregon	71.2
38	Pennsylvania	76.3
28	Rhode Island	79.0
6	South Carolina	83.0
24	South Dakota	80.6
3	Tennessee	83.9
23	Texas	80.8
39	Utah	75.8
36	Vermont	76.9
32	Virginia	77.5
44	Washington	72.4
9	West Virginia	82.7
20	Wisconsin	81.2
33	Wyoming	77.3

RANK ORDER

RANK	STATE	PERCENT
1	Alabama	85.5
2	Mississippi	85.4
3	Tennessee	83.9
4	Ohio	83.2
5	Indiana	83.1
6	South Carolina	83.0
7	Louisiana	82.8
7	Michigan	82.8
9	West Virginia	82.7
10	Arkansas	82.6
10	Kansas	82.6
12	Oklahoma	82.5
13	Kentucky	82.1
14	Nebraska	82.0
14	North Dakota	82.0
16	Missouri	81.8
17	Delaware	81.4
17	New Mexico	81.4
17	North Carolina	81.4
20	Wisconsin	81.2
21	New Hampshire	81.1
22	Iowa	81.0
23	Texas	80.8
24	South Dakota	80.6
25	Florida	79.7
25	Maine	79.7
27	Georgia	79.6
28	Rhode Island	79.0
29	Connecticut	78.4
30	Minnesota	78.1
31	Nevada	77.8
32	Virginia	77.5
33	Wyoming	77.3
34	Arizona	77.1
34	Idaho	77.1
36	Vermont	76.9
37	Colorado	76.5
38	Pennsylvania	76.3
39	Utah	75.8
40	Montana	74.5
41	California	73.9
42	Maryland	73.8
43	Illinois	73.6
44	Washington	72.4
45	New Jersey	71.8
46	Oregon	71.2
47	Massachusetts	70.2
48	Alaska	67.9
49	Hawaii	67.4
50	New York	52.7

District of Columbia	33.6

Source: U.S. Bureau of the Census
"2015 American Community Survey-Table R0802" (http://www.census.gov/programs-surveys/acs/)
*Workers 16 and older who traveled to work by car, truck or van.

Percent of Commuters Who Drive to Work in Carpools in 2015

National Percent = 9.0%*

ALPHA ORDER			RANK ORDER		
RANK	STATE	PERCENT	RANK	STATE	PERCENT
22	Alabama	9.0	1	Hawaii	13.5
2	Alaska	12.6	2	Alaska	12.6
6	Arizona	10.6	3	Utah	11.2
4	Arkansas	10.8	4	Arkansas	10.8
12	California	10.0	4	Idaho	10.8
38	Colorado	8.4	6	Arizona	10.6
45	Connecticut	7.8	7	Nevada	10.5
42	Delaware	7.9	8	Montana	10.4
27	Florida	8.9	9	Oklahoma	10.2
14	Georgia	9.9	9	Oregon	10.2
1	Hawaii	13.5	9	Texas	10.2
4	Idaho	10.8	12	California	10.0
42	Illinois	7.9	12	Wyoming	10.0
34	Indiana	8.6	14	Georgia	9.9
34	Iowa	8.6	15	Washington	9.8
27	Kansas	8.9	16	Kentucky	9.7
16	Kentucky	9.7	16	Rhode Island	9.7
22	Louisiana	9.0	18	North Carolina	9.4
30	Maine	8.7	19	South Carolina	9.3
27	Maryland	8.9	20	Mississippi	9.2
49	Massachusetts	7.4	21	Virginia	9.1
30	Michigan	8.7	22	Alabama	9.0
40	Minnesota	8.3	22	Louisiana	9.0
20	Mississippi	9.2	22	Nebraska	9.0
30	Missouri	8.7	22	New Mexico	9.0
8	Montana	10.4	22	Tennessee	9.0
22	Nebraska	9.0	27	Florida	8.9
7	Nevada	10.5	27	Kansas	8.9
47	New Hampshire	7.5	27	Maryland	8.9
47	New Jersey	7.5	30	Maine	8.7
22	New Mexico	9.0	30	Michigan	8.7
50	New York	6.6	30	Missouri	8.7
18	North Carolina	9.4	30	West Virginia	8.7
34	North Dakota	8.6	34	Indiana	8.6
45	Ohio	7.8	34	Iowa	8.6
9	Oklahoma	10.2	34	North Dakota	8.6
9	Oregon	10.2	37	Pennsylvania	8.5
37	Pennsylvania	8.5	38	Colorado	8.4
16	Rhode Island	9.7	38	South Dakota	8.4
19	South Carolina	9.3	40	Minnesota	8.3
38	South Dakota	8.4	41	Vermont	8.2
22	Tennessee	9.0	42	Delaware	7.9
9	Texas	10.2	42	Illinois	7.9
3	Utah	11.2	42	Wisconsin	7.9
41	Vermont	8.2	45	Connecticut	7.8
21	Virginia	9.1	45	Ohio	7.8
15	Washington	9.8	47	New Hampshire	7.5
30	West Virginia	8.7	47	New Jersey	7.5
42	Wisconsin	7.9	49	Massachusetts	7.4
12	Wyoming	10.0	50	New York	6.6
				District of Columbia	5.2

Source: U.S. Bureau of the Census
   "2015 American Community Survey-Table R0803" (http://www.census.gov/programs-surveys/acs/)
*Workers 16 and older who traveled to work by car, truck or van.

Percent of Commuters Who Travel to Work by Public Transportation in 2015

National Percent = 5.2%*

ALPHA ORDER

RANK	STATE	PERCENT
49	Alabama	0.3
26	Alaska	1.5
22	Arizona	2.1
45	Arkansas	0.5
9	California	5.2
15	Colorado	3.0
10	Connecticut	4.9
17	Delaware	2.7
20	Florida	2.2
19	Georgia	2.3
6	Hawaii	7.0
38	Idaho	0.8
4	Illinois	9.3
32	Indiana	1.1
29	Iowa	1.4
43	Kansas	0.6
32	Kentucky	1.1
26	Louisiana	1.5
43	Maine	0.6
5	Maryland	9.0
3	Massachusetts	10.6
30	Michigan	1.3
14	Minnesota	3.6
49	Mississippi	0.3
25	Missouri	1.6
38	Montana	0.8
38	Nebraska	0.8
13	Nevada	3.7
36	New Hampshire	0.9
2	New Jersey	11.6
36	New Mexico	0.9
1	New York	28.6
32	North Carolina	1.1
47	North Dakota	0.4
24	Ohio	1.8
47	Oklahoma	0.4
11	Oregon	4.8
8	Pennsylvania	5.7
16	Rhode Island	2.9
45	South Carolina	0.5
38	South Dakota	0.8
38	Tennessee	0.8
26	Texas	1.5
17	Utah	2.7
30	Vermont	1.3
12	Virginia	4.7
7	Washington	6.2
32	West Virginia	1.1
23	Wisconsin	1.9
20	Wyoming	2.2

RANK ORDER

RANK	STATE	PERCENT
1	New York	28.6
2	New Jersey	11.6
3	Massachusetts	10.6
4	Illinois	9.3
5	Maryland	9.0
6	Hawaii	7.0
7	Washington	6.2
8	Pennsylvania	5.7
9	California	5.2
10	Connecticut	4.9
11	Oregon	4.8
12	Virginia	4.7
13	Nevada	3.7
14	Minnesota	3.6
15	Colorado	3.0
16	Rhode Island	2.9
17	Delaware	2.7
17	Utah	2.7
19	Georgia	2.3
20	Florida	2.2
20	Wyoming	2.2
22	Arizona	2.1
23	Wisconsin	1.9
24	Ohio	1.8
25	Missouri	1.6
26	Alaska	1.5
26	Louisiana	1.5
26	Texas	1.5
29	Iowa	1.4
30	Michigan	1.3
30	Vermont	1.3
32	Indiana	1.1
32	Kentucky	1.1
32	North Carolina	1.1
32	West Virginia	1.1
36	New Hampshire	0.9
36	New Mexico	0.9
38	Idaho	0.8
38	Montana	0.8
38	Nebraska	0.8
38	South Dakota	0.8
38	Tennessee	0.8
43	Kansas	0.6
43	Maine	0.6
45	Arkansas	0.5
45	South Carolina	0.5
47	North Dakota	0.4
47	Oklahoma	0.4
49	Alabama	0.3
49	Mississippi	0.3

District of Columbia — 35.8

Source: U.S. Bureau of the Census
"2015 American Community Survey-Table R0804" (http://www.census.gov/programs-surveys/acs/)
*Workers 16 and older.

Annual Miles per Vehicle in 2015

National Annual Average = 11,742 Miles*

ALPHA ORDER				RANK ORDER		
RANK	STATE	MILES		RANK	STATE	MILES
15	Alabama	12,454		1	Mississippi	19,281
50	Alaska	6,190		2	Oklahoma	15,965
26	Arizona	11,552		3	New Mexico	15,046
14	Arkansas	12,588		4	Georgia	14,514
28	California	11,404		5	North Carolina	14,110
39	Colorado	10,077		6	Maryland	13,909
33	Connecticut	11,117		7	Tennessee	13,662
36	Delaware	10,298		8	Utah	13,280
11	Florida	12,852		9	Maine	13,251
4	Georgia	14,514		10	Indiana	13,038
48	Hawaii	8,291		11	Florida	12,852
44	Idaho	8,987		12	Missouri	12,788
41	Illinois	9,931		13	New Jersey	12,696
10	Indiana	13,038		14	Arkansas	12,588
43	Iowa	9,118		15	Alabama	12,454
20	Kansas	11,909		16	South Carolina	12,426
24	Kentucky	11,723		17	Louisiana	12,349
17	Louisiana	12,349		18	West Virginia	12,289
9	Maine	13,251		19	New York	11,959
6	Maryland	13,909		20	Kansas	11,909
25	Massachusetts	11,689		21	Texas	11,805
22	Michigan	11,797		22	Michigan	11,797
34	Minnesota	10,868		23	Wyoming	11,776
1	Mississippi	19,281		24	Kentucky	11,723
12	Missouri	12,788		25	Massachusetts	11,689
49	Montana	7,504		26	Arizona	11,552
37	Nebraska	10,145		27	Virginia	11,414
31	Nevada	11,194		28	California	11,404
38	New Hampshire	10,102		29	Wisconsin	11,355
13	New Jersey	12,696		30	North Dakota	11,266
3	New Mexico	15,046		31	Nevada	11,194
19	New York	11,959		32	Vermont	11,160
5	North Carolina	14,110		33	Connecticut	11,117
30	North Dakota	11,266		34	Minnesota	10,868
35	Ohio	10,767		35	Ohio	10,767
2	Oklahoma	15,965		36	Delaware	10,298
40	Oregon	9,979		37	Nebraska	10,145
42	Pennsylvania	9,524		38	New Hampshire	10,102
45	Rhode Island	8,951		39	Colorado	10,077
16	South Carolina	12,426		40	Oregon	9,979
47	South Dakota	8,615		41	Illinois	9,931
7	Tennessee	13,662		42	Pennsylvania	9,524
21	Texas	11,805		43	Iowa	9,118
8	Utah	13,280		44	Idaho	8,987
32	Vermont	11,160		45	Rhode Island	8,951
27	Virginia	11,414		46	Washington	8,870
46	Washington	8,870		47	South Dakota	8,615
18	West Virginia	12,289		48	Hawaii	8,291
29	Wisconsin	11,355		49	Montana	7,504
23	Wyoming	11,776		50	Alaska	6,190
					District of Columbia	11,015

Source: CQ Press using data from U.S. Department of Transportation, Federal Highway Administration
"Highway Statistics 2015" (Tables MV-1 and VM-2, http://www.fhwa.dot.gov/policyinformation/statistics/2015/)
*Includes automobiles, trucks, buses and motorcycles.

Average Miles per Gallon in 2015

National Average = 17.9 Miles per Gallon*

ALPHA ORDER

RANK	STATE	MILES PER GALLON
5	Alabama	20.2
49	Alaska	13.2
12	Arizona	19.1
25	Arkansas	18.0
9	California	19.5
19	Colorado	18.4
17	Connecticut	18.8
6	Delaware	19.9
1	Florida	21.6
12	Georgia	19.1
2	Hawaii	21.4
33	Idaho	17.4
40	Illinois	16.1
19	Indiana	18.4
44	Iowa	15.4
19	Kansas	18.4
35	Kentucky	17.1
37	Louisiana	16.6
42	Maine	16.0
31	Maryland	17.7
14	Massachusetts	19.0
19	Michigan	18.4
11	Minnesota	19.2
29	Mississippi	17.8
24	Missouri	18.1
38	Montana	16.4
43	Nebraska	15.9
17	Nevada	18.8
34	New Hampshire	17.3
40	New Jersey	16.1
16	New Mexico	18.9
7	New York	19.6
3	North Carolina	21.0
50	North Dakota	12.7
29	Ohio	17.8
28	Oklahoma	17.9
25	Oregon	18.0
39	Pennsylvania	16.3
23	Rhode Island	18.3
45	South Carolina	15.2
47	South Dakota	14.0
14	Tennessee	19.0
47	Texas	14.0
7	Utah	19.6
4	Vermont	20.4
35	Virginia	17.1
25	Washington	18.0
32	West Virginia	17.5
9	Wisconsin	19.5
46	Wyoming	14.4

RANK ORDER

RANK	STATE	MILES PER GALLON
1	Florida	21.6
2	Hawaii	21.4
3	North Carolina	21.0
4	Vermont	20.4
5	Alabama	20.2
6	Delaware	19.9
7	New York	19.6
7	Utah	19.6
9	California	19.5
9	Wisconsin	19.5
11	Minnesota	19.2
12	Arizona	19.1
12	Georgia	19.1
14	Massachusetts	19.0
14	Tennessee	19.0
16	New Mexico	18.9
17	Connecticut	18.8
17	Nevada	18.8
19	Colorado	18.4
19	Indiana	18.4
19	Kansas	18.4
19	Michigan	18.4
23	Rhode Island	18.3
24	Missouri	18.1
25	Arkansas	18.0
25	Oregon	18.0
25	Washington	18.0
28	Oklahoma	17.9
29	Mississippi	17.8
29	Ohio	17.8
31	Maryland	17.7
32	West Virginia	17.5
33	Idaho	17.4
34	New Hampshire	17.3
35	Kentucky	17.1
35	Virginia	17.1
37	Louisiana	16.6
38	Montana	16.4
39	Pennsylvania	16.3
40	Illinois	16.1
40	New Jersey	16.1
42	Maine	16.0
43	Nebraska	15.9
44	Iowa	15.4
45	South Carolina	15.2
46	Wyoming	14.4
47	South Dakota	14.0
47	Texas	14.0
49	Alaska	13.2
50	North Dakota	12.7

District of Columbia 29.1

Source: CQ Press using data from U.S. Department of Transportation, Federal Highway Administration
"Highway Statistics 2015" (Table VM-2, http://www.fhwa.dot.gov/policyinformation/statistics/2015/)
*Total vehicle-miles for 2015 divided by total highway motor-fuel use. Includes gasoline, gasohol, diesel, and other "special fuels."

Airports in 2013

National Total = 13,174 Airports*

ALPHA ORDER

RANK	STATE	AIRPORTS	% of USA
32	Alabama	180	1.4%
2	Alaska	554	4.2%
30	Arizona	189	1.4%
26	Arkansas	215	1.6%
3	California	522	4.0%
21	Colorado	265	2.0%
47	Connecticut	51	0.4%
49	Delaware	31	0.2%
4	Florida	501	3.8%
15	Georgia	336	2.6%
48	Hawaii	32	0.2%
25	Idaho	227	1.7%
5	Illinois	478	3.6%
9	Indiana	405	3.1%
28	Iowa	199	1.5%
16	Kansas	333	2.5%
34	Kentucky	150	1.1%
24	Louisiana	229	1.7%
38	Maine	115	0.9%
35	Maryland	149	1.1%
43	Massachusetts	75	0.6%
13	Michigan	355	2.7%
17	Minnesota	327	2.5%
31	Mississippi	186	1.4%
12	Missouri	363	2.8%
23	Montana	231	1.8%
29	Nebraska	198	1.5%
40	Nevada	97	0.7%
46	New Hampshire	54	0.4%
39	New Jersey	100	0.8%
37	New Mexico	135	1.0%
10	New York	388	2.9%
14	North Carolina	338	2.6%
22	North Dakota	256	1.9%
6	Ohio	450	3.4%
19	Oklahoma	294	2.2%
18	Oregon	325	2.5%
8	Pennsylvania	432	3.3%
50	Rhode Island	9	0.1%
33	South Carolina	158	1.2%
36	South Dakota	143	1.1%
27	Tennessee	212	1.6%
1	Texas	1,466	11.1%
42	Utah	91	0.7%
45	Vermont	61	0.5%
20	Virginia	291	2.2%
11	Washington	370	2.8%
43	West Virginia	75	0.6%
7	Wisconsin	435	3.3%
41	Wyoming	95	0.7%

RANK ORDER

RANK	STATE	AIRPORTS	% of USA
1	Texas	1,466	11.1%
2	Alaska	554	4.2%
3	California	522	4.0%
4	Florida	501	3.8%
5	Illinois	478	3.6%
6	Ohio	450	3.4%
7	Wisconsin	435	3.3%
8	Pennsylvania	432	3.3%
9	Indiana	405	3.1%
10	New York	388	2.9%
11	Washington	370	2.8%
12	Missouri	363	2.8%
13	Michigan	355	2.7%
14	North Carolina	338	2.6%
15	Georgia	336	2.6%
16	Kansas	333	2.5%
17	Minnesota	327	2.5%
18	Oregon	325	2.5%
19	Oklahoma	294	2.2%
20	Virginia	291	2.2%
21	Colorado	265	2.0%
22	North Dakota	256	1.9%
23	Montana	231	1.8%
24	Louisiana	229	1.7%
25	Idaho	227	1.7%
26	Arkansas	215	1.6%
27	Tennessee	212	1.6%
28	Iowa	199	1.5%
29	Nebraska	198	1.5%
30	Arizona	189	1.4%
31	Mississippi	186	1.4%
32	Alabama	180	1.4%
33	South Carolina	158	1.2%
34	Kentucky	150	1.1%
35	Maryland	149	1.1%
36	South Dakota	143	1.1%
37	New Mexico	135	1.0%
38	Maine	115	0.9%
39	New Jersey	100	0.8%
40	Nevada	97	0.7%
41	Wyoming	95	0.7%
42	Utah	91	0.7%
43	Massachusetts	75	0.6%
43	West Virginia	75	0.6%
45	Vermont	61	0.5%
46	New Hampshire	54	0.4%
47	Connecticut	51	0.4%
48	Hawaii	32	0.2%
49	Delaware	31	0.2%
50	Rhode Island	9	0.1%
	District of Columbia	3	0.0%

Source: U.S. Department of Transportation, Bureau of Transportation Statistics
"State Transportation Statistics 2015" (Table 1-10, http://www.bts.gov/publications/state_transportation_statistics/)
*This table comprises all U.S. public use and private use airports. Public use facilities are open to the public with no prior authorization or permission required. Private use facilities are not open to the general public and include medical, law enforcement, corporate, and other such facilities.

Inland Waterway Mileage in 2013

National Total = 29,620 Miles*

ALPHA ORDER

RANK	STATE	MILES	% of USA
6	Alabama	1,270	4.3%
1	Alaska	5,500	18.6%
40	Arizona	0	0.0%
3	Arkansas	1,860	6.3%
26	California	290	1.0%
40	Colorado	0	0.0%
31	Connecticut	120	0.4%
34	Delaware	100	0.3%
5	Florida	1,540	5.2%
14	Georgia	720	2.4%
40	Hawaii	0	0.0%
33	Idaho	110	0.4%
8	Illinois	1,100	3.7%
24	Indiana	350	1.2%
19	Iowa	490	1.7%
31	Kansas	120	0.4%
4	Kentucky	1,590	5.4%
2	Louisiana	2,820	9.5%
37	Maine	70	0.2%
18	Maryland	530	1.8%
35	Massachusetts	90	0.3%
40	Michigan	0	0.0%
27	Minnesota	260	0.9%
12	Mississippi	870	2.9%
10	Missouri	1,030	3.5%
40	Montana	0	0.0%
25	Nebraska	320	1.1%
40	Nevada	0	0.0%
39	New Hampshire	10	0.0%
23	New Jersey	360	1.2%
40	New Mexico	0	0.0%
22	New York	390	1.3%
7	North Carolina	1,150	3.9%
40	North Dakota	0	0.0%
21	Ohio	440	1.5%
30	Oklahoma	150	0.5%
15	Oregon	680	2.3%
27	Pennsylvania	260	0.9%
38	Rhode Island	40	0.1%
20	South Carolina	480	1.6%
36	South Dakota	80	0.3%
11	Tennessee	950	3.2%
13	Texas	830	2.8%
40	Utah	0	0.0%
40	Vermont	0	0.0%
17	Virginia	670	2.3%
9	Washington	1,060	3.6%
15	West Virginia	680	2.3%
29	Wisconsin	230	0.8%
40	Wyoming	0	0.0%

RANK ORDER

RANK	STATE	MILES	% of USA
1	Alaska	5,500	18.6%
2	Louisiana	2,820	9.5%
3	Arkansas	1,860	6.3%
4	Kentucky	1,590	5.4%
5	Florida	1,540	5.2%
6	Alabama	1,270	4.3%
7	North Carolina	1,150	3.9%
8	Illinois	1,100	3.7%
9	Washington	1,060	3.6%
10	Missouri	1,030	3.5%
11	Tennessee	950	3.2%
12	Mississippi	870	2.9%
13	Texas	830	2.8%
14	Georgia	720	2.4%
15	Oregon	680	2.3%
15	West Virginia	680	2.3%
17	Virginia	670	2.3%
18	Maryland	530	1.8%
19	Iowa	490	1.7%
20	South Carolina	480	1.6%
21	Ohio	440	1.5%
22	New York	390	1.3%
23	New Jersey	360	1.2%
24	Indiana	350	1.2%
25	Nebraska	320	1.1%
26	California	290	1.0%
27	Minnesota	260	0.9%
27	Pennsylvania	260	0.9%
29	Wisconsin	230	0.8%
30	Oklahoma	150	0.5%
31	Connecticut	120	0.4%
31	Kansas	120	0.4%
33	Idaho	110	0.4%
34	Delaware	100	0.3%
35	Massachusetts	90	0.3%
36	South Dakota	80	0.3%
37	Maine	70	0.2%
38	Rhode Island	40	0.1%
39	New Hampshire	10	0.0%
40	Arizona	0	0.0%
40	Colorado	0	0.0%
40	Hawaii	0	0.0%
40	Michigan	0	0.0%
40	Montana	0	0.0%
40	Nevada	0	0.0%
40	New Mexico	0	0.0%
40	North Dakota	0	0.0%
40	Utah	0	0.0%
40	Vermont	0	0.0%
40	Wyoming	0	0.0%
	District of Columbia	10	0.0%

Source: U.S. Department of Transportation, Bureau of Transportation Statistics
   "State Transportation Statistics 2015" (Table 1-16, http://www.bts.gov/publications/state_transportation_statistics/)
*Waterway mileage was determined by including the length of channels 1) with a controlling draft of nine feet or greater, 2) with commercial cargo traffic reported for 1998 and 1999, but 3) were not offshore. Channels within major bays are included (e.g., Chesapeake Bay, San Francisco Bay, Puget Sound, Long Island Sound, and major sounds and straits in southeastern Alaska). Channels in the Great Lakes are not included. Approximately 4,600 miles are counted twice as several are state boundaries.

Percent of Recreational Boating Accidents Involving Alcohol in 2015

National Percent = 7.4% of Accidents*

ALPHA ORDER

RANK	STATE	PERCENT
14	Alabama	11.4
11	Alaska	12.0
22	Arizona	8.2
22	Arkansas	8.2
40	California	4.3
34	Colorado	5.6
37	Connecticut	5.2
47	Delaware	0.0
38	Florida	4.5
19	Georgia	9.4
47	Hawaii	0.0
17	Idaho	10.3
8	Illinois	13.6
20	Indiana	9.3
34	Iowa	5.6
25	Kansas	8.0
5	Kentucky	17.1
7	Louisiana	13.8
42	Maine	3.1
12	Maryland	11.6
29	Massachusetts	6.7
29	Michigan	6.7
13	Minnesota	11.5
41	Mississippi	3.3
36	Missouri	5.5
6	Montana	14.3
42	Nebraska	3.1
28	Nevada	7.9
46	New Hampshire	1.9
44	New Jersey	2.5
47	New Mexico	0.0
25	New York	8.0
9	North Carolina	12.3
4	North Dakota	18.2
25	Ohio	8.0
10	Oklahoma	12.1
15	Oregon	10.8
31	Pennsylvania	5.8
24	Rhode Island	8.1
32	South Carolina	5.7
2	South Dakota	26.7
20	Tennessee	9.3
38	Texas	4.5
44	Utah	2.5
3	Vermont	25.0
32	Virginia	5.7
17	Washington	10.3
1	West Virginia	36.4
16	Wisconsin	10.7
47	Wyoming	0.0

RANK ORDER

RANK	STATE	PERCENT
1	West Virginia	36.4
2	South Dakota	26.7
3	Vermont	25.0
4	North Dakota	18.2
5	Kentucky	17.1
6	Montana	14.3
7	Louisiana	13.8
8	Illinois	13.6
9	North Carolina	12.3
10	Oklahoma	12.1
11	Alaska	12.0
12	Maryland	11.6
13	Minnesota	11.5
14	Alabama	11.4
15	Oregon	10.8
16	Wisconsin	10.7
17	Idaho	10.3
17	Washington	10.3
19	Georgia	9.4
20	Indiana	9.3
20	Tennessee	9.3
22	Arizona	8.2
22	Arkansas	8.2
24	Rhode Island	8.1
25	Kansas	8.0
25	New York	8.0
25	Ohio	8.0
28	Nevada	7.9
29	Massachusetts	6.7
29	Michigan	6.7
31	Pennsylvania	5.8
32	South Carolina	5.7
32	Virginia	5.7
34	Colorado	5.6
34	Iowa	5.6
36	Missouri	5.5
37	Connecticut	5.2
38	Florida	4.5
38	Texas	4.5
40	California	4.3
41	Mississippi	3.3
42	Maine	3.1
42	Nebraska	3.1
44	New Jersey	2.5
44	Utah	2.5
46	New Hampshire	1.9
47	Delaware	0.0
47	Hawaii	0.0
47	New Mexico	0.0
47	Wyoming	0.0

District of Columbia   0.0

Source: CQ Press using data from United States Coast Guard
"Boating Statistics 2015" (http://www.uscgboating.org/statistics/accident_statistics.php)
*Alcohol involvement in a boating accident includes any accident in which alcoholic beverages are consumed in the boat and the investigating official has determined that the operator was impaired or affected while operating the boat.

Railroad Accidents and Incidents in 2015

National Total = 11,776*

ALPHA ORDER					RANK ORDER			

RANK	STATE	ACCIDENTS	% of USA		RANK	STATE	ACCIDENTS	% of USA
16	Alabama	211	1.8%		1	New York	1,431	12.2%
41	Alaska	47	0.4%		2	Illinois	985	8.4%
33	Arizona	102	0.9%		3	California	868	7.4%
29	Arkansas	140	1.2%		4	Texas	806	6.8%
3	California	868	7.4%		5	New Jersey	726	6.2%
25	Colorado	165	1.4%		6	Pennsylvania	696	5.9%
27	Connecticut	144	1.2%		7	Indiana	362	3.1%
39	Delaware	73	0.6%		8	Florida	324	2.8%
8	Florida	324	2.8%		9	Ohio	311	2.6%
10	Georgia	284	2.4%		10	Georgia	284	2.4%
50	Hawaii	0	0.0%		11	Louisiana	261	2.2%
43	Idaho	45	0.4%		12	Missouri	222	1.9%
2	Illinois	985	8.4%		13	Minnesota	220	1.9%
7	Indiana	362	3.1%		14	Massachusetts	217	1.8%
20	Iowa	180	1.5%		15	Washington	213	1.8%
21	Kansas	174	1.5%		16	Alabama	211	1.8%
28	Kentucky	143	1.2%		17	Virginia	203	1.7%
11	Louisiana	261	2.2%		18	North Carolina	197	1.7%
48	Maine	13	0.1%		19	Nebraska	189	1.6%
26	Maryland	149	1.3%		20	Iowa	180	1.5%
14	Massachusetts	217	1.8%		21	Kansas	174	1.5%
22	Michigan	168	1.4%		22	Michigan	168	1.4%
13	Minnesota	220	1.9%		23	Tennessee	167	1.4%
35	Mississippi	100	0.8%		24	Wisconsin	166	1.4%
12	Missouri	222	1.9%		25	Colorado	165	1.4%
36	Montana	91	0.8%		26	Maryland	149	1.3%
19	Nebraska	189	1.6%		27	Connecticut	144	1.2%
44	Nevada	34	0.3%		28	Kentucky	143	1.2%
49	New Hampshire	3	0.0%		29	Arkansas	140	1.2%
5	New Jersey	726	6.2%		30	Oregon	117	1.0%
33	New Mexico	102	0.9%		31	South Carolina	114	1.0%
1	New York	1,431	12.2%		32	Oklahoma	110	0.9%
18	North Carolina	197	1.7%		33	Arizona	102	0.9%
37	North Dakota	87	0.7%		33	New Mexico	102	0.9%
9	Ohio	311	2.6%		35	Mississippi	100	0.8%
32	Oklahoma	110	0.9%		36	Montana	91	0.8%
30	Oregon	117	1.0%		37	North Dakota	87	0.7%
6	Pennsylvania	696	5.9%		38	West Virginia	84	0.7%
44	Rhode Island	34	0.3%		39	Delaware	73	0.6%
31	South Carolina	114	1.0%		40	Wyoming	66	0.6%
47	South Dakota	31	0.3%		41	Alaska	47	0.4%
23	Tennessee	167	1.4%		41	Utah	47	0.4%
4	Texas	806	6.8%		43	Idaho	45	0.4%
41	Utah	47	0.4%		44	Nevada	34	0.3%
46	Vermont	33	0.3%		44	Rhode Island	34	0.3%
17	Virginia	203	1.7%		46	Vermont	33	0.3%
15	Washington	213	1.8%		47	South Dakota	31	0.3%
38	West Virginia	84	0.7%		48	Maine	13	0.1%
24	Wisconsin	166	1.4%		49	New Hampshire	3	0.0%
40	Wyoming	66	0.6%		50	Hawaii	0	0.0%
						District of Columbia	121	1.0%

Source: U.S. Department of Transportation, Federal Railroad Administration, Office of Safety Analysis
"Railroad Accidents and Incidents" (Table 1.11, http://safetydata.fra.dot.gov/OfficeofSafety/Default.aspx)
*Accidents or incidents include all events reportable to the U.S. Department of Transportation. These include train accidents causing damage above an established threshold; highway-rail grade crossing incidents involving impact between railroad equipment and highway users at crossings; and all other reportable incidents that cause a fatality or injury to any person or an occupational illness to a railroad employee. There were 753 fatalities involving railroads.

Railroad Mileage Operated in 2012

National Total = 138,524 Miles of Railroad*

ALPHA ORDER

RANK	STATE	MILES	% of USA
21	Alabama	3,194	2.3%
45	Alaska	506	0.4%
36	Arizona	1,643	1.2%
25	Arkansas	2,698	1.9%
3	California	5,295	3.8%
26	Colorado	2,662	1.9%
46	Connecticut	364	0.3%
48	Delaware	250	0.2%
24	Florida	2,900	2.1%
7	Georgia	4,653	3.4%
50	Hawaii	0	0.0%
37	Idaho	1,623	1.2%
2	Illinois	6,986	5.0%
9	Indiana	4,075	2.9%
11	Iowa	3,869	2.8%
6	Kansas	4,855	3.5%
28	Kentucky	2,608	1.9%
23	Louisiana	2,927	2.1%
40	Maine	1,116	0.8%
43	Maryland	758	0.5%
42	Massachusetts	973	0.7%
12	Michigan	3,542	2.6%
8	Minnesota	4,450	3.2%
29	Mississippi	2,452	1.8%
10	Missouri	3,957	2.9%
20	Montana	3,200	2.3%
15	Nebraska	3,375	2.4%
39	Nevada	1,192	0.9%
47	New Hampshire	344	0.2%
41	New Jersey	981	0.7%
34	New Mexico	1,837	1.3%
14	New York	3,447	2.5%
18	North Carolina	3,258	2.4%
16	North Dakota	3,330	2.4%
4	Ohio	5,288	3.8%
17	Oklahoma	3,273	2.4%
30	Oregon	2,396	1.7%
5	Pennsylvania	5,151	3.7%
49	Rhode Island	19	0.0%
31	South Carolina	2,311	1.7%
35	South Dakota	1,753	1.3%
27	Tennessee	2,649	1.9%
1	Texas	10,469	7.6%
38	Utah	1,343	1.0%
44	Vermont	590	0.4%
19	Virginia	3,215	2.3%
22	Washington	3,192	2.3%
32	West Virginia	2,226	1.6%
13	Wisconsin	3,449	2.5%
33	Wyoming	1,860	1.3%

RANK ORDER

RANK	STATE	MILES	% of USA
1	Texas	10,469	7.6%
2	Illinois	6,986	5.0%
3	California	5,295	3.8%
4	Ohio	5,288	3.8%
5	Pennsylvania	5,151	3.7%
6	Kansas	4,855	3.5%
7	Georgia	4,653	3.4%
8	Minnesota	4,450	3.2%
9	Indiana	4,075	2.9%
10	Missouri	3,957	2.9%
11	Iowa	3,869	2.8%
12	Michigan	3,542	2.6%
13	Wisconsin	3,449	2.5%
14	New York	3,447	2.5%
15	Nebraska	3,375	2.4%
16	North Dakota	3,330	2.4%
17	Oklahoma	3,273	2.4%
18	North Carolina	3,258	2.4%
19	Virginia	3,215	2.3%
20	Montana	3,200	2.3%
21	Alabama	3,194	2.3%
22	Washington	3,192	2.3%
23	Louisiana	2,927	2.1%
24	Florida	2,900	2.1%
25	Arkansas	2,698	1.9%
26	Colorado	2,662	1.9%
27	Tennessee	2,649	1.9%
28	Kentucky	2,608	1.9%
29	Mississippi	2,452	1.8%
30	Oregon	2,396	1.7%
31	South Carolina	2,311	1.7%
32	West Virginia	2,226	1.6%
33	Wyoming	1,860	1.3%
34	New Mexico	1,837	1.3%
35	South Dakota	1,753	1.3%
36	Arizona	1,643	1.2%
37	Idaho	1,623	1.2%
38	Utah	1,343	1.0%
39	Nevada	1,192	0.9%
40	Maine	1,116	0.8%
41	New Jersey	981	0.7%
42	Massachusetts	973	0.7%
43	Maryland	758	0.5%
44	Vermont	590	0.4%
45	Alaska	506	0.4%
46	Connecticut	364	0.3%
47	New Hampshire	344	0.2%
48	Delaware	250	0.2%
49	Rhode Island	19	0.0%
50	Hawaii	0	0.0%
	District of Columbia	20	0.0%

Source: Association of American Railroads
    "Railroads and States" (https://www.aar.org/data-center/railroads-states)
*Includes Class I and non-Class I miles. Excludes trackage rights. Synonymous with route-miles, so that a mile of single track is counted the same as a mile of double track.

Sources

ACT, Inc.
500 ACT Drive, P.O. Box 168
Iowa City, IA 52243-0168
319-337-1000
www.act.org

Administration for Children and Families
U.S. Department of Health and Human Services
330 C Street, SW
Washington, DC 20201
202-401-9215
www.acf.hhs.gov

American Cancer Society, Inc.
250 Williams Street, NW
Atlanta, GA 30303
800-227-2345
www.cancer.org

American Dental Association
211 E. Chicago Avenue
Chicago, IL 60611-2678
312-440-2500
www.ada.org

American Hospital Association
155 N. Wacker Drive
Chicago, IL 60606
312-422-3000
www.aha.org

American Medical Association
330 N. Wabash Avenue
Chicago, IL 60611-5885
800-621-8335
www.ama-assn.org

Association of American Railroads
425 Third Street, SW, Suite 1000
Washington, DC 20024
202-639-2100
www.aar.org

Bureau of Economic Analysis
U.S. Department of Commerce
4600 Silver Hill Road
Washington, DC 20233
301-278-9004
www.bea.gov

Bureau of Justice Statistics
U.S. Department of Justice
810 Seventh Street, NW
Washington, DC 20531
202-307-0765
www.bjs.gov

Bureau of Labor Statistics
U.S. Department of Labor
2 Massachusetts Avenue, NE
Washington, DC 20212-0001
202-691-5200
www.bls.gov

Bureau of Transportation Statistics
U.S. Department of Transportation
1200 New Jersey Avenue, SE
Washington, DC 20590
800-853-1351
www.rita.dot.gov

Census Bureau
4600 Silver Hill Road
Washington, DC 20233-0001
800-923-8282
www.census.gov

Centers for Disease Control and Prevention
1600 Clifton Road
Atlanta, GA 30329-4027
800-232-4636
www.cdc.gov

Centers for Medicare and Medicaid Services
7500 Security Boulevard
Baltimore, MD 21244-1850
877-267-2323
www.cms.hhs.gov

College Board
250 Vesey Street
New York, NY 10281
212-713-8000
www.collegeboard.org

Economic Research Service
U.S. Department of Agriculture
1400 Independence Avenue, SW
Mail Stop 1800
Washington, DC 20250-0002
202-694-5139
www.ers.usda.gov

Energy Information Administration
U.S. Department of Energy
1000 Independence Avenue, SW
Washington, DC 20585
202-586-8800
www.eia.doe.gov

Environmental Protection Agency
Ariel Rios Building
1200 Pennsylvania Avenue, NW
Washington, DC 20460
202-272-0167
www.epa.gov

Federal Bureau of Investigation
J Edgar Hoover Building
935 Pennsylvania Avenue, NW
Washington, DC 20535-0001
202-324-3000
www.fbi.gov

Federal Highway Administration
U.S. Department of Transportation
1200 New Jersey Avenue, SE
Washington, DC 20590
202-366-4000
www.fhwa.dot.gov

Federation of Tax Administrators
444 North Capitol Street, NW, Suite 348
Washington, DC 20001
202-624-5890
www.taxadmin.org

Food and Nutrition Service
U.S. Department of Agriculture
3101 Park Center Drive
Alexandria, VA 22302
703-305-2062
www.fns.usda.gov

General Services Administration
1800 F Street, NW
Washington, DC 20450
844-472-43111
www.gsa.gov

Health Resources and Services Administration
Division of Practitioner Data Banks
5600 Fishers Lane
Rockville, MD 20857
301-443-3376
www.hrsa.gov

Institute of Museum and Library Services
955 L'Enfant Plaza North, SW, Suite 4000
Washington, DC 20024-2135
202-653-4657
www.imls.gov

Internal Revenue Service
U.S. Department of the Treasury
1111 Constitution Avenue, NW
Washington, DC 20224
202-283-1710
www.irs.gov

Medical Expenditure Panel Survey
Agency for Healthcare Research and Quality
5600 Fishers Lane
Rockville, MD 20857
301-427-1364
www.meps.ahrq.gov

National Agricultural Statistics Service
1400 Independence Avenue, SW
Washington, DC 20250
800-727-9540
www.nass.usda.gov

National Assembly of State Arts Agencies
1200 18th Street, NW, Suite 1100
Washington, DC 20036
202-347-6352
www.nasaa-arts.org

National Center for Education Statistics
U.S. Department of Education
550 12th Street, SW
Washington, DC 20036
202-403-5551
https://nces.ed.gov/

National Center for Health Statistics
U.S. Department of Health and Human Services
3311 Toledo Road
Hyattsville, MD 20782
800-232-4636
www.cdc.gov/nchs/

National Conference of State Legislatures
7700 E. First Place
Denver, CO 80230
303-364-7700
www.ncsl.org

National Education Association
1201 16th Street, NW
Washington, DC 20036-3290
202-833-4000
www.nea.org

National Highway Traffic Safety Administration
1200 New Jersey Avenue, SE
Washington, DC 20590
888-327-4236
www.nhtsa.gov

National Institute on Alcohol Abuse and Alcoholism
5635 Fishers Lane, MSC 9304
Bethesda, MD 20892-9304
301-443-3860
www.niaaa.nih.gov

National Oceanic & Atmospheric Administration
U.S. Department of Commerce
1401 Constitution Avenue, NW, Room 5128
Washington, DC 20230
202-482-6090
www.noaa.gov

Office of Management and Budget
725 17th Street, NW
Washington, DC 20503
202-395-3080
www.USAspending.gov

Project on Student Debt
Institute for College Access and Success
405 14th Street, 11th Floor
Oakland CA 94612
510-318-7900
http://ticas.org/posd/home

Social Security Administration
Office of Public Inquiries
1100 West High Rise
6401 Security Boulevard
Baltimore, MD 21235
800-772-1213 (information)
www.ssa.gov

Storm Prediction Center
National Weather Service
120 David Boren Boulevard
Norman, OK 73072
405-579-0771
www.spc.noaa.gov

Tax Foundation
1325 G Street, NW, Suite 950
Washington, DC 20005
202-464-6200
www.taxfoundation.org

U.S. Department of Defense
Directorate for Public Inquiry and Analysis
Room 2E565 The Pentagon
1400 Defense Pentagon
Washington, DC 20301-1400
703-571-3343
www.defense.gov

U.S. Department of Veterans Affairs
810 Vermont Avenue, NW
Washington, DC 20420
800-827-1000
www.va.gov

U.S. Geological Survey
12201 Sunrise Valley Drive
Reston, VA 20192
888-275-8747
www.usgs.gov

Index